Engineering Chemistry

Engineering Chemistry

Dr. O. P. Aggarwal
M.Sc., Ph.D.,
Reader in Chemistry
M.M. (P.G) College, Modinagar (U.P.)

Dr. Pooja Gupta
Assistant Professor in Department of Chemistry
Government Motilal Vigyan Mahavidyalaya, Bhopal.

KHANNA PUBLISHERS®
Operational Office Investing in Learning®
4575/15, Onkar House, Opp. Happy School,
Ground Floor, Daryaganj, New Delhi-110002
Phones : 011-45033819 • *Mob.* 09811541460
email : contactus@khannapublishers.in

Published by :

Romesh Chander Khanna & Vineet Khanna
for KHANNA PUBLISHERS
2-B, Nath Market, Nai Sarak
Delhi- 110 006 (India)

Website : www.khannapublishers.in

Hologram & Description

To all readers of our books, to prevent yourself from being defrauded by piraters, please make sure that there is an Hologram on the cover of our books with the below specifications. If you find any book without Hologram and Description, please mail us at **contactus@khannapublishers.in**

Thanking you

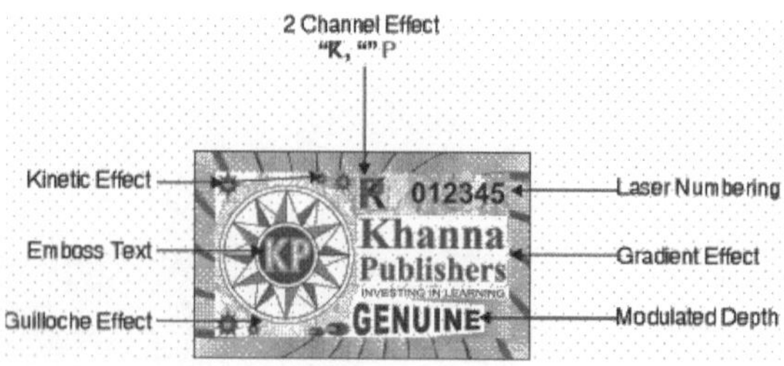

ISBN No. : 978-81-7409-103-1

***Fourth Edition :* 2026**

Price : Rs. 599.00

Preface

This book is written for first year undergraduate engineering students. The objective of this book is to provide a broad understanding of the concepts in a clear and concise manner. Great care has been taken to render accurate diagrams that clearly illustrate the topics. The text includes a number of examples and numerical problems with solutions giving a deep understanding of each topic. This book contains 15 chapters and each chapter is provided with different types of questions (multiple type questions (MCQs), short and long answer type questions.) and numerical wherever necessary.

We hope this book will be useful to the students as well as teachers. We would also be happy to invite suggestions and comments for improvement of this book at gupta9pooja@gmail.com.

Dr. O.P Aggarwal

Dr. Pooja Gupta

Acknowledgement

First of all I would like to thank god for giving me the knowledge and guidance for writing this book. This book has only been possible because of Dr. O.P. Aggarwal who lent his enormous experience and skill for writing this book.

I would also like to thank my brother, Deepak Agarwal and my sister Dr. Priyanka Goyal for inspiring me to write this book.

I am also grateful to my mother in law, Mrs. Sunita Gupta and my mother Mrs. Kanta Agarwal for their constant inspiration, blessings and faith in me.

I am highly grateful to my husband, Mr. Jayant Gupta and my sons, Aman Gupta and Kanishk Gupta for showing immense patience and understanding during the course of this work.

I dedicate this book to the two pillars of my life Justice S.K. Mittal and Mrs Manju Mittal.

—Authors

Contents

Chapter 1 Molecular Structure and Bonding

1.1 INTRODUCTION

It is a well-known fact that matter is made up of atoms but under normal conditions (except noble gases) the atoms are not capable of independent existence. However, the smallest particle of matter capable of independent existence is the molecule. The molecule is a group of atoms of the same or different elements behaving as a single unit and having characteristic properties, for example, H_2, O_2, P_4, S_8, H_2O, NH_3 etc. These molecules consist of groups of atoms, which are held together by some attractive forces. In addition to these, there are certain other molecules, which contain ions instead of atoms (*e.g.* NaCl, CaF_2 etc.). The attractive force that holds various constituents (atoms, ions etc.) together in molecules is called as chemical bond. From the limited number of elements, there are derived millions of known compounds and there are an infinite number possible. This is because there are so many possible ways in which atoms combine to form molecules. The existence of a large number of molecules or compounds raises many questions, such as

1. Why do atoms combine to form compounds?
2. Why are only certain combinations possible for example existence of H_2 and non-existence of H_3?
3. Why do some atoms combine while others do not, for example H-atoms combine to form H_2 but He-atoms do not combine to form He_2?
4. Why do molecules possess definite shapes, for example CO_2 is linear, while H_2O is bent shaped?

To answer the above questions, different theories have been put forward from time to time. Some of the theories are:

1. Kossel-Lewis approach
2. Valence Shell Electron Pair Repulsion (VSEPR) Theory
3. Valence Bond Theory (VBT)
4. Molecular Orbital Theory (MOT)

1.2 KOSSEL-LEWIS APPROACH TO CHEMICAL BONDING (ELECTRONIC THEORY OF VALENCY)

In early days, a number of attempts were made to explain the formation of chemical bond in terms of electrons but first satisfactory explanation was given by Lewis and Kossel, while working independently. They visualized that noble gas atoms had a stable electronic configuration (*i.e.* had 8 electrons in their valence shell), while atoms of all other elements had unstable or incomplete electronic configuration (*i.e.* had 1 to 7 electrons in their valence shell).

Kossel-Lewis in 1916 proposed the **octet rule** or the electronic theory of valency, which states that 'in chemical bond formation atoms interact by losing, gaining or sharing of electrons in order to complete their respective octets so as to acquire a stable noble gas configuration'. According to electronic theory of valency, the interaction of valence electrons can occur by following ways.

1. By complete transference of one or more electrons from one atom to another. This type of bond is called as **ionic bond/electrovalent bond**.
2. By sharing of electrons. This can occur in two ways:
   (*i*) When the shared electrons are contributed by the two combining atoms equally, the bond formed is called as **covalent bond**.
   (*ii*) When the shared electrons are contributed entirely by one of the atoms but shared by both, the bond formed is called as **coordinate bond or dative bond**.

1.2.1 Ionic Bond/Electrovalent Bond

When a bond is formed by complete transference of electrons from one atom to another so as to complete their octets is called as **ionic bond/electrovalent bond**. This type of bond usually comes into existence between a metal and a non-metal.

For example, formation of sodium chloride:

Electronic configuration of sodium = 2, 8, 1

So, when sodium loses one electron of its outermost shell, it acquires the noble gas configuration of neon and changes to Na^+.

$$\underset{(2,8,1)}{Na} \longrightarrow \underset{(2,8)}{Na^+} + e^-$$

On the other hand, electronic configuration of chlorine = 2, 8, 7. Chlorine accepts one electron released by sodium to complete its octet and acquires a noble gas configuration of argon and changes to Cl^-.

$$\underset{(2,8,7)}{Cl} + e^- \longrightarrow \underset{(2,8,8)}{Cl^-}$$

Now the two species, one positively charged (Na^+) and the other negatively charged (Cl^-) approach each other and are held together by strong electrostatic forces of attraction. Formation of NaCl takes place in the following manner:

$$[Na]^+ + [Cl]^- \longrightarrow [Na]^+ [Cl]^-$$

Thus, sodium is assigned a positive electrovalency of 1 while chlorine is assigned a negative electrovalency of 1. Other examples of ionic compounds are CaF_2, MgO, $MgBr_2$, CaS, Na_2S, Al_2O_3 etc.

Electrovalency is the number of electrons lost or gained by the atom during the formation of an electrovalent bond.

1.2.2 Covalent Bond

The combining atoms which are short of electrons than the nearest noble gas configuration may form bond by sharing of electrons between the atoms. Each combining atom contributes one electron to form a common pair of electron which is then shared by both. Such type of bond which is formed between the atoms by mutual sharing of electrons is called as **covalent bond**.

For example, formation of chlorine molecule (Cl_2)

Electronic configuration of chlorine = $[Ne]3s^23p^5$

Each chlorine atom is one electron short of attaining a stable noble gas configuration of argon. Each chlorine atom contributes one electron to form a common shared pair. In this process, both chlorine atoms attain the outer shell octet of a noble gas **(Fig. 1.1)**.

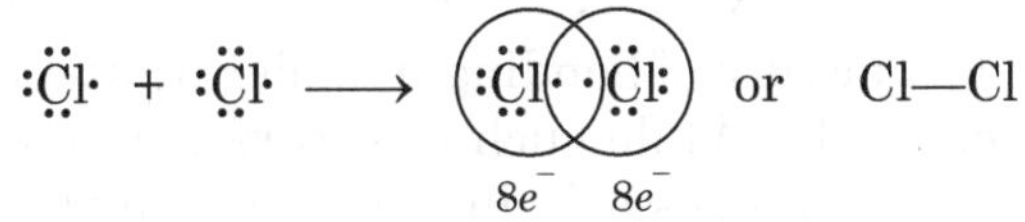

Fig. 1.1. Formation of chlorine molecule.

The dots represent electrons. Such structures are referred to as **Lewis structures**.

Other examples of covalent compounds are HCl, H_2, H_2O, NH_3, CH_4 etc.

The number of pairs of electrons shared between two atoms determines the type of the covalent bond formed between them. A covalent bond is said to be **single covalent bond**, when the two combining atoms share only one pair of electrons. However, if two electron pairs are shared by the atoms, the bond formed is **double covalent bond**. Similarly, when the combining atoms share three electron pairs, the bond formed is called as **triple bond**.

1.2.3 Coordinate/Dative Bond

In a normal covalent bond each of the two bonded atoms contribute one electron to make the shared pair. In some cases, a bond is formed when both the electrons are contributed entirely by one atom but shared by both atoms. Such bonds are called as **coordinate covalent/dative bond**. The atom which donates the electron pair is called as **donor** and the atom which accepts this electron pair is called as an **acceptor**. The coordinate bond is represented by an arrow (→) pointing from the donor towards the acceptor.

For example, formation of NH_4^+ ion: In ammonia molecule, the nitrogen atom has a complete octet around it with an unshared or lone pair of electrons and H^+ ion has no electron. The nitrogen atom, therefore donates its lone pair of electrons to H^+ ion. Thus, NH_3 behaves as donor by donating its unshared electrons to H^+ (which behaves as an acceptor), forming ammonium ion **(Fig. 1.2)**.

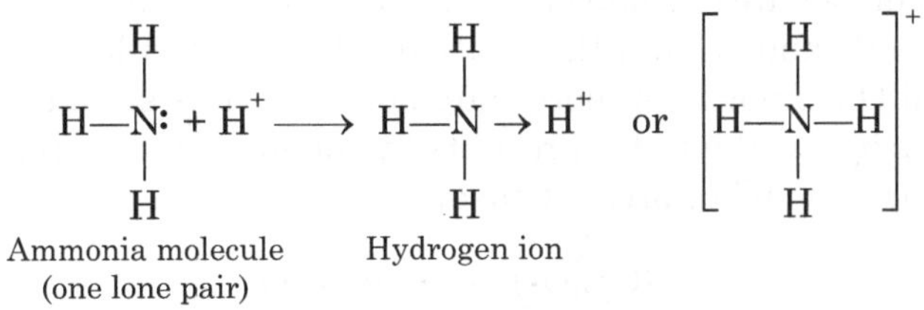

Fig. 1.2. Formation of NH_4^+ ion.

The bond formed is indistinguishable from a normal covalent bond because all electrons are alike irrespective of their source. Thus, in the modern terminology, there is no distinction between a covalent and a coordinate bond. Other examples of coordinate covalent bond are H_3O^+, BF_4^-, BCl_3 and NH_3 addition compound, SO_2, SO_3, Al_2Cl_6, SO_4^{2-}, O_3, CO etc.

Lewis Structures

In the formation of a molecule, only the valence electrons are involved as the inner electrons are well protected and are generally not involved in the bond formation.

G.N. Lewis introduced simple symbols to denote the valence shell electrons in an atom. The valence shell electrons are represented by dots placed around the letter symbol of the atom. Each dot represents an electron. These symbols are known as Lewis symbols or electron dot symbols. A few examples are

·Li ·Be· ·B· ·C· ·N· O: ·F: :Ne:

The Lewis structures provide a picture of bonding in molecule and ions in terms of the shared pair of electrons and the octet rule. While such a picture may not explain the bonding and behavior of a molecule completely, it does help in understanding the formation and properties of the molecule to a large extent. Lewis dot structures can be written by adopting the following basic steps:

- Calculate the total number of electrons available in the valence shell of all the atoms present. In case of ionic species, add number of electrons equal to the negative charge if the species is an anion and if the species is a cation, subtract the number of electrons equal to the units of positive charge.
- Select the central atom (usually the least electronegative atom) and draw the skeletal structure by guessing which atom is linked to which other atom. Also remember hydrogen and fluorine usually occupies terminal positions.
- Put one shared pair of electrons between every two atoms to represent a single bond and use remaining electron pair either for multiple bonding or to show them as lone pairs keeping in mind that octet of each atom is completed.

For example, Lewis structure of CO molecule

Number of valence electrons of carbon = 4

Number of valence electrons of oxygen = 6

Total number of valence electrons of C and O = 4 + 6 = 10

The skeleton structure of CO is written as CO

Drawing of a single bond (one shared e^- pair) between C & O and completing the octet on O, the remaining two electrons are the lone pair on C.

:C: :O:

However, the above structure does not have an octet on carbon and oxygen atom has an extra pair of electrons. Oxygen donates its one electron pair to carbon and this electron pair becomes common to both atoms (C and O) and thus satisfies the octet rule for atoms. This new bond formed between C and O is known as coordinate bond which is similar to covalent bond in all respects. It is indicates by $\rightarrow$; the tail represents the donor atom (O in present case) and head represents the acceptor atom (C in present case)

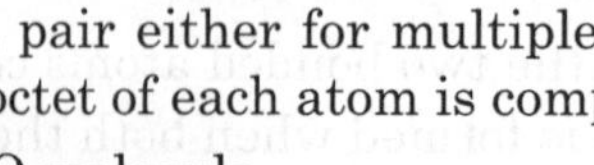

Thus, carbon and oxygen atoms are bonded by a triple bond in CO molecule.

Limitations of Octet Rule

Though the octet rule is very useful, is not universal. It is quite useful for understanding the structures of most of the compounds but there are some exceptions to this rule. These are

1. There are some compounds where central atom has less than 8 electrons **(electron deficient compounds)** and does not satisfy the octet rule. For example, $BeCl_2$, BF_3, $AlCl_3$ etc.
2. A number of compounds are known in which central atom has more than 8 electrons (*i.e.*, **expanded octet or hypervalent compounds**). Obviously the octet rule does not apply in such cases. For example, PCl_5, SF_6, IF_7 etc.
3. According to octet rule, which is based upon the chemical inertness of the noble gases, atoms of noble gases are inert and should not form any compound but various compounds of noble gases like XeF_2, XeF_4, XeF_6, KrF_2 etc. are well known and have been actually prepared.
4. The octet rule is not satisfied for all the atoms in compounds having odd number of electrons. For example, NO (nitric oxide), NO_2 (nitrogen dioxide) etc.
5. This rule does not account for the shape of molecules.
6. This rule is unable to predict the energy changes during the formation of a covalent bond.

1.3 VALENCE SHELL ELECTRON PAIR REPULSION (VSEPR) THEORY

The first simple theory that was put forward to explain the shape of molecules is known as **Valence Shell Electron Pair Repulsion (VSEPR) theory**. This theory was given by **Sidgwick and Powell** in 1940 and was further improved by **Nyholm and Gillespie** in 1957.

1.3.1 Postulates of VSEPR Theory

The main postulates of VSEPR theory are:

1. The electron pairs in the valence shell around the central atom of a molecule repel each other because their electron clouds are negatively charged. As a result, they tend to orient in space as far as possible in order to minimize the repulsions and maximize the distance between them.
2. There are two types of valence shell electron pairs *viz.*, bond pairs and lone pairs. The shared pairs of electron are called as **bond pairs** while the electron pairs which are not involved in bond formation are called as the **lone pairs**. Presence of lone pairs on the central atom in the molecule causes certain distortions in the expected regular geometry of the molecule. The order of repulsion between different types of electron pairs is as follows:

   Lone pair – Lone pair > Lone pair – Bond pair > Bond pair – Bond pair.

   The repulsive forces decrease sharply as the angle between the electron pairs increases. The repulsion is strong at 90°, much weaker at 120° and weakest at 180°.
3. In VSEPR theory, a multiple bond is treated as if it is a single bond. The electron pairs in multiple bonds are treated collectively as a single super pair.

   The repulsion caused by bonds increases with increase in the number of bonded pairs between two atoms *i.e.* a triple bond causes more repulsion than a double bond which in turn causes more repulsion than a single bond.
4. The shape of a molecule depends upon the number and type of valence shell electron pairs around the central atom. When the valence shell of central atom contains only bond pairs, the molecule assumes symmetrical geometry due to even repulsions between them. For example, the molecules such as CH_4, PF_5, SF_6 etc. have regular geometries.

However, the geometry is distorted when lone pairs are also present along with bond pairs due to uneven repulsive forces. For example, NH_3, H_2O etc.

5. When two or more resonance structures can depict a molecule, the VSEPR model is applicable to any such structure.

The **Table 1.1** shows the shapes of some molecules and ions on the basis of number and type of electron pairs around the central atom.

Table 1.1: Shapes of Some Simple Molecules on the Basis of VSEPR Theory.

Type of molecule	Number of bond pairs (B)	Number of lone pairs (E)	Shape of the molecule	Approximate bond angles	Example
AB_2	2	0	Linear	180°	$BeCl_2$, $HgCl_2$, CO_2
AB_3	3	0	Trigonal planar	120°	BF_3, CO_3^{2-}, NO_3^-, $AlCl_3$, SO_3
AB_2E	2	1	Angular	120°	SO_2, $SnCl_2$, O_3, NO_2^-
AX_4	4	0	Tetrahedral	109.28°	CH_4, SiF_4, NH_4^+, PO_4^{3-}, SO_4^{2-}, ClO_4^-
AB_3E	3	1	Trigonal pyramidal	—	PCl_3, NCl_3, PH_3, H_3O^+
AB_2E_2	2	2	Angular	109.28°	H_2O, SCl_2, Cl_2O, OF_2, H_2S, NH_2^-
AX_5	5	0	Trigonal bipyramidal	120° and 90°	PCl_5, $SbCl_5$, AsF_5
AB_4E	4	1	Distorted tetrahedral	—	SF_4, $TeCl_4$
AB_3E_2	3	2	T-Shape	90°	ClF_3, BrF_3
AB_2E_3	2	3	Linear	180°	XeF_2, I_3^-, ICl_2^-
AB_6	6	0	Octahedral	90°	SF_6
AB_5E	5	1	Square pyramidal	90°	ClF_5, IF_5, BrF_5, ICl_5
AB_4E_2	4	2	Square planar	90°	XeF_4
AB_7	7	0	Pentagonal bipyramidal	72° and 90°	IF_7
AB_6E	6	1	Pentagonal pyramidal	Around 72° and 90°	$XeOF_5^-$, IOF_5^{2-}

In the above table, the molecule is represented by "ABE" notation, where (A = Central atom, B = Bond pair, E = Lone pair).

Calculation of electron pairs, bond pairs and lone pairs in a molecule

1. **Electron pairs:** Total number of electron pairs around the central atom
   = 1/2 (Number of valence electrons of central atom
   + Number of atoms linked to central atom by single bonds)

For ions carrying negative charge, add number of electrons equal to the negative charge on the ion to the valence electrons of the central atom, while for ions carrying positive charge, subtract number of electrons equal to the positive charge from the valence electrons of the central atom.

2. **Bond pairs:** Number of atoms linked to central atom by single bonds.
3. **Lone pairs:** Total number of electron pairs – number of bond pairs.

1.3.2 Illustration and Applications of VSEPR Theory

1. In $BeCl_2$ molecule (AB_2 type molecule), the central atom Be has two bond pairs of electrons and no lone pair of electrons. According to VSEPR theory, the only way to keep them as far apart as possible is to arrange them at an angle of 180° to each other. Thus, the $BeCl_2$ molecule adopts a linear geometry **(Fig. 1.3)**. In general, all molecules of type AB_2 having only two bond pairs and no lone pair are linear.

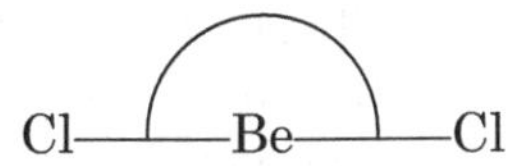

Fig. 1.3. $BeCl_2$ molecule.

2. In $SnCl_2$ molecule (AB_2E type molecule), there are three electron pairs around the Sn atom (one lone pair and two bond pairs), the overall arrangement is trigonal planar with a bond angle of 120°. Since the lone pair occupies one of the positions, the $SnCl_2$ molecule has a bent shape and because of lp-bp and bp-bp repulsions, Cl—Sn—Cl bond angle is less than 120°.
3. In NH_3 molecule (AB_3E type molecule), there are four electron pairs around the nitrogen atom *viz.*, three bond pairs and one lone pair. The overall arrangement of four electron pairs should be tetrahedral but because of lp-bp repulsions the HNH bond angle is less than 109.28° and therefore, the geometry of NH_3 is pyramidal **(Fig. 1.4)**.

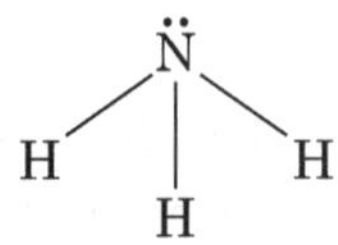

Fig. 1.4. NH_3 molecule.

4. In H_2O molecule (AB_2E_2 type molecule), the central oxygen atom also contains four bond pairs *i.e.* two bond pairs and two lone pairs of electron. The overall arrangement of four electron pairs is tetrahedral, but because of lp-lp and lp-bp repulsions, the HOH bond angle in H_2O is less than 109.28° (normal tetrahedral angle) and the molecule has a bent or angular shape **(Fig. 1.5)**.

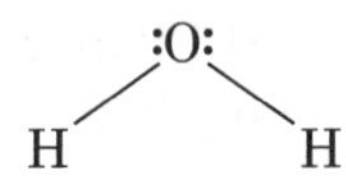

Fig. 1.5. H_2O molecule.

5. In SF_4 molecule (AB_4E type molecule), the central sulphur atom has five electron pairs whose arrangement should be trigonal bipyramidal in which a lone pair occupies one of the positions. However, it may be noted that the lone pair can either occupy an axial position **[Fig. 1.6(*a*)]** or an equatorial position **[Fig. 1.6(*b*)]** as shown below:

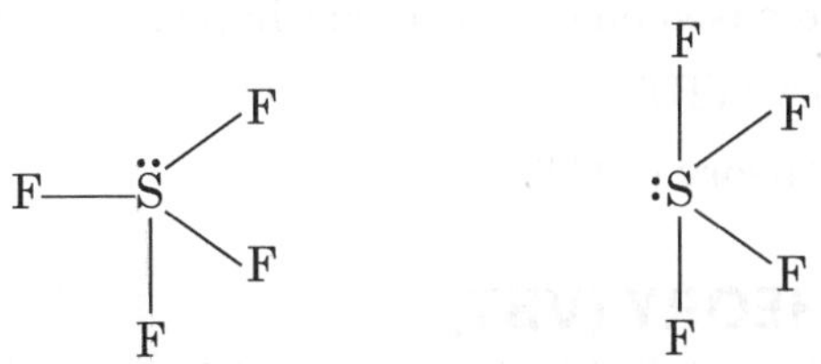

(*a*) *lp* in axial position (*b*) *lp* in equatorial position (Sea-saw structure)

Fig. 1.6. The position of lone pair in SF_4 molecule.

This can be easily decided by counting the repulsions at these positions. In arrangement (*a*), the lone pair is present in an axial position, which leads to three lp-bp repulsions at 90° and one lp-bp repulsion at 120°, whereas in arrangement (*b*), the lone pair is in an equatorial position and there are two lp-bp repulsions at 90° and two lp-bp repulsions 120°. According to VSEPR theory (postulate number 2) the repulsions between neighbouring electron pairs decrease with increase in bond angle. Therefore, the repulsions between electron pairs at 120° can be neglected in comparison to one at 90°. Hence, arrangement (*b*) is preferred over (*a*).

6. ClF_3 molecule (AB_3E_2 type molecule), also contains five electron pairs like SF_4 molecule. It is also expected to have trigonal bipyramidal geometry in which two positions are occupied by the lone pairs **(Fig. 1.7)**. The two lone pairs can occupy the following three positions:

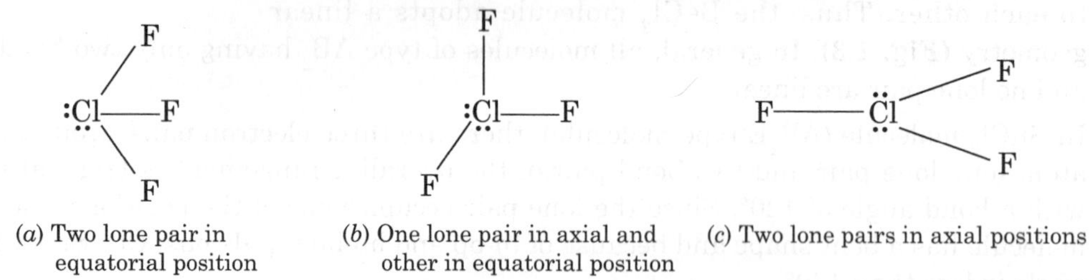

Fig. 1.7. Position of lone pairs in ClF_3 molecule.

On the basis of repulsions at different positions, the structure (*a*) appears to be the most stable. If we compare arrangement (*a*) with (*b*) it has no lp-lp repulsions and in comparison to arrangement (*c*) it has less lp-bp repulsions (postulate 2 of VSEPR theory). Thus, ClF_3 adopts geometry (*a*) and is having T-shaped structure.

1.3.3 Limitations of VSEPR Theory

The VSEPR model is successful in predicting geometries of a large number of molecules, yet it has many limitations. These are

1. This theory is not useful for predicting the shapes of transition metal complexes.
2. It does not help in predicting the exact bond angle in molecules having distorted geometries.
3. This theory is applicable only to simple covalent compounds and is not useful for ionic compounds.

To explain the above limitations, two important theories called modern theories of covalent bond formation based on quantum mechanical principles have been proposed.

(*i*) Valence Bond Theory (VBT)

(*ii*) Molecular Orbital Theory (MOT).

1.4 VALENCE BOND THEORY (VBT)

The valence bond theory was introduced by **Heitler and London** in 1927 and modified later by **Pauling and Slater** in 1931. Pauling was awarded the 1954 Chemistry Nobel prize for developing this theory.

1.4.1 Postulates of Valence Bond Theory

1. For the formation of a covalent bond, two atoms must come close to each other so that the orbitals of one atom overlap with that of another.
2. Overlapping orbitals must have (*a*) unpaired electron (*b*) opposite spin of electrons.
3. After overlapping, a now localized bond orbital is formed which has maximum probability of finding electrons.
4. Strength of the bond depends upon the extent of orbital overlapping. Greater overlapping results in
   (*i*) More attraction, therefore more bond energy, high bond strength and high bond stability
   (*ii*) Shorter bond length.
5. The extent of overlapping depends upon the nature of orbitals involved and the type of overlapping. For example, *s*-orbitals are spherically symmetrical and thus only head on overlapping is possible. On the other hand, *p*-orbitals are directionally concentrated and thus show higher extent of overlapping *i.e.,* either head on overlapping or lateral overlapping

$$2s\text{-}2s < 2s\text{-}2p < 2p\text{-}2p.$$

Two types of bonds are formed on account of overlapping *viz.* sigma (σ) bond and pi (π) bond.

1. **Sigma (σ) bond:** When a bond is formed between two atoms by the overlap of their atomic orbitals along the internuclear axis (end to end or head on overlap), the bond formed is called **sigma bond**. In sigma bond formation, maximum overlap is possible between electron clouds and hence, it is a strong bond.

   Sigma bonds can be formed by three types of the overlapping.
   (*i*) *s-s* overlapping (*ii*) *s-p* overlapping (*iii*) *p-p* overlapping.

(*i*) ***s-s* overlapping:** Here, overlapping takes place between atoms having half filled s-orbitals in their outermost energy shell.

For example, formation of hydrogen molecule (Fig. 1.8)

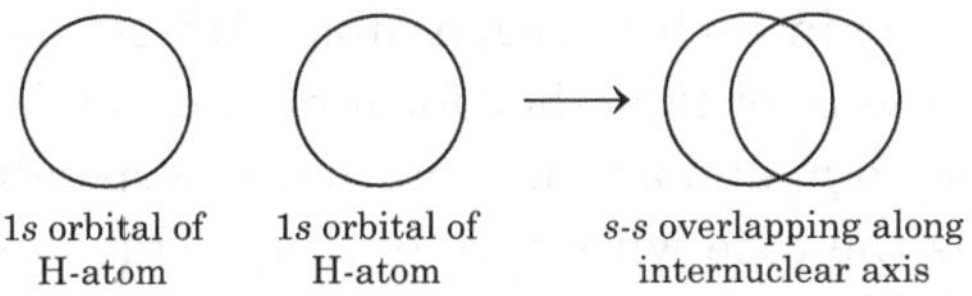

Fig. 1.8. Formation of Hydrogen molecule.

Other example, LiH

(*ii*) ***s-p* overlapping:** In this type of overlapping, half filled *s*-orbitals of one atom overlaps with the half filled *p*-orbital of another atom.

For example, formation of hydrogen fluoride **(Fig. 1.9)**

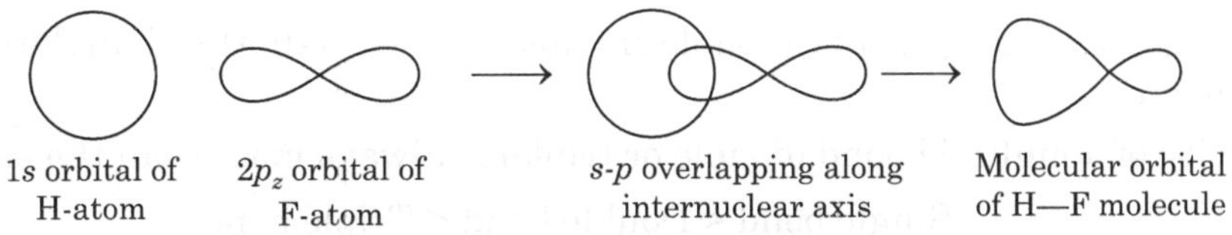

Fig. 1.9. Formation of HF molecule.

Other examples, HCl, H_2O, NH_3 etc.

(*iii*) *p-p* Overlapping: Here, half filled *p*-orbital of one atom overlaps with the half filled *p*-orbital of the other, as in case of fluorine molecule.

Electronic configuration of F = $1s^2\,2s^2\,2p_x^2\,2p_y^2\,2p_z^2$.

The fluorine molecule is produced by the overlapping of $2p_z$ orbitals of two fluorine atoms (Fig. 1.10).

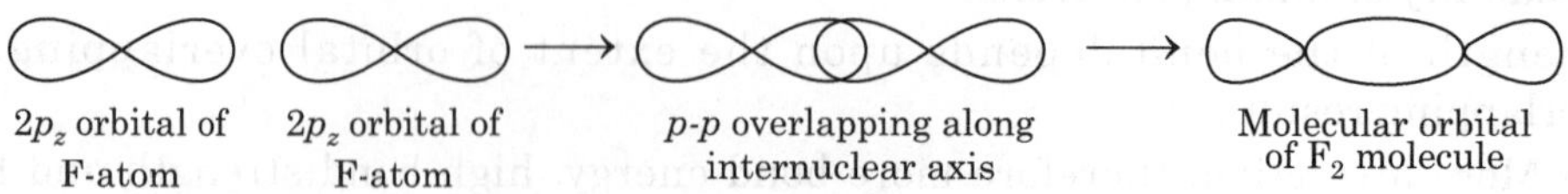

Fig. 1.10. Formation of F_2 molecule.

Other examples, Cl_2, Br_2 etc.

Note: If *z* axis is chosen as the internuclear axis, no overlapping can take place between *s* and p_x or p_y orbital or p_x and p_y orbitals *i.e.,* there is zero overlap.

2. Pi (π) bond: This type of bond is formed by the sideways or lateral overlapping of the half filled *p*-orbitals. This type of overlapping takes place perpendicular to the internuclear axis.

For example, Formation of nitrogen molecule (Fig. 1.11)

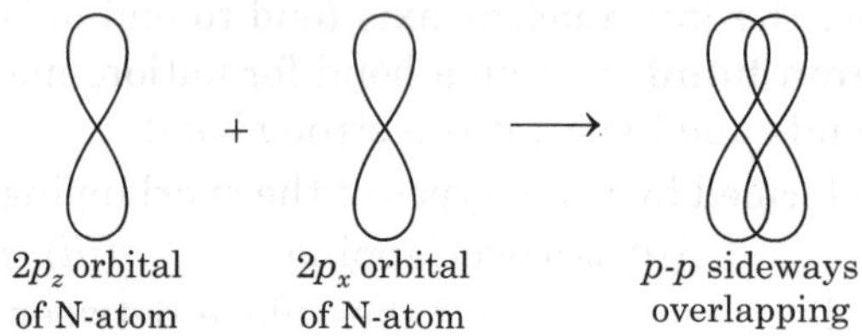

Fig. 1.11. Formation of nitrogen molecule

There are three *p*-electrons in each nitrogen atom ($1s^2\,2s^2\,2p_x^1\,2p_y^1\,2p_z^1$). The p_z orbital of one nitrogen overlaps with the p_z of the other forming a σ bond. On the other hand. p_x and p_y orbitals are perpendicular to p_z and are also mutually perpendicular. So, the p_x-p_x overlap occurs laterally and same is the case with p_y-p_y overlap. This lateral or sideways overlap of orbitals gives rise to pi bond. Thus, the nitrogen molecule has one sigma and two pi bond.

All single bonds are sigma bonds. A double bond comprises of one σ and one π bond while, a triple bond comprises of one σ and two π bonds.

1. Bond energy and bond strength increases from a single bond to a triple bond.

   Single bond < Double bond < Triple bond

2. Bond length of a multiple bond (double or triple) is always shorter than the corresponding single bond.

3. Reactivity of a multiple bond (double or triple) is always more than the single bond.

   Single bond < Double bond < Triple bond

The various points of differences between sigma and pi bond are summarized in **Table 1.2.**

Table 1.2 : Differences between Sigma and pi Bonds

	Sigma (σ) bond		Pi (π) bond
1.	It arises due to head on or end to end overlapping. It includes *s-s*, *s-p* or *p-p* overlapping.	1.	It arises due to sideways or lateral overlapping. It includes *p-p* overlapping.
2.	Stronger bond.	2.	Less strong than σ bond.
3.	Bond energy of σ bond is greater than π bond.	3.	Bond energy less than σ bond.
4.	More stable and less reactive bond.	4.	More reactive and less stable bond.
5.	It can exist independently.	5.	It always exists with a σ bond.
6.	The electron cloud is symmetrical about the internuclear axis.	6.	The electron cloud is above and below the plane of internuclear axis *i.e.*, unsymmetrical.
7.	There can be free rotation of atoms around this bond.	7.	Free rotation is not possible around this bond.

1.5 HYBRIDIZATION OF ATOMIC ORBITALS

Originally, according to valence bond theory, only unpaired electrons in atoms can participate in covalent bonding. As such, it can explain the formation of covalent bonds in simple molecules like H_2, Cl_2 and HCl but not in complex molecules like $BeCl_2$, BCl_3 and CH_4. On the basis of electronic configuration, Be ($1s^2 2s^2$) should be inert (no unpaired electron therefore no bond formation), B ($1s^2 2s^2 2p^1$) should be monovalent as it has one impaired electron and C ($1s^2 2s^2 2p^2$) having two unpaired electrons should be divalent. However, beryllium is divalent in its compounds (*e.g.*, BeF_2, BeH_2, $BeCl_2$ etc.), boron is trivalent (*e.g.*, BF_3, BH_3, BCl_3 etc.) and carbon is tetravalent (*e.g.*, CH_4, CCl_4, etc.). Therefore, it is not possible to explain the valencies of these atoms on the basis of simple valence bond theory. To explain these observations, the valence bond theory has been supplemented by the concept of hybridization proposed by **Pauling and Slater**.

Let us understand this concept by taking an example of CH_4 molecule. The ground state electronic configuration of C = $1s^2 2s^2 2p^2$. The valence shell of carbon can be represented by

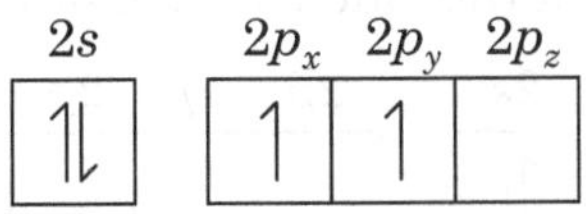

There are only two half filled orbitals in carbon, therefore its should have bonding capacity of two (*i.e.*, bivalent) but in actual practice it has bonding capacity of four (*i.e.*, tetravalent) in all its compounds like CH_4, CCl_4 etc. In order to explain this tetravalency, it was proposed that one of the electrons from 2*s* filled orbital is promoted to the empty 2*p* orbital which is higher in energy state. After promotion of electron (in excited state), the configuration of carbon is represented by

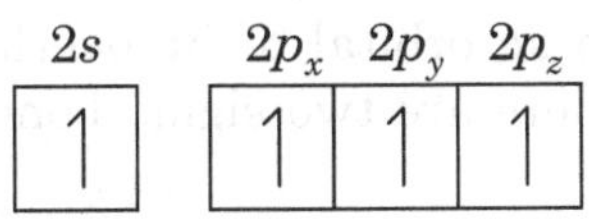

As a result, four half filled orbitals are formed in the valence shell which accounts for the tetravalency of carbon, but the four bonds formed will not be equivalent. This is because one C—H bond will be formed by the overlap of 2*s* orbitals and three C—H bonds by the overlap of 2*p* orbitals. But in actual practice, most of the carbon compounds have all the four bonds equivalent. The equivalent character of the bonds can be explained with the concept of hybridization.

Hybridization is defined as the intermixing of the atomic orbitals belonging to the same atom but having slightly different energies so that a redistribution of energy takes place between them, resulting in the formation of new orbitals of equal energies and identical shapes. The new orbitals thus formed are known as **hybrid orbitals.**

1.5.1 Types of Hybridization

1. ***sp* Hybridization (linear or diagonal hybridization):** In *sp* hybridization, one *s* and one *p*-orbital belonging to the same main shell of an atom mix together to form two new equivalent *sp*-hybrid orbitals as shown in **Fig. 1.12.**

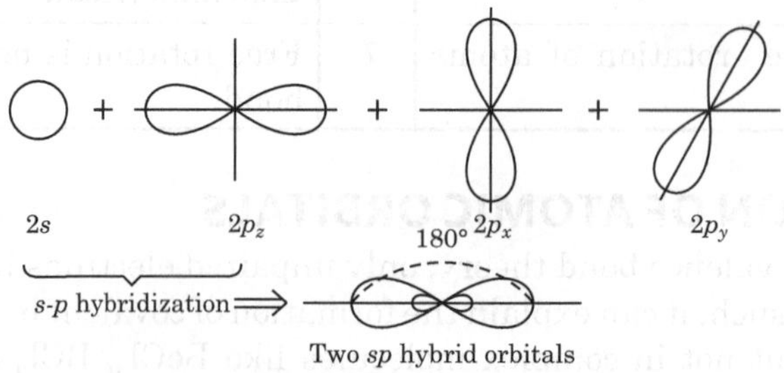

Fig. 1.12. Formation of *sp* hybrid orbitals.

The *sp* hybrid orbitals try to remain as far apart as possible and therefore, adopts linear geometry, making a bond angle of 180° between the two orbitals. Each of *sp*-hybridized orbital has 50% *s*-character and 50% *p*-character. It may be noted that each *sp*-hybridized orbital contains one large lobe and one small lobe. The size of large lobe is much bigger than the original *p*-orbital. The remaining two *p*-orbitals, which do not participate in hybridization, remain as such. The geometry of molecules such as $BeCl_2$, BeH_2, BeF_2 etc. can be explained by *sp* hybridization.

For example, Be in $BeCl_2$

The electronic configuration of the valence shell of Be is

2s	$2p_x$	$2p_y$	$2p_z$
⇅			

The 2*s* electrons are decoupled and one electron is promoted to the *p*-orbital.

2s	$2p_x$	$2p_y$	$2p_z$
1	1		

The *s* and *p* orbital, each now containing one unpaired electron, hybridized to give two *sp* hybridized orbitals. Each *sp* orbital of Be overlaps with a *p*-orbital of chlorine to form a sigma bond. Thus, there are two sigma bonds in $BeCl_2$. This is represented in **Fig. 1.13.**

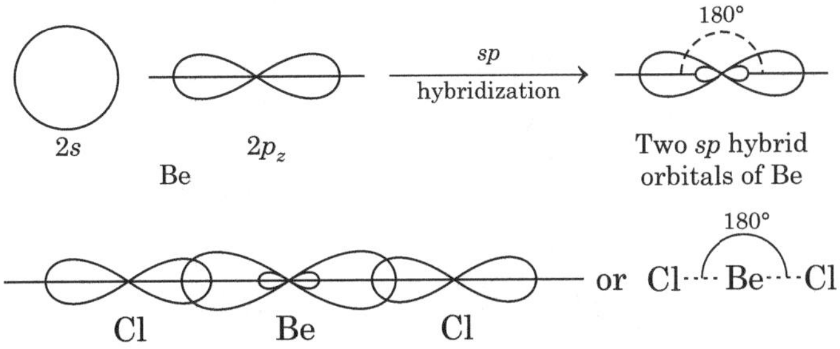

Fig. 1.13. Formation of $BeCl_2$ molecule.

The molecule is linear and the bond angle is 180°. *Other examples are:* C_2H_2, CO_2, BeF_2, BeH_2 etc.

2. ***sp*² Hybridization (Trigonal planar hybridization):** In sp^2 hybridization, one *s* and two *p*-orbitals of the same shell of an atom mix to form three new equivalent sp^2 hybrid orbitals **(Fig. 1.14)**. The three hybrid orbitals trying to remain as far apart as possible thus, adopts trigonal planar arrangement making an angle of 120° with one-another. Each sp^2 hybrid orbital has 33% *s*-character and 67% *p*-character.

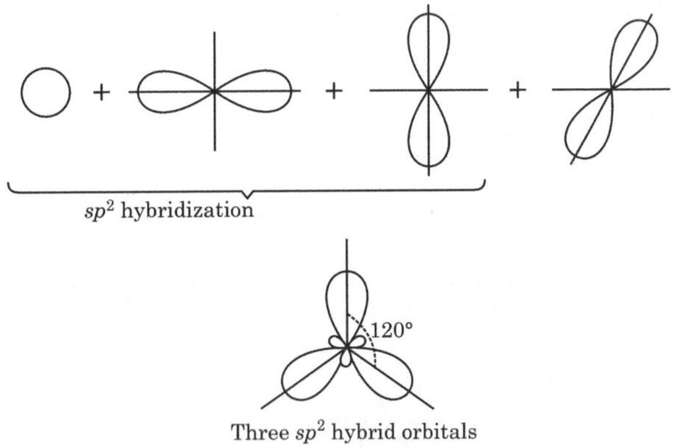

Fig. 1.14. Formation of sp^2 hybrid orbitals.

For example, BF_3

Outermost shell electronic configuration of Boron = $2s^2 2p^1$

2s	$2p_x$	$2p_y$	$2p_z$
⇅	1		

After decoupling and promotion

2s	$2p_x$	$2p_y$	$2p_z$
1	1	1	

The three orbitals *i.e.,* one 2*s* orbital and two 2*p*-orbitals hybridize to give three sp^2 hybrid orbitals. In BF_3 molecule, the three-sp^2 orbitals of boron overlap with the half filled *p*-orbitals of fluorine to form three sigma bonds as shown in **Fig. 1.15**.

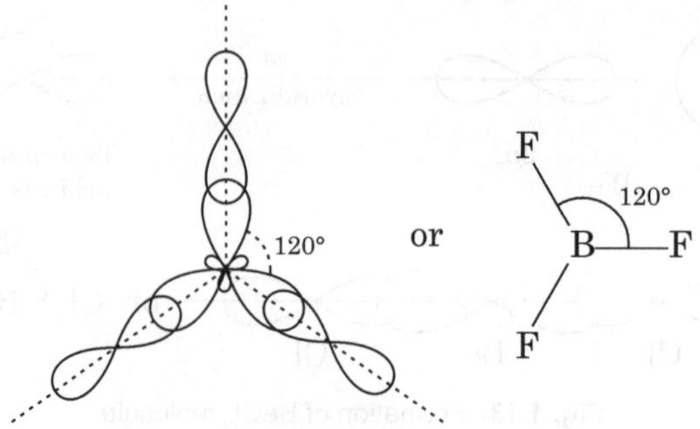

Fig. 1.15. Formation of BF_3 molecule.

Thus, BF_3 molecule is trigonal planar and the bond angle is 120°. *Other examples are:* BH_3, NO_3^-, C_2H_4 etc.

3. ***sp*³ hybridization (tetrahedral hybridization):** In sp^3 hybridization, one *s* and three *p*-orbitals belonging to the same shell of an atom mix together to form four new equivalent sp^3 hybrid orbitals **(Fig. 1.16)**. These four hybrid orbitals are directed towards the four corners of a regular tetrahedron and make an angle of 109.28° with one another. Each sp^3 hybrid orbital has 25% *s*-character and 75% *p*-character.

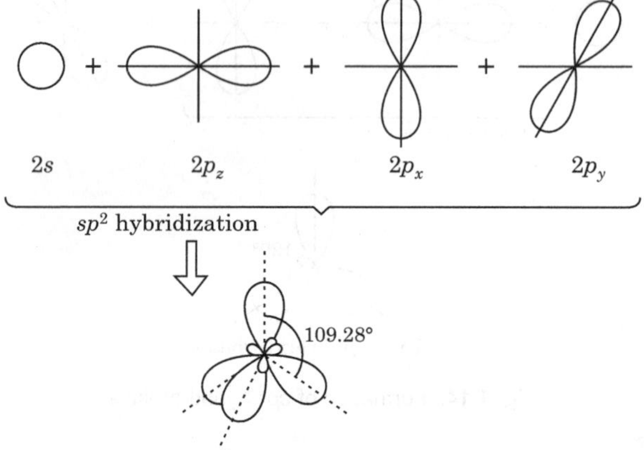

Fig. 1.16. Formation of sp^3 hybrid orbitals.

For example, CH_4

Outermost shell electronic configuration of C = $2s^2 2p^2$

$2s$	$2p_x$	$2p_y$	$2p_z$
⇅	↑	↑	

After decoupling and promotion

$2s$	$2p_x$	$2p_y$	$2p_z$
↑	↑	↑	↑

In carbon, one 2*s* orbital and three 2*p*-orbitals overlap to give four sp^3 hybrid orbitals. Each sp^3 hybrid orbital of C overlaps with the half filled *s*-orbital of hydrogen to form a sigma bond. Thus, there are four sigma bonds in CH_4 **(Fig. 1.17)**.

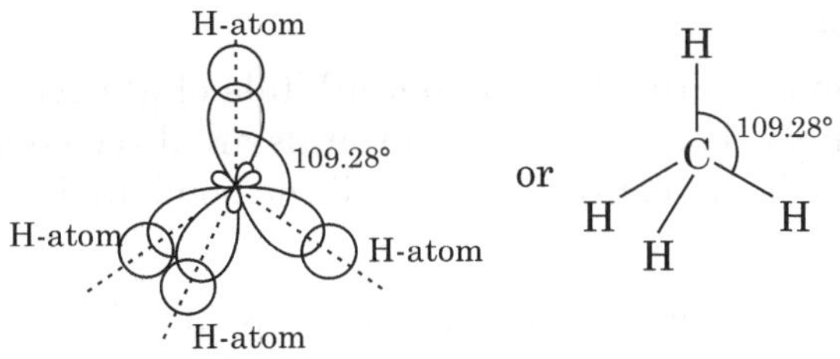

Fig. 1.17. Formation of CH_4 molecule.

Thus, CH_4 is tetrahedral molecule with a bond angle of 109.28°. *Other examples are:* NH_3, SO_4^{2-}, ClO_4^-, C_2H_6 etc.

Hybridization Involving *d*-orbitals

There are several types of hybridization involving *d*-orbitals. Since the *d*-orbitals have a relatively complex shape, we will consider here only some of the common types. The most important of these are sp^3d and sp^3d^2 hybridization.

1. sp^3d Hybridization

In this type of hybridization one *s*-orbital, three *p*-orbitals and one *d*-orbital of almost equal energy hybridize to give five equivalent sp^3d hybrid orbitals.

For example, PCl_5

The outermost shell electronic configuration of P = $3s^2\ 3p^3$

3s	3p			3d				
↑↓	↑	↑	↑					

In the excited state, the configuration is

3s	3p			3d				
↑	↑	↑	↑	↑				

sp^3d^2 Hybridization

Each of the five sp^3d hybrid orbital overlaps with the half filled *p*-orbital of chlorine forming five P-Cl bonds having trigonal bipyramidal geometry **(Fig. 1.18)**. It may be noted here that all the bond angles are not equal. Three bonds (equatorial bonds) lie in the same plane making an angle of 120° with each other and the other two bonds (axial bonds) lying above and below the plane of equatorial bonds making an angle of 90° with the plane.

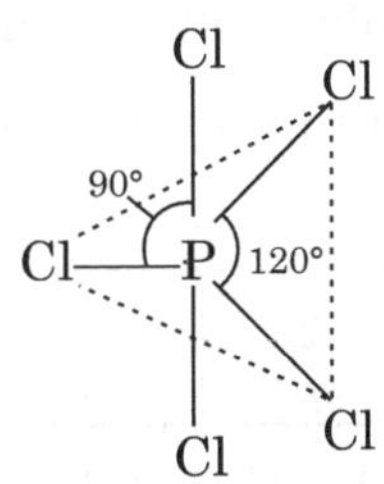

Fig. 1.18. PCl_5 molecule (Trigonal bipyramidal geometry).

Other examples are: XeF_2, $SbCl_5$, SF_4, ClF_3, I_3^- etc.

2. sp^3d^2 Hybridization

In sp^3d^2 hybridization, one *s*, three *p* and two *d*-orbitals of almost same energy hybridize to give six sp^3d^2 hybrid orbitals. These six hybrid orbitals are directed towards the corners of an octahedron. All the six bonds are equivalent and all the bond angles are equal to 90°.

For example: SF_6

The outermost shell electronic configuration of $S = 3s^2 3p^4$

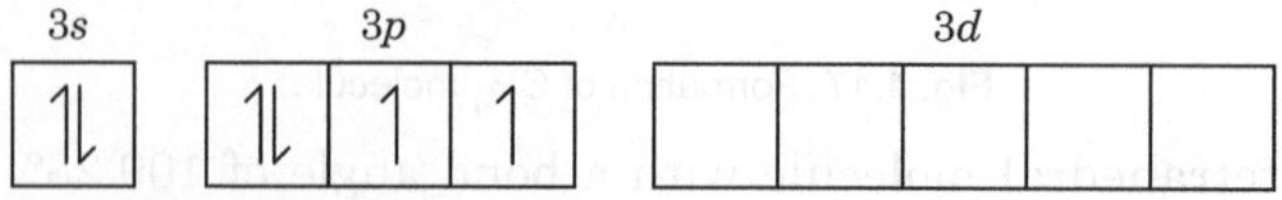

In the excited state, the configuration is

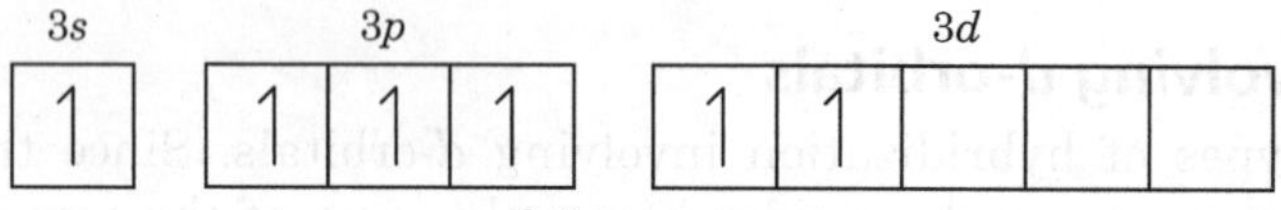

sp^3d^2 Hybridization

Each of the six hybrid orbitals overlaps with the 2*p*-orbitals of fluorine to form SF_6 molecule having octahedral geometry **(Fig. 1.19)**.

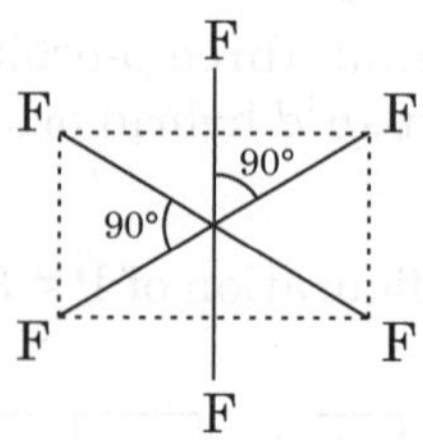

Fig. 1.19. SF_6 molecule (Octahedral geometry).

Other examples are, IF_5, SeF_4, SiF_6, BrF_5 etc.

Predicting the hybrid state of the central atom:

$$\text{Number of hybrid orbitals (X)} = \frac{1}{2}\,[\text{VE} + \text{MA} - c + a]$$

where VE = Number of valence electrons of the central atom

MA = Number of monovalent atoms surrounding the central atom

c = charge on the cation (if the given species is polyatomic cation)

a = charge on the anion (if the given species is polyatomic anion)

Note: Only monovalent atom (MA) are to be considered. For divalent atom like Oxygen, MA = 0 (zero).

Value of X	2	3	4	5	6	7
Hybridization	sp	sp^2	sp^3	sp^3d	sp^3d^2	sp^3d^3

A few examples to predict the hybridization of the central atom and shape of the molecule/ion are given below in **Table 1.3**.

Table 1.3: Hybridization and Shape of Some Common Molecules

Molecule/ species	Number of hybrid orbitals (*X*)	Hybridization	Hybrid orbitals containing lone pairs	Shape
CO_2	= 1/2 [4] = 2	*sp*	0	Linear
BeH_2	= 1/2 [2 + 2] = 2	*sp*	0	Linear
BCl_3	= 1/2 [3 + 3] = 3	sp^2	0	Triangular planar
CH_3^+	= 1/2 [4 + 3 – 1] = 3	sp^2	0	Triangular planar
H_2O	= 1/2 [6 + 2] = 4	sp^3	2	*V*-shape (bent)
CCl_4	= 1/2 [4 + 4] = 4	sp^3	0	Tetrahedral
NH_4^+	= 1/2 [5 + 4 – 1] = 4	sp^3	0	Tetrahedral
SO_4^{2-}	= 1/2 [6 + 2] = 4	sp^3	0	Tetrahedral
H_3O^+	= 1/2 [6 + 3 – 1] = 4	sp^3	1	Pyramidal
PCl_5	= 1/2 [5 + 5] = 5	sp^3d	0	Trigonal bipyramidal
I_3^-	= 1/2 [7 + 2 + 1] = 5	sp^3d	3	Linear
SF_6	= 1/2 [6 + 6] = 6	sp^3d^2	0	Octahedral
IF_5	= 1/2 [7 + 5] = 6	sp^3d^2	1	Square pyramidal
IF_7	= 1/2 [7 + 7] = 7	sp^3d^3	0	Pentagonal bipyramidal

1.5.2 Limitations of Valance Bond Theory

Although VBT was very successful in explaining the properties and behavior of many compounds, yet it suffers from certain drawbacks. These are

1. It does not explain the electronic spectra of complexes.
2. It failed to explain the paramagnetic character of oxygen.
3. It does not discuss energies of electrons.

1.6 MOLECULAR ORBITAL THEORY

Molecular orbital theory is more rational and more useful in comparison to valence bond theory. This theory was given by **F. Hund and R.S. Mulliken** in 1932.

1.6.1 Postulates of the Molecular Orbital Theory

1. When nuclei of two individual atoms come close to each other, their atomic orbitals (AOs) interact leading to the formation of molecular orbitals (MOs). After the formation of molecular orbitals, the atomic orbitals completely lose their identity.
2. Only those atomic orbitals can combine to form molecular orbitals, which have comparable energies and proper orientation. For example, 1*s* atomic orbital can overlap with 1*s* and not with 2*s*. Likewise, 2*s* atomic orbital can overlap either with 2*s* or $2p_z$ (if *z* is the internuclear axis); $2p_z$ with $2p_z$, $2p_y$ with $2p_y$ and so on.
3. The number of molecular orbitals formed is equal to the number of combining atomic orbitals. When two atomic orbitals combine, two molecular orbitals are formed, one

is known as **bonding molecular orbital** and the other is called as **antibonding molecular orbital**.

4. Molecular orbitals of a molecule are obtained by LCAO (Linear combination of atomic orbitals) of the bonded atoms. The LCAO can take place either by addition (constructive interaction) or subtraction (destructive interaction) of the wave functions of atomic orbitals involved.
5. If two identical waves are added, they combine constructively to produce bonding molecular orbitals. The amplitude of the bonding molecular orbital is denoted by ψ

$$\Psi(MO) = \psi_A + \psi_B$$

where ψ_A and ψ_B represents the amplitudes (or wave functions) of the electron waves of the atomic orbitals of the two atoms A and B respectively.

6. If two identical waves are subtracted, they combine destructively to produce antibonding molecular orbitals. The amplitude of the antibonding molecular orbital is denoted by ψ^*

$$\Psi^*(MO) = \psi_A - \psi_B$$

7. Probability of formation of molecular orbital is given by the square of the amplitude, we have

$$\psi^2 = (\psi_A + \psi_B)^2 = \psi_A^2 + \psi_B^2 + 2\psi_A\psi_B \quad \text{(for bonding molecular orbitals)}$$

$$\psi^{*2} = (\psi_A - \psi_B)^2 = \psi_A^2 + \psi_B^2 - 2\psi_A\psi_B \quad \text{(for antibonding molecular orbitals)}$$

Thus, $\psi^2 > (\psi^{*2})$

8. The bonding molecular orbitals are represented by σ, π, δ etc. and the corresponding antibonding molecular orbitals are represented by putting an asterisk *i.e.*, σ^*, π^*, δ^* etc.
9. The bonding molecular orbital has lower energy and greater stability whereas antibonding molecular orbital has higher energy and lesser stability than the energies and stability of the combining atomic orbitals.
10. The molecular orbitals are filled in the same way as atomic orbitals are filled and in accordance with Aufbau principle (MO are filled in order of increasing energy), Pauli's exclusion principle (MO may possess maximum of two electrons with opposite spins) and Hund's rule (pairing of electrons in degenerate molecular orbitals does not take place until each of them is singly filled).

Differences between bonding and antibonding molecular orbitals are given in **Table 1.4.**

Table 1.4 : Bonding Molecular Orbital *vs.* Antibonding Molecular Orbital.

Bonding Molecular Orbital (BMO)	Antibonding Molecular Orbital (ABMO)
A bonding atomic orbital is formed by the addition overlap of AOs.	An antibonding molecular orbital is formed by the subtraction overlap of AOs.
It has lower energy than the AOs from which it is formed.	It has higher energy than the AOs from which it is formed.
In BMO, the electron density is more in between the two nuclei of bonded atoms and hence the repulsion between the nuclei is very less. It therefore stabilizes the molecule.	In ABMO, the electron density is less in between the two nuclei of bonded atoms and hence the repulsion between the nuclei is high. It therefore destabilizes the molecule.

1.7 ENERGY LEVEL DIAGRAM FOR MOLECULAR ORBITALS

The relative energies of molecular orbitals depend upon:

1. The energies of combining atomic orbitals
2. The extent of overlapping between the atomic orbitals.

The greater the overlap, the more the bonding orbital is lowered and antibonding orbital is raised in energy relative to the atomic orbitals. For example, the overlapping is more effective in case of σ orbital (formed by head on overlapping) than that in π orbital (formed by lateral overlapping). As a result, the σMO is lower in energy than $\pi 2p_x$ or $\pi 2p_y$ MOs.

The energies of various MOs have been determined experimentally by spectroscopic studies. The MOs obtained by the combination of 1*s*, 2*s* and 2*p* orbitals can be arranged in order of increasing energy as follows:

$$\sigma 1s < \sigma^* 1s < \sigma 2s < \sigma^* 2s < \sigma 2p_z < \pi 2p_x = \pi 2p_x < \pi^* 2p_x = \pi^* 2p_y < \sigma^* 2p_z$$

$\rightarrow$ Increasing energy

However, experimental evidences have revealed that the above sequence of energy levels of MOs is not correct for all molecules. The molecular orbitals of O_2, F_2 and Ne_2 follow the above mentioned order of energy levels whereas for molecules upto N_2 (*i.e.*, Li_2, Be_2, B_2, C_2 and N_2), the $\sigma 2p_z$ MO is higher in energy than the $\pi 2p_x$ and $\pi 2p_y$ MOs. This change in sequence of energy levels of MOs is due to the fact that in some cases, there is a very small energy gap between 2*s* and $2p_z$ atomic orbitals, as a result their mixing takes place which leads to change in energies of the MOs.

Mixing of Orbitals

We have seen that when 2*s* AOs of two atoms combine, two molecule orbitals *viz.* $\sigma 2s$ and $\sigma^* 2s$ MOs are formed and when $2p_z$ AOs of two atom combine, $\sigma 2p_z$ and $\sigma^* 2p_z$ MOs are formed. However, if the energy difference between 2*s* and 2*p* atomic orbitals is quite less (as in case of Li_2, Be_2, B_2, C_2 and N_2), there is a possibility of mixing of 2*s* AOs of one atom with the $2p_z$ AOs of other atom as they are of same symmetry. Hence, due to this mixing of 2*s* and 2*p* atomic orbitals, the energies of all the four MOs *i.e.*, $\sigma 2s$ and $\sigma^* 2s$, $\sigma 2p_z$ and $\sigma^* 2p_z$ change and $\sigma 2p_z$ becomes higher in energy as compared to $\pi 2p_x$ and $\pi 2p_y$ MOs.

Note: It is important to note here that π MOs are not involved in mixing and secondly the energy difference between 2*s* and 2*p* atomic orbitals is significantly high in case of O_2 and F_2, therefore mixing of AOs is ruled out in these molecules.

Thus, for homonuclear diatomic molecules, the sequence of energy levels of MOs is as follows:

- **For H_2 to N_2:** $\sigma 1s < \sigma^* 1s < \sigma 2s < \sigma^* 2s < [\pi 2p_x = \pi 2p_y], < \sigma 2p_z < [\pi^* 2p_x = \pi^* 2p_y] < \sigma^* 2p_z$
- **For O_2 to Ne_2:** $\sigma 1s < \sigma^* 1s < \sigma 2s < \sigma^* 2s < \sigma 2p_z < [\pi 2p_x = \pi 2p_y] < [\pi^* 2p_x = \pi^* 2p_y] < \sigma^* 2p_z$

1.8 RELATIONSHIP BETWEEN ELECTRONIC CONFIGURATION AND MOLECULAR BEHAVIOUR

Molecular orbital energy level diagram provides important information regarding the behaviour of molecules. The electronic configuration conveyed the following informations regarding the molecules:

I. Stability of a Molecule

If N_a and N_b represent number of electrons present in antibonding and bonding molecular orbitals respectively, then

1. the molecule is stable if $N_b > N_a$ (because there is net force of attraction due to the presence of greater number of electrons in bonding MO over antibonding MO).
2. the molecule is unstable if $N_b < N_a$ (because there is net force of repulsion due to the presence of greater number of electrons in antibonding MO over bonding MO)
3. If $N_b = N_a$, the molecule is again unstable because there is no net force of attraction.

II. Bond Order

Bond order of a molecule is a measure of the strength of the bond between two atoms. Mathematically,

$$BO = \frac{N_b - N_a}{2}.$$

The bond order provides the following informations:

1. If the value of BO is positive, the molecule is stable and if the BO is negative or zero, the molecule is unstable and does not exist. Fractional BO indicates that the molecule exists but it is unstable.
2. Knowing the BO, the number of covalent bonds between the atoms in the molecule can be predicted. The bond orders of 1, 2 and 3 indicates the presence of single, double and triple bonds, respectively in the molecule.
3. Dissociation energy of a molecule is directly proportional to its bond order and greater the bond dissociation energy, more stable will be the molecule. For example, nitrogen molecule having BO of 3 has greater bond dissociation energy than oxygen molecule that has a BO of 2.

$$\text{Stability} \propto \text{BO} \propto \text{Bond dissociation energy.}$$

4. BO is inversely proportional to the bond length.

$$BO \propto \frac{1}{\text{bond length}}$$

i.e., Higher the bond order, smaller is the bond length.

III. Magnetic Character of the Molecule

If all the electrons in a molecule are paired, the molecule is diamagnetic. On the other hand, if a molecule has some unpaired electrons, it is paramagnetic in nature.

Magnetic moment $\mu = \sqrt{n(n+1)}$ BM

where n is the number of unpaired electrons present in a molecule.

More the number of unpaired electrons in a molecule more will be its paramagnetic character.

1.9 BONDING IN HOMONUCLEAR DIATOMIC MOLECULES

1.9.1 Hydrogen Molecule (H_2)

Hydrogen molecule is formed by the combination of two hydrogen atoms. Therefore, H_2 molecule has a total of 2 electrons, so its molecular orbital configuration is $\sigma 1s^2$. The energy level diagram for hydrogen molecule is shown in **Fig. 1.20**. The bond order is given by

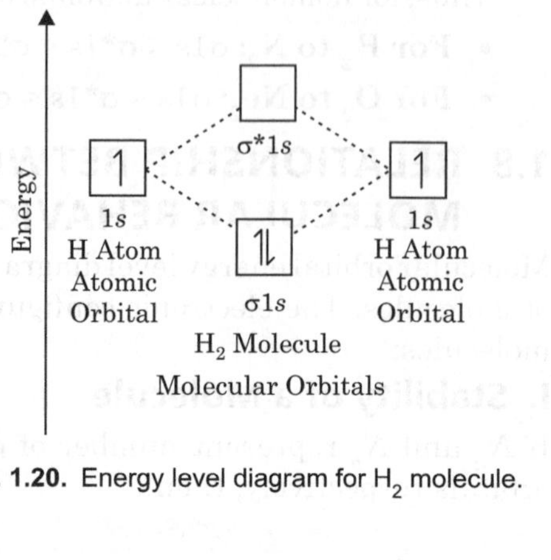

Fig. 1.20. Energy level diagram for H_2 molecule.

$$BO = \frac{1}{2}(2 - 0) = 1$$

(BO value 1 indicates single covalent bond between two H-atoms). As all the electrons in bonding as well as antibonding MO are paired, therefore, it is diamagnetic in nature.

1.9.2 Helium Molecule (He_2)

He_2 molecule has total of 4 electrons (two in each He-atom), so its molecular orbital configuration is

$$\sigma 1s^2 \sigma^* 1s^2.$$

The molecular orbital energy level diagram for helium molecule is shown in **Fig. 1.21**.

The bond order is given by

$$BO = \frac{1}{2}(2 - 2) = 0$$

(BO value zero indicates that no bond is formed between two He-atoms *i.e.*, He_2 molecule does not exist).

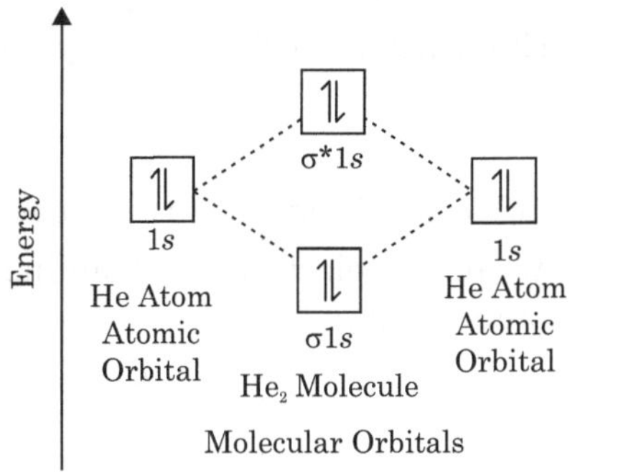

Fig. 1.21. Energy level diagram for He_2 molecule.

1.9.3 Lithium Molecule (Li_2)

Li_2 molecule has total of 6 electrons (three in each Li-atom), so its molecular orbital configuration is: $\sigma 1s^2 \sigma^* 1s^2 \sigma 2s^2$.

The molecular orbital energy level diagram for lithium molecule is shown in Fig. 1.22

$$BO = \frac{1}{2}(N_b - N_a) = \frac{1}{2}(4 - 2) = 1$$

(BO value 1 indicates single covalent bond between two Li-atoms).

As all the electrons in bonding as well as antibonding MO are paired, therefore, it is diamagnetic in nature.

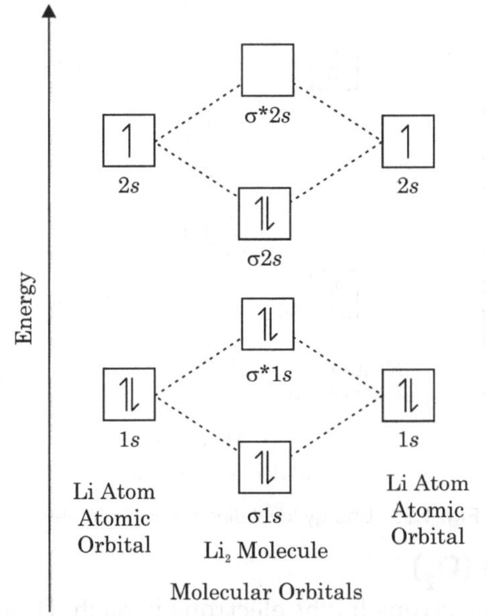

Fig. 1.22. Energy level diagram for Li_2 molecule.

1.9.4 Nitrogen Molecule (N_2)

Nitrogen molecule has total of 14 electrons [seven in each N-atom-electronic configuration = $1s^2\ 2s^2\ 2p^3$], so its molecular orbital configuration is:

$$\sigma 1s^2\ \sigma^* 1s^2\ \sigma 2s^2\ \sigma^* 2s^2\ [\pi 2p_x^2 = \pi 2p_y^2]\ \sigma 2p_z^2.$$

The configuration, $\sigma 1s^2 \sigma^* 1s^2$, indicates a closed K shell structure. Therefore, it is usually represented as KK. Hence, the electronic configuration of nitrogen molecule can also be written as KK $\sigma 2s^2\ \sigma^* 2s^2\ \pi 2p_x^2 = \pi 2p_y^2\ \sigma 2p_z^2$.

The molecular orbital energy level diagram for nitrogen molecule is shown in **Fig. 1.23**

$$\text{BO} = \frac{1}{2}(10 - 4) = 3$$

(BO value 3 indicates triple covalent bond between two N-atoms).

As all the electrons in bonding as well as antibonding MOs are paired, therefore, it is diamagnetic in nature.

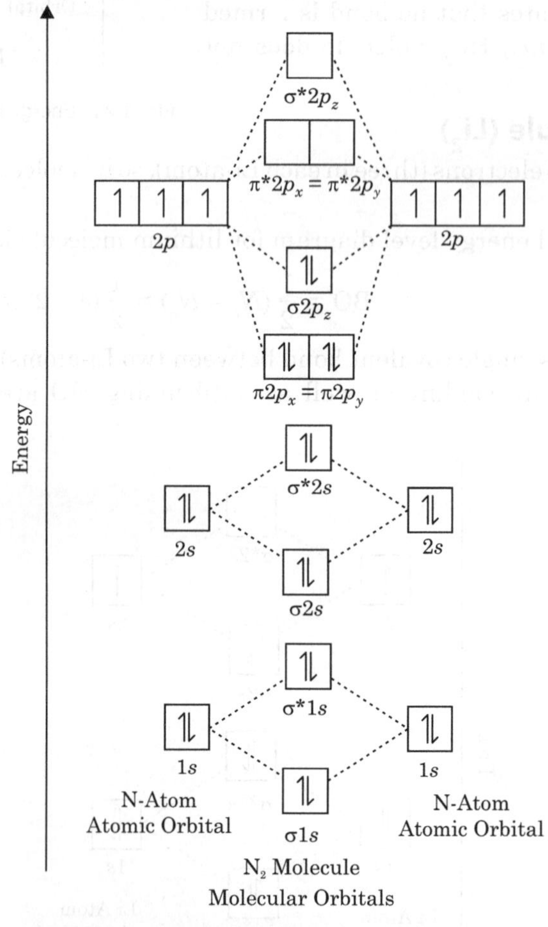

Fig. 1.23. Energy level diagram for N_2 molecule.

1.9.5 Oxygen Molecule (O_2)

O_2 molecule has total of 16 electrons [eight electrons in each O-atom (electronic configuration = $1s^2 2s^2 2p^4$)], so its molecular orbital configuration is:

$$\sigma 1s^2\ \sigma^*1s^2\ \sigma 2s^2\ \sigma^*2s^2\ \sigma 2p_z^2[\pi 2p_x^2 = \pi 2p_y^2][\pi^*2p_x^1 = \pi^*2p_y^1]$$

or $$\text{KK}\ \sigma 2s^2\ \sigma^*2s^2\ \sigma 2p_z^2[\pi 2p_x^2 = \pi 2p_y^2][\pi^*2p_x^1 = \pi^*2p_y^1]$$

The molecular orbital energy level diagram for oxygen molecule is shown in **Fig. 1.24.**

$$\text{BO} = \frac{1}{2}\ (10 - 6) = 2$$

(BO value 2 indicates double covalent bond between two O-atoms).

The presence of two unpaired electrons, one in each π^*2p_x and π^*2p_y MOs indicate that O_2 is paramagnetic in character.

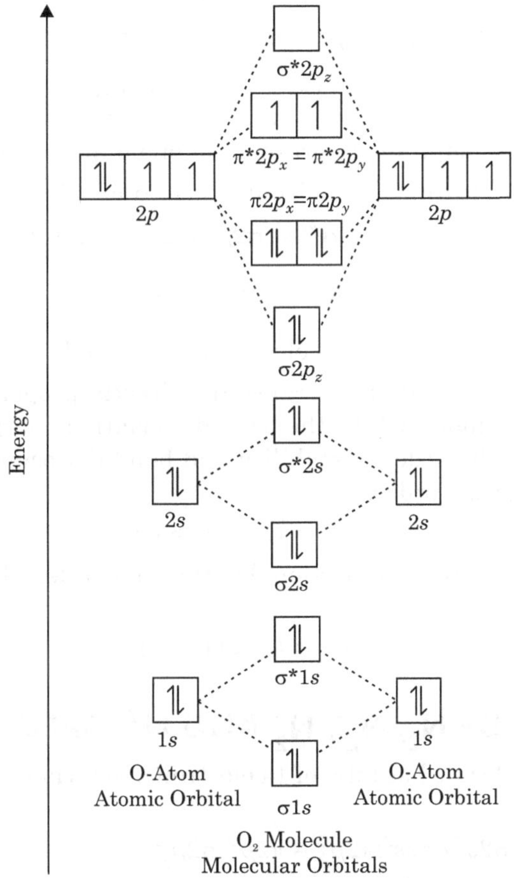

Fig. 1.24. Energy level diagram for O_2 molecule.

1.10 COMPARISON OF O_2, O_2^+, O_2^- AND O_2^{2-} SPECIES

1. **O_2 molecule:** O_2 molecule has total of 16 electrons. The electronic configuration of O_2 is

$$\sigma 1s^2\ \sigma^*1s^2\ \sigma 2s^2\ \sigma^*2s^2\ \sigma 2p_z^2\ [\pi_x^2 p_x^2 = \pi 2p_y^2][\pi^*2p_x^1 = \pi^*2p_y^1]$$

and $$\text{BO} = \frac{1}{2}\ (10 - 6) = 2$$

(paramagnetic in character due to presence of two unpaired electrons)

2. **O_2^+ ion:** O_2^+ ion is formed by the loss of one electron from O_2 molecule, thus O_2^+ ion has total of 15 electrons.

The electronic configuration of O_2^+ is

$$\sigma 1s^2\ \sigma^*1s^2\ \sigma 2s^2\ \sigma^*2s^2\ \sigma 2p_z^2\ [\pi 2p_x^2 = \pi 2p_y^2][\pi^*2p_x^1 = \pi^*2p_y^0]$$

or $\sigma 1s^2\ \sigma^*1s^2\ \sigma 2s^2\ \sigma^*2s^2\ \sigma 2p_z^2[\pi 2p_x^2 = \pi 2p_y^2][\pi^*2p_x^0 = \pi^*2p_y^1]$

and $$BO = \frac{1}{2}(10 - 5) = 2.5$$

(paramagnetic in character due to presence of one unpaired electron in either π^*2p_x or π^*2p_y)

3. **O_2^- ion (superoxide ion):** O_2^- ion is formed by the addition of one electron in O_2 molecule thus it has total of 17 electrons. The electronic configuration of O_2^- ion is

$$\sigma 1s^2\ \sigma^*1s^2\ \sigma 2s^2\ \sigma^*2s^2\ \sigma 2p_z^2[\pi 2p_x^2 = \pi 2p_y^2][\pi^*2p_x^2 = \pi^*2p_y^1]$$

$$BO = \frac{1}{2}(10 - 7) = 1.5$$

(paramagnetic in character due to presence of one unpaired electron in π^*2p_y)

4. **O_2^{2-} ion (peroxide ion):** O_2^{2-} molecule has total of 18 electrons. The electronic configuration of O_2^{2-} is $\sigma 1s^2\ \sigma^*1s^2\ \sigma^*2s^2\ \sigma 2p_z^2[\pi 2p_x^2 = \pi 2p_y^2][\pi^*2p_x^2 = \pi^*2p_y^2]$

$$BO = \frac{1}{2}\ (10 - 8) = 1$$

(diamagnetic in character as all the electrons are paired)

Stability and bond dissociation energies are directly proportional to the bond order. More the bond order, more will be the bond dissociation energy and greater will be the stability. Therefore, the order of stability and bond dissociation energies of the above oxygen species are in the order:

$$O_2^+ > O_2 > O_2^- > O_2^{2-}$$

The bond length is inversely proportional to the bond order, therefore, the order of their bond lengths is:

$$O_2^- < O_2 < O_2^- < O_2^{2-}$$

1.11 COMPARISON OF N_2, N_2^+, N_2^- AND N_2^{2-} SPECIES

1. **N_2 molecule:** N_2 molecule has total of 14 electrons, so its molecular orbital configuration is:

$$\sigma 1s^2\ \sigma^*1s^2\sigma 2s^2\ \sigma^*2s^2[\pi 2p_x^2 = \pi 2p_y^2]\sigma 2p_z^2$$

$\therefore$ $$BO = \frac{1}{2}\ (10 - 4) = 3$$

(diamagnetic in character as all the electrons are paired)

2. **N_2^+ ion:** N_2^+ ion has total of 13 electrons, so its molecular orbital configuration is:

$$\sigma 1s^2\ \sigma^*1s^2\ \sigma 2s^2\ \sigma^*2s^2[\pi 2p_x^2 = \pi 2p_y^2]\sigma 2p_z^1$$

$$BO = \frac{1}{2} = (9 - 4) = 2.5$$

(paramagnetic in character)

3. **N_2^- ion:** N_2^- ion has total of 15 electrons, so its molecular orbital configuration is:

$$\sigma 1s^2\ \sigma^*1s^2\ \sigma 2s^2\ \sigma^*2s^2[\pi 2p_x^2 = \pi 2p_y^2]\sigma 2p_z^2\ [\pi^*2p_x^1 = \pi^*2p_y^0]$$

$$BO = \frac{1}{2}(10 - 5) = 2.5$$

(paramagnetic in character)

4. **N_2^{2-} ion:** N_2^{2-} ion has total of 16 electrons, so its molecular orbital configuration is:

$$\sigma 1s^2 \sigma^* 1s^2 \sigma 2s^2\ \sigma^* 2s^2 [\pi 2p_x^2 = \pi 2p_y^2][\sigma 2p_z^2 \pi^*][2p_x^1 = \pi^* 2p_y^1]$$

$$BO = \frac{1}{2}(10 - 6) = 2$$

(paramagnetic in character)

Therefore, the order of stability and bond dissociation energies of the above nitrogen species follows the following order:

$$N_2 > N_2^+ = N_2^- > N_2^{2-}$$

The bond length is inversely proportional to the bond order, therefore, the order of their bond lengths in $N_2 < N_2^+ = N_2^- < N_2^{2-}$.

1.12 BONDING IN HETERONUCLEAR DIATOMIC MOLECULES

In heteronuclear diatomic molecules, two different atoms are bonded together. The principles involved in the distribution of electrons are the same as in case of homonuclear diatomic molecules. In case of homonuclear bonds, the atomic orbitals of the bonding atom are at the same energy. However, the heteronuclear bonds will be formed between two atoms with orbitals at different energies due to electronegativity difference between the two atoms. In such cases, the bonding electrons will be more stable in the presence of the nucleus of the atom having the greater attraction for electrons (*i.e.,* atom with higher electronegativity and lower atomic energy levels). The electrons in the bonding molecular orbital are closer to more electronegative atom and antibonding molecular orbitals are closer to the less electronegative atom. Let us discuss the electronic configurations and molecular orbital diagrams for some common heteronuclear diatomic molecules.

1. **CO molecule:** The electronic configurations of C and O atoms are $1s^2\ 2s^2\ 2p^2$ and $1s^2\ 2s^2\ 2p^4$, respectively. Thus, there are total 14 electrons in CO molecule. Because of higher electronegativity of oxygen atom than carbon, its atomic orbitals would be of lower energy than atomic orbitals of carbon. The bonding molecular orbitals will resemble more with the atomic orbitals of oxygen whereas; the antibonding molecular orbitals resemble more with the atomic orbitals of carbon. The molecular orbital electronic configuration of CO molecule is $\sigma 1s^2\ \sigma^* 1s^2\ \sigma 2s^2\ \sigma^* 2s^2\ [\pi 2p_x^2 = \pi 2p_y^2]\ \sigma 2p_z^2$

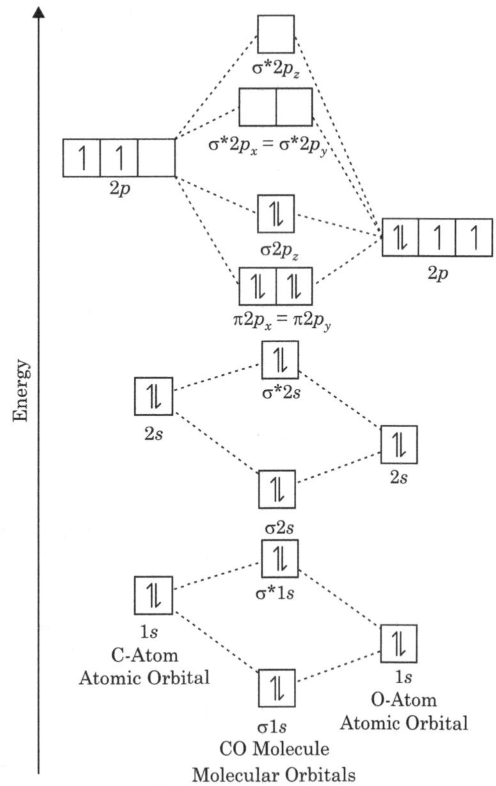

Fig. 1.25. Energy level diagram for CO molecule.

The energy level diagram for CO is shown in the **Fig. 1.25.**

$$BO = \frac{1}{2}(10 - 4) = 3.$$

The molecule, CO is diamagnetic in nature as all the electrons in bonding as well as antibonding MO are paired.

2. **Nitric oxide (Nitrogen monoxide, NO):** The electronic configurations of N and O atoms are $1s^2\ 2s^2\ 2p^3$ and $1s^2\ 2s^2\ 2p^4$, respectively. Thus, there are total 15 electrons in NO molecule. The electronic configuration of NO molecule is:

$$\sigma 1s^2\ \sigma^*1s^2\ \sigma 2s^2\ \sigma^*2s^2\ \sigma 2p_z^2\ [\pi 2p_x^2 = \pi 2p_y^2]\ [\pi^*2p_x^{\ 1} = \pi^*2p_y^0]$$

The energy level diagram for NO molecule is shown in **Fig. 1.26.**

$$BO = \frac{1}{2}(10 - 5) = 2.5$$

The presence of one unpaired electron in π^*2p_x or π^*2p_y indicates that NO is paramagnetic in character.

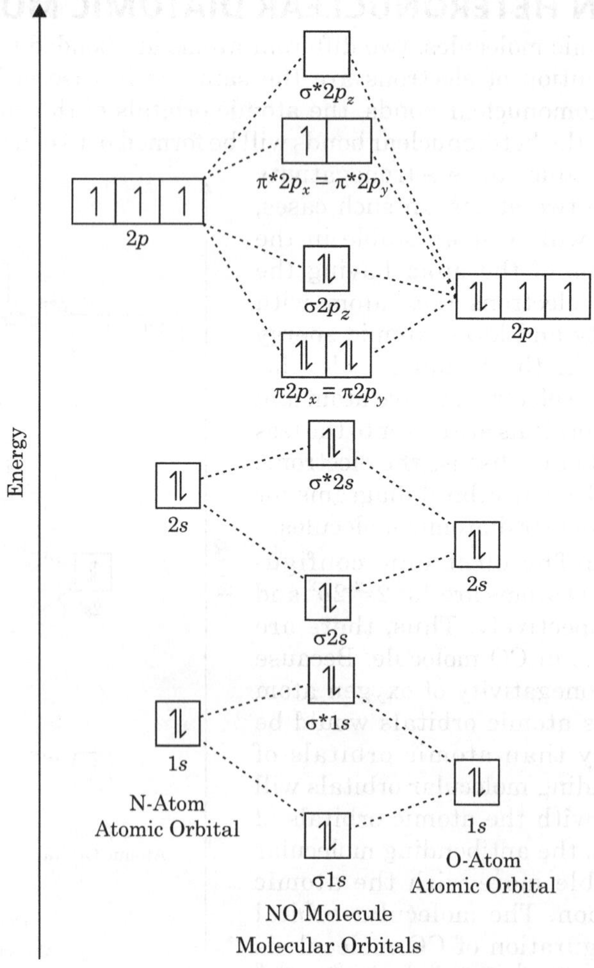

Fig 1.26. Energy level diagram for NO molecule.

3. **HF molecule:** The electronic configuration of hydrogen and fluorine atoms are $1s^1$ and $1s^2 2s^2 2p^5$, respectively. HF molecule is formed by the linear combination of 1*s* atomic orbital of hydrogen and 2*p* orbitals of fluorine atom. The $1s^2$ and $2s^2$ orbitals of fluorine do not take part in bonding as their energy is low. The combination of a p_x or p_y orbital with an *s*-orbital is ruled out on symmetry consideration. However, $2p_z$ orbital of fluorine overlap effectively with the *s*-orbital of H-atom. The molecular orbitals formed in the case of HF molecule will not be symmetrical due to difference in energies of the *s*-orbital of H-atom and $2p_z$ orbital of F-atom. The MO diagram for HF can be shown in **Fig. 1.27**.

$$BO = \frac{1}{2}(N_b - N_a) = \frac{1}{2}(2-0) = 1$$

It may be noted here that there are only 2 electrons in bonding MOs and the electrons in non-bonding MOs should not be counted for calculating bond order.

(BO value 1 indicates single bond between two H and F-atoms).

As all the electrons in MO are paired, therefore, it is diamagnetic in nature.

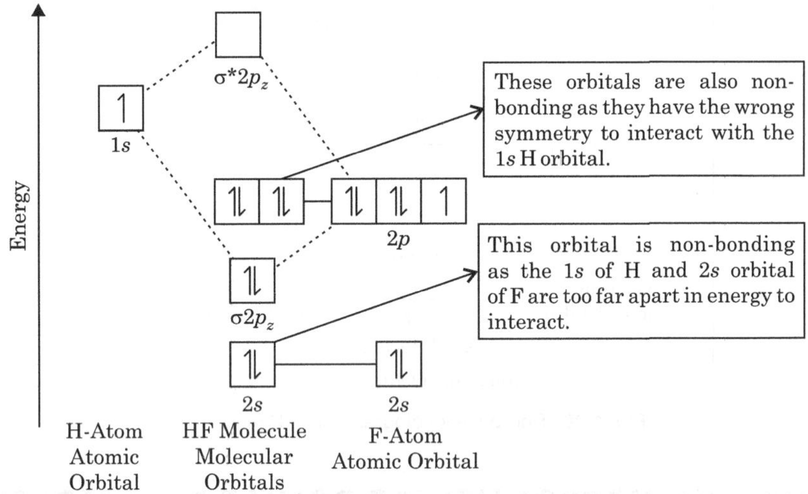

Fig 1.27. Energy level diagram for HF molecule.

4. **CN^- ion (cyanide ion):** The electronic configurations of C and N atoms are $1s^2\ 2s^2\ 2p^2$ and $1s^2\ 2s^2\ 2p^3$, respectively.

In CN^- ion, there are 6 electrons in C-atom, 7 electrons in N-atom and 1 electron for the negative charge, this makes total 14 electron count in the molecule. The molecular orbital electronic configuration for this molecule can be written as:

$$\sigma 1s^{2-}\ \sigma^* 1s^2\ \sigma 2s^2\ \sigma^* 2s^2\ [\pi 2p_x^{\ 2} = \pi 2p_y^{\ 2}]\ \sigma 2p_z^{\ 2}$$

The molecular orbital diagram is shown in **Fig. 1.28**

$$BO = \frac{1}{2}(10-4) = 3$$

(thus, there is triple bond between C and N).

As all the electrons in bonding as well as antibonding MO are paired, therefore, it is **diamagnetic** in nature.

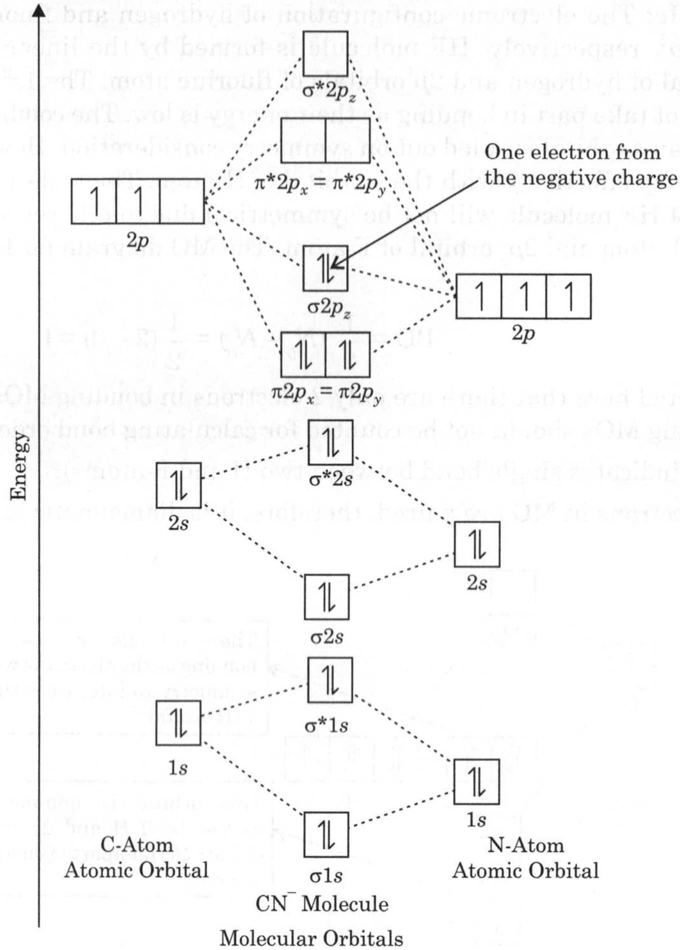

Fig. 1.28. Energy level diagram for CN^- molecule.

1.13 BONDING IN HETERONUCLEAR POLYATOMIC MOLECULES

In this section, we shall illustrate the application of molecular orbital theory only to a couple of simple polyatomic molecules like BeH_2 and NH_3

1. **BeH_2 (Beryllium hydride):** BeH_2 is the simplest example of triatomic molecule. The molecular orbitals for BeH_2 are formed from the 1s orbitals on the hydrogen atoms (labelled H and H') and the 2*s* and $2p_z$ orbitals of beryllium (as *z* is the internuclear axis and $2p_z$ is directed along the H—Be—H bond axis). The remaining 2*p* orbitals (*i.e.*, $2p_x$ and $2p_y$) of beryllium cannot enter into the bonding because they are perpendicular to the molecular axis and therefore have no net overlap with the hydrogen orbitals.

   Bonding in BeH_2 involves two stages. In the first stage, the orbitals of two hydrogen atoms combine together to form group orbitals. In the second stage, these group orbitals interact with the suitable orbitals on the central beryllium atom.

   The atomic orbitals of the two hydrogen atoms combine to form group orbitals which are consistent with the linear geometry of the molecule and with the symmetries of atomic orbitals of beryllium. The group orbitals are formed simply by LCAO (Linear

Combination of Atomic Orbitals) *i.e.*, combination of Is orbitals of two H-atoms. There are only two possibilities of the formation of group orbitals *i.e.*, $\psi_H + \psi_H'$ and $\psi_H - \psi_H'$. The beryllium 2*s* orbitals being spherical is positive everywhere, therefore, it overlaps with the $\psi_H + \psi_H'$ group orbital to form σ_g molecular orbital. The $2p_z$ orbital of beryllium (which has one positive and one negative lobe) overlaps efficiently with the $\psi_H - \psi_H'$ group orbitals to form σ_u molecular orbital. The antibonding molecular orbitals will be formed by opposite combinations to form σ_g^*.

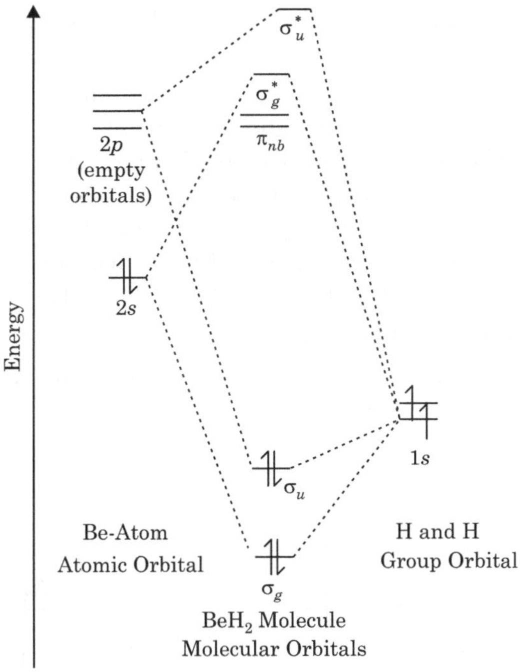

Fig 1.29. Energy level diagram for BeH_2 molecule.

Bonding molecular orbitals:

$$\psi_g = a\,\psi_{2s} + b\,(\psi_H + \psi_{H'}) = \sigma_g$$
$$\psi_u = c\,\psi_{2pz} - c\,(\psi_H - \psi_{H'}) = \sigma_u$$

Antibonding molecular orbitals:

$$\psi_g^* = b\,\psi_{2s} - a\,(\psi_H + \psi_{H'}) = \sigma_g^*$$
$$\psi_u^* = d\,\psi_{2pz} - c\,(\psi_H - \psi_{H'}) = \sigma_u^*$$

The coefficients *a*, *b*, *c* and *d* are necessary because of electronegativity difference between beryllium (1.5) and hydrogen (2.1). The molecular orbital diagram for BeH_2 is represented in **Fig. 1.29.**

The molecular orbital configuration of BeH_2 is $\sigma_g^2\,\sigma_u^2$. None of the antibonding and non-bonding orbitals are occupied.

2. **NH_3 (Ammonia):** The ammonia molecule is a trigonal pyramidal, belonging to C_{3v} point group. The 2*s* and 2*p* orbitals of the N-atom and the 1*s* orbital group combination of three H-atoms transform w.r.t. point group of NH_3 to give

2*s* orbitals of nitrogen $\rightarrow a_1$

$2p_x$ and $2p_y$ orbitals of nitrogen $\rightarrow e$

$2p_z$ orbitals of nitrogen $\rightarrow a_2$

Three 1*s* orbitals of hydrogen $\rightarrow a_1 + e$.

The 2*s* and $2p_z$ orbitals of N-atom are of the same symmetry *i.e.*, a_1 and thus they can hybridize together to form two a_1 hybrid orbitals, while $2p_x$ and $2p_y$ are of '*e*' symmetry. As we discussed earlier, the bonding in NH_3 also takes place in two stages. In the first stage, the atomic orbitals of three H-atoms combine to form group orbitals. In the second stage, these group orbitals interact with the suitable orbitals on the central nitrogen atom.

The atomic orbitals of the three hydrogen atoms combine to form group orbitals which are consistent with the trigonal pyramidal geometry of the molecule and also with the symmetries of the atomic orbitals on nitrogen. The group orbitals are formed by SALCO (*i.e.*, Symmetry Adapted Linear Combination of Orbitals). The bonding molecular orbitals are formed by the appropriate combination of orbitals to form $1a_1$ and l*e* molecular orbitals whereas, the antibonding molecular orbitals formed are $3a_1$ and 2*e*. The $2a_1$ is the non-bonding molecular orbital. Thus, the molecular orbital electronic configuration of NH_3 is $\sigma_{1a_1}^{2}\,\sigma_{11e}^{4}\,\sigma_{2a_1}^{2}$.

No antibonding molecular orbitals are occupied. The molecular orbital diagram of NH_3 given in **Fig. 1.30.**

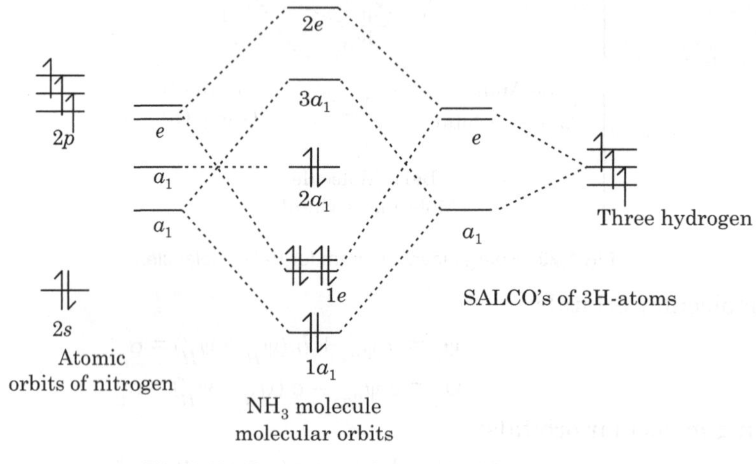

Fig. 1.30. Energy level diagram for NH_3 molecule.

Table 1.5: Comparison between Valence Bond Theory and Molecular Orbital Theory

Valence bond theory (VBT)	Molecular orbital theory (MOT)
In VBT, only valence electrons take part in the bond formation.	In MOT, all the electrons of interacting atoms take part in bond formation.
In VBT, the bonding in molecules is localized between the combining atoms.	In MOT, the bonding in molecules is not localized between the combining atoms but it spreads throughout the molecule.
In VBT, the atoms constituting the molecules do not lose their identity when linked to each other.	In MOT, the atoms constituting the molecules lose their identity when linked to each other.

It fails to explain the paramagnetic character of O_2 molecule.	It gives a satisfactory explanation for the paramagnetic character of O_2 molecule.
Resonance plays an important role in VBT theory.	MOT does not involve the concept of resonance.
For most of the molecules, the wave function in original VBT does not give any weightage to the ionic structures (later on the ionic term was incorporated as a modification to the original theory).	MOT inherently gives equal weightage to the covalent and ionic structures.
Mathematically, VBT is simple to apply.	The calculations involved in MOT are much more tedious than those involved in VBT.

Inspite of all these differences, both these theories have some **similarities**. These are:

1. According to both the theories, the formation of bond takes place by the overlapping of atomic orbitals. The overlapping atomic orbitals must have proper symmetry and comparable energies.
2. Both the theories are approximations.
3. Both the theories predict the non-existence of helium (He_2) and neon (Ne_2) molecules.
4. The basic principles involved in distribution of electron are same in both the theories. Thus, the electrons in atomic or molecular orbitals are filled in accordance with the Hund's rule, Aufbau rule and Pauli's exclusion principle.
5. Both the theories account for the directional nature of the covalent bond.

EXERCISES

I. SHORT ANSWER TYPE QUESTIONS

1. Explain *sp*, sp^2 and sp^3 hybridization with examples.

2. Describe the structures of H_2O, NH_3 and CH_4 molecules in terms of the valance shell electron pair repulsion theory. Also explain why the bond angles are different in the three molecules.

3. Discuss the shape of PCl_5, SF_4 and ClF_3 on the basis of VSEPR theory.

4. Differentiate between bonding and antibonding molecular orbitals.

5. Explain structures of the following pairs of molecules in terms of valence bond theory.

(*a*) NH_3 and BF_3 (*b*) H_2S and H_2O.

6. Nitrogen molecule is diamagnetic while, oxygen molecule is paramagnetic. Explain on the basis of molecular orbital theory.

7. Explain the non-existence of Ne_2 and He_2 on the basis of molecular orbital theory.

8. Arrange the following set of molecules in the increasing order of bond angle

(*a*) $AlCl_3$, H_2S, BeH_2, H_2O (*b*) NH_4^+, H_2O, BF_3, NH_3

(*c*) CH_4, CCl_4, NH_3, H_2O.

Hint: (a) $H_2S < H_2O < AlCl_3 < BeH_2$

(b) $H_2O < NH_3 < NH_4^+ < BF_3$

(c) $H_2O < NH_3 < CH_4 = CCl_4$

9. Compare bond order and bond length of peroxide and superoxide ion.

10. On the basis of molecular orbital theory, predict which of the following species is diamagnetic: H_2^+, O_2, O_2^{2+}.
11. Differentiate between valence bond theory and molecular orbital theory.
(*RGPV, CBCS Scheme, Dec., 2015*)
12. Calculate the bond order of CO and N_2.
(*RGPV, CBCS Scheme, Dec., 2015*)
13. Arrange the following species in the decreasing order of their bond dissociation enthalpies: O_2, O_2^+ and O_2^-. (*RGPV, CBCS Scheme, June, 2016*)
14. Explain why N_2 has greater bond dissociation energy than N_2^+ whereas O_2 has lesser bond dissociation energy than O_2^{+}? (*RGPV, DDI PG program, June, 2016*)
15. Using VSEPR theory, how will you show that?
(*i*) ClF_3 is T-shaped? (*ii*) SF_4 is see-saw shaped?
16. What are the limitations of VSEPR theory.
17. What is hybridization? Discuss the structures of following molecules on the basis of hybridization PF_5, $SnCl_2$, NH_3, ClF_3.
18. Discuss the relationship between electronic configuration and molecular behavior.
19. All the P—F bonds in PCl_5 molecule are not equivalent. Explain.
20. Write various points of similarities and dissimilarities between valence bond theory and molecular orbital theory.
21. Bond order in O_2^+ is more than in O_2 whereas bond order in N_2^+ is less than that in N_2 molecule. Explain on the basis of molecular orbital theory.
22. Give the hybridization of the central atom in the following species:

$$H_3O^+, I_3^-, IF_7, CH_3^+, NO_3^-, PO_4^{3-}, XeF_4, ClO_4^-.$$

II. LONG ANSWER TYPE QUESTIONS

1. What is VSEPR theory of molecular model? Explain with suitable examples.
2. What is hybridization of atomic orbitals ? Describe the shapes of *sp*, *sp*^{2} and *sp*^{3} hybrid orbitals. (*RGPV, DDI PG program, June, 2016*)
3. Discuss with the help of molecular orbital theory, the formation of N_2, O_2 and F_2 molecules. How does this theory explain the difference in reactivity of these molecules?
4. Discuss briefly the molecular orbital theory. On the basis of MOT, explain the formation of N_2 and CO molecules.
5. Draw molecular orbital diagram for nitric oxide and boron molecule.
(*RGPV, CBCS Scheme, Dec., 2015*)
6. Explain various postulates of valence bond theory taking at least two examples.
(*RGPV, CBCS Scheme, June, 2016*)
7. Explain molecular orbital theory. Draw the molecular orbital diagram for CO and also calculate its bond order. (*RGPV, CBCS Scheme, June, 2016*)
8. Write the various postulates of molecular orbital theory? Draw the molecular orbital diagram for F_2 and also calculate its bond order.
9. Discuss molecular orbital theory. Explain on the basis of molecular orbital theory that N_2 molecule is diamagnetic and O_2 molecule is paramagnetic.

10. Draw molecular orbital diagram of cyanide ion. Calculate its bond order.
11. Discuss the molecular orbital diagrams for heteroatomic molecules. Explain and draw the molecular orbital diagram for HF molecule.
12. Write various postulates of molecular orbital theory. Draw and explain the molecular orbital diagram of NO molecule.
13. Discuss the molecular orbital diagram of BeH_2.
14. Explain the molecular orbital diagram of a polyatomic molecule, NH_3.

III. MULTIPLE CHOICE QUESTIONS

1. The molecule with the highest bond order among CO, CN, NO and O_2 is:
   (*a*) CO (*b*) O_2 (*c*) CN (*d*) NO.
2. The molecule He_2 does not exist because
   (*a*) $N_b = N_a$ (*b*) $N_b > N_a$ (*c*) $N_a > N_b$ (*d*) None of these.
3. The paramagnetic character of O_2 molecule can be explained by:
   (*a*) Valence bond theory (*b*) Molecular orbital theory
   (*c*) Hybridization (*d*) None of the above.
4. Which of the following has a zero bond order?
   (*a*) Ne_2 (*b*) H_2 (*c*) N_2 (*d*) O_2.
5. Which among the following species is diamagnetic ?
   (*a*) O_2^+ (*b*) O_2 (*c*) O_2^{2-} (*d*) O_2^-.
6. In NO_3^- ion, the number of bond pairs and lone pairs of electrons on nitrogen atom are:
   (*a*) 3, 1 (*b*) 2, 2 (*c*) 4, 0 (*d*) 3, 1.
7. Which of the following species has tetrahedral geometry?
   (*a*) NH_2^- (*b*) BH_4^- (*c*) H_3O^+ (*d*) CO_3^{2-}
8. Which of the following species contain unpaired electrons?
   (*a*) O_2 (*b*) N_2 (*c*) O_2^{2-} (*d*) F_2.
9. Which of the following options represent the correct bond order
   (*a*) $O_2^+ > O_2 > O_2^-$ (*b*) $O_2^- > O_2 > O_2^+$ (*c*) $O_2 > O_2^- > O_2^+$ (*d*) $O_2^+ > O_2^- > O_2$.
10. In which of the following species all bond are not equal?
    (*a*) SiF_4 (*b*) BH_4^- (*c*) C_2H_4 (*d*) XeF_4.
11. Molecular orbital theory was proposed by
    (*a*) Hund and Mulliken (*b*) Pauling and Slater
    (*c*) Heitler and London (*d*) Kossel and Lewis.
12. Which of the following molecular orbitals has the highest energy?
    (*a*) $\sigma 2p_z$ (*b*) $\sigma^* 2p_z$ (*c*) $\pi 2p_x$ (*d*) $\pi^* 2p_y$.
13. Central atom is sp^2 hybridized in which of the following:
    (*a*) NH_4^+ (*b*) PCl_3 (*c*) C_2H_2 (*d*) BF_3.
14. CO is isoelectronic with
    (*a*) N_2 (*b*) NO^+ (*c*) CN^- (*d*) All of the above

15. The types of hybrid orbitals of nitrogen in NO_2^+, NO_3^- and NH_4^+ respectively are expected to be

(*a*) *sp*, sp^2 and sp^3 (*b*) sp^2, *sp* and sp^3 (*c*) sp^3, sp^2 and *sp* (*d*) *sp*, sp^2 and *sp*.

16. Among the following species identify the isostructural pairs

(*a*) NF_3 and BF_3 (*b*) BH_4^- and NH_4^+ (*c*) NH_3 and NO_3^- (*d*) BCl_3 and $BrCl_3$.

17. Which of the following relations is correct?

(*a*) Bond order $\propto \dfrac{1}{\text{bond length}} \propto$ bond energy

(*b*) Bond order $\propto \dfrac{1}{\text{bond energy}} \propto$ bond length

(*c*) Bond order $\propto \dfrac{1}{\text{bond length}} \propto \dfrac{1}{\text{bond energy}}$

(*d*) Bond order $\propto$ bond length $\propto$ bond energy.

18. Which of the following species has a pyramidal shape?

(*a*) NH_4^+ (*b*) CO_3^{2-} (*c*) NO_3^- (*d*) PCl_3.

19. The Xe atom in $XeOF_2$ involves

(*a*) sp^3 hybridization (*b*) sp^3d hybridization

(*c*) sp^3d^2 hybridization (*d*) sp^3d^3 hybridization.

20. Which of the following is least polar?

(*a*) HF (*b*) HBr (*c*) HCl (*d*) HI.

21. Which of the following statements regarding covalent bond is not true?

(*a*) The electrons are shared between two atoms

(*b*) The bond is non-directional

(*c*) The strength of the bond depends upon the extent of overlapping

(*d*) The bond formed may or may not be polar.

22. In XeF_2, XeF_4 and XeF_6, the number of lone pairs on Xenon are respectively

(*a*) 2, 3, 1 (*b*) 3, 2, 1 (*c*) 1, 2, 3 (*d*) 3, 1, 2.

23. Covalent bond implies:

(*a*) attraction

(*b*) repulsion

(*c*) attraction and repulsion balanced at a particular distance

(*d*) attraction and repulsion.

24. The number of sigma (σ) bonds in 1-butene is:

(*a*) 12 (*b*) 11 (*c*) 10 (*d*) 8.

25. When a chemical bond is formed between two atoms, the potential energy of the system?

(*a*) increases (*b*) decreases (*c*) unchanged (*d*) cannot be predicted.

Answers

1. (*a*)	2. (*a*)	3. (*b*)	4. (*a*)	5. (*c*)	6. (*c*)	7. (*b*)	8. (*a*)	9. (*a*)	10. (*c*)
11. (*a*)	12. (*b*)	13. (*d*)	14. (*d*)	15. (*a*)	16. (*b*)	17. (*a*)	18. (*d*)	19. (*b*)	20. (*d*)
21. (*b*)	22. (*b*)	23. (*c*)	24. (*b*)	25. (*b*)					

Chapter 2 Electrochemistry

2.1 INTRODUCTION

Electrochemistry is the branch of chemistry which is concerned with the conversion of chemical energy to electrical energy end vice-versa.

The importance of electrochemistry is undeniable, we literally cannot live without it for proper functioning of cell and transmission of signals through nervous system. Electrochemistry is also vital in a wide range of important technological applications

1. Batteries are important in storing energy for mobile devices, vehicles etc.
2. It is of huge economical importance because of costly destruction caused by corrosion.
3. New emerging technology such as fuel cells generate electricity directly from fuel.
4. It provides techniques for measuring the thermodynamical state functions and for predicting equilibrium concentrations of dissolving and reacting ions.

2.2 ARRHENIUS THEORY OF ELECTROLYTIC DISSOCIATION/ IONIZATION

In order to explain the properties of electrolytic solutions, **Arrhenius** in 1884, put forth, a comprehensive theory which is known as **theory of electrolytic dissociation**. The main points of the theory are as follows.

1. When an electrolyte (acid, base or salt) is dissolved in water, it splits up into two types of charged particles, one carrying a positive charge and the other a negative charge. These charged particles were called as ions and the process was termed **ionization**. The positively charged ions were termed **cations** while those having negative charge were called ***anions***.

   For examples:
   $$AB \longrightarrow \underset{\text{cation}}{A^+} + \underset{\text{anion}}{B^-}$$
   $$NaCl \longrightarrow \underset{\text{cation}}{Na^+} + \underset{\text{anion}}{Cl^-}$$

   Arrhenius theory in its modern form assumes that solid electrolytes are composed of ions which are held together by electrostatic forces of attraction. When an electrolyte is dissolved in water, the forces between the ions get weakened and the electrolyte dissociate to form separate cations and anions.

2. It has been observed that all electrolytes do not ionize to the same extent. Some are almost completely ionized whereas others are feebly ionized. The degree of ionization or degree of dissociation of an electrolyte is given by

$$\alpha = \frac{\text{Number of molecules dissociated into ions}}{\text{Total number of molecules}}.$$

3. The ions present in solution constantly reunite to form neutral molecules and thus, there is a state of dynamic equilibrium between the ionized and the unionized molecules

$$AB \rightleftharpoons A^+ + B^-$$

According to law of mass action, the dissociation constant (K) for the above equilibrium is given by the formula

$$K = \frac{[A^+][B^-]}{[AB]}$$

High value of K indicates strong electrolytes whereas lower value of K indicates weak electrolytes.

4. When an electric current is passed through the electrolytic solution, the positive ions (cations) start moving towards cathode whereas negative charge (anions) towards the anode.
5. Each ion behaves osmotically as molecule *i.e.*, each ion that is formed from electrolytic dissociation produce the same effect on colligative properties as an undissociated molecule.

Colligative properties: The properties of the solution which depend only on the number of solute particles but not on the nature of the solute *e.g.*, relative lowering of vapour pressure, elevation in boiling point, depression in freezing point and osmotic pressure.

6. Inspite of the presence of charged particles, the electrolytic solution is always neutral in nature as the total charge on cations is always equal to the total charge on anion. However, it is not necessary that the number of cation and anion must be equal always

For example, $NaCl \rightleftharpoons Na^+ + Cl^-$ Both ions are equal

$BaCl_2 \rightleftharpoons Ba^{2+} + 2Cl^-$ [Anions are double than cations]

7. The properties of electrolytes in solution are the properties of the ions. All cobalt salts solutions are pink because of presence of cobalt ions which are pink in colour Similarly, all chromium salts solution are green due to the green colour of chromium ions.

2.2.1 Factors Affecting the Degree of Ionization

1. **Nature of the electrolyte:** Weak electrolytes are only partly ionized and therefore, their degree of ionization is low. Strong electrolytes which are almost completely ionized have high degree of ionization.
2. **Nature of the solvent:** The nature of the solvent also plays an important role in the dissociation of electrolytes. Generally, the solvents having high dielectric constant have high solvating power as compared to solvents having low dielectric constant.

For example, Water (having dielectric constant = 80.4) ionize the electrolytes to a greater extent as compared to benzene (dielectric constant = 2.27).

Dielectric constant: Dielectric constant of a solvent is defined as its capacity to weaken the forces of attraction between the oppositely charged ions immersed in that solvent. It is a dimensionless quantity.
Water = 80.4, methyl alcohol = 35, ethyl alcohol = 27, acetone = 21 etc.

3. **Temperature:** The degree of ionization increases with increase in temperature. This is due to the fact that at higher temperature molecular speed increases which overcomes the forces for attraction between the ions.
4. **Concentration of the electrolyte:** The degree of ionization of an electrolyte is inversely proportional to its concentration. This is due to the fact that at higher dilution, the solvent molecules make more molecules of the solute to break into ions.
5. **Presence of other ions/electrolytes:** The degree of ionization of a weak electrolyte is suppressed in the presence of a strong electrolyte having a common ion. This effect is called as **common ion effect**. For example, Solubility of AgCl decreases in the presence of NaCl or dissociation of H_2S decreases in the presence of HCl. However, when applied to strong electrolytes many discrepancies have been observed

2.2.2 Limitations of Arrhenius Theory

Various limitations of Arrhenius theory are listed below:

1. Ostwald's dilution law which is based on Arrhenius theory fails completely when applied to strong electrolytes.
2. As strong electrolytes conduct electricity in molten state also, it means that their ionization must have taken place even in the absence of water.
3. Arrhenius theory simply assumes the independent existence of ions in solution but does not take into account that the mobility of ions can be changed by electrostatic forces between oppositely charged ions lying side by side, particularly in solutions of moderate concentration.
4. Arrhenius theory could not explain the variation of transport number with concentration.
5. Arrhenius theory states that conductance increases with dilution because the dissociation of electrolyte increases. This makes no sense for strong electrolytes which dissociates almost completely at moderate concentrations.

2.3 OSTWALD DILUTION LAW

According to Arrhenius theory of electrolytic dissociation, the weak electrolytes are ionized only partially. The ions formed on the dissociation of weak electrolytes are present in a dynamic equilibrium with the unionized molecules of the electrolyte in solution. It was pointed out by Ostwald that like chemical equilibrium, law of mass action can be applied to such system also.

Consider a binary electrolyte AB which dissociates into A^+ and B^- ions and the equilibrium state is represented by the equation:

$$\begin{array}{lccc} & AB & \rightleftharpoons A^+ & + \quad B^+ \\ \text{At } t = 0 & C & 0 & 0 \\ \text{At equilibrium} & C(1-\alpha) & C\alpha & C\alpha \end{array}$$

where C moles of the electrolyte are dissolved per litre of the solution and α is the degree of dissociation.

Applying the law of mass action to the above equilibrium, we get

$$K = \frac{[A^+][B^-]}{[AB]} = \frac{C\alpha \,.\, C\alpha}{C(1-\alpha)} = \frac{C\alpha^2}{(1-\alpha)}$$

Where K is called the dissociation or ionization constant.

For weak electrolytes, such as acetic acid or ammonium hydroxide, the value of degree of dissociation is very small

$$\therefore \qquad 1 - \alpha \cong 1$$

and the above equation simplifies to

$$K = C\alpha^2$$

$$\alpha = \sqrt{\frac{K}{C}}.$$

From the above equation, it is clear that degree of ionization increases on dilution. The value of α can be determined by conductivity measurements.

This law holds good only for weak electrolytes and fails completely in the case of strong electrolytes like KCl, HCl, NaOH etc.

The behaviour of strong electrolytes is better explained by Debye Huckel Theory.

2.3.1 Types of Conductors

All substances do not conduct electric current. The substances which allow the passage of electric current through them are called as conductors. For example, Cu, Ag etc. On the other hand, the substances which do not allow the passage of electric current through them are called as non-conductors or insulators. For example, wood, wax, glass, ceramics.

Conductors are broadly classified into two types:

1. **Metallic conductors or Electronic conductors:** Conductors which allow electricity to pass through them without undergoing any chemical change are called as **metallic conductors**. The flow of electric current through metallic conductors is due to the flow of electrons in the metal atoms. For example, pure metals, graphite, most alloys, carbon etc.
2. **Electrolytic conductors or Electrolytes:** Electrolytes are the substances which allow the electricity to pass through them in their molten states or in the form of their aqueous solution and undergo chemical decomposition. For example aqueous solutions of acids, bases and salts etc. In this type of conduction, the current is due to the movement of ions. As the conduction is due to movement of ions, these substances do not conduct electricity in solid state where ions are not free to move. The main points of difference between metallic and electrolytic conductors are given in **Table 2.1**. Electrolytes can be further divided into strong and weak electrolytes.

(*i*) **Strong electrolytes:** The electrolytes which are almost completely dissociated into their ions in aqueous solution are called **strong electrolytes** for example HCl, H_2SO_4, NaCl, KOH, NaOH, NH_4Cl etc.

(*ii*) **Weak electrolytes:** The electrolytes which are partially dissociated in their aqueous solutions are called as **weak electrolytes**. For example NH_4OH, CH_3COOH etc.

Table 2.1. Differences between metallic conductors and electrolytic conductors.

	Metallic conductors		Electrolytic conductors
1.	Conduction through metals is carried by the movement of electrons.	1.	Conduction through electrolytes is carried by the movement of ions.
2.	It involves no change in the chemical properties of the conductor.	2.	It involves the decomposition of the electroyte as a result of the chemical reaction.
3.	Metallic conduction decreases with increase in temperature due to the resistance offered to the moving electrons by the vibration of atoms.	3.	Electrolytic conduction increases with increase in temperature due to increase in the mobility of ions and also due to increase in degree of dissociation of an electrolyte.
4.	Metallic conduction does not involve any transfer of matter.	4.	It involves transfer of matter in the form of ions.

The electrolytic conductance of a solution depends upon:

(*i*) Nature of solute (*ii*) Valency of its ions

(*iii*) Concentration of the solution (*iv*) Temperature.

2.3.2 Conductance in Electrolytic Solutions

Flow of electricity through solution of electrolytes is due to the movement of ions when potential difference is applied between the two electrodes. Like metallic conductors, electrolytic conductors also obey ohm's law. According to **Ohm's law**, current I (Amperes) passing through a metallic conductor is directly proportional to the potential difference, V (volts) applied across it.

$$I = \frac{V}{R} \qquad \therefore \quad V = IR$$

Where R is the constant of proportionality and is known as **resistance of** the conductor. It is expressed in ohms (Ω). The resistance of any conductor is directly proportional to the length (l) and inversely proportional to the area of cross-section (a), so that

$$R \propto \frac{l}{a} \qquad \text{or} \qquad R = \rho\,\frac{l}{a}$$

Where ρ is the another proportionality constant called as **resistivity or specific resistance.**

If $l = 1$ cm , $a = l$ cm^2, then R = ρ.

Thus, resistivity is defined as the resistance of a conductor of 1 cm length and having area of cross-section equal to 1 cm^2. Value of ρ depends upon the material of the conductor.

Units of ρ: $\rho = R\frac{a}{l} = \Omega\,\frac{\text{cm}^2}{\text{cm}} = \Omega$ cm or ohm cm

[SI unit is Ω m]

Conductance: It is a measure of the ease with which electricity flows through a solution It is expressed as 'G'. It is reciprocal of the resistance *i.e.*

$$G = \frac{1}{R} \quad \therefore \quad G = \frac{1}{\Omega} = \Omega^{-1} \text{ or ohm}^{-1}$$

[SI unit is siemens (S) = Ω^{-1}]

Specific Conductance or Conductivity

The inverse of resistivity is called **conductivity or specific conductance.** It is expressed as κ (Kappa).

$$\kappa = \frac{1}{\rho} = \frac{1}{R}\frac{l}{a} = \frac{1}{\Omega}\frac{\text{cm}}{\text{cm}^2} = \Omega^{-1}\text{cm}^{-1} \text{ [In SI} \longrightarrow \text{Sm}^{-1}]$$

Other Relations

If κ is in Ω^{-1Z} cm^{-1}, then

$$\Lambda_m = \frac{1000 \times \kappa}{M}$$

Λ_m = molar conductivity (Ω^{-1} cm^2 mol^{-1})

$$\Lambda_{eq} = \frac{1000 \times \kappa}{N}$$

Λ_{eq} = equivalent conductivity (Ω^{-1} cm^2 eq^{-1})

$$\text{Cell constant} = \frac{l}{a} = \text{cm}^{-1}$$

$$= \frac{R}{\rho}.$$

2.3.3 Variation of Conductivity and Molar Conductivity with Concentration

Both the conductivity and molar conductivity of a solution varies with concentration of the electrolyte. The conductivity or specific conductance (κ) increases with increase in concentration whereas the molar conductivity (Λ_m) increases with decrease in concentration (or we can say molar conductivity increases on dilution). This can be explained as follows:

Specific conductance is the conductance of unit volume of the solution. On diluting the solution (or decreasing the concentration), the concentration of ions per unit volume decreases and therefore, the conductivity decreases.

Molar conductivity on the other hand, is the product of conductivity (κ) and the volume of the solution containing one mole of the electrolyte.

$$\Lambda_m = \kappa \times V$$

On dilution, the conductivity (κ) decreases but volume containing one mole of an electrolyte increases much more. Hence, their product *i.e.* molar conductivity increases on dilution. The variation of Λ_m on dilution for strong and weak electrolytes shows altogether different behaviour **(Fig. 2.1).**

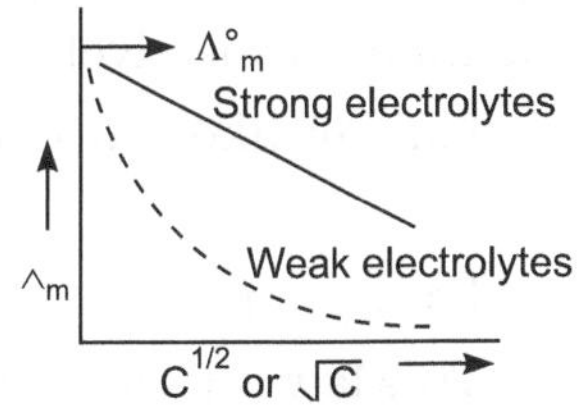

Fig. 2.1. Variation of molar conductivity on dilution.

(i) **For strong electrolytes:** It is found that for strong electrolytes there is a tendency for molar conductance to approach a certain limiting value when the concentration approaches zero. At this point, the molar conductance is called as **molar conductance at infinite dilution.** It is represented by $\Lambda°_m$ or Λ^{∞}_m. The variation of molar conductivity with concentration is given by **Debye Huckel Onsager equation**

$$\Lambda_m = \Lambda°_m - AC^{1/2}$$

where A is a constant.

It has been observed that for strong electrolytes, the variation of Λ_m with concentration $C^{1/2}$ is small, therefore the plot can be extrapolated to zero concentration. When the concentration approaches zero, the intercept gives the limiting value of molar conductivity $\Lambda°_m$.

(ii) **For weak electrolytes:** The molar conductivity of weak electrolytes is low as compared to strong electrolytes because they dissociate to a smaller extent in comparison to strong electrolytes. The variation of Λ_m with $C^{1/2}$ is very rapid and large, thus it becomes difficult to obtain molar conductance at infinite dilution by extrapolation of the graph (Fig. 2.1). Hence, the $\Lambda°_m$ values for weak electrolytes are determined using **Kohlrausch law.**

2.4 KOHLRAUSCH'S LAW

Kohlrausch (1857) determined the molar conductivity at infinite dilution for various electrolytes and concluded that at infinite dilution, each ion makes a definite contribution to the total molar conductivity of an electrolyte. For example, if we take two salts KCl and KNO_3 and compare their molar conductivity at infinite dilution (at 25°*C*) with those of corresponding sodium salts NaCl and $NaNO_3$, we have

$$\Lambda°_{(KCl)} = 149.9 \qquad \Lambda°_{(KNO_3)} = 145.0$$

$$\Lambda°_{(NaCl)} = 126.5 \qquad \Lambda°_{(NaNO_3)} = 121.6$$

$$\Lambda°_{(KCl)} - \Lambda°_{NaCl} = 23.4$$

$$\Lambda°_{(KNO_3)} - \Lambda°_{(NaNO_3)} = 23.4$$

$$\Lambda°_{(K^+)} - \Lambda°_{(Na^+)} = 23.4 \text{ S cm}^2\text{mol}^{-1}.$$

This means that the difference between molar conductivities of K^+ and Na^+ is 23.4 S cm^2 mol^{-1} irrespective of the anion.

Therefore, he generalized his observation as "At infinite dilution when the dissociation is complete, each ion of the electrolyte makes a definite contribution towards conductivity of the electrolyte and is independent of the presence of other ions of the electrolyte. Molar conductance at infinite dilution ($\Lambda°_m$) for an electrolyte is given by

$$\Lambda°_m = \upsilon_+ \lambda^{\infty}_+ + \upsilon_- \lambda^{\infty}_-$$

Where υ_+ and υ_- are the number of cations and anions per formula unit of the electrolyte *e.g.* $HCl \longrightarrow \upsilon_+ = \upsilon_- = 1$, $MgCl_2 \longrightarrow \upsilon_+ = 1, \upsilon_- = 2$ and λ_+^0 and λ_-^0 are molar conductance of cation and anion respectively at infinite dilution. It is expressed as $S\ cm^2\ mol^{-1}$ or $S\ m^2\ mol^{-1}$.

For salt like NaCl, molar conductivity at infinite dilution can be written as

$$\Lambda^\circ_{(NaCl)} = \lambda^\circ_{(Na^+)} + \lambda^\circ_{(Cl^-)}$$

For example, $MgCl_2$ $\quad \Lambda^\circ_{(MgCl_2)} = \lambda^\circ_{(Mg^{2+})} + 2\lambda^\circ_{(Cl^-)}$

This law is used to calculate the molar conductivity at infinite dilution for weak electrolytes whose Λ°_m cannot be obtained graphically.

2.4.1 Applications of Kohlrausch Law

1. **Calculation of molar conductance at infinite dilution for weak electrolytes:** It is not possible to determine the Λ°_m for weak electrolytes since we cannot obtain the limiting value of the molar conductivity for a weak electrolyte. However, this can be calculated by applying Kohlrausch law. For example, molar conductance of acetic acid (CH_3COOH) at infinite dilution can be calculated from the molar conductance at infinite dilution for HCl, CH_3COONa and NaCl as follows.

$$\Lambda^\circ_{m(HCl)} = \lambda^\circ_{(H^+)} + \lambda^\circ_{(Cl^-)} \quad \ldots(i)$$

$$\Lambda^\circ_{(CH_3COONa)} = \lambda^\circ_{(CH_3COO^-)} + \lambda^\circ_{(Na^+)} \quad \ldots(ii)$$

$$\Lambda^\circ_{(NaCl)} = \lambda^\circ_{(Na^+)} + \lambda^\circ_{(Cl^-)} \quad \ldots(iii)$$

Add equations (*i*) and (*ii*) and subtract (*iii*), we get

$$\lambda^\circ_{(CH_3COO^-)} + \lambda^\circ_{(H^+)} = \left[\lambda^\circ_{(CH_3COO^-)} + \lambda^\circ_{(Na^+)}\right] + \left[\lambda^\circ_{(H^+)} + \lambda^\circ_{(Cl^-)}\right] - \left[\lambda^\circ_{(Na^+)} + \lambda^\circ_{(Cl^-)}\right]$$

$$\Lambda^\circ_{(CH_3COOH)} = \Lambda^\circ_{(CH_3COONa)} + \Lambda^\circ_{(HCl)} - \Lambda^\circ_{(NaCl)}.$$

2. **Calculation of degree of dissociation and dissociation constant of weak electrolytes:** The degree of dissociation of weak electrolytes such as NH_4OH, CH_3COOH can be determined by measuring the molar conductivity of the solution of an electrolyte at any given dilution. For example, the degree of dissociation (α) of a weak electrolyte at concentration C moles/litre may be given by the following relation $\alpha = \dfrac{\Lambda^c}{\Lambda^\circ}$, where Λ^c is the molar conductance at concentration C and Λ° is the molar conductance at infinite dilution for the same electrolyte.

   Dissociation constant, $K = \dfrac{C\alpha^2}{1-\alpha}$

   K can be determined, if α is known.

2.5 CONCENTRATION CELLS

In simple words, a concentration cell is the one in which both the electrodes are of the same type but the electrolyte solution in which they dip have different concentration.

In the case of galvanic cells, the electrical energy is produced from the chemical reaction which takes place in the cells whereas in case of concentration cells, the EMF arises due to the transfer of matter from one half cell to the another due to different concentration of the species in the two cells.

The concentration cells are of two types:

(1) Electrode concentration cells.

(2) Electrolyte concentration cells.

2.5.1 Electrode Concentration Cells

In these cells, two similar electrodes of different concentrations are dipped in the same electrolyte solution containing ions of the electrode material. For example, electrode concentration cells consist of two hydrogen electrodes at unequal gas pressures immersed in the same solution of H^+ ions.

The cell may be represented as:

$$Pt/H_{2(P_1)}/HCl/H_{2(P_2)}/Pt$$

The cell reactions occurring are:

At anode:

$$H_{2(P_1)} \longrightarrow 2H^+ + 2e^- \quad \text{(Oxidation)}$$

At cathode:

$$2H^+ + 2e^- \longrightarrow H_{2(P_2)} \quad \text{(Reduction)}$$

Overall cell reaction

$$H_{2(P_1)} \longrightarrow H_{2(P_2)}$$

This reaction is evidently independent of the electrolyte concentration.

The Nernst equation for the above change can be written as

$$E = E° - \frac{0.0591}{2} \log \frac{(P_2)}{(P_1)}, \text{ at } 25°C$$

$E°$ = 0 for concentration cells as the two half reactions are identical written in opposite directions so the standard half cell potential of the two reactions cancels each other and $E° = 0$.

Therefore, we have

$$E = -\,0.02955 \log \frac{(P_2)}{(P_1)} = 0.02955 \log \frac{P_2}{P_1}.$$

The reaction will be spontaneous when $P_1 > P_2$ and hence EMF will become positive.

Other examples: gaseous electrodes, amalgam electrodes.

2.5.2 Electrolyte Concentration Cells

In these cells, the two electrodes are identical and are immersed in solutions of the same electrolyte but at different concentrations. As the concentration of electrolyte is different at the two electrodes, their electrode potential will be different.

For example, $Zn \mid Zn^{2+}_{(C_1)} \mid\mid Zn^{2+}_{(C_2)} \mid Zn$

The cell reactions occurring are:

At anode: $Zn(s) \longrightarrow Zn_{C_1}^{2+} + 2e^-$ (Oxidation)

At cathode: $Zn_{C_2}^{2+} + 2e^- \longrightarrow Zn(s)$ (Reduction)

Overall reaction: $Zn^{2+}_{(C_2)} \longrightarrow Zn^{2+}_{(C_1)}$

The Nernst equation can be written as

$$E = E^\circ \frac{-RT}{nF} \ln \frac{C_1}{C_2} \quad [E^\circ = 0 \text{ as discussed earlier}]$$

$$\therefore \qquad E = \frac{-RT}{nF} \ln \frac{C_1}{C_2} = \frac{RT}{nF} \ln \frac{C_2}{C_1}.$$

The process will be spontaneous, when $C_2 > C_1$ and thus EMF will become positive.

With the advent of time the two concentrations tend to become equal. Thus, in the beginning the emf of the cell is maximum and it gradually falls to zero.

2.6 ELECTROCHEMICAL CELLS

An electrochemical cell is a device which converts chemical energy into electrical energy. They are also called as **galvanic cells or voltaic cells.**

Such cells, usually consist of two electrodes immersed in one or more suitable electrolytes. When these electrodes are connected externally (and internally if required), a chemical reaction occurs in the cell. The electrode at which oxidation occurs is called **anode** while the reduction occurs at **cathode**.

The well known example of electrochemical cell is the **Daniel cell** (Fig. 2.2).

It consist of two beakers, one containing 1 M solution of $ZnSO_4$ while other containing 1 M solution of $CuSO_4$. A zinc rod is dipped into $ZnSO_4$ solution and a Cu rod is dipped into $CuSO_4$ solution. These metallic rods (Cu and Zn) are called as **electrodes**. These two electrodes are connected through an ammeter and the two solutions (*i.e.*, $ZnSO_4$ and $CuSO_4$ solution) are connected through a slat bridge (an inverted *U*-shaped glass tube filled with a solution of KCl, KNO_3 or NH_4NO_3 which does not undergo any chemical change during process). As soon as the circuit is completed by inserting a key in the circuit, the current starts flowing through external circuit which is indicated by the deflection in the ammeter.

It has been observed that the flow of electrons in the external circuit is from zinc rod to copper rod by convention. Therefore, the current flows from copper rod to zinc rod as the direction of flow of electric current is opposite to that to flow of electrons. A simple galvanic cell is shown in **Fig. 2.2.**

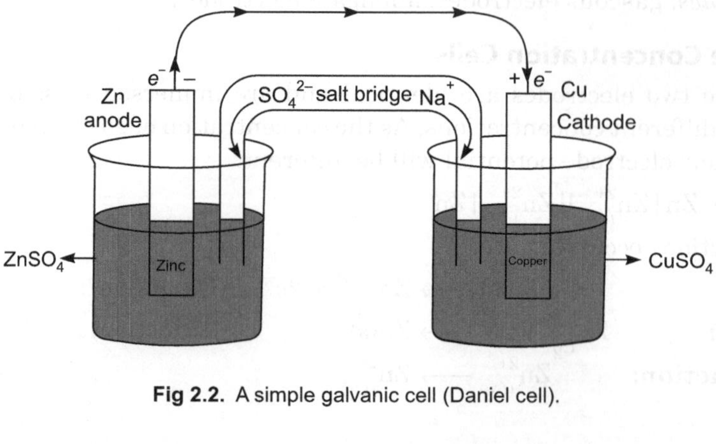

Fig 2.2. A simple galvanic cell (Daniel cell).

The following reactions takes place

At anode,

$$Zn_{(s)} \longrightarrow Zn^{2+}_{(aq)} + 2e^- \text{ (Oxidation)}$$

At cathode,

$$Cu^{2+}_{(aq)} + 2e^- \longrightarrow Cu_{(s)} \text{ (Reduction)}$$

Overall cell reaction is

$$Zn_{(s)} + Cu^{2+}_{(aq)} \longrightarrow Zn^{2+}_{(aq)} + Cu_{(s)}$$

As the electron move from Zn rod to the copper rod, the Zn rod is regarded as a negative terminal (Anode) whereas copper rod is regarded as positive terminal (Cathode). With the passage of time, the concentration of Zn^{2+} ion increases while that of Cu^{2+} decreases. This pushes the cell reaction in the backward direction. Ultimately, a state of equilibrium is reached and cell stops producing electricity.

2.6.1 Representation of an Electrochemical Cell

Connection used in representing an electrochemical cell are:

1. Anode (where oxidation occurs) is always written on the left hand side, whereas cathode (where reduction occurs) on the right hand side.
2. The anode is represented by writing metal or solid phase first and then the electrolyte (or cation) while the cathode is represented by writing the electrolyte first (or cation) and then metal or solid phase.
3. The concentration of the electrolytes is also mentioned within the bracket after the cation.
4. The metal and the cation are separated by a semicolon (;) or by a vertical line.
   For example: the above anode reaction can be written as
   $$Zn; Zn^{2+} \text{ or } Zn \mid Zn^{2+}$$
5. The salt bridge which separates the two half cells is represented by two vertical lines, *i.e.* ||
   For Daniel cell $Zn \mid Zn^{2+}_{(1M)} \parallel Cu^{2+}_{(1M)} \mid Cu$

Functions of salt bridge:

(*i*) It connect oxidation half cell with the reduction half cell to complete the electrical circuit.

(*ii*) It avoids any transference of the solution of the two half cells.

(*iii*) It prevents or minimizes liquid-liquid junction potential (liquid-liquid junction potential develops between the two solutions in contact with each other).

(*iv*) It maintains electrical neutrality of the two half cell solutions.

Standard Electrode Potential (Electrochemical series): The potential of an electrode at a given temperature depends upon the concentration of the ion in the surrounding solution. If the concentration of the ions is unity and the temperature is 25°C, the potential of the electrode is termed as the **standard electrode potential.**

The standard electrode potential value of large number of electrodes are given in table 2.2. These values are said to be on hydrogen scale since in these determinations, the potential of the standard hydrogen electrode, used as a reference electrode, has been taken as zero. The arrangement of elements in order of increasing electrode potential values is called as **electrochemical series or activity series.**

Table 2.2. Standard reduction potential at 25°C

Electrode	Electrode Reaction	$E°$(Volts)
$F_2(g)$; $2F^-$	$F_2(g) + 2e^- \rightleftharpoons 2F^-$	+ 2.87
Co^{3+}, Co^{2+}; Pt	$Co^{3+} + e^- \rightleftharpoons Co^{2+}$	+ 1.82
Ce^{4+}, Ce^{3+}; Pt	$Ce^{4+} + e^- \rightleftharpoons Ce^{3+}$	+ 1.61
Mn^{2+}, MnO_4^-; Pt	$MnO_4^- + 8H^+ + 5e^- \rightleftharpoons Mn^{2+} + 4H_2O$	+ 1.51
Au^{3+}, Au	$Au^{3+} + 3e^- \rightleftharpoons Au$	+ 1.50
Cl_2 (g), $2Cl^-$; Pt	$Cl_2(g, 1atm) + 2e^- \rightleftharpoons 2Cl^-$	+ 1.36
Cr^{3+}, $Cr_2O_7^{2-}$	$Cr_2O_7^{2-} + 14H^+ + 6e^- \rightleftharpoons Cr^{3+} + 7H_2O$	+ 1.33
Tl^{3+}, Tl^+	$Tl^{3+} + 2e^- \rightleftharpoons Tl^+$	+ 1.25
$Br_2(l)$, $2Br^-$; Pt	$Br_2(l) + 2e^- \rightleftharpoons 2Br^-$	+ 1.06
Hg^{2+}, Hg_2^{2+} ; Pt	$2Hg^{2+} + 2e^- \rightleftharpoons Hg_2^{2+}$	+ 0.92
Ag^+, Ag	$Ag^+ + e^- \rightleftharpoons Ag$	+ 0.80
Fe^{3+}, Fe^{2+} ; Pt	$Fe^{3+} + e^- \rightleftharpoons Fe^{2+}$	+ 0.77
Hg_2SO_4 (s), SO_4^{2-}; Hg	$Hg_2SO_4 (s) + e^- \rightleftharpoons 2Hg + SO_4^{2-}$	+ 0.61
I_2 (s) ; $2I^-$; Pt	$I_2(s) + 2e^- \rightleftharpoons 2I^-$	+ 0.53
Cu^+, Cu	$Cu^+ + e^- \rightleftharpoons Cu$	+ 0.52
Cu^{2+}, Cu	$Cu^{2+} + 2e^- \rightleftharpoons Cu$	+ 0.34
Hg_2Cl_2 (s), Cl^-; Hg	$Hg_2Cl_2 (s) + 2e^- \rightleftharpoons 2Hg + 2Cl^-$	+ 0.28
AgCl (s), Cl^-; Ag	$AgCl (s) + e^- \rightleftharpoons Ag (s) + Cl^-$	+ 0.22
Sn^{4+}, Sn^{2+}; Pt	$Sn^{4+} + 2e^- \rightleftharpoons Sn^{2+}$	+ 0.15
Cu^{2+}, Cu^+	$Cu^{2+} + e^- \rightleftharpoons Cu^+$	+ 0.15
$Hg_2Br_2(s)$, Br^-; Hg	$Hg_2Br_2 (s) + 2e^- \rightleftharpoons 2Hg + 2Br^-$	+ 0.13
AgBr (s), Br^- ; Ag	$AgBr (s) + e^- \rightleftharpoons Ag(s) + Br^-$	+ 0.07
$2H^+$, $H_2(g)$; Pt	$2H^+ + 2e^- \rightleftharpoons H_2(g, 1 atm)$	+ 0.00
Pb^{2+}, Pb	$Pb^{2+} + 2e^- \rightleftharpoons Pb$	– 0.13
Sn^{2+}, Sn	$Sn^{2+} + 2e^- \rightleftharpoons Sn$	– 0.15
AgI(s), I^-; Ag	$AgI(s) + e^- \rightleftharpoons Ag(s) + I^-$	– 0.15
Ni^{2+}, Ni	$Ni^{2+} + 2e^- \rightleftharpoons Ni$	– 0.24
Co^{2+}, Co	$Co^{2+} + 2e^- \rightleftharpoons Co$	– 0.27
TI^+, TI	$TI^+ + e^- \rightleftharpoons TI$	– 0.34
Cd^{2+} , Cd	$Cd^{2+} + 2e^- \rightleftharpoons Cd$	– 0.40
Fe^{2+}, Fe	$Fe^{2+} + 2e^- \rightleftharpoons Fe$	– 0.44
Cr^{3+}, Cr	$Cr^{3+} + 3e^- \rightleftharpoons Cr$	– 0.74
Zn^{2+} , Zn	$Zn^{2+} + 2e^- \rightleftharpoons Zn$	– 0.76
Mn^{2+}, Mn	$Mn^{2+} + 2e^- \rightleftharpoons Mn$	– 1.18
Al^{3+}, Al	$Al^{3+} + 3e^- \rightleftharpoons Al$	– 1.66

Mg^{2+}, Mg	$Mg^{2+} + 2e^- \rightleftharpoons Mg$	– 2.52
Na^+, Na	$Na^+ + e^- \rightleftharpoons Na$	– 2.71
Ca^{2+}, Ca	$Ca^{2+} + 2e^- \rightleftharpoons Ca$	– 2.87
Ba^{2+}, Ba	$Ba^{2+} + 2e^- \rightleftharpoons Ba$	– 2.90
K^+, K	$K^+ + e^- \rightleftharpoons K$	– 2.92
Li^+, Li	$Li^+ + e^- \rightleftharpoons Li$	– 3.04

2.6.2 EMF of Electrochemical Cells

The electrochemical series include a variety of electrodes (half cells) alongwith their electrode reaction and their standard electrode potential. Any two suitable half cells can be combined to form a galvanic cell. The EMF of the cell and the feasibility of the cell reaction can be easily determined with the help of information given in electrochemical series. For this purpose, the following rules have been suggested:

1. **Representation of the cell:** Write the two half cell reactions in such a way that the reaction taking place at the left hand side electrode is written as an oxidation reaction and reduction is written at the right hand side electrode.
2. Multiply one of the equation if necessary by suitable number to equate the number of electrons in the two half cell equations. Electrode potential is an **intrinsic property** therefore, $E°$ **values are not multiplied**.
3. The emf of the cell ($E°_{cell}$) is equal to the difference between the standard electrode potential of the cathode and cathode and the standard electrode potential of the anode. Thus

$$E°_{cell} = E°_{(Cathode)} - E°_{(Anode)} \text{ or } E°_{cell} = E_R - E_L$$

Both electrode potential are taken to be reduction potentials. If the emf of the cell is positive, the reaction is feasible in the given direction. If the value of emf comes out to be negative, the cell reaction is not possible and the electrodes needs to be reversed to bring about the chemical reaction.

2.7 NERNST EQUATION FOR ELECTRODE POTENTIAL

Nernst equation relates electrode potential to the concentration of ions in the electrolyte of concentration 1 M.

For the general reversible reaction,

$$M^{n+}_{(eq)} + ne^- \rightleftharpoons M_{(s)}$$

For an electrochemical cell, the free energy change (ΔG) for the cell reaction is given by the relation

$$\Delta G = -nFE \quad ...(1)$$

where n = number of electrons transferred in the half reaction

F = Faraday of electricity (96500)

E = EMF of the cell.

The free energy change for any chemical change can be expressed as:

$$\Delta G = \Delta G^\circ + RT \ln Q \qquad ...(2)$$

$$Q = \text{Activity quotient}$$

$$= \frac{a_{\text{M}}}{a_{\text{M}^{n+}}}$$

(Where a_M and $a_{M^{n+}}$ are the activities of products and reactants respectively)

From above equations (1) and (2), we have

$$-nFE = -nFE^\circ + RT \ln \frac{a_{\text{M}}}{a_{\text{M}^{n+}}} \qquad ...(3)\ (\because \Delta G^\circ = -nFE^\circ)$$

Dividing both sides of the equation (3) by nF, we get

$$-E = -E^\circ + RT \frac{RT}{nF} \ln \frac{a_{\text{M}}}{a_{\text{M}^{n+}}} \qquad ...(4)$$

On rearranging equation (4),

$$E = E^\circ - \frac{RT}{nF} \ln \frac{a_{\text{M}}}{a_{\text{M}^{n+}}} \qquad ...(5)$$

The activity or molar concentration of solids is taken as unity.

Therefore, Q can be written as

$$Q = \frac{[\text{Reduced state}]}{[\text{Oxidised state}]}$$

Equation (5) can also be written as

$$E = E^\circ - \frac{2.303\, RT}{nF} \log \frac{[\text{Reduced state}]}{[\text{Oxidised state}]}$$

or

$$E = E - \frac{2.303\, RT}{nF} \log \frac{[\text{M}_{(s)}]}{[\text{M}^{n+}_{(aq)}]}$$

where E = Electrode potential

$[M^{n+}]$ = Molar concentration of M^{n+} ion

$[M_{(s)}]$ = Molar concentration of pure solid = 1

E° = Standard electrode potential

R = Gas constant (8.314 JK^{-1})

T = Temperature (in Kelvin).

On substituting the values of R, F and T at 25°, the above equation becomes

$$E = E^\circ - \frac{0.0591}{n} \log \frac{[\text{M}]}{[\text{M}^{n+}]}$$

$$E = E^\circ - \frac{0.0591}{n} \log \frac{1}{[\text{M}^{n+}]}$$

For a general reaction, $aA + bB \longrightarrow xX + yY$

$$E_{\text{cell}} = E^\circ - \frac{0.0591}{n} \log \frac{[\text{X}]^x [\text{Y}]^y}{[\text{A}]^a [\text{B}]^b}$$

Relationship between cell EMF and Equilibrium constant (K_c):

$$E^\circ_{cell} = \frac{2.303\,RT}{nF} \log K_c$$

At equilibrium, $E^\circ_{cell} = 0$

$$E^\circ_{cell} = \frac{0.059}{n} \log K_c$$

Relationship between cell EMF and Gibbs energy of the reaction

$$\Delta G = -nF\,E_{cell}$$

Also, $$\Delta G^\circ = -RT \ln K_c.$$

2.8 REFERENCE ELECTRODES

The electrode whose potential is arbitrarily fixed or is exactly known at a given constant temperature is known as a **reference electrode**. The half cell potential of such electrodes is completely insensitive to the composition of the solution. The reference electrode can act as both cathode or anode depending upon the nature of other electrodes. Using reference electrode unknown potential of any other single electrode can be determined.

The reference electrodes are classified into two types:

1. **Primary reference electrode:** The standard hydrogen electrode (SHE) is called as primary reference electrode.
2. **Secondary reference electrode:** The electrode whose potential is determined by connecting to the SHE is called as **secondary reference electrode**. For example, calomel electrode, glass electrode, quinhydrone electrode etc.

2.8.1 Standard Hydrogen Electrode (SHE)

SHE is used to determine the electrode potential of individual half cells. This is assigned zero potential at all temperatures. It consists of a platinum wire sealed into a glass tube and carrying a platinum foil at one end **(Fig. 2.3)**. The platinum foil is coated with finely divided platinum called as platinum black. The electrode is immersed in an aqueous solution of some acid (like HCl, H_2SO_4 etc.) having one molar concentration of H^+ ions. Hydrogen gas at 1 atmospheric pressure and 298 K is continuously bubbled into the solution through the side tube. Platinum foil adsorbs H_2 gas and equilibrium is maintained between H_2 gas and H^+ ion in the solution. Thus, oxidation or reduction takes place at platinum foil. As a result, it can act as both cathode or anode and may be represented as:

$$\text{Pt, } H_2 \text{ (1 atm)/}H^+ \text{ (1 M); } E^\circ = 0\text{V}$$

If SHE acts as anode, oxidation will take place as

$$H_2\,(g) \rightleftharpoons 2H^+ + 2e^-$$

If it acts as cathode, reduction will take place as

$$2H^+(aq) + 2e^- \rightleftharpoons H_2\,(g)$$

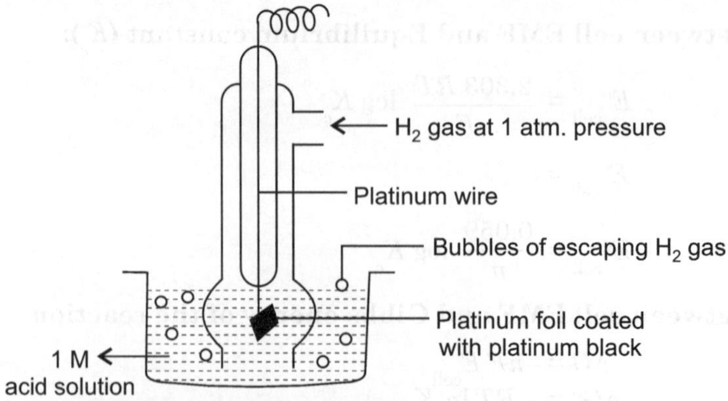

Fig. 2.3. Standard Hydrogen Electrode (SHE).

To determine the electrode potential using SHE: The half cell whose electrode potential is to be determined is connected to a SHE (having 1M H^+ ions) with the help of salt bridge. In this way, a galvanic cell is set up. Now, measure the cell potential of the resulting galvanic cell according to the following formula

$$E^\circ_{cell} = E^\circ_{cathode} - E^\circ_{anode}$$

Knowing the E°_{cell} and electrode potential of one of the electrodes (SHE), the electrode potential of other can be calculated.

Limitations of SHE

1. It is difficult to obtain pure and dry hydrogen gas. If it contains impurities of sulphur the platinum foil gets poisoned. This will disturb the equilibrium and also affects the developed potential.
2. It cannot be employed in solutions containing redox systems.
3. It is difficult to maintain a pressure of 1 atmosphere throughout the experiment.

2.8.2 Calomel Electrode (Hg – Hg_2Cl_2 – KCl Electrode)

This is the most commonly used reference electrode. It consist of mercury (Hg) in contact with a paste of mercurous chloride (Hg_2Cl_2). A solution of KCl is introduced above the paste through the side tube as shown in **Fig. 2.4.** A platinum wire sealed into a glass tube serves to make electrical contact of the electrode with the circuit.

Like SHE it can act as cathode as well as anode. If the electrode acts as anode, the following reaction will take place

Oxidation: $2\,Hg\,(l) + 2Cl^- \rightleftharpoons Hg_2Cl_2(s) + 2e^-$

If it acts as cathode, the reaction is

Reduction: $Hg_2Cl_2\,(s) + 2e^- \rightleftharpoons 2Hg\,(l) + 2Cl^-$

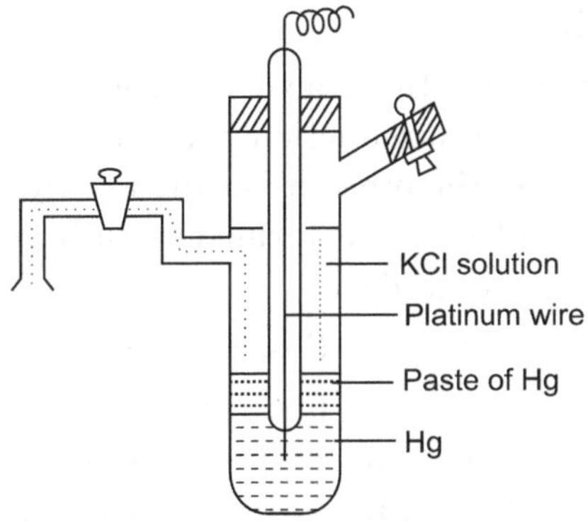

Fig. 2.4. Calomel electrode.

The potential of calomel electrode depends on the concentration of KCl solution taken in the half cell. The **Table 2.3** shows the potential of electrode at different KCl concentrations.

Table 2.3

Conc. of KCl	Reduction potential of calomel electrode
Saturated	+ 0.2415 V
1 M	+ 0.2800 V
0.1M	+ 0.3338 V

Determination of standard electrode potential using calomel electrode.

Let us determine the electrode potential of $Zn \mid Zn^{2+}$ electrode.

For this, the zinc electrode is dipped in $ZnSO_4$ (1M) solution and the calomel electrode (1M KCl solution) is set up as shown in **Fig. 2.5.**

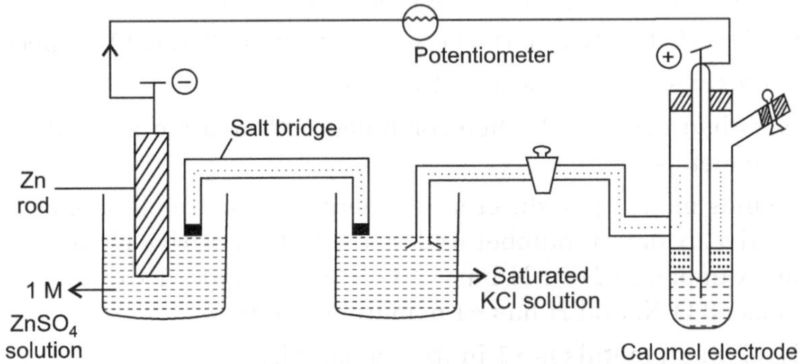

Fig. 2.5. Calomel electrode connected with other electrode.

The $E°$ of the above cell is found to be 1.083 V at 298 K. The direction of current indicates that zinc acts as anode and calomel electrode as cathode. The EMF of the cell is

$$E°_{cell} = E°_{cathode} - E°_{anode}.$$

$E°_{cell}$ and $E°_{cathode}$ are known so $E°_{anode}$ can be calculated.

The net reaction of the cell is

$$Zn(s) + Hg_2^{2+} \longrightarrow Zn^{2+}(aq) + 2Hg(l).$$

2.9 REDOX REACTIONS

Oxidation and reduction reactions constitute a very important class of chemical reactions. The electronic concept look at oxidation and reduction in terms of electron transfer. When an atom or ion loses one or more electron to the other it is called **oxidation** and the process in which an atom or ion gains one or more electrons is termed as **reduction**.

In the formation of NaCl from Na and Cl

$$Na \longrightarrow Na^+ + e^- \quad \text{(loss of } e^- \text{ by Na; oxidation)}$$

$$Cl + e^- \longrightarrow Cl^- \quad \text{(gain of } e^- \text{ by Cl; reduction)}$$

Sodium undergoes oxidation and chlorine undergoes reduction. Here, sodium helps chlorine to undergo reduction and therefore it is called as **reducing agent or reductant**.

Chlorine on the other hand accepts electron, therefore it is an **oxidising agent or oxidant.**

Thus, a **reductant** is a species in a chemical reaction which loses its electron to another reactant whereas an **oxidant** is a species which accepts electrons.

It may be noted that oxidation and reduction processes do not take place independently but occur simultaneously and are thus called **oxidation-reduction reaction** or **redox reactions**.

Rules for assigning oxidation number: There are certain rules that are to be followed for computing the oxidation number (O.N.) of an atom in a molecule or an ion.

1. O.N. is taken as zero if atoms are a present in elemental from. For example, O_2, Na, S_8, P_4, C (diamond or graphite), Br_2, N_2 etc. They have zero oxidation number.
2. The oxidation number of a monoatomic charged species is same as the charge on it. For example, Na^+, Mg^{2+}, Cl^-, SO_4^{2-}, N^{3-} will have oxidation number +1, + 2, –1, –2, –3 respectively.
3. The oxidation number of oxygen is –2 in most of its compounds except in
   (*i*) Peroxides like H_2O_2, BaO_2 where its O.N. is –1.
   (*ii*) In OF_2 and O_2F_2 where the O.N. of oxygen is +2 and +1 respectively.
   (*iii*) Superoxides like KO_2 where it is –1/2.
4. The O.N. of hydrogen is +1 when combined with non-metals and –1 when combined with active metals.
5. In compounds made up of different elements, the more electronegative element will have negative oxidation number and more electro positive element will have positive O.N. For example, in NF_3, N has +3 O.N. and F has –1 oxidation state whereas in NH_3, N has –3 O.N. and H has +1 oxidation number.
6. The O.N. of alkali metals is +1 in its compounds.
7. The sum of the O.N. of all the atoms in a neutral compound is zero.
8. In a polyatomic ion, the sum of the O.N. of all the atoms is equal to the charge on the ion. For example in ClO_4^-, the sum of O.N. of Cl and O is –1.

2.9.1 Balancing Redox Reaction

The redox reaction can be balanced by any of the following **two** methods:

1. Oxidation number method.
2. Half reaction method.

1. Balancing by oxidation number method: The steps involved in balancing redox reaction by this method are as follows:

1. Write skeletal equation of the reaction *i.e.* chemical equation without the stoichiometric coefficients and indicate the oxidation number of each atom above its symbol in the equation.
2. Identify the atoms undergoing change in oxidation number and calculate the increase or decrease in oxidation number per atom for the atom undergoing a change in oxidation number. If more than one atom is involved, multiply the increase or decrease in number with the number of atoms undergoing the change to determine the total change in oxidation number.
3. Balance the equation with respect to all the atoms except hydrogen and oxygen.
4. Finally, balance hydrogen and oxygen also.
   (*i*) If the reaction is taking place in acidic medium balance the oxygen atoms by adding required number of H_2O molecules on the side where O atoms are less in number. Balance the H atoms by adding H^+ to the side deficient in H atoms.
   (*ii*) In the basic medium, deficiency in hydrogen atoms can be made up by adding H_2O molecules on the deficient side and adding equal number of OH^- ions on the other side of the equation.

Finally, the equation is balanced by cancelling common species present on both sides of the equation.

(*i*) Balance the following reaction by oxidation number method taking place in acidic medium.

$MnO_4^- (aq) + Fe^{2+} (aq) \longrightarrow Mn^{2+} (aq) + Fe^{3+} (aq)$

Solution:

Step 1: $\overset{+7\ -2}{MnO_4^-} (aq) + \overset{+2}{Fe^{2+}} (aq) \longrightarrow \overset{+2}{Mn^{2+}} (aq) + \overset{+3}{Fe^{3+}} (aq)$ ...(*i*)

Step 2: $\overset{+7}{MnO_{4(aq)}} + \overset{+2}{Fe^{2+}_{(aq)}} \longrightarrow \overset{+2}{Mn^{2+}_{(aq)}} + \overset{+3}{Fe^{3+}_{(aq)}}$ ...(*ii*)

Decrease in O.N. = 5 (Mn: +7 → +2)

Increase in O.N. = 1 (Fe: +2 → +3)

Step 3: Equating the increase/decrease in oxidation number. The total decrease in O.N. is 5 and increase is 1, therefore, multiply Fe^{2+} on the LHS of equation (ii) by 5

$\therefore \quad MnO_4^- (aq) + 5Fe^{2+} (aq) \longrightarrow Mn^{2+} (aq) + Fe^{3+} (aq)$ ...(*iii*)

Step 4: Balance all atoms other than H and O.

$MnO_4^- (aq) + 5Fe^{2+} (aq) \longrightarrow Mn^{2+} (aq) + 5Fe^{3+} (aq)$ ...(*iv*)

Step 5: Balance O atoms by adding H_2O molecules. Since there are 4 oxygen atoms on LHS and none on the RHS of equation (*iv*), therefore add $4H_2O$ on the RHS. We have

$MnO_4^- (aq) + 5Fe^{2+} (aq) \longrightarrow Mn^{2+} + 5Fe^{3+} (aq) + 4H_2O$ ...(*v*)

Step 6: Balance H atoms by adding H^+ ions, as the reaction occurs in acidic medium. Since there are 8 H atoms on RHS and none on LHS in equation (*v*), therefore add $8H^+$ ions on the LHS of equation (*v*).

$MnO_4^- (aq) + 5Fe^{2+} (aq) + 8H^+ \longrightarrow Mn^{2+} + 5Fe^{3+} + 4H_2O$ ..(*vi*)

Thus, equation (*vi*) represents the correct balanced equation.

(*ii*) Balance the following reaction by oxidation number method taking place in basic medium.

$$Cr(OH)_3 + IO_3^- \longrightarrow I^- + CrO_4^{2-}$$

Solution: Step 1: $\overset{+3}{Cr}(OH)_3 + \overset{+5}{I}O_3^- \longrightarrow \overset{-1}{I^-} + \overset{+6}{Cr}O_4^{2-}$ ...(*i*)

Step 2:

O.N. increases by 3 per atom

$$\overset{+3}{Cr}(OH)_3 + \overset{+5}{I}O_3^- \longrightarrow \overset{-1}{I^-} + \overset{+6}{Cr}O_4^{2-} \quad ...(ii)$$

O.N. decreases by 6 per atom

Steps 3: To equate increase or decrease in O.N. multiply $Cr(OH)_3$ by 2 and IO_3^- by one.

$$2Cr(OH)_3 + IO_3^- \longrightarrow I^- + CrO_4^{2-} \quad ...(iii)$$

Step 4: Balance all atoms other than H and O.

$$2Cr(OH)_3 + IO_3^- \longrightarrow I^- + 2CrO_4^{2-} \quad ...(iv)$$

Step 5: Add OH^- to RHS to balance O atoms (as the reaction occurs in basic medium)

$$2Cr(OH)_3 + IO_3^- \longrightarrow I^- + 2CrO_4^{2-} + OH^- \quad ...(v)$$

Step 6: To balance H atoms add H_2O molecules on the RHS and equal number of OH on the LHS.

$$2Cr(OH)_3 + IO_3^- + 5OH^- \longrightarrow I^- + 2\,CrO_4^{2-} + OH^- + 5H_2O$$

or $$2Cr\,(OH)_3 + IO_3^- + 4OH^- \longrightarrow I^- + 2\,CrO_4^{2-} + 5H_2O$$

2. Balancing by Ion Electron Method or Half Reaction Method

The steps involved in balancing redox reaction by this method are as follows:

(*i*) Write the skeletal equation and indicate the O.N. of all the elements in the equation above their respective symbols.

(*ii*) Find out the species which are oxidized and reduced in the reaction.

(*iii*) Split the complete equation into two half reactions *i.e.* oxidation half reaction and reduction half reaction.

(*iv*) Balance two half equations by the following steps:

(*a*) In each half reaction, first balance the atoms of the elements which have undergone a change in O.N.

(*b*) Balance the O.N. by adding electrons to whichever side is necessary to make up the difference.

(*c*) Balance charge by adding H^+ ion (if reaction occurs in acidic medium) and OH^- ion (if reaction occurs in basic medium).

(*d*) Balance oxygen atoms by adding required number of water molecules to the side deficient in O atoms.

(*e*) Balance hydrogen atoms by adding H^+ ions if reaction is occurring in acidic medium. In basic medium, H atoms are balanced by adding H_2O molecules equal to the deficiency of H atoms and an equal number of OH^- ion added on the opposite side of the reaction.

(*v*) Add two balanced half cell reactions. Multiply one or both half cell reaction by suitable integers so that on adding the two equations, the electrons are balanced.

Example (i). Balance the following reaction by half reaction method in basic medium.

$$\mathbf{Zn + NO_3^- \longrightarrow Zn^{2+} + NH_4^+}$$

Solution:

O.N. increases by 2 per atom

Step 1:

$$\overset{0}{Zn} + \overset{+5}{N}\overset{-2}{O_3^-} \longrightarrow \overset{+2}{Zn^{2+}} + \overset{-3}{N}\overset{+1}{H_4^+} \qquad ...(i)$$

O.N. decreases by 8 per atom

Step 2: O.N. of Zn is increasing therefore it is undergoing oxidation and O.N. of N is decreasing so it undergoes reduction.

Step 3: Splitting of reaction into two half reactions.

(Reduction half reaction:)

$$NO_3^- \longrightarrow NH_4^+ \qquad ...(ii)$$

Oxidation half reaction:

$$Zn \longrightarrow Zn^{2+} \qquad ...(iii)$$

Step 4: Balance the reduction half reaction first

$$NO_3^- \longrightarrow NH_4^+$$

(*a*) Balance all atoms other than H and O (already done).

(*b*) O.N. of nitrogen decreases from + 5 to – 3 *i.e.* there is a difference of 8 electrons. To balance the electrons,

$$NO_3^- + 8e^- \longrightarrow NH_4^+ \qquad ...(iv)$$

(*c*) The reaction is taking place in basic medium so balance the charge by adding OH^- ions. The total charge on LHS is – 9 and on RHS is + 1. Therefore add 10 OH^- to RHS of equation (*iv*)

$$NO_3^- + 8e^- \longrightarrow NH_4^+ + 10\,OH^- \qquad ...(v)$$

(*d*) Add water molecules to balance the O atoms. As there are 10 oxygen atoms on RHS and 3 on LHS, so add 7 H_2O on LHS.

$$NO_3^- + 8e^- + 7H_2O \longrightarrow NH_4^+ + 10\,OH^- \qquad ...(vi)$$

The H atoms get automatically balanced. Equation (*iv*) is the balanced reduction half reaction.

Step 5: Balancing oxidation half reaction.

$$Zn \longrightarrow Zn^{2+}$$

(*a*) Balance all atoms other than H and O (already done).

(*b*) O.N. of Zn increases by 2 so add $2e^-$ to make up the difference in O.N.

$$Zn \longrightarrow Zn^{2+} + 2e^- \qquad ...(vii)$$

(*c*) Balance the charges (already done).

(*d*) As there are no H and O to balance, so there is no need of adding H_2O.

The balanced oxidation half reaction is

$$Zn \longrightarrow Zn^{2+} + 2e^- \qquad ...(viii)$$

Step 6: Multiply equation (*viii*) by 4 to balance the electrons and then add the two half cell reactions

$$4Zn \longrightarrow 4Zn^{2+} + 8e^-$$

$$NO_3^- + 8e^- + 7H_2O \rightarrow NH_4^+ + 10OH^-$$

$$4Zn + NO_3^- + 7H_2O \rightarrow 4Zn^{2+} + NH_4^+ + 10\,OH^-$$

This gives the final balanced reaction.

Example (ii). Balance the following reaction by half reaction method in acidic medium.

$$Cr_2O_{7\,(aq)}^{2-} + Fe^{2+}(aq) \longrightarrow Cr^{3+}(aq) + Fe^{3+}(aq)$$

Step 1: Writing of O.N of atoms above their symbols.

O.N. of Fe increases by 1 per atom

$$\overset{+6}{Cr_2}O_7^{2-}\ (aq) + \overset{+2}{Fe^{2+}}(aq) \longrightarrow \overset{3+}{Cr^{3+}}(aq) + \overset{3+}{Fe^{3+}}(aq) \qquad ...(i)$$

O.N. of Cr decreases by 3 per atom

Step 2: O.N. of Fe^{2+} is increasing therefore it is undergoing oxidation and O.N. of Cr is decreasing so it is undergoing reduction.

Step 3: Splitting of reaction into two half reactions:

Reduction half reaction: $Cr_2O_7^{2-} \longrightarrow Cr^{3+}$ ...(*ii*)

Oxidation half reaction: $Fe^{2+} \longrightarrow Fe^{3+}$ ...(*iii*)

Step4: Balance the reduction half reaction first

$$Cr_2O_7^{2-} \longrightarrow Cr^{3+}$$

(*a*) Balance the atoms undergoing change in O.N., *i.e.* Cr

$$Cr_2O_7^{2-} \longrightarrow 2Cr^{3+}$$

(*b*) Balance the O.N. by adding electrons. Here, each Cr atom undergoes change in O.N. by 3 therefore 2Cr atoms undergo change in O.N by 6.

$$Cr_2O_7^{2-} + 6e^- \longrightarrow 2Cr^{3+}$$

(*c*) As the reaction is taking place in acidic medium, the charge will be balanced by adding H^+ ions on LHS. The total charge on LHS is – 8 whereas on RHS. it is + 6. Therefore, 14 H^+ ions are added to LHS to balance the charge.

$$Cr_2O_7^{2-} + 6e^- + 14H^+ \longrightarrow 2Cr^{3+}$$

(*d*) Balance the H and O by adding H_2O molecules: As there as 7 Oxygen atoms on LHS so add $7H_2O$ molecules on RHS.

$$Cr_2O_7^{2-}\ (aq) + 14H^+ + 6e^- \longrightarrow 2Cr^{3+} + 7H_2O \qquad ...(iv)$$

The H atoms get automatically balanced.

Step 5: Balancing oxidation half reaction

$$Fe^{2+} \longrightarrow Fe^{3+}$$

(*a*) Atoms are balanced on both sides

(*b*) Oxidation number is balanced by adding electrons.

$$Fe^{2+} \longrightarrow Fe^{3+} + e^- \qquad ...(v)$$

(*c*) Charge is also balanced, therefore no need to add H^+ ions.

Step 6: Add the two half reactions: To balance the number of electrons lost in oxidation half reaction and number of e^- gained in reduction half reaction multiply equation (v) by 6.

$$\begin{aligned} Cr_2O_7^{2-} + 14H^+ + 6e^- &\longrightarrow 2Cr^{3+} + 7H_2O \\ 6Fe^{2+} &\longrightarrow 6Fe^{3+} + 6e^- \\ \hline Cr_2O_7^{2-} + 6Fe^{2+} + 14H^+ &\longrightarrow 2Cr^{3+} + 6Fe^{3+} + 7H_2O \end{aligned}$$

This gives the final balanced reaction.

2.10 TRANSPORT NUMBER

We have seen earlier that the current in an electrolytic solution is carried by cations and anions. The fraction of the total current carried by the anion or the cation is called its **transport number or transference number**.

If u_+ represents the speed of migration of cation and u_- that of that anion, then

$$\text{Transport number of cation} = \frac{\text{Current carried by cation}}{\text{Total current passed through the solution}}$$

$$t_+ = \frac{u_+}{u_+ + u_-}.$$

$$\text{Similarly, transport number of anion} = \frac{\text{Current carried by an anion}}{\text{Total current passed through the solution}}$$

$$t_- = \frac{u_-}{u_+ + u_-}.$$

From the above relation,

$$\frac{t_+}{t_-} = \frac{u_+}{u_-} \quad \text{and} \quad t_+ + t_- = 1.$$

Hence, if the transport number of one of the ions is known, that of the other can be easily calculated. Thus, transport number of an ion depends on the mobility, concentration of the ions and temperature of the electrolytic solution.

There are two basic methods for the determination of transport number. These are:

1. Hittorf's method
2. Moving boundary method

2.10.1 Hittorf's Method

This method is based on the Hittorf's rule, according to which when electric current is passed through an electrolyte solution, the fall in concentration around any electrode is proportional to the speed of the ion moving away from that electrode. Thus, according to this rule, the transport number is given by

$$t_+ = \frac{u_+}{u_+ + u_-} = \frac{\text{Fall in concentraion around anode}}{\text{Total fall in concentraion around both electrodes}}$$

If the concentration is expressed in terms of gram equivalents then,

$$t_+ = \frac{\text{Number of gram equivalents lost from anode}}{\text{Number of gram equivalents lost from both the electrodes}}$$

$$t_+ = \frac{\text{Number of gram equivalents lost from anode}}{\text{Number of gram equivalents deposited on each electrode}} \quad \ldots(iii)$$

Similarly transport number of anion can also be defined. The denominator in equation (*ii*) can be determined by placing a copper or silver coulometer in series with the electrolysis apparatus used for determining the transport number. According to Faraday's law, the number of gram equivalents deposited on each electrode must be equal to the number of gram equivalents of coppper or silver deposited in a copper or silver coulometer. Thus,

$$t_+ = \frac{\text{Number of gram equivalents lost from anode}}{\text{Number of gram equivalent of Cu or Ag deposited in coulometer}} \quad \ldots(iv)$$

Knowing the value of t_+, we can easily determine t_-

$$t_- = 1 - t_+$$

Apparatus and procedure used in Hittorf's method: The Hittorf's apparatus consists of three compartments; The cathode compartment, the middle compartment (a U-tube which separates anodic and cathodic compartments) and an anodic compartment as shown in **Fig. 2.6.** All the three compartments are provided with the stop cocks at the bottom. The electrodes are made of suitable metals and some mercury is placed in the tubes to make adequate contacts. Suppose we need to determine the transport number of Ag^+ ions. For this, the apparatus is filled with $AgNO_3$ solution in which the electrodes (of either Ag or Pt) are dipped. A steady current of about 0.01 ampere is passed through the electrolytic solution for about 2-3 hours. The whole of the solution from the anodic compartment is carefully withdrawn into a weighed flask. The silver content of the anodic compartment can be determined by titrating against a standard solution of KCl. The weight of silver or copper deposited in the silver or copper coulometer is also determined. There should be no appreciable change in the concentration of the solution in the U-tube.

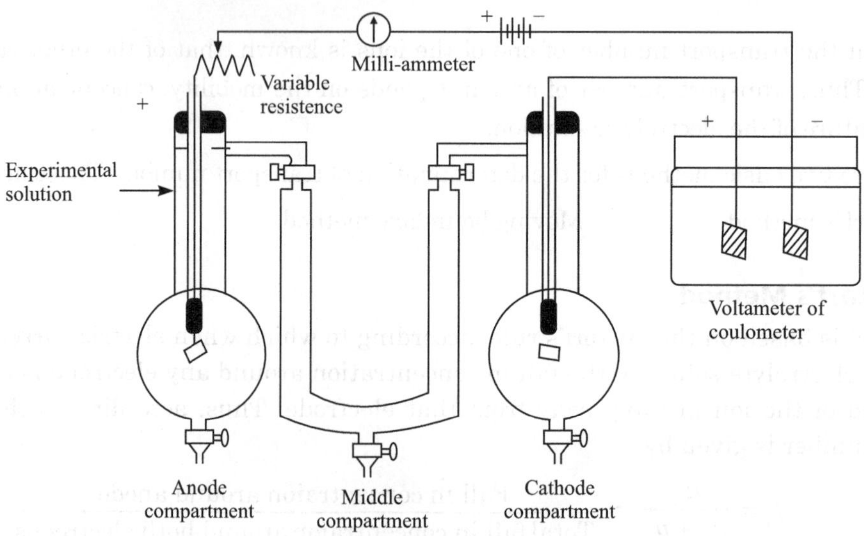

Fig 2.6. Hittorf's apparatus.

Depending on the type of electrodes (Ag electrodes or Pt electrodes) used, two different cases may arise:

(a) When non-attackable or inert electrodes (Pt electrodes) are used: After passing electric current

Let the weight of anodic solution withdrawn = x g

Weight of $AgNO_3$ present in it by titration = y g

Weight of water = $(x - y)$g

Thus, $(x - y)$g of water contains = y g of $AgNO_3$

$$= \frac{y}{170} \text{ g eq. of } AgNO_3 \text{ or } Ag^+ \qquad [\text{Mol. wt. of } AgNO_3 = 170]$$

$$= Z \text{ g eq}$$

Before passing electric current.

Let 'a' g of anodic solution contains 'b' g of $AgNO_3$

Weight of water = $(a - b)$g

Thus, $(a - b)$g of water contains = 'b' g of $AgNO_3$

Fall in concentration of anodic solution = $(b - y)$g of $AgNO_3$

$$= \frac{(b-y)}{170} \text{ g eq. of } AgNO_3 \text{ or } Ag^+$$

$$= C \text{ g eq.}$$

In Silver coulometer

Let the weight of Ag deposited in silver coulometer = w g

$$= \frac{w}{108} \text{ g eq or Ag (Mol. wt of Ag = 108)} = D \text{ g eq}$$

Now according to Hittorf's method [equation (*iv*)], transport number of ions will be given by

$$t_{Ag+} = \frac{\text{Fall in concentration around anode in g eq}}{\text{Amount of Ag deposited in geq}} = \frac{C}{D}$$

And
$$t_{NO_3^-} = 1 - t_{Ag+} = 1 - \frac{C}{D}.$$

(b) When attackable electrodes (Ag electrodes) are used: If Ag electrodes are used here, the nitrate ions attack the silver anode. Thus, there is an increase in concentration of Ag^+ ions rather than decrease. So,

Increase in concentration of anodic solution

$$= (y - b) \text{ g of } AgNO_3$$

$$= \frac{(y-b)}{170} \times 108 \text{ g of Ag}$$

$$= \frac{(y-b)}{170} \text{ g eq. of Ag} = d \text{ g eq. of Ag.}$$

If no Ag^+ ions are migrated from anode, the increase in concentration of Ag^+ ions would have been equal to D g eq. Thus, fall in concentration because of migration of Ag^+ ions = $D - d$

Here,

$$t_{Ag^+} = \frac{D-d}{D}$$

And

$$t_{NO_3^-} = 1 - \frac{D-d}{D}$$

2.10.2 Moving Boundary Method

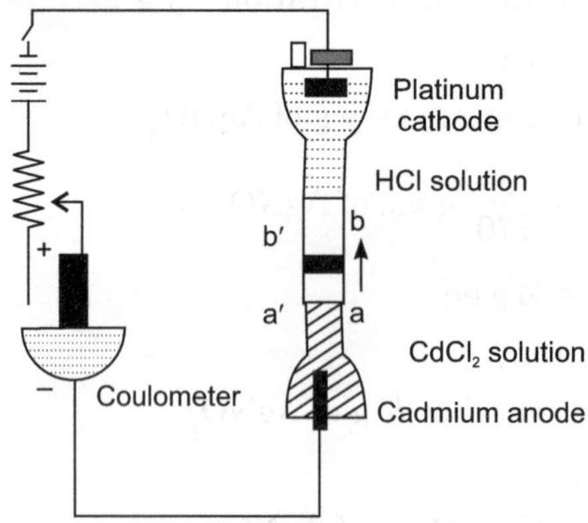

Fig. 2.7. The Moving Boundary Method.

The moving boundary method is based on the direct observation of migration of ions in an electric field. Thus, the speeds of cations and anions are determined. The transport number of ions are given by the following formulas:

$$t_+ = \frac{u_+}{u_+ + u_-} \quad \text{and} \quad t_- = \frac{u_-}{u_+ + u_-}.$$

The principle can be explained with reference to determination of transport number of H^+ ions in hydrochloride acid. Hydrochloric acid is the main electrolyte whereas $CdCl_2$ serves as an indicator electrolyte to enable formation of a boundary. The apparatus consists of a long vertical tube fitted with two electrodes at the two ends **(Fig. 2.7)**. The tube is filled with $CdCl_2$ solution at the lower end and HCl at the upper end in a way that a sharp boundary appears between the two solutions due to difference in their refractive indices. The selection of the indicator electrolyte has to be made carefully. It's cation should not move faster than the cation whose transport number has to be determined and it should have the same anion as the main electrolyte. Cadmium chloride fulfills both these requirements. The mobility of Cd^{2+} ions is less than that of H^+ ion and it has a common anion with HCl *i.e.* Cl^- ions.

The cathode at the top is a platinum foil while anode is of cadmium metal present at the bottom. On passing electric current through the cell, the chloride ions move towards the anode whereas H^+ ions followed by Cd^{2+} ions move towards the cathode. The boundary separating the two solutions move upwards due to the movement of ions *i.e.* from $a - a'$ to $b - b'$. If the boundary comes through a distance l cm *i.e.*, from $a - a'$ to $b - b'$, then the volume of the liquid that has moved up is lA cm^3 (A = area of cross-section of the tube in cm^2). Let 'C' be the concentration of the acid in gram equivalents per ml. Then, the number of gram equivalents of H^+ ions moving towards the cathode = $l\,AC$.

The fraction of current carried by H^+ ions = $n \times t_{A^+}$

$$n \times t_{A^+} = lAC$$

Hence, $$t_{A^+} = \frac{l\,AC}{n}$$

Where $n = \frac{Q}{F}$, and Q is the quantity of electricity passed and F is one Faraday, *i.e*, 96500 coulmbs

$$t_{A^+} = \frac{l\,AC \times F}{Q}.$$

2.11 SOLUBILITY EQUILIBRIUM AND SOLUBILITY PRODUCT

A solubility product is a special type of equilibrium constant. It gives us information about the equilibrium between a solid and the ions it furnishes in solution. The most important point about solubility product is that it applies only to springily soluble salts. Substances like, AgCl, $BaSO_4$, $PbSO_4$, $Al(OH)_3$, $Ca_3(PO_4)_2$, etc., which dissolve in water to an extremely small extent are called as **sparingly soluble salts**. When a sparingly soluble salt is added to water, there exists a dynamic equilibrium between the undissolved solid salt and the ions which it furnishes in the solution. For example in case of saturated solution of AgCl, there exists an equilibrium between undissolved salt and its ions.

Thus,

$$AgCl_{(s)} \underset{\text{Precipitation}}{\overset{\text{Dissolution}}{\rightleftharpoons}} AgCl_{(aq)} \rightleftharpoons Ag^+_{(aq)} + Cl^-_{(aq)}$$

or we may write directly as

$$AgCl_{(s)} \rightleftharpoons Ag^+_{(aq)} + Cl^-_{(aq)}$$

Applying law of chemical equilibrium to the above ionic equilibrium, we have

$$K = \frac{[Ag^+][Cl^-]}{[AgCl]}$$

Since, the solution is saturated, the concentration of undissociated solid remains almost constant, we can write

$$K[AgCl] = [Ag^+][Cl^-]$$

$$K_{sp} = [Ag^+][Cl^-]$$

where K_{sp} is the solubility product and is equal to ionic product for a saturated solution.

In general, for any electrolyte A_xB_y, the equilibrium may be written as,

$$A_xB_y \rightleftharpoons xA^{y+} + yB^{x-}$$

$$K_{sp} = [A^{y+}]^x\,[B^{x-}]^y$$

Solubility product of a salt is constant at constant temperature. By using the general formula for the solubility product, the solubility product for certain substance may be expressed as:

$$BaSO_4\,(s) \rightleftharpoons Ba^{2+} + SO_4^{2-} \qquad K_{sp} = [Ba^{2+}][SO_4^{2-}]$$

$$Al(OH)_3(s) \rightleftharpoons Al^{3+} + 3OH^- \qquad K_{sp} = [Al^{3+}][OH^-]^3$$

$$Ca_3(PO_4)_2(s) \rightleftharpoons 3Ca^{2+} + 2PO_4^{3-} \qquad K_{sp} = [Ca^{2+}]^3\,[PO_4^{3-}]^2$$

Ionic product has a broad meaning since it is applicable to all types of solutions, i.e., saturated as well as unsaturated, However, solubility product has restricted meaning as it applies only to a saturated solution in which there exists a dynamic equilibrium between the undissolved salt and the ions present in solution. Solubility product is in fact, the ionic product for a saturated solution.

2.11.1 Applications of Solubility Product

1. **Calculation of solubility of sparingly soluble salts:** Knowing the solubility product of a sparingly soluble salt at any given temperature, we can easily calculate its solubility. The relationship between solubility (*s*) and solubility product depends upon the nature of the salt. For example:

   (*i*) For salts of the type *AB* (*e.g.* AgCl, $BaSO_4$, $PbSO_4$ etc.)

$$\underset{S}{AB} \rightleftharpoons \underset{S}{A^+} + \underset{S}{B^-} \qquad K_{sp} = [A^+][B^-] = s \times s = s^2$$

   (*ii*) For salts of type AB_2 (*e.g.* $PbCl_2$, CaF_2, etc.)

$$\underset{S}{AB_2} \rightleftharpoons \underset{S}{A^{2+}} + \underset{2S}{2B^-} \qquad K_{sp} = [A^{2+}][B^-]^2 = s \times (2s)^2 = 4s^3$$

Similarly for salts of the type A_2B (*e.g.* Ag_2CrO_4, Ag_2SO_4 etc.) also $K_{sp} = 4s^3$.

   (*iii*) For salts of the type AB_3 (*e.g.* $Fe(OH)_3$, $Al(OH)_3$ etc.)

$$\underset{S}{AB_3} \rightleftharpoons \underset{S}{A^{3+}} + \underset{3S}{3B^-} \qquad K_{sp} = [A^{3+}][B^-]^3 = s \times (3s)^3 = 27s^4.$$

2. **Predicting ionic or precipitation reaction:** If the ionic product *i.e.*, the product of the concentration of ions in the solution exceeds the value of the solubility product of a sparingly soluble salt, the excess ions will combine resulting in the formation of precipitate.

   If, ionic product > K_{sp} ⟶ precipitation occurs
   ionic product < K_{sp} ⟶ no precipitation occurs

   Thus, by the knowledge of solubility product of any sparingly soluble salt, we can predict whether the salt will precipitate out or not when two solutions containing a known concentration of its ions are mixed together.

3. **In explaining salting out or precipitation of soluble salts:** For example: On passing HCl gas through a saturated solution of NaCl, the concentration of chloride ions will be increased. This increases the ionic product of NaCl and the solid salt will be precipitated. Thus the equilibrium

$$NaCl(s) \rightleftharpoons Na^+_{(aq)} + Cl^-_{(aq)}$$

$$K_{sp} = [Na^+_{(aq)}]\,[Cl^-_{(aq)}]$$

   In presence of some common ions, the concentration of ions are disturbed and in place of K_{sp} we use the symbol Q_{sp}.

   Now, Cl^- ion concentration will increase so that $Q_{sp} > K_{sp}$. In order that Q_{sp} becomes equal to K_{sp} equilibrium will shift in backward direction *i.e.*, pure NaCl will precipitate out.

   Salting out of soap: Soap is a sodium salt of higher fatty acids. From the solution, soap is precipitated by the addition of concentrated solution of NaCl.

$$\underset{\text{Soap}}{RCOONa} \rightleftharpoons RCOO^- + Na^+$$

$$NaCl \rightleftharpoons Na^+ + Cl^-$$

   Thus, the concentration of Na^+ ions increases considerably on addition of NaCl solution. Hence, the ionic product of soap $[RCOO^-]\,[Na^+]$ exceeds the solubility product of soap and therefore, soap precipitates out from the solution.

4. **In qualitative analysis:** The separation and identification of various basic radicals into different groups in based on:

(i) Solubility product principle: According to this principle, a precipitate is formed if ionic product is greater than the solubility product.

(ii) Common ion effect: According to this, if to the solution of a weak electrolyte, a strong electrolyte having a common ion is added the ionization of weak electrolyte is further suppressed. The phenomena of suppression of the degree of dissociation of a weak electrolyte (acid or base) by the addition of a strong electrolyte having a common ion is called as common ion effect.

(a) Precipitation of sulphides of groups II: Cations of group II (Hg^{2+}, Cu^{2+}, Bi^{3+}, Cd^{2+}) are precipitated as their sulphides by passing H_2S gas through the solution containing dil HCl. H_2S being a weak electrolyte ionizes only slightly, while HCl being a strong electrolyte ionizes almost completely

$$H_2S \rightleftharpoons 2H^+ + S^{2-}$$
$$HCl \longrightarrow H^+ + Cl^-$$

Due to common ion effect, the degree of dissociation of H_2S decreases sufficiently and the concentration of S^{2-} ions in the solution becomes very small. But with this low concentration of S^{2-} ions, the ionic product of the cations of II group and the sulphide ions exceeds the very low solubility products of their corresponding sulphides. Therefore, the cations of group II are precipitated as their insoluble sulphides.

On the other hand, the sulphides of the cations of the other groups (III, IV, V and Mg) are not precipitated under these conditions because their solubility products are quite high.

(b) Precipitation of hydroxides of group III: Cations of group III (Al^{3+}, Fe^{3+} and Cr^{3+}) are precipitated as their hydroxides by adding excess of solid NH_4OH in presence of NH_4Cl. Being a weak electrolyte, NH_4OH is only slightly ionized, whereas NH_4Cl being a strong electrolyte, ionizes almost completely to give a large concentration of NH_4^+ ions.

$$NH_4OH \rightleftharpoons NH_4^+ + OH^-$$
$$NH_4Cl \longrightarrow NH_4^+ + Cl^-$$

Due to the common ion effect, the degree of dissociation of NH_4OH gets suppressed and hence the concentration of OH^- ions in solution decreases appreciably. But even with this low concentration of OH^- ions, the ionic product of the cations of group III and OH^- ions exceeds the low value of their solubility products. As a result, the cations of group III get precipitated as their insoluble hydroxides. On the other hand cations of other groups do not precipitate because of high values of their solubility products.

(c) Precipitation of sulphides of group IV: Cations of group IV (Zn^{2+}, Mn^{2+}, $Ni^{2+}$and CO^{2+}) are precipitated as their sulphides by passing H_2S gas through solution containing NH_4OH.

Both H_2S and NH_4OH are weak electrolytes and ionize slightly.

$$H_2S \rightleftharpoons 2H^+ + S^{2-}$$
$$NH_4OH \rightleftharpoons NH_4^+ + OH^-$$

The H^+ and OH^- ions combine to produce practically unionized molecules of H_2O.

$$H^+ + OH^- \longrightarrow H_2O$$

As a result, the above dissociation equilibrium gets shifted in the forward direction, hence the concentration of S^{2-} ions goes on increasing. Ultimately the ionic product of the cations of the group IV and S^{2-} ions exceed the solubility product of their corresponding metal sulphides and hence get precipitated.

(*d*) **Precipitation of carbonates of group V:** Cations of group V are precipitated as their carbonates by adding $(NH_4)_2CO_3$ solutions to the extract of group III in the presence of NH_4OH and NH_4Cl.

$(NH_4)_2CO_3$ being a weak electrolyte ionizes only slightly to give a small concentration of CO_3^{2-} ions.

$$(NH_4)_2CO_3 \rightleftharpoons 2NH_4^+ + CO_3^{2-}$$

On the other hand, NH_4Cl being a strong electrolyte ionizes almost completely to give a large concentration of NH_4^+ ions. Due to the common ion (NH_4^+) effect, the dissociation of $(NH_4)_2CO_3$ is suppressed and hence the concentration of CO_3^{2-} ions in the solution decreases considerably. But even with this low concentration of CO_3^{2-} ions, the ionic products of group V cations and CO_3^{2-} ions exceed the low values of the solubility products of their corresponding metal carbonates and thus get precipitated.

SOLVED EXAMPLES

Example 2.1. *The ionization constant of acetic acid is 1.8 × 10^{-5} mol l^{-1} at 298 K. Calculate the degree of dissociation of the acid in 0.01M solution.*

Solution: Given:

$$K = 1.8 \times 10^{-5} \text{ mol } l^{-1}$$

$$C = 0.01 \text{ M}$$

$$K = C\alpha^2$$

$$\alpha = \sqrt{\frac{K}{C}} = \sqrt{\frac{1.8 \times 10^{-5}}{0.01}} \; 4.24 \times 10^{-2} = 4.24\%.$$

Example 2.2. *At 25°C, the molar concentration of propanoic acid at infinite dilution is 386.65 S cm^2 mol^{-1}. If its ionization constant is 1.4 × 10^{-5}, calculate molar conductance of 0.05 M propanoic acid solution at 25°C.*

Solution: We know that $K = C\alpha^2$

$$\alpha = \sqrt{\frac{K}{C}} = \sqrt{\frac{1.4 \times 10^{-5}}{0.05}} = 0.0167$$

$$\alpha = \frac{\Lambda^c}{\Lambda^\circ}, \text{ therefore}$$

$$\Lambda^c = \alpha\,\Lambda^\circ = 0.0167 \times 386.6 \text{ S cm}^2 \text{ mol}^{-1}$$

$$= 6.47 \text{ S cm}^2 \text{ mol}^{-1}.$$

Example 2.3. *Molar conductivities at infinite dilution at 25°C of NH_4Cl, NaOH and NaCl are 129.8, 217.4 and 108.9 S $cm^2 mol^{-1}$. For 0.01 M NH_4OH, molar conductance is 9.33 S cm^2 mol^{-1}. Calculate ionization constant of NH_4OH.*

Solution: $NH_4OH \rightleftharpoons NH_4^+ + OH^-$

By Ostwald dilution law:

$$K = \frac{C\alpha^2}{(1-\alpha)}$$

By Kohlrausch law:

$$\Lambda^\circ_{(NH_4OH)} = \Lambda^\circ_{(NH_4Cl)} + \Lambda^\circ_{(NaOH)} - \Lambda^\circ_{(NaCl)}$$

$$= 129.8 + 217.4 - 108.9$$

$$= 238.3 \text{ S cm}^2 \text{ mol}^{-1}$$

$$\alpha = \frac{\Lambda^c}{\Lambda^\circ} \quad \Lambda^C = 9.33 \text{ S cm}^2 \text{ mol}^{-1} \text{ at concentration of 0.01 M}$$

$$\alpha = \frac{9.33}{238.3} = 0.0392$$

$$K = \frac{C\alpha^2}{(1-\alpha)} = \frac{0.01 \times (0.0392)^2}{(1-0.0392)} = 1.6 \times 10^{-5}.$$

Example 2.4. *The solubility product of lead bromide is 8×10^{-5} at 298 K. If the slat is 80% dissociated in saturated solution, calculate the solubility of the salt (in gram/litre).*

Solution: The solubility equilibrium is

$$PbBr_{2(s)} \rightleftharpoons Pb^{2+}_{(aq)} + 2Br^-$$

Suppose, the solubility of $PbBr_2$ is '*s*' moles per litre. Then,

$$[Pb^{2+}] = s \; [Br^-] = 2s$$

Now,

$$K_{sp} = [Pb^{2+}][Br^-]^2$$

$$8 \times 10^{-5} = s \times (2s)^2 = 4s^3$$

$$s^2 \times \frac{8 \times 10^{-5}}{4} = 2 \times 10^{-5}$$

$$s = (2 \times 10^{-5})^{1/3} = 2.714 \times 10^{-2} \text{ mol L}^{-1}.$$

This is the solubility of $PbBr_2$ if it is 100% dissociated.

Solubility of $PbBr_2$, if it is 80% dissociated.

$$\frac{2.714 \times 10^{-2} \times 80}{100} = 2.192 \times 10^{-2} \text{ mol L}^{-1}.$$

Mol. wt. of $PbBr_2$ = 367.

$$\text{Solubility of } PbBr_2 = 2.192 \times 10^{-2} \text{ mol L}^{-1}$$

$$= 2.192 \times 10^{-2} \times 367 \text{ g L}^{-1}$$

$$= 8.04 \text{ g L}^{-1}$$

Example 2.5. *In a moving boundary experiment with 0.1 N KCl using 0.65 N LiCl a indicator electrolyte, a constant current of 0.006 ampere was passed for 1900 sec and the boundary was observed to move through 5 cm in a tube of 0.1142 cm² cross-section. Calculate the transport number of K^+ and Cl^- ions.*

Solution: Given:

$$A = 0.1142 \text{ cm}^2$$

$$Q = I\,t = 0.006 \times 1900 \text{ C}$$

$$C = 0.1 \text{ N} = 0.1\, g \text{ eq } L^{-1} = \frac{0.1}{1000} \text{ g eq ml}^{-1}$$

$$F = 96500 \text{ C}$$

$$l = 5 \text{ cm.}$$

Transport number of ions can be calculated as:

$$t_{K^+} = \frac{AlC \times F}{Q} = \frac{0.1142 \times 5 \times 0.1 \times 96500}{1000 \times 0.006 \times 1900}$$

$$= 0.4833$$

$$t_{Cl^-} = 1 - 0.4833 = 0.5167.$$

Example 2.6. *In a moving boundary experiment with 0.02 N NaCl using $CdCl_2$ as an indicator electrolyte, a current of 0.0020 ampere in 2020 seconds moved the boundary through a distance of 5.7 cm in a tube of 0.1250 cm² area of cross-section. Determine the transport number of Na^+ and Cl^- ions.*

Solution: Given

$$A = 0.1250 \text{ cm}^2$$

$$l = 5.7 \text{ cm}$$

$$C = 0.02 \text{ N} = 0.02 \text{ g eq/l} = \frac{0.02}{1000} \text{ g eq ml}^{-1}$$

$$Q = I \times t = 0.0020 \times 2020 = 4.04 \text{ C}$$

Transport number of t_{Na^+} is given by

$$t_{Na^+} = \frac{AlC \times F}{Q}$$

$$= \frac{0.1250 \times 5.7 \times 0.02 \times 96500}{4.04 \times 1000}$$

$$= 0.340$$

$$t_{Cl^-} = 1 - 0.340 = 0.66.$$

Example 2.7. *What is the minimum volume of water required to dissolve 1 g of $CaSO_4$ at 298 K. K_{sp} for $CaSO_4$ is 9.1×10^{-6}.*

Solution: K_{sp} for $CaSO_4 = 9.1 \times 10^{-6}$

Let solubility of $CaSO_4$ be *s*.

$$CaSO_4 \rightleftharpoons Ca^{2+} + SO_4^{2-}$$

$$[Ca^{2+}] = s \quad [SO_4^{2-}] = s$$

$$K_{sp} = [Ca^{2+}][SO_4^{2-}] = s \times s = s^2$$
$$s^2 = K_{sp} = 9.1 \times 10^{-6}$$
$$s = (9.1 \times 10^{-6})^{1/2} = 3.016 \times 10^{-3} \text{ mol L}^{-1}$$
$$1 \text{ mol of } CaSO_4 = 136 \text{ g}$$
$$\text{Solubility} = 3.016 \times 10^{-3} \times 136 = 0.410 \text{ g L}^{-1}$$

0.41 g is dissolved in 1L

$\therefore$ 1 g can be dissolved in $\frac{1}{0.41} = 2.44\text{L}.$

Example 2.8. *The concentration of Ca^{2+} ion in blood is 0.0025 M. If an oxalate solution with oxalate ion concentration 1×10^{-7} is added to it, state whether precipitation occurs or not. Solubility product of calcium oxalate = 2.3×10^{-9}.*

Solution: In the given solution $[Ca^{2+}] = 0.0025$ M

$$\text{Oxalate } [C_2O_4^{2-}] = 1 \times 10^{-7} \text{ M}$$

$$\therefore \quad \text{Ionic product of calcium oxalate} = [Ca^{2+}][C_2O_4^{2-}]$$
$$= [0.0025]\ [1 \times 10^{-7}]$$
$$= 0.0025 \times 10^{-7}$$
$$= 2.5 \times 10^{-10}$$

Thus, ionic product of calcium oxalate is less than its solubility product (2.3×10^{-9}) therefore precipitation of calcium oxalate will not occur.

Example 2.9. *Specific conductance of a decimolar solution of KCl at 18°C is 1.10 Sm^{-1}. The resistance of a conductivity cell containing the solution at 18°C was found to be 55 Ω. Find out the cell constant?*

Solution: Given: $R = 55\ \Omega$

Specific conductance, $\kappa = 1.10\ Sm^{-1}$

$$\rho = \frac{1}{\kappa} = \frac{1}{1.10}\ \Omega\text{m}$$

$$\text{Cell constant} = \frac{l}{a} = \frac{R}{\rho}$$

$$= \frac{55 \times 1.10}{1} = 60.5 \text{ m}^{-1}.$$

Example 2.10. *Calculate the equivalent conductivity if 1M H_2SO_4 solution whose conductivity is $26 \times 10^{-2}\ \Omega^{-1}\ cm^{-1}$.*

Solution:
$$\Lambda_{eq} = \frac{1000 \times \kappa}{N}$$

Now,
$$\text{normality of } H_2SO_4 = 2 \times \text{molarity}$$
$$= 2 \times 1 = 2 \text{ N}$$
$$\kappa = 26 \times 10^{-2}\ \Omega^{-1}\ \text{cm}^{-1}$$

$$\therefore \quad \Lambda_{eq} = \frac{1000 \times 26 \times 10^{-2}}{2} = 130\ \Omega^{-1}\ \text{cm}^2\ \text{equiv}^{-1}.$$

Example 2.11. *The resistance of a 0.1 N solution of an electrolyte was found to be 200 Ω at 25°C. Calculate the equivalent conductance of the solution at 25°C, if the electrodes in the cell are 0.9 cm apart and have an area of 0.82 sq. cm.*

Solution: Given: $R = 200\ \Omega$, $l = 0.9$ cm

$$a = 0.82\ \text{cm}^2$$

$$\Lambda_{eq} = \frac{1000 \times \kappa}{N} \qquad \kappa = \frac{1}{\rho} = \frac{1}{R}\frac{l}{a}$$

$$\kappa = \frac{1}{200} \times \frac{0.9}{0.82} = 5.48 \times 10^{-3}\ \Omega^{-1}\ \text{cm}^{-1}$$

$$\Lambda_{eq} = \frac{1000 \times 5.48 \times 10^{-3}}{0.1} = 54.8\ \Omega^{-1}\ \text{cm}^2\ \text{equiv}^{-1}.$$

Example 2.12. *When a certain cell was filled with 0.02N KCl solution, the resistance was 300 Ω. When the same cell was filled with 0.1 N sodium acetate solution, the resistance was 1150 Ω. If the specific conductance of 0.02 N KCl solution is $27.7 \times 10^{-4}\ \Omega^{-1}cm^{-1}$. Calculate the equivalent conductance of the sodium acetate solution.*

Solution: Given: (*i*) For KCl solution:

$$N = 0.02,\ R = 300\Omega,\ \kappa = 27.7 \times 10^{-4}\ \Omega^{-1}\text{cm}^{-1}.$$

As the cell is same in both the cases therefore, cell constant will also be same. Cell constant can be calculated as:

$$R = \frac{\rho l}{a} \text{ or } \frac{l}{a} = \frac{R}{\rho} = R\kappa \because \frac{1}{\rho} = \kappa$$

$$\frac{l}{a} = 300 \times 27.7 \times 10^{-4} = 0.831\ \text{cm}^{-1}.$$

(*ii*) For sodium acetate solution: $N = 0.1$, $R = 1150\ \Omega$

$$\left(\frac{l}{a}\right) \text{cell} = 0.831\ \text{cm}^{-1}$$

$$\therefore \qquad \rho = R\,\frac{a}{l} = 1150 \times \frac{1}{0.831} = 13.83 \times 10^2\ \text{cm}^{-1}$$

And

$$\kappa = \frac{1}{\rho} = \frac{1}{13.83 \times 10^2} = 7.23 \times 10^{-4}\ \Omega^{-1}\ \text{cm}^{-1}$$

$$\Lambda_{eq} = \frac{\kappa \times 1000}{N} = \frac{7.23 \times 10^{-4} \times 1000}{0.1} = 7.23\ \Omega^{-1}\text{cm}^2\text{eq}^{-1}.$$

Example 2.13. *The molar conductance of NaOH, NaCl and $BaCl_2$ at infinite dilution are 2.481×10^{-2}, 1.265×10^{-2}, and 2.8×10^{-2} $Sm^2\ mol^{-1}$ respectively. Calculate molar conductivity of $Ba(OH)_2$ at infinite dilution.*

Solution: Molar conductivity of $Ba(OH)_2$ at infinite dilution can be calculate as:

$$\Lambda^\circ_{(Ba(OH)_2)} = \Lambda^\circ_{(NaOH)} + \Lambda^\circ_{(BaCl_2)} - \Lambda^\circ_{(NaCl)}$$

Given:

$$\Lambda^\circ_{(NaOH)} = 2.481 \times 10^{-2}\ \text{Sm}^2\ \text{mol}^{-1}$$

$$\Lambda^\circ_{(NaCl)} = 1.265 \times 10^{-2}\ Sm^2\ mol^{-1}$$

$$\Lambda^\circ_{(BaCl_2)} = 2.8 \times 10^{-2}\ Sm^2\ mol^{-1}.$$

Substitute these values in above equation:

$$\Lambda^\circ_{(Ba(OH)_2)} = (2.481 + 2.8 - 1.265) \times 10^{-2}$$
$$= 5.232 \times 10^{-2}\ Sm^2\ mol^{-1}.$$

Example 2.14. *Conductivity of 0.00241 M acetic acid is 7.896×10^{-5} Scm^{-1}. Calculate its molar conductivity and if Λ° for acetic acid is 390.5 $Scm^2\ mol^{-1}$, what is its dissociation constant?*

Solution: Molar conductivity

$$\Lambda_m = \frac{1000 \times \kappa}{M}$$

where, $\kappa = 7.896 \times 10^{-5}\ S\ cm^{-1}$

$M = 0.00241$ M

$$\Lambda_m = \frac{1000 \times 7.896 \times 10^{-5}}{0.00241} = 32.76\ S\ cm^2\ mol^{-1}$$

Dissociation constant,

$$K = \frac{C\alpha^2}{1-\alpha}, \quad \text{where } \alpha = \frac{\Lambda_m^c}{\Lambda_m^\circ}$$

$$\Lambda^\circ_m = 32.76 \quad S\ cm^2\ mol^{-1}, \Lambda^\circ_m = 390.5 \quad S\ cm^2\ mol^{-1}$$

$$\alpha = \frac{32.76}{390.5} = 0.0839$$

and
$$K = \frac{C\alpha^2}{1-\alpha} = \frac{0.00241 \times (0.0839)^2}{(1-0.0839)} = 1.85 \times 10^{-5}$$

Example 2.15. *Calculate the EMF of the cell:*

$$Zn\,|\,Zn^{2+}\ (0.001\ M)\ ||\ Ag^+\ (0.1M)\,|\,Ag$$

The standard potential of Ag^+ | Ag half cell is 0.80 V and Zn^{2+} | Zn is – 0.76 volt.

Solution: The reactions involved are:

At anode

$$Zn \longrightarrow Zn^{2+} + 2e^- \qquad E^\circ = -0.76\ V$$

At cathode

$$2Ag^+ + 2e^- \longrightarrow Ag \qquad E^\circ = 0.80\ V$$

$$E^\circ = E_R - E_L = 0.80 - (-0.76)\ V$$

$$E = E^\circ - \frac{0.0591}{2} \log \frac{[Zn^{2+}]}{[Ag^+]^2}$$

$$= 1.56 - \frac{0.0591}{2} \log \frac{[10^{-3}]}{[10^{-1}]^2}$$

$$= 1.56 - \frac{0.0591}{2} \log 10^{-1}$$

$$= 1.56 - \frac{0.0591}{2} (-1 \log 10) = 1.56 - \frac{0.0591(-1)}{2}$$

$$= 1.56 + \frac{0.0591}{2}$$

$$= 1.589 \text{ V.}$$

Example 2.16. *Calculate the reduction potential for the following half cell at 298 K. $Ag^+_{(0.1\,M)} + e^- \longrightarrow Ag_{(s)}$. Given E° of cell is 0.80 V.*

Solution:

$$E = E° - \frac{0.0591}{n} \log \frac{1}{[Ag^+]}$$

$$= 0.80 - \frac{0.0591}{1} \log \frac{1}{0.1}$$

$$= 0.80 - 0.0591 \log 10$$

$$= 0.80 - 0.0591$$

$$= 0.741 \text{ V.}$$

Example 2.17. *A dilute solution of $AgNO_3$ was electrolysed using platinum electrodes. After passing small current for 3 hrs, a fall of 0.00064 g equivalent of electrolyte occurred in the anionic solution. The weight of copper deposited was found to be 0.05122 gm. Calculate the transport number of Ag^+ ions and nitrate ions.*

Solution:

$$\text{Transport number of } Ag^+ = \frac{\text{Fall in conc. around anode in g eq.}}{\text{Amt. of Cu deposited in g eq.}}$$

Fall in concentration around anode = 0.00064 g eq.

Amt. of Cu deposited = 0.05122 g

$$= \frac{0.05122}{31.5} \text{ geq.}$$

$$\text{as Eq. wt. of Cu} = \frac{63}{2} = 31.5$$

$$t_{Ag+} = \frac{0.00064 \times 31.5}{0.05122} = 0.394$$

$$t_{NO_3^-} = 1 - 0.394 = 0.606.$$

Example 2.18. *The solubility of AgCl in water at 25°C is found to be 1.06×10^{-5} moles/litre. Calculate the solubility product of AgCl at this temperature.*

Solution: AgCl ionizes in the solution as

$$\underset{1\text{ mole}}{AgCl} \longrightarrow \underset{1\text{ mole}}{Ag^+} + \underset{1\text{ mole}}{Cl^-}$$

i.e., 1 mole of AgCl gives 1 mole of Ag^+ and one mole of Cl^- ions. Now, as the solubility of AgCl = 1.06×10^{-5} moles/litre.

$$[Ag^+] = 1.06 \times 10^{-5} \text{ moles/litre}$$
$$[Cl^-] = 1.06 \times 10^{-5} \text{ moles/litre}$$
$$K_{sp} \text{ of AgCl} = [Ag^+][Cl^-]$$
$$= (1.06 \times 10^{-5})(1.06 \times 10^{-5})$$
$$= 1.1 \times 10^{-10} \text{ mol}^2\text{L}^{-2}.$$

Example 2.19. *A saturated solution of sparingly soluble lead chloride on analysis was found to contain 12.2 g/litre of the slat at room temperature. Calculate the solubility product constant at room temperature (At mass Pb = 207, Cl = 35.5)*

Solution: Solubility of $PbCl_2$ = 12.2 g/*L*

$$\text{Mol. wt. of } PbCl_2 = 207 + 2\,(35.5) = 278$$

$$\text{Solubility of } PbCl_2 = \frac{12.2}{278} \text{ mol L}^{-1} = 4.38 \times 10^{-2} \text{ mol/L}$$

$$PbCl_2 \longrightarrow Pb^{2+} + 2Cl^-$$
$$K_{sp} = [Pb^{2+}][Cl^-]^2$$
$$= [4.38 \times 10^{-2}][2 \times 4.38 \times 10^{-2}]^2$$
$$= [4.38 \times 10^{-2}][76.74 \times 10^{-4}]$$
$$= 336.11 \times 10^{-6} = 3.36 \times 10^{-4} \text{ mol}^3\text{ L}^{-3}.$$

Example 2.20. *Given that the solubility product of $BaSO_4$ is 1×10^{-10}. Will a precipitate form when*

(*a*) *Equal volumes of 2×10^{-3} M $BaCl_2$ solution and 2×10^{-4} Na_2SO_4 solution are mixed.*

(*b*) *Equal volumes of 2×10^{-8} M $BaCl_2$ solution and 2×10^{-3} M Na_2SO_4 solution are mixed.*

Solution: (*a*) $BaCl_2$ ionizes completely in the solution as

$$BaCl_2 \longrightarrow Ba^{2+} + 2Cl^-$$
$$[Ba^{2+}] = [BaCl_2] = 2 \times 10^{-3} \text{ M (given)}$$

Na_2SO_4 ionizes completely in the solution as

$$Na_2SO_4 \longrightarrow 2Na^+ + SO_4^{2-}$$
$$[SO_4^{2-}] = [Na_2SO_4] = 2 \times 10^{-4} \text{ M (given)}$$

Since, equal volumes of the two solutions are mixed together, therefore the concentration of Ba^{2+} ions and SO_4^{2-} ions after mixing will be

$$[Ba^{2+}] = \frac{2 \times 10^{-3}}{2} = 10^{-3} \text{ M}$$

$$[SO_4^{2-}] = \frac{2 \times 10^{-4}}{2} = 10^{-4} \text{ M}$$

Ionic product of $BaSO_4 = [Ba^{2+}][SO_4^{2-}] = 10^{-3} \times 10^{-4} = 10^{-7}$ is greater than the solubility product (1×10^{-10}) of $BaSO_4$.

$\therefore$ a precipitation of $BaSO_4$ will be formed.

(*b*) $[Ba^{2+}] = 2 \times 10^{-8}$ M $[SO_4^{2-}] = 2 \times 10^{-3}$ M

After mixing equal volumes of the two, the concentrations of Ba^{2+} and SO_4^{2-} ions will be

$$[Ba^{2+}] = \frac{2 \times 10^{-8}}{2} = 10^{-8} \text{ M} \qquad [SO_4^{2-}] = \frac{2 \times 10^{-3}}{2} = 10^{-3} \text{ M}$$

Ionic product of

$$BaSO_4 = [Ba^{2+}][SO_4^{2-}] = 10^{-8} \times 10^{-3} = 10^{-11} \text{ M}$$

is less than the solubility product 1×10^{-10} of $BaSO_4$, therefore no precipitates will be formed in this case.

Example 2.21. *A solution of $AgNO_3$ containing 0.51 g of the slat in 60.40 g of the solution was electrolysed using Ag electrodes. After electrolysis 64 g of the anode solution was found to contain 0.56 g of $AgNO_3$. A current of 0.04 Ampere was passed for 2950 sec. Calculate the transport number of Ag^+ and NO_3^- ions.*

Solution: Before electrolysis: wt. of solution = 60.40 g

wt. of $AgNO_3$ = 0.51 g

wt. of H_2O = 60.40 – 0.51 = 59.89 g

After electrolysis: wt. of anodic solution = 64 g

wt. of $AgNO_3$ = 0.56 g

wt. of H_2O = 64 – 0.56 = 63.44 g

59.89 g of water before electrolysis contains 0.51 g of $AgNO_3$

63.44 g of H_2O before electrolysis contains $\dfrac{0.51}{59.89} \times 63.44$

= 0.540 g of $AgNO_3$ Mol. wt. of $AgNO_3$ = 170

$= \dfrac{0.540}{170}$ g eq of $AgNO_3$

= 0.003177 g eq of $AgNO_3$

And 63.44 g of H_2O after electrolysis contains $\longrightarrow$ 0.56 g of $AgNO_3$

$= \dfrac{0.56}{170}$ g eq of $AgNO_3$

= 0.003294 g eq of $AgNO_3$

Increases in weight of $AgNO_3$ in anodic compartment

= 0.003294 – 0.003177 = 0.000117 g eq

Weight of Ag deposited in coulometer

$$Ag^+ + e^- \longrightarrow Ag$$

From I law of electrolysis Q = It = 0.04 × 2950 = 118 coulombs

96500 coulombs will deposit = 108 g of Ag

$$118 \text{ C of current will deposit} = \frac{108}{96500} \times 118$$

$$= 0.1321 \text{ g of Ag}$$

$$= \frac{0.1321}{180} \text{ g eq of Ag [At. wt. of Ag = 108]}$$

$$= 0.00122 \text{ g eq of Ag}$$

If no Ag^+ ions has migrated from anodic compartment, the increases in anodic concentration would have been equal to Ag deposited in the coulometer = 0.00122 g eq.

But actual increase in concentration in anodic compartment = 0.000117 g eq. Therefore fall in concentration around anode due to migration of Ag^+ ions.

$$= 0.00122 - 0.000117 = 0.00111 \text{ g eq}$$

Thus,
$$t_{Ag^+} = \frac{\text{Fall in concentration around anode}}{\text{Wt. of metal deposited in coulometer}}$$

$$t_{Ag^+} = \frac{0.00111}{0.00122} = 0.909$$

$$t_{No_3^-} = 1 - 0.909 = 0.091.$$

Example 2.22. *In the Hittorf's method for the determination of transport number using Ag electrodes and $AgNO_3$ solution it was found that the concentration of $AgNO_3$ in the anodic compartment increased by 0.0264 g. During the experiment, 0.0468 g of silver was deposited in silver coulometer. Calculate the transport number of Ag^+ and NO_3^- ions.*

Solution: When Ag electrodes are used, then the concentration of Ag^+ in the anodic compartment increases after electrolysis.

Increase in concentration of $AgNO_3$ in anodic compartment after electrolysis

$$= 0.0264 \text{ g}$$

$$= \frac{0.0264}{170} = 0.000155 \text{ g eq}$$

$$\text{Number of equivalents of Ag deposited in Ag coulometer} = \frac{0.0468}{108}$$

$$= 0.000433 \text{ g eq.}$$

If no Ag^+ has migrated from anodic compartment, the increase in concentration of anodic compartment would have been equal to the silver deposited in the coulometer = 0.000433 g eq.

But actual increase in concentration in anodic compartment = 0.000155 g eq.

Hence, fall in concentration around anode due to migration of Ag^+

$$= 0.000433 - 0.000155$$

$$= 0.000278 \text{ g eq.}$$

Therefore, $t_{Ag^+} = \dfrac{\text{Fall in conc. around anode}}{\text{Wt. of metal deposited in coulometer}}$

$$= \frac{0.000278}{0.000433} = 0.642$$

$$t_{NO_3^-} = 1 - 0.642 = 0.358.$$

Example 2.23. *Copper sulphate solution was electrolysed using copper electrodes and the total mass of copper deposited at the cathode in the coulometer was 0.145 g. The mass of copper per unit volume of the anode solution before and after passing electric current were 0.80 and 0.93 g respectively. Calculate the transport number of Cu^{2+} and SO_4^{2-} ions.*

Solution: Before passing electric current, wt. of Cu in anodic compartment = 0.80 g

After passing electric current, wt. of Cu in anodic compartment = 0.93 g

Increase in wt. of Cu in anodic compartment = 0.93 – 0.80 = 0.13 g

If no Cu^{2+} ions has migrated from anodic compartment, the increase in wt. of anodic compartment would have been equal to the copper deposited in the coulometer

= 0.145 g

But the actual increase in wt. in anodic compartment

= 0.13 g

= 0.145 – 0.13 = 0.015 g.

Hence, fall in concentration around anode due to migration of Cu^{2+}

Thus, $t_{Cu^{2+}} = \dfrac{\text{Fall in conc. around anode}}{\text{Wt. of metal deposited in coulometer}}$

$$= \frac{0.015}{0.145} = 0.104$$

$$t_{SO_4^{2-}} = 1 - 0.104 = 0.896.$$

EXERCISES

I. SHORT ANSWER TYPE QUESTIONS

1. What are the main postulates of Arrhenius theory of electrolytic dissociation?
2. Write various limitations of Arrhenius theory of ionization.
3. State Kohlrausch's law of independent migration of ions. Mention one application of Kohlrausch's law.
4. Explain various factors which affect the ionization of an electrolyte.
5. State and explain Ostwald's dilution law.
6. How will you distinguish between (*a*) Metallic conduction and electrolytic conduction (*b*) Strong and weak electrolytes.
7. What is a salt bridge? Describe the functions of salt bridge in an electrochemical cell.

8. What are concentration cells? Give their different types.
9. Define transport number. How is it related to velocity of ions?
10. Write the half cell reactions for electrochemical cells involving the following cell reactions.
    (*a*) $Fe^{2+} + Ag^{+} \rightleftharpoons Fe^{3+} + Ag$ (*b*) $Zn(s) + 2AgCl \rightleftharpoons 2Ag(s) + ZnCl_2$
11. Define specific conductance, molar conductance and equivalent conductance. Also give their SI units.
12. How the emf of a cell is related to
    (*a*) Free energy change (*b*) Equilibrium constant.
13. Write Nernst equation for the following cell reaction;
    (*i*) $2Al(s) + 3Fe^{2+}(aq) \longrightarrow 2Al^{3+}(aq) + 3Fe(s)$
    (*ii*) $Sn^{4+}(aq) + Zn(s) \longrightarrow Sn^{2+}(aq) + Zn^{2+}(aq)$
14. State Kohlrausch law. How will you calculate Λ^{∞} for $Al(OH)_3$ using this law?
15. While Zn can liberate hydrogen from dilute HCl, Cu fails to do so? Explain.
16. Explain the terms (*a*) Solubility product (*b*) Common ion effect.
17. How does solubility product differ from ionic product? Discuss two important application of solubility product.
18. Write the expression for molar conductivity at infinite dilution for $Al_2(SO_4)_3$.
19. Draw a graph showing variation in molar conductivity of weak and strong electrolytes.
20. Give units of specific conductance and molar conductance.
21. Define and classify reference electrode.

II. LONG ANSWER TYPE QUESTIONS

1. What is transport number? Describe briefly the Hittorf's method for the determination of transport number of Ag^{+} and NO_3^{-} ions in $AgNO_3$ solution when
    (*a*) the electrodes of silver are used
    (*b*) the electrodes of platinum are used.
2. State and explain Arrhenius theory of ionization. What are the various limitation of Arrhenius theory?
3. What is Kohlrausch's law? Write various applications of this law.
4. What is an electrochemical cell? Explain its construction and working. How is it represented?
5. Explain the term solubility product. Discuss its application in
    (*a*) calculation of solubility of a sparingly soluble salt
    (*b*) qualitative analysis.
6. What are redox reactions? Write various steps for balancing a redox reaction by oxidation number method.
7. Define oxidation and reduction in terms of electrons. Write various steps for balancing a redox reaction by half reaction methods.
8. Draw a labelled diagram of the Daniel cell. Discuss its working.
9. Balance the following redox reactions by the half reactions method:

(a) $MnO_4^-(aq) + I^-(aq) \longrightarrow MnO_2(s) + I_2(s)$ in basic medium.

(b) $Cl_2(g) + OH^-(g) \longrightarrow Cl^-(aq) + ClO_3^-(aq)$ in basic medium

(c) $As_2S_3(s) + NO_3^-(aq) + H^+(aq) \longrightarrow AsO_4^{3-}(aq) + S(s) + NO(g) + H_2O(l)$ in acidic medium

(d) $Cr_2O_7^{2-}(aq) + SO_2(g) \longrightarrow Cr^{3+}(aq) + SO_4^{2-}(aq)$ in acidic medium.

10. Define transport number. Explain the moving boundary method to determine the transport number.

11. Balance the following redox reactions by oxidation number method:

(a) $FeS_2 + O_2 \longrightarrow Fe_2O_3 + SO_2$

(b) $Zn(s) + NO_3^-(aq) \longrightarrow Zn^{2+}(aq) + NH_4^+(aq)$

(c) $Mg(aq) + HNO_3(aq) \longrightarrow Mg(NO)_2(aq) + N_2O(g) + H_2O(l)$

12. Define transport number. Explain the Hittorf's method for the calculation of transport number.

13. Write a short note in determination of transport number by moving boundary method.

14. What do you mean by solubility product and sparingly soluble salts?

15. What is the cause of electrolytic conduction?

16. Write the Nernst equation and calculate the emf of the following cell:

$Mg(s) \mid Mg^{2+}$ (0.001 M) $\|$ Cu^{2+} (0.0001 M) $\mid Cu(s)$

Given $\quad E°Cu^{2+} \mid Cu = +0.337$ V

$E°Mg^{2+} \mid Mg = -2.37$ V.

Also determine the value of standard free energy change for the cell.

17. What is reference electrode? How to determine electrode potential using calomel as reference electrode?

18. What is Nernst equation ? What is its importance in computing the EMF of the cell? *(HMTU 2017)*

19. Explain the construction of calomel electrode. What are advantages and disadvantages of calomel electrode? *(HMTU 2017)*

III. NUMERICAL PROBLEMS

1. In a moving boundary experiment 0.01 N HCl solution was floated on a lithium chloride solution. The tube used has a diameter of 1 cm. When a current of 11.0 mA was passed for 20 minutes, the H^+ ion–Li^+ ion boundary moved through 13.9 cm. Calculate the transport number of H^+ and Cl^- ions in HCl solution used.

2. A solution of $AgNO_3$ containing 6.07 g silver in 25 ml solution was electrolyzed between platinum electrodes. After electrolysis, 5.77 g of silver was present in 25 ml of anode solution while 0.625 g of metallic silver was deposited on the cathode. Calculate the transport number of silver and nitrate ions.

3. Calculate the equilibrium constant for the following reaction.

$$Fe^{2+} + Ce^{4+} \longrightarrow Fe^{3+} + Ce^{3+}$$

Given $\quad E°_{Ce^{4+} \mid Ce^{3+}} = 1.44V, \; E°_{Fe^{3+} \mid Fe^{2+}} = 0.68$ V.

4. Find the solubility product of a saturated solution of Ag_2CrO_4 in water at 298 K if the emf of the cell:

   $Ag \mid Ag^+$ (std. Ag_2 CrO_4) $\parallel$ Ag^+ (0.1M)/Ag is 0.164 V at 298 K.

5. At 25°C, the equivalent conductivity of 0.1 M solution of a weak electrolyte is 1.20 mhos cm^2 and at infinite dilution it is 90.90 mhos cm^2. Calculate the dissociation constant of weak electrolyte at 25°C.

6. In a moving boundary experiment 0.01 M HCl solution was treated on a LiCl solution. The tube used has a diameter of 1 cm, when a current of 11.0 mA was passed for 20 min, the H^+ ions— Li^+ ions boundary moved through 13.9 cm. Calculate the transport number of H^+ and Cl^- ion in HCl solution used?

7. Represent the cell in which the following reaction takes place

   $$Mg(s) + 2Ag^+ \text{ (0.0001 M)} \longrightarrow Mg^{2+} \text{ (0.130 } M\text{)} + 2Ag(s)$$

   Calculate its E_{cell} if E°_{Cell} = 3.17 V.

8. The electrical resistance of a column of 0.05 mol L^{-1} NaOH solution of diameter 1 cm and length 50 cm is 5.55×10^3 ohm. Calculate the resistivity, conductivity and molar conductivity.

9. Molar conductance of 1.5 M solution of an electrolyte was found to be 15.45 S m^2 mol^{-1}. Calculate specific conductivity for this solution.

10. The equivalent conductivity of 0.1 M weak acid is 100 times less than that at infinite dilution. Calculate the degree of dissociation of the acid.

11. 0.05M NaOH solution offered a resistance of 31.6 Ω in a conductivity cell at 298 K. If the cell constant of the cell is 0.367 cm^{-1}, calculate the molar conductivity of the NaOH solution.

12. The equivalent conductance of NH_4Cl, NaOH and NaCl at infinite dilution are 149.7, 248.11 and 126.45 Ω^{-1} cm^2 $equiv^{-1}$ respectively. Calculate the equivalent conductance of NH_4OH at infinite dilution.

13. The conductivity of 0.5 N solution of an electrolyte *XY* at 25°C is 0.054 Ω^{-1} cm^{-1}. Its equivalent conductance at infinite dilution is 130.4 Ω^{-1} cm^2 $equiv^{-1}$. Calculate the apparent degree of dissociation of 0.5 N solution of *XY* at 25°C.

14. Write the Nernst equation and calculate the emf of the following cell. Mg/Mg^{2+}(0.001 M) $\parallel$ Cu^{2+} (0.001 M)/Cu(*s*). Given

    $$E^\circ_{(Cu^{2+}/Cu)} = +\,0.337 \text{ V}$$

    $$E^\circ_{(Mg^{2+}/Mg)} = --2.37 \text{ V.}$$

15. The dissociation constant of NH_4OH is 1.8×10^{-5}. Calculate the concentration of OH^- ions in 0.2 M NH_4OH solution.

16. The specific conductance of 0.02 N solution of KCl at 25°C is 0.002765 Ω^{-1} cm. If the resistance of cell containing this solution is 210 Ω. Calculate the cell constant.

17. 0.5N salt solution placed between two platinum electrodes 50 cm apart and area of cross-section 10 cm^2 has a resistance of 50 Ω. Calculate the equivalent conductance of the slat solution.

18. During electrolysis of a solution of KCl using platinum electrodes 0.0140 g of chloride was lost from the anodic compartment and 0.0901 g of silver was deposited in the silver coulometer. Calculate the transport number of K^+ and Cl^- ion.

19. A solution of $AgNO_3$ was electrolyzed using Ag electrodes. Before electrolysis, 10 g of the solution contained 0.01788 g of $AgNO_3$. After electrolysis, 20.09 g of the anodic solution contained 0.06227g of $AgNO_3$. At the same time, 0.009479 g of Cu was deposited in the coulometer. Determine the transport number Ag^+ and NO_3^- ions.

20. Copper sulphate solution was electrolyzed using copper electrodes and the total mass of Cu deposited at cathode was 0.153 g. The mass of copper per unit volume of the anode solution before and after electrolysis was 0.79 and 0.91 g respectively. Calculate the transport number of Cu^{2+} ions.

21. A solution of $AgNO_3$ was electrolyzed using platinum electrodes. Before electrolysis, 50 ml of the solution contained 12.14 g of silver. After electrolysis, 50 ml of the anodic solution contained 11.55 g of silver, while 1.20 g of metallic silver was deposited at the cathode. Determine the transport number of Ag^+ and NO_3^- ions.

22. In a moving boundary experiment with 0.12 N KCl solution, the boundary moved 4.50 cm during 3600 seconds when a current of 5.15 mA was used. The cross-sectional area of the tube was 0.20 cm^2. Determine the transport number of K^+ and Cl^- ions.

IV. MULTIPLE CHOICE QUESTIONS

1. In a galvanic cell, which one of the following statements is not correct?

(*a*) Anode is negatively charged. (*b*) Cathode is positively charged.

(*c*) Reduction takes place at the anode. (*d*) Reduction takes place at the cathode.

2. For the electrode reaction:

$M^{n+}(aq) + ne^- \longrightarrow M(s)$, Nernst equation is

(*a*) $E = E° + \dfrac{RT}{nF} \log \dfrac{1}{[M^{n+}]}$ (*b*) $E° = E° + RT \ln [M^{n+}]$

(*c*) $E = E° + \dfrac{RT}{nF} \ln [M^{n+}]$ (*d*) $\dfrac{E}{E°} = \dfrac{RT}{nF} \ln[M^{n+}]$

3. The emf of the cell $Cu(s)/Cu^{2+}$ (1M) || Ag^+(1M)/Ag is 0.46 V. The standard reduction potential of Ag^+/Ag is 0.80 V. The standard reduction potential of Cu^{2+}/Cu is:

(*a*) – 0.34 V (*b*) 1.26 V (*c*) – 1.26 V (*d*) 0.34 V.

4. An electrochemical cell stops working after some time because:

(*a*) One electrode is eaten up

(*b*) Electrode potential of both electrodes decreases

(*c*) The reduction potential of one electrode becomes equal to that of the other

(*d*) None of these.

5. Saturated solution of KNO_3 is used to make salt bridge because:

(*a*) Velocity of K^+ is greater than that of NO_3^-

(*b*) Velocity of both K^+ and NO_3^- are nearly the same

(*c*) Velocity of NO_3^- is greater than that of K^+

(*d*) KNO_3 is highly soluble in water.

6. The standard reduction potentials of the three metallic cations *X*, *Y*, and *Z* are + 0.52, – 3.03 and – 1.18 V respectively. The order of reducing power is:

(*a*) $Y > Z > X$ (*b*) $X > Y > Z$ (*c*) $Z > Y > X$ (*d*) $Z > X > Y$.

7. Through the salt bridge

(*a*) Electrons move (*b*) The cations and anions move

(*c*) Only cations move (*d*) Only anions move.

8. Which of the following statements is correct?

(*a*) $\Delta G = \dfrac{nF}{E_{cell}}$

(*b*) In galvanic cell chemical energy is transformed into electrical energy

(*c*) Oxidation state of Cr in potassium dichromate is + 7

(*d*) The unit of the cell emf is $V\,cm^{-1}$.

9. According to Kohlrausch law, the limiting value of molar conductivity of an electrolyte A_2B is:

(*a*) $\lambda^{\alpha}_{(A^+)} + \lambda^{\alpha}_{(B^-)}$ (*b*) $\lambda^{\alpha}_{(A^+} - \lambda^{\alpha}_{(B^-)}$

(*c*) $2\lambda^{\alpha}_{(A^+)} + \frac{1}{2}\lambda^{\alpha}_{(B^-)}$ (*d*) $2\lambda^{\alpha}_{(A^+} + \lambda^{\alpha}_{(B^{2-})}$.

10. The increase in the value of molar conductivity of acetic acid with dilution is due to:

(*a*) Decrease is interionic force

(*b*) Increase in degree of ionization

(*c*) Increase in self ionization of water

(*d*) None of these.

11. Given that:

$$I_2 + 2e^- \longrightarrow 2I; \quad E° = 0.54 \text{ V}$$
$$Br_2 + 2e^- \longrightarrow 2Br^-; \quad E° = 1.09 \text{ V}$$

Predict which of the following is true:

(*a*) I^- ions will be able to reduce bromine

(*b*) Br^- ions will be able to reduce iodine

(*c*) Iodine will be able to reduce bromide ions

(*d*) Bromine will be able to reduce iodide ions.

12. The solubility of A_2X_3 is y mol dm^{-3}. Its solubility product is:

(*a*) $6y^4$ (*b*) $64y^4$ (*c*) $36y^5$ (*d*) $108\,y^5$.

13. What is the correct representation for the solubility product of SnS_2?

(*a*) $[Sn^{2+}][S^{2-}]^2$ (*b*) $[Sn^{4+}][S^{2-}]^2$ (*c*) $[Sn^{2+}][2S^{2-}]^2$ (*d*) $[Sn^{4+}][2S^{2-}]^2$.

14. ZnS is not precipitated by passing H_2S in acidic medium but CuS is precipitated. The reason for this is

(*a*) K_{sp} CuS << K_{sp} ZnS (*b*) K_{sp} CuS >> K_{sp} ZnS

(*c*) K_{sp} CuS = K_{sp} ZnS (*d*) None of these.

15. The standard electrode potential values of the elements *A*, *B* and *C* are 0.68, – 2.50 and – 0.50 V respectively. The order of their reducing power is:

(*a*) $A > B > C$ (*b*) $A > C > B$ (*c*) $C > B > A$ (*d*) $B > C > A$.

16. The order of increasing conductivity in 0.1 N aqueous solution is:

(*a*) $C_2H_5OH < CaBr_2 < AlBr_3$ (*b*) $AlBr_3 < CaBr_2 < C_2H_5OH$

(*c*) $AlBr_3 < C_2H_5OH < CaBr_2$ (*d*) $CaBr_2 < C_2H_5OH < AlBr_3$.

17. What would be the cell constant when the conductance and specific conductance of a solution are equal?

(*a*) 0 (*b*) 0.5 (*c*) 1.0 (*d*) 0.1.

18. The flow of electrons in an electrochemical cell is from

(*a*) anode to cathode through external supply

(*b*) cathode to anode through external supply

(*c*) anode to cathode through internal supply

(*d*) cathode to anode through internal supply.

19. The equivalent conductivity of a weak acid having 0.1 M concentration is 100 times less than that at infinite dilution. The degree of dissociation is:

(*a*) 0.01 (*b*) 0.001 (*c*) 0.1 (*d*) 100.

20. The number of coulombs required for the deposition of 108 g of Ag is:

(*a*) 48250 (*b*) 96500 (*c*) 24125 (*d*) 10800.

21. The units of molar conductivity are:

(*a*) Sm^{-2} mol (*b*) Sm^{-2} mol^{-1} (*c*) Sm mol^{-1} (*d*) Sm^{-2} mol^{-1}.

22. Which of the following is not a redox reaction?

(*a*) $BaCl_2 + H_2SO_4 \longrightarrow BaSO_4 + 2HCl$ (*b*) $CuO + H_2 \longrightarrow Cu + H_2O$

(*c*) $Fe_2O_3 + 3CO \longrightarrow 2Fe + 3CO_2$ (*d*) $2K + F_2 \longrightarrow 2KF$.

23. $E°$ value of some redox couples are given below:

(*a*) $E°$ value for $Br_2 \mid Br^- = +1.90$ V; $Ag^+ \mid Ag(s) = +0.80$ V

(*b*) $Cu^{2+} \mid Cu(s) = +0.34$ V; $I_2(s) \mid I^- = +0.54$ V_r

Choose the correct option

(*a*) Cu will reduce Br_2 (*b*) Cu will reduce I^-

(*c*) Cu will reduce Ag (*d*) Cu will reduce Br^-.

24. If Λ^{∞} and Λ^{∞} are the equivalent conductances at infinite dilution and at concentration C, then the degree of dissociation is given by the following relation:

(*a*) $\alpha = \dfrac{\Lambda^{\infty}}{\Lambda^{c}}$ (*b*) $\alpha = \dfrac{\Lambda^{c}}{\Lambda^{\infty}}$

(c) $\alpha = \dfrac{\Lambda^{c} \times \Lambda^{\infty}}{1000}$ (d) None of these.

25. The units of cell constant are

(*a*) $ohm^{-1}cm^{-1}$ (*b*) cm (*c*) cm^{-1} (*d*) ohm^{-1} cm.

Answers

III. NUMERICAL PROBLEMS

1. $t_{H+} = 0.798$, $t_{Cl-} = 0.202$
2. $t_{Ag^+} = 0.48$, $t_{NO_3^-} = 0.520$
3. $K = 7.61 \times 10^{12}$
4. $K_{sp} = 2.29 \times 10^{-12}$
5. 1.767×10^{-5}
6. $t_{H^+} = 0.7988$, $t_{Cl^-} = 0.2012$
7. + 2.96 V
8. Conductivity = 0.01148 S cm^{-1}
   Resistivity = 87.135 ohm cm
   Molar conductivity = 229.6 S cm^2 mol^{-1}
9. 23.17×10^3 S m^{-1}
10. $\alpha = 0.01$
11. $\Lambda_m = 232$ S cm^2 mol^{-1}
12. $\Lambda^{\circ}_{eq} = 271.36\ \Omega^{-1}\ cm^2\ equiv^{-1}$
13. $\alpha = 0.828$
14. $E_{cell} = 2.68$ V
15. 6×10^{-4} moles per litre
16. Cell constant = 0.5806 cm^{-1}
17. $\Lambda_{eq} = 200\ \Omega^{-1}\ cm^{-1}\ equiv^{-1}$
18. $t_{K^+} = 0.472$, $t_{Cl^-} = 0.528$
19. $t_{Ag+} = 0.4794$ $t_{NO_3^-} = 0.5206$
20. $t_{Cu^{2+}} = 0.215$
21. $t_{Ag+} = 0.495$, $t_{NO_3^-} = 0.505$
22. $t_{K^+} = 0.562$ $t_{Cl-} = 0.438$.

IV. MULTIPLE CHOICE QUESTIONS

1. (*c*)	**2.** (*c*)	**3.** (*d*)	**4.** (*c*)	**5.** (*b*)	**6.** (*a*)	**7.** (*b*)	**8.** (*b*)	**9.** (*d*)	**10.** (*b*)
11. (*b*)	**12.** (*d*)	**13.** (*b*)	**14.** (*a*)	**15.** (*c*)	**16.** (*a*)	**17.** (*c*)	**18.** (*a*)	**19.** (*a*)	**20.** (*b*)
21. (*b*)	**22.** (*a*)	**23.** (*a*)	**24.** (*b*)	**25.** (*c*)					

Chapter 3 The Phase Rule and Corrosion

3.1 INTRODUCTION

Phase rule deals with the heterogeneous equilibria. During the study of chemical systems, we generally deal with the systems containing two or more phases (solid, liquid, gas) in equilibrium which are called **heterogeneous systems**. For example,

$$\underset{\text{(solid)}}{\text{Ice}} \rightleftharpoons \underset{\text{(liquid)}}{\text{Water}}$$

Here, the two phases, ice and liquid water are in equilibrium with each other. Water system consists of following equilibrium:

$$\underset{(s)}{\text{Ice}} \rightleftharpoons \underset{(l)}{\text{Water}} \rightleftharpoons \underset{(g)}{\text{Water vapour}}$$

This is a heterogeneous equilibrium where three phases *i.e.,* solid, liquid and gas co-exist. The number of phases that can co-exist at equilibrium depends upon the conditions of temperature, pressure and composition of different phases. J.W. Gibbs, while studying heterogeneous equilibria (1876), gave an important generalization called as **phase rule**. With the help of phase rule, it has been possible to predict qualitatively, by means of a diagram, the effect of changing temperature, pressure and concentration on a heterogeneous system in equilibrium. **Gibbs phase rule** may be **defined as**:

In every heterogeneous system in equilibrium, the sum of the number of phases and degrees of freedom is greater than the number of components by 2, provided the equilibrium is not influenced by external factors such as gravity, electrical or magnetic forces, surface tension etc. It is applicable to all heterogeneous systems in equilibrium.

Mathematically, the phase rule is given by the expression.

$$P + F = C + 2$$

or

$$F = C - P + 2$$

where,

F = number of degrees of freedom

C = number of components

P = number of phases.

Before we proceed to derive phase rule, it is necessary to define and explain the terms involved in it.

3.2 DEFINITION OF PHASE, COMPONENT AND DEGREES OF FREEDOM

Phase: A phase is a homogeneous and physically distinct portion of a system separated from other parts of the system by definite boundaries.

When a system consists of only one phase, it is called as **homogeneous system**. For example, a solution of NaCl in water is a homogeneous system which consists of only one phase *i.e.*, solution phase. This is so, because NaCl and water present in the system are neither distinct nor mechanically separable. On the other hand, when a system consists of more than one phase, it is called as **heterogeneous system**. For example, a system consisting of benzene and water is heterogeneous system which consists of two phases *i.e.*, water phase and benzene phase. Each phase is homogeneous in itself (*i.e.*, distinct) and mechanically separable.

Some examples of Systems Containing Different Number of Phases

1. A mixture of two or more gases are completely miscible at normal pressures. Thus, they constitute a single phase. But at high pressure, they may exhibit limited solubility.
2. Immiscible liquids constitute two different phases. For example:
   (*a*) $CCl_4 + H_2O$ (*b*) $C_6H_6 + H_2O$
   (*c*) Aniline + H_2O (*d*) Oil + H_2O etc.
3. Two miscible liquids (water and milk) constitute a single phase. Other examples are benzene and $CHCl_3$, water and ethanol etc.
4. A system consisting of a liquid in equilibrium with its vapour is said to have 2 phases *i.e.*, a liquid phase and a vapour phase.
5. In a mixtures of solids, every solid in a systems is an individual phase which is separated from other solids by a definite boundary. Hence, a heterogeneous mixture of solids consists of as many phases as the number of solid substances present in the mixture. For example, consider decomposition of $CaCO_3$

   $$CaCO_3(s) \rightleftharpoons CaO(s) + CO_2(g)$$

   It is a 3-phase system *i.e.*, $CaCO_3(s)$, $CaO(s)$ and $CO_2(g)$. Here, $CaCO_3$ and CaO, both are solids, so they constitute two different phases.
6. **Pure substances:** A pure substance (solid, liquid, gas) consisting of only one chemical species constitutes a single phase. For example, O_2, benzene, ice etc. are all one phase systems.
7. A solute completely dissolved in a solvent molecule constitutes one phase. For example, aqueous solution of NaCl, aqueous solution of sugar etc.

   However, a saturated solution of sugar in water in contact with excess sugar is a 2-phase system *i.e.*, aqueous sugar solution and solid sugar.
8. Water system containing ice, water and vapour in equilibrium is a three phase system.

   $$\text{Solid (Ice)} \rightleftharpoons \text{Liquid (Water)} \rightleftharpoons \text{Gas (Water vapour)}$$
9. The decomposition of ammonium chloride in a closed container constitutes a two-phase system.

   $$NH_4Cl(s) \rightleftharpoons NH_3(g) + HCl(g)$$

   Two phase are:

   (*i*) $NH_4Cl(s)$

   (*ii*) Mixture of $NH_3(g)$ and $HCl(g)$: As said earlier that a mixture of two gases are completely miscible with each other at normal temperature therefore they constitute one phase.

3.3 COMPONENTS

The number of components of a system at equilibrium is defined as the smallest number of independent chemical constituents in terms of which the composition of each phase can be expressed either directly or in terms of chemical equations. It is important to note that the number of components may be or may not be equal to the actual number of constituents present in the system. Let us consider a few examples:

1. **Water system** has three phases, *viz.* ice, water and water
$$\text{Ice }(s) \rightleftharpoons \text{Water }(l) \rightleftharpoons \text{Vapour }(g)$$
However, the composition of each phase can be expressed in terms of one chemical constituent *i.e.* H_2O. Hence, water is a **one-component system.**
2. **Sulphur system** exists in four different phases *viz.* rhombic sulphur (*s*), monoclinic sulphur (*s*), liquid sulphur (*l*) and sulphur vapour (*g*). The composition of all the four phases can be expressed in terms of sulphur only. Thus, it is a **one-component system.**
3. **Aqueous sodium chloride system:** Aqueous solution of sodium chloride is a **one-phase system** as discussed earlier. But since its composition can be expressed in terms of two chemical constituents *i.e.*, NaCl and H_2O. Hence, it is a **2-component system.**
However, saturated NaCl solution is a 2-phase system (aqueous NaCl solution and solid NaCl) as well as 2-component system. This is because the composition of each phase can be expressed in terms of two components NaCl and H_2O.
4. The system,
$$CuSO_4.5H_2O(s) \rightleftharpoons CuSO_4.3H_2O(s) + 2H_2O(g)$$
is a **three phase system**. The number of components is 2, as the composition of each phase can be expressed in terms of $CuSO_4$ and H_2O.
5. Decomposition of $CaCO_3$ on heating can be expressed as:
$$CaCO_3(s) \rightleftharpoons CaO(s) + CO_2(g)$$
It is a **three phase system** *i.e.*, $CaCO_3(s)$, CaO(*s*) and $CO_2(g)$ but the composition of each phase can be expressed in terms of any two constituents as shown below:

Phase	When CaO and CO_2 are considered as components	When $CaCO_3$ and CaO are considered as components	When $CaCO_3$ and CaO are considered as components
$CaCO_3$	$CaO + CO_2$	$CaCO_3 + 0CaO$	$CaCO_3 + 0CO_2$
CaO	$CaO + 0CO_2$	$CaO + 0CaCO_3$	$CaCO_3 - CO_2$
CO_2	$CO_2 + 0CaO$	$CaCO_3 - CaO$	$CO_2 + 0CaCO_3$

Thus, it is a **2-component system.**
6. Decomposition of NH_4Cl occurs as follows:
$$NH_4Cl(s) \rightleftharpoons NH_3\,(g) + HCl(g)$$
But, actually this equilibrium exists as
$$NH_4Cl(s) \rightleftharpoons NH_4Cl(g) \rightleftharpoons NH_3\,(g) + HCl(g)$$
It is a two phase system as discussed earlier. Now, two cases can arise:
(*i*) **When the reaction is carried out in a closed vessel:** If the reaction is carried out in a closed vessel or vacuum, then the gaseous mixture HCl and NH_3 are

present in the same proportion in which they are combined in NH_4Cl. Thus, the composition of both the phases [($NH_4Cl(s)$ and gaseous mixture (NH_3 + HCl)] can be expressed in terms of only one component NH_4Cl.

(ii) **When excess of NH_3 and HCl are added into the vessel:** If an excess of NH_3 or HCl is introduced into the system, the composition of gaseous phase can no longer be the same and therefore, the composition of gaseous phase can no longer be represented by NH_4Cl alone, but one more component is required. Thus, it becomes a **2-component system.**

7. **Sodium sulphate-H_2O system:** In this system, various phases present are $Na_2SO_4.10H_2O$, Na_2SO_4. $7H_2O$, $Na_2SO_4(s)$ aqueous Na_2SO_4 solution, ice, water, vapour, but the composition of each phase can be expressed in terms of two constituents *i.e.* Na_2SO_4 and H_2O.

Phase	Constituent
$Na_2SO_4.10H_2O$	$Na_2SO_4 + 10H_2O$
$Na_2SO_4.7H_2O$	$Na_2SO_4 + 7H_2O$
Na_2SO_4 Aqueous solution	$Na_2SO_4 + xH_2O$
$Na_2SO_4(s)$	$Na_2SO_4 + 0H_2O$
Ice	$0Na_2SO_4 + H_2O$
Water	$0Na_2SO_4 + H_2O$
Vapour	$0Na_2SO_4 + H_2O$

Hence, it is a **2-component system.**

8. Rusting of iron can be represented by

$$Fe(s) + H_2O(g) \rightleftharpoons FeO(s) + H_2(g)$$

This is a **three phase system** *i.e.*, Fe(*s*), FeO(*s*) and [$H_2O(g) + H_2(g)$]. Out of four constituents, any three may be considered as components to explain the system. Thus, it is a **3-component system.**

3.3.1 Calculation of Number of Components in a Chemically Reactive System

1. The number of components (*C*) in a chemically reactive system is calculated by the formula

$$C = S - R \quad ...(i)$$

where *S* is the total number of constituents present in the system and *R* is the number of independent chemical equations which the various species can undergo.

2. When ions are also present in the system, then the condition that a solution be electricity neutral also counts as one equation, and the equation (*i*) modifies to

$$C = S - (R + 1) \quad ...(ii)$$

***(i)* Consider the system NaBr – KCl – H_2O:** The system consists of following species: NaBr, KCl, H_2O, NaCl, KBr, K^+, Na^+, Br^- and Cl^-

(Dissociation of H_2O is ignored)

Thus, $S = 9$.

Now, number of independent equilibrium reactions can be

$$NaBr \rightleftharpoons Na^+ + Br^-$$
$$KCl \rightleftharpoons K^+ + Cl^-$$
$$Na^+ + Cl^- \rightleftharpoons NaCl$$
$$K^+ + Br^- \rightleftharpoons KBr$$

Thus, $R = 4$, as, ions are involved, there is one more condition of electroneutrality, thus the number of components in the system can be calculated using following formula

$$C = S - (R + 1)$$
$$C = 9 - (4 + 1) = 4.$$

Hence, it is a **4-component system.**

(ii)

KCl–NaCl–H_2O system	KCl–NaBr–H_2O system
(a) The system consists of following species KCl, NaCl, H_2O, K^+, Na^+, Cl^- *i.e.*, $S = 6$	The system consists of following species KCl, NaBr, H_2O, KBr, NaCl, K^+, Na^+, Cl^-, Br^-, *i.e.*, $S = 9$
(b) Number of independent equilibrium reactions are 2 viz. $NaCl \rightleftharpoons Na^+ + Cl^-$ $KCl \rightleftharpoons K^+ + Cl^-$	Number of independent equilibrium reactions is 4, viz. $NaBr \rightleftharpoons Na^+ + Br^-$ $KCl \rightleftharpoons K^+ + Cl^-$ $Na^+ + Cl^- \rightleftharpoons NaCl$ $K^+ + Br^- \rightleftharpoons KBr$
(c) As ions are involved, so one condition of electroneutrality is also present. Therefore, number of components is given by $C = S - (R + 1)$ $= 6 - (2 + 1) = 3$ Thus, it is a **3-component system.**	Here also, one condition of electroneutrality is present: $C = S - (R + 1) = 9 - (4 + 1) = 4$ Thus, it is a **4-component system.**

3.3.2 Degree of freedom (F)

The degree of freedom of a system is defined as the minimum number of intensive variables (such as temperature, pressure, concentration) which must be specified in order to define the system completely. For examples, consider the following equilibrium,

$$\text{Ice } (s) \rightleftharpoons \text{Water } (l) \rightleftharpoons \text{Vapour } (g)$$

All the three phases of water co-exist at temperature of 0.0075°C and a pressure of 4.58 mm Hg. If any one of the conditions, *viz.* temperature or pressure is disturbed, then the system may convert to 2-phase or 1-phase system. Thus, this system has zero degree of freedom *i.e.*

invariant or **non-variant**, which means that no variable can be changed if we want to retain this three phase equilibrium. It can also be predicted by using phase rule *i.e.*

$F = C - P + 2$ For H_2O system, $C = 1$

$\therefore$ $F = 1 - 3 + 2$ $P = 3$

$= 0$ *i.e.*, zero degrees of freedom.

Let us consider one more example:

$$\text{Water}(l) \rightleftharpoons \text{Vapour}(g)$$

It is a 2-phase system. We know that vapour pressure of water has a definite value at a particular temperature. If the temperature is fixed, the pressure will get automatically fixed. Hence, we need only one variable to define the system *i.e.* the system is having one degree of freedom **(univariant)**. This can also be deduced from phase rule

$F = C - P + 2$ Here $C = 1$

$= 1 - 2 + 2$ $P = 2$

$= 1$ *i.e.*, one degree of freedom.

Thus, systems having degrees of freedom zero, one, two and three are called as invariant, univariant, bivariant and trivariant systems, respectively.

3.4 DERIVATION OF THE PHASE RULE

Consider a heterogeneous system having 'P' phases and C components. Now, by definition the degree of freedom of system is the minimum number of independent variables which must be fixed arbitrarily to define the system completely. But the number of these variables is equal to the total number of variables minus the number of relations between them at equilibrium, since each relation diminishes the number of independent variables by one.

Now, let us first calculate the number of independent variables:

(*i*) **Temperature:** At equilibrium, temperature of every phase is same. Hence, there is only one temperature variable for the whole system.

(*ii*) **Pressure:** Like temperature, at equilibrium each phase has the same pressure, so there is only one pressure variable for the whole system.

(*iii*) **Concentration:** Concentration of each component is generally expressed in terms of mole fractions (Mole fractions can be used to determine the number of moles also). As a rule, the number of concentration variables required for each phase are C-1, since the concentration of all the components may be expressed by stating the mole fraction of all except one of the components. For example, if there are two components A and B in one phase and if we know the concentration or mole fraction of one component (say A), then the concentration of other *i.e.*, 'B' can be automatically found, because the sum of mole fractions of all the components in a system is unity. [For example, In a solution of water and ethyl alcohol, if the mole fraction of ethyl alcohol is 0.9, then the mole fraction of water will be 0.1]. Thus, if the mole fraction of A is 0.3, then that of B will be (1 – 0.3) or 0.7. Similarly, if we have three components and if the composition of any two is known then the composition of the third can be easily found out. Thus, if we have C components, we must know the concentration of C –1 components. So, for 'P' phases, the total concentration variables are $P(C - 1)$.

$\therefore$ Total number of variables = 1 (for temperature) + 1 (for pressure) + $P(C - 1)$ (for concentration) = $P(C - 1) + 2$.

Now, let us calculate the number of relations at equilibrium: From thermodynamic considerations, when a system is in equilibrium, the chemical potential of each constituent is same in all the phases.

Consider a system having *i*th component distributed in 3-phases 1, 2 and 3. The chemical potential (μ_i) of *i*th component must be same in all the three phases in equilibrium, *i.e.*,

$$(\mu_i)_1 = (\mu_i)_2 = (\mu_i)_3.$$

Consequently, there are two equilibrium relationships for each component if there are three phases. Hence, for P phases, the number of such relationships for each component are $(P-1)$. If there are C components present in P phases, then such relationships will be $C(P-1)$.

As said earlier

Degrees of freedom (F) = Total number of independent variables – Number of relationships between these variables.

$$F = [P(C-1)+2] - [C(P-1)]$$

$$F = PC - P + 2 - (PC - C)$$

$$F = C - P + 2$$

This is the **phase rule equation** given by Gibbs.

3.5 PHASE DIAGRAM

A phase diagram is a graphical presentation which gives the conditions of equilibrium between various phases of a given system. When the system is in equilibrium, the number of phases that exist together depends upon the conditions of temperature and pressure of the system (if concentration in kept constant). These conditions of pressure and temperature are determined experimentally and plotted as pressure-temperature diagrams. These phase diagrams contain a number of lines, areas and points with the help of which we are able to know the conditions under which various phases will be present in the system.

Phase diagram can be of various types depending on the number of components present in the system.

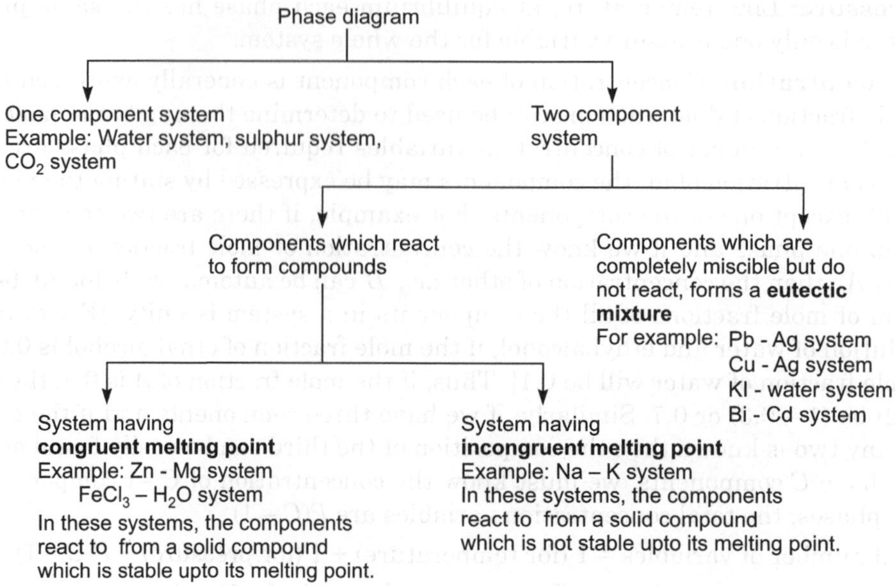

3.5.1 One Component System

System which contains only on component is called as one component system. For example, H_2O system, sulphur system etc.

3.5.1.1 Water system

Under normal conditions, the water system is a three phase and one component system. The three phase involved are liquid water, ice and water vapour.

$$\text{Ice}(s) \rightleftharpoons \text{Water}(l) \rightleftharpoons \text{Water vapour}(g)$$

All the three phases can be represented by a single component water, so it is a **one-component system**. The number of phase which can exist in equilibrium at any time depends on the conditions of temperature and pressure. The phase diagram of water system is shown in **Fig. 3.1**.

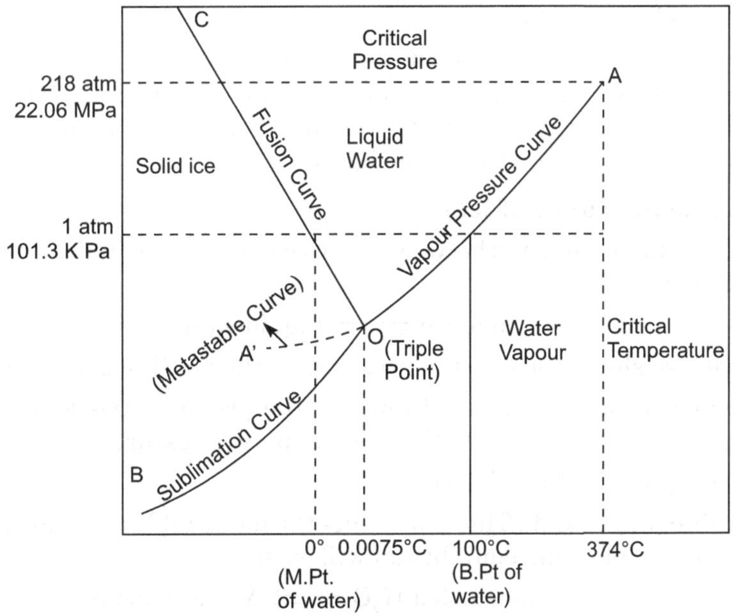

Fig. 3.1. Phase diagram of water system.

The phase diagram of water consists of

(*i*) Three stable curves: *OA*, *OB* and *OC*

(*ii*) One metastable curve *OA′*

(*iii*) Three areas *AOC*, *AOB* and *BOC*

(*iv*) A point '*O*' called the triple point.

(*i*) Curves (*OA*, *OB* and *OC*): There are three stable curves in this phase diagram, *OA*, *OB* and *OC*. Along each of these curves, two phases exist in equilibrium with each other. Therefore, according to phase rule, degrees of freedom along these curves will be given by

$$F = C - P + 2 = 1 - 2 + 2 = 1.$$

This shows that the system is **univariant or monovariant** along each of these curves, which means that for any given vapour pressure on these curves, there is only one value of temperature and vice-versa. Therefore, to define the system completely at any point along these curves, only one variable, either pressure or temperature needs to the specified. The various curves are discussed below:

Curve *OA* (The vapour pressure curve of water)

- This curve represents the equilibrium between liquid water and water vapour at different temperatures. Along this curve the two phases, liquid water and water vapour are in equilibrium.

$$\text{Liquid water} \rightleftharpoons \text{Water vapour.}$$

- This curve will extend upto the critical point (218 atm pressure and 374°C temperature).
- At point *A*, *i.e.*, the **critical point**, the liquid water and water vapour are no longer distinguishable from each other and there is left only one phase *i.e.* water vapour.

Curve *OB* (The sublimation curve of ice)

- This curve represents the equilibrium between ice and water vapour at different temperatures and pressures.

$$\text{Solid ice} \rightleftharpoons \text{Water vapour.}$$

- The curve will extend upto the absolute zero (– 273°C) where only solid ice will be present and no vapour phase exists. It shows that as the temperature is lowered, the vapour pressure of ice tends to be negligible.

Curve *OC* (The fusion curve of ice)

- It represents the equilibrium between solid ice and liquid water at different temperatures and pressures.

$$\text{Solid ice} \rightleftharpoons \text{Liquid water}$$

- This curve also shows the effect of pressure on the melting point of ice.
- The curve *OC* is slightly inclined towards the pressure axis which indicates that the melting point of ice decreases with the increase in pressure.
- There is no upper limit for this curve.

***(ii)* Metastable, curve *OA′*:** This represents the metastable curve for water or metastable equilibrium where the following equilibrium will exist

$$\text{Supercooled } H_2O \rightleftharpoons \text{Water vapour.}$$

Sometimes, its is possible with due care to cool water below its freezing point without the separation of ice, the water is then said to be **supercooled**. The supercooled state is not stable and is therefore called as **metastable state.**

On the slightest disturbance (like introducing a small crystal of ice) the supercooled water at once changes to solid ice and the temperature rises to 0°C.

The curve *OA* is above *OB* (the vapour pressure curve of ice) which indicates that the metastable supercooled water has a higher vapour pressure as compared to ice.

***(iii)* Areas (*AOC*, *AOB* and *BOC*):** The areas *AOC*, *AOB* and *BOC* in the phase diagram show the conditions of temperature and pressure at which a single phase ice, liquid water or water vapour can exist.

Area *AOC*– single phase liquid water is present

Area *BOC*– single phase ice is present.

Area *AOB*– single phase water vapour is present.

Therefore, all these three areas are **one component** and **one phase system**. Hence, according to phase law, we have

$$F = C - P + 2 = 1 - 1 + 2 = 2$$

Thus, the system in each of these areas is **bivariant** (*i.e.*, having 2 degrees of freedom) which means that in order to specify any point on these areas, both the variables-temperature and pressure are to be specified.

***(iv)* Triple point '*O*':** The point '*O*' in the phase diagram represents the triple point of water, where all the three curves *OA*, *OB* and *OC* meet. At this point, all the three phases namely ice, liquid water and water vapour co-exist in equilibrium. According to phase rule at point '*O*'

$$\text{Ice } (s) \rightleftharpoons \text{Water } (l) \rightleftharpoons \text{Vapour } (g)$$

$$F = C - P + 2 = 1 - 3 + 2 = 0$$

Thus, the degree of freedom at point '*O*' is **zero** and the system is said to be **non-variant** or **invariant**. This means that if either pressure or temperature is varied slightly, then at least one of the phases will disappear and all the three phases will no longer co-exist.

- The triple point corresponds to a definite temperature of 0.0075°C and a pressure of 4.58 mm of Hg.

3.5.1.2 Sulphur system

Sulphur system is **one component** and **four phase** system. It consist of following four phases.

(*i*) Rhombic sulphur (S_R)
(*ii*) Monoclinic sulphur (S_M)
(*iii*) Liquid sulphur (S_L)
(*iv*) Vapour sulphur (S_V).

All the four phases can be represented by a single chemical compound, sulphur, so it is a one-component system.

According to phase rule

$$F = C - P + 2 = 1 - P + 2 = 3 - P.$$

Therefore, the maximum number of phases that can co-exist in this system is only 3. It may be noted that all the four phases of sulphur cannot co-exist. This is forbidden by the phase rule as follows:

$$F = C - P + 2$$

As this system is one component system

$\therefore$ $\quad F = 1 - P + 2$

When $\quad P = 4$

$$F = 1 - 4 + 2 = -1.$$

Degree of freedom becomes negative which is not possible. The actual number of phases which can coexist depends upon the conditions of temperature and pressure.

Sulphur system exhibit phenomena of **polymorphism** [the existence of a substance in more than one crystalline/allotropic form and each form possessing different physical properties is known as **polymorphism**. In sulphur system, sulphur exists in two crystalline forms, namely rhombic and monoclinic where one allotropic form transforms into the other.

$$S_R \xrightleftharpoons{95.6°C} S_M$$

Rhombic sulphur is stable at ordinary temperature below 95.6°C while the monoclonic variety is stable above 95.6°C. At 95.6°C both forms are in equilibrium with each other.

The phase diagram of sulphur system is shown in Fig. 3.2.

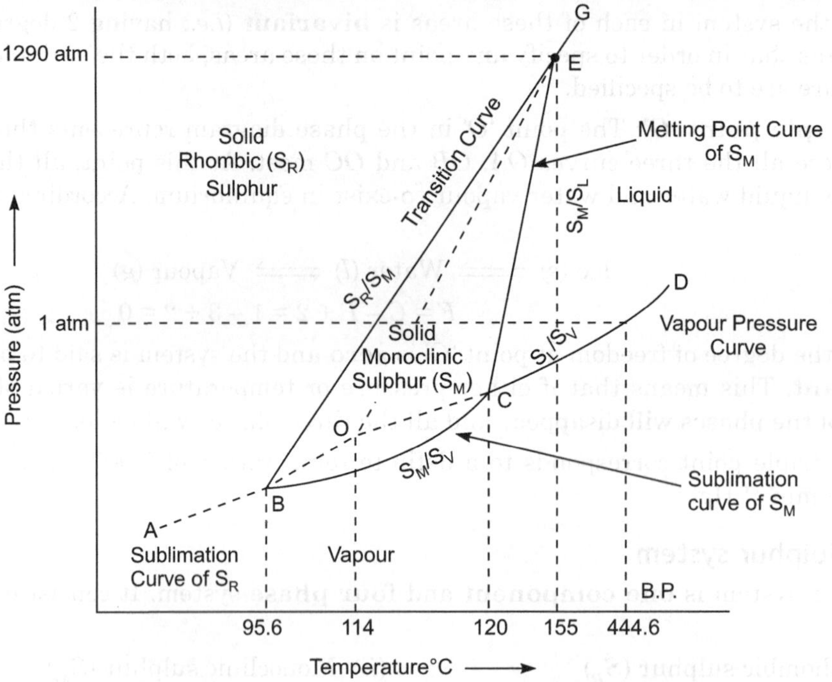

Fig. 3.2. Phase diagram of sulphur system

The phase diagram of sulphur system consists of:

(*i*) Six curves (*AB, BC, CD, BE, CE* and *EG*).

(*ii*) Four areas *ABG, BECB, GECD* and *ABCD*

(*iii*) Three triple points

(*iv*) Three metastable equilibrium.

The curves: The six curves of phase diagram are: Curve *AB*, the sublimation/vapour pressure curve of rhombic sulphur: It shows the variation of vapour pressure of rhombic sulphur with temperature. Along this curve, two phases S_R and S_V exist in equilibrium ($S_R \rightleftharpoons S_V$). S_R is stable upto 95.6°C (point *B*), above which S_R changes to S_M.

Point *B* is known as the transition temperature.

Curve BC, the sublimation/vapour pressure cure of monoclinic sulphur: This curve represents variation of vapour pressure of S_M with temperature. Along this curve, two phases S_M and S_V exist in equilibrium ($S_M \rightleftharpoons S_V$). Point *C* represents the melting point of monoclinic sulphur (120°C).

Curve *CD*, the vapour pressure/sublimation curve of liquid sulphur: This curve shows the variation of vapour pressure of S_L with temperature. Along this curve, S_L and S_V exist in equilibrium ($S_L \rightleftharpoons S_V$). This curve terminates at point *D* which is the **critical point** beyond which only S_V exists.

Curve *BE*, the transition curve: This curve represents the equilibrium between S_R and S_M. It shows the effect of pressure on the transition temperature of S_R and S_M. The curve *BE* is inclined away from the pressure axis shows that the transition temperature can be raised with increase in pressure.

Curve *CE*, the melting point or fusion cure of S_M: This curve represents the effect of change of pressure on the melting point of S_M. Along this curve, the two phases S_M and S_L exist in equilibrium. This curve slopes away from the pressure axis which shows that the melting point is raised by the increase in pressure.

Curve *EG*, the melting point or fusion curve of S_R: This curve represents the effect of change of pressure on the melting point of S_R. Along this curve, the two phases S_R and S_L exist in equilibrium.

Along all the six curves, two phases are in equilibrium. Therefore, the degree of freedom along all the curves can be calculated as follows.

$$C = 1 \text{ and } P = 2$$

$$\therefore \quad F = C - P + 2 = 1 - 2 + 2 = 1.$$

Hence, the system is univariant along all these curves which means that only one variable *i.e.*, temperature or pressure is sufficient to express the system completely at any point along these curves.

The Areas: The phase diagram of sulphur system has four areas:

(*i*) *ABG* (rhombic sulphur)

(*ii*) *BECB* (monoclinic sulphur)

(*iii*) *GECD* (liquid sulphur)

(*iv*) *ABCD* (vapour sulphur).

All these four areas contain only one phase indicated in bracket. Therefore, according to phase rule.

$$C = 1 \text{ and } P = 1$$

$$\therefore \quad F = C - P + 2 = 1 - 1 + 2 = 2.$$

System is **bivariant** in these areas which means both temperature an pressure are required to define the system completely at and point within these areas.

The triple points: There are three triple points in this system.

Point *B*: At this point three cures *AB*, *BC* and *BE* meet and the three phases S_R, S_M and S_V co-exist in equilibrium.

Thus, according to phase rule,

$$F = C - P + 2 \qquad \text{Phases} = 3$$

$$\text{Component} = 1$$

$$\therefore \quad F = 1 - 3 + 2 = 0.$$

it is a **non-variant point** which means that if any one variable either pressure or temperature is altered then one of the phases disappears. This point corresponds to temperature of 95.6°C and pressure 0.006 mm.

Point *C*: At this point three cures *BC*, *CD* and *CE* meet and the three phases namely S_M, S_L and S_V co-exist in equilibrium. According to phase rule, it is also a non-variant point.

This point corresponds to temperature 120°C and pressure 0.04 mm.

Point *E*: At this point, three curves *CE, BE* and *EG* meet and three phases S_R, S_M and S_L co-exist in equilibrium. The point is non-variant and corresponds to temperature 155°C and pressure 1290 mm.

Metastable equilibria: Besides the stable equilibria discussed above there are certain metastable equililbria represented by the **dotted lines** in the phase diagram.

Curve *BO*, the metastable curve of S_R: This is a continuation of sublimation curve of S_R (*AB*). If S_R is heated rapidly, it will bypass the transition point *B* without changing to S_M and finally melt to liquid sulphur at point *E*. This curve represents the metastable equilibrium between S_R and S_V ($S_R \rightleftharpoons S_V$). It represents a univariant system.

Curve CO, the metastable vapourisation curve of liquid sulphur: This curve is obtained by suddenly cooling S_L without changing into monoclinic form. It represents the metastable equilibrium between supercooled S_L and S_V ($S_L \rightleftharpoons S_V$).

Curve *EO*, the metastable melting point curve of S_R: This curve represents the equilibrium between two phases S_R and S_L. If S_L is cooled rapidly at a pressure of 1290 atm, we get S_R without the formation of S_M.

Along all the three metastable curves, two phases are in equilibrium. Thus, according to phase rule, the system is univariant along these metastable curves.

$$F = C - P + 2 = 1 - 2 + 2 = 1 \therefore \text{univariant.}$$

Metastable triple point *O*: The metastable curves *BO, CO* and *EO* meet at this point and the three phases S_R, S_L and S_V are in equilibrium at this point. This point *O* represents the melting point of metastable rhombic sulphur (114°C). This point is non-variant ($F = C - P + 2 = 1 - 3 + 2 = 0$).

3.5.2 Two Component System or Multi-component Equilibria

- When a single phase is present in a 2-component system, then the number of degrees of freedom is three *i.e.*,

$$F = C - P + 2 = 2 - 1 + 2 = 3.$$

This indicates that three variables *i.e.,* pressure, temperature and composition of the system must be specified in order to define the system. Since, it is difficult to represent three variables on a graph, we generally consider only two variables, the third one being a constant. In this way, three types of phase diagrams are possible,

(*i*) Pressure–Temperature ($P - T$) diagram

(*ii*) Temperature–Composition ($T - C$) diagram

(*iii*) Composition–Pressure ($C - P$) diagram.

For example, for a solid/liquid equilibrium, the gas phase is generally absent and the effect of pressure on the equilibrium is negligible.

Thus, the systems in which only the solid and liquid phases are considered and the gas phase is ignored are called as **condensed systems**. In condensed systems, experiments are usually carried out at 1 atmospheric pressure.

With this restriction of constant pressure, the degree of freedom is reduced by one and the phase rule for condensed system becomes $F' = C - P + 1$.

This equation is known as **reduced phase rule equation**.

- Based on the solubility and reactive ability, the 2-component systems are classified as
  - (*i*) Simple eutectic formation
  - (*ii*) Formation of compound with congruent MPt
  - (*iii*) Formation of compound with incongruent MPt. We will consider here only simple eutectic system.

3.5.2.1 Simple Eutectic System

A binary system having two substances, which are miscible in all proportions in the liquid phase but do not react chemically is called as an **eutectic system**.

These two substances have the property to lower each other freezing point. A solid solution of two or more substances having the minimum freezing point of all the possible mixtures of the components is termed as an **eutectic mixture**. The minimum freezing point attainable corresponding to the eutectic mixture is called as the **eutectic point** or **eutectic temperature**.

Examples of Eutectic Systems

- Ag (melting point – 961°C) and Cu(melting point – 1083°C) forms a eutectic mixture at composition 71.9% Ag and 28.1% Cu having a eutectic point at 778°C.
- KI (melting point 682°C) and H_2O (melting point 0°C) forms a eutectic mixture at composition 52% KI and 48% H_2O with eutectic point at – 22°C.
- Bi (melting point 273°C) and Cd (melting point 323°C) forms a eutectic mixture at composition 60% Bi and 40% Cd with a eutectic point at 140°C.

Characteristics of Eutectic Point

- It represents the lowest freezing point of the system, below which the liquid phase does not exist. In other words, the melting point of the eutectic mixture is lower than that of the components.
- Eutectic point has definite values of temperature and composition and it represents an invariant system, *i.e.*,

$$F = C - P + 1 \quad C = 2 \text{ (for two components system)}$$
$$= 2 - 3 + 1 \quad P = 3 \text{ (two solids and one is their solution)}$$
$$= 0.$$

- If the liquid is cooled below its eutectic point, both the components of the eutectic simultaneously solidify without change in composition.
- Eutectics are mixtures and not compounds.

Significance of Eutectic

- Eutectic point is of great importance in metallurgy and material science. It is the required point in casting and in foundry as it is the lowest possible temperature of the system and it also helps to reduce the energy cost. At this point, the alloys exhibit greater strength than their individual components.

It is of great value in semiconductor industry. For example, in items like pressure cookers, automobiles, boilers etc.

Eutectic mixtures are commonly used in drug designing and delivery processes for various routes of administration.

Cu-Ag Eutectic system

Cu-Ag system is a binary alloy system. When two metals are added together in an alloy, usually they are not completely soluble with each other so they create separate phase.

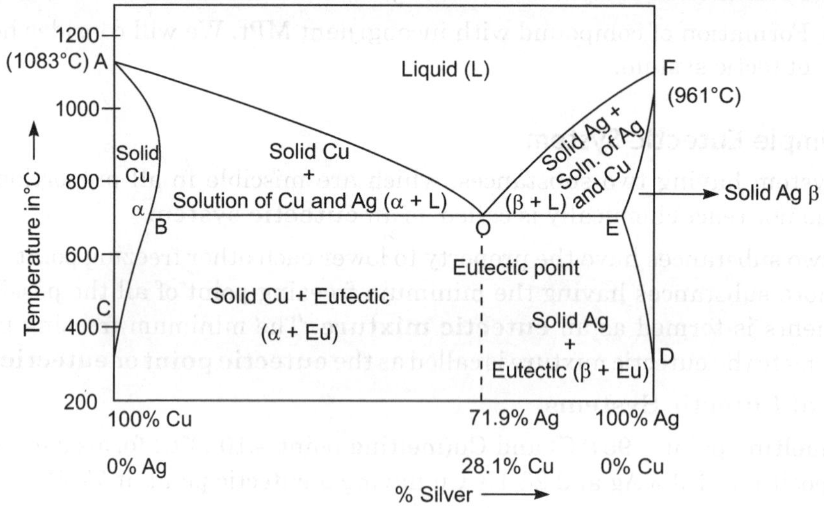

Fig. 3.3. Phase diagram of Cu-Ag eutectic system

- This may be due to different atomic radii or different crystal structure. In case of Cu–Ag system, both Cu and Ag are *FCC* but their atomic radii differ so they have limited solubility in the solid state.

The phase diagram of Cu-Ag system **(Fig. 3.3)** consists of various curves, areas and lines. These are described below.

α-Phase is a solid solution rich in copper. It has silver as the solute component. 100% pure copper is also considered as α-phase. β-Phase is a solid solution rich in silver. It has copper as the solute component. 100% pure silver is also considered as β-phase.

1. Curve *AO*, the freezing point curve of Cu: Point *A* is the freezing point of Cu (1083°C). The curve *AO* shows that the addition of Ag to Cu, decreases the freezing point of Cu. Thus, the freezing point of Cu falls along this curve. Along this curve solid Cu exists in equilibrium with liquid solution of Ag in Cu. Thus, there are two phases: Solid Cu and liquid solution. The degree of freedom calculated by reduced phase rule is

$$F' = C - P + 1 = 2 - 2 + 1 = 1 \text{ (univariant)}$$

So, curve *AO* represents a univariant system. This *AO* curve is also called as **Liquidus** as above this curve the alloy is present in liquid phase only.

2. Curve *FO*, the freezing point curve of Ag: Point *F* represents the freezing point of Ag (961°C). Curve *FO* shows the fall in freezing point of Ag on addition of Cu.

Along this curve solid Ag exists in equilibrium with liquid solution of Cu in Ag. Thus, there are two phases *i.e.* solid Ag and liquid solution. From the reduced phase rule.

$$F' = C - P + 1 = 2 - 2 + 1 = 1 \text{ (univariant)}$$

This curve *FO* also represent **Liquidus line**.

3. Curve *CBA*: *CBA* line represents the solubility limit for the α-phase or Cu-phase. The solubility of Cu increases with temperature to a maximum (with 8.0% wt. Ag at 779°C) at point *B* and decreases back to zero at the melting temperature of pure Cu at point *A* (1083°C). Below 779°C, the solubility limit line *BC* is called as **solvus line**. The boundary *AB* is called as **solidus line**.

4. Curve *DEF*: *DEF* line represents the solubility limit for the β-phase or Ag-phase. The solubility of Ag increases with temperature to a maximum with 8.8% wt. of Cu (779°C) at point *E* and decreases back to zero at the melting temperature of pure Ag at point *F* (961°C). Below 779°C, the solubility limit line *ED* is called **solvus** and *EF* is the **solidus line**.

5. Eutectic point *O*: The curve *AO* and *FO* meet at point *O*. At this point, solid Cu and solid Ag exist in equilibrium with liquid solution (solution of Cu and Ag). The number of phases is three [2 solids (Cu and Ag) and one liquid solution of Cu and Ag] by applying reduced phase rule equation.

$$F' = C - P + 1 = 2 - 3 + 1 = 0.$$

Hence, *O* is an **invariant point**. In other words, both the temperature and composition of the system are fixed at point *O*. The mixture of Ag and Cu melts at the lowest temperature at point *O*, which is called as **eutectic point**. Temperature and composition corresponding to eutectic point are called as **eutectic temperature** and **eutectic composition** (779°C , 71.9% Ag and 28.1% Cu).

6. Area above curve *AOF*: In area above curve *AOF*, Cu and Ag are present as liquid solutions having varying composition. The solution of Cu and Ag is homogeneous, thus they constitute a single phase. According to reduced phase rule,

$$F' = C - P + 1 = 2 - 1 + 1 = 2 \text{ (bivariant)}$$

So, to specify the system at any point in this region, both the variables, temperature and composition have to be specified.

7. Line *BOE*: The horizontal line *BOE* is parallel to the composition line and connects the maximum solubility positions of Cu and Ag. Below this line only solid phases will be present.

It represents the lowest temperature at which liquid phase may exist for any Cu-Ag alloy that is at equilibrium.

8. Area *AOB*: In this area, solid Cu and solution (solution of Cu and Ag) are present. As there are two phases, so it represents a univariant system ($F' = C - P + 1 = 2 - 2 + 1 = 1$).

9. Area *FOE*: In this area, solid Ag and solution (solution of Ag and Cu) are present. Again two phases are present, so it is also a **univariant system**.

Cooling of solution: Upon cooling, the liquid phase is transformed into two solids (α and β or Cu and Ag) phases at the eutectic temperature (T_E), the opposite reaction occurs upon heating. This is called as an **eutectic reaction**.

$$L \text{ (71.9 wt.\% Ag)} \underset{\text{heating}}{\overset{\text{Cooling}}{\rightleftharpoons}} \alpha \text{ (8\% wt. Ag)} + \beta \text{ (8.8\% wt. Cu)}$$

Lead-silver system

The phase diagram of Pb-Ag system is represented by **Fig. 3.4.**

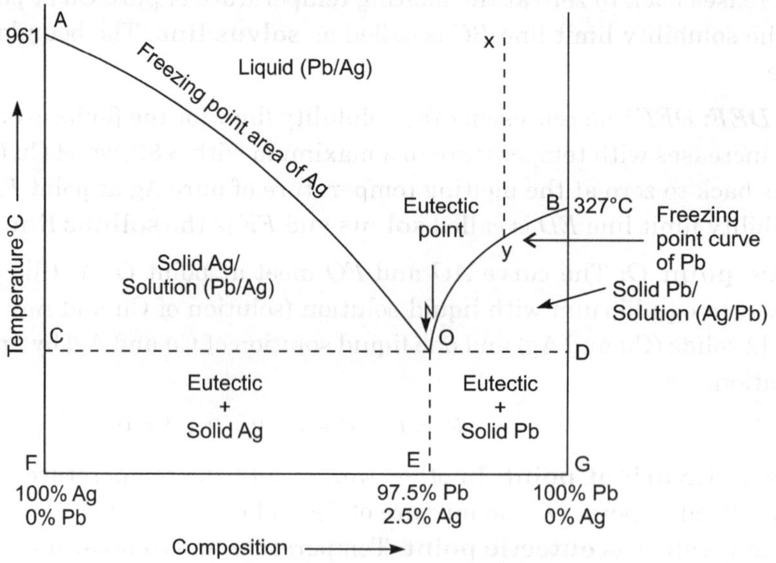

Fig. 3.4. Phase diagram of lead-silver system.

It is a two component system containing lead and silver having four phases. The four phases are:

(*i*) Solid lead

(*ii*) Solid silver

(*iii*) Solution of molten lead and silver

(*iv*) Vapour.

The boiling points of lead and silver are considerably high and the vapour pressure of the system is very low (low V.P. means strong intermolecular forces of attraction). So the vapour phase can be ignored and the Pb-Ag system can be considered as a condensed system with three phases. As the vapour phase is ignored so there will be no effect of pressure on equilibrium and hence this system can be easily studied with the help of temperature-composition diagram as shown in above figure.

Pb-Ag system consists of

(*i*) Curves *AO* and *BO*

(*ii*) Eutectic point *O*

(*iii*) Area above *AOB*, area *AOC*, area *BOD*, *COEF* and *DOEG*.

The Curves

Curve *AO* (freezing point curve of Ag)

Curve *AO* represents the variation of melting point of silver on addition of small quantities of molten lead. Point *A* represents the freezing point of Ag (961°C). On addition of molten lead to molten silver, the added Pb dissolves in Ag forming Pb-Ag solution and the melting point of Ag is lowered. The lowering of melting point of Ag continued till point *O* (Eutectic point) is reached. At this point, the solution becomes saturated with lead and therefore the melting point of Ag does not fall any further.

It is observed that along this curve, the added lead goes into the solution and silver separates out and the separation of Ag continues till point *O*.

On applying the reduced phase rule,

$$F' = C - P + 1 \qquad C = 2$$
$$= 2 - 2 + 1 = 1 \qquad P = 2\text{(solid Ag and liquid solution of Pb-Ag)}$$

Thus, the system is univariant and all along this curve solid Ag exist in equilibrium with liquid solution of Pb in Ag.

Curve *BO* (Freezing point curve of Pb)

This curve represents the variation of melting point of Pb on addition of Ag. The melting point of pure lead is 327°C. On gradual addition of Ag, the melting point of Pb is lowered along *BO*. Along this curve, the added silver goes into the solution and the separation of solid lead takes place. Hence, along this curve two phase solid lead and Pb-Ag solution are in equilibrium.

On applying reduced phase rule,

$$F' = C - P + 1$$
$$= 2 - 2 + 1 = 1.$$ Thus, it is a univariant system.

Eutectic point *O*: The point *O* is called the **eutectic point** where the two fusion curves *AO* and *BO* meet. This point *O* corresponds to temperature 303°C and fixed composition *i.e.* 97.4% Pb and 2.6% Ag. At this point, three phases namely solid silver, solid lead and silver-lead solution co-exist in equilibrium. According to reduced phase rule,

$$F' = C - P + 1 = 2 - 3 + 1 = 0$$

The system is **invariant** (zero degree of freedom).

This eutectic point *O* corresponds to the minimum melting point or freezing point of the system and hence no mixture of lead and silver has a melting point lower than the eutectic temperature.

Areas

Area above *AOB*: This region represents the liquid state and consist of single phase of liquid solution of lead and silver. Thus, on applying reduced phase rule,

$$F' = C - P + 1 = 2 - 1 + 1 = 2.$$

The system is bivariant. Both the temperature and composition have to be specified to define the system completely.

Area *AOC*: This region consist of two phases namely solid silver and liquid solution of silver and lead. On applying condensed phase rule,

$$F' = C - P + 1 = 2 - 2 + 1 = 1$$ *i.e.,* univariant system.

Area *BOD*: This region consist of phases solid lead and liquid solution of silver and lead. It is also a univariant area.

Area *COEF*: This region consist of eutectic (mix of Ag-Pb) and solid silver. It is a monovariant area.

Area *DOEG*: This region consist of eutectic (mix of Ag-Pb) and solid lead. It is also a monovariant area.

Application of lead-silver system to Desilverisation of lead (Pattison's process)

Galena (PbS) an ore of lead is usually contaminated with 0.1% silver. This lead is therefore called as argentiferous lead. For separating silver from the argentiferous lead, the above principle is applied.

For separation process, the galena is heated much above the melting point of lead so that the system consist of only one phase *i.e.,* liquid melt of Pb-Ag represented by point x in the **Fig. 3.4.**

This liquid melt at point x is cooled slowly the temperature of liquid melt falls along the line xy. As soon as point y is reached, lead will begin to crystallize and the percentage of silver will increase in the solution. If cooling is continued, the system shifts along the curve yO and the melt continues to be richer and richer in Ag until point O is reached. At point O, the percentage of Ag rises to 2.6%. Thus, the original argentiferous lead which might have contained 0.1% of Ag can now have upto 2.6% of Ag. This process of increasing the relative proportion of Ag in galena is called as **Pattison's process.**

3.5.2.2 Formation of Compounds with Congruent Melting Point

In certain cases, the two components of a system a react to form solid compound which exist in equilibrium with liquid phase. The solid compound is said to have a **congruent melting point** if it melts at a constant temperature to yield a liquid of the same composition as that of the solid. This constant temperature is known as the **congruent temperature.** Examples of such system are zinc-magnesium system, mercury-thallium system, gold-tin system, ferric chloride-water system etc.

Zinc-magnesium System

It is a typical two-component system and possess a congruent melting point. The two components are zinc and magnesium. Zinc melts at 420°C and magnesium at 650°C and are represented by points B and A in the diagram **(Fig. 3.5).** Both metals combine to form an intermetallic compound $MgZn_2$ which melts at 590°C to give a liquid of the same composition as that of solid. Thus, 590°C is the congruent melting point of the system.

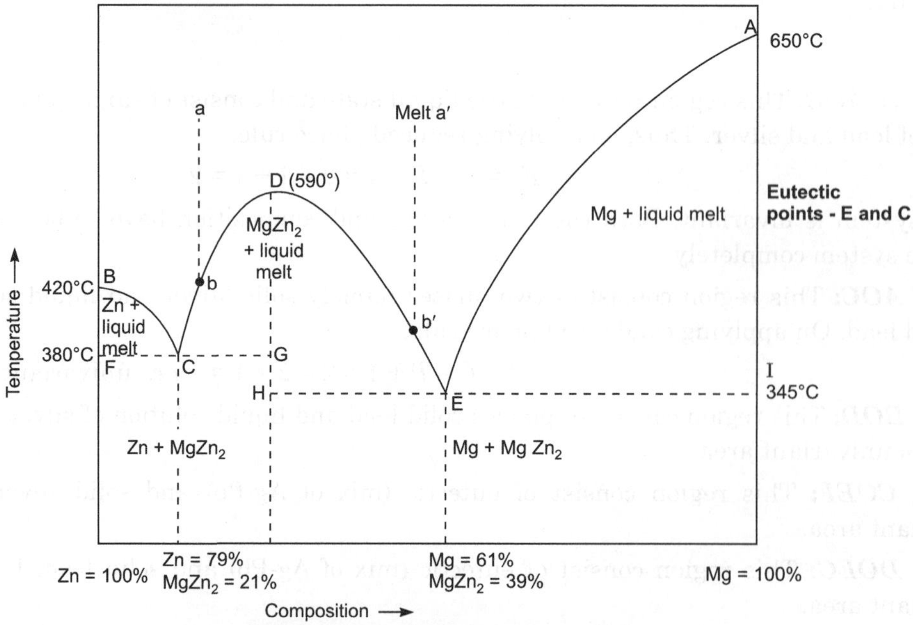

Fig. 3.5. Phase diagram of Zn-Mg system.

The experiments are carried out at constant pressure, therefore, the vapour phase is not considered. Hence condensed phase rule is applied.

$$F' = C - P + 1$$

In the condensed phase rule, this system has four phases namely solid magnesium, solid zinc, solid $MgZn_2$ and liquid melt of Zn and Mg.

The phase diagram of this system consists of:

(*i*) Curves-*BC*, *AE*, *CDE*

(*ii*) Points-*A*, *B*, *C*, *D* and *E*.

(*iii*) Areas-Area above *BCDEA*

area *BCF*, *CDG*, *DHE*, *AEI*

area below *FCG*, *HEI*.

(*i*) Curves

(*a*) Curve *BC* (Freezing point curve of zinc): This curve shows that the freezing point of Zn decreases on gradual addition of magnesium till point '*C*' is reached where solid $MgZn_2$ separates out. Along this curve two phases solid zinc and the liquid melt of Zn and Mg co-exist together. Thus, on applying reduced phase rule ($C = 2$, $P = 2$)

$\therefore$ $F' = 2 - 2 + 1 = 1$ *i.e.*, the system is unvariant.

(*b*) Curve *AE* (Freezing point curve of magnesium): This curve shows that the freezing point of magnesium decreases on gradual addition of zinc. Along this curve, solid magnesium and liquid melt of Zn and Mg are in equilibrium with each other. Hence, the system is univariant.

(*c*) Cures *CDE*: The point *D* of this curve represents the melting point of solid $MgZn_2$. The *DE* portion of the curve represents the lowering of melting point of $MgZn_2$ with increase in percentage of magnesium whereas the portion *DC* represents the decrease in melting point of $MgZn_2$ with increase in percentage of zinc. All along this curve, two phases are in equilibrium solid $MgZn_2$ and liquid melt of Zn and Mg. Hence, the system is univariant ($F' = 2 - 2 + 1$).

(*ii*) Points:

(*a*) Point *A*: It is melting point of pure magnesium (650°C)

(*b*) Point *B*: It is the melting point of pure zinc (420°C).

(*c*) Point *C* (Eutectic point): This point is called the eutectic point which corresponds to temperature 380°C and composition Zn-79% and 21% $MgZn_2$. At this point, three phases, i.e., solid Zn, solid $MgZn_2$ and liquid melt of Zn and Mg are in equilibrium. Hence,

$$F' = C - P + 1 = 2 - 3 + 1 = 0, \text{ the system is invariant.}$$

(*d*) Point *E* (Eutectic point): This is the second eutectic point of the system which corresponds to 345°C and 61% Mg and 39% $MgZn_2$. At this point, three phases *i.e.* solid magnesium, solid $MgZn_2$ and liquid melt of Zn and Mg are in equilibrium. Hence, the system is invariant.

(*e*) Point *D*: At this point, the composition of solid $MgZn_2$ and that of liquid melt are same, hence point *D* is called as the **congruent melting point** of the system. It corresponds to temperature of 590°C. At this point, the two component system reduced to one component system because of the presence of one compound $MgZn_2$ in both solid and liquid phases.

$$\therefore \quad F' = C - P + 1 = 1 - 2 + 1 = 0 \text{ i.e., a non-variant system.}$$

***(iii)* Areas**

(*a*) Area above *BCDEA*: It represent a single phase consisting of liquid melt of Zn and Mg. Therefore, it is a bivariant system ($F' = C - P + 1 = 2 - 1 + 1 = 2$).

(*b*) Area *BCF*: This area contains solid Zn and liquid melt of Zn and Mg ($F' = 2 - 2 + 1 = 1$) (Univariant).

(*c*) Area *CDG*: This area contains solid $MgZn_2$ and liquid melt ($F' = 2 - 2 + 1 = 1$). Here, the composition of solid $MgZn_2$ and liquid melt are different, hence, it is a 2-component system [Difference from Eutectic point D-where composition of solid $MgZn_2$ and liquid melt are same.]

(*d*) Area *DHE*: This area contains two phase solid $MgZn_2$ and liquid melt (Univariant).

(*e*) Area *AEI*: This area contains solid magnesium and liquid melt (Univariant).

(*f*) Area below *FCG*: It is an area containing solid mixture of zinc and $MgZn_2$ ($F' = 2 - 2 + 1 = 1$) *i.e.,* Univariant.

(*g*) Area below *HEI*: This area corresponds to solid mixture of magnesium and $MgZn_2$ (Univariant).

Study of Cooling Effect on Curves

Consider a melt of composition represents by a point *a*. If the liquid is cooled along line *ab* (Fig. 3.5) then at point *b*, solid $MgZn_2$ starts to separate out from the liquid melt and the composition varies along the curve *bC*. ($F' = 2 - 2 + 1 = 1$). At point *C*, zinc also separate out.

Similarly if a melt of composition *a'* is cooled along *a'b'* line, then at point *b'* solid $MgZn_2$ starts to separate out from the liquid melt and the composition varies along *b'E*. At point *E*, magnesium also separate out ($F' = 2 - 2 + 1 = 1$).

The phase diagram of this system can be considered to be made up of two simple eutectic diagrams, one on the left represents the eutectic system Zn-$MgZn_2$ while the other on the right represents the eutectic system Mg-$MgZn_2$. These two systems meet at point *D*. In general, the position of *D* can be higher, lower or may have an intermediate value as compared to *A* and *B*. Further, the shape of the curve *CDE* depends on the stability of the compound formed. The bend of the curve will be sharper if the compound formed is stable whereas a flat curve indicates the greater degree of dissociation of the compound.

3.5.2.3 Formation of a Compound with Incongruent Melting Point

In certain cases, the components of a system combine together to form one or more compounds which are unstable and do not possess congruent melting point. This unstable compound decomposes on heating below its melting point and forms a new solid phase and a solution having different composition from the corresponding solid state. Such a compound is said to have an **incongruent melting point**. The temperature at which the decomposition takes place is called a **transition/peritectic/meritectic temperature**. Examples of such system are NaCl–H_2O system, sodium sulphate–H_2O system, gold-antimony system, sodium-bismuth system, potassium chloride-copper chloride system etc.

NaCl–Water System

It is a two component system. Sodium chloride forms only one hydrate *i.e.*, a dihydrate ($NaCl \cdot 2H_2O$). This dehydrate is not stable upto its melting point (0.15°C) but it starts decomposing above 0.15°C. Hence, sodium dihydrate $NaCl.2H_2O$ shows incongruent melting point of 0.15°C.

The phase diagram (temperature-composition) of sodium-chloride water system is shown in **Fig. 3.6**. The various possible phases in $NaCl \cdot H_2O$ system are:

(*i*) $NaCl \cdot 2H_2O$ (*ii*) NaCl (*iii*) ice (*iv*) solution.

All the phases are studied at atmospheric pressure, therefore vapour phase is not taken into consideration and the system is regarded as reduced/condensed system.

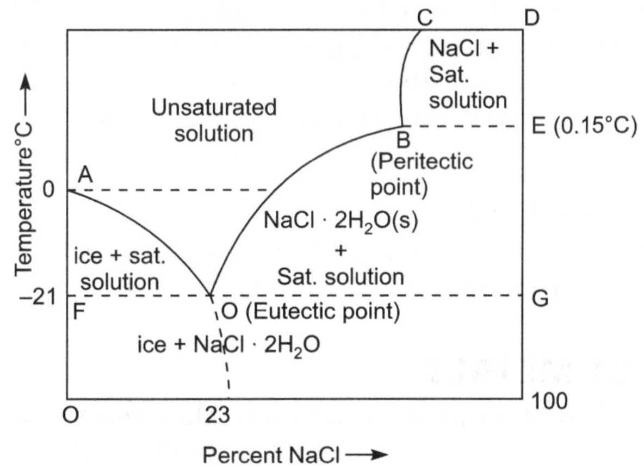

Fig. 3.6. Phase diagram of sodium chloride-water system.

The $NaCl - H_2O$ phase diagram consists of

(*i*) the curves *AO*, *OB* and *BC* (*ii*) eutectic point *O*

(*iii*) peritectic point *B* (*iv*) Area below *FOG*.

(*i*) The curves:

(*a*) Curve *AO* (Freezing point curve of water): The point *A* represents the freezing point of water or the melting point of ice (0°C) at 1 atmospheric pressure. When sodium chloride is added to water, the freezing point of water is lowered along the curve *AO*, till point *O* is reached. Along this curve, two phases ice and saturated solution are in equilibrium. Therefore, according to reduced phase rule,

$$F' = C - P + 1 = 2 - 2 + 1 = 1 \quad i.e., \text{ Univariant system}$$

(*b*) Curve *OB* (the solubility curve of the $NaCl \cdot 2H_2O$): At point *O*, the solution is saturated with $NaCl \cdot 2H_2O$. Thus, the curve *OB* shows the effect of temperature on the solubility of the hydrated sodium chloride ($NaCl.2H_2O$). Along this curve, two phase solid $NaCl \cdot 2H_2O$ and saturated solution are in equilibrium ($F' = 2 - 2 + 1 = 1$ *i.e.*, Univariant system).

(*c*) Curve *BC* (the solubility curve of anhydrous NaCl): When the system at *B* is heated, all the dihydrate changes into anhydrous sodium chloride and solution as we move along curve *BC*. Along this curve, anhydrous NaCl and solution are in equilibrium. Thus, it is also a univariant system ($F' = 2 - 2 + 1 = 1$).

***(ii)* Eutectic point *O*:** Point *O* is the **eutectic** or **cryohydric point** (– 21°C) where three phases *viz.*, ice, incongruent melting compound ($NaCl.2H_2O$) and the solution are in equilibrium. The temperature at this point is the lowest temperature (– 21°C) that can be attained in this system. Hence, this point is called the **eutectic point**. According to reduced phase rule,

$$F' = C - P + 1 = 2 - 3 + 1 = 0$$

The system is **invariant (non-variant)**.

Here both, the temperature (– 21°C) and the composition are fixed. (23% NaCl + 77% ice).

***(iii)* Peritectic point *B*:** At point B, the dihydrate $NaCl.2H_2O$ decomposes into anhydrous NaCl and solution. The temperature at peritectic point is 0.15°C and is called as incongruent melting point of $NaCl \cdot 2H_2O$ because the composition of solution is different from that of the solid $NaCl \cdot 2H_2O$ in equilibrium. At this point *B*, the three phases $NaCl \cdot 2H_2O$ water and NaCl are in equilibrium. Hence, according to reduced phase rule,

$$F' = C - P + 1 = 2 - 3 + 1 = 0$$

i.e., the system at point *B* is invariant.

***(iv)* Area below *FOG*:** Below the line *FOG i.e.,* below – 21°C, only ice and $NaCl.2H_2O$ exist and the system is univariant ($F' = 2 - 2 + 1 = 1$).

3.6 CORROSION OF METALS

When metals are exposed to atmospheric conditions, they react with air or water present in the environment to form undesirable compounds (usually oxides). This process is referred as **corrosion**. Almost all metals except the least active metals such as gold, platinum and palladium undergo corrosion when exposed to environment. For example, rusting of iron, tarnishing of silver, development of a green coating on Cu, etc.

Thus, corrosion is a process of destruction of a metal as a result of its reaction with air or water present in the environment surrounding it.

In case of iron, corrosion has been given a special name **rusting**. Chemically, rust is hydrated ferric oxide $Fe_2O_3.xH_2O$. Rusting of iron is usually due to moisture, CO_2 and oxygen present in air. The damage due to corrosion can be realised by the fact that nearly 25% of the steel production of the US is utilized for the replacement of corroded material.

Why Does Corrosion Occurs?

Apart from few least reactive metals (like gold, platinum, palladium etc.), metals do not occur in nature in their pure form: They are usually bound to other substances in ores, like sulphides, oxides etc. Energy must be supplied (*e.g.,* in blast furnace) to extract the metals from their ores to obtain pure metals. Thus, pure metals contain more bound energy, representing a higher energy state as compared to their oxides, sulphides etc. from which they are extracted. Therefore, these oxides, and sulphides of metals are thermodynamically more stable than the pure metals and all materials in the universe strives to return to its lowest energy state. Thus, most of the pure metals rapidly react with oxygen to form oxides. For example, iron, copper, aluminium etc. react with oxygen to form corresponding oxides:

$$4Fe + 3O_2 \longrightarrow 2Fe_2O_3$$

$$4Cu + O_2 \longrightarrow 2Cu_2O$$
$$4Al + 3O_2 \longrightarrow 2Al_2O_3$$

Although corroded metal is thermodynamically more stable than the pure metal but due to corrosion, some useful properties of metals like malleability, ductility, hardness, luster and electrical conductivity are lost.

3.6.1 Factors Affecting Corrosion

The corrosion of a metal depend upon several factors. These factors are categorised into 2 parts. These are (1) nature of the metal (2) corroding environment.

1. Nature of the Metal

(*i*) **Position of the metal in electrochemical series:** The reactivity of a metal depends upon its position in the, electrochemical series. The more active metal suffers corrosion. In general, the metal with lower electrode potential is more reactive and therefore more susceptible to corrosion as compared with metals having high electrode potential. For example, metals like Na, K, Mg, Zn etc. have low electrode potential and therefore undergo corrosion very easily.

(*ii*) **Presence of impurities in metals:** The pure metals are sufficiently corrosion resistant. However, the presence of impurities help in setting up small electrochemical cells and thus initiates corrosion at the anodic part. For example, presence of lead or iron in zinc as an impurity causes corrosion of zinc.

(*iii*) **Relative areas of anodic and cathodic part:** When two dissimilar atoms are in contact, the corrosion of anodic part is directly proportional to the ratio of the areas of the cathodic and the anodic part. Corrosion is fast when the anodic area is small (e.g. a steel pipe fitted in a large copper tank). This is due to the reason that the current density at small anodic area is much greater and the demand of electrons for cathode can be met by smaller anode only through a rapid corrosion rate.

(*iv*) **Removal of corroded part:** The process of corrosion becomes fast if the corroded part is removed from the surface either by vapourisation or its solubility in the medium. In both the cases, fresh surface is exposed for further attack and thus, leads to further corrosion.

(*v*) **Surface state of the metals:** Corrosion is a surface phenomenon, larger the surface area more will be the corrosion. Corrosion takes place rapidly at bends, scratches and cuts in the metal due to formation of large number of air concentration cells with cathodic and anodic regions.

(*vi*) **Hydrogen (over-voltage:** Hydrogen over-voltage is the potential difference that can be found between an electrode and a reversible hydrogen electrode within a single solution. The metal with lower hydrogen over-voltage on its surface is more susceptible to corrosion, when cathodic reaction is hydrogen evolution type. Since, at lower hydrogen over-voltage, liberation of hydrogen gas is easy. The cathodic reaction is very fast, which in turn makes anodic reaction also fast, thus increasing the rate of corrosion. Higher the over-voltage, lesser is the corrosion.

(*vii*) **Nature of surface film:** In presence of air, most of metals are covered with a layer of oxides which slows down their corrosion. The ratio of volume of metal oxide to that of metals is called as **specific volume ratio**. If the specific volume ratio of the metal is more than one, then the metal will not undergo corrosion but if the specific volume ratio is less than one, the film will be unstable and the underlying metal will undergo corrosion.

2. Corroding Environment

There are certain environmental factors which also affects the rate of corrosion to a considerable extent. The major environmental factors are:

(*i*) **Temperature:** With increase in temperature, the rate of diffusion increases and hence corrosion also increases.

(*ii*) **Humidity:** Corrosion increases with increase in humidity of the atmosphere because the gases (CO_2, O_2 etc.) and vapours present in the atmosphere furnish water to the electrolyte for setting up an electrochemical corrosion cell.

(*iii*) **pH of the medium:** The rate of corrosion is affected by change in pH of the solution. As the pH of the solution decreases, the evolution of H_2 gas also decreases and as a result, ionization of oxygen increases as the cathode reaction. Acidic media are usually more corrosive than alkaline and neutral media.

(*iv*) **Presence of impurities in air:** Presence of impurities like HCl, SO_2 etc. in air affects the rate of corrosion. SO_2 is a serious air pollutant (which is formed by the combustion of coal) has greater solubility in water (about 100 times) as compared to oxygen and is the reason for the formation of sulphuric acid and the so called **acid rain**. In the presence of SO_2, iron objects corrode according to the following reactions:

$$Fe + SO_2 + O_2 \longrightarrow FeSO_4$$

$$4FeSO_4 + O_2 + 6H_2O \longrightarrow 2Fe_2O_3.H_2O + 4H_2SO_4$$

$$4H_2SO_4 + 4Fe + 2O_2 \longrightarrow 4FeSO_4 + 4H_2O$$

The sulphuric acid formed in the reactions is difficult to remove and this is the reason that even after cleaning the iron objects carefully, corrosion continues as long as sulphates are present.

(*v*) **Conductance of the medium:** Presence of conducting species in the medium/ atmosphere increases the rate of corrosion. This is an important factor for corrosion in underground or submerged structure. Dry sandy soils have lower conductance as compared with clayey and mineralised soils. Metallic structures which are buried under clayey or mineralised soil are more susceptible to corrosion than under dry soil.

Certain other factors which also influence corrosion are nature of cations and anions present in the medium, flow velocity of process stream, formation of oxygen concentration cells etc.

3.7 TYPES OF CORROSION

3.7.1 Electrochemical/Wet Corrosion

Electrochemical corrosion takes place under moist or wet conditions due to the formation of short circuited galvanic or electrochemical cells. Wet corrosion is more common than dry corrosion. Wet corrosion involves:

1. the formation of cathodic and anodic area
2. the presence of conducting medium
3. occurrence of oxidation at anodic areas

4. formation of corrosion product somewhere between anodic and cathodic areas and flow of electrons between the anodic and cathodic areas.

Anodic reactions: At anodic areas, oxidation takes place *i.e.*, the metal loses electrons and passes into the solution. Thus, the metal at anode is destroyed by dissolving or by changing into metal ions. Corrosion always takes place at anodic areas.

$$\underset{\text{Metal}}{M} \longrightarrow \underset{\text{metal ion (dissolves in solution or forms compounds such as oxides)}}{M^{n+}} + ne^-$$

Cathodic reactions: The electrons released in the anodic reaction are consumed in the cathodic reactions. Generally, cathodic reactions do not affect the cathode, since metals are already present in their most reduced state, thus cannot be reduced further. So, at cathodic part, dissolved constituents in the conducting medium accept electrons to form 'ions' like OH^-, O^{2-} etc.

$$2H^+ + e^- \longrightarrow H_2\uparrow \text{(in acidic medium)}$$

$$2H_2O + 2e^- \longrightarrow H_2 + 2OH^- \text{ (in basic medium)}$$

The ions formed at the cathode and anode more towards each other through the conducting medium and forms a corrosion product.

Wet corrosion can be of various types:

(*i*) Galvanic corrosion
(*ii*) Differential aeration corrosion
(*iii*) Intergranular corrosion
(*iv*) Underground corrosion
(*v*) Stress corrosion
(*vi*) Erosion corrosion
(*vii*) Selective leaching

(*i*) Galvanic Corrosion/Bimetallic Corrosion (Corrosion by hydrogen Evolution and Oxygen Absorption): It is the most important type of corrosion. It takes place when two different metals or coatings are joined together in presence of an electrolyte, the metal higher in electrochemical series undergoes corrosion. In this process, the metal with more negative electrode potential acts as anode and undergoes corrosion, while the metal with less negative electrode potential acts as cathode. For example, if Zn and Cu are connected, Zn forms the anode and undergoes corrosion wheres Cu acts a cathode.

Mechanism: At anode: $Zn \longrightarrow Zn^{2+} + 2e^-$

The reaction at the cathode depends upon the environment. In acidic solution, corrosion occurs by the evolution of hydrogen gas

$$2H^+ + 2e^- \longrightarrow H_2$$

Whereas if the solution is alkaline or neutral, oxygen absorption takes place.

$$\frac{1}{2}O_2 + H_2O + 2e^- \longrightarrow 2OH^-$$

Hence, Zn dissolves and Cu (cathode) is protected form the attack.

Examples:

- It may be found at the junction of a water main, where a copper pipe meets a steel pipe.
- In a microelectronic device, where different metals and semiconductors are present together.
- On a ship, where the various components immersed in water are made of different metal alloys.

***(ii)* Differential Aeration Corrosion:** It occurs when one part of metal is exposed to different air concentration than the other part (Fig. 3.7.). This causes a potential difference between differently aerated areas. The part of metal exposed to high air/oxygen concentration acts as cathode whereas the metal part which is exposed to low air concentration acts as anode and corrosion occurs at anode.

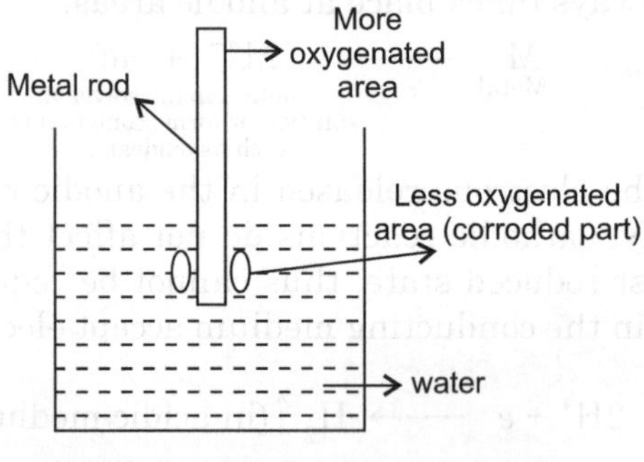

Fig. 3.7. Differential aeration corrosion.

Examples:

***(a)* Pitting corrosion:** A drop of water, oil, sand, dust etc. on a metal surface discussed later **(Fig. 3.8)**.

***(b)* Water line corrosion:** A metal part immersed in H_2O or in a conducting liquid.

(c) Joints of iron metals by iron washer.

***(d)* Crevice corrosion:** Discussed in later section.

***(e)* Pipeline corrosion:** The buried pipelines passes from one type of soil to another, say from clayey soil (less aerated) to sandy solid (more aerated) may get corroded due to differential aeration.

***(f)* Corrosion on wire fence:** In a wire fence, the areas where the wires cross are less aerated (and acts as anode) than the other parts of the fence. Hence, corrosion takes place at the wire crossings.

Pitting Corrosion

Consider a drop of water on the surface of iron metal. The point beneath the centre of the water droplet is poorly oxygenated and acts as anode whereas the rest part of the metal acts as cathode.

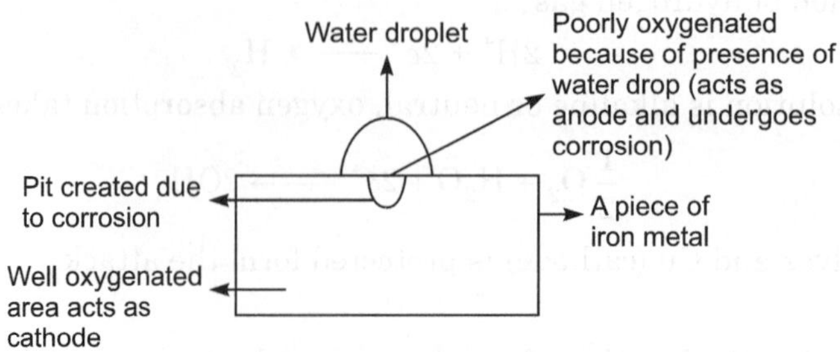

Fig. 3.8. Pitting corrosion.

- We have learnt earlier that when the anodic area is very small as compared to the cathodic area, the anode undegoes rapid corrosion. Therefore, more and more metal is removed from the same spot. It is called as **pitting corrosion** as a small pit is formed on the surface of the metal.

Reaction Mechanism

At anode: $Fe \longrightarrow Fe^{2+} + 2e^-$

At cathode: $\frac{1}{2} H_2O + O_2 + 2e^- \longrightarrow 2OH^-$

Net reaction: $Fe^{2+} + 2OH^- \longrightarrow Fe(OH)_2$

In the presence of excess oxygen, yellow rust is formed.

$$4Fe(OH)_2 + O_2 + 2H_2O \longrightarrow \underset{\text{Ferric hydroxide (yellow rust)}}{4Fe(OH)_3}$$

- Pitting is a localized attack, which occurs in areas of a hole and the area around the metal is unattacked.

Crevice Corrosion

If a crevice (a crack forming a narrow opening) between metallic and non-metallic material is in contact with a liquid, the crevice which is deficient in oxygen becomes anode and undergoes corrosion. The exposed area has high oxygen supply and acts as cathode **(Fig. 3.9)**.

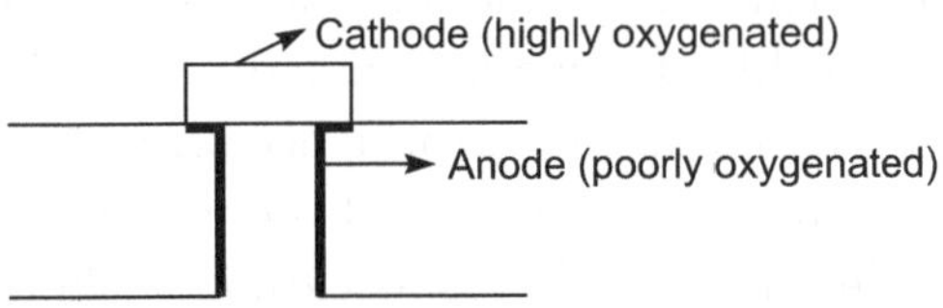

Fig. 3.9. Crevice corrosion.

The crevices can be formed due to one of the following reasons:

(*a*) The geometry of the structure.

(*b*) Contact of metal with non-metallic solids.

(*c*) Deposits of sand, dirt or permeable corrosion products on the metal surface.

For example: Bolts, nuts, rivets, joints etc. in contact with liquids.

(*iii*) Inter-granular corrosion: Virtually all engineering alloys are fabricated by solidifying a melt composed of a mixture of elements. During this solidification process, crystals nucleate and grow together, forming the solid. As a result of this process, the chemical composition and the properties of the region between the crystals can differ significantly from those inside the crystals grains. Thus, the structure of the metal inside the grain/crystal is slightly different from the grain boundary. As a result, a potential difference is created between the grain boundary (which acts as anode) and grain centre (which acts as cathode) which leads to corrosion at anodic grain boundry.

For example: The precipitation of chromium carbide ($Cr_{23}C_6$) at the grain boundries of stainless steel during welding is a suitable example.

The inter-granular corrosion takes place at micro level. There will be no signs of corrosion but it may progress slowly and may cause sudden failure of the material due to loss of cohesive forces between the grain boundries.

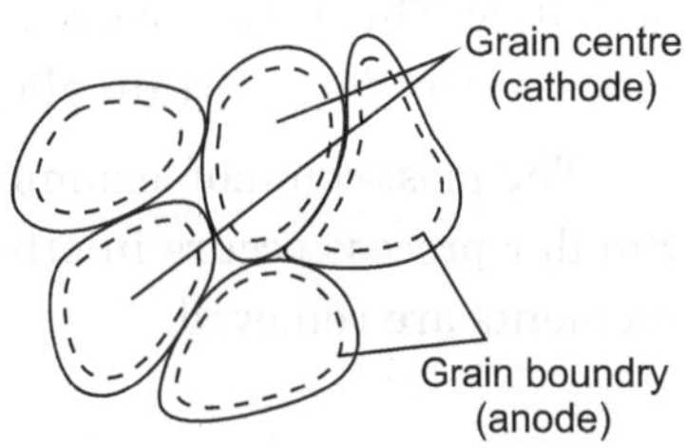

Fig. 3.10. Intergranular corrosion

***(iv)* Underground/Soil Corrosion:** Soil corrosion may be considered to encompass all corrosion that takes place on underground structures.

For example, underground storage tanks, gas and oil pipeline and many other similar structures buried in soil are susceptible to soil corrosion.

The corrosiveness of the soil depends upon the acidity of soil, degree of aeration, moisture content, mineral content, presence of bacteria and other microorganisms, presence of organic matter etc.

In highly acidic soils, metals undergo corrosion accompanied by liberation of hydrogen. In neutral and mildly alkaline soils, the mineral and moisture content of the soil greatly influence the rate of corrosion. Soils having high mineral and moisture content also have high electrical conductivity which promotes corrosion.

In water logged soil, various bacteria and micro-organisms can grow, leading to microbiological corrosion.

***(v)* Stress Corrosion:** This type of corrosion takes place due to combined effect of tensile stress and corrosive environment on the metal. A metal is subjected to tensile stress either during manufacturing process (like quenching, annealing, bending etc.) or fabrication process or heat treatment process. The metal also experience stress under service conditions. There will be difference in potential between the parts of the metal under stress (acts as anode) and the parts which are not under stress (behaves as cathode). Thus, the part of the metal under stress acts as anode and becomes highly reactive which is attacked even by a mild corrosive environment resulting in the formation of a crack. The corroding medium is selective while attacking the parts under stress.

For example, a solution of ammonia can corrode stressed parts of brass, stainless steel can be attacked by chloride ions and alkalies.

Stress corrosion also includes season cracking (stress corrosion of copper alloys like brass) and caustic embrittlement.

***(vi)* Erosion Corrosion:** It is also called as **flow assisted** or **flow accelerated corrosion**. There is an increase in rate of corrosion because of relative movement between a corrosive fluid and the metal surface. In this type of corrosion, the protective layer of the metal or metallic surface itself is removed due to the movement of liquid at high velocity. This type of corrosion is frequently observed in pump impellers, agitators and piping at bends and elbows.

It also includes fretting and cavitation corrosion.

***(vii)* Selective leaching/Dealloying:** Different elements have different chemical activities. This type of corrosion involves the selective removal of one metal (electrochemically more active) from certain alloys under certain environmental conditions.

The most common example is the selective removal of zinc in brass alloys (dezincification). Similar process occurs in other alloys in which aluminium, cobalt, chromium, iron and other elements are removed.

3.7.2 Dry Corrosion/Chemical Corrosion

This type of corrosion occurs due to the direct chemical attack of metal surfaces by the atmospheric gases such as oxygen (O_2), halogen (Cl_2, Br_2) hydrogen sulphide (H_2S), sulphur dioxide (SO_2), nitrogen (N_2) anhydrous inorganic liquid etc.

A solid film of the corrosion product is formed on the surface of the metal which protects the metal from further corrosion attack. If a soluble or volatile corrosion product is formed, then the metal is exposed to further attack. For example, chlorine and iodine attack silver generating a protecting film of silver halide.

There are three main types of chemical corrosion.

(*a*) Oxidation corrosion

(*b*) Corrosion by other gases

(*c*) Liquid metal corrosion.

(*a*) Oxidation Corrosion/Corrosion by Oxygen: Direct attack of metals by oxygen at low or high temperatures, in the absence of moisture leads to oxidation corrosion. Highly reactive alkali and alkaline earth metals undergo oxidation corrosion at low temperature whereas other metals require higher temperature.

Mechanism: The following type of reactions may take place during oxidation corrosion:

(*i*) Oxidation takes place at the surface of the metal forming metal ions

$$M \longrightarrow M^{2+} + 2e^-$$

(*ii*) Oxygen is converted into O^{2-} due to transfer of electrons from metal

$$\frac{1}{2} O_2 + 2e^- \longrightarrow O^{2-}$$

Net reaction is the combination of metal ions with oxide ions forming metal oxide.

$$M + \frac{1}{2} O_2 \longrightarrow M^{2+} + O^{2-} \rightarrow MO$$

Oxidation occurs first at the surface of the metal and the resulting metal oxide scale forms a barrier which restricts further oxidation of metal surface. For oxidation to continue, either the oxygen may diffuse inward through the scale to the underlying metal or the metal may diffuse outwards through the scale to the metal surface. Outward diffusion of metal is much more rapid than the inward diffusion of oxygen, since the metal ion is appreciably smaller than the oxygen and consequently of high mobility. In this type of corrosion the oxide layer formed at the surface decides the further course of corrosion. The oxide layer formed on the metal surface can be of four types. These are:

(*i*) Stable oxide layer: If the oxide layer is stable, it adhere tightly to the metal surface. Hence, such type of oxide layers are impervious in nature, which stops further oxygen attack. Thus, the stable film acts as a protective coating. For example, Al, Sn, Pb, Cu etc.

(*ii*) Unstable oxide film: Noble metals like Au, Ag, Pt forms unstable oxide layer *i.e.*, the oxide layer formed decomposes back into the metal and oxygen.

$$\text{Metal oxide} \rightleftharpoons \text{Metal} + \text{Oxygen}$$

At any point of time, the metal does not have oxide coat on it. Hence, oxidation corrosion is not possible in such cases. This is the reason that Ag, Au, Pt do not undergo oxidation corrosion.

(*iii*) **Volatile oxide layer:** When the metal reacts with oxygen, sometimes a volatile oxide layer is formed which volatilizes as soon as it is formed. The fresh metal surface is kept exposed all the time for further attack, leading to excessive corrosion. For example, molybdenum oxide (MoO_3).

(*iv*) **Porous oxide layer:** Reactive metals like alkali and alkaline earth metals form a porous oxide layer (*i.e.*, layer having pores and cracks). In such cases, oxygen can easily move into the underlying surface of metal through the pores and cracks, thus the corrosion continues unobstructed till the entire metal is completely converted into its oxide.

The protective and non-protective nature of oxide layer at metal surface is governed by **Pilling-Bedworth rule**. According to this rule, specific volume ratio is calculated as follows:

$$\text{Specific volume ratio} = \frac{\text{Volume of metal oxide}}{\text{Volume of metal}}.$$

- If the volume of oxide formed is equal to or greater than the volume of the metal from which it is formed, the oxide layer is tightly adhering, non-porous and therefore protective in nature. In such case, specific volume ratio ≥ 1, as in case of copper-oxygen system (the volume ratio of Cu_2O to Cu is 1.71) the oxide is able to cover the surface or metal effectively. Other examples are oxides of Al, Sn, Pb, Fe, Ni, Zn etc.
- If the volume of oxide formed is less than the volume of metal from which it is formed, the oxide layer is porous (or non-continuous) and hence non-protective. In such cases, specific volume ratio < 1, for instance, the specific volume ratio of CaO to Ca is 0.64 and hence the oxide cannot protect the metal from further corrosion. Other examples, oxides of alkali (Li, Na, K) and alkaline earth metals (Ca, Mg, Sr), etc.

(*b*) **Corrosion by Other Gases:** In the absence of moisture of atmosphere a few gases like SO_2, Cl_2, F_2, H_2S attack the metal by dry corrosion and the extent of corrosion depends mainly on the chemical affinity of the metal and the gas involved. The gases chemically react with the metal surface forming either the protective or non-protective layer.

- If the layer formed is non-porous and protective, the extent of corrosion decreases, because the layer formed protects the metal surface from further attack. For example, formation of AgCl layer on the silver metal by the attack of chlorine.
- If a non-protective, porous layer is formed on the metal surface, the extent of corrosion increases for *e.g.*, attack of dry Cl_2 on tin forming $SnCl_4$, attack of H_2S on steel forming scales of FeS etc.

(*c*) **Liquid Metal Corrosion:** Liquid-metal corrosion occurs due to the chemical action of flowing liquid metal at high temperature on solid metal or alloy. As a result of this corrosion, the solid metal becomes weak as it involves either dissolution of solid metal by a liquid metal or due to penetration of the liquid metal into the solid metal. Such type of corrosion has been found to occur in devices used for nuclear power.

3.7.3 Corrosion of Metals by Acids

Metals are generally exposed to the action of bases or acids in the industries. Acids being corrosive causes severe damage to properties of metal resulting in sudden failure of material in service without any warning.

- The corrosion cost in most of the countries are in the range of 2-4% of the gross national product.
- All metals above hydrogen in the electrochemical series have a tendency to get dissolved in acidic solution with simultaneous evolution of hydrogen. For example, when iron metal comes in contact with non-oxidizing acids like H_2SO_4, HCl, evolution of hydrogen occurs.

At anode: Iron undergoes dissolution to give ferrous ion with the liberation of electrons.

$$Fe \longrightarrow Fe^{2+} + 2e^- \text{ (oxidation)}$$

These electrons flow through the metal from anode to cathode, where H^+ ions of acidic solution takes up the electrons and get reduced to H_2.

At cathode: $2H^+ + 2e^- \longrightarrow H_2 \uparrow$ (Reduction)

Overall reaction is $Fe + 2H^+ \longrightarrow Fe^{2+} + H_2$

- Let us discuss the corrosive tendency of certain metals like Al, Cu and mild steel in various concentrations of hydrochloric acid and sulphuric acid.

Aluminium is more corrosion resistant as composed to Cu and mild steel due to formation of compact, tightly adherent and continuous thin film of aluminium oxide (Al_2O_3) on its surface. This oxide film is **resistant to corrosion** in the pH range 4 to 9. Aluminium corrode more in HCl than H_2SO_4. This is due to the presence of Cl^- ions in HCl, which accelerate the process of corrosion, whereas SO_4^{2-} ions are found to show inhibitive effect.

Mild steel was observed to be more corroded in H_2SO_4 as compared to Cu and Al because iron (which is present in steel) is more reactive than Cu as per the galvanic series. Aluminium being passive is not affected much initially as sulphate ions are inert but with due passage of time, the oxide film dissolves which leads to corrosion.

- With increase in acid strength, the corrosion rate also increase.

3.8 CORROSION CONTROL

As we have seen that corrosion is very harmful and losses incurred are tremendous, therefore it becomes necessary to minimize or control corrosion of metals. It is not possible to stop corrosion completely, however, it can be minimized considerably. Since the types of corrosion are so numerous and the conditions under which corrosion occurs are so different, diverse methods are used to control corrosion. As the corrosion is a reaction between the metal or alloy with the environment, any method of corrosion control must be aimed at either modifying the metal /alloy or the environment. The various methods used for the protection of metal against corrosion are summarised below in the form of chart.

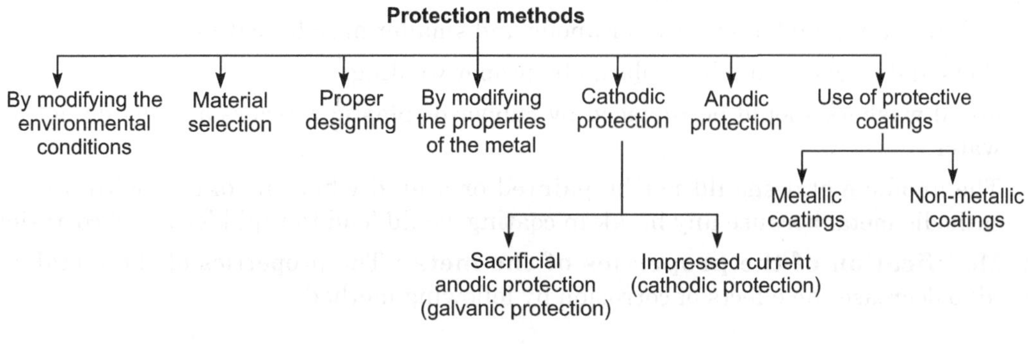

1. Modifying the environmental conditions: Environment plays a major role in the corrosion of metals. Hence, we can prevent corrosion to a great extent by modifying the environment. Some of the methods are given below:

(i) **Deaeration:** The presence of increased amounts of oxygen is harmful, as it increases the corrosion rate. Deaeration aims at the removal of dissolved oxygen. Dissolved oxygen (DO) can be removed by adding some chemicals like Na_2CO_3.

(ii) **Dehumidification:** In this method, moisture present in the air is removed by lowering the relative humidity of the surrounding air. This can be achieved by adding alumina or silica gel which has a tendency to absorb moisture.

(iii) **Inhibitors:** Corrosion inhibitors may be defined as substances which when added in small quantities to the corrosive medium decrease the corrosion of metal. The inhibitors provide protection against corrosion by retarding either anodic or cathodic reaction or both. On this basis, inhibitors can be anodic (for example, chromates, phosphates, tungstates etc.) or cathodic (for example, amines, mercaptans, substituted ureas and thiourea etc.).

2. Material selection:

(*i*) The first choice is to use noble metals such as silver, gold and platinum. They are most resistant to corrosion, therefore used in ornaments but too expensive to be used for general purposes.

(*ii*) The next choice is to use purest possible metal, as pure metals have higher corrosion resistance. Even a small amount of impurity may lead to severe corrosion,

(*iii*) The next choice is to use corrosion resistant alloys. Corrosion resistant alloys have been developed for specific purposes and environment. For example, stainless steel containing chromium, cupro-nickel alloys, highly stressed nimonic alloy (Ni-Cr-Mo alloys), german silver, duralumin etc.

3. Proper designing: It is important to design the metal structures properly in order to prevent corrosion of equipments and structures. The important design principles are:

(*i*) To use simple design, structure and shapes. As far as possible crevices (gap or crack) should be avoided between adjacent parts of a structure.

(*ii*) If two dissimilar metals are in contact, it may lead to galvanic corrosion. In such a case, galvanic corrosion can be prevented by the following methods:

- (*a*) The metals chosen should be as close as possible in the electrochemical series.
- (*b*) By inserting an insulating material between the two metals. For example, metal washers should be covered with plastic or rubber washers to avoid direct contact between the two metals.
- (*c*) By providing larger area for anode and smaller area for cathode.

(*iii*) Bolts and rivets should be replaced by proper welding.

(*iv*) Metal washers should be replaced by rubber or plastic washers as they do not adsorb water.

(*v*) The anodic metal should not be painted or coated when in contact with a different cathodic metal because any break in coating would lead to rapid localized corrosion.

4. Modification of the properties of the metal: The properties of the metal can be modified to decrease the effects of corrosion by following method.

(*i*) **Refining:** Refining is done to decrease the concentration of impurities. For example, lowering of sulphur, phosphorus and carbon in steels increases the corrosion resistance of steels.

(*ii*) **Alloying:** Alloying is another way to improve the corrosion resistance of metals. For example, Al, Be, Mg etc. are added to copper to improve its oxidation resistance.

(*iii*) **Annealing:** Annealing is a type of heat treatment for metals to reduce residual stress.

5. Cathodic protection: The reduction or prevention of corrosion by making metallic structure as cathode in the electrolytic cell is called **cathodic protection**. Since, there will not be any anodic area on the metal, corrosion does not occur. This can be done in two ways:

(*i*) Sacrificial anodic protection (galvanic protection)

(*ii*) Impressed current cathodic protection.

(*a*) Sacrificial anodic protection: We know that the corrosion starts at anode. In this technique, the metallic structure to be protected is made cathode by connecting it with a more active metal which behaves as anode. Hence, all the corrosion is concentrated at more active metal (*i.e.*, anodic part) and the cathodic part is protected. The more active metal so employed is called **sacrificial anode**. The sacrificial anode is a metal alloy which has more negative electrochemical potential than the metal to be protected. Metals that are commonly employed as sacrificial anodes are magnesium, zinc, aluminium and their alloys. This method is used for the protection of sea going vessels such as ships and boats.

Sheets of zinc and magnesium behave as sacrificial anode and are hung around the hull of the ship. Zinc and magnesium being anodic to iron get corroded and iron is protected. The corroded sacrificial anode is replaced by a fresh one when consumed completely.

This method of sacrificial anodic protection is also used for the protection of underground pipelines and cables from soil corrosion.

(*b*) Impressed current cathodic protection method: In this method, current from an external source is applied in opposite direction to nullify the corrosion current and convert the corroding metal from anode to cathode. Once the metal becomes cathodic, it is protected from undergoing corrosion. The impressed current is derived from direct current sources (like battery or rectifier on AC line) with an insoluble, inert anode (like graphite, scrap iron, stainless steel, platinum or high silica iron). This type of protection is of particular importance is case of buried structures such as oil or water pipelines, water tanks, transmission line powers etc.

6. Anodic protection: Passivity is quite common for certain metals like Al, Cr, Ni, Ti etc. and in such cases, cathodic protection technique cannot be used. In this technique, the metal structure to be protected from corrosion is made more anodic. An external impressed DC is applied to the anodic part, which makes it more anodic. As a result, a thin oxide film is formed on the surface of metal which protects it from further corrosion.

7. Use of protective coatings: Protecting the metal surface by the application of coating is probably the oldest of the common procedures for corrosion prevention. These coating acts as a physical barrier between the metal and the environment.

Various types of protective coatings on metals

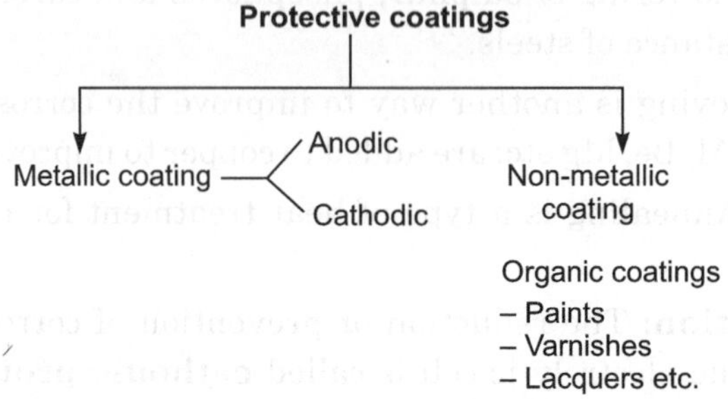

Metallic Coating

The metal structure to be protected is coated with a layer of other metal which may be either more noble or less noble than it. For example, steel structures can be coated either with copper (which is more noble than steel) or with zinc (which is less noble than steel). Two important protective coatings are:

(*a*) Anodic coating (*b*) Cathodic coating

(***a***) **Anodic metal coating:** In this technique, the base metal is coated with a more active metal so that the coating metal behaves as an anode and undergoes corrosion in preference to the base metal. The anodic coating has an advantage that if any crack or pore appears on the coating metal than a galvanic cell is created between the base metal and the coating metal. As a result corrosion occurs at coating metal and the base metal is protected. For example: galvanization.

(***b***) **Cathodic metal coating:** The metal surface can be protected from corrosion by coating the base metal with a more noble metal which has lower tendency for corrosion than the base metal in the galvanic series.

The cathodic coating thus formed on the surface of the base metal protects it from corrosion because of high corrosion resistance of coating metal than the base metal. For example, a thin film coating of metals like tin, copper, nickel etc. are deposited on the base metal iron by this technique. The cathodic coating provides an effective protection against corrosion only if the surface of base metal is continuous and not defective, because defective coating causes more corrosion damage when the base metal is made anodic. **Tinning** is a good example of cathodic coating.

There are various methods by which these metallic coatings are applied on a metal surface. Few of them are discussed here:

1. Hot dipping: In this method, the metal to be coated (base metal) is dipped in the molten bath of coating metal, covered by a molten flux layer. The flux cleans the base metal and prevents oxidation of the molten coating metal. For example, applying coating of low melting metals and alloys such as Zn, Pb, Sn, solder etc. The process providing tin coating is called **tinning** and that providing zinc coating is called **galvanizing**.

(***a***) **Tinning:** It is the method of coating iron or steel structures with tin. In this process, first the base metal is cleaned by pickling with dilute sulphuric acid. Then it is passed through molten tin, covered with zinc chloride flux. The tin coated article is finally passed through a series of rollers immersed in palm oil bath to remove excess tin. Tin coated utensils are used for storing foodstuffs, pickles, oils etc.

(*b*) **Galvanizing:** It is the process of coating iron or steel articles (base metal) with a thin coat of zinc to prevent them from rusting.

As, Zn is higher up in the corrosion series, the Zn coating acts as anode with respect to the base metal which acts as cathode. With repeated exposure of the galvanized metal to the environment, only the coated actve zinc metal gets corroded. In this way the base metal is protected from rusting.

The galvanization process is carried out in following steps:

1. The metal is first cleaned and degreased using organic solvents.
2. The cleaned and degreased metal is treated with dilute sulphuric acid at 60–90°C for about 15-20 minutes (pickling process) to remove any rust or scales if present.
3. The metal is then treated with flux materials like $ZnCl_2$, NH_4Cl.
4. After this, the metal part is immersed into the molten zinc bath maintained at 430–470°C.
5. The coated base metal is then passed through rollers to remove excess zinc and produce the film of uniform thickness. Excess zinc can also be removed by wiping or air blow technique.

This method is used to protect roofing sheets, wires, pipes, nails etc.

Galvanizing is preferred over tinning because zinc is anodic to iron whereas tin is cathodic. So, if the protective layer of the coating has any cracks, iron will corrode. But if zinc coating has any cracks, iron being cathodic does not get corrode. The corrosion products fill up the cracks, thus preventing corrosion.

2. Metal cladding: It is the process by which a dense, homogeneous layer of coating metal is bonded firmly and permanently to the base metal on one or both sides.

In this method, the base metal is sandwiched between two layers of the coating metal which is then passed through rollers under the action of heat and pressure. Metal cladding is used in aircraft industry. For example, Al-clad sheeting which is prepared by sandwiching duralumin between two layers of 99.5% pure aluminium.

3. Electroplating: It is the most important and frequently used method of producing metal coating industrially. Electroplating is the technique by which the coating metal is deposited on the base metal by passing a direct current through an electrolytic solution containing the soluble salt of the coating metal.

In this method, the base metal is made cathode and anode is either inert (like graphite) or made of the coating metal. When direct current is passed, coating metal ions moved towards cathode and get deposited there. Thus, a thin layer of coating material is formed on the article made as cathode. For example, coating of silver on copper material. Other metals that can be electroplated are Au, Cr, Ni, Cu, Sn etc.

4. Electroless plating: Electroless plating is a technique of depositing a more noble metal (such as copper, silver, gold, palladium etc.) on a catalytically active surface of a less noble metal by employing a reducing agent without using electrical energy.

This process is also called as **"autocatalytic plating"** as the reduction of metal ions by the reducing agent is catalyzed by the metal atoms being plated. In this process, the metal ions are reduced to metal atoms by a suitable reducing agent. The metal atoms get deposited on the active sites of the coating metal. The process can be represented as :

$$\text{Metals ions } (M^{n+}) + \text{Reducing agent} \longrightarrow \text{Metal (M)} + \text{oxidised product}$$

This type of plating is used for following purposes:

Machinery where metal to metal wear applications are needed and the use of routine lubricants is not possible.

- Non metal and plastics can also be coated by this process.
- Plating of printed circuit boards.

Steps Involved in Electroless Plating

Following steps are involved in electroless plating:

(*i*) Preparation of active surface of the substrate

(*ii*) Preparation of plating bath.

(*i*) Preparation of active surface of the substrate: Active surface can be prepared by any one of the following methods:

- **Etching:** (by acid treatment) In this process the unwanted particles present on the surface of the substrate are removed by treatment with an acid.
- **Electroplating:** A thin layer of the metal to be plated or any other suitable metal. This is usually followed by heat treatment.
- **Treatment with stannous chloride followed by dipping in palladium chloride:** This process gives a thin layer of palladium on the treated surface. This process is usually followed in case of plastics and printed circuit boards.

(*ii*) Preparation of plating bath: The electroless plating bath will have the following composition:

1. Metal salt solution to provide metal ions for deposition.
2. A reducing agent (for example sodium hypophosphite or formaldehyde) for reducing the metal ions to metal atoms.
3. A complexing agent like EDTA, trisodium citrate etc. to complex with the metal ions so as to prevent bulk deposition of metal ions.
4. Buffer (e.g., sodium acetate, sodium hydroxide + rochelle salt etc.) is added to maintain the pH of the bath.
5. A stabilizer like thiourea to prevent the decomposition of the plating bath solution.
6. An accelerator like succinate, fluoride, glycinate etc to enhance the plating rate.

Comparison of Electroless Plating and Electroplating

Table 3.1. Comparison of Electroplating and Electroless plating

S.No.	Electroplating	Electroless plating
1.	External current source is needed.	No external current source is required.
2.	It is a non-catalytic process.	It is an autocatalytic process.
3.	As it uses electric current, it only works with conductive material.	It works both with conductive and non-conductive materials.
4.	Less throwing power of the electrolytic bath.	Better throwing powers of the electrolytic bath *i.e.,* capable to plate even on irregular and non-uniform structures.
5.	It is a cheaper technique as compared to electroless plating.	It is an expensive technique as it employes expensive chemicals.
6.	It produces thick layer of metals.	It produces thinner layer of metal as compared to electroplating.

Throwing power is a measure of an electroplating solution's ability to plate to a uniform thickness over an irregularly shaped cathode.

Electroless plating is applicable to a large number of metals but copper and nickel are important in view of the extent of their application.

Electroless plating of nickel: Electroless nickel plating is the deposit of a nickel alloy coating by chemical reduction without the electric current. The majority of electroless nickel plating for engineering purpose is a nickel-phosphorus deposit containing 2-14% phosphorus.

The process involves the following steps:

***(i)* Preparation of active surface of the substrate:** The surface to the plated is first degreased using organic solvent or by alkali treatment followed by treatment with an acid.

- Aluminum, iron, copper, brass etc. can be directly nickel plated without preparation of active surface.
- Stainless steel is activated by dipping in 50% H_2SO_4 solution.
- Magnesium alloys are given a thin coating of Zn and Cu over it.
- Non-metallic surfaces like plastics, glass, quartz etc. are activated by dipping in $SnCl_2$ and then $PdCl_2$ to get a thin activating layer of Pd on their surfaces.

***(ii)* Plating bath composition:** Plating bath solution comprises of:

- Nickel chloride ($NiCl_2$) coating solution = 20 g/L
- Sodium hypophosphite ($NaPO_2H_2$), reducing agent = 20 g/L
- Sodium acetate buffer = 10 g/L
- Sodium succinate ($C_4H_4Na_2O_4$) complexing agent = 15 g/L
- Optimum temperature range = 85–95°C
- Optimum pH range = 4–6.

Process: The prepared surface is immersed in the plating bath. The reduction of nickel ions occurs and the nickel gets deposited over the surface. The following reactions takes place at the surface.

At anode: $$H_2PO_2^- + H_2O \longrightarrow H_2PO_3^- + 2H^+ + 2e^-$$

At cathode: $$Ni_2^+ + 2e^- \longrightarrow Ni$$

Net Redox reaction: $$Ni^{2+} + H_2PO_2^- + H_2O \longrightarrow Ni + H_2PO_3^- + 2H^+$$

- In the above redox reaction, H^+ ions are released and hence pH tends to decrease which may affect the quality of plating. Hence, the addition of buffer is very essential.

Applications of Electroless Nickel Plating

- It is extensively used in electronic appliances like knobs of equipements.
- Plastic cabinets coated with Cu and Ni finds applications in electronic as well as digital instruments.
- It finds application in automotive as well as domestic field like tops of perfume bottles, car trims etc.
- It is also used in several valves, piston, pumps, compressors etc.

ELECTROLESS PLATING OF COPPER

Electroless copper plating is a chemical process that deposits an even layer of copper on the surface of a solid substrate like metal or plastics.

The process involves in the following steps:

***(i)* Preparation of active surface of the substrate:** The surface to be coated is first degreased using organic solvents or by alkali treatment followed by treatment with an acid.

- Iron, cobalt, nickel etc. can be directly copper plated without any preparation of active surface.
- Non-metallic surfaces are activated by dipping in $SnCl_2$ solution followed by dipping in $PdCl_2$ solution.

***(ii)* Plating both composition:** Plating both solution is composed of

- Copper sulphate solution ($CuSO_4.5H_2O$) coating solution = 12 g/L
- Formaldehyde (HCHO), reducing agent = 8 g/L
- Sodium hydroxide (15 g/L) + Rochelle salt (14 g/L) = Buffer
- EDTA (Ethylene diamine tetra acetic acid), complexing agent = 20 g/L

Optimum pH = 11

Optimum temperature = 25°C.

Process: The prepared surface is immersed in the plating bath. The reduction of cupric ions to metallic copper occurs with the action of reducing agent, formaldehyde under a strongly basic medium. The copper gets deposited over the surface. The following reactions take place at the surface.

At Anode:	$2HCHO + 4OH^- \longrightarrow 2HCOO^- + 2H_2O + H_2 + 2e^-$
At cathode:	$Cu^{2+} + 2e^- \longrightarrow Cu$
Net redox reaction:	$Cu^{2+} + 2HCHO + 4OH^- \longrightarrow Cu + 2HCOO^- + 2H_2O + H_2$

- In the above redox reaction, OH^- ions are released which tends to increase the pH of solutions, therefore addition of buffer is essential.

Applications of Electroless Copper Plating

- Finds application in printed circuit boards especially double sided and multilayered boards in which plating through holes is required.
- Used for plating insulators.
- Used as a base for subsequent conventional electroplating.

3.9 NON-METALLIC COATINGS

Non-metallic coatings may be organic or inorganic.

Inorganic Coatings: The commonly used inorganic coatings are:

(*a*) Phosphate coating: Phosphate coatings are produced by the reaction between base metal and aqueous solution of phosphoric acid in the presence of accelerators. Accelerators enhance the rate of the reaction. These coatings are applied on iron, steel, zinc, aluminium, cadmium and tin surfaces. The phosphate coating is not corrosion resistant but it provides a good base for painting or impregnation with oils.

(*b*) Chromate coating: Chromate coating is formed on base metals like Zn, Cd, Mg, Al by the action of sodium chromate and dil. sulphuric acid. The dissolution of the base metal in the dilute sulphuric acid raises the pH of solution and at a particular pH value, basic chromium chromate ($Cr_2O_3.CrO_3.xH_2O$) is precipitated on the metal surface forming the chromate coating.

Organic coatings: Important organic coatings include paints (a mixture of pigment, dry oil and thinner), varnishes (paints without pigment), lacquers (a soln. of resin and plasticizer) etc. When applied on cleaned metal surfaces, they act as effective inert barriers which protect the metal from corrosion.

EXERCISES

I. SHORT ANSWER TYPE QUESTIONS

1. What do you mean by component? What is the maximum number of phases that can be in equilibrium at one point of one-component system (T and P constant)?

2. Find out the number of phases in the following systems:

(*a*) $NH_4Cl(s) \rightleftharpoons NH_3(g) + HCl(g)$
(*b*) $N_2(g) + 3H_2(g) \rightleftharpoons 2NH_3(g)$
(*c*) $CuSO_4.5H_2O(s) \rightleftharpoons CuSO_4.3H_2O(s) + 2H_2O(g)$
(*d*) $C(s) + H_2O(g) \rightleftharpoons CO(g) + H_2(g)$

Hint: (*a*) 2 (*b*) 1 (*c*) 3 (*d*) 4

3. Calculate the degrees of freedom for a two phase, one component system.
4. What is corrosion? What are the factors which affect corrosion?
5. Why galvanization is preferred over tinning? *[HMTU 2017]*
6. Write short notes on the following:
   (*a*) Galvanic corrosion
   (*b*) Differential aeration corrosion
   (*c*) Inter-granular corrosion
   (*d*) Erosion corrosion.
7. Write a short note on prevention of corrosion by cathodic protection.
8. On the basis of phase rule, calculate the number of components present in the following systems:
   (*a*) $H_2O(s) \rightleftharpoons H_2O(l)$
   (*b*) Cu and Ag at eutectic point.
   (*c*) $MgCO_3(s) \rightleftharpoons MgO(s) + CO_2(g)$
   (*d*) Saturated solution of NaCl.
9. How many degrees of freedom will be present in the following systems?
   (*a*) $N_2O_4(g) \rightleftharpoons NO_2(g)$
   (*b*) A gas in equilibrium with its solution in a liquid
   (*c*) $NH_4Cl\ (s) \rightleftharpoons NH_3\ (g) + HCl(g)$, When $P_{NH_3} = P_{HCl}$
   (*d*) $NH_4Cl(s) \rightleftharpoons NH_3(g) + HCl(g)$, When $P_{NH_3} \neq P_{HCl}$
10. Write short notes on
    (*a*) Galvanization
    (*b*) Electroplating
    (*c*) Non-metallic coatings for corrosion prevention
    (*d*) Tinning.
11. What is meant by invariant system? Explain with an example.
12. Explain why the fusion curve of ice in phase diagram of H_2O is slightly inclined towards pressure axis?
13. Explain triple point in water system.
14. Define the following terms :
    (*a*) Eutectic system
    (*b*) Eutectic temperature
    (*c*) Eutectic composition.
15. Draw well labelled phase diagram of water system.
16. Draw well labelled phase diagram of Cu-Ag system.
17. Explain the electrochemical theory of corrosion.
18. Explain the corrosion of metals by oxygen.

19. How can corrosion be controlled by modifying the environment.
20. How corrosion can be prevented by cathodic coatings?
21. Define eutectic system and write significance of eutectic.
22. Define eutectic point and write the characteristics of eutectic point.
23. What is galvanization? Write various steps involves in it. Also writes it applications.
24. What is electroless plating? Write various steps involved in it.
25. Differentiate between anodic and cathodic coatings. ...[*HMTU 2017*]

II. LONG ANSWER TYPE QUESTIONS

1. State and derive the phase rule. Also define the terms involved in it.
2. With the help of well labelled diagram explain the phase diagram of water system and discuss the importance of triple point.
3. Draw and explain the phase diagram for Cu-Ag eutectic system.
4. Find out the number of components in KCl-NaCl-H_2O system and KCl-NaBr-H_2O system.
5. Define corrosion. Explain various types of electrochemical corrosions.
6. What is dry corrosion? Explain its various types.
7. Write various methods of corrosion control. (*RTU 2020, 2017*)
8. Explain the following terms:
   (*a*) Galvanizing
   (*b*) Tinning
   (*c*) Pilling-Bedworth rule. (*RTU 22*)
9. Explain sacrificial anodic protection method of controlling corrosion.
10. List all the methods of prevention of corrosion and explain in detail the use of protective coatings in the prevention of corrosion.
11. Define electroless plating. What are the differences between electroplating and electroless plating? (*VTU Dec 2011, 2018*)
12. Discuss the mechanism of electrochemicals corrosion by hydrogen evolution and oxygen absorption. (*RTU 2022*)
13. Explain impressed current catholic protection method of controlling corrosion. (*RTU 2022*)
14. Discuss about the chemical corrosion. (*RTU 2020*)
15. Explain electroless plating of Cu. What are application of electroless Cu plating?
16. Explain electroless plating of Ni. What are applications of electroless Ni plating?
17. Iron does not rust if the zinc coating is broken in a galvanized iron pipe but rusting occurs much faster if the tin coating over iron is broken. Explain. (*RTU 2022*)
18. Explain theory of wet electrochemical corrosion of metals. (*RTU 2017*)
19. Draw and explain the phase diagram of sulphur system.

20. State the phase rule. Draw and briefly explain the phase diagram of Pb-Ag system.
21. What is congruent melting point? Explain the phase diagram of Zn-Mg system with neat and lebelled diagram.
22. Define non-congruent melting point. Draw and explain the phase diagram of NaCl-water system.

III. MULTIPLE CHOICE QUESTIONS

1. For water system, the maximum number of degrees of freedom is:
   (*a*) 0 (*b*) 3
   (*c*) 2 (*d*) 4.
2. Number of phases in saturated NaCl solution:
   (*a*) 1 (*b*) 2
   (*c*) 3 (*d*) 0.
3. The condensed phase rule is applicable for:
   (*a*) Bi-Cd system (*b*) sulphur system
   (*c*) water system (*d*) none of these.
4. The number of degrees of freedom at the triple point for the water system is:
   (*a*) 1 (*b*) 2
   (*c*) 3 (*d*) 0.
5. According to Gibbs phase rule:
   (*a*) $F = C - P + 2$ (*b*) $F = C + P + 2$
   (*c*) $F = C - P - 2$ (*d*) $C = F - P + 2$.
6. The corrosion of metals due to direct chemical attack of the environment on the metal surface in the absence of moisture is:
   (*a*) chemical corrosion (*b*) dry corrosion
   (*c*) electrochemical corrosion (*d*) both (*a*) and (*b*).
7. According to Pilling-Bedworth rule a metal undergoes continuous corrosion when the volume of the oxide film formed is:
   (*a*) less than the volume of the metals from which it is formed.
   (*b*) more than the volume of the metals from which it is formed.
   (*c*) equal to the volume of the metals from which it is formed.
   (*d*) none of the above.
8. Triple point of water corresponds to:
   (*a*) 5.58 mm, 0.0065°C (*b*) 2.18 mm, 0.0065°C
   (*c*) 4.58 mm, 0.0075°C (*d*) 1 mm, 0.0078°C.
9. Dissociation of ammonium chloride in a closed vessel is a:
   (*a*) 1-component system (*b*) 2-component system
   (*c*) 3-component system (*d*) none of the above.

10. According to the electrochemical theory, corrosion occurs at:

(*a*) cathode (*b*) anode

(*c*) both cathode and anode (*d*) neither at anode nor at cathode.

11. The corrosion rate is high if:

(*a*) area of anode is large and cathode is small

(*b*) area of anode is small and cathode is large

(c) both anodic and cathodic areas are large

(*d*) does not depend upon the anodic and cathodic area.

12. In electroplating, the metal to be coated is made:

(a) cathode (*b*) anode

(*c*) either anode or cathode (*d*) neither anode nor cathode.

13. In electroplating, the article to be electroplated serves as:

(*a*) cathode (*b*) electrolyte

(*c*) anode (*d*) conductor.

14. Prevention of corrosion of iron by Zn is called as:

(*a*) galvanization (*b*) cathode protection

(*c*) sacrificial anodic protection (*d*) metal cladding.

15. Rusting of iron is:

(*a*) 1-phase system (*b*) 2-phase system

(*c*) 3-phase system (*d*) none of the above.

16. In electrochemical corrosion, which type of chemical reaction is observed at cathode?

(*a*) oxidation (*b*) reduction

(*c*) peritectic (*d*) eutectic.

17. Chemical formula of rust is:

(*a*) Fe_2O_3 (*b*) Fe_3O_4

(*c*) FeO (*d*) $Fe_2O_3.xH_2O$.

18. At the triple point of water system, the system is:

(*a*) univariant (*b*) invariant

(*c*) bivariant (*d*) trivariant.

19. At the freezing point of water the number of degree of freedom is:

(*a*) 0 (*b*) 1

(*c*) 2 (*d*) 3.

20. In water system, the critical point corresponds:

(*a*) $T = -373°C, P = 18.4$ atm (*b*) $T = 374°C, P = 218$ atm

(*c*) $T = 100°C, P = 1.48$ atm (*d*) $T = -374°C, P = 1$ atm.

21. Eutectic system has lower melting point than its individual components because:

(*a*) one of the component has very low melting point.

(*b*) all the components are of same size and forms a homogeneous mixture.

(*c*) due to presence of impurities in the eutectic system

(*d*) distortion and strain result in poor interface bonding.

22. Eutectic Cu-Ag system has the following composition

(*a*) Cu (50%) + Ag (50%) (*b*) Cu (28.1%) + Ag (71.9%)

(*c*) Cu (71.9%) + Ag (28.1%) (*d*) Cu (60 %) + Ag (40%).

23. The eutectic temperature of Cu-Ag system is

(*a*) 779°C (*b*) 1083°C

(*c*) 961°C (*d*) 373°C

24. Eutectic point is

(*a*) non-variant (*b*) monovariant

(*c*) bivariant (*d*) trivariant.

25. Which of the following is not a eutectic point?

(*a*) Fe-C (b) Bi-Cd

(*c*) Ag-Cu (*d*) Zn-Cd.

Answers

MULTIPLE CHOICE QUESTIONS

1. (*c*)	**2.** (*b*)	**3.** (*a*)	**4.** (*d*)	**5.** (*a*)	**6.** (*d*)	**7.** (*a*)	**8.** (*c*)	**9.** (*a*)	**10.** (*b*)
11. (*b*)	**12.** (*a*)	**13.** (*a*)	**14.** (*a*)	**15.** (*c*)	**16.** (*b*)	**17.** (*d*)	**18.** (*b*)	**19.** (*b*)	**20.** (*b*)
21. (*d*)	**22.** (*b*)	**23.** (*a*)	**24.** (*a*)	**25.** (*a*)					

Chapter 4 Chemical Kinetics

4.1 INTRODUCTION

Chemical kinetics is a branch of chemistry which deals with the **rate of chemical reactions,** the factors affecting the reaction rate and the mechanism by which these reactions occur. Thermodynamics tells us only about the spontaneity or feasibility of a chemical reaction whereas chemical kinetics tells us about the rate of a reaction. For example, the reaction between hydrogen and oxygen to give water at room temperature is thermodynamically feasible. However, this conversion takes place so slowly that unless we are willing to wait indefinitely, practically no water results. Hence, chemical kinetics is a technique complementary to thermodynamics for studying a given reaction.

Chemical kinetics is concerned with the following aspects:

(*a*) The rate of reaction and the rate laws.

(*b*) The effect of various factors (like temperature, pressure, catalyst etc.) on the rate of reaction.

(*c*) The mechanism of the chemical reaction.

4.2 RATE OF REACTION

When the reactants are mixed to perform a reaction there are no products present initially. As time passes, the concentration of the products increases and that of the reactants decreases. This change in concentration of any of reactant or product per unit time is called as the **rate of reaction**. For example:

Consider a simple reaction: $A \longrightarrow B$

$$\text{Rate of chemical reaction} = \frac{\text{Change in concentration of a reactant or a product}}{\text{time taken}}$$

$$= \frac{\text{mol litre}^{-1}}{\text{second}} = \text{Mol L}^{-1}\text{s}^{-1}$$

Thus, the rate of reaction can be expressed either as rate of disappearance of a reactant or rate of appearance of a product per unit time.

$$\text{Rate of reaction} = \frac{\text{Decrease in concentration of } A}{\text{Time taken}} = \frac{-\Delta[A]}{\Delta t}$$

Negative sign indicates the decrease in concentration of reactant with time.

or $$\text{Rate of reaction} = \frac{\text{Increase in concentration of } B}{\text{Time taken}} = \frac{\Delta[B]}{\Delta t}.$$

Positive sign indicates the increase in concentration of product with time.

The rate of disappearance of reactant is equal to the rate of appearance of product. Thus

$$\text{Rate of reaction} = \frac{-\Delta[A]}{\Delta t} = \frac{\Delta[B]}{\Delta t}$$

For a general reaction,

$$aA + bB \longrightarrow cC + dD$$

The rate of reaction may be expressed as

$$-\frac{1}{a}\frac{d[A]}{dt} = -\frac{1}{b}\frac{d[B]}{dt} = \frac{1}{c}\frac{d[C]}{dt} = \frac{1}{d}\frac{d[D]}{dt}.$$

Units of rate of a reaction: If concentration is in mol l^{-1} and time is in seconds then the units be mol l^{-1} s^{-1}.

However in gaseous reactions, the units of rate of reaction will be atm sec^{-1}.

4.2.1 Average Rate and Instantaneous Rate

The rate expressions discussed so far give the average rate of reactions over a time interval (Δt). Thus, mathematically,

$$\text{Rate} = \frac{\text{Change in concentration}}{\text{Time interval}} = \frac{\Delta x}{\Delta t}.$$

According to law of mass action, the rate of reaction depends upon the concentration of reactants. As the reaction proceeds, the concentration of reactants decrease continuously with time, therefore it is not possible to find the rate of reaction at a particular time with the help of average rate expression. Therefore, the rate of reaction is expressed as the instantaneous rate which measures the rate of reaction at a particular time (t). For this purpose, the time interval Δt is made as small as possible so that the rate of reaction remains almost constant during that time interval. Mathematically,

$$\text{Rate} = \left[\frac{\Delta x}{\Delta t}\right]_{\Delta t \to 0} = \frac{dx}{dt}.$$

When concentration of any of the reactants or products is plotted against time, then the instantaneous rate can be determined by drawing a tangent to the curve at a particular time. The slope of the tangent gives the rate of reaction at that time **Fig. 4.1.**

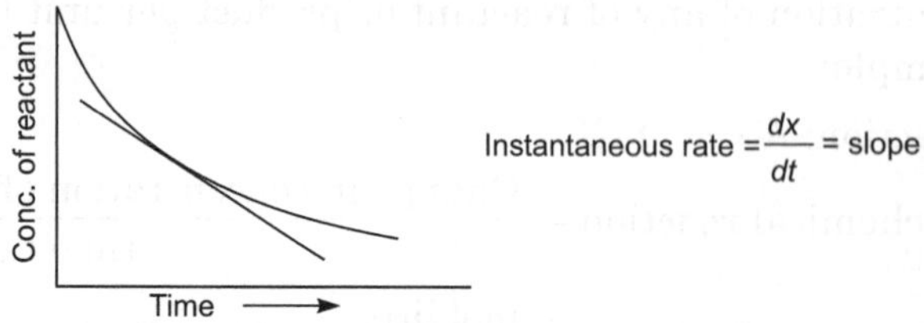

Fig. 4.1. Graphical method for determining rate.

For the reaction

$$2N_2O_5(g) \longrightarrow 2NO_2(g) + O_2(g)$$

$$\text{Average rate} = \frac{-1}{2}\frac{\Delta[N_2O_5]}{\Delta t} = \frac{\Delta[O_2]}{\Delta t}$$

$$\text{Instantaneous rate} = \frac{-1}{2}\frac{d[N_2O_5]}{dt} = \frac{1}{2}\frac{d[NO_2]}{dt} = \frac{d[O_2]}{dt}.$$

4.2.2 Factors Influencing Rates of Chemical Reaction

1. **Temperature of the system:** In general, almost all chemical reactions are accelerated by increase in temperature. In most cases, the rate of a chemical reaction becomes almost double for every 10°C rise in temperature Fig. 4.2.

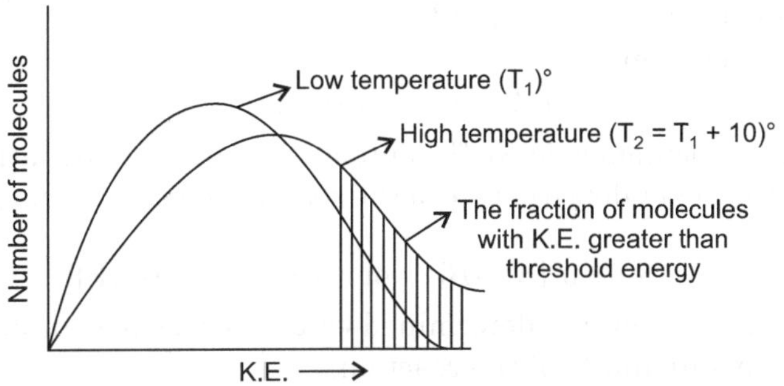

Fig. 4.2. Distribution of molecular energies at temperatures T_1 and T_2.

2. **Concentration of reactants:** Rate of a reaction is directly proportional to the concentration of reactants. When the concentration of reactants is increased, the number of molecules per unit volume increases, thereby increasing the collision frequency, which ultimately causes the increase in reaction rate.

3. **Nature of reactant:** A chemical reaction involves the breaking of old bonds and formation of new bonds. The reactivity of a substance can, therefore, be related to the ease with which the particular bonds are broken or formed and also on the number of such bonds involved. For example, ionic reactions which do not involve any bond cleavage proceed instantaneously, whereas reactions involving covalent bonds proceed rather slowly depending upon the strength of the bonds.

4. **Presence of catalyst:** Catalysts are substance that increase reactions rate by lowering the activation energy needed for the reaction to occur. A catalyst is not destroyed or changed during a reaction so it can be used again. For example, at ordinary conditions H_2 and O_2 do not combine. However, they combine in the presence of a small quantity of finely divided platinum, which acts at a catalyst and the reaction then occurs rapidly.

5. **Surface area of the reactants:** The larger the surface area of the reactants faster is the rate of reaction. It has been observed that if one of the reactants is solid then the rate of the reaction depends upon the state of subdivision of the solid. Finely divided solid reacts faster than massive solids as the former has larger surface area than the latter.

   For example, a log of wood burns slowly, but if it is cut into small wooden chips, the burning takes place rapidly.

6. **Exposure to radiations:** In some cases, the rate of a chemical reaction is considerably increased by the use of certain radiations. Such reactions are called as **photochemical reactions**. For example, when a mixture of hydrogen and chlorine gases kept in dark nothing happens whereas, an explosive reaction takes place when this mixture is subjected to a pulse of ultraviolet (UV) light.

4.3 RATE LAW

The rate of a chemical reaction at a given temperature may depend on the concentration of one or more reactants and sometimes even on the concentration of the products or some foreign substances.

The mathematical expression that relates the rate of reaction to the concentration of either reactants or products is known as the **rate law**.

Consider a general reaction

$$aA + bB \longrightarrow \text{Products}$$

where a and b are the stoichiometric coefficients of the balanced equation. From the kinetic study of the reaction, the dependence of rate of the reaction on the concentration of the reactant is found to be

$$\text{Rate} \propto [A]^x [B]^y \quad \text{or} \quad \text{Rate} = k\, [A]^x [B]^y$$

where x and y are the experimentally determined values. These may or may not be equal to the stoichiometric coefficients (a and b) of the reaction.

k, is the proportionality constant called as **rate constant** or **velocity constant** for the reaction. It is numerically equal to the rate of reaction if all the concentrations were set equal to unity.

$$\text{Rate} = k\, [1]^x [1]^y$$

$$\text{Rate} = k$$

It means that rate constant is a measure of the rate of the reaction.

Larger the value of k, faster is the reaction. Similarly smaller value of k indicates slow reaction.

For example:

(*i*) $2NO_2\,(g) + F_2\,(g) \longrightarrow 2NO_2F\,(g)$

The experimental observations reveal that the rate law expression for the above reaction is given by the expression

$$\text{Rate} = k[NO_2]\,[F_2]$$

(*ii*) $2N_2O_5\,(g) \longrightarrow 4NO_2\,(g) + O_2(g)$

The experimentally determined values show that the rate of this reaction is proportional to $[N_2O_5]$ and not to $[N_2O_5]^2$. Thus, the rate law expression is thus

$$\text{Rate} = k[N_2O_5]$$

Generally, the rate law expressions are not simple. These may differ even for the same reaction depending on the conditions under which the reaction has been carried out.

For example, for the reaction:

$$H_2(g) + I_2(g) \longrightarrow 2HI(g)$$

$$\text{Rate} = k\,[H_2][I_2]$$

However, for a similar type of reaction:

$$H_2(g) + Br_2(g) \longrightarrow 2HBr$$

$$\text{Rate} = \frac{k_a[H_2][Br_2]^{1/2}}{1 + k_b \left\{ \dfrac{[HBr]}{[Br_2]} \right\}}$$

where k_a and k_b are the constants and depend upon the reaction temperature.

4.4 ORDER OF A REACTION

The powers to which the concentration terms are raised in the rate law expression describes the order of the reaction with respect to that particular reactant.

Consider the following reaction:

$$aA + bB \rightarrow \text{Products}$$

In the rate law—

$$\text{Rate} = k[A]^x\,[B]^y$$

the values of x and y are order of the reaction with respect to the reactants A and B respectively. The overall order (n) of the reaction is $x + y$.

If $n = 1$, the reaction is said to be **first order reaction**, If $n = 2$, the reaction is said to be **second order** and so on. The order of reaction can be in fractions as well. For example—

$$CH_3CHO(g) \xrightarrow{723\text{ K}} CH_4(g) + CO(g)$$

Rate law expression of this reaction:

$$\text{Rate} = k[CH_3CHO]^{3/2}$$

Reaction rate constant: The rate is the change in concentration with time. Therefore,

$$\text{Units of rate} = \frac{\text{Concentration}}{\text{time}} = \frac{\text{mol L}^{-1}}{\text{s}} = \text{mol L}^{-1}\text{s}^{-1}$$

For a zero order reaction

$$\text{Rate} = k[A]^\circ$$

$$\text{Rate} = k_0$$

$$\frac{\text{molL}^{-1}}{s} = k_0$$

$$k_0 = \text{mol L}^{-1}\text{s}^{-1}$$

For first order reaction—

$$\text{Rate} = k_1[A]^1$$

$$\frac{\text{mol L}^{-1}}{s} = k_1(\text{mol L}^{-1})$$

$$k_1 = \text{s}^{-1}$$

For second order reaction—

$$\text{Rate} = k_2[A]^2$$

$$\frac{\text{mol L}^{-1}}{\text{s}} = k_2(\text{mol L}^{-1})^2$$

$$k_2 = \frac{1}{\text{mol L}^{-1}\text{s}} = \text{L mol}^{-1}\text{s}^{-1}$$

For third order reaction—

$$\text{Rate} = k_3[A]^3$$

$$\frac{\text{mol L}^{-1}}{\text{s}} = k_3(\text{mol L}^{-1})^3$$

$$k_3 = \text{L}^2\,\text{mol}^{-2}\,\text{s}^{-1}$$

In general, for any order 'n', the unit for rate constant is given by $k_n = (\text{mol L}^{-1})^{1-n}\,\text{s}^{-1}$ where, n = order of reaction.

4.5 MOLECULARITY OF A REACTION

According to **'collision theory'**, for a chemical reaction to occur, the reacting molecules must collide with each other. The number of reacting species which collide simultaneously to bring about a chemical reaction is called **molecularity of a reaction**.

To understand the concept of molecularity, let us classify the chemical reaction into two types—

1. Elementary reactions/Simple reactions
2. Complex reactions.

4.5.1 Elementary Reactions

A chemical reaction that takes place in a single step is called as an **elementary reaction**.

In general, molecularity of an elementary reaction is equal to the sum of the number of molecules of reactants involved in the balanced stoichiometric equation.

Depending on the number of reactant molecules taking part in an elementary reaction, the reaction can be of three types.

(i) **Unimolecular reactions:** Reactions which involve only one reactant molecule are called as **unimolecular reactions.** (Molecularity = 1)

Examples:

$$\text{(a)} \quad H_2O_2 \longrightarrow H_2O + \frac{1}{2}O_2$$

$$\text{(b)} \; NH_4NO_2 \longrightarrow N_2 + 2H_2O$$

(ii) **Bimolecular reactions:** Reaction which involves two reacting molecules (or collision of two species) are called as **bimolecular reactions.** (Molecularity = 2)

Examples:

(a) $2HI(g) \rightarrow H_2(g) + I_2(g)$

(b) $2NOCl \rightarrow 2NO(g) + CO_2(g)$

(c) $CO(g) + NO(g) \rightarrow NO_2(g) + CO_2(g)$

(iii) **Trimolecular reactions:** If a reaction involves three reacting molecules (or collision of three species) then the reaction is called as **trimolecular reactions.** (Molecularity = 3)

Examples:

(1) $2NO(g) + O_2(g) \rightarrow 2NO_2(g)$

(2) $2NO + Cl_2 \rightarrow 2NOCl$

Trimolecular reactions are not common.

Pseudo chemical reactions (Pseudo first order reactions)

From a study of the kinetics of a number of elementary reactions, it is found that in some cases, the order of a reaction is same as its molecularity. But, this is not always the case. In several reactions, the order is different from molecularity. This is particularly in the case of reactions where one of the reactants is present in large excess. For example—hydrolysis of esters

$$CH_3COOC_2H_5 + H_2O \xrightarrow[\text{(large excess)}]{H^+} CH_3COOH + C_2H_5OH$$

The molecularity of this reactions is 2 but the order of reaction is 1. The reason for this being the first order reaction is that the water is present in such a large amount that its concentration remains practically unchanged. Therefore, the rate of reaction varies only with the concentration of the ester and hence the order of reaction is one. Thus, such reactions which appears to be of higher order but actually follow lower order kinetics are called **pseudochemical reactions.**

For example, the above reaction of hydrolysis of ester is **pseudo first order reaction**. or pseudo unimolecular reactions. (where the molecularity of the reaction is 2 but the actual order is one) Another example of pseudo first order reaction is the inversion of cane sugar.

$$\left\{\underset{\text{Sugar}}{C_{12}H_{22}O_{11}} + \underset{\text{(Large excess)}}{H_2O} \longrightarrow \underset{\text{Glucose}}{C_6H_{12}O_6} + \underset{\text{Fructose}}{C_6H_{12}O_6}\right\}$$

In this case also, the molecularity of the reaction is 2, while the order of reaction is one as water is present in large excess.

4.5.2 Complex Reactions

A complex reaction is that which occurs in a sequence of two or more steps. Each step of the complex reaction is an elementary step reaction. Most chemical reactions are complex reactions. The sequence of steps through which a complex reaction takes place is called **reaction mechanism.** In any mechanism, some of the reaction steps are fast whereas others are slow. A reaction cannot proceed faster than its slowest step. Thus, it is the **slowest step which is the rate determining step** in any reaction.

For example, decomposition of hypochlorite ion (ClO^-) can be represented by the following reaction

$$3ClO^- \longrightarrow ClO_3^- + 2Cl^-$$

but actually it is a complex reaction that takes place in 2 steps:

$$ClO^- + ClO^- \longrightarrow ClO_2^- + Cl^- \quad \text{Slow}$$

$$ClO_2^- + ClO^- \longrightarrow ClO_3^- + Cl^- \quad \text{Fast}$$

$$3ClO^- \longrightarrow ClO_3^- + 2Cl^- \quad \text{Overall reaction}$$

Each elementary reaction in the above mechanism has molecularity equal to the number of molecules or atoms participating in it. The molecularity of the overall reaction has no meaning as it consist of various elementary reactions. Since, the first step is slow, it is the rate determining step. **Table 4.1** shows the difference between molecularity and order of reaction.

Table 4.1. Distinction between molecularity and order of reaction

	Molecularity	Order of reaction
1.	It is the number of reacting species undergoing simultaneous collision in a simple reaction.	It is the sum of the powers of the concentration in the rate law expression.
2.	It is applicable to elementary reactions only. For complex reactions, it has no meaning.	It is applicable to elementary as well as complex reactions.
3.	It is always a whole number *i.e.,* 1, 2, 3, etc.	It need not be a whole number. It can have fractional value also.
4.	It is a theoretical concept.	It is determined experimentally.
5.	It is invariant for a chemical reaction.	It can change with the conditions like temperature, pressure, concentration.
6.	Molecularity of a reaction cannot be zero.	Order of a reaction can be zero.

Why High Molecularity Reactions are Rare?

Most of the chemical reactions involve one, two or three molecules. Reactions involving higher molecularity *i.e.,* molecularity of 4 or more is rare. According to kinetic theory, the rate of a chemical reaction is proportional to the number of collisions taking place between the reacting molecules and the possibility of simultaneous collision of reacting molecules decreases with increase in number of molecules. As a result, the chances of four or more molecules coming closer and colliding with each other (with proper orientation) is much less than that of tri and bimolecular collisions. Hence, the reactions having molecularity more than three are rare or we can say practically impossible. Therefore, reactions which involve more than three molecules proceed through a series of steps, where each step involves collision of one, two or three molecules.

4.6 DETERMINATION OF ORDER OF REACTION

There are number of methods available for determining rate law or order of a reaction. The following methods are commonly used:

1. Integration method
2. Half life reaction method
3. Ostwald isolation method
4. Initial rate method.

4.6.1 Integration Method

This is the most common method for studying the kinetics of chemical reactions. The integrated rate equations for different order reactions can be derived as below:

4.6.1.1 Zero Order Reactions

Zero order reaction means that the rate of the reaction is proportional to zero power of the concentration of reactants. Consider the reaction.

$$\text{X} \longrightarrow \text{Products}$$

At $t = 0$ $\quad [A]_0 \quad 0$

$t = t$ $\quad [A]_0 - [A] \quad [A]$

$$\text{Rate} = \frac{-d[X]}{dt} = k_0[X]^0 = k_0 \qquad \text{...(4.1)}$$

k_0 = rate constant for the zero order reaction. Rearranging the above equation, we get

$$-d[X] = k_0 dt$$

Integrating both sides

$$-\int d[X] = k_0 \int dt$$
$$-[X] = k_0 t + I$$

where I is the constant of integration. At $t = 0$, the concentration of reactant $X = [A]_0$. i.e. the initial concentration of the reactant

$$-[A]_0 = k_0 \times 0 + I$$
$$I = -[A]_0$$

Substituting value of (I) in equation (4.2), we get

$$-[A] = k_0 t - [A]_0$$
$$k_0 t = [A]_0 - [A]$$
$$[A] = -k_0 t + [A]_0 \qquad ...(4.2)$$

Comparing equation 4.2 with the equation of straight line, $y = mx + c$, if we plot $[A]$ against, t, we get a straight line **(Fig. 4.3)** with slope = $-k_0$ and intercept = $[A]_0$

On simplifying equation 4.2, we get

or
$$k_0 = \frac{[A]_0 - [A]}{t} \qquad ...(4.3)$$

For the reaction—

$$X \rightarrow \text{products}$$

if $\quad [A]_0 = a$ and $[A] = a - x$

then $\quad [A]_0 - [A] = a - (a - x)$

Equation (4.3) becomes

$$k_0 = \frac{x}{t} \quad \text{or} \quad x = k_0 t$$

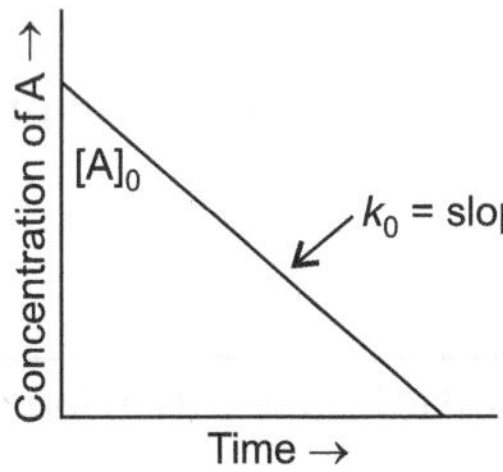

Fig. 4.3. Variation of concentration of reactant with time for a zero order reaction.

Thus, rate constant can be calculated if we know the concentration of reactant X at any time t and $[A]_0$.

Zero order reactions are relatively uncommon. They generally take place in heterogeneous systems.

Examples of zero order reactions

(*i*) the decomposition of gaseous ammonia on a hot platinum surface is a zero order at high pressure

$$2NH_3(g) \xrightarrow[\text{Pt catalyst}]{1130\text{ K}} N_2(g) + 3H_2(g)$$

(*ii*) Photochemical reaction between hydrogen and chlorine

$$H_2(g) + Cl_2(g) \xrightarrow{h\nu} 2HCl(g)$$

4.6.1.2 First Order Reaction

Consider the general first order reaction

$$A \rightarrow \text{Products}$$

Rate of a first order reaction is given by

$$\text{Rate} = \frac{-d[A]}{dt} = k_1[A]$$

Rearranging the above equation, we get

$$\frac{-d[A]}{[A]} = k_1 dt \qquad ...(4.4)$$

Integrating both sides

$$-\int d\frac{[A]}{[A]} = k_1 \int dt$$

$$-\ln[A] = k_1 t + I \qquad ...(4.5)$$

Where the constant of integration, I can be evaluated by putting $t = 0$ and $[A] = [A]_0$

$$I = -\ln [A]_0$$

Substituting the value of I in equation (4.5), we get

$$-\ln[A] = k_1 t - ln\ [A]_0$$

$$\ln[A]_0 - \ln[A] = k_1 t$$

$$k_1 = \frac{1}{t} \ln \frac{[A]_0}{[A]} \qquad ...(4.6)$$

Changing the above expression to log base 10, we get

$$k_1 = \frac{2.303}{t} \log \frac{[A]_0}{[A]} \qquad ...(4.7)$$

If initial concentration of reactant A is 'a' moles/L. If after time t, x moles of A have reacted then the concentration of A left at time, t will be $(a - x)$.

So, equation (4.7) will become,

$$k_1 = \frac{2.303}{t} \log \frac{a}{(a-x)}$$

When the experiment is performed at two different times t_1 and t_2 having concentrations $[A]_1$ and $[A]_2$ respectively, then the integrated rate law in the following form is used—

$$k_1 = \frac{2.303}{t_2 - t_1} \log \frac{[A]_1}{[A]_2} \qquad ...(4.8)$$

Now, for first order reaction—

$$k_1 = \frac{2.303}{t} \log \frac{[A]_0}{[A]}$$

$$\log[A] = \frac{-k_1}{2.303} t + \log[A]_0.$$

This equation is comparable to straight line equation $y = mx + c$, where slope $= \frac{-k_1}{2.303}$ and intercept = log $[A]_0$ **(Fig. 4.4)**

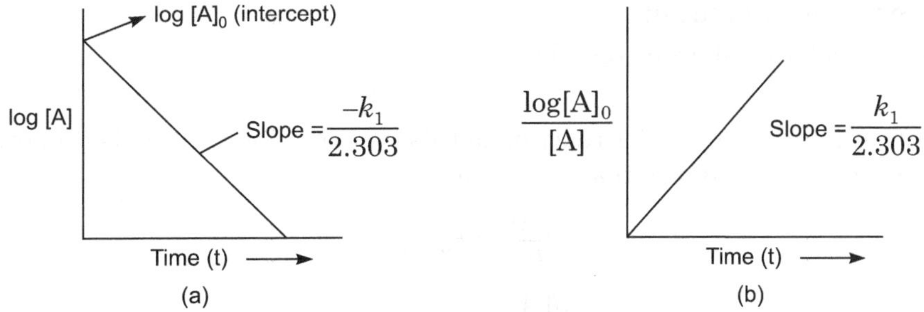

Fig. 4.4. I order reaction plots.

Examples of first order reaction—

(*a*) Hydrogenation of ethene follows first order kinetics.

$$C_2H_4(g) + H_2(g) \longrightarrow C_2H_6(g)$$

(*b*) All natural and artificial radioactive decay take place by first order kinetics.

$$^{226}_{88}Ra \longrightarrow {}^{226}_{88}Rn + {}^{4}_{2}He$$

(*c*) Decomposition of N_2O_5

$$N_2O_5 \longrightarrow 2NO_2 + \frac{1}{2}O_2$$

(*d*) Decomposition of hydrogen peroxide: Decomposition of H_2O_2 is a first order reaction and takes place according to the following equation.

$$2H_2O_2 \longrightarrow 2H_2O + O_2$$

The progress of this reaction can be studied by following two methods :

(*i*) By measuring the volume of oxygen liberated at regular time intervals and the rate constant can be calculated using the equation,

$$k_1 = \frac{2.303}{t}\log\frac{V_\infty}{V_\infty - V_t}$$

where,

V_∞ = Volume at infinite time

V_t = Volume at time, *t*.

(*ii*) By estimating the concentration of H_2O_2 by titrating against standard $KMnO_4$. The volume of $KMnO_4$ used will be directly proportional to the concentration of H_2O_2 left at any particular time (*t*). The rate constant can then be calculated using following equation:

$$k_1 = \frac{2.303}{t}\log\frac{V_0}{V_t}$$

where,

V_0 = Volume of $KMnO_4$ used at time, $t = 0$

V_t = Volume of $KMnO_4$ used at time, $t = t$.

(*e*) Decomposition of ammonium nitrite

At room temperature, decomposition of ammonium nitrite follows the following reaction

$$NH_4NO_{2(aq)} \rightarrow 2H_2O + N_2.$$

The progress of reaction is studied by measuring volume of nitrogen produced at different time intervals. The rate constant can be calculated by the following equation:

$$k = \frac{2.303}{t}\log\frac{V_\infty}{V_\infty - V_t}$$

4.6.1.3 Second order reaction:

Consider the general second order reaction

$$2A \rightarrow \text{Products}$$

We know that for a second order reaction of this type, rate of reaction is proportional to the square of the concentration of the reactants, thus

$$-\frac{d[A]}{dt} = k_2[A]^2$$

$$\frac{d[A]}{[A]^2} = k_2 dt \qquad \text{...(4.9)}$$

Integrating the above equation, we get

$$-\int\frac{d[A]}{[A]^2} = k_2\int dt \text{ where } -\int\frac{d[A]}{[A]^2} = +\frac{1}{[A]}$$

so,

$$\frac{1}{[A]} = k_2 t + I \qquad \text{...(4.10)}$$

The integration constant (I) can be evaluated by putting $[A] = [A]_0$ at $t = 0$, we get

$$+\frac{1}{[A]_0} = k_2 \times 0 + I$$

so,

$$I = +\frac{1}{[A]_0}$$

Substituting the value of I in equation (4.10), we get

$$+\frac{1}{[A]} = k_2 t + \frac{1}{[A]_0} \qquad \text{...(4.11)}$$

$$k_2 t = \frac{1}{[A]} - \frac{1}{[A]_0} \qquad \text{...(4.12)}$$

$$k_2 = \frac{1}{t}\left[\frac{1}{[A]} - \frac{1}{[A]_0}\right] \qquad \text{...(4.13)}$$

This is the integrated form of rate equation for a second order reaction. On rearranging,

$$\frac{1}{[A]} = k_2 t + \frac{1}{[A]_0} \qquad \text{...(4.14)}$$

Comparing this equation with straight line equation $y = mx + c$, we get $\frac{1}{[A]}$ vs. t a straight line graph **(Fig. 4.5)** with slope = k_2 and intercept = $\frac{1}{[A]_0}$.

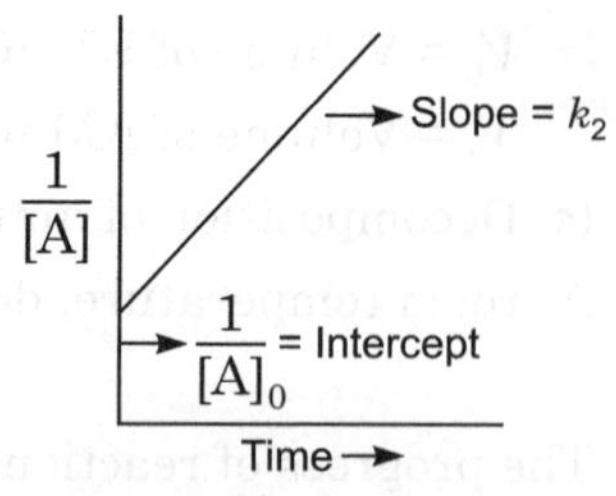

Fig. 4.5. Plot of $\frac{1}{[A]}$ Vs. t for II order reaction.

If initial concentration of reactant A is 'a' moles/L. If after t, x moles of A have reacted then the concentration of A left at time, t will be $(a - x)$. So, the equation (4.13) will become

$$k_2 = \frac{1}{t}\left[\frac{1}{(a-x)} - \frac{1}{a}\right] = \left(\frac{x}{a(a-x)}\right)$$

Examples of second order reaction:

(*a*) Thermal decomposition of acetaldehyde

$$CH_3CHO(g) \xrightarrow{791K} CH_4(g) + CO(g)$$

(*b*) Saponification of esters

$$CH_3COOC_2H_5 + NaOH \longrightarrow CH_3COONa + C_2H_5OH$$

The reaction is carried out in a vessel at constant temperature by taking equimolar quantities of ethyl acetate and NaOH. As the reaction proceeds, concentration of NaOH decreases. The concentration of NaOH at any time can be determined by titrating the reaction mixture with a standard acid. The amount of unused NaOH is equal to the unreacted ethyl acetate.

Thus, for saponification of ester with NaOH the second order rate equation becomes:

$$k_2 = \frac{1}{t}\frac{(V_i - V_t)}{V_i\, V_t}$$

where V_i is the volume of acid used at $t = 0$ (*i.e.*, corresponds to initial concentration of NaOH $[A]_0$) and V_t is the volume of acid used at time, t (*i.e.* corresponds to concentration of NaOH [A] at time t).

4.6.2 Half Life Period

The time taken for a reaction to reach the half way stage *i.e.*, when half of the starting material has reacted is called **half-life period** of the reaction. It is generally denoted by $\boldsymbol{t_{1/2}}$.

4.6.2.1 First order reactions

For first order reaction, the integrated rate equation is:

$$t = \frac{2.303}{k_1}\log\frac{[A]_0}{[A]} \qquad \text{...(4.15)}$$

At $t = t_{1/2}$, $[A] = \frac{1}{2}[A]_0$ (Reaction reduce to the half way of the initial concentration)

Substitute these values in equation (4.15), we get

$$t_{1/2} = \frac{2.303}{k_1}\log\frac{[A]_0}{[A]_0/2} = \frac{2.303}{k_1}\log 2 \qquad [\log 2 = 0.3010]$$

$$= \frac{2.303 \times 0.3010}{k_1} = \frac{0.693}{k_1} \quad \text{or} \quad \boxed{t_{1/2} = \frac{0.693}{k_1}}$$

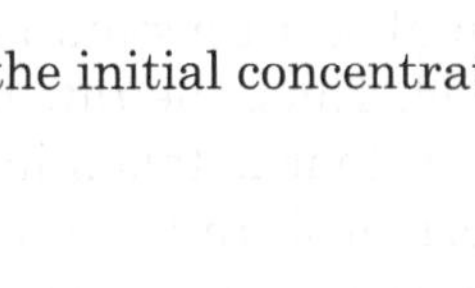

Fig. 4.6. Variation of half life with concentration for I order reaction.

Thus, half life period of a first order reaction is independent of the initial concentration of the reactant **(Fig. 4.6)**.

4.6.2.2 Second order reactions

The integrated rate equation for a second order reaction is:

$$k_2 t = \frac{1}{[A]} - \frac{1}{[A]_0} \qquad \text{...(4.15)}$$

$$\text{at } t = t_{1/2} \qquad [A] = \frac{1}{2}[A]_0$$

Substitute the values in equation (4.15), we get

$$k_2 t_{1/2} = \left[\frac{2}{[A_0]} - \frac{1}{[A]_0}\right] = \left(\frac{1}{[A]_0}\right)$$

$$\boxed{t_{1/2} = \frac{1}{k_2[A]_0}}$$

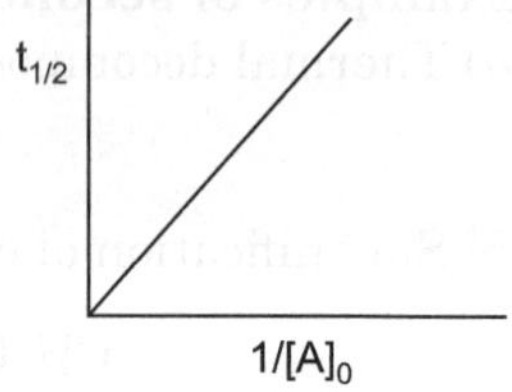

Fig. 4.7. Variation of half life with concentration for II order reaction.

Zero order reaction:

$$k_0 t = [A]_0 - [A]$$

At $t = t_{1/2}$, $[A] = \frac{1}{2}[A]_0$

$$k_0 t_{1/2} = [A]_0 - \frac{[A]_0}{2} \Rightarrow t_{1/2} = \frac{[A]_0}{2k_0}.$$

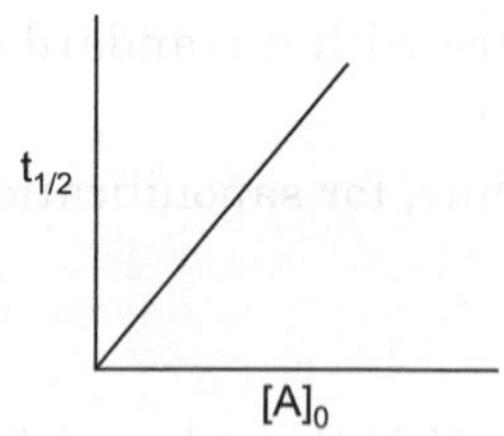

Fig. 4.8. Variation of half life with concentration for Zero order reaction.

Conclusion

If we plot the concentration of a reactant versus time, we can see the differences in half lives for reactions of different orders in the graphs. We can identify zero, first or second order reaction from a plot of $[A]$ versus t by the variation in the time it takes the concentration of a reactant to change by half.

- For a first order reaction, the half life is constant *i.e.*, independent of the concentration. **(Fig. 4.6)**
- For a second order reaction, the half life increases with decreasing concentration. **(Fig. 4.7)**
- For a zero order reaction, the half life decreases with decreasing concentration. **(Fig. 4.8)**

4.6.3. Ostwald Isolation Method

Some reactions involve a large number of reactants. In order to determine the order of such reactions, Ostwald in 1902 developed a method called as **Ostwald isolation method**. This method is based on the principle that the contribution of the reactant taken in excess to the order of reaction can be neglected. In this method, the concentration of all the reactants are taken in excess except one. Then the concentration of those reactants taken in excess will remain almost constant and the concentration of the reactant present in small concentration is varied. Thus, the rate of reaction will vary with the concentration of the isolated reactant (reactant that is taken in smaller quantity). Hence, the order of reaction w.r.t. one reactant is determined. In the similar fashion, the order w.r.t. other reactants can be determined by isolating them one by one. The sum of the orders calculated by the isolated reactions gives the overall order of the reaction. Consider the following reaction,

$$A + B + C \rightarrow \text{Products}$$

the order of reaction will be determined with respect to all of the reactants *i.e.*, A, B and C one by one. For the determination of order of the reaction with respect to A, we have to take B and C in large excess. The order of reaction with respect to A can be determined by either of the methods described above (integrated method or half life method). Likewise, the order of reaction with respect to B and C is determined. If n_A, n_B and n_C are the orders of the reaction with respect to A, B and C respectively, then the overall order of the reaction (n) is given by-

$$n = n_A + n_B + n_C$$

4.6.4 Initial Rate Method

This method is applied for the reactions which involve more than one reactant. The initial rate of a reaction is the instantaneous rate at the moment the reaction begins. In this method, the initial rate of the reaction (which corresponds to the slope of the tangent in the concentration versus time graph at $t = 0$) is measured when the concentrations of reactants have not changed considerably. Then, the experiments are conducted in which the initial concentration of only one of the reactants is changed (keeping the concentration of all other reactants constant) and the initial rate is determined. The experiment gives the order of reaction w.r.t. that particular reactant. The experiment is similarly repeated for each reactant until the overall rate is fully determined. The sum of the individual orders w.r.t. each reactant gives the overall order of the reaction. This method can be illustrated with the help of the following reaction:

$$2NO(g) + Br_2(g) \longrightarrow 2NOBr(g).$$

whose rate law has the form

$$\text{Rate} = k[NO]^a\,[Br_2]^b$$

Using the following initial rate data, it is possible to calculate the order of the reaction for both nitric oxide (NO) and bromine (Br_2):

Experiment	[NO]	$[Br_2]$	Initial rate (mol L^{-1} s^{-1})
I	0.10	0.10	1.3×10^{-6}
II	0.20	0.10	5.2×10^{-6}
III	0.20	0.30	1.56×10^{-5}

To calculate the order of the reaction for bromine, notice that experiments II and III holds the concentration of NO constant while tripling the concentration of bromine. The initial rate of the reaction becomes triple by tripling the concentration of the bromine, so the reaction is of first order w.r.t. bromine.

Mathematically, we can prove this by taking the ratio of the rates from experiments II and III

$$\frac{\text{Rate}_2}{\text{Rate}_3} = \frac{k[NO]^a\,[Br_2]^b}{k[NO]^a\,[Br_2]^b} = \frac{(0.20)^a\,(0.10)^b}{(0.20)^a\,(0.30)^b} = \frac{5.2\times10^{-6}}{1.56\times10^{-5}}$$

$$\left[\frac{1}{3}\right]^b = \frac{1}{3} \text{ or } \left[\frac{1}{3}\right]^b = \left[\frac{1}{3}\right]^1.$$

Thus, $b = 1$.

By similar reasoning, we can conclude that the order of reaction w.r.t. NO is 2 as the rate of reaction is quadrupled when the concentration of NO was doubled [in experiments I and II]

$$\frac{\text{Rate}_1}{\text{Rate}_2} = \frac{k[NO]^a\,[Br_2]^b}{k[NO]^a\,[Br_2]^b} = \frac{k[0.10]^a\,[0.10]^b}{k[0.20]^a\,[0.10]^b} = \frac{1.3\times10^{-6}}{5.2\times10^{-6}}$$

$$\left[\frac{1}{4}\right]^a = \frac{1}{4} \text{ or } \left[\frac{1}{2}\right]^a = \left[\frac{1}{2}\right]^2$$

$\therefore$ $a = 2$

Thus, the rate law expression for the above reaction is

$$\text{rate} = k[NO]^2\,[Br_2]$$

The overall order of the reaction is

$$n = 2 + 1 = 3$$

The value of k can be calculated by putting the rate of the reaction and concentrations in the rate law expression from any one of the experiments. All the three experiments should give the same value of k.

$$\text{Rate} = k[NO]^2\,[Br_2] \quad \text{or} \quad k = \frac{\text{Rate}}{[NO]^2[Br_2]}$$

According to I experiment:

$$k = \frac{1.3 \times 10^{-6}}{[0.10]^2\,[0.10]} = 1.3 \times 10^{-3}\ \text{mol}^{-2}\ \text{L}^2\ \text{s}^{-1}$$

According to II experiment:

$$k = \frac{5.2 \times 10^{-6}}{[0.20]^2\,[0.10]} = 1.3 \times 10^{-3}\ \text{mol}^{-2}\ \text{L}^2\ \text{s}^{-1}$$

According to III experiment:

$$k = \frac{1.56 \times 10^{-5}}{[0.20]^2\,[0.30]} = 1.3 \times 10^{-3}\ \text{mol}^{-2}\ \text{L}^2\ \text{s}^{-1}.$$

SOLVED EXAMPLES

Example 4.1. *Express the rate of the following reactions in terms of the concentration of reactants and products*

(*i*) $2O_3 \rightleftharpoons 3O_2$

(*ii*) $4NH_3(g) + 5O_2(g) \longrightarrow 4NO(g) + 6H_2O(g)$

(*iii*) $2N_2O_5 \rightleftharpoons NO_2 + O_2$

Solution: (*i*) $2O_3 \rightleftharpoons 3O_2$

$$\text{Rate of reaction} = \frac{-1}{2}\frac{d[O_3]}{dt} = \frac{1}{3}\frac{d[O_2]}{dt}$$

(*ii*) $4NH_3(g) + 5O_2(g) \longrightarrow 4NO(g) + 6H_2O(g)$

$$\text{Rate of reaction} = \frac{-1}{4}\frac{d[NH_3]}{dt} = \frac{-1}{5}\frac{d[O_2]}{dt} = \frac{1}{4}\frac{d[NO]}{dt} = \frac{1}{6}\frac{d[H_2O]}{dt}$$

(*iii*) $2N_2O_5 \rightleftharpoons 4NO_2 + O_2$

$$\text{Rate of reaction} = -\frac{1}{2}\frac{d[N_2O_5]}{dt} = \frac{1}{4}\frac{d[NO_2]}{dt} = \frac{d[O_2]}{dt}$$

Example 4.2. *The thermal decomposition of N_2O_5 occurs in the following steps:*

(*i*) $N_2O_5 \xrightarrow{\text{Slow}} NO_2 + NO_3$

(*ii*) $N_2O_5 + NO_3 \xrightarrow{\text{Fast}} 3NO_2 + O_2$

Suggest the rate expression for the reaction.

Solution: Rate of reaction = $k[N_2O_5]$

As the slowest step in the reaction determines the reaction rate.

Example 4.3. *In the reaction* $2O_3(g) \longrightarrow 3O_2(g)$

If the rate at which O_2 *appears is* 6.0×10^{-5} *M/s at a particular instant, at what rate is* O_3 *disappearing at the same time?*

Solution: Rate of reaction for the above reaction is given by

$$= \frac{-1}{2}\frac{d}{dt}[O_3] = \frac{1}{3}\frac{d}{dt}[O_2]$$

$$= -\frac{1}{2}\frac{d}{dt}[O_3] = \frac{1}{3}(6.0 \times 10^{-5})\ \text{M/s}$$

So,
$$= -\frac{d}{dt}[O_3] = \frac{2}{3} \times 6.0 \times 10^{-5}\ \text{M/s}$$

$$= 4.0 \times 10^{-5}\ \text{M/s.}$$

Example 4.4. *The decomposition of* N_2O_5 *proceeds according to the following reaction:*

$$2N_2O_5(g) \longrightarrow 4NO_2(g) + O_2(g)$$

If the rate of decomposition of N_2O_5 *at a particular instant in a reaction vessel is* 4.2×10^{-7} *M/s. What is the rate of appearance of (a)* NO_2 *(b)* O_2.

Solution:

$$\text{Rate of reaction} = \frac{-1}{2}\frac{d}{dt}[N_2O_5] = \frac{1}{4}\frac{d}{dt}[NO_2] = \frac{d}{dt}[O_2]$$

Given
$$\frac{-d}{dt}[N_2O_5] = 4.2 \times 10^{-7}\ \text{M/s}$$

(*a*) Rate of appearance of NO_2

$$\frac{-1}{2}\frac{d}{dt}[N_2O_5] = \frac{1}{4}\frac{d}{dt}[NO_2]$$

So,
$$\frac{d}{dt}[NO_2] = \frac{4}{2}(4.2 \times 10^{-7}) = 8.4 \times 10^{-7}\ \text{M/s.}$$

(*b*) Rate of appearance of O_2

$$-\frac{1}{2}\frac{d}{dt}[N_2O_5] = \frac{d}{dt}[O_2]$$

$$\frac{d}{dt}[O_2] = \frac{1}{2}(4.2 \times 10^{-7}) = 2.1 \times 10^{-7}\ \text{M/s.}$$

Example 4.5. *The reaction* $2N_2O_5(g) \rightleftharpoons 4NO_2(g) + O_2(g)$ *takes place in a closed container. It is found that the concentration of* NO_2 *increases by* 1.6×10^{-2} *mol* L^{-1} *in four seconds. Calculate the rate of reaction and rate of change of concentration of* N_2O_5.

Solution: Rate of reaction $= \frac{-1}{2}\frac{\Delta[N_2O_5]}{\Delta t} = \frac{1}{4}\frac{\Delta[NO_2]}{\Delta t} = \frac{\Delta[O_2]}{\Delta t}$

$$\Delta[NO_2] = 1.6 \times 10^{-2} \text{ mol L}^{-1}$$

$$\Delta t = 4 \text{ sec.}$$

$\therefore$ Rate of reaction $= \frac{1}{4}\frac{\Delta[NO_2]}{\Delta t} = \frac{1}{4}\times\frac{1.6\times10^{-2}}{4} = 1.0\times10^{-3}\text{mol L}^{-1}\text{s}^{-1}$

and rate of change of conc. of N_2O_5

$$\text{Rate of reaction} = \frac{-1}{2}\frac{\Delta[N_2O_5]}{\Delta t}$$

and rate of reaction $= 1.0 \times 10^{-3}$ mol L^{-1} s^{-1}

$\therefore$ $\frac{-\Delta[N_2O_5]}{\Delta t} = 1.0 \times 10^{-3} \times 2 = 2 \times 10^{-3}$ mol $L^{-1}s^{-1}$.

Example 4.6. Reaction $2A + B + C \rightarrow D + 2E$ is found to be I order in A, II order in B and zero order in C. *(a) Write the rate expression (b) What is the overall order of the reaction (c) What is the effect on rate on increasing the concentration of A, B and C two times?*

Solution: (*a*) Rate expression $= k\,[A]^1\,[B]^2\,[C]^0$

(*b*) Order of the reaction : from the rate expression

$$\text{Order of reaction} = 1 + 2 + 0 = 3$$

$\therefore$ The reaction is of third order.

(*c*) Suppose the initial concentrations are:

$$[A] = a \text{ mol L}^{-1}$$

$$[B] = b \text{ mol L}^{-1}$$

$$[C] = c \text{ mol L}^{-1}.$$

Now, if the concentration A, B and C are doubled *i.e.* $2a$, $2b$ and $2c$ respectively, then

Rate $= k\,(2a)^1\,(2b)^2\,(2c)^0 = 8\,k\,abc$ *i.e.*, the rate of reaction is increased by 8 times.

Example 4.7. *The decomposition of NH_3 on platinum surface*

$2NH_3(g) \rightarrow N_2(g) + 3H_2(g)$ *is a zero order reaction with $k = 3.2 \times 10^{-4}$ Ms^{-1}. What are the rates of production of* N_2 *and* H_2*?*

Solution: For zero order reaction, Rate $= k$.

$$\text{Rate} = \frac{-1}{2}\frac{d}{dt}[NH_3] = \frac{d}{dt}[N_2] = \frac{1}{3}\frac{d}{dt}[H_2] = k = 3.2\times10^{-4}\ \text{Ms}^{-1}$$

Rate of production of $N_2 = \frac{d}{dt}[N_2] = 3.2\times10^{-4}\ \text{Ms}^{-1}$

Rate of production of H_2

$$= \frac{d}{dt}[H_2] = 3k = 3 \times 3.2 \times 10^{-4}\ \text{Ms}^{-1}$$

$$= 9.6 \times 10^{-4}\ \text{Ms}^{-1}.$$

Example 4.8. *The rate of decomposition of hydrogen peroxide at a particular temperature was measured by titrating its solution with potassium permanganate solution. The results obtained were:*

Time, t(min)	*0*	*5*	*15*	*25*
Volume of $KMnO_4$ used	*37.0*	*29.8*	*19.6*	*12.3*

(i) Show that the reaction is of first order.

(ii) Calculate the rate constant.

Solution: (*i*) As the reaction is of first order, it must obey the equation

$$k = \frac{2.303}{t}\log\frac{a}{a-x} \quad \text{or} \quad k = \frac{2.303}{t}\log\frac{V_0}{V_t}$$

Volume of $KMnO_4$ used is proportional to the amount of H_2O_2 present. Here $V_0 = 37.0$ ml and the value of k can be calculated by substituting the value of V_t at different times.

At $t = 5$ min $V_t = 29.8$ ml $k = \frac{2.303}{5}\log\frac{37}{29.8}$ (log 37 = 1.5682, log 29.8 = 1.4742)

$$k = \frac{2.303}{5}\log 37 - \log 29.8 = \frac{2.303}{5}(1.5682 - 1.4742)$$

$$= 0.0433 \text{ min}^{-1}$$

at $t = 15$ min $V_t = 19.6$ ml; $k = \frac{2.303}{15}\log\frac{37}{19.6}$ (log 19.6 = 1.2923)

$$= \frac{2.303}{15}(1.5682 - 1.2923)$$

$$= 0.0424 \text{ min}^{-1}$$

at $t = 25$ min, $V_t = 12.3$ ml; $k = \frac{2.303}{15}\log\frac{37}{12.3}$ log 12.3 = 1.0899

$$k = \frac{2.303}{25}(1.5682 - 1.0899)$$

$$= 0.0441 \text{ min}^{-1}.$$

Since the value of k comes out to be nearly constant, the reaction therefore, follows Ist order kinetics.

(*ii*) The average value of rate constant $= \frac{0.0433 + 0.0424 + 0.0441}{3}$

$$= 0.0432 \text{ min}^{-1}.$$

Example 4.9. *A first order reaction is 50% completed in 1.26 × 10^{14}s. How much time would it take for 80% completion?*

Solution: For the first order reaction

$k = \frac{2.303}{t}\log\frac{[A]_0}{[A]}$ Where, $[A]$ = amount of reactant left after time t.

Case I: Let $[A]_0 = 100$

$[A] = 100 - 50 = 50 \quad t = 1.26 \times 10^{14}$ s

$$k = \frac{2.303}{1.26\times10^{14}}\log\frac{100}{50} = \frac{2.303}{1.26\times10^{14}}\log 2$$

$$= \frac{2.303}{1.26\times10^{14}} \times (0.3010) = 0.55 \times 10^{-14}\ \text{s}^{-1} = 5.5 \times 10^{-15}\ \text{s}^{-1}.$$

Case II: $[A]_0 = 100 \quad [A] = 100 - 80 = 20 \quad t = ?$

Put the value of k from Case I, $k = 5.5 \times 10^{-15}\ \text{s}^{-1}$.

$$t = \frac{2.303}{5.5\times10^{-15}}\log\left(\frac{100}{20}\right) = \frac{2.303}{5.5\times10^{-15}}\log 5 = \frac{2.303}{5.5\times10^{-15}}\times 0.6990 \log 5 = 0.6990$$

$$t = 0.293 \times 10^{15}\ \text{sec} = 2.93 \times 10^{14}\ \text{s}.$$

Alternate solution: For 50% completion: $k = \dfrac{0.693}{t_{1/2}} = \dfrac{0.693}{1.26\times10^{14}} = 5.5\times10^{-15}\text{s}^{-1}$

Put the value of k in first order equation to find the time taken for 80% completion.

Example 4.10. *Show that for a first order reaction, time required for 99% completion is twice the time required for the completion of 90% of the reaction.*

Solution: For 99% completion

$$t_{99\%} = \frac{2.303}{k}\log\frac{100}{100-99} = \frac{2.303}{k}\log 100 \qquad ...(i)$$

For 90% completion :

$$t_{90\%} = \frac{2.303}{k}\log\frac{100}{100-90}$$

$$= \frac{2.303}{k}\log 10 \qquad ...(ii)$$

from equations (*i*) and (*ii*)

$$\frac{t_{99\%}}{t_{90\%}} = \frac{\frac{2.303}{k}\log 100}{\frac{2.303}{k}\log 10} = \frac{\log 100}{\log 10} = \frac{2}{1} = 2$$

$$\therefore \quad \boxed{t_{99\%} = 2 \times t_{90\%}}$$

Example 4.11. *A first order reaction is 50% completed in 100 minutes. How much time would it take for 100% completion?*

Solution: For the first order reaction.

As the time required for 50% completion is 100 min. It is taken as $t_{1/2}$ for the reaction.

$$k = \frac{0.693}{t_{1/2}} = \frac{0.693}{100}$$

$$k = 0.693 \times 10^{-2}\ \text{min}^{-1}$$

For 100% completion

$a = 100 \qquad a - x = 100 - 100 = 0 \qquad$ [For 100% completion x is also 100]

$$k = \frac{2.303}{t}\log\frac{a}{a-x}$$

$$t = \frac{2.303}{k}\log\frac{100}{0}$$

$$= \frac{2.303}{k}\log\infty \qquad (\log\infty = \infty)$$

$$t = \frac{2.303}{k}\infty = \infty$$

$$t = \infty.$$

Example 4.12. *The rate constant for a first order reaction is 80 s^{-1}. How much time will it take to reduce the concentration of the reactant to $1/10^{th}$ of its initial value?*

Solution: For a first order reaction

$$t = \frac{2.303}{k}\log\frac{[A]_0}{[A]} \qquad [A] = [A]_0/10$$

or $$\frac{[A]_0}{[A]} = 10 \qquad k = 80\ s^{-1}$$

$$t = \frac{2.303}{k}\log 10$$

$$= \frac{2.303}{80}\log 10 = \frac{2.303}{80}\times 1 = 2.878\times 10^{-2}\ \text{sec.}$$

Example 4.13. *The following data were obtained for the reaction:*

$$2NO(g) + Br_2(g) \longrightarrow 2NOBr(g)$$

Experiment	**Initial concentration**		**Initial rate (mol L^{-1} min^{-1})**
	[NO]	**[Br_2]**	
I	0.20	0.20	2.6×10^{-6}
II	0.40	0.20	10.4×10^{-6}
III	0.40	0.60	3.13×10^{-5}

Determine : (*i*) *The orders with respect to* NO *and* Br_2.

(*ii*) *The rate law*

(*iii*) *Rate constant.*

Solution: (*i*) The rate law may be written as

$$\text{Rate} = k[NO]^a\,[Br_2]^b$$

On comparing experiments I and II, we get

$$\text{Rate}_1 = k(0.20)^a\,(0.20)^b = 2.6 \times 10^{-6} \qquad ...(i)$$

$$\text{Rate}_2 = k(0.40)^a\,(0.20)^b = 10{,}4 \times 10^{-6} \qquad ...(ii)$$

$$\text{Rate}_3 = k(0.40)^a\,(0.60)^b = 3.13 \times 10^{-5} \qquad ...(iii)$$

From equations (*i*) and (*ii*)

$$\frac{\text{Rate}_2}{\text{Rate}_1} = \frac{k(0.40)^a\ (0.20)^b}{k(0.20)^a\ (0.20)^b} = \frac{10.4\times10^{-6}}{2.6\times10^{-6}}$$

$$\frac{(0.40)^a}{(0.20)^a} = 4 \qquad \text{or} \qquad (2)^a = 4$$

$$2^a = 2^2$$

$$\therefore \qquad a = 2$$

From equations (*ii*) and (*iii*)

$$\frac{\text{Rate}_3}{\text{Rate}_2} = \frac{k(0.40)^a\ (0.60)^b}{k(0.40)^a\ (0.20)^b} = \frac{3.13\times10^{-5}}{10.4\times10^{-6}} = \frac{31.3\times10^{-6}}{10.4\times10^{-6}}$$

$$\left(\frac{0.60}{0.20}\right)^b = 3 \qquad \text{or} \qquad (3)^b = 3$$

$$3^b = 3^1 \qquad \therefore \qquad b = 1$$

Thus, order with respect to NO = a = 2

Br_2 = b = 1.

(*ii*) The rate law is given by

$$\text{Rate} = k\ [\text{NO}]^2\ [\text{Br}_2]^1.$$

(*iii*) Rate constant for the reaction can be calculated by substituting the values of rate, [NO] and $[Br_2]$ in any of the three experiments:

From experiment I—

$$k = \frac{\text{Rate}}{[\text{NO}]^2\ [\text{Br}_2]} = \frac{2.6\times10^{-6}}{(0.20)^2\ (0.20)} = \frac{2.6\times10^{-6}}{4\times10^{-2}\times2\times10^{-1}}$$

$$k = 3.25 \times 10^{-4}\ \text{mol}^{-2}\ \text{L}^2\ \text{min}^{-1}.$$

Example 4.14. *The following data were obtained for the reaction*

$$2NO_2(g) + F_2(g) \longrightarrow 2NO_2F$$

Experiment	***Initial concentration***		***Initial rate*** **mol L^{-1} s^{-1}**
	$[NO_2]$	**$[F_2]$**	
I	*0.01*	*0.02*	*2.40×10^{-4}*
II	*0.03*	*0.02*	*2.16×10^{-3}*
III	*0.03*	*0.04*	*4.32×10^{-3}*

Determine: (i) Order of reaction with respect to NO_2 *and* F_2.

(ii) rate law

(iii) rate constant.

Solution: (i) The rate for the above reaction can be written as

$$\text{Rate} = k[\text{NO}_2]^a[\text{F}_2]^b$$

On comparing experiments I and II, we get

$$\frac{\text{Rate}_2}{\text{Rate}_1} = \frac{(0.03)^a\,(0.02)^b}{(0.01)^a\,(0.02)^b} = \frac{2.16\times10^{-3}}{2.4\times10^{-4}}$$

$$\frac{\text{Rate}_2}{\text{Rate}_1} = 3^a = 9 \quad \text{or} \quad 3^a = 3^2 \therefore a = 2$$

From experiments (II) and (III), $\dfrac{\text{Rate}_3}{\text{Rate}_2} = \dfrac{(0.03)^a\,(0.04)^b}{(0.03)^a\,(0.02)^b} = \dfrac{4.32\times10^{-3}}{2.16\times10^{-3}}$

$$\frac{\text{Rate}_3}{\text{Rate}_2} = 2^b = 2$$

$\therefore \qquad b = 1$

Thus, order with respect to $NO_2 = 2$

and order w.r.t. $F_2 = 1$.

(*ii*) The rate law is given by

$$\text{Rate} = k[NO_2]^2\,[F_2]^1.$$

(*iii*) Rate constant for the reaction can be calculated by substituting the values of rate, $[NO_2]$ and $[F_2]$ in any the three experiments.

From experiment I:

$$k = \frac{\text{Rate}}{[NO_2]^2[F_2]} = \frac{2.40\times10^{-4}}{[0.01]^2\,[0.02]} = \frac{2.40\times10^{-4}}{2\times10^{-6}}$$

$$k = 1.2 \times 10^2 \text{ mol}^{-2}\text{ L}^2\text{ s}^{-1}.$$

Example 4.15. *The half life for the reaction*

$$N_2O_5 \longrightarrow 2NO_2 + \frac{1}{2}O_2 \text{ is 3.2 hours.}$$

(*a*) *Starting with 120 g of* N_2O_5, *how many grams will remain after a period of 10.4 hours?*

(*b*) *What time would be required to reduce* 5×10^{10} *molecules of* N_2O_5 *to* 2.5×10^8 *molecules?*

Solution: For a first order reaction

$$k = \frac{0.693}{t_{1/2}} = \frac{0.693}{3.2} = 0.216 \text{ hr}^{-1}.$$

(*a*) $[A]_0 = 120$ g $\qquad [A] = x$ g $\qquad t = 10.4$ hr

$$t = \frac{2.303}{k}\log\frac{[A]_0}{[A]} = \frac{2.303}{0.216}\log\frac{(120)}{x} = 10.4$$

$$\log\frac{120}{x} = \frac{10.4\times0.216}{2.303} = 0.9754$$

$\dfrac{120}{x}$ = anti log 0.9754 = 9.550 $\qquad \therefore x = \dfrac{120}{9.550} = 12.56$ g.

Example 4.16. *Decomposition of a gas follows second order kinetics. When the initial concentration of the gas is* 11.5×10^{-2} *moles/litre, it takes 60 minutes for 50% decomposition of the gas. Calculate the specific rate constant.*

Solution: Given, $t_{1/2} = 60$ min

$[A]_0 = 11.5 \times 10^{-2}$ moles/L $\qquad k_2 = ?$

For a second order reaction

$$k_2 = \frac{1}{t_{1/2}[A]_0} = \frac{1}{60\times 11.5\times 10^{-2}}$$

$$= 0.0145 \text{ mol}^{-1} \text{ L min}^{-1}.$$

Example 4.17. *In a second order reaction, the initial concentration of both the reactants is same, the rate constant is 5.2×10^{-3} L mol^{-1} min^{-1}. If half of the reactants are consumed in 60 minutes, determine the initial concentration of the reactants.*

Solution: Given, $t_{1/2} = 60$ min

$$[A]_0 = ?\ k_2 = 5.2 \times 10^{-3} \text{ L mol}^{-1} \text{ min}^{-1}$$

For a second order reaction

$$t_{1/2} = \frac{1}{k_2[A]_0} \quad \text{or} \quad [A]_0 = \frac{1}{t_{1/2}\times k_2}$$

$$= \frac{1}{5.2\times 10^{-3}\times 60} = 3.205 \text{ mol L}^{-1}$$

Example 4.18. *In the saponification of ethyl acetate by* NaOH, *the following data were obtained, using equimolar concentration of ester and alkali:*

Time (min)	*0*	*4.89*	*10.07*	*23.66*
Volume of acid used (ml)	*47.65*	*38.92*	*32.62*	*23.00*

Show that the saponification of ethyl acetate follows second order kinetics.

Solution: Volume of acid used ∝ Amount of unreacted NaOH in the reaction mixture

for a second order reaction, rate constant is also given by

$$k_2 = \frac{1}{t}\frac{(V_i - V_t)}{V_i\, V_t}$$

Given: $V_i = 47.65$ ml.

The second order rate constant (k_2) can be calculated as follows:

T(min)	$\boldsymbol{V_t}$	$\boldsymbol{V_i - V_t}$	$k_2 = \frac{1}{t}\frac{(V_i - V_t)}{V_i V_t}$ **Lmol^{-1} min^{-1}**
4.89	38.92	8.73	$k_2 = \frac{1}{4.89}\times\frac{8.73}{47.65\times 38.92} = 0.000963$
10.07	32.62	15.03	$k_2 = \frac{1}{10.07}\times\frac{15.03}{47.65\times 32.62} = 0.000960$
23.66	23.00	24.65	$k_2 = \frac{1}{23.66}\times\frac{24.65}{47.65\times 23} = 0.000951$

The value of k_2 is fairly constant, hence the reaction is of second order.

4.7 EFFECT OF TEMPERATURE ON RATE OF REACTION (ARRHENIUS EQUATION)

The velocity of most of the chemical reactions increase with increase in temperature. For example, in decomposition of N_2O_5, the time taken for half of the original amount of material to decompose is 12 minutes at 50°C, 5 hrs at 25°C and 10 days at 0°C.

It has been found that the rate of a chemical reaction becomes almost double for every 10°C rise in temperature.

In 1889, Arrhenius gave the quantitative relationship between temperature and the rate constant and hence the rate of reaction. The relationship is called as Arrhenius equation and can be written as

$$k = Ae^{-E_a/RT} \qquad ...(i)$$

where A is a constant called as Arrhenius factor or the frequency factor or pre-exponential factor. It is a constant specific to a particular reaction. E_a is the activation energy, R is the gas constant and T is the absolute temperature. The factor $e^{-Ea/RT}$ corresponds to the fraction of molecules that have kinetic energy greater than E_a. The E_a represents the minimum energy that the reacting molecules must possess before undergoing a chemical reaction. Activation energy cannot be measured directly but can be calculated using Arrhenius equation. Taking logarithms on both sides of equation (*i*), we get

$$\ln k = \ln A - \frac{E_a}{RT} \qquad ...(ii)$$

When $\ln k$ is plotted against $\frac{1}{T}$, we get a straight line **(Fig. 4.9)**. The intercept of this line is equal to $\ln A$ and the slope is equal to $\frac{-E_a}{R}$.

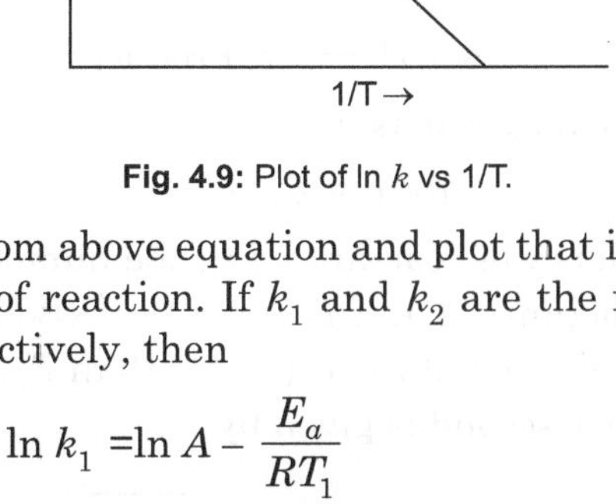

Fig. 4.9: Plot of ln k vs 1/T.

Thus, it has been found from above equation and plot that increasing the temperature will result in an increase in rate of reaction. If k_1 and k_2 are the rate constants at two different temperatures T_1 and T_2 respectively, then

$$\ln k_1 = \ln A - \frac{E_a}{RT_1} \qquad ...(iii)$$

$$\ln k_2 = \ln A - \frac{E_a}{RT_2} \qquad ...(iv)$$

Subtracting equations (*iii*) from (*iv*), we get

$$\ln k_2 - \ln k_1 = \frac{-E_a}{RT_2} - \left(\frac{-E_a}{RT_1}\right)$$

$$\ln \frac{k_2}{k_1} = \frac{E_a}{RT_1} - \frac{E_a}{RT_2}$$

$$\ln \frac{k_2}{k_1} = \frac{E_a}{R}\left[\frac{1}{T_1} - \frac{1}{T_2}\right]$$

$$\log \frac{k_2}{k_1} = \frac{E_a}{2.303R}\left[\frac{1}{T_1} - \frac{1}{T_2}\right] \quad \text{...(v)}$$

Hence, knowing the values of rate constants k_1 and k_2 at two different temperatures T_1 and T_2, the activation energy can be calculated.

4.8 THEORY OF REACTION RATES

There are two main theories to explain the rate of chemical reactions

(*i*) Collision theory

(*ii*) Transition state theory or the theory of absolute reaction rates.

(*i*) Collision theory: Arrhenius equation is applicable under a wide range of circumstances but collision theory which was developed by Max Trautz and William Lewis (1916-18) provides a better insight into the energetic and mechanistic side of the reactions. It is based on kinetic theory of gases. According to this theory, the reactant molecules are assumed to be hard spheres and the reaction occurs when molecules undergo collision with each other.

The collision theory is based on two postulates. These are:

(*a*) The products are formed only when the reactant molecules collide with each other.

(*b*) For collisions to be effective, the molecules should possess sufficient activation energy as well as proper orientation.

Let us consider a reaction between two dissimilar reactants *A* and *B* (*i.e.*, a bimolecular reaction)

$$A + B \longrightarrow \text{Products}$$

The rate of reaction can be expressed as

$$\text{Rate} = Z_{AB}\, e^{-E_a/RT} \quad \text{...(i)}$$

where Z_{AB} is the collision frequency of reactants. *i.e.*, the number of binary collisions per unit volume per second between reactants *A* and *B* and $e^{-E_a/RT}$ (Boltzmann factor) represents the fraction of molecules with energies equal to or greater than E_a. From kinetic theory of gases, the collisions per unit volume per second is given by

$$Z_{AB} = \sigma_{AB}^2 \sqrt{\frac{8\pi KT}{\mu}}\, n_A n_B$$

where σ_{AB} is the distance of closest approach or the effective molecular diameter for collision between A and B, and is equal to $\frac{\sigma_A + \sigma_B}{2}$ n_A and n_B are the number of molecules of A and B and μ is the reduced mass and is equal to

$\mu = \frac{m_A m_B}{m_A + m_B}$, m_A and m_B are mass of single molecule A and single molecule B respectively.

K is Boltzmann constant and T is the temperature.

Substituting values of Z_{AB} and μ, in eq. (i) we get

$$\text{Rate} = \sigma_{AB}^2 \sqrt{8\pi KT\left(\frac{m_A + m_B}{m_A m_B}\right)}\, n_A n_B \cdot e^{-E_a/RT} \quad \text{...(ii)}$$

Also, in terms of molar masses, we can put $m_A = \frac{m_A}{N}$ & $m_B = \frac{m_B}{N}$ and $K = \frac{R}{N}$ where N is Avogadro's number, equation (ii) becomes

$$\text{Rate} = \sigma_{AB}^2 \sqrt{8\pi RT\left(\frac{m_A + m_B}{m_A m_B}\right)}\, n_A n_B\, e^{-E_a/RT} \quad \text{...(iii)}$$

Equation (*iii*) predicts the rate constants fairly accurately for the reactions which involve simple molecules but for reactions involving complex molecules, significant deviations are observed.

Modification of Collision theory: The collision theory predicts accurately the rate constant for biomolecular reactions involving simple molecules in gas phase and in solution. However, for reactions involving complex molecules, the experimental values for rate constant are smaller than those predicted from equation (iii). This is because, according to kinetic theory all the molecules that have energy greater than or equal to activation energy (Ea) leads to effective collision. However, if the energetic molecules do not have proper orientation while collision, the product formation will not take place (Fig. 4.10). Thus, to account for effective collisions, another factor called as probability factor or steric factor (P) is introduced and the equation for the rate constant is modified as

$$\text{Rate} = PZ_{AB}\, e^{-E_a/RT}.$$

This steric factor takes into account the fact that in a collision, the molecules must be properly oriented.

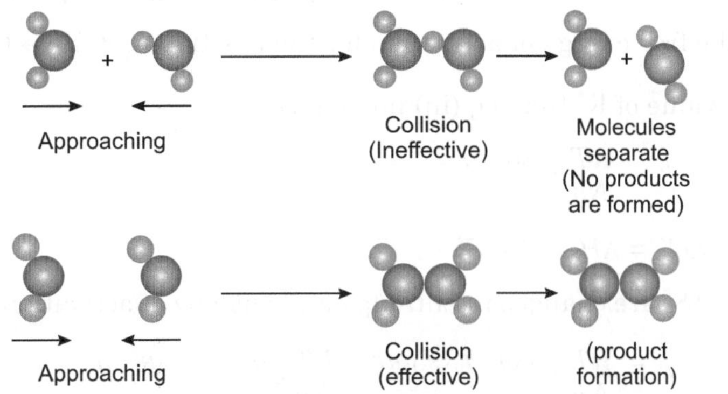

Fig. 4.10 Effective and Ineffective collision due to orientation of molecules.

Hence, in collision theory both the factors activation energy and proper orientation of molecules together determine the criteria of an effective collision and therefore, the rate of a chemical reaction.

Collision theory also has a major drawback that it considers the reacting molecules to be hard spheres and ignores their structural aspect. Also, the collision diameters calculated from this theory are not precise.

Transition state theory or the theory of Absolute reaction rates:

According to this theory, it is believed that before the reacting molecules changes into products, they form an intermediate called transition state or activated complex which has higher energy than both the reactants and products. It is for this reason that the theory is called as transition state theory or the activated complex theory. This energy was developed by Eyring, Polanyi and Evans in 1935. The activation complex cannot be isolated and exists in equilibrium with the reacting molecules. The rate of reaction is given by the rate of decomposition of the activated complex to form products.

Consider a reaction between reactants X_2 and Y_2

$$X_2 + Y_2 \rightleftharpoons (X_2Y_2)^* \rightarrow 2XY$$

or

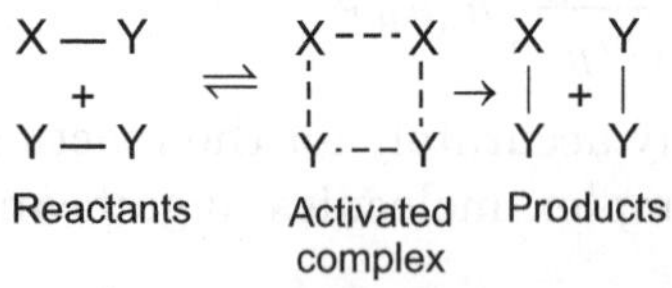

It was shown by Eyring that the rate constant (k) for any reaction is given by

$$k = \frac{RT}{Nh} K^* \qquad ...(i)$$

where R is the gas constant, T is absolute temperature, N is Avogadro's number, n is Planck's constant and K^* is the equilibrium constant for the formation of activated complex from the reacting molecules.

$$K^* = \frac{[X_2Y_2]^*}{[X_2][Y_2]} \qquad ...(ii)$$

From thermodynamics, we know that

$$\Delta G^* = -RT \ln K^*$$

or $\quad \ln K^* = -\Delta G^*/RT \quad$ or $\quad K^* = e^{-\Delta G^*/RT} \qquad ...(iii)$

where ΔG^* is the free energy of activation for the reaction $X_2 + Y_2 \rightarrow (X_2Y_2)^*$

Substitute the value of K^* from eq (iii) into eq (i)

$$k = \frac{RT}{Nh} e^{-\Delta G^*/RT} \qquad ...(iv)$$

Also $\quad \Delta G^* = \Delta H^* - T\Delta S^*$

where ΔH^* and ΔS^* are changes in enthalpy and entropy of activation respectively we get

$$k = \frac{RT}{Nh} e^{-(\Delta H^* - T\Delta S^*)/RT} = \frac{RT}{Nh} e^{\Delta S^*/R} \cdot e^{-\Delta H^*/RT} \qquad ...(v)$$

Equation (v) is known as **Eyring equation.**

Advantages of transition state theory

The transition state energy is superior over the collision theory of reaction rates in following aspects:

(*i*) The concept of the formation of an activated complex seems to be more appropriate than assuming that the molecules just collide together and form products.

(*ii*) Transition state theory is thermodynamics in nature, it justifies the steric factor (P) of the collision theory in terms of entropy of activation.

Example 4.19. *The rate constant for a reaction is* 1.72×10^{-5} sec^{-1} *at 273 K and* 2.85×10^{-5} sec^{-1} *at 303K. Calculate the activation energy.*

Solution: Given,

$k_1 = 1.72 \times 10^{-5}$ sec^{-1} $\quad T_1 = 273$ K

$k_2 = 2.85 \times 10^{-5}$ sec^{-1} $\quad T_2 = 303$ K

$R = 8.314$ JK^{-1} mol^{-1}

Apply the equation

$$\log \frac{k_2}{k_1} = \frac{E_a}{2.303R}\left[\frac{1}{T_1} - \frac{1}{T_2}\right]$$

Substituting the values in above equation

$$\log \frac{2.85 \times 10^{-5}}{1.72 \times 10^{-5}} = \frac{E_a}{2.303 \times 8.314}\left[\frac{1}{273} - \frac{1}{303}\right]$$

$$\log \frac{2.85 \times 10^{-5}}{1.72 \times 10^{-5}} = \frac{E_a}{2.303 \times 8.314}\left[\frac{30}{273 \times 303}\right]$$

$$E_a = \frac{2.303 \times 8.314 \times 273 \times 303}{30} \log \frac{2.85 \times 10^{-5}}{1.72 \times 10^{-5}}$$

$$E_a = 52794.4\ (\log 2.85 \times 10^{-5} - \log 1.72 \times 10^{-5})$$

$$= 52794.4\ [0.4548 - 5 - (0.2355 - 5)]$$

$$= 52794.4\ (-4.5452 + 4.7645)$$

$$= 52794.4\ (0.2193)$$

$$= 11577.8 \text{ J/mol} = 11.578 \text{ kJ/mol.}$$

Example 4.20. *The first order rate constant for the decomposition of ethyl iodide at 600 K is* 1.60×10^{-5} s^{-1}. *Its activation energy is 212 kJ/mol. Calculate the rate constant of the reaction at 710 K.*

Solution: Given,

$k_1 = 1.60 \times 10^{-5}$ s^{-1} $\quad T_1 = 600$ K

$k_2 = ?$ $\quad T_2 = 710$ K

$E_a = 212$ kJ/mol $= 212000$ J/mol $\quad R = 8.314$ J./K/mol

$$\log \frac{k_2}{k_1} = \frac{E_a}{2.303\ R}\left[\frac{1}{T_1} - \frac{1}{T_2}\right]$$

$$\log k_2 = \log(1.60\times10^{-5}) + \frac{212000}{2.303\times8.314}\left[\frac{1}{600}-\frac{1}{710}\right]$$

$$= (0.2041-5)+11072.23\left(\frac{110}{600\times710}\right)$$

$$= -4.796 + 2.86$$

$$\log k_2 = -1.936$$

$$k_2 = \text{antilog} - 1.936$$

$$k_2 = 1.159 \times 10^{-2}\ s^{-1}$$

antilog – 1.936
– 1 + 1
– 1.936
– 2.064

look into antilog .064 and put 10^{-2} with that = 1.159×10^{-2}.

Example 4.21. *The activation energy of a reaction is 225 cal/mol and the rate constant at 313 K is 1.8 × 10*$^{-5}$ *sec*$^{-1}$*. Calculate the Arrhenius factor.*

Solution: Given, $E_a = 225$ cal/mol

$k = 1.8 \times 10^{-5}\ s^{-1}$, T = 313 K

$R = 1.987$ cal/mol.

$$\log k = \frac{-E_a}{2.303\ RT} + \log A$$

$$\log A = \log k + \frac{E_a}{2.303\ RT}$$

$$= \log 1.8\times10^{-5} + \frac{225}{2.303\times1.987\times313}$$

$$= (-5 + 0.2553) + 0.157$$

$$= -4.745 + 0.157 = -4.588$$

$$A = \text{antilog} - 4.588$$

$$= 2.582 \times 10^{-5}.$$

EXERCISES

I. SHORT ANSWER TYPE QUESTIONS

1. Explain the term order of a reaction. Write down the rate equations for zero, first and second order reactions.
2. Define the term rate constant. Derive integral expressions for the rate constant of first and second order reactions.
3. What is meant by half life period of a reaction? Show that for a first order reaction, $t_{1/2} = 0.693/k_1$.
4. List the three factors that affect the rate of a chemical reaction.
5. For the following reaction:

$$C_2H_4(g) + I_2(g) \longrightarrow C_2H_4I_2(g)$$

The rate equation is

$$\text{Rate} = k[C_2H_4][I_2]^{3/2}$$

(*a*) What is the order of reaction with respect to each reactant?

(*b*) What is the overall order of reaction?

(*c*) What is the unit of k, if concentrations are measured in mol dm^{-3} s^{-1}?

6. For a chemical reaction, $R \longrightarrow P$, the variation in the concentration (R) *vs.* time (t), plot is given as

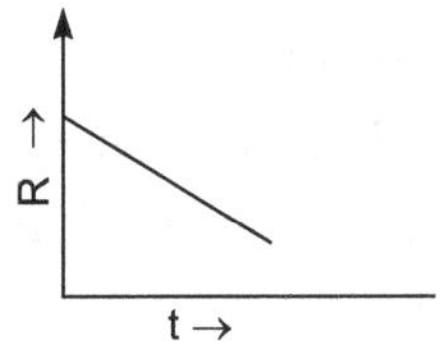

(*i*) Predict the order of the reaction.

(*ii*) What is the slope of the curve?

7. For the assumed reaction $A_2 + 2B_2 \longrightarrow 2AB_2$, Write the rate equation in terms of the rate of disappearance of reactants A_2 and B_2.

8. What are pseudochemical reactions? Give one example of a pseudo first order reaction.

9. State any one condition under which a bimolecular reaction may be kinetically of first order.

10. Slowest step in the mechanism of a reaction determines the rate of a reaction. Explain.

11. Derive the expression for determining the half life of first order reaction.

12. Define rate constant of a reaction. If the concentration is expressed in mol L^{-1} and time in seconds. What would be the units of k,

(*i*) for a first order reaction?

(*ii*) for a second order reaction?

13. Explain Ostwald's method for the determination of order of a reaction.

14. Why high molecularity reactions are rare?

15. Define order of reaction. How it is different from molecularity of a reaction?

16. Derive a second order rate equation for the reaction

$$2X \longrightarrow \text{Products}$$

Explain that half life period depends upon initial concentration of the reactants.

17. Derive an expression for the half life period of the following reactions:

$$A \longrightarrow B, \text{ Rate} = k[A].$$

II. LONG ANSWER TYPE QUESTIONS

1. Briefly explain various methods used to determine the order of a reaction.

2. Derive an expression for the rate constant of a first order reaction by integral method. What are the units of rate constant for first order reactions? Prove that for first order reactions, half life period is independent of initial concentration.

3. Describe various factors which affect the rate of chemical reactions.

4. Derive an expression for the rate constant of a second order reaction by integral method. What are the units of rate constant for second order constant? Explain how the half life period of a second order reaction varies with initial concentration.

III. NUMERICAL PROBLEMS

1. $2A + B \rightarrow A_2B$

   The rate law is given by the expression

   $r = k\,[A]^2$ with rate constant equal to 0.60 $mol^{-1}\ Ls^{-1}$. Calculate the rate of the reaction when

   (*i*) $[A] = 0.50\ mol\ L^{-1}$, $[B] = 0.08\ mol\ L^{-1}$

   (*ii*) When concentration of *A* and *B* have been reduced to 1/2.

2. A first order reaction is 20% complete in 10 minutes. Calculate the time taken for the reaction to go to 80% completion.

3. For a first order reaction, prove that the time taken for three fourth completion of the reaction is double the time taken for half completion of the reaction *i.e.*, $t_{3/4}/t_{1/2} = 2$.

4. The thermal decomposition of a compound follows first order kinetics. If 50% of the compound is decomposed in 120 minutes, how long will it take for 90% of the compound to decompose?

5. The three fourth of a first order reaction is completed in 32 minutes. What is the half life period of the reaction?

6. A first order reaction was 75% completed in 32 minutes. When was its half completed?

7. Derive an expression for the half life period of the following reactions:

   $$A \rightarrow B,\ \text{rate} = k[A]$$

8. If 20% of a substance decomposes in first 15 minutes in a first order reaction, calculate how much of it would remain undecomposed after one hour?

9. For a certain reaction, it takes 5 minutes for the initial concentration of 0.5 $mol\ L^{-1}$ to become 0.25 $mol\ L^{-1}$ and another 5 minutes to become 0.125 $mol\ L^{-1}$. Find out the

   (*i*) order of the reaction.

   (*ii*) rate constant of the reaction.

10. The reaction $SO_2Cl_2 \xrightarrow{k_1} SO_2 + Cl_2$ is a first order reaction with a half life of 3.15×10^4 s at 570 K. What percentage of SO_2Cl_2 would be decomposed on heating at 570 K for 90 minutes.

11. The rate constant for a first order reaction is 60 s^{-1}. How much time will it take to reduce the concentration of the reactant to 1/10th of its initial value?

12. For a first order reaction, calculate the ratio between the time taken to complete three fourth of the reaction and the time taken to complete half of the reaction.

13. In a second order reaction, half life period is 60 min. When the initial concentration of reactants is 0.02 moles per litre. Calculate the value of rate constant.

14. In a second order reaction, the initial concentration of reactants is 0.1 $mol\ L^{-1}$. The reaction takes 40 min. for 20% completion. Determine the rate constant and the half-life period of the reaction.

15. 100 cm^3 each of ethyl acetate and NaOH (each of 0.1 M concentration) were mixed and hydrolysed in a thermostat. When some volumes of mixture were withdrawn at different time intervals and titrated against standard HCl solution (0.1 M), the following data were obtained.

Time (min)	0	4	6	10	15	20
Volume of acid used (ml)	8.04	5.30	4.58	3.50	2.74	2.22

Show that the reaction follows second order kinetics and also calculate the value of rate constant.

16. The rate of decomposition of H_2O_2 at a particular temperature was measured by titrating its solution with $KMnO_4$ solution. The results obtained were:

Time (sec.)	0	300	600	1200
Volume of $KMnO_4$ used (mL)	46	37	30	20

Show that the reaction follows first order kinetics. Also calculate rate constant of the reaction.

17. Following data was obtained in decomposition of H_2O_2 by titrating it with standard $KMnO_4$ at different intervals. Show that it is a first order reaction. Calculate the rate constant.

Time (min.)	0	5	15	25	45
Volume of $KMnO_4$ used (mL)	37	29.8	19.6	12.3	5.0

18. Iodine atoms combine to form molecular iodine in the gas phase:

$$I(g) + I(g) \longrightarrow I_2(g)$$

The reaction follows second order kinetics and has the high rate constant of 7×10^9 moles $L^{-1}s^{-1}$ at 23°C.

(*a*) If the initial concentration of 1 was 0.086 moles L^{-1}. Calculate the concentration after two min.

(*b*) Calculate the half-life of the reaction, if the initial concentration of iodine is 0.60 mol L^{-1}.

19. Rate data were obtained for the following reaction at 25°C. What is the rate law (including k) for the reaction?

$$2A + B + 2C \longrightarrow D + 2E$$

Expt.	**Initial [*A*]**	**Initial [*B*]**	**Initial [*C*]**	**Initial rate of *D* (mol/min.)**
I	0.10	0,20	0.10	5×10^{-4}
II	0.20	0.20	0.30	1.5×10^{-3}
III	0.30	0.20	0.10	5.0×10^{-4}
IV	0.40	0.60	0.30	4.5×10^{-3}

20. The first order rate constant for the radioactive decay of radium – 223 is 0.0606 day^{-1}. What is the half life of the reaction?

21. The reaction of nitric oxide with hydrogen at 1280 °C is

$$2NO(g) + 2H_2(g) \longrightarrow N_2(g) + 2H_2O(g)$$

From the following data collected at this temperature, determine.

(*a*) rate law

(*b*) the rate constant (with units)

(*c*) the rate of reaction when
$[NO] = 1.20 \times 10^{-3}$ M and $[H_2] = 6.0 \times 10^{-3}$ M.

22. The rate constants of a reaction at 500 K and 700 K are 0.02 s^{-1} and 0.07 s^{-1} respectively. Calculate the values of E_a and A.

23. The values of E_a and A for a chemical reaction are 98.6 kJ/mol and 4.0×10^{13} s^{-1}, respectively. If the reaction is of first order, then using the Arrhenius equation, calculation the temperature at which its half life period will be 600 sec.

24. Calculate the activation energy of a reaction if the slope of the Arrhenius plot of log K against $1/T$ for a chemical reaction is found to be –20.62.

IV. MULTIPLE CHOICE QUESTIONS

1. The inversion of cane sugar using excess water in the presence of acid catalyst is a reaction of

(*a*) Third order

(*b*) Second order

(*c*) Zero order with respect to cane sugar.

(*d*) First order with respect to cane sugar.

2. Units of second order rate constant are:

(*a*) sec^{-1} (*b*) mol L^{-1} sec^{-1}

(*c*) L mol^{-1} sec^{-1} (*d*) mol^2 L^{-2} sec^{-1}.

3. Which one of the following statements about the order of a reaction is true?

(*a*) It increases with increase in temperature.

(*b*) It can only be determined by experiment.

(*c*) It can be determined from the balanced equation.

(*d*) A second order reaction is always bimolecular.

4. A radioactive decay follows

(*a*) First order kinetics (*b*) Second order kinetics

(*c*) Zero order kinetics (*d*) Third order kinetics.

5. What is the order of the absorption process for alcohol through the lining of the stomach and small intestine.

(*a*) First order (*b*) Second order

(*c*) Third order (*d*) Zero order.

6. Which of the following does not affect the rate of a chemical reaction?

(*a*) Concentration of reacting molecules

(*b*) Surface area

(*c*) Temperature

(*d*) Enthalpy of the reaction.

7. The decomposition of N_2O_5 can be represented as

$$N_2O_5(g) \longrightarrow 2NO_2(g) + \frac{1}{2}O_2(g)$$

The rate of the reaction can be expressed as

(a) $-\frac{d[N_2O_5]}{dt} = \frac{2d[NO_2]}{dt} = \frac{1}{2}\frac{d[O_2]}{dt} = k[N_2O_5]$

(b) $\frac{1}{2}\frac{d[N_2O_5]}{dt} = \frac{1}{2}\frac{d[NO_2]}{dt} = \frac{d}{dt}[O_2] = k[N_2O_5]$

(c) $-\frac{d[N_2O_5]}{dt} = \frac{1}{2}\frac{d[NO_2]}{dt}\frac{2d[O_2]}{dt} = k[N_2O_5]$

(d) $\frac{-d[N_2O_5]}{dt} = \frac{1}{2}\frac{d[NO_2]}{dt} = \frac{1}{2}\frac{d[O_2]}{dt} = k[N_2O_5]$.

8. The unit of the rate of reaction is the same as that of the rate constant for a

(a) First order reaction (b) Second order reaction
(c) Third order reaction (d) Zero order reaction.

9. The unit of the rate constant depends upon the

(a) Temperature of the reaction (b) Order of the reaction
(c) Molecularity of the reaction (d) Activation energy of the reaction.

10. The half life period for the first order reaction whose rate constant is 1.052×10^{-3} sec^{-1} is:

(a) 659 sec (b) 1.528 sec
(c) 0.526 sec (d) 0.693 sec.

11. What will happen for the rate of an elementary reaction, $2NO + O_2 \longrightarrow 2NO_2$, when the volume of the reaction vessel is doubled:

(a) It will grow eight times of its initial rate.
(b) It will reduce to one eighth of its initial rate.
(c) It will grow four times of its initial rate.
(d) It will reduce to one fourth of its initial rate.

12. A reaction $X_2 + Y_2 \longrightarrow 2XY$ occurs by the following mechanism.

$$X_2 \longrightarrow X + X \quad \text{...(slow)}$$

$$X + Y_2 \longrightarrow XY + Y \quad \text{...(fast)}$$

$$X + Y \longrightarrow XY \quad \text{...(fast)}$$

The order of the reaction would be

(a) 3/2 (b) Zero
(c) 2 (d) 1.

13. The rate of an elementary reaction, $R \longrightarrow P$, increases by a factor of 100 when the concentration of R is increased ten times. The order of reaction is:

(a) 1 (b) 2
(c) 10 (d) 100

14. If 75% of a radioactive element disintegrates in 60 seconds, the half life of the radio element is:

(a) 20 sec (b) 30 sec
(c) 25 sec (d) 45 sec.

15. On increasing the temperature of the system, the rate of reaction increases. The most appropriate reason for this is:

(*a*) Collision frequency increases

(*b*) The value of threshold energy decreases

(*c*) The fraction of molecules having energy equal to threshold energy or more increases

(*d*) Activation energy decreases by increase in temperature.

16. If the rate of reaction between *A* and *B* is expressed as $k\,[A]^2\,[B]^1$, the reaction is

(*a*) Second order w.r.t. *A* (*b*) First order w.r.t. *B*

(*c*) Overall order is three (*d*) All are correct

17. For the first order reaction, time required for completion of 99% of the reaction is

(*a*) Twice the time required for 90% completion of reaction

(*b*) Thrice the time required for 90% completion of reaction

(*c*) Half time required for 90% completion of reaction

(*d*) None of these.

18. Which of the following plot is not correct?

(*a*)
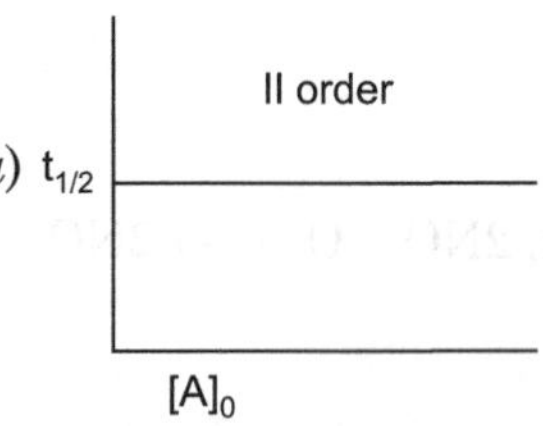

(*b*)
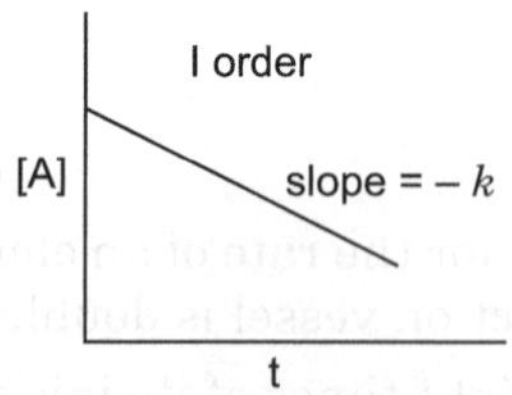

(*c*)
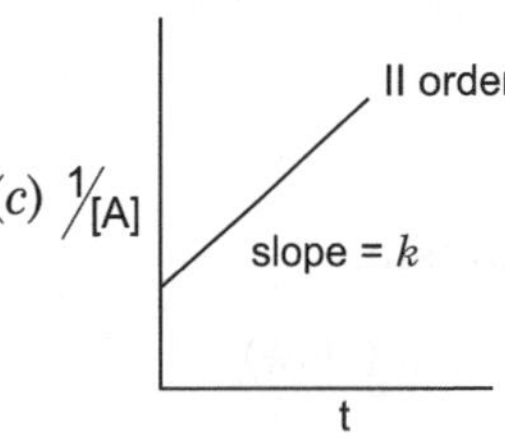

(*d*)
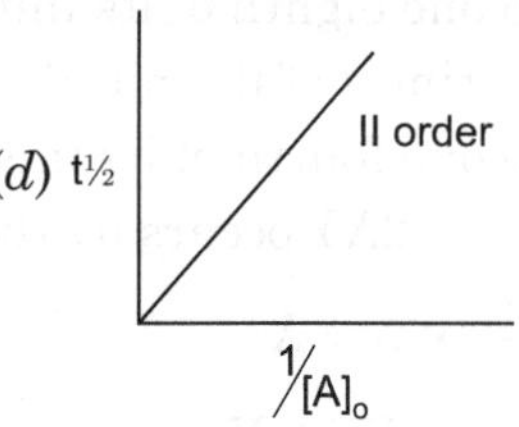

19. A first order reaction requires 8.96 months for the concentration of reactant to be reduced to one fourth of its initial concentration. The half life of the reaction is

(*a*) 17.9 months (*b*) 4.48 months

(*c*) 8.96 months (*d*) 35.84 months.

20. With increase in temperature, the rate of reaction

(*a*) Increases (*b*) Decreases

(*c*) Stays same (*d*) Cannot be predicted.

21. The half life period of any second order reaction is:

(*a*) directly proportional to the initial concentration of the reactant

(*b*) inversely proportional to the initial concentration of the reactant

(*c*) independent of the initial concentration of the reactant

(*d*) half the specific rate constant.

22. The rate constant of a reaction is 2.3×10^{-3} mol^{-2} L^{-2} sec^{-1}. The order of reaction is

(*a*) zero order (*b*) first order

(*c*) second order (*d*) third order

23. The units of concentration are mol dm^{-3} and of time are s, then the units of the rate constant for a first order reaction will be

(*a*) mol dm^{-3} s^{-1} (*b*) mol^{-1} dm^3 s^{-1}

(*c*) s^{-1} (*d*) mol^{-1} dm^{-3} s^{-1}

24. The rate constant of a reaction does not depend upon

(*a*) Nature of reactants (*b*) Temperature

(*c*) Concentration of reactants (*d*) All of the above.

25. For a zero order reaction, the integrated rate equation is

(*a*) $kt = [A] - [A]_0$ (*b*) $[A] = -kt + [A]_0$

(*c*) $kt = [A]/[A]_0$ (*d*) $[A] = kt - [A]_0$

Answers

III. NUMERICAL PROBLEMS

1. (*i*) 0.15 mol L^{-1} s^{-1}, (*ii*) 0.0375 mol $L^{-1}s^{-1}$.

2. 72.18 min. **4.** 399 min. **5.** 16 min.

6. 16 min. **8.** 41.17% **9.** (*i*) First order, (*ii*) 0.136 min^{-1}

10. 11.2% **11.** 3.8×10^{-2} s. **12.** $\frac{t_{3/4}}{t_{1/2}} = 2$

14. $k_2 = 6.25 \times 10^{-2}$ mol^{-1} Ls^{-1}, $t_{1/2} = 160$ min **15.** $k = 0.01602$ L mol^{-1} min^{-1}

16. $k = 0.00072$ s^{-1} **17.** $k = 4.355 \times 10^{-2}$ min^{-1}

18. (*a*) 1.17×10^{-12} M (*b*) $t_{1/2} = 1.66 \times 10^{-9}$ sec.

19. Rate = $k\,[A]^0\,[B]\,[C] = 0.025\,[A]^0\,[B]\,[C]$ **20.** $t_{1/2} = 11.4$ day

21. (*a*) Rate = 260 $[NO]^2$ $[H_2]$, (*b*) $k = 260$ mol^{-2} L^2 s^{-1}, (*c*) Rate = 2.2×10^{-4} M/s

22. $E_a = 18.23$ kJ, A = 1.61 **23.** T = 311.35 K **24.** $E_a = 171.4$ J/mol.

IV. MULTIPLE CHOICE QUESTIONS

1. (*d*)	**2.** (*c*)	**3.** (*a*)	**4.** (*a*)	**5.** (*a*)	**6.** (*d*)	**7.** (*a*)	**8.** (*a*)	**9.** (*b*)	**10.** (*a*)
11. (*b*)	**12.** (*b*)	**13.** (*b*)	**14.** (*b*)	**15.** (*c*)	**16.** (*d*)	**17.** (*a*)	**18.** (*a*)	**19.** (*b*)	**20.** (*a*)
21. (*b*)	**22.** (*d*)	**23.** (*c*)	**24.** (*c*)	**25.** (*b*)					

Chapter 5 Polymers and Polymerization

5.1 INTRODUCTION

In today's world, polymers are an integral part of everyone's life style. They have very diverse structures and applications ranging from domestic articles, clothes, furniture, children's toys, automobile tyres, electrical insulating materials, etc to space aircraft, scientific and medical instruments.

Polymers in Greek-*poly* means many and *mer* means part or segment) are high molecular weight ($10^3 - 10^7$ u) substances consisting of large number of repeating structural units called as **monomers**. The process by which the monomers are converted into polymers is called as **polymerization**. For example, polythene

$$\underset{\text{Ethylene}}{n(CH_2 = CH_2)} \longrightarrow \underset{\text{Polyethylene}}{(-CH_2-CH_2-)_n}$$

Several ethylene molecules combine to form a giant molecule of polyethylene. Here, n is the number of monomers in the polymeric chain.

- Polymers which are formed from one type of monomers are called as **homopolymers** (*e.g.* polythene, polypropylene, PVC, PAN, etc.).
- Polymers which are formed from two or more different monomers are called as **copolymers** or **mixed polymers**. For example nylon-66, buna-S, bakelite, melamine etc.

Examples of Typical Polymers

(*i*) Natural inorganic polymers-*e.g.* sand, clay.

(*ii*) Synthetic inorganic polymers-fibre glass, ceramics.

(*iii*) Natural organic polymers (Biopolymers)

e.g., polysaccharide (wood, starch), polypeptides (proteins), polyisoprene (natural rubber), nucleic acid (DNA, RNA).

(*iv*) Synthetic organic polymers -

Polyolefins, Polyesters, Polyamides etc.

The number of repeating units (n) in a polymer chain is called as the **degree of polymerization** of the polymer. Polymers with a high degree of polymerization (of the order of $10^4 - 10^6$)

are called as **high polymers** while those with low degree of polymerization are called as **oligomers** (*e.g.*, dimers, trimers, tetramers etc.).

Classification of Polymers

Polymers are classified in a number of ways

1. According to origin
2. On the basis of structure
3. On the basis of configuration (tacticity)
4. On the basis of molecular forces
5. On the basis of method of synthesis.

1. According to origin:

(*i*) Natural polymers

(*ii*) Synthetic polymers

(*iii*) Semi-synthetic polymers.

(*i*) **Natural polymers:** Polymers which are obtained from nature are called as **natural polymers**. *Examples*: starch (polymers of α-*D* glucose), cellulose (β-*D* glucose), natural rubber (isoprene), proteins (α-amino acids), nucleic acids (nucleotides), wool (protein fibre), cotton (vegetable fibre), etc.

(*ii*) **Synthetic polymers:** Polymers which are prepared in the laboratory are called as **synthetic polymers**. These are also called as **man-made polymers. Examples:** fibres (nylon, terylene, polyesters), plastic (polythene, polystyrene), rubbers (neoprene, polystyrene), etc.

(*iii*) **Semi-synthetic polymers:** Semi-synthetic polymers are derived from naturally occurring polymers by chemical modifications such as hydrogenation, halogenation, hydrohalogenation etc. Cellulose derivatives such as cellulose acetate (rayon) and cellulose nitrate, methyl cellulose, vulcanized rubber (derived from the chemical modifications in the structure of natural rubber) etc.

2. On the basis of structure:

(*i*) Linear polymers

(*ii*) Branched chain polymers

(*iii*) Cross linked/3-Dimensional polymers.

(*i*) **Linear polymers:** Polymers in which monomer units are joined together to form long straight and closely packed chains are called **linear polymers**. Due to the close packing of polymer chains, these polymers have high melting point, high density and high tensile strength. For example, nylon, polyesters, PVC, high density polythene etc.

(*ii*) **Branched chain polymers:** In these polymers, the monomers are joined to form not only linear chains (called the main chain) but also possess some branches along the main chain. These polymer molecules do not pack well due to the presence of branches. Due to poor packing of polymer chains, they have lower boiling point, lower density, lower tensile strength as compared to linear polymers. For example, low density polythene (LDPE), glycogen, amylopectin etc.

(*iii*) **Three dimensional network polymers:** Polymers in which monomers units are connected to each other by covalent bonds forming a 3-dimensional network structure are called as **cross linked polymers.**

They are giant molecules in which movement of individual monomeric units is prevented by strong cross-links. Due to the presence of strong cross links they are hard, rigid, brittle and do not melt but burn or heating. For example: bakelite, urea-formaldehyde resin, melamine formaldehyde resin, rubber etc.

3. **On the basis of tacticity:** Tacticity means orientation of side groups around the main backbone chain in 3-dimensional structure of a polymer. On the basis of tacticity, polymers can be

   (*i*) Isotactic polymers

   (*ii*) Syndiotactic polymers

   (*iii*) Atactic polymers.

(*i*) **Isotactic polymers:** In isotactic polymers, the side groups are all on the same side. **Giulio Natta** and his coworkers observed that ziegler-type catalysts could polymerise propylene ($CH_2 = CHCH_3$) to yield a polymer having all the methyl (CH_3) groups on the same side of the polymer chain.

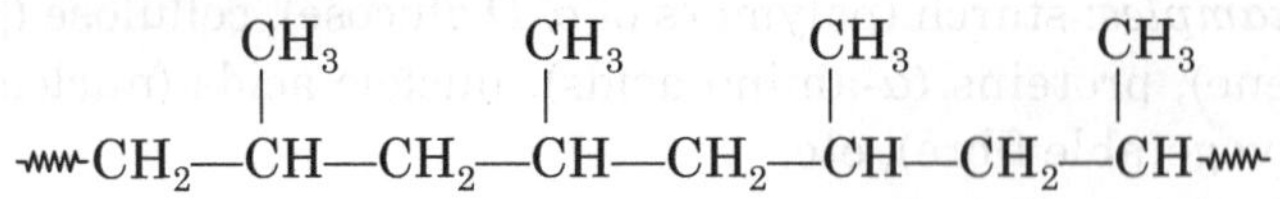

(*ii*) **Syndiotactic polymers:** In these polymers, the side groups are arranged in alternate manner around the main backbone chain. Natta synthesized polypropylene containing methyl groups arranged in alternate manner with the help of vanadium containing catalysts.

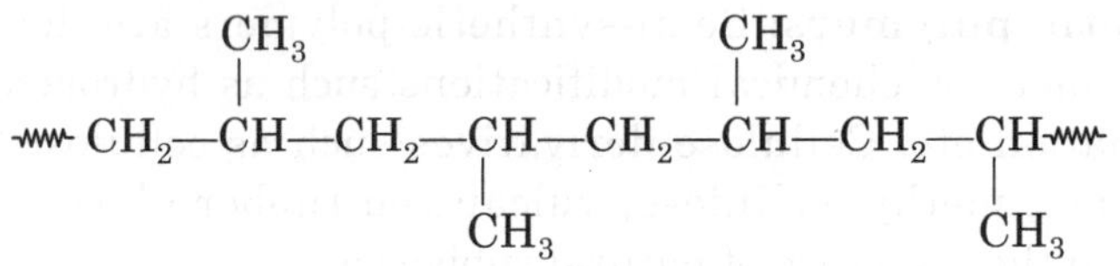

(*iii*) **Atactic polymers:** In atactic polymers, the side groups are randomly oriented around the main backbone chain.

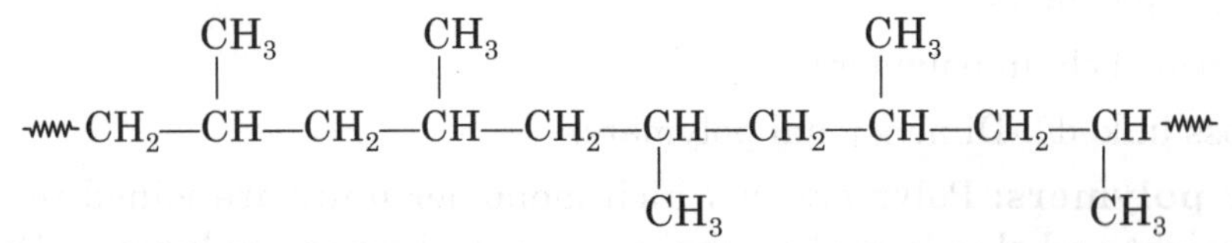

- Isotactic and syndiotactic polymers have regular arrangement of side groups along the main chain. Because of this uniform arrangement, the polymer chains are closely packed. Due to this close packing, isotactic and syndiotactic polymers generally have high melting point, high tensile strength and less solubility as compared to atactic polymers.
- Isotactic and syndiotactic polymers are also generally more crystalline than atactic polymers.
- It should be noted that formation of isotactic, syndiotactic and atactic polymers depend mainly on the presence of complex catalysts used for the polymerization.

4. **On the basis of molecular forces:** On the basis of magnitude of intermolecular forces present, the polymers can be classified into following 4 types

(*i*) Elastomers (*ii*) Fibres

(*iii*) Thermoplastic polymers (*iv*) Thermosetting polymers

(*i*) Elastomers: Polymers in which the polymer chains are held together by weakest intermolecular forces are called as **elastomers**. Due to the weak intermolecular forces, these polymers can be easily stretched by application of small stress and regains their original shape after the removal of stress. Elastomers are commonly known as rubbers. Natural rubber is a popular elastomer. Various synthetic elastomers include vulcanized rubber, polybutadiene, styrene butadiene rubber (Buna-S), polyurethane, silicon rubbers, butyl rubber etc.

(*ii*) Fibres: Polymers in which polymer chains are held together by strong intermolecular forces of attraction like hydrogen bonds or dipole-dipole interactions are called as **fibres**.

Due to the strong intermolecular forces, these polymer chains are closely packed in fibres which imparts crystalline nature. Also they have high tensile strength, less elasticity and sharp melting point.

These polymers are long, thin and thread like which can be woven in fabrics. Fibres may be natural (such as cotton, wool, silk etc.) and synthetic (like nylon, polyester, acrylics etc.).

(*iii*) Thermoplastics: Polymers in which the intermolecular forces of attraction between polymeric chain are intermediate between elastomers and fibres are called as **thermoplastic polymers**.

These polymers are linear, long chain which can be softened on heating and hardened on cooling. They can be melted or processed again and again without any change. For example, polythene, polystyrene, polyvinyl chloride, teflon etc.

(*iv*) Thermosetting polymers: Polymers which undergo permanent change on heating are called as thermosetting polymers. On heating, these polymers undergo extensive cross linking in moulds and become infusible and form an insoluble hard mass, therefore, they cannot be reused. For example: bakelite, phenol-formaldehyde resin, melamine-formaldehyde resin, vulcanized rubber, polyamides etc.

Table 5.1: Difference between thermoplastic and thermosetting polymers

	Thermoplastic polymers	Thermosetting polymers
1.	These are formed by addition or condensation polymerization.	These are formed by condensation polymerization.
2.	They can be softened on heating and hardened on cooling any number of times.	They do not soften at all when heated but stay hard and rigid.
3.	Theromoplastic polymers are composed mainly of linear and branched molecules.	Thermosetting polymers are made up of cross-linked network structure.
4.	These polymers have low molecular weight.	These polymers have high molecular weight.
5.	Thermoplastic polymers are soluble in organic solvents.	Thermosetting polymers are insoluble in almost all the solvents.

6.	In thermoplastics, the polymer chains are free to slide past one another as the molecules of chains are not chemically tied together.	In thermosettings, the chains are cross-linked *i.e.* neighbouring chains are linked together therefore the chains will not flow freely even under the application of heat and pressure.
7.	They can be remoulded, reused and recycled.	They cannot be remoulded, reused and recycled.
8.	Neighbouring polymer chains are held together by weak intermolecular forces of attraction.	Neighbouring polymer chains are held together by strong chemical bonds.
9.	These polymers range from soft, flexible meterials to those which are hard and rigid.	These polymers are generally rigid and brittle.
10.	*Examples:* PE, PVC, PMMA, polystyrene, etc.	*Examples:* bakelite, urea formaldehyde resin, melamine etc.

5. **On the basis of method of synthesis:** On the basis of method of synthesis, Carothers (1925) classified the polymers into two groups: (*i*) Addition polymers, (*ii*) Condensation polymers.

   (*i*) Addition polymers: Polymers formed by direct addition of repeated monomers without elimination of by product molecules are called as **addition polymers**. The monomers used are unsaturated compounds such as alkenes, alkadines and their derivatives. For example,

$$\underset{\text{ethene}}{n(CH_2{=}CH_2)} \longrightarrow \underset{\text{polyethylene}}{(\text{—}CH_2\text{—}CH_2\text{—})_n}$$

   Other examples are: polypropylene, polyvinyl chloride, polystyrene etc.

   (*ii*) Condensation polymers: Polymers which are formed by the condensation of two different bifunctional or polyfunctional monomers having functional groups which have affinity for each other are called as *condensation polymers*. Simple molecule like H_2O, NH_3, CH_3OH etc. are eliminated during the process. The monomers used carry functional groups like —OH, —COOH, —NH_2, —NCO etc. For example

$$\underset{\text{Hexamethylene diamine}}{nH_2N\text{—}(CH_2)_6\text{—}NH_2} + \underset{\text{Adipic acid}}{n\,HOOC\text{—}(CH_2)_4\text{—}COOH}$$

$$\Big\downarrow$$

$$\underset{\text{Nylon-66}}{(HN\text{—}(CH_2)_6\text{—}NHCO\text{—}(CH_2)_4\text{—}CO)_n} + nH_2O$$

   Other examples are: Nylon-6, polyethylene terephthalate (PET), etc.

5.2 POLYMERIZATION

Polymerization is the union of two or more smaller molecules of same or different types, with or without elimination of simple molecules (often H_2O) leading to the formation of new C—C bonds or linkages. On this basis, polymerization can proceed according to two different mechanisms called as

1. Chain growth polymerization or addition polymerization
2. Step growth polymerization or condensation polymerization.

1. **Chain growth or Addition polymerization:** Addition polymers are formed when the molecules of monomers simply add together and this process is called **addition**

polymerization. No by product is formed and the product has the same empirical formula as the monomer. Addition polymerization pass through successive stages of initiation, propagation and termination common to chain reactions, therefore it is also called as **chain growth polymerization.**

During addition polymerization, three different types of reactive species (free radicals, carbanions and carbocation) have been found to be formed. So, depending upon these reactive species, three types of mechanism are found:

(*i*) Free radical addition polymerization
(*ii*) Cationic addition polymerization
(*iii*) Anionic addition polymerization

(*i*) **Free radical addition polymerization:** A variety of unsaturated compounds like alkenes and their derivatives are polymerized via free radical mechanism. **A free radical** may be defined as an intermediate compound containing an odd number of electrons but do not carry any charge.

Free radical addition mechanism involves three processes mentioned earlier-chain initiation, propagation and termination.

Chain initiation: Addition polymerization can be initiated by one of the following methods:

(*a*) Photochemically using UV light
(*b*) Thermally or by heating
(*c*) By initiators: Initiators are compounds which readily decomposes into free radicals so that monomer molecules can interact with these compounds for activation. These are irreversibly consumed in the process. For example, azo compounds (AIBN-azo bis- isobutyronitrile), hydroperoxides, peresters, peracids, peroxides (benzoyl peroxide, ditert-butyl peroxide, H_2O_2) etc.

Some commonly used initiators and the free radicals formed by their decomposition are given below

AIBN:

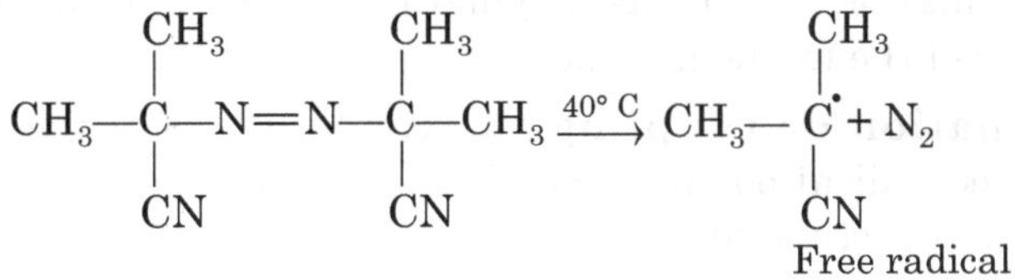

Benzoyl peroxide:

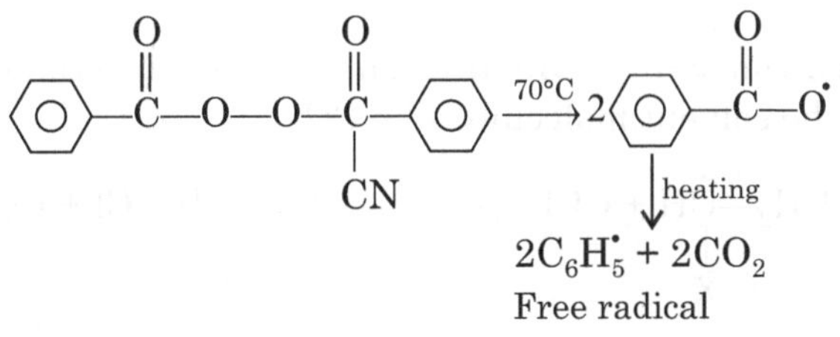

Hydrogen peroxide:

$$\mathrm{H{-}O{-}O{-}H} \xrightarrow{\Delta} \underbrace{\mathrm{\dot{O}H + \dot{O}H}}_{\text{Free radicals}}$$

The larger the amount of initiator present, the larger will be the number of free radicals formed and more will be the rate of polymerization (but the average molecular weight of polymer decrease with increase in amount of initiator).

In general, decomposition of initiator to free radical can be written as:

$$\text{Peroxides} \longrightarrow 2\dot{\mathrm{In}}$$

As free radical $\dot{\mathrm{In}}$ contains lone electron, it is extremely reactive and attacks the double bond of the monomer unit, forming a new free radical, which is called the **activated monomer**.

$$\underset{\text{Free radical}}{\dot{\mathrm{In}}} + \underset{\text{Monomer}}{\mathrm{CH_2{=}CH(X)}} \longrightarrow \underset{\text{Activated monomer}}{\mathrm{In{-}CH_2{-}\dot{C}H(X)}}$$

The attack of free radical on the monomer is an **exothemic process.**

Chain propagation: In this stage, the activated monomer attacks the other monomer molecule to form another new free radical, which further adds to another fresh monomer molecule to form another new free radical and so on. Hence, the chain propagates by successive addition of monomers

$$\mathrm{In{-}CH_2{-}\dot{C}H(X) + CH_2{=}CH_2 \longrightarrow In{-}CH_2{-}CH(X){-}CH_2{-}\dot{C}H(X)}$$

or

$$\mathrm{In{-}CH_2{-}\dot{C}H(X) + \mathit{n}CH_2 = CH_2 \longrightarrow In{-}(CH_2{-}CH(X))_{\mathit{n}}\, CH_2{-}\dot{C}H(X)}$$

During a chain reaction, most of the time is spent in the propagation phase as the polymer chain grows.

Chain termination: The chain reaction cannot go on forever. It must terminate somewhere. The termination of growing polymer chain can be brought about by deactivation of free radicals by any of the following reaction:

(*a*) **By recombination or coupling** *i.e.*, combination of two free radicals. When a propagating free radical polymer combines with another growing free radical polymer, both of them get deactivated.

$$\mathrm{In{-}CH_2{-}\dot{C}H(X) + \dot{C}H(X){-}CH_2{-}In \longrightarrow In{-}CH_2{-}CH(X){-}CH(X){-}CH_2{-}In}$$

(*b*) **Reaction with the solvent molecule:** The growing free radical chain may terminate by reacting with the solvent molecules like CCl_4.

$$\mathrm{{-}CH_2{-}\dot{C}H(X) + CCl_4 \longrightarrow {-}CH_2{-}CH(X){-}Cl + \dot{C}Cl_3}$$

The new free radical species $\dot{C}Cl_3$ can either react with another free radical or can react with the monomer molecule.

$$\dot{C}Cl_3 + \dot{C}Cl_3 \longrightarrow C_2Cl_6$$

$$\dot{C}Cl_3 + -CH_2-\underset{X}{\underset{|}{\dot{C}H}} \longrightarrow CCl_3-\underset{X}{\underset{|}{CH}}-CH_2-$$

(c) By disproportionation of free radicals: In this reaction, a hydrogen atom of one free radical is transferred to another producing a polymer with a terminal unsaturated group and another with a terminal saturated group.

$$n\ -CH_2-\underset{X}{\underset{|}{\dot{C}H}} + \underset{X}{\underset{|}{\dot{C}H}}-CH_2 \xrightarrow[\text{tionation}]{\text{Dispropor-}} \underset{\text{Saturated polymer}}{-CH_2-\underset{X}{\underset{|}{CH_2}}} + \underset{\text{Unsaturated polymer}}{\underset{X}{\underset{|}{CH}}=CH-}$$

(d) Reaction with polymerization inhibitors: Polymerization inhibitors stop or slow down polymerization by reacting either with the growing polymer chain or with the initiator. For example: quinones, hydroquinones, phenols, aromatic nitro compounds, aromatic amines, trinitrobenzene etc. Oxygen is also a powerful polymerization inhibitor as it reacts with growing free radical polymer to form unreactive peroxy radical.

$$In-CH_2-\underset{X}{\underset{|}{CH}}-CH_2-\underset{X}{\underset{|}{\dot{C}H}} + O_2 \longrightarrow \underset{\text{Unactive peroxy radical}}{In-CH_2-\underset{X}{\underset{|}{CH}}-CH_2-\underset{X}{\underset{|}{CH}}-\underset{\dot{O}}{\underset{|}{O}}}$$

This peroxy radical forms inactive products by coupling with another growing radical.
Examples: Ethylene and other vinyl derivatives; for example: PVC, PMMA, PAN, polythene, polypropylene, polystyrene, etc. polymerize *via* free radical addition mechanism.

(*ii*) Cationic addition polymerization: In cationic addition polymerization, the reactive species are positively charged carbocations. Chain initiation is brought about by addition of an electrophile to the double bond of the monomer.

Compounds used to initiate cationic polymerization are:

(*a*) Protonic acids with unreactive counter ions, for example H_2SO_4, H_3PO_4, $HClO_4$ etc. because if, counter ions will be active then they will also attack double bond of the monomer and polymerization will not take place.

(*b*) Lewis acids such as BF_3, $AlCl_3$, $TiCl_4$, $SnCl_4$ etc. in the presence of co-catalysts (co-catalysts are usually proton donating compounds such as alcohol, water, cyclic ethers and acids). Double bonds cannot form bond directly with lewis acids therefore, co-catalysts are required. For example:

$$AlCl_3 + H_2O \rightleftharpoons [AlCl_3OH]^- H^+ \rightarrow$$
$$BF_3 + H_2O \rightleftharpoons [BF_3OH]^- H^+$$

> This is not a very good nucleophile so it would not be able to attack the double bond and therefore H^+ will be the only active species.

Chain initiation: Formation of cationic chain involves the attack of carbonium ions (carbocations) on the π electrons of the double bond of the monomer.

$$[BF_3OH]^- H^+ + CH_2{=}\underset{X}{\underset{|}{CH}} \rightarrow CH_3{-}\underset{X}{\underset{|}{\overset{+}{C}H}} + [BF_3OH]^-$$

Here, H^+ ion is an initiating cationic species and $[BF_3OH]^-$ is the counter ion.

Note: It must be noted that cationic polymerization is effective only when X is an electron donating group. As electron donating groups can stabilize the carbocation formed. More the stability of the carbocation intermediate, more **facile** is the cationic polymerization. Thus, alkenes containing electron releasing groups are preferably polymerized *via* cationic addition mechanism. For example isobutylene *i.e.*

$$CH_2{=}\overset{\overset{CH_3}{|}}{\underset{\underset{CH_3}{|}}{C}}$$

It has two electron donating—CH_3 groups which help to stabilize the positive charge of the carbocation formed. Thus, isobutylene polymerizes *via* cationic mechanism.

Chain propagation: The carbocation formed attacks the other monomer unit and a new carbocation is formed. As more and more monomer units are added up, the chain keeps on growing.

$$CH_3{-}\underset{X}{\underset{|}{\overset{+}{C}H}} + CH_2{=}\underset{X}{\underset{|}{CH}} \longrightarrow CH_3{-}\underset{X}{\underset{|}{CH}}{-}CH_2{-}\underset{X}{\underset{|}{\overset{+}{C}H}}$$

OR

$$CH_3{-}\underset{X}{\underset{|}{CH}}{-}CH_2{-}\underset{X}{\underset{|}{\overset{+}{C}H}} + nCH_2{=}\underset{X}{\underset{|}{CH}} \longrightarrow CH_3{-}\underset{X}{\underset{|}{CH}}{-}\left(CH_2{-}\underset{X}{\underset{|}{CH}}\right)_n{-}CH_2{-}\underset{X}{\underset{|}{\overset{+}{C}H}}$$

When n molecules of monomers are added.

$$CH_3{-}\underset{X}{\underset{|}{\overset{+}{C}H}} + nCH_2{=}\underset{X}{\underset{|}{CH}} \longrightarrow CH_3{-}\underset{X}{\underset{|}{CH}}{-}\left(CH_2{-}\underset{X}{\underset{|}{CH}}\right)_{n-1}{-}CH_2{-}\underset{X}{\underset{|}{\overset{+}{C}H}}$$

Chain termination: Chain termination takes place when there is a collision between the propagating carbocation either from the counter ion of another growing chain or from some added anion. Chain termination can take place by two methods.

(*a*) By coupling: Chain termination can take place by coupling *i.e.* reaction between carbocation and the counter ion.

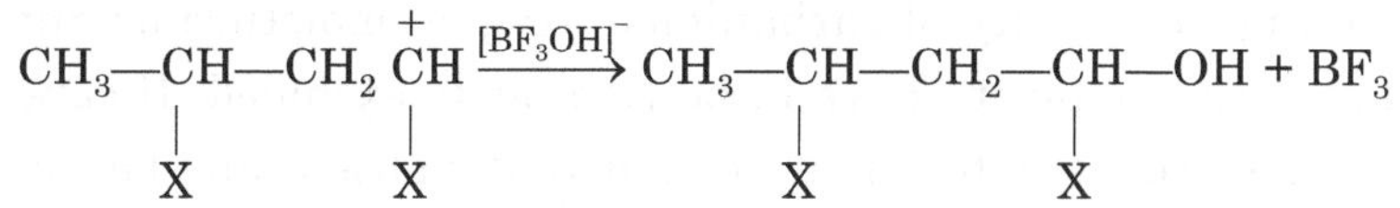

Initiator is regenerated in this process.

(b) Ion-pair precipitation: In this step, the counter ion abstracts a proton from the growing polymer chain, as a result a double bond in formed at the end of growing polymer and the chain growth is arrested.

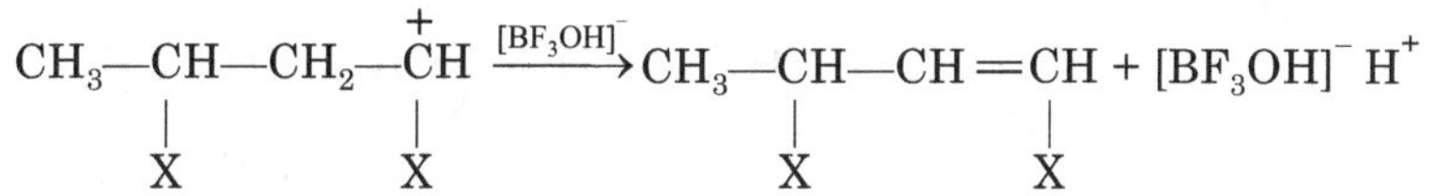

This process of proton abstraction and reformation of BF_3 hydrate is called as **ion pair precipitation**. In this method also, the initiator is regenerated.

Example: monomers capable of undergoing cationic polymerization are isobutylene, α-methyl styrene, styrene and many vinyl ethers.

(iii) Anionic Addition polymerization: In this type of polymerization, the initiation step is the formation of a negatively charged carbanion which acts as a chain carrier. Monomers bearing anion stabilizing substituents (eg. phenyl, vinyl, ester, nitro, cyano etc.) or electron attracting substituents undergo anionic addition mechanism.

Chain initiation: Typical initiators used for this mechanism are alkali metal amides (*e.g.* $LiNH_2$, KNH_2 etc), alkali metal alkyls (*e.g.* (C_4H_9Li) butyl lithium) grignard reagent, naphthalene radical anion, alkali metals (*e.g.* Na, Li) etc. Because of cheapness of naphthalene, it is widely used in industrial applications.

$$KNH_2 \rightleftharpoons K^+ + NH_2^-$$

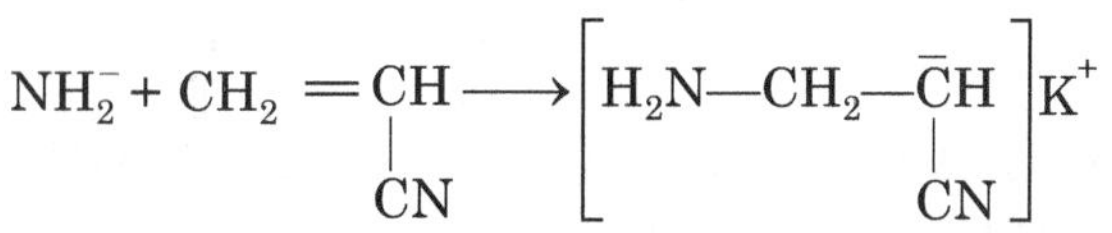

Note: As mentioned earlier, anionic polymerization occurs in vinyl polymers having electron withdrawing group. Greater the stability of carbanion intermediate, more easy will be the polymerization.

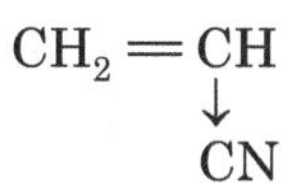

Acrylonitrile having — CN group

Chain propagation: Propagation proceeds in the usual manner

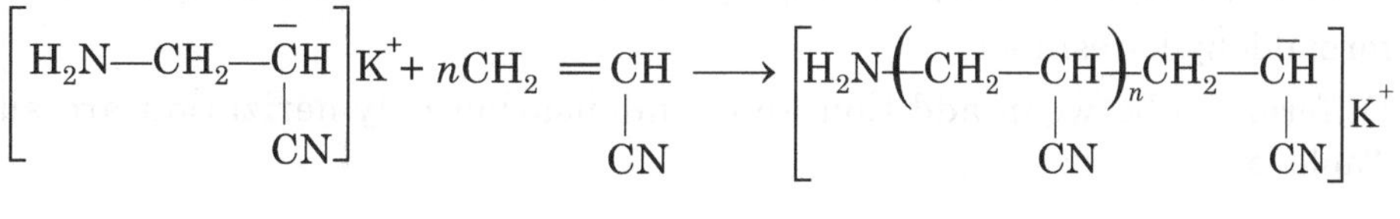

As result of high reactivity of carbanions, oxygen, moisture or any other protic or carbanion-sensitive impurity have to be rigorously excluded. If care is taken during an anionic polymerization, termination is virtually absent and because of this reason, it is also called as **living polymerization**. The polymerization can be quenched with the help of terminating agents (such as H_2O, NH_3) which can donate H^+ ions to the propagating polymer.

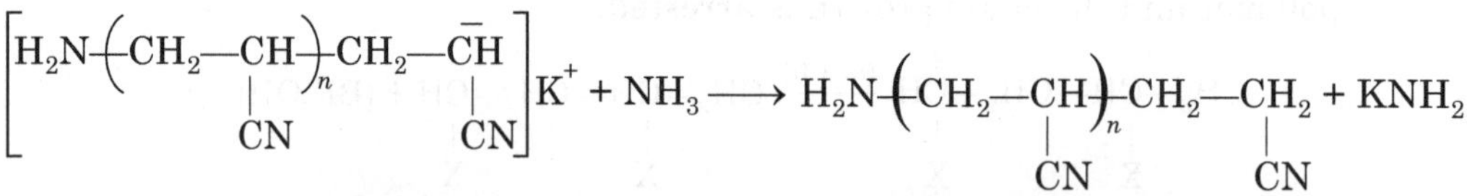

This type of polymerization forms polymers of desired molecular weight and polymerization can be stopped at any stage by adding a terminating agent. Examples are PMMA, PAN, Polystyrene etc.

5.2.1 Step Growth Polymerization or Condensation Polymerization

Condensation polymerization generally involves a repetitive condensation reaction between two different bi-functional or polyfunctional monomers having functional group which have affinity for each other. This polymerization reaction may result in loss of simple molecules like H_2O, HCl, alcohol etc. In this polymerization reaction, the product of each step is again a bi-functional species and the process of condensation goes on. Since, each step produces a distinct functionalised species which is independent of other species, this process is also known as **step growth polymerization.**

The formation of Dacron by the reaction between terephthalic acid and ethylene glycol is an example of this type of polymerization.

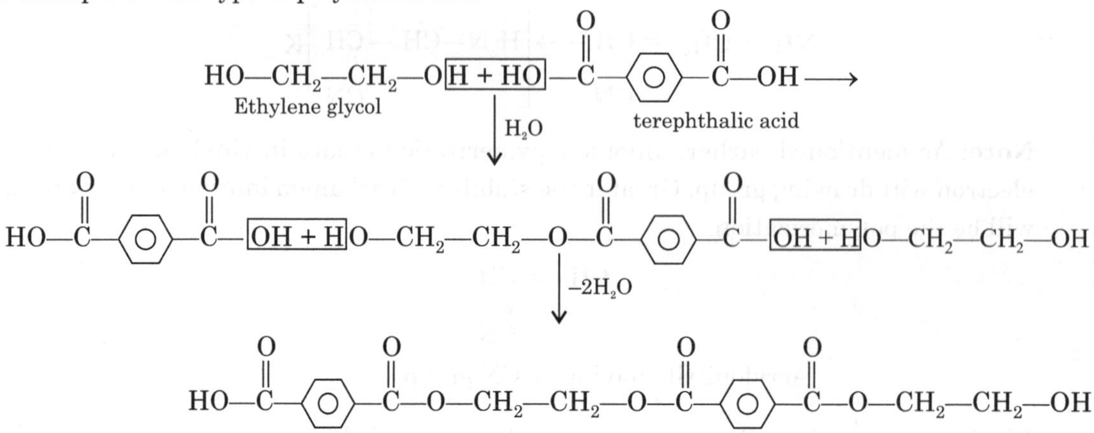

Other example are nylon-66, nylon-6, phenol formaldehyde resin, melamine formaldehyde-resin etc.

Differences between addition and condensation polymerization are summarised in Table 5.2.

Table 5.2: Differences between Addition and Condensation Polymerization

Addition Polymerization	Condensation Polymerization
1. The essential condition is the presence of double bond in the monomer.	The essential condition is the presence of reactive functional group at both ends of the monomer. There should be atleast two different monomers having functional groups with affinity for each other.
2. Nothing is lost during polymerization.	Small molecules like H_2O, NH_3, HCl etc. are lost during polymerization
3. Generally it involves one monomer, therefore a homochain polymer or a thermoplastic is obtained.	It involves two different monomers, therefore a heterochain polymer is obtained which can be thermoplastic or thermosetting in nature.
4. The growth of chain is at one active centre.	The growth of chain occurs at minimum of two active centres.
5. **Examples:** PVC, PS (polystrene), polyethene, polypropylene etc. Polymerization of vinyl chloride to form PVC: $n\underset{\text{Vinyl Chloride}}{CH_2=\underset{\underset{Cl}{\mid}}{CH}} \xrightarrow{\text{Ploymerization}} \underset{\text{PVC}}{\left(CH_2-\underset{\underset{Cl}{\mid}}{CH}-\right)_n}$	**Examples:** Nylon-66, terylene, bakelite etc. formation of nylon-66: $nH_2N-(CH_2)_6-NH_2 + nHO-\overset{\overset{O}{\parallel}}{C}-(CH_2)_4-\overset{\overset{O}{\parallel}}{C}-OH$ $\downarrow$ $\left(\overset{\overset{H}{\mid}}{N}-(CH_2)_6-\overset{\overset{H}{\mid}}{N}-\underset{\underset{O}{\parallel}}{C}-(CH_2)_4-\overset{\overset{O}{\parallel}}{C}\right)_n-$

Co-polymerization and Co-polymers: When two or more different monomers are allowed to polymerize together, a **copolymer** is formed. The process of formation of a coplymer is called as **copolymerization**. The copolymer can be made not only by chain growth polymerization but also by step growth polymerization. For example copolymerization of a mixture of 1, 3-butadiene and styrene gives styrene butadiene rubber (SBR) or Buna-S (In Buna-S, Bu stands for butadiene, Na for sodium which is the polymerizing agent and S for styrene).

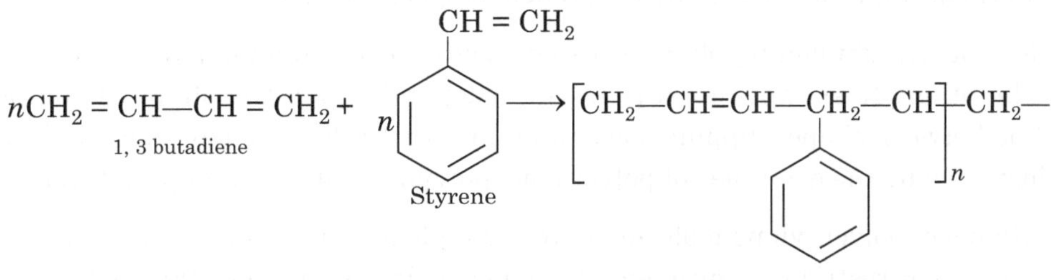

Co-polymers have properties quite different from the homopolymers. For example, polystyrene which is a homopolymer of styrene is a good electrical insulator and can be moulded into toys, combs, radio parts etc. In contrast SBR is a copolymer of styrene and butadiene is quite tough and is a good substitute for natural rubber. It is used for the manufacture of automobile tyres, floor tiles, cable insulation etc. Other examples are nitrile rubber, styrene-acrylonitrile, ethylene-vinyl acetate etc. The reaction proceeds step by step and the chain elongates.

5.3 PROPERTIES OF POLYMERS

5.3.1 Strength

The properties of polymers are mainly determined by the magnitude and distribution of attractive forces between polymer molecules. These forces may be primary (chemical bond) and secondary (intermolecular forces).

In straight chain and branched chain polymers, the individual chains are held together by weak intermolecular forces of attraction. The magnitude of these force increases with the chain length (Fig. 5.1).

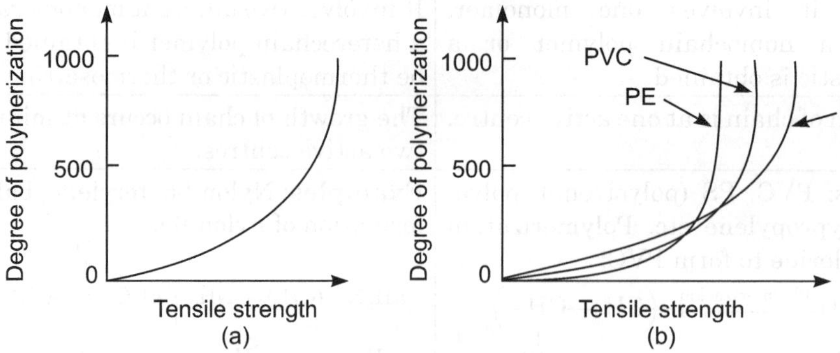

Fig. 5.1. Effect of degree of polymerization (DP) on strength.

Such polymers exhibit mechanical strength only when chain length is greater than 150 to 200 atoms in a line. Such high polymers are tough and more heat resistant than polymers of small chain length which are quite soft, gummy and brittle to impact at low temperatures.

Thus it is evident that physical properties of polymers can be changes from soft and flexible to hard and horn like by controlling the chain length of the polymer. Polar groups like —COOH, —OH, —Cl, —F, —CN etc. present along the chain length also increases the intermolecular forces as in nylons, teflon, polyester etc.

Strength of straight chain polymers also depends on the slipping power of one molecule over the other. Resistance to slip, in turn, depends upon the shape of the polymer. Relation between shape, slipping power and thus strength of the molecule can beautifully be illustrated by the examples of polyethene, polyvinyl chloride and polystyrene.

(*i*) Shape of polyethylene molecule is very simple and uniform and hence there is only limited or restricted movement of one molecule over another (Fig. 5.2).

(*ii*) Since, polyvinyl chloride molecule has large lumps of chlorine atoms periodically along its chain, the movement between molecules is greatly restricted. Moreover, chlorine atom causes stronger vander Waals attractive forces.

(*iii*) In polystyrene, presence of bulky phenyl group further restricts the movement of molecules over each other.

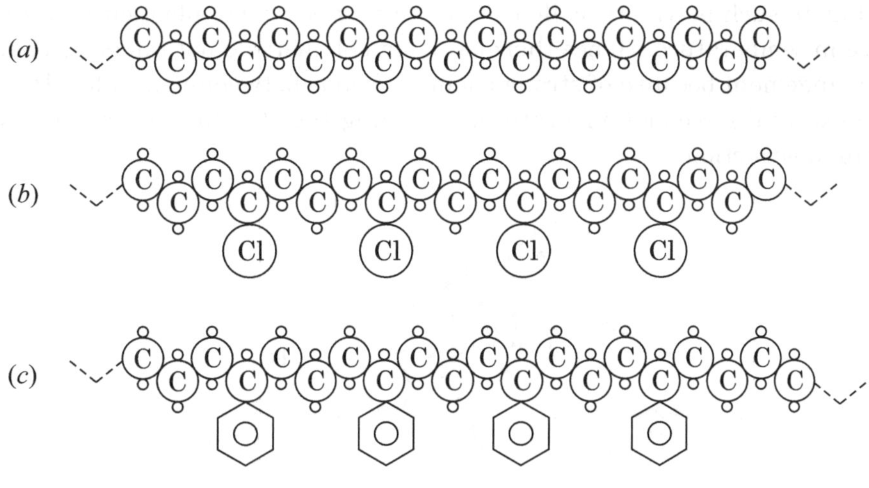

Fig. 5.2. Schematic representation of (a) polyethylene, (b) polyvinyl chloride and (c) polystyrene molecules.

The complexity of shape from polyethylene to polystyrene explains the increasing toughness and strength of the three types of polymers.

On the same pattern we can also explain that cross-linked polymers are the most strong and tough because in these molecules, the movement of intermolecular chains is totally restricted as the structural units are connected by strong covalent forces, resulting is a giant solid molecule, extending in three dimensions.

5.3.2 Plastic Deformation

Structure of thermoplastics (which soften on heating) is deformed when the former is subjected to heat, pressure or both. This property of thermoplastics has been used to prepare articles of the desired shape.

When sufficient load is applied on a thermoplastic which is simple in structure (e.g. polyethylene), weaker secondary intermolecular forces present between adjacent molecules are destroyed causing slippage of the layers leading to permanent deformation of the molecule. (Fig. 5.3) Thus thermoplastic polymers in heated state readily take the shape of the mould. On cooling, the material becomes rigid because plasticity of the material decreases with decrease in temperature.

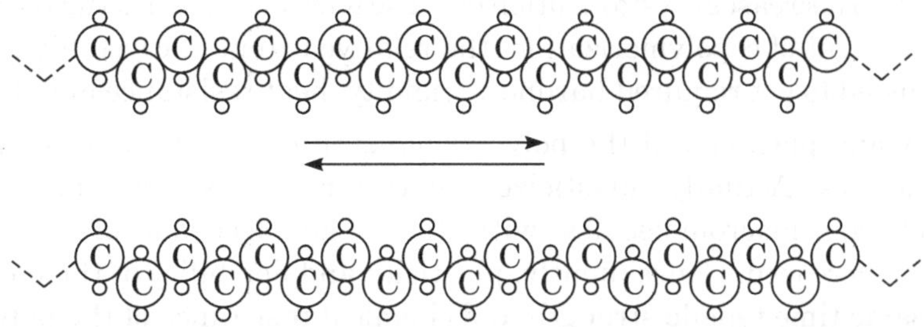

Fig. 5.3. Schematic representation of the slippage between linearly aligned polymer molecules.

However, in case of giant cross-linked polymers, since only primary strong covalent bonds are present throughout the entire structure, no slippage occurs between adjacent molecules

(Fig. 5.4). Thus in such polymers, called *thermosetting polymers*, plasticity does not increase with increase in temperature. Hence thermosetting polymers do not under-go change in their molecular arrangement because of strong chemical bonds between molecules. However, when considerable external force or temperature, exceeding the stability of material is applied, it results in total destruction.

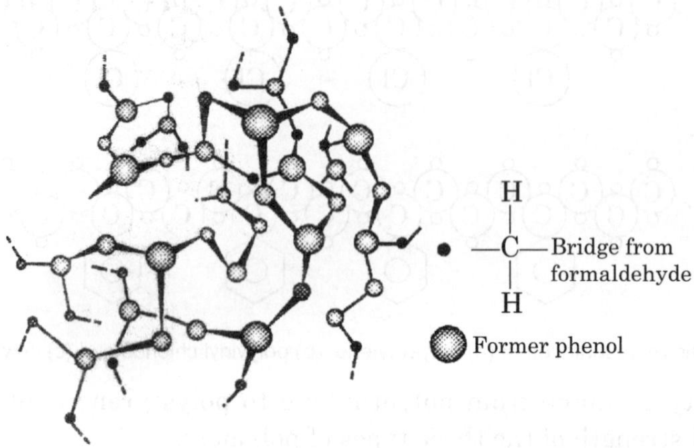

Fig 5.4. Giant three-dimensional framework of thermosetting resin.

5.3.3 Physical State of Polymers

Relative arrangement of the polymers with respect to each other may result in *amorphous* or *crystalline state of polymer.* Arrangement of molecules in a highly ordered manner leads to crystalline region (*crystallinity*), while random arrangement of polymer chains leads to amorphous region. *Polymers with a long repeating unit or with a low degree* of symmetry do not crystallise easily and therefore they generally from *amorphous structures, e.g.* polystyrene, polyvinyl acetate and polymethyl methacrylate.

Crystallization imparts a denser packing of molecules, thereby increasing the intermolecular forces of attraction. This accounts for a higher and sharper softening point, greater rigidity and strength and greater density. A completely crystalline polymer tends to acquire brittleness.

In actual practice, many polymers consist of crystallites embedded in an amorphous matrix. In such polymers, the crystallites provide required hardness, rigidity and heat resistance, while the amorphous matrix areas provide flexibility.

Copolymerization decreases crystallization because it lowers the structural symmetry. Hence, by controlling the extent of copolymerization, the relative extent of crystallites and amorphous region can be adjusted to get required hardness, rigidity, heat resistance and flexibility.

The flexibility and plasticity of the polymer (crystalline or amorphous) can be increased by adding plasticizers. Actually, plasticizers partly neutralise the intermolecular forces of attraction between macromolecules with the result freedom of movement between macromolecules is increased. Consequently, plasticity and flexibility of the polymer increases, although at the same time tensile strength and chemical resistance of the polymer decreases.

5.3.4 Elastic Character

When a stress is applied to a polymer, its shape is deformed; *the recoverance of the original shape on releasing the stress is a measure of the elastic character of the polymer.* Elastomers or rubber like polymers have the greatest elasticity. The elastic deformation in elastomers is due to the fact that elastomer consists of very long chain of molecules having free rotating groups. In the normal unstressed state, these groups have a peculiar configuration of irregularly coiled and entangles *snaris* (Fig. 5.5). Under normal conditions, these snaris are in a random arrangement leading to amorphous state of the polymer. However, on stretching, the snaris start disentangling and thus chains become oriented. Chain orientation causes crystallization which in turn enhances the attractive forces between different chains, thereby producing stiffness. However, when the strain is release, the stretched snaris return to their original arrangement.

(a) Snaris in normal outstretched condition. (b) Snaris oriented in chains in stretched condition

Fig. 5.5.

5.3.5 Chemical Reactivity and Solubility

The chemical reactivity of a polymer depends upon the chemical nature of monomeric units and their molecular configuration. Generally, chemical attack is internal and causes swelling, softening and loss in strength of the polymeric substance.

According to the general law like dissolves like, a polymer is more soluble in structurally similar solvents, thus polymers containing polar groups (—OH, —COOH etc.) undergo swelling or even dissolve in water, alcohol and ketones (all polar solvents) but they are almost chemically inert to benzene, toluene, carbon tetrachloride (all non-polar solvents). On the other hand, polymers having non-polar groups like $—CH_3$ $—C_6H_5$ etc. undergo swelling or even dissolve in benzene, toluene, carbon tetrachloride but they are chemically resistance to polar solvents like water, alcohol etc. Further polymers of more aliphatic character are more soluble in aliphatic water, alcohol etc. Further, polymers of more aliphatic character are more soluble in aliphatic solvents, while those of aromatic character are more soluble in aromatic solvents. In general,

(*i*) The solubility of polymers in a particular solvent decreases with increase in molecular weight of the polymer.

(*ii*) Crystalline polymers show higher chemical resistance than the less crystalline polymers of similar chemical character.

(*iii*) Greater the degree of cross linking in the polymer, lesser is its solubility.

5.3.6 Glass Transition Temperature (T_g)

The temperature below which an amorphous polymer becomes hard, brittle and glassy and above which it is softer and flexible is known as **glass transition temperature** (T_g). The hard and the brittle state is called the **glassy state** as the random arrangement of polymeric chains is similar to one found in glass. On the other hand, the soft and the flexible state is called the rubbery or viscolastic state. On further heating, the polymer (if it is not cross-linked) becomes highly viscous and starts flowing and this state is called viscofluid state and the temperature at which this transition occurs is called as **flow temperature** (T_f)

Glassy state	Rubbery or viscoelastic state	Viscofluid state
Brittle plastics	Tough plastics and rubber	Polymer melts
T_g	T_f	

Glass temperature can be calculated by using **Flory-Fox equation:**

$$T_g = T_g^{\alpha} - \frac{K}{M_n}$$

where T_g^{α} is the maximum glass transition temperature that can be achieved at a theoretical infinite molecular weight and K is an empirical parameter that is related to the free volume present in the polymer sample.

Glass transition temperature is the property of amorphous polymers (PMMA, PVC etc.) due to their disordered or random arrangement of molecules. At T_g, they take the glassy state properties like brittleness, stiffness and rigidity. They have a lower T_g, than semi-crystalline polymers. This is because the polymeric chains of amorphous polymers are physically entangled and have spaces between them or at the chain ends. This space is known as **free volume** which helps polymer chains to move at low temperatures. Higher the **free volume**, lower is the glass transition temperature.

On the other hand, crystalline polymers have highly ordered molecular structure. They do not soften on increase in temperature but rather have a defined and narrow melting point (T_m). This melting point is generally above the upper range of amorphous polymers.

Semi-crystalline polymers have a combination of random and ordered structures. These ordered structures are crystals that restrict the movement of polymer chains resulting in higher T_g.

Factors affecting glass transition temperature (T_g)

1. **Chain flexibility and rigidity:** Stiffening groups in the polymer chain reduce the flexibility of the chain and increase the value of glass transition temperature (T_g). In other words, we can say that the greater the *intrinsic chain flexibility*, the smaller will be the value of glass transition temperature.
2. **Intermolecular Forces:** Stronger intermolecular forces due to dipole forces, H-bonding, etc. decreases the mobility of the chain which increases the value of T_g. For example. *T_g of PVC is greater than T_g of polypropylene* because PVC has stronger intermolecular forces than polypropylene because of the dipole-dipole forces from the C—Cl bond.
3. **Molecular weight:** Glass transition temperature is directly proportional to the molecular weight of the polymer *i.e.* when the molecular weight of the polymer increases, T_g also increases.
4. **Cross-linking:** The greater the degree of cross-linking, the higher will be the T_g because the presence of cross-links between chains restricts rotational motion.
5. **Plasticizers:** Plasticizers are low molecular weight compounds that are added to plastics to increase their flexibility and workability. This weakens the intermolecular forces between the polymer chains and increases the mobility thus *decreasing* the glass transition temperature.

6. **Copolymerization:** Random copolymers have lower T_g since it tends to promote the disorder, reduce molecular packing, the inter-chain forces of attraction.
7. **Polar groups:** The presence of polar groups increases intermolecular forces, interchain attraction and cohesion. This leads to a decrease in free volume resulting in an increase in T_g.

Significance of glass transition temperature (T_g)

1. Glass transition temperature is used as measure for evaluating the *flexibility of a polymer* and the type of response the polymeric material would exhibit to mechanical stress.
2. Glass transition temperature tells us that, above it, a polymer will be soft and flexible and exhibit viscoelasticity (delayed elastic response) and below it, a polymer will be hard and brittle and will possess dimension stability.
3. The glass transition temperature value alongwith the T_m value indicates the temperature region at which a polymeric material transforms from a rigid state to a soft viscous state. This helps in choosing the right processing temperature which is the temperature region in which the material can be converted into the finished products through different processing techniques molding, calendaring and extrusion.

5.4 RUBBER OR ELASTOMERS

Elastomer is a high polymer having elastic properties in excess of 300%. On stretching it elongates to 200% of its original dimensions and quickly returns to its original state after the stretching force is removed. It was first used by South American Indians who called it **caoutchouc**. Priestly discovered that it can be used to rub pencil marks and henceforth it was known as **rubber**. Rubber has been commonly used for over 1000 years, in earlier days it came entirely from natural sources; but now it is also prepared artificially in chemical plants. This is because we can't produce enough natural rubber to meet all our needs. Thus, elastomers can be naturally occuring polymers like natural rubber, gutta percha or they can be synthetically produced such as butyl rubber, neoprene rubber etc. Natural rubber is obtained as latex from a wide variety of plants like Hevea brasiliensis, guayule found in tropical and sub tropical countries. The plants would be "tapped", *i.e.*, an incision made into the bark of the tree and the sticky, milk coloured latex sap collected and refined into a usable rubber. Natural rubber is a polymer of isoprene (2-methyl buta-1, 3-diene). An isoprene rubber can have all *cis*(*z*-configration) or all trans configuration (*E*-configuration of polymer chains) about the double bond. Natural rubber obtained from rubber tree (Hevea brasiliensis) is *cis*-polyisoprene and has the following structure.

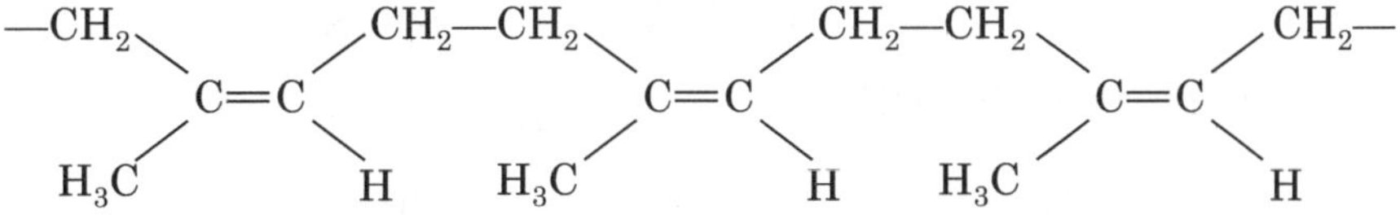

cis-polyisoprene

There is another variety of natural rubber called gutta percha which is obtained from the leaves of trees known as palaquium gutta and dichopsis gutta. This is all *trans* configuration and has the following structure.

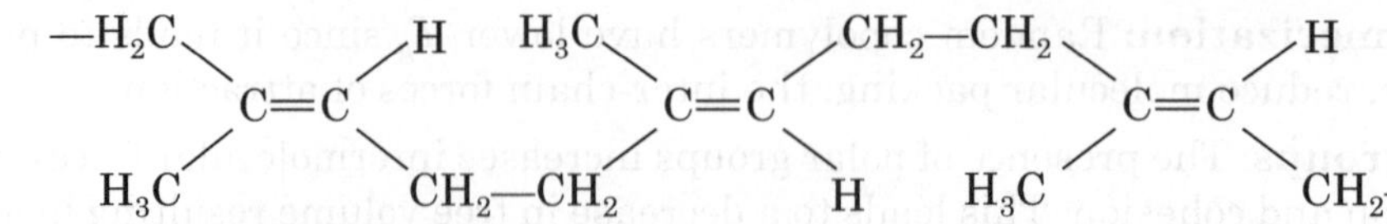

Trans-polyisoprene

Natural rubber is soft and elastic whereas gutta percha is tough and non-elastic.

5.4.1 Vulcanization of Rubber

Natural rubber has certain disadvantages because of which it cannot be used directly. The various disadvantages are:

1. It's elasticity is less and is plastic in nature which means that when stretched to a great extent it undergoes permanent deformation.
2. It has low tensile strength of the order of 200 kg/cm^2 and its load bearing capacity is low.
3. Natural rubber becomes soft and sticky in hot summer while in cold weather it becomes hard and brittle, therefore its usage temperature is very low *i.e.*, 10 – 60°C.
4. It is non-resistant to non-polar solvents therefore it is not recommended for use in alcohols, esters or among the aromatic solution.
5. It has high water absorption capacity therefore, it becomes weak.
6. It has poor resistance to attack by petroleum oils, ozone, UV-radiation etc.
7. It is highly unsaturated (*i.e.* presence of double bonds), therefore it can be easily attacked by chemicals-like HCl, H_2SO_4, HNO_3.
8. It exhibit the property of tackiness which means that under pressure, two fresh raw rubber surfaces coalesce together to form a single piece. Because of this tendency, we cannot carry it to different places as it can coalesce.

These undesirable properties of natural rubber were overcome by an American Scientist Charles Goodyear, who accidentally placed a sample of rubber mixed with sulphur and litharge (PbO) on a hot stove. The operation converted rubber into highly cross-linked insoluble and infusible, thermosetting polymer.

The properties of natural rubber can be modified and improved by the process of ***vulcanization***. For this, natural rubber is heated with certain chemicals like sulphur, hydrogen sulphide etc. at a temperature of 373 to 415K. The added sulphur combines chemically at the double bonds of different rubber chains and provides cross-linking between the chains. As a result, rubber gets stiffened and inter-molecular movement of rubber chains is prevented.

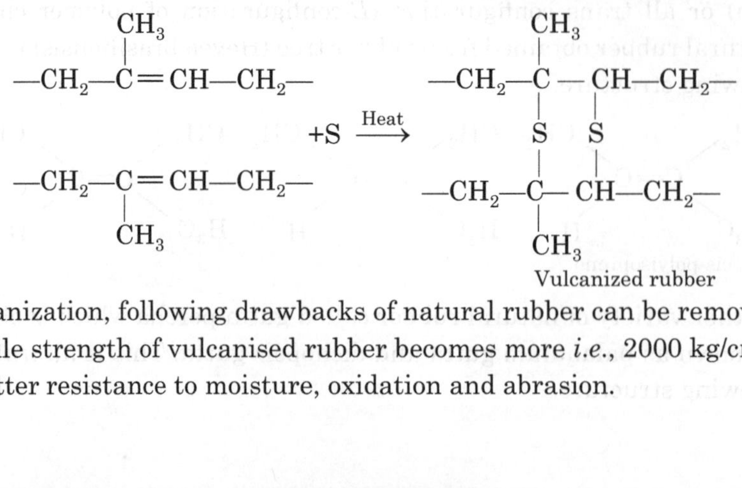

Vulcanized rubber

Due to vulcanization, following drawbacks of natural rubber can be removed.

1. The tensile strength of vulcanised rubber becomes more *i.e.*, 2000 kg/cm^2.
2. It has better resistance to moisture, oxidation and abrasion.

3. It has low water absorption capacity.
4. It's electrical insulation properties get enhanced.
5. It can be used over a wide range of temperatures *i.e.*, – 40°C to 100°C.
6. It has only little or slight tackiness.

As the demand for elastomers for a variety of applications increased therefore, new synthetic rubbers derived from polymers were developed.

5.5 SYNTHETIC RUBBER

Synthetic rubber is an artificial rubber which is capable of getting stretched to about twice of its length. However, it regains its original shape and size as soon as the external force is removed. Usually synthetic rubber is an improvement over natural rubber specially with respect to its resistance to oils, gas, solvent etc. Some common synthetic rubbers are neoprene, styrene-butadiene rubber, nitrile rubber, butyl rubber, thiokol etc.

5.5.1 Styrene-Butadiene Rubber (SBR) or Buna-S or GR-S

SBR is most widely used elastomer in the world. It is manufactured by the copolymerization of 1, 3-butadiene with styrene in the ratio of 3:1.

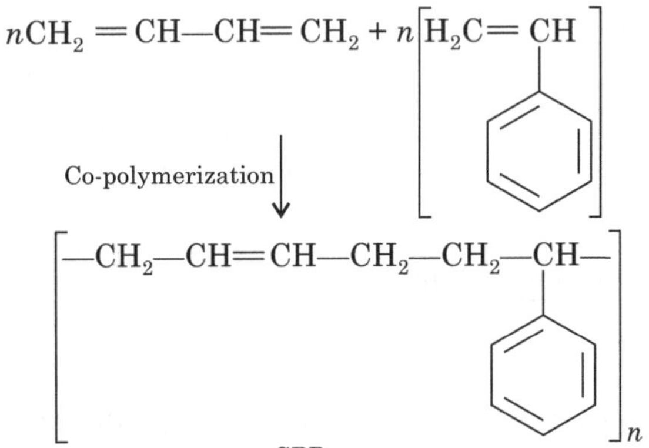

SBR

Under the American synthetic rubber research programme, all different types of synthetic rubbers got new fancy names, all of which start with GR (Government rubber),
Buna-S is known as GR-S (S for styrene)
Buna-N is known as GR-A (Acrylonitrile)
Butyl rubber-GR-I (I for Isobutylene) etc.

Properties:

1. It posseses high abrasion resistance, high load bearing capacity and good resilience.
2. They get readily oxidised especially in the presence of O_3 present in the atmosphere.
3. SBR swells in oils and solvents.
4. Since SBR contains double bond, vulcanisation can be done either by sulphur or sulphur monochloride.

Applications:

1. It is mainly used for making light duty tyres.
2. It is also used in floor tiles, gaskets, footwear components, shoe soles, carpet backing, tank lining, insulation of wire and cable etc.

5.5.2 Nitrile Rubber (Buna-N or GR-A)

Buna-N rubber is obtained by copolymerization of 1, 3-butadiene (75%) and acrylonitrile (25%) in presence of a peroxide catalyst.

$$nCH_2=CH-CH=CH_2 + nCH_2=\underset{\displaystyle CN}{\underset{|}{CH}} \xrightarrow[\text{peroxide, heat}]{\text{copolymerization}} \left(-CH_2-CH=CH-CH_2-\underset{\displaystyle CN}{\underset{|}{CH}}-CH_2-\right)_n$$

Properties:

1. It is resistant to action of petrol, lubricating oils and organic solvents.
2. It has excellent resistance to heat, sunlight, oils, acids and salts but is less resistant to alkalies than natural rubber.
3. It has low tensile strength.
4. It has less resilience than natural rubber.
5. It can be vulcanized with sulphur. Vulcanized nitrile rubber is more resistant to heat and ageing than natural rubber.

Applications:

Nitrile rubber find applications in

(*a*) Conveyer belts
(*b*) Hoses and tank linings
(*c*) Gaskets
(*d*) Printing rollers
(*e*) Oil seals
(*f*) High altitude aircraft components
(*g*) Automobile parts, etc.

*Nitrile rubber is unsuitable for making tyres.

5.5.3 Neoprene

(GR-M): (Government Rubber-Mono vinyl-acetylene). It is produced by the free radical addition polymerization of chloroprene (2-chloro 1, 3-butadiene). It is also called as polychloroprene.

$$\underset{\text{mono vinyl acetylene}}{CH_2=CH-C\equiv CH} \xrightarrow{HCl} \underset{\text{chloroprene}}{CH_2=\underset{\displaystyle Cl}{\underset{|}{C}}-CH=CH_2}$$

$$n[CH_2=\underset{\displaystyle Cl}{\underset{|}{C}}-CH=CH_2] \xrightarrow{\text{Polymerization}} \left[CH_2-\underset{\displaystyle Cl}{\underset{|}{C}}=CH-CH_2\right]_n$$

chloroprene → neoprene

Properties:

1. Neoprene can tolerate higher temperatures upto (200°F) as compared to natural rubber.
2. It is water, fire and thermal resistant.
3. It is resistant to oxidizing agents like O_2, O_3 etc.
4. It is resistant to vegetable and mineral oils.
5. It is soluble in polar solvents.
6. It can be vulcanized to a considerable extent by heat alone. Properly vulcanized neoprene rubber is extremely resistant to oxidative degradation.

Applications:

1. Chemical inertness, one of neoprene's key property, makes the polymer especially useful in industrial applications, including corrosion-resistant coatings and as a base for various adhesives.
2. It is used in power transformers and other electrical applications as it is fire resistant.
3. It is an effective source of padding and reinforcement for certain fragile applications.
4. It is also used in wet suits and diving suits.

5.5.4 Butyl Rubber (GR-I or IIR) IIR (Isobutylene Isoprene Rubber)

Butyl rubber is manufactured by copolymerization of isobutylene (97%) with small amounts of isoprene (around 3%). Isoprene is added to introduce the ethylene linkages for vulcanization.

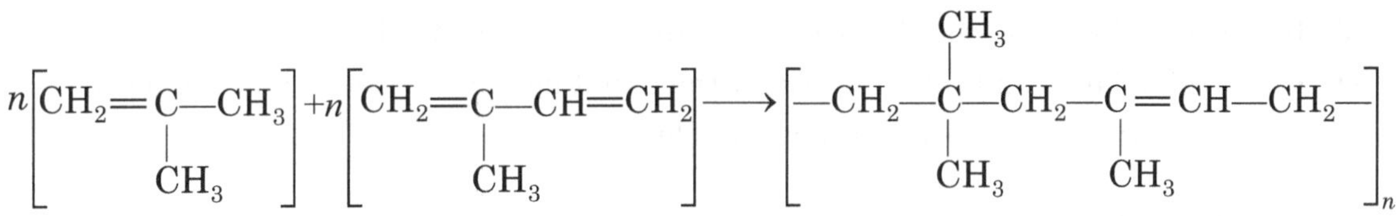

Isobutylene Isoprene Butyl rubber

Because of small percentage of isoprene, the percentage of double bonds (unsaturation) is very little in butyl rubber.

Properties:

1. It is resistant to oxidation, chemicals, heat, abrasion etc.
2. It has high tensile strength.
3. It is very impermeable to air and other gases.
4. As butyl rubber contains hydrocarbon chain, it is soluble in hydrocarbon solvents (like dissolves like) such as benzene, oils etc. but has excellent resistance to polar solvents.
5. It has excellent electrical insulating properties.
6. It can also be vulcanised, but cannot be hardened much due to low unsaturation.

Applications: Butyl rubber is used in making:

(*a*) Tubes and tyres of vehicles
(*b*) Hoses*
(*c*) Conveyer belts for food and other materials
(*d*) Tank linings
(*e*) Insulation of high voltage wires and cables etc.

*__Hoses-__ A flexible tube conveying water, used chiefly for watering plants and in fire fighting.

5.5.5 Thiokol (Polysulphide rubber) (GR-P)

Thikol is a condensation polymer which is obtained by the reaction between sodium tetrasulphide and ethylene dichloride

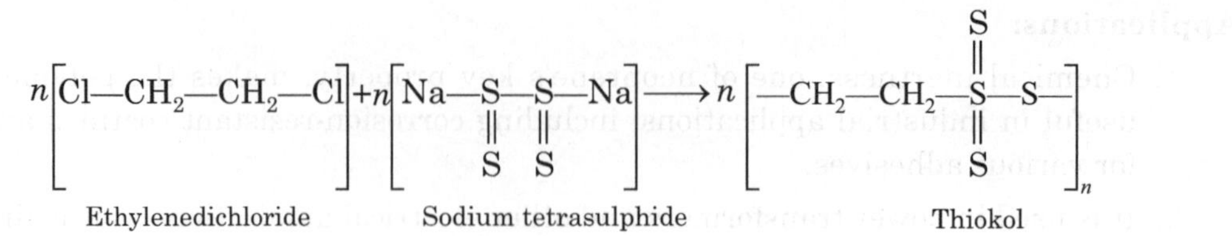

Properties:

1. It has good resistance to mineral oils, solvent and gases such as O_2 and O_3.
2. It has low gas permeability, therefore they are advantageous in balloon fabrics.
3. It has poor strength and poor abrasion resistance.

Applications:

1. Thiokol rubber is used in printing textile.
2. Thiokol mixed with oxidizing agents can be used as a fuel in rocket engines.
3. It is used in lining of vessels used in manufacture of chemicals.
4. It is used in hoses and tank linings for the handling and storage of oils and solvents.
5. It is used for coating fabrics for making life rafts, jackets.

5.6 SILICONES

Silicone polymers, also called **polysiloxanes** do not have carbon as part of the backbone structure. Although silicon belongs to the same group as carbon, but it has quite different chemistry. Many silanes are known which are analogous to hydrocarbons with Si—Si bonds. These compounds are not very useful as they are not stable. Silicones, on the other hand have Si—O—Si linkages *i.e.*, contains alternate Si and O atoms in which the Si atoms are joined to various organic groups like methyl, benzene ring etc. They have the general formula $(R_2SiO)_n$.

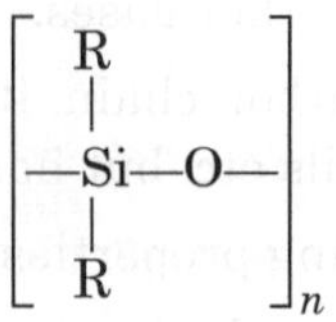

The simultaneous presence of organic groups attached to inorganic backbone gives silicones a combination of unique properties and allows their use in fields as different as aerospace, electronics, health care, construction etc.

Silicones can be divided into 4 classes:

1. Silicone oils or silicone fluids.
2. Silicone gels.
3. Silicone rubber.
4. Silicone resin.

5.6.1 Silicone Fluids

Silicone fluids are usually straight chains of polysiloxanes of 50–200 units having low molecular weight.

They have the repeating unit -

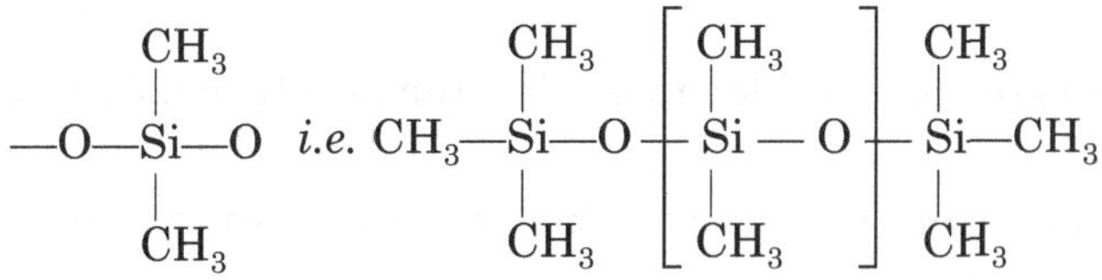

and they usually have $Si(CH_3)_3$ group at the end of each chain.

Properties:

1. Silicone oils are inert and non-toxic materials.
2. They have low surface tension.
3. They have anti-foaming properties.

Applications:

1. Used as lubricant in polishes, paints etc.
2. They can be used in cooking oils and processing of fruit juices as they are inert and non-toxic.
3. They are used as water repellents for treating masonry, buildings, glassware and fabrics.
4. Silicone oil can be used as anti-foaming and hydrophobizing in sewage disposal plants, textile dyeing, beer making and frothing of cooking oils.

5.6.2 Silicone Gels

Silicone gels are based on the polysiloxane chains but with a few cross links between the chains, giving it an open 3-dimensional network structure.

Pads containing silicone gels are used as shock absorbers in shoes, particularly in high performance trainers and running shoes. Silicone gel also acts as an electrical insulator.

5.6.3 Silicone Rubber (elastomer)

Silicone rubbers are made of long-chain polymers (dimethyl polysiloxanes) having 6000–600,000 silicone units, mixed with SiO_2 or graphite as a filler. The filler is added to make the elastomers stronger and hard.

- They have high molecular weight of the order or 10^5–10^7.
- Silicone rubbers can be vulcanised by organic peroxides at 120°–130°C to form cross links between two adjacent chains:

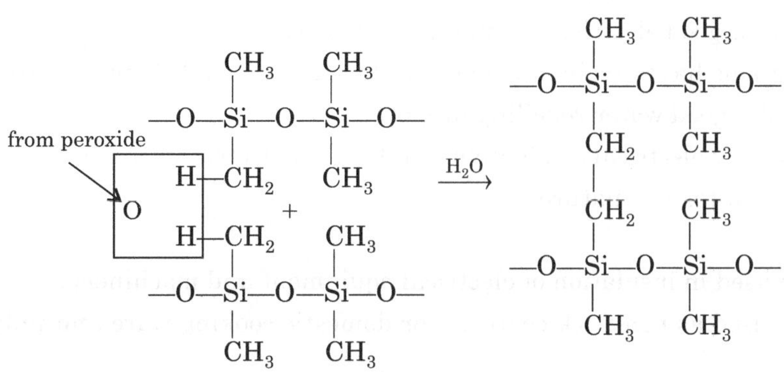

Properties:

1. Silicone rubbers are more stable at both low temperature (200 K) and high temperature (450–600 K).
2. They are generally more resistant to chemical attack than natural rubber.
3. They have high thermal stability.
4. They are abrasion resistant.

Applications:

1. Silicone rubbers are used for making boots at very low temperature since they are less affected by temperature variation.
2. They are used as a sealing material in search light and in aircraft engines.
3. Used for insulating electrical wiring in ships and washing machines.
4. Used as adhesives in electronic industry.
5. They are also used for making protective coatings for fabric finishing.

5.6.4 Silicone Resins

Silicone resins have a 3 dimensional structure with the atoms arranged tetrahedrally about the silicone atoms.

About 10% silicones produced are resins. Silicone resins are made by dissolving a mixture of phenyl substituted trichlorosilane, $PhSiCl_3$ and dichlorosilane, Ph_2SiCl_2 in toluene and hydrolysing with water. The partly polymerized product is washed with HCl and can then be shaped or moulded. Finally, the product is heated with a quaternary ammonium salt as catalyst to condense any remaining OH groups in the product. The product thus formed is extensively cross-linked and therefore, silicone resins are rigid polymers like bakelite.

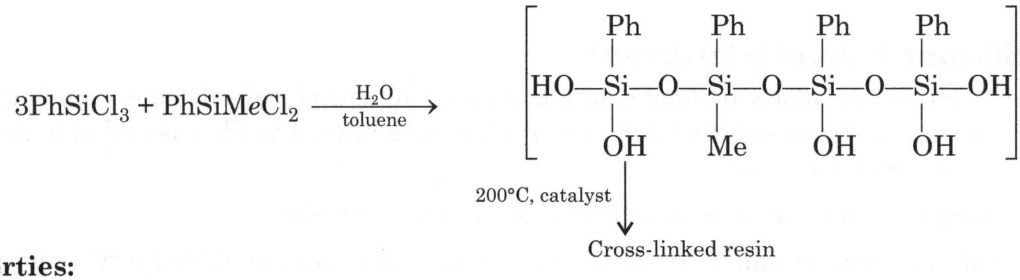

Properties:

1. They are thermosetting polymers.
2. They possess good electrical insulating properties.
3. Silicone resins have excellent oxidation, thermal, UV and chemical resistance.
4. They exhibit good water repelling property.
5. They have low electrical conductivity and high dielectric strength.
6. They are non-toxic in nature.

Applications:

1. They are used in insulation of electrical equipment and machinery.
2. They are used as non-stick coatings for domestic cooking ware and industrial car tyre moulds.

3. They are used in electronics as laminates for printed circuit boards and also used for the encapsulation of components such as resistors and integrated circuit by means of transfer moulding.
4. They are used as protective coatings for bridges and municipal water towers.
5. They are also used in formulation of pressure sensitive adhesives, release coatings etc.

5.7 INDIVIDUAL POLYMERS

5.7.1 Teflon (Fluon): (Polytetrafluorothylene)

It is an addition polymer of tetrafluorthylene ($F_2C{=}CF_2$). It is prepared by heating tetrafluoroethylene with a free radical or persulphate catalyst at high pressures.

$$nCF_2 = CF_2 \xrightarrow[\text{Heat}]{\text{Catalyst}} \underset{\text{Teflon}}{\left(CF_2 - CF_2 \right)_n}$$

Properties: Teflon has a twisted, zig-zag structure in which fluorine atoms are packed tightly in spiral manner around the carbon-carbon skeleton. Different polymer chains are held by strong attractive forces because of highly electronegative fluorine atoms in the chains. The presence of fluorine atoms gives unique properties to teflon. Teflon is called as **wonder plastic** because of a number of technologically important properties.

1. It is practically insoluble in all solvents.
2. It is having high resistance to corrosive chemicals, oxidising and reducing agents, strong mineral acids etc.
3. It is thermally stable and has a good electrical insulating property.
4. It has high melting point (above 350°C).
5. It does not absorb moisture or oil.
6. It has very low coefficient of friction.

Applications:

1. It is used for insulation of motors, generators, transformers, coils, capacitors, wires and cables.
2. Teflon is an ideal lubricant as it stays slippery over a wide range of temperatures (–40 to 300°C).
3. Oil and water do not wet teflon therefore it is used in coating non-stick cooking pans, bakery trays and other non-stick utensils.
4. Teflon is used for anticorrosive coating, a property which is widely used for army weapons.
5. Teflon is used for making stop cocks for burettes as it is resistant to chemicals.
6. It is also used for making variety of seals, gaskets, pump parts etc.

5.7.2 PMMA (Polymethyl methacrylate) (Plexiglass/lucite)

PMMA is manufactured by the polymerization of methyl methacrylate $CH_2{=}C\,(CH_3)\,COOCH_3$ in the presence of peroxides as initiators

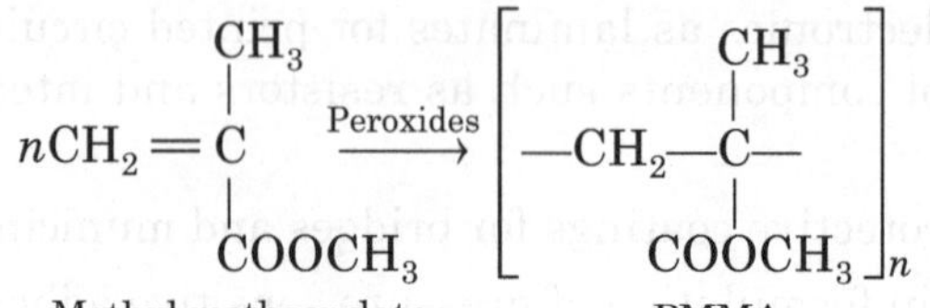

Methyl methacrylate PMMA

Properties:

1. PMMA is a colourless transparent thermoplastic, capable of transmitting 100% of sunlight including UV light without any loss of intensity.
2. It is an amorphous polymer because of presence of bulky side groups.
3. It has excellent chemical resistivity but soluble in many organic solvents.
4. It is very hard and is highly scratch resistant.
5. It exhibits low moisture and water absorbing capacity.
6. PMMA is a combustible material which continues burning even after the removal of flame.
7. It has high softening point of about 400 – 410°C but becomes a viscous mass at about 65°C and hence can be moulded into any desired shape.

Applications:

1. It used for making attractive signboards, instruments and appliances covers.
2. It is used for making windscreen in automobiles and aircraft.
3. It is an excellent substitute for glass.
4. It is used in healthcare and medical industry in making blood sample tubes, diagnostic dishes and toothbrushes.
5. Due to its good optical properties, it is extensively used in production of sunglasses, watch glasses and diffuser panels.
6. It is used in manufacturing of windows, port holes and domes for the buildings.

5.7.3 Polyethylene (PE)

It is the simplest homopolymer and a thermoplastic. It is formed by the addition polymerization of ethylene. It has the following structure.

$$\left[CH_2—CH_2 \right]_n$$

There are two varieties of polyethylene:

(*i*) Low density polyethylene (LDPE)

(*ii*) High density polyethylene (HDPE)

At present about 65% of the global production of polyethylene is LDPE and 35% HDPE.

(*i*) **Low density polyethylene (LDPE):** LDPE is manufactured by the free radical addition polymerization of ethylene at 250°C and high pressure of about 1000–3000 atm in presence of O_2 or any peroxide as catalyst.

$$CH_2{=}CH_2 \xrightarrow[\text{Peroxide}]{250°C\ 1000–3000\ \text{atm}} \left[CH_2—CH_2 \right]_n$$

Properties:

1. It is waxy solid and has linear structure with extensive branching. Due to branching, the molecules are not efficiently packed, therefore, their density is low.
2. It is chemically inert and tough.
3. It has low degree of crystallinity, low density and low melting point.
4. It has low tensile strength.
5. It swells when exposed to oils and organic solvents, such as C_6H_6, CCl_4 etc.
6. As it is non-polar, it has outstanding electrical insulating properties.

Applications: LDPE finds use in a wide variety of products such as:

1. Table cloth
2. Packaging materials in the form of films, sheets, bags, coated paper etc.
3. Squeeze bottles.
4. Pipes for water supply.
5. Wire and cable coating.

(*ii*) **High Density Polyethylene (HDPE):** HDPE is manufactured by the coordination polymerization of ethylene in a hydrocarbon solvent and an organometallic complex catalyst, **Ziegler Natta catalyst** [$TiCl_4$ + $(C_2H_5)_3Al$] at 50 – 70°C and a pressure of 2 – 6 atm.

$$\underset{\text{Ethylene}}{nCH_2{=}CH_2} \xrightarrow[50-70^\circ C]{TiCl_4 + Al(C_2H_5)_3} \underset{\text{HDPE}}{\left[\!-CH_2-CH_2-\!\right]_n}$$

Properties:

1. HDPE molecules are linear with practically no branching therefore, their density is high and also have high degree of crystallinity.
2. HDPE is more stiff, hard and possesses greater tensile strength as compared to LDPE.
3. It has excellent chemical resistance and also does not swell or dissolve in solvents.
4. It has higher melting point (140°C) as compared to LDPE (110°C).

Application: It is used in manufacturing of:

1. Bottle caps, crates
2. Food storage containers
3. Fuel tanks for vehicles
4. Domestic water and gas piping etc.

A comparative study of the properties and applications of LDPE and HDPE is given in the Table 5.3.

Table 5.3: Differences between LDPE and HDPE

LDPE	HDPE
1. It is produced by chain polymerization using peroxides as catalysts.	It is produced by coordination polymerization using Ziegler Natta catalyst.
2. It has linear structure with extensive branching.	It is a linear polymer with practically no branching.

3. It has low melting point (110°C).	It has high melting point (140°C).
4. It has low density (0.912 – 0.925) g/cm^3.	It has high density (0.95 – 0.97) g/cm^3.
5. It has low chemical resistance.	It has high chemical resistance.
6. It has low degree of crystallinity (40%).	It has high degree of crystallinity (90%).

5.7.4 PVC (Polyvinyl chloride)

Polyvinyl chloride is a thermoplastic polymer. It is prepared by the polymerization of vinyl chloride ($CH_2 = CHCl$). It is extensively used polymer especially for electrical insulation. It is of two types:

1. Rigid PVC
2. Plasticized PVC

1. **Rigid PVC:** In this process, a mixture of vinyl chloride (say 1 part), water (1 part), small amount of catalyst (like persulphate) and an emulsifier (like sodium lauryl sulphate) is vigorously stirred and then introduced into an autoclave at temperature 40–45°C. The polymerization is completed in about 72 hours. The polymer is recovered by spray drying or coagulation by an acid. The polymer can be moulded according to the desired properties with the help of plasticizers, pigments, stabilizers, fillers and lubricants.

$$\underset{\text{Vinyl chloride}}{nCH_2 = CHCl} \xrightarrow{\text{polymerization}} \underset{\text{PVC}}{\left(-CH_2-\underset{\underset{Cl}{|}}{CH}- \right)_n}$$

Properties:

(*i*) Rigid PVC is an unmodified polymer and exhibits high rigidity.

(*ii*) It is colourless, odourless and non-inflammable.

(*iii*) It is chemically inert and not attacked by dilute acids and alkalis, petrol, oils, fats, greases and salt solutions.

(*iv*) It is not resistant to aromatic and chlorinated hydrocarbons ($CHCl_3$, CCl_4) strong alkalis, nitric acid etc.

Applications:

(*i*) Rigid PVC is used in applications such as:

  (*a*) Door and window frames.

  (*b*) Pipe fittings and conduit.

  (*c*) Credit cards.

  (*d*) Building panels and sidings.

(*ii*) It is widely used in chemical processing, electroplating, chemical drainage and various water handling and distribution systems.

(*iii*) It is widely used in packaging market for fruit juices and beverages as well as bathroom toiletry.

2. **Plasticized PVC:** It is generally prepared by adding plasticizers such as dibutyl phthalate, dioctyl phthalate, diisodecyl phthalate (DIDP), diisononyl phthalate (DINP), tricresyl phosphate etc. to rigid PVC.

Properties:

1. It is tough and even rubbery at high plasticizer content.

   Plasticizer: It is a substance which when added to a material (usually a plastic) makes it flexible, resilient and easier to handle.

2. It is very good insulator for direct current and low frequency AC current.
3. Plasticized PVC is flexible and water proof.

Applications:

1. The largest application of plasticized PVC are cable and wire insulation.
2. Plasticized PVC is used for making leather clothes which find application in upholstery and trim in car application, houses furnishings (*e.g.* kitchen upholstery, printed sheets, bathroom curtains.)
3. It is used for making plastic rain wear, beach wear shoes etc.

5.7.5 PVA (Poly vinyl acetate)

PVA is prepared by heating vinyl acetate in the presence of small amount of benzoyl peroxide as catalyst.

$$\underset{\text{Vinyl acetate}}{nCH_2{=}CH{-}COOCH_3} \longrightarrow \underset{\text{PVA}}{\left(-CH_2-\underset{\displaystyle COOCH_3}{\underset{|}{CH}}- \right)_n}$$

Properties:

1. PVA is colourless and transparent polymer.
2. PVA is a soft and sticky polymer.
3. It is resistant to atmospheric oxygen, water and chemicals.
4. PVA is an amorphous polymer and has low glass transition temperature. Hence, under the influence of compressive and tensile forces, products made of PVA are distorted even at room temperature.
5. It is soluble in organic acids as well as organic solvents.

Applications:

1. It is used for large scale manufacture of gramophone records.
2. It is used for making chewing gums, surgical dressings, plastic coatings, emulsions etc.
3. PVA emulsions are used as adhesives which are used for bonding of textile to textile, paper to paper, paper to textile, leather to leather, metal to metal etc.

5.7.6 Nylon

Nylon is a generic name for synthetic polyamides, which are characterized by a repeating amide linkage $(NHCO)$. Nylons are described by a unique numbering system indicating the number of carbon atoms in the repeating unit.

5.7.7 Nylon-6

Nylon 6 or **polycaprolactum** is a semi-crystalline polyamide. Unlike most other nylons, it is not a condensation polymer but instead formed by ring opening polymerization. It has the monomer caprolactam, which is obtained from cyclohexane as follows:

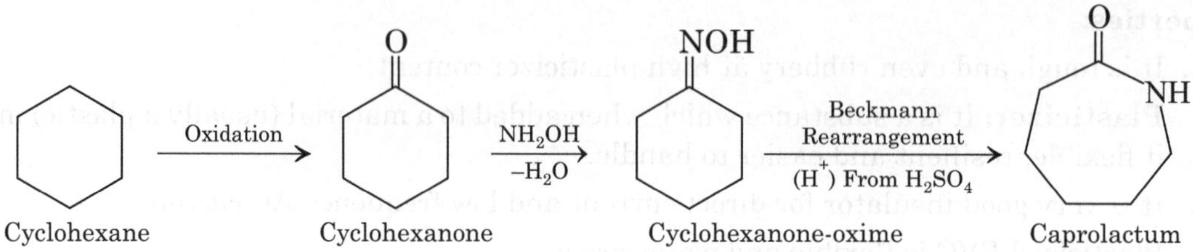

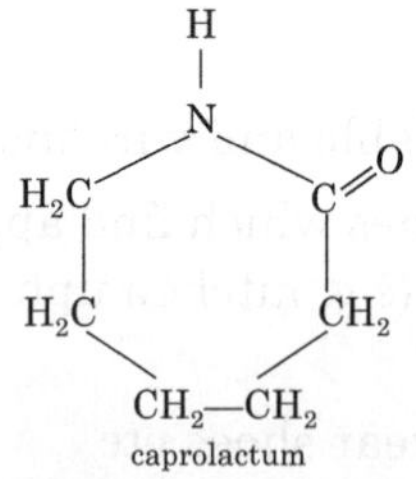

Carolactum is a seven-membered ring having 6-C-atom

Caprolactum, on heating with traces of water undergoes ring opening and form ε-amino caproic acid, which polymerises to form nylon-6.

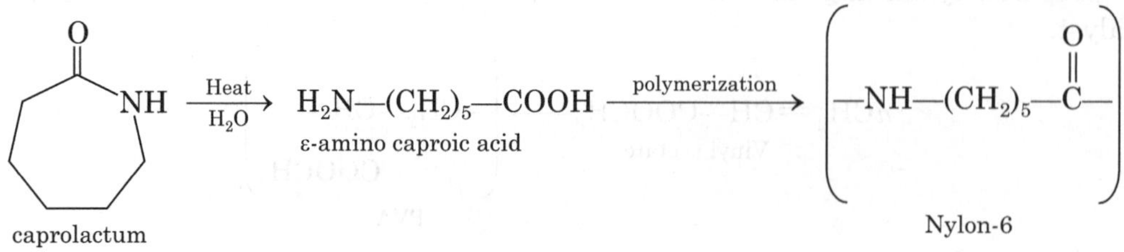

Properties:

1. It is a crystalline polymer which softens around 210°C.
2. It is soluble in mineral acids and organic solvents.
3. It has good abrasion and chemical resistance.
4. It has high tensile strength, elasticity and toughness but lower than nylon-66.

Applications: It is used in manufacturing of:

1. Automobile tyre cords
2. Non-woven fabrics.
3. Ropes, belts, carpets, industrial fabrics.
4. It is also used for moulding purposes for gears, bearings, electrical mountings etc. Nylon gears and bearings work quickly without any lubrication.

5.7.8 Nylon-66

It is the polymer which was developed by Carothers at DuPont's research unit Nylon 66 is manufactured by the condensation polymerization of adipic acid ($HOOC—(CH_2)_4—COOH$) and hexamethylene diamine ($H_2N—(CH_2)_6—NH_2$), both having 6 carbon atoms in their chain.

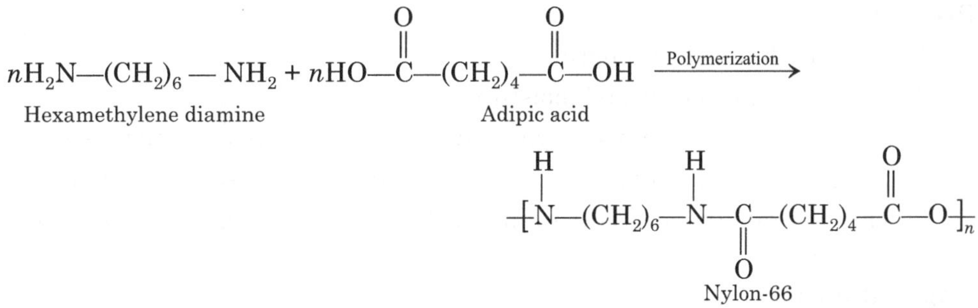

Properties:

1. In nylons, polymer chains are held together by H-bonds, therefore, they have high-tensile strength, elasticity, toughness and melting point.
2. It has good resistance to acids and alkalies except hot mineral acids and alkalies under extreme conditions.
3. It is mostly insoluble in all organic solvents except some phenolic solvents.

Applications:

1. It is used in mechanical engineering and other applications like drive gears, bearings, bushes, fish plates for railways line tubing.
2. It is used in making bristles for brushes.
3. It is used in textiles. It is blended with wool to make socks and sweaters.
4. It is a light material therefore, suitable to be used for parachutes.
5. It is resistant to water or it is waterproof so used to make swim wears.

5.8 POLYESTERS

Polyesters are the polymers having ester linkages of $-\!(\overset{O}{\overset{\|}{C}}-O)\!-$. They are formed by the condensation polymerization of dihydroxy alcohols (*e.g.* ethylene glycol) and dibasic acids (*e.g.* phthalic acid, terephthalic acid). The important members of this class are terylene and glyptal resins.

5.8.1 Terylene/Dacron

Terylene is synthesized by the condensation of ethylene glycol with terephthalic acid or its ester dimethyl terephthalate in presence of Sb_2O_3 as catalyst.

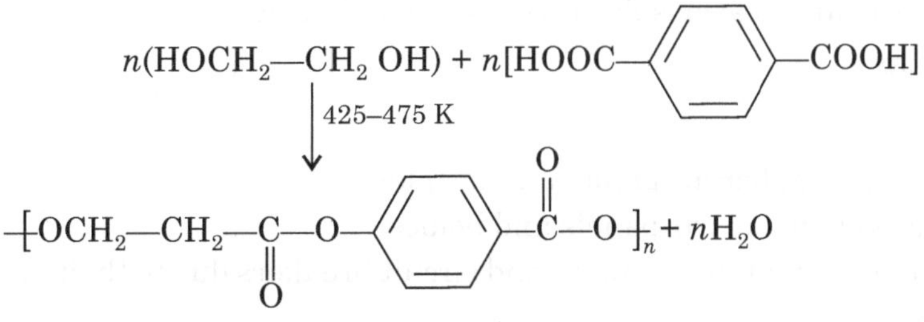

Poly (ethylene terephthalate)
or PET or Terylene

Properties:

1. It has high tensile strength.
2. It is resistant to heat and moisture and melts around 265°C.
3. It is a good fibre forming polymer due to the presence of numerous polar groups.
4. Terylene fibres are highly stretch resistant, high crease and wrinkle resistant.
5. They are highly resistant to mineral and organic acids but are readily attacked by alkalies.

Applications:

1. It is extensively used for making textile fibres.
2. Garments made from terylene fibres are wrinkle resistant, have low moisture absorption property and are not attacked by insects.
3. Glass reinforced polymer is used in safety helmets, aircrafts, battery boxes, toasters etc.
4. PET is also used in the manufacturing of bottles and containers.
5. It is also made into films which are used in manufacturing of magnetic recording tapes, transparencies for overhead projectors.

5.8.2 Glyptal

Glyptal is a general name of all polymers obtained by condensation of di-basic acids and polyhydroxy alcohols. The simplest glyptal is obtained by a condensation polymerization between ethylene glycol and o-phthalic acid and is called as **polyethlene glycol phthalate.**

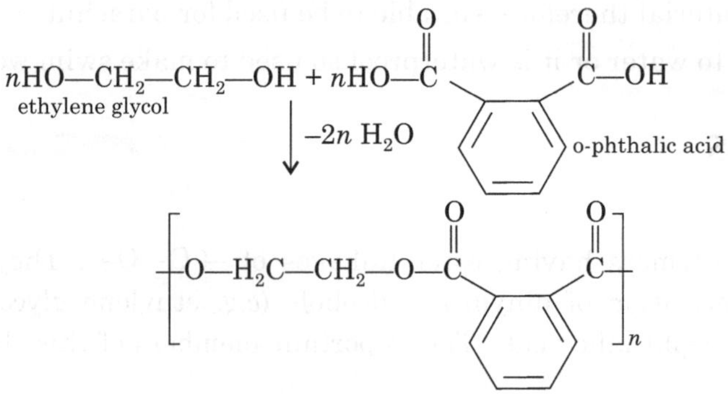

Glyptals can also be prepared by reaction between phthalic acid and glycerol.

Properties:

1. Glyptals are 3-dimensional cross-linked polymers.
2. They are resistant to atmospheric corrosion and acids.
3. They are hard.

Applications:

1. They are used in adherent paints and lacquers.
2. They are used to make car panels and bodies.
3. They are used for making switches and circuit breakers due to their electrical insulating properties.
4. They are also used as a binding materials for cements, asbestos etc.

5.9 BAKELITE (PHENOL-FORMALDEHYDE RESIN)

- Bakelite is a phenol-formaldehyde resin prepared by condensing phenol with formaldehyde in presence of either an acid or a base.
- The reaction actually involves the initial formation of ortho and/ or para-hydroxy methyl phenol derivatives.

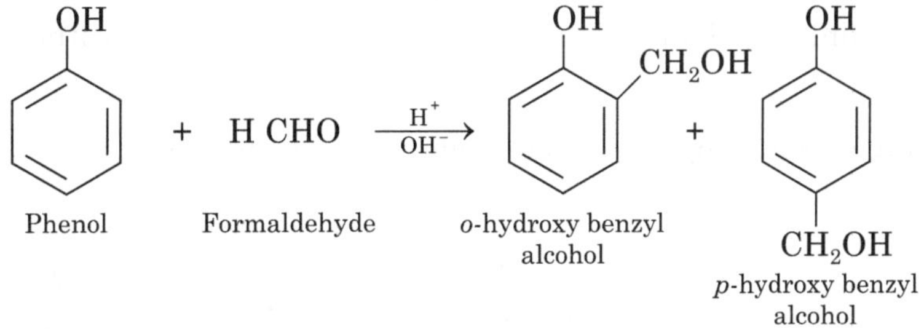

- These *o*- and *p*-isomers react further with phenol to form compounds having methlene (—CH_2) bridges either at *o* or *p*-position or both at *o* & *p*– positions w.r.t. phenolic group. The initial product is linear and called **novolac**.

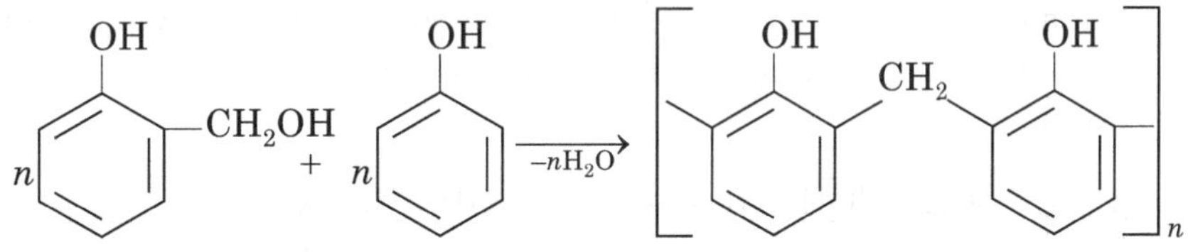

novolac

- Novolac on further heating with excess of formaldehyde, paraformaldehyde or hexamethylenetetramine undergoes cross-linking to form a 3-dimensional polymer.

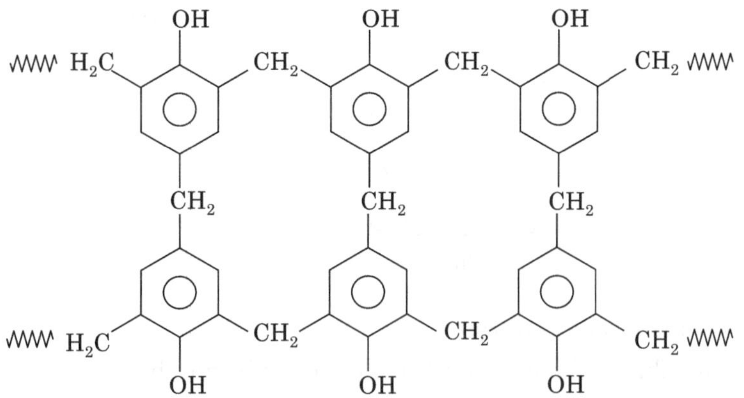

Bakelite

Properties:

1. It is hard, rigid and scratch resistant.
2. It is insoluble in water and many organic solvents due to its cross-linked structure.
3. It has good resistance to acids and oxidizing agents but readily attacked by strong alkalies due to the presence of phenolic groups.
4. It possess excellent electrical insulating character.

Applications:

1. Bakelite is used in making plugs, switches, handle of utensils, washing machine agitators, fountain pens, phonograph records.

2. It is used in paints, varnishes and protective coatings.
3. It is used for the production of ion exchange resins for softening of water.
4. It is used as adhesive for grinding wheels and brake linings.

5.10 UREA-FORMALDEHYDE RESIN (UF RESIN)

UF resin is a cross-linked polymer of urea and formaldehyde. It's synthesis takes place in 2 stages:

In the first stage, urea is hydroxy methylolated by the addition of formaldehyde to form mono and di methylolurea.

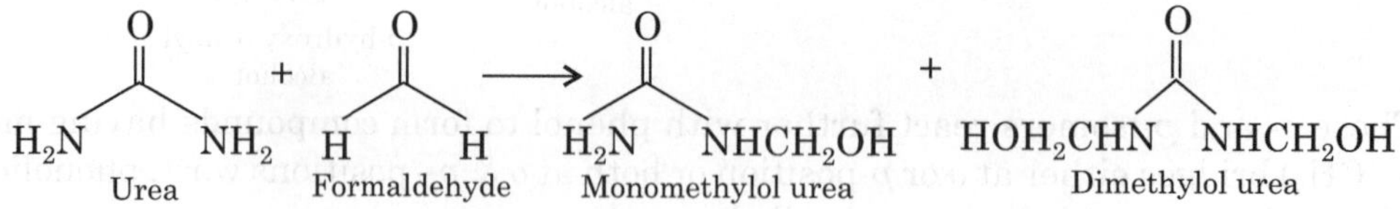

In the second stage, methylol ureas are compounded with plasticizers, fillers, pigments, catalysts etc. and then cured by applying heat and pressure. During curing, 3-dimensional network of UF resin is formed.

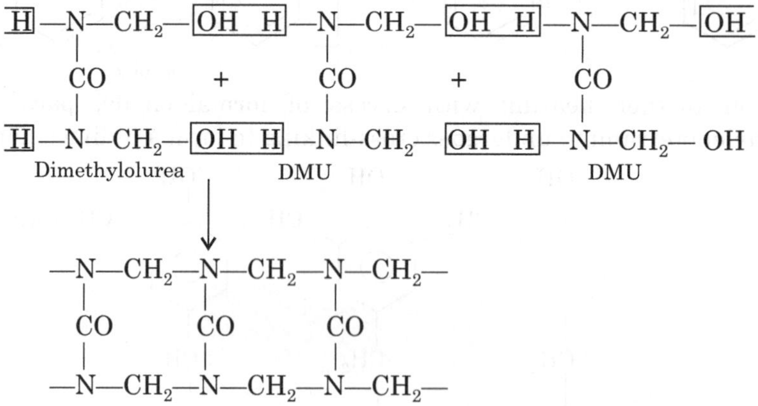

UF Resin

Properties:

1. UF resin is transparent material.
2. It is hard, infusible and has better tensile strength than bakelite.
3. It has good electrical insulation properties.
4. It has good chemical and abrasion resistance.
5. It has high heat-distortion temperature and low water absorption capacity.
6. It has high surface hardness.

Applications:

1. UF resins are used in kitchen appliances like stove hardware, enamels for refrigerator etc.
2. They are used for the preparation of lacquers.
3. They are used for making coloured toilet seats.

4. They are used for the finishing of cotton textiles. (They impart stiffness, crease resistance, water repellancy, fire retardation to the fabric).
5. UF resins are also used as adhesives for plywood and furniture.
6. UF resins are used for making vacuum flask cups arid jugs.
7. They are used in moulded plastic industries.

5.11 BIOPOLYMERS

Biopolymers are polymeric materials produced from renewable resource such as plants, animals and micro-organisms. The monomeric units of these biopolymers are joined via covalent bonding to form large structures. Some examples of biopolymers are DNA, RNA, fatty acids, gelatin, keratin, cellulose, starch etc.

The biopolymers are found to be biocompatible and biodegradable, making then useful in different applications such as edible films, emulsions, packaging materials in the food industry and as drug transport materials, medical implants like medical implant organs, wound healing tissue scaffolds and dressing materials in pharmaceutical industries.

5.11.1 Classification

Biopolymers can be classified differently based on their origin, the repeating unit and their degradability Fig. 5.6 shows all these classes.

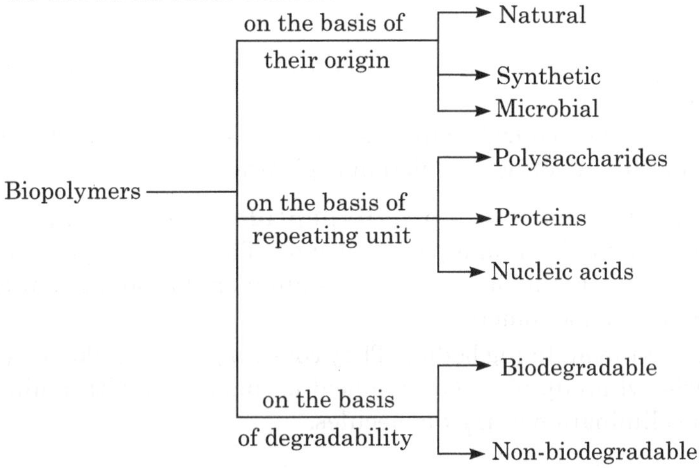

Fig 5.6 Classification of Biopolymers

Based on their origin, biopolymers can be classified into natural, synthetic and microbial.

(*i*) **Natural biopolymers:** These are the biopolymers that are naturally produced by living organisms. For example, proteins (like collagen, fibrinogen), polysaccharide (like cellulose, chitin, starch) etc.

(*ii*) **Synthetic biopolymers:** These are man-made biopolymers not naturally synthesized and are produced from renewable sources.
For example, polylactic and PCL, PVA etc.

(*iii*) **Microbial biopolymers:** Different micro-organisms synthesize these biopolymers including molds, yeast and bacteria. For example xanthan, welan, succinoglucan, chitosan, EPS (extracellular polymeric substance), PHA's (polyhydroxy alkanoates), EPS are high molecular weight substances composed of mainly polysaccharides and proteins and their biosynthesis takes place inside the microbe using different precursor molecules.

Based on the repeating unit (monomer), biopolymers can be classified into polysaccharides, proteins and nucleic acids

(*i*) **Polysaccharides:** These are the most abundant natural biopolymer. The monosaccharides (building blocks) and the glycosidic linkages forms the backbone of these polymers and determine the diversity and complexity of the polysaccharides.

For example, cellulose, starch, glycogen, chitin etc.

Starch is the main storage polysaccharide of plants. Its main sources are wheat, rice maize, potato etc.

Cellulose is a major polysaccharide in higher plants, where it constitutes the cell walls. It is the most abundant carbohydrate which serves as structural material in living organisms.

Functions:

1. Cellulose and chitin are structural polyaccharides *i.e.*, cellulose makes the cell wall of plants and chitin is present in the shells of crustaceans like crabs, lobsters etc.
2. Starch and glycogen are storage polysaccharides. Glycogens is the energy stored in animals, whereas starch is the energy stored in plants.
3. Polysaccharides are used in food industry for functions such as thickners and protective coating.
4. In industries, polysaccharides are used in cosmetics, textiles, medicines, paper, breweries etc.
5. Ribose (a monosaccharide) is an essential component of ATP which acts as an energy currency of the cell.
6. Agar is a heteropolysaccharide which is gelatinous in nature and chiefly used as a solid substrate to culture medium for microbiological work.

(*ii*) **Proteins:** Proteins, also called as **polypeptides**, are complex copolymers of amino acids covalently linked through peptide bonds. They are composed of upto 20 different amino acids. There are virtually a limitless number of proteins that can be formed from these 20 amino acid monomers.

Proteins are present in all living bodies. They contain peptide linkage -(CO—NH)- which is formed when carboxyl group of one amino acid is condensed with amino group of another amino acid with the elimination of H_2O molecules.

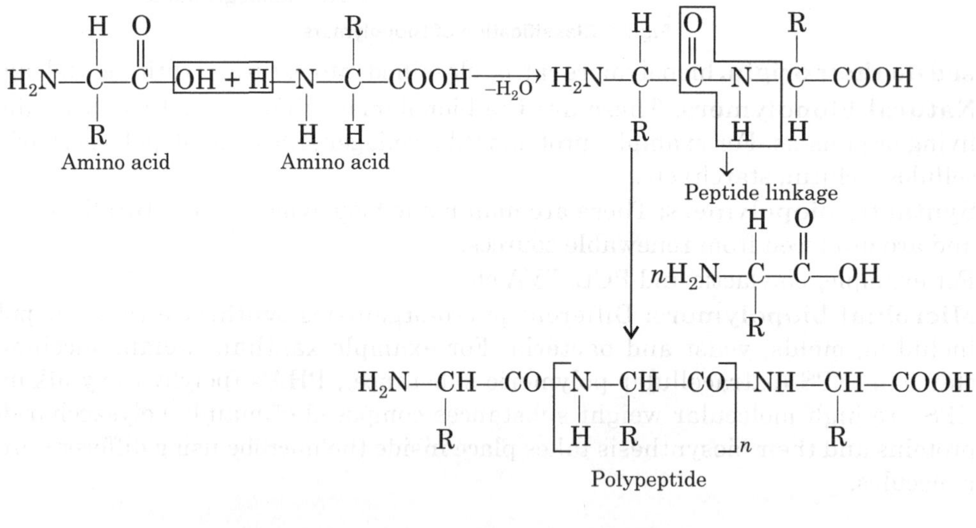

Function: Proteins perform essential functions throughout the system of human body. They serve various functions.

S. No.	Proteins class	Functions	Examples
1.	Structural proteins	They are used to construct the biological buildings.	α-Keratin of fur, feathers, hair and claws, collagens of skin, bone and cartilage.
2.	Carrier proteins	They carry metabolites from one site to another to make biological process a reality.	**Haemoglobin** carries oxygen, **transferrin** transports iron.
3.	Storage proteins or nutrient proteins	They serve as store houses to preserve nutritional proteins which act as source of essential amino acids.	Casein of milk, ovalbumins and ovomucoid of eggs and gluten of wheat and ferritin.
4.	Enzyme proteins	They act as biological catalysts.	Digestive enzymes trypsin and pepsin.
5.	Hormone proteins	They act as biological signals and regulate various physiological processes.	Insulin, glucagons, adrenocorticotropic hormone etc.
6.	Defence proteins	These proteins fight against foreign particles like bacteria, viruses etc.	Antibodies, thrombin, lysozyme etc.
7.	Proteins as toxins or poisons	They are toxic/poisonous to others but provide a defence tool to organism they belong to.	Snake venoms, diphtheria toxin, gossypin of cotton seed etc.

***(iii)* Nucleic Acids (Polynucleotides):** Nucleic acids are biopolymers of high molecular weight with mononucleotide as their repeating unit. Each nucleotide consists of the following:

1. Nitrogenous bases
2. Phosphate group
3. Pentose sugar.

There are two types of nucleic acids:

(*i*) DNA (Deoxyribonucleic acid)

(*ii*) RNA (Ribonucleic acid)

(*i*) DNA: DNA consists of

(*a*) **Nitrogenous bases:** Adenine, guanine, cytosine and thymine

(*b*) Deoxy ribose sugar

(*c*) Phosphate group

DNA is the genetic material in all organisms except some virus where RNA is the genetic material. In prokaryotic cells, DNA occurs in the cytoplasm, whereas in eukaryotic cells, DNA is mainly confined to nucleus. It is double stranded.

Functions:

1. It carries hereditary character from parents to offspring.
2. It enables the cell to maintain, grow and divide by directing the synthesis of structural proteins.
3. It brings about differentiation of cells during development.
4. It contributes to the evolution of the organism by undergoing gene mutation.

***(ii)* RNA:**

– RNA is a single standared, long, unbranched molecule.

– RNA is synthesized from DNA in a process called **transcription**.

– RNA consists of

(*a*) Nitrogenous bases-Adenine, guanine, cytosine and uracil (instead of thymine in DNA).

(*b*) A ribose sugar

(*c*) Phosphate group

In all prokaryotic and eukaryotic organisms, three main classes of RNA molecule exist *i.e.*, rRNA, mRNA and tRNA

Ribosomal RNA (rRNA): These are the components of ribosomes and hence their name. They constitute 80% of total RNA. This is the most stable form of RNA. rRNA, moves along the mRNA and helps in building the proteins.

Messenger RNA (mRNA): mRNA's are intermediates for carrying information from DNA to ribosomes for protein synthesis. It is synthesized in the nucleus during the process of transcription. It is very unstable and forms only about 5% of total RNA.

Transfer RNA (tRNA): tRNA serves as adapter molecule in translating the language of nucleic acids in mRNA into the language of proteins. They do so by serving as carriers of specific amino acids to specific sites on ribosomes (*i.e.* protein synthesizing template). It contributes to 15% of total RNA.

Carbohydrates, proteins, nucleic acid and lipids all are considered as macromolecules. Of these macro molecules, carbohydrates, nucleic acids and proteins are polymers while lipids are not. This is because polymers are made up of monomers which lipids do not contain.

Based on degradability, biopolymers can be biodegradable and non-biodegradable.

***(i)* Biodegradable Polymers:** The polymers are finding extensive use in our daily life. Although high chemical stability of polymers is a blessing, it becomes a curse due to its disposal problem. Such problem however can be controlled to certain extent through recycling of these plastics. Frequently, plastics are simply thrown away rather then recycled, which in turn creates a serious environmental problem. The best solution is therefore, to produce the polymers which will disintegrate spontaneously after its use for some period of time. Such polymers which are degraded naturally by micro-organisms through enzymatic hydrolysis are called as **biodegradable polymers**.

In biological systems, biopolymers degrade mainly by enzymatic hydrolysis and to some extent by chemical oxidation. Therefore, in view of the above said problem of disposal of polymers waste, attempts have been made to develop biodegradable synthetic polymers.

Aliphatic polyesters are an important class of such type of polymers. For example PLA (poly lactic acid), PHB (polyhydroxy butyrate), poly-β-hydroxybutyrate-co-β-poly hydroxyvalerate (PHBV), polyglycolic acid (PGA), poly ε-caprolactone (PCL) etc. Let us discuss them one by one.

1. **Polylactic Acid (PLA):** It can be obtained either by polymerization of the cyclic dimer of lactic acid or by microbiological synthesis of lactic acid followed by the poly-condensation with the removal of water molecule.

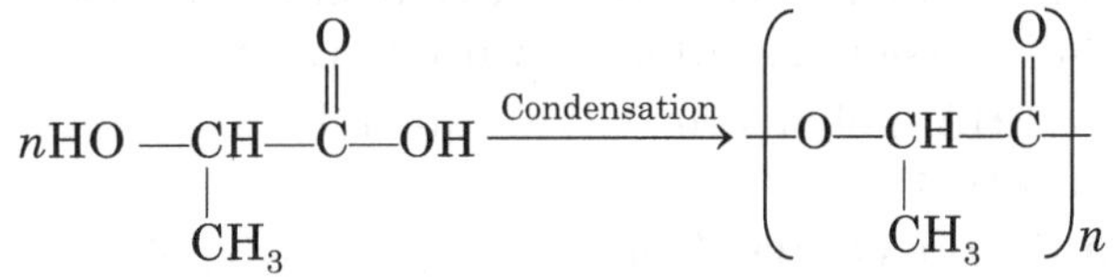

It is a crystalline polymer. It has a glass transition temperature of 60 – 65°C and a melting temperature of approximately 175°C.

PLA is a significant commercial polymer which is used in recyclable and biodegradable packaging like bottles, yoghurt cups etc. It also has biomedical applications like drug delivery, biodegradable medical devices etc.

2. **Poly-β-hydroxy butyrate-Co-β-hydroxyvalerate (PHBV):** It is an aliphatic polyester formed by copolymerization of 3-hydroxybutanoic acid and 3-hydroxypentanoic acid.

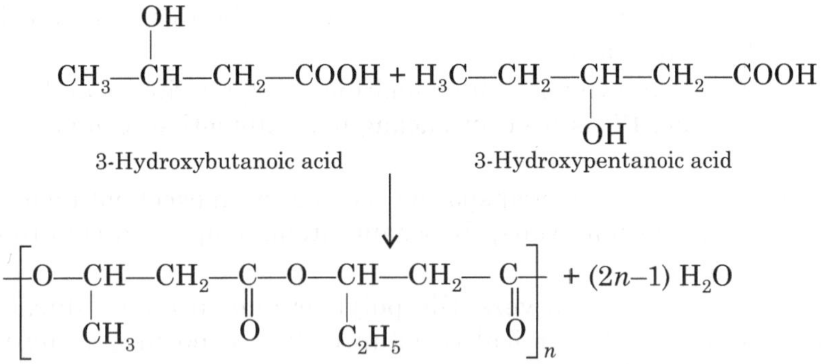

PHBV

PHBV is a non-toxic, biocompatible and biodegradable plastic produced naturally by bacteria.

It is used in special packaging, orthopaedic devices and in controlled drug delivery systems.

3. **PGA (Polyglycolic acid):** It is obtained by the chain polymerization of dimer of glycolic acid.

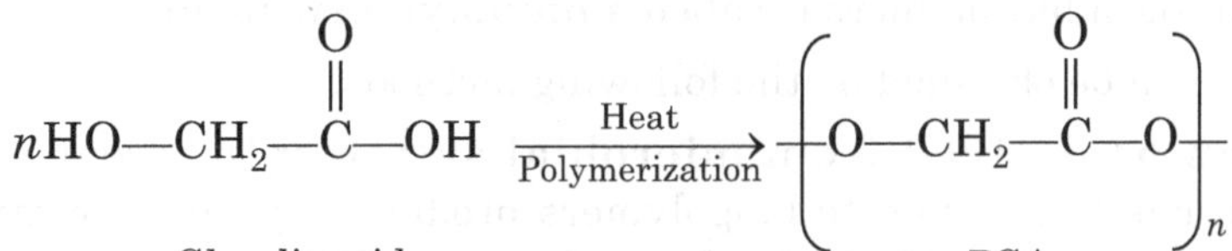

Glycolic acid PGA

It is a crystalline polymer and exhibits a high tensile modulus with a very low solubility in organic solvents.

PGA was one of the very first degradable polymers ever investigated for biomedical use.

4. **PCL (Poly ε-caprolactone):** It is a synthetic biodegradable polyester obtained by the chain polymerization of the lactone, of 6-hydroxyhexanoic acid.

$$\underset{\text{6-Hydroxyhexanoic acid}}{HO{-}(CH_2)_5{-}\overset{\overset{\Large O}{\|}}{C}{-}OH} \xrightarrow{\text{Polymerization}} PCL$$

It finds applications in biomedical areas of controlled release drug delivery systems, surgical sutures, 3-dimensional scaffolds for use in tissue engineering etc.

Other examples are PHA (polyhydroxyalkanoates), PBS (polybutylene succinate), PHUs (polyhydroxy urethanes etc.)

(*ii*) **Non-biodegradable polymers:** These are synthetic polymers that do not undergo significant degradation by natural biological processes. These polymers remain in the environment for long periods of time. Such polymers cause negative impact on the environment and human health. They are a major cause of pollution and cause damage to the ecosystem.

Examples: polyethylene (PE), polypropylene (PP), polystyrene (PS), polyvinyl chloride (PVC), polyethylene terephthalate (PET), teflon etc.

Polyethylene is one of the most widely used non-biodegradable polymer. It is a versatile plastic which has high strength, durability and resistance to chemicals. PE is used in various applications including packaging, plastic bags, bottles, pipes etc. It is also used in orthopedic implants and catheters.

Polypropylene (PP) is known for its high melting point, toughness and resistance to heat, chemicals and fatigue. PP is used in packaging, automotive components, textiles and medical devices.

Polystyrene (PS) is a rigid and transparent polymer with excellent insulation properties. It is used in packaging materials, disposable items (cups and containers), insulation boards, foam products etc.

Polyvinyl chloride (PVC) is a versatile polymer known for its durability, electrical insulation properties and chemical resistance. It is used in making pipes, electrical cables, flooring, window frames etc.

Polyethylene terephthalate (PET) is a strong and light weight polymer. It is used in the production of beverage bottles, food packaging, polyester fibres etc.

Teflon (polytetrafluroethylene) is chemically and biologically inert polymer having high lubricity. It is used in cooking wares, wiring in aerospace etc.

5.12 BIOPOLYMERIZATION

Process of synthesis of biopolymers is called a **biopolymerization.**

Biopolymers can be obtained by the following methods:

1. **They can be derived from microbial systems:** In recent years, considerable attention has been given to biopolymers produced by micro-organisms. It is on the microbial level, where the tools of genetic engineering can be readily applied. Various polymers synthesized by this method are now being developed and introduced into the market. These are: polyesters, proteins and polysaccharides. Among polyesters are PHA's (Poly hydroxy alkanoates), PHB (Poly-β-hydroxy butyrate), PHBV (polyhydroxy butyrate-co-β-polyhydroxy valerate) etc.

Chemical synthesis of proteins is a quite expensive process and typically does not yield product with sufficient physical and chemical uniformity. In contrast the recombinant DNA technology allows for the production of protein polymers that have high purity of specific molecular weight etc. For example pronectin F (pronectin-F shows excellent adhesion properties to plastic surfaces like polystyrene and therefore can be used to attach cells to synthetic substrates), bacteriorhodopsin (BR) (used in optical data storage, image processing, holography etc.).

Polysaccharides: Cellulose (a polysaccharide) is traditionally extracted from plant tissues, can also be produced by certain bacteria (like acetobacter) by fermentation yielding a pure cellulose product with unique properties. Others are xanthen (from xanthomonas campestris), dextrans (from Leuconostoc mesenteroides), pollulan (from Aureobasidium pullulans), glucans (from saccharomyces cerevisiae *i.e.* baker's yeast) etc.

2. **They can be extracted from higher organisms and plants:** Starch is the principal carbohydrate extracted from plants like corn, potatoes, rice, barley, sorghum and wheat.
    - **Cellulose:** Among the plant cellulose, cotton fibre is the most pure, containing around 90% cellulose, wood contains 50% cellulose.
    - **Lignin:** found in woody and herbaceous plants.
    - **Chitin:** Important structural component of the exoskeleton of a great number of organisms such as insects and shell fish.
3. **They can be prepared by chemical methods:** Polymers that are produced by the chemical polymerization of naturally occurring monomers are attracting enormous commercial interest. These polymers are not produced by biological systems but are derived from basic biological building blocks. For example:

    1. Polymers synthesized from Lactic acid: This includes polylactide homopolymers (PLA) and copolymers with glyclolic acid (PLA-GLA) 2. Polyamino-acids.

5.12 CONDUCTING POLYMERS/ORGANIC POLYMERIC CONDUCTORS

Polymers were considered to be electrical insulators before the invention of conducting polymers but these organic polymeric conductors have unique electrical and optical properties similar to those of inorganic semiconductors.

The idea that a polymer can conduct electricity as good as metals, was accidentally discovered by **H. Shirakawa, A. Heeger** and **A. M. Diarmid** in 1947 at the plastic research laboratory of BASF, Germany. **Polyacetylene** prepared using Ziegler Natta catalyst was the first conducting polymer but its conductivity was very less. Later in the year 1977, they discovered that oxidation with halogen vapour producers a much more conductive polyacetylene film and its conductivity was much higher (about million times) than other previously available conducting polymers. This led to the development of many other conducting polymers. These three scientists received the Noble prize in the year 2000 for their discovery and development of electrically conductive polymers. Some common conductive polymers are polyaniline, polythiophene, trans-poly-acetylene, polypyrole, polyfuran etc.

Classification of conducting polymers:

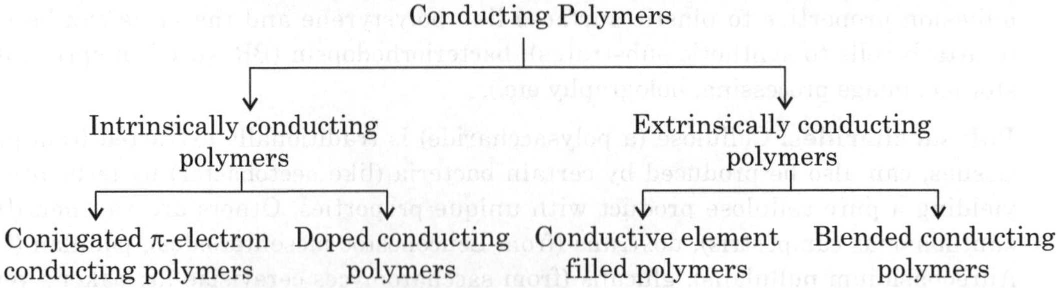

5.13.1 Intrinsically Conducting Polymers

The conductance in these polymers is because of presence of conjugation in the backbone of the polymer. These are further classified into:

5.13.2 Conjugated π-electrons Conducting Polymers

In these type of polymers, conduction of electricity is due to the presence of double bonds and lone pair of electrons. Overlapping of orbitals of conjugated π-electrons over the entire backbone results in the formation of valence and conduction band. Generally, conductivity increases with decreasing band gap between conduction and valance band. This band gap is the amount of energy needed to excite an electron from the highest occupied energy level (valence band) to the empty band (conduction band) immediately above it. Presence of conjugation in the system decreases the band gap and thus increases conductivity. However, the conductivity of these polymers is not sufficient for their use in various industrial applications.

For example

Polypyrolle -

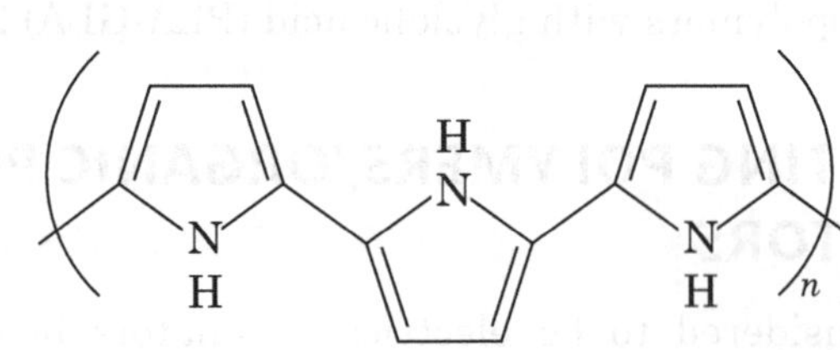

Transpolyacetylene -

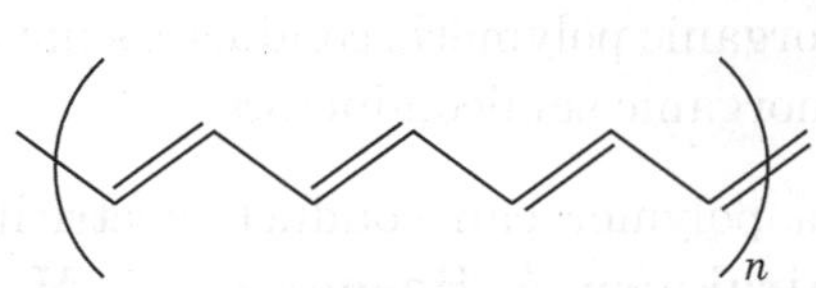

Polythiophene -

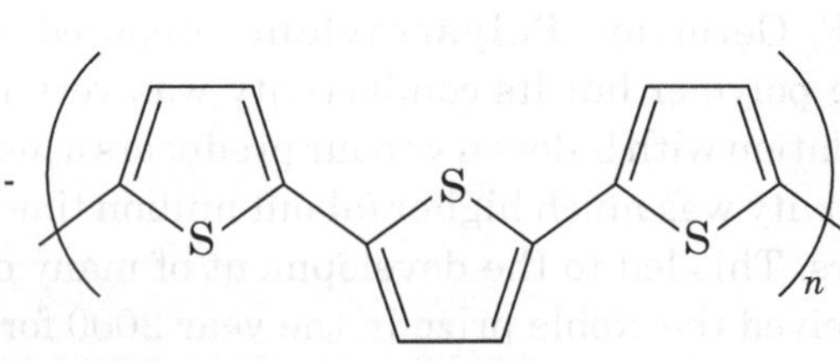

Polyaniline (HCl)-

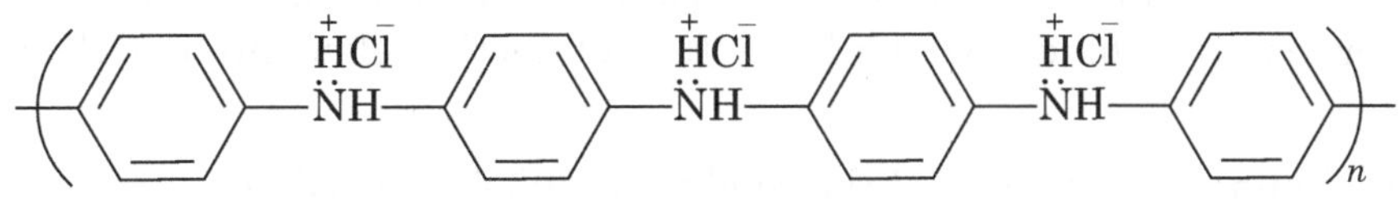

5.13.3 Doped Conducting Polymer

Polymers with conjugated double bonds (*i.e* conjugated π electron conducting polymers) can be easily oxidised or reduced, therefore they are doped either by electron donor or electron acceptors to increase their conductivity.

Doping can be

(*a*) **P-type doping:** When polymers with conjugated double bonds are treated with electron deficient species (Lewis acids), its oxidation takes place and a positive charge or hole is created in the molecule. This results in delocalization of positive charge which causes electrical conduction. Commonly used dopants of this category are $FeCl_3$, I_2 vapour, I_2/CCl_4, Br_2, AsF_5 etc.

$$\text{polymer} + p\text{-type dopant} \longrightarrow \underset{\text{(oxidative coupling)}}{p\text{-doped polymer}}$$

For example,

$$\underset{\text{Polyacetylene}}{(C_2H_2)_n} + 2\,FeCl_3 \longrightarrow (C_2H_2)_n^+\,FeCl_4^- + FeCl_2$$

$$\underset{\text{Polyacetylene}}{2(C_2H_2)_n} + 3I_2 \longrightarrow 2\left[(C_2H_2)_n^+ I_3^-\right]$$

(*b*) ***n*-type doping:** When polymers with conjugated double bonds are doped with electron rich species (Lewis bases), reduction takes place and negative charge is created in the polymer chain. As a result, conduction takes place. Some common *n*-type dopant's are Li, Na, sodium naphthalide etc.

$$\text{Polymer} + n\text{-type dopant} \longrightarrow \underset{\text{(reductive coupling)}}{n\text{-doped polymer}}$$

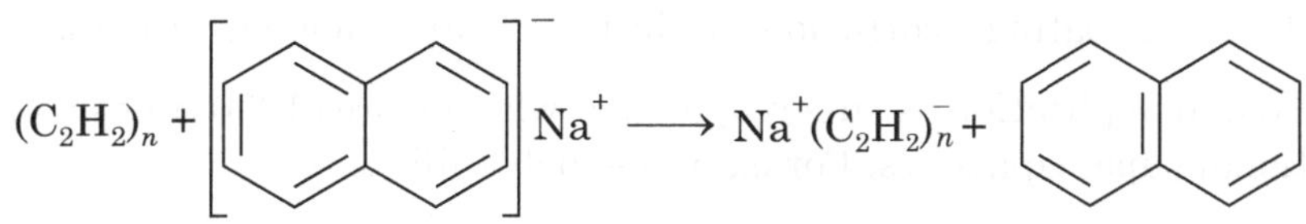

Advantages of intrinsically conducting polymers

(*i*) Good electrical conductivity

(*ii*) Capability to store charge

(*iii*) Capacity to exchange ions

(*iv*) Ability to absorb visible radiation to give coloured products

(*v*) X-ray transparent.

5.13.4 Extrinsically Conducting Polymers

Conducting polymers whose conductivity is due to the presence of externally added ingredients are called as **extrinsically conducting polymers**. They are of two types.

(*i*) **Conductive element filled polymer:** They are formed when a polymer is filled with conducting elements such as carbon black, metallic fibres, metal oxides etc. Here, the polymer acts as a binder which holds the conducting elements together in the solid entity.

The minimum concentration of the conductive filler required for an insulating polymer to make it conducting is called **percolation threshold**.

The conductivity of this type of polymer is not due to the matrix polymer but due to conductive fillers which are added.

These polymers have reasonably good conductivity. They are low in cost, light weight and mechanically durable and strong. It has been observed that if excess of conducting filler is used then it affects the properties of a polymer like tensile strength, impact strength etc. greatly. This problem can be resolved by blending conventional polymer with a conducting polymer.

(*ii*) **Blended conducting polymer:** Such polymers are obtained by blending a conventional polymer with a conducting polymer either chemically or physically. These blended polymers have improved mechanical, electrical, physical and chemical properties.

5.13.5 Applications of Conducting Polymers

1. Polymer based delivery systems such as Intrinsically conducting polymers (ICPs) shows enormous benefits in drug delivery and release. For example, polypyrole, poly (3, 4-ethylene dioxythiophiene) (PEDOT), Polyaniline (PANI) and their derivatives.
2. They are used for producing photovoltaic devices/organic solar cells etc. For example, Al/polymer/Au photovotlaic cell.
3. They find application as electrode material in rechargeable batteries. For example, polypyrrole lithium cell.
4. Literature reveals that conductive polymers find application in large number of areas which include photocatalysis, electrochromic windows, fuel cells, non linear optics, colour changing coatings, corrosion inhibition, organic field effect transistors etc.
5. They also find application as supercapacitors which stores 1000 times more energy than conventional supercapacitors. For example, polyaniline.
6. Conductive polymers have potential application in the field of biosensors and chemical sensors.
7. They are also used in biomedical and antimicrobial application. Conductive polymers like polyaniline, polypyrrole, PDOT etc. have outstanding capability for absorbing IR and they have notably less cytotoxicity. Therefore, these polymers are widely used for both in vivo and in vitro cell studies.
8. Conducting polymers are also used as flexible display devices in mobile phones, personal digital assistants, watches etc. They are also used in multicolour displays.
9. Conducting polymers also find extensive application in tele-communication systems, micro-electronic devices etc.

EXERCISES

I. SHORT ANSWER TYPE QUESTIONS

1. Differentiate between LDPE and HDPE polymers.
2. Explain the differences between chain growth and step growth polymerization.
3. What is a copolymer? Give one example.
4. What are elastomers? Give the chemical equation for the preparation of butyl rubber.
5. Write the name and structures of monomers of the following polymers:
   (*a*) Bakelite (*b*) Dacron (*c*) Nylon-6 (*d*) PMMA
   (*e*) Neoprene (*f*) Nitrile rubber.
6. How will you prepare the following? Give chemical reaction only:
   (*a*) PMMA (*b*) Nylon 6 (*c*) Polystyrene (*d*) UF resin
   (*e*) Bakelite.
7. Explain natural and synthetic polymers? Give two examples of each type.
8. How are buna-S and nitrile rubber synthesized? Give chemical equations.
9. Explain *cis* and *trans* natural rubber.
10. Arrange the following polymers in the increasing order of their intermolecular forces. Nylon 66, Buna-S, Polyethene

    Hint: Nylon66 (Condensation polymer) > Buna-S (Addition polymer) > Polythene (Addition polymer)
11. Give IUPAC names and structures of monomers of the following polymers:
    (*a*) Natural rubber (*b*) PMMA (*c*) Neoprene.
12. What is PHBV?
13. What is tacticity? Explain its various types? **(HMTU, 2016)**
14. Write three initiators alongwith their structures used in free radical polymerization.
15. What does LDPE and HDPE represent? Write two uses of each one of these.
16. Explain the term co-polymerization and give two examples.

    Hint: SBR, Nitrile rubber.
17. Differentiate between addition and condensation polymerization. **(HMTU, 2016)**

II. LONG ANSWER TYPE QUESTIONS

1. How are polymers classified into different categories on the basis of intermolecular forces? Give one example of a polymer of each of these categories.
2. What are biodegradable polymers? Give two examples of biodegradable aliphatic polyesters.

   Hint: Biodegradable aliphatic polyesters are: Poly-(β-hydroxy butyrate-Co-β-hydroxy valerate (PHBV) and PGA (Poly glycolic acid).
3. Differentiate between thermosetting and thermoplastic polymers. **(HMTU, Dec., 2016)**

4. What is vulcanization of rubber? Write various advantages of vulcanized rubber over natural rubber. **(RTU, 2020)**
5. Give preparation, properties and uses of the following polymers:
   (*a*) Orlon (*b*) Nylon 6 (*c*) PMMA (*d*) Nitrile rubbber
   (e) Silicone rubber (*g*) Glyptal (*h*) UF resin.
6. Define and explain the following:
   (*a*) Fibers (*b*) Elastomers (*c*) Natural rubber.
7. Describe the mechanism of free radical addition polymerization.
8. Explain cationic addition mechanism of polymerization?
9. What is addition polymerization? Explain anionic addition mechanism of polymerization.
10. What is silicone rubber? Explain various classes of silicone rubber.
11. Define biopolymers. Explain classification of biopolymers.
12. What is biopolymerization? Explain various methods of biopolymerization.
13. What is condensation polymerization? Write various steps involved in formation of dacron.
14. What do you mean by synthetic rubbers? Explain the manufacturing properties and uses of Buna-S and Buna-N rubbers. **(RTU, 2017)**
15. What is anionic polymerization? What are its conditions? Discuss its mechanism. **(HMTU, 2016)**

III. MULTIPLE CHOICE QUESTIONS

1. Biodegradable polymers find use in
   (*a*) controlled drug delivery (*b*) orthopaedic fixation devices
   (*c*) plastic bags manufacturing (*d*) all of these.
2. Which of the following is a natural polymer?
   (*a*) Teflon (*b*) Cellulose
   (*c*) Polyethene (*d*) Nylon.
3. Which of the following is not a condensation polymer?
   (*a*) Dacron (*b*) Glyptal
   (*c*) Melamine (*d*) Neoprene.
4. Polymer which is coated on non-stick utensils is
   (*a*) Orlon (*b*) Dacron
   (*c*) Teflon (*d*) PVC.
5 Of the following which one is a polyester polymer?
   (*a*) Terylene (*b*) Bakelite
   (*c*) Nylon-66 (*d*) Melamine.
6. Natural polymers are
   (*a*) Starch and Nylon (*b*) Protein and Nylon
   (*c*) Protein and Glyptal (*d*) Starch and Cellulose.

7. Which is not a synthetic rubber?
   (*a*) *Cis*-1, 4, Polyisoprene (*b*) Buna-S
   (*c*) Butyl rubber (*d*) Buna-N.
8. The monomers of buna-S rubber are
   (*a*) Styrene and butadiene (*b*) Isoprene and butadiene
   (*c*) Vinyl chloride and sulphur (*d*) Butadiene.
9. Which of the following is prepared by condensation polymerization?
   (*a*) Teflon (*b*) Rubber
   (*c*) Styrene (*d*) Nylon-6, 6.
10. Which of the following monomers give the polymer neoprene on polymerization?
   (*a*) $CH_2 = CHCl$ (*b*) $CCl_2 = CHCl$
   (*c*) $CH_2 = CCl—CH = CH_2$ (*d*) $CF_2 = CF_2$.
11. Which of the following glucose polymer is stored by animals?
   (*a*) Glycogen (*b*) Cellulose
   (*c*) Amylose (*d*) Amylopectin.
12. Polyacrylonitrile is an example of
   (*a*) Addition polymer (*b*) Natural polymer
   (*c*) Condensation polymer (*d*) Biodegradable polymer.
13. Example of fibres is
   (*a*) Bakelite (*b*) Buna-N
   (*c*) Nylon-66 (*d*) PVC.
14. Which one of the following is a synthetic polymer?
   (*a*) Starch (*b*) Neoprene
   (*c*) Silk (*d*) Protein.
15. Natural rubber is an example of
   (*a*) Condensation polymer (*b*) Addition polymer
   (*c*) Co-ordination polymer (*d*) None of these.
16. Caprolactam polymerises to form
   (*a*) Nylon-6 (*b*) Nylon-66
   (*c*) Dacron (*d*) Teflon.
17. A polymer which is used for coating electric wires is
   (*a*) Buna-N (*b*) Neoprene
   (*c*) Gutta percha (*d*) PVC.
18. Caprolactum used for nylon-6 manufacturing is obtained by Beckmann rearrangement of
   (*a*) Acetophenone oxime (*b*) Cyclohexanone oxime
   (*c*) Any one of (*a*) and (*b*) (*d*) None of these.

19. Among the following polymers, the weakest intermolecular forces are present in

(*a*) Thermosetting (*b*) Thermoplastic

(*c*) Fibres (*d*) Elastomers.

20. LDPE is prepared by

(*a*) Anionic addition polymerization

(*b*) Cationic addition polymerization

(*c*) Ziegler Natta polymerization

(*d*) Free radical addition polymerization.

21. Which of the following polymer is biodegradable?

(*a*) 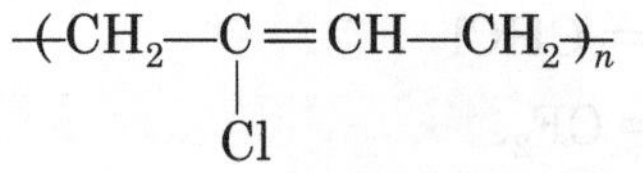

(*b*) 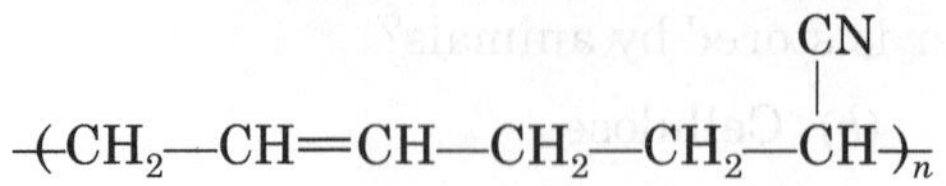

(*c*) 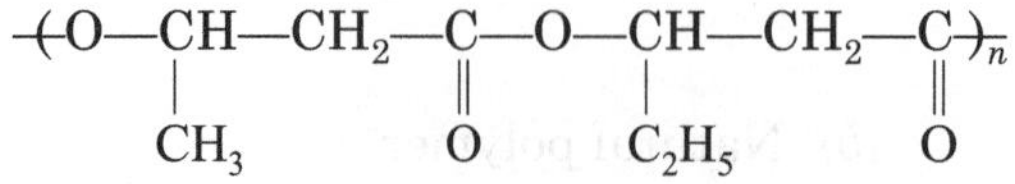

(*d*) 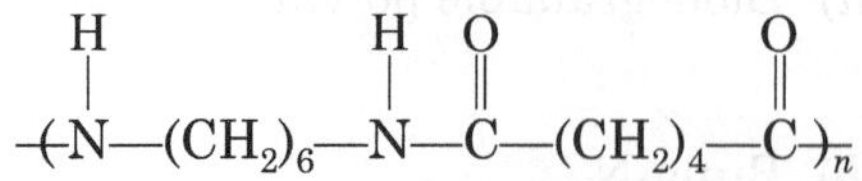

22. Which of the following fibres are made of polyamides?

(*a*) Orlon (*b*) Nylon (*c*) Rayon (*d*) Dacron.

23. Which of the following set contains only addition polymer?

(*a*) PMMA, Polythene, Teflon (*b*) Polythene, Nylon, Teflon

(*c*) PVA, PVC, Buna-S (*d*) Bakelite, PVC, PAN.

24. Ziegler Natta catalyst is

(*a*) R_3Al (*b*) $(C_2H_5)_3Al$ and $TiCl_4$

(*c*) $(C_2H_5)_3$ Ti and $TiCl_4$ (*d*) $TiCl_4$ and $(C_2H_5)_3Mg$.

25. Nitrile rubber is a copolymer of butadiene and

(*a*) Styrene (*b*) Acrylonitrile

(*c*) Acetonitrile (*d*) Isobutylene.

Answers

MULTIPLE CHOICE QUESTIONS

1. (*d*)	2. (*b*)	3. (*d*)	4. (*c*)	5. (*a*)	6. (*d*)	7. (*a*)	8. (*a*)	9. (*d*)	10. (*c*)
11. (*a*)	12. (*a*)	13. (*c*)	14. (*b*)	15. (*b*)	16. (*a*)	17. (*d*)	18. (*b*)	19. (*d*)	20. (*b*)
21. (*c*)	22. (*b*)	23. (*a*)	24. (*b*)	25. (*b*)					

Chapter 6 Photochemistry

6.1 INTRODUCTION

Many reactions that do not proceed under ordinary conditions can take place if the reactants are irradiated with visible or ultraviolet light.

Photochemistry is the branch of chemistry that deals with the study of chemical reactions which are caused by the absorption of light radiations. The light radiations of visible and UV region lying between 200–800 nm wavelength are generally used to bring about photochemical reactions, because these radiations possess sufficient energy to raise the atom or molecule from the ground state to an excited state. In the excited state, the molecule is more likely to undergo chemical reaction than in ground state. If a molecule undergoes a chemical reaction in the excited state in this manner, the reaction is called as **photo chemical reaction**.

The energy supplied by a particular wavelength of light can be calculated using the following equation.

$$E = h\nu = \frac{hc}{\lambda}$$

In CGS units,

$$h = 6.626 \times 10^{-27} \text{ erg s} \quad C = 3 \times 10^{10} \text{ cm s}^{-1}$$

$$\therefore \quad E = \frac{6.626 \times 10^{-27} \times 3 \times 10^{10}}{\lambda(\text{in cm})} \text{ erg} = \frac{1.988 \times 10^{-16}}{\lambda(\text{in cm})} \text{ erg}$$

To calculate energy per mole (multiply by N_A)

$$E = \frac{6.023 \times 10^{23} \times 1.988 \times 10^{-16}}{\lambda(\text{in cm})} = \frac{1.197 \times 10^{8}}{\lambda(\text{in cm})} \text{ erg mol}^{-1}$$

In calories : 1 calorie = 4.184×10^7 erg

$$\therefore \quad E = \frac{1.197 \times 10^{8}}{4.184 \times 10^{7}\, \lambda(\text{cm})} \text{ cal/mol}$$

$$= \frac{2.860}{\lambda(\text{cm})} \text{ cal/mol.}$$

This energy is sufficient to break most of the chemical bonds. Photochemical reactions depend on the absorption of electromagnetic radiations rather than on collision for the generation of reactive intermediate as in thermal or dark reactions. The main points of difference between thermal and photochemical reactions are given Table 6.1.

Table 6.1: Difference between Photochemical and Thermal Reactions

Thermal Reactions	Photochemical Reactions
• These reaction proceed in presence of light radiations.	• These reactions can take place both in the presence of light or in the dark. Light is not an essential requirement for these reactions.
• These reactions involve the absorption of light radiations in the range of 200–800 nm.	• These reactions involve either absorption of heat endothermic reactions) or evolution of heat (exothermic reactions)
• For these reactions, free energy change (ΔG) may not be always negative. For example ozonization of oxygen, polymerization of anthracene, photo synthesis etc. proceed by an increase in free energy *i.e.*, ΔG is positive.	• Thermal reactions are always accompanied by a decrease in free energy *i.e.* ΔG is negative.
• Photochemical reactions are usually independent of temperature. However, the rate of photochemical reaction is affected by the intensity of radiations employed.	• The rate of thermal reaction depends on temperature and generally increase with increase in temperature.
• Photochemical reactions are highly selective *i.e.* absorbed photon of light activates only a particular atom or molecule and the neighbouring atoms/molecules are not affected. For example, when a mixture of H_2 and Br_2 is exposed to light radiations of 450–550 nm wavelength, only bromine molecules get excited.	• These reactions are not selective. Thermal reactions causes the activation of all molecules to the same extent. For example, when H_2 and Br_2 are heated, both hydrogen and bromine gets excited.

6.2 INTERACTION OF MATTER WITH RADIATION

When a molecule is exposed to light, it absorbs photons of sufficient energy and gets activated. However, it is not essential that the light absorbed must bring about a photochemical change. The absorption of light may result in two types of photo processes:

1. Photophysical processes
2. Photochemical processes

1. **Photophysical processes:** In these processes, the light absorbed by molecules does not bring about any chemical change. The light absorbed is re-emitted by the matter instantaneously (fluorescence) or very slowly in the form of light radiation (phosphorescence). Fluorescence stops as soon as the light radiation is cut off whereas the phosphorescence continues even after the removal of light radiation. Apart from fluorescence and phosphorescence, the excited molecule may also lose energy by colliding with the surrounding molecules. This type of energy decay does not involve emission of light and is called **radiation less decay** or **non-radiative emission**.
2. **Photochemical processes:** In photochemical processes, when a photon of sufficient energy is absorbed by a molecule, a chemical reaction takes place *i.e.*, the molecule either dissociates, isomerises, rearranges or reacts with another molecule. Some common photochemical reactions are:

(*i*) Photosynthesis:

$$6\ CO_2 + 6\ H_2O \xrightarrow[\text{chlorophyll}]{\text{light}} C_6H_{12}O_6 + 6\ O_2$$

(*ii*) Reaction between H_2 and Br_2 in presence of light.

$$H_2 + Br_2 \longrightarrow 2\ HBr$$

(*iii*) Dimerization of anthracene

$$\underset{\text{Anthracene}}{2(C_4H_{10})} \xrightarrow[h\nu]{\text{light}} \underset{\text{Dianthracene}}{C_{28}H_{20}}$$

6.3 LAWS GOVERNING ABSORPTION OF LIGHT

There are two laws which govern the absorption of light. These are:

6.3.1 Lambert's law

Lambert's law states that "when a beam of monochromatic light passes through a transparent medium, the rate of decrease in intensity of radiation with the thickness of the absorbing medium is directly proportional to the intensity of the incident light".

Mathematically,

$$\frac{-dI}{dl} \propto I$$

$$\frac{-dI}{dl} = KI \qquad \text{...(6.1)}$$

where, K is the constant of proportionality, I = Intensity of radiation.

dI = decrease in intensity of light when it passes through a small thickness '*dl*' of the absorbing medium (Fig. 6.1).

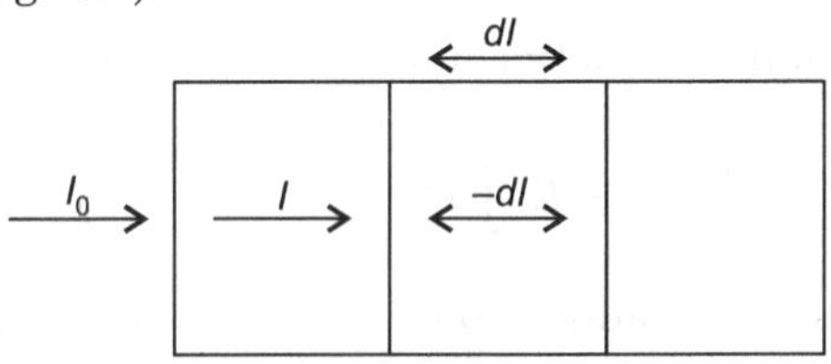

Fig. 6.1. Decrease in intensity of light with thickness of medium.

Equation (6.1) can be written as

$$\frac{-dI}{I} = Kdl \qquad \text{...(6.2)}$$

Equation (6.2) can be integrated between the limits of thickness medium = 0 to l and $I = I_0$ to I, we get

$$\int_{I_0}^{-I} \frac{-dI}{I} = \int_0^l Kdl$$

$$-\ln \frac{I_0}{I} = Kl$$

$$-\ln \frac{I}{I_0} = Kl \quad \text{or} \quad \frac{I}{I_0} = e^{-Kl}$$

$$I = I_0\, e^{-kl}$$

where I_0 is the intensity of radiation before entering the absorbing medium (where $l = 0$) and I is the intensity when the beam has travelled the thickness l of the absorbing medium.

$$2.303 \log_{10} \frac{I_0}{I} = Kl$$

$$\log_{10} \frac{I_0}{I} = \frac{Kl}{2.303}$$

$$\log_{10} \frac{I_0}{I} = \varepsilon l; \ \varepsilon = \text{Absorption coefficient} = \frac{K}{2.303}$$

$$\log_{10} \frac{I_0}{I} = A; \ A = \text{Absorbance or optical density} = \varepsilon l.$$

6.3.2 Beer's Law

Lambert's law shows that there is a relationship between the absorbance and thickness 'l' of the medium. Beer observed that a similar relationship hold between absorbance and concentration of a solution.

Beer's law states that,"the intensity of beam of monochromatic light decreases exponentially with the increase in concentration of absorbing substance."

Mathematically,

$$\frac{-dI}{I} \propto dc \qquad ...(6.3)$$

$$\frac{-dI}{I} = K'dc \qquad ...(6.4)$$

On integrating the equation (6.4) between the limits $c = 0$ to c and $I = I_0$ to I, we get

$$-\int_{I_0}^{I} \frac{dI}{I} = K' \int_0^c dc$$

where $c = 0$ when no solute was added to the solvent and $c = c$ when whole of the solute is added.

$$\ln \frac{I_0}{I} = K'c \qquad ...(6.5)$$

On combing the two laws, Lambert's law and Beer's law, the Lambert Beer's law can be formulated as:

$$\frac{-dI}{I} = K''cdl \qquad ...(6.6)$$

On integrating the equation (6.6) between the limits $l = 0$ to l and $I = I_0$ to I, we get

$$-\int_{I_0}^{I} \frac{-dI}{I} = K''c \int_0^l dl$$

$$-\ln \frac{I}{I_0} = K''cl \qquad ...(6.7)$$

$$2.303 \log \frac{I}{I_0} = -K''cl$$

$$\log \frac{I}{I_0} = \frac{-K''}{2.303} cl = -\varepsilon cl \qquad ...(6.8)$$

where $\varepsilon = \dfrac{K''}{2.303}$, it is called **molar absorption coefficient** (or molar extinction coefficient or molar absorptivity). Equation (6.8) can also be written as

$$\log \frac{I}{I_0} = -\varepsilon cl \text{ or } \log \frac{I_0}{I} = \varepsilon cl \text{ or } A = \varepsilon cl$$

$$\left[-\log \frac{I}{I_0} = \log \frac{I_0}{I} = A\right], \text{ where } A \text{ is absorbance}$$

or $$\frac{I}{I_0} = 10^{-\varepsilon cl} \left[\text{transmittance } T = \frac{I}{I_0}\right] \qquad \therefore \quad T = 10^{-\varepsilon cl}$$

or $$I = I_0 \times 10^{-\varepsilon cl}$$

A plot of $-\log \dfrac{I}{I_0}$ vs. c is a straight line (Fig. 6.2) passing through origin, having slope ε

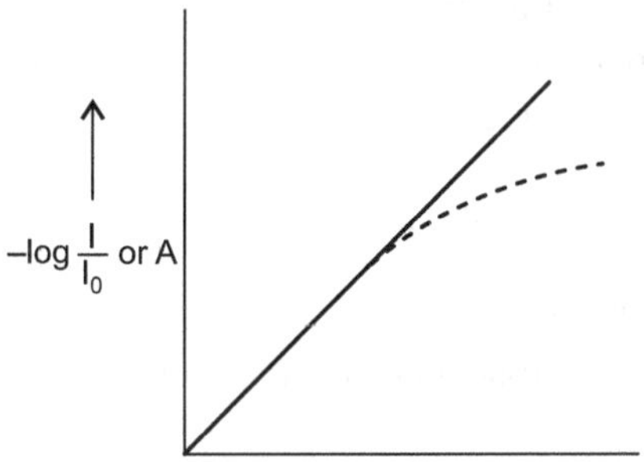

Fig. 6.2. Plot of absorbance (A) vs. concentration (c) of solution.

This curve shows the deviation of Lambert Beer's law at high concentration of the solution.

6.3.3 Limitations of Lambert Beer's Law

This law holds good:

1. For dilute solution only as deviations are observed for solutions of high concentration.
2. Only for light of single wavelength (*i.e* for monochromatic radiation).
3. If temperature remains constant during measurement.

6.4 LAWS OF PHOTOCHEMISTRY

There are basically two laws that govern the effect of radiation on a particular chemical reaction. These are:

6.4.1 Grothus Draper Law: (Ist Law of Photochemistry)

Grothus and Draper in 19th century made a generalization after studying a number of photochemical reactions. It states that "when an incident light falls on any substance only that fraction of incident light which is absorbed by the substance brings about a chemical reaction, reflected and transmitted light has no role in the reaction". This does not mean that all the absorbed radiations must necessarily bring about a chemical reaction. Chemical reaction takes place only if conditions are favourable. If conditions are not favourable for a chemical reaction, the absorbed light remains unused. It may be re-emitted as radiation of the same or different frequency.

This law is purely qualitative and gives no idea of the relation between the amount of light absorbed by a system and the number of reacting molecules.

6.4.2 Stark-Einstein Law of Photochemical Equivalence: (IInd Law of Photochemistry)

This law is based on quantum theory of light. This law was enunciated independently by Stark in 1908 and Einstein in 1912. According to this law, "in a photochemical reaction, each molecule of the reacting substance absorbs one photon of radiations, gets excited and causes the reaction".

Here it is important to note that one photon (or one quantum) of light has energy equal to $h\nu$.

i.e. $$E = h\nu$$

where υ is the frequency of radiation and h is the Plank's constant. The energy absorbed by one mole of the reacting substances is given by the expression,

$$E = N_A h\nu$$

$$= N_A h \frac{c}{\lambda} \quad \therefore \quad \nu = \frac{c}{\lambda}$$

where N_A = Avogadro's number

The quantity, 'E' is the energy absorbed per mole of the reacting substance and it is called as **one Einstein.**

Energy per Einstein $= N_A h\nu = N_A h \frac{c}{\lambda}$.

Substituting the values, in SI units,

$$N_A = 6.023 \times 10^{23} \text{ molecules, } h = 6.624 \times 10^{-34} \text{ Js}$$

$$c = 3 \times 10^8 \text{ ms}^{-1}$$

$$E = \frac{6.023 \times 10^{23} \times 6.624 \times 10^{-34} \times 3 \times 10^8}{\lambda(\text{m})}$$

$$= \frac{0.1196}{\lambda(\text{m})} \text{ J mol}^{-1}$$

$$E = \frac{0.1196}{\lambda(\text{Å})} \times 10^{10} \text{ J mol}^{-1}$$

In CGS units

$$c = 3 \times 10^{10} \text{ cms}^{-1}, h = 6.624 \times 10^{-27} \text{ergs}$$

$$E = \frac{6.023 \times 10^{23} \times 6.624 \times 10^{-27} \times 3 \times 10^{10}}{\lambda(\text{cm})}$$

$$E = \frac{1.196 \times 10^8}{\lambda(\text{cm})} \text{ erg mol}^{-1}$$

$$E = \frac{0.1196 \times 10^{10}}{\lambda(\text{Å})} \text{ Jmol}^{-1}$$

$$E = \frac{1.196 \times 10^{8} \times 10^{8}}{\lambda(\text{Å})} \text{ erg mol}^{-1}$$

$$E = \frac{1.196 \times 10^{16}}{\lambda(\text{Å})} \text{ erg mol}^{-1}$$

As $$1 \text{ cal} = 4.184 \times 10^{7} \text{ ergs}$$

$\therefore$ $$E = \frac{1.196 \times 10^{16}}{4.184 \times 10^{7}\ \lambda(\text{Å})} \text{ cal mol}^{-1}$$

$$= \frac{2.859 \times 10^{8}}{\lambda(\text{Å})} \text{ cal mol}^{-1}.$$

It is evident from the above equation that the value of E is inversely proportional to the wavelength of light absorbed. The longer the wavelength, the lesser is the energy absorbed.

6.5 QUANTUM YIELD

It has been shown that a photochemical reaction does not always obey the Einstein's law. The number of molecules reacted or decomposed is often found to be markedly different from the number of quanta or photons of light absorbed in a given time. The number of molecules reacted or formed per photon of light absorbed is called as **quantum yield (ϕ)**.

$$\phi = \frac{\text{Number of molecules reacted or formed in a given time}}{\text{Number of photons absorbed in same time}}$$

or $$\phi = \frac{\text{Rate of chemical reaction}}{\text{Number of Einsteins absorbed}}.$$

According to Stark-Einstein law, one molecule reacts or decomposes per photon of light absorbed. Hence, ideally the quantum yield for all photochemical reactions should be unity. However, the quantum efficiency of a photochemical reaction is either greater than one or less than one.

If the number of molecules formed or decomposed per photon of light absorbed is less than one, then $\phi < 1$, the reaction is said to have **low quantum yield**. If the number of molecules formed or decomposed is more than one per photon of light absorbed, then $\phi > 1$ and the reaction is said to have **high quantum yield**.

Few phtochemical reactions and their quantum yields are given below:

Reaction	Quantum Yield
1. **Reactions having low quantum yield ($\phi < 1$).** (*i*) Hydrogen-bromine reaction $H_2 + Br_2 \xrightarrow[510\text{ nm}]{h\nu} HBr$	0.01
(*ii*) Photolysis of maleic acid Maleic acid $\xrightarrow{200-180\text{ nm}}$ fumaric acid	0.04

(*iii*) Photolysis of ammonia $2NH_3 \xrightarrow[500\text{ atm}]{160-200\text{ nm}} N_2 + 3H_2$	0.25
(*iv*) Dimerization of anthracene. $2C_{14}H_{10} \xrightarrow[360\text{ nm}]{h\nu} C_{28}H_{20}$	0.5
(*v*) Decomposition of nitric oxide (NO_2) $2NO_2 \longrightarrow 2NO + O_2$	0.7
2. Reactions having high quantum yield (ϕ > 1) (*i*) Hydrogen-chlorine reaction $H_2(g) + Cl_2(g) \xrightarrow[400-460\text{ nm}]{h\nu} 2HCl(g)$	$10^4 - 10^6$
(*ii*) Photochemical formation of phosgene $CO + Cl_2 \xrightarrow{400-436\text{ nm}} COCl_2$	10^3
(*iii*) Photochemical decomposition of H_2O_2 $2H_2O_2 \xrightarrow{310\text{ nm}} 2H_2O + O_2$	> 7
(*iv*) Photochemical formation of ozone: $3O_2 \xrightarrow{170-190\text{ nm}} 2O_3$	3
(*v*) Photochemical decomposition of HBr $2HBr \xrightarrow{207-253\text{ nm}} H_2 + Br_2$	2
3. Reactions having quantum yield equal to 1 (*i*) Photochemical decomposition of H_2S $H_2S \xrightarrow{208\text{ nm}} H_2 + S$	1
(*ii*) Photochemical reaction between SO_2 and Cl_2 $SO_2 + Cl_2 \xrightarrow{420\text{ nm}} SO_2 + Cl_2$	1
(*iii*) Iodine sensitized oxidation of ferrous ions. $2Fe^{2+} + I_2 \xrightarrow{579\text{ nm}} 2Fe^{3+} + 2I^-$	1

6.5.1 Reasons for High and Low Quantum Yields

In order to explain the exceptions to Einstein's law of photochemical equivalence, Bodenstein and others pointed out that photochemical reactions generally involve two processes. These are called as primary process and the secondary process.

1. **Primary process:** This step of photochemical reaction follows the Einstein's law. In this process, each molecule absorbs one quantum of radiation ($h\nu$) and gets excited to higher energy state.

$$AB + h\nu \longrightarrow \underset{\text{Excited molecule}}{[AB]^*}$$

The excited molecule may associate, dissociate, lose energy by collisions with other molecules or may undergo phosphorescence or fluorescence.

2. **Secondary process:** In the secondary process, the species formed in the primary process may undergo further reaction. Sometimes, the excited molecules initiates a chain reaction which results in high quantum yield.

   It follows from the above points that the value of quantum yield will depend upon secondary process as the primary process remains the same for every reaction. We will now discuss the reasons for different quantum yields of different reactions on the basis of secondary process.

6.5.2 Reasons for High Quantum Yield

The main reasons for high quantum yield are:

1. **Reactions subsequent to the primary process:** When the excited species formed in the primary process undergo secondary processes, each such process gives rise to some further excited particles or species, this process continues unless it is checked due to one or other reason. Thus, by absorbing only one quanta, a large number of reactant molecules undergo reaction. Hence, the quantum yield of such reactions is greater than 1.
2. **Initiation of a chain reaction:** Sometimes the species like free radicals formed in the primary process, initiate a series of chain reactions. For example, in the combination of H_2 and Cl_2 to give HCl the quantum yield are of the order of $10^4 - 10^6$.
3. **Activation of other molecules:** If the secondary reaction is exothermic, the heat liberated may activate other molecules and thereby increase the quantum yield.

Examples of High Quantum Yield Reactions

1. **The hydrogen-chlorine reaction:** The photochemical formation of HCl from H_2 and Cl_2 is given by the overall reaction

$$H_2(g) + Cl_2(g) \xrightarrow{h\nu} 2HCl$$

The quantum yield of this reaction is very high of the order of $10^4 - 10^6$. This reaction has been found to proceed by the following mechanism;

(*a*) $Cl_2 + h\nu \longrightarrow 2Cl$ Initiation (1° process)

(*b*) $Cl + H_2 \longrightarrow HCl + H$ Exothermic (2° process) (propagation)

(*c*) $H + Cl_2 \longrightarrow HCl + Cl$ Propagation (2° process)

(*d*) 2Cl at the walls $\longrightarrow Cl_2$ Termination

In the primary (1°) process (*i*), Cl_2 absorbs one photon and dissociates into two Cl atoms. Reaction (*ii*) is a secondary (2°) process but takes place very rapidly because of its exothermic nature. Reaction (*iii*) depends on the ease of formation of H in step (*ii*) and therefore occurs quickly. In this way Cl radical/atom consumed in step (*ii*) is regenerated in step (*iii*). Thus, absorption of one photon of radiation leads to the formation of large number of molecules as a result. of repetition of steps (*ii*) and (*iii*). Therefore, the quantum yield of the above reaction is very high. The chain reaction is terminated, when the Cl atoms recombine at the walls of the vessel and lose their excess energy.

2. **Photochemical decomposition of HI:** The decomposition of HI occurs by the absorption of light of wavelength less than 400 nm.

$$2\,HI \xrightarrow{h\nu} H_2 + I_2$$

Mechanism for the photolysis of HI has been proposed as under:

$$HI + h\nu \longrightarrow H + I \text{ (Primary process)}$$

Secondary processes

(*a*) $HI + H \longrightarrow H_2 + I$ (*b*) $I + HI \longrightarrow I_2 + H$ (endothermic)

(*c*) $H + H \longrightarrow H_2$ (exothermic) (*d*) $I + I \longrightarrow I_2$

(*e*) $H + I \longrightarrow HI$ (exothermic)

In the above proposed mechanism, steps (*c*) and (*e*) are highly exothermic and the heat produced causes the dissociation of the products of these reactions. Step (*b*) is endothermic and hence takes place slowly. Therefore, the only important secondary processes are steps (*a*) and (*d*).

Thus the decomposition of HI can be written as,

Primary process $HI \xrightarrow{h\nu} H + I$

Secondary process $H + HI \longrightarrow H_2 + I$

$I + I \longrightarrow I_2$

Overall reaction $2HI \xrightarrow{h\nu} H_2 + I_2$

Thus, the absorption of one photon of radiation leads to the decomposition of two molecules of HI. Therefore, the quantum yield of this reaction is 2.

6.5.3 Reasons for Low Quantum Yield

When the number of molecules decomposed is less than one per photon, then the reaction is said to have **low quantum yield**. The main reasons for low quantum yield are:

1. **Deactivation of the reacting molecules:** The activated molecule formed in the primary process may be deactivated before they form products. They get deactivated either by emitting energy in the form of fluorescence or phosphorescence or by collision with the surrounding molecules and lose energy in the form of heat.
2. **Primary photochemical reaction may be reversible:** The atoms or radicals formed in the primary process may recombine to give back the reactant molecules, till an equilibrium is attained. As a result, a polymer a formed. In other words, many atoms or molecules combine to give one big molecule, hence, the quantum yield decreases.

$$2A \rightleftharpoons A_2$$

3. **Recombination of dissociated fragments:** The reactant molecule dissociates to form small fragments in a primary process. These fragments recombine to give back the reactant without the formation of products. Hence, the quantum yield will decrease.

Example of Low Quantum Yield Reactions

1. **Photolysis of ammonia**

$$2NH_3 \xrightarrow{160-200\text{ nm}} N_2 + 3H_2$$

The quantum yield of this reaction is quite low *i.e* about 0.25 at ordinary temperature and pressure. The probable mechanism is as follows,

Primary process: $NH_3 \xrightarrow{h\nu} NH_2 + H$

Secondary process:

(*a*) $NH_2 + NH_2 \longrightarrow N_2 + 2H_2$ (*b*) $NH_2 + NH_2 \longrightarrow N_2H_4$

(*c*) $H + H \longrightarrow H_2$ (*d*) $NH_2 + H \longrightarrow NH_3$

Studies show that the secondary reactions (*a*), (*b*) and (*c*) occur only to a small extent while the secondary reaction (*d*) involves the reversal of the primary process. Therefore, a low quantum yield is observed for this reaction,

2. **Dimerization of anthracene in benzene solution:** When a solution of anthracene and benzene are exposed to light in the UV region, dimerization of anthracene occurs.

$$2C_{14}H_{10} \xrightarrow{h\nu} \underset{\text{Dianthracene}}{C_{28}H_{20}}$$

The quantum yield for the reaction should be 2 but actually it is 0.5. This can be understood with the help of the following mechanism:

Primary process: $A \xrightarrow{h\nu} A^*$ (A = Anthracene)

Secondary process:

(*a*) $A^* \longrightarrow A + h\nu'$ fluorescence ($\nu' < \nu$)

(*b*) $A^* + A \longrightarrow A_2$ Dimerization

Due to fluorescence, the activated molecule returns back to ground state *i.e* gets deactivated and therefore the quantum yield decreases. Furthermore, the secondary reaction (*b*) is reversible *i.e.* the transformation of products back to the reactant continues till an equilibrium is attained. This further decreases the quantum yield.

3. **The hydrogen-bromine reaction:**

$$H_2(g) + Br_2(g) \xrightarrow{h\nu} 2HBr(g)$$

The following mechanisms has been proposed for the above reaction

Primary process: $Br_2 \xrightarrow{h\nu} 2Br$

Secondary processes:

(*a*) $Br + H_2 \longrightarrow HBr + H$ (endothermic) (*b*) $H + Br_2 \longrightarrow HBr + Br$

(*c*) $H + HBr \longrightarrow H_2 + Br$ (*d*) $Br + Br \longrightarrow Br_2$

Reaction (*a*) is highly endothermic and thus takes place very slowly at ordinary temperature. Reactions (*b*) and (*c*) depend upon the formation of H atoms in reaction (*a*), consequently reactions (*b*) and (*c*) are very slow. Step (*d*) is just the reversal of primary process in which the bromine atoms recombine to form Br_2 rather than HBr. As a result of all these secondary processes, the quantum yield of the reaction is quite low at ordinary temperature. However, with increase of reaction temperature, the quantum yield increases. This is because of the reason that the reaction (*a*) which is endothermic requires high activation energy which becomes available at higher temperatures. As a results, more H atoms are produced in reaction (*a*) thereby increasing the rate of reaction of (*b*) and (*c*) also.

6.6 PHOTOPHYSICAL PROCESSES

The processes in which the light absorbed by a molecule does not bring about any photochemical change are classified as photophysical processes. Three common photophysical processes are:

1. Fluorescence
2. Phosphorescence
3. Chemiluminescence

The fluorescence and phosphorescence can be best explained using Jablonski diagram.

6.6.1 Jablonski Diagram

Alexander Jablonski was a polish academician who devoted his life to the study of molecular absorbance and emission of light. Jablonski diagram is a representation that shows possible consequences of absorption of photon from visible light by the molecules.

In order to understand Jablonski diagram, we first need to go through some basic terms. Most molecules have an even number of electrons and thus in the ground state, all electrons are spin paired. The quantity $2S + 1$ (S = total electronic spin) is called as the **spin multiplicity** of a state. As both the electron are a paired in the ground state *i.e.* $\uparrow\downarrow$, therefore total spin, $S = +\frac{1}{2} + \left(-\frac{1}{2}\right) = 0$ and hence multiplicity $(2S + 1) = 2 \times 0 + 1 = 1$. Thus, spin multiplicity of the molecules is 1 and is called as **singlet ground state** and is represented as S_0.

When this molecule absorbs photon of light, the electron is promoted to higher electronic energy level, where it can have spin parallel or antiparallel to the spin of electron in the ground state (Fig. 6.3).

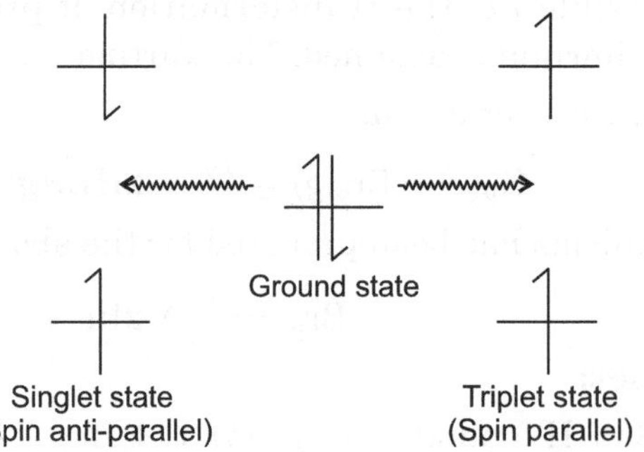

Fig. 6.3. Excited singlet and triplet states.

Case I: When spin of both the electrons are parallel.

$$\text{Total spin } (S) = +\frac{1}{2} + \left(+\frac{1}{2}\right) = 1$$

Thus multiplicity $(2S + 1) = 2 \times 1 + 1 = 3$

Thus, the molecule is said to be in **triplet excited state (*T*)**

Case II: When spins of two electrons are antiparallel

$$\text{Total spin } (S) = +\frac{1}{2} + \left(-\frac{1}{2}\right) = 0$$

Thus multiplicity $(2S + 1) = 2 \times 0 + 1 = 1$

Therefore, it is a **singlet excited state (*S*)**

There are many singlet and triplet states which are available to the electron. Excited singlet states are denoted by S_1, S_2. S_3, S_4,... and excited triplet states are represented by T_1, T_2, T_3, T_4 .... For each excited singlet state there is a corresponding triplet excited state. In accordance with Hund's rule, triplet excited state has lower energy and more stability as compared to singlet excited state.

When a molecule absorbs light, its electrons can jump from S_0 to S_1, S_2 or S_3 singlet excited state depending upon the amount of photons or energy absorbed (Fig. 6.4). The excited molecule returns to the ground state by dissipating energy through the following general types of processes:

1. Non-radiative transitions
2. Radiative transitions
3. Chemical reactions.

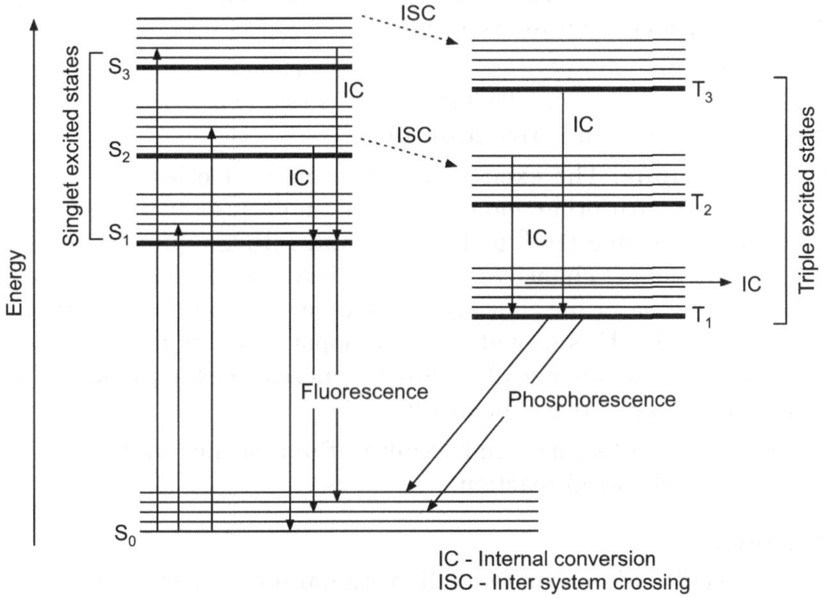

Fig. 6.4. Jablonski diagram.

1. **Non-radiative transitions:** These transitions do not involve emission of any radiations, therefore called as **non-radiative transitions**.

   Non-radiative transitions can occur via two processes:

   (*i*) **Internal conversion**: These transitions involve the return of excited electron from higher excited states (S_3, S_2 or T_3, T_2) to the first excited state (S_1 or T_1,) having same multiplicity *i.e.* $S_3 \rightarrow S_1$, $S_2 \rightarrow S_1$, $T_3 \rightarrow T_1$, $T_2 \rightarrow T_1$. The energy of the excited molecule is lost through molecular collisions in the form of heat. Spectroscopically, this is an allowed transition. It occurs very fast and its life time is less than 10^{-11} sec.

(*ii*) **Inter system crossing (ISC):** The excited molecule may also lose energy by ISC, which involves transition between states of different multiplicity *i.e.* $S_2 \rightarrow T_2$, $S_1 \rightarrow T_1$ etc. This is possible through spin inversion. Such transitions are spectroscopically forbidden, so they occur at comparatively lower rates.

The direct excitation from $S_0 \rightarrow T_1$ is forbidden, therefore triplet states are populated *via.* ISC.

2. **Radiative transitions:** These transitions involve the return of excited molecules from the excited singlet state S_1 and excited triplet state T_1 to the ground state S_0. These transitions are accompanied by the emission of radiations, therefore, these are also called as **radiative transitions.**

   Spectroscopically, $S_1 \rightarrow S_0$ transitions are allowed and occur in about 10^{-8} sec. This emission of radiation from first excited singlet state to ground state is called as **fluorescence**.

   The transition $T_1 \rightarrow S_0$ are forbidden spectroscopically and takes place slowly. The life time is much longer than fluorescence being of the order of 10^{-4} sec or more, because these transitions involve spin inversion (from $T_1 \rightarrow S_0$) which needs time for its occurrence. This emission of radiation from first excited triplet state (T_1) to the ground state (S_0) is called as **phosphorescence**.

   Both fluorescence and phosphorescence are of shorter frequency than the absorbed light used for excitation of electrons. This is so because some part of light energy is lost in the form of heat during non-radiative transitions.

3. **Chemical reactions:** The excited molecule may also lose energy by undergoing chemical reaction with other molecules. The molecules in the excited singlet state have very short life time (10^{-9} to 10^{-6} sec) and returns quickly to the ground state, therefore they do not get chance to react chemically. However, molecules in the excited triplet state have greater life time (10^{-4} to few seconds) and return to the ground state comparatively slowly. This provides ample opportunity to the activated molecules in the triplet state to react chemically. Thus it is necessary for a molecule to be in excited triplet state before it can react chemically.

   Benzophenone is a substance that exhibits fluorescence and phosphorescence and undergoes a photo chemical reaction.

6.6.2 Fluorescence

Certain atoms or molecules when exposed to light radiation of short wavelength (high energy) emit light of longer wavelength (less energy) instantaneously (within 10^{-8} sec). The process is called as **fluorescence** and the atoms or molecules that exhibit fluorescence are called as **fluorescent substances**. The colour of fluorescence depends on the wavelength of light emitted.

Fluorescence starts as soon as the molecules are exposed to light and stops as soon as the incident light is cut-off. The wavelength of emitted light in fluorescence is longer than the incident light because the excited molecules loses some of its energy in the form of heat during collision with other molecules.

Few examples of substances that show fluorescence on exposure to radiations are given below:

1. Quinine sulphate solution
2. Fluorspar
3. Chlorophyll solution in ether
4. Solution of uranyl sulphate etc.

Applications: Fluorescence is widely use in analytical techniques and finds applications in the medical and biological field.

Some common applications are:

1. Fluorescent lamps are used for lighting purposes.
2. Fluorescent microscopes are used in testing of food products and also for detecting the presence of ring worms and other similar types of bacteria.
3. Fluorescent indicators such as fluorescein, eosin, acridine are widely used in acid base titrations of coloured substances.
4. Fluorescence spectroscopy is used in analysis of drugs and dyes, textiles and paper, fuels and chemicals etc.

6.6.3 Phosphorescence

The phenomena of phosphorescence is almost similar to that of fluorescence. It is a type of **delayed fluorescence**, where the molecule emits light continuously even after the removal of source of light. Substances exhibiting this phenomena are called as **phosphorescent substances**.

This phenomena is more pronounced in solids. For example minerals (like ruby, emerald), sulphates of alkaline earth metals, zinc sulphate etc.

Applications: Phosphorescence also finds applications in medicine, biology and in analytical analysis.

1. In determination of cocaine and atropine in urine.
2. Phosphorescence also finds application in television tubes.
3. Certain phosphorescent pigments of alkaline earth metals are used in manufacturing paint, ink, plastic, rubber films etc. These phosphorescent pigments are especially suitable for the production of afterglow safety products like warning, mandatory and escape-route signs.

Although there are lot of similarities between fluorescene and phosphoresene there are many differences which are listed below in Table 6.2.

Table 6.2: Differences between Fluorescence and Phosphorescence

Fluorescence	Phosphorescence
• Fluorescence is an instantaneous emission of light by an excited molecule.	• Phosphorescence is a delayed emission of light by an excited molecule.
• The emission of light suddenly stops on removal of source of excitation.	• The emission of light remains for some time even after the removal of source of excitation.
• In fluorescence, the excited atom has comparatively short life time (10^{-6} to 10^{-9} sec) before its transition to lower energy states,	• In phosphorescence the excited atom has comparatively long life time (10^{-4} to few sec) before its transition to lower energy states,
• Fluorescence involves transition from excited singlet state S_1 to ground state S_0.	• It involves transition from excited triplet state T_1 to ground state S_0.
• It involves allowed transitions.	• These transitions are spectroscopically forbidden.

• Fluorescence can be observed in solutions at room temperature,	• Phosphorescence is not observed in solution at room temperature.
• Fluorescence spectrum is the mirror image of the absorption spectrum.	• Phosphorescence spectrum is not the mirror image of the absorption spectrum.
• Jelly fish, chlorophyll fluorspar etc. fluoresce.	• Glow of clock dial, bulbs after switching off the light in room, sulphates of alkaline earth metals etc. shows phosphorescence.
• 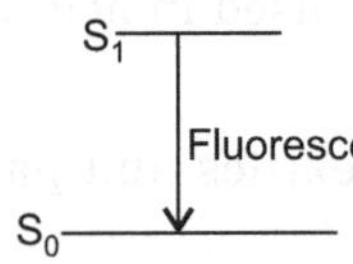	• 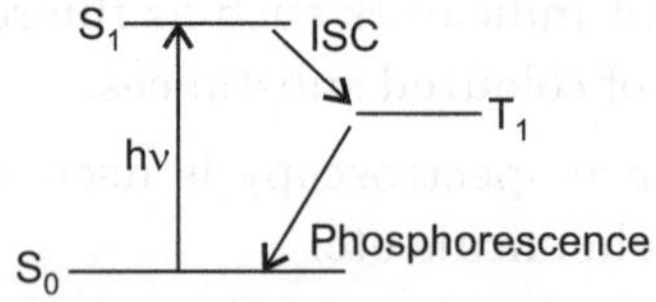

6.6.4 Chemiluminescence

Chemiluminescence is the phenomenon of production of light by a chemical reaction. Therefore, it can be considered as a reverse of a photochemical reaction in which absorption of light brings about chemical change.

For a chemical reaction to produce light, it must furnish sufficient energy to excite at least one of the reactants or intermediates to a higher electronic state so that when it returns to ground state, the absorbed energy may be re-emitted in the form of radiation. Chemiluminescent reactions do not usually release much heat. Some examples of chemiluminescent reactions are:

(*i*) Luminescence produced by phosphorus and its oxides.

(*ii*) Electron transfer reactions

(*iii*) The decay of luminous jelly fish observed at night in the ocean.

(*iv*) "Cold light" emission by glow worms or fireflies. This biochemical reaction involves the oxidation of a protein 'luciferin' by atmospheric oxygen in presence of enzyme luciferase.

Applications:

1. Chemiluminescent substances are used in lighting objects like glow sticks, emergency light, toys etc.
2. Chemiluminescence find various applications in analytical field like analysis of inorganic species in liquid phase, gas analysis etc.
3. Use of luminol in forensics to detect the presence of blood. Luminol reacts with tiny amounts of iron to generate luminescence. Detectives also use luminol at crime scenes.

6.7 PHOTOSENSITIZATION

There are many substances which do not react directly when exposed to radiations. However, if a foreign substance is added the photochemical reaction starts. This foreign substance apparently does not undergo any chemical change. It simply absorbs the light energy and transfers it to one of the reactants. Such a foreign substance which when added to a reaction mixture helps to starts a photochemical reaction, without itself undergoing any chemical change is called as **photosensitizer** and the reaction is called as **photosensitized reaction** or simply **photosensitization**. Commonly used photosensitizers are mercury, cadmium, zinc, benzophenone, sulphur dioxide etc.

Let 'P' denote the photosensitizer and A is the reactant, then the mechanism of photosensitization can be represented as:

(*i*) $P + h\nu \xrightarrow{\text{excitation}} P^*$

(*ii*) $P^* + A \xrightarrow[\text{transfer}]{\text{energy}} P + A^*$

(*iii*) $A^* \longrightarrow \text{Products}$

A few examples of photosensitized reactions are:

1. The most common example of photosensitization is photosynthesis in plants in presence of chlorophyll as a photosensitizer. The photosynthesis can be represented by the following reaction:

$$nCO_2 + nH_2O + h\nu \xrightarrow{\text{chlorophyll}} (CH_2O)_n + nO_2$$

Both CO_2 and H_2O do not absorb light in the visible region and thus do not react with each other independently. The green pigment, chlorophyll absorbs light in the visible region of 600 – 700 nm and transfers it to CO_2 and H_2O molecules which in turn react to form carbohydrates.

2. **Dissociation of hydrogen molecule in presence of mercury vapours:** Hydrogen molecules are not affected when exposed to UV light. However, when a mixture of hydrogen gas and mercury vapours is exposed to UV light, it undergoes dissociation and forms hydrogen atoms. Thus, mercury acts as photosensitizer. This is represented by the following reactions.

(*i*) $Hg + h\nu \xrightarrow{\text{excitation}} Hg^*$

(*ii*) $Hg^* + H_2 \xrightarrow[\text{transfer}]{\text{energy}} H_2^* + Hg$

(*iii*) $H_2^* \longrightarrow 2H$

3. **Isomerization of 2-butene in presence of SO_2:** The *cis*-2-butene undergoes isomerization to give *trans*-2-butene when exposed to radiation of 253.7 nm wavelength in presence of SO_2 which acts as a photosensitizer.

(*i*) $SO_2 \xrightarrow[\text{excited}]{h\nu} SO^*_2$

(*ii*) $SO_2^* + cis\text{-2-Butene} \xrightarrow[\text{transfer}]{\text{energy}} SO_2 + cis\text{-2-Butene}^*$

(*iii*) $cis\text{-2-Butene}^* \longrightarrow trans\text{-2-Butene}$

4. **Decomposition of oxalic acid in the presence of uranyl ions:** Oxalic acid undergoes decomposition in presence of a photosensitizer uranyl ions (UO_2^{2+}), The schematic reactions are:

(*i*) $UO_2^{2+} + h\nu \xrightarrow{\text{excitation}} (UO_2^{2+})^*$

(*ii*) $(UO_2^{2+})^* + H_2C_2O_4 \xrightarrow[\text{transfer}]{\text{energy}} UO_2^{2+} + H_2C_2O_4^*$

(*iii*) $H_2C_2O_4^* \longrightarrow CO_2 + CO + H_2O$

Other examples are dissociation of ethylene in presence of mercury vapours, decomposition of diazomethane in the presence of benzophenone, combination of CO and H_2 in presence of mercury vapours etc.

6.8 PHOTOLYSIS OF CARBONYL COMPOUNDS

Carbonyl compounds can undergo various photochemical reactions the most important of which are Norrish type reactions which are named after a chemist Ronald G.W. Norrish.

Norrish type reactions: These are photochemical reactions which involve excitation of a carbonyl compound. They are of two types, one being a cleavage reaction (Norrish type I) and the other a hydrogen abstract reaction that can further lead to cleavage of the compound (Norrish type II).

Norrish type I reactions: The bond dissociation energy of carbon-cabon bond adjacent to a carbonyl group is comparatively small and consequently photochemical excitation of ketones generally results in homolytic fission of the C—CO bond followed by elimination of carbon monoxide. This process is known as **α-cleavage** or **Norrish type I reaction.** An extensively studied reaction is the photolysis of acetone in vapour phase, the products of the reaction depend on the temperature of the experiment. Absorption of light results in the excitation of acetone which then undergoes carbon-carbon cleavage giving a methyl and an acetyl radical.

$$CH_3{-}\overset{O}{\overset{\|}{C}}{-}CH_3 \xrightarrow{h\nu} [CH_3{-}\overset{O}{\overset{\|}{C}}{-}CH_3]^* \longrightarrow CH_3^{\bullet} + CH_3{-}\overset{O}{\overset{\|}{C}}{}^{\bullet}$$

The radicals proceed to form final products by a number of secondary reactions

1. **At room temperature:** At room temperature the products are diacetyl, acetaldehyde, methane and hexane-2, 5-dione.

$$CH_3{-}\overset{O}{\overset{\|}{C}}{}^* + CH_3{-}\overset{O}{\overset{\|}{C}}{-}CH_3 \longrightarrow CH_3\overset{O}{\overset{\|}{C}}{-}H + \overset{*}{C}H_2{-}\overset{O}{\overset{\|}{C}}{-}CH_3$$

$$CH_3^* + CH_3{-}\overset{O}{\overset{\|}{C}}{-}CH_3 \longrightarrow CH_4 + CH_3{-}\overset{O}{\overset{\|}{C}}{-}CH_2^*$$

$$2CH_3{-}\overset{O}{\overset{\|}{C}}{}^* \longrightarrow CH_3{-}\overset{O}{\overset{\|}{C}}{-}\overset{O}{\overset{\|}{C}}{-}CH_3$$

$$2CH_3{-}\overset{O}{\overset{\|}{C}}{-}CH_2^* \longrightarrow CH_3{-}\overset{O}{\overset{\|}{C}}{-}CH_2{-}CH_2{-}\overset{O}{\overset{\|}{C}}{-}CH_3$$

2. **At elevated temperature:** Above 100°C, acetyl radicals decarbonylate with the production of carbon monoxide and ethane.

$$CH_3{-}\overset{O}{\overset{\|}{C}}{}^* \longrightarrow CH_3^* + CO$$

$$2CH_3^* \longrightarrow CH_3{-}CH_3$$

Acetone is a symmetrical ketone but when the ketone is unsymmetrical, fission takes place in a way as to generate mainly the more stable radical. For example, photodissociation of ethyl methyl ketone gives predominantly ethyl radical and small amount of methyl radical.

$$CH_3{-}\overset{O}{\overset{\|}{C}}{}^* + {}^*CH_2{-}CH_3 \xleftarrow{h\nu} CH_3\overset{O}{\overset{\|}{C}}{-}CH_2{-}CH_3 \xrightarrow{h\nu} CH_3^* + {}^*\overset{O}{\overset{\|}{C}}{-}CH_2{-}CH_3$$

Norrish type II reaction: When the length and complexity of alkyl group increases, the products of photolysis becomes more complicated. Thus, when ketones possessing γ-hydrogen atom are heated, a six-membered cyclic transition state is found which results into the formation of an alkene and an enol (of a smaller ketone). The enol tautomerises to the carbonyl compound. This type of photolysis of ketones and aldehydes is called as **Norrish type II reaction**.

For example: Hexan-2-one

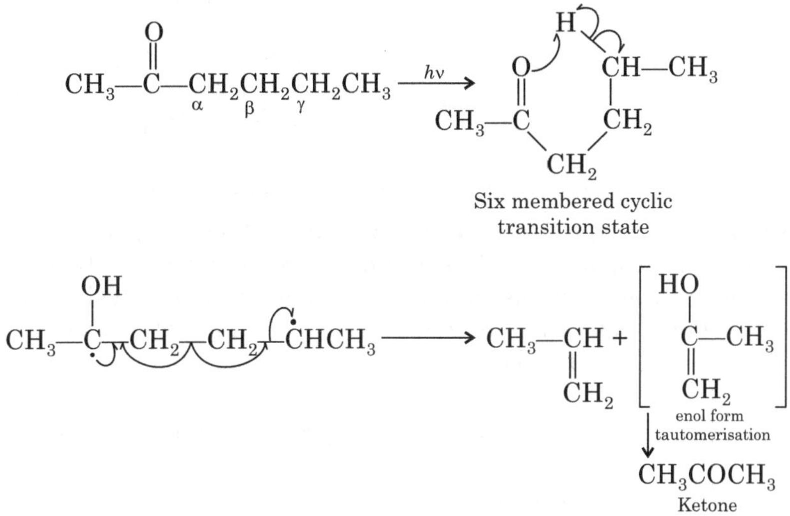

6.9 PHOTOEXCITATION OF ORGANIC MOLECULES

Organic molecules undergo photochemical reactions because of electron transitions of $\pi - \pi^*$ or $n - \pi^*$ or intramolecular charge transfer excitation. Most widely studied organic molecules are carbonyl compounds therefore, they are largely used to describe the various types of photochemical reactions. Organic molecules undergo following types of photochemical reactions on exposure to light.

1. **Photochemical elimination/cleavage reaction:** These include Norrish type I, Norrish type II, Barton reaction etc.
2. **Photochemical reduction reaction:** In these reactions, a H-atom is abstracted from the solvent or from other reactant to generate two free radicals. For example irradiation of benzophenone in alcoholic solvent.

$$Ph_2CO \xrightarrow{h\nu} Ph_2CO^*$$
$$Ph_2CO^* + (CH_3)_2\,CHOH \longrightarrow Ph_2C - OH + (CH_3)_2C^* - OH$$
$$(CH_3)_2\,C^* - OH + Ph_2CO \longrightarrow (CH_3)_2CO + Ph_2C^* - OH$$
$$2Ph_2\,{}^*COH \longrightarrow Ph_2C(OH)C(OH)Ph_2$$

   Quantum yield for this reaction is 2.
3. **Photochemical oxidation reaction:** This is a **photosensitized reaction**. Some organic compounds undergo oxidation in presence of oxygen to form peroxides, hydroperoxides etc. Oxygen adds to organic compounds both in the presence or absence of a sensitizer. Example: Photo-oxidation of anthracene.

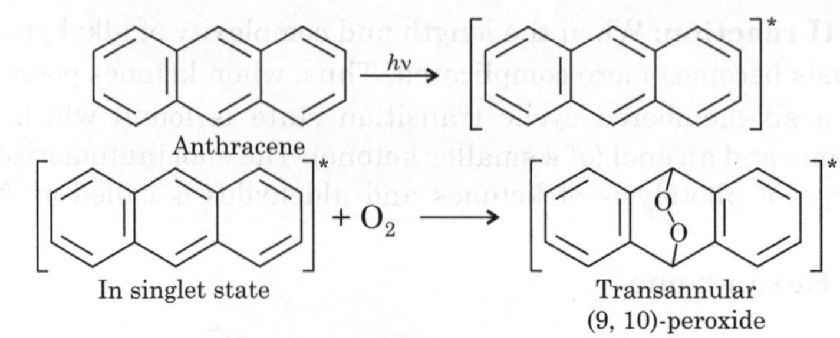

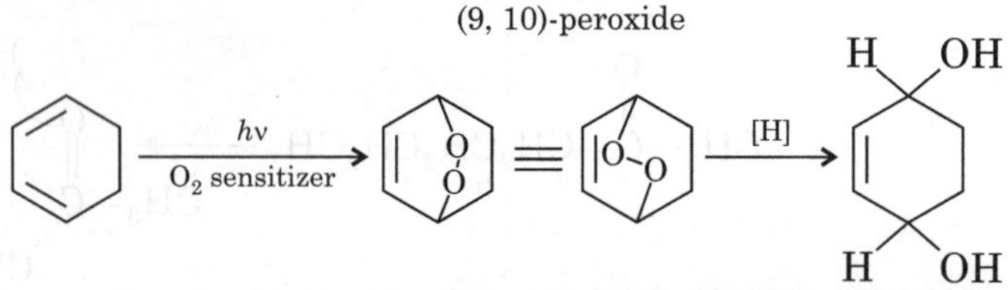

The synthetic utility of this reaction is due to the reduction of peroxides to diols.

Photochemical *cis-trans* isomerization: Alkenes display a characteristic photochemical interconversion of *cis* and *trans* isomers. Generally, the *trans*-isomer is thermodynamically more stable than the *cis*-isomer and photolysis gives a mixture rich in *cis*-isomer. Photolysis, thus provides a useful method of converting a *trans*-alkene to *cis*-alkene. It can be carried out by irradiation alone or in presence of a catalyst or a sensitizer.

For example, isomerization of stilbene in the presence of benzophenone as sensitizer.

$$\underset{\text{Benzophenone}}{Ph_2CO} \xrightarrow{h\nu} [Ph_2CO]^*$$

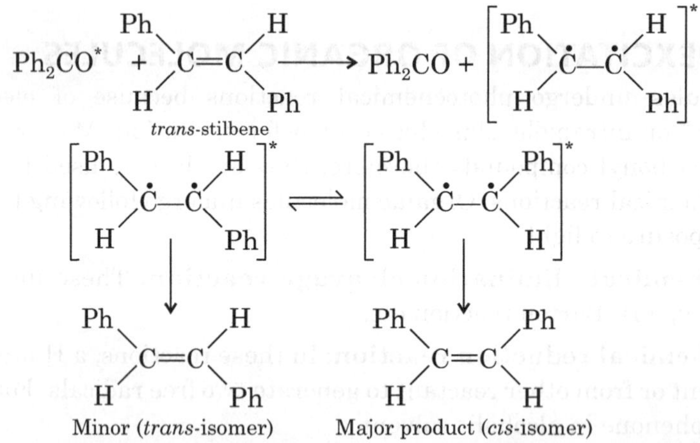

4. **Photochemical rearrangements:** Organic compounds like α, β unsaturated ketones and alkenes undergo various types of rearrangements when irradiated with light.

For example,

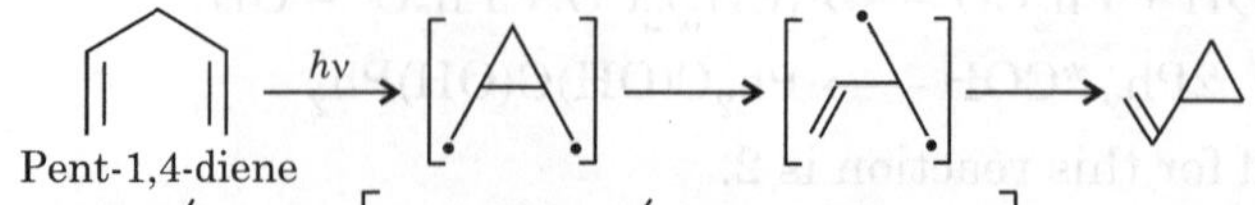

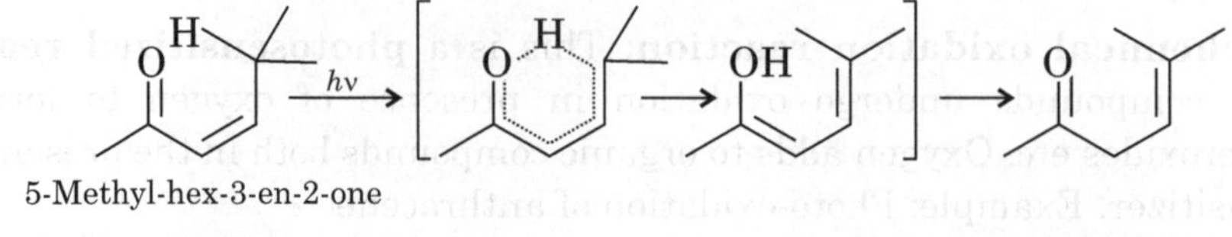

5. Photochemical dimerization and cycloaddition reactions

$$\underset{\text{Anthracene}}{2(C_{14}H_{10})} \xrightarrow{h\nu} \underset{\text{Dianthracene}}{C_{28}H_{20}}$$

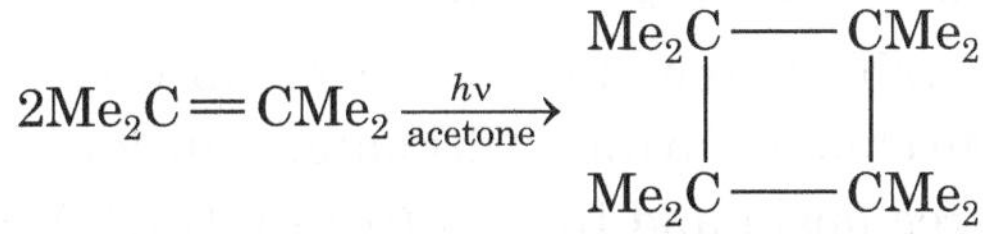

It involves certain electrocyclic reactions which have very complicated mechanism. Example: Dies-Alder reaction.

6.10 CHEMISTRY OF VISION

Vision is without doubt, the most important of all our senses. 40% of all sensory information about our world comes to us through our eyes. **But how do we see ?** The answer to this question lies in the following paragraphs.

The retina of our eyes is lined with many millions of photoreceptor cells that consist of two types of light sensitive cells: **rods** and **cones**. The rods are receptors for black and white light and are the dominant receptors in dim light, cones on the other hand are necessary for colour vision and are dominant receptor cells in bright light only. Rhodopsin is the only photoreceptor protein (a visual pigment) in the outer segment of rod cells. **Rhodopsin** has 11-*cis* retinal as its chromophore, which precisely fits into a cavity in a protein called **opsin**. Sources of 11-cis retinal are vitamin A and β-carotene. A diet lacking in vitamin A can lead to night blindness and a diet rich in β-carotene (found in carrots) can improve vision.

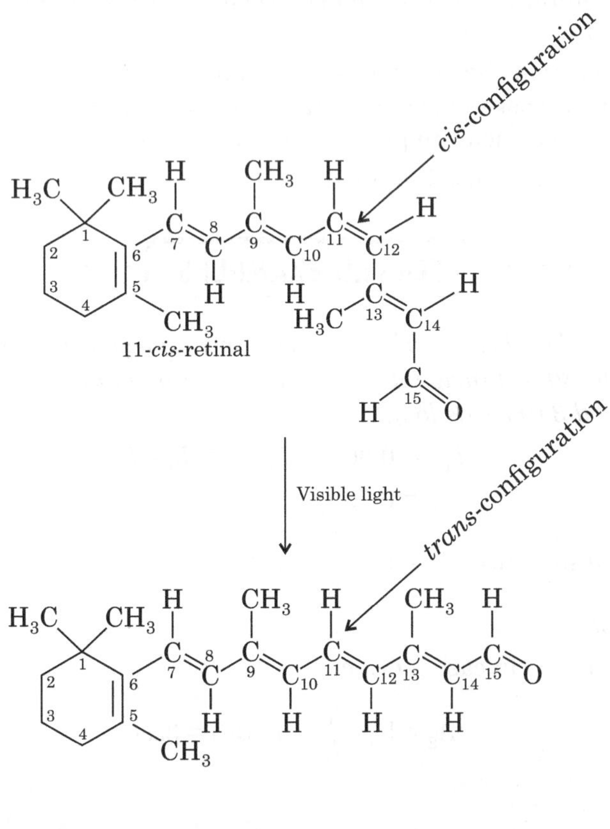

When light strikes the retina of our eyes, the 11-*cis* retinal portion of rhodopsin absorbs a photon and a *cis-trans* photo isomerization occurs leading to the formation of all *trans*-retinal. This *trans*-retinal docs not fit well into the protein opsin and so a series of geometrical changes begins in the protein. The resulting complex is called as **bathrhodopsin**.

Bathrhodopsin is too unstable to remain in this configuration for long. Within 10^{-9} sec, the shape of the protein begins to change further. Ultimately, all *trans* retinal molecule is expelled from the protein, giving a free opsin and free all *trans* retinal At intermediate temperature, certain intermediates have been isolated. These are:

Rhodopsin → Bathrhodopsin → Lumirhodopsin → Metarhodopsin I → Metarhodopsin II → *trans*-Retinal free.

For vision to occur, the important intermediate is metarhodopsin II. This intermediate activates the enzyme transducin, which starts the impressive signal transduction cascade, resulting in production of nerve impulse to the brain.

Applications of Photochemistry: Photochemistry finds applications in various fields.

1. Photophysical phenomena of fluorescence and phosphorescence find useful applications in the development of X-ray and television screens, fluorescent lamps, optical brightners in paints and white dress material, luminescent dials for watches etc.
2. The development of LASER technology is a recent marvellous application of photochemistry. LASERS are intense source of monochromatic and coherent radiations used in medical field, industries, construction etc.
3. Photochemistry also finds increasing application in solving the energy crisis by conversion and storage of solar energy. (Solar batteries operate on the principle of photovoltaic cells).
4. Photochemical reactions have been used to manufacture certain chemicals like vitamin D_2 (by irradiating ergosterol), caprolactam (from cyclohexene and NOCl), gammexane, which are otherwise difficult to produce *via.* thermal reactions.
5. Photochemistry is widely used in photography.

SOLVED EXAMPLES

Example 6.1. *In a Lambert-Beer's law cell, the aqueous solution of a substance of concentration 'c' absorbs 30% of incident light. What fraction of incident light will be absorbed by same solution in a cell 3 times as long?*

Solution: Case 1: $I_{abs} = 0.30 \qquad I_0 = I_t = I_0 - I_{abs}$

$$I = 0.70\ I_0$$

$$\text{(Absorbance) } A_1 = \log \frac{I_0}{I_t} = \varepsilon cl \qquad ...(i)$$

Case 2: Here $l' = 3l$

Concentration is same as in case 1 *i.e.*, c

$$\therefore \qquad A_2 = \log \frac{I_0}{I_t} = \varepsilon\ c(3l) = 3\varepsilon cl \qquad ...(ii)$$

From equations (*i*) and (*ii*), we get

$$\frac{A_2}{A_1} = \frac{3\varepsilon cl}{\varepsilon cl} = 3$$

$$A_2 = 3A_1 = 3\log\left(\frac{I_0}{I_t}\right) = 3\log\left(\frac{100}{70}\right)$$

$$A_2 = 3(\log 100 - \log 70) = 3(2 - 1.845)$$

$$= 3(0.155) = 0.465$$

$$A_2 = \log\frac{I_0}{I_t}$$

$$\log\frac{I_0}{I_t} = 0.465 \text{ or } \frac{I_0}{I_t} = \text{antilog } 0.465 = 2.917$$

$$I_t = \frac{I_0}{2.917} = \frac{100}{2.917}\ 34.28$$

$$I_{abs} = 100 - 34.28 = 65.72$$

Therefore, fraction of light absorbed = 0.657.

Example 6.2. *Calculate the energy per mole of light having wavelength (i) 2000 Å, (ii) 4000 Å, (iii) 8000 Å.*

Solution: Energy per mole = $\frac{N_A hc}{\lambda}$ where $N_A = 6.02 \times 10^{23}$ mol^{-1}, $h = 6.626 \times 10^{-34}$ Js, $c = 3 \times 10^8$ m/s.

(*i*) $\lambda = 2000$ Å $= 2000 \times 10^{-10}$ m

$$E = \frac{(6.02\times10^{23}\ \text{mol}^{-1})\times(6.626\times10^{-34}\ \text{Js})\times(3\times10^{8}\ \text{ms}^{-1})}{2000\times10^{-10}\ \text{m}}$$

$$= 5.98 \times 10^5 \text{ J/mol.}$$

(*ii*) $\lambda = 4000$ Å $= 4000 \times 10^{-10}$ m

$$E = \frac{(6.02\times10^{23}\ \text{mol}^{-1})\times(6.626\times10^{-34}\ \text{Js})\times(3\times10^{8}\ \text{ms}^{-1})}{4000\times10^{-10}\ \text{m}}$$

$$= 2.99 \times 10^5 \text{ J/mol.}$$

(*iii*) $\lambda = 8000$ Å – 8000×10^{-10} m

$$E = \frac{(6.02\times10^{23}\ \text{mol}^{-1})\times(6.626\times10^{-34}\ \text{Js})\times(3\times10^{8}\ \text{ms}^{-1})}{8000\times10^{-10}\ \text{m}}$$

$$= 1.49 \times 10^5 \text{ J/mol.}$$

Example 6.3. *A solution shows a transmittance of 22% when taken in a cell of 3.0 cm thickness. Calculate its concentration, if the molar absorptivity is 12000 dm^3 mol^{-1}cm^{-1}.*

Solution: Transmittance = $\frac{I}{I_0} = 22\% = 0.22$ or $\frac{I_0}{I} = \frac{1}{0.22} = 4.5$

$$\varepsilon = 12000 \text{ dm}^3 \text{ mol}^{-1} \text{ cm}^{-1},\ l = 3.0 \text{ cm}$$

$$\log\frac{I_0}{I}. = \varepsilon\, cl$$

$$\log 4.5 = (12000 \text{ dm}^3 \text{ mol}^{-1} \text{ cm}^{-1}) \times c \times 3.0 \text{ cm}$$

$$0.6532 = (36000 \text{ dm}^3 \text{ mol}^{-1}) \times c$$

$$= \frac{0.6532}{36000} \text{ mol dm}^{-3} = 1.814 \times 10^{-5} \text{ mol dm}^{-3}.$$

Example 6.4. *Intensity of light of wavelength 2600 Å when passed through a 1.0 mm cell containing 0.05 M benzene solution, the light intensity is reduced to 16% of its initial value. Calculate the absorbance and molar absorption coefficient of the sample. Also calculate the transmittance through a 2.0 mm cell.*

Solution: $\frac{I}{I_0} = 16\% = 0.16,\ c = 0.05 \text{ M},\ l = 1.0 \text{ mm} = 0.1 \text{ cm}$

$$\log \frac{I_0}{I} = \varepsilon cl$$

$$\log \frac{1}{0.16} = \varepsilon \times 0.05 \times 0.1$$

or $\log 100 - \log 16 = \varepsilon \times 0.005$

$$2 - 1.204 = \varepsilon \times 0.005$$

$$= \frac{0.796}{0.005} = 159.2 \text{ M}^{-1} \text{ cm}^{-1}$$

Absorbance, $A = \varepsilon cl = 159.2 \times 0.05 \times 0.1 = 0.796$

when, $l = 2 \text{ mm} = 0.2 \text{ cm}$

ε will be the same, as the solution is same.

∴ $\varepsilon = 159.2 \text{ M}^{-1} \text{ cm}^{-1},\ c = 0.05 \text{ M}$

$$\log \frac{I_0}{I} = \varepsilon cl = 159.2 \times 0.05 \times 0.2 = 1.592$$

$$\frac{I_0}{I} = \text{antilog } 1.592$$

$$\frac{I_0}{I} = 39.08$$

or $\text{transmittance} = \frac{I}{I_0} = \frac{1}{39.08} = 0.025 \text{ or } 2.5\%.$

Example 6.5. *A wavelength of 520 nm was used to decompose a gas substance. When 280 joules of energy was found to decompose 1.5 × 10*$^{-3}$ *moles of substance. Calculate the quantum yield for the dissociation of the gas.*

Solution: Wavelength of light used = 520 nm

Number of moles of substances decomposed = 1.5×10^{-3}

Number of molecules of substances decomposed = $1.5 \times 10^{-3} \times 6.02 \times 10^{23}$

1 mol contains 6.02×10^{23} molecules

Energy of quantum of radiation having wavelength 520 nm is

$$E = \frac{hc}{\lambda} = \frac{6.624 \times 10^{-34} \times 3 \times 10^{8}}{520 \times 10^{-9}}$$

$$= 3.821 \times 10^{-19} \text{ Joules}$$

$$\text{No. of Photon} = \frac{\text{Total energy}}{\text{Energy of one photon}}$$

The number of quanta absorbed (N_{abs}) by the substance is

$$E_{abs} = N_{abs} \frac{hc}{\lambda}$$

$$N_{abs} = \frac{E_{abs}\lambda}{hc} = \frac{280}{3.821 \times 10^{-19}} = 7.33 \times 10^{20}$$

$$\text{Quantum yield} = \frac{\text{Number of molecules decomposed}}{\text{Number of quanta absorbed}}$$

$$= \frac{1.5 \times 10^{-3} \times 6.02 \times 10^{23}}{7.33 \times 10^{20}} = 1.23.$$

Example 6.6. *0.05 moles of a substance reacted in 20 minutes. The number of photons absorbed per second is 2.0 × 10^6. Calculate the quantum yield of the reaction.*

Solution: No. of moles of substance reacted = 0.05

Number of molecules of substance reacted = 0.05 × 6.02 × 10^{23}

Number of photons absorbed per second = 2.0 × 10^6

Number of photons absorbed in 20 minutes = 2.0 × 10^6 × 20 × 60

= 24 × 10^8

$$\text{Quantum yield} = \frac{\text{Number of molecules reacted}}{\text{Number of photons absorbed}}$$

$$= \frac{0.05 \times 6.02 \times 10^{23}}{24 \times 10^{8}} = 1.25 \times 10^{13}.$$

Example 6.7. *Calculate the energy associated with (i) one photon, (ii) one Einstein of radiation of wavelength 6200 Å.*

Solution: (*i*) Energy of one photon = $\frac{hc}{\lambda}$

$$= \frac{6.62 \times 10^{-34} \text{ Js} \times 3 \times 10^{8} \text{ ms}^{-1}}{6200 \times 10^{-10} \text{ m}} = 3.20 \times 10^{-19} \text{ J}.$$

(*ii*) Energy per einstein = $\frac{N_A hc}{\lambda}$ = 6.02 × 10^{23} × 3.20 × 10^{-19} J

= 1.93 × 10^5 J.

Example 6.8. *Photobromination of cinnamic acid to dibromocinnamic acid was carried out in a light of wavelength 440 nm. Using light intensity of 2.1 × 10^{-3} Js^{-1}, an exposure of 18 minutes decrease 0.069 millimole of bromine. The solution absorbed 78% of the light passing through it. Calculate the quantum yield of the reaction.*

Solution: Energy associated with a quantum of light of wavelength 440 nm = $\frac{hc}{\lambda}$

$$= \frac{6.626 \times 10^{-34}\ \text{Js} \times 3 \times 10^{8}\ \text{ms}^{-1}}{440 \times 10^{-9}\ \text{m}} = 4.51 \times 10^{-19}\ \text{J}$$

Intensity of light = 1.5×10^{-3} Js^{-1}

Radiation energy absorbed per second (78% absorption)

$$= 1.5 \times 10^{-3}\ \text{Js}^{-1} \times \frac{78}{100} = 1.17 \times 10^{-3}\ \text{Js}^{-1}$$

Radiation energy absorbed in 18 minutes

$$= 1.17 \times 10^{-3}\ \text{Js}^{-1} \times 18 \times 60\ \text{s}$$

$$= 1.26\ \text{J}$$

Number of quanta absorbed = $\frac{1.26\ \text{J}}{4.51 \times 10^{-19}\ \text{J}}$ = 2.79×10^{18} J.

Number of moles of bromine reacted = 0.069 millimole = 6.9×10^{-5} mole

Number of molecules of bromine reacted = $6.9 \times 10^{-5} \times 6.02 \times 10^{23}$

$$= 41.54 \times 10^{18}$$

$$\text{Quantum yield} = \frac{\text{Number of molecules reacted}}{\text{Number of quantum absorbed}}$$

$$= \frac{41.54 \times 10^{18}}{2.79 \times 10^{18}} = 14.88.$$

EXERCISES

I. SHORT ANSWER TYPE QUESTIONS

1. Explain the photophysical laws governing absorption of light.
2. Write a note on the following process:
   (*a*) Fluorescence (*b*) Phosphorescence
   (*c*) Internal conversion (*d*) Intersystem crossing.
3. Explain the term chemiluminescence. Give some examples.
4. Write an explanatory note on photosensitization, giving two examples.
5. How does a photochemical reaction differs from a thermal reaction?
6. Write various applications of photochemistry.
7. State Grothus Draper law of photochemistry.
8. What are photosensitized reactions. Explain photosynthesis in plants is a photosensitized reaction.
9. What is meant by quantum yield of a photochemical reaction? Discuss it.
10. What are primary and secondary process in photochemistry?
11. Write a note on singlet and triplet state.

12. Write a note on photodimerization of anthracene in benzene solution.
13. What do you mean by one Einstein of energy? How is it related to wavelength?
14. Define Lambert Beer's law. Write its various limitations.
15. Define photochemistry. What are photophysical and photochemical processes?

II. LONG ANSWER TYPE QUESTIONS

1. Draw Jablonski's diagram. Discuss the radiative and non-radiative transitions.

   [**Hint:** Non-radiative transitions include internal conversion and intersystem crossing. Radiative transitions include fluorescence and phosphorescence.]
2. Give the mechanism of photolysis of ammonia. What is the quantum yield of the process? Give reasons for your answer.
3. Write various differences between fluorescence and phosphorescence.
4. State and derive Lambert-Beer law for light absorption by solutions.
5. State and explain the Stark Einstein's law of photochemical equivalence. How would you explain very high and very low quantum yield of some photochemical reactions? Explain giving examples.
6. Define quantum yield of a photochemical reaction. How will you classify photochemical reactions on the basis of quantum yield?
7. Discuss the photochemistry of vision.
8. Explain Norrish type I and Norrish type II photochemical reactions of carbonyl compounds.
9. Give various types of photochemical reactions of organic compounds.
10. The quantum yield for the photochemical formation of HBr is low, around 2, while in case of HCl it is unusually high. Explain,
11. Discuss fluorescence and phosphorescence in terms of excitation of electrons (Jablonski diagram)
12. What are the various pathways available to a molecule excited by absorbing photon of light?
13. Give reasons for abnormal quantum yield.

III. NUMERICAL PROBLEMS

1. Calculate the absorbance, transmittance and absorption coefficient of a solution which absorbs 90% of a certain wavelength of light passed through 1 cm cell containing 0.25 M solution.
2. Calculate the energy associated with radiations having wavelength 4000 Å. Give answer in kcal mol^{-1} and kJ mol^{-1}.
3. When an incident light of wavelength 3000 Å was allowed to pass through 2 mm thick glass, the intensity of the radiation was reduced to $\frac{1}{10^{th}}$ of its initial value. What part of the same radiation will be absorbed by 1 mm thick glass?

4. Calculate the molar absorptivity of a 1×10^{-4} M solution, which has an absorbance of 0.20, when the path length is 2.5 cm.
5. A solution of thickness 2 cm transmits 40% incident light. Calculate the concentration of the solution. Given $\varepsilon = 6000\ dm^3\ mol^{-1}\ cm^{-1}$.
6. For the photochemical reaction $X \rightarrow Y$, 1.0×10^{-5} moles of B were formed on absorption of 6.0×10^7 ergs at 360 nm. Calculate the quantum efficiency.
7. When irradiated with light of 4000 Å wavelength, 2×10^{-4} mole of a substance is decomposed. Calculate the number of photons absorbed during the reactions, if its quantum efficiency is 8.0.
8. Irradiation of propionaldehyde with light of wavelength 3020 Å, decomposed it to form CO according to the reaction $CH_3CH_2CHO \rightarrow CH_3CH_3 + CO$
   The quantum yield of the reaction is 0.54. The light energy absorbed is 15000 erg mole in a given time. Find the amount of CO formed in moles in the same time.
9. A sample of gaseous HI was irradiated with light of wavelength 253.7 nm. When 307 J of energy was found to decompose 1.3×10^{-3} moles of HI, calculate the quantum yield for the decomposition reaction.
10. Calculate the optical density, if 20% of incident light is transmitted.

    $\left[\textbf{Hint: } \text{Optical density} = \log \dfrac{I_0}{I}.\right]$

IV. MULTIPLE CHOICE QUESTIONS

1. The process through which electronically excited molecules return to ground state having same multiplicity is called as
   (*a*) Fluorescence (*b*) Phosphorescence
   (*c*) Chemiluminescence (*d*) Photosensitization
2. Mathematical expression for Beer Lambert's Law is
   (*a*) $I_0 = I_t e^{-\varepsilon lc}$ (*b*) $I_0 = I_t e^{-\varepsilon cl}.\ Kc$ (*c*) $I_t = I_0 I_t e^{-\varepsilon cl}$ (*d*) $I_t = I_0 e^{-\varepsilon cl}$.
3. Light that is formed from a chemical reaction is called as
   (*a*) Luminescence (*b*) Chemiluminescence
   (*c*) Bioluminescence (*d*) All of the above.
4. Which of the following decay with change in multiplicity is called as *ISC*?
   (*a*) $S_1 \rightarrow S_0$ (*b*) $S_2 \rightarrow S_1$ (*c*) $T_2 \rightarrow T_1$ (*d*) $S_1 \rightarrow T_1$.
5. Photochemical reaction are accompanied by
   (*a*) Decrease in free energy
   (*b*) Increase in free energy
   (*c*) Both increase and decrease in free energy
   (*d*) Neither increase nor decrease in free energy.
6. The excitation of a molecule with spin inversion gives rise to:
   (*a*) Singlet excited state (*b*) Triplet excited state
   (*c*) Both (*a*) and (*b*) (*d*) None of the above.

7. The energy of one Einstein is given by

(*a*) $E = \frac{Nhc}{\lambda}$ (*b*) $E = h\lambda$ (*c*) $E = \frac{Nhc}{\upsilon}$ (*d*) $E = \frac{Nh\nu}{c}$

8. The quantum efficiency of a reaction which obey the law of photochemical equivalence is equal to:

(*a*) Unity (*b*) Less than unity

(c) Greater than unity (*d*) Unpredictable.

9. According to Grothus Draper law, a chemical change is produced only by those radiations which are:

(*a*) Emitted (*b*) Reflected (*c*) Absorbed (*d*) None of the above.

10. The quantum yield of the dimerization of anthracene is equal to:

(*a*) 2 (*b*) 1 (*c*) 0.5 (*d*) 10.

11. Intersystem crossing is a transition between

(*a*) States of same multiplicity (*b*) States of different multiplicity

(*c*) States of different energy (*d*) States of same energy.

12. Photosensitizer is substance which

(*a*) Increases the rate of a photochemical reaction

(*b*) Decreases the rate of a photochemical reaction

(*c*) Undergoes a chemical change and also initiates a photochemical change in other substances.

(*d*) Does not undergo any chemical change but initiates a photochemical change in other substances.

13. If a photochemical reaction has higher quantum yield than unity, it indicates

(*a*) Reversible reaction (*b*) Chain reaction

(*c*) Elementary reaction (*d*) None of these.

14. During the photolysis of ketones in Norrish type II reaction,

(*a*) CO is produced.

(*b*) Dimerization of radicals that are formed.

(*c*) A homolytic fission leads to the formation of a radical intermediate.

(*d*) Photoexcited carbonyl group abstracts *a* γ-hydrogen in primary process.

15. The quantum yield of the following reaction is

$$2HBr \longrightarrow H_2 + Br_2.$$

(*a*) 1.5 (*b*) 1.0 (*c*) 2.0 (*d*) 10.

16. Which one of the following decay takes place in phosphorescence?

(*a*) $S_1 \to S_0$ (*b*) $T_2 \to T_1$ (*c*) $T_1 \to S_0$ (*d*) $T_2 \to S_1$.

17. The units of molor absorption coefficient are:

(*a*) m^3 mol (*b*) m^2 mol (*c*) m^2 mol^{-1} (*d*) m mol^{-1}.

18. The wavelength range of radiations generally used for photochemical reaction is:

(*a*) 2000 – 8000 Å (*b*) 4000 – 6000 Å (*c*) 2000 – 4000 Å (*d*) 6000 – 8000 Å.

19. The thermal reactions are always accompanied by
- (*a*) A decrease in free energy
- (*b*) An increase in free energy
- (*c*) Free energy remains constant
- (*d*) Neither increase nor decrease in free energy.

20. In fluorescence which one of the following decay of excited state takes place?
(*a*) $T_2 \rightarrow T_1$ (*b*) $S_1,\rightarrow S_2$ (*c*) $T_1 \rightarrow S_0$ (*d*) All of the above.

21. The rate of a photochemical reaction depends on
- (*a*) Concentration of photochemical product
- (*b*) Intensity of light radiation
- (*c*) Both (*a*) and (*b*)
- (*d*) None of the above.

22. Organic dyes like eosin, chlorophyll etc show .... in the UV or visible region
(*a*) Chemiluminescence (*b*) Phosphorescence
(*c*) Fluorescence (*d*) None of the above.

23. In photochemical reactions the light absorption occurs in
- (*a*) Primary process only
- (*b*) Secondary process only
- (*c*) Both primary and secondary process
- (*d*) Either primary or secondary process.

24. In some photochemical reactions, low quantum yield is obtained. Its due to
- (*a*) Recombination of dissociated fragments
- (*b*) Deactivation of reacting molecules
- (*c*) Occurance of reverse primary reaction
- (*d*) All of these.

25. A photochemical reaction takes place by the absorption of
(*a*) Visible and UV light (*b*) IR light
(*c*) Heat energy (*d*) None of these.

Answers

III. Numerical Problems

1. $A = 1$, $T = 0.10$, $\varepsilon = 0.4\ L\ mol^{-1}\ cm^{-1}$
2. $E = 71.6$ kcal/mol, $E = 299.5$ kJ/mol
3. $I_{ab} = 0.684\ I_0$
4. $\varepsilon = 8000\ dm^3\ mol^{-1}\ cm^{-1}$
5. $c = 3.32 \times 10^{-5}\ mol\ dm^{-3}$
6. $\phi = 0.5$
7. 1.57×10^{19}
8. 2.04×10^{-9} moles.
9. $\phi = 2$
10. 0.699.

IV. Multiple Choice Questions

1. (*a*)	2. (*d*)	3. (*b*)	4. (*d*)	5. (*c*)	6. (*b*)	7. (*a*)	8. (*a*)	9. (*c*)	10. (*c*)
11. (*b*)	12. (*d*)	13. (*b*)	14. (*d*)	15. (*c*)	16. (*c*)	17. (*c*)	18. (*a*)	19. (*a*)	20. (*c*)
21. (*b*)	22. (*c*)	23. (*a*)	24. (*d*)	25. (*a*)					

Chapter 7 Thermodynamics

7.1 INTRODUCTION

Many physical and chemical processes are accompanied by energy changes which, ordinarily, appear in the form of evolution or absorption of heat.

The branch of physical science which deals with the study of different forms of energy and the quantitative relationship between them is called as thermodynamics.

The complete study of thermodynamics is based on three laws called first, second and third law of thermodynamics. These laws apply only where the systems is in equilibrium or shifts from one equilibrium state to another equilibrium state. These are based purely on human experience and there is no formal proof for these laws. However, the validity of these laws is, supported by the fact that nothing contrary to these laws has been found so far and nothing contrary is expected.

The word "Thermodynamics" implies flow of heat.

7.2 SIGNIFICANCE OF THERMODYNAMICS

Thermodynamics is a fundamental subject of great importance not only in physical chemistry but also in other branches of science like engineering, medicine, biotechnology, biochemistry, space sciences etc.

Some of the ways in which thermodynamics can be useful are as follows:

(*a*) It helps us to predict the spontaneity or feasibility of a process under the given set of conditions.

(*b*) It helps to predict the extent up to which a reaction can proceed before the equilibrium is attained.

(*c*) Most of the important laws of physical chemistry including Van't Hoff law of dilute solutions, Raoult's law of lowering of vapour pressure, distribution law, phase rule, laws of chemical equilibrium etc. can be deduced from the laws of thermodynamics.

7.3 LIMITATIONS OF THERMODYNAMICS

(*a*) These laws are applicable only to matter in bulk (system of large number of molecules) and not to individual molecules.

(*b*) Thermodynamics can predict the feasibility of a given process or a chemical reaction but does not tell anything about the rate at which the reaction proceeds.

(*c*) It deals only with the initial and final stages of a system but does not tell anything about the mechanism of the process.

7.4 SOME THERMODYNAMIC TERMS

1. **System and surroundings:** The part of the universe chosen for thermodynamic consideration (*i.e.* to study the effect of temperature, pressure, volume etc.) is called as a **system.**

   The remaining portion of the universe, excluding the system, is called as **surroundings.** In simple cases, surroundings generally mean air or a water bath in which a system under examination is immersed.

   Universe = System + Surroundings

   Types of systems: On the basis of exchange of matter and energy with the surroundings, there are 3 types of systems:

   1. **Open system:** A system is said to be an open system, if it can exchange both matter and energy with the surroundings. For example; hot tea in an open cup is an example of open system as it can exchange both matter and energy.
   2. **Closed system:** A system is said to be closed if it can exchange energy but not matter with the surroundings.

      For example; hot tea in a stainless steel flask is an example of closed system because heat is gradually lost and the liquid cools but there is no exchange of matter.
   3. **Isolated system:** A system which can neither exchange energy nor matter with the surroundings is called an isolated system. For example; hot tea in a thermos flask is an example of an isolated system. In this case, there is no exchange of matter or energy with the surroundings. However, a perfectly isolated system does not exist.

Homogeneous and Heterogeneous Systems: A system is said to be **homogeneous** when it is completely uniform throughout. A homogeneous system consists of only one phase. For example a pure solid, a pure liquid, a solution of two completely miscible liquids, a mixture of gases etc.

On the other hand, a system is said to be **heterogeneous**, when it is not uniform throughout. In other words, a heterogeneous system consists of two or more phases. For example; a mixture of oil and water, a mixture of solid and liquid, a mixture of two or more solids, a mixture of two or more immiscible liquids etc.

2. **Macroscopic property:** A system containing a large number of particles is called **macroscopic system**. The word macroscopic implies large quantities and the properties of a macroscopic system are called as bulk or macroscopic properties. For example; pressure, temperature, volume, density, melting point, etc. Macroscopic properties can be further divided into two types.

   (1) Extensive (2) Intensive.

   ***(a)* Extensive Properties**

   (*i*) The property of the system that depends on the amount of matter present in the system under consideration is called as an **extensive property**.

   (*ii*) They depend on the size (or extent) of the system.

   (*iii*) Extensive property is additive for independent and non-interacting sub systems.

(*iv*) They are not very helpful in identifying a sample as they can change according to sample size or other conditions.

(*v*) **Examples:** Mass, volume, enthalpy, entropy, internal energy, free energy, heat capacity, surface area, etc.

(*b*) Intensive Properties

(*i*) The property of the system that does not depend on the amount of matter present in the system is called as an **intensive property**.

(*ii*) They are independent of the size or extent of the system.

(*iii*) Intensive property is not additive but a bulk property.

(*iv*) They are very helpful in identifying a sample because they neither depend upon the amount of the sample nor do they change according to the conditions.

Examples: Temperature, pressure, concentration, density, freezing point, boiling point, viscosity, refractive index, surface tension, specific heat capacity etc.

3. **State of a system and state variables:** When macroscopic properties of the system like temperature, pressure, volume etc. have definite values, then the system is said to be in a particular state. If there is a change in any one of these properties, the system is said to change into a different state. Thus, the state of a system is defined by its macroscopic properties. The fundamental properties like temperature, pressure, volume, composition etc. that describe the state of a system are called as **state variables**. In actual practice, it is not essential to specify all the state variables to specify the state of a system because these variables are inter-dependent.

These variables are inter-related by a relationship called ideal gas equation ($PV = nRT$). Thus, for one mole of a pure ideal gas, the equation becomes.

$$PV = RT$$

where R is a constant. If out of the three variables P, V and T, any two variables are specified, the value of third becomes automatically fixed and can be calculated by using the gas equation. Hence, only two variables are required to define the state of a system.

4. **Thermodynamic processes:** The operation by which a system changes from one state to another state is called as **thermodynamic process**. On the basis of conditions under which the change of state is brought about, the thermodynamic process can be of following types:

(*a*) **Isothermal process:** A process is said to be isothermal, if the temperature of the system remains constant during each stage of the process. During this process, heat can flow from system to the surroundings and vice-versa to keep the temperature of the system constant.

(*b*) **Isobaric process:** A process is said to be isobaric, if the pressure of the system remains constant during each stage of the process. This is usually obtained by allowing the volume to expand or contact in such a way to neutralize any pressure change that is caused by heat transfer.

(*c*) **Isochoric process/Isometric or Isovolumetric process:** A process is said to be isochoric, when the volume of the system remains constant.

(*d*) **Adiabatic process:** A process is said to be adiabatic, when no heat is gained or lost by the system although the temperature of the system may change.

In an adiabatic process, if the process is endothermic, there is fall in temperature of the system, whereas the temperature of the system rises, if the process is exothermic.

(*e*) **Cyclic process:** A process in which the system returns to the original state after undergoing a series of changes is called as a cyclic process.

Reversible process: A process is said to be reversible, when it is carried out infinitesimally slowly through a series of steps so that the system remains almost in equilibrium and the process may be reversed at any stage by merely a small change in variables like temperature, pressure etc.

Characteristics of reversible process:

(*a*) The process is carried out infinitesimally slowly.

(*b*) The force driving this operation is only infinitesimally greater than the opposing force.

(*c*) It is an ideal process and takes infinite time.

(*d*) In such a process, the system and the surroundings are almost always in equilibrium with each other.

(*e*) It is difficult to realise in practice

(*f*) A reversible process can be made to go in either direction.

(*g*) Work obtained in this process is maximum.

Irreversible process: A process is said to be irreversible, when it is carried out rapidly so that the equilibrium with the surroundings is never maintained. All spontaneous processes are irreversible in nature.

Characteristics of irreversible process:

(*a*) The process is carried out rapidly.

(*b*) The driving force is much greater than the opposing force.

(*c*) It is a spontaneous process and takes finite time.

(*d*) System does not remain in equilibrium with the surroundings.

(*e*) It can be performed in practice.

(*f*) An irreversible process can proceed only in one direction.

(*g*) Work obtained is not maximum.

5. Internal energy and internal energy change: Every substance possesses a definite quantity of energy, called the internal energy or intrinsic energy. This internal energy depends upon factors such as nature of the substance, temperature, pressure and volume. It is represented by the symbol '*U*' and is made up of kinetic and potential energies of the constituent particles. The kinetic energy of particles is because of their motion, therefore it also includes their translational, rotational and vibrational energy. The *P.E* arises from various types of interactions between the particles and includes nuclear energy, electronic energy etc.

The exact magnitude of internal energy cannot be determined because it involves certain quantities which cannot be measured. However, fortunately in different processes, it is simply the change in internal energy that is required and not the absolute value. This change in internal energy is easily measurable quantity and is represented by ΔU, If U_1 and U_2 are the internal energies in initial and final state respectively, then the change in internal energy (ΔU) may be given by

$$\Delta U = U_2 - U_1,$$

Thus, internal energy is a state function as it depends only upon the initial and final states and is independent of the method by which this state has been attained.

6. **Some thermodynamic quantities:** Chemical reactions are accompanied by the change in energy. The exchange of energy between the system and the surroundings can occur is various ways. Two important means by which a system can exchange energy with the surroundings are heat and work.

   (*i*) **Heat:** Heat is a mode of exchange of energy between the system and the surroundings as a result of the difference of temperature between them. When the system is at higher temperature than the surroundings, then the heat is lost by the system to the surroundings whereas, if the temperature of the system is lower than that of the surroundings, then heat is gained by the system from the surroundings. The amount of heat lost or gained by the system is represented by the letter '*q*'.

   Sign convention of heat '*q*': When heat is absorbed or gained by the system from the surroundings, it is given a positive sign.

   When heat is lost by the system to the surroundings, it is given a negative sign.

   Heat is usually measured in term of 'calories', whereas the SI unit of heat is Joule (J).The two types of units are related to each other as:

   $$1 \text{ Calorie} = 4.184 \text{ Joules}$$

   or $$1 \text{ Joule} = 0.2390 \text{ Calories.}$$

   (*ii*) **Work:** It is another mode of exchange of energy. Work is said to be done if the point of application of force moves in the direction of the force. In other words, if f is the force and dl is the displacement of the point of application in the direction of force acts, then work done is given by the following expression.

   $$W = f \times dl$$

   In thermodynamics, we will come across generally two types of work. These are: (*i*) electrical work, (*ii*) pressure-volume work.

   Electrical work: Electrical work is defined as the product of E.M.F. and the quantity of electricity flowing through the circuit *i.e.*

   Electrical work = E.M.F. × Quantity of electricity.

   (*iii*) **Pressure-volume work or work of expansion/compression:** This type of work is involved in system consisting of gases. Pressure-volume work is said to be done when the gas expands or contracts against the internal pressure (usually atmospheric pressure). It is a kind of mechanical work. Consider a gas enclosed in a cylinder fitted with a frictionless piston (Fig.7.1) having '*a*' as the area of cross-section and the pressure on the piston is P_{ext} which is slightly less than the internal pressure of the gas. This pressure difference allows the gas to expand against the external pressure by moving the piston through a distance dl. Then, force acting on the piston is given by $f = P_{ext} \times a$.

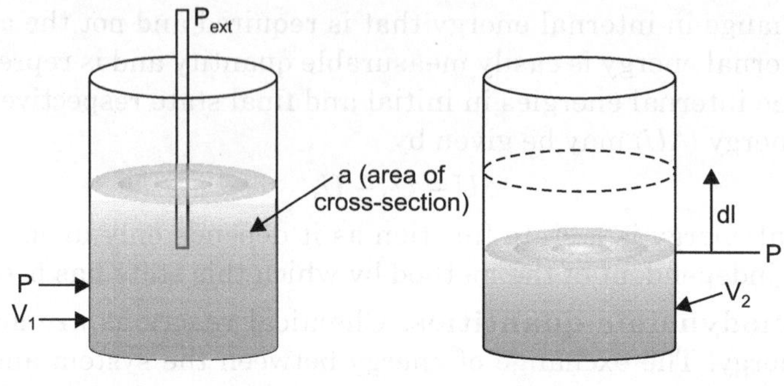

Fig. 7.1. Pressure volume work

By the definition of the work done by the system (*i.e.* gas)

$$W = f \times dl = P_{ext} \times a \times dl, \text{ but } aX\, dl = dV,$$

dV is a small increase in volume of the gas due to expansion

$$\therefore \quad dW = P_{ext} \times dV$$

If the gas expands from initial volume V_1 to final volume V_2, then the total work done can be obtained by integrating the above expression

$$W = \int_{V_1}^{V_2} P_{ext}\, dV \quad \text{where } P_{ext} = \text{constant}$$

$$= P_{ext} \int_{V_2}^{V_1} dV = P_{ext}\,(V_2 - V_1) = P_{ext}\,\Delta V$$

(*iv*) **Sign convention of W:** If work is done by the system (*i.e.*, during expansion), then it is given a negative sign.

If work is done on the system (*i.e* during contraction), then it is given a positive sign.

The general expression for the work done is written as.

$$W = -P_{ext}\,\Delta V = -P_{ext}\,(V_f - V_i)$$

(*v*) **Units of work:** Work is measured in units of ergs or joules.

$$1\text{ J} = 1\text{ Nm} = 1\text{ kg m}^2\text{ s}^{-2}$$

$$1\text{ J} = 10^7\text{ergs.}$$

Joules is the SI unit of work.

(*a*) Work done in an isothermal reversible expansion of an ideal gas is given by the expression

$$W = -2.303\, nRT \log \frac{V_2}{V_1}$$

$$= -2.303\, nRT \log \frac{P_1}{P_2}$$

Maximum work is done by the system when the process of expansion is carried out in a reversible manner.

(*b*) Work done during free expansion of an ideal gas, *i.e.* expansion against vacuum $\Delta P_{ext} = 0$ (for free expansion), therefore

$$W = P_{ext}\,\Delta V = 0$$

Thus, for a free expansion of an ideal gas against vacuum, the work done is zero.

(*c*) Work and heat are not state functions as their values do not depend merely on initial and final states but also upon the path followed.

7.5 FIRST LAW OF THERMODYNAMICS

First law of thermodynamics is sometimes called as the **law of conservation of energy** which states that **"energy can neither be created nor destroyed, although if can be transformed from one form to another"**. Thus, whenever energy in one form disappears an equal amount of energy in some other form must appear so that the total energy of the universe remains constant. The first law has been stated in various other ways also, but the basic idea remains the same. Some of its other statements are:

(*i*) The total energy of the universe (*i.e.* system + surroundings) remains constant, however, it may change from one form to another.

(*ii*) The energy of the system which is isolated form its surroundings is constant *i.e.* the energy of an isolated system is constant, although it may be transformed from one form to another.

The validity of first law is based on the fact that it is impossible to construct a perpetual motion machine, *i.e.* a machine which can produce energy without consuming energy. If the first law were not true, it would have been possible to construct such a machine.

Mathematical Expression of the First Law

Let us suppose that U_1 is the initial internal energy of the system. Again let us suppose that work (W) is performed on the system and at the same time heat (q) is supplied to the system. The heat absorbed by the system increases the internal energy of the system from U_1 to U_2. Thus, from the first law, we get

Heat supplied to the system = Increase in internal energy + Work done on the system.

$$q = U_2 - U_1 - W \qquad ...(7.1)$$

$$q = \Delta U - W \quad \text{or} \quad \Delta U = q + W \qquad ...(7.2)$$

This is the mathematical expression of the first law of thermodynamics.

If the work done is the work of expansion (*i.e.*, if work is done by the system) then equation (7.2) becomes

$$q = \Delta U + W$$

$$\Delta U = q - W$$

Work done by the system $W = -P\Delta V$

$$\therefore \qquad \Delta U = q - (-P\Delta V) = q + P\Delta V$$

If a system absorbs q amount heat and work (W) is done on the system then W is taken as positive and the change in internal energy becomes

$$\Delta U = q + (+W) = q + W.$$

Important Informations Derived From First Law

The equation of first law of thermodynamics takes different forms under different set of conditions.

(*i*) When the process is carried out at constant volume (isochoric process), then $\Delta V = 0$, therefore $W = 0$ and $\Delta U = q_v$ ...(7.3)
i.e Change in internal energy is equal to the heat absorbed at constant volume.

(*ii*) In an adiabatic process, where there is no exchange of heat between the system and the surroundings, $q = 0$

$$\Delta U = W_{ad}$$

It implies that if work is done on the system, its internal energy will increase. On the other hand, if work is done by the system, its internal energy will decrease. Thus, in an adiabatic process work is done by the system at the expense of its internal energy. This is the reason that in an adiabatic expansion of a gas, cooling effect is observed and during adiabatic compression, heating effect is observed.

(*iii*) In an isothermal process, where the temperature remains constant, the internal energy of the system does not change *i.e.* $\Delta U = 0 \therefore q = -W$ (as it is a function of temperature only).

Thus, during an isothermal process, the heat absorbed by the system is equal to the work done by the system.

(*iv*) When an ideal gas expand against vacuum or during free expansion of an ideal gas, $P = 0$ therefore $W = 0$ and, the internal energy change will be $\Delta U = q$.

7.6 ENTHALPY AND ENTHALPY CHANGE

The change in internal energy (ΔU) is equal the heat absorbed at constant volume (q_v) [Equation (7.3)]. But in laboratory, the experiments are usually performed at constant pressure and volume is allowed to change. So, the measured value of ΔU cannot account for the actual heat exchanged between the system and surroundings at constant pressure. Hence, there is a need of a new function that can account for the total heat content. This new function is called **heat content or enthalpy**. Thus, enthalpy is defined as:

$$H = U + PV$$

Where P is the pressure and V is the volume of the system.

(*a*) Enthalpy of a system is a state property *i.e.* it depends only on the initial and final states of the system and is independent of the path followed.

(*b*) Enthalpy is an extensive property as its value depends on the amount of substance present in the system.

(*c*) The absolute value of enthalpy of a system cannot be determined as the absolute value of internal energy is not known. However, change in enthalpy of a system can be determined.

Change in enthalpy may be expressed as

$$\Delta H = \Delta U + \Delta (PV)$$

$$\Delta H = \Delta U + P\Delta V + V\Delta P$$

Now, if the process is carried out at constant P *i.e.* $\Delta P = 0$, then ($\Delta H = \Delta U + P\Delta V$)

Thus, enthalpy change may be defined as sum of the increase in internal energy of the system and the pressure volume work done.

Depending upon the sign of ΔH, the chemical reactions are classified into two types—endothermic and exothermic.

The main points of difference between exothermic and endothermic reactions are given here.

Endothermic Reactions

(*i*) A reaction which proceeds with the absorption of heat energy is called as *endothermic reactions.*

(*ii*) Change in enthalpy (ΔH) is always positive $\Delta H = H_P - H_R$.

(*iii*) The enthalpy of products will be more than the enthalpy of reactants *i.e.* $\Delta H = H_P - H_R$ = positive.

(*iv*) Endothermic reactions cool their surroundings.

(*v*) Graphically:

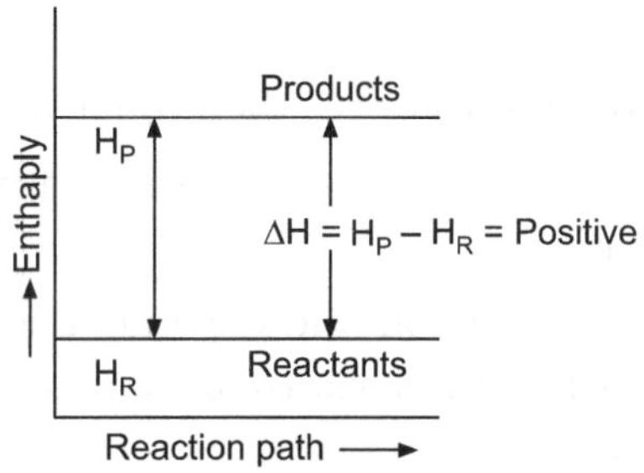

(*vi*) For endothermic reactions, ΔU is also positive.

(*vii*) Photosynthesis – plants absorb heat energy from sunlight to convert CO_2 and H_2O into glucose and oxygen

$$CO_2 + H_2O + \text{heat} \longrightarrow C_6H_{12}O_6 + 6O_2$$

Exothermic Reactions

(*i*) A reaction which proceeds with the evolution of heat energy is called as *exothermic reaction.*

(*ii*) Change in enthalpy (ΔH) is always negative.

(*iii*) The enthalpy of products will be less than the enthalpy of reactants.

$$\Delta H = H_p - H_R = \text{Negative}$$

(*iv*) Exothermic reactions make surroundings hotter.

(*v*) Graphically,

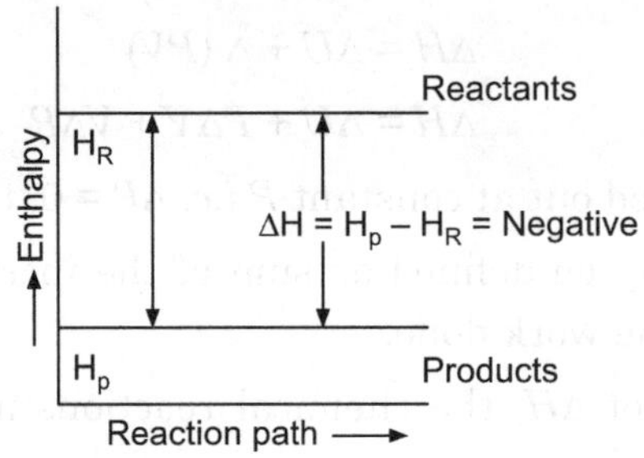

(*vi*) For exothermic reactions, ΔU is also negative.

(*vii*) Burning of carbon containing compounds uses oxygen from air and produces CO_2, H_2O and lots of heat.

$$CH_4 + 2O_2 \longrightarrow CO_2 + 2H_2O + \text{heat}$$

7.7 HEAT CAPACITY

The heat capacity of a system is defined as the amount of heat required to raise the temperature of the system by one degree. If '*q*' is the heat absorbed by the system and temperature of the system rises form T_1 to T_2, then the heat capacity (*C*) is given by expression,

$$C = \frac{q}{T_1 - T_2} = \frac{q}{\Delta T} \qquad ...(7.4)$$

For small changes, $C = \dfrac{dq}{dT}$

It q is in Joule and ΔT is in Kelvin (*K*) or °C, then the heat capacity will be in JK^{-1} or J/°C.

1. Heat capacity is an extensive property because the heat needed to raise the temperature of the system depends on its size.
2. Heat capacity is not a state function and depends upon the path followed. Hence, its value can be determined when the path conditions are specified. Consequently, there are two types of heat capacities:
   (*i*) Heat capacity at constant volume (represented by C_V)
   (*ii*) Heat capacity at constant pressure (represented by C_P)

According to first law of thermodynamics,

$$dq = dU + PdV \qquad ...(7.5)$$

Substitute this value in equation (7.4), we get

$$C = \frac{dU + PdV}{dT} \qquad ...(7.6)$$

At constant volume, $dV = 0$, therefore equation (7.6) becomes

$$C_V = \left(\frac{dU}{dT}\right)_V$$

Thus, heat capacity at constant volume may be defined as the rate of change of internal energy with temperature.

When the pressure of the system is kept constant, the equation (7.6) becomes

$$C_P = \frac{dU + PdV}{dT} \quad ...(7.7)$$

Also, we know that the enthalpy of a system is given by

$$H = U + PV$$

or at constant pressure,

$$dH = dU + PdV \quad ...(7.8)$$

Substitute equation (7.8) in equation (7.7), we get

$$C_P = \left(\frac{dH}{dT}\right)_P \quad ...(7.9)$$

Hence, heat capacity at constant pressure may be defined as the rate of change of enthalpy with temperature.

7.8 RELATION BETWEEN C_P AND C_V

1. Heat capacity at constant volume C_V and heat capacity at a pressure C_P are not equal for a given system.
2. When a gas is heated at constant volume, no external work is done by the gas because $\Delta V = 0$. Therefore, all the heat supplied to the system is used in increasing its internal energy.
3. However, when a gas is heated at constant pressure, $\Delta V \neq 0$, *i.e.* there will be increase in volume and the gas will expand and do some external work equal to PdV. Therefore, some extra heat (in addition to the heat required by system to increase the internal energy of its molecules) must be supplied to the gas to enable it to perform this external work.

Thus, for raising the temperature of the system by same value, the amount of heat absorbed at constant pressure is more than that at constant volume because at constant pressure some extra amount of heat is required to perform the work of expansion.

Thus $C_P > C_V$

For an ideal gas,

$$H = U + PV$$

Also, $PV = nRT$ for an ideal gas.

$$\therefore \quad H = U + nRT$$

Differentiate the above equation with respect to temperature

$$\frac{dH}{dT} = \frac{dU}{dT} + nR$$

$$C_P = C_V + nR$$

$$C_P - C_V = nR$$

For one mole of an ideal gas, $n = 1$

$$\therefore \quad C_P - C_V = R$$

Thus, the difference between the heat capacities at constant pressure and constant volume becomes equal to the universal gas constant, R whose value is 1.987 cal or 8.314 J.

This relation

$C_P - C_V = R$ is also called as **Meyer's relation.**

7.9 CALCULATION OF W, q, ΔU AND ΔH FOR ISOTHERMAL AND ADIABATIC EXPANSION OF AN IDEAL GAS

First law of thermodynamics can be used to calculate the changes in thermodynamic properties like q, W, ΔU and ΔH when an ideal gas undergoes expansion. The expansion of an ideal gas can be carried out either isothermally or adiabatically. Further, the expansion may be carried out reversibly or irreversibly.

Reversible isothermal expansion of an ideal gas

Internal energy of an ideal gas depends only on temperature, therefore for an isothermal process there will be no change in internal energy *i.e.* $\Delta U = 0$. Therefore, if an ideal gas expands isothermally (*i.e.* work is done by the system) then according to the first law of thermodynamics,

(*i*) $\Delta U = 0 \Rightarrow \Delta U = q + W = 0 \Rightarrow q = -W$

$$W = -2.303\, nRT \log \frac{V_2}{V_1}$$

$$= -2.303\, nRT \log \frac{P_1}{P_2}$$

$$\therefore \quad q = 2.303\, nRT \log \frac{P_1}{P_2} \qquad (\because q = -W)$$

(*ii*) Like ΔU the ethalpy change (ΔH) is also zero in reversible isothermal expansion process.

$$\Delta H = \Delta U + \Delta(PV) \qquad (\therefore PV = nRT \text{ for an ideal gas})$$

$$\Delta H = \Delta U + \Delta(nRT)$$

for an isothermal process

$$\Delta T = 0, \Delta U = 0$$

$$\therefore \quad \Delta H = 0 + 0 = 0.$$

Irreversible Isothermal Expansion

Irreversible isothermal expansion can be performed in two ways:

(*a*) Expansion against zero pressure (free expansion).

(*b*) Expansion against a constant external pressure (intermediate expansion).

- During free expansion of an ideal gas (*i.e.* when external pressure is zero) or expansion of an ideal gas against vacuum. Here, $P_{ext} = 0$

$$W = P_{ext}\, \Delta V = 0$$

- $\Delta U = 0$ as temperature remains constant in an isothermal process.

Also, $\Delta H = 0$ for an isothermal process

Now since $\Delta U = q + W$

$$0 = q + 0$$

$$\Delta q = 0 \qquad (\because \text{ Here, } W = 0)$$

Hence, for free expansion of an ideal gas.

$$W = 0, q = 0, \Delta U = 0 \text{ and } \Delta H = 0$$

- **During intermediate expansion:** Here, the gas expands against a constant external pressure. If the volume of the gas changes from V_1 to V_2, then work done is given by,

$$W = -\int_{V_1}^{V_2} P_{ext}\, dV$$

$$W = -P_{ext}(V_2 - V_1)$$

$$q = -W = P_{ext}(V_2 - V_1).$$

Reversible Adiabatic Expansion

In an adiabatic process, there is no exchange of heat between the system and the surroundings *i.e.*, $\Delta q = 0$, then according to first law of thermodynamics.

$$\Delta U = 0 + W$$

or

$$\Delta U = W$$

$$\Delta U = -P_{ext}\Delta V = -P_{ext}(V_2 - V_1)$$

We know that during expansion volume increases *i.e.* ΔV is positive and as a result ΔU becomes negative. This indicates that during adiabatic expansion, the internal energy of the system decreases. As a result, the temperature of the system falls. In other words, we can say that in an adiabatic expansion, work is done at the cost of internal energy of the gas.

$$\Delta U = C_V \Delta T$$

$$\Delta H = C_P \Delta T.$$

Irreversible Adiabatic Expansion

Irreversible adiabatic expansion can be performed in two ways:

(*a*) Free expansion

(*b*) Intermediate expansion

In free expansion $P_{ext} = 0 \therefore W = 0$

$$W = 0,\ q = 0,\ \Delta U = 0,\ \Delta H = 0$$

In intermediate expansion

$$W = -P_{ext}\Delta V$$

$$= -P_{ext}(V_2 - V_1).$$

7.10 VARIOUS HEAT OF REACTION

The enthalpy changes taking place during the chemical reactions have been given different names dependent upon the nature of the reaction. Some of then are:

Heat of reaction (ΔH)

The amount of heat absorbed or evolved in a chemical reaction, when molar quantities of the reactants as represented by the balanced chemical equation have completely reacted, is called the **heat of reaction or enthalpy of reaction**

$$\Delta H = \text{Sum of enthalpies of products} - \text{Sum of enthalpies of reactants.}$$

$$\Delta H = \sum a_i H_P - \sum b_i H_R$$

a_i and b_i represent coefficients of the products and reactants respectively and H_p and H_R represents enthalpies of products and reactants respectively. Let us consider the following example:

$$CH_4(g) + 2O_2(g) \longrightarrow CO_2(g) + 2H_2O(l); \Delta H = -890.4 \text{ kJ/mol}$$

This reaction indicates that when one mole of methane combines completely with two moles of oxygen, 890.4 kJ of heat is produced.

If the reactions is reversed, the sign of ΔH changes.

Enthalpy of Combustion

The enthalpy change, when one mole of a substance is completely burnt in excess of air or oxygen is called as **enthalpy of combustion**. For example

$$C(s) + O_2(g) \longrightarrow CO_2(g); \Delta H = \Delta H_C = -393.5 \text{ kJ}$$

Combustion reactions are always exothermic, therefore, heat of combustion is always negative.

Enthalpy of Formation

The enthalpy change when one mole of a substance is formed from its elements in their commonly or naturally occuring state is called as **heat of formation**. For example

$$C(s) + 2H_2(g) \longrightarrow CH_4(g); \Delta H = \Delta H_f = -74.8 \text{ kJ}$$

When one mole of methane is formed from its elements, C and H_2, 74.8 kJ of heat is evolved which is called as heat of formation of methane.

Standard enthalpy of formation is the enthalpy change of a reaction, when a substance is formed from its constituent elements, the reactants and products all being in a given standard state (*i.e.* 298 K and 1 bar pressure). For free elements in their standard state, the standard enthalpy of formation (ΔH_f^0) is taken as zero.

Enthalpy of Neutralization

The amount of heat evolved when one gram equivalent of an acid (or a base) is completely neutralized by one gram equivalent of a base (or an acid) in dilute solution is called as **enthalpy of neutralization**. For example,

$$NaOH(aq) + HCl(aq) \longrightarrow NaCl(aq) + H_2O(aq); \Delta H = 57.1 \text{ kJ/mol}$$

Thus, the enthalpy of naturalization of HCl with NaOH or vice-versa is 57.1 kJ/mol or 13.7 kcal. Enthalpies of neutralization of some strong bases with strong acids are given in the table:

S.No.	Acid	Base	Enthalpy of neutralization
1.	HNO_3	NaOH	– 57.1
2.	HCl	NaOH	– 57.1
3.	HCl	KOH	– 57.1
4.	HCl	LiOH	– 57.1

Heat of neutralization of a strong acid and strong base in dilute solution is always 57.1 kJ/mol. This constant value is due to the reason that heat of neutralization of a strong acid with strong base is actually the heat of formation of H_2O from H^+ of an acid and OH^- of a base,

For example,

$$H^+(aq) + OH^-(aq) \longrightarrow H_2O(l); \qquad \Delta H = -57.1 \text{ kJ/mol}$$

$$Na^+ + OH^- + H^+ + Cl^- \longrightarrow Na^+ + Cl^- + H_2O; \Delta H = -57.1 \text{ kJ/mol}$$

In case either the acid or the base or both are weak the enthaply of neutralization is generally less than 57.1 kJ.

Enthalpies of Phase Transition

(*a*) **Enthalpy of fusion:** Enthalpy change accompanying the conversion of one mole of a solid substance into its liquid state at its melting point is called as enthalpy of fusion. For example,

$$\underset{\text{(Ice)}}{H_2O(s)} \longrightarrow \underset{\text{(Water)}}{H_2O(l)} \qquad \Delta H_{fus} = 6.0 \text{ kJ/mol}$$

If water freezes, then the process is reversed and the enthalpy of freezing has same value as enthalpy of fusion but with opposite sign.

$$H_2O(l) \longrightarrow H_2O(s) \qquad \Delta H_{freezing} = -6.0 \text{ kJ/mol}$$

(*b*) **Enthalpy of vapourization:** Enthalpy change accompanying the conversion of one mole of liquid water into its vapour state at its boiling point is called as **enthalpy** of **vapourization**.

For example,

$$H_2O(l) \longrightarrow H_2O(g) \qquad \Delta H_{vap} = 40.7 \text{ kJ/mol.}$$

Condensation is the reverse of vapourization, therefore the enthalpy of condensation has same value as the enthalpy of vapourization but with opposite sign.

$$H_2O(g) \longrightarrow H_2O(l) \qquad \Delta H_{cond} = -40.7 \text{ kJ/mol.}$$

(*c*) **Enthalpy of sublimation:** Enthalpy change involved in conversion of one mole of a solid directly into its vapour state at a given temperature below its melting point. For example,

$$I_2(s) \longrightarrow I_2(g) \qquad \Delta H_{sub} = 62.4 \text{ kJ/mol.}$$

$$\Delta H_{sub} = \Delta H_{fus} + \Delta H_{vap}.$$

(*d*) **Enthalpy of atomisation:** Enthalpy change involved in the dissociation of one mole of a given substance into gaseous atoms is known as **enthalpy of atomisation** of that element.

$$H_2(s) \longrightarrow 2H(g) \qquad \Delta H_a = 435.0 \text{ kJ/mol}$$

$$CH_4(g) \longrightarrow C(g) \qquad \Delta H_a = 1665 \text{ kJ/mol}$$

7.11 HESS'S LAW OF CONSTANT HEAT SUMMATION

G.H. Hess in 1840 proposed an important law regarding enthalpies of reaction called as Hess's law. It states that the enthalpy change in a chemical reaction is same whether the reaction takes place in a single step or in a number of steps.

In other words, the amount of heat evolved or absorbed in a given chemical reaction depends only upon the enthalpy of initial reactants and final products irrespective of the path or the method by which the change has taken place.

For example; consider the formation of CO_2. Carbon can be burnt directly to CO_2 in a single step, where the amount of heat released is 393.5 kJ/mol.

$$C(s) + O_2(g) \longrightarrow CO_2(g) \qquad \Delta H = -393.5 \text{ kJ/mol}$$

Another way is to convert carbon to carbon monoxide and then to carbon dioxide.

$$C(s) + \frac{1}{2} O_2(g) \longrightarrow CO(g) \qquad \Delta H = -110.5 \text{ kJ/mol}$$

$$CO(g) + \frac{1}{2} O_2(g) \longrightarrow CO_2(g) \qquad \Delta H = -283.0 \text{ kJ/mol}$$

$$\text{Net reaction} = C(s) + O_2(g) \longrightarrow CO_2(g) \quad \Delta H = -393.5 \text{ kJ/mol}$$

Thus, the heat evolved is same *i.e.* – 393.5 kJ/mol whether the reaction takes place in a single step or in two steps.

Bond Enthalpy: Amount of energy released when one mole of bonds are formed from the dissociation of a molecule in the gaseous state. Amount of energy required to break one mole of bonds of a particular type between the atoms in the gaseous state of a compound.

For example,

$$H_2(g) \longrightarrow 2H(g) \qquad \Delta H = 435.0 \text{ kJ/mol}$$

For H_2 molecule, bond dissociation energy and bond enthalpy are same *i.e.* 435.0 kJ/mol. Similarly, for other diatomic molecules like O_2, N_2, Cl_2, HCl etc., the bond enthalpies are equal to their bond dissociation energies.

In case of polyatomic compounds, the bond enthalpy of a particular bond differs in different type of compounds. For example bond enthalpy of C—H bond differs slightly from compound to compound as in CH_4, CH_3Cl, CH_2Cl_2 and $CHCl_3$ etc. but the difference is not large. The bond enthalpies can be calculated by the application of Hess's law.

Applications of Hess's Law

The main practical use of Hess's law lies in the fact that the thermochemical equations can be added and subtracted just like algebric equations. As a result, it is possible to calculate the enthalpy change for a reaction whose direct measurement is not possible because either the reaction is incomplete or the reactants do not combine easily or the reaction may be too slow or dangerous. This gives rise to a mathematical method for calculating

(*a*) heat of reaction (*b*) heat of transition (*c*) heat of formation

Let us describe these one by one.

1. **Heat of reaction:** Hess's law makes it possible to calculate heat of many reactions which cannot be determined experimentally. For example, it is extremely difficult to measure the heat evolved when carbon burns in oxygen to give carbon monoxide *i.e.*

$$C(s) + \frac{1}{2} O_2(g) \longrightarrow CO(g) \qquad \Delta H = ? \qquad \text{...(7.10)}$$

But, the heat of combustion of CO to form CO_2 can be measured and has been found to be – 282.0 kJ/mol. *i.e.*

$$CO(g) + \frac{1}{2} O_2(g) \longrightarrow CO_2(g) \qquad \Delta H = -282 \text{ kJ/mol} \qquad \text{...(7.11)}$$

Also the heat of combustion of carbon to give (CO_2) is also known *i.e.*

$$C(s) + O_2(g) \longrightarrow CO_2(g) \qquad \Delta H = -393.5 \text{ kJ/mol} \qquad ...(7.12)$$

According to Hess's law,

Subtracting equation (7.11) from (7.12), we get

$$C(s) + \frac{1}{2} O_2(g) \longrightarrow CO(g)$$

$$\Delta H_{\text{reaction}} = -393.5 + 282.0 = -111.5 \text{ kJ/mol}$$

In general,

$$\Delta H_{(\text{reaction})} = \sum \Delta H_{(f)} \text{ (products)} - \sum \Delta H_{(f)} \text{ (reactants)}$$

also,

$$\Delta H_{\text{reaction}} = \sum \text{Bond enthalpies of reactants} - \sum \text{Bond enthalpies of products.}$$

2. **Heat of transition:** Transition of an element from one allotropic form to another takes place extremely slowly, as it requires heating of one allotropic form for a long period and at constant temperature. So, it becomes difficult to directly measure the heats of transition of elements experimentally. They are however, determined indirectly with the help of Hess's law. For example, we intend to determine the heat of transition of rhombic sulphur into monoclinic sulphur, the heat of combustion of rhombic and monoclinic sulphur are – 297.5 and – 300.0 kJ/mol, respectively, *i.e.*

$$S_{(\text{rhombic})} + O_2(g) \longrightarrow SO_2(g) \qquad \Delta H = -297.5 \text{ kJ} \qquad ...(7.13)$$

$$S_{(\text{monoclinic})} + O_2(g) \longrightarrow SO_2(g) \qquad \Delta H = -300.0 \text{ kJ} \qquad ...(7.14)$$

On subtracting equation (7.14) from (7.13), we get

$$S_{(\text{rhombic})} \longrightarrow S_{(\text{monoclinic})} \qquad \Delta H = +2.5 \text{ kJ}$$

Thus, transition of one mole of rhombic sulphur into monoclinic sulphur requires 2.5 kJ of heat.

3. **Heat of formation:** Several compounds like CH_4, CO, C_6H_6 etc. cannot be prepared directly by the combination of their elements, therefore, it is impossible to determine experimentally the enthalpy of formation of these compounds. However, it can be calculated by using Hess's law. For example, enthalpy of formation of methane can be determined from the heats of formation of CO_2 and H_2O and the heat of combustion of CH_4 as follows.

$$C(s) + 2H_2(g) \longrightarrow CH_4(g) \qquad \Delta H = ? \qquad ...(7.15)$$

$$C(s) + O_2(g) \longrightarrow CO_2(g) \qquad \Delta H = -393.5 \text{ kJ/mol} \qquad ...(7.16)$$

$$H_2(g) + \frac{1}{2} O_2(g) \longrightarrow H_2O(l) \qquad \Delta H = -285.9 \text{ kJ/mol} \qquad ...(7.17)$$

$$CH_4(g) + 2O_2(g) \longrightarrow CO_2(g) + 2H_2O(l) \quad \Delta H = -890.5 \text{ kJ/mol} \qquad ...(7.18)$$

Equation (7.15) can be derived by first multiplying equation (7.16) by 2, then adding equations (7.16) and (7.17) and subtracting equation (7.18), we get

$$C(s) + 2H_2(g) \longrightarrow CH_4(g) \qquad \Delta H = -74.8 \text{ kJ/mol.}$$

Thus, the heat of formation of methane is – 74.8 kJ/mol.

Kirchhoff's Equation: The heat evolved or absorbed in a chemical reaction depends on the temperature at which it is carried out, Kirchoff's in 1858 deduced a mathematical expression depicting the effect of temperature on the heat of let reaction.

$$\frac{\Delta H_2 - \Delta H_1}{T_2 - T_1} = \Delta C_P \quad \text{or} \quad \left[\frac{d(\Delta H)}{dT}\right]_P = \Delta C_P$$

This is the Kirchhoff's equation for a reaction carried out at constant pressure.

7.12 LIMITATIONS OF FIRST LAW OF THERMODYNAMICS: (NEED OF THE SECOND LAW)

1. The first law establishes a definite relationship between the heat absorbed and work performed by a system. However, it does not indicate the direction of flow of heat.

   For example, heat naturally flow from hot end to cold end and not in the reverse direction, but first law is silent about it.
2. The first law gives no information regarding spontaneity or feasibility of a reaction.
3. The first law is a qualitative statement that fails to prelude the possibility of existence of either a refrigerator or a heat engine. This law does not contradict the existence of 100% efficient heat engine or a self-acting refrigerator. In practice, both the situations are not attainable.

   Heat engine is mainly concerned with the conversion of heal energy into mechanical energy whereas refrigerator is a device to cool a certain area below the temperature of the surroundings.
4. The first law does not explain why chemical reactions do not proceed to 100% completion. Consider the following reaction.

$$CO(g) + H_2O(g) \longrightarrow CO_2(g) + H_2(g)$$

   If one mole each of CO_2 and H_2O were taken then one mole each of CO_2, and H_2 should be formed but practically the yield is less than 100%.
5. It fails to explain the expansion of gases in vacuum when

$$\Delta E = 0, \Delta H = 0, W = 0.$$

   Thus, the first law of thermodynamics is not sufficient and therefore an additional law *i.e.* the second law of thermodynamics is necessary which would explain the above limitations.

7.13 THE SECOND LAW OF THERMODYNAMICS

The second law is applicable to reversible cyclic processes only. The second law of thermodynamics can be stated in a number of ways. The various statements are as follows:

(*i*) **Kelvin-Plank Statement:** it is impossible to convert heat into work completely without producing changes in some other parts of the system.

(*ii*) **Clausius Statement:** It is impossible for a self acting machine to transfer heat from a body at low temperature to a body at higher temperature without use of an external agency.

7.14 CARNOT'S HEAT ENGINE/CARNOT CYCLE

The Carnot cycle was first devised by a French engineer, Sadi Carnot. Carnot employed a reversible cycle to demonstrate the maximum convertibility of heat into work. The system consists of one mole of an ideal gas filled in a cylinder which is insulated and fitted with a frictionless piston. The gas is brought in contact with two heat reservoirs maintained at constant temperature *i.e.* a source at temperature T_1 and a sink at temperature T_2 where $T_1 > T_2$.

The Carnot cycle involves four reversible steps as shown is Fig. 7.2

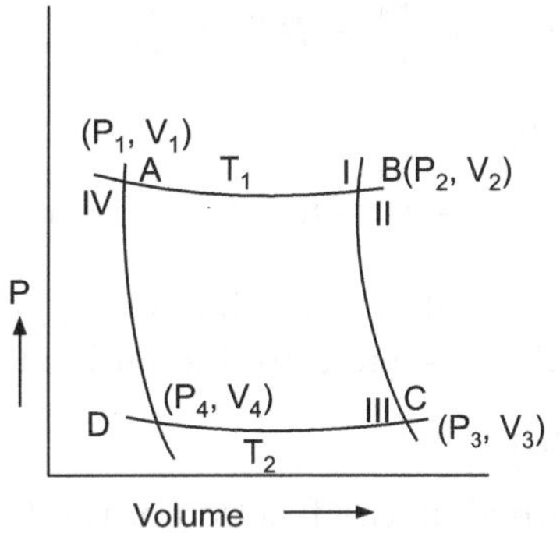

Fig. 7.1. The four steps in Carnot cycle

***Step I:* Isothermal Expansion:** The cylinder containing one mole of an ideal gas occupying volume V_1 is placed is contact with the source at temperature T_1, The gas absorbs 'q_1' amount of heat and undergoes reversible isothermal expansion to volume V_2 as indicated by curve *AB*. The work done (W_1) by the system on its surrounding is given by:

$$q_1 = -W_1 = RT_1 \ln V_2/V_1$$

In isothermal process, $\Delta U = 0$. Therefore, work done (W_1) is equal to heat absorbed (q_1).

***Step II:* Adiabatic Expansion:** Now, the cylinder is removed form the source and is kept on the insulated base. The gas is allowed to expand reversibly and adiabatically from the volume V_2 to V_3 as indicated by curve *BC*. As work is done by the system adiabatically, it is not in a position to absorb heat ($dq = 0$). Therefore, the temperature of the system falls from T_1 to T_2. From the first law, it follows that $\Delta U = W$ (as $\Delta q = 0$). Therefore, the amount of work done, W_2 by the gas will be

$$-W_2 = -C_v (T_1 - T_2) \quad \text{or} \quad -W_2 = C_v (T_2 - T_1).$$

***Step III*: Isothermal compression:** Now, the cylinder is removed from insulated base and is placed is contact with the sink at temperature T_2. The gas is subjected to a reversible and isothermal compression till the volume decreases from V_3 to V_4 as indicated by curve *CD*. In this step, the work is done on the system, therefore, heat (q_2) will be produced and given up to the surroundings. As a convention work done (W_3) will be positive and is given by

$$-q_2 = W_3 = RT_2 \ln \frac{V_4}{V_3}$$

During isothermal compression, q_2 amount of heat is given out to the surrounding ($W_3 = -q_2$).

***Step IV*: Adiabatic Compression:** Finally, the gas is restored to its initial volume V_1 and temperature T_1, by an adiabatic reversible compression along the curve *DA*. In this case, work is done on the system, hence it is positive. According to first law, for an adiabatic process $\Delta U = W$(as $q = 0$), thus work done (W_4) is given by

$$\Delta U = W_4 = C_V (T_1 - T_2)$$

Net Work Done in the Carnot Cycle

After these four operations, the system returns to its initial state and the Carnot cycle is completed. The net work done in the cycle in given by

$$W = (-W_1) + (-W_2) + W_3 + W_4$$

$$= RT_1 \ln \frac{V_2}{V_1} - C_v(T_1 - T_2) + RT_2 \ln \frac{V_4}{V_3} + C_v(T_1 - T_2)$$

$$W = RT_1 \ln \frac{V_2}{V_1} + RT_2 \ln \frac{V_4}{V_3} \qquad \text{...(7.19)}$$

Net heat absorbed q is given by

$$q = q_1 + (-q_2) = RT_1 \ln \frac{V_2}{V_1} + RT_2 \ln \frac{V_3}{V_4} \qquad \text{...(7.20)}$$

From equations (7.19) and (7.20), it is clear that $W = q$. Thus, the essential condition for a cyclic process that the net work done is equal to the net heat absorbed is fully satisfied.

Efficiency of Heat Engine (η)

Efficiency of a heat engine is defined as the fraction of the heat absorbed by an engine which can be converted into work. So, for the above Carnot cycle efficiency (η) is given by

$$\eta = \frac{W}{q_1} = \frac{T_1 - T_2}{T_1}$$

As $\frac{T_1 - T_2}{T_1}$ is invariably less than 1, therefore the efficiency of a heat engine is always less l.

For an engine to have an efficiency of 1, T_2 must be zero (*i.e.* at absolute zero). As absolute zero temperature cannot be realised in actual practice, a heat engine with an efficiency of 1 is not possible. No heat engine has yet been constructed whose efficiency is equal to unity.

7.15 ENTROPY

During the formulation of the second law of thermodynamics, Clausius introduced a new thermodynamic function called as entropy. Entropy of a system is a measure of its randomness or disorder and is denoted by the symbol '*S*'. It is a state function (*i.e.* the change in entropy is independent of path).

Entropy Change in a Reversible Process

Total entropy change of the universe is the sum of entropy change of the system plus that of the surroundings.

$$\Delta S_{\text{universe}} = \Delta S_{\text{system}} + \Delta S_{\text{surroundings}}$$

If an ideal gas undergoes an isothermal reversible expansion and absorbs heat equal to q_{rev} at temperature T, then the entropy change of the system is given by

$$\therefore \qquad \Delta S_{\text{system}} = \frac{q_{\text{rev}}}{T}$$

As the expansion is reversible, the surroundings lose an equivalent amount of heat (*i.e.* q_{rev}) as absorbed by the system. Then, the entropy change of the surroundings is given by

$$\Delta S_{\text{surrounding}} = \frac{-q_{\text{rev}}}{T}$$

The total entropy change of the universe is,

$$\Delta S_{\text{universe}} = \Delta_{\text{system}} + \Delta_{\text{surroundings}}$$

$$= \frac{q_{\text{rev}}}{T} - \frac{q_{\text{rev}}}{T} = 0$$

$$\Delta S_{\text{universe}} = 0$$

Thus, the total entropy change for a reversible isothermal cycle is zero.

Entropy Change in an Irreversible Process

If any part of the cyclic process is irreversible, the whole process becomes irreversible. We know that whatever might be the path followed in going from one state to another, the entropy change is always evaluated using a reversible path connecting the two states.

Let q_{irrev} be the amount of heat lost by the surroundings. This amount of heat will be absorbed by the system, but according to definition, the entropy change of the system depends only on the heat absorbed reversibly.

$$\therefore \quad \Delta S_{\text{system}} = \frac{q_{\text{rev}}}{T}$$

$$\Delta S_{\text{surrounding}} = \frac{-q_{\text{irrev}}}{T}$$

The net change in entropy of the universe will be

$$\Delta S_{\text{universe}} = \Delta_{\text{system}} + \Delta S_{\text{surroundings}}$$

$$= \frac{q_{\text{rev}}}{T} - \frac{q_{\text{irrev}}}{T} \qquad \text{...(7.21)}$$

For reversible process, according to first law

$$\Delta U = q_{\text{rev}} + W_{\text{rev}} \qquad \text{...(7.22)}$$

When the same process is carried out irreversibly, then

$$\Delta U = q_{\text{irrev}} - W_{\text{irrev}} \qquad \text{...(7.23)}$$

ΔU = is a state function, therefore is remains same whether the process is carried out reversibly or irreversibly, therefore

$$q_{\text{rev}} - W_{\text{rev}} = q_{\text{irrev}} - W_{\text{irrev}} \qquad \text{...(7.24)}$$

We know that work done in reversible process is maximum,

$$\therefore \quad W_{\text{rev}} > W_{\text{irrev}} \qquad \text{...(7.25)}$$

From equations (7.24) and (7.25)

$$q_{\text{rev}} > q_{\text{irrev}}$$

$$\therefore \quad \frac{q_{\text{rev}}}{T} > \frac{q_{\text{irrev}}}{T}$$

$$\text{or} \quad \frac{q_{\text{rev}}}{T} - \frac{q_{\text{irrev}}}{T} > 0$$

$$\therefore \quad \Delta S_{\text{univ}} > 0.$$

Thus, in an irreversible process, the entropy of the universe increases.

Entropy Changes During Phase Transitions

The change of matter from one state (solid, liquid or gas) to another is called as *phase transition*. The entropy change during phase transition can occur in any of the following processes.

(*i*) When a solid melts or a liquid freezes (*Entropy of fusion*).

(*ii*) When a liquid vapourizes or a gas condenses (*Entropy of vaporization*)

(*iii*) When a solid changes form one crystalline form to another (*Entropy of Transition*)

1. Entropy of fusion:

$$\text{Solid} \xrightarrow{\text{Fusion}} \text{Liquid}$$

When a solid changes into liquid at its fusion point, heat is absorbed. Consider melting of one mole of a solid reversibly at the fusion point (T_f) at constant pressure. The entropy change of the process ΔS_f is given by

$$\Delta S_f = \frac{\Delta H_f}{T_f}$$

where ΔH_f is the molar heat of fusion or latent heat effusion.

2. Entropy of vapourization:

$$\text{Liquid} \xrightarrow{\text{Vapourization}} \text{Vapour}$$

Consider the vapourization of one mole of a liquid reversibly at its boiling points (T_b) under constant pressure. The entropy change (ΔS_v) accompanying the process is given by

$$\Delta S_v = \frac{\Delta H_V}{T_b}$$

where ΔH_v is the latent heat of vapourization or molar heat of vapourization.

It may be noted that both fusion and vapourization processes are endothermic, therefore ΔH_f and ΔH_v are both positive and are both accompanied by increase of entropy.

3. Entropy of transition: When one mole of a substance undergoes change of state from one crystalline form to another, the entropy change is given by

$$\Delta S_{tr} = \frac{\Delta H_{tr}}{T}$$

where ΔH_{tr} is the molar heat of transition and T is the transition temperature.

ΔH_{tr} may be positive or negative, thus the entropy of transition may be positive or negative.

4. Entropy change for an ideal gas with change in P, V and T: We know that entropy is a state function, therefore its value for an ideal gas changes as the state variables P, V and T changes. We will consider the variation of entropy with change in two variables at one time *i.e.* T and V or T and P.

(*i*) **Entropy as a function of T and V:** Consider n moles of an ideal gas expands reversibly. If the volume of the gas changes from V_1 to V_2 and the temperature changes form T_1 to T_2, then the change in entropy of an ideal gas is given by

$$\Delta S = nC_v \ln \frac{T_2}{T_1} + nR \ln \frac{V_2}{V_1}.$$

(*ii*) **Entropy as a function of T and P:** For n moles of an ideal gas, if P_1 and P_2 are the initial and final pressures at temperature T_1 and T_2, then during reversible expansion of an ideal gas, the change in entropy is given by the expression:

$$\Delta S = nC_p \ln \frac{T_2}{T_1} + nR \ln \frac{P_2}{P_1}.$$

5. **Entropy Change of an Ideal Gas in Different Process:**

(*i*) **Isothermal process:** When temperature is kept constant *i.e.* $T_1 = T_2$

$$\Delta S = nR \ln \frac{V_2}{V_1} = nR \ln \frac{P_1}{P_2}$$

If $V_2 > V_1$ (during isothermal expansion), ΔS will be positive *i.e.* entropy of the system increases.

If $V_2 < V_1$ (during isothermal compression), ΔS will be negative *i.e.* entropy of the system decreases.

(*ii*) **Isobaric process:** When pressure is kept constant *i.e.* $P_1 = P_2$

$$\Delta S = nC_v \ln \frac{T_2}{T_1}$$

(*iii*) **Isochoric process:** When volume is kept constant *i.e.* $V_1 = V_2$

$$\Delta S = nC_v \ln \frac{T_2}{T_1}.$$

6. **Entropy Change on Mixing of an Ideal Gas:** When different gases are mixed together at constant temperature and pressure, there is an increase in entropy. The entropy change of mixing of ideal gases is given by the expression:

$$\Delta S_{mix} = -R\, \Sigma n_i \ln x_i$$

Where n_i and x_i represents the number of moles and the mole fraction, respectively of each constituent of the mixture. For a total of one mole of the gaseous mixture $\Sigma n_i = \Sigma x_i$, the entropy change of mixing is given by $\Delta S_{mix} = -R\, \Sigma\, x_i \ln x_i$.

As x_i is a fraction, therefore the entropy of mixing is always positive.

Physical Significance of Entropy

The entropy of a substance is real physical quantity and is a definite function of the state of the system like temperature, pressure, volume etc. We can readily infer it from the following aspects:

1. **Entropy as a measure of the disorder of the system:** Entropy is a measure of the disorder or randomness in the system. The greater the randomness in a system, higher is the entropy. All spontaneous processes such as expansion of gas in vacuum, flow of water down the hill, diffusion of solute from a concentrated to a dilute solution etc. are accompanied by increase in disorder as well as entropy of the system.

   Similarly, it has been seen that the melting of solid, vapourization of liquid are the processes in which disorder increases and hence, entropy also increases. Solids have a definite crystalline structure therefore they have lowest disorder and lowest entropy. Entropy follows the order:

   gaseous state > liquid state > solid state.

2. **Entropy as a measure of unavailable energy:** According to second law of thermodynamics, the whole amount of internal energy of a substance is not convertible into useful work. The amount of energy which cannot be converted into useful work is the unavailable energy. Entropy is a measure of unavailable energy. In fact, entropy is the unavailable energy per unit temperature.

$$\text{Entropy} = \frac{\text{Unavailable evergy}}{\text{Temperature}}.$$

3. **Entropy as measure of probability:** All spontaneous processes are accompanied by increase in disorder and entropy of the system. When a process is spontaneous it means that it is proceeding form a less probable to a more probable state (Fig.7.3).

   Boltzmann's entropy equation gives the relationship between *thermodynamic probability* (w) and the entropy (S) of the system, *i.e.*

$$S = K \ln w$$

   where K is the Boltzmann constant.

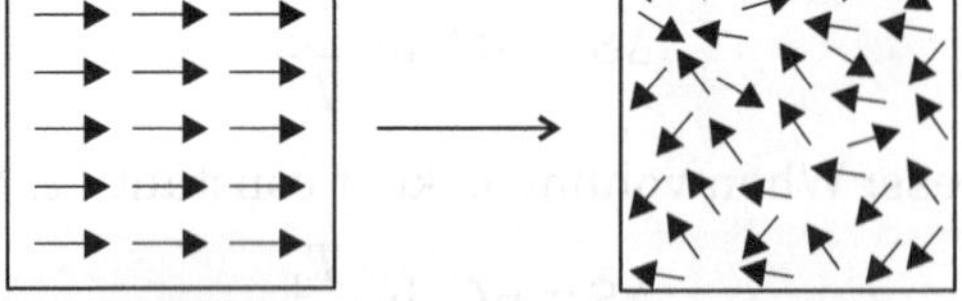

Fig. 7.3. Illustration of the concept of entropy.

The general criteria for spontaneous processes is that the entropy of the universe ($\Delta S_{\text{universe}} = \Delta S_{\text{system}} + \Delta S_{\text{surroundings}}$) must increase. If $\Delta S_{\text{universe}} > 0$, the process is spontaneous or irreversible. If $\Delta S_{\text{universe}} = 0$, the process is reversible *i.e.* the system remains in a state of equilibrium. In order to decide about the spontaneity of a process, we must know the entropy change of the system as well as that of the surroundings. This is not always convenient. Therefore, some other state functions are needed which depend on the state of the system only and can be conveniently determined. Two such functions are the work function (A) and the free energy function (G). Let us discuss then one by one.

(*i*) **Work function (Helmholtz function/Helmholtz free energy):** The work function is represented by the symbol A (derived from German word Arbeit which means work). It is defined by the equation.

$$A = U - TS$$

As the internal energy (U), entropy (S) and the temperature (T) are state functions, therefore, the work function (A) is also a state function.

Consider a process taking place isothermally at temperature T, from initial state (A_1, U_1, S_1) to final state (A_2, U_2, S_2). Then,

$$A_1 = U_1 - TS_1 \quad \text{...(7.26)}$$

$$A_2 = U_2 - TS_2 \quad \text{...(7.27)}$$

The change in work function at constant temperature is

$$A_2 - A_1 = (U_2 - TS_2) - (U_1 - TS_1) \quad \text{...(7.28)}$$

$$= (U_2 - U_1) - T(S_2 - S_1) \quad \text{...(7.29)}$$

$$\Delta A = \Delta U - T\Delta S \qquad ...(7.30)$$

$\therefore\ \Delta S = \frac{q_{rev}}{T}$ (q_{rev} is the amount of heat taken up during a reversible process)

Substitute the value of ΔS in equation (7.30), we get

$$\Delta A = \Delta U - q_{rev} \qquad ...(7.31)$$

From the first law of thermodynamics, for a reversible isothermal process.

$$\Delta U = q_{rev} + W_{rev} \qquad ...(7.32)$$

If work is done by the system W_{rev} is negative and

$$\Delta U = q_{rev} - W_{rev} \qquad ...(7.33)$$

Substitute the value of ΔU from equation (7.33) into equation (7.31), we get

$$\Delta A = q_{rev} - W_{rev} - q_{rev}$$

$$\Delta A = -W_{rev}$$

or

$$-\Delta A = W_{rev} = W_{max}$$

As the process is carried out reversibly, W_{rev} represents the maximum work done. Thus, decrease in work function, *i.e*, ΔA represents the maximum work that can be done by the system during the given change. The function A, is therefore called as *work function* or the *Helmholtz free energy*.

7.16 GIBBS FREE ENERGY

Gibbs free energy is represented by the symbol G and is defined as

$$G = H - TS \qquad ...(7.34)$$

Where H and S are enthalpy of the system respectively at a constant temperature T. H, T and S are state functions so G is also a state function.

If G_1, H_1 and S_1 are the thermodynamic functions in the initial state and G_2, H_2 and S_2 in the final state for an isothermal process occuring at temperature T. We have,

$$G_1 = H_1 - TS_1$$

$$G_2 = H_2 - TS_2$$

and the change in Gibbs free energy will be

$$G_2 - G_1 = H_2 - TS_2 - (H_1 - TS_1)$$

$$\Delta G = (H_2 - H_1) - T(S_2 - S_1)$$

$$\Delta G = \Delta H - T\Delta S \qquad ...(7.35)$$

For a reversible process,

$$\Delta S = \frac{q_{rev}}{T}$$

$$\therefore \qquad T\Delta S = q_{rev}.$$

Further at constant pressure,

$$\Delta H = \Delta U + P\Delta V \qquad ...(7.36)$$

Put the value of ΔH in equation (7.35), we get

$$\therefore \qquad \Delta G = \Delta U + P\Delta V - T\Delta S$$

$$= \Delta U + P\Delta V - q_{rev}$$

$$= (\Delta U - q_{rev}) + P\Delta V$$

For a reversible process, first law equation is $\Delta U = q_{rev} + W_{rev}$. If work is done by the system then $\Delta U = q_{rev} - W_{rev}$ and $\Delta U - q_{rev} = - W_{rev}$

$$\therefore \qquad \Delta G = -W_{rev} + P\Delta V$$

$$\text{As} \qquad W_{rev} = W_{max} \quad \therefore \quad -\Delta G = W_{max} - P\Delta V$$

$P\Delta V$ is the work done by the gas during expansion against a constant external pressure P. Thus, $-\Delta G$ is the maximum work attainable from the system other than pressure volume work. The work so obtained at constant temperature and pressure is called as the *net work*. Therefore,

$$-\Delta G = W_{net} = W_{max} - P\Delta V$$

Thus, the decrease of Gibb's free energy for a reversible process is equal to the net amount of non-mechanical work (electrical work, chemical work etc.) that can be obtained from a system.

7.17 GIBBS HELMHOLTZ EQUATION

(*i*) $\Delta G = \Delta H + T\left[\frac{\partial(\Delta G)}{\partial T}\right]_P$

(*ii*) $\left[\frac{\partial}{\partial T}\left(\frac{\Delta G}{T}\right)\right]_P = \frac{-\Delta H}{T^2}$.

7.18 CHEMICAL POTENTIAL

The chemical potential is the partial molar free energy which is defined as

$$\mu_i = \left(\frac{\partial G}{\partial n_i}\right)_{T,P,n_i,\ldots,n_j} \qquad \ldots(7.37)$$

For a pure substance, the chemical potential is equal to its molar Gibbs free energy, *i.e*, $\mu_i = G$

The chemical potential tells us that how the Gibbs free energy varies with the number of moles n_i of the component i keeping temperature, pressure and the number of moles of all other components constant.

$$\mu_i = \bar{G}_i = \left(\frac{\partial G}{\partial n_i}\right)_{T,P,n_i,\ldots,n_j} \qquad \ldots(7.38)$$

Thus, the change in free energy of the system may be written as

$$dG = \left(\frac{\partial G}{\partial T}\right)_{P,N} dT + \left(\frac{\partial G}{\partial P}\right)_{T,N} dP + \mu_1\, dn_1 + \mu_2\, dn_2 + \ldots + \mu_j\, dn_j \qquad \ldots(7.39)$$

where μ_1, μ_2 ...μ_j represents the chemical potentials of the components 1, 2 ..., j respectively.

If T and P remain constant, than

$$(dG)_{T,P} = \mu_1\, dn_1 + \mu_2\, dn_2 + \ldots + \ldots\mu_j\, dn_j \qquad \ldots(7.40)$$

For a system of definite composition having n_1, n_2, ...,n_j moles of constituents 1, 2, ... j, respectively, then on integrating above equation we get.

$$(G)_{T,P,N} = + n_1\mu_1 + n_2\mu_2 + \ldots + \ldots n_j\mu_j \qquad \ldots(7.41)$$

The chemical potential of a given substance is the change in free energy of the system that results on addition of 1 mole of that particular substance at constant pressure and temperature to such a large quantity of the system that there is no appreciable change in the overall composition of the system.

Variation of Chemical Potential with Temperature

Variation of chemical potential of any constituent i of a system with temperature can be derived by differentiating equation (7.38) with respect to temperature.

$$\frac{\partial^2 G}{\partial n_i\, \partial_T} = \left(\frac{\partial \mu_i}{\partial T}\right)_{P,N} \quad ...(7.42)$$

By definition, partial molar entropy

$$-\bar{S}_i = -\left(\frac{\partial S}{\partial n_i}\right)_{T,P,n_i...n_j} = \left(\frac{\partial^2 G}{\partial T \partial n_i}\right) \quad ...(7.43)$$

So, from these equations, we get

$$\left(\frac{\partial \mu_i}{\partial T}\right)_{P,N} = -\bar{S}_i \quad ...(7.44)$$

Thus, equation (7.44) gives the variation of chemical potential of any constituent i of the system with temperature.

The chemical potential would decrease with increase in temperature as the entropy of a substance is always positive.

Variation of Chemical Potential with Pressure

Variation of chemical potential of any constituent i of a system with pressure can be derived by differentiating equation (7.38) with respect to pressure.

$$\frac{\partial^2 G}{\partial P \partial n_i} = \left(\frac{\partial \mu_i}{\partial P}\right)_{T,N} \quad ...(7.45)$$

By definition, partial molar volume of the component i is given by

$$\overline{V}_i = \frac{\partial^2 G}{\partial n_i \partial P} = \left(\frac{\partial V}{\partial n_i}\right)_{T,P,n_i...n_j} \quad ...(7.46)$$

From equation (7.45) and equation (7.46),

$$(\partial \mu_i / \partial P)_{T,N} = \overline{V_i} \quad ...(7.47)$$

Equation (7.47) gives the variation of chemical potential with pressure.

Physical Significance of Chemical Potential

(*i*) Chemical potential represents the partial change in free energy w.r.t. number of moles at constant temperature and pressure.

$$(dG)_{T,P} = \mu_1 dn_1 + \mu_2 dn_2 + ...\mu_j dn_j$$

If the system has a definite composition, then on integrating above equation, we get

$$(G)_{T,P,N} = n_1\mu_1 + n_2\mu_2 + ...n_j\mu_j$$

Thus, chemical potential is the contribution of each particular component of the mixture to the total free energy of the system at constant temperature and. pressure.

(*ii*) Chemical potential is an **extensive property** and may be regarded as the driving force which compels the system to attain equilibrium.

(*iii*) For a pure substance, the chemical potential is equal to its molar Gibbs free energy, $\mu = G$.

(*iv*) At equilibrium state, the chemical potential of a substance has the same value throughout the system

$$\sum \mu_i dn_i = 0.$$

SOLVED EXAMPLES

Example 7.1. *Two moles of an ideal gas are compressed isothermally and reversibly at 298 K from 1 atm to 200 atm. Calculate q, w, ΔH and for the process.*

Solution: For an isothermal reversible process,

$$W = -2.303\, nRT \log \frac{P_1}{P_2}$$

Given, $n = 2$, $T = 298$ K, $P_1 = 1$ atm and $P_2 = 200$ atm

$$W = -2.303 \times 2 \times 8.314 \times 298 \log \frac{1}{200}$$

$$= -2.303 \times 2 \times 8.314 \times 298 (\log 1 - \log 200)$$

$$= -2.303 \times 2 \times 8.314 \times 298 (0 - 2.3010)$$

$$= -2.303 \times 2 \times 8.314 \times 298 (-2.3010)$$

$$= 26258.31\text{J} = 26.26 \text{ kJ}.$$

For an isothermal process

$$q = -W = -26.26 \text{ kJ}$$

$$\Delta H = 0,$$

(As temperature remains constant during the process therefore, $\Delta U = 0$).

Example 7.2. *One mole of an ideal gas at 300 K expands isothermally and reversibly from 5 to 20 litres. Calculate the work done and heat absorbed by the gas.*

Solution: Work done by the system during reversible isothermal expansion of an ideal gas is gives by

$$W = -2.303\, nRT \log \frac{V_2}{V_1}$$

Given $T = 300\, K$, $V_1 = 5L$, $V_2 = 20L$, $n = 1$ mole

$$R = 8.314 \text{ JK}^{-1}\text{mol}^{-1}$$

$$= -2.303 \times 1 \times 8.314 \times 300 \log \frac{20}{5}$$

$$= -2.303 \times 8.314 \times 300 \log 4$$

$$= -3458.3 \text{ J} = -3.458 \text{ kJ}$$

for reversible isothermal expansion,

$$q = -W \text{ as } \Delta U = 0$$

$$\therefore \quad q = -(-3.458) \text{ kJ}$$

$$q = 3.458 \text{ kJ}.$$

Example 7.3. *Calculate the maximum work done when the pressure on 12 g of hydrogen is reduced from 18 to 2 atm at a constant temperature of 273 K. Will there be any change in internal energy? Also calculate 'q'. Assume the gas behaves ideally.*

Solution: For an isothermal reversible expansion of an ideal gas,

$$W = -2.303\, nRT \log \frac{P_1}{P_2}$$

Given $T = 273$ K, $P_1 = 18$ atm, $P_2 = 2$ atm

Mass of hydrogen gas = 12 g

$$\text{Number of moles} = \frac{\text{mass ring}}{\text{mol. wt.}}$$

$$n = \frac{12}{2} = 6$$

$$W = -2.303 \times 6 \times 8.314 \times 273 \log \frac{18}{2}$$

$$= -2.303 \times 6 \times 8.314 \times 273 \log 9$$

$$= -29926.59 \text{ J}$$

$$= -29.926 \text{ kJ}$$

As the temperature remains constant in isothermal process,

$$\therefore \quad \Delta U = 0$$

and from first law

$$q = \Delta U - W \text{ (for expansion)}$$

$$q = -W$$

$$q = -(-29.926) \text{ kJ} = 29.926 \text{ kJ.}$$

Example 7.4. *Calculate the internal energy change when a gas absorbs 200 J of heat and expands against the external pressure of 1.10 atm from a volume of 2.0 to 5.0 L.*

Solution: According to first law of thermodynamics,

$$\Delta U = q + W,\ q = 200 \text{ J},\ P = 1 \text{ atm}$$

As the gas is expanding,

$$W = -P\Delta V$$

$$W = -1.10(5.0 - 2.0)$$

$$= -1.10 \times 3 \text{ L atm}$$

$$= -3.30 \text{ L atm. (1 L atm = 101.3 J)}$$

$$= -3.30 \times 101.3 \text{ J}$$

$$= -334.29 \text{ J}$$

$$\Delta U = q + W$$

and

$$\Delta U = 200 + (-334.29) = -134.29 \text{ J.}$$

Example 7.5. *Calculate the internal energy change and work done when 1 mole of water at 373 K vapourizes against an atmospheric pressure of 1.0 atm. Heat of vapourization of water at 373 K is 40.670 kJ/mol. Assume ideal gas behaviour.*

Solution: $P = 1$ atm

V_1 = Volume of 1 mole of liquid water at 1 atm = 18 mL

$= 18 \times 10^{-3}$ L.

V_2 (Volume of 1 mole of steam at 373 K and 1 atm.) = ?

Assuming ideal gas behaviour,

$$PV_2 = nRT$$

$$V_2 = \frac{nRT}{P} = \frac{1 \times 0.0821 \times 373}{1} \quad (R = 0.0821 \text{ L atm K}^{-1} \text{ mol}^{-1})$$

$$= 30.6 \text{ L}$$

$$\Delta V = V_2 - V_1 = 30.6 - 0.018 = 30.582 \text{ L}$$

(Work done is negative as it is the work of expansion).

Work done, $W = -P\Delta V$

$$= -1 \text{ atm} \times 30.582 \text{ L}$$

$$= -30.582 \text{ L atm}$$

$$= -30.582 \times 101.3 \text{ J}$$

$$= -3098 \text{ J} = -3.098 \text{ kJ}$$

According to first law of thermodynamics

$$\Delta U = q + W = 40.670 - 3.098 = 37.57 \text{ kJ.}$$

Example 7.6. *Calculate the standard enthalpy of formation of $C_2H_4(g)$ from the following thermo chemical equations:*

$$C_2H_4(g) + 3O_2(g) \longrightarrow 2CO_2(g) + 2H_2O(g) \quad \Delta H = -1323 \text{ kJ}$$

Given that standard heat of formation of $CO_2(g)$ and $H_2O(g)$ are – 393.5 and – 249 kJ/mol respectively.

Solution: To find

$$2C(s) + 2H_2(g) \longrightarrow C_2H_2(g) \qquad \Delta H = ? \qquad ...(i)$$

Standard enthalpy of formation is the enthalpy change when one mole of a substance is formed from its elements in their commonly or naturally occurring state.

Given:

$$C_2H_4(g) + 3O_2(g) \longrightarrow 2CO_2(g) + 2H_2O(g) \quad \Delta H = -1323 \text{ kJ/mol} \qquad ...(ii)$$

$$C(s) + O_2(g) \longrightarrow CO_2(g) \quad \Delta H = -393.5 \text{ kJ/mol} \qquad ...(iii)$$

$$H_2(s) + \frac{1}{2} O_2(g) \longrightarrow H_2O(g) \quad \Delta H = -249 \text{ kJ/mol} \qquad ...(iv)$$

Multiply equation (*iii*) and equation (*iv*) by 2 and then add them.

$$2C(s) + 2O_2(g) \longrightarrow 2CO_2(g) \quad \Delta H = -393.5 \times 2 \text{ kJ/mol}$$

$$2H_2(g) + O_2(g) \longrightarrow 2H_2O(g) \quad \Delta H = -249 \times 2 \text{ kJ/mol}$$

$$2C(g) + 2H_2(g) + 3O_2(g) \longrightarrow 2CO_2(g) + 2H_2O(g) \quad \Delta H = -1285 \text{ kJ/mol} \qquad ...(v)$$

Subtract equation (*ii*) form above equation (*v*) and we get the required equation (*i*)

$$2C(s) + 2H_2(g) + 3O_2(g) \longrightarrow 2CO_2(g) + 2H_2O(g) \quad \Delta H = -1285 \text{ kJ/mol}$$

$$-C_2H_4(g) + \underline{3O_2(g)} \longrightarrow \underline{2CO_2(g) + 2H_2O(g)} \quad \Delta H = +1323 \text{ kJ/mol}$$

$$2C(s) + 2H_2(g) \longrightarrow C_2H_4(g) \quad \Delta H = 38 \text{ kJ/mol}$$

Example 7.7. *The molar heat of formation of NH_4NO_3 (s) is – 367.54 kJ and those of $N_2O(g)$, $H_2O(l)$ are 81.46 and – 285.8 kJ, respectively at 25°C and 1 atmospheric pressure. Calculate ΔH and ΔE for the following reaction:*

$$NH_4NO_3(s) \longrightarrow N_2O(g) + 2H_2O(l)$$

Solution: $NH_4NO_3(s) \longrightarrow N_2O(g) + 2H_2O(l) \qquad \Delta H = ?$

Given

$$\Delta H_f\,(NH_4NO_3) = -\,367.54 \text{ kJ}$$
$$\Delta H_f\,(N_2O) = 81.46 \text{ kJ}$$
$$\Delta H_f\,(H_2O) = -\,285.8 \text{ kJ}$$
$$\Delta H_{\text{ reaction}} = \Delta H_{f\,(\text{Products})} - \Delta H_{f\,(\text{reactants})}$$
$$\Delta H_{\text{ reaction}} = \Delta H_f\,(N_2O) + 2 \times \Delta H_f(H_2O) - \Delta H_f(NH_4NO_3)$$
$$= 81.46 + 2 \times (-\,285.8) - (-\,367.54)$$
$$= 81.46 - 571.6 + 367.54$$
$$= -\,122.60 \text{ kJ}$$
$$= -\,122600 \text{ J}$$

Now, $\Delta H = \Delta E + \Delta nRT$

Δn = Number of moles of gaseous products – Number of moles of gaseous reactants.

$\Delta n = 1 - 0 = 1$

$R = 8.314 \text{ JK}^{-1} \text{ mol}^{-1}$

ΔH should also be in J and not kJ.

$$-\,122600 = \Delta E + 1 \times 8.314 \times 298$$
$$\Delta E = -\,122600 - 2477.57$$
$$= -\,120122.43 \text{ J}$$
$$\Delta E = -\,120.12 \text{ kJ.}$$

Example 7.8. *The enthalpy change for the reaction.*

$$N_2(g) + 3H_2(g) \longrightarrow 2NH_3(g)$$

is – 92.38 kJ at 298 K. Calculate the change in internal energy at this temperature.

Solution: We know that

$$\Delta H = \Delta U + \Delta n_g RT$$

For the reaction,

$$N_2(g) + 3H_2(g) \longrightarrow 2NH_3(g)$$
$$\Delta n_g = 2 - (1 + 3) = -\,2 \text{ mole}$$

Given:

$$\Delta H = -\,92.38 \text{ kJ} = -\,92380 \text{ J}$$
$$R = 8.314 \text{ JK}^{-1} \text{ mol}^{-1}$$

Substitute these values in above equation, we get

$$-\,92380 = \Delta U + (-\,2 \times 8.314 \times 298)$$
$$-\,92380 = \Delta U - 4955.14$$
$$\Delta U = -\,87424.8 \text{ J} = -\,87.425 \text{ kJ.}$$

Example 7.9. *The enthalpy change for the transition of liquid water to steam is 40.8 kJ/mol at 373 K. Calculate the entropy of vapourisation of water.*

Solution: $\Delta S_v = \dfrac{\Delta H_v}{T}$ Given : $\Delta H_v = 40.8$ kJ/mol

$$T = 373 \text{ K}$$

$$\therefore \qquad \Delta S_v = \frac{40.8 \times 10^3 \text{ J mol}^{-1}}{373 \text{ K}} = 109.4 \text{ JK}^{-1} \text{ mol}^{-1}.$$

Example 7.10. *At 0°C, ice and water are in equilibrium and enthalpy change for the process, $H_2O(s) \longrightarrow H_2O(l)$ is 6.0×10^3 J/mol. What will be ΔS and ΔG for the conversion of ice into liquid water?*

Sol. For the process:

$$H_2O(s) \rightleftarrows H_2O(l)$$

Given: $\Delta H = 6.0 \times 10^3$ J/mol

$$T = 0°\text{C} = 273 \text{ K}$$

$$\Delta G = 0 \text{ (for a process in equilibrium)}$$

$$\therefore \qquad \Delta G = \Delta H - T\Delta S$$

$$\text{or} \qquad 0 = \Delta H - T\Delta S$$

$$\Delta S = \frac{\Delta H}{T} = \frac{6.0 \times 10^3 \text{ J mol}}{273 \text{ K}} = 21.9 \text{ JK}^{-1} \text{ mol}^{-1}.$$

Example 7.11. *Calculate ΔG and ΔG° for the following equilibrium reaction $X + Y \longrightarrow Z + A$ at 300 K. Equilibrium constant for the above reaction is 10^2.*

Solution: $\Delta G = 0$ (for a process in equilibrium) $K = 10^2$ $T = 300$ K

$$\Delta G° = -2.303\, RT \log K, \quad R = 8.314 \text{ JK}^{-1} \text{ mol}^{-1}$$

$$\Delta G° = -2.303 \times 8.314 \times 300 \times \log 10^2$$

$$= -11.48 \times 10^3 \text{ J}.$$

Example 7.12. *Calculate the value of equilibrium constant for the following reaction at 25°C:*

$$2NH_3(g) + CO_2(g) \rightleftharpoons NH_2\,CO\,NH_2(aq) + H_2O(l)$$

Standard Gibbs free energy change for the reaction is – 13.6 kJ/mol.

Solution: $\Delta G = -RT \ln K = -2.303\, RT \log K$

$$\log K = \frac{-\Delta G}{2.303\, RT}$$

Given: $\Delta G = -13.6$ kJ/mol = 13600 J/mol

$$R = 8.314 \text{ JK}^{-1}\text{mol}$$

$$T = 25 \text{ °C} = 298 \text{ K}$$

$$\log K = \frac{-13600}{2.303 \times 8.314 \times 298}$$

$$\log K = 2.38$$

$$K = \text{antilog } 2.38 \text{ (antilog } 2.38 = 2.399 \times 10^2)$$

$$K = 2.399 \times 10^2.$$

Example 7.13. *Calculate ΔH°_r for the reaction*

$$\begin{array}{c} \text{H} \\ | \\ \text{H—C—Cl}(g) \\ | \\ \text{Cl} \end{array} \longrightarrow C(s) + 2H(g) + 2Cl(g)$$

Average bond enthalpies of C — H and C — Cl bond are 414 and 330 kJ/mol respectively.

Solution:

$$\begin{array}{c} \text{H} \\ | \\ \text{H—C—Cl}(g) \\ | \\ \text{Cl} \end{array} \longrightarrow C(s) + 2H(g) + 2Cl(g)$$

In this reaction, 2C — H and 2C — Cl bonds are broken but no new bond is formed.

Therefore,

$$\Delta H^\circ_r = [2 \times (\text{bond enthalpy of C — H}) + 2 \times (\text{bond enthalpy of C — Cl bond})]$$
$$= 2 \times 414 + 2 \times 330 = 1488 \text{ kJ/mol.}$$

Example 7.14. *The bond dissociation energy of gaseous H_2, Cl_2 and HCl are 430, 242 and 427 kJ/mol respectively. Calculate the enthalpy of formation of HCl gas.*

Solution: Given that

$$H_2(g) \longrightarrow 2H(g) \qquad \Delta H = 430 \text{ kJ/mol}$$
$$Cl_2(g) \longrightarrow 2Cl(g) \qquad \Delta H = 242 \text{ kJ/mol.}$$
$$HCl(g) \longrightarrow H(g) + Cl(g) \quad \Delta H = 427 \text{ kJ/mol}$$

To find

$$\frac{1}{2} H_2(g) + \frac{1}{2} Cl_2(g) \longrightarrow HCl(g) \qquad \Delta H = ?$$

The $\Delta H_{\text{reaction}}$ is given by the following relation:

$$\Delta H_{\text{reaction}} = \Sigma \text{ bond energies of reactants} - \Sigma \text{ bond energies of products}$$
$$= \frac{1}{2} B.E\,(H_2) + \frac{1}{2} B.E(Cl_2) - B.E\,(HCl)$$
$$= \frac{1}{2} \times 430 + \frac{1}{2} \times 242 - 427$$
$$= -91 \text{ kJ/mol.}$$

EXERCISES

I. SHORT ANSWER TYPE QUESTIONS

1. Define thermodynamics. What are its limitations?

2. Define the following thermodynamic processes

(*a*) Adiabatic process (*b*) Isothermal process

(*c*) Isochoric process (*d*) Isobaric process.

3. Derive an expression for work done during adiabatic reversible expansion of an ideal gas.
4. State and explain first law of thermodynamics.
5. Why is the heat of neutralization of a strong acid with a strong base is constant? Explain.
6. Derive the relationship between heat of reaction at constant pressure (C_P) and that at constant volume (C_V).
7. What are the limitations of first law of thermodynamics? Justify the need of second law.
8. Differentiate between the following pairs:
   (*a*) Endothermic and exothermic reactions.
   (*b*) Extensive and intensive properties.
   (*c*) Reversible and irreversible processes.
9. Explain the concept of entropy. Write the physical significance of entropy.
10. How chemical potential varies with temperature and pressure?
11. What do you mean by free energy and work function? What are their needs in thermodynamics?
12. Explain the following terms (*a*) Gibbs free energy function, (*b*) Helmholtz free energy function, (*c*) Chemical potential.
13. State and explain second law of thermodynamics.
14. Give the criteria of spontaneity of a reaction and thermodynamic equilibrium.
15. Predict the increase or decrease in entropy in the following cases:
    (*a*) $H_2(g) \longrightarrow 2H(g)$
    (*b*) $2NaHCO_3(s) \longrightarrow Na_2CO_3(s) + CO_2(g) + H_2O(g)$
    (*c*) A liquid crystallizes into a solid.

II. LONG ANSWER TYPE QUESTIONS

1. Derive expressions for W, q, ΔU and ΔH when an ideal gas which undergoes
   (*a*) Isothermal reversible expansion
   (*b*) Isothermal irreversible expansion.
2. Explain entropy change during phase transition.
3. Explain that work done by a system in a reversible process is the maximum work for a given expansion.
4. Define the term Helmholtz function. Prove that for an isothermal process, the decrease in Helmholtz function 'A' is equal to the maximum work that can be done by a system.
5. State and explain Hess's law of constant heat summation. Discuss its important applications.
6. Explain the Carnot's cycle. Calculate its efficiency.
7. What do you mean by chemical potential? What is its physical significance?

III. NUMERICAL PROBLEMS

1. Calculate the internal energy change for each of the following processes:
   (*a*) A system absorbs 536 J of energy and does work equivalent to 376 J on its surroundings.
   (*b*) 15 kJ of work is done on the system and 25 kJ of heat is given out by the system.
2. 3 moles of hydrogen gas are compressed isothermally and reversibly form 80 L to 40 L and 7.5 kJ of work is done on it. Calculate the temperature of the gas, assuming ideal gas behaviour.
   $$\left[\textbf{Hint: } W = 2.303\, nRT \log \frac{V_2}{V_1}\right]$$
3. Calculate the work done when 1 mole of an ideal gas is compressed reversibly from 1 bar to 5 bar at a constant temperature of 300 K.
4. Calculate the work done when 10 moles of an ideal gas at initial pressure of 1 atmosphere at 273 K is expanded reversibly under isothermal conditions to a final pressure of 0.1 atmosphere.
5. The molar heats of combustion of $C_2H_2(g)$, $C_{(graphite)}$ and $H_2(g)$ are 310.62, 94.05 and 68.32 kcal respectively. Calculate the heat of formation of C_2H_2.
6. Calculate standard heat of formation of CS_2. Given that standard heat of combustion of C, S and CS_2 are – 393.3, – 293.72 and – 1108.76 kJ/mol respectively.
7. Heat of combustion of H_2, C_2H_4 and C_2H_6 are – 68.4 kcal, – 337 kcal and – 373 kcal, respectively. Calculate the enthalpy change when ethylene is reduced to ethane. .
8. Calculate the standard enthalpy change for the reaction:
   $$CO(g) + H_2(g) \longrightarrow CO(g) + H_2O(g)$$
   given that standard heat of formation for $CO_2(g)$, $H_2O(g)$ and $CO(g)$ are – 393.15, – 241.8 and – 113.3 kJ/mol, respectively.
9. Calculate the heat of combustion of glucose from the following data:
   (*i*) $C_{(Graphite)} + O_2(g) \longrightarrow CO_2(g)$ $\quad \Delta H = -395.0$ kJ
   (*ii*) $H_2(g) + \frac{1}{2}O_2(g) \longrightarrow H_2O(l)$ $\quad \Delta H = -269.4$ kJ
   (*iii*) $6C_{(Graphite)} + 6H_2(g) + 3O_2(g) \longrightarrow C_6H_{12}O_6(s)$ $\quad \Delta H = -1169.8$ kJ
10. The standard enthalpies of formation of $SO_2(g)$ and $SO_3(g)$ are – 296.6 kJ and –395.6 kJ respectively, Calculate enthalpy change for the following reaction.
    $$SO_2(g) + \frac{1}{2}O_2(g) \longrightarrow SO_3(g)$$
11. The enthalpy of formation of CO and steam are – 110.5 and – 243.0 kJ and – 395.6 kJ respectively. Calculate the heat of the reaction, when steam is passed over coke
    $$C(s) + H_2O(g) \longrightarrow CO(g) + H_2(g)$$
12. It is planned to carry out the reaction:
    $$CaCO_3(s) \rightleftarrows CaO(s) + CO_2(g)$$
    at 1273 K and 1 bar pressure. $\Delta H° = 176$ kJ/mol and $\Delta S° = 157.2$ kJ/mol.
    Predict the spontaneity of the process at 1273 K and 1 bar pressure.

13. Two moles of an ideal gas at 2 atm at 300 K is compressed isothermally to one half of its volume by an external pressure of 4 atm. Calculate q, W and ΔU.

14. What would be the work done on/by the system if the internal energy of the system falls by 100 J even when 200 J of heat is supplied to it ?

15. Two litres of an ideal gas at a pressure of 10 atmosphere expands isothermally into a vacuum until its total volume is 10 L. Calculate

(*i*) the amount of heat absorbed and work done during the expansion.

(*ii*) the amount of heat absorbed when the system expands against a constant external pressure of 1 atm.

(*iii*) the amount of heat absorbed when the expansion is done reversibly at 298 K.

[**Hint:** (*i*) Expansion occurs in vacuum $\therefore P_{ext} = 0$

(*iii*) $q = -W = -2.303\, RT \log \frac{V_2}{V_1}$]

16. Calculate the bond energy of $S — F$ bond. The standard heat of formation values of $SF_6(g)$, $S(g)$ and $F(g)$ are – 1100 kJ/mol, 275 kJ/mol and 80 kJ/mol respectively.

17. The enthalpy change for the following reactions at 298 K are given below:

$$\frac{1}{2} H_2(g) + \frac{1}{2} O_2(g) \longrightarrow OH(g) \quad \Delta H = -10.06 \text{ kcal}$$

$$H_2(g) \longrightarrow 2H(g) \quad \Delta H = 104.18 \text{ kcal}$$

$$O_2(g) \longrightarrow 2O(g) \quad \Delta H = 118.32 \text{ kcal}$$

Calculate OH bond energy in hydroxy radical.

18. Calculate the enthalpy of formation of water, given that the bond energies of H—H, O = O and O—H bond are 433, 492 and 464 kJ/mol respectively.

[**Hint:** Required reaction is $H_2 + \frac{1}{2} O_2 \longrightarrow H_2O; \Delta H = ?$

$$\Delta H = B.E\,(H_2) + \frac{1}{2} B.E(O_2) - 2B.E(OH).]$$

19. Calculate the enthalpy change for the reaction

$$H_2(g) + Br_2(g) \longrightarrow 2HBr(g)$$

Given that the bond energies of H—H, Br—Br and H—Br are 435, 192 and 364 kJ/mol respectively.

[**Hint:** $\Delta H = B.E\,(H_2) + B.E\,(Br_2) - 2\,B.E\,(H—Br)$]

20. Enthalpies of the formation of $CO(g)$, $CO_2(g)$ and $N_2O(g)$ are –110, – 393.81 and 9.7 kJ/mol respectively. Calculate heat of reaction for the following reaction:

$$N_2O_4(g) + 3CO(g) \longrightarrow N_2O(g) + 3CO_2(g)$$

21. The standard enthalpy of formation of $C_2H_6(g)$, $H_2O(l)$ and $CO_2(g)$ are – 21.1, – 68.3 and – 94.1 kcal/mol respectively. Determine the standard enthalpy change for the following reaction:

$$2C_2H_6(g) + 7O_2(g) \longrightarrow 4CO_2(g) + 6H_2O(l)$$

IV. MULTIPLE CHOICE QUESTIONS

1. Gibbs Helmholtz equation is:

(a) $\Delta G = \Delta H - T\Delta S$
(b) $\Delta G = \Delta H - T\left[\frac{\partial G}{\partial T}\right]_P$
(c) $\Delta G = \Delta H + T\left[\partial\frac{(\Delta G)}{\partial T}\right]_P$
(d) $\Delta G = \Delta H - T\left[\partial\frac{(\Delta U)}{\partial T}\right]_P$.

2. The Helmholtz free energy is also called as Helmholtz work function because:

(a) It so equal to Gibbs free energy.
(b) It is equal to maximum work done by the system.
(c) It is equal to maximum work done on the system.
(d) None of the above.

3. Pick the incorrect expression.

(a) $\Delta G = \Delta H - T\Delta S$
(b) $-\Delta G° = RT \ln K$
(c) $\Delta A = \Delta U - T\Delta S$
(d) $\Delta S = R \ln W$.

4. Which of the following is not a state function:

(a) S (b) W (c) H (d) U.

5. Identify the intensive quantity from the following:

(a) enthalpy and volume
(b) volume and temperature
(c) enthalpy and temperature
(d) temperature and refractive index.

6. In exothermic reactions

(a) $\Delta S = 0$ (b) $\Delta H = -$ ve (c) $\Delta E = 0$ (d) $\Delta H = +$ ve.

7. The amount of heat liberated when one mole of NH_4OH is treated with one mole of HCl is:

(a) 13.7 kcal (b) > 13.7 kcal (c) < 13.7 kcal (d) Cannot be predicted.

8. Heat of neutralization of strong acid against strong base is constant and is equal to:

(a) 13.7 kcal (b) 57 kJ (c) 5.7×10^4 J (d) All of the above.

9. Which of the following processes is accompanied by decrease in entropy.

(a) Crystallisation of sucrose from solution
(b) Conversion of ice to water
(c) Rusting of iron
(d) Vapourisation of camphor.

10. The maximum efficiency of a steam engine operating between 100°C and 75°C is:

(a) 20% (b) 22.2% (c) 25% (d) 30%.

11. The mathematical expression of the first law of thermodynamics when q is the heat supplied and W is the work done by the system is:

(a) $\Delta U = q - W$ (b) $\Delta U = -q - W$ (c) $\Delta U = q + W$ (d) $\Delta U = W - q$.

12. Chemical potential tells us how the

(*a*) Enthalpy varies with number of moles

(*b*) Entropy varies with number of moles

(*c*) Gibbs free energy varies with number of moles

(*d*) Helmholtz free energy varies with number of moles.

13. Variation of chemical potential with temperature is given by the following expression

(*a*) $\left[\frac{\partial \mu_i}{\partial T}\right]_{P,N} = -\bar{S}_i$ (*b*) $\left[\frac{\partial \mu_i}{\partial T}\right]_{P,N} = \bar{V}_i$

(*c*) $\left[\frac{\partial \mu_i}{\partial T}\right]_{P,N} = \bar{S}_i$ (*d*) $\left[\frac{\partial \mu_i}{\partial T}\right]_{P,N} = -\bar{V}_i$.

14. In an adiabatic expansion of an ideal gas:

(*a*) $\Delta T = 0$ (*b*) $W = 0$ (*c*) $\Delta U = 0$ (*d*) $q = 0$.

15. For a reaction to occurs spontaneously

(*a*) ΔS must be negative (*b*) $(\Delta H - T\Delta S)$ must be negative

(*c*) ΔH must be positive (*d*) $(\Delta H - T\Delta S)$ must be positive.

16. A system absorbs 500 kJ of heat and does 250 kJ of work on the surroundings. The increase in internal energy of the system is:

(*a*) 750 kJ (*b*) 250 kJ (*c*) 500 kJ (*d*) 1000 kJ.

17. The heat required to raise the temperature of a body by 1° is called as:

(*a*) Specific heat (*b*) Heat capacity

(*c*) Water equivalent (*d*) None of the above.

18. According to Hess's law

(*a*) Enthalpy change of a reaction is always negative

(*b*) Enthalpy change of a reaction is always positive

(*c*) Enthalpy change of a reaction is same whether it takes place in one or several steps

(*d*) No change in enthalpy during a reaction.

19. Heat of transition is the heat absorbed or released when a substance is converted into

(*a*) Solid to liquid

(*b*) Solid to vapour

(*c*) Liquid to vapour

(*d*) One allotropic form to another allotropic form.

20. During isothermal expansion of an ideal gas, its

(*a*) Enthalpy decreases (*b*) Enthalpy reduces to zero

(*c*) Internal energy increases (*d*) Enthalpy remains unaffected.

Answers

III. Numerical Problems

1. (*a*) $U = 160$ J, (*b*) $\Delta U = -10$ kJ
2. $T = 273.6$ K
3. $W = 4.01$ kJ
4. $W = -52.27$ kJ
5. $\Delta H_f(C_2H_2) = +54.2$ k cal
6. $\Delta H_f(CS_2) = +128.02$ kJ/mol
7. $\Delta H = -32.4$ kcal.
8. $\Delta H = +38.05$ kJ/mol
9. $\Delta H = -28I6.6$ kJ.
10. $\Delta H° = -99.0$ kJ
11. $\Delta H_r = +132.5$ kJ
12. $\Delta G° = -24.10$ kJ
13. $q = -4.984$ kJ, $W = -4.984$ kJ, $\Delta U = 0$
14. $W = -300$ J
15. (*i*) $q = 0$, (*ii*) $q = 8$ litre atm, (*iii*) $q = 39.3$ litre atm
16. Bond energy of S—F bond = 309.17 kJ/mol
17. Bond energy = 121.31 k cal
18. $\Delta H = -249$ kJ/mol.
19. $\Delta H = -101$ kJ/mol.
20. $\Delta H_r = -777.7$ kJ/mol
21. $\Delta H° = -744.5$ kcal.

IV. Multiple Choice Questions

1. (*c*)	**2.** (*b*)	**3.** (*d*)	**4.** (*b*)	**5.** (*d*)	**6.** (*b*)	**7.** (*c*)	**8.** (*d*)	**9.** (*a*)	**10.** (*c*)
11. (*a*)	**12.** (*c*)	**13.** (*a*)	**14.** (*d*)	**15.** (*b*)	**16.** (*b*)	**17.** (*b*)	**18.** (*c*)	**19.** (*d*)	**20.** (*d*)

Chapter 8 Water Analysis Techniques

8.1 INTRODUCTION

Water is the most precious, wonderful and useful gift of nature. It is the most abundant natural resource. All animals and vegetables possess water as an essential constituent.

The earth has an abundance of water but unfortunately, only a small percentage about 1% is available as fresh water in rivers, lakes, streams and ground water which is suitable for human consumption. The other 99% is in the oceans and glaciers.

Water can be obtained from variety of sources.

Surface Water: The visible bodies of water are referred to as surface water. For example, lakes, ponds, reservoirs, streams, rivers, sea.

Underground Water: Water that is accumulated under the ground through seepage. For example, springs, wells, tubewells.

Rain Water: It is the purest form of water. However, due to pollution, the rain water dissolves many gases before it reaches to the ground and hence the first rain water usually possess very high amount of dissolved gases.

Common Impurities of Water

Water is a very good solvent, it dissolves a large number of substances in it. Water may contain various impurities due to

(*a*) the ground or soil with which it comes in contact (For example, garbage, soil particles etc.)

(*b*) the decomposition of dead plants and animals.

(*c*) the growth of microorganisms like bacteria, algae etc.

(*d*) its contact with sewage or industrial wastes.

The common impurities present in natural water can be classified into three types:

1. Physical Impurities
2. Chemical Impurities
3. Bacteriological Impurities.

Physical Impurities

They can be:

(*a*) **Colloidal impurities:** Those impurities whose particle size varies from 1 to 100 nm. Finely divided clay, silica, ferric hydroxide, colouring matter, waste products, complex proteins, amines etc. These impurities impart colour, odour and taste to the water.

(b) Suspended impurities: Those impurities whose particle size is greater than 100 nm and can be removed by filtration or settling. For example, clay, sand, decayed vegetable and animal matter, wood pieces, leaves etc. These impurities make the water turbid.

Chemical Impurities

It include dissolved impurities like dissolved gases and dissolved salts.

(a) Dissolved salts: Carbonates, bicarbonates, nitrates, sulphates and chlorides of Ca, Mg, Na, K, Fe, Mn, Al etc.

– $CaCl_2$, $CaSO_4$, $Ca(HCO_3)_2$, $MgCl_2$, $MgSO_4$, $Mg(HCO_3)_2$ make the water hard.

– $Mg(HCO_3)_2$, $Ca(HCO_3)_2$, Na_2CO_3, $NaHCO_3$ etc. make the water alkaline.

(b) Dissolved gases: O_2, CO_2, H_2S, SO_2, NH_3 and oxides of nitrogen also fall in this category.

– O_2 accelerates the rate of corrosion.

– CO_2, H_2S make the water acidic and corrosive.

Bacteriological Impurities

These include various types of pathogenic micro-organisms like bacteria, fungi, algae, protozoa etc.

8.2 TYPES OF WATER

Water is classified into two types based on the property of it forming lather with soap solution. They are:

(i) Soft water: Water which produces lather with soap solution readily is called soft water

$$\underset{\text{Soap}}{2RCOONa} + \underset{\text{Soft water}}{H_2O} \longrightarrow \underset{\text{Foam}}{2R\,COOH + 2NaOH}$$

For example, rain water, distilled water etc.

(ii) Hard water: Water which does not produce lather with soap solution readily but forms an insoluble precipitate like white scum is called as hard water.

$$\underset{\text{Soap}}{RCOONa} + \underset{\substack{\text{Hard water}\\ \text{(Containing}\\ CaCl_2, MgCl_2\\ \text{etc.)}}}{H_2O} \longrightarrow \underset{\text{Insoluble Soap}}{(RCOO)_2Ca} + 2NaCl$$

For example, river water, sea water, tap water etc.

8.3 HARDNESS OF WATER

The characteristic property which prevents water from forming lather with soap is termed as **hardness of water**. Hardness of water is due to the presence of certain soluble salts of calcium and magnesium in water. Hard water containing calcium and magnesium ions when treated with soap, does not produce lather or foam but forms an insoluble precipitate or scum instead.

$$\underset{\substack{\text{Sodium stearate}\\ \text{(Soap)}}}{2C_{17}H_{35}COONa} + \underset{\substack{\text{(From hard}\\ \text{water)}}}{CaCl_2} \longrightarrow \underset{\substack{\text{Calcium stearate}\\ \text{(Insoluble)}}}{(C_{17}H_{35}COO)_2Ca} + 2\,NaCl$$

Classification of Hardness

Hardness is classified into:

1. Temporary hardness
2. Permanent hardness

1. Temporary hardness: The temporary hardness of water is due to the soluble bicarbonates of calcium and magnesium. This type of hardness is also known as **carbonate hardness**. When water is boiled, the bicarbonates present in it decompose to form insoluble carbonates ($CaCO_3$) or hydroxides ($Mg(OH)_2$). Therefore, temporary hardness of water can be removed by boiling.

$$\underset{\text{Calcium bicarbonate}}{Ca(HCO_3)_2} \xrightarrow{\text{boil}} \underset{\text{Insoluble}}{CaCO_3\downarrow} + H_2O + CO_2\uparrow$$

$$\underset{\text{Magnesium bicarbonate}}{Mg(HCO_3)_2} \xrightarrow{\text{boil}} \underset{\text{Insoluble}}{Mg(OH)_2\downarrow} + H_2O + 2CO_2\uparrow$$

Salts responsible for temporary hardness are $Ca(HCO_3)_2$, $Mg(HCO_3)_2$.

2. Permanent hardness: Permanent hardness of water is due to the presence of chlorides, sulphates and nitrates of calcium, magnesium, iron and other heavy metals. This type of hardness is also called as **non-carbonate** or **non-alkaline hardness**. It cannot be removed by simple boiling but can be removed by certain special methods like lime-soda process, ion-exchange process, zeolite method etc.

For example, $CaSO_4 + \underset{\text{Soda ash}}{Na_2CO_3} \longrightarrow CaCO_3\downarrow + Na_2SO_4$

Salt responsible for permanent hardness:

$MgCl_2$, $MgSO_4$, $Mg(NO_3)_2$, $CaCl_2$, $CaSO_4$, $Ca(NO_3)_2$ etc.

We know that hardness of water is because of presence of salts of calcium and magnesium in water but for comparison of hardness of different samples of water, it is necessary to choose a reference. For this purpose, hardness of water is expressed in terms of equivalents of $CaCO_3$. There are two main reasons for choosing $CaCO_3$ as reference.

(*i*) It is a completely insoluble salt, thus it can be easily precipitated completely during water treatment.

(*ii*) Molecular weight of $CaCO_3$ is 100 and equivalent weight is 50, therefore, calculations become easy.

Hence, to determine the hardness of a given water sample, it is first converted into calcium carbonate equivalents by using the following formula:

$$\text{Equivalent of } CaCO_3 = \frac{\text{Equivalent weight of } CaCO_3 \times \text{Weight of hardness producing substance in mg/L}}{\text{Equivalent weight of hardness causing substance}}$$

$$\text{Equivalent of } CaCO_3 = \frac{\text{Mol. wt. of } CaCO_3 \times \text{Weight of hardness producing substance in mg/L}}{\text{Mol. wt. of hardness causing substance}}$$

$$\text{The ratio} = \frac{\text{Equivalent weight of } CaCO_3}{\text{Equivalent weight of hardness causing substance}}$$

The above ratio is constant for a particular substance. This ratio is called as **multiplication factor**.

Thus, Equivalents of $CaCO_3$ = Weight of hardness producing substance in mg/L × multiplication factor.

Salts responsible for hardness and their multiplication factor are given in Table 8.1.

Table 8.1: Calculation of Multiplication Factor

Dissolved Salt or ion	Molecular Mass (*M*)	Equivalent weight or Chemical equivalent (*E*)	Multiplication factor $= \frac{100/2}{E}$
$Ca(HCO_3)_2$	162	162/2	$\frac{100/2}{162/2} = \frac{100}{162}$
$Mg(HCO_3)_2$	146	146/2	$\frac{100/2}{146/2} = \frac{100}{146}$
$CaSO_4$	136	136/2	$\frac{100/2}{136/2} = \frac{100}{136}$
$CaCl_2$	111	111/2	$\frac{100/2}{111/2} = \frac{100}{111}$
$MgSO_4$	120	120/2	$\frac{100/2}{120/2} = \frac{100}{120}$
$MgCl_2$	95	95/2	$\frac{100/2}{95/2} = \frac{100}{95}$
$CaCO_3$	100	100/2	$\frac{100/2}{100/2} = \frac{100}{100}$
$MgCO_3$	84	84/2	$\frac{100/2}{84/2} = \frac{100}{84}$
CO_2	44	44/2	$\frac{100/2}{44/2} = \frac{100}{44}$
$Ca(NO_3)_2$	164	164/2	$\frac{100/2}{164/2} = \frac{100}{164}$
$Mg(NO_3)_2$	148	148/2	$\frac{100/2}{148/2} = \frac{100}{148}$
HCO_3^-	61	61/1	$\frac{100/2}{61/1} = \frac{100}{122}$
CO_3^{2-}	60	60/2	$\frac{100/2}{60/2} = \frac{100}{60}$
OH^-	17	17/1	$\frac{100/2}{17/1} = \frac{100}{34}$
H^+	1	1	$\frac{100/2}{1} = \frac{100}{2}$

Ca^{2+}	40	40/2	$\frac{100/2}{40/2} = \frac{100}{40}$
Mg^{2+}	24	24/2	$\frac{100/2}{24/2} = \frac{100}{24}$
HCl	36.5	36.5/1	$\frac{100/2}{36.5/1} = \frac{100}{73}$
H_2SO_4	98	98/2	$\frac{100/2}{98/2} = \frac{100}{98}$
$FeSO_4.7H_2O$	278	278/2	$\frac{100/2}{278/2} = \frac{100}{278}$
$NaAlO_2$	82	82/1	$\frac{100/2}{82/1} = \frac{100}{164}$
$Al_2(SO)_3$	342	342/6	$\frac{100/2}{342/6} = \frac{100 \times 3}{342}$

Units of Hardness

Various units used for expressing hardness of water are given below:

1. **Parts per million (ppm):** It is defined as the parts of calcium carbonate equivalent hardness per 10^6 parts of water.

   1 ppm hardness means 1 part of $CaCO_3$ equivalent hardness in 10^6 parts of water.
2. **Milligrams per litre (mg/L):** It is the number of milligrams of $CaCO_3$ equivalent hardness present per litre of water.

   1 mg/L means 1 milligram of $CaCO_3$ equivalent hardness in 1 L of water.
3. **Degree Clarke (°Cl):** It is the number of parts of $CaCO_3$ equivalent hardness present per 70,000 parts of water.
4. **Degree French (°Fr):** It is the number of parts of $CaCO_3$ equivalent hardness present per 10^5 parts of water.

Relationship between various units of hardness: 1 ppm = 1 mg/L = 0.07 °Cl = 0.1 °Fr

Disadvantages of Using Hard Water

There are many disadvantages of using hard water for domestic and industrial purposes:

1. **For industrial use:**

   (*a*) **Textile industry:** In textile industries, dyeing of clothes is an important process. With hard water, uniform dyeing is not possible as hard water decreases the solubility of acidic dyes and precipitation of basic dyes. Also, if water contains Fe, Mn, colour or turbidity, it causes uneven dyeing and leave stains on fabrics.

   (*b*) **Laundries:** Hardness increases consumption of soaps. If hard water contains Fe, Mn as impurity then they can impart grey or yellow shade to the fabric.

   (c) **Paper industry:** The presence of various impuries has impact on the properties and quality of paper and their products.

   Presence of:

   (*i*) SiO_2 – produces cracks in the paper.

   (*ii*) Fe, Mn, colour, turbidity – affect the colour and brightness of paper.

(*iii*) hardness-increases the ash content of paper.

(*iv*) alkalinity-increase the cost of production as alkaline water consumes alum.

(*d*) **Beverage industry:** It require water which is free from alkalinity because presence of alkalinity modifies or destroys the taste by neutralization of fruit acids.

(*e*) **Sugar industry:** If hard water containing impurities of sulphates, nitrates etc. is used then it can cause difficulty in crystallization of sugar.

(*f*) **Dairies and pharmaceutical industry:** Such industries require ultrapure water. Use of hard water in pharmaceutical industry can lead to formation of drugs which are harmful or even poisonous.

(*g*) **Boilers:** Boilers require soft water as hard water causes various problems in boilers like corrosion, scale and sludge formation, priming and foaming and caustic embrittlement. It also leads to wastage of fuel.

2. **For domestic use:**

(*a*) **Cooking:** Because of the presence of various salts in hard water, the boiling point of water is increased. Hence, more fuel and more time are required for cooking.

(*b*) **Washing and bathing:** Hard water does not form lather with soap easily, because of this the cleansing action of soap is decreased and a lot of soap is wasted.

(*c*) **Drinking:** Hard water causes bad effect on our digestive system. Sometimes, it leads to formation of calcium oxalate crystals which causes various urinary problems.

Considering all the problems associated with hard and alkaline water, it can be concluded that water need to be treated to remove all the undesirable impurities. This water can be made fit for domestic and industrial use by using various available processes like lime soda, zeolite, carbonate conditioning etc.

8.4 BOILER FEED WATER

In industries, water is mainly used in boilers for the generation of steam. For such water, all the impurities are not necessarily eliminated and only those impurities which lead to objectionable phenomenon in boilers are eliminated or kept within the prescribed range. A boiler feed water should fulfill the following criteria:

(*i*) Its hardness should be below 0.2 ppm.

(*ii*) Its caustic alkalinity should lie in between 0.15 and 0.45 ppm

(*iii*) Its soda alkalinity should be in the range 0.45 to 1 ppm.

Excess of impurities, if present in boiler feed water generally cause the following problems:

1. Scale and sludge formation
2. Boiler corrosion
3. Priming and foaming
4. Caustic embrittlement.

Let us discuss these one by one

Scale and Sludge Formation

Continuous evaporation of water in the boilers increases the concentration of dissolved salts. Finally a stage is reached when the ionic product of these salts exceeds their solubility product and hence they are thrown out as precipitates. If these precipitates are loose ands slimy, these are known as **sludges**; while if the precipitates are hard and adhere on the inner walls of the boiler, these are called as **scales.**

***(i)* Sludge:** It is a soft, slimy and loose precipitate formed on the inner walls of the boiler.

Formation of sludge: Sludges are formed by substances which have greater solubilities in hot water than in cold water, *e.g.* $CaCl_2$, $MgSO_4$, $MgCl_2$, $MgCO_3$ etc. They are formed at relatively colder portions of the boiler and get collected at places where the flow rate is slow.

They can be easily scrapped off with a wire brush.

Disadvantages of sludge formation:

(*i*) Sludges are poor conductors of heat therefore, they tend to waste a portion of heat generated. As a result of this, the efficiency of boiler decreases.

(*ii*) Excessive sludge formation hinders the working of the boiler. It settles in the region of poor water circulation such as plug opening, pipe connection, gauze-glass connection, thereby chocking the pipes.

Prevention of sludge formation:

(*i*) by feeding softened water

(*ii*) by frequently blow down operation *i.e.* partial removal of concentrated water from the boiler and replacing it with fresh water.

***(ii)* Scales:** Scales are hard deposits, which stick firmly to the inner walls of the boiler.

Formation of scales: Scales are formed inside the boiler due to following reasons:

(a) Decomposition of calcium bicarbonate $Ca(HCO_3)$: Calcium bicarbonate present in hard water is converted into carbonate (which gets precipitated) by giving off CO_2.

$$Ca(HCO_3)_2 \longrightarrow \underset{\text{(Scale)}}{CaCO_3}\downarrow + H_2O + CO_2\uparrow$$

This is the main cause of scale formation in low pressure boilers. However, in high pressure boilers, $CaCO_3$ is soluble due to formation of soluble calcium hydroxide.

$$CaCO_3 + H_2O \longrightarrow Ca(OH)_2 + CO_2\uparrow.$$

(*b*) Decomposition of calcium sulphate ($CaSO_4$): The solubility of $CaSO_4$ in water decreases with rise in temperature. As a result, $CaSO_4$ gets precipitated as hard scale on the heated portions of the boiler. This is the main reason for the scale formation in high pressure boilers. $CaSO_4$ scale is quite adherent to the inner portions of the boiler and is difficult to remove even with the help of hammer and chisel.

(*c*) Hydrolysis of magnesium salts: At high temperature inside the boiler, the dissolved magnesium salts undergo hydrolysis, forming magnesium hydroxide precipitate which forms a soft type of scale. For example:

$$MgCl_2 + 2H_2O \longrightarrow \underset{\text{Scale}}{Mg(OH)_2}\downarrow + 2\,HCl\uparrow$$

(*d*) Presence of silica: Silica comes in water through sand filters. Even if small quantities of silica are present in hard water, they react with Ca and Mg ions to form calcium silicate ($CaSiO_3$)/magnesium silicate (Mg SiO_3) which stick very tightly on the inner walls of the boiler surface and are extremely difficult to remove.

Disadvantages of scale formation

(*i*) Wastage of fuel: Scales, being poor conductor of heat, hinders the flow of heat from the source to the water. Therefore, the consumption of fuel for producing steam will be much more than usual.

(*ii*) **Lowering of boiler safety:** Due to scale formation, heat available to water is reduced and hence more heat is required to produce steam. This causes overheating of boiler plates and tubes and thus their life is reduced.

(*iii*) **Danger of explosion in boilers:** Under high pressure of steam inside the boiler, the boiler metal expands and a stage is reached when the scale deposited on it gets cracked. When the scale cracks, the water comes suddenly in contact with overheated portion and large amount of steam is formed instantaneously. The sudden high pressure thus produced (due to formation of steam) may cause the boiler to burst.

(*iv*) **Decrease in efficiency of boilers:** Tubes, valves and condensers of the boiler may be clogged (chocked) by the deposition of scales. This results in decrease in efficiency of the boilers.

Prevention of scale formation: Formation of scales can be prevented by following methods:

1. External treatment: It includes efficient softening of water (*i.e.,* removal of hardness producing substances of water). This topic will discussed separately in later sections of the chapter.

2. Internal treatment: It is also called as sequestration or conditioning. In this method, chemicals are added to the hard water in the boiler. The added chemicals may function as precipitating or sequestering agents to form more soluble complex compounds with metal ions (*e.g.*, Ca^{2+}, Mg^{2+} etc.). This method helps to convert hard deposits into loose deposits which are easily removed by blow-down operation. Important internal treatment methods are:

(*i*) **Colloidal conditioning:** This method is suitable for low pressure boilers. Colloidal substances like kerosene, tannins, agar-agar, linseed extract etc. are added to the boiler water. These substances acts as protective colloids which get coated over the scale forming articles and thus the coalescence or joining together of these particles to a compact scale is prevented. Thus, the scale formed remains loose and non-sticky and can be removed from time to time by blow down operation.

(*ii*) **Carbonate conditioning:** In this method, sodium carbonate is added to boiler water so that salts like $CaSO_4$ etc. are converted into $CaCO_3$.

$$CaSO_4 + Na_2CO_3 \longrightarrow CaCO_3 \downarrow + Na_2SO_4$$

$CaCO_3$ is loose sludge and can be removed by blow down operation.

This method is used only for low pressure boiler. In high pressure boiler, the excess Na_2CO_3 might be converted into NaOH due to hydrolysis.

$$Na_2CO_3 + 2H_2O \rightleftharpoons 2NaOH + H_2CO_3$$

$$H_2CO_3 \rightleftharpoons H_2O + CO_2$$

NaOH causes caustic embittlement in high pressure boilers, therefore this method is not preferred very much.

(*iii*) **Phosphate conditioning:** This method is applicable to high pressure boilers. In this method, soluble phosphate is added to boiler water, which reacts with calcium and magnesium salts to form soft sludge of Ca and Mg phosphate which can be removed by blow down operation.

$$3\ MCl_2 + 2\ Na_3PO_4 \longrightarrow M_3(PO_4)_2\downarrow + 6\ NaCl$$
$$3\ MSO_4 + 2\ Na_3PO_4 \longrightarrow M_3(PO_4)_2\downarrow + 6\ Na_2SO_4$$

where $M = Ca^{2+}$ or Mg^{2+}.

Phosphates used for this method are Na_3PO_4 (sodium phosphate), Na_2HPO_4 (disodium hydrogen phosphate), NaH_2PO_4 (sodium dihydrogen phosphate), $NaPO_3$ (sodium metaphosphate), $Na_4P_2O_7$ (sodium pyrophosphate) etc. The choice of phosphate salt depends upon the alkalinity of the boiler feed water. For example, if the boiler feed water tends to produce an acidic condition in the boiler, Na_3PO_4 should be chosen. If the boiler feed water produces the right alkalinity as desired in the boiler, it is preferable to use Na_2HPO_4 which is practically neutral. If the boiler water becomes too alkaline then acidic NaH_2PO_4 would be used.

$Na_4P_2O_7$ and $NaPO_3$ undergo rapid hydrolysis under boiler water temperature to orthophosphates.

$$Na_4P_2O_7 + H_2O \longrightarrow NaH_2PO_4 \text{ (acidic)}$$
$$Na_4P_2O_7 + H_2O \longrightarrow 2Na_2HPO_4 \text{ (neutral)}$$

Hence, they show the similar behaviour as other phosphates mentioned above.

(*iv*) **Calgon conditioning:** Addition of small amount (0.5 – 5 ppm) of sodium hexametaphosphate $Na(PO_3)_6$ also called as calgon, presents scale formation in the following ways:

- at low temperature and pressure, calgon forms quite stable and soluble compounds with calcium salts.

$$2CaSO_4 + [Na_4(PO_3)_6]^{2-} \longrightarrow \underset{\text{Soluble complex}}{[Ca_2(PO_3)_6]^{2-}} + 2Na_2SO_4$$

- at high temperature and pressure, calgon is converted into sodium orthophosphate which reacts with calcium salts to form calcium orthophosphate.

$$2Na_2[Na_4(PO_3)_6] + 6H_2O \longrightarrow 6Na_2P_2O_7 + 6H_2\uparrow$$
$$Na_2P_2O_7 + CaSO_4 \longrightarrow \underset{\substack{\text{Calcium orthophosphate} \\ \text{(loose sludge)}}}{CaP_2O_7} + Na_2SO_4$$

Calcium orthophosphate appears as loose sludge and thus can be removed by blow down operation.

(*v*) **Treatment with sodium aluminate ($NaAlO_2$):** Sodium aluminate gets hydrolysed producing NaOH and a gelatinous precipitate of $Al(OH)_3$. Thus,

$$NaAlO_2 + 2H_2O \longrightarrow NaOH + Al(OH)_3\downarrow$$

The sodium hydroxide formed in above reaction, precipitates some of the magnesium (present in hard water) as $Mg(OH)_2$

$$2\ NaOH + MgCl_2 \longrightarrow Mg(OH)_2\downarrow + 2\ NaCl$$

The flocculant precipitate (loose and wooly precipitate) of $Mg(OH)_2$ and $Al(OH)_3$ produced inside the boiler entraps the suspended and colloidal impurities alongwith silica. The loose precipitates can be removed by blow down operation. Sodium aluminate is available in plenty and at a very cheap rate from bauxite refining units.

Boiler Corrosion

Decay or disintegration of boiler material due to chemical or electrochemical reaction with its environment. Corrosion is the most serious problem created by the use of unsuitable water in boilers. Nearly all the parts of boilers may be corroded.

Disadvantages of corrosion:

(*i*) shortening of boiler life

(*ii*) leakages of the joints and rivets

(*iii*) Increased cost of repairs and maintenance.

Causes of boiler corrosion: Corrosion in boilers is due to the

1. Dissolved oxygen: This is the most usual corrosion causing factor. Dissolved oxygen reacts with the iron of boiler in presence of water and under prevailing high temperatures to form ferric oxide (rust)

$$4Fe + 2H_2O + O_2 \longrightarrow 4Fe(OH)_2$$

$$2Fe(OH)_2 + O_2 \longrightarrow \underset{\text{(Rust)}}{Fe_2O_3}$$

In boilers, oxygen is introduced through the raw water supply. As water is heated, the dissolved oxygen is set free and the boiler starts corroding.

Removal of dissolved oxygen:

(*i*) **By adding chemicals:** Oxygen can be removed by adding certain chemicals to the boiler feed water like sodium sulphite, sodium sulphide, hydrazine etc. These chemicals combine with oxygen in the following way.

$$2\,Na_2\,SO_3 + O_2 \longrightarrow 2\,Na_2SO_4$$

$$Na_2S + 2\,O_2 \longrightarrow Na_2\,SO_4$$

$$NH_2NH_2 + O_2 \longrightarrow N_2 + 2\,H_2O$$

Sodium sulphide (Na_2S) and sodium sulphite (Na_2SO_3) are suitable for boilers operating at low pressures. Na_2SO_3 and Na_2S reacts with dissolved oxygen to form Na_2SO_4.

These cannot be used in high pressure boiler due to:

(*i*) increasing dissolved salts concentrations produce foaming and priming, (*ii*) $Na_2\,SO_4$ decomposes and liberates SO_2 and / or H_2S.

Hydrazine (NH_2NH_2) is now extensively used to remove dissolved oxygen in high pressure boilers. It reacts with oxygen to form nitrogen and water. Nitrogen is harmless. One important advantage of NH_2NH_2 is that it removes oxygen without increasing the concentration of dissolved salts.

The amount of hydrazine added must be closely controlled. Any excess reagent decomposes in the boiler, liberating ammonia.

$$3\,N_2H_4 \longrightarrow 4\,NH_3 + N_2$$

Dissolved ammonia can cause corrosion of some alloys, *e.g.* copper alloy condenser tubes.

(*ii*) **By mechanical de-aeration:** Oxygen can also be removed by mechanical de-aeration method. The method consists in spraying water in a tower provided with perforated plates. Tower is heated by steam jacket provided on the sides. Vacuum is created inside the tower using vacuum pump. Large exposed surface, high temperature and low pressure reduce the dissolved oxygen content of water.

2. Carbon dioxide: There are two sources of carbon dioxide in boiler water, *viz.* dissolved carbon dioxide in raw water and CO_2 formed by the decomposition of dissolved bicarbonates

$$\underset{\text{Dissolved bicarbonates}}{Mg(HCO_3)_2} \longrightarrow MgCO_3 + H_2O + CO_2$$

Carbon dioxide in presence of water forms carbonic acid which has a corrosive effect on the boiler material

$$H_2O + CO_2 \longrightarrow \underset{\text{Carbonic acid}}{H_2CO_3}$$

Moreover, some of the dissolved carbon dioxide is released on heating and carried alongwith the steam to other parts of the boiler and thus corrodes such parts.

Removal of carbon dioxide.

(*i*) **Mechanical de-aeration:** CO_2 alongwith O_2 can be removed by mechanical de-aeration method, already discussed.

(*ii*) **Filtration through limestone ($CaCO_3$):** CO_2 can be removed by filtering through limestone.

$$CaCO_3 + H_2O + CO_2 \longrightarrow Ca(HCO_3)_2$$

However, this method leads to hardness of water as calcium bicarbonate ($Ca(HCO_3)_2$) is formed which causes temporary hardness.

(*iii*) **Addition of aqueous ammonia:** CO_2 can also be removed by addition of aqueous ammonia

$$CO_2 + 2NH_3 + H_2O \longrightarrow (NH_4)_2\,CO_3$$

But ammonia, being corrosive to copper and its alloys, is replaced by amines.

3. Mineral acids: Magnesium chloride if present in boiler feed water undergoes hydrolysis producing hydrochloric acid.

$$MgCl_2 + 2H_2O \longrightarrow Mg(OH)_2\downarrow + 2HCl$$

Free hydrochloric acid, present in boiler water, reacts with iron material of the boiler to form ferrous hydroxide which in turn is converted into rust in the following way:

$$Fe + 2HCl \longrightarrow FeCl_2 + H_2$$
$$FeCl_2 + 2H_2O \longrightarrow Fe(OH)_2 + 2HCl$$
$$2Fe(OH)_2 + O_2 \longrightarrow \underset{\text{(Rust)}}{Fe_2O_3.H_2O}$$

Thus, a small amount of HCl may cause continuous corrosion since HCl is again produced in the reaction. However, the boiler water is generally alkaline and thus the acid is usually neutralized. In case, the amount of acid is more, calculated amount of alkali is added from outside to neutralize the acid.

Priming and Foaming

Priming: When steam is produced rapidly in the boilers, some droplets of the liquid water are carried alongwith the steam. This process of formation of 'wet steam' is called as **priming**.

Priming is caused by:

(*i*) The presence of dissolved impurities particularly the suspended ones.

(*ii*) High velocity of steam which carries water droplets alongwith it in the steam pipe.

(*iii*) Sudden boiling

(*iv*) Faulty design of the boiler

(*v*) Very high water level in the boiler.

Priming can be prevented by:

(*i*) Using water having no suspended impurities.

(*ii*) Providing ample steam space by maintaining low water level in the boiler.

(*iii*) Avoiding rapid changes in steam rate.

(*iv*) Changing boiler water from time to time.

(*v*) Using a properly designed boiler.

(*vi*) Blowing off scales or sludge from time to time.

(*vii*) Fitting mechanical steam purifiers. They return the boiler water carried-over to the boiler.

Foaming: Priming is generally associated with *foaming* which is defined as 'the production of continuous foam or bubbles in boilers which do not break easily'.

Foaming is caused by the presence of an oil and alkali in boiler feed water. Actually, oils and alkalis react to form soaps which greatly reduce the surface tension of water and thus cause foaming.

Foaming can be prevented by:

(*i*) The addition of anti-foaming chemicals such as caster oil which spreads on the surface of water and therefore reduces its surface tension.

(*ii*) Blow down operations at appropriate time.

(*iii*) The removal of oil (foaming agent) from boiler water. Traces of oil are generally introduced in boiler feed water through the lubricating materials used for pumps etc. Oil can be removed by the addition of aluminium compounds like sodium aluminate ($NaAlO_2$) and aluminium sulphate [$(NH_4)_2SO_4$]. The aluminium compounds are hydrolysed to form flocks of $Al(OH)_3$ which entraps oil drops. The flocks of $Al(OH)_3$ containing droplets are removed by filtration through anthrafilt filter bed.

Caustic Embrittlement

Caustic embrittlement is the phenomena during which boiler material becomes brittle due to the accumulation of caustic substances.

It is a well known fact that slight excess of sodium carbonate is used during the softening of water (lime soda process) for the complete removal of calcium and magnesium salts in the form of carbonates. Due to evaporation of water in boilers, the concentration of sodium carbonate increases and thus it undergoes hydrolysis to form sodium hydroxide in the boiler.

$$Na_2CO_3 + H_2O \longrightarrow 2NaOH + CO_2$$

This together with the natural alkalinity in water make boiler water caustic. Water containing caustic soda enters the minute cracks by capillary action. Inside the cracks, water evaporates and the amount of caustic goes on increasing with time. The concentrated alkali then attacks the nearest intergranular cracks thereby dissolving iron of boiler as sodium ferroate (Na_2FeO_2).

$$Fe + 2NaOH \longrightarrow Na_2FeO_2 + H_2\uparrow$$

$$3Na_2\,FeO_2 + 4H_2O \longrightarrow 6NaOH + Fe_3O_4 + H_2\uparrow$$

$$6Na_2\,FeO_2 + 6H_2O + O_2 \longrightarrow 12NaOH + 2Fe_3O_4$$

It has been seen that sodium hydroxide is regenerated in this process and its concentration keeps on increasing maintaining the required environment.

Prevention of caustic embrittlement:

(*i*) By adding sodium nitrate ($NaNO_3$) as it neutralizes the excess amount of alkali, therefore, prevents caustic embrittlement.

(*ii*) By adding tannin or lignin to the boiler water. These prevent caustic cracking by blocking up the hair cracks and thus preventing the infiltration of sodium hydroxide.

(*iii*) Caustic embrittlement may also be checked by using sodium phosphate in place of sodium carbonate for softening of the boiler water.

(*iv*) pH of boiler water should b adjusted between 8 – 9.

(*v*) By adding sodium sulphate to boiler water.

8.5 SOFTENING OF WATER

The process of removal of hardness producing salts, which are present in the water is known as **softening of water**. The important processes used for the softening of water are:

1. Lime-soda precess
2. Zeolite process
3. Ion-exchange process.

The details of these methods are discussed below:

Lime-soda Process

In this process, lime [$Ca(OH)_2$] and soda (Na_2CO_3) are the reagents used to precipitate the dissolved salts of Ca^{2+} and Mg^{2+} as $CaCO_3$ and $Mg(OH)_2$ which are later on filtered off. The precipitates formed are finely divided, which do not settle down and cause difficulty in filtration. So, it is necessary to add small amounts of coagulants like alum [$K_2SO_4 \cdot Al_2(SO_4)_3 \cdot 24H_2O$], sodium aluminate ($NaAlO_2$) and ferrous sulphate($FeSO_4$) which hydrolyse to flocculent, gelatinous precipitate of $Al(OH)_3$ and entraps the fine precipitates of $CaCO_3$ and $Mg(OH)_2$.

Calculation of lime and soda requirement: The amount of lime and soda required can be calculated by keeping in mind the following points:

(*i*) **Lime requirement:** Lime removes

(*a*) Temporary calcium hardness

(*b*) Temporary magnesium hardness

(*c*) Permanent magnesium hardness

(*d*) Hardness caused by Fe^{2+}, Al^{3+}, dissolved gases. (CO_2, H_2S) and mineral acids (HCl, H_2SO_4 and $NaHCO_3$).

(*ii*) **Soda requirement:** Soda removes permanent calcium hardness which is introduced during the removal of permanent Mg^{2+} hardness, Fe^{2+}, Al^{3+}, HCl and H_2SO_4 by lime in water due to the formation of calcium salts.

(*iii*) If any $NaHCO_3$ is present in the water, it will be converted into Na_2CO_3 (*i.e.* soda) by lime. Therefore, it has to be subtracted form the soda requirement.

(*iv*) Sodium aluminate, $NaAlO_2$ required neither lime nor soda. However, it undergoes hydrolysis to produce one equivalent of NaOH, which precipitate some of the magnesium as $Mg(OH)_2$.

Therefore, the quantity of $NaAlO_2$ in equivalent is subtracted while calculating lime requirement.

(*v*) The impurities such as NaCl, KCl, SiO_2, Fe_2O_3, $FeCl_3$, Na_2SO_4 etc. should be ignored as they do not consume any lime or soda.

(*vi*) When impurities are given as $CaCO_3$ or $MgCO_3$, these should be considered as temporary hardness because of their bicarbonates.

A given hard water sample can have different combination of salts or ions. Accordingly, it requires different amount of lime and soda for effective softening. The various constituents and their chemical reactions with lime and soda are given in Table 8.2.

Table 8.2: Chemical Reactions Involved and Requirement of Lime and Soda

S.No.	Constituent	Chemical reactions	Requirement of lime (L) and Soda (S)
1.	Temporary calcium hardness $Ca(HCO_3)_2$	$Ca(HCO_3)_2 + Ca(OH)_2 \longrightarrow 2CaCO_3 + 2H_2O$	1 L (means 1 equivalent of lime is required to remove 1 equivalent of $Ca(HCO_3)_2$)
2.	Temporary magnesium hardness $Mg(HCO_3)_2$	$Mg(HCO_3)_2 + 2Ca(OH)_2 \longrightarrow 2CaCO_3 + Mg(OH)_2 + 2H_2O$	2 L
3.	Permanent calcium hardness ($CaCl_2$, $CaSO_4$ etc.)	$CaCl_2 + Na_2CO_3 \longrightarrow CaCO_3\downarrow + 2NaCl$ $CaSO_4 + Na_2CO_3 \longrightarrow CaCO_3\downarrow + Na_2SO_4$	1 S
4.	Permanent magnesium hardness ($MgCl_2$, $MgSO_4$ etc.)	$MgCl_2 + Ca(OH)_2 \longrightarrow Mg(OH)_2 + CaCl_2$ (Causes permanent hardness) $MgSO_4 + Ca(OH)_2 \longrightarrow Mg(OH)_2 + CaSO_4$ (Causes permanent hardness) $CaCl_2 + Na_2CO_3 \longrightarrow CaCO_3 + 2\ NaCl$ $CaSO_4 + Na_2CO_3 \longrightarrow CaCO_3 + Na_2SO_4$	1 L + 1 S lime removes permanent magnesium hardness but imparts calcium hardness which is removed by soda.
5.	HCO_3^- (*e.g.* $NaHCO_3$)	$2NaHCO_3 + Ca(OH)_2 \longrightarrow CaCO_3\downarrow + H_2O + Na_2CO_3$	1 L – 1 S
6.	CO_2	$CO_2 + Ca(OH)_2 \longrightarrow CaCO_3\downarrow + H_2O$	1 L
7.	H^+ (From free acids like HCl, H_2SO_4 etc.)	$2\ HCl + Ca(OH)_2 \longrightarrow CaCl_2 + 2H_2O$ ($CaCl_2$ ↓ removed by soda) $H_2SO_4 + Ca(OH)_2 \longrightarrow CaSO_4 + 2H_2O$ ($CaSO_4$ ↓ removed by soda) $CaCl_2 + NaCO_3 \longrightarrow CaCO_3\downarrow + 2NaCl$ $CaSO_4 + Na_2CO_3 \longrightarrow CaCO_3 + Na_2SO_4$	1 L + 1 S

8.	$FeSO_4$	$FeSO_4 + Ca(OH)_2 \longrightarrow Fe(OH)_2 + CaSO_4$ $\downarrow$ removed by soda $CaSO_4 + Na_2CO_3 \longrightarrow CaCO_3\downarrow + Na_2SO_4$	1 L + 1 S
9.	$Al_2(SO_4)_3$	$Al_2(SO_4)_3 + 3Ca(OH)_2 \longrightarrow 2Al(OH)_3\downarrow + 3CaSO_4$ $3CaSO_4 + 3Na_2CO_3 \longrightarrow 3\,CaCO_3\downarrow + 3Na_2SO_4$	1 L + 1 S
10.	$NaAlO_2$	$NaAlO_2 + 2H_2O \longrightarrow Al(OH)_3\downarrow + NaOH$ $MgCl_2 + 2NaOH \longrightarrow Mg(OH)_2 + 2NaCl$	– 1 L (NaOH produces precipitates some of magnesium as $Mg(OH)_2$ $\therefore$ it needs to be subtracted

Note: Aluminium and iron salt (*e.g.* $Al_2(SO_4)_3$, $FeSO_4$) may be present in water as contributor of hardness or they may be added as coagulants.

Thus, lime required for softening is given by the following formula:

$$= \frac{74}{100}\left\{\begin{array}{l} Ca(HCO_3)_2 + 2Mg(HCO_3)_2 + MgCl_2 + MgSO_4 + \\ FeSO_4 + Al_2(SO_4)_3 + CO_2 + HCl + H_2SO_4 + \\ NaHCO_3 - NaAlO_2 \end{array}\right\} \text{mg/L or ppm}$$

Soda required for softening

$$= \frac{106}{100}\left\{\begin{array}{l} CaCl_2 + CaSO_4 + MgCl_2 + MgSO_4 \\ + Al_2(SO_4)_3 + FeSO_4 + HCl + H_2SO_4 - \\ NaHCO_3 \end{array}\right\} \text{mg/L or ppm}$$

Concentration of all the dissolved salts is in terms of $CaCO_3$ equivalents. If lime and soda used is impure then while calculating lime and soda requirement, we have to consider their percentage purity also. So,

Lime required for softening (in mg/L or ppm)

$$= \frac{74}{100}\left\{\begin{array}{l} Ca(HCO_3)_2 + 2Mg(HCO_3)_2 + MgCl_2 + MgSO_4 \\ + FeSO_4 + Al_2(SO_4)_3 + CO_2 + HCl + H_2SO_4 \\ + NaHCO_3 - NaAlO_2 \end{array}\right\} \times \frac{100}{\%\text{ purity of lime}} \text{ ppm}$$

and soda required for softening (in mg/L or ppm)

$$= \frac{106}{100}\left\{\begin{array}{l} CaCl_2 + CaSO_4 + MgCl_2 + MgSO_4 \\ + Al_2(SO_4)_3 + FeSO_4 + HCl + H_2SO_4 - NaHCO_3 \end{array}\right\} \times \frac{100}{\%\text{ purity of lime}} \text{ ppm}$$

To calculate the lime and soda requirement in kg, lime requirement (in kg)

$$= \frac{74}{100}\left\{\begin{array}{l} Ca(HCO_3)_2 + 2Mg(HCO_3)_2 + MgCl_2 \\ + MgSO_4 + FeSO_4 + Al_2(SO_4)_3 + CO_2 \\ + HCl + H_2SO_4 + NaHCO_3 - NaAlO_2 \end{array}\right\} \times \frac{\text{volume of water}}{10^6} \times \frac{100}{\%\text{purity of lime}} \text{ kg}$$

Similarly soda requirement (in kg)

$$= \frac{106}{100}\begin{Bmatrix} CaCl_2 + CaSO_4 + MgCl_2 + MgSO_4 \\ + Al_2(SO_4)_3 + FeSO_4 + HCl + H_2SO_4 \\ - NaHCO_3 \end{Bmatrix} \times \frac{\text{Volume of water}}{10^6} \times \frac{100}{\%\text{ purity of soda}} \text{ kg.}$$

Types of Lime Soda Process

There are two types of lime soda precess:

(*i*) Cold lime soda process (*ii*) Hot lime soda process.

Cold Lime Soda Process

In this process, water is treated with chemicals at room temperature. There are two types of cold-lime soda softeners which work either in batch precess or in continuous process. These are briefly discussed below:

(*a*) Intermittent type (Batch precess): In this precess, a pair of tanks are used for softening water. Each tank is provided with a mechanical stirrer, inlets for raw water and chemicals and outlets for softened water and sludge. Raw water is passed from one side and a mixture of lime and soda is passed simultaneously from the opposite side and stirring is started. A small amount of sludge/precipitate (from a previous operation) is added during stirring which act as nucleus for the fresh precipitation. By the time the tank fill up, the reaction is complete and thus stirring is stopped and the precipitate is allowed to settle down. The precipitate (sludge), taken out through the outlet provided at the bottom while the clear softened water is taken out through a floating pipe so that no sludge can go with clear water. The softened water is further filtered at the filtering station. By using a pair of tanks planned for alternate cycles of reaction and settling, continuous supply of softened water may be ensured.

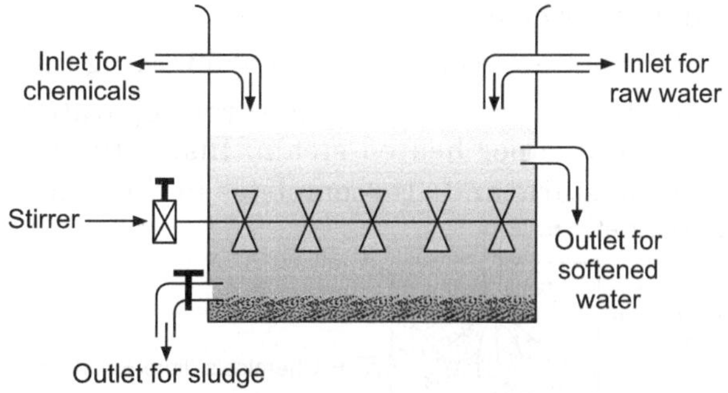

Fig. 8.1. Intermittent type of cold lime soda softener.

(*b*) Continuous softener for cold precess: In the continuous process, there is a continuous feed of raws water and chemicals and again there is uninterrupted outflow of soft water.

The softener consists of a big steel tank with two chambers. The inner chamber is provided with a stirrer having a number of paddles while the outer chamber has two wood fiber filters to remove the last particles of sludge.

Raw water and calculated amount of lime, soda and a coagulant (alum, aluminium sulphate, sodium aluminate etc.) are fed through two opposite inlets into the inner chamber at room temperature and stirring is started. Due to continuous stirring, the raw water and the chemicals flowing down the chamber come in close contact and softening of water takes place in the inner chamber. Sludge (precipitate) formed settles down at the bottom in the outer chamber and the softened water goes upward in the outer chamber where it passes through the wood fibre filters to ensure complete removal of the sludge. Filtered soft water finally comes out continuously through the outlet provided for the purpose.

Cold lime-soda process provides water containing a residual hardness of 50–60 ppm.

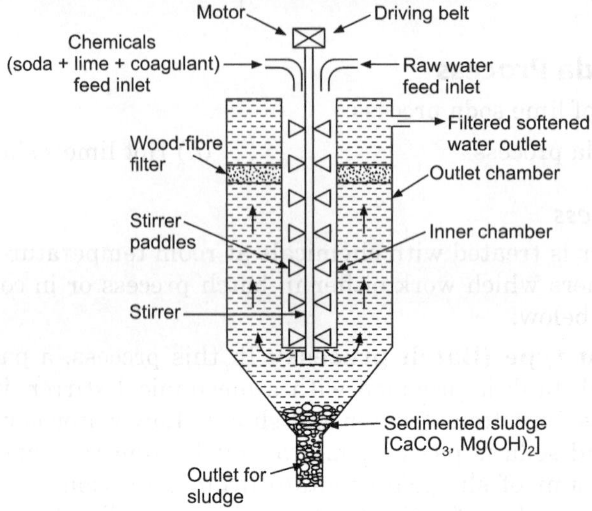

Fig. 8.2. Continuous cold lime soda softener.

Hot Lime Soda Process

In this process, water is treated at a temperature of 80°– 150°C, The softeners used may be of intermittent type or continuous type.

1. The intermittent type softener is of the same type as in the cold process except that the heating coils are installed in it for heating water.

2. Continuous softener for hot process: It consists of following three parts:

   (*i*) **Reaction tank:** This reaction tank has three separate inlets, one each for raw water, chemicals and super heated steam. Inside the tank, they are thoroughly mixed. The reaction starts and also completes in this tank.

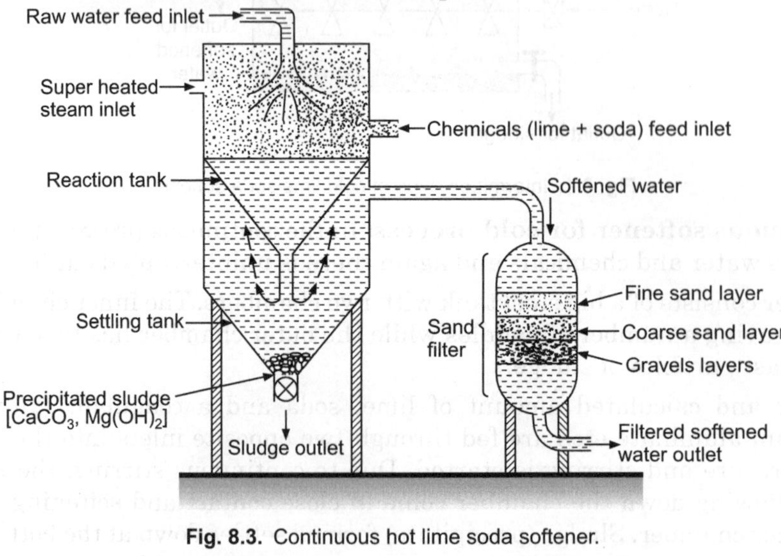

Fig. 8.3. Continuous hot lime soda softener.

(*ii*) **Settling tank:** From the reaction tank, the contents go to the conical settling tank in which sludge settles down.

(*iii*) **Sand filter:** Clear and softened water from the settling tank passes to filter vessel having layers of fine and coarse sand. The sand layers act as filters and remove any suspended impurity or precipitate.

This process provides soft water containing a residual hardness of 15 – 30 ppm.

Advantages of hot lime soda precess over cold lime soda process are:

(*i*) As the precipitation takes place rapidly, the reaction completes in less time (only 15 minutes) than the cold process which takes several hours for completion.

(*ii*) Residual hardness is far less than the cold precess.

(*iii*) The precipitate and sludge formed settle down rapidly and hence no coagulant is needed.

(*iv*) Most of the dissolved gases such as CO_2 and H_2S are removed from the solution.

(*v*) Quantity of chemicals required for softening is low and hence softening capacity of the process is high.

(*vi*) Viscosity of softened water becomes low and hence its filtration becomes easier.

(*vii*) The residual hardness of water obtained from hot lime soda process (15–30 ppm) is less than that obtained from cold lime soda process (upto 60 ppm).

Advantages of Lime Soda Process

(*i*) It is very economical as compared to other processes available for softening of water.

(*ii*) This process increases the pH of the treated water, thereby corrosion of the distribution pipes is reduced.

(*iii*) Besides the removal of hardness, the quantity of minerals in the water is reduced.

(*iv*) To some extent iron and manganese are also removed from the water.

(*v*) Due to the alkaline nature of treated water, amount of pathogenic bacteria in water is considerably reduced.

Disadvantages of Lime-soda Process

1. For efficient and economical softening, careful operation and skilled supervision is required.
2. Disposal of large amounts of sludge poses a great problem.
3. The softened water is not completely free from hardness and therefore it cannot be used in high pressure boilers.

Zeolite Process (Permutit Process)

Zeolites, also known as **permutits** *i.e.* boiling stone (in greek). Zeolites are **hydrated sodium alumino silicate minerals** of the general formula $Na_2O\ .\ Al_2O_3\ xSiO_2\ .\ yH_2O$ (where $x = 2 - 10$ and $y = 2 - 6$) capable of exchanging reversibly its sodium ions with the hardness producing ions like Ca^{2+}, Mg^{2+} in water. Zeolites are of two types:

1. **Natural zeolites:** These are non-porous, amorphous and durable. *e.g.* natralite ($Na_2O\ .\ Al_2O_3\ .\ 3SiO_2\ .\ 2H_2O$), laumonite ($CaO\ .\ Al_2O_3\ .\ 4SiO_2\ .\ 4H_2O$) etc.
2. **Synthetic zeolites:** These are generally porous and have gel like structure. Synthetic zeolites are obtained in the form of coarse sand by fusing together sodium

carbonate (Na_2CO_3), alumina (Al_2O_3) and silica (SiO_2). For example, sodium zeolite ($Na_2O \cdot Al_2O_3 \cdot x\,SiO_2 \cdot yH_2O$) where $x = 2 - 10$ and $y = 2 - 6$).

Synthetic zeolites have higher exchange capacity as compared to natural zeolites.

Process

Zeolite softener consists of a steel tank packed with a thick layer of permutit. A slow stream of hard water is passed through a bed of zeolite stacked in a cylindrical column. As a result, calcium and magnesium ions present in hard water are removed in the form of insoluble zeolites. The outgoing water contains sodium salts which do not cause hardness. The chemical reactions occur in the process are as follows:

$$Ca(HCO_3)_2 + Na_2Ze \longrightarrow CaZe + 2NaHCO_3$$
$$Mg(HCO_3)_2 + Na_2Ze \longrightarrow MgZe + 2NaHCO_3$$
$$CaCl_2 + Na_2Ze \longrightarrow CaZe + 2NaCl$$
$$CaSO_4 + Na_2Ze \longrightarrow CaZe + Na_2SO_4$$
$$MgCl_2 + Na_2Ze \longrightarrow MgZe + 2NaCl$$
$$MgSO_4 + Na_2Ze \longrightarrow MgZe + Na_2SO_4$$

where Na_2Ze is the zeolite. This process removes both temporary and permanent hardness. Over a period of time, zeolite gets converted into a mixture of calcium and magnesium alumina silicates which is unable to soften water further. At this stage, the zeolite is said to be exhausted and it has to be regenerated for further use.

Regeneration

Regeneration of exhausted zeolite can be done by percolating a concentrated solution of brine (10% NaCl) through it. This operation converts calcium or magnesium zeolite back into sodium zeolite according to the equation:

$$CaZe + 2NaCl \longrightarrow Na_2Ze + CaCl_2$$
$$MgZe + 2NaCl \longrightarrow Na_2Ze + MgCl_2$$

Regeneration of exhausted zeolite can also be carried out using $NaNO_3$, KCl, KNO_3 etc., but NaCl is most commonly used because of its low cost and the products of regeneration process *i.e.* $CaCl_2$ and $MgCl_2$ are highly soluble and can be easily rinsed out from the zeolite bed.

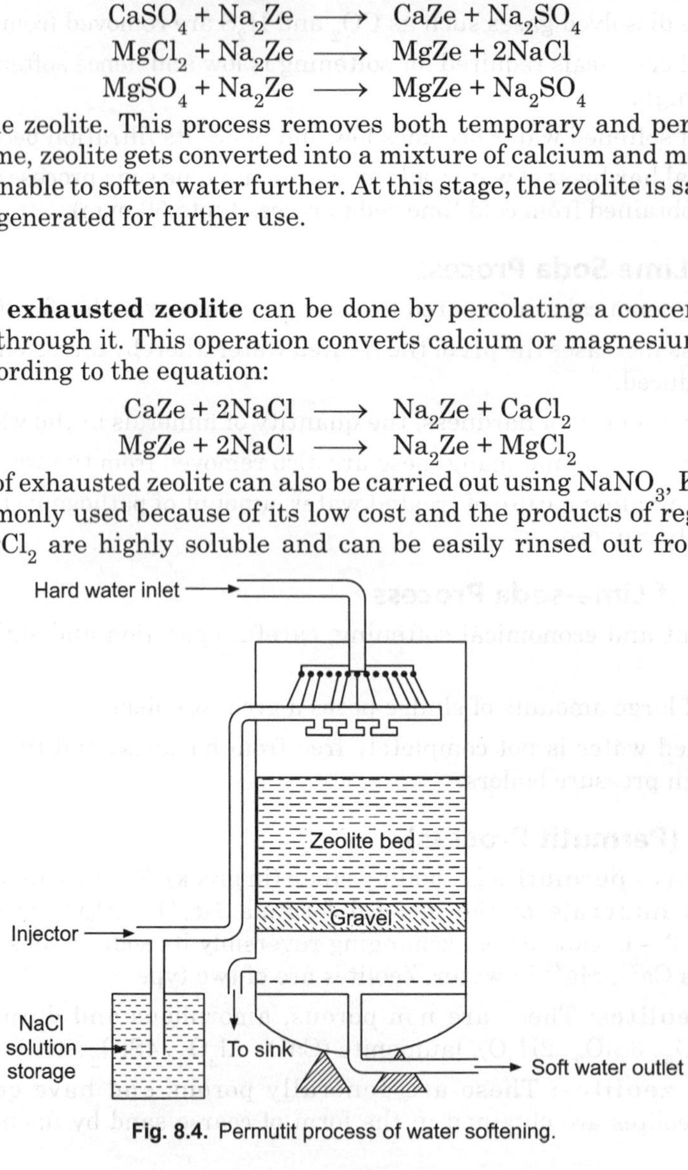

Fig. 8.4. Permutit process of water softening.

By knowing the amount of NaCl used for the regeneration of zeolite, the hardness of given water sample can be calculated using the formula:

$$\text{Hardness} = \frac{mV_2 \times 50 \times 1000}{V_1 \times 58.5} \text{ mg/L or ppm}$$

$$= \frac{854.7 mV_2}{V_1} \text{ ppm}$$

where

m = amount of NaCl (in g/L) present in volume V_2

V_1 = Volume of water to be softened (in L)

V_2 = Volume of NaCl required for regeneration of zeolite. (in L).

Advantages of Zeolite Process

1. Hardness is almost completely removed. It contains the residual hardness of about 10 ppm.
2. The equipment is compact and occupies less space.
3. In this process, the hardness causing ions are simply exchanged with sodium ions. Therefore, it does not involve any precipitation or sludge formation.
4. This method is very cheap because the regenerated permutit can be used again and the process can be repeated a number of times. The consumption being only of sodium chloride which is always inexpensive.
5. It automatically adjusts to waters of different hardness.

Limitations of Zeolite Process

1. If the water to be processed is turbid, it must be made clear by removing the suspended impurities by filtration, coagulation etc. Otherwise the suspended impurities will clog the pores of zeolite bed and these restrict the flow of water.
2. Mineral acids if present in water destroy the zeolite bed, therefore, they must be neutralized before passing to the zeolite bed.
3. If water contains large amounts of coloured ions (*e.g.* Fe^{2+} and Mn^{2+}), they must be removed first because they produce iron and manganese zeolites which are very difficult to be regenerated.
4. The water fed to the zeolite should not be hot as zeolite tends to dissolve in it.
5. Zeolite treatment removes only the cations like Ca^{2+} and Mg^{2+}, leaving all the anions like HCO_3^- and CO_3^{2-} in the treated water. Such treated water containing large amount of anions cause following problems in boilers.

(*i*) When such water is fed to boilers, carbon dioxide is liberated

$$NaHCO_3 \longrightarrow NaOH + CO_2\uparrow$$

Free CO_2 is weakly acidic in nature and extremely corrosive to boiler material.

(*ii*) Due to the formation of NaOH, the water becomes alkaline and can cause caustic embrittlement in boilers.

However, both the above problems (CO_2 and NaOH) can be overcome by neutralizing the water (to be used in boilers) with calculated amount of sulphuric acid.

$$2\ NaHCO_3 + H_2SO_4 \longrightarrow Na_2SO_4 + 2H_2O + 2CO_2$$

The liberated CO_2 is removed by de-aeration.

6. The treated water contains 25% more dissolved solids as compared to lime-soda process.

Table 8.3: Comparison between the Zeolite Process and the Lime-soda Process

S.No.	Lime-soda process	Permutit or Zeolite process
1.	Water obtained is not perfectly pure. It contains about 15–50 ppm hardness.	Water of almost zero hardness is obtained.
2.	The plant occupies more space.	The plant occupies less space.
3.	Capital cost is lower but the operational expenses are high.	Capital cost is higher but the operational expenses are low.
4.	It can be used for softening acidic water, hot water and turbid water (water having suspended impurities).	It cannot be used for softening acidic water (acids destroy zeolites), hot water (dissolves zeolites) and turbid water (impurities block the pores of zeolite bed).
5.	It involves difficult steps like coagulation, settling and filtration.	It does not involve these steps.
6.	It cannot operate under pressure	It can operate under pressure and can be made fully automatic.
7.	Treated water contains lesser amount of sodium salts than the hard water.	Treated water contains larger amounts of sodium salts than the hard water.
8.	This process removes cations as well as anoins	This process removes only the cations like Ca^{2+} and Mg^{2+}.
9.	Large amounts of sludge is formed.	No sludge is formed so it is a clean process.
10.	In order to meet the changing hardness of incoming water, adjustment of reagent doses is needed.	The process adjusts itself to water of different hardness.

Ion Exchange Process (Demineralization or Deionization)

Deionization is the process of complete removal of all ions *i.e.*, cations and anions present in water by using ion-exchange resins. An ion-exchange resin is a cross linked organic polymer network having some ionizable groups. Usually polystyrene-divinylbenzene, phenol-formaldehyde resin, polymethacrylic acid-divinyl benzene etc. are used as ion-exchange resins. Ion-exchange resins are of two types depending upon the nature of the ionizable group:

Cation Exchange Resins or Cation Exchanger

Such resins have $-SO_3H$, $-COOH$ group as the ionizable group. They are capable of exchanging their cationic part or H^+ ions with the cations present in hard water. They are usually copolymer of styrene and divinyl benzene which on carboxylation or sulphonation become cation exchanger. They can be represented as:

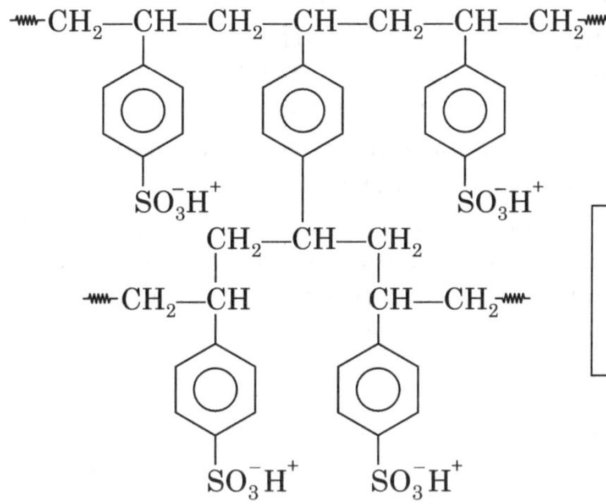

Commercially available cation exchangers are Dowex-50 Amberlite IRC-120 etc.

Fig 8.4. Structure of cation exchanger

They are represented by RH^+ where *R* represents the resin network.

Anion Exchange Resins or Anion Exchanger

These resins have $—NH_2$, $—NHCH_3$, $—N(CH_3)_2$ or —OH group. They are capable of exchanging their anionic part or –OH ions with the anions present in hard water. They are usually copolymers of styrene and divinyl benzene having amine or substituted amines as their hydroxide salts. They can be represented as:

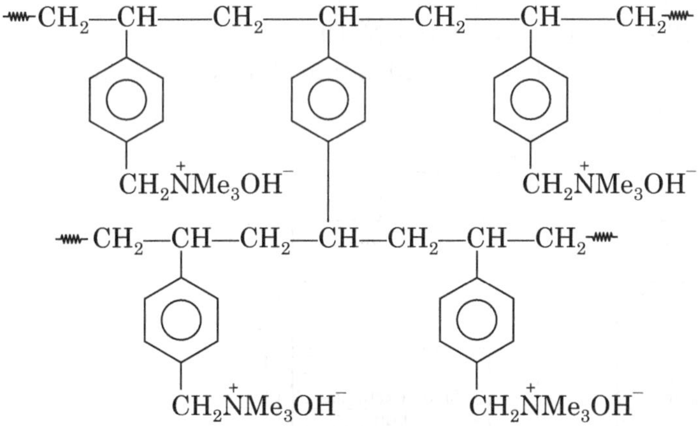

Amberlite IRA-400 and Dowex-3 are commercially available anion exchangers.

Fig. 8.5. Structure of anion exchange resin.

In general it is represented as R′OH where R′ represents resin network.

Process

Water is first passed through a tank having cation exchanger (hydrogen exchanger) which absorbs all the cations present in water and releases H^+ ions in the water.

$$2RH + Ca^{2+} \longrightarrow R_2Ca + 2H^+$$

$$2RH + Mg^{2+} \longrightarrow R_2Mg + 2H^+$$

The water coming out of cation exchanger is highly acidic due to the presence of H^+ ions. The cation free water is now passed through another tank having anion exchanger which absorbs all the anions present in water and releases OH^- in the water.

$$R'OH + Cl^- \longrightarrow R'Cl + OH^-$$
$$2\,R'OH + SO_4^{2-} \longrightarrow R_2SO_4 + 2OH^-$$

The anion exchanger not only removes anions like Cl^- and SO_4^{2-} but also introduces OH^- ions just sufficient to neutralize the H^+ ions produced in the cation exchanger.

$$H^+ + OH^- \longrightarrow H_2O$$

Thus, the water coming out from exchanger is free from all ions and is also free from acidity or alkalinity. Thus, it is as pure as distilled water and is called as **deionized or demineralised water**. Finally, the demineralised water is passed through a degasifier, which reduces the amount of dissolved gases like CO_2 and O_2 in water.

Regeneration

When the cation and anion exchangers are used for some period, they are exhausted and stop working. However, they can be regenerated as below:

Cation exchange resins are usually regenerated by passing dilute HCl or H_2SO_4 solution into the bed. The H^+ ions of the acid are exchanged with the cations (Ca^{2+} and Mg^{2+}) present in the cation exchanger.

$$R_2Ca + H_2SO_4 \longrightarrow 2RH + CaSO_4$$
$$R_2Mg + 2HCl \longrightarrow 2RH + MgCl_2$$

The washings containing Ca^{2+} and Mg^{2+} ions ($CaSO_4$, $CaCl_2$, $MgSO_4$, $MgCl_2$) are passed to sink.

Similarly, the exhausted anion exchange resins are regenerated by treatment with dil. NaOH solution.

$$R_2'SO_4 + 2NaOH \longrightarrow 2R'OH + Na_2SO_4$$
$$R'Cl + NaOH \longrightarrow R'OH + NaCl$$

The washings containing Na_2SO_4 and NaCl are discarded into sink. The deionization and regeneration are the alternate process.

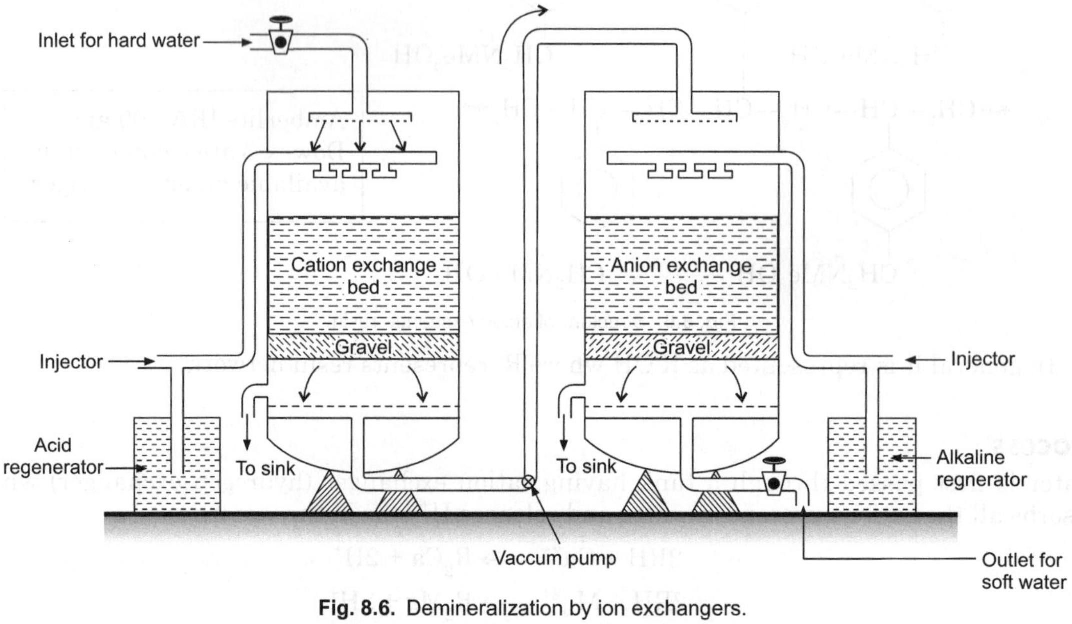

Fig. 8.6. Demineralization by ion exchangers.

Advantages of Ion Exchange Process

1. Highly acidic or highly alkaline water can also be softened.
2. The softened water is of very low hardness *i.e.* about 2 ppm.

Disadvantages of the Process

1. The process is very expensive as the cost of ion exchange resins and the equipment is very high.
2. The resins need to be regenerated again and again, thus making the process inconvenient and complex.
3. Turbid water reduces the efficiency of the process.

Table 8.4: Difference between Zeolite Process and Ion Exchange Process.

S.No.	Zeolite process	Ion exchange process
1.	It removes only cations from hard water.	It removes both cations and anions from hard water.
2.	It cannot be used for softening acidic water.	It can be used to soften acidic water.
3.	Treated water has high content of TDS therefore cannot be used in boilers.	Treated water is free from TDS, hence can be used in boilers.
4.	It produces soft water containing sodium salts.	It produces demineralised water (free from salts).

8.6 MUNICIPAL WATER SUPPLY

Municipal water is what many people refer to as tap water. In most locations, throughout the country, municipal water is supplied to homes and industries with the help of underground pipes. Municipal water is not as clean and healthy to drink as purified and filtered water, therefore, it needs to be treated and processed so that it meets the *standard* of drinking water that have been set by Environmental Protection Agency.

Water for domestic purposes should be obtained from a source which is least contaminated like rivers, lakes and wells. The common requirements for drinking or potable water are:

1. It should be sparkling clear and odourless.
2. It should be good in taste.
3. It should be free from disease causing micro-organisms.
4. It's turbidity should not exceed 10 ppm.
5. It's pH should be about 6.5 to 8.5.
6. The TDS (total dissolved solids) in potable water should be less than 500 ppm.
7. It should be free from harmful chemicals such as poisonous gases (*e.g.*, H_2S), lead, arsenic, chromium salts, radioactive elements etc.
8. It should be reasonably soft and total hardness should not exceed 500 ppm.
9. It should be free from chlorides, fluorides, sulphates and phenolic compounds.

In order for a municipality to provide water for domestic use, they must first treat the water and have it tested. Water treatment for domestic use employs the following steps:

(*i*) Screening (*ii*) Sedimentation (*iii*) filtration (*iv*) disinfection

Screening

The first step in purifying surface water is to remove large debris such as leaves, wood pieces, sticks and other large particles which may interfere with subsequent purification steps. Deep ground water does not need screening before other purification steps.

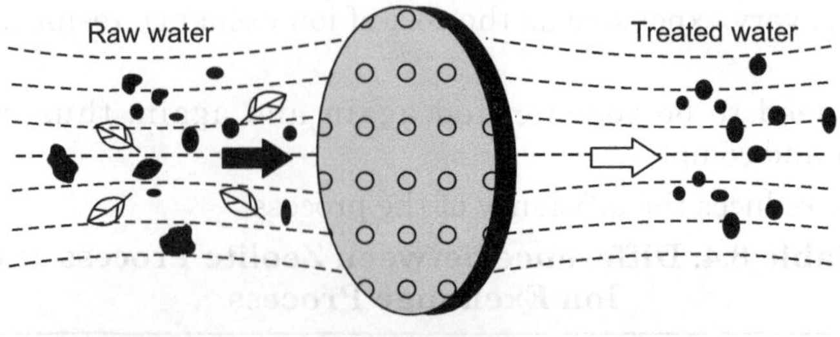

Fig. 8.7. Screening.

Sedimentation (Settling)

Sedimentation is the process of removing suspended impurities by allowing water to stand undisturbed for some hours or even days in order to facilitate the settling down of the coarse suspended particles under the action of gravity. The rate of settling of the particles being removed varies with their diameter and specific gravity. The bigger particles settle down quickly in still water whereas smaller particles such as silt, may require few days to settle down. The longer the water is held undisturbed, the more the suspended solids and pathogens will settle to the bottom of the tank. The clear supernatant liquid is then drawn from the tank with the help of pumps.

Fine suspended particles like mud, clay and other colloidal impurities do not settle down easily, therefore, it is difficult to remove them simply by sedimentation. However, they can be removed by adding certain chemicals called coagulants before sedimentation process *i.e* sedimentation with coagulation.

Sedimentation with coagulation: Every colloidal particle carries a definite charge and same charge repel each other. The colloidal particles like mud, clay, organic matter particles carry a negative charge. Due to repulsion of like charges, these particles are not able to come closer and do not grow in size. As a result, these colloidal particles do not settle down under the influence of gravity. However, the addition of coagulants cause the small suspended particles to coagulate into bigger ones, which due to their weight, settle down more quickly. Commonly used coagulants are alum $[K_2SO_4 . Al_2(SO_4)_3 . 24H_2O]$, sodium aluminate ($NaAlO_2$) and ferrous sulphate ($FeSO_4.7H_2O$).

Alum, when added to water breaks into different salts.

$$[K_2SO_4 . Al_2(SO_4)_3 . 24H_2O] \longrightarrow K_2SO_4 + Al_2(SO_4)_3 + 24H_2O$$

The $Al_2(SO_4)_3$ further reacts with calcium or magnesium carbonate to give $Al(OH)_3$, which acts as coagulant.

$$Al_2(SO_4)_3 + 3Mg(HCO_3)_2 \longrightarrow 2Al(OH)_3 + 3MgSO_4 + 6CO_2$$
$$Al_2(SO_4)_3 + 3Ca(HCO_3)_2 \longrightarrow 2Al(OH)_3 + 3CaSO_4 + 6CO_2$$

$Al(OH)_3$ is an insoluble, flocculante precipitate which capture very fine suspended impurities forming bigger flocs, which settle down easily. Moreover, alum also provides Al^{3+} ions, which neutralizes the negatively charged colloidal particles, which when come closer results in bigger particles. These bigger particles settle down due to force of gravity. Sodium aluminate is generally used with aluminium sulphate for the treatment of acidic waters.

$$6NaAlO_2 + Al_2(SO_4)_3 + 12H_2O \longrightarrow 8Al(OH)_3 + 3Na_2SO_4$$

Ferrous sulphate is generally used as a coagulant for alkaline waters. If water is not alkaline then sufficient lime is to be added. If forms a precipitate of ferric hydroxide which acts as a coagulant.

$$FeSO_4 + 2H_2O \longrightarrow Fe(OH)_2 + H_2SO_4$$

$$4Fe(OH)_2 + \underset{\text{Dissolved oxygen in water}}{O_2} + 2H_2O \longrightarrow 4Fe(OH)_3$$

The $Fe(OH)_3$ formed, facilitates the colloidal particles to grow in size which finally settle down.

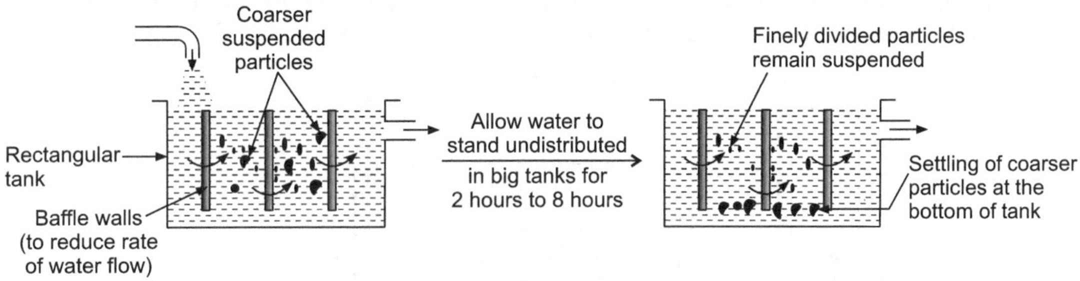

Fig. 8.8. Sedimentation for removal of suspended impurities.

Filtration

After separating most floc, the water is filtered at the final step to remove the remaining suspended particles and unsettled floc.

Filtration is the process of clarification of water by passing the water through a porous material, which is capable of retaining coarse impurities on its surface and in the pores. Filtration of water takes place due to the difference between the pressures at the bed of the filtering material and that underneath it. The filters used consist of several layers of sand particles of different size. Following two types of filters are commonly used in water treatment:

(*i*) Gravity sand filter, (*ii*) pressure filter.

***(i)* Gravity sand filter:** Gravity sand filtration can be slow or rapid. The sand filter used for water treatment consists of three main layers as shown in Fig. 8.9. The top layer consists of fine sand and is thick. The middle layer is made up of coarse sand and the bottom layer consists of gravels. Below the gravels are drains through which filtered water goes out.

Sedimented water enters the sand filter from the top and is evenly distributed over the fine sand layer. As water percolates (due to gravity) through the fine sand bed, most of the objectionable materials are absorbed by it and clear (filtered) water collects in the under drain channel, from where it is drawn out.

Slow sand filters may be used where there is sufficient land and space as the water must be passed at very slow rates.

Rapid sand filters are more commonly used. The only difference between the slow and rapid filters is the presence of an extra layer above the top layer of sand. This extra layer can be of activated carbon or anthracite coal. This layer removes organic compounds which contribute to taste and odour.

Gravity sand filters are used where a large quantity of water is to be filtered. These are best suited for municipal water.

In both the filters, after some time the rate of filtration becomes very slow because of clogging of pores of the top layer by the impurities retained in the pores. Therefore, to regain the speed of filtration, the top sand layer of few centimeters is removed and is replaced with the fresh sand. In this way, they are ready to be reused.

***(ii)* Pressure filters:** Pressure filters are used for the filtration of water where a small amount of water is required because these are not economical for large scale supplies. Thus, these filters are used for filtering water for industrial plants and for small scale water supply schemes.

A typical pressure filter consist of cylindrical steel shell containing there layers of filtering media: pebbles, coarse sand and fine sand layer one above the other.

Impure sedimented water is mixed with a small quaintly of alum and the water is then passed through filter bed under pressure. Alums forms an artificial slimy layer above the filter bed so that the colloidal and bacteriological impurities are removed. Filtered water, as it comes out from the bottom of filter, is under pressure and hence, can be pumped directly.

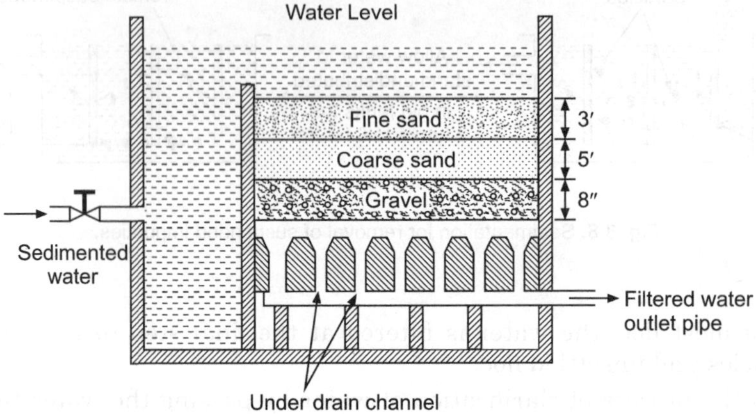

Fig. 8.9. Gravity sand filter.

Disinfection/sterilization (Removal of Micro-Organisms)

Although most of the bacteria and micro-organisms present in water are removed by coagulation followed by settling and filtration through sand beds, yet water contains a small percentage of pathogenic bacteria. These bacteria must be completely removed from water supplied by municipality for drinking purposes, otherwise water borne diseases may be produced.

The process of killing or destroying pathogenic bacteria (disease causing bacteria) and other micro-organisms is known as **sterilization or disinfection.** The chemicals used for sterilization are known as **sterilizers.** Water can be sterilized by a number of methods. Some of them are given below:

(i) Boiling	*(ii)* UV rays	*(iii)* Ozone
(iv) Bleaching powder	*(v)* Potassium permanganate	*(vi)* Chloramine
(vii) Chlorination		

***(i)* Boiling:** Boiling is a good method of sterilizing water since boiling of water for 20–30 minutes destroys all the disease causing bacteria. Although this is the simplest and easiest method but it is useful only for household purposes because the process is very expensive for municipal water supply. In addition, a large amount of fuel is required to boil water on a large scale. It kills the bacteria only at the time of boiling and does not provide any protection against future contamination.

***(ii)* Ultra-violet rays:** This is an excellent method for sterilizing water. In this method, water is exposed to UV rays which are generated from mercury lamp enclosed in a quartz globe placed under water. This method is used for cleaning swimming pool water. The method is quite expensive and cannot be applied for municipal work.

Sunlight also provides UV rays but it cannot penetrate large depths of water and hence sunlight is not an efficient method for sterilization of water.

***(iii)* By Ozone (O_3):** Ozone is an excellent disinfectant and the process of destroying the pathogens by ozone is called **ozonization**. Ozone is an unstable compound and decomposes to molecular oxygen and nascent oxygen.

$$O_3 \longrightarrow O_2 + [O]$$

The nascent oxygen thus released is very effective and kills all the germs and bacteria. During ozonization, ozone is injected through an injector into water in a contact tank and the sterilized water is collected from the top. The commonly used dose strength of ozone is 2–3 ppm.

Advantages of using Ozone as sterilizing agent:

- Ozone acts not only as a sterilizing agent but also as a bleaching, decolourising and deodourizing agent.
- It improves the taste of water.
- It's excess is not harmful since it is unstable and releases O_2 on decomposition.

It is an expensive treatment but still used for the sterilization of municipal water supply.

***(iv)* By adding bleaching powder ($CaOCl_2$):** Bleaching powder is a good sterilizer for small water works. It reacts with water to produce hypochlorous acid which further releases nascent oxygen. This nascent oxygen deactivates the enzymes of pathogens, as a result of which their metabolic activities stop and the pathogens get killed.

$$CaOCl_2 + H_2O \longrightarrow Ca(OH)_2 + Cl_2$$

$$Cl_2 + H_2O \longrightarrow HOCl + HCl$$

$$HOCl \longrightarrow HCl + [O]$$

Bleaching power should be used only in calculated amount because excess of it will give a bad taste and disagreeable odour, while lesser amount of it will not sterilize the water completely. About 1 kg of bleaching powder is sufficient to sterilize 1000 kilolitres of water.

The use of $CaOCl_2$ has certain disadvantages:

- It introduces calcium in water, which increases the hardness of water.
- If used in excess amount, it imparts a bad taste and disagreeable odour to water.
- It is not stable, therefore, if deteriorates due to its continuous decomposition during storage.

***(v)* By adding potassium permanganate ($KMnO_4$):** $KMnO_4$ is a strong oxidant and is used widely for taste and odour control and manganese removal. It is a weak disinfectant, therefore, the contact time and concentration required for adequate primary disinfection are quite large. As a result, it has limited use as a disinfectant.

***(vi)* By chloramine:** Ammonia and chlorine when mixed in the ratio of 1:2 by volume produces a compound known as chloramine.

$$Cl_2 + NH_3 \longrightarrow \underset{\text{Cloramine}}{NH_2Cl} + HCl$$

Chloramine is a quite stable compound and does not impart any disagreeable smell or bad taste to water, hence it is considered as better germicidal then chlorine alone.

$$NH_2Cl + H_2O \longrightarrow HOCl + NH_3$$

$$HOCl \longrightarrow HCl + [O]$$

***(vii)* Chlorination:** Chlorine is the most commonly used sterilizer in municipal water treatment. Chlorine may be added in the from of bleaching powder (already discussed), directly as a gas or in the form of concentrated solution in water (called as chlorine water). It's germicidal action is based on its reaction with water. It reacts with water to from hypochlorous acid and nascent oxygen, both of which are powerful germicides.

$$Cl_2 + H_2O \longrightarrow HOCl + HCl$$
$$HOCl \longrightarrow HCl + [O]$$

Treated water should not contain more than 0.1 – 0.2 ppm of free chlorine.

Advantages of using chlorine as a sterilizing agent:

Chlorine as a sterilizer has several advantages

- It does not decompose on standing and can be stored in a very little space.
- It is more effective and economical.
- No impurity is introduced into water.

Disadvantages of using chlorine as a sterilizing agent:

- If excess of chlorine is used, it imparts characteristic unpleasant taste and odour in water.
- Excess chlorine produces irritation on mucous membranes.

8.7 PROCESS OF CHLORINATION

Water is treated with chlorine in a tower known as chlorinater, provided with a number of baffle trays. Chlorine and water are introduced at the top. During their passage through the tower, they get thoroughly mixed. The treated water is taken out from the bottom.

Break Point Chlorination

It is a controlled chlorination process in which water is treated with such quantity of chlorine which is just enough to destroy bacteria, oxidise organic matter and leave some slight excess of free chlorine that could act as disinfectant during the storage of water.

When chlorine is added to a sample of water and its amount is estimated after a few minutes, it will be found that the amount of available chlorine (also called as free residual chlorine) is less than the added chlorine. The difference is due to the fact that some chlorine is used up in oxidizing organic impurities, reducing substance and killing the pathogens present in water. The point at which free residual chlorine (or simply residual chlorine) begins to appear is called **break point chlorination**.

If a graph is plotted between the amount of chlorine added and the residual chlorine a plot as shown in Fig. 8.10 is obtained:

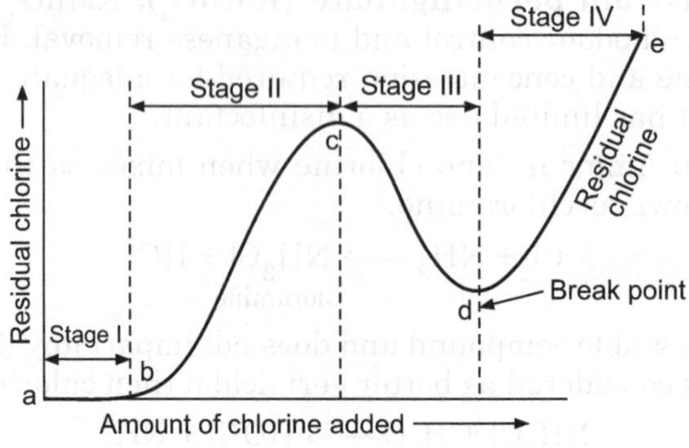

Fig. 8.10. Break point chlorination curve.

This graph has four stages:

Stage I: In the beginning, with the lower dosage of chlorine, there is no free residual chlorine since all the added chlorine gets used up in oxidising the reducing compounds in water. It is represented by line *ab* in the graph.

Stage II: As the amount of added chlorine increases, the amount of residual chlorine also shows steady increase. This stage corresponds to the formation of chloro-organic and chloramine compounds without oxidising them. Chloramine acts as a chlorine reserve and contribute in the chlorine test as free chlorine does. Hence, the graph shows steady increase in residual chlorine. It is shown by part *bc* in the graph.

Stage III: With further addition of chlorine, the *oxidation* of chloramines and chloro-organic compounds takes place. The added chlorine is used up in oxidation process, therefore. the amount of residual chlorine decreases and reaches a minimum as shown in graph (point *d*). This point *d* is called as **break point**. This stage is represented by part *cd* in the graph.

Stage IV: After minima, the added chlorine is not used in any reaction as the water is now free from all the disinfectants. Hence, the residual chlorine keeps on increasing in direct proportion to the added chlorine. This is represented by part *de* in the graph.

Advantages of Break-Point Chlorination

- It prevents the development of any weeds in water.
- It completely destroys all the disease causing bacteria, organic matter and dissolved ammonia present in water.
- It removes all compounds that impart colour, bad odour and unpleasant taste to water.

Superchlorination

When excess amount of chlorine is used for the disinfection of water, it is called as superchlorination. It destroys all the pathogenic micro-organisms as well as organic impurities by oxidation.

8.8 DECHLORINATION

Over-chlorination after the break point produces unpleasant taste and odour of chlorine in water. The excess of chlorine may be removed by filtering the over chlorinated water through a bed of granular carbon or activated carbon. Alternatively, dechlorination can also be achieved by adding sulphur dioxide (SO_2), sodium sulphite (Na_2SO_3) or hypo ($Na_2S_2O_3$) to the superchlorinated water.

$$SO_2 + Cl_2 + 2H_2O \longrightarrow H_2SO_4 + 2HCl$$
$$Na_2SO_3 + Cl_2 + H_2O \longrightarrow Na_2SO_4 + 2HCl$$
$$Na_2S_2O_3 + 4Cl_2 + 5\,H_2O \longrightarrow 2NaHSO_4 + 8HCl$$

Desalination of Brackish water: The process of removal of dissolved slats (mostly NaCl) from water is called as **desalination**. The salinity of water is expressed in terms of ppm or mg/L of dissolved salts. On the basis of salinity, water is classified into three groups:

(*i*) **Fresh water:** less than 1000 ppm of dissolved salts.

(*ii*) **Brackish water:** 1000 – 35000 ppm of dissolved salts.

(*iii*) **Sea water:** more than 35000 ppm of dissolved salts.

Brine is water containing more dissolved solids than sea water. Desalination of water is an expensive process but to meet the growing demand of water, we need to desalinate the brackish water.

The desalination process can be carried out by following methods:

(*i*) Reverse Osmosis (*ii*) Electrodialysis

8.9 REVERSE OSMOSIS

Osmosis is a spontaneous process which involves the flow of the solvent particles from a dilute solution to a more concentrated solution through a semi-permeable membrane.

The minimum excess pressure that has to be applied on the solution to prevent the flow of solvent molecules through semi-permeable membrane is called as **osmotic pressure**. If an external pressure equal to the osmotic pressure is applied on the concentrated solution, the solvent molecules ceases to flow. If external pressure higher than osmotic pressure is applied, then the flow of solvent molecules get reversed *i.e.* from a concentrated solution to dilute solution, the process is called as **reverse osmosis.**

Reverse osmosis process can also be used in purification of sea water. For this purpose, sea water is delivered under pressure through the semi-permeable membrane where water permeate the minute pores of the membrane and is delivered as purified water.

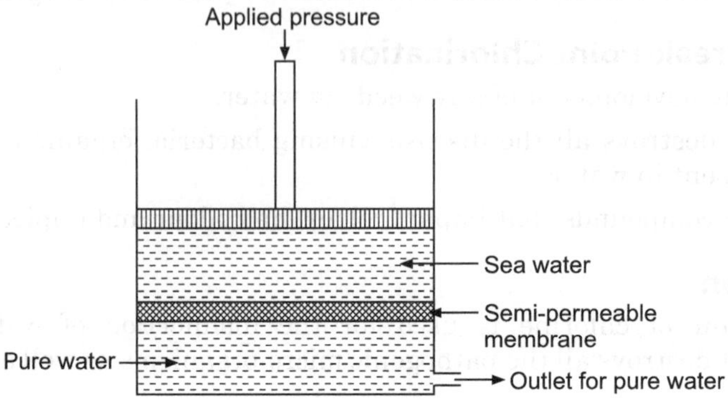

Fig. 8.11. Reverse Osmosis cell.

Reverse osmosis is also called as super filtration or hyper filtration.

Advantages of Reverse Osmosis:

- It is a low energy consumption process as compared to other processes.
- Reverse osmosis system have low maintenance requirement.
- It removes colloidal silica which is not removed by demineralization.
- It is suitable for converting sea water into drinking water.

Disadvantages of Reverse Osmosis:

- The primary disadvantage of reverse osmosis is the amount of water wasted by the process. For each gallon of water produced, about 2 – 20 gallons of water are lost as waste.
- Reverse osmosis units are expensive.
- The RO membranes are subject to decay and require periodic replacement.

8.10 ELECTRODIALYSIS

It is a method in which the ions (of the salts present) are taken out of the salt water by passing direct current, using electrodes and thin rigid ion selective semi-permeable membrane (natural or synthetic).

An etectrodialysis cell consists of a large number of alternate cation and anion-permeable membranes, the anode is being placed near the anion permeable membrane while cathode is placed near the cation permeable membrane. When an e.m.f. is applied across the electrodes, the cations (Na^+) move towards the cathode and the anions (*e.g.*, Cl^-) move towards the anode.

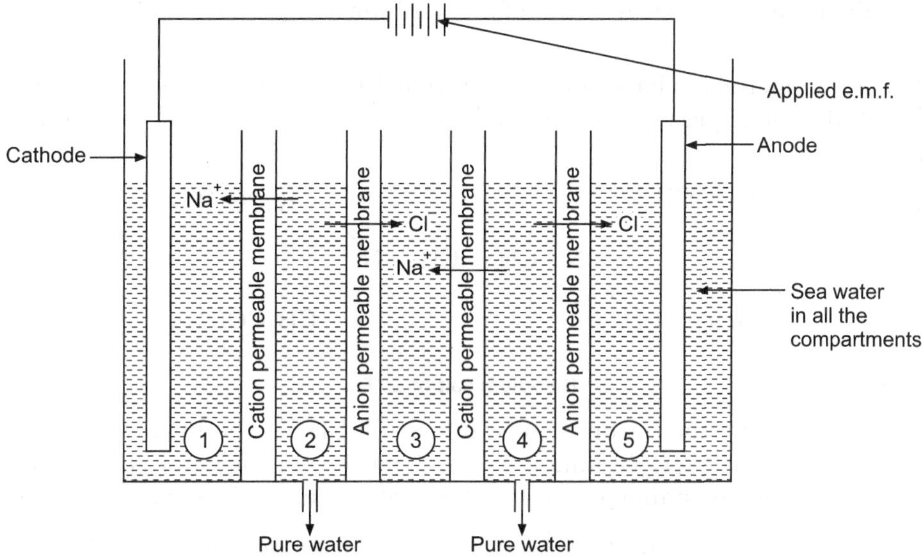

Fig. 8.12. Desalination by electrodialysis.

Cl^- ions can more from compartment (2) to (3) but those in (3) are not allowed to move into (4) towards the anode because of the presence of cation permeable membrane (which allows only the movement of cations). Similarly, Na^+ ions can move from compartment (2) to (1) but those in compartment (3) are not allowed to move into (2) towards the cathode because of the anoion permeable membrane (which allows only the movement of anions). As a result, there is depletion of ions in the even numbered compartments and concentration of ions in the odd numbered compartment. If saline water is fed into the ion losing compartments (even numbered compartments) and brine is collected from the ion concentrating compartments (odd numbered compartments), the saline water can be demineralized electrochemically in a continuous fashion. Sea water requires very high energy, therefore at present this process is restricted to brackish water only.

Advantages:

- It is a compact, cost effective and economical unit.
- This method is used when very high purified water is not required.

8.11 CHEMICAL ANALYSIS OF WATER

8.11.1 Determination of Hardness

The hardness of water is determined by the following methods:

1. EDTA titration method (complexometric-titration)
2. O. Hehner's method
3. Soap titration method

EDTA Titration Method

The hardness of water is most commonly determined by complexometric titration by using ethylene diamine tetraacetic acid (EDTA). This method is commonly known as EDTA method.

This is the most important and more accurate method of determining the hardness of water. EDTA has limited solubility in water, therefore disodium salt of EDTA is used which is soluble in water.

EDTA titration method is based on the fact that EDTA forms stable and soluble complex with Ca^{2+} and Mg^{2+} ions present in hard water. Therefore, it is called as **complexometric titration**.

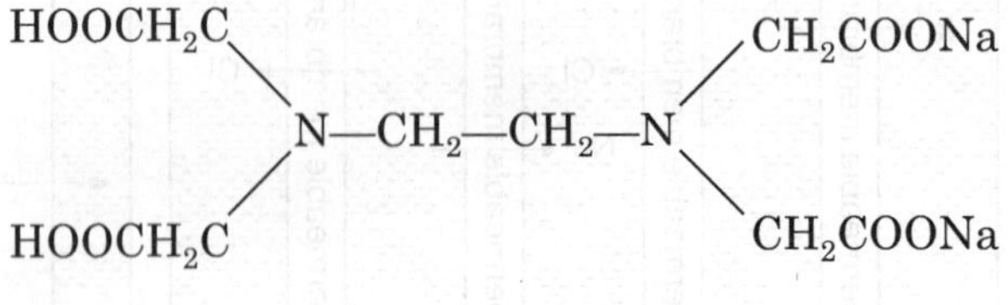

Disodium salt of EDTA

In order to determine the hardness of water using EDTA, the hard water is buffered to a pH of 10 using NH_4OH—NH_4Cl buffer. When few drops of indicator, Eriochrome Black-*T* (EBT) are added, a weak unstable metal – EBT complex is formed which is wine red in colour.

$$\underset{\text{(From hard water)}}{Ca^{2+} \text{ or } Mg^{2+}} + \underset{\text{Blue}}{EBT} \xrightarrow{\sim pH = 10} \underset{\substack{\text{Unstable complex} \\ \text{(wine red)}}}{[Ca^{2+}\text{—}EBT] \text{ or } [Mg^{2+}\text{—}EBT]}$$

During the course of titration of water sample (containing buffer, EBT) against EDTA, EDTA first combines with any Ca^{2+} or Mg^{2+} ions present in the water sample to form a stable metal-EDTA complex which is colourless. After all the free Ca^{2+} or Mg^{2+} ions are consumed by EDTA, the next drop of EDTA starts displacing EBT from the metal-EBT complex and form metal-EDTA complex because the equilibrium constant for the formation of EDTA-metal ion complex is larger than that for the indicator metal ion complex. Thus, at the end point a sudden change in colour *i.e.* from wine red to blue is observed.

$$[Ca^{2+} - EBT] \text{ or } [Mg^{2+} - EBT] + EDTA \xrightarrow{\text{Titration}} \underset{\text{Colourless Complex}}{[Ca^{2+} - EDTA]}$$

$$\text{or} \quad \underset{\text{Colourless complex}}{[Mg^{2+}\text{—}EDTA]} + \underset{\text{Blue}}{EBT}$$

The blue colour at the end point is due to free EBT.

Role of Buffer of pH 8 – 10 in the titration:

1. EDTA has two amine groups which are weekly basic. The reason for adding a basic buffer is to keep these amine groups as free amines. If instead of basic, we use acidic medium, then due to availability of protons from the acid, the lone pair on the amines will get protonated. As a result, EDTA will not be able to form complex with metal ions (Ca^{2+} and Mg^{2+}).
2. EBT is an indicator which gives different colour at different pH values.

   At $\quad pH < 6 \rightarrow$ red colour

   $pH = 7 - 11 \rightarrow$ blue colour

   $pH \geq 12 \rightarrow$ yellow – orange colour

The metal-EBT complex is wine red in colour, therefore to distinguish end point, it is most desirable to use pH 8 – 10 (as blue colour is observed at end point). However, if we use pH < 6 red colour or pH ≥ 12 yellow-orange colour, then the colours are not so easy to distinguish from the original wine red colour.

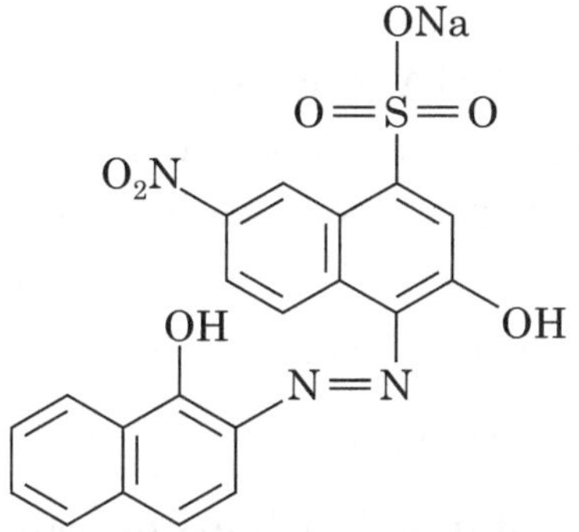

Calmagite indicator can also be used in place of EBT. Unlike EBT, calmagite is stable in aqueous solution. Calmagite gives the same colour change *i.e.* from red to blue but with a sharper end point.

Fig. 8.13. Structure of EBT

The metal-EDTA complex may be represented as:

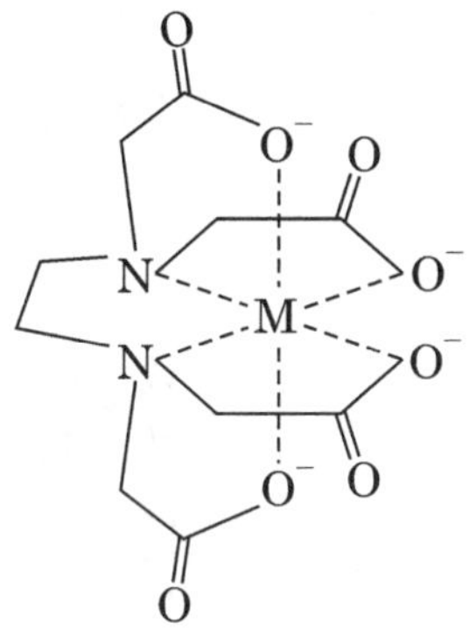

Fig. 8.14. Metal–EDTA complex

Procedure

Step I: Standardization of EDTA solution: Though both the disodium salt and the free EDTA can be used as primary standards, it may be necessary to standardize the EDTA solution to cross check its purity.

Rinse and fill the burette with EDTA solution. Take out 50 mL of standard hard water (1 mg of $CaCO_3$ equivalent hardness in 1 mL of solution) with pipette in a conical flask. Add 10 – 15 mL of ammonia buffer and 2–3 drops of indicator, EBT. Titrate the solution against the EDTA solution till the colour changes from wine red to blue, it is end point. Repeat the procedure to get 2 concordant readings. Let the volume of EDTA used be V_1 mL.

Step II: Determination of total hardness of water: Titrate 50 mL of unknown hard water sample with EDTA by the same procedure as done in step 1. Let the volume of EDTA used here is V_2 mL.

Step III: Determination of permanent hardness of water: Take 250 mL of water sample in a 500 mL beaker and boil gently till the volume is reduced to about 50 mL (all the bicarbonates are decomposed into insoluble $CaCO_3$ and $Mg(OH)_2$). Filter and wash the precipitate with distilled water, collecting filtrate and washing in a 250 mL measuring flask and make the volume up to the mark with distilled water. Titrate 50 mL of boiled water sample against EDTA solution as done in step 1. Let the volume of EDTA used be V_3 mL.

Calculation

Step 1: Standardization of EDTA solution:

Volume of EDTA solution used = V_1 mL

V_1 mL of EDTA Solution = 50 mL of standard hard water

= 50 mg of the $CaCO_3$

(as 1 mL of standard hard water = 1 mg of $CaCO_3$)

Or 1 mL of EDTA solution = $\frac{50}{V_1}$ mg of $CaCO_3$. ...(*i*)

Step 2: Determination of total hardness of water:

Volume of EDTA solution used = V_2 mL

Volume of unknown water sample taken for titration = 50 mL

Now,

50 mL of unknown water sample = V_2 mL of EDTA

$$= V_2 \times \frac{50}{V_1} \text{ mg of } CaCO_3$$

$$\left(\text{as 1 mL EDTA} = \frac{50}{V_1} \text{ mg of } CaCO_3\right)$$

1 mL of unknown water sample $= \frac{V_2}{50} \times \frac{50}{V_1}$ mg of $CaCO_3$

1 L (1000 mL) of unknown water sample $= \frac{V_2}{V_1} \times 1000$ mg/L or ppm

Therefore, total hardness of water $= \frac{V_2}{V_1} \times 1000$ mg/L

Step 3: Determination of permanent hardness of water:

Volume of hard water sample taken after boiling and filtering = 50 mL

Volume of EDTA used = V_3 mL.

50 mL of boiled water = V_3 mL of EDTA

$$= V_3 \times \frac{50}{V_1} \text{ mg of } CaCO_3$$

(as 1 mL of EDTA = $50/V_1$ mg of CaCO)

1 mL of boiled water $= \frac{V_3}{50} \times \frac{50}{V_1}$ mg of $CaCO_3$

1 L (1000 mL) of boiled water $= \frac{V_3}{V_1} \times 1000$ mg/L

$$\text{Permanent hardness} = \frac{V_3}{V_1} \times 1000 \text{ mg/L}$$

$$\text{Temporary hardness} = \text{Total hardness} - \text{Permanent hardness}$$

$$= \frac{V_2}{V_1} \times 1000 - \frac{V_3}{V_1} \times 1000 \text{ mg/L}$$

or

$$\text{Temporary hardness} = \frac{(V_2 - V_3)\,1000}{V_1} \text{ mg/L or ppm.}$$

O. Hehner's Method

This method is based on the fact that temporary hardness can be removed be boiling

$$Ca(HCO_3)_2 \xrightarrow{\text{boil}} CaCO_3 \downarrow + H_2O + CO_2$$

$$Mg(HCO_3)_2 \xrightarrow{\text{boil}} MgCO_3 \downarrow + H_2O + CO_2$$

Thus it can be determined by estimating the alkalinity of the water before and after boiling.

Procedure. Take 50 mL of the sample water in a conical flask and to it 2 – 3 drops of methyl orange. Titrate it against N/50 HCl solution and note the volume of HCl consumed.

Now take 100 mL of the same sample water in a pyrex beaker and evaporate it to dryness. To the residue, add 50 mL of distilled water, warm and then stir to dissolve the soluble portions. Filter off the insoluble material (carbonates), wash the residue with distilled water and then make up the filtrate to 100 mL in a measuring flask by adding more distilled water. Titrate 50 mL of this solution against *N*/50 HCl using methvl orange as indicator and note the volume of acid used.

Calculations: Let volume of N/50 acid by 50 mL of water before boiling = V_1 mL.

and vol. of N/50 acid used by 50 mL of water after boiling = V_2 mL.

∴ Volume of *N*/50 HCl used by temporary hardness present in 50 mL of water = $(V_1 + V_2)$ mL.

According to normality formula

$$1000 \text{ mL } N/50 \text{ HCl} \equiv 1000 \text{ mL of N/50 } CaCO_3$$

(Hardness in terms of $CaCO_3$)

$$\therefore \quad 1000 \text{ mL of N/50 } CaCO_3 \equiv \frac{50 \times 1}{50} = 1 \text{ gm of } CaCO_3$$

[∵ Eq. wt. of $CaCO_3$ = 50]

$$\therefore \quad 1000 \text{ mL of N/50 HCl} \equiv 1 \text{ gm of } CaCO_3$$

$$(V_1 - V_2) \text{ mL of N/50 HCl} = \frac{1 \times (V_1 - V_2)}{1000} \text{ gm of } CaCO_3$$

$$\text{Now 50 mL of water} = \frac{(V_1 - V_2)}{1000} \text{ gm of } CaCO_3$$

$$10^6 \text{ mL of water} = \frac{(V_1 - V_2) \times 10^6}{1000 \times 50} \text{ gm of } CaCO_3$$

$$= 20(V_1 - V_2) \text{ gm of } CaCO_3$$

$$\therefore \text{ Temporary hardness} = 20\,(V_1 - V_2) \text{ ppm.}$$

Determination of *permanent hardness* is based on the fact that it can be removed by boiling with sodium carbonate with which chlorides and sulphates of calcium and magnesium form insoluble carbonates.

$$CaCl_2 + Na_2CO_3 \longrightarrow CaCO_3\downarrow + 2NaCl$$
$$MgSO_4 + Na_2CO_3 \longrightarrow MgCO_3\downarrow + Na_2SO_4$$

In practice, an excess but known amount of standard sodium carbonate is used and the residual sodium carbonate is then determined by titrating against a standard acid solution. The amount of Na_2CO_3 used is equivalent to permanent hardness of water.

Procedure

Boil 50 mL of the water sample with 50 mL of *N*/50 sodium carbonate solution in a beaker. Cool the resulting solution, filter off the precipitate and then wash it with distilled water, collecting all the filtrate and washings in the conical flask. Titrate the contents of the conical flask against *N*/50 HCl using methyl orange as indicator.

Calculations: Let the volume of *N*/50 HCl used during titration = *V* mL.

$\therefore$ Volume of *N*/50 Na_2CO_3 used for removing permanent hardness of the water sample

$$= (50 - V) \text{ mL}$$

According to normality formula

1000 mL of *N*/50 $Na_2CO_3 \equiv$ 1000 mL of *N*/50 $CaCO_3$

But 1000 mL of *N*/50 $CaCO_3$ contains $50 \times \frac{1}{50} = 1$ gm of $CaCO_3$ [$\because$ Eq. wt. of $CaCO_3 = 50$]

$\therefore$ 1000 mL of *N*/50 $Na_2CO_3 \equiv 1$ gm of $CaCO_3$

$(50 - V)$ mL of *N*/50 $NaCO_3 \equiv \dfrac{1 \times (50 - V)}{1000}$ gm of $CaCO_3$

Now 50 mL of hard water $\equiv \dfrac{(50 - V)}{10^3}$ gm of $CaCO_3$

10^6 mL of hard water $\equiv \dfrac{(50 - V) \times 10^6}{10^3 \times 50}$ gm of $CaCO_3 = \dfrac{(50 - V) \times 10^6}{10^3 \times 50}$ ppm

$\therefore$ Permanent hardness $\equiv 20\,(50 - V)$ ppm.

Magnesium hardness of water can be estimated by treating sample water with an excess but known amount of standard caustic soda solution, when magnesium chloride and sulphate are precipitated as magnesium hydroxide.

$$MgCl_2 + 2NaOH \longrightarrow Mg(OH_2)\downarrow + 2NaCl$$
$$MgSO_4 + 2NaOH \longrightarrow Mg(OH_2)\downarrow + Na_2SO_4$$

The amount of unreacted NaOH is then determined by titration against a standard acid. Thus the amount of NaOH consumed which is equivalent to the magnesium hardness can be determined.

It is important to note that caustic soda decomposes bicarbonates (temporary hardness) to form sodium carbonate which in turn will react with calcium salts to form insoluble calcium carbonate.

$$Ca(HCO_3)_2 + 2NaOH \longrightarrow CaCO_3\downarrow + Na_2CO_3 + 2H_2O$$
$$Mg(HCO_3)_2 + 2NaOH \longrightarrow Mg(OH)_2\downarrow 2Na_2CO_3 + 2H_2O$$

To avoid this, it is therefore necessary that prior to boiling with caustic soda, the sample water is neutralized with HCl (using methyl orange as indicator) to convert bicarbonate into chloride.

$$Ca(HCO_3)_2 + 2HCl \longrightarrow CaCl_2 + 2H_2O + 2CO_2$$
$$Mg(HCO_3)_2 + 2HCl \longrightarrow MgCl_2 + 2H_2O + 2CO_2$$

Procedure: Take 50 ml of sample water in a beaker. Neutralise it to methyl orange end point with *N*/10 HCl. Boil off carbon dioxide gas. Add 50 mL of *N*/50 NaOH solution. Boil the contents to precipitate out magnesium hardness. Cool and filter the solution. Titrate the filtrate against *N*/50 HCl solution using methyl orange as indicator.

Calculations: Let the volume of *N*/50 HCl used = V mL.

∴ Vol. of *N*/50 NaOH used for removing magnesium hardness in 50 mL of water

$$= (50 - V) \text{ mL.}$$

∴ Strength of magnesium hardness in terms of $CaCO_3$ equivalent

$$= \frac{(50 - V) \times 50}{50 \times 50} \text{ gm/L}$$

$$\therefore \quad \text{Magnesium hardness} = \frac{(50 - V) \times 50 \times 10^6}{50 \times 50 \times 10^3} \text{ ppm} = 20\,(50 - V) \text{ ppm.}$$

Soap Titration Method

This method is based on the fact that soluble soap (sodium or potassium salt of a higher fatty acid) when added to hard water first forms insoluble compounds with the metal ions producing hardness and thus does not produce any lather. But as soon as all such metal ions are precipitated out, addition of further drop of soap solution will produce lather.

$$\underset{\text{Sodium stearate (soap)}}{2C_{17}H_{35}COONa} + Ca(HCO_3)_2 \longrightarrow \underset{\text{Calcium stearate}}{(C_{17}H_{35}COO)_2Ca} \downarrow + 2NaHCO_3$$

$$2C_{17}H_{35}COONa + MgCl_2 \longrightarrow (C_{17}H_{35}COO)_2Mg \downarrow + 2NaCl$$

$$2C_{17}H_{35}COONa + CaSO_4 \longrightarrow (C_{17}H_{35}COO)_2Ca \downarrow + 2Na_2SO_4$$

Thus the total hardness can be determined by titrating the water sample against a standard soap solution. On the other hand, permanent hardness can be determined by first precipitating the temporary hardness by boiling and then titrating the filtrate against standard soap solution. The end point is the appearance of a stable lather at least for two minutes.

Procedure

1. Preparation of standard hard water: Dissolve 1.0 gm of pure and dry calcium carbonate in the minimum amount of dil. HCl Evaporate the solution to dryness. Dissolve the residue in one litre of distilled water. The hardness of this solution is 1 g/litre or 1000 mg/litre or 1000 ppm or 1 mg/mL.

2. Preparation and standardization of soap solution: Dissolve 10 gm of pure and dry soap in one litre of 80% alcohol. Take this solution in the burette. Take 50 mL of hard water in a stoppered bottle and add to it soap solution from the burette dropwise and with constant shaking till a permanent (at least for a minute) lather is formed. Let the volume of soap used be V_1 mL.

3. Lather factor of distilled water: Titrate 50 mL of distilled water against the above solution of soap till permanent lather is formed. Let the volume of soap used is V mL. This is lather factor and must be subtracted from all the titre values.

4. Total hardness: Titrate 50 mL of hard water against the soap solution as above. Let the volume of soap used is V_2 mL.

5. Permanent hardness: Boil 250 mL of the water sample in a pyrex beaker till the volume is reduced to 50 mL to convert all bicarbonates to carbonates. Filter off the precipitate, wash the ppt. with the distilled water and collect all the filtrate and washings in a 250 m measuring flask. Make up the solution with distilled water. Titrate 50 ml of this solution against soap solution and let V_3 mL of soap solution is used.

Calculations

***(i)* Strength of soap solution.** Since 1 mL of standard hard water contains 1 mg of hardness causing substances in terms of $CaCO_3$.

$$50 \text{ mL of standard hard water} \equiv 50 \text{ mg of } CaCO_3$$

Also $$50 \text{ mL of standard water} = (V_1 - V) \text{ mL of soap solution}$$

$$(V_1 - V) \text{ mL of soap solution} = 50 \text{ mg of } CaCO_3$$

or $$1 \text{ mL of soap solution} = \frac{50}{(V_1 - V)} \text{ mg of } CaCO_3$$

***(ii)* Calculation of total hardness**

$$\text{Since 1 mL of soap solution} = \frac{50}{(V_1 - V)} \text{ mg of } CaCO_3$$

$$(V_2 - V) \text{ mL of soap solution} = \frac{(V_2 - V) \times 50}{(V_1 - V)} \text{ mg } CaCO_3$$

$$\text{Thus 50 mL of the sample water contains} = \frac{(V_2 - V) \times 50}{(V_1 - V)} \text{ mg of } CaCO_3$$

$$\therefore \quad 1000 \text{ mL (1 litre) of water sample} = \frac{(V_2 - V) \times 1000 \times 50}{(V_1 - V) \times 50} \text{ mg of } CaCO_3$$

$$\therefore \quad \text{Total hardness of water sample} = \frac{(V_2 - V) \times 1000}{(V_1 - V)} \text{ mg/litre}$$

$$= \frac{(V_2 - V) \times 1000}{(V_1 - V)} \text{ ppm.}$$

[$\because$ 1000 mg/litre = 1000 ppm]

***(iii)* Calculation of permanent hardness**

$$\text{Again, since 1 mL of soap solution} = \frac{50}{(V_1 - V)} \text{ mg of } CaCO_3$$

$$(V_3 - V) \text{ mL of soap solution} = \frac{(V_3 - V) \times 50}{(V_1 - V)} \text{ mg of } CaCO_3$$

$$\text{Thus 50 mL of the given water contains} = \frac{(V_3 - V) \times 50}{(V_1 - V)} \text{ mg of } CaCO_3$$

$$\therefore \quad 1000 \text{ mL of boiled water} = \frac{(V_3 - V) \times 1000 \times 50}{(V_1 - V) \times 50} \text{ mg of } CaCO_3$$

$$\therefore \quad \text{Permanent hardness} = \frac{(V_3 - V) \times 1000}{(V_1 - V)} \text{ mg/litre}$$

$$= \frac{(V_3 - V) \times 1000}{(V_1 - V)} \text{ ppm}$$

(iv) **Temporary hardness** = Total hardness – Permanent hardness

$$= \frac{(V_2 - V) \times 1000}{(V_1 - V)} - \frac{(V_3 - V) \times 1000}{(V_1 - V)}$$

$$= \frac{1000}{V_1 - V} [(V_2 - V) - (V_3 - V)] \text{ppm}$$

$$= \frac{1000 \times (V_2 - V_3)}{(V_1 - V)} \text{ ppm}$$

$$\text{In short, Total hardness} = x \times \frac{V_2 - V}{V_1 - V} \times 1000 \text{ ppm}$$

$$\text{Permanent hardness} = x \times \frac{(V_3 - V)}{(V_1 - V)} \times 1000 \text{ ppm}$$

Temporary hardness = Total hardness – Permanent hardness

where, x = Amount of $CaCO_3$ in gm per litre or mg per mL in standard hard water.

V = Volume of soap solution required by 50 mL of distilled water.

V_1 = Volume of soap solution used by 50 mL of standard hard water.

V_2 = Volume of soap solution used by 50 mL of the given hard water solution.

V_3 = Volume of soap solution used by 50 mL of the boiled hard water.

8.11.2 Alkalinity of Water

By alkalinity of water we mean the total content of those species in it which causes an increased hydroxide ion concentration (OH^-) upon dissociation or due to hydrolysis.

In engineering terms, alkalinity frequently is expressed in unit of mg/L of $CaCO_3$ based upon the following acid neutralization reaction.

$$CaCO_3 + 2\,H^+ \longrightarrow Ca^{2+} + CO_2 + H_2O$$

1. Caustic alkalinity: This is due to the presence of OH^- and CO_3^{2-} ions.

2. Temporary hardness: When alkalinity is due to the presence of bicarbonate ions (HCO_3^-), it is also called as temporary hardness.

Theory: These alkalinity causing ions (*i.e.* OH^-, CO_3^{2-} and HCO_3^-) can be estimated separately be titration against a standard acid with the help of phenolphthalein and methyl orange as indicators. This is a type for **acid-base titration**.

With respect to constituents causing alkalinity, the following situations may arise:

(*i*) Hydroxides only (OH^-)

(*ii*) Carbonates only (CO_3^{2-})

(*iii*) Bicarbonates only (HCO_3^-)

(*iv*) Hydroxides and bicarbonate (OH^- and CO_3^{2-})

(*v*) Carbonates and bicarbonate (CO_3^{2-} and HCO_3^-)

The possibility of OH^- and HCO_3^- ions together is ruled out. Because they combine instantaneously to form carbonates

i.e.
$$OH^- + HCO_3^- \longrightarrow CO_3^{2-} + H_2O$$

On the basis of same reasoning all the three ions (*i.e.* OH^-, CO_3^{2-} and HCO_3^-) cannot exist together.

The determination is based on the following reactions:

$$\left.\begin{array}{l}\left.\begin{array}{l}(i)\ OH^- + H^+ \longrightarrow H_2O \\ (ii)\ CO_3^{2-} + H^+ \longrightarrow HCO_3^-\end{array}\right\} P \\ (iii)\ HCO_3^- + H^+ \longrightarrow H_2O + CO_2\end{array}\right\} M \qquad \begin{array}{l}P = \text{Phenolphthalein} \\ M = \text{Methyl orange}\end{array}$$

The titration of the alkaline water sample against a standard acid upto phenolphthalein end point corresponds to the completion of reactions (*i*) and (*ii*) only. This amount of acid used thus corresponds to hydroxides plus one half of the normal carbonate present.

On the other hand, titration of alkaline water sample against standard acid to methyl orange end point corresponds to the completion of all the three reactions (*i*), (*ii*) and (*iii*).

Hence, the amount of acid used after phenolphthalein end point corresponds to one half of normal carbonates plus bicarbonatcs and the total amount of acid used from beginning of the experiment till the methyl orange end point represents the total alkalinity (or methyl orange alkalinity).

Question: Why do we need two indicators in alkalinity?

Answer: Alkalinity in water is mainly due to carbonate and bicarbonate salts in water. The carbonate ion has two end points, one from carbonate to bicarbonate and another form bicarbonate to CO_2, *i.e.*

$$CO_3^{2-} + H^+ \longrightarrow HCO_3^- \qquad \text{I end-point}$$

$$HCO_3^- + H^+ \longrightarrow CO_2 + H_2O \qquad \text{II end-point}$$

The first end point can be detected by phenolphthalein but for second end point we need methyl orange.

- Hydroxides can be easily detected by both the indicators
- If only methyl orange is used, then we can only determine the total alkalinity of the water sample and we will not be able to know the extent and amount of alkalinity causing ions.
- If only phenolphthalein is used, then we will not be able to determine the bicarbonates and half of the carbonates.

Thus, to determine alkalinity, both the indicators are necessary.

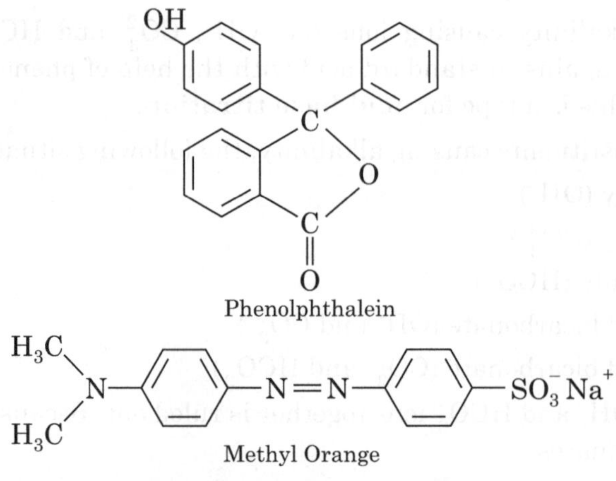

Fig. 8.15. Structure of indicators.

Procedure: A known volume of water sample is titrated against standard H_2SO_4 by using phenolphthalein indicator. The end point is disappearance of pink colour. Let the volume of H_2SO_4 used till phenolphthalein end point is V_1 mL. Then, to the same solution, add 2–3 drops of methyl orange indicator (the solution becomes yellow). Continue the titration until the pink colour reappears. Let the extra volume of acid used from phenolphthalein end point to methyl orange end point is V_2 mL.

Calculations:

(*i*) Phenolphthalein alkalinity (*P*):

$$N_P V_w = N_1 V_1$$

$$N_p = \frac{N_1 V_1}{V_w}$$

where, N_p = Normality of phenolphthalein alkalinity

V_w = Volume of water taken for titration

N_1 = Normality of acid (H_2SO_4)

V_1 = Volume of acid used till phenolphthalein end point.

Now, strength of alkalinity upto phenolphthalein end point in terms of $CaCO_3$ equivalents.

$$\text{Strength } (P) = \text{Normality } (N_p) \times \text{Eq. wt. of } CaCO_3$$

$$= \frac{N_1 V_1}{V_W} \times 50 \text{ g/L} = \frac{N_1 V_1}{V_W} \times 50 \times 1000 \text{ mg/L}$$

$$\therefore \quad P = \frac{N_1 V_1}{V_W} \times 50000 \text{ ppm or mg/L.}$$

(*ii*) Methyl orange alkalinity (*M*):

$$N_m V_w = N_1 (V_1 + V_2)$$

$$N_m = \frac{(V_1 + V_2)}{V_w} N_1$$

where

N_m = Normality of methyl orange alkalinity

V_2 = Volume of acid used from phenolphthalein end point to methyl orange end point.

Strength of alkalinity upto methyl orange end point in term of $CaCO_3$ equivalents.

Strength (*M*) = Normality (N_m) × Eq. wt. of $CaCO_3$

$$= \frac{(V_1 + V_2) N_1}{V_w} \times 50 \text{ g/L}$$

$$= \frac{(V_1 + V_2) N_1}{V_w} \times 50 \times 1000 \text{ mg/L or ppm}$$

$$\therefore \quad M = \frac{(V_1 + V_2)}{V_w} N_1 \times 50{,}000 \text{ mg/L or ppm.}$$

Depending on the values of *P* and *M* we can determine the type and extent of alkalinity.

Table 8.5: Type and Extent of Alkalinity

Value of P and M	Alkalinity as $CaCO_3$ due to		
	OH^-	CO_3^{2-}	HCO_3^-
$P = 0$	O	O	M
$P = \frac{1}{2}M$ (or $V_1 = V_2$)	O	$2P$	O
$P > \frac{1}{2}M$	$2P - M$	$2(M - P)$	O
$P < \frac{1}{2}M$	$2M$	O	$(M - 2P)$
$P = M$	M	O	O

8.11.3 Estimation of Free Chlorine

It is a well known fact that water supplied by municipality for drinking purpose is sterilized with a calculated amount of chlorine gas. However, free chlorine should not be present in water beyond a certain limit (0.1 – 0.2 ppm), because it is injurious to human metabolism. Thus, it becomes necessary to know the amount of chlorine in water and adjust it to a certain amount.

The estimation of free chlorine is based on the fact that it oxidises potassium iodide to an equivalent amount of free iodine which can be titrated against hypo solution using starch as an indicator.

$$2KI + Cl_2 \longrightarrow 2KCl + I_2$$

$$\underset{\text{hypo}}{Na_2S_2O_3} + I_2 \longrightarrow 2NaI + \underset{\text{sod. tetrathionate}}{Na_2S_4O_6}$$

$$\text{Starch} + I_2 \longrightarrow \text{Deep blue colour}$$

The end point is the disappearance of blue colour.

Procedure: Take 50 mL of water in a stoppered bottle and slowly add to it 10% solution of potassium iodide. Shake the contents well, remove the stopper and wash it well collecting all the washings in the bottle. Titrate the solution against *N*/50 hypo solution using starch as an indicator till the blue colour disappears.

Calculations: N_1V_1 (water sample) = N_2V_2 (Hypo solution)

$$N_1 \times 50 = \frac{N}{50} \times V_2$$

$$N_1 \text{ (Normality of water sample or free chlorine)} = \frac{N}{50} \times \frac{1}{50} V_2$$

and Strength of free chlorine = Normality of free chlorine × eq. wt. of chlorine

$$\text{Strength of free chlorine} = \frac{1}{50} \times \frac{V_2}{50} \times 35.5 \text{ g/L}$$

$$= \frac{V_2}{2500} \times 35.5 \times 1000 \text{ mg/L}.$$

8.11.4 Dissolved Oxygen

Dissolved oxygen refers to the level of free, non-compound oxygen present in water. Dissolved oxygen enters water through the air or as a waste product of photosynthesis from algae, sea weed or other aquatic plants. It is an important parameter in assessing water quality because of its influence on the living organisms present in various water bodies.

It is usually determined by **Winkler's method** (an iodometric technique). This method is based on the fact that dissolved oxygen present in water oxidises potassium iodide. On oxidation, iodine is liberated which is titrated against a standard hypo solution (sodium thiosulphate $Na_2S_2O_3$) using starch as an indicator.

Dissolved oxygen present in water is in the molecular state (O_2) and therefore, not capable of oxidising KI. Hence, an oxygen carrier such as manganese hydroxide ($Mn(OH)_2$) is used. This oxygen carrier reacts with dissolved oxygen to form brown precipitates of basic manganic oxide $MnO(OH)_2$.

$$MnSO_4 + 2KOH \longrightarrow Mn(OH)_2 + K_2SO_4$$

$$2Mn(OH)_2 + O_2 \longrightarrow \underset{\text{Brown precipitate}}{2MnO(OH)_2}$$

Manganic oxide ($MnO(OH)_2$) reacts with conc. sulphuric acid to liberate nascent oxygen which helps in oxidation of KI to I_2.

$$MnO(OH_2) + H_2SO_4 \longrightarrow MnSO_4 + 2H_2O + [O]$$

$$2KI + H_2SO_4 + [O] \longrightarrow K_2SO_4 + H_2O + I_2$$

The liberated iodine is finally titrated against standard hypo solution using starch as an indicator.

$$2Na_2S_2O_3 + I_2 \longrightarrow \underset{\substack{\text{Sodium}\\ \text{tetrathionate}}}{Na_2S_4O_6} + 2NaI$$

On addition of starch, the solution becomes blue. At the end point of the titration, one drop is often enough to turn the solution from blue to colourless. At this stage the acid has been neutralized and the amount of hypo used is exactly proportional to the amount of oxygen in the original sample.

Sources of error in Winkler's method:

- The oxidising agents present in water such as nitrites oxidises I^- to I_2 and therefore give positive error. To overcome this problem, sodium azide (NaN_3) is used to decompose the nitrite.

$$2NO_2^- + 2I^- + 4H^+ \longrightarrow 2NO + I_2 + 2H_2O$$

$$2NaN_3 + H_2SO_4 \longrightarrow 2HN_3 + Na_2SO_4$$

$$HNO_2 + HN_3 \longrightarrow N_2O\uparrow + N_2\uparrow + H_2O$$

- The reducing agents present in water such as sulphite, sulphide reduces I_2 to I^- and produces negative error. To overcome this problem, $KMnO_4$ is used for pretreatment.

Reagents used and procedure:

- Manganous sulphate solution– 400 g $MnSO_4$ in 1 L of distilled water.
- Alkaline azide solution– 150 g KI + 500 g NaOH + 20 g NaN_3 in 1 L of distilled water.
- Hypo solution– *N*/100
- Starch indicator– 1%.

Take 250 mL of water sample in a stoppered bottle avoiding contact with air as far as possible. Add 2 mL of $MnSO_4$ solution and 2 mL of alkaline azide solution immediately. Stopper the bottle and shake the contents thoroughly. When the precipitate settle down, add

2 mL of conc. sulphuric acid. Shake the bottle again to dissolve the precipitate. Allow the yellow solution to stand for 5 minutes. Take 100 mL of this solution and titrate it against $N/100$ hypo solution using starch as an indicator. The disappearance of blue colour marks the end point. Let the volume of hypo solution used till end point is V_2 mL.

Calculation: As we said the amount of hypo used is exactly equal to the amount of oxygen in the water sample. Therefore,

$$\underset{O_2 \text{ in water sample}}{N_1V_1} = \underset{\text{Hypo}}{N_2V_2}$$

$$N_1 \times 100 = \frac{1}{100} \times V_2$$

$$\therefore \quad N_1 = \frac{1}{100 \times 100} \times V_2$$

Strength of O_2 in water = Normality of O_2 in water × Equivalent weight of O_2

$$\text{Strength of } O_2 = \frac{V_2}{10000} \times 8 \text{ g/L}$$

$$= \frac{V_2}{10000} \times 8 \times 1000 \text{ mg/L}$$

$$= 0.8\ V_2 \text{ mg/L} = 0.8\ V_2 \text{ ppm.}$$

8.11.5 Biological Oxygen Demand (BOD)

The BOD is an important measure of water quality. It measures the extent of pollution of waste water, sewage and industrial effluents.

BOD is a measure of the amount of oxygen needed (in ppm or mg/L) by bacteria and other micro-organisms to oxidize the organic matter present in water under aerobic conditions.

The demand for oxygen is proportional to the amount of organic waste to be decomposed aerobically. High BOD means low oxygen is available. When low oxygen is available, aquatic organisms become stressed, suffocate and die.

Polluted waters will continue to absorb oxygen for many months, till the oxidation gets completed and therefore, it is not practical to determine the ultimate oxygen demand that would require on extremely long period of time. Therefore, we simply measure the oxygen over a shorter time period of 5 days. This type of test is known as **5 day BOD test**. It indicates the amount of oxygen consumed by bacteria or other micro-organisms during the first five days of biodegradation.

Determination of BOD

A known volume of sample water is diluted with a known volume of distilled water. The diluted sample is taken in two stoppered bottles. The dissolved oxygen content of one of the bottles is immediately determined (DO_b). The second bottle is incubated at 20°C for 5 days, after which unused oxygen is determined (DO_i). The difference between the original oxygen content in the blank (DO_b) and unused oxygen content of sample water after 5 days (DO_i) gives the BOD.

Thus, BOD = ($DO_b - DO_i$) × dilution factor

$$\text{Dilution factor} = \frac{\text{Volume of sample after dilution}}{\text{Volume of sample before dilution}}$$

Significance of BOD

Biochemical oxygen demand find its importance in various fields. These are:

- It determines the rate of respiration in living beings.
- It is of primary importance in sewage treatment plants. It gives the respiration rate of sewage, sludge, soil, garbage etc.
- It measures the extent of pollution of waste water, sewage, industrial effluents etc.
- It finds application in medical and pharmaceutical industries to measure the oxygen consumption of cell cultures.

8.11.6 Chemical Oxygen Demand (COD)

BOD value takes into account only biodegradable organic impurities and does not account for non-biodegradable organic impurities. Therefore, COD (Chemical oxygen demand) is introduced to measure the total organic matter (biodegradable and non-biodegradable) present in water. It is defined as the amount of oxygen used while oxidising the total organic content of a water sample with a strong chemical oxidant (*e.g.* $K_2Cr_2O_7$ in acidic medium).

As it is measure of total organic content therefore, COD is always higher than BOD. COD is a rapidly measurable parameter and requires about three hours for completion.

Determination of COD: A known volume of waste water sample (V_1) is refluxed with a known excess of standard $K_2Cr_2O_7$ solution in acidic (*e.g.* H_2SO_4) medium in the presence of silver sulphate (Ag_2SO_4) and mercuric sulphate ($HgSO_4$) as catalysts. $K_2Cr_2O_7$ oxidizes all oxidisable impurities. $AgSO_4$ helps in oxidation of straight chain organic compounds, aromatics etc. while $HgSO_4$ suppress the interference of Cl^- ions by forming complex with them. The excess dichromate ($K_2Cr_2O_7$) remaining unreacted in the solution is titrated with a standard ferrous ammonium sulphate solution $[FeSO_4 \cdot (NH_4)_2SO_4 \cdot 6H_2O]$ or Mohr's salt using **ferroin** as an indicator. The amount of $K_2Cr_2O_7$ consumed is used to calculate the equivalent oxygen required by the waste water for the degradation of pollutants. Let V_3 be the volume of FAS consumed.

A blank experiment is performed by titrating known volume of acidified $K_2Cr_2O_7$ with the same FAS using same indicator. Let the volume of FAS used in blank titration is V_4.

Thus, Net volume of FAS consumed

$$= (V_4 - V_3) \text{ mL}$$

Applying normality equation:

$$\underset{\text{Waste water sample}}{N_1V_1} = \underset{\text{FAS}}{N_2V_2}$$

$$N_1V_1 = N_2(V_4 - V_3)$$

$$N_1 = \frac{N_2(V_4 - V_3)}{V_1}$$

$$\text{COD} = \text{Normality of waste water sample} \times \text{Eq. wt. of oxygen}$$

$$= \frac{N_2(V_4 - V_3)}{V_1} \times 8 \text{ g/L}$$

$$= \frac{N_2(V_4 - V_3)}{V_1} \times 8 \times 1000 \text{ mg/L or ppm.}$$

N_2 = Normality of FAS

V_1 = Volume of waste water sample taken

V_3 and V_4 are the volumes of FAS in the blank and test experiments respectively.

SOLVED EXAMPLES

Example 8.1. *A water sample contains 170 mg of $CaSO_4$ per litre. Calculate the hardness in terms of $CaCO_3$ equivalents.*

Solution: Hardness = Strength of $CaSO_4$ (mg/L) × Multiplication factor

$$= \text{Strength of } CaSO_4 \text{ (mg/L)} \times \frac{\text{eq. wt. of } CaCO_3}{\text{eq. wt. of } CaSO_4}$$

$$= 170 \times \frac{50}{68} \text{ mg/L} = 125 \text{ mg/L} = 125 \text{ ppm.}$$

Example 8.2. *How many grams of $MgCO_3$ dissolved per litre gives 90 ppm of hardness?*

Solution: Hardness = Strength of $MgCO_3$ (in mg/L) × Multiplication factor

$$= \text{Strength of } MgCO_3 \text{ (in mg/L)} \times \frac{\text{eq . wt. of } CaCO_3}{\text{eq . wt. of } MgCO_3}$$

$$= \frac{\text{Mass of } MgCO_3 \text{(in mg)}}{1 \text{ litre}} \times \frac{\text{eq . wt. of } CaCO_3}{\text{eq . wt. of } MgCO_3}$$

$$\text{Mass of } MgCO_3 = \text{Hardness} \times \frac{\text{eq . wt. of } MgCO_3}{\text{eq . wt. of } CaCO_3}$$

$$= 90 \text{ ppm} \times \frac{42}{50} = 75.6 \text{ mg}$$

or $= 75.6 \times 10^{-3}$ g

Thus, 75.6×10^{-3} gm of $MgCO_3$ dissolved per litre gives 90 ppm of hardness.

Example 8.3. *Calculate the temporary and permanent hardness of a sample of water containing:*

$$Mg(HCO_3)_2 = 7.3 \text{ mg/L};\ Ca(HCO_3)_2 = 16.2 \text{ mg/L}$$
$$MgCl_2 = 9.5 \text{ mg/L};\ CaSO_4 = 13.6 \text{ mg/L}$$

Solution: Conversion into $CaCO_3$ equivalents

Constituent	Multiplication factor	Amount (mg/L)	$CaCO_3$ equivalent (mg/L)
$Mg(HCO_3)_2$	$\frac{100}{146}$	7.3	$7.3 \times \frac{100}{146} = 5$
$Ca(HCO_3)_2$	$\frac{100}{162}$	16.2	$16.2 \times \frac{100}{162} = 10$
$MgCl_2$	$\frac{100}{95}$	9.5	$9.5 \times \frac{100}{95} = 10$
$CaSO_4$	$\frac{100}{136}$	13.6	$13.6 \times \frac{100}{136} = 10$

$$\text{Temporary hardness} = Mg(HCO_3)_2 + Ca(HCO_3)_2$$
$$= 5 + 10 \text{ mg/L} = 15 \text{ mg/L} = 15 \text{ ppm}$$

Permanent hardness = $MgCl_2 + CaSO_4$

$= 10 + 10$ mg/L $= 20$ mg/L $= 20$ ppm.

Example 8.4. *A sample of water was found to contain the following impurities.*

$Ca(HCO_3)_2 = 81.0$ mg/L $\quad CaSO_4 = 68$ mg/L

$Mg(HCO_3)_2 = 73.0$ mg/L $\quad CaCl_2 = 55.5$ mg/L

$MgSO_4 = 60$ mg/L $\quad NaCl = 20$ mg/L

Calculate the temporary and permanent hardness of the water sample.

Solution: Conversion into $CaCO_3$ equivalents

Constituent	Multiplication factor	Amount (mg/L)	$CaCO_3$ equivalent (mg/L)
$Ca(HCO_3)_2$	$\frac{100}{162}$	81	$81 \times \frac{100}{162} = 50$
$Mg(HCO_3)_2$	$\frac{100}{146}$	73	$73 \times \frac{100}{146} = 50$
$MgSO_4$	$\frac{100}{120}$	60	$60 \times \frac{100}{120} = 50$
$CaSO_4$	$\frac{100}{136}$	68	$68 \times \frac{100}{136} = 50$
$CaCl_2$	$\frac{100}{111}$	55.5	$55.5 \times \frac{100}{111} = 50$

NaCl does not cause any type of hardness

Temporary hardness = $Ca(HCO_3)_2 + Mg(HCO_3)_2$

$= 50 + 50$ mg/L

$= 100$ mg/L $= 100$ ppm

Permanent hardness = $MgSO_4 + CaSO_4 + CaCl_2$

$= 50 + 50 + 50$ mg/L

$= 150$ mg/L $= 150$ ppm

Lime required for softening (in mg/L)

$$= \frac{74}{100}\begin{bmatrix} Ca(HCO_3)_2 + 2Mg(HCO_3)_2 + MgCl_2 + MgSO_4 + FeSO_4 \\ + Al_2(SO_4)_3 + CO_2 + HCl + H_2SO_4 + NaHCO_3 - NaAlO_2 \end{bmatrix}$$

All in terms of $CaCO_3$ equivalents. This equation is for 100% pure lime. If lime is 90% pure, then we have to multiply above equation by 100/90.

Soda required of softening (in mg/L)

$$= \frac{106}{100}\begin{bmatrix} CaCl_2 + CaSO_4 + MgCl_2 + MgSO_4 + Al_2(SO_4)_3 \\ + FeSO_4 + HCl + H_2SO_4 - NaHCO_3 \end{bmatrix}$$

All in terms of $CaCO_3$ equivalents.

Example 8.5. *A sample of polluted water on analysis gave the following results:*

Suspended matter = 200 mg/L $CaSO_4$ *= 250 mg/L*

$MgSO_4$ *= 240 mg/L* $MgCl_2$ *= 190 mg/L*

Organic matter = 750 mg/L H_2SO_4 *= 98 mg/L*

(i) Calculate the total hardness of water sample.

(ii) Calculate the amount of lime and soda needed per litre for its treatment (purity of lime is 90% and that of soda is 98%).

Solution: Calculation of $CaCO_3$ equivalents:

Constituent	Multiplication factor	Amount (mg/L)	$CaCO_3$ equivalent (mg/L)
$MgCl_2$	$\frac{100}{95}$	190	$190 \times \frac{100}{95} = 200$
$CaSO_4$	$\frac{100}{136}$	250	$250 \times \frac{100}{136} = 183.82$
$MgSO_4$	$\frac{100}{120}$	240	$240 \times \frac{100}{120} = 200$
H_2SO_4	$\frac{100}{98}$	98	$98 \times \frac{100}{98} = 100$

Lime required – Lime is 90% pure

$$= \frac{74}{100} [MgCl_2 + MgSO_4 + H_2SO_4] \times \frac{100}{90} \text{ ppm}$$

$$= \frac{74}{100} [200 + 200 + 100] \times \frac{100}{90} \text{ ppm}$$

$$= \frac{74}{100} (500) \times \frac{100}{90} = \frac{74 \times 50}{9} = 411.11 \text{ ppm}$$

Soda required – soda is 98% pure.

$$= \frac{106}{100} [MgCl_2 + CaSO_4 + MgSO_4 + H_2SO_4] \times \frac{100}{98} \text{ ppm}$$

$$= \frac{106}{100} [200+183.82 + 200+100] \times \frac{100}{98} \text{ ppm}$$

$$= \frac{106}{100} (683.82) \times \frac{100}{98} \text{ ppm}$$

$$= \frac{106 \times 683.82}{98} = 739.64 \text{ ppm}$$

Total hardness in terms of $CaCO_3$ equivalents

$= (MgCl_2 + CaSO_4 + MgSO_4)$

$= (200 + 183.82 + 200)$

$= 583.82$ ppm.

Example 8.6. *Calculate the carbonate and non-carbonate hardness of sample of water containing dissolved solids (mg/L) given as follows:*

$$Mg(HCO_3)_2 = 7.3 \qquad Ca(HCO_3)_2 = 40.5$$
$$CaSO_4 = 13.6 \qquad MgCl_2 = 21.75$$
$$NaCl = 60.$$

Solution: Conversion into $CaCO_3$ equivalents

Constituent	Multiplication factor	Amount (mg/L)	$CaCO_3$ equivalent (mg/L)
$Mg(HCO_3)_2$	$\frac{100}{146}$	7.3	$7.3 \times \frac{100}{146} = 5$
$Ca(HCO_3)_2$	$\frac{100}{162}$	40.5	$40.5 \times \frac{100}{162} = 25$
$CaSO_4$	$\frac{100}{136}$	13.6	$13.6 \times \frac{100}{136} = 10$
$MgCl_2$	$\frac{100}{95}$	21.75	$21.75 \times \frac{100}{95} = 22.9$

NaCl does not contribute any hardness to water. Carbonate hardness (due to the presence of bicarbonate of Ca and Mg)

$$= [Ca(HCO_3)_2 + Mg(HCO_3)_2] = 5 + 25 \text{ mg/L}$$
$$= 30 \text{ mg/L}$$

Non-carbonate hardness (due to the presence of chloride and sulphates of Ca, Mg and other heavy metal ions)

$$= (CaSO_4 + MgCl_2) = 10 + 22.9 \text{ mg/L} = 32.9 \text{ mg/L}.$$

Example 8.7. *100 mL of water sample has a hardness equivalent to 12.5 mL of 0.08N $MgSO_4$. What is its hardness in ppm?*

Solution: Applying the Normality equation

$$\underbrace{N_1 V_1}_{\text{Water}} = \underbrace{N_2 V_2}_{MgSO_4}$$

$$N_1 \times 100 = 0.08 \times 12.5$$

$$N_1 = \frac{0.08 \times 12.5}{100}$$

$$= \frac{1}{100}$$

$$\text{Strength (g/L)} = N \times \text{eq. wt. of } CaCO_3$$

$$= \frac{1}{100} \times 50 \text{ g/L}$$

$$= \frac{1}{100} \times 50 \times 1000 \text{ mg/L}$$

$$= 500 \text{ mg/L or } 500 \text{ ppm.}$$

Example 8.8. *A sample of water was found to contain the following impurities:*

$$Ca(HCO_3)_2 = 84\ mg/L \qquad Mg(HCO_3)_2 = 93\ mg/L$$
$$MgSO_4 = 80\ mg/L \qquad CaSO_4 = 88\ mg/L$$
$$CaCl_2 = 55.5\ mg/L \qquad NaCl = 20\ mg/L.$$

Calculate the temporary and permanent hardness along with the amount of lime and soda require for treatment of 40000 litre of water.

Solution: Conversion into $CaCO_3$ equivalents

Constituent	Multiplication factor	Amount (mg/L)	$CaCO_3$ equivalent (mg/L)
$Ca(HCO_3)_2$	$\frac{100}{162}$	84	$84 \times \frac{100}{162} = 51.85$
$Mg(HCO_3)_2$	$\frac{100}{146}$	93	$93 \times \frac{100}{146} = 63.69$
$MgSO_4$	$\frac{100}{120}$	80	$80 \times \frac{100}{120} = 66.66$
$CaSO_4$	$\frac{100}{136}$	88	$88 \times \frac{100}{136} = 64.71$
$CaCl_2$	$\frac{100}{111}$	55.5	$55.5 \times \frac{100}{111} = 50$

NaCl does not impart hardness and therefore, does not consume any lime or soda.

$$\text{Temporary hardness} = [Ca(HCO_3)_2 + Mg(HCO_3)_2]$$
$$= 51.85 + 63.69 \text{ mg/L}$$
$$= 115.54 \text{ mg/L} = 115.54 \text{ ppm}$$

$$\text{Permanent hardness} = (MgSO_4 + CaSO_4 + CaCl_2)$$
$$= (66.66 + 64.71 + 50) \text{ mg/L}$$
$$= 181.37 \text{ mg/L} = 181.37 \text{ ppm}$$

Lime requirement:

$$= \frac{74}{100}\{Ca(HCO_3)_2 + 2[Mg(HCO_3)_2] + MgSO_4\}$$

$$= \frac{74}{100}(51.85 + (2 \times 63.69) + 66.66)\text{mg/L}$$

$$= \frac{74}{100}(245.89) = 181.95 \text{ mg/L} = 181.95 \text{ ppm}$$

Soda requirement:

$$= \frac{106}{100}[CaSO_4 + CaCl_2 + MgSO_4]$$

$$= \frac{106}{100}(64.71 + 50 + 66.66) \text{ mg/L}$$

$$= 192.25 \text{ mg/L} = 192.25 \text{ ppm}$$

For 40,000 litre of water

Soda required:

For 1 litre of water, soda required = 192.25 mg

For 40,000 litre = 192.25 × 40,000 mg

= 7690000 mg

= 7690 g

Lime required:

For 1 litre of water, lime required = 181.95 mg

For 40,000 litre = 181.95 × 40,000 mg

= 7278,000 mg

= 7278 g.

Example 8.9. *Analysis of water gave the following results:*

$Ca(HCO_3)_2 = 40.5$ *ppm* $\quad Mg(HCO_3)_2 = 36.5$ *ppm*

$MgSO_4 = 30.0$ *ppm* $\quad CaCl_2 = 27.75$ *ppm*

$MgCl_2 = 91$ *ppm* $\quad NaCl = 10$ *ppm*

$KCl = 35$ *ppm* $\quad CaSO_4 = 30.4$ *ppm.*

Water is to be supplied to the town of population of one lac only. The daily consumption of H_2O *is 50 litres per head. Calculate the cost of lime and soda required for softening of hard water for the town for the month of January 2012. If cost of lime (84% pure) is ₹ 20.0 per kg and soda (92% pure) is ₹ 35.0 per kg.*

Solution: Conversion into $CaCO_3$ equivalents.

Constituent	Multiplication factor	Amount (mg/L)	$CaCO_3$ equivalent (mg/L)
$Ca(HCO_3)_2$	$\frac{100}{162}$	40.5	$40.5 \times \frac{100}{162} = 25$
$Mg(HCO_3)_2$	$\frac{100}{146}$	36.5	$36.5 \times \frac{100}{146} = 25$
$MgSO_4$	$\frac{100}{120}$	30	$30 \times \frac{100}{120} = 25$
$CaSO_4$	$\frac{100}{136}$	30.4	$30.4 \times \frac{100}{136} = 22.35$
$CaCl_2$	$\frac{100}{111}$	27.75	$27.75 \times \frac{100}{111} = 25$
$MgCl_2$	$\frac{100}{95}$	91	$91 \times \frac{100}{95} = 95.79$

NaCl and KCl does not contribute to hardness.

Daily consumption of water per head = 50 litres

Population of town = 1 lac = 10^5

Daily consumption of water for the whole town = $10^5 \times 50$ litres

For January, 2012 (*i.e.* 31 days), the consumption of water for whole town

$$= 31 \times 10^5 \times 50 = 155 \times 10^6 \text{ litres}$$

Lime required (84% Pure):

$$= \frac{74}{100}\left[Ca(HCO_3)_2 + 2(Mg(HCO_3)_2 + MgCl_2 + MgSO_4)\right] \times \frac{100}{84}$$

$$= \frac{74}{100}[25 + (2 \times 25) + 95.79 + 25] \times \frac{100}{84} = 172.48 \text{ mg/L}$$

∴ For 1 litre of water; lime required = 172.48 mg

For 155×10^6 litres of water lime required will be

$$= 172.48 \times 155 \times 10^6 \text{ mg}$$

$$= 26734.4 \times 10^6 \text{ mg}$$

$$= 26.73 \times 10^3 \text{ kg}$$

The cost of 1 kg lime = ₹20

Cost of 26.73×10^3 kg lime will be = $20 \times 26.73 \times 10^3$ ₹

= ₹ 534680

Soda required (92% pure)

$$= \frac{106}{100}[CaCl_2 + CaSO_4 + MgCl_2 + MgSO_4] \times \frac{100}{92}$$

$$= \frac{106}{100}(25 + 22.35 + 95.79 + 25) \times \frac{100}{92}$$

$$= \frac{106}{100}(168.14) \times \frac{100}{92} = 193.72 \text{ mg/L}$$

For 1 litre of water, soda required = 193.72 mg

For 155×10^6 litre of water, soda required will be –

$$= 193.72 \times 155 \times 10^6 \text{ mg}$$

$$= 30{,}026.6 \times 10^6 \text{ mg}$$

$$= 30{,}026.6 \text{ kg}$$

The cost of soda for 1 kg = ₹ 35.0

Then, for 30,026.6 kg of soda, the cost will

= 35 × ₹ 30,026.6

= ₹ 1050931

Example 8.10. *Calculate the quantity of lime and soda required for softening 5,00,000 litres of water using 42.8 ppm of sodium aluminate as a coagulant. The analysis of raw water is as follows:* ***(RGPV, Nov. – Dec., 2013)***

$Ca^{2+} = 140$ *ppm*	$HCO_3^- = 132$ *ppm*
$CO_2 = 24$ *ppm*	$NaCl = 20$ *ppm*
$Fe_2O_3 = 40$ *ppm*	$Mg^{2+} = 42$ *ppm*

Solution: Conversion into $CaCO_3$ equivalents:

Constituent	Multiplication factor	Amount (mg/L)	$CaCO_3$ equivalent (mg/L)
Ca^{2+}	$\frac{100}{40}$	140	$140 \times \frac{100}{40} = 350$
Mg^{2+}	$\frac{100}{24}$	42	$42 \times \frac{100}{24} = 175$
HCO_3^-	$\frac{100}{122}$	132	$132 \times \frac{100}{122} = 108.13$
CO_2	$\frac{100}{44}$	24	$24 \times \frac{100}{44} = 54.55$
$NaAlO_2$	$\frac{100}{164}$	42.8	$42.8 \times \frac{100}{164} = 26.09$

NaCl and Fe_2O_3 are ignored as they do not cause any hardness.

Lime required:

$$= \frac{74}{100} [Mg^{2+} + HCO^-_3 + CO_2 - NaAlO_2]$$

$$= \frac{74}{100} (175 + 108.19 + 54.55 - 26.09)$$

$$= 230.621 \text{ mg/L}$$

For 1 litre water, lime required = 230.621 mg.

∴ For 5,00,000 litres of water lime required will be

$$= 230.621 \times 5,00,000 \text{ mg}$$

$$= 1153.105 \times 10^5 \text{ mg}$$

$$= 115.31 \times 10^6 \text{ mg}$$

$$= 115.31 \text{ kg.}$$

Soda required:

$$= \frac{106}{100} (Ca^{2+} + Mg^{2+} - HCO_3^-)$$

$$= \frac{106}{100} (350 + 175 - 108.19)$$

$$= \frac{106}{100} (416.81) = 441.81 \text{mg/L}$$

For 1 litre of water soda required = 441.81 mg

For 5,00,00 litre of water soda required will be

$$= 441.81 \times 5,00,000 \text{ mg}$$

$$= 2209.05 \times 10^5 \text{ mg}$$

$$= 220.91 \text{ kg}$$

Example 8.11. *The analysis of a sample of water has produced follow concentrations (mg/l):*

(UIT – RGPV, Dec. 20)

Cations	***Anions***
$Ca^{2+} = 80$	$Cl^{-} = 100$
$Mg^{2+} = 30$	$SO_4^{2-} = 201$
$Na^{+} = 72$	$HCO_3^{-} = 165$
$K^{+} = 6$	

If a drinking water plant treats 3×10^6 L water per day to its maximum softness before distribution, how much lime and soda the plant would require daily?

Solution: Conversion into $CaCO_3$ equivalents

Constituent	Multiplication factor	Amount (mg/L)	$CaCO_3$ equivalent (mg/L)
Ca^{2+}	$\frac{100}{40}$	80	$80 \times \frac{100}{40} = 200$
Mg^{2+}	$\frac{100}{24}$	30	$30 \times \frac{100}{24} = 125$
HCO_3^{-}	$\frac{100}{122}$	165	$165 \times \frac{100}{122} = 135.25$

Lime required:

$$= \frac{74}{100}[Mg^{2+} + HCO_3^{-}] = \frac{74}{100}(125 + 135.25) = \frac{74}{100} \times 260.25$$

$$= 192.58 \text{ mg/L}$$

For 1 litre of water, lime required = 192.58 mg

For 3×10^6 litres of water, lime required will be

$$= 192.58 \times 3 \times 10^6 \text{ mg}$$
$$= 192.58 \times 3 \text{ kg}$$
$$= 577.74 \text{ kg}$$

Thus daily requirement of lime = 577.74 kg

Soda required

$$= \frac{106}{100}(Ca^{2+} + Mg^{2+} - HCO_3^{-}) \text{ mg/L}$$

$$= \frac{106}{100}(200 + 125 - 135.25)$$

$$= \frac{106}{100} \times 189.75 = 201.14 \text{ mg/L}$$

For 3×10^6 litre of water soda required will be

$$= 201.14 \times 3 \times 10^6 \text{ mg}$$
$$= 201.14 \times 3 \text{ kg}$$
$$= 603.42 \text{ kg}$$

Thus, daily requirement of soda = 603.42 kg.

Example 8.12. *Calculate the quantities of lime and soda required for softening 10,000 litres of water, the percentage purity of lime and soda being 80% and 85% respectively, containing the following salts per litre.* **(UIT – RGPV, June, 2015)**

$Ca(HCO_3)_2 = 8.1\ mg/L$ $Mg(HCO_3)_2 = 7.5\ mg/L$

$CaSO_4 = 13.6\ mg/L$ $MgSO_4 = 12.8\ mg/L$

$MgCl_2 = 2.5\ mg/L$ $HCO_3^- = 8.5\ mg/L$

$NaAlO_2 = 10.5\ mg/L$ $CO_2 = 12.5\ mg/L$

$HCl = 11.5\ mg/L.$

Solution: Conversion into $CaCO_3$ equivalents

Constituent	Multiplication factor	Amount (mg/L)	$CaCO_3$ equivalent (mg/L)
$Ca(HCO_3)_2$	$\frac{100}{162}$	8.1	$8.1 \times \frac{100}{162} = 5$
$Mg(HCO_3)_2$	$\frac{100}{146}$	7.5	$7.5 \times \frac{100}{146} = 5.14$
$CaSO_4$	$\frac{100}{136}$	13.6	$13.6 \times \frac{100}{136} = 10$
$MgSO_4$	$\frac{100}{120}$	12.8	$12.8 \times \frac{100}{120} = 10.67$
$MgCl_2$	$\frac{100}{95}$	2.5	$2.5 \times \frac{100}{95} = 2.63$
HCO_3^-	$\frac{100}{122}$	8.5	$8.5 \times \frac{100}{122} = 6.97$
$NaAlO_2$	$\frac{100}{164}$	10.5	$10.5 \times \frac{100}{164} = 6.40$
CO_2	$\frac{100}{44}$	12.5	$12.5 \times \frac{100}{44} = 28.41$
HCl	$\frac{100}{73}$	11.5	$11.5 \times \frac{100}{73} = 15.75$

Lime required:

$$= \frac{74}{100}[Ca(HCO_3)_2 + 2Mg(HCO_3)_2 + MgSO_4 + MgCl_2 + HCO_3^- + CO_2 + HCl - NaAlO_2] \times \frac{100}{80}\ mg/L$$

$$= \frac{74}{100}(5 + (2 \times 5.14) + 10.67 + 2.63 + 6.97 + 28.41 + 15.75 - 6.40) \times \frac{100}{80}\ mg/L$$

$$= \frac{74}{100}(73.31) \times \frac{100}{80}\ mg/L = 67.81\ mg/L$$

For 1 litre of water, lime required = 67.81 mg.

For 10,000 litre of water, lime required will be

$$= \frac{67.81 \times 10000}{1000 \times 1000} = 0.6781 \text{ kg}$$

Soda required

$$= \frac{106}{100}\left(CaSO_4 + MgCl_2 + MgSO_4 + HCl - HCO^-_3\right) \times \frac{100}{85} \text{ mg/L}$$

$$= \frac{106}{100} (10 + 2.63 + 10.67 + 15.75 - 6.97) \times \frac{100}{85} \text{ mg/L}$$

$$= \frac{106}{100} (32.08) \times \frac{100}{85} \text{ mg/L} = 40.01 \text{ mg/L}$$

For 1 litre of water, soda required = 40.01 mg

For 10,000 litres of water soda required will be

$$= \frac{40.01 \times 10,000}{1000 \times 1000} = 0.40 \text{ kg.}$$

Example 8.13. *Calculate the amount of lime and soda required for softening 1 million litres of water with the following analysis using 10 ppm of sodium aluminate as a coagulant*

$Ca^{2+} = 95$ *ppm* $Mg^{2+} = 40$ *ppm*

$CO_2 = 66$ *ppm* $HCO_3^- = 264$ *ppm* $H^+ = 2$ *ppm.*

(RGPV, Mar–Apr/2010)

Solution: Conversion into $CaCO_3$ equivalents:

Constituent	Multiplication factor	Amount (mg/L)	$CaCO_3$ equivalent (mg/L)
Ca^{2+}	$\frac{100}{40}$	95	$95 \times \frac{100}{40} = 237.50$
Mg^{2+}	$\frac{100}{24}$	40	$40 \times \frac{100}{24} = 166.67$
CO_2	$\frac{100}{44}$	66	$66 \times \frac{100}{44} = 150$
HCO_3^-	$\frac{100}{122}$	264	$264 \times \frac{100}{122} = 216.39$
H^+	$\frac{100}{2}$	2	$2 \times \frac{100}{2} = 100$
$NaAlO_2$	$\frac{100}{164}$	10	$10 \times \frac{100}{164} = 6.09$

Lime required

$$= \frac{74}{100}[Mg^{2+} + HCO_3^- + CO_2 + H^+ - NaAlO_2] \text{ mg/L}$$

$$= \frac{74}{100}[166.67 + 216.39 + 150 + 100 - 6.09] \text{ mg/L}$$

$$= \frac{74}{100}(626.97)\text{mg/L} = 463.95 \text{ mg/L}$$

Fir 1 litre of water, lime required = 463.95 mg/L

For 1 million litre of water *i.e.* 10^6 litre, the lime required will be

$$= 463.95 \times 10^6 \text{ mg}$$

$$= 463.95 \text{ kg}$$

Soda required:

$$= \frac{106}{100}[Ca^{2+} + Mg^{2+} + H^+ - HCO_3^-] \text{ mg/L}$$

$$= \frac{106}{100}[237.50 + 166.67 + 100 - 216.39] \text{ mg/L}$$

$$= \frac{106}{100}(287.78) \text{ mg/L} = 305.05 \text{ mg/L}$$

For 1 litre of water soda required = 305.05 mg

for 1 million litre of water, soda required will be

$$= 305.05 \times 10^6 \text{ mg}$$

$$= 305.05 \text{ kg.}$$

Example 8.14. *A water sample using $FeSO_4 \cdot 7H_2O$ as a coagulant at the rate of 278 ppm, gave the following results on analysis:* **(RGPV, June, 2014)**

$$Ca^{2+} = 320 \text{ ppm} \qquad Mg^{2+} = 144 \text{ ppm}$$

$$CO_2 = 88 \text{ ppm} \qquad HCO_3^- = 488 \text{ ppm}$$

Calculate the lime and soda required for softening 1,00,000 litres of water.

Solution: Conversion into $CaCO_3$ equivalents

Constituent	Multiplication factor	Amount (mg/L)	$CaCO_3$ equivalent (mg/L)
Ca^{2+}	$\frac{100}{40}$	320	$320 \times \frac{100}{40} = 800$
Mg^{2+}	$\frac{100}{24}$	144	$144 \times \frac{100}{24} = 600$
CO_2	$\frac{100}{44}$	88	$88 \times \frac{100}{44} = 200$
HCO_3^-	$\frac{100}{122}$	488	$488 \times \frac{100}{122} = 400$
$FeSO_4 \cdot 7H_2O$	$\frac{100}{278}$	278	$278 \times \frac{100}{278} = 100$

Lime required

$$= \frac{74}{100} [Mg^{2+} + CO_2 + HCO_3^- + FeSO_4 \cdot 7H_2O] \text{ mg/L}$$

$$= \frac{74}{100} [600 + 200 + 400 + 100] \text{ mg/L}$$

$$= \frac{74}{100} \times 1300 \text{ mg/L} = 962 \text{ mg/L}$$

For 1 litre of water, lime required = 962 mg

For 1,00,000 litres lime required will be

$$= 962 \times 1,00,000 \text{ mg}$$

$$= 96.2 \text{ kg}$$

Soda required

$$= \frac{106}{100} [Ca^{2+} + Mg^{2+} - HCO_3^- + FeSO_4 \cdot 7H_2O] \text{ mg/L}$$

$$= \frac{106}{100} (800 + 600 - 400 + 100)$$

$$= \frac{106}{100} \times 1100 = 1166 \text{ mg/L}$$

For 1 litre of water, soda required = 1162 mg

For 1,00,000 litres of water, soda required will be

$$= 1162 \times 1,00,000 \text{ mg}$$

$$= 116.2 \text{ kg.}$$

Example 8.15. *The hardness of 10000 litres of a sample of water was completely removed by zeolite softener. The zeolite softener required 60 litres of NaCl solution containing 1.5 kg/litre of NaCl for regeneration. Calculate the hardness of the sample of water.*

Solution: Hardness of water can be calculated using the following formula:

$$\text{Hardness} = \frac{mV_2 \times 50 \times 1000}{V_1 \times 58.5} \text{ mg/L}$$

Here,

$$m = 1.5 \text{ kg/L} = 1.5 \times 10^3 \text{ g/L}$$

$$V_1 = 10,000 \text{ litres}$$

$$V_2 = 60 \text{ litres.}$$

Thus,

$$\text{Hardness} = \frac{1.5 \times 10^3 \times 60 \times 50 \times 1000}{10000 \times 58.5} = 7.6923 \times 10^3 \text{ mg/L.}$$

Example 8.16. *An exhausted zeolite softener was regenerated by passing 140 litres of NaCl solution, having a strength of 140 g/L of NaCl. How many litres of hard water sample, having hardness of 600 ppm can be softened, using this softener?*

Solution: Hardness of water sample to be softened by zeolite process is given by

$$\text{Hardness} = \frac{mV_2 \times 50 \times 1000}{V_1 \times 58.5} \text{ mg/L}$$

Here, $m = 140$ g/L, $V_1 = ?$ $V_2 = 140$ litres

Hardness = 600 ppm

By substituting these values,

$$V_1 = \frac{140 \times 140 \times 50 \times 1000}{600 \times 58.5} = 27920.2 \text{ litres.}$$

Therefore, the amount of hard water that can be softened by this softener is 27920.2 litres.

Example 8.17. *(i) 100 mL of water sample has a hardness equivalent to 6.25 mL of 0.08 N $MgSO_4$. What is its hardness in ppm?*

(ii) An exhausted zeolite softener was regenerated by passing 250 litres of NaCl solution, having a strength of 200 g/L of NaCl. If the hardness of water is 500 ppm, calculate the total volume of water that is softened by this softener. **(UIT – RGPV Nov./Dec., 2015)**

Solution: (*i*) Applying the normality equation:

$$\underbrace{N_1V_1}_{\text{Water}} = \underbrace{N_2V_2}_{MgSO_4}$$

$$N_1 \times 100 = 0.08 \times 6.25$$

$$N_1 = \frac{0.08 \times 6.25}{100} = 0.005 \text{ N}$$

Strength (g/L) = Normality × eq. weight of $CaCO_3$

$$= 0.005 \times 50 = 250 \times 10^{-3} \text{ g/L}$$

Hardness/Strength (mg/L) = $250 \times 10^{-3} \times 10^3$ mg/L

$$= 250 \text{ mg/L} = 250 \text{ ppm.}$$

(*ii*) Hardness of water sample to be softened by zeolite process in given by:

$$\text{Hardness} = \frac{mV_2 \times 50 \times 1000}{V_1 \times 58.5} \text{ mg/L}$$

Here, $m = 200$g/L

$V_1 = ?$

$V_2 = 250$ L

Hardness = 500 ppm

∴ The amount of hard water that can be softened by this method is

$$V_1 = \frac{200 \times 250 \times 50 \times 1000}{500 \times 58.5} \text{ litres}$$

$$= 85470.08 \text{ litres.}$$

Example 8.18. *A Zeolite softener was 80% exhausted when 50,000 litres of water sample was passed through it. If it requires 400 litres of 4.6% NaCl solution for complete regeneration Calculate the hardness of given water sample.* **(UIT–RGPV Nov./Dec., 20)**

Solution: Hardness of water sample is given by:

$$\text{Hardness} = \frac{mV_2 \times 50 \times 1000}{V_1 \times 58.5} \text{ mg/L}$$

Here, m = 4.6% = 4.6 g of NaCl per 100 mL of solution

∴ 46 g/L

$$V_1 = 50{,}000 \text{ litres}$$
$$V_2 = 400 \text{ litres}$$
$$\text{Hardness} = \frac{46 \times 400 \times 50 \times 1000}{50000 \times 58.5} \text{ mg/L}$$
$$= 314.5 \text{ mg/L.}$$

Example 8.19. *400 mL of a sample of water on EDTA titration with EBT as an indicator consumed 30 mL of 0.05M EDTA till point is reached. Calculate the hardness of water.*

Solution: Applying the molarity equation here

$$\underbrace{M_1V_1}_{\text{Hard Water}} = \underbrace{M_2V_2}_{\text{EDTA}}$$

$$V_1 = 400 \text{ mL}, M_2 = 0.05 \text{ M}, V_2 = 300 \text{ mL}, M_1 = ?$$
$$M_1 \times 400 = 0.05 \times 30$$
$$M_1 = \frac{0.05 \times 30}{400} = 0.00375 \text{ M}$$
$$\text{Molarity of Hard Water} = 0.00375 \text{ M}$$
$$\text{Hardness/strength in (mg/L)} = \text{Molarity} \times \text{Molar mass of } CaCO_3 \times 1000 \text{ mg/L}$$
$$= 0.00375 \times 100 \times 1000 = 375 \text{ mg/L}$$

∴ Hardness of water 375 mg/L = 375 ppm.

Example 8.20. *100 mL of standard hard water containing 1 mg of pure $CaCO_3$ per ml consumed 25 mL of EDTA. 50 mL of water sample consumed 25 mL of the same EDTA solution, using EBT as an indicator, calculate the total hardness of water sample in ppm.*

(RGPV, June 2011)

Solution: (*i*) Standard hard water vs. EDTA.

Applying the molarity equation

$$\underbrace{M_1\ V_1}_{\text{Standard hard water}} = \underbrace{M_2\ V_2}_{\text{EDTA}}$$

$$\text{Molarity of standard hard water} = M_1 = \frac{1 \times 10^{-3}}{100} \times \frac{1000}{1} = 0.01 \text{ M}$$

$$M_2 = \frac{M_1V_1}{V_2} \quad \text{or} \quad M_2 = \frac{0.01 \times 100}{25} = 0.04 \text{ M}$$

∴ Molarity of EDTA = 0.04 M

(*ii*) Water sample Vs. EDTA

Applying the molarity equation:

$$\underbrace{M_1\ V_1}_{\text{Water Sample}} = \underbrace{M_2\ V_2}_{\text{EDTA}}$$

$$M_1 \times 50 = 0.04 \times 25$$
$$M_1 = \frac{0.04 \times 25}{50} = 0.02$$

$$\text{Hardness (mg/L)} = \text{Molarity} \times \text{Molar mass of } CaCO_3 \times 1000 \text{ mg/L}$$
$$= 0.02 \times 100 \times 1000$$
$$= 2000 \text{ mg/L} = 2000 \text{ ppm.}$$

Example 8.21. *1 g of $CaCO_3$ was dissolved in dil. HCl and diluted to 1000 mL. 25 mL of this solution required 25 mL of EDTA solution for titration. 50 mL of sample hard water required 45 mL of EDTA solution. In another titration, 50 mL of same hard water sample on boiling, cooling and filtering etc. required 20 mL of EDTA solution using eriochrome black-T as an indicator. Calculate temporary and permanent hardness of water in different units.*

Solution: First titration: (*i*) Standard hard water vs. EDTA solution

$$\underbrace{M_1 V_1}_{\text{Water}} = \underbrace{M_2 V_2}_{\text{EDTA}}$$

Molarity of standard Hard water (M_1)

$$= \frac{1}{100} \times \frac{1000}{1000} = 0.01 \text{ M}$$

$$\therefore \quad 0.01 \times 25 = M_2 \times 25$$

$$M_2 = \frac{0.01 \times 25}{25} = 0.01 \text{ M}$$

i.e., Molarity of EDTA = 0.01 M.

Standard hard water means, the hard water whose strength is known with accuracy. For example, if 1 g of $CaCO_3$ was dissolved in dil HCl and diluted to 1000 mL means 1 g $CaCO_3$/1000 mL.

(*ii*) Sample hard water Vs. EDTA

$$\underbrace{M_1 V_1}_{\text{Water}} = \underbrace{M_2 V_2}_{\text{EDTA}}$$

$$50 \times M_1 = 0.01 \times 45$$

$$M_1 = \frac{0.01 \times 45}{50} = 0.009 \text{ M}$$

Total Hardness of the sample (mg/L)

$$= \text{Molarity} \times \text{Molar Mass of } CaCO_3 \times 1000$$
$$= 0.009 \times 100 \times 1000 = 900 \text{ mg/L}$$
$$= 900 \times 0.1° \text{ Fr} = 90° \text{ F}$$
$$= 900 \times 0.07° \text{ Cl} = 63° \text{ Cl.}$$

Second titration: Now, when we boil the hard water, temporary hardness is removed and only permanent hardness left.

So,

$$\underbrace{M_1 V_1}_{\text{Water}} = \underbrace{M_2 V_2}_{\text{EDTA}}$$

$$M_1 \times 50 = 0.01 \times 20$$

$$M_1 = \frac{0.01 \times 20}{50} = 0.004 \text{ M}$$

Thus, permanent hardness (mg/L)

$$= \text{Molarity} \times \text{Molar Mass of } CaCO_3 \times 1000$$
$$= 0.004 \times 100 \times 1000 = 400 \text{ mg/L}$$
$$= 40°\text{Fr}$$
$$= 28°\text{Cl}$$

$$\text{Temporary Hardness} = \text{Total hardness} - \text{Permanent hardness}$$
$$\text{Temporary Hardness} = 900 - 400 \text{ ppm}$$
$$= 500 \text{ ppm} = 500 \text{ mg/L}$$
$$= 50°\text{Fr}$$
$$= 35°\text{Cl.}$$

Example 8.22. *A sample of water was alkaline to both phenolphthalein and methyl orange. 100 mL of this sample required 10 mL of N/50 H_2SO_4 for phenolphthalein end point and 10 mL of the acid to methyl orange end point on separate titration. Determine the types and extent of alkalinity present.* **(RGPV, June 20)**

Solution: (*i*) Phenolphthalein alkalinity (*P*): This is the strength of alkalinity upto phenolphthalein end point.

Water sample *Vs.* Acid titration (till *P* end point)

Applying the normality equation

$$\underbrace{N_P\, V_1}_{\text{Water sample}} = \underbrace{N_2\, V_2}_{\text{Acid}}$$

$$V_1 = 100 \text{ mL}$$
$$N_1 = \frac{N}{50}$$
$$V_2 = 10 \text{ mL}$$
$$N_p \times 100 = \frac{N}{50} \times 10$$
$$\therefore \quad N_p = \frac{N}{50} \times \frac{10}{100}$$

Now, the strength of alkalinity upto phenolphthalein end point

$$= N_p \times \text{eq. wt. of } CaCO_5 \times 1000 \text{ mg/L}$$
$$= \frac{1}{50} \times \frac{10}{100} \times 50 \times 1000 \text{ mg/L}$$
$$P = 100 \text{ mg/L} = 100 \text{ ppm}$$

(*ii*) Methyl orange Alkalinity (*M*) *i.e.* the strength of alkalinity upto methyl orange end point.

As the titration has been performed separately with methyl orange.

Applying the Normality equation:

$$\underbrace{N_m\, V_1}_{\text{Water Sample}} = \underbrace{N_2\, V_2}_{\text{Acid}}$$

$$V_1 = 100 \text{ mL}, N_2 = \text{N/50}, V_2 = 20 \text{ mL}, N_m = ?$$
$$N_m \times 100 = \frac{N}{50} \times 20$$

$$N_m = \frac{N}{50} \times \frac{20}{100}$$

Now, the strength of alkalinity upto Methyl orange end point

$$= N_m \times \text{Eq. wt of } CaCO_3 \times 1000 \text{ mg/L}$$

$$= \frac{1}{50} \times \frac{20}{100} \times 50 \times 1000 \text{ mg/L}$$

$$M = 200 \text{ mg/L} = 200 \text{ ppm} \therefore M = 200 \text{ ppm.}$$

$\therefore$ $$P = \frac{1}{2} M \quad \therefore \quad \text{Only } CO_3^{2-} \text{ ions are present}$$

Hence, $$CO_3^{2-} = 2P = 2 \times 100 = 200 \text{ ppm or } 200 \text{ mg/L}$$

Example 8.23. *A sample of water is alkaline to both phenolphthalein as well as methyl orange. 100 mL of the water sample on titration with* $\frac{N}{50}$ *HCl required 4.7 mL of the acid to phenolphthalein end point. When a few drops of methyl orange are added to the same solution and the titration further continued the yellow colour of the solution just turned red after addition of another 10.3 mL of the acid solution. Determine the type and extent of alkalinity present in the water sample.*

Solution: (*i*) Phenolphthalein alkalinity (*P*)

Water sample Vs. Acid titration (upto *P* end point)

According to law of equivalence

$$\underbrace{N_p V_1}_{\text{Water}} = \underbrace{N_2 V_2}_{\text{Acid}}$$

$$V_1 = 100 \text{ mL}, \quad N_2 = \frac{N}{50}, \quad V_2 = 4.7 \text{ mL}, \quad N_P = ?$$

$\therefore$ $$N_p \times 100 = \frac{N}{50} \times 4.7$$

$$N_p = \frac{N}{50} \times \frac{4.7}{100}$$

Now, Phenolphthalein alkalinity

$$P = N_p \times \text{eq. wt. of } CaCO_3 \times 1000 \text{ mg/L}$$

$$= \frac{1}{50} \times \frac{4.7}{100} \times 50 \times 1000 \text{ mg/L}$$

$$= 47 \text{ mg/L} = 47 \text{ ppm}$$

(*ii*) Methyl Orange alkalinity/total alkalinity

$$\underbrace{N_M V_1}_{\text{Water}} = \underbrace{N_2 V_2}_{\text{Acid}}$$

$$V_1 = 100, \ N_2 = \frac{N}{50}$$

$$V_2 = 10.3 + 4.7 \text{ mL}$$

$$= 15.0 \text{ mL}$$

As methyl orange alkalinity is also called as total alkalinity, we have to use total volume that is used from beginning till *M* point.

$$N_M \times 100 = \frac{N}{50} \times 15 \quad \text{or} \quad N_M = \frac{N}{50} \times \frac{15}{100}$$

Now,

$$M = N_M \times \text{eq. wt. of } CaCO_3 \times 1000 \text{ mg/L}$$

$$= \frac{N}{50} \times \frac{15}{100} \times 50 \times 1000 = 150 \text{ mg/L} = 150 \text{ ppm}$$

Now, $P = 47$ ppm

$M = 150$ ppm

Thus, $P < \frac{1}{2} M$

Therefore CO_3^{2-} and HCO_3^- ions are present

$$P = \frac{1}{2} CO_3^{2-} \qquad CO_3^{2-} = 2P = 2 \times 47 \text{ ppm} = 94 \text{ ppm}$$

$$HCO_3^- = M - 2P = 150 - 94 \text{ ppm} = 56 \text{ ppm}$$

Thus, $CO_3^{2-} = 94$ ppm and $HCO_3^- = 56$ ppm.

Example 8.24. *100 mL of a raw water sample on titration with $\frac{N}{50}$ H_2SO_4 required 12.8 ml of the acid to phenolphthalein end point and 16.0 mL of the acid to methyl, orange end point. Determine the type and extent of alkalinity present in the water sample.*

Solution: (*i*) Phenolphthalein alkalinity: Water sample *Vs.* Acid titration (till phenolphthalein end point)

According to the law of equivalence

$$\underbrace{N_p V_1}_{\text{Water}} = \underbrace{N_2 V_2}_{\text{Acid}}$$

$$N_2 = \frac{N}{50}, \; V_1 = 100 \text{ mL}, \; V_2 = 12.8 \text{ mL}$$

$$N_p = \frac{N}{50} \times \frac{12.8}{100}$$

Phenolphthalein Alkalinity (*P*)

$$= N_p \times \text{eq. wt. of } CaCO_3 \times 1000 \text{ mg/L}$$

$$P = \frac{1}{50} \times \frac{12.8}{100} \times 50 \times 1000 \text{ mg/L}$$

$$= 128 \text{ mg/L} = 128 \text{ ppm.}$$

(*ii*) Methyl orange alkalinity: Water sample Vs. Acid titration (till methyl orange end point)

According to law of equivalence

$$N_M V_1 = N_2 V_2$$

$$N = \frac{N}{50} \times \frac{16}{100}$$

Methyl orange alkalinity (*M*)

$$= N_M \times \text{eq. wt. of } CaCO_3 \times 1000 \text{ mg/L}$$

$$= \frac{N}{50} \times \frac{16}{100} \times 50 \times 1000 = 160 \text{ mg/L} = 160 \text{ ppm}$$

$$P = 128 \text{ ppm}$$

$$M = 160 \text{ ppm}$$

$\therefore P > \frac{1}{2} M$ therefore, OH^- and CO_3^{2-} ions present.

$$OH^- \text{ alkalinity} = 2P - M = 2 \times 128 - 160 = 96 \text{ ppm}$$

$$CO_3^{2-} \text{ alkalinity} = 2(M - P) = 2(160 - 128) = 64 \text{ ppm.}$$

Example 8.25. *100 mL of water sample required 20 mL of N/50 H_2SO_4 for neutralization to phenolphthalein end point. After this, methyl orange indicator was added to this and further acid required was 15 mL. Calculate the type and the extent of alkalinity.*

(RGPV. Jan/Feb., 2008, Dec., 2012)

Solution: (*i*) Phenolphthalein alkalinity (*P*)

Water sample *Vs.* Acid titration (till *P* end point)

According to law of equivalence

$$\underbrace{N_P V_1}_{\text{Water}} = \underbrace{N_2 V_2}_{\text{Acid}}$$

$$N_2 = \frac{N}{50}, \; V_1 = 100 \text{ mL}, \; V_2 = 20 \text{ mL}$$

$$N_P = \frac{N}{50} \times \frac{20}{100}$$

$$P = N_P \times \text{eq. wt. of } CaCO_3 \times 1000 \text{ mg/L}$$

$$= \frac{1}{50} \times \frac{20}{100} \times 50 \times 1000 = 200 \text{ mg/L} = 200 \text{ ppm.}$$

(*ii*) Methyl orange alkalinity (*M*)

Water sample *Vs.* Acid titration (till *M* end point)

$$\underbrace{N_M V_1}_{\text{Water}} = \underbrace{N_2 V_2}_{\text{Acid}}$$

$$V_1 = 100 \text{ mL}, \; N_2 = \frac{N}{50}, \; V_2 = 20 + 15 \text{ mL} = 35 \text{ mL}$$

$$N_M = \frac{N}{50} \times \frac{35}{100}$$

$$M = N_M \times \text{eq. wt. of } CaCO_3 \times 1000 \text{ mg/L}$$

$$= \frac{1}{50} \times \frac{35}{100} \times 50 \times 1000 = 350 \text{ mg/L} = 350 \text{ ppm}$$

Now, $M = 350$ ppm, $P = 200$ ppm, $\therefore P > \frac{1}{2} M$

Thus OH^- and CO_3^{2-} ions are present

N_M is the normality and M is the strength.

OH^- alkalinity = $2P - M = 2 \times 200 - 350 = 50$ ppm

CO_3^{2-} alkalinity = $2(M - P) = 2(350 - 200) = 300$ ppm

Thus, OH^- alkalinity = 50 ppm

CO_3^{2-} alkalinity = 300 ppm.

Example 8.26. *A 100 mL of sample contains 210 ppm of dissolved oxygen. After 5 days the dissolved oxygen value becomes 40 ppm after the sample has been diluted to 500 mL. Calculate the BOD of the sample.*

Solution: Given DO_b = 210 ppm dilution factor = $\frac{500}{100}$

$$DO_i = 40 \text{ ppm}$$

$$\therefore \quad BOD = (DO_b - DO_i) \times \text{dilution factor}$$

$$= (210 - 40) \times \frac{500}{100}$$

$$= 170 \times 5 = 850 \text{ ppm.}$$

Example 8.27. *50 cm³ of waste is diluted to 800 cm³ and equal volumes are filled in two BOD bottles. A blank titration was performed using 100 cm³ of diluted waste water. It required 14 cm³ of 0.05 N hypo solution for neutralization, 100 cm³ of the incubated sample was titrated again after 5 days. It required 8 cm³ of the same hypo solution. Determine the BOD of waste water.*

Sol. Initially (Blank titration)

$$\text{Volume of waste water} = 50 \text{ cm}^3$$

$$\text{Volume of diluted waste water} = 800 \text{ cm}^3$$

$$\therefore \quad \text{Dilution factor} = \frac{800}{50}$$

$$\underset{\text{Sample water}}{N_1 V_1} = \underset{\text{hypo}}{N_2 V_2}$$

$$N_1 = ?$$

$$N_2 = 0.05 N$$

$$V_1 = 100 \text{ cm}^3$$

$$V_2 = 14 \text{ cm}^3$$

$$N_1 = \frac{0.05 \times 14}{100}$$

Strength of dissolved oxygen = N_1 × eq. wt. of oxygen × 1000 mg/L

$$DO_b = \frac{0.05 \times 14}{100} \times 8 \times 1000 = 56 \text{ mg/L}$$

After 5 days

$$\underset{\text{Waste water}}{N_3 V_3} = \underset{\text{hypo}}{N_4 V_4}$$

$$N_3 = ?$$

$$V_3 = 100 \text{ cm}^3$$

$$N_4 = 0.05 \text{ N}$$

$$V_4 = 8 \text{ cm}^3$$

$$\therefore \quad N_3 = \frac{0.05 \times 8}{100}$$

$$\text{Strength of DO [i.e., } (DO_i)] = \frac{0.05 \times 8}{100} \times 8 \times 1000 = 32 \text{ mg/L}$$

Hence,

$$\text{BOD} = (DO_b - DO_i) \times \text{dilution factor}$$

$$= (56 - 32) \times \frac{800}{50} \text{ mg/L}$$

$$= 24 \times 16 \text{ mg/L} = 384 \text{ mg/L.}$$

Example 8.28. *25 mL of sewage water sample was refluxed with 10 mL of 0.50 M $K_2Cr_2O_7$ in presence of dil H_2SO_4, $AgSO_4$ and $HgSO_4$. The unreacted dichromate required 8.5 mL of 0.1 N FAS. 10 mL of the same $K_2Cr_2O_7$ solution and 25 mL of distilled water, under the same conditions as the sample required 30 mL of 0.1 N FAS. Calculate the COD of sewage water sample.*

Solution: Given: Volume of FAS consumed in blank titration = 30 mL = V_4

Volume of FAS consumed in test experiments = 8.5 mL = V_3

Normality of FAS = 0.1 N = N_2

Volume of effluent sample taken = 25 mL = V_1

According to the formula,

$$\text{COD} = \frac{V_4 - V_3}{V_1} \times N_2 \times 8 \times 1000$$

$$= \frac{(30 - 8.5) \times 0.1 \times 8 \times 1000}{25}$$

$$= 688 \text{ mg/L or ppm.}$$

EXERCISES

I. SHORT ANSWER TYPE QUESTIONS

1. Define hardness of water. Explain different types of hardness of water.
2. Define hardness of water. Explain various units of hardness of water. Also give the relationship between different units.
3. Explain why hardness of water is expressed in terms of $CaCO_3$ equivalents.
4. What do you mean by alkalinity of water? Why alkalinity of water cannot be due to the presence of OH^-, CO_3^{2-} and HCO_3^- at a time?
5. What are the main types of alkalinity in water?
6. Write the structures of:
   (*a*) EDTA (*b*) EBT
   (*c*) Methyl orange (*d*) Phenolphthalein.
7. Discuss various chemical reactions involved in lime-soda process. **(RGPV, 2003, 2004, 2006, 2008)**
8. Name the various methods used for softening of water. Explain with equations which is the best method and why? **(RGPV, 2008)**

9. In the deionization process, water is first passed through a cation exchanger and then through anion exchanger. Give reason.
10. Write short note on scale and sludge formation. **(RGPV, 2004, 2006)**
11. Name the problems faced by using hard water in boilers. Explain any one.
12. Write short note on:
    (*a*) Priming and foaming (*b*) Boiler corrosion
    (*c*) Caustic embrittlement (*d*) Phosphate conditioning.
13. What is calgon? Explain its role in water treatment.
14. How does the formation of scale and sludge affect boiler performance?
15. How are the exhausted resins regenerated in ion exchange method of water softening?
16. Explain break point chlorination.
17. Write short notes on:
    (*a*) Dissolved oxygen (*b*) Biochemical oxygen demand
    (*c*) Chemical oxygen demand.
18. Differentiate between lime soda process and zeolite process.
19. Give the names of various external treatment methods of water softening.
20. Explain BOD and COD alongwith their significance.
21. CO_2 should not be present in boiler feed water. Why? **(RGPV, 2015)**

II. LONG ANSWER TYPE QUESTIONS

1. Discuss the chemistry involved in complexometric titration for the determination of the hardness of water.
2. Why phenolphthalein and methyl orange both indicators are needed to determine the alkalinity of the water?
3. Define hardness of water. How is hardness of water determined by EDTA method?
4. Describe with the help of neat labelled diagram cold lime-soda process of softening of hard water.
5. What are zeloites? How softening of hard water is carried out by zeolite process? Also write advantages and disadvantages of the process. **(RGPV, 2010)**
6. Describe with the help of neat and labelled diagram ion exchange process of softening of hard water.
7. Discuss formation, causes and harmful effects of scales and sludges in boilers.
8. Explain boiler corrosion and caustic embrittlement. **(RGPV, 2014)**
9. Explain the term reverse osmosis. How can it be used to obtain soft water from sea water.
10. What are the essential requirements of domestic water? Explain various steps involved in the supply of water in a municipality for domestic use.
11. What is desalination of water? Write various methods for desalination and explain any one of them.

III. NUMERICAL PROBLEMS

1. A sample of water on analysis has been found to contain the following impurities

   $Ca(HCO_3)_2$ = 48.6 mg/L $CaSO_4$ = 68.0 mg/L

   $MgSO_4$ = 84.0 mg/L.

   Calculate the temporary and permanent hardness of the water sample.

2. A sample of water on analysis was found to contain:

   $Ca(HCO_3)_2$ = 40 mg/L $Mg(HCO_3)_2$ = 60 mg/L

   $CaSO_4$ = 80.0 mg/L $MgSO_4$ = 10 mg/L

   Calculate the temporary, permanent and total hardness of water in ppm, °Fr and °Cl.

3. Calculate the amount of lime (84% pure) and soda (92% pure) required for treatment of 20,000 litres of water whose analysis is as follows:

   $Ca(HCO_3)_2$ = 40.5 mg/L $Mg(HCO_3)_2$ = 36.5 mg/L

   $MgSO_4$ = 30 mg/L $CaSO_4$ = 34.0 mg/L

   $CaCl_2$ = 27.75 mg/L   NaCl = 10.0 mg/L

   Also calculate the temporary and permanent hardness of the water sample.

4. Calculate the amount of lime and soda required for softening 10,000 litres of hard water containing. **(RGPV, Dec., 2011)**

   Mg $(HCO_3)_2$ = 146 ppm $Ca(HCO_3)_2$ = 81 ppm

   $MgCl_2$ = 95 ppm $CaCl_2$ = 111 ppm

   NaCl = 20 ppm   KCl = 30 ppm.

5. A turbid water using $FeSO_4.7H_2O$ as a coagulant at the rate of 278 ppm, gave the following results on analysis:

   Ca^{2+} = 240 ppm Mg^{2+} = 96 ppm

   CO_2 = 44 ppm HCO_3^- = 732 ppm

   SiO_2 = 40 ppm   NaCl = 58 ppm

   Calculate the lime and soda required for softening one million litres of water.

   [**Hint:** NaCl and SiO_2 are ignored as they do not cause any hardness.]

6. Calculate the quantities of lime (84% pure) and soda (92% pure) in kg for softening 3,00,000 litres of water using 32.8 ppm of sodium aluminate as a coagulant. The impurities present in water are as follows: **(RGPV, Dec., 2003, 2008)**

   Ca^{2+} = 240 mg/L Mg^{2+} = 96 mg/L

   HCO_3^- = 732 mg/L   Dissolved CO_2 = 44 mg/L

   NaCl = 60 mg/L   and Fe_2O_3 = 160 mg/L

   [**Hint:** NaCl and Fe_2O_3 are ignored, as they do not cause any hardness.]

7. A water sample has the analytical report as under:

   $MgCO_3$ = 84 ppm $CaCO_3$ = 80 ppm

   $MgSO_4$ = 30 ppm $CaSO_4$ = 34 ppm

   NaCl = 10 ppm Fe_2O_3 = 56 ppm

   Calculate the amount of lime and soda needed for the treatment of 80000 litres of water.

8. A hard water sample has the following compositional data.

$Ca(HCO_3)_2$ = 162 ppm $Mg(HCO_3)_2$ = 73 ppm

$CaCl_2$ = 111 ppm $MgCl_2$ = 95 ppm

$CaSO_4$ = 136 ppm $MgSO_4$ = 120 ppm

$FeSO_4.7H_2O$ = 139 ppm CO_2 = 44 ppm

Calculate temporary and permanent hardness and the quantity of lime and soda required for softening one million litres of water.

9. Water sample on analysis, gave the following data:

$MgCl_2$ = 95 ppm $CaSO_4$ = 272 ppm

$MgSO_4$ = 120 ppm H_2SO_4 = 49 ppm

SiO_2 = 7 ppm.

Calculate the amount of lime (95% pure) and soda (97% pure) needed for treating 1 million litres of water. If the costs of lime and soda are ₹ 40 and ₹ 2000 per 100 kg each respectively. Calculate the cost of lime and soda needed for treating 1 million litres of the water.

10. A zeolite softener was completely exhausted and regenerated by passing 100 litres of NaCl solution containing 200 g/L of NaCl. How many litres of sample of water of hardness 500 ppm can be softened by this softener.

11. An exhausted zeolite softener was regenerated by passing 150 litres of NaCl solution, having a strength of 150 g/L of NaCl. How many litres of hard water sample having hardness of 600 ppm, can be softened, using this softener.

12. A totally exhausted zeolite softener required 50 mL of NaCl solution containing 351 g of NaCl/litre. How many litres of hard water sample containing 70° Clarke hardness can be softened by this process. **(UIT–RGPV, May/June 2015, RGPV, Dec., 2005)**

13. A zeolite softener was 95% exhausted, when 10,000 L of hard water was passed through it. The softener required 150 litres of NaCl solution of strength 50 g NaCl/L to regenerate. What is the hardness of water?

14. Hardness of standard hard water in terms of $CaCO_3$ is 1 g/L. 50 mL of this solution required 50 mL of EDTA solution for titration. 50 mL of sample hard water required 40 mL of EDTA solution for titration. In another titration, 50 mL of same hard water sample on boiling, cooling and filtering required 20 mL of EDTA solution. Calculate the temporary and permanent hardness of water sample.

15. 50 mL of standard hard water containing 1000 mg of pure $CaCO_3$ per litre, consumed 20 mL of EDTA. 50 mL of water sample consumed 25 mL of the same EDTA solution. Using eriochrome black-*T* as an indicator, calculate the total hardness of water sample in ppm. **(RGPV, Dec., 2011)**

16. 10 mL of a sample of water required 1 mL of 0.01 N HCl using methyl orange as an indicator but did not give any coloration with phenolphthalein. What type and amount of alkalinity is present? Express the result in ppm.

[**Hint:** $P = 0$ M can be determined using normal procedure.]

17. 100 mL of water sample, on titration with $\frac{N}{50}$ H_2SO_4, gave a titre value of 5.0 mL to phenolphthalein end point and 10 mL to methyl orange end-point. Calculate the alkalinity of the water sample in terms of $CaCO_3$ and comment on the type of alkalinity present.

$\left[\textbf{Hint.}\ P = \frac{1}{2}M\right]$

18. 5 mL of water sample on titration with $\frac{N}{50}$ HCl required 10 mL of the acid to phenolphthalein end point and 15 mL of the acid to methyl orange end point. Calculate the type and extent of alkalinity present in the water sample.

19. A sample of hard water was alkaline to both phenolphthalein and methyl orange alkalinity. 200 mL of water sample on titration with $\frac{N}{50}$ HCl required 9.4 mL of the acid to phenolphthalein end point. When a few drops of methyl orange are added to the same solution and the titration further continued, end point comes after addition of another 21 mL of acid. Elucidate the type and extent of alkalinity present in the water.

(RGPV, Jan., 2012)

20. A water sample contains 500 mg of $CaSO_4$ per litre. Calculate the hardness in terms of $CaCO_3$ equivalents.

21. How many grams of $FeSO_4$ dissolved per litre gives 210.5 ppm of hardness (Fe = 56).

22. 50 cm^3 of acidified $K_2Cr_2O_7$ was mixed with 50 cm^3 of waste water sample and refluxed. 20.4 cm^3 of FAS solution was required by unreacted acidified $K_2Cr_2O_7$ solution. Blank titration was carried out to estimate the amount of $K_2Cr_2O_7$ at the beginning of the reaction. 50 cm^3 of acidified $K_2Cr_2O_7$ required 40.8 cm^3 of the same 0.2 N FAS solution. Determine the COD of the waste water sample.

23. A 100 mL of sample contains 230 ppm of dissolved oxygen. After 5 days the dissolved oxygen value becomes 30 ppm after the sample has been diluted to 500 mL. Calculate the BOD of the sample.

III. MULTIPLE CHOICE QUESTIONS

1. Water is hard due to the presence of

   (*a*) Salts of Ca and Mg (*b*) Salts of Na and K

   (*c*) Salts of iron (*d*) All of the above.

2. Lime-Sods method uses

   (*a*) $Ca(OH)_2$ alone (*b*) Na_2CO_3 alone

   (*c*) Both $Ca(OH)_2$ and Na_2CO_3 (*d*) None of these.

3. Alkalinity in water is due to the presence of:

   (*a*) CO_3^{2-} (*b*) OH^-

   (*c*) HCO_3^- (*d*) All of the above.

4. The purest form of natural water is:

   (*a*) River water (*b*) Sea water

   (*c*) Rain water (*d*) Underground water.

5. A sample of water contains 40 mg of Ca^{2+} per litre. The hardness of the water sample in terms of $CaCO_3$ equivalents is:
(a) 200 mg/L (b) 100 mg/L
(c) 50 mg/L (d) 40 mg/L.

6. The total hardness of water sample is 8.82 mg/L. It's hardness in °Fr will be:
(a) 0.088 °Fr (b) 0.88 °Fr
(c) 0.62 °Fr (d) 0.062 °Fr.

7. EDTA method is used for determining
(a) Temporary hardness (b) Alkalinity
(c) Permanent hardness (d) Both (a) and (c).

8. When phenolphthalein alkalinity, $P = \frac{1}{2} M$, then alkalinity is due to
(a) OH^- (b) CO_3^{2-}
(c) HCO_3^- (d) OH^- and CO_3^{2-}.

9. Permutit is chemically
(a) Sodium silicate (b) Aluminium silicate
(c) Hydrated sodium alumino silicate (d) None of the above.

10. Which of the following causes both alkalinity and hardness in natural water?
(a) $CaCO_3$ (b) $Ca(HCO_3)_2$
(c) $MgCO_3$ (d) All of the above.

11. Process which is not used for desalination.
(a) Electrodialysis (b) Distillation
(c) Lime soda process (d) Reverse Osmosis.

12. Disinfection of water removes
(a) Salts from water (b) Hardness from water
(c) Pathogenic bacteria from water (d) Dissolved oxygen from water.

13. Water can be sterilized by using
(a) O_2 (b) O_3
(c) H_2O_2 (d) KOH.

14. Ultraviolet rays are used in water treatment for
(a) Illumination (b) Sterilization
(c) Sedimentation (d) Coagulation.

15. 1 ppm = ———
(a) 0.01 °Fr (b) 0.1 °Fr
(c) 0.7 °Fr (d) 0.07 °Fr.

16. Zeolite softening process removes both temporary and permanent hardness of water. In this process, the Ca and Mg salts present in water are precipitated as
(a) Insoluble carbonates (b) Insoluble zeolites
(c) Insoluble chlorides (d) Insoluble sulphates.

17. At break point of chlorination
(a) Chlorine is used to oxidise chloramine (b) Residual chlorine is zero
(c) Residual chlorine is maximum (d) Residual chlorine reappears.

18. Foaming is caused by the formation of ________
    (*a*) Acids (*b*) Alcohols
    (*c*) Oils and alkalis (*d*) Ketones.
19. Ion exchange process is also called as
    (*a*) Zeolite process (*b*) Demineralization
    (*c*) Permutit's process (*d*) Lime soda process.
20. Ion exchange process is a clean process due to ________
    (*a*) Sludge formation (*b*) No sludge formation
    (*c*) Little sludge formation (*d*) Formation of other precipitates.
21. Zeolites are complex compounds of ________
    (*a*) Silica and soda (*b*) Aluminium, silica and soda
    (*c*) Lime and soda (*d*) Aluminium and lime.
22. The chemical formula of permutit is
    (*a*) $SiOAl_2\ O_3\ Na_2O$ (*b*) $SiO_2\ Al_2O_3\ Na_2O$
    (*c*) $SiO_2\ Al_2O_3\ NaO$ (*d*) $SiO_3\ .Al_2O_3.Na_2O$.
23. Concentrated sea water is called as
    (*a*) Permeate (*b*) RO water
    (*c*) Brine (*d*) Salt water.
24. BOD is a measure of
    (*a*) Industrial waste passed into water bodies
    (*b*) Extent of pollution with organic matter
    (*c*) Amount of oxygen required by aquatic plants during night
    (*d*) All of the above.
25. ———— is the amount of oxygen required to oxidise both organic and inorganic matter in sewage.
    (*a*) Turbidity (*b*) DO
    (*c*) BOD (*d*) COD.

Answers

III. NUMERICAL PROBLEMS

1. Temporary hardness = 30 mg/L
   Permanent hardness = 120 mg/L
2. Temporary hardness = 65.78 ppm, 6.578 °Fr and 4.605 °Cl
   Permanent hardness = 67.15 ppm, 6.715 °Fr and 4.701 °Cl
   Total hardness = 132.93 ppm, 13.29 °Fr and 9.305 °Cl
3. Lime = 1.762 kg, Soda = 1.728 kg, Temporary hardness = 50 ppm,
   Permanent hardness = 75 ppm
4. Lime = 2.59 kg, Soda = 2.12 kg
5. Lime = 888 kg, Soda = 530 kg
6. Lime = 285.4 kg, Soda = 138.26 kg
7. Lime = 18.06 kg. Soda = 4.24 kg
8. Temporary Hardness = 150 ppm, Permanent Hardness = 450 ppm, Lime = 407 kg, Soda = 477 kg.

9. Lime = 194.74 kg. Total cost of lime required = ₹ 77.91, Soda = 491.75 kg,
Total cost of soda required = ₹ 9835.05

10. 4,000 litres **11.** 32051 litres

12. 15 litre **13.** 641 mg/L

14. Temporary hardness = 400 ppm, Permanent hardness = 400 ppm

15. Total hardness = 1250 ppm

16. HCO_3^{2-} = 50 ppm

17. CO_3^{2-} alkalinity = 100 ppm.

18. P = 2000 ppm, OH^- = 1000 ppm, M = 3000 ppm, CO_3^{2-} = 2000 ppm.

19. P = 47 ppm, CO_3^{2-} = 94 ppm, M = 152 ppm, HCO_3^- = 58 ppm.

20. 367.75 mg/L **21.** 0.3199 g

22. 652.8 mg/L **23.** 1000 ppm.

IV. MULTIPLE CHOICE QUESTIONS

1. (*a*)	**2.** (*c*)	**3.** (*d*)	**4.** (*c*)	**5.** (*b*)	**6.** (*b*)	**7.** (*d*)	**8.** (*c*)	**9.** (*c*)	**10.** (*d*)
11. (*c*)	**12.** (*c*)	**13.** (*b*)	**14.** (*b*)	**15.** (*b*)	**16.** (*b*)	**17.** (*d*)	**18.** (*c*)	**19.** (*b*)	**20.** (*b*)
21. (*c*)	**22.** (*b*)	**23.** (*b*)	**24.** (*b*)	**25.** (*d*)					

Chapter 9 Lubricants

9.1 INTRODUCTION

Whenever a machine works its moving, sliding or rolling parts rub against each other, with the result a friction is developed. Friction cause a lot of wear and tear of the concerned surfaces and hence such parts require replacement at frequent intervals. Furthermore, due to friction large amount of energy are dissipated in the form of heat and thus causes loss in the efficiency of machine. Moreover, the heat produced due to friction heats up and thus causes damage to the moving parts.

However, the above ill effects of frictional resistance can be minimized by applying a thin layer of certain substances called as lubricant in between the moving parts. Thus, lubricant may be defined as a substance which reduces the friction between the two moving or sliding surfaces. The process of applying the lubricant in between the moving or sliding surfaces is called as lubrication.

The surfaces of all materials, no matter how smooth they appear, are not truly smooth on an atomic scale. If we look at the metallic surface on a molecular/atomic scale even the best polished surface has irregularities as shown in Fig. 9.1.

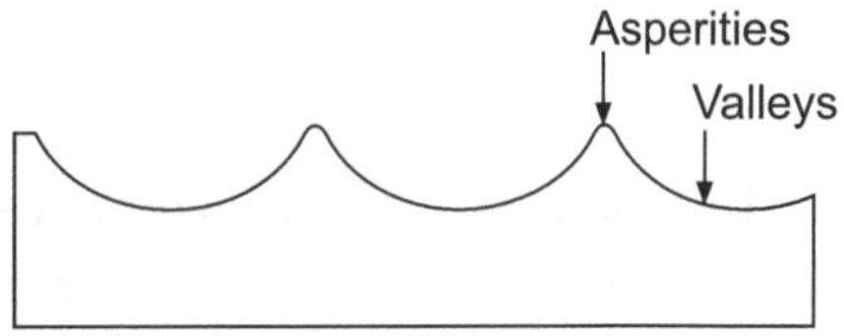

Fig. 9.1. An enlarged look of metallic surface.

When two metallic or any two solid surfaces come in contact with each other, a real contact between them occurs only at certain limited number of asperities and thus the real contact area is always a very small fraction of the apparent contact area is shown in Fig. 9.2. The depth and the height of valleys and asperities differ and hence whenever two surface comes in contact with each other, they bear high local pressure on asperities and cause adhesion.

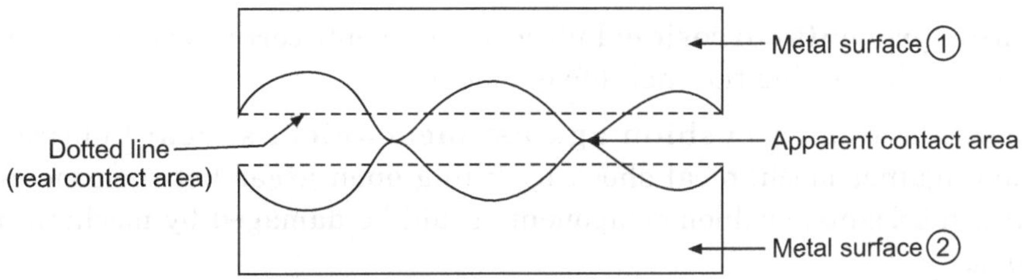

Fig 9.2. Real and apparent contact area when two metals come in contact with each other.

The wear of metal surface actually depends on the nature of metal surfaces which are in contact with each other. Suppose one of the two metal surfaces is hard and the other soft then the asperities of the hard metal will form *indentions* in the softer metal. There are times when the asperities at the surface of two metals weld strongly and nothing happens at the junction of two asperities. The problem arises when two metallic surfaces move over one another and friction becomes operative. This is the case where lies the importance of lubrication.

9.2 FUNCTIONS OF LUBRICANTS

A lubricant performs the following functions:

1. **Lubricant reduces friction:** The primary function of a lubricant is to reduce friction between the moving surfaces by keeping them apart. It also avoids direct contact between the surfaces so that the asperities do not interlock.
2. **Lubricant carry away excess heat and acts as coolant:** Frictional heat is produced in all machines at the point of contact between the rubbing surfaces/parts. When lubricant is applied, it flows over the heated surface where it absorbs the generated heat and acts as a coolant.

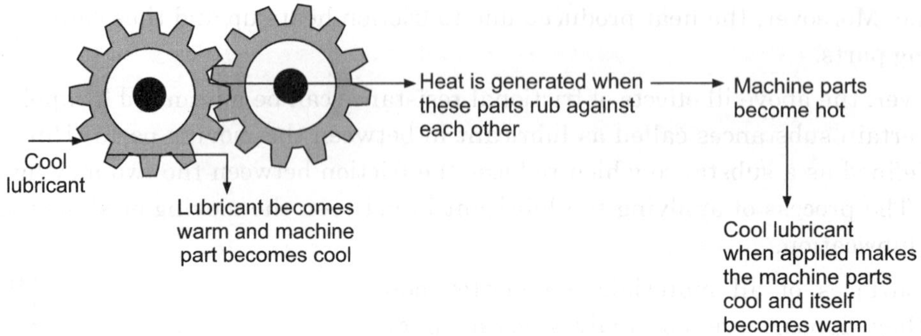

3. **Lubricants reduces wear, tear and surface deformation:** Wear, tear and surface deformations are reduced by preventing direct contact between the moving/rubbing surfaces.
4. **Lubricants keep out dirt and clean surfaces:** Lubricants flush debris from surfaces and carry it away. This can then be filtered out of the lubricant. By carrying away debris, lubricants prevent it from blocking oil passages and damaging parts.
5. **Lubricants acts as a seal:** Fluid lubricants fill open areas between moving surfaces. This provides a seal that prevents foreign matter from passing between moving surfaces. Also, this seal prevents the leakage of gases under high pressure from the cylinder.
6. **Lubricants prevents corrosion:** Lubricants prevents corrosion and rusting of machine parts, thereby increasing the shelf life of machine.
7. **Lubricants acts as a cushion against mechanical shock:** Lubricants provides a cushion against mechanical shock by filling open areas between moving surfaces. Without a lubricants, cushion components could be damaged by mechanical shock and vibrations.
8. Lubricants reduce noise of the machines.

9. **Lubricants improve the efficiency of the machine:** Lubricants reduces the frictional heat therefore it prevents seizure of moving surfaces and expansion of metal. It also reduces wear and tear of the machine parts. Hence, it improves the efficiency of machines.

9.3 LUBRICATION

Lubrication is a technique employed to reduce friction between two relatively sliding/moving surfaces by applying a lubricant between the surfaces to carry or help carry the load between the opposing surfaces. Considering the nature of motion between moving or sliding surfaces, there are three different types of mechanisms by which the lubrication is done. These are:

1. Fluid film/thick film/hydrodynamic lubrication
2. Thin film/boundary lubrication
3. Extreme pressure lubrication.

Fluid Film/Thick Film/Hydrodynamic Lubrication

This type of lubrication is said to exist when the moving surfaces are separated by the pressure of a continuous unbroken film or a layer of lubricant. The layer of lubricant should be around ~1000 Å thick so that it prevents direct surface to surface contact in a way that small peaks and valleys do not interlock. Since, the lubricant layer or film comes in contact with the moving surface, it offers resistance to motion due to its viscosity. Thus, the viscosity of the liquid lubricant should be sufficient to maintain the lubricant layer/fluid film in its place.

Fluid film or hydrodynamic lubrication is the term given when a shaft rotating in a bearing is supported by a layer or wedge of oil so that the shaft is not in contact with the bearing material. Consider a steady load *F*, a foxed bearing and a rotating journal. There are three stages in its mechanism:

Stage I: At rest, the bearing clearance space is filled with lubricants, but the load F has squeezed out the oil film at the bottom. (Fig. 9.3)

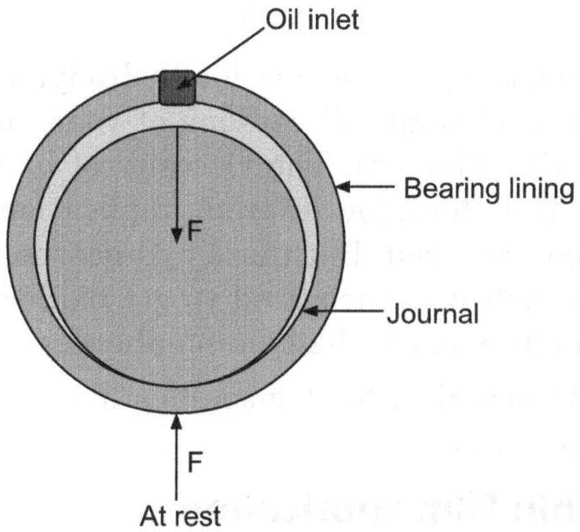

Fig. 9.3

Stage II: When the journal starts rotating slowly in clockwise direction, the journal starts to climb the wall of the bearing surface due to friction. (Fig. 9.4)

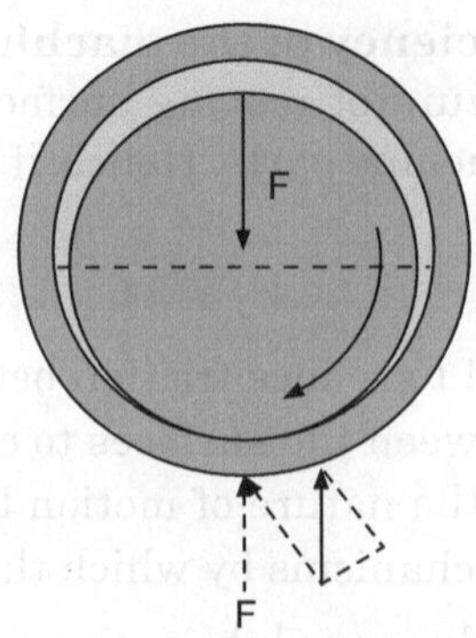

Fig. 9.4

The wear generally take place during this stage. However, the journal rotation draws the lubricant/oil between the surfaces and they separate. Boundary lubrication operates here.

Stage III: As the speed of the journal increase, more oil/lubricant is drawn in and enough pressure is builds up in the contact zone to float the journal. (Fig. 9.5).

As the speed of journal increases further, the additional pressure of the converging oil flow to the right of the minimum film thickness position moves the shaft little to the left of center. As a result, complete separation of bearing and journal surface occurs which reduces the friction between the surfaces.

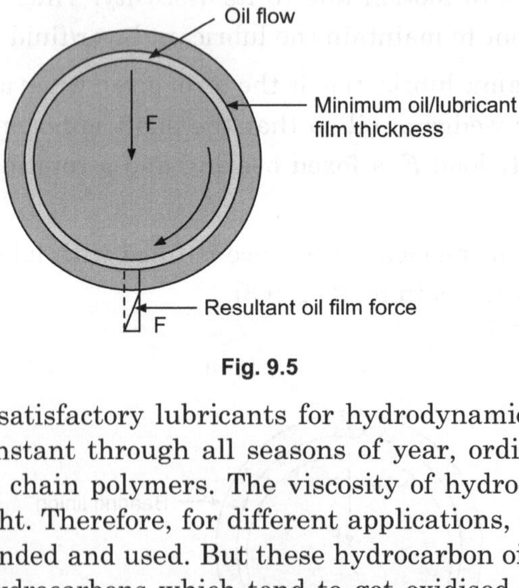

Fig. 9.5

Hydrocarbon oils are satisfactory lubricants for hydrodynamic lubrication. To maintain the viscosity of the oil constant through all seasons of year, ordinary hydrocarbon oils are blended with certain long chain polymers. The viscosity of hydrocarbon oils increases with increasing molecular weight. Therefore, for different applications, appropriate fractions from petroleum refining are blended and used. But these hydrocarbon oil fractions contain a small amount of unsaturated hydrocarbons which tend to get oxidised forming gummy products. Hence, they are blended with antioxidants like amino-phenols.

Such type of lubrication is useful in light machines like sewing machine, watches, fans, delicate and scientific instruments etc.

Boundary Lubrication/Thin Film Lubrication

When the load is high and/or the speed is low, the hydrodyanamic pressure may not be sufficient to fully support the load and the surfaces come into contact. Hence, a thin layer of lubricant, consisting of one or two molecular layers (20–30 Å) is absorbed on the surface of metal which avoid metal to metal contact. The adsorption of lubricant on the metal surface occurs due to physical or chemical forces or both. In some cases, the lubricant may chemically react with the metal surface leading to formation of a thin film of metal soap which acts as a lubricant. In boundary lubrication, the lubrication film is too thin to provide total surface separation. Therefore, under boundary lubrication conditions, interaction between the metallic surfaces takes place in the form of asperities colliding with each other. These collisions produce a number of consequences at the asperity level, *i.e.* from elastic deformation to plastic deformation to fracture. These collision leads to friction, heat and some times wear. Chemical reactions between lubricant and metal surface usually accompany such collisions producing organic and inorganic films. Some fims provides protection against wear, some are benign and some films are detrimental.

Boundary lubrication is undesirable as the metal surfaces are not fully separated and leads to increased friction, wear and tear, material damage etc. However, it is inevitable during the operating life of a machine usually when

- a shaft moves from its resting position
- the load is very high
- the speed is very slow
- lubricant/oil has low viscosity.

For boundary lubrication, the lubricant molecule should have following properties:

- Good oiliness (oiliness is the property of an oil by virtue of which it sticks to the surface of machine parts even at high temperature and heavy loads).
- Long hydrocarbon chains and the lateral attraction between the chains.
- They should have active polar or functional groups to promote spreading and to form the linkage with the metallic surface at high pressure.
- Resistance to heat and oxidation
- Low cloud and pour point

Lubricants used for boundary lubrication are:

- Vegetable oils, animal oils and their soaps posses good oiliness property. They also posses great property of adsorption at the metal surface, forming a thin film of metallic soap which acts as lubricants. For example oleic acid, stearic acid etc.
- Graphite and molybdenum disulphide (MoS_2) either as solid or stable emulsion in oil are used for boundary lubrication. These substances form a thin film on the metallic surfaces which reduces the friction and can bear high temperature as well as compression.

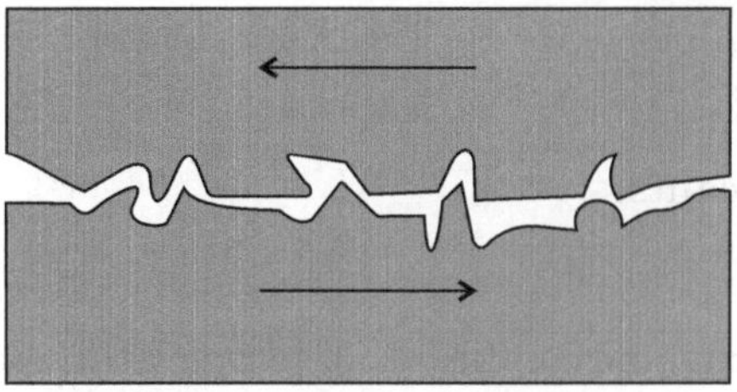

Fig. 9.6. Boundary lubrication.

Applications of boundary lubrication:

- Railway track joints
- Hydraulic pumps

- Aircraft landing gears
- Door hinge joints
- Tractors

Extreme Pressure Lubrication

If the moving surfaces are subjected to very high pressure and speed, a large amount of heat is produced and temperature becomes very high. At high temperature, the commonly used liquid lubricants decompose or even vapourises and fails to stick over the metallic surface. In order to provide effective lubrication under these conditions, special additives called "extreme pressure additives" are used alongwith the lubricants.

The extreme pressure additives are the organic compounds possessing the active functional groups such as sulphur, phosphorus, chlorine etc. At high temperature, these additive react with metal surface forming durable films of sulphates, phosphates and chlorides thereby reducing the friction. These films have a relatively low shear strength so that rubbing between the interacting surfaces occur in the additive film and thus protects the underlying metal from damage. The melting points of the extreme pressure layers are very high so that they remain attached to the metal surface even under conditions of high temperature and pressure. Further, these extreme pressure lubricants have an additional advantage that if the low shear strength films formed on moving parts are broken by the rubbing action, they are immediately replenished.

Applications where extreme pressure additives are used:

- Wire drawing of titanium (it requires chlorine containing additive).
- In "cutting fluids" in machining of tough metals.
- In hypoid gears used in rear axle drive of cars.
- Aircrafts, spacecrafts etc.

9.4 CLASSIFICATION OF LUBRICANTS

According to the physical state of lubricants, they are mainly classified into three types:

1. Solid lubricants
2. Semi-solid lubricants
3. Liquid lubricants.

Other than these three classes, lubricants can be

1. Synthetic lubricants
2. Lubricating emulsions
3. Biodegradable lubricants.

9.4.1 Solid Lubricants

Solid lubricants are used in extreme conditions of temperature, load, vacuum etc. where liquid and semi-solid lubricants do not work satisfactorily. For example, at low temperature if liquid lubricants (*e.g.* oils) and semi solid lubricants (*e.g.* greases) are used, they gets solidified and thus moving parts of machine are jammed and at very high temperature, oxidation of oil occurs and volatile components evaporate. Similarly, under conditions of high vacuum, the oil lubricant evaporates.

Solid lubricants are used either in dry powder form or mixed with oil or water. Sometimes they are combined with binders (*e.g.* phenolics, epoxy, polyamide resins, fused ceramics etc.) so that they can stay at the target surface.

Most commonly employed solid lubricants are graphite and molybdenum disulphide. Others are talc, mica, boron nitride $(BN)_x$, polytetrafluoroethylene, wax, tungsten disulphide WS_2, $CdCl_2$, borax, ZnO, CaF_2 etc.

Graphite: Graphite consist of a stack of carbon atom sheets each sheet having a hexagonal arrangement of atoms (Fig. 9.7). Each carbon atom within a sheet is sp^2 hybridised and forms strong bonds to three other carbons atoms. However, the stacked sheets are held together by weak van der Waal's forces of interaction due to which the sheets has a tendency to readily slide over each other and imports lubricating property to graphite.

Graphite is soapy to touch, non-inflammable and not oxidised in air below 375°C. It is used either in powdered form or as suspension. Suspension of graphite when dispersed in oil is called as **"Oildag"** and when it is dispersed in water, it is called as **"Aquadag"**. Oildag finds application in internal combustion engine as it gives a tight fit contact by forming a film between the cylinder and the piston rings thereby increasing compression. On the other hand aquadag is used where an oil free lubricants is required, *e.g.* foodstuff industry. Graphite when mixed with greases is used at high temperatures.

Graphite is used as a lubricant in food stuff industry, general machine shop works, open gears, chains, railway track joints, cast iron bearings, air compressors etc.

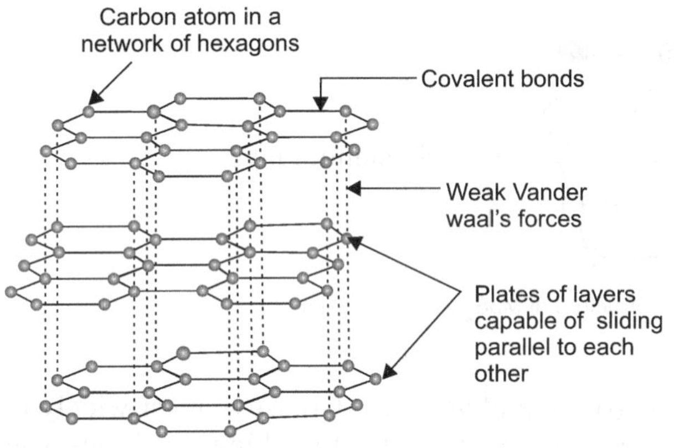

Fig. 9.7. Structure of graphite

Graphite acts as good lubricant on the surface of moon. Why?

The temperature on the moon is 110°C and – 150°C during day and night respectively. Oils and greases are not able to withstand such temperature changes but graphite is unaffected within this temperature range. Hence, it acts as a good lubricants on the surface of moon.

Molybdenum disulphide: Molybdenum disulphide has a sandwich like structure in which hexagonal molybdenum planes are sandwiched between two sulphur planes. The atoms in each plane are strongly covalently bonded to each other whereas the different planes are bonded by weak van der waal's interactions. The layered structure allows sliding movement of the parallel planes. Weak bonding between the different planes provides low shear strength in the direction of the sliding movement but high compression strength in the direction perpendicular to the sliding movement. This imparts the combination of low coefficient of friction and high load carrying capacity to molybdenum disulphide.

The sulphur layers of the MoS_2 have an affinity for tight adherence to the metal atoms, therefore a strong film is formed on the metal surfaces. The lubrication film provides good wear resistance and seizure resistance.

In contrast to graphite, moist atmosphere is not required for MoS_2. Hence, it shows low friction in dry atmosphere and in vacuum where its coefficient of friction is even lower than in the presence of moisture.

Application of Molybdenum disulphide in open air at elevated temperatures is limited up to around 400°C. Higher temperatures cause oxidation of MoS_2 to MoO_3 and SO_2. The oxides attract moisture resulting in increase coefficient of friction.

MoS_2 is an excellent lubricant in vacuum, therefore it is used in space vehicles. For space vehicles 70% MoS_2 + 7% graphite bonded with 23% silicates is used as a lubricant as it can withstand extreme temperatures, low pressures and nuclear radiations.

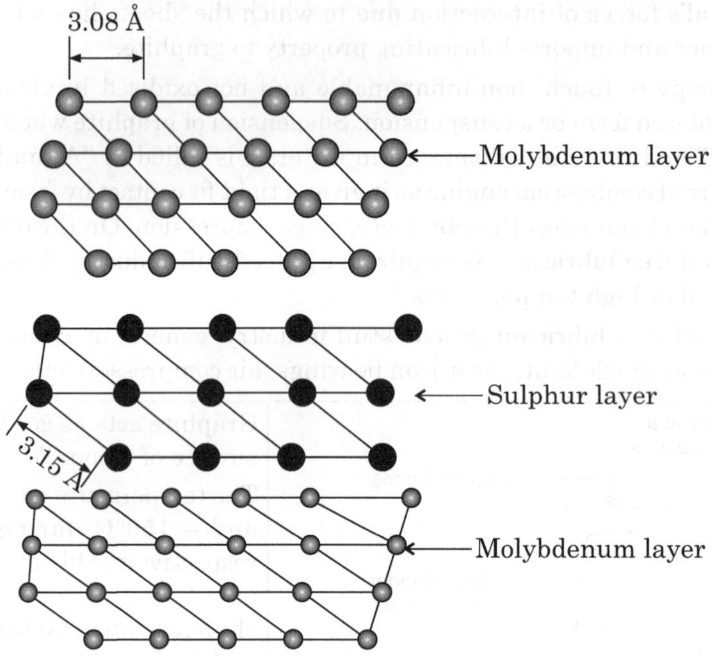

Fig. 9.8. Structure of MoS_2.

9.4.2 Semi-solid Lubricants

The most common semi-solid lubricants are grease and vaseline. Grease is most widely used semi-solid lubricant. Semi-solid lubricants or greases are used under working conditions where-

(*a*) Oil cannot remain in place due to high load, low speed intermittent operation of machine parts, sudden jerks etc. In such cases greases can be used due to higher frictional resistance than oils. Example: rail axle boxes.

(*b*) Dripping of oil is undesirable, Grease are semi solid and if used, do not splash or drip over articles being prepared by the machine. Example: machines used in textile mills, food industry, paper industry etc.

(*c*) Bearing has to be sealed against entry of dirt, water and grit and grease are less liable to contaminate by these particles.

(*d*) Bearing and gears work at high temperatures.

Grease is a dispersion of soap in a liquid lubricating oil (*e.g.* mineral oil, synthetic oil or blended oil). To improve the heat resistance property of grease, certain inorganic thickening agents are added such as finely divided clay, colloidal silica, carbon black, bentonite etc.

Preparation of Greases

Greases are prepared by the saponification of fat with a metal base and adding hot lubricating oil with constant stirring of a mixture under controlled temperature conditions. The metal bases commonly used are hydroxides of sodium, lithium, calcium, aluminium and named as corresponding grease, like soda based grease, lithium grease, calcium grease etc. The physical properties of the grease depend primarily on the metal base used in its preparation. The nature of soap decides the consistency of soap and to improve heat resistance, thickening agents are used.

Table 9.1: Types of Greases

	Types of Grease	Chemical Composition	Properties and Uses
1.	Sodium-Soap grease [Soda-based grease]	Sodium soap as thickening agent in petroleum oils.	Sodium soap content is soluble in water therefore, these grease are not water resistance. They can be used upto 175°C and are suitable for use in high temperature lubrication in ball bearings.
2.	Calcium soap grease [Cheapest and Most commonly used]	Calcium soap as thickening agent in petroleum oils.	Water resistance and can be used upto 80°C as above this temperature oil and soap separates. Used for lubricating water pumps, tractors, caterpillar treads etc.
3.	Lithium based greases [most expensive grease]	Lithium soap as thickening agent in petroleum oils.	Water and heat resistant. They have high mechanical and oxidation stability. Used for aircraft lubrication at extreme heights and low temperature (– 55°C).
4.	Axle grease (Resin grease) [very cheap]	Lime added to resin and fatty oils. Talc and mica are added as fillers.	Water resistant and used for less delicate instruments under high load and low speed.
5.	Non-soap greases	Non-soap thickeners such as carbon black, silica gel, organic dyes etc. added to mineral oils.	Used in tredmills, laser printers, computer equipments, rail axle boxes, machine bearings, tractors, rolling equipment etc.

Drop point: Drop point of a grease is defined as the temperature at which the grease passes from semi-solid state to the liquid state. It determines the upper temperature limit of the applicability of the grease.

9.4.3 Lubricating Oils/Liquid Lubricants

These lubricants exist in liquid form and are used to reduce friction or wear between two sliding metallic surfaces by providing a uniform film between them. They are widely used in several machine tools. They are of following three types:

(*i*) Animal and Vegetable oils

(*ii*) Mineral oils or Petroleum oils

(*iii*) Blended oils

Animal and Vegetable oils

Animal and vegetable oils are very important and are extracted from animal and vegetable matter containing glycerides of higher fatty acids. Before the advent of the petroleum industry, oils of animal and vegetable origin were the most commonly used lubricants.

These lubricants posses good oiliness (a property of lubricant by virtue of which the oil sticks to the surface of machine parts even under the conditions of high temperature and heavy loads) and viscosity properties.

Commonly used animal oils-Lard oil, neats foot oil, sperm oil, whale oil, seal oil etc.

Commonly used vegetable oils-castar oil, palm oil, mustard oil, olive oil etc.

These oils have very limited use at present because

- They are very costly
- They have less resistance to oxidation and on oxidation they form gummy and acidic products.
- They gets hydrolysed in aqueous medium or moist air.

Therefore, the properties of these lubricants may be improved by adding certain chemicals. They are actually used as blending agents for mineral oils to improve the properties of later.

Mineral Oils or Petroleum Oils

These oils are obtained by fractional distillation of crude petroleum. Fractional distillation of crude petroleum produces three fractions of oils *i.e.* light, medium and heavy oils. But these oils can not be used as such as lubricants because of the presence of wax, asphalt, coloured substances and other oxidisable impurities and hence they need to be purified before use:

(*a*) The wax, if not removed, raises the pour points and renders the lubricating oil unfit for use at low temperatures. Wax can be removed by chilling the oil fraction.

(*b*) The asphaltic material if present tends to leave carbonaceous deposits on the engine parts and can be removed by solvent extraction, Solvents used for this purpose are phenol, o-cresol, nitrobenzene, furfural, dichloroethyl ether etc.

(*c*) The coloured matter can be removed by filtration through fuller's earth or activated clay

(*d*) Certain constituents get easily oxidised under working conditions and cause sludge formation.

These mineral oils are basically lower molecular weight hydrocarbons with 12–50 carbon atoms. Their viscosity increases as the length of the hydrocarbon chain increases. Although they have poor oiliness yet they are widely used as lubricants because they are: (*i*) cheap, (*ii*) available in abundance and (*iii*) quite stable under operating conditions. Their oiliness can be increased by adding high molecular weight compounds like oaleic acid, stearic acid to the petroleum oils.

Blended Oils

No single oil serves as the most ideal lubricant for many of the modern machineries. Certain specific additives can be added to petroleum oil to improve their properties. The oil thus obtained are called as blended oils or compounded oils. The various additives used are as follows:

(*i*) Surface Protective Additives

These additives when added to petroleum oil improves their ability to protect the metal surface from damage. Table 9.2 lists surface protective additives and their functions.

Table 9.2: Surface protective additives and their functions

S.No.	Additives	Chemicals used	Function
1.	Corrosion/rust inhibitor	Organometallic compounds, Zinc dithiophosphates, sulphurized terpenes, phosphoric terpenes, amine phosphates etc.	Forms a strong durable film on the metal surface therefore, prevents rusting and corrosion of metal parts in contact with the lubricant.

2.	Anti-wear additives	Zinc dialkyl dithio-phosphate, tricresyl phosphate, alkyl earth phenolates	Reduce friction and wear [Prevent metal to metal contact by chemical reaction with metal surface to form a film with less shear strength than the metal.]
3.	Detergents and Deflocculents	Calcium and barium salts of phosphates and sulphonates	Neutralize the sludge and varnish precursors and keep them soluble thereby keeping the surface deposit free.
4.	Dispersants	Alkyl succinimides, polymeric alkyl thio phosphonates, high molecular weight amine and amide polymers etc.	They prevent or retard sludge formation and deposition
5.	Extreme pressure additives	Sulphurized fats, phosphorus compounds, chlorinated hydrocarbons etc	They either gets adsorbed on the surface of metal or react chemically with the metal forming a surface layer of low shear strength which prevents tearing up of the metals.

(*ii*) Lubricant Protective Additives

These additive when added to lubricants protect them from oxidation, foam formation etc. Table 9.3 lists various lubricant protective additives and their functions.

Table 9.3: Lubricant Protective Additives and their Functions

S.No	Additives	Chemicals used	Functions
1.	Antioxidant	Aromatic phenolic or amino compounds.	They retard the oxidation of lubricating oil by getting themselves preferentially oxidised.
2.	Antifoaming agents	Silicon polymers, oil insoluble liquids like glycerol, glycol etc	They prevent formation of stable foam.
3.	Metal deactivators	Sulphides, amines, triaryl phosphites etc.	They stop the catalytic effect of metals on oxidation and corrosion.

(*iii*) Performance Additives

There are certain additives which when added of the lubricants improves their properties like viscosity oiliness, pour point etc., are called as performance additives. Table 9.4 lists various performance additives and their functions.

Table 9.4: Performance additives and their Functions

S.No.	Additives	Chemicals used	Functions
1.	Oiliness carriers	Vegetable oils (*e.g.* mustard oil, castor oil etc.) and fatty acids (stearic acid, palmitic acid etc.)	They increase the strength of the oil film and prevent the rupture of the oil film.
2.	Pour point depressants	Alkylated naphthalenes, phenolic polymers, polymethacrylates.	These reduce the pour point of lubricants and inhibit the lubricant for becoming solid.
3.	Viscosity index improvers	Hexanol, polymers like polystyrene, polyesters, polyisobutylene etc	These reduces the rate of change of viscosity with temperature.
4.	Emulsifiers	Sodium salts of sulphonic acid, sodium salts of organic acids, fatty amine salts, monoesters of polyhydric alcohols.	They help in formation of emulsions of lubricating oils with water and make mineral oils miscible in water.

9.4.4 Synthetic Lubricants

Mineral oil lubricants are widely used lubricants due to their easy availability, low cost and desirable viscosity-temperature characteristics. However, under various extreme conditions like high speed machinery, wide variations in temperature conditions, heavy load, fire risks, conventional mineral oils cannot be employed as they tend to get oxidized at higher temperatures whereas at low temperatures wax separation takes place. Thus, to meet these extreme conditions, synthetic lubricants came into existence. Synthetic lubricants are engineered products which are synthesized by chemical reactions.

The commonly used synthetic lubricants are:

(*i*) **Dibasic acid esters:** Diesters of the the type ROOC—$(CH_2)_n$—COOR are derived from adipic acid (n = 4) and sebacic acid (n = 8) esterified with C_8 or C_9 branched alcohols such as iso-octyl alcohols, 2-ethyl hexanol etc. These lubricants perform satisfactory in the temperature range of – 50°C to 230°C. They have low pour point, high flash point, low volatility, high viscosity index, non-corrosive, non-toxic and stable to hydrolysis. They are used in jet engines and military equipments.

(*ii*) **Phosphate esters:** Phosphate esters of the type $PO(OR)_3$ (where R can be alkyl, aryl or any other group) are fire resistant. They are used as hydraulic fluids.

(*iii*) **Silicones:** The general structure of silicone oil is:

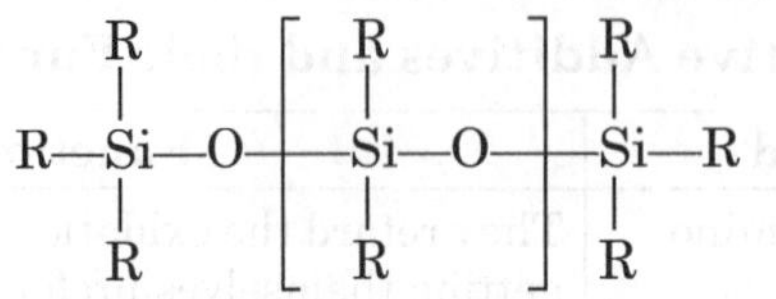

R = methyl or phenyl group

They are excellent synthetic lubricants as they do not oxidise below 200°C and posses high viscosity index. Silicones are prone to oxidation at high temperature forming gels, therefore they are used for low temperature lubrication purpose. For example; moisture repellent dielectric lubricants for clocks, timers and other electronic devices.

(*iv*) **Chlorofluoro hydrocarbons:** Fluorocarbons are extensively used these days as lubricants for machines that handle reactive elements and compounds due to their good thermal stability, hydrolytic stability and fire resistance. For example, they are used in equipments for manufacturing and handling liquid oxygen and hydrogen peroxide. They have general structure

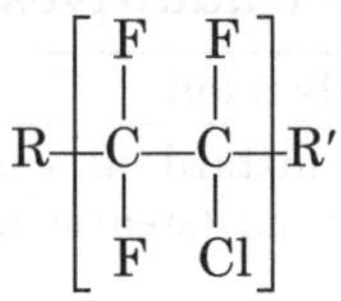

The presence of fluorine in these compounds make them highly resistant to acids, alkalies and oxidising compounds.

(*v*) **Polyglycols and related compounds:** Lubricants used under this categories are:

(*a*) polyethylene glycol

(*b*) polypropylene glycol and its derivatives

(*c*) higher polyalkylene oxides

(*d*) polyglycidyl ethers.

Polyethylene and polypropylene glycols are water soluble. So, water diluted lubricants can be prepared from these for use in rubber bearings and joints. The basic advantage with these lubricants is that they can be easily removed from metal surface by flushing with water. Also, they are thermally stable, posses high shear resistance, high viscosity index and free from corrosive action. Higher polyalkylene oxides and polyglycidyl ethers are water insoluble but adsorb lot of water. Their viscosity is not affected by temperature. They decompose into volatile parts under high temperature and oxidation of these volatile parts take place. They are used in roller bearing of sheet glass machinery.

(*vi*) **Amines, Imines and amides:** Organic amines, imines and amides have high viscosity index and low pour point.

9.4.5 Lubricating Emulsions

An emulsion is a two phase system which consist of fairly coarse dispersion of two immiscible liquids, the one being dispersed as fine droplets in the other. The liquid that is broken into droplets is the disperse phase and the surrounding liquid forms the dispersing medium. The size of dispersed droplets is very fine and varies in the range 1–6 μm.

An emulsion is usually unstable, however its stability can be increased by adding certain agents called as **emulsifying agents or emulsifiers** such as sodium palmitate ($C_{15}H_{31}COONa$). Emulsifiers have a long hydrocarbon chain (non-polar end) and a polar end. The hydrocarbon end is hydrophobic in nature whereas polar end is hydrophilic. The hydrophobic end is liked by oil while hydrophilic end is linked by water. Because of adsorption of these emulsifiers at the interface of two immiscible liquids, a protective film is formed around the dispersed phase and the emulsion become stable.

Generally two type of emulsions are recognised depending on the percentage of oil in an emulsion:

(*i*) **Oil in water emulsion (Aqueous emulsions):** When the percentage of oil is less than 26%. These emulsions are obtained by adding 3–20% water soluble emulsifiers (*e.g.*, sodium soap and sodium and potassium salts of sulphonic acids) to a suitable amount of water. Such emulsions are used as cooling as well as lubricating liquid for cutting tools. They are also used in heavy sliding components of various machine parts such as piston of diesel engines. Such emulsions also behaves as rust protecting agents.

(*ii*) **Water in oil emulsion:** When the percentage of oil is more than 74%. These emulsions are prepared by mixing water containing about 1–10% water soluble emulsifiers (*e.g.* calcium stearate) with oil. Such emulsions have high viscosity as compared to oil from which they are formed and that of oil in water emulsion. These emulsions are very useful as compressor and pneumatic tool lubricant as they provide internal cooling effect due to the evaporation of water.

9.4.6 Biolubricants or Biodegradable Lubricants

They are usually considered to be lubricants that have high biodegradability and low human and environmental toxicity. Biodegradable lubricants can be made from plant oils such as soyabean, sunflower, rapseed, palm oil, coconut oil, wax esters and plant polymeric carbohydrates like starch, cellulose, chitosan etc. Biodegradable lubricants offers various advantages as well as certain disadvantages.

Advantages of Biolubricants

- They are less toxic to the environment.
- They posses good oiliness, high viscosity index and can be used under high pressure conditions.
- They posses high flash and fire point therefore can be used under conditions of high temperature.
- They posses good vapourisation stability.
- They can be used for environmental protection *e.g.* aquatic, mountain, agricultural and forest environments.

Disadvantages of Biolubricants

- Generally biolubricants posses high pour point and low oxidation stability hence, they are not suitable for use at low temperatures and high oxidative environment.
- In some cases, biolubricants alone cannot serve as good lubricants so certain additives are mixed with them. The mixed additives are either not completely biodegradable or not biodegradable at all and reduces the overall degradability of the lubricants. In addition to this, the additives also increase the overall toxicity of the environment.

In times to come, because of new developments, more stable oil seed will be developed which will offer many benefits in prices, application and in the safety concern for the environment.

9.5 PROPERTIES OF LUBRICATING OIL

A lubricant is a substance introduced between two moving surfaces to reduce the friction between them. Therefore, the properties of a lubricant needs to be well understood so that we can select best lubricant for desired end use. Some of the important properties of lubricants normally tested are:

(*i*) Viscosity
(*ii*) Viscosity index
(*iii*) Flash and fire point
(*iv*) Cloud and pour point
(*v*) Aniline point
(*vi*) Steam emulsion number
(*vii*) Saponification number
(*viii*) Carbon residue
(*ix*) Neutralization number.

9.5.1 Viscosity

Viscosity is the most important property determining the behaviour of lubricants. It is a property of liquid by virtue of which it offers resistance to its own flow. A liquid contains a number of layers, each upper layer moves with higher velocity in comparison with the lower layer. This is due to internal force of cohesion between the molecules of liquid. Consider two layers of liquid separated by a distance '*d*' and moving with a relative velocity 'v' then, the force required to maintain the velocity difference between the two layers is given by

$$F = \eta \frac{v}{d}$$

Where η is a constant of liquid, called the coefficient of velocity. If $v = 1$ cm/sec and $d = 1$ cm, then

$$F = \eta$$

So, coefficient of viscosity is the force per unit area, required to maintain a unit velocity gradient, between two parallel layers of a liquid.

The unit of η is "Poise" or "centipoise" but a more common practical measure of the viscosity of an oil is the "time" required in seconds for a given quantity of an oil to flow through a standard orifice under the specified set of conditions. Thus, viscosities are generally determined with Redwood Viscosities in commonwealth countries, Engler's viscometer in Europe and Saybolt's viscometer and kinematic viscometer in USA. In these commercial viscometers, a fixed volume of the liquid is allowed to flow through the standard orifice of the apparatus used. It is also necessary to mention the temperature used for measuring viscosity.

Different instruments used to measure the viscosity of a lubricating oil are:

1. Redwood Viscometer No. 1
2. Redwood Viscometer No. 2] generally used in common wealth countries
3. Saybolt's Viscometer
4. Kinematic Viscometer] generally used in USA
5. Engler's Viscometer - Europe

Determination of viscosity by Redwood Viscometer: The apparatus used is shown in fig. 1.

The flask used for receiving oil is called as Kohlrausch flask. The oil is filled into the oil cup till the tip of the pointer taking care to close the orifice with the brass value. The oil is heated. When the oil reaches the required temperature, the valve is removed and the time taken for the flow of 50 ml of the oil sample is noted. This gives the redwood viscosity in seconds at the test temperature.

Redwood viscometer are of two types:

(*i*) Redwood viscometer No. 1 Generally used for low viscous oils.

(*ii*) Redwood viscometer No. 2 Used for high viscous oils.

The various differences between the two instruments are given in Table 9.5.

Table 9.5: Difference between Viscometer 1 and 2

Redwood Viscometer No. 1	Redwood Viscometer No. 1
Used for fluids having low viscosity *i.e.* corresponds to Redwood seconds less than 2000. For *e.g.* kerosene oil, mustard oil etc.	Used for fluids having high viscosity *i.e.* corresponds to Redwood seconds greater than 2000. For *e.g.* fuel oil, mobil oil etc.
The mouth of Kohlrausch flask is small.	The mouth of Kohrausch flask is wide.
Dimensions of orifice: Length = 10 mm Diameter = 1.62 mm	Dimensions of Orifice Length = 50 mm Diameter = 3.8 mm.

Fig. 9.8. Redwood Viscometer

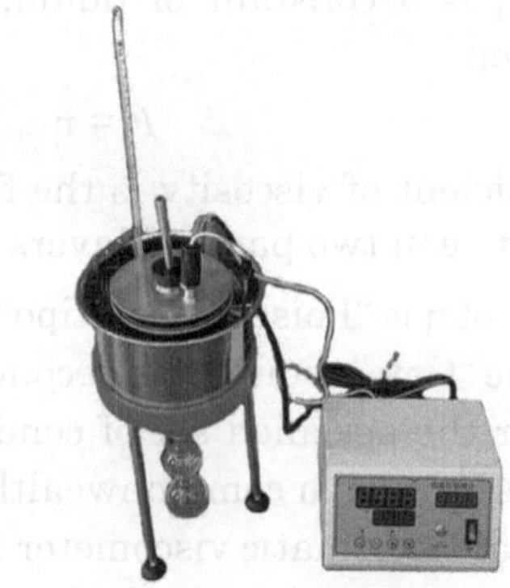

Fig. 9.9. Engler's Viscometer

Significance of Viscosity

Viscosity is the most important characteristic of an oil as it is directly related to its load carrying capacity. The greater an oil's viscosity, the greater the load it can withstand. The viscosity of an oil must be adequate to separate moving parts under normal operating conditions.

If the oil is light (i.e. having low viscosity).

- Metal to metal contact increases (friction and wear)
- Poor sealing
- Increased oil consumption, to maintain operating conditions

If the oil is too heavy (i.e. having very high viscosity).

- Increased fluid friction
- Reduced energy efficiency
- higher operating temperatures
- hard starting particularly at cold temperatures

Thus, the key is to select on oil that is not too light and not too heavy.

Viscosity-Temperature Relation: Viscosity of a lubricating oil is inversely proportional to the temperature *i.e.*, viscosity of oils decrease with increase in temperature. As the temperature increases, the free volume available for the molecules to move about also increases therefore, viscosity decreases. For a good lubricating oil, viscosity should not change much with temperature.

9.5.2 Viscosity Index

Viscosity index is an arbitrary scale for lubricating oils that indicates the extent of variation in viscosity with variation of temperature. If the viscosity of an oil falls rapidly with small increase in temperature, the oil is said to have *Low viscosity index.* (*e.g.* Naphthenic oils). *High viscosity index* oils on the other hand are those whose viscosity does not change appreciably with moderate change in temperature (*e.g.* paraffinic oils).

Hence, it is always necessary to mention the temperature at which the viscosity is measured.

Determination of viscosity index: For the determination of viscosity index of an experimental oil, the viscosities of testing oil at 100°F and 210°F are first determined. For a good oil, the difference between the two values should be minimum. If the difference is high, then the oil has poor viscosity. The difference is generally compared with two standard oils, one with the highest viscosity index (*VI* = 100) and another with the lowest viscosity index (*VI* = zero). Paraffinic-base Pennsylvanian oils (also called high viscosity Index Standard or *H* oils) have highest viscosity index (*VI* = 100) whereas naphthenic base Gulf oils (also called Low viscosity Index standard or *L* oils) have lowest viscosity index (*VI* = Zero), their viscosities at 100°F and 200°F are marked. Now, from the list of *H*-oils, we choose the oil which has the same viscosity at 210°F as the experimental oil (*i.e.* oil under test) and its corresponding viscosity at 100°F is noted. It is represented by *H*. Likewise, from the list of *L*-oils, we choose the one which has the same viscosity at 210°F as the experimental oil and its corresponding viscosity at 100°F is noted. It is represented by *L*. Now, the viscosity index may be calculated as:

$$VI = \frac{L-U}{L-H} \times 100$$

VI is the viscosity index of the experimental oil.

L = Viscosity of the low-viscosity reference oil (at 100°F) and also having the same viscosity at 210°F as the experimental oil.

H = Viscosity of the high viscosity reference oil (at 100°F) and also having the same viscosity at 210°F as the experimental oil.

U = Viscosity of the experimental oil at 100°C.

The change of viscosity of a liquid with temperature can be seen by plotting a graph between viscosity and temperature. (Fig. 9.10)

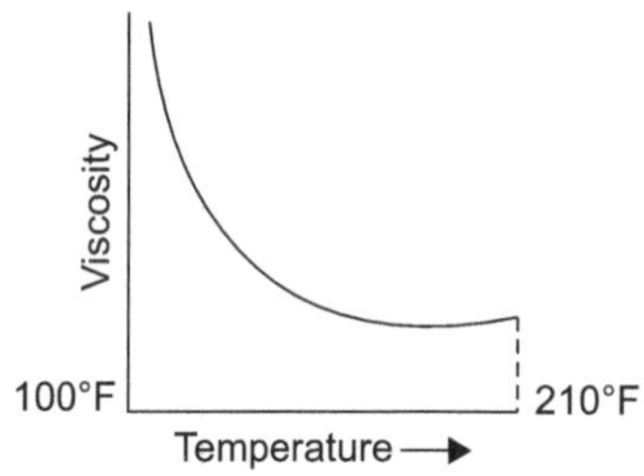

Fig. 9.10. Viscosity Temperature curve

In case of automotive lubricants, an oils having a high viscosity index resists excessive thickening when the engine is cold and, consequently, promotes rapid starting and prompt circulation. Therefore, it also resists excessive thinning when the motor is hot and thus provides full lubrication, prevents excessive oil consumption and retain its properties over a long period.

Consider the case of military aircrafts, where the hydraulic control system may be exposed to temperature ranging from below –65°F at high attitudes to over 100°F on the ground. For the proper operation of the hydraulic control system, the hydraulic fluid must have a sufficiently high viscosity index to perform its functions at the extremes of the expected temperature range.

Thus, in various industries, the lubricating oils of high viscosity index are preferred as they can be used continuously under varying conditions of temperature without undergoing any appreciable change in their viscosity.

9.5.3 Flash and Fire Point

During use, lubricants are also be subjected to high temperatures and at high temperatures, they have a tendency to volatilize and cause loss of lubricant. A good lubricant is one that does not volatilize under the working temperatures. If, however, they volatilize, the vapours formed should not catch fire under the working conditions. Therefore, a good lubricant should form inflammable vapours only at a temperature which is higher than the working temperature of the lubricant.

Flash point of an oil is the minimum temperature at which the lubricating oil gives off enough vapours which when mixes with air or oxygen forms an ignition mixture which ignite for a moment when a small flame is brought in contact with it.

Fire point of an oil is the minimum temperature at which the vapours of the lubricating oil burn continuously for at least 5 seconds, when a tiny flame is brought near it. Usually, it has been observed that the fire points are 5 to 40°C higher than the flash points.

The flash and fire points are generally determined by the following apparatus:

(*a*) Pensky Marten's apparatus: It is a ***closed cup apparatus.***

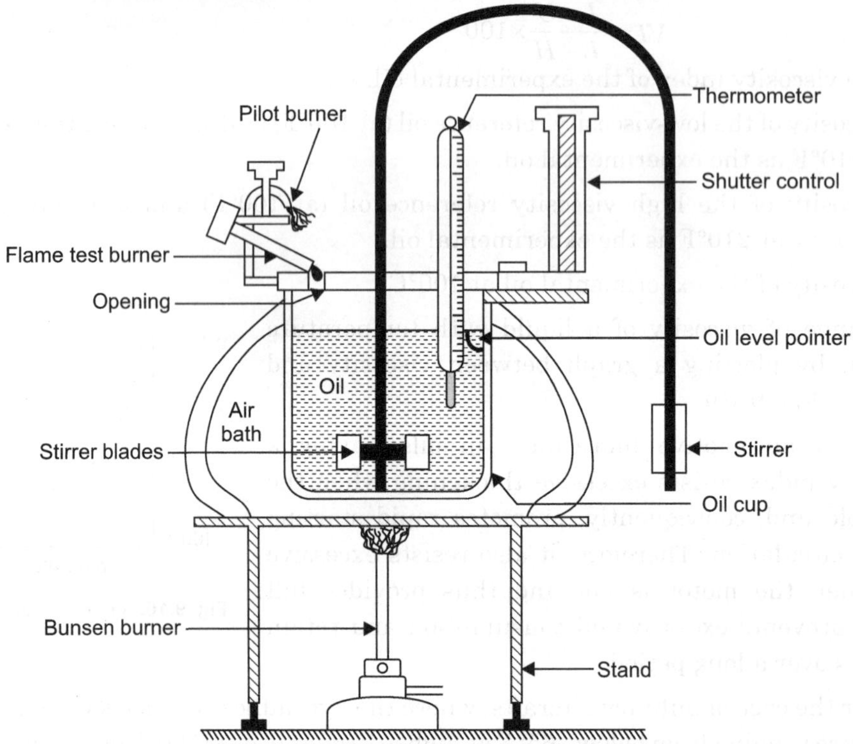

Fig. 9.11. Pensky Marten's Apparatus

In this apparatus, the oil is heated by a burner through an air bath.

The oil sample is filled in a cup till the tip of the pointer. The thermometer is inserted in the sample and then the sample is heated. The test flame is applied at every 1° rise in temperature. The temperature at which a distinct flash is observed is noted as the flash point and the temperature at which the flame continues to burn for at least 5 seconds in the fire point of the lubricating oil.

(b) Cleveland apparatus: It is an ***open cup apparatus***.

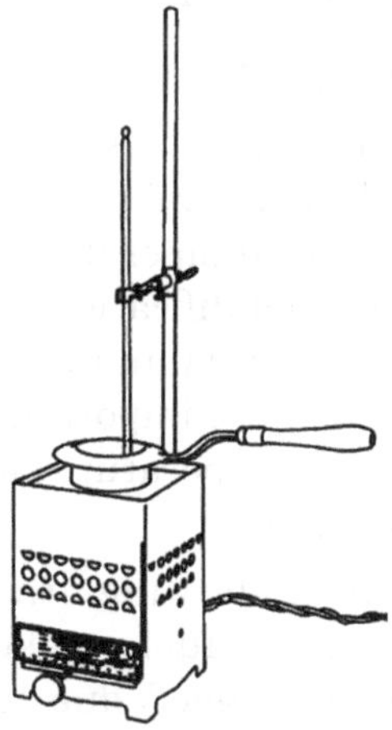

Fig. 9.12. Cleveland Apparatus

In this apparatus, the oil is directly heated on a heating plate.

(c) Abel's apparatus: It is also a ***closed cup apparatus***.

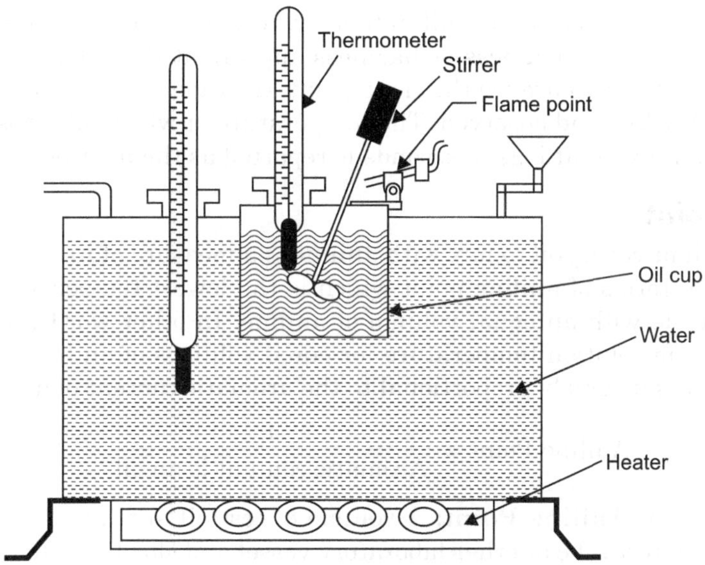

Fig. 9.13. Abel's Apparatus

In this apparatus, the oil is heated by a burner through a water bath.

9.5.4 Cloud and Pour Point

Petroleum oils are complex mixtures of chemical compounds and do not show a fixed freezing point. They become more or less plastic solids when cooled to sufficiently low temperatures. This is due to the formation of solid crystals or the congealing of the various hydrocarbons which constitute the oil.

The ***cloud point*** of a petroleum oil is the temperature at which solidifiable substances like paraffin wax present in the oil begin to crystallize or separate from solution when the oil is cooled gradually under standard conditions.

The ***pour point*** of a petroleum oil is the temperature at which the oil just ceases to flow when cooled at a standard rate in a standard apparatus.

Significance of Cloud and Pour Point

The cloud and pour points can be used to access the suitability of lubricants in cold conditions. Lubricants which are used in machines working at low temperatures should have low pour point, otherwise solidification of lubricant will take place which will result in jamming of the machine. The pour point, however, is more important as it indicates the approximate lowest temperature at which the oil can be transferred by pouring.

Fig. 9.14. Cloud and Pour Point Apparatus

The cloud point is useful for indicating the temperature at which filter screens in the fuel intake system of diesel engines might become clogged due to wax separation. The apparatus used for determine cloud and pour point is shown in (Fig. 9.14)

To determine the cloud point, a sample of oil is poured into a tube enclosed in an air jacket. It is then placed in a freezing mixture (ice + NaCl or $CaCl_2$). As the oil cools, the temperature falls continuously. With every degree fall in temperature, the tube is taken out and observed. The temperature at which cloudiness or haziness appears at the bottom of tube is the cloud point of the oil. After the appearance the cloud point, the tube is now taken out at every 3° fall of temperature. It is tilted and observed. The temperature at which oil stops flowing when the tube is kept horizontally for at least 5 seconds is reported as the pour point of the oil.

9.5.5 Aniline Point

The tendency of a lubricating oil to mix with aniline is a measure of its aromatic content. This can be expressed in terms of aniline point which is the lowest temperature at which the oil is completely miscible with an equal volume of aniline. In other words, aniline point is the minimum equilibrium solution temperature for equal volumes of aniline and the lubricating oil the aniline point is inversely proportional to the aromatic content of a lubricating oil.

i.e. $$\text{Aniline Point} \propto \frac{1}{\text{Aromatic content is an oil}}$$

Determination of Aniline Point: A volume of test oil and an equal volume of aniline are mix together in a test tube or other laboratory vessel and slowly heated while being gently agitated until a homogeneous solution is obtained. Then the tube or vessel is allowed to cool at a controlled rate. The temperature at which the two phases separate distinctively is taken as the aniline point.

Significance of Aniline Point

Aniline point is important primarily for oils that may come into contact with natural rubber.

Oils with a high concentration of aromatics are less suitable for use in systems or machinery that have rubber parts because the aromatic hydrocarbons gradually break down natural rubber, potentially causing failure in gaskets, seals and other components.

More the content of aromatic hydrocarbon in an oil, more are the chance of deterioration of an oil when it comes in contact with rubber sealings, packing etc.

Thus, low aromatic content or high aniline point is desirable in a lubricating oil.

High aniline point is also an indication of higher content of paraffins. Since paraffins give easy starting and a minimum of knock in a diesel engine, high aniline point usually indicates high cetane number.

9.5.6 Emulsification and Steam Emulsion Number

Emulsification is the property of oils to get intimately mixed with water, forming a mixture, called emulsion. Generally, emulsions are the product of two immiscible liquids in which one liquid acts as the dispersion medium and the other as he dispersed phase. For example, certain oils form emulsions with water easily.

Emulsions have a tendency to collect dirt, grit, foreign matter thus causing an abrasion and wearing out of the lubricated parts of the machinery. So, a good lubricating oil should form an emulsion with water, which breaks off quickly. The tendency of this emulsion (oil-water emulsion) to break is determined by A.S.T.M text.

A.S.T.M. is a standard test method in which a known volume of oil is taken in a test tube and steam is bubbled through it, till the temperature is raised to 90°C. The formation of oil-water emulsion takes place and the test tube is placed in a water bath maintained at 90°C. The hot test tube is allowed to stand and the time in seconds in which the oil and water emulsion separate out in distinct layers is called as "Steam emulsion number" (SEN). A good lubricant should have low steam emulsion number *i.e.* the oil and water emulsion breaks quickly or separates quickly.

9.5.7 Saponification Number

Many lubricating oils are "compounded" with fatty materials to increase their film strength or water-displacing qualities. The degree of compounding is indicated by the saponification number of the lubricating oil.

Determination of saponification number is based on the fact that these fatty materials can be saponified *i.e.* converted to soap by reaction with an alkali usually at an elevated temperature.

$$\underset{\text{fat/Oil}}{RCOOR'} + \underset{\substack{\text{or} \\ \text{KOH Alkali}}}{NaOH} \longrightarrow \underset{\text{Alkanel}}{R'OH} + \underset{\substack{\text{or} \\ RCOO^- K^+}}{RCOO^- Na^+}$$

Thus, saponification number is defined as "the number of milligrams of potassium hydroxide required to saponify the fatty materials present in one gram of the oil."

Determination of Saponification number: It is usually determined when a known amount of oil is allowed to react with a known excess of standard KOH or NaOH solution and determining the alkali consumed by titrating the unreacted alkali with standard acid using phenolphthalein as an indicator. Mineral oils, being mixtures of hydrocarbons do not react with KOH and so are not saponifiable. Vegetable and animal oils, however are mixture of glyceryl esters of fatty acids and therefore, require large amounts of alkali to get hydrolysed. Thus, they have high saponification value. Hence, the determination of saponification value help to ascertain the presence of animal and vegetable oil .8 in a lubricant. Conversely, all the fined oils possess their own characteristic saponification number, therefore, any departure from this value in a given oil sample indicates the probability and extent of adulteration.

9.5.8 Carbon Residue

Many lubricating oils contain high percentage of carbon in combined form. When used in internal combustion engines and air compressors, they decompose due to high temperature or heat and carbon residue deposits on machines, causing numerous problems. A good lubricant should deposit the least amount of carbon when used in various machines. Carbon residue can be estimated generally by Conradson apparatus (Fig. 9.15) In this method, a known amount of oil is placed in a silica crucible which in turn is put into a skidmore crucible which is provided with a lid having a small opening for the escape of volatile matter. The crucibles are then placed in a wrought iron crucible covered with a chimney shaped iron hood. Heat is supplied from a burner at prescribed rates till vapours of all volatile matter are burnt completely. Apparatus is then allowed to cool and weight of residue left is determined.

$$\% \text{ carbon residue} = \frac{\text{weight of residue in crucible}}{\text{weight of original oil sample}} \times 100.$$

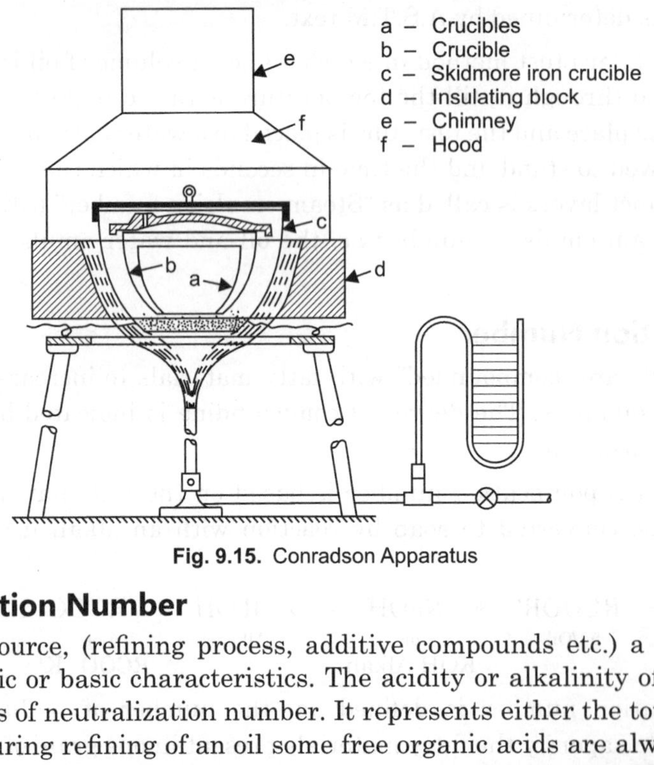

Fig. 9.15. Conradson Apparatus

9.5.9 Neutralization Number

Depending on its source, (refining process, additive compounds etc.) a lubricating oil may exhibit certain acidic or basic characteristics. The acidity or alkalinity of a lubricating oil is determined in terms of neutralization number. It represents either the total acid value or the total base value. During refining of an oil some free organic acids are always associated with the oil, so acidity is more common and it is expressed in acid value or acid number.

Total acid value or total acid number (TAN) is the number of milligrams of potassium hydroxide required to neutralize any free acid present in 1 g of the oil. Generally, free acid are not present in the oils or lubricants unless they are refined in a wrong manner. Acid value of a lubricating oil should be less than 0.1. Acid value greater than 0.1 indicates that the oil is oxidized and as a result sludge formation and corrosion may occurs.

Determination of acid value or neutralization number: For the determination of acid value, a known amount of oil sample (3–4 mL) is taken in a titration flask. The oil sample is then dissolved in minimum quantity of a solvent like ethyl methyl ketone. Add few drops of phenolphthalein indicator and titrate it against standard solution of alcoholic KOH. The appearance of pink colour indicates the end point. The acid value can be calculated using the following formula:

$$\text{Acid value} = \text{Vol. of KOH used (mL)} \times \text{Normality of KOH} \times \frac{\text{Eq. wt. of KOH}}{\text{wt. of Oil Sample}}$$

SOLVED EXAMPLES

Example 9.1. *An oil sample under test has a Saybolt universal viscosity of 64 seconds at 210°F and 560 seconds at 100°F. The low viscosity standard (Gulf oil) possesses a Saybolt universal viscosity values of 64 seconds at 210°F and 770 seconds at 100°F. The high viscosity standard (Pennsylvanian gave the Saybolt universal viscosity values of 64 seconds at 210°F and 410 at 100°F. Calculate the viscosity in of oil sample under test.*

Solution:
$$VI = \left(\frac{L-U}{L-H}\right) \times 100$$

Here

$$L = 770 \text{ seconds}$$
$$U = 560 \text{ seconds}$$
$$H = 450 \text{ seconds}$$
$$VI = \left(\frac{770-560}{770-410}\right) \times 100 = \left(\frac{210}{360}\right) \times 100 = 58.35$$

Viscosity index is a unit less quantity.

Example 9.2. *An oil sample under test has a Saybolt universal viscosity same as that of standard Gulf oil (low viscosity standard and Pennsylvanion oil (high viscosity standard) at 210. Their Saybolt universal viscosities at 100°F are 50, and 450 respectively. Calculate viscosity index of the sample.* **(RGPV, Dec., 2020)**

Solution:
$$VI = \left(\frac{L-U}{L-U}\right) \times 100$$

$$L = 750 \text{ seconds}$$
$$U = 50 \text{ seconds}$$
$$H = 450 \text{ seconds}$$
$$VI = \left(\frac{750-50}{750-450}\right) \times 100 = \left(\frac{750}{300}\right) \times 100 = 233.3$$

Viscosity index of the oil sample = 233.33.

Example 9.3. *A lubricating oil has a S.U.V of 58 seconds at 210 F ans 600 seconds at 100°F. The high viscosity index standard (i.e. Pennsylvanion oil) has S.U.V of 58 seconds at 2 F and 400 seconds at 100°F. The low viscosity in standard (i.e. Gulf oil) oil has a S.U.V of 58 second 210°F and 800 seconds at 100°F. Calculate the viscosity index of the oil.*

(RGPV, Dec., 2003, Jan./Feb., 2020)

Solution: In USA, the time required for 60 ml of the oil to flow of an orifice in a Saybolt Viscometer is known as Saylbolt universal viscosity (S.U.V) or Saybolt universal secoand (S.U.S.).

$$VI = \left(\frac{L-U}{L-H}\right) \times 100$$

$$L = 800 \text{ seconds}$$
$$U = 600 \text{ seconds}$$
$$H = 400 \text{ seconds}$$
$$VI = \left(\frac{800 - 600}{800 - 400}\right) \times 100 = \left(\frac{200}{400}\right) \times 100 = 50$$

$\therefore$ Viscosity index of the oil sample = 50.

Example 9.4. *The three oil samples A, B and C under test have a Saybolt universal viscosity of 64 sec at 210°F and 570, 579, 589 sec. at 100°F respectively. The low viscosity standard (Gulf oil) possess a Saybolt universal viscosity of 64 seconds 210°F and 780 sec at 100°F. The high viscosity standard (Pennsylvanion oil) gave a Saybolt universal viscosity 64 sec. at 210°F and 450 sec. at 100°F. Calculate compare viscosity index of the oil sample under test.*

(RGPV, Jan., 2020)

Solution: Here, $L = 780$ sec, $H = 450$ sec

For sample *A*:
$$VI_A = \left(\frac{L - U}{L - H}\right) \times 100$$
$$U = 570 \text{ sec.}$$
$$VI_A = \left(\frac{780 - 570}{780 - 450}\right) \times 100 = \left(\frac{210}{330}\right) \times 100 = 63.64$$

For sample *B*:
$$VI_B = \left(\frac{L - U}{L - H}\right) \times 100$$
$$U = 579 \text{ sec.}$$
$$VI_B = \left(\frac{780 - 579}{780 - 450}\right) \times 100 = \left(\frac{201}{330}\right) \times 100 = 60.91$$

For sample *C*:
$$V_{IC} = \left(\frac{L - U}{L - H}\right) \times 100$$
$$U = 589 \text{ sec.}$$
$$V_{IC} = \left(\frac{780 - 589}{780 - 450}\right) \times 100$$
$$= \left(\frac{191}{330}\right) \times 100 = 57.88$$

$$\therefore \qquad VI_A > VI_B > VI_C$$

Viscosity index of simple A in highest whereas sample C is having lowest viscosity index among all the three samples.

EXERCISES

I. SHORT ANSWER TYPE QUESTIONS

1. Define lubricant and mention the important functions of a lubricant.
   (RGPV, June, 2008)
2. Define lubrication. Give classification of lubricants with examples.
   (RGPV, June, 2003, Jan., 2007)

3. Name the additives mixed with lubricant used for extreme pressure lubrication. **(RTU, May, 2019)**
4. What are lubricants? Explain thick layer mechanism of lubrication. **(RTU, Dec., 2018, Dec., 2017, 2014, 2013)**
5. What is hydrodynamic lubrication? Explain the phenomena with the help of a suitable diagram.
6. What are greases? Explain different type of greases. **(RGPV, June, 2007)**
7. Explain extreme pressure lubrication.
8. What are synthetic lubricants? Write name and functions of two synthetic lubricants.
9. Explain and discuss the significance of the following properties of the lubricants.
   (*a*) Flash and fire point
   (*b*) Saponification number.
10. Define and write the significance of following:
   (*a*) Viscosity and viscosity index
   (*b*) Aniline point
11. Write short notes on the following:
   (*a*) Carbon residue
   (*b*) Cloud and pour point
   (*c*) Oiliness
   (*d*) Neutralization number.
12. Write a note on solid lubricants. **(RGPV, June, 2005, Jan, 2008, April, 2010)**
13. Explain why a lubricant should have high aniline point? **(RGPV, April, 2009)**
14. Discuss the method of flash point determination by Abel's apparatus. **(RGPV, June, 2008)**
15. Write a brief note on greases? **(RGPV, April, 2009)**
16. What are biodegradable lubricants? Discuss the need of these lubricants in present scenario.
17. What are the advantages of greases over other lubricants?

II. LONG ANSWER TYPE QUESTIONS

1. Explain the term lubricants. Discuss the mechanism of lubrication. **(RTU, Dec., 17, RGPV(CBCS) May, 2019)**
2. What are lubricants? What are their functions? Explain thin film lubrication. **(JNTU, April, 2018)**
3. Explain the following:
   (*a*) Steam emulsification number
   (*b*) functions of lubricants
   (*c*) Viscosity index
   (*d*) thin layer lubrication. **(RTU Dec., 2016)**
4. What is viscosity of oil? Describe viscosity measurement of oil by redwood viscometer. **(RTU, Dec., 2018)**
5. Write a short note on viscosity and viscosity index. Write various instruments used for determining viscosity. Draw neat and labelled diagram of any one instrument.
6. What is flash and fire point of a lubricating oil? How is it determined by Pensky Martin's apparatus? Also give it significance. **(RTU, May, 2019, RGPV Dec., 2008)**

7. What is neutralization number? How is it determined?
8. Define aniline number. Explain the method of determination of aniline number.
9. What is viscosity? Differentiate between redwood viscometer 1 and 2.
10. Define flash and fire point of a lubricating oil. What are various instruments used to determine flash and fire point. Explain determination of flash and fire point by any one of them.
11. Define lubrication. Explain the mechanism of boundary Lubrication in detail. **(RGPV, Dec., 2015)**
12. What are solid lubricants? Explain the types of solid lubricants and give their applications.
13. What are blended oils? Write various additives and their functions used in blended oils.

III. NUMERICAL PROBLEMS

1. A lubricating oil has Saybolt universal viscosity of 58 sec at 210°F and 564 seconds at 100°F. The low *V.I* standards oil has saybolt universal viscosity of 58 seconds at 210°F and 758 seconds at 100°F. The high *V.I* standards Pennsylvanian oil gave the Saybolt universal viscosity value of 58 seconds at 210°F and 420 seconds at 100°F. Calculate *V.I* of the lubricating oil. **(RGPV, Jan., 2008)**
2. A lubricating oil has the same viscosity as standard naphthenic and paraffinic type oils at 210°F. Their viscosities at 38°C are 325 S.U.S, 430 S.U.S and 260 S.U.S respectively. Find the viscosity index of the oil. **(RGPV, April, 2010)**
3. An oil sample under test has a Saybolt universal viscosity same as that of standard Gulf oil (low viscosity standard) and Pennsylvanian oil (high viscosity standard) at 210°F. Their Saybolt universal viscosities at 100°F are 700, 900 and 600 respectively. Calculate viscosity index of the oil sample.
4. An oil sample under test has a Saybolt universal viscosity same as that of standard Gulf oil (low viscosity standard) and Pennsylvanian oil (high viscosity standard) at 210°F. Their universal viscosities at 100°F are 61, 758 and 420—respectively. Calculate viscosity index of the sample oil.
5. Lubricating oil of an unknown viscosity index has a viscosity of 80 redwood seconds (RWs) at 210°F and 740 RWs at 100°F. The high viscosity standard oil having a viscosity of 80 RWs at 201°F and 300 RWs at 100°F. The low viscosity standard oil having a viscosity of 80 RWs at 210°F and 830 RWs at 100°F. Calculate the viscosity index of unknown oil.
6. An oil of unknown viscosity index has a saybolt universal viscosity of 58 seconds at 210°F and of 600 seconds at 100°F. The high viscosity index standard oil (Pennyslavian oil) has saybolt viscosity of 58 seconds at 210°F and 430 seconds at 100°F. The low viscosity index standard (Gulf oil) has a saybolt universal viscosity of 58 seconds at 210°F and 780 seconds at 100°F. Calculate the viscosity index of unknown oil.
7. An oil of unknown viscosity index has a redwood viscosity of 70s at 210°F and 500s at 100°F. The high viscosity standard oil has a redwood viscosity of 70s at 210°F and 600 RWs at 100°F. The low viscosity standard oil has a redwood viscosity of 70 s at 210°F and 760 RWs at 100°F. Calculate the viscosity index of unknown oil.

IV. MULTIPLE CHOICE QUESTIONS

1. Select the incorrect statement from the following option:
   (*a*) lubricant acts as a seal (*b*) lubricant reduces friction
   (*c*) lubricant keeps out dirt (*d*) lubricant enhance corrosion.
2. The science of friction, lubrication and wear is called:
   (*a*) Geology (*b*) Surface science
   (*c*) tribology (*d*) lubrology.
3. Oil emulsions are the most effective lubricants in:
   (*a*) heavy cutting (*b*) light cutting
   (*c*) engines (*d*) gears.
4. Beside graphite, the other solid lubricants are:
   (*a*) soapstone (*b*) molybdenum disulphide
   (*c*) tungsten disulphide (*d*) all of the above.
5. The lubrication under condition of high load and slow speed is:
   (*a*) Thin film (*b*) Thick film
   (*c*) high pressure (*d*) all of the above.
6. The purpose of lubrication is:
   (*a*) to reduce friction (*b*) to reduce wear
   (*c*) transfer heat produced (*d*) All of the above
7. Viscosity index can defined as:
   (*a*) $\frac{L-U}{L-H}\times 100$ (*b*) $\frac{L+U}{L-H}\times 100$
   (*c*) $\frac{L-H}{L-U}\times 100$ (*d*) $\frac{L-H}{L+U}\times 100$.
8. Antiwear additive in extreme pressure additive is:
   (*a*) Graphite (*b*) Mica
   (*c*) Tricrecyl phosphate (*d*) Soapstone.
9. Animal and vegetable oil posses
   (*a*) good oiliness (*b*) poor oiliness
   (*c*) optimum oiliness (*d*) none of the above.
10. Cleveland's apparatus is used to find out the:
   (*a*) Cloud point (*b*) Pour point
   (*c*) Viscosity (*d*) Flash and fire point.
11. Unit of viscosity is:
   (*a*) Poise (*b*) cm
   (*c*) Ohm (*d*) cm^{-1}.
12. Aniline point is related to:
   (*a*) Octane number (*b*) Cetane number
   (*c*) Smoke (*d*) Pour point.

13. Acid value of a good lubricant should be:
(*a*) Least (*b*) High
(*c*) Moderate (*d*) Can be high or low.

14. With the increase in temperature, the viscosity of a lubricant oil:
(*a*) Increases (*b*) Decreases
(*c*) Can increase or decrease (*d*) Neither increase nor decrease.

15. The suitability of a lubricant in cold conditions depend on:
(*a*) Steam emulsion number (*b*) Cloud and pour point
(*c*) Flash and fire point (*d*) Neutralization number.

16. The property of a lubricating oil that helps to estimate the percentage of aromatic hydrocarbons in an oil is:
(*a*) Saponification value (*b*) Aniline point
(*c*) Cloud and pour point (*d*) Steam emulsion number.

17. The property of a lubricant that determines its resistance to flow:
(*a*) Viscosity (*b*) Viscosity index
(*c*) Oiliness (*d*) None of the above.

18. The rate of change of viscosity with temperature is called as:
(*a*) Coefficient of viscosity (*b*) Viscosity index
(*c*) Viscosity gradient (*d*) none of the above.

19. The viscosity of lubricating oil is determined by:
(*a*) Ostwald's viscometer (*b*) Pensky Marten apparatus
(*c*) Cleveland's apparatus (*d*) Engler's viscometer.

20. Apparatus used to determine the flash and fire points of lubricating oils is known as:
(*a*) Redwood apparatus (*b*) Saybolt apparatus
(*c*) Abel's apparatus (*d*) Engler's apparatus

21. Acid value is also known as:
(*a*) Saponification number (*b*) Neutralization number
(*c*) Steam emulsion number (*d*) Iodine number.

22. Engler's viscometer is generally used in:
(*a*) USA (*b*) India
(*c*) Europe (*d*) Commonwealth countries.

23. The temperature at which the lubricating oil ceases to flow.
(*a*) Cloud point (*b*) Pour point
(*c*) Flash point (*d*) Fire point.

24. _______ is the open cup apparatus for determining flash and fire point of a lubricating oil
(*a*) Abel's apparatus (*b*) Cleveland's apparatus
(*c*) Pensky Marten's apparatus (*d*) All of the above.

25. A good lubricating oil should posses:
(*a*) High viscosity index (*b*) High aniline point
(*c*) Low carbon residue (*d*) All of the above.

Answers

III. NUMERICAL PROBLEMS

1. $VI = 57.39$ 2. $VI = 61.76$ 3. $VI = 66.67$ 4. $VI = 206.2$

5. $VI = 33.96$ 6. $VI = 51.43$ 7. $VI = 162.5$

IV. MULTIPLE CHOICE QUESTIONS

1. (*d*)	**2.** (*c*)	**3.** (*b*)	**4.** (*d*)	**5.** (*a*)	**6.** (*d*)	**7.** (*a*)	**8.** (*c*)	**9.** (*a*)	**10.** (*d*)
11. (*a*)	**12.** (*b*)	**13.** (*a*)	**14.** (*b*)	**15.** (*b*)	**16.** (*b*)	**17.** (*a*)	**18.** (*c*)	**19.** (*d*)	**20.** (*c*)
21. (*b*)	**22.** (*c*)	**23.** (*b*)	**24.** (*b*)	**25.** (*d*)					

Chapter 10 Cement and Refractories

10.1 CEMENT

Cement is the general term given to the powdered materials which initially have plastic flow but when mixed with water or other liquid has the property of setting into a hard solid structure in several hours with varying degree of strength and bonding properties. Cements are capable of joining rigid masses like stones, bricks, tiles etc. into coherent structures.

The cements generally used in engineering construction are of the following types:

1. Natural cement
2. Puzzolana cement
3. Slag cement
4. Portland cement.

1. Natural cement: It is prepared by calcination (heating of solid at high temperature) and pulverization (crushing something to a powdered mass) of naturally occurring argillaceous limestone at high temperature. During calcination, calcium silicates and aluminates are formed.

Natural cement is hydraulic which posses quick setting property and relatively low strength. Combination of natural cement and sand is called as **mortar**.

Mortar is used in various applications like:

- Binding of bricks or stones in masonry work.
- Hiding the joints and improving appearance in plastering works.
- Moulding and ornamental purpose.
- Construction of dams and foundations as bulk masses of concrete.

2. Puzzolana Cement: This is among the oldest cementing materials known. It was invented by Romans and can be still seen is some Roman structures *e.g.* the pantheon in Rome. It was first made from volcanic ash from Mount Vesuvius situated near a place called Pozzuoli. When volcanic ash (consisting of silicates of calcium, iron and aluminium) is mixed with lime and heated, puzzolanic cement is formed. Puzzolana cement develop strength slowly but its ultimate strength is very high.

3. Slag Cement: It is a mixture of lime and blast furnace slag (a mixture of calcium and aluminium silicates). The blast furnace slag is granualated by pouring it into a stream of cold water. It is then dried and mixed with hydraulic lime and finally it is pulverized. Slag cement *harden* very slowly hence, an accelarator like clay, salt or caustic soda is sometimes added. They have low strength and poor abrasion resistance.

4. Portland Cement: It is one of the most important construction materials in the present time. In 1824, William Aspdin found that a strongly heated mixture of clay and limestone, when mixed with a small amount of water, set to a hard stone like substance in few hours. After setting, the stone like substance resembled famous portland rock of England and therefore, it was named as Portland cement.

Portland cement is also called as **magic powder**. It mainly consists of compounds of lime, silica, alumina and iron. On mixing with water it forms a paste which hardens and binds the aggregates (crushed rock, sand, gravel etc.) together to form a hard and durable mass known as **concrete**. Thus, cement is one of the ingredient of concrete.

All Portland cements are hydraulic as they set and harden under water.

10.2 MANUFACTURE OF PORTLAND CEMENT

Raw materials Required: The raw materials required for the manufacturing of Portland cement are:

(*i*) **Calcareous materials:** These material provide calcium in the form of calcium oxide (CaO). For example, limestone ($CaCO_3$), chalk, marlstone, etc.

(*ii*) **Argillaceous materials:** These materials provide alumina (Al_2O_3), silica (SiO_2), iron oxide (Fe_2O_3) aluminium ore refuse, clay, sand, marlstone, shale etc.

(*iii*) Gypsum ($CaSO_4.2H_2O$)

(*iv*) Powdered coal or fuel oil.

Manufacturing Process: Portland cement is manufactured by mixing together the argillaceous and calcareous materials in the required ratio. The mixture is heated to around 1450°C in a rotary kiln. The various steps involved in the manufacturing process are as follows:

(*i*) mixing (*ii*) burning (*iii*) grinding (*iv*) packing

(*i*) **Mixing:** Mixing of raw material can be done either by

(*a*) Dry process (*b*) Wet process.

Dry Process: In the dry process, the raw materials are separately crushed in gyrotary crushers, ground in suitable machines (ball mills/tube mills) and then dried using rotary dries. These are then mixed in proper proportions, pulverised in ball mills and finally homogenised. (*i.e.* made uniform by means of compressed air mixing arrangement). The resulting mass is called as "**raw mix**" which is stored in the storage bins (called **silos**) and kept ready to be fed in a rotary kiln.

Wet Process: In the wet process, the calcareous raw material (limestone) is crushed in gyrotary crushers to particles of suitable size and the argillaceous material (*i.e.* clay) is washed with water in wash mills to remove foreign material such as flint and a slurry containing nearly 60% water is obtained. Crushed limestone and clay slurry are mixed in right proportion and led to the grinding mill (tube mill/ball mill). The resulting slurry is called **raw slurry**. This slurry in then led into the correcting basin where its chemical composition is adjusted to the proper ratio (*i.e.* containing about 30–40% water). The slurry is finally stored in storage tanks and kept ready for feeding to a rotary kiln.

The dry process was invented in America and still used there while the wet process is older and used mostly in India and Europe. Table 10.1 provides a tabulated comparison of these two processes.

Table 10.1: Comparison between dry and wet process of mixing

S. No.	Dry Process	Wet Process
1.	In dry process, no water is added to the raw material in grinding and thus no slurry is made.	It wet process, water is added to the raw material in grinding and a slurry is formed.
2.	If the raw materials (*i.e.* limestone and clay) are hard, dry process is employed.	It can be used for any kind of raw material *i.e.* hard or soft both.
3.	The process is slow and fuel consumption is less.	The process is fast and fuel consumption is high.
4.	Cement produced is of inferior quality.	Superior quality cement is produced.
5.	Overall process is expensive.	The process is inexpensive.
6.	In general, dry process is not used much for the manufacture of cement.	Wet process is most common and is almost universally applied for the manufacture of cement.

(*ii*) **Burning:** The raw slurry from the wet process and raw mix from the dry process is now fed into the hopper (funnel shaped device) provided on the upper part of rotary kiln which consists of an inclined cylinder (Fig. 10.1) made of steel. The cylinder is about 30–160 metres long and 2–4 metres in diameter. Its inside surface is lined with refractory bricks. The kiln is laid in slightly inclined position as shown in Fig. 10.1. The kiln rest on roller bearings therefore it can be rotated at desired speeds. Burning fuel and air are injected at the lower end. Due to slope and slow rotation of the kiln, the material (raw slurry or raw mix) passes slowly from the upper to the lower end at a controlled rate. As the mixture or slurry gradually descends, the temperature increases and the actual chemical reactions takes place. The chemical reactions taking place in different parts/zones of rotary kiln are as follows:

(*a*) **Drying zone:** In the upper part of the kiln where the temperature is about 100–500°C, most of the water in the slurry gets evaporated and the raw material becomes completely dry. Thus, this zone is called as drying zone.

(*b*) **Calcination zone:** The middle part of the kiln is called as calcination zone, where the temperature is around 1000°C. In the zone, calcination of limestone takes place.

$$CaCO_3 \longrightarrow CaO + CO_2\uparrow$$

(*c*) **Burning zone:** In the lower part of the kiln, the temperature is between 1500–1700°C. In the zone, actual chemical reaction takes place yielding calcium aluminates and silicates.

$$2CaO + SiO_2 \longrightarrow \underset{\text{Dicalcium silicate } (C_2S)}{2CaO.SiO_2 \text{ or } Ca_2SiO_4}$$

$$3CaO + SiO_2 \longrightarrow \underset{\text{Tricalcium silicate } (C_3S)}{3CaO.SiO_2 \text{ or } Ca_3SiO_5}$$

$$3CaO + Al_2O_3 \longrightarrow \underset{\text{Tricalcium aluminate } (C_3A)}{3CaO.Al_2O_3 \text{ or } Ca_3Al_2O_6}$$

$$4CaO + Al_2O_3 + Fe_2O_3 \longrightarrow \underset{\text{Tetracalcium aluminoferrite } (C_4AF)}{4CaO.Al_2O_3Fe_2O_3 \text{ or } Ca_4Al_2Fe_2O_{10}}$$

Where C = CaO,	$S = SiO_2$,
$A = Al_2O_3$ and	$F = Fe_2O_3$.

These aluminates and silicates fuse together to form small, hard, greyish stones called **clinkers**. These clinkers are very hot and can be cooled by passing a stream of cool air. The cooled clinkers are collected and the hot air so produced is used for drying the coal before pulverization.

(iii) Grinding: The cooled clinkers are ground to a fine powder in grinding mills (ball mills/ tube mills). Finely grounded clinkers sets very fast by absorption of moisture from the atmosphere. Thus, a small quantity *i.e.* 2–3% of powdered gypsum($CaSO_4 . 2H_2O$) is added to the cement to control or retard the setting time of cement. Gypsum, thus, acts as a retarding agent for early setting of cement. This is due to the formation of calcium sulpho aluminate (by reaction between gypsum and C_3A) which does not show any tendancy of rapid hydration.

$$\underset{(C_3A)}{3CaO.Al_2O_3} + \underset{\text{gypsum}}{xCaSO_4.2H_2O} \longrightarrow \underset{\text{tricalcium sulphoaluminate}}{3CaO.Al_2O_3.xCaSO_4.2H_2O}$$

The mixture of clinker and gypsum (*i.e.* tricalcium sulpho-aluminate) is called as **Portland cement**.

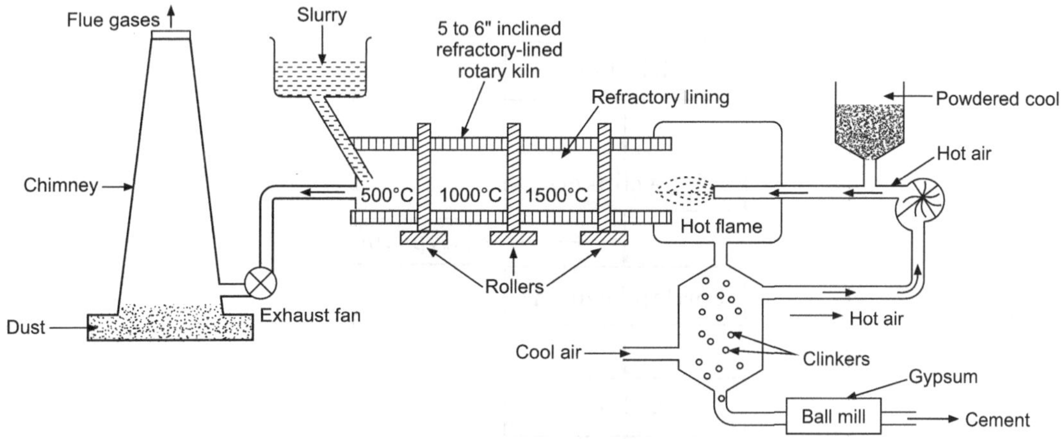

Fig. 10.1. Rotary Kiln.

(iv) Packing: The cement is stored in silos from which it is bagged or loaded for shipment. Each bag usually contains 50 kg of cement.

The manufacturing process of portland cement can be summarized in a flow chart as follows.

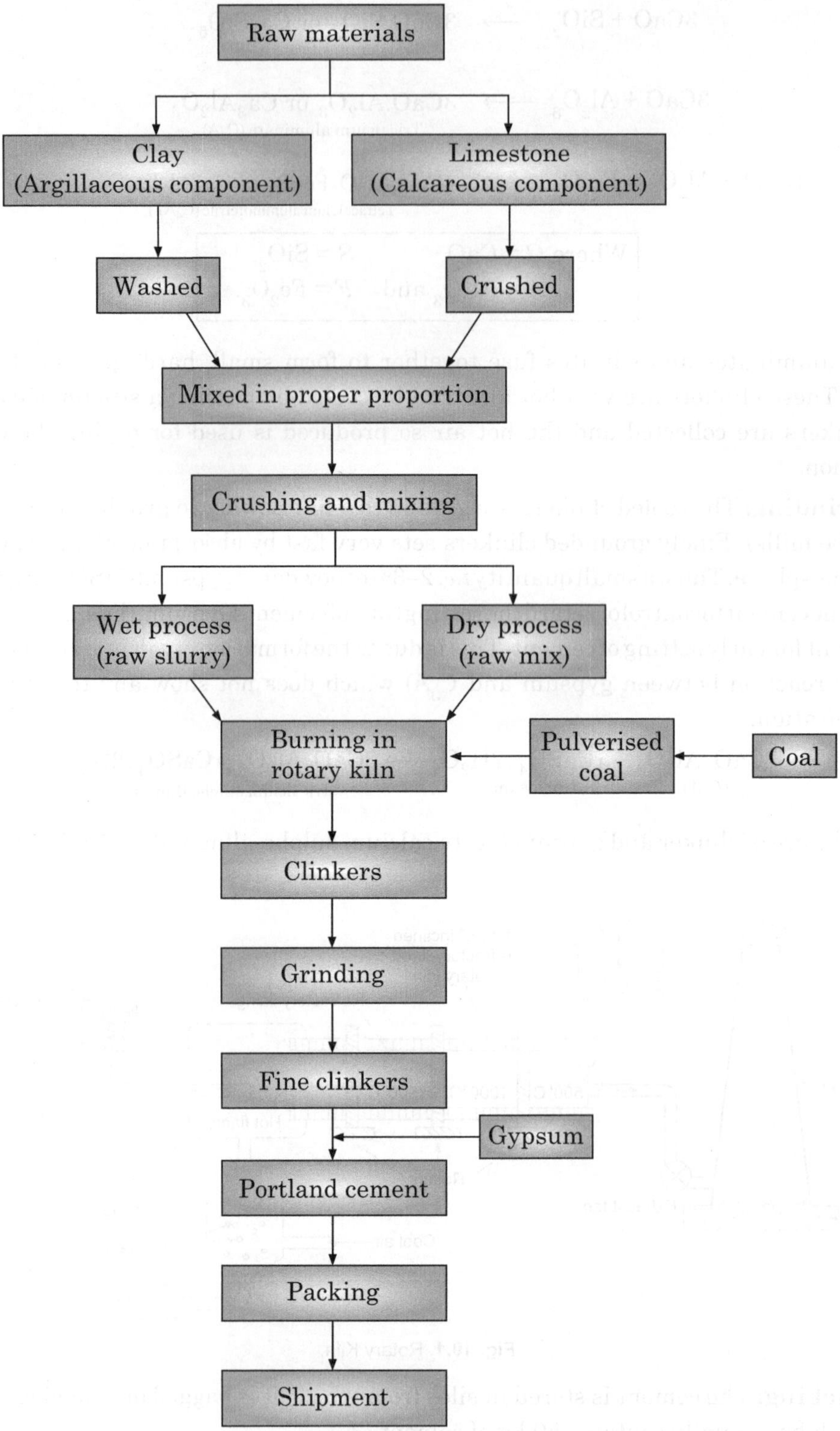

Fig. 10.2. Flow chart for the manufacture of Portland cement.

10.3 CHEMICAL COMPOSITION OF PORTLAND CEMENT

Portland cements are composed of following major chemical compounds.

Table 10.2: Main Constituents of Portland Cement

S.No.	Name	Chemical Formula	Abbreviation	Average %
1	Dicalcium silicate	$2CaO.SiO_2$ or Ca_2SiO_4	C_2S	25
2	Tricalcium silicate	$3CaO.SiO_2$ or Ca_3SiO_5	C_3S	45
3	Tricalcium aluminate	$3CaO.Al_2O_3$ or $Ca_3Al_2O_6$	C_3A	1
4	Tetra calcium Aluminoferrite	$4CaO.Al_2O_3.Fe_2O_3$ or $Ca_4Al_2Fe_2O_{10}$	C_4AF	9

Each component exhibit particular special behaviour. Hence, the bevahiour/properties of cement can be altered by changing or modifying the relative percentage of these compounds. The importance of various components are given below:

(*a*) **Dicalcium silicates(C_2S):** Due to slow reaction with water, it gets hardened slowly and strengthen after one week. It has low early strength but develops ultimate strength slighty less than C_3S. It possesses the heat of hydration of 420 kJ/kg.

(*b*) **Tricalcium silicate (C_3S):** It has medium range of hydration and develops high ultimate strength quite rapidly. It's ultimate strength is highest *among* all the constituents. Heat of hydration is about 880 kJ/kg.

(*c*) **Tricalcium aluminate (C_3A):** It hydrates very rapidly and its hydration is a highly exothermic reaction. It has good early strength but low ultimate strength.

(*d*) **Tetra calcium alumino ferrite (C_4AF):** It hydrates very slowly and does not contribute much to the strength of cement as it has poorest early as well as ultimate strength *amongst* all the constituents.

Apart from these four constituents cement also contains calcium sulphate ($CaSO_4$), magnesium oxide (MgO) and calcium oxide (CaO) in minute quantities.

Setting and Hardening of Cement

When water is added to cement, it converts into a paste and then hardens. This process is known as setting and hardening of cement. Setting is regarded as stiffening of the original paste mass due to initial gel formation while hardening is regarded as development of strength due to crystallization. The strength of the cement depends on the amount of gelation and the extend of crystallization. The process of setting and hardening of cement can be explained as follows:

Setting of cement can be divided into two stages-initial set and final set.

Initial set is the hydration and gel formation from the different constituents of cement. Initially hydration and hydrolysis of tricalcium aluminate and tetracalcium aluminoferrite takes place to give hydrated crystalline products alongwith the formation of gels.

1. **Hydration of tricalcium aluminate:**

$$3CaO\,.\,Al_2O_3 + 6H_2O \longrightarrow \underset{\text{Hydrated tricalcium aluminate crystals}}{3CaO.Al_2O_3.6H_2O} + 880\ \text{kJ/kg}$$

Due to hydration, the cement sets in the early stages. To avoid early setting of cement, gypsum is added

$$\underset{\text{Tricalcium aluminate}}{3CaO.Al_2O_3} + xH_2O + \underset{\text{Gypsum}}{yCaSO_4.2H_2O} \longrightarrow \underset{\text{Calcium sulphoalumiante (insoluble)}}{3CaO.Al_2O_3.3CaSO_4.(30-32)H_2O}$$

calcium sulphoaluminate so formed is **insoluble** and does not hydrate rapidly.

2. Hydrolysis of tetracalcium aluminoferrite: Tetracalcium aluminoferrite undergoes hydrolysis according to the following reaction:

$$\underset{\text{Tetra calcium aluminoferrite}}{4CaO.Al_2O_3.Fe_2O_3} + 7H_2O \longrightarrow 3CaO.Al_2O_3.6H_2O + CaO.Fe_2O_3.H_2O + 420\text{kJ/kg}$$

After hydration of tricalcium aluminate, C_3S (tricalcium silicate) begins to hydrate to give tobermorite gel and crystalline $Ca(OH)_2$ which imparts initial strength to the cement.

$$2[3CaO.SiO_2] + 6H_2O \longrightarrow \underset{\text{Tobermorite gel}}{3CaO.2SiO_2.3H_2O} + 3Ca(OH)_2 + \text{Heat}$$

The hydration of C_3S gets completed within 7 days.

Final setting refers to the beginning of hardening and gain of strength.

Dicalcium silicate reacts slowly with water and gets completed in 7 to 28 days.

$$\underset{\text{Dicalcium silicate}}{2[2CaO.SiO_2]} + 4H_2O \longrightarrow \underset{\text{Tobermorite gel}}{3CaO.2SiO_2.3H_2O} + \underset{\text{Crystalline}}{Ca(OH)_2} + \text{Heat}$$

Increase of strength of cement is due to the formation of tobermorite gel and crystalline $Ca(OH)_2$ from hydrolysis of both C_3S and C_2S. The strength and hardness of cement increases with time. The process takes nearly 28 days to complete.

Testing and ISI Specifications of Portland Cement

In order to ascertain the quality of cement, various chemical and physical tests re conducted from raw material stage to the final finished product. Different type of cements have to satisfy their relevant specifications. Some important specifications for ordinary portland cement as per Indian Standards Institute (ISI) are given below:

Chemical Requirement of Cement

(*i*) Ratio of percentage of alumina to that of iron oxide should not be less than 0.66

$$\text{Alumina ratio} = \frac{Al_2O_3}{Fe_2O_3} \geq 0.66$$

(*ii*) Ratio of percentage of lime to that of silica, alumina and iron oxide (called as **lime saturation factor**) should not be less than 0.66 and not more than 1.02 when calculated by the following formula:

$$\text{Lime saturation factor} = \frac{CaO - 0.7SO_3}{2.8SiO_2 + 1.2Al_2O_3 + 0.65Fe_2O_3} = 0.66 \text{ to } 1.02.$$

(*iii*) The weight of insoluble residue shall not exceed 2%.

(*iv*) Weight of magnesia shall not exceed 6%.

(*v*) Total sulphur content, calculated as SO_3, shall not be more than 2.75%.

(*vi*) Total loss on ignition shall not exceed 4%.

Physical Requirements of Cement

Following are some of the physical measurements used to test the quality of cement:

(*i*) Setting time: 30 minutes as initial setting time and 600 minutes (10 hours) as final setting time.

(*ii*) **Fineness:** It should be not be less than 215 m^2/kg. The finer the cement, the more is the surface area and faster is the rate of reaction and hence strength develops early. However, the cement should not be ground too finely because there is possibility of prehydration due to accidental contact with moisture during manufacturing and storage. This result in cracks in the cement.

(*iii*) **Soundness:** It refers to the ability of a cement to maintain a stable volume after setting. It is related to the excessive amount of free lime or magnesia in the cement. On hydration, if a cement produces very small volume changes which are well within tolerance limits laid down in the specifications, the cement is said to be "**sound**". The soundness is determined by Le Chatelier's method which expresses the expansivity of the cement set in 24 hours between 25°C to 100°C. Recently, this test is replaced by "**Autoclave test**". In autoclave test, a sample of hardened cement paste is boiled for a fixed time so that any tendency to expand is speeded up and can be detected.

By Le Chatelier's method : maximum expansion for
unaerated cement = 10 mm
Aerated cement = 5 mm

By autoclave method : Maximum expansion = 0.8%.

(*iv*) **Compressive strength:** Compressive strength of 1:3 mortar cube of cement and Ennore sand:

Not less than 1.6 kg/mm^2 after 3 days

Not less than 2.2 kg/mm^2 after 7 days.

(*v*) **Specific gravity:** It should lie between 3.1 to 3.2. Specific gravity more than 3.2 indicates that cement was not properly minced into powder form during its production or cement has more moisture content.

(*vi*) **Tensile strength:** It refers to the capacity of cement to resist cracking or breaking under tension. It should not be less than 300 lbs/sq inch after 72 hours.

(*vii*) **Heat of hydration:** When water is mixed with portland cement, some amount of heat is liberated due to hydration and hydrolysis reaction. It should not be more than 65 cal/g after 7 days and not more than 75 cal/g after 28 days.

(*viii*) **Composition:** The approximate composition of an Indian Portland cement is:

Constituent	CaO	SiO_2	Al_2O_3	Fe_2O_3	SO_3	MgO	Losses
%	64.86	23	5.97	2.19	1.75	1.0	0.75

10.4 OTHER TYPES OF CEMENTS

Certain cements differ from conventional portland cements in their chemical and phase composition as well as in their properties. Their properties can be achieved by using an additive, modifying raw material mix or by adjusting the grinding fineness of the cement.

(*i*) **High alumina cement:** It is essentially a calcium aluminate cement and can be manufactured by heating a mixture of limestone and bauxite at 1550 – 1600°C. This cement has a very rapid rate of development of strength and superior resistance to sea and sulphate waters.

(*ii*) **Super sulphate cement:** This cement is prepared by fusing together blast furnace slag, calcium sulphate (gypsum) and lime in a kiln. This cement is exceptionally resistant to chemical corrosion and expands very little on setting therefore, it is used in construction of dams and highways.

(*iii*) **Waterproof cement:** The moisture loving property (hydrophilic property) of portland cement can be decreased by mixing it with varying amounts of calcium and aluminium stearates. The cement thus formed is called as waterproof cement. This cement find application in construction of structures like water tanks, swimming pools, casting basement wall etc.

(*iv*) **White cement:** The colour of ordinary portland cement is greyish-black due to the presence of iron oxide (Fe_2O_3) and other colouring ions like Mn^{3+}, Mn^{4+}, Cr^{6+} etc. By reducing the content of these colouring ions in the raw material it is possible to get white cement. It is mainly used for decorative construction. It is also used for repairing of cracks in swimming pools, flood control ducts and other underwater structures.

(*v*) **Coloured cement:** It can be manufactured by mixing ordinary portland cement (grey cement) with suitable coloured pigments. It is used to enhance the appearance and beauty of various monuments.

10.5 OTHER CEMENTING MATERIALS

1. Plaster of Paris, 2. Gypsum, 3. Lime

1. Plaster of Paris ($CaSO_4 \cdot \frac{1}{2} H_2O$)

It is a hemihydrate of calcium sulphate *i.e.* $CaSO_4 \cdot \frac{1}{2} H_2O$ or $2CaSO_4 \cdot H_2O$. It is prepared by heating gypsum ($CaSO_4.2H_2O$) to a temperature of 120°C to 160°C.

$$CaSO_4.2H_2O \xrightarrow[120° - 160°C]{Heat} \underset{\text{Plaster of Paris}}{CaSO_4.\frac{1}{2}H_2O}$$

The preparation involves following steps:

1. crushing and grinding of gypsum
2. calcination of grounded gypsum
3. pulverization of calcined product

During the preparation of plaster of paris if temperature increases above 200°C, it loses all its water and form anhydrous salt ($CaSO_4$) called as **dead burnt plaster**, which does not have any setting properties.

Properties:

When mixed with water, plaster of Paris forms a plastic mass which quickly hardens (5–10 min). During this process, it expands slightly and regains the closely packed crystalline structure of gypsum. Also, due to expansion, plaster of Paris takes the shape of the mould in which it is placed.

The process of setting of plaster of Paris can be accelerated by adding alums or alkali sulphates (K_2SO_4, Na_2SO_4 etc.).

Applications:

(*i*) It is used for making moulds, statues, black board chalk, etc.

(*ii*) In labs, it is used for making the apparatus air tight.

(*iii*) It is also used in plastering the walls, interior ceilings etc.

(*iv*) It is used in manufacturing of surgical bandages, structural tiles and castings.

2. Gypsum ($CaSO_4 . 2H_2O$)

Gypsum is a soft non-metallic natural mineral of the chemical formula $CaSO_4 . 2H_2O$. Gypsum is usually found in beds or bands in the sedimentary rocks such as limestone, sandstone and shales. Sometimes, they are found as scattered crystals and grains in clays. Gypsum is also obtained as a by product during the manufacture of salt from sea water by direct solar evaporation.

Properties:

(*i*) It is colourless to white mineral but due to mixing of impurities it may be grey, brown, red or pink in colour.

(*ii*) It is very soft and can be scratched with a fingernail.

(*iii*) On heating gypsum, a number of cementing materials related to $CaSO_4$ are formed due to partial or complete dehydration.

$$CaSO_4 \cdot 2H_2O \xrightarrow[120°-150°C]{Heat} \underset{\text{Plaster of Paris}}{CaSO_4 \cdot \frac{1}{2}H_2O} \xrightarrow[200°C]{Heat} \underset{\text{Dead burnt plaster}}{CaSO_4}$$

$$CaSO_4 \underset{}{\overset{800°C}{\rightleftharpoons}} CaO + SO_3$$

Applications:

(*i*) Gypsum is used for carving images and other art pieces due to its soft, dense and fine textured nature.

(*ii*) It is used in the preparation of plaster of Paris, crayons, chalk pencils etc.

(*iii*) It is used in the manufacture of cement to prevent rapid setting.

(*iv*) It is used in the manufacturing of tiles, plasters, baking powder etc.

(*v*) It is used in paints, pharmaceutical products, paper filling, insecticides, water treatment etc.

(*vi*) It is used in the manufacture of fertilizers.

(*vii*) It is used to lower the pH of water brewery.

3. Lime

Chemically, lime is calcium oxide and is obtained by heating a natural mineral, limestone ($CaCO_3$) in a special type of rotary kiln at about 895°C.

$$CaCO_3 \rightleftharpoons CaO + CO_2$$

The temperature of the process should not increase beyond 1200°C otherwise silica (SiO_2) present in limestone (as an impurity) will react with CaO to form $CaSiO_3$ (calcium silicate)

$$CaO + SiO_2 \xrightarrow{>1200°C} CaSiO_3$$

There are different varieties of lime depending on the percentage of calcium oxide. The different varieties are:

(*i*) **Fat limes:** Contains about 95–98% CaO. Rest 2–5% are impurities like SiO_2, Al_2O_3 and MgO.

(ii) **Lean limes:** Contains about 70–80% CaO. Impurities are MgO (about 5%), SiO_2 and Fe_2O_3 etc. Also known as **poor limes.**

(iii) **Hydraulic limes:** Contains about 70 – 80% CaO and rest is the impurity in the form of silica and alumina (5–30%) and less than 2% MgO.

(iv) **Dolomite limes:** These are obtained by heating dolomite ($CaCO_3$ + $MgCO_3$) in presence of limited supply of air. These contain less percentage of SiO_2 and Al_2O_3 but 30–40% of MgO as impurity.

Properties:

(i) Lime is a white solid with high melting point.

(ii) When pure lime (CaO) or quick lime is treated with water, the water is readily absorbed through the pores of quicklime lumps and $Ca(OH)_2$ (slaked lime) is formed

$$CaO + H_2O \longrightarrow Ca(OH)_2 + 15.9 \text{ kcal}$$

This process is accompanied by

- evolution of considerable amount of heat
- 2 – 2.5 times increase in volume
- development of hissing and cracking sound due to conversion of water → steam and lime → slaked lime.

(iii) When lime is mixed with silica or sand, it can be used as mortar or plaster because silica decreases the shrinkage of lime during setting and increases the plasticity of lime. It makes the mixture more economical.

(iv) When placed in air, lime slowly absorbs moisture and CO_2 from the atmosphere and swells as well as disintegrates into fine powder (called air soaked time).

$$CaO + H_2O \longrightarrow Ca(OH)_2$$

$$Ca(OH)_2 + CO_2 \longrightarrow CaCO_3 + H_2O$$

Due to formation of $CaCO_3$, this lime is not suitable for the manufacture of mortars and plasters. Mortars made from soaked lime will not harden.

Applications:

(i) It is used to soften water through lime soda process.

(ii) It is used in agriculture as a fertilizer and also for liming soil.

(iii) It is used in construction as a plaster, whitewash, mortar when mixed with sand, lime-concrete when mixed with sand and coarse aggregates, sand lime bricks etc.

(iv) It is used in industries as a flux in metallurgy, refractory material for lining metallurgical furnaces, raw material for glass manufacture etc.

(v) Lime is used to control pollution caused by emission of oxides of sulphur from various industries. Lime absorbs and neutralizes sulphur oxides from these industries and thus helps to prevent acid rain and reducing emission of hazardous air pollutants including mercury.

$$CaO(s) + SO_2(g) \longrightarrow CaSO_3(s)$$

(vi) It is also used in paper industry for pulping.

(vii) It is used as reagent in laboratories.

10.6 REFRACTORIES

Refractories are inorganic materials which can withstand very high temperature without undergoing physicochemical changes (*e.g.* softening, melting, deformation in shape etc.) while remaining in contact with molten slag, metals and gases. They are mostly used in lining of furnaces, kilns, crucibles etc. which are usually heated to a very high temperature.

Characteristics and Selection of a Good Refractory

A good refractory should possess the following characteristics:

(*i*) It should not melt or undergo large dimensional changes at high temperature (due to expansion or contraction).

(*ii*) It should be chemically inert even at high temperature, it should not react with reactants or products in the furnace like metallic liquids, slags etc.

(*iii*) It should have good thermal strength or resistance to thermal shock due to rapid fluctuating temperature (*i.e.* should not crack).

(*iv*) It should have high fusion temperature.

(*v*) It should have excellent heat, corrosion and abrasion resistance.

(*vi*) It should be able to withstand the overlying load of structure at severe operating conditions.

In general, no single substance can satisfy all of these above mentioned characteristics of a refractory, therefore, a refractory is formulated from a mixture of compounds.

Classification of Refractories

Refractories are classified into three main types on the basis of the nature of their constituents:

(*a*) Acid refractories: These are made up of acidic oxides like alumina (Al_2O_3), silica (SiO_2). These are not attacked by acidic substances but are easily attacked by basic substances. For example, alumina, silica, fireclay refractories etc.

(*b*) Basic Refractories: These are made up of basic oxides such as calcium oxide (CaO), magnesium oxide (MgO). Hence, these are not attached by basic substances but are easily attacked by acidic substances. For example dolomite, magnesite, chrome magnesite etc.

(*c*) Neutral refractories: These are made up of weakly acidic/basic substances like carbon, zirconia(ZrO_2), chromite ($FeOCrO_2$). For example graphite, chromite.

These refractories are discussed in detail in later sections.

On the basis of oxide content, refractories can also be:

- **Simple oxide refractory:** The oxide content is simple oxide. For example, alumina, magnesia, zirconia etc.
- **Mixed oxide refractories:** The oxide content is mixed oxide. For example, mullite, spinel etc.
- **Non-oxide refractory:** The refractory does not contain any oxide. For example carbides, nitrides, silicide, borides etc.

On the basis of operating temperature, refractories can be:

- **Low temperature refractories:** Fusin range is 1600–1800°C. For example fire-clay refractory.
- **Medium temperature refractory:** Fusion range is 1800–2000°C. For example chromite refractory.
- **High temperature refractory:** Fusion range > 2000°C. For example, zirconia refractory.

Properties of refractories: The important properties of refractories are:

- Refractoriness
- Strength or refractoriness under load
- Dimensional stability
- Chemical inertness
- Thermal expansion
- Thermal conductivity
- Porosity
- Thermal spalling
- Resistance to abrasion or corosion
- Electrical conductivity
- Heat capacity
- Texture
- Permeability.

1. Refractoriness: It is the ability of a material to withstand the heat without appreciable deformation or softening under particular service conditions. Refractoriness is generally measured as the softening or melting temperature of the material.

Softening temperature of the material to be used as refractory >> Operating temperature of the furnace

Measurement of refractoriness (Pyrometric cone test or Seger Cone test):

As already mentioned most of the refractory materials are mixture of several metallic oxides, therefore, they do not have sharp fusion temperature. Hence, softening temperature of refractories rather than fusion temperature is determined. The softening temperature of the refractory material are generally determined by using pyrometric cone test (Seger cone test).

The refractories is usually determined by comparing the behaviour of heat on cone (triangular cone) of material to be tested with that of a series of Seger cones of standard dimensions (3.8 cm high and 1.9 cm long sides or base). Seger cones melt or fuse at a definite temperature when heated under standard conditions of 10°C/min.

Now, the test refractory in the form of cone is kept along side similar sized standard Seger cones. and are heated uniformly at 10°C/min. When the test cone softens and loses its shape, one of the standard Seger cone also softens and losses its shape provided its refractoriness is close to that of the test cone. The temperature at which the cone finally touches the plaque is known as **softening temperature or refractoriness**. This is the PCE (Pyrometric cone equivalent) value of the test cone. For example, if the test cone softens alongwith Seger cone no.11, then the PCE value of the test cone is 11 and the softening temperature also corresponds to that of Seger cone no. 11. If more than one Segar cone softens alongwith the test cone then the PCE value of the test sample is approximated as the average of the two. The fusion temperature of some Seger cones at 10°C/min heating rate are given in Table 10.3.

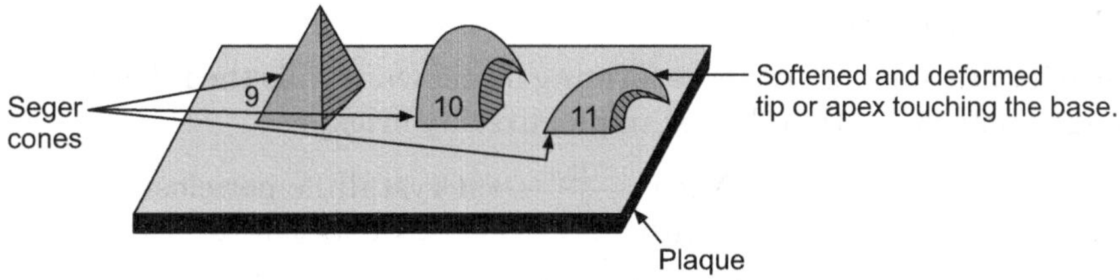

Fig. 10.3 Seger cone test

Table 10.3: Seger Cone Number and Fusion Temperature

Seger cone. no.	1	2	3	4	5	6	7	8	9	10	15	20	30
Fusion temp. (°C)	1110	1120	1140	1160	1180	1200	1230	1250	1280	1300	1435	1530	1670

2. Strength of refractoriness under load: It is the resistance of the refractory to compressive loads, tension and shear stresses in the cold as well as under high temperature. Some refractories like fire clay and alumina brick collapse under appreciable load far below their fusion point. However, a good refractory material must possess high mechanical strength to bear the maximum possible load without breaking.

Measurement: This test is performed to measure the safe upper temperature limit upto which the refractories can be used. Seger cone test is not applicable for the measurement of strength because some refractories soften gradually over a range of temperature but under high load, they collpase far below their true fusion temperature. Therefore, for good results refractoriness under load (R.U.L.) test is performed by applying a constant load of 1.75 or 3.5 kg/cm^2 to the refractory specimen of standard size 5 cm^2 base and 75 cm height. The sample is then kept in carbon resistant furnace and heated at a rate of 10°C/min. During heating, the sample will soften, as a result its height will keep decreasing under the load. The height of the sample is plotted versus temperature and R.U.L. is expressed as the temperature at which 10% deformation (height is decreased by 10% of its original height) takes place. On the basis of R.U.L. test, a refractory can be

(*a*) **High heat duty brick:** RUL → 1350°C *i.e.* it does not deform more than 10% at 1350°C.

(*b*) **Intermediate heat duty brick:** RUL → 1300°C *i.e.* it does not deform more than 10% at 1300°C.

(*c*) **Moderate heat duty brick:** RUL → 110°C *i.e.* it does not deform more than 10% at 1100°C.

3. Dimensional stability: It is the resistance of a material to any change in volume when it is exposed to high temperatures over a prolonged time.

Dimensional changes can be of two type:

***(i)* Permanent contraction:** When a refractory material is subjected to high temperatures for long duration, permanent contraction takes place due to:

- transformation of one crystalline form of material into another of low density. For example magnesite brick.
- melting of low fusible constituents forming liquid which fills the refractory pores causing shrinkage and vitrification. For example, fireclay brick.

$$\underset{\text{(Specific gravity = 3.05)}}{\text{Amorphous MgO}} \xrightarrow[\text{Temp.}]{\text{High}} \underset{\text{(Specific gravity = 3.54)}}{\text{Crystalline periclose}}$$

***(ii)* Permanent expansion:** When a refractory material is subjected to high temperature, it undergoes transformation from one crystalline from to another of low density causing expansion. For example silica bricks

$$\underset{\text{(Specific gravity = 2.65)}}{\text{Quartz}} \longrightarrow \underset{\text{(Specific gravity = 2.26)}}{\text{tridymite}} \longrightarrow \underset{\text{(Specific gravity = 2.23)}}{\text{Cristobalite}}$$

4. Chemical inertness: Slags, fuel, ashes, furnace gases and products formed in refractories may react with refractory material. Acid refractories react with basic products and basic refractories react with acidic products. Hence, chemical reactions of the products formed in refractory must be considered before using a particular refractory. Therefore, such a refractory should be selected that the above mentioned reacting substances have the least effect on the refractory.

5. Thermal expansion: Practically all solids expand on heating and contract on cooling. A good refractory material should expand or contract minimally.

Expansion of refractories may produce following two effects:

(*i*) Expansion decreases the capacity of the furnace.

(*ii*) Repeated expansion and contraction may lead to wear and tear and even breakage of the refractory material.

6. Thermal conductivity: Refractories of low as well as high thermal conductivity are used in industries depending upon the type of furnace. In most cases, furnace is lined with refractories of low heat conductivity to reduce the heat loss to the outside by radiation (for example blast furnace, open hearth furnace). However, refractories used in muffle furnace walls, coke oven furnace require high thermal conductivity.

7. Porosity: Porosity of a refractory material is the ratio of its pores volume to the bulk volume. Thus,

Porosity, $$P = \frac{W - D}{W - A} \times 100$$

where,

W = weight of sample saturated with moisture

D = weight of same dry sample

A = weight of saturated sample and submerged in water.

Pores are present in all refractory materials and can be open or closed. Porosity is an important property of refractories because it effects several other characteristics. In general, high porosity refractory is not preferred much because.

- It will allow the gases and molten material to enter the pores thereby decreasing the strength as well and resistance to abrasion.
- It is also susceptible to corrosion.

All these factors reduces the life of the refractory. However, air is entrapped in the pores and hence increase the resistance to thermal spalling as the entrapped air acts as a non-heat conducting material.

On the other hand low porosity refractory will have greater strength, higher heat capacity and thermal conductivity. A good refractory in general has low porosity.

8. Thermal spalling: Spalling is breaking or fracturing of a refractory due to uneven expansion and contraction of a refractory on account of heating or cooling. Spalling may also be due to slag penetration into the refractory brick, thereby causing variation in the coefficient of expansion leading to the development of internal stress. Spalling may be reduced in the following ways:

By using refractory bricks having high porosity, low coefficient of expansion and good thermal conductivity. All these factors resist the development of internal stress.

By avoiding sudden temperature changes.

By modifying the furnace design.

9. Resistance to corrosion and erosion: During the course of the reaction (in metallurgy) as the temperature increases, the viscosity of slag decreases which accelerates the chemical reaction between the slag and refractory lining. This might lead to corrosion of refractory lining. Similarly, greater wetting of the refractory by the slag also increases corrosion (a carbonaceous refractory is not wet by slags).

Erosion is gradual wearing away of a material from its surface and arises due to mechanical action inside the furnace Erosion produces cavities and pot holes on the refractory surface which in turn increases the probability of corrosion. Zircon refractories are high-density compacted refractories which resist erosion very well.

For a refractory to last longer, it should have excellent corrosion and erosion resistance.

10. Electrical conductivity: Refractories used for lining electric furnaces should have low electrical conductivity. All refractories except graphite are poor conductors of electricity.

11. Heat capacity: Heat capacity of a furnace depends on thermal conductivity, specific heat and specific gravity of the refractory. Heavy and dense refractory bricks (*e.g.*, fire clay refractories) have high heat capacity and therefore, find use in regenerative checker brick work of coke ovens, glass furnaces and blast furnace stoves. On the other hand, light weight refractory bricks due to their low heat capacity are used in intermittently operated furnaces to achieve the working temperature in a short time with lesser fuel consumption.

12. Texture: Refractories can be
- coarse or light textured
- fine or dense textured

The fine or dense textured refractories have less porosity and hence have more weight. Due to this property, they are not easily attacked by chemicals and do not undergo corrosion easily. But, these fine refractories cannot withstand sudden temperature fluctuations. Conversely, coarse textured bricks due to high porosity are susceptible to chemical attack and corrosion. However, these coarse bricks have an advantage of withstanding sudden temperature fluctuations.

13. Permeability: Permeability is the rate of diffusion of molten solids, liquids and gases through the pores. Permeability is directly proportional to porosity *i.e.* more the porosity, higher will be the permeability.

A good refractory should have low permeability.

10.7 MANUFACTURE OF REFRACTORIES

Manufacture of refractories consists of the following steps:

1. Grinding: The materials are properly ground so that the ratio of coarse particles to the one is 55 : 45.

2. Mixing: The ground particles are thoroughly mixed. It is done for two purposes, viz.,

(*i*) Distributing evenly the coarse and fine particles, and

(*ii*) For making moulding easy.

3. Moulding: Moulding may be done is two ways.

(*i*) **By hand:** When moulding is done by hand, the density and strength of the refractory is comparatively low.

(*ii*) **Mechanical moulding:** During mechanical moulding, de-airing of refractory is essential. De-airing increases the density of the refractory since the air with lower density than the refractory is excluded. De-airing is carried out by the following methods:

(*a*) Air inside the voides in the refractory is allowed to escape by decreasing the rate of pressure application and release.

(*b*) The material is first pressed and allowed to crack. It is repressed to close the voids.

(*c*) By passing a gas such as butane to the mould in order to displace the air. When pressure is applied, the a gas is absorbed by clay.

(*d*) By applying vacuum through vents in the moulds.

4. Drying: The moulded refractory is dried to remove its moisture. Drying should be so modulated that neither voids are left in the refractory nor the refractory is shrunk to produce internal stresses. Generally drying is carried out very slowly and under particular set of conditions of humidity and temperature depending upon the type of refractory.

5. Burning: The dried refractory is burnt for vitrification and development of stable mineral forms. Burning of refractory produces following changes.

(*i*) Removal of water of hydration (Dehydration)

(*ii*) Calcination of carbonates and oxidation of Fe^{2+} to Fe^{3+}.

(*iii*) Shrinkage in volume may also take place which in turn produces stresses in the refractory. However, this can be avoided by the use of pre-stabilised material. Pre-stabilization consists of appropriate sizing and pressing.

The refractories are generally fired at a temperature higher than the temperature at which they are used. Firing is done in down draught kilns or tunnel kiln.

10.8 ACID REFRACTORIES

Acid refractories may be of two types, *viz.*, fire-clay and silica.

10.8.1 Fire-clay Refractories

Fire-clay is a clay which is more refractory than any other clay and has a softening temperature of 1580°C. Raw materials employed for the manufacture of fire-clay refractories are:

(*i*) Raw fire-clay.

(*ii*) *Burnt fire-clay (grog):* Addition of grog has following advantages:

(*a*) It decreases the amount of water added to get a workable plasticity.

(*b*) It decreases shrinkage of the article produced.

(*c*) It increases the strength of fired material.

(*d*)It increases apparent porosity and apparent specific gravity.

(*e*) It increases resistance to sudden change of temperature.

Manufacture of Fire-clay Refractories

Raw fire-clay is dried, crushed by gyratory crushers, ground finely in an edge runner and mixed with ground grog. The mixture is soaked in water for about 34 hours or more so that water is properly distributed throughout the whole mass. After soaking, the mixture is transferred to a pug mill where the whole mass is throughly mixed. The whole mass is now transferred to a coal cellar where it is allowed to mature for a number of days. The completely matured mixture is moulded (by hand or by machines) into bricks and blocks etc. The moulded refractories are dried evenly and properly at room temperature.

Dried refractories are arranged in a kiln which may be down draught, up draught, horizontal draught type, single kilns or continuous kilns. Temperature is raised slowly upto 1300°C and then cooled slowly.

Properties of Fire-clay Refractories

(*i*) Fire-clay refractories are generally light yellow to reddish brown in colour.

(*ii*) These are as hard as steel; the exact hardness depends upon the firing temperature.

(*iii*) They possess low porosity (8 to 24%); the exact porosity depends upon the temperature to which the refractory is fired.

(*iv*) They have better resistance to thermal spalling than silica bricks. This makes fire-clay bricks very suitable for making a checker work of regenerative furnaces and charging doors etc. which are subjected to temperature fluctuations.

(*v*) Fire-clay bricks have specific heat as low as 0.25. It rises rapidly with rise in temperature and is 0.264 at 1300°C.

(*vi*) Chemical properties: Fire-clay refractories are slightly acidic in character; hence they combine with alkalies such as soda, potash, lime, magnesia, iron oxide, etc. at high temperature.

(*vii*) Strength or resistance to crushing: Crushing strength varies with temperature. An ordinary fire-clay has crushing strength as 950 kg/cm^2 at room temperature, but it decreases with temperature as is evident from the following data.

Temperature	Crushing load (kg/cm^2)	Temperature	Crushing load (kg/cm^2)
800°C	755	1300°C	360
1000°C	575	1500°C	65

(*viii*) **Refractoriness:** They have low refractoriness than silica bricks. On the basis of refractoriness, fire-clay refractories have been grouped in three grades.

(*a*) First grade having softening temperature between 1770° and 1790°C.

(*b*) Second grade having softening temperature between 1670° and 1770°C.

(*c*) Third grade having softening temperature between 1580° and 1670°C.

(*ix*) Refractoriness under load: Most of the fire-clay refractories have softening point of 1350°C under a load of 50 lbs/square inch.

(*x*) Effect of heat: Fire-clay refractories undergo following changes on heating:

(*a*) **Baking:** It involves heating of clay till it is decomposed and there is no more loss of water. Baking takes place between 500 – 650°C.

(*b*) **Vitrification:** It involves heating of clay till some of its ingredients are fused and fill the pores. During vitrification kaolinite, $Al_2O_3 . 2SiO_2(2H_2O)$ is changed to mullite, $3Al_2O_3 . 2SiO_2$. It takes place between 1250 and 1400°C.

(*c*) **Squatting or softening:** It involves heating of clay till it begins to loose its shape. It takes place between 1550 and 1770°C.

(*d*) **Fusion:** Fusion is that stage of heating during which material changes from solid to liquid state. It takes place above 1770°C.

(*xi*) Thermal conductivity: Thermal conductivity of fire-clay refractories varies with temperature. Fire clay refractories are although bad conductor of heat, they possess a high power of radiation. So materials placed in fire chambers mode of fire-clay may be heated to a very high temperature though the conductivity of fire-clay is very low.

Applications of fire-clay Refractories

- Fire-clay bricks are most widely used of all the refractives because they are very cheap and have properties of ideal refractories.
- They are used for the construction of furnaces (blast, open-hearth, etc.), kilns, stoves, ovens, flues, boiler settings and any other structures in which heat is generated or through which hot gases pass.
- They are used for making checker works of regenerative furnaces because these bricks have better resistance to thermal spalling than silica bricks.

10.8.2 Silica Refractories

Silica refractories consist of silica (90–95%) and lime (about 2% as binding material).

Silica: Crystalline silica mainly in the form of quartz (rock crystal, quartzite and sands-to constitute the raw material for silica.

Binding material: Since crushed silica has no plasticity, it cannot be shaped into materials; hence some binding material is added to furnish the bond and thus to bind the silica particles. Common binding materials are lime, clay, sodium silicate, alum, aluminium sulphate, calcium chloride, complex silicates, plaster of Paris, barium sulphate, calcium phosphate, etc.

Manufacture of silica refractories

Silica rocks are crushed in gyratory crushers, ground with appropriate amount (2%) of lime and then mixed with water in an edge runner. Mixing (tempering) is done till a uniform paste is obtained. The thick paste is then moulded into bricks either by hand or machine pressing. Moulded bricks are dried in air or in heated rooms. The dried bricks any burnt in a kiln;

the temperature of kiln is slowly raised to about 1500°C which is maintained for nearly 12 hours. This causes conversion of quartzite to trydymite or cristobalite (other form of crystalline silica). During burning of silica refractory, following changes take place :

(*a*) Any moisture and organic matter is removed.

(*b*) Lime and other bases are converted into silicates which are then fused.

(*c*) Quartz is converted into cristobalite or tridymite which ensures constant volume in the brick.

The kiln is slowly cooled. During cooling some of the cristobalite is slowly changed into tridymite hence silica bricks are finally mixtures of tridymite and cristobalite.

Properties

(*i*) Silica bricks are yellowish in colour with brown speck throughout the body.

(*ii*) Its specific gravity varies from 2.2 to 2.6 depending upon the temperature to which silica is burnt.

(*iii*) Silica refractories expand on heating: However, this effect is reversible and the bricks contract to its original size when cooled. These volume changes are due to allotropic changes occurring in silica. Actually, these allotropic changes cause changes in specific gravity which in turn causes change in volume.

$$\underset{\text{(sp. gr. = 2.65)}}{\text{Quartzite}} \xrightleftharpoons{870°C} \underset{\text{(sp. gr. = 2.26)}}{\text{Tridymite}} \xrightleftharpoons{1470°C} \underset{\text{(sp. gr. = 2.23)}}{\text{Cristobalite}}$$

Thus at 870°C when tridymite is formed, there is increase in volume of 14 to 16%. On the other hand, heating of silica refractory upto 1470°C (*i.e.* conversion of silica to cristobalite) is accompanied by an increase in volume by 20%.

(*iv*) Silica bricks are homogeneous in texture; these are free from air-pockets and moulding defects.

(*v*) Mechanical strength: Their mechanical strength varies from 900 to 3700 lbs/inch^2 depending upon the composition. The crushing strength of silica brick is proportional to fineness of quartz used, the proportion of binding material and water added to make paste.

(*vi*) Refractoriness under load: Silica brick when heated under a load of 50 lbs/inch^2 will disintegrate between 1350 and 1470°C. The maximum working temperature of silica brick under load is usually 1680°C.

(*vii*) Refractoriness: The best silica refractory has softening temperature from 1750°C to 1760°C. The refractoriness depends upon the following factors:

(*a*) Proportion of lime, soda, potash and alumina present in the refractory.

(*b*) Texture of refractory.

(*c*) Mode and extent to which refractory is burnt.

(*viii*) Spalling: Silica bricks have low resistance to thermal spalling and a sudden change in temperature causes fine cracks in the brick The spalling is due to following factors.

(*a*) Spalling occurs in the refractory when the conversion from quartz to cristobalite or tridymite is either complete or occurs suddenly due to rapid rise in temperature of the refractory. However, this type of spalling can be avoided by repeatedly raising the temperature of the refractory at a slow rate up to 800°C and then cooling it slowly

(*b*) Spalling occurs due to reversible expansion and contraction occurring too rapidly. This can also be avoided by heating the refractory slowly.

(*c*) Spalling may also occur due to the action of slags.

In general, spalling can be decreased in silica refractory by the following instruction:

(*i*) By using a coarse-grained refractory

(*ii*) By increasing the porosity and decreasing the density.

(*iii*) By repeatedly heating the refractory to 800°C and then cooling it slowly. This causes conversion of quartz to tridymite rather than cristobalite.

(*ix*) Thermal conductivity: It is higher than fire-clay bricks.

(*x*) Action of chemical agents: Among acids, silica is effected only by hydrofluoric acid in cold and phosphoric acid at 400°C.

Alkalies and bases react with silica refractory, particularly at high temperatures, forming silicates.

Silica reacts with carbon at about 1200°C to form Si and CO or SiC in some cases.

Applications of silica refractories

Silica bricks are used in the roof and lining of furnaces, kilns, convertors, etc.

- Silica bricks are extensively used in steel and iron industries.

10.9 BASIC REFRACTORIES

Important basic refractories are alumina, magnesite, dolomite, etc.

10.9.1. Alumina Bricks

Pure alumina is the best refractory material but because of its high cost it is rarely used as such for manufacturing refractories. Generally, bauxite (naturally occurring alumina) is used for the manufacture of alumina refractories. Binding materials used for uniting bauxite particles are fire-clay, silica, lime, magnesia, plaster of Paris, sodium silicate, etc.

Properties:

(*i*) **Porosity:** Alumina bricks are highly porous which decreases their durability in furnace.

(*ii*) **Shrinkage:** Bauxite refractories show great shrinkage even at high temperature. However, this drawback can be eliminated by making the refractory from fused bauxite.

(*iii*) **Resistance to abrasion:** These have great resistant to abrasion.

(*iv*) **Mechanical strength:** Bauxite refractories have high mechanical strength.

(*v*) **Refractoriness:** Bauxite refractories are heat resistant from 1790° to 1880°C. Under a pressure of 50 lbs/inch^2 bauxite refractories soften at about 1500°C.

(*vi*) **Spalling:** Bauxite refractories have very little tendency to spall.

(*vii*) **Chemical reactions:** Bauxite is inert to gases like CO_2, H_2 and also to oxidizing and reducing agents. Being basic in character, bauxite is not attacked by basic slags. This property of bauxite makes it superior to fire-clay refractories which are subject to such attacks.

Applications of Bauxite Refractories:

(*i*) Bauxite refractories are used in furnaces in which molten metals, basic slags and metallic oxides are heated to a very high temperature. Such types of furnaces include steel furnaces and rotatory cement kilns.

(*ii*) Since bauxite is unaffected by alkalies, bauxite bricks arc used for lining furnaces resistant to alkalies.

(*iii*) Fused bauxite bricks are used for roofs of electric furnaces.

10.9.2 Magnesia Bricks

The main raw material for magnesia bricks is magnesia (MgO) which is obtained from naturally occurring mineral known as magnesite ($MgCO_3$). The binding material for magnesia particles may be clay, sodium silicate, silica, caustic soda, iron oxide, gum, dextrin, starch, etc.

Calcined magnesite (MgO) is powdered to a proper size, mixed with finely powdered binding material, ground with required quantity of water and then placed in a warm place for about three days for souring. When the mixture attains proper uniformity and plasticity, it is moulded into bricks. The bricks are dried slowly and then burnt in a kiln slowly raising the temperature to 1350°C. This temperature is kept for some time and then allowed to fall slowly

Properties:

(*i*) Magnesia bricks are usually grey or dark brown in colour with a specific gravity of 3.05 to 3.58.

(*ii*) Magnesia bricks have good crushing strength but have low resistance to abrasion.

(*iii*) They show little shrinkage.

(*iv*) They show great spalling.

(*v*) These are resistant to slags. However, being basic in nature, they react with acid refractories. They also react with iron oxide and carbon.

(*vi*) Magnesia bricks can be used upto 2000°C without load and upto 1500°C under a load of 3.5 kg/cm^2.

(*vii*) Heat conductivity of magnesia refractory is very low, so it is very useful for raising and maintaining high temperature in furnace.

Applications of magnesia refractory:

(*i*) Magnesia refractories are used mainly in the steel industry for the lining of basic convertors and open hearth furnaces.

(*ii*) Magnesia bricks are also used for constructing furnaces for melting lead, antimony and copper.

(*iii*) These are also used for gold, silver and platinum refining furnaces.

(*iv*) Bottom and side walls of electric furnaces are constructed with magnesia bricks.

(*v*) Magnesia bricks are used for covering fire-clay bricks.

10.9.3 Dolomite Refractories

Dolomite is magnesium lime stone with the composition. Ca Mg $(CO_3)_2$. It occurs in nature. Calcined dolomite particles are united with the help of magnesium silicate, iron ore, basic slags, tar, etc. (binding materials).

Dolomite is calcined, powdered and mixed with binding material and water. Mixing is performed in edge runner and then allowed to age by keeping it in wet condition. The mixture is moulded to bricks which are air-dried and burnt to a temperature ranging between 1200° to 1650°C.

Stabilised dolomite bricks: For preparing such bricks, dolomite is mixed with serpentine $(MgO.SiO_2)$ and the mixture is calcined to form di- and tri-calcium silicates which do not absorb water and carbon dioxide. The calcined mixture is mixed with a binding agent (usually silicate) and moulded into bricks which when burnt at about 1500°C for about a day gives stabilized dolomite bricks. Such bricks are quite stable towards basic slags.

Properties:

(*i*) Dolomite bricks are more porous and possess more softness, shrinkage and less strength than magnesia bricks.

(*ii*) They can be used upto 2300°C without load and upto 1650°C under a load of 3.5 kg/cm^2.

(*iii*) Dolomite bricks are corroded by silica. However, stabilized dolomite bricks are more resistant to slags and spalling than magnesia bricks because the former contains dicalcium silicate which is more resistant than magnesium silicate to dust and slag containing lime and iron compounds.

Applications of dolomite refractory: Dolomite is generally used as a repairing material rather than as a direct refractory because of its defects like great porosity, shrinkage and softness. However, stabilized dolomite bricks are used in electric furnaces, Bessemer convertors, open-hearth furnaces, etc. and as a cheap substitute for magnesia bricks.

10.10 NEUTRAL REFRACTORIES

The important neutral refractories are carbon, silicon carbide (carborundum) and chromites.

10.10.1 Carbon Refractories

Carbon refractories are again of two types depending upon the nature of the raw material.

(*a*) **Carbon refractories from coke.** These are commonly known as carbon refractories (carbon bricks).

(*b*) **Carbon refractories from graphite.** These are commonly known as graphite bricks.

(A) Carbon Bricks: (Carbon bricks from coke). Blast furnace coke is crushed and ground in edge runner mill. It is mixed with the required amount of tar (binding agent). Mixture is passed through pug mill heated with a steam jacket. The mixture is now moulded into bricks which are first dried in a cool room and then fired in a kiln from 1100°C to 1300°C.

Properties:

(*i*) They are light grey in colour,

(*ii*) They possess high crushing strength.

(*iii*) If not exposed to air, they can withstand high temperatures. However, when heated in presence of air, they burn.

(*iv*) They are not attacked by acids, alkalies and slags.

Applications:

Carbon bricks are used at bottom and sides of iron and steel furnaces. They are also used in furnaces for smelting copper, lead and aluminium.

(B) Graphite bricks: (Carbon bricks from graphite). Graphite (plumbago or black lead are other names) is the refractory material, while fire-clay is the binding material.

Pure graphite (impurities are removed by flotation) is crushed, finely powdered and mixed with fire-clay. It is then processed for the manufacture of bricks as in fire-clay bricks.

Properties and Uses:

Graphite bricks have closer texture. They arc not easily attacked by corrosive slag and bases. They allow the heat to pass through them. This property makes graphite bricks useless for furnace linings but makes them useful for partition, etc.

10.10.2 Silicon Carbide (Carborundum) Bricks

Although carbides of other elements like tantalum, zirconium, titanium and boron are useful as refractory materials, their cost restricted their use only for special purposes.

Raw materials for silicon carbide refractories:

(*i*) **Silicon carbide (SiC):** It is produced by heating sand (SiO_2) with coke in presence of saw dust and salt in electric furnaces at 1300 – 2200°C

$$SiO_2 + 3\,C \longrightarrow SiC + 2\,CO$$

(*ii*) **Binding material:** It may be plaster of Paris, lime, aluminium sulphate, felspar, glue, tar, molasses, etc.

Manufacture: The finely powdered silicon carbide is mixed with a little water in a pan. The mixture is moulded into bricks which are dried and fired in electric furnace upto 1400° to 2000°C.

Recently self-bonded silicon carbide bricks have been prepared. For this, silicon carbide is mixed with a temporary binding agent (*e.g.* glue), pressed and fired at 2000°C when the inter-crystalline bond of silicon carbide develops.

Properties:

(*i*) Silicon carbide bricks are dark grey to blue black in colour.

(*ii*) These can be used upto 1750°C.

(*iii*) They have high thermal conductivity and very low co-efficient of expansion.

(*iv*) When heated in air at a temperature range of 900–1000°C, they get oxidised to silica. However, this oxidation can be prevented by coating them with a thin layer of zirconium.

Self bonded silicon carbide has very useful properties like high density, greater resistance to abrasion, great strength, high refractoriness and higher resistance to chemicals.

Applications: Carborundum refractories are useful because of its hardness, low co-efficient of expansion, great strength and toughness. They are used for partition walls of chamber kilns, coke ovens and muffle furnaces. They are also used as heating elements in furnaces in the form of rods and bars.

EXERCISES

I. SHORT ANSWER TYPE QUESTIONS

1. What are the constituents of cement? Explain the role of each constituent.
2. Explain the reactions involved in setting and hardening of cement.
3. Distinguish between dry process and wet process in the manufacturing of cement.
4. Write short notes on:
   (*i*) Puzzolana cement (*ii*) Slag cement
   (*iii*) White cement (*iv*) Portland cement.
5. What are the I.S.I. specifications of Portland cement? **(RGPV, 2007)**
6. What is the role of gypsum in cement. **(RGPV, 2003)**
7. Define refractory. How are they classified?
8. What is meant by thermal spalling? How it can be avoided? **(Anna Univ. 2012)**
9. What are the essential requirements of a good refractory?
10. Explain the following properties of refractories:
    (*i*) Refractoriness (*ii*) Porosity
    (*iii*) R.U.L. (*iv*) Resistance to corrosion and erosion
    (*v*) Dimensional stability.
11. What is soundness of a cement?
12. Define cement. Explain fineness of a cement.
13. Write short note on R.U.L. test.
14. Write preparation and properties of following:
    (*i*) Magnesia bricks (*ii*) Dolomite bricks
    (*iii*) Alumina bricks (*iv*) Carbon refractories.
15. Write a short note on plaster of paris.
16. Write a short note on gypsum.
17. Differentiate between acidic and basic refractories.

II. LONG ANSWER TYPE QUESTIONS

1. How can you manufacture Portland cement by rotary kiln method? Draw neat and labelled diagram and also write chemical reactions involved in it.
2. Explain in brief the manufacture of cement by wet process. **(Anna Univ. 2016, RGPV 2008)**
3. Describe the chemistry of setting and hardening of cement. **(RGPV, 2009)**
4. What is plaster of Paris? Give its manufacture and important applications. **(RGPV, 2008)**
5. What is gypsum? Give its properties and important applications.

6. What is lime? Write its various properties and applications.
7. What is refractoriness? How is it measured by Seger cone test?
8. What are refractories? Explain any five of their important properties. **(Anna Univ., 2016)**
9. What are refractories? How are they classified? Give essential requirements of a good refractory material. **(Anna Univ., 2014)**
10. Define refractory. Discuss the significance of the following in the evaluation of a refractory brick:

    (*i*) Refractoriness (*ii*) R.U.L. (*iii*) Thermal spalling.
11. What are acidic refractories? Explain the preparation, properties and uses of silica bricks.
12. What are fire-clay refractories? How are they manufactured? Explain their properties and uses.

III. MULTIPLE CHOICE QUESTIONS

1. Which stone provides the calcareous component required for the manufacture of cement

   (*a*) Marble (*b*) Granite

   (*c*) Lime (*d*) Limestone.
2. The most common type of cement is:

   (*a*) Puzzolana cement (*b*) Portland cement

   (*c*) Slag (*d*) Natural cement.
3. The purpose of adding gypsum in cement is:

   (*a*) To improve strength (*b*) To increase the setting rate of cement

   (*c*) To delay the setting rater of cement (*d*) To increase the hardening rate of cement.
4. The whole process of setting and hardening of cement requires ———

   (*a*) 7 days (*b*) 30 days

   (*c*) 60 days (*d*) 90 days.
5. Chemically gypsum is:

   (*a*) $CaSO_4$ (*b*) $CaCO_3 . 2\,H_2O$

   (*c*) $CaSO_4 . 2\,H_2O$ (*d*) $CaSO_4 . \frac{1}{2}\,H_2O$
6. Plaster of Paris is:

   (*a*) $CaSO_4 . 2\,H_2O$ (*b*) $CaSO_4 . \frac{1}{2}\,H_2O$

   (*c*) $CaCO_3 . 2\,H_2O$ (*d*) $CaSO_4$.
7. A sample of cement is said to be sound when it does not contain free

   (*a*) Lime (*b*) Silica

   (*c*) Iron oxide (*d*) Alumina.

8. Gypsum added in cement manufacturing acts as

(*a*) Accelerator (*b*) Plasticizer

(*c*) Retarder (*d*) All of the above.

9. A good quality cement should have higher percentage of ———.

(*a*) Di-calcium silicate (*b*) Tricalcium silicate

(*c*) Silica (*d*) Lime.

10. The initial setting of cement is caused due to ———.

(*a*) C_2S (*b*) C_3S

(*c*) C_3A (*d*) C_4AF.

11. What is the meaning of soundness of cement?

(*a*) Ability to flow when mixed

(*b*) Ability to make noise when struck

(*c*) Ability to retain volume after setting

(*d*) Ability to form strong and sound structure.

12. What is the initial setting time of cement as per I.S.I. specifications?

(*a*) 1 hour (*b*) 30 minutes

(*c*) 15 minute (*d*) 2 hours.

13. The expansion of Portland cement can be tested by

(*a*) Fineness test (*b*) Setting time test

(*c*) Soundness test (*d*) None of the above.

14. Which of the following is acidic refractory?

(*a*) Chromite (*b*) Magnesite

(*c*) Silica (*d*) Dolomite.

15. Silica bricks belong to ——— refractory.

(*a*) Acidic (*b*) Basic

(*c*) Neutral (*d*) None of the above.

16. Spalling of refractory material can be reduced by

(*a*) Using good thermal conductivity refractory material

(*b*) Using refractory material of high coefficient of expansion.

(*c*) Using porous refractory material

(*d*) Rapid changes in temperature.

17. An ideal refractory should have high

(*a*) Spalling rate (*b*) Shrinkage ability

(*c*) Fusion point (*d*) None of these.

18. ——— is not a basic refractory.

(*a*) Magnesite (*b*) Dolomite

(*c*) Silicon carbide (*d*) Chrome magnesia.

19. Pyrometric test is performed to measure

(*a*) Porosity (*b*) Permeability

(*c*) Spalling (*d*) Refractoriness.

20. Bauxite is a/an

(*a*) Acidic refractory (*b*) Basic refractory

(*c*) Neutral refractory (*d*) silica refractory.

21. Permeability of bricks is a measure of the

(*a*) fusion point

(*b*) refractoriness

(*c*) rate at which a fluid will pass trough the pores

(*d*) expansion during heating.

22. Seger cone test is used to measure ———.

(*a*) Spalling resistance (*b*) Softening temperature

(*c*) Electrical conductivity (*d*) Resistance to slag attack

23. R.U.L. test is used to determine

(*a*) Refractoriness (*b*) Refractoriness under load

(*c*) Dimensional stability (*d*) Porosity.

24. The breaking, cracking and fracturing of refractory material due to temperature changes is called as

(*a*) Thermal spalling (*b*) Thermal cracking

(*c*) Thermal fracturing (*d*) Thermal expansion.

25. ——— refractory undergoes permanent contraction on heating.

(*a*) Graphite bricks (*b*) Dolomite bricks

(*c*) Silica bricks (*d*) Magnesite bricks.

Answers

MULTIPLE CHOICE QUESTIONS

1. (*d*)	**2.** (*b*)	**3.** (*c*)	**4.** (*b*)	**5.** (*c*)	**6.** (*b*)	**7.** (*a*)	**8.** (*c*)	**9.** (*b*)	**10.** (*c*)
11. (*c*)	**12.** (*b*)	**13.** (*c*)	**14.** (*c*)	**15.** (*a*)	**16.** (*c*)	**17.** (*c*)	**18.** (*c*)	**19.** (*d*)	**20.** (*b*)
21. (*c*)	**22.** (*b*)	**23.** (*b*)	**24.** (*a*)	**25.** (*d*)					

Chapter 11 Fuels and Combustion

11.1 INTRODUCTION

Fuel is a combustible substance containing carbon as a main constituent which when burnt in air (or oxygen) produces heat or energy that can be used economically for domestic and industrial purposes. For example, wood, kerosene, diesel, petrol, coal etc. The principal constituents of any fuel are carbon and hydrogen. During combustion, carbon, hydrogen and other combustible atoms (sulphur etc.) combine with oxygen and liberate heat.

$$\text{Fuel} + O_2 \longrightarrow \text{Products} + \text{heat}$$

$$C + O_2 \longrightarrow CO_2 + 94 \text{ kcal}$$

$$2H_2 + O_2 \longrightarrow 2H_2O + 68.5 \text{ kcal.}$$

Fuels are one of the most important substances on earth. They cook our food, heat our home, keep the cars and trains running and may more.

11.2 CLASSIFICATION OF FUELS

The fuels have been classified in two ways *i.e.*

1. **According to their occurance:** According to occurance, fuels can be primary and secondary.

   Primary or natural fuels which are found in nature as such they are used *e.g.* wood, coal petroleum, natural gas etc. Secondary or artificial fuels which are derived from primary fuels through chemical or physical processes. These are fuels that are not found as a natural resource. *e.g.* charcoal, coke, kerosene, producer gas, water gas, coal gas, coal tar etc.

2. **According to the physical state:** Solid, liquid or gaseous. The important examples of above categories (1) and (2) are given below.

Physical state	Primary fuels	Secondary fuels
Solid fuels	Wood, peat, lignite, coal	Coke, charcoal
Liquid fuels	Petroleum	Various fractions of petroleum *viz.* petrol, diesel, kerosene
Gaseous fuels	Natural gas	Water gas, coal gas, oil gas, biogas

The main characteristic points of difference between solid, liquid and gaseous fuel is given in Table 11.1.

Table 11.1: Comparison of Solid Liquid and Gaseous Fuels

S. No.		Solid fuel	Liquid fuel	Gaseous fuel
1.	Calorific value	Their caloric value is low.	Their calorific value is high.	They have highest calorific value.
2.	Cost	Their production cost is low.	Their production cost is higher than solid fuel	They are more costly as compared to solid and liquid fuels.
3.	Transportation	They are easy to transport through normal carriage.	They can be transported through pipelines.	They can also be transported through pipelines.
4.	Storage	Don't need container for storage.	Should be stored in closed containers only.	Must be stored in leak proof voluminous storage tanks.
5.	Ash and smoke	Their ash content is high and they produce lot of smoke on burning.	Their ash content is low and they burn without smoke.	They burn without smoke and less ash.
6.	Ignition temperature	They have moderate ignition temperature.	They have low ignition temperature.	They have very low ignition temperature.
7.	Thermal efficiency	They have low thermal efficiency	Their thermal efficiency is higher than solid fuels.	They have highest thermal efficiency.
8.	Risk towards fire hazards	Less	High	Very high since these fuels are highly inflammable.
9.	Combustion	It is a slow process but cannot be controlled easily.	It is very rapid and can be controlled or stopped when necessary.	Very fast and can be controlled or stopped easily.
10.	Use in internal combustion engine	It cannot be used.	It can be used.	It can also be used.

11.3 CHARACTERISTICS OF A GOOD FUEL

Ideally a good fuel should have the following characteristic:

1. **High calorific value:** The calorific value of a fuel is the direct measure of its efficiency as a fuel. Higher the calorific value, more is the efficiency of the fuel. A good fuel therefore, must have high calorific value.
2. **Moderate ignition temperature:** Ignition temperature is the lowest temperature to which the fuel must be heated to start combustion. A **good fuel must have moderate ignition temperature** because low ignition temperature can cause fire hazard during their handling, storage and transportation and high ignition temperature causes difficulty in igniting and burning the fuel.
3. **Low ash content/Low non-combustible matter:** Ash is the non-combustible matter obtained by burning coal. The non-combustible water remains in form of ash or clinker,

after combustion. High ash content lowers the calorific value and also poses problems in its disposal. Therefore, a good fuel should have low ash content.

4. **Low moisture content:** The presence of high moisture content in the fuel lower the efficiency of a fuel. It also lowers the calorific value since most of the heat produced in the process is utilized in vapourising the moisture content. It is also a loss of money, since it is paid at the same rate as fuel.
5. **Combustion products should be harmless:** An ideal fuel must not emit harmful gaseous products like CO, SO_2, NO, H_2S and other poisonous gases. Emission of such gases can pollute the environment and also cause harmful effects on health.
6. **Easy availability with low cost:** Fuel must be readily available in abundant amount and its cost must be low.
7. **Easy to store and transport:** An ideal fuel should be easy to store and transport.
8. **Combustion control:** The combustion process should be controllable. It means that it can be started and stopped when necessary.

11.4 CALORIFIC VALUE

Calorific value is the most important parameter of fuels. It gives useful information about the heating efficiency of a fuel.

It is defined as total quantity of heat liberated by the complete combustion of a unit weight of the fuel.

- The calorific value is normally expressed in calorie per gram in cgs units. It is also expressed in joules per kg for solid fuels and joules per cubic meter for gaseous fuels in SI units.
- British thermal unit (B. Th. U) is the English system unit and is defined as the quantity of heat required to raise the temperature of one pound of water by one degree fahrenheit.

$$1 \text{ B.Th. U} = 252 \text{ cal.}$$

A fuel can have two calorific values.

1. **Gross or higher calorific value (GCV/HCV):** Generally, all fuels contain some hydrogen and during the experimental determination of calorific value, this hydrogen is converted into steam. If the products of combustion are condensed to the room temperature, the latent heat of condensation of steam also gets included in the measured heat. So, gross or higher calorific value is defined as the total amount of heat generated when a unit quantity (mass/volume) of fuel is completely burnt and the products of combustion are cooled to room temperature (15°C or 60°F).

2. **Lower or net calorific value (LCV/NCV):** In actual combustion practice, the products of combustion are not condensed and escape as such alongwith hot combustion gases. Thus, a lesser amount of heat is available than expected. The amount of heat so available is called as lower or net calorific value. Thus, net calorific value is defined as the amount of heat generated when a unit quantity (mass/volume) of fuel is completely burnt and the products of combustion are allowed to escape.

Lower calorific value = Higher calorific value – Latent heat of water vapours formed

Conversion of hydrogen into steam takes place according to the following equation:

$$H_2 + \frac{1}{2} O_2 \longrightarrow H_2O$$

	H_2	$\frac{1}{2}O_2$	H_2O
	2g	16g	18g
for burning of unit mass	1g	8g	9g

The latent heat of steam = 587 cal/gm

1 part by mass of hydrogen produces 9 parts by mass of water.

∴ Lower calorific value = Higher calorific value – 9 × H × 587 cal/gm

$$\text{LCV} = \text{HCV} - 9 \times H \times 587 \text{ cal/gm}$$

where H = weight of hydrogen in fuel.

Theoretical Calculation of Calorific Value of a Fuel

Theoretically, the calorific value of a fuel can be calculated, if the percent content of the constituent elements are known. Dulong assumed that the heat liberated by a fuel comes from the combustion of the constituent elements *i.e.* carbon, hydrogen and sulphur.

Constituent element	C	H	S
Higher calorific value kcal/kg	8080	34500	2240

Sometimes oxygen is also present in the fuel, but it combines with hydrogen to form H_2O. Thus, the hydrogen in combined from (*i.e.,* H_2O) is not available for combustion and is called as fixed hydrogen. Therefore, amount of hydrogen available for combustion

= Total mass of hydrogen – hydrogen combined with oxygen.

Calculation of hydrogen available for combustion:

$$\begin{array}{cccc} H_2 + & \frac{1}{2}O_2 & \longrightarrow & H_2O \\ 2 & 16 & & 18 \\ 1 & 8 & & 9 \end{array}$$

8 parts of oxygen combines with one part of hydrogen which means for every 8 parts of oxygen 1 part of hydrogen gets fixed.

∴ Amount of hydrogen available for combustion

$$= \text{Total mass of hydrogen} - \frac{1}{8} \text{ mass of oxygen in fuel.}$$

If H is the mass of hydrogen and O is the mass of oxygen then,

$$\text{Amount of hydrogen available} = \text{H} - \frac{1}{8} \times \text{O} = \text{H} - \frac{\text{O}}{8}$$

Dulong formula for calculation of calorific value is given by the following expression

$$\textbf{HCV} = \frac{1}{100}\left[8080\%\,\text{C} + 34500\left(\%\text{H} - \frac{\%\text{O}}{8}\right) + 2240\%\,\text{S}\right] \textbf{ cal/gm or kcal/kg}$$

Where C, H, O and S are the percentages of carbon, hydrogen, oxygen and sulphur in the fuel respectively.

$$\text{LCV} = [\text{HCV} - 0.09\ \%\ \text{H} \times 587] \text{ kcal/kg or cal/gm.}$$

Determination of Calorific Value

1. **Bomb Calorimeter:** The calorific value of solid and non-volatile liquid fuels is best determined by Bomb calorimeter.

Construction

The apparatus consists of a strong cylindrical stainless steel bomb, resistant to corrosion and capable of withstanding high pressures upto 50 atmosphere.

This bomb is provided with a stainless steel lid which can be screwed as desired (this screw is a rubber ring to avoid corrosion troubles). The lid has three holes in it : two for stainless steel electrodes and one oxygen inlet valve.

The sample crucible (placed at the bottom of the bomb) is made of nickel or stainless steel which is supported by a small ring attached to one of the electrodes.

The bomb is lined inside with platinum to avoid corrosive action of HNO_3 and H_2SO_4 vapours formed due to burning of fuel.

2. The bomb is immersed in a rectangular copper calorimeter containing a known mass of water. The bomb is surrounded by air and water jackets to minimize heat losses due to radiation.
3. The calorimeter is provided with an electrical stirrer and Beckmann thermometer to measure the rise in temperature accurately to $\frac{1}{100^{\text{th}}}$ of a degree.

A schematic diagram of the apparatus is shown in Fig. 11.1

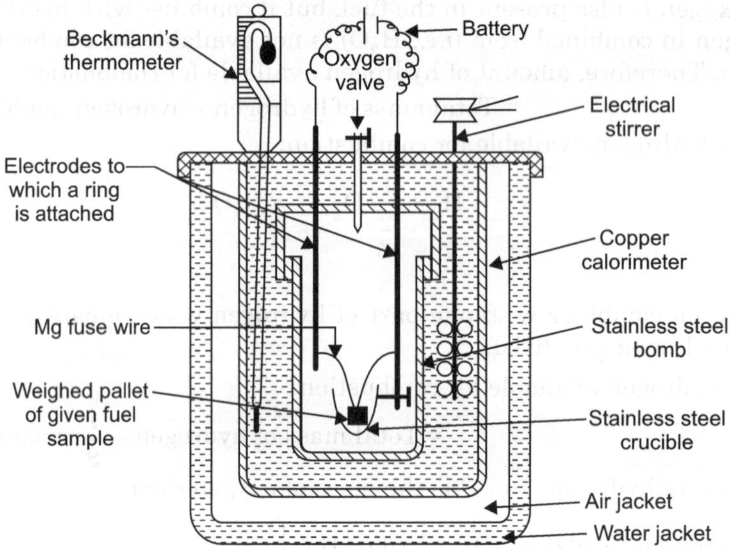

Fig. 11.1. Bomb calorimeter.

Working

A known amount of fuel (0.5 – 1 g) is taken in a clean crucible supported over the ring. A fine magnesium fuse wire is placed on the fuel sample and stretched across the electrodes. About 10 mL of distilled water is introduced into the bomb to absorb vapours of sulphuric acid and nitric acid formed during the combustion. The lid of the bomb is tightly screwed and through the inlet value, oxygen is filled into the bomb upto a pressure of about 25 atmosphere. The bomb is then lowered into the calorimeter containing a known mass of water. The stirrer is started and the initial temperature of water is noted. The electrodes are then connected to a 6 volt battery to complete the circuit. The fuel sample burns and the heat liberated causes a rise in temperature of stirred water in the calorimeter. The maximum temperature shown by the thermometer is recorded. The calorific value of fuel can be calculated as follows:

Weight of fuel taken = x gm

Weight of water in calorimeter = W gm

Water equivalent of the calorimeter, stirrer, thermometer and bomb = w gm.

Initial temperature of water in the calorimeter = $t_1°C$

Final temperature of water in the calorimeter = $t_2°C$

Let the higher calorific value of fuel = C cal/gm

Calculations

$$\text{Heat gained by water} = W \times \Delta T \times \text{specific heat of water}$$
$$= W(t_2 - t_1) \times 1 \text{ cal}$$
$$= W(t_2 - t_1)$$
$$\text{Heat gained by calorimeter} = w\,(t_2 - t_1)$$
$$\text{Total heat gained by water and calorimeter} = W(t_2 - t_1) + w\,(t_2 - t_1)$$
$$= (W + w)(t_2 - t_1)$$
$$\text{Heat liberated by fuel} = x \times C$$

But,

Heat liberated by the fuel = Total heat gained by water and calorimeter

$$x \times C = (W + w)(t_2 - t_1)$$
$$C = \frac{(W + w)(t_2 - t_1)}{x} \text{ cal/gm.}$$

To calculate lower calorific value (LCV):

$$\text{LCV} = \text{HCV} - \frac{9}{100} \times H \times 587 \text{ cal/gm}$$

H = percentage of hydrogen in fuel

$$\text{HCV} = C \;\therefore\; \text{LCV} = C - 0.09\,H \times 587 \text{ cal/gm.}$$

The theoretical values calculated using this formula were found to differ with experimental values. Therefore, for more accurate calculation of gross calorific value, it is necessary to apply following corrections:

1. **Acid correction:** During combustion, the nitrogen and sulphur present in the fuel gets oxidized to corresponding acids.

$$S + O_2 \longrightarrow SO_2$$
$$2\,SO_2 + O_2 + 2\,H_2O \longrightarrow 2\,H_2SO_4 + \text{Heat}$$
$$2\,N_2 + 5O_2 + 2\,H_2O \longrightarrow 4\,HNO_3 + \text{Heat}$$

   These reactions are exothermic therefore, the heat liberated will also be used to raise the temperature of water. Thus, a correction is required in this case. As these reactions are exothermic therefore, it should be subtracted from the obtained value of GCV.

2. **Fuse wire correction:** The magnesium fuse wire which is used for the ignition of fuel also gives some heat therefore, this amount of heat should also be subtracted from the obtained value of GCV.

3. **Cooling correction:** Inspite of all insulation in calorimeter, some heat is lost. The amount of heat lost can be corrected by applying cooling correction. To determine its value, the time taken to cool the water in calorimeter from maximum temperature to

room temperature is noted and the rate of cooling is calculated in degree/minute (say *dt*/min). The cooling correction is then calculated by multiplying the rate of cooling (*dt*/min) with the total time taken (*T*) to cool the water in calorimeter from the maximum temperature to room temperature in minutes (cooling correction = $dt \times T$).

After incorporating these corrections, the formula becomes

$$\text{HCV} = \frac{(W + w)(t_2 - t_1 + \text{cooling correction}) - (\text{acid correction} + \text{fuse wire correction})}{\text{wt. of coal sample/fuel taken}}$$

The cooling correction simply indicates that the higher temperature would have reached to the room temperature in time *T*. Thus, the actual difference in temperature ($t_2 - t_1$) should be higher. Therefore, the cooling correction needs to be added.

2. Junker's Calorimeter: It is used for measuring the calorific value of gaseous and volatile liquid fuels.

Construction

1. **Combustion Chamber:** It consists of a vertical cylindrical combustion chamber where combustion of fuel is carried out with the help of *Bunsen* burner. Around this combustion chamber, there is an annular space where water is made to circulate at constant rate. To reduce the heat loss by radiation and convection, the calorimeter is provided with an outer jacket which is coated by nickel or chromium and is fine polished. Supply of gaseous fuel is regulated by pressure governor.
2. **Bunsen burner:** It is used for the combustion of fuel in the combustion chamber.
3. **Gasometer:** It is attached with a manometer fitted with a thermometer to record the pressure and temperature of the gas before burning. Gasometer measures the volume of gas burnt per unit time.
4. **Thermometers:** Two thermometers are placed at appropriate places to measure the temperature of inlet and outlet water.

Schematic diagram of Junker's calorimeter is shown in Fig. 11.2.

Working

A known volume of gas is burnt at a constant rate is the presence of excess air. The heat produced by combustion of gases is absorbed by the cold water flowing through water jacket. The gases are cooled upto room temperature as far as possible so that entire heat biberated from the burning of fuel may be absorbed by the circulating water.

To determine the calorific value, the temperature of inlet and outlet water are noted. The weight of water flowing is also recorded.

Calculations

Temperature of inlet water = t_1°C

Temperature of outlet water = t_2°C

Weight of water circulated in coil in time $t = W$ g

Weight of water condensed in time $t = m$ kg.

The heat absorbed by the circulating water = $W(t_2 - t_1)$

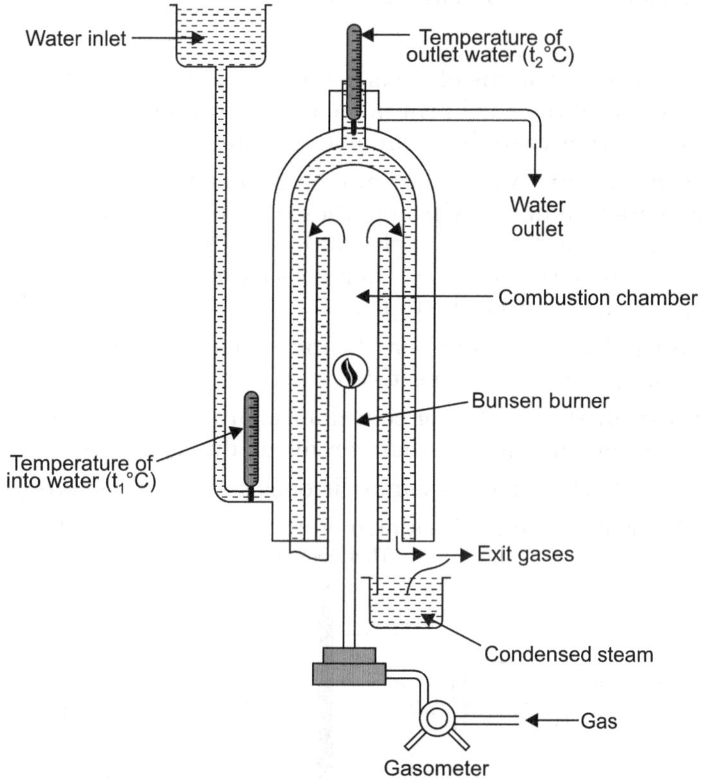

Fig. 11.2. Junker's calorimeter.

If C is the higher calorific value and V is the volume of gas burnt at given temperature and pressure then the heat produced by the combustion of fuel = $V \times C$

If there is no heat loss, then

Heat liberated by the fuel = Heat gained by the water.

$$V \times C = W(t_2 - t_1)$$

$$C = \frac{W(t_2 - t_1)}{V} \text{ kcal/m}^3.$$

To calculate net or lower calorific value:

Weight of water condensed per m^3 of gas = $\frac{m}{V}$ kg

Latent heat of steam per m^3 of gas = $\frac{m \times 587}{V}$ kcal

$$\therefore \quad \text{LCV} = \left[\text{HCV} - \frac{m \times 587}{V}\right] \text{kcal/m}^3$$

$$= \left[C - \frac{m \times 587}{V}\right] \text{kcal/m}^3.$$

3. Boy's Gas Calorimeter: The calorific value of volatile liquid fuels and gaseous fuels is determined by Boy's gas calorimeter. The calorimeter consists of the following parts:

Construction

1. **Gas Burner:** A known volume of a gas is burnt at a uniform rate with the help of a gas burner. The volume of the gas burnt is measured by a meter fitted near the inlet of the gas. Around the burner there is a combustion chamber.
2. **Combustion chamber:** A chamber having copper tubes coiled inside and outside is called as combustion chamber. Through these copper tubes, water is flown at a constant rate. Water enters from the top of the outer coil, passes through the outer coils and moves to the bottom of the chimney, then goes through the inner coil and finally leaves the combustion chamber from the top exit.
3. **Thermometers:** Two thermometers t_1 and t_2 are fitted to note the temperature of incoming and outgoing water respectively.
4. **Container:** A graduated beaker or container is provided for collecting the water which is formed due to condensation of steam produced during combustion.
5. **Insulated Jacket:** The whole assembly is enclosed in an insulated jacket.

The schematic diagram of the Boy's calorimeter is shown in Fig. 11.3.

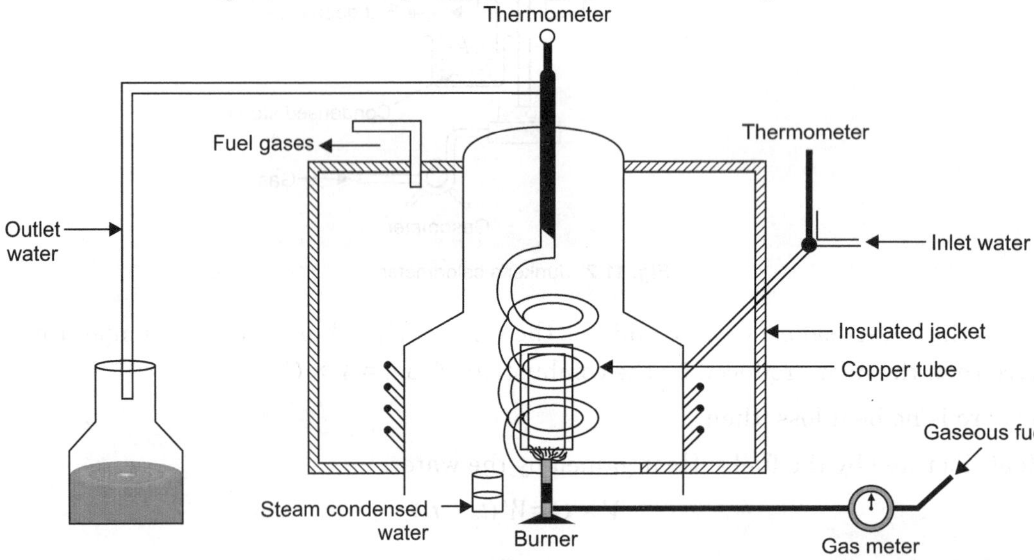

Fig.11.3. Boy's calorimeter.

Working

The working of Boy's calorimeter is similar to Junker's calorimeter. Burning of fuel and water circulation are continued for about 15 minutes to provide an initial warming period. When the calorimeter gets warmed, the rate of flow of the gas is so adjusted that the water leaves the apparatus nearly at atmospheric pressure. The heat energy produced is taken up by running water, whose temperature increases to t_2°C and the steam formed inside the combustion chamber during combustion gets condensed to water which is collected. The increase in temperature, volume of gas burnt, volume of circulated water and the mass of condensed steam are used to find out the calorific value of a fuel. **Observations and calculations are similar to Junker's calorimeter.**

11.5 SOLID FUELS

Major solid fuels include wood, coal, coke, charcoal etc.

Common solid fuels are discussed below:

Wood

Wood has been used as a fuel since ancient times. In present scenario, it is used extensively in countries where forests exist and where other fuels are not readily and cheaply available.

Wood consists of cellulose $(C_6H_{10}O_5)_n$, lignin, resins, inorganic materials and water. Water content of wood varies from 15–60% depending upon whether the wood is dry (~ 15%) or freshly cut (25–50%). Dry wood is more combustible, easily handled and burns with a long non-smoky flame. The composition of dry wood is 50% C, 35% O, 7% N, 6% H and 2% ash. The calorific value of dry wood varies from 4000 to 4500 kcal/kg. Wood is largely used as a domestic fuel. As the calorific value of wood is very low, it is *hardly* used in industries. The main advantages of wood as a fuel are the ready inflammabily, fairly good non-smoky flame and low ash content, the only requirement is that the wood should be dry.

Coal

It is a combustible sedimentary rock primarily composed of carbon with varying amounts of hydrogen, nitrogen, oxygen and sulphur. Coal is regarded as a fossil fuel produced from the remains of decaying tress and vegetation under the influence of temperature, pressure and limited supply of air over millions of years.

Coal is the largest source of energy for generating electricity in the world and an essential input for steel production. According to a survey (2018) based on statistical review of world energy, China is the highest coal producing country followed by India and then USA. Jharkhand, Odisha and Chhattisgarh are top three coal producing states in India (2018 survey).

Classification of coal: Coal is classified on the basis of their rank. The rank is defined as the degree of extent of maturation and is therefore a quantitative measure of the % of carbon in a coal. Coal is found in various forms, which denotes the different stages of the transformation of vegetable matter. These are

$$\text{Wood} \longrightarrow \text{Peat} \longrightarrow \text{Lignite} \longrightarrow \text{Bituminous} \longrightarrow \text{Anthracite}$$

Peat represents the first stage of the conversion of vegetable matter to coal. It has lower calorific value due to high percentage of moisture about 90%. It is not actually coal but rather the precursor to coal.

Lignite is referred to as brown coal because of its colour. It burns with a long smoky flame due to the presence of high volatile matter content in it. It is the **lowest rank of coal**. It is the least mature of all the coal types and is mainly used to generate electricity. Lignite is the **youngest coal**.

Bituminous coal is the most common and widely used variety of coal. Bituminous coal looks smooth and shiny.

Anthracite is quite dense and lusturous in appearance. It is the **highest rank coal** and it contains about 95% carbon content and is the **hardest** among all the varieties of cool. It has low moisture and volatile matter content. Because of low volatile matter content, it ignites without much difficulty, burns without smoke and provide intense local heating. It has low percentage of ash. It is used for domestic purposes, raising steam, metallurgical purposes etc. Anthracite is the **oldest coal**. The variation in average composition in different varieties of coal are summarised in the Table 11.2.

Table 11.2: Different Varieties of Coal and their Characteristics

Fuel	Characteristics	Calorific value	% Moisture	% Volatile matter	% of C, H, O	Uses
Peat	Highly fibrous and light brown in colour. Precursor of coal.	4000 – 5400 kcal/kg	70 – 90	45 – 75	C – 57 H – 5.7 O – 35.3	Domestic fuel.
Lignite	Brown coal, lowest rank of coal.	6500 – 7100 kcal/kg	30 – 50	45 – 60	C – 67 H – 5.0 O – 26.5	Power generation.
Sub bituminous	Black in colour and dull appearance.	7000 – 7500 kcal/kg	10 – 20	11 – 50	C – 77 H – 5.0 O – 16.2	Manufacturing of gaseous fuels.
Bituminous	Shiny and smooth	8000 – 8500 kcal/kg	4	10 – 15	C – 83 H – 5.0 O – 10.0	In industries for making metallurgical coke, coal gas etc. Fuel in steel and iron industries.
Anthracite	Hard, brittle and black lusturous coal Highest rank coal.	8500 – 8700 kcal/kg	1.5 – 3.5	3.8 – 10	C – 93.3 H – 3.0 O – 3.0	Boilers, metallurgical processes, domestic purposes

Analysis of Coal

The composition of coal varies widely from mine to mine and therefore, it is necessary to analyse and interpret the results for the purpose of commercial classification, price fixation and industrial fulfillment. The quality of cool is ascertained by the following analysis:

1. Proximate analysis
2. Ultimate analysis

Proximate analysis: Proximate analysis involves the determination of moisture content, volatile matter, ash and fixed carbon. This gives quick and valuable information regarding type of coal and its practical utility. The data obtained by proximate analysis are not absolute **but** varies with the procedure adopted. The constituents of coal that can be determined with proximate analysis are: (*a*) moisture content, (*b*) volatile matter, (*c*) ash, (*d*) fixed carbon.

***(a)* Moisture Content:** The moisture content in coal is determined by drying off the moisture in an air over. A known weight (about 1 g) of powdered and air-dried coal is taken in a silica crucible. Heat the crucible to 105 – 110°C in an electric hot air-oven for one hour.

The crucible is then taken out and cooled in a desiccator and weighed. The loss in weight of the sample is found out and the percentage of moisture is calculated according to the formula:

Weight of the empty crucible = w_1 g

Weight of the crucible + sample (before heating) = w_2 g

Weight of the crucible + sample (after heating) = w_3 g

$$\% \text{ moisture} = \frac{w_2 - w_3}{w_2 - w_1} \times 100$$

$$= \frac{\text{Loss in weight}}{\text{Weight of coal taken}} \times 100.$$

Significance: Presence of moisture in a fuel reduces its calorific value and increases the transportation cost. A considerable amount of heat is wasted in evaporating the moisture present in coal during combustion. Therefore, high percentage of moisture is undesirable.

Lesser the moisture content, better will be the quality of coal as a fuel.

***(b)* Volatile Matter:** Volatile matter obtained during the heating of coal consists of gases such as methane, hydrogen, carbon monoxide and other hydrocarbons. It also contain some non-combustible gases like CO_2, oxides of nitrogen, oxides of sulphur, steam etc. The percentage of volatile matter present in the fuel depends upon the rank of coal.

It is determined by taking the dried sample of coal, obtained ofter determining the moisture content in a silica or platinum crucible. The crucible is then covered with a lid and placed in an electric furnace maintained at 925° ± 20°C. The crucible is taken out of the oven after 7 minutes of heating. The crucible is cooled first in air then inside a desiccator and weighed. The loss in weight of the sample corresponds to the volatile matter present in a fuel and can be calculated as follows:

Weight of empty crucible = w_1 g

Weight of crucible + sample (before heating) = w_2 g

Weight of crucible + sample (after 7 min heating) = w_3 g

$$\% \text{ of volatile matter} = \frac{w_2 - w_3}{w_2 - w_1} \times 100$$

$$= \frac{\text{Loss in weight}}{\text{Weight of coal taken}} \times 100.$$

Significance: Volatile matter is directly related to coal rank. As the rank increases, volatile matter content decreases.

Coal having high percentage of volatile matter burns with a long flame and high smoke and has low calorific value. Therefore, the lesser the volatile content, the better is the quality of coal. Coal containing lesser volatile content burn with a shorter flame. Therefore, higher the volatile matter content, the larger is the combustion space required. Hence, the percentage of volatile matter in a coal sample influences the furnace design.

The percentage of volatile matter in a coal denotes the portion of coal that can be converted into gas and tar products by heat.

High volatile matter content is preferable in coal gas manufacture and in carbonization plant especially when the main aim is the recovery of by product. For the manufacture of metallurgical coke, coal with low volatile matter content is preferred.

(c) Ash: Ash is the useless, non-combustible, inorganic material that is left behind when all the combustible substances have been burnt off from the coal. It is usually composed of silica (SiO_2), alumina (Al_2O_3), iron oxide (Fe_2O_3) and small amounts of lime [$Ca(OH)_2$], magnesia [$Mg(OH)_2$] etc.

It is determined by heating 1 g of dried coal sample in a silica/platinum crucible at 725 ± 25°C in a electric furnace for half an hour. The crucible is then taken out, cooled first in air and then in desiccator and weighed. From the weight of residue, the percentage of ash can be calculated as

$$\%\text{ of ash} = \frac{\text{Weight of ash formed}}{\text{Weight of coal sample taken}} \times 100$$

> Crucible is a ceramic or metallic container in which metal or other substances may be melted or subjected to very high temperature.
>
> They can be made from any material which can withstand very high temperatures. For example porcelain, stainless steel, nickel, zirconium, silica, platinum etc.

Significance: Ash is a non-combustible matter therefore, it reduces the calorific value of coal. The presence of ash increases the transportation, handling and storage costs.

- Ash also causes hindrance to the flow of air and heat. It also creates trouble during firing by forming clinkers which block the inter spaces of the chimney/grate.
- Ash deposition also causes problems in the furnace walls or the burning apparatus and also the disposal of ash is a big problem.
- The percentage of ash in a given coal sample determines its quality. Lesser the percentage of ash in a coal sample, the better is the quality of coal.
- Indian coals have high percentage of ash.

(*d*) Fixed Carbon: Fixed carbon is the solid combustible residue that remains after a coal sample is heated and the volatile matter is expelled. It is the pure carbon present in coal. It is calculated by subtracting the sum of moisture, volatile matter and ash content

$$\%\text{ fixed carbon} = 100 - (\%\text{ moisture} + \%\text{ volatile matter} + \%\text{ ash})$$

Fixed carbon varies inversely with volatile matter.

Significance: Fixed carbon gives a rough estimate of the calorific value of coal. Higher the percentage of fixed carbon in coal, higher is its calorific value and better is the quality of coal.

Ultimate Analysis (Elemental Analysis)

Ultimate analysis is an absolute method for the determination of the elemental composition of coal. Typical ultimate analysis include carbon, hydrogen, sulphur, nitrogen and oxygen contents but other elements can also be analysed if present. Since it is used for the determination of elements in coal, it is also called as **elemental analysis.** This analysis gives exact results (in terms of percentage of elements) which are useful in calculating the calorific value of coal using Dulong's formula. It involves following determinations.

1. Carbon and hydrogen: Both carbon and hydrogen are estimated together in one operation. For the determination of % of carbon and hydrogen, a known amount (about 1–2 g) of coal sample is burnt in excess supply of oxygen in a combustion apparatus. Carbon and hydrogen of the coal are oxidised to CO_2 and H_2O respectively.

$$\underset{12}{C} + \underset{32}{O_2} \longrightarrow \underset{44}{CO_2} \qquad \underset{2}{H_2} + \underset{16}{\frac{1}{2} O_2} \longrightarrow \underset{18}{H_2O}$$

These gaseous products of combustion (CO_2 and H_2O) are absorbed by previously weighed tubes containing KOH and anhydrous $CaCl_2$. The increase in weight of KOH bulb gives the weight of CO_2 formed whereas the increase in weight of $CaCl_2$ bulb represents the weight of water formed

$$2\,KOH + CO_2 \longrightarrow K_2CO_3 + H_2O$$
$$CaCl_2 + 7\,H_2O \longrightarrow CaCl_2 \cdot 7H_2O$$

The percentage of C and H is calculated as follows:

Let, the weight of coal sample taken = x g

Increase in weight of KOH bulb (due to CO_2) = y g

Increase in weight of $CaCl_2$ bulb (due to H_2O) = z g

From the above reactions, we know that

44 g of CO_2 contains – 12 g of carbon

$$\therefore \ \% \text{ of C} = \frac{12}{44} \times \frac{\text{Increase in weight of KOH}}{\text{Weight of coal sample taken}} \times 100 = \frac{12}{44} \times \frac{y}{x} \times 100 .$$

Similarly,

18 g of H_2O contains – 2 g of hydrogen

$$\therefore \ \% \text{ H} = \frac{2}{18} \times \frac{\text{Increase in weight of CaCl}_2}{\text{Weight of coal sample taken}} \times 100 = \frac{2}{18} \times \frac{z}{x} \times 100$$

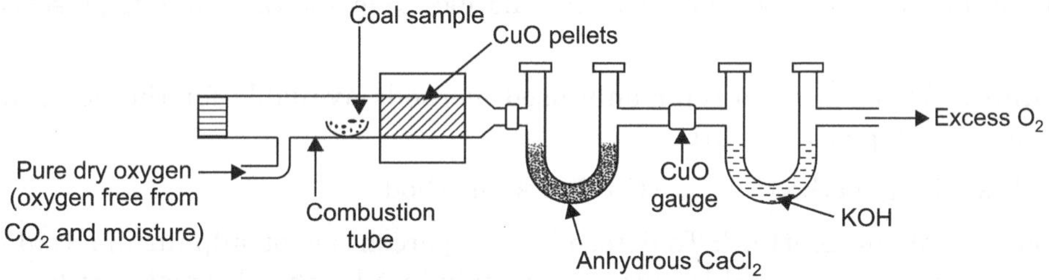

Fig. 11.4. Combustion apparatus for estimation of C and H.

Significance: Carbon is a major constituent of coal. Higher the percentage of carbon, higher is the calorific value of the coal. Higher is the percentage of carbon better is the quality of coal.

The percentage of hydrogen in a coal sample reflects greatly in its calorific value. Calorific value of hydrogen is four times more than that of carbon. Hydrogen is mostly associated with the volatile matter of coal and hence is a deciding factor in the design of combustion furnace.

2. Nitrogen: Nitrogen is an unwanted constituent in coal and it does not contribute towards calorific value. It is determined by **Kjeldahl's method**. In this method about 1 g accurately weighed powdered coal is taken in a long necked flask called Kjeldahl's flask and heated with conc. H_2SO_4 in the presence of catalysts like selenium powder, K_2SO_4 etc. Nitrogen present in coal is converted into ammonium sulphate and a clear solution is obtained.

$$N_2 + H_2\,SO_4 \longrightarrow (NH_4)_2\,SO_4$$

This clear solution is then treated with excess of KOH or NaOH and NH_3 is liberated.

$$(NH_4)_2 SO_4 + 2 NaOH \longrightarrow 2 NH_3 \uparrow + Na_2SO_4 + 2 H_2O$$

The liberated NH_3 is then distilled over and absorbed in a known excess of standard acid solution. The unused acid is determined by back titration with standard NaOH solution. From the volume of acid used by liberated ammonia, the percentage of nitrogen in coal is calculated by the following equation:

$$\% \text{ of Nitrogen} = \frac{\text{Volume of acid consumed} \times \text{Normality of acid}}{\text{Weight of coal sample}} \times 1.4$$

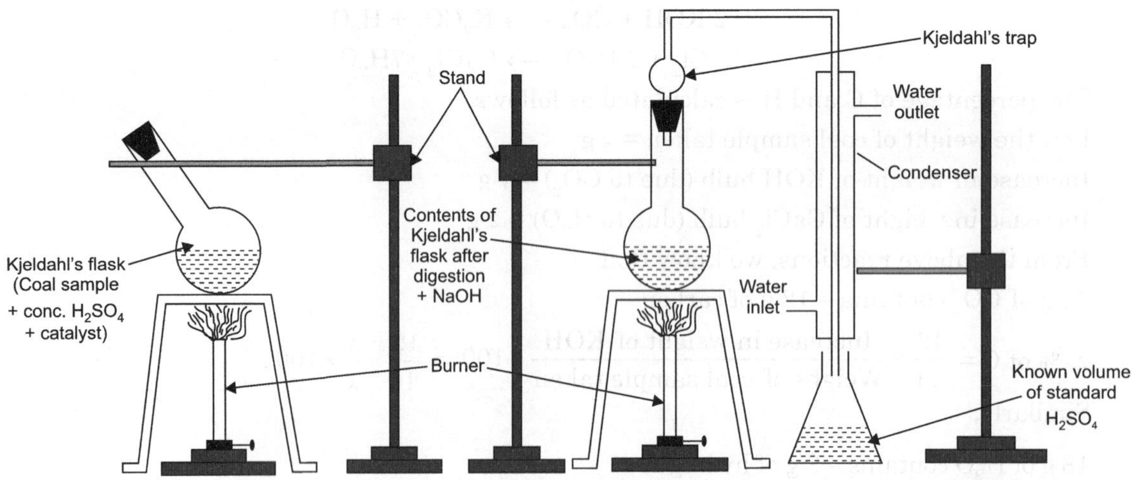

Fig. 11.5. Estimation of nitrogen by Kjeldahl's method.

Significance: Nitrogen does not have any calorific value and therefore its presence is not of much significance.

3. Sulphur: There are two commonly used methods available for the determination of sulphur in a coal sample. These are:

(*i*) Bomb washing method (*ii*) Eschka method

(*i*) Bomb washing method: To determine the percentage of sulphur in a coal sample, a known amount of powdered coal is burnt completely in a bomb calorimeter at high pressure of oxygen. Entire sulphur present in the coal gets oxidised to sulphur dioxide. The SO_2 gas thus formed dissolves in the water in the calorimeter and treated with $BaCl_2$ solution, the sulphate will get precipitated as $BaSO_4$. The precipitate is collected over a Whatmann filter paper, washed, dried and ignited in a silica crucible to burn off the filter paper (the filter paper used should be ash less). The precipitate of $BaSO_4$ is weighed accurately and the percentage of sulphur can be determined as follows:

Let the weight of coal sample = w g

Weight of $BaSO_4$ = x g

Now, 233 g of $BaSO_4$ contains = 32 g of S

1 g of $BaSO_4$ contains = $\frac{32}{233}$ g of S

and x g of $BaSO_4$ contains $= \frac{32}{233} \times x$ g of S

% of sulphur in w g of coal is

$$\% \text{ of sulphur} = \frac{32}{233} \times \frac{x}{w} \times 100$$

or

$$= \frac{32}{233} \times \frac{\text{Weigth of } BaSO_4}{\text{Weight of coal taken}} \times 100.$$

***(ii)* Eschka method:** In this method, the sulphur in coal is converted into soluble sulphate by incinerating coal with a 1 : 2 mixture of sodium carbonate and calcined magnesium carbonate. It is further treated with barium chloride solution and the sulphates are precipitated as $BaSO_4$. From the weight of $BaSO_4$ formed, the percentage of sulphur in coal sample is calculated according to the following formula.

$$\% \text{ of sulphur} = \frac{32}{233} \times \frac{\text{Weigth of } BaSO_4 \text{ obtained}}{\text{Weight of coal taken}} \times 100.$$

Calcined Magnesium Carbonate: Calcination is heating of solids at high temperature for the purpose of removing volatile substances. When $MgCO_3$ is calcined, it decomposes to

$$MgCO_3 \longrightarrow MgO + CO_2$$

Eschka's mixture: 1 part of Na_2CO_3 + 2 parts of MgO

Significance: Sulphur increases the calorific value of coal but its combustion products SO_2 and SO_3 have corrosive effects on the equipments specially in presence of moisture. Also these gases SO_2 and SO_3 causes environmental pollution. Coal having sulphur is not suitable for the preparation of metallurgical coke as it adversely affects the properties of the metal. So, the presence of sulphur in coal is undesirable.

4. Ash: Ash content is determined in the same way as in proximate analysis.

5. Oxygen: The percentage of oxygen in coal is determined by the difference method as follows:

% of oxygen = 100 – % of (C + H + N + S + Ash)

Significance: The presence of oxygen in coal decreases the calorific value as it is usually associated with moisture, thereby decreasing available hydrogen for combustion. Therefore, a good quality coal should have lower percentage of oxygen.

Carbonization of Coal

When coal is heated in the absence of air, it loses volatile matter and converted into white, dense, lusturous, porous, strong and coherent mass called as **coke**. The process of converting coal into coke is called as **carbonization**. Depending upon the temperature, carbonization is classified into three categories:

1. Low temperature carbonization
2. Medium temperature carbonization
3. High temperature carbonization.

1. Low temperature carbonization: In this process, the heating of coal is carried out at 500 – 700°C. The yield of coke is about 75 to 80% and it contains 5 to 15% volatile matter.

The various products of low temperature carbonisation are semicoke, low temperature tar, spirit and gas. The coke so produced is not mechanically strong therefore cannot be used as a metallurgical coke. However, it burns easily giving a smokeless and radiant fire and hence is an ideal fuel for household purposes. The gas obtained has high calorific value therefore it is a valuable gaseous fuel. Tar obtained contains paraffinic hydrocarbons, aromatic hydrocarbons, phenols etc.

This process gives low yield of spirit.

2. Medium temperature carbonisation: Medium temperature carbonisation is carried out in the temperature range of 700 to 900°C. It is carried out to recover a variety of products like ammonia tar, light oils containing paraffinic and diolefinic hydrocarbons and phenols in good yield. Medium temperature carbonisation is rarely practiced these days.

3. High temperature carbonisation: In this process the heating of coal is carried out at high temperature of 900 – 1200°C. The yield of coke is about 65 – 75% and it contains 1 – 3% volatile matter. The coke obtained is porous, hard, pure and strong and thus can be used in metallurgy. The by products obtained by this process are coal gas, coal tar, liquor ammonia etc.

Metallurgical Coke

Metallurgical coke is produced from coal by heating it for 70–80 hrs in absence of air at a temperature of 1100°C. The resulting coke is obtained in hard, porous, lusturous and strong coherent mas consisting of about 70–90% of fixed carbon and 10–25% of ash.

Most metallurgical coke is used in steel and iron industry processes such as blast furnaces, sinter plants and foundries to reduce iron ore to iron. About 90 % of the total metallurgical coke production is used in blast furnace operations. A good metallurgical coke should have the following requisites:

1. **Purity:** It should have low moisture, ash and other impurities mainly sulphur and phosphorus content. Presence of moisture reduces the calorific value of the coke and high percentage of ash hinders the heating process and forms slag. Sulphur and phosphorus impurities produce unwanted products such as SO_2, P_2O_5, P_2O_3 etc. which affect the quality of coke. Also, high percentage of sulphur *makes* the coal brittle.
2. **Size:** It should neither be too big nor too small. Uniform heating is not obtained with large size coke and if the size is too small choking will *take* place.
3. **Strength:** It should be compact, hard and strong to withstand high pressure of the overlaying material in the furnace.
4. **Porosity:** It should be porous so that oxygen can easily come in contact with the carbon of coke, thereby *helping* in complete combustion at high rate.
5. **Calorific value:** It should have a high calorific value.
6. **Transportation cost and availability:** It should be cheap and readily/easily available near the metallurgical plant site so that the transportation *cost is reduced.*
7. **Combustibility:** Coke should burn easily. Its combustibility depends on the nature of coal, carbonisation temperature and reaction temperature.
8. **Reactivity:** The reactivity of coke should not be very high because reactive cokes do not produce intense heat.

Manufacture of Metallurgical Coke

There are two methods available for the manufacture of metallurgical coke. These are:

1. Beehive oven method
2. Otto-Hoffmann's oven/by-product oven method

1. Beehive oven method: It is the earliest and the cheapest method for the carbonisation of coal.

A Beehive oven is a dome shaped brick, structure (Fig. 11.6) that looks a bit like an insect's nest, hence the name "Beehive". It is about 4 m wide and 2.5 m high. There are two openings one at the top from where the coal is *fed* into the oven and the other at the side from where the coke is removed after the process of carbonisation. The side door also acts as an air inlet.

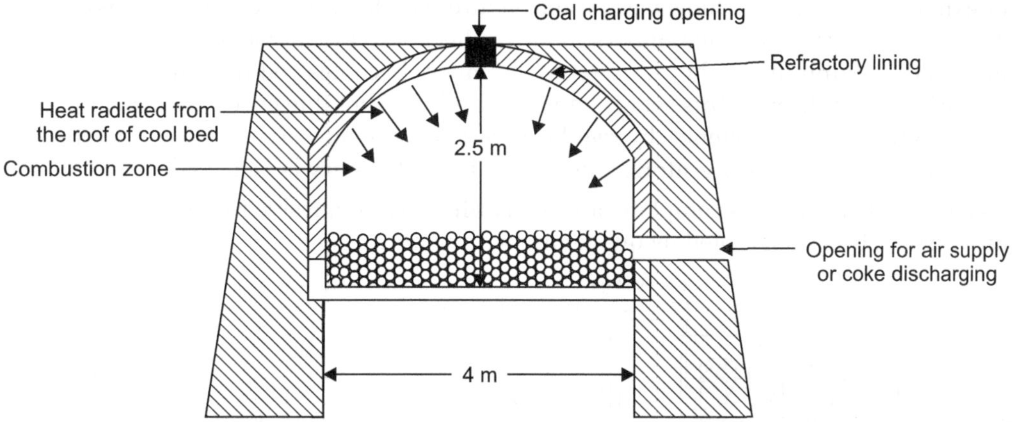

Fig. 11.6. Beehive coke oven.

Working

Coal is fed into the oven through the opening at the top and the charge is evenly levelled by means of a rake to produce a layer about 0.6 – 0.9 m deep. Air is supplied through the side opening and the coal is ignited. Volatile matter escapes and burns inside. Therefore, heat for carbonisation is supplied partly by burning of volatile matter and partly by coal itself. Carbonisation proceeds from top to bottom. This may last for nearly 3 – 4 days. When the carbonisation is complete, the hot coke is quenched with water and discharged manually through the side door. The oven is hot enough to continue the process with a fresh batch. The coke produced has a yield of about 80%. No by-products are recovered in this method. Beehive method is now an obsolete process because of low productivity and high pollution but it is still in practice because it produces a special type of coke very much demand in foundries.

Beehive oven method has certain disadvantages. These are:

(*i*) There is no recovery of by products

(*ii*) Yield of coke is not good due to partial combustion of coal.

(*iii*) The coking time of the process is long, 3 – 4 days.

(*iv*) This process cannot be used to produce good coke from blends of inferior coals.

(*v*) The exhaust gases causes high pollution.

2. Otto-Hoffmann's Oven/By-product oven method: In order to increase the thermal efficiency of the carbonisation process and to recover the valuable by products (like coal gas, ammonia, benzene etc), Otto-Hoffmann developed modern by product coke oven.

Otto-Hoffmann's oven consists of a number of narrow rectangular silica chambers, each having 12 m length, 4 m height and 0.5 m width. The chambers are tightly closed so that no air is admitted. The chambers are also fitted with charging doors having 3 – 4 openings at the top and discharging doors at the bottom.

Working

Coal is introduced into the silica chambers and the chambers are then tightly closed at both ends so as to prevent the entry of air.

The chambers are heated upto a temperature of 1200°C by burning pre-heated air and the producer gas mixture in the interspaces between the chambers. The gas and air both are preheated with the help of regenerators.

Hot exhaust gases or the flue gases produced after combustion are made to pass through one of the two sets of regenerators (chambers made of checkered brick work) placed below the ovens. After about 20 – 30 minutes, when this set of chambers becomes red hot, the air flue mixture is preheated by passing through this set of chambers while the hot flue gases are heating the another set of regenerator chambers. Hence, by regular reversal of the flow of inlet gases and the flue gases through these two sets of regenerators, substantial heat efficiency is achieved.

When the carbonisation is complete, an electrically driven massive ram pushes out the red hot coke into a truck. It is then cooled by quenching with water.

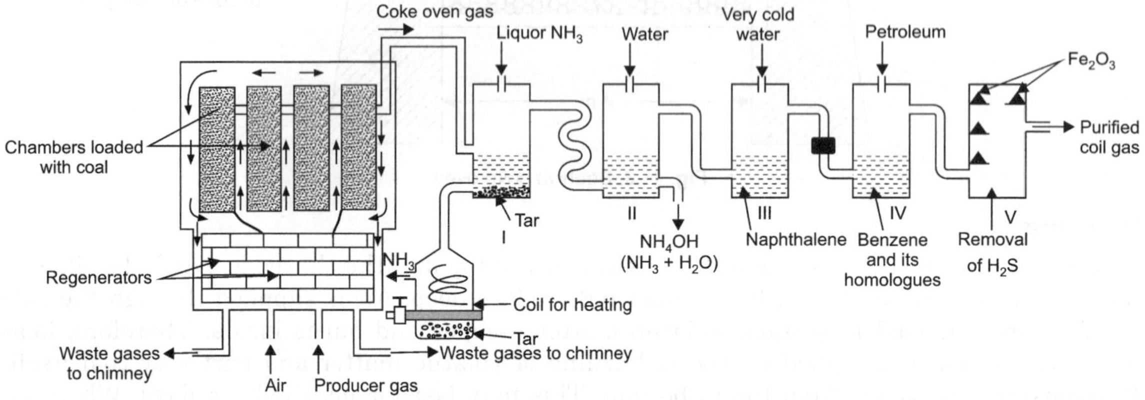

Fig. 11.7. Otto-Hoffmann's oven for manufacturing of coke.

Recovery of by products: The volatile matter coming out of the oven is in the form of gas popularly known as **coke oven gas** and is mainly composed of tar, ammonia, naphthalene, benzene and its homologues and H_2S. These products are separated from each other.

1. **Recovery of tar:** The coke oven gas is allowed to pass through I tower where liquor ammonia is sprayed. Dust and tar gets collected in a tank which is heated by heating coils to recover ammonia back.

   Tar pitch is used for making roads. It is also used for preserving timber.

2. **Recovery of ammonia:** The gas free from tart is sent to II tower where water is sprayed. Ammonia goes into solution as NH_4OH. On boiling NH_4OH with milk of lime, it yields NH_3 which is converted into ammonium sulphate which is used as a fertilizer.

3. **Recovery of naphthalene:** The gas free from tar and ammonia is then passed through III tower where water is sprayed at a very low temperature. Condensation of some gases takes place and naphthalene is recovered.

4. **Recovery of Benzene:** The gas in then passed through IV tower where petroleum is sprayed. Here benzene and its homologues are recovered.
5. **Removal of H_2S:** The H_2S in the residual gas is removed by passing the gas through a purifier packed with moist Fe_2O_3. Here H_2S is retained.

$$Fe_2O_3.3\ H_2O(s) + 3H_2S(g) \longrightarrow Fe_2S_3(s) + 6H_2O(l)$$

After some time the whole iron oxide gets converted into iron sulphide, it is taken out and exposed to air/ atmosphere when Fe_2O_3 is regenerated

$$2\ Fe_2S_3\ (s) + 3\ O_2\ (g) \longrightarrow 2\ Fe_2O_3 + 6\ S\ (s)$$

Advantages of Otto-Hoffmann Method

(*i*) Valuable by products like coal gas, NH_3, naphthalene, benzene etc. are all recovered.

(*ii*) Higher yield of coke is produced.

(*iii*) This process has high thermal efficiency

(*iv*) It is a fast process.

11.6 LIQUID FUEL

Liquid fuels are becoming more and more important these days due to their usefulness and economical nature. Major liquid fuel includes crude oil or petroleum.

Crude Oil/Petroleum

Crude oil at present is the world's main source of organic chemicals. Petroleum is a fossil fuel because it was formed millions of years ago by the decomposition of plants and animal remains under high temperature and pressure deep below the earth's surface. As the formation of crude oil takes million of years therefore it is a non-renewable source of energy.

It is a dark, greenish brown, viscous oil mainly composed of paraffinic, olefenic and aromatic hydrocarbons with small amounts of organic compounds containing O, N and S. Depending upon the source of extraction, the composition of petroleum varies. The average composition of crude oil varies as:

$$C \rightarrow 80 - 87\%,\ H \rightarrow 11 - 15\%,\ S \rightarrow 0.1 - 3.5\%,\ N \text{ and } S \rightarrow 0.1 - 0.5\%$$

India produces about $1/3^{rd}$ of its total petroleum requirement within the country (Trombay, Visakhapatnam, Cochin, Manali) and the rest is imported from various middle east countries (Iraq, Iran, Kuwait, Saudi Arabia, Indonesia etc.)

Crude oil is classified into three classes depending upon the nature of hydrocarbons present in it. They are:

1. **Paraffinic based crude oils:** These oils are mainly composed of straight chain hydrocarbons from CH_4 to $C_{35}\ H_{72}$ with a smaller amount of naphthenes ad aromatics. This type of crude oil deposits are usually found in Iraq, Iran, Rumania [Pennsylvanian and Gulf oil].
2. **Asphaltic or Naphthene based crude oils:** These oils are mainly composed of cycloparaffins or naphthenes alongwith small amounts of paraffins and aromatic hydrocarbons.

This type of crude oil deposits are found in Russia, Venezuela, California.

3. **Mixed based crude oils:** These oils contain both paraffinic and asphaltic hydrocarbons Mixed based crude oils are found in Texas, Mexico etc.

Origin of petroleum

Several theories have been put forward to explain the formation of crude oil but none of them is able to account for its origin very convincingly. Still, these are three main theories which explains the origin of crude oil to large extent. These are.

1. Carbide or Mendeleev's theory
2. Organic or Engler's theory
3. Modern theory.

1. Carbide or Mendeleev's theory: This is also known as **inorganic theory** of origin of petroleum. According to this theory, hydrcarbons present in petroleum are formed by the action of steam or water on inorganic carbides (which are formed from a reaction between carbon and metals at high temperature and pressure inside the earth crust). Various steps of this theory are:

(*i*) The molten metals in the earthcrust come in contact with coal under high temperature and pressure to form carbides:

$$\underset{\text{from coke}}{Ca + 2C} \longrightarrow \underset{\text{Calcium carbide}}{CaC_2}$$

$$\underset{\text{from coke}}{4Al + 3\,C} \longrightarrow \underset{\text{Aluminium carbide}}{Al_4C_3}$$

(*ii*) The carbides so formed are acted upon by steam under high pressure and temperature to form hydrocarbons

$$CaC_2 + 2H_2O \longrightarrow Ca(OH)_2 + \underset{\text{Acetylene}}{C_2H_2}$$

$$Al_4C_3 + 12H_2O \longrightarrow 4Al\,(OH)_3 + \underset{\text{Methane}}{3CH_4}$$

(*iii*) From the second step lower hydrocarbons are formed which undergo hydrogenation and polymerization to give higher aliphatic and cyclic hydrocarbons and aromatic hydrocarbons.

$$C_2H_2 + H_2 \longrightarrow \underset{\text{ethene}}{C_2H_4}$$

$$C_2H_4 + H_2 \longrightarrow \underset{\text{ethane}}{C_2H_6}$$

Hydrogenation takes place in presence of metallic catalyst at high temperature

$$3C_2H_2 \longrightarrow \underset{\text{benzene}}{C_6H_6}$$

$$3C_2H_4 \longrightarrow$$

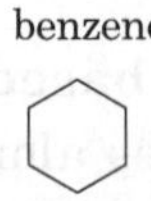

cyclohexane

Polymerization takes place in the presence of hot metals

This theory provides us a proof of the inorganic origin of the petroleum but it failed to explain the following points:

1. Natural petroleum contains S and N compounds, chlorophyll, haemin etc. This theory failed to explain their presence in petroleum.

2. Petroleum contains optically active compounds but this theory also failed to explain their presence in petroleum.

2. **Engler theory (Organic theory):** According to this theory, the dead marine animals were buried under the deeper parts of earth due to various reasons like volcanic eruption, earthquake etc. Later these have undergone decay and then decomposed to form petroleum. This theory was further supported by the fact that when destructive distillation of fish oil and other animal fats under high pressure and temperature was carried out, a petroleum like liquid consisting of S, N and optically active compound was obtained. This theory account for the presence of S, N and optically active compounds in the petroleum but fails to trace the origin of chlorophyll in petroleum.

3. Modern theory: Modern theory is a combination of two theories proposed above. According to this theory, petroleum is formed by the decay and decomposition of both marine animals and vegetable organisms by radioactive elements or bacteria at high temperature and pressure. This theory explains the presence of compounds of N and S as well as the presence of chlorophyll and haemin in petroleum.

Mining of Crude Oil

Crude oil deposits are found deep below the earth crust. Usually natural gas is found above petroleum deposits. Extraction of crude oil from its deposits below the earth's crust is called as **mining of crude oil**. Mining is done by drilling holes in the earth's crust and dropping/sinking pipes upto the impervious rocks bearing oil (Fig. 11.8). The oil rushes up itself through the pipes due to the hydrostatic pressure exerted by the natural gas inside. When the pressure becomes too low, the oil is brought to the surface by mechanical pumping using lift pump. The crude oil from these wells is conveyed to refineries through a system of underground pipelines for refining.

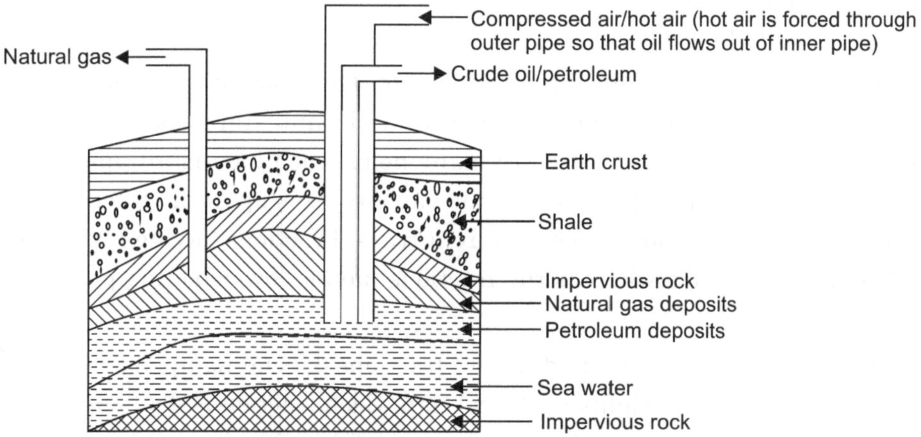

Fig. 11.8. Mining of crude oil/petroleum.

Impervious rock: Rocks that do not permit water to pass through them freely are called as impervious rocks. They can be porous or non-porous.

Refining of petroleum: The crude oil or petroleum obtained from mining is a dark, viscous liquid having unpleasant smell (due to the presence of compounds containing sulphur) and is usually associated with various impurities like sand, salts. Chemically, it is a complex mixture of hydrocarbons, so it is necessary to separate these hydrocarbon from impurities to get various useful fraction. After removal of sand, water, sulphur and other impurities the crude oil is subjected to fractional distillation. The process of separating crude oil into various useful fractions with different boiling points is called **refining of crude oil** and the plants set up for carrying out such process are called as **oil refineries**. The refining process involves the following steps:

1. **Separation of water by Cottrell's process (De-emulsification):** The crude oil from the oil well is an extremely stable emulsion of oil and salt water. To remove water from oil, various methods can be used like mechanical, thermal, chemical, thermochemical and electrical methods. The electrical method is the widely **employed**. In this method the crude oil is allowed to flow between two highly charged electrodes,where the colloidal water droplets coalesce (combine) to form large drops, which separate out form the oil.
2. **Removal of harmful impurities:**
   (*i*) Crude oil contains valuable sulphur compounds. These can be separated by treating crude oil with copper oxide and the copper sulphide formed can be filtered off.
   (*ii*) Crude oil also contain NaCl and $MgCl_2$ impurities. These impurities can corrode the refining equipment and also cause scale formation in the heating pipes. Electrical desalting and dehydration is done to remove these impurities.
3. **Fractional distillation:** After passing through steps (1) and (2), the crude oil is then heated to about 400°C in an iron retort (a device used for distillation) whereby all volatile components are evaporated. The components which are non-volatile like tar and asphalt settle at the bottom of the column. The hot vapours are then passed through a distillation column.

The distillation column is a cylindrical structure of steel, about 31 metres high and 3 metres in diameter. It is provided with a large number of horizontal stainless steel trays separated by short distances. In every tray, there are many holes, each having an up-going short tube with a bubble cap on each (Fig. 11.9). When the vapours rises up in the fractionating column, they become cooler and get condensed at different trays. Fractions having higher boiling point condenses first at lower trays whereas the fractions having lower boiling points condense at higher trays.

Crude oil thus gets fractioned into different fractions depending upon their boiling ranges and are collected at different heights of the column. Each fraction is drained out through the respective outlet. Each fraction is actually a mixture of hydrocarbons with a range of boiling points, Each fraction may be further separated to get products of the desired properties. For example, high boiling fractions which are collected at the bottom can be subjected to cracking to get more useful low boiling fractions.

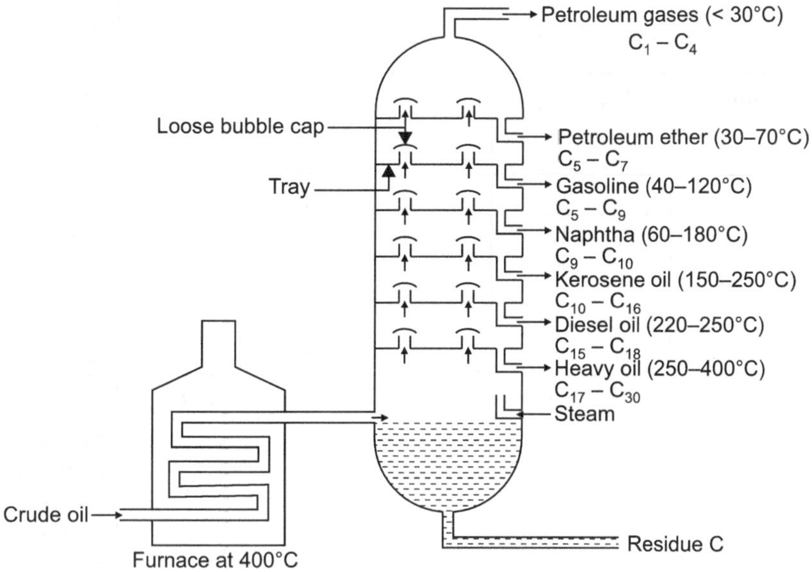

Fig. 11.9. Fractional distillation of crude oil.

The major fractions, their approximate composition, boiling range and uses are listed in Table 11.3.

Table 11.3: Various Crude Oil Fractions and their Specifications

S.No.	Fraction	Composition	Approximate %	Boiling point range (°C)	Uses
1.	Petroleum gases	$C_1 - C_4$	2	< 30	Used as a domestic fuel under the name LPG, feedstock for organic chemicals.
2.	Petroleum ether	$C_5 - C_7$	2	30 – 70	As a solvent in pharmaceuticals, dry cleaning.
3.	Gasoline or petrol	$C_5 - C_9$	32	40 – 120	As a motor fuel, solvent, and in dry cleaning
4.	Naphtha	$C_9 - C_{10}$	2	60 – 180	As a solvent for paints and varnishes, for production of organic chemicals.
5.	Kerosene oil	$C_{10} - C_{16}$	18	150 – 250	Domestic fuel in stove, aviation turbine fuel, illuminant, jet engine fuel for making oil gas.
6.	Diesel oil	$C_{15} - C_{18}$	20	220 – 250	Diesel engine fuel, power generation,
7.	Heavy oil On *vacuum distillation* it gives various fractions	$C_{17} - C_{40}$	–	250 – 400	Fuel for ships and used to get more gasoline and other varieties of lubricants and greases by the process of cracking.

	(*a*) Lubricating oil	$C_{17} - C_{20}$	–	–	Ass a lubricant
	(*b*) Petroleum jelly	$C_{20} - C_{30}$	–	–	In cosmetic and medicines as a lubricant.
	(*c*) Greases		–	–	Semi-solid lubricant.
	(*d*) Paraffin wax	$C_{20} - C_{30}$	–	–	In the manufacturing of candles, ointment, toilet soaps, polish, varnishes, waxed papers.
8.	Residue	C_{30} and above	–	> 400	
	(*a*) Asphalt				In manufacture of points for water proofing of roofs and for road making.
	(*b*) Petroleum coke				For moulding electrode rods for cells and arc lamps and as a fuel.

Cracking of Petroleum

Cracking means that higher molecular weight hydrocarbons of the crude oil decompose or break apart into ligher, more volatile hydrocarbons by means of heat and usually pressure and sometimes catalyst. The gasoline (straight run motor spirit) obtained by the fractional distillation of crude oil is in low yield which is not sufficient to meet the market demand. The present day gasoline demand is heavily supplemented by the cracking process. Cracking basically converts high boiling fractions for which there is less demand into high demand gasoline. For example,

$$\underset{\text{pentadecane}}{C_{15}H_{32}} \longrightarrow \underbrace{\underset{\text{ethene}}{2C_2H_4} + \underset{\text{propene}}{C_3H_6}}_{\substack{\text{Important materials}\\ \text{for making plastics}}} + \underbrace{\underset{\text{octane}}{C_8H_{18}}}_{\substack{\text{One of the molecules}\\ \text{found in gasoline (petrol)}}}$$

$$\underset{\text{Decane}}{C_{10}H_{22}} \longrightarrow \underset{\text{paraffin}}{C_5H_{12}} + \underset{\text{olefin}}{C_5H_{10}}$$

Applications of cracking:

1. Most important application of cracking is the production of gasoline from gas oils.
2. Production of olefins from naphthas and gas oils. Olefins so produced are used as raw materials for petrochemical industries.
3. Conversion of heavy residual fractions into coke and lighter products

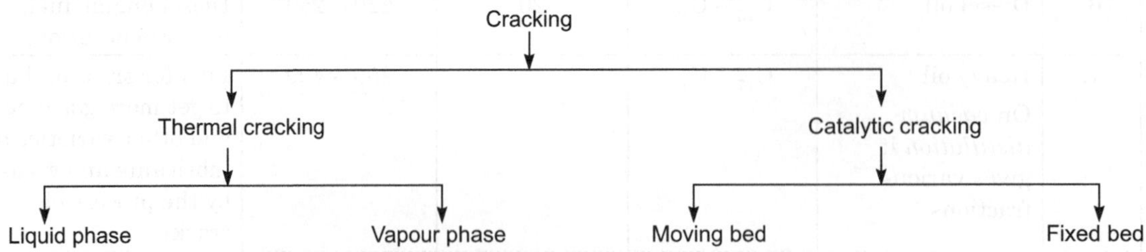

1. Thermal cracking: In this process, the heavy oil is subjected to high temperature (400 – 650°C) and pressure in the absence of air and catalyst. The vapours obtained are fractionated to get gasoline and other low molecular weight paraffins and olefins. This method is old and seldom used now because there is no control over the products of cracking and moreover the efficiency is also low.

Depending upon the cracking conditions it can be:

(*i*) **Liquid phase cracking:** Heavy oil is cracked by heating to a temperature of 420–550°C under a pressure of about 7 – 10 atmosphere. The heavy oil is converted into gasoline to the extent of 60 – 65% of the oil. This method can be used to crack any type of oil.

(*ii*) **Vapour phase cracking:** The oil is heated to a temperature of 600 – 650° under a pressure of about 3 – 4 atmosphere. As compared to liquid phase cracking, the time required for this process is less and the products obtained has less stability and higher octane rating. This method can be used for only those oils which can vaporize at low temperatures.

2. Catalytic cracking: This is the best method to get more gasoline having high octane number. Catalytic cracking is actually the decomposition of hydrocarbons in the presence of catalysts at low temperature and pressure. Usually catalysts like silica, alumina, molecular sieves, aluminosilicates or zeolites are used as catalysts for cracking. Catalytic cracking offers various advantages over thermal cracking. These are:

(*i*) Gasoline produced is in high yield and is of better quality.

(*ii*) No external fuel is required for cracking as the heat required is derived from the coal present in the catalyst.

(*iii*) It can be controlled to ensure the formation of desired products.

(*iv*) Products with low sulphur content are obtained. Sulphur is the undesirable content in gasoline products.

(*v*) It requires low temperature and pressure.

(*vi*) Catalysts are highly specific in nature and only long chain hydrocarbons are cracked.

(*vii*) The products of cracking undergoes isomerization, due to which branched hydrocarbons with better anti-knock properties will result.

Catalytic cracking can be of two types:

Moving bed or fluidized bed: In this method, the heavy oil fraction is heated to 400°C in a preheater and the vapours are mixed with finely divided catalyst powder. This mixture behaves like a fluidized bed and is forced into a large reactor maintained at 500°C. In the reactor, catalyst break down the long chain hydrocarbons into smaller chain and the reaction is highly exothermic. There is a centrifugal separator (also called as cyclone) near the top of the reactor which allows only cracked oil vapours to pass through and retains the catalyst in the reactor only. The hot vapours are subjected to fractionation. The cracked gases and gasoline (petrol) are removed from the top of the fractionating column and is further cooled using water cooler. It is then sent to a chamber where stabilizer is added to prevent the polymerization of dissolved gases like ethylene, propylene etc. The carbon formed during cracking will deposit on the catalyst surface and becomes deactivated. The carbon coated catalyst can be ejected out into the regenerator by an air blast where carbon is oxidized to CO_2 and the catalyst is regenerated.

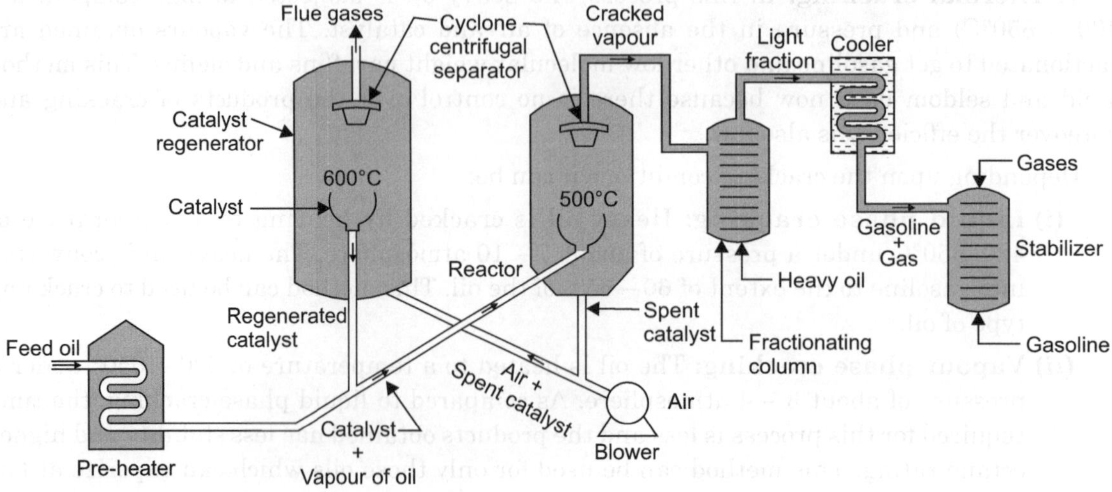

Fig. 11.10. Moving bed catalyst cracking

Fixed bed cracking: In this method, the heavy oil is heated in a per-heater maintained at a temperature of about 425 – 450°C. The vapours of oil are then passed through the catalytic chamber (where bauxite catalyst is mixed with clay and zirconium oxide and arranged on the fixed racks) which is also maintained at a temperature of 425 – 450°C and a pressure of about 1.5 kg/cm^2. The cracking of hydrocarbons takes place in the catalyst chamber and the cracked vapours are sent into the fractionating column to separate the various components. In the fractioning column, gasoline vapours and other gaseous products are recovered from the top while the heavy gas oil fractions are collected from the bottom of the column. The gasoline and other gaseous products are then cooled and sent to a chamber containing stabilizer where gasoline is recovered and all the dissolved gases are removed. After cracking a certain amount of oil, the catalyst stops functioning as a black layer of carbon is deposited on the catalyst. The catalyst can be reactivated by burning off the carbon deposited in a steam of hot air.

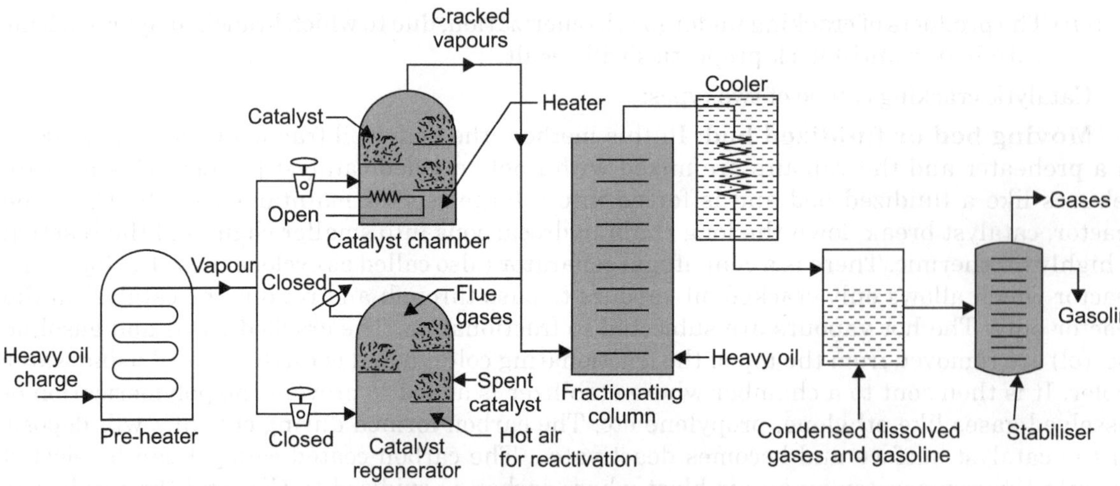

Fig. 11.11. Fixed bed catalytic cracking.

Syntheses of Gasoline or Petrol

Gasoline can be synthesized by any one of the following methods:

1. Polymerization 2. Alkylation
3. Hydrogenation of coal: (*a*) Bergius process (*b*) Fischer Tropsch process.

1. Polymerization

Gasoline obtained by the cracking process contains certain quantities of lower alkanes (like ethane, propane, butane etc.) and alkenes (like ethene, isopropylene, isobutylene etc.). When they are subjected to high temperature and pressure with or without catalyst they undergo polymerization to yield higher hydrocarbons resembling gasoline, which is called **polymer gasoline**.

$$\underset{\text{Propene}}{CH_3CH=CH_2} + \underset{\text{But-1-ene}}{CH_3CH_2CH=CH_2} \xrightarrow[\text{Pressure, catalyst}]{\text{Heat}} \underset{\text{5-methyl-hex-1-ene}}{CH_2=CHCH_2CH_2\,CH(CH_3)_2}$$

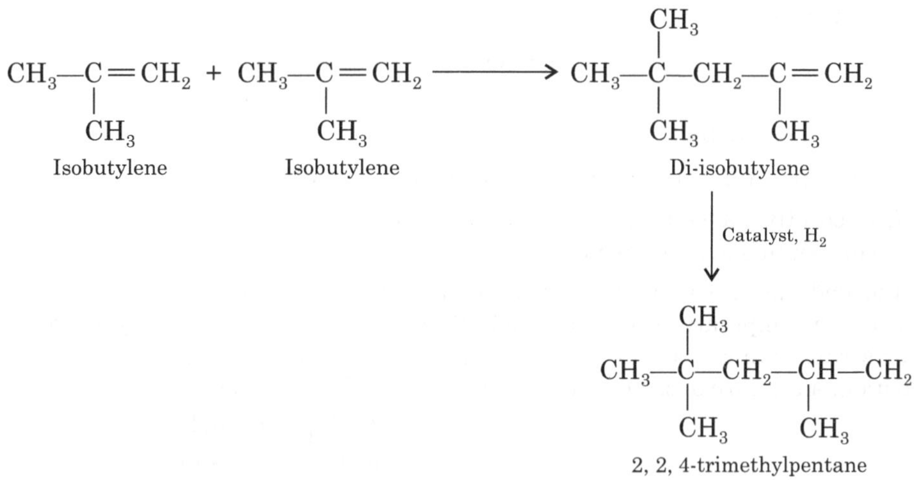

The polymerization of olefins provides a gasoline of high octane number.

Polymerization is of two types:

(*i*) **Thermal polymerization:** Polymerization of cracked goses is carried out at a temperature of 500 – 600°C and pressure 70 – 350 kg/cm^2. The product of polymerization is a mixture of gasoline and oil gas which can be separated through fractionation.

(*ii*) **Catalytic polymerization:** The polymerization is carried out in the presence of catalysts like H_2SO_4, H_3PO_4 or Kieselguhr earth at a low temperature and pressure. In the presence of catalysts, the rate of reaction is increased and also the polymerization unit can be made big or small as per the requirement.

2. Alkylation

This is another important method of converting olefins into gasoline. In the process of alkylation, an olefin reacts with an isoparaffin in the presence of catalyst (*e.g.* H_2SO_4, BF_3, anhyd. HF, $AlCl_3$ etc.) at about 40°C temperature. The most important example is the reaction of isobutene and isobutane in the presence of catalyst to give iso-octane.

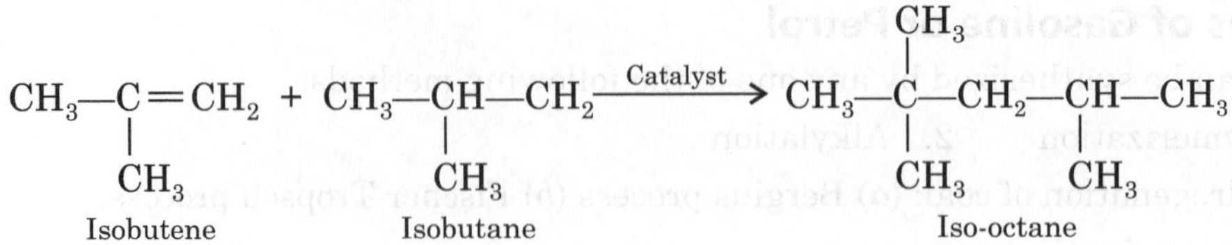

3. Hydrogenation of Coal

Coal is considered as black diamond because of its high utility value. It is therefore not surprising that coal can be used to produce gasoline. Coal is a hydrogen deficient compound and if it is made to react with hydrogen at high temperature and pressure, it can be converted into liquid fuels. The process is called as hydrogenation of coal. So, coal can be converted into gasoline by two processes:

(*i*) **Fischer-Tropsch process:** In this process, coal is first converted into coke. Over heated coke is mixed with hydrogen and steam is passed through it, water gas is formed.

$$C + H_2O \xrightarrow{1200°C} \underset{\text{(Water gas)}}{CO + H_2}$$

Water gas is purified by:

(*i*) First passing through $Fe_2O_3 \rightarrow H_2S$ is removed here

(*ii*) Secondly passed through a mixture of Fe_2O_3 and $Na_2CO_3 \rightarrow$ organic sulphur compounds are removed.

The purified gas is compressed to 5 –10 atm pressure and sent to a catalytic converter maintained at a temperature of about 200 300°C (Fig. 11.12). The catalyst used is a mixture of 200 parts Kieselguhr, 100 parts cobalt, 8 parts magnesia and 5 parts thoria. As a result of hydrogenation, a mixture of saturated and unsaturated hydrocarbons is formed.

$$nCO + 2nH_2 \longrightarrow \underset{\text{Unsaturated hydrocarbon}}{C_n H_{2n}} + nH_2O$$

$$nCO + (2n + 1)\, H_2 \longrightarrow \underset{\text{Saturated hydrocarbon}}{C_nH_{2n+2}} + nH_2O$$

The reactions are highly exothermic therefore, the products or gases formed are sent to a cooler. A liquid resembling crude oil is obtained which is passed through a fractionating column to yield gasoline, diesel and heavy oil. Heavy oil on cracking gives gasoline.

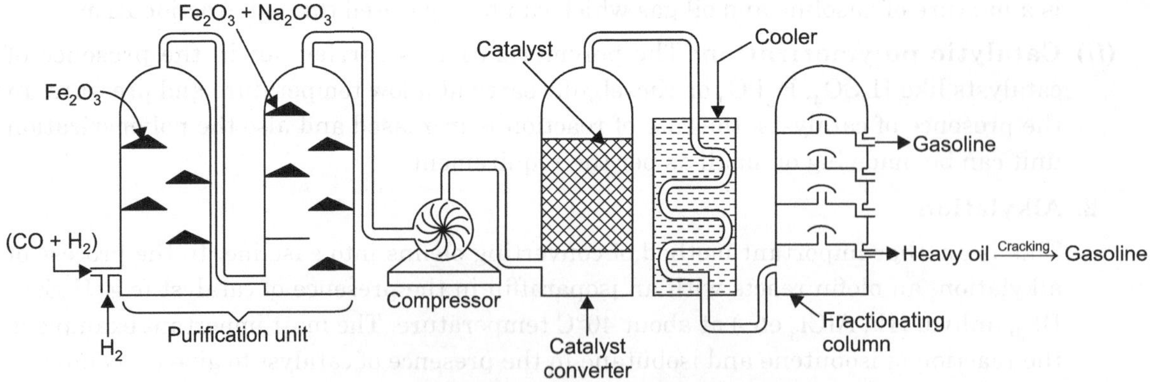

Fig. 11.12. Fischer Tropsch process.

(*ii*) **Bergius process:** In this process, the finely powdered coal is converted into a paste with a heavy oil and a catalyst (tin or nickel oleate). This paste is sent to a converter where it is heated with hydrogen at 400 – 450°C temperature and 200 – 250 atmosphere pressure for about two hours. Here, hydrogen reacts with coal to give higher saturated hydrocarbons. These higher saturated hydrocarbons undergo cracking (because of high pressure and temperature prevailing in the converter) to produce low molecular weight hydrocarbons. When these low molecular weight hydrocarbons are sent to a cooler, a liquid resembling crude oil is formed which on fractional distillation yield gasoline, middle oil and heavy oil. Heavy oil is used further for making paste with fresh batch of coal whereas the middle oil is hydrogenated in vapour phase to give gasoline. The schematic diagram of the process is shown in Fig. 11.13.

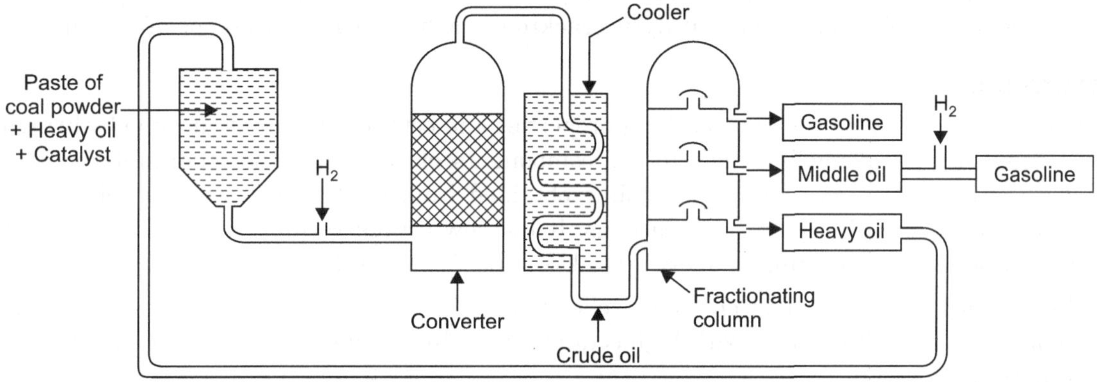

Fig. 11.13. Bergius process.

Refining of gasoline: The straight run gasoline (petrol) obtained from fractional distillation of crude oil of by synthesis contains some undesirable unsaturated olefins and sulphur compounds. The unsaturated olefins if present undergo oxidation and polymerization and therefore causes gum and sludge formation. Accumulation of these products can cause engine wear and can have adverse effects on engine efficiency, performance, emission and durability. On the other hand, sulphur containing gasoline when used as a fuel gives off SO_2 which not only leads to corrosion of the internal combustion engine but also pollutes the atmosphere and imparts objectionable odours to gasoline. Therefore, these impurities must be removed from gasoline. The following methods are used for the removal of such undesirable impurities from the gasoline.

(*i*) **Removal of sulphur compounds (Desulphurisation):** Gasoline may contain sulphur as H_2S or as mercaptans (RSH). Gasoline containing mercaptans are called as **sour gasoline** and their removal as disulphides is called **"sweetening"**. Sweetening can be achieved by Doctor's treastment, where gasoline is treated with an alkaline solution of sodium plumbite (Na_2PbO_4) with controlled amount of sulphur.

$$\underset{\text{Sodium plumbite, (Doctor's solution)}}{Na_2PbO_4} + \underset{\text{Mercaptans}}{2\,RSH} \longrightarrow \underset{\text{Lead mercaptide}}{(RS)_2Pb} + 2\,NaOH$$

$$(RS)_2\,Pb + S \longrightarrow \underset{\text{disulphides}}{RS - RS} + PbS$$

The sulphur impurities in the gasoline are converted into PbS which can be removed by filtration and disulphides can be extracted with a suitable solvent.

(*ii*) **Removal of Olefins:** Olefins present as an impurity in the gasoline can be removed by treating it with 80% cold H_2SO_4. Olefins get converted into a tar like substance which can be removed by filtration. The gasoline fraction is then washed with sodium hydroxide solution.

Olefins can also be removed when the gasoline is passed through Kieselgugr, fuller's earth, clay etc. They also adsorb any colouring matter present in the gasoline.

(*iii*) **Addition of inhibitors:** After removal of impurities, some inhibitors are added to the gasoline to retard oxidation of olefins. Common inhibitors used for this purpose are butylamino phenols, benzyl aminophenols and phenylene diamines.

(*iv*) **Blending:** Even after the removal the impurities the gasoline does not have good combustion qualities. Therefore, to improve the quality of gasoline it is blended with high octane fractions from catalytic cracking to achieve the desired specifications.

Reforming

The process of improving the antiknocking properties and octane number of gasoline by bringing about some structural modifications in the components of gasoline either thermally or in the presence of a catalyst. Straight run gasoline obtained from fractional destillation of crude oil contains mainly straight chain hydrocarbons. It has low octane rating ($\simeq$ 60). But IC engines require gasoline of octane number above 90 in USA and 75 – 85 in India.

Reforming converts straight chain or cyclic hydrocarbons with low octane rating to branched chain or aromatic hydrocarbons with high octane rating. Reforming can be carried out thermally or catalytically.

In thermal reforming, the straight run gasoline is heated to a temperature of about 500 – 600°C and pressure about 85 atmosphere. The amount and quality of gasoline after reforming depends significantly on the temperature of the furnace. As a thumb rule, with increase in temperature of the furnace, the octane number of gasoline increases but at the expense of gasoline yield. The octane number of gasoline achieved in this process is only 65 – 80. Thermal cracking is less effective and less economical than catalytic reforming.

In catalytic reforming, the gasoline is heated at a temperature of about 500°C and 50 atmospheric pressure in the presence of catalyst. There are two main types of catalytic reforming **moving bed** and **fixed bed types**. Catalyst employed in the catalytic reforming process depends upon the type of process. Various catalysts used are metal oxides supported over alumina like $MoO_2 - Al_2O_3$, $Cr_2O_3 - Al_2O_3$ (used mainly for moving bed reforming) and platinum supported over alumina (for fixed bed reforming). Catalytic reforming achieves octane number of gasoline as 90 –95. In general, the quality as well as quantity of the gasoline obtained from catalytic reforming is far better than the one obtained from thermal reforming.

The main reactions taking place during reforming process are:

1. Dehydrogenation, 2. Dehydrocyclisation, 3. Isomerisation, 4. Hydro cracking.

1. **Dehydrogenation:** Cyclic alkanes undergo dehydrogenation to form aromatic compounds.

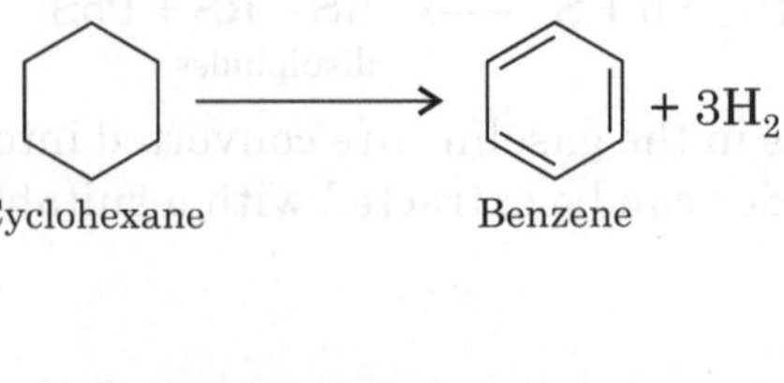

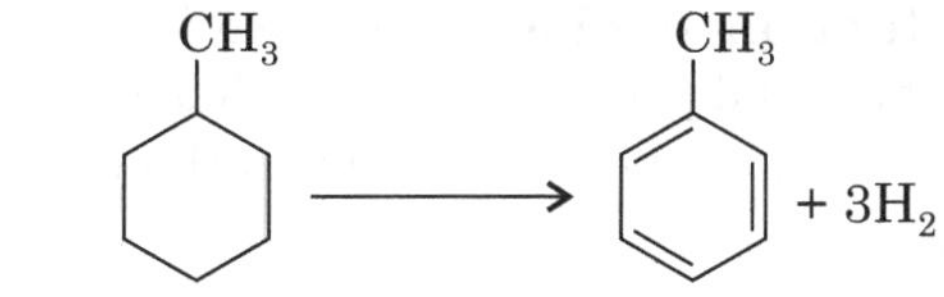

Methylcyclohexane Toluene

2. **Dehydrocyclisation:** Straight chain hydrocarbons undergo cyclisation followed by dehydrogenation to form aromatic compounds.

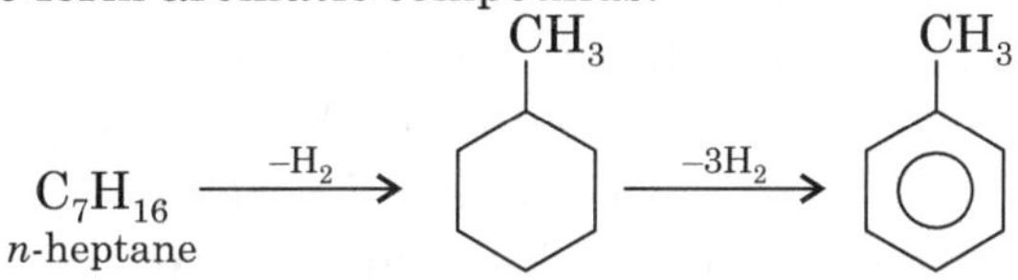

Methyl cyclohexane Toluene

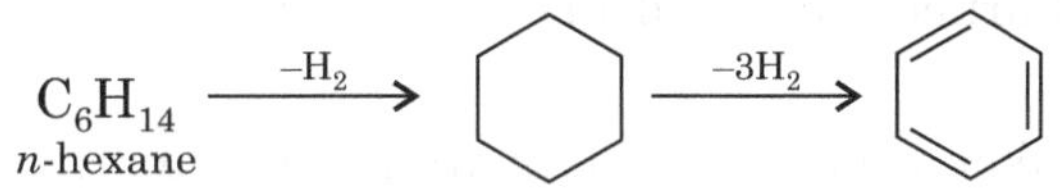

3. **Isomerisation:** Straight chain hydrocarbons undergo isomerisation to form branched chain hydrocarbons.

$CH_3—CH_2—CH_2—CH_2—CH_2—CH_3$ (*n*-hexane) →

→ $CH_3—CH(CH_3)—CH_2CH_2—CH_3$ 2-methylpentane

→ $CH_3—CH(CH_3)—CH(CH_3)—CH_3$ 2,2-dimethylbutane

4. **Hydrocracking:** Paraffins undergo cracking in the presence of H_2 and catalyst, two light gases are produced that are removed from gasoline to improve octane number.

$$\underset{n\text{-decane}}{C_{10}H_{22}} + H_2 \xrightarrow[\text{Pt}]{\text{Catalyst}} \underset{n\text{-pentane}}{2C_5H_{12}}$$

$$\underset{n\text{-hexane}}{C_6H_{14}} + H_2 \xrightarrow{\text{Pt}} \underset{\text{propane}}{2C_3H_8}$$

$$\underset{n\text{-hexane}}{C_6H_{14}} + H_2 \xrightarrow{\text{Pt}} \underset{\text{ethane}}{C_2H_6} + \underset{n\text{-butane}}{C_4H_{10}}$$

Heat engine: Engine which converts chemical energy of the fuel into thermal energy which is then utilized to perform mechanical work is called as **heat engine**. They are classified as:

(*i*) **Internal Combustion Engines (IC Engines):** In IC engines, heat is produced by burning the fuel inside the engine. For example: Diesel engine, petrol engine etc.

(*ii*) **External Combustion Engines (EC Engines):** In EC engines, heat is produced by burning the fuel outside the engine. For example: steam engine.

An IC engine uses either diesel or gasoline as a fuel. Let us discuss about petrol engines where gasoline (petrol) is used as a fuel. In petrol engine, the running of engine involves the continuous repetition of four operations or stroke that make up what is called the cycle of operations. The four strokes occur in the following order.

1. **Suction stroke (Induction stroke):** The space in the cylinder above the piston is filled with a mixture of air and petrol vapours (called as charge). This mixture of air and petrol vapours in able to enter the cylinder when the piston move down. This is called as **suction stroke**.
2. **Compression stroke:** During the compression stroke, the mixture which was sucked into the cylinder during the suction stroke is compressed into the top end of the cylinder (called the combustion chamber) thus raising its temperature. This is achieved by the upward movement of the piston. Due to the high pressure and temperature the mixture gets heated up and vaporised. It is here that a low octane rating fuel might ignite and cause knocking. The ratio of initial volume *i.e.* volume at induction stroke to final volume *i.e* volume at compression stroke is called as **compression ratio**.
3. **Power stroke:** Now when the gases are pushed up, the petrol vapour is ignited by an electric spark and burned. The resulting increase in pressure drives the piston down the cylinder.
4. **Exhaust Stroke:** When the burnt gases are pushed up, the piston goes up. The burnt gases are expelled from the cylinder. The piston moves down again and a fresh mixture of air and petrol is again drawn into the cylinder. The cycle of four strokes *viz.* suction, compression, power and exhaust strokes is then repeated.

Knocking

In an internal combustion engine, the air-petrol mixture should normally burnt smoothly. This mixture is compressed and ignited by an electric spark to have maximum efficiency. Under certain conditions there may be spontaneous combustion before it is ignited by the spark, which may result in explosive burning of fuel and a characteristic metallic sound is produced called as **knocking**. Knocking results in a decreased power output besides causing mechanical damage by overheating the cylinder parts.

The tendency of a fuel to knock depends mainly on the engine design, running conditions and also on the chemical structure of the hydrocarbons present in fuel.

The knocking tendency decreases with increase in the compactness of the molecule, double bonds and cyclic structure. The knocking tendency decreases in the following order:

Straight chain paraffins > branched chain paraffins > olefins > cycloparaffins > Aromatics.

- In straight chain paraffins, knocking increases with the increase in the length of the hydrocarbon chain:

  n-heptane > *n*-hexane > *n*-pentane > *n*-butane

- In branched chain paraffins, the one having less branching have more knocking characteristics. For example

  n-heptane > 2-methyl hexane > 2, 2-dimethyl pentane

- Aromatic hydrocarbons such as benzene and toluene have very high antiknock properties.

Octane number or octane rating: The knocking characteristics of the fuel cannot be expressed in absolute terms. Graham Edgar in 1926 developed an arbitrary scale to express the knocking characteristics of fuel. It has been observed than *n*-heptane due to its straight chain structure knocks very badly and therefore assigned an octane number of zero, while iso-octane a highly branched paraffin gives very little knocking and has been assigned an octane number of 100.

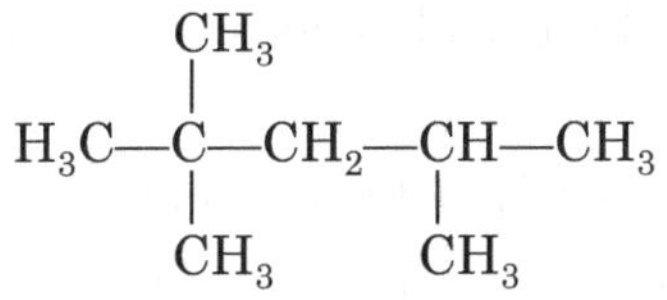

Iso-octane
(2, 2, 4-trimethylpentane)
(Octane number = 100)

$CH_3—CH_2CH_2CH_2CH_2CH_2—CH_3$

n-heptane
(Octane number = 0)

More the octane number, less is the knocking tendency.

Octane number of a fuel is defined as the percentage of iso-octane present in a mixture of iso-octane and *n*-heptane which has the same knocking characteristics as the fuel under investigation under the same set of conditions. Let us understand this with the help of an example—a fuel with octane number 90, would give the same knocking as a mixture of iso-octane and *n*-heptane containing 90% of iso-octane and 10% *n*-heptane.

It is possible for a fuel to have octane number higher than 100. This is because iso-octane is not the most knock-resistant substance available. LPG, racing fuels and alcohol fuels (*e.g.* methanol, ethanol etc.), may have octane ratings of around 110 or significantly higher. The octane number of some fuels are given below:

Fuel	**Octane number**
Toluene	118
Benzene	106
Ethanol	129
2, 2, 3-trimethyl pentane	125

Antiknocking agents: Knocking can be decreased by adding certain agents /compounds to the fuel and these agents are called as **antiknocking agents**. Thus, the compounds which when added to gasoline increase its octane number and decrease knocking are called as **antiknocking agents**. Antiknocking agents improve the quality of the fuel. The most effective antiknocking agents are tetraethyl lead (TEL) – $(C_2H_5)_4$ Pb, tetramethyl lead (TML) – $(CH_3)_4$ Pb.

It is believed that knocking is a free radical process. The antiknocking agents TEL and TML undergo dissociation to produce ethyl and methyl free radical respectively.

$$(C_2H_5)_4\,Pb \longrightarrow 4C_2H_5^{\bullet} + Pb$$

$$(CH_3)_4\,Pb \longrightarrow 4CH_3^{\bullet} + Pb$$

These free radicals combine with the radicals formed by branching chain reaction during the combustion of gasoline and form stable hydrocarbons. Thus, these ethyl and methyl free radicals act as chain inhibitors and therefore the chain reaction which leads to knocking does not take place.

During combustion TEL and TML get converted to Pb or PbO. PbO rapidly reduces to lead which gets deposited on the spark plug, cylinder walls and other engine parts causing damages. In order to solve these problems, TEL and TML are used alongwith ethylene dichloride or dibromide. During this process, lead and lead oxide are converted into $PbCl_2$ or $PbBr_2$ which are volatile and escape into the environment causing pollution and also these lead halides are poisonous to human beings and animals.

$$Br - CH_2 - CH_2 - Br + Pb \longrightarrow CH_2 = CH_2 + PbBr_2 \text{ (volatile)}$$
$$Cl - CH_2 - CH_2 - Cl + Pb \longrightarrow CH_2 = CH_2 + PbCl_2 \text{ (volatile)}$$

Therefore, it is better to avoid use of organolead compounds.

It is highly recommended to use lead free petrol. Therefore, now a days methyl tertiary butyl ether (MTBE) is used instead of tetraethyl lead.

Unleaded Petrol

The petrol whose octane number is increased without the addition of lead compounds is referred as **unleaded petrol**. This can be achieved by

1. **Reforming:** reforming increases the content of molecules having branched and aromatic ring structures. Thus, by this process, the contents of isopentane, isooctane, ethyl benzene and isopropyl benzene increases in the given fuel.
2. **Adding compounds which have high octane number:** For example, methyl tertiary butyl ether (MTBE), ethyl tertiary butyl ether (ETBE) etc. are added to petrol in place of TEL. MTBE has oxygen in the form of ether and supplies oxygen for the combustion of petrol in internal combustion engine thereby reducing the formation of peroxy compound.

   The compelling reasons for using unleaded petrol are:

   (*i*) **Lead is toxic:** Lead salts are poisonous to animals and human beings.

   (*ii*) Another factor for reducing tetra ethyl lead is the requirement of vehicles to be fitted with catalytic convertors to control pollution. These catalytic convertors convert the low octane rating straight chain compounds present in gasoline to branched chain compounds having high octane rating. Only lead free petrol (unleaded petrol) can be used for vehicles fitted with catalytic convertors because lead inactivates the catalyst used in convertors.

Diesel Oil (Diesel Fuel)

Diesel oil is that fraction of petroleum distillation which is collected in the temperature range of 300 – 350°C. It is heavier than gas oil and lighter than the residual oil. Its specific gravity lies between 0.86 – 0.95. Its calorific value is about 10350 kcal/kg. It is used as fuel in diesel engines.

Diesel fuel is used in engines where the fuel is directly ignited into cylinders and is atomised there before it is ignited and burnt. In a diesel engine the fuel is exploded by the application of heat and pressure and not by a spark. The main characteristic of a diesel engine fuel is that is should easily ignite below compression temperature. The induction lag should be as short as possible. Chemically, diesel engine fuels (diesel oils) consist of straight-longer chain hydrocarbons with a minimum amount of branched chain and aromatic hydrocarbons.

Thus in contrast to gasoline, the desirable characteristic of the diesel oil (used as fuel in diesel engines) is a low spontaneous ignition temperature. Thus a separate scale is necessary for grading the diesel oils as they cannot be rated on octane number scale. The number used for rating diesel oil is called **cetane number** which represents the spontaneous ignition temperature of a particular diesel fuel. The hydrocarbon **cetane (*n*-hexadecane)** ignites more rapidly than any other commercial fuel and thus has been assigned an arbitrary cetane number of 100. On the other hand, since α-methylnaphthalene ignites slowly than any other fuel, it has been assigned a cetane number of zero.

$CH_3(CH_2)_{14}CH_3$
n-Hexadecane
(cetane)
(spontaneously ignites)
Cetane No. = 100

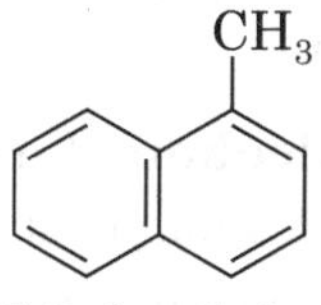

α-Methylnapthalene
(Ignites very slowly)
Cetane No. = 0

Mixture of these two hydrocarbons forms a standard scale for studying the spontaneous ignition temperature of a diesel fuel, *i.e.* its cetane number. Thus the *cetane number of a diesel fuel is defined as the percentage of cetane present is a mixture of cetane and α-methylnaphthalene which matches the fuel (diesel fuel) in question in ignition property.* For example, a diesel fuel is said to have a cetane number of 80 when is matches in ignition property to a mixture of 80% cetane and 20% α-methylnaphthalene. The cetane number of a diesel fuel can be increased by the addition of a small amount (1 – 5%) of certain compounds called additives. The commonly used additives are ethyl nitrate, isoamyl nitrate, acetone, nitronaphthalene, etc. The usual diesel fuel is diesel oil, a fraction obtained between 250 – 320°C during the fractional distillation of crude petroleum.

Benzol: Benzol is the fraction obtained at a temperature range of 70 – 150° during coal-tar distillation. Chemically, it is a mixture of the following hydrocarbons (mainly aromatic).

Benzene = 70%, Toluene = 18%, Xylene = 6%

Paraffins, naphthenes and unsaturated hydrocarbons = 4 – 6%.

Since benzol has mainly aromatic hydrocarbons, it has high octane number (87 – 90) and thus constitutes a good fuel for internal combustion engines. Its calorific value is very high (10,200 kcal/kg). Ortho or para-cresols either alone or mixed with catechol are added to prevent gum formation.

Power alcohol: *Alcohol used for the generation of power is called power alcohol.* Absolute alcohol (100% ethyl alcohol) and rectified spirit (93 –95% ethyl alcohol) are not used as prime fuels but they are only used as additives to petrol. Generally, power alcohol has petrol and alcohol in the ratio of 4 : 1. In industries, ethanol is prepared from molasses. Molasses are byproduct, obtained from the refining of sugarcane into sugar. Molasses is converted into ethyl alcohol by the following steps.

(*i*) **Dilution:** Since the high concentration of sugars is undesirable for the fermentation reaction, molasses is first of all diluted with water to get about 8 – 10% solution of sugars.

(*ii*) **Addition of dilute sulphuric acid:** The diluted molasses is acidified with small amount of dilute sulphuric acid. Dilute sulphuric acid checks the growth of undesirable bacteria which would otherwise form lactic acid and acetic acid.

(*iii*) **Addition of ammonium salts:** To the above solution a small quantity of ammonium salts (ammonium sulphate and ammonium phosphate) is added. Ammonium salts act as a food for the ferment and hence these are added only when molasses contain insufficient yeast food.

(*iv*) **Addition of yeast (alcoholic fermentation):** The above solution of molasses is taken in a fermentation tank and yeast is now added to it (approximately 5% of the liquid). the mixture is maintained at about 30°C and kept for 2 – 3 days. During this period, the enzymes *invertase* and *zymase*, present in yeast decompose sugars to ethyl alcohol with the evolution of carbon dioxide (alcoholic fermentation).

(*a*) $$\underset{\text{sucrose}}{C_{12}H_{22}O_{11}} + H_2O \xrightarrow{\text{invertase}} \underset{\text{glucose}}{C_6H_{12}O_6} + \underset{\text{fructose}}{C_6H_{12}O_6}$$

(*b*) $$\underset{\text{glucose or fructose}}{C_6H_{12}O_6} \xrightarrow{\text{zymase}} \underset{\text{ethyl alcohol}}{2C_2H_5OH} + 2CO_2$$

The process of fermentation is completed in 2 – 3 days. When the evolution of carbon dioxide ceases, the yeast is filtered off. The filtrate, commonly known as *wash* or *wort* contains nearly 6 – 10% ethyl alcohol, 3 – 5% glycerol, some acetaldehyde, higher alcohols etc. It is distilled for obtaining ethyl alcohol.

(*v*) **Distillation:** Wash is distilled in a specially designed continuous plant known as *coffey still.* It consists of two tall fractionating columns called the *analyser* and the *rectifier* provided with a number of perforated plates with values opening upwards. It works on the principle of counter current, since steam and alcohol travel in opposite directions.

Preheated wash is admitted near the top of the rectifier while a current of steam is introduced at the bottom end of the analyser. As the steam comes in contact with wash, it vapourises the alcohol present in the wash and carries the alcohol vapours to the rectifier, condensation of steam (b.p. 100°C) takes place while the uncondensed alcohol vapours (b.p. 78.3°C) leave the rectifier at its top end and are condensed separately with the help of a condenser. The alcohol thus obtained is 90% pure and is subjected to fractional distillation. The process being known as rectification.

(*vi*) **Rectification:** Rectification of 90% alcohol gives following three fractions.

(*a*) **First fraction:** This fraction consists mainly of low boiling liquids like acetadehyde

(*b*) **Middle fraction:** It contains 93 – 95% ethyl alcohol. It is sold under the name of *rectified spirit* or *commercial alcohol.*

(*c*) **Last fraction (b.p. 125 – 140°C) or fusel oil:** It contains water and fusel oil. Fusel oil is a mixture of *n*-propyl, *n*-butyl, *n*-amyl, isoamyl and optically active amyl alcohols.

In modern plants, both distillation and rectification are done in one operation.

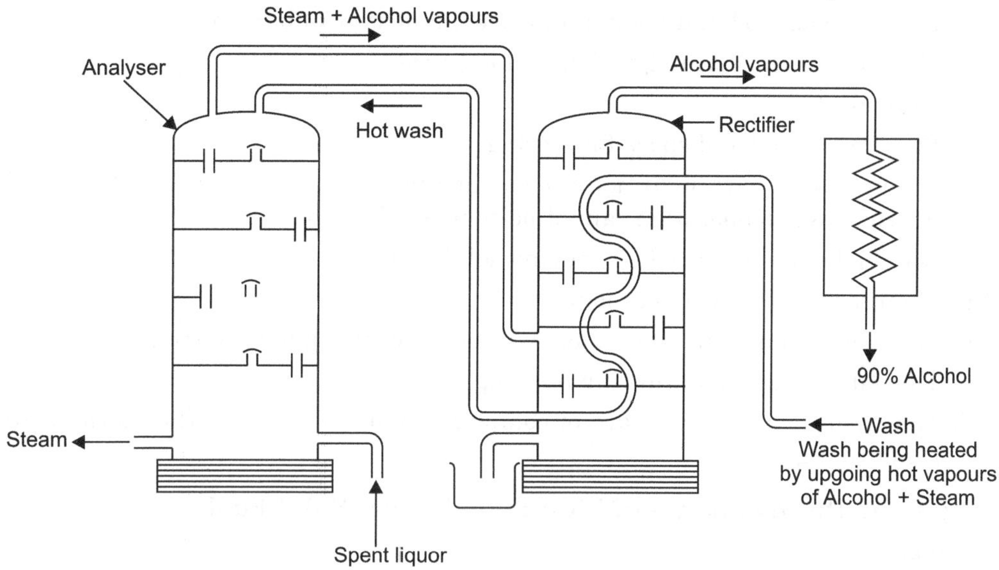

Fig. 11.14. Distillation of wash.

Advantages of Alcohol Blended Petrol

(*i*) Since alcohol has high octane number (90) than the petrol (60 – 70), its presence in petrol increases the octane number. Hence, alcohol blended petrol has better anti-knock properties.

(*ii*) There is no decrease in power output or increase in specific fuel consumption.

(*iii*) There is no starting difficulty.

(*iv*) Alcohol is capable of absorbing any traces of moisture which may otherwise enter into the petrol system.

Disadvantages of Alcohol Blended Petrol

(*i*) The calorific value of alcohol is low hence alcohol blended petrol has low calorific value.

(*ii*) Alcohol is easily oxidised to acids. Hence it is liable to cause corrosion.

(*iii*) The ratio of flow of blend is to be increases to 1.56 times to that of pure petrol by altering the size of carburettor jet.

(*iv*) Since the alcohol-blended petrol requires less air than the pure gasoline, the air entering the cylinders is to be regulated either by modifying air inlet or by operating choke.

(*v*) Due to higher specific gravity of the blend, the float is to be weighed down to the correct level.

(*vi*) At low temperatures (below 70°C) starting difficulty arises due to lower vapour pressure of alcohol. Hence specific arrangement must be provided for heating the carburettor.

Advantages and Disadvantages of Solid Fuels

Advantages:

(*i*) Solid fuels occur widely and their cost of production is cheap.

(*ii*) Their transportation is very easy.

(*iii*) They can be stored conveniently without any risk of explosion.

(*iv*) They are easy to handle and require a simple type of burning.

(*v*) They possess moderate ignition temperature.

Disadvantages:

(*i*) They require a lot of space for storing.

(*ii*) The process of burning is not as clean as that of liquid and gaseous fuels. Moreover the combustion operation cannot be controlled easily.

(*iii*) Lot of labour is required for moving solid fuel.

(*iv*) Their large portion of heat is wasted.

(*v*) They form a large amount of ash whose disposal is a big problem.

(*vi*) They also form clinker during burning.

(*vii*) They require lot of excess air for complete combustion. Hence the thermal efficiency is not so high.

Advantages and Disadvantages of Liquid Fuels Over Solid Fuels

Advantages:

(*i*) Liquid fuels occupy less volume than solid fuels. hence they require less space for storing.

(*ii*) They have high calorific value than the solid fuels.

(*iii*) Their combustion is uniform and can be controlled or extinguished easily by regulating or stopping the liquid fuel supply.

(*iv*) They can be easily transported through pipes.

(*v*) They are clean in use and economic in labour.

(*vi*) They do not leave any ash or residue after burning.

(*vii*) They require less air for complete combustion than the solid fuel. Hence the thermal efficiency is very high and the final temperature is attained immediately.

(*viii*) Due to uniform heating, there is no wear and tear of the plates or tubes of the apparatus.

Disadvantages:

(*i*) The liquid fuels are less abundant than the solid fuels.

(*ii*) Their cost is relatively higher as compared to solid fuels.

(*iii*) They have bad and sometimes harmful odours.

(*iv*) Special and costly tanks are required for storing liquid fuels.

(*v*) They are inflammable and hence great precaution has to be taken during their storage.

(*vi*) For efficient burning of liquid fuels, specially constructed burners and spraying apparatus are required which need the service of a mechanic.

11.7 GASEOUS FUELS OR FUEL GASES

Gaseous fuels are considered to be the best fuels because they possess several advantages over solid and liquid fuels. Actually gaseous fuels have all the advantages of liquid fuels alongwith some additional advantages. The important advantages are given below.

Advantages of Gaseous Fuels Over Solid and Liquid Fuel

(*i*) Fuel gases can flow through pipes and hence can be easily transported (conveyed) to the place of need without any manual labour.

(*ii*) They can be lighted at a moment's notice.

(*iii*) They burn with high efficiency and high temperature flame is obtained in no time.

(*iv*) The gaseous fuels on burning, do not produce any smoke and ash. Moreover, they burn freely in presence of air.

(*v*) the fuel gases possess high calorific value and produce high temperature.

(*vi*) The burning of the gaseous fuel can be controlled and hence the temperature can be maintained as required.

(*vii*) They can be preheated by the heat of waste gases and hence their use is economical as far as heat is concerned.

(*viii*) The flame can be made oxidising, reducing or neutral by regulating the air supply. This is of great significance in metallurgical operations.

(*ix*) The supply of gas to the burners can be easily controlled.

(*x*) Gaseous fuel can be produced by the poorest quality of solid fuel (coal).

(*xi*) They burn in slight excess of air.

However, **gaseous fuels have following two disadvantages.**

(*i*) Since gases occupy a large volume, they require large tanks for storing.

(*ii*) They are highly inflammable and hence fire hazard chances are more in their use.

Due to the above advantages gaseous fuels are becoming popular day by day for the domestic as well as industrial purposes. The important gaseous fuels are: natural gas (methane), coal gas, oil gas, water gas, producer gas, semi-water gas, blast furnace gas, gobar gas, etc.

1. Natural gas: Natural gas is formed by the decomposition of organic matter. It is found in regions rich in petroleum. It is a very cheap and convenient fuel consisting of methane and other saturated hydrocarbons. Its calorific value is 12000 to 14000 kcal/m^2. A typical natural gas has the following composition.

(*i*) Methane = 85%, (*ii*) Ethane = 8%,

(*iii*) Propane = 4% (*iv*) Butane = 1.5%,

(*v*) Higher hydrocarbons = 1.5%.

However, the exact amounts of the various gases vary from one gas fields to another, but methane is always the main constituent.

It is an excellent gaseous fuel and burns with a hot blue flame. It is used as a fuel for industrial and domestic purposes.

2. Water gas: Water gas is a mixture of carbon monoxide and hydrogen alongwith a small amount of carbon dioxide. It is obtained by the action of steam on a bed of coke heated to 1000°C.

$$C + H_2O \longrightarrow \underbrace{CO + H_2}_{\text{Water gas}} - 28 \text{ kcal}$$

Since the above reaction is endothermic, the coal cools down after a few minutes and the reaction proceeds in a different way to form carbon dioxide and hydrogen instead of water gas ($CO + H_2$).

$$C + 2H_2O \longrightarrow CO_2 + 2H_2 - 19 \text{ kcal}$$

In order to avoid the above undesirable reaction, the current of steam is intermittently replaced by a blast of air. The following reactions now occur.

(*i*) $C + O_2 \longrightarrow CO_2 + 97$ kcal (*ii*) $2C + O_2 \longrightarrow 2CO + 59$ kcal.

Thus due to exothermic reaction, the temperature of carbon again rises and when the temperature increases to 1000°C air entry is stopped and steam is again passed. Thus in modern gas plants, steam and air are blown alternatively. The period of *steam blow (cold blow)* is usually 4 minutes while the period of air blow (*hot blow*) is very short (about 1–2 minutes). The durations of these periods are adjusted in such a way that the maximum yield of water gas is obtained.

A water gas generator is a cylindrical vessel made of steel. It is bout 4 – 5 m in height and 2 – 3 m in diameter. At the top it is provided with a hopper for adding coke. Water gas outlet is provided near the top. It has two separate inlets for blowing steam and air at will. At the bottom, it is provided with an arrangement of taking out ash formed.

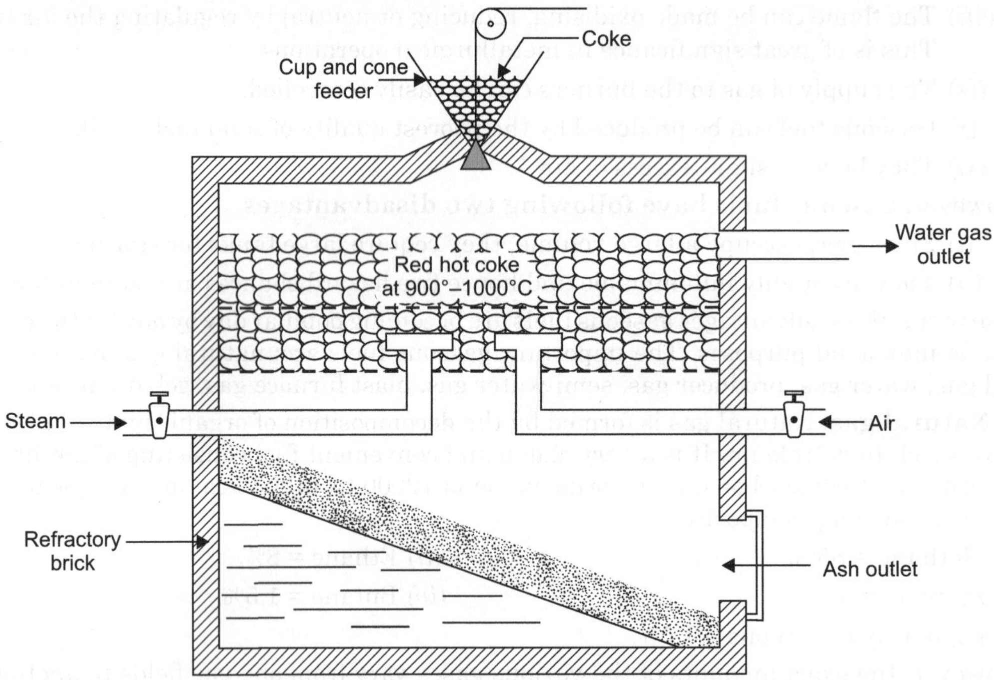

Fig. 11.15. Manufacture of water gas.

During the steam blow, water gas is produced. This is led out through the water gas outlet. On the other hand, nitrogen carbon dioxide and carbon monoxide are formed during the air blow. These are allowed to escape into the atmosphere. Thus the manufacture of water gas is intermittent.

Properties and composition: Water gas burns with a non-luminous blue flame and hence it is also called **blue water gas**. Its calorific value is about 3255 kcal/m^3. It burns with a high temperature flame about 1200°C. The approximate composition of the water gas is as below.

(*i*) Hydrogen = 48.0%,
(*ii*) Nitrogen = 3%,
(*iii*) Carbon monoxide = 44.0%,
(*iv*) Methane = 0.8%,
(*v*) Carbon dioxide = 4.2%.

Uses: (*i*) Because of its high calorific value, water gas is used as a good fuel.

(*a*) $2CO + O_2 \longrightarrow 2CO_2 + \text{Heat}$ (*b*) $H_2 + \frac{1}{2}O_2 \longrightarrow H_2O + \text{Heat}$

(*ii*) It is a good source of hydrogen on commercial scale.

(*iii*) A mixture of water gas and producer gas is used for the manufacture of ammonia by Haber's process.

(*iv*) Mixed with hydrogen, it is used in the manufacture of methyl alcohol.

$$CO + 2H_2 \xrightarrow[200-300 \text{ atmos pressure}]{\text{ZnO (catalyst)}} CH_3OH$$

(*v*) Water gas is also used for the preparation of carburetted water gas (water gas + gaseous hydrocarbons) which can be used for lighting and heating purposes.

(*vi*) It is also used for welding purposes.

3. Producer gas: Producer gas is a mixture of carbon monoxide and nitrogen. It is produced by burning a solid carbonaceous fuel (coke, etc.) in a limited supply of air. Since a low grade coal can be used in producing producer gas, its cost comes out to be low. Actually, it is considered as the cheapest gaseous fuel. But due to the presence of a large proportion of nitrogen, its calorific value is the lowest (1209 kcal/m^3) of all gaseous fuels.

Manufacture: The furnace used for the manufacture of producer gas is known as *producer* (Fig. 11.16). It consists of a large air-tight cylindrical vessel of mild steel lined inside with fire bricks. It is about 2 – 4 m in diameter and 3 – 5 m in height. At the bottom, it is provided with pipe for blowing air and an arrangement for removing ash. Coal is added through a hopper at the top and producer gas comes out from an exit near the top.

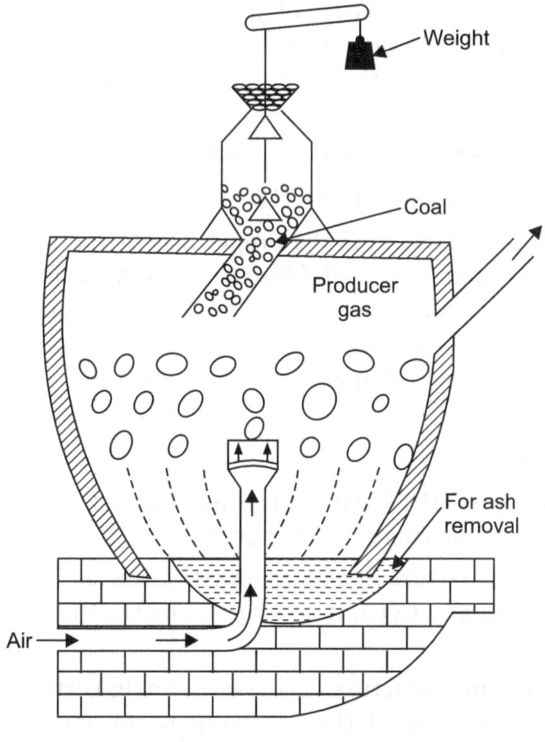

Fig. 11.16. Manufacture of producer gas.

When air mixed with a little steam is passed through the inlet, carbon (of the coal) combines with oxygen (of the air) in the lower part of the furnace to form carbon dioxide. Carbon dioxide, so formed rises up through the red hot coal and gets reduced to carbon monoxide during its passage.

$$C + O_2 \longrightarrow CO_2 + 97 \text{ kcal } (\textit{In the lower part})$$
$$CO_2 + C \longrightarrow 2CO - 39 \text{ kcal } (\textit{In the upper part})$$

Nitrogen (of air) remains unaffected throughout the process. Thus a mixture of carbon monoxide and nitrogen with traces of carbon dioxide and hydrocarbons comes out through the exit at the upper end of the producer. Since more heat is liberated than absorbed in the above two reactions, in the long run some excess heat is obtained which keeps the coal hot in the product.

Composition and uses: It is a poisonous gas, insoluble in water and heavier than air. The average composition of producer gas is as below.

(*i*) $CO = 22 - 30\%$, (*ii*) $H_2 = 8 - 12\%$,

(*iii*) $N_2 = 52 - 55\%$ (*iv*) $CO_2 = 3\%$,

(*v*) Methane = Small amount.

As mentioned earlier it is the cheapest fuel gas and used for the following purposes.

(*i*) It is used as a fuel for heating open-hearth furnaces (used in steel and glass manufacture), muffle furnaces, retorts (used in coke and coal gas manufacture), etc.

$$2CO + O_2 \longrightarrow 2CO_2 + \text{Heat}$$

(*ii*) It provides a reducing atmosphere in certain metallurgical operations.

4. Semi-water gas: Since the action of air on carbon (combustion of carbon) is an exothermic reaction, about 3% of the heat generated in the manufacture of producer gas is lost unless the gas is used on the spot. On the other hand, the action of steam on red hot carbon is an endothermic reaction.

$$2C + O_2 \longrightarrow 2CO \quad + 54 \text{ kcal (In producer gas)}$$
$$C + H_2O \longrightarrow CO + H_2 \quad - 28 \text{ kcal (In water gas)}$$

Hence if a mixture of air and steam in the proper proportion is passed over red hot carbon, whole of the heat generated can be utilized, Moreover, the heat liberated by the combustion of carbon is sufficient to maintain the temperature necessary for the formation of water gas by the action of steam on carbon. The gas mixture, thus obtained, may be considered as a mixture of the water gas and producer gas. Its approximate composition is as below.

(*i*) $CO = 25 - 28\%$, (*ii*) $CO_2 = 4 - 5\%$,

(*iii*) Methane etc. = 1 – 1.5%, (*iv*) $N_2 = 50 - 55\%$.

Its calorific value is 160 – 180 B.T.U./ ft^3. It is used as a fuel in the steel industry and also for the production of power in internal combustion engines.

5. Coal gas: Coal gas is a mixture of 95% combustible gases (H_2, CH_4, CO, C_2H_4, C_2H_2) and 5% non-combustible gases (N_2 and CO_2). It is obtained by the destructive distillation of coal at about 1000°C.

The modern plant for the manufacture of coal–gas, using vertical retorts is shown diagram matically in Fig. 11.17. It consists of the following parts: (*i*) retorts, (*ii*) hydraulic main. (*iii*) condensers, (*iv*) tar-well, (*v*) scrubber, (*vi*) purifier and (*vii*) gas-holder.

Manufacture: The vertical retorts made of fireclay are loaded with coal. These are heated to about 1300°C by means of preheated producer gas being prepared at the site. Coal is decomposed into volatile products which leave the retorts at the top and are led to the *hydraulic main* containing water where some coal tar and ammonical liquor condense. The gases then pass through **condensers** cooled by air where most of coal tar and ammonical salts are condensed and collected in a *tar-well* below the condensers. The tar and the ammonical layer form two separate layers in the well and hence can be easily separated.

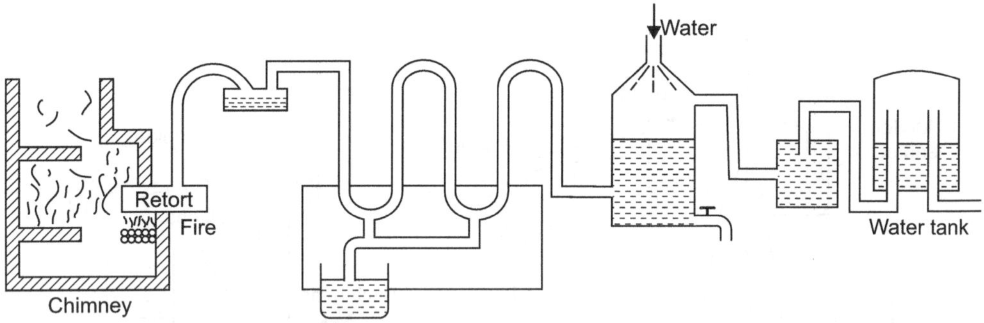

Fig. 11.17. Manufacture of coal gas.

The gases are then passed through *scrubbers or washing towers* under pressure with the help of an exhaust pump. Scrubbers are filled with coke and water is sprayed over it continuously. Here most of the ammonia and little amount of CO_2, H_2S, CS_2 and HCN are removed. The cooled gases are then scrubbed with *creosote oil*, which dissolves benzole, naphthalene, etc. The gases are then passed to the *purifiers* containing trays of moist ferric oxide and lime. It removes hydrogen sulphide and other impurities like CS_2, CO_2 and HCN.

$$2Fe(OH)_3 + 3H_2S \longrightarrow Fe_2S_3 + 6H_2O$$

$$Ca(OH)_2 + H_2S \longrightarrow CaS + 2H_2O \; ; \; CaS + CS_2 \longrightarrow \underset{\text{Cal. thiocarbonate}}{CaCS_3}$$

The gas thus purified is collected in the *gas holder*.

Composition: Coal gas is a colourless gas with characteristic odour. It is lighter than air and somewhat soluble in water. Its calorific value is quite high, about 5208 kcal/m^3. Its average composition is as below.

Hydrogen	= 45 – 48%	Acetylene	= 2%
Methane	= 32 – 35%	Nitrogen	= 4 – 8%
Carbon monoxide	= 5 – 10%	Carbon dioxide	= 1%
Ethylene	= 3%	Remaining gases	= 4%

Uses: (*i*) It is mainly used as a heating fuel.

(*ii*) It is also used as an illuminant. Illuminating power of coal gas flame is due to the presence of unsaturated hydrocarbons, *e.g.*, ethylene and aromatic hydrocarbons, *e.g.*, benzene.

(*iii*) It is also used for providing an inert or reducing atmosphere in various metallurgical operations.

(*iv*) Owing to its high calorific value, it is also used in smelting of metals and alloys.

6. Oil gas: Oil gas is a mixture of gaseous hydrocarbons. It is prepared by the thermal cracking of kerosene oil.

Manufacture: The plant used for the manufacture of oil gas is shown in Fig. 11.18. A thin stream of kerosene oil is allowed to drop on the red hot surface of an iron retort. As each drop falls down it decomposes (cracks) and vapourises into a mixture of simpler gaseous hydrocarbons like methane, ethylene, acetylene, ethane, etc.

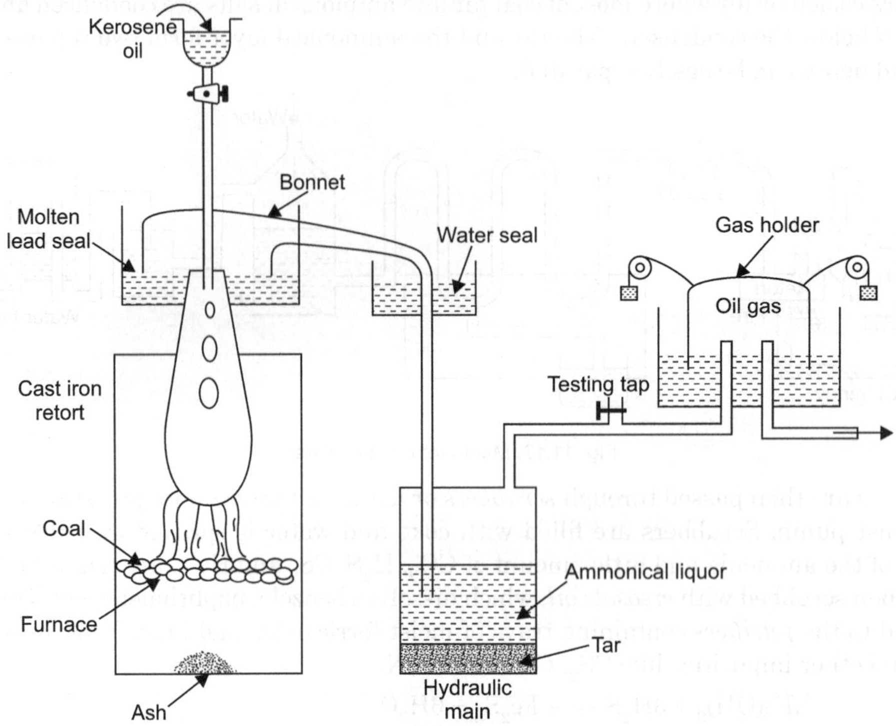

Fig. 11.18. Manufacture of oil gas.

The gases so obtained rise up and pass to the hydraulic main containing water through the bonnet. The hydraulic main retains the tar and ammonical liquor. The pure gas is then collected in the gas holder and mixed with the required quantity of air and supplied to the laboratory. The quality of the gas is tested by taking a sample through the testing cap provided before gas holder.

Oil gas is colourless with a calorific value of about 4185 kcal/m^3. Its average composition is as below.

Methane	= 25 – 30%	Carbon monoxide = 10 – 15%
Hydrogen	= 50 – 55%	Carbon dioxide = 3%
Ethylene	= 10 – 20%.	

It is used as a laboratory gas.

7. Gobar gas: Gobar gas is obtained by the fermentation of gobar (dung) in absence of air.

A simple gobar gas plant developed by I.A.R.I. New Delhi is sketched in Fig. 11.19. The dung in the form of slurry is introduced into a brick-lined well (3.7 m deep and 1.7 m wide), called **fermentation well**. An inverted drum of about 1.5 m diameter and 1.2 m height is placed air-tightly on the *fermentation well.* It acts as a gas holder and can be made up and down with the help of pulleys.

Formation of gas starts in a week. As the gas starts collecting in the drum, the latter begins to rise and float. The gas is taken out from the exit provided at the top of the drum. It is devoid of its condensed moisture and used as a domestic fuel. The spent slurry overflows from the top of the well. It is taken out and used as a valuable manure.

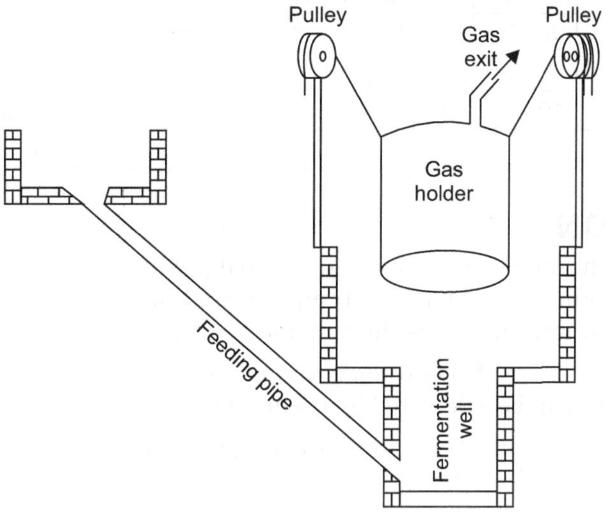

Fig. 11.19. Preparation of gobar gas.

An average composition of the gobar gas is as below.

(*i*) Methane = 60% (*ii*) Carbon dioxide = 30% (*iii*) Hydrogen = 10%.

Uses:

(*i*) It is used as a domestic fuel especially in villages where dung is available in plenty. About 45 kg of dung per day is required to produce 2.8 m^3 of the gas which is sufficient for an average family.

(*ii*) Gobar gas can also be used for lighting and power purposes like running water pumps, chaff cutting machines etc.

(*iii*) The spent slurry is a richer manure than the original gobar.

8. Blast furnace gas: Blast furnace gas is obtained as a by-product during the reduction of iron ore by coke in the blast furnace. It contains about 20 – 25% of carbon monoxide along with CO_2 and N_2. Its calorific value is 100 kcal/m^3. It is used for the following purposes.

(*i*) It is mainly used for preheating air used in blast furnace.

(*ii*) It is also used for heating boilers.

(*iii*) After cleaning it may be used in gas engines.

(*iv*) It is also used in special type of stoves called *Cowper's stove.*

Table 11.4: Approximate Percentage Composition of the Various Fuel Gases

S. No.	Name of the gas	CO%	H_2%	CH_4%	N_2%	CO_2%	%Other gases
1	Natural gas	–	–	85	–	–	$C_2H_6 = 8$ $C_3H_8 = 4$ Butane = 1.5 Higher hydrocarbons = 1.5
2.	Water gas	44	48	0.8	3	4.2	–

3.	Producer gas	22 – 30	8 – 12	small	52 – 55	3	–
4.	Semi water gas	25 – 28	10 – 12	1 – 1.5	50 – 55	4 – 5	–
5.	Coal gas	5 – 10	45 – 48	32 – 35	4 – 8	1	Ethylene = 3 Acetylene = 2
6.	Oil gas	10 – 15	50 – 55	25 – 30	–	3	Ethylene = 10 – 12
7.	Gobar gas	30	10	60	–	–	–

11.8 COMBUSTION

Combustion is an exothermic chemical reaction during which combustible elements or gases when brought to their kindling or ignition temperature burn in presence of air instantly with the development of heat and thus considerable increase in temperature.

The amount (volume or weight) of oxygen and air required for the complete combustion of a given quantity of the fuel can be calculated by taking the following points in consideration.

1. Substances always combine in definite proportions which are determined by their molecular weights. Thus, to determine the amount of oxygen required for the combustion of an element or a gas, we must know its combustion reaction. For example, the combustion reaction of carbon indicates that

$$\begin{array}{lcccccc} & C & + & O_2 & \longrightarrow & CO_2 \\ \text{(by wt.)} & 12 & & 32 & & 44 \\ \text{(by vol.)} & \text{(1 vol.)} & & \text{(1 vol.)} & & \text{(1 vol.)} \end{array}$$

12 parts by weight of *C* require 32 parts by weight of O_2

and 44 parts by weight of CO_2 is produced by 12 parts by weight of *C*.

OR

1 volume of carbon require 1 volume of oxygen

and 1 volume of CO_2 is produced by 1 volume of carbon.

The most commonly involved combustion reactions are given below. From these, the amount of oxygen required by the substance may be calculated easily as above.

(*i*) $2H_2 + O_2 \longrightarrow 2H_2O$ (*ii*) $S + O_2 \longrightarrow SO_2$

(*iii*) $2CO + O_2 \longrightarrow 2CO_2$ (*iv*) $CH_4 + 2O_2 \longrightarrow CO_2 + 2H_2O$

(*v*) $2C_2H_6 + 7O_2 \longrightarrow 4CO_2 + 6H_2O$ (*vi*) $C_2H_4 + 3O_2 \longrightarrow 2CO_2 + 2H_2O$

(*vii*) $2C_2H_2 + 5O_2 \longrightarrow 4CO_2 + 2H_2O$.

Nitrogen, ash and carbon dioxide (if any) present in the fuel or air are incombustible matters and hence they do not take any oxygen during combustion. The total amount of oxygen consumed by the fuel will thus be given by the sum of the amounts of oxygen required by the individual combustible constituent present in the fuel.

2. Air contains 21% oxygen (rest being nitrogen) by volume and 23% of oxygen (77% being nitrogen) by weight. Hence from the amount of oxygen required by the fuel, the amount of air can be calculated.

3. Weight can be converted into volume, if required, in the following ways:

(*i*) At N.T.P. (*i.e.* 0°C and 760 mm pressure) 22.4 litres or 22400 mL of any gas weights equal to its one gram molecule, *i.e.* its molecular weight in grams. For example, 22.4 litre of CO_2 at N.T.P. will weight 44 gm (44 being the molecular weight of CO_2).

(*ii*) The relative weights of the two or more gases may be converted to the proportional volumes by the following relation.

$$\text{Proportional volume of the gases} = \frac{\text{Weight of a gas}}{\text{Its molecular weight}} : \frac{\text{Weight of other gas}}{\text{Its molecular weight}}, \text{ and so on.}$$

11.9 ANALYSIS OF FLUE GASES

Analysis of flue gases give idea about the complete or incomplete combustion process. Thus the presence of a high percentage of carbon monoxide in the flue gases shows incomplete combustion of the fuel and also indicates the short supply of oxygen. On the other hand, if the flue gases contain a considerable amount of oxygen, it indicates an excess supply of oxygen and possibility of complete combustion.

The analysis of flue gases generally deals with the determination of CO_2, O_2 and CO by absorbing them in the respective solution of KOH, alkaline pyrogallic acid and alkaline cuprous chloride respectively. Though in some rare cases percentage of hydrogen is also determined. Analysis of flue gases is carried out by Orsat's apparatus.

Description of Orsat Apparatus

It consists of a horizontal tube having a three-way stopcock at one end and a water-jacketed measuring burrette at the other end. The three way stop-cock end of the horizontal tube is further connected to a U-tube having fused calcium chloride. The lower end of the burette which is water-jacketed in order to keep the temperature of the gas constant during the experiment is connected to a water reservoir by means of a rubber tube. The level of the water in water reservoir can be raise or lowered by raising or lowering the water reservoir. By changing the level of water, the flue gas can be moved into various parts of the apparatus during its working.

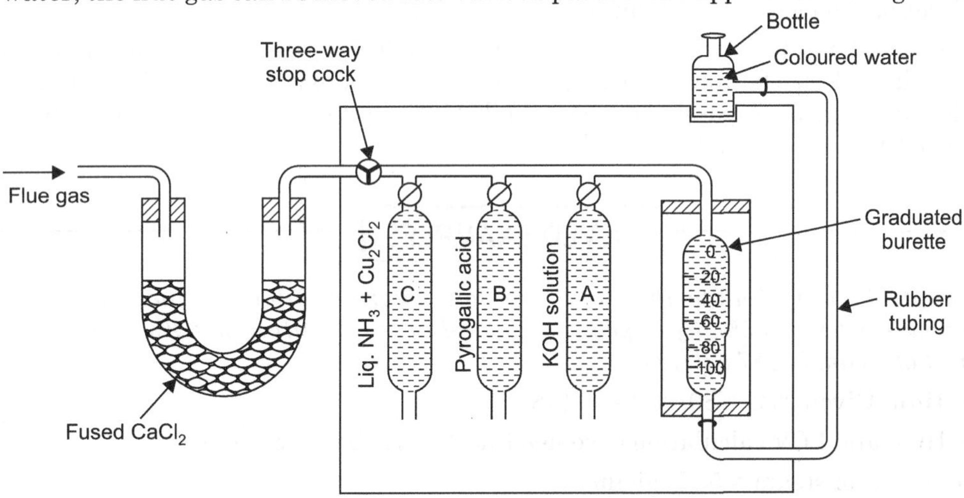

Fig. 11.20. Orsat apparatus.

The central portion of the horizontal tube is also connected to three different absorption bulbs *A*, *B* and *C* for the absorption of carbon dioxide, oxygen and carbon monoxide respectively. Bulb *A* contains potassium hydroxide solution (250 gm of KOH in 500 mL of freshly boiled distilled water) to absorb CO_2. Bulb *B* contains an alkaline pyrogallol (25 gm pyrogallic acid + 200 gm KOH + 500 mL distilled water) to absorb oxygen. Bulb *C* contains a solution of ammonical cuprous chloride (100 gm cuprous chloride + 125 mL liquor ammonia + 375 mL distilled water) to absorb carbon monoxide.

Working of Orsat Apparatus

The thoroughly cleaned and properly greased parts of the air tight apparatus are filled with their respective reagents or water or the case may be. The stop-cock of the bulbs *A*, *B* and *C* are closed while the three-way stop-cock is opened to the atmosphere and burette is completely filled with water by raising the water reservoir to remove air present in the burette. Now the three-way stop-cock is connected to the flue gases to be analysed and the reservoir is lowered for giving entry to the flue gases to the burette. However, this gas is expelled to the atmosphere by opening the three-way stop-cock and raising the reservoir since it is mixed with air present in the apparatus. This process is repeated 3 – 4 times for completely removing the air present in the apparatus.

Now the flue gases are sucked as earlier by opening the three-way stop-cock and by lowering the water reservoir. The volume of the gases taken in burette is 100 mL at atmospheric pressure which is done carefully by bringing the level of water in the reservoir at the same height as in burette which stands at 100 mL mark. The three way stop-cock is now closed.

Flue gases are now passed in the bulb *A via* its stop cock by raising the water reservoir. Carbon dioxide present in the flue gases is absorbed by KOH. The gas is again sent to the burette and then again sent to bulb *A*. The process is repeated several times by raising and lowering the water reservoir so as to ensure complete absorption of CO_2 in KOH solution. The unabsorbed gases are finally taken back to the burette by raising the liquid in the bulb *A*, till it is filled completely. Now the stopper of bulb *A* is closed. The reading of the volume of residual gases in the burette is taken by equalising th water level both is the burette and the water reservoir.

The absorption process is again repeated in bulb *A* and the burette reading of residual gas is again taken. In case the reading is constant, it shows CO_2 has been completely absorbed. But if there is any difference in reading, the absorption process is repeated till the two consecutive readings are constant. The difference between the original volume (100 c.c) and the volume of gas after CO_2 absorption gives the volume of CO_2 absorbed.

Stop-cock of bulb *A* is closed and the stop-cock of bulb *B* is opened. The absorption process is repeated as in bulb *A*. The volume of gas absorbed here is of oxygen. Similarly, volume of carbon monoxide is determined by passing the gas to bulb *C*. The gas remaining in burette after removing CO_2, O_2 and CO is taken as nitrogen.

SOLVED EXAMPLES

Example 11.1. *Calculate the high and low calorific values of fuel having following composition: Carbon = 85%, hydrogen = 8%, sulphur = 6%, nitrogen = 2%, ash = 4% and the latent heat of steam is 587 cal/gm.*

Solution: Given: %C = 80, %H = 8, %S = 6

[For HCV and LCV calculations, we need % of C, H, O and S only]

Latent heat of steam = 587 cal/gm

$$\text{HCV} = \frac{1}{100}\left[8080\%\,\text{C} + 34500\left(\%\,\text{H} - \frac{\%\text{O}}{8}\right) + 2240\%\,\text{S}\right] \text{ cal/gm or kcal/gm}$$

$$\text{HCV} = \frac{1}{100}[8080 \times 85 + 34500\,(8 - 0) + 2240 \times 6] \text{ cal/gm}$$

$$= \frac{1}{100}[686800 + 27600 + 13440] \text{ cal/gm}$$

$$= 9762.40 \text{ cal/gm}$$

$$\begin{aligned} \text{LCV} &= [\text{HCV} - 0.09\ \%\ \text{H} \times \text{latent heat of steam}] \\ &= 9762.40 - 0.09 \times 8 \times 587 \text{ cal/gm or kcal/kg} \\ &= 9339.76 \text{ cal/gm.} \end{aligned}$$

Example 11.2. *A sample of coal has the following composition: Carbon = 83%, H = 7.5%, S = 1.5%, N = 0.6%, O = 8.4%. Find the gross calorific value using Dulong's formula.*

Solution: Given %C = 83, %H = 7.5, %S = 1.5, %O = 8.4

$$\text{GCV} = \frac{1}{100}\left[8080\%\ \text{C} + 34500\left(\%\ \text{H} - \frac{\%\text{O}}{8}\right) + 2240\ \%\ \text{S}\right] \text{ cal/gm}$$

$$= \frac{1}{100}\left[8080 \times 83 + 34500\left(7.5 - \frac{8.4}{8}\right) + 2240 \times 1.5\right] \text{ cal/gm}$$

$$= \frac{1}{100}[670640 + 258750 - 36225 + 3360]$$

$$= 8965.25 \text{ cal/gm.}$$

Example 11.3. *The ultimate analysis of coal gave the following results: C = 72%, H = 6.5%, O = 9.4% and S = 1.5%. Calculate the gross and net calorific value of coal using Dulong's formula.*

Solution: Given: %C = 72, %H = 6.5, %O = 9.4, %S = 1.5

$$\text{GCV} = \frac{1}{100}\left[8080\ \%\ \text{C} + 34500\left(\%\text{H} - \frac{\%\text{O}}{8}\right) + 2240\%\ \text{S}\right]$$

$$= \frac{1}{100}\left[8080 \times 72 + 34500\left(6.5 - \frac{9.4}{8}\right) + 2240 \times 1.5\right]$$

$$= \frac{1}{100}[581760 + 224250 - 40537.5 + 3360]$$

$$= 7688.32 \text{ cal/gm.}$$

$$\begin{aligned} \text{NCV} &= (\text{GCV} - 0.09\ \%\ \text{H} \times 587) \text{ cal/gm} \\ &= 7688.32 - 0.09 \times 6.5 \times 587 \\ &= 7688.32 - 343.39 \\ &= 7344.93 \text{ cal/gm.} \end{aligned}$$

Example 11.4. *A coal sample has the following composition by weight: C = 87%, O = 4%, S = 1% and ash = 2.5 %. Net calorific value of the coal was found to be 8629 kcal/kg. Calculate the percentage of hydrogen and gross calorific value of coal.*

Solution: Given % C = 87, % O = 4, % *S* = 1, NCV = 8629 kcal/kg

$$\text{GCV} = \frac{1}{100}\left[8080\ \%\ \text{C} + 34500\left(\%\text{H} - \frac{\%\text{O}}{8}\right) + 2240\ \%\ \text{S}\right] \text{ kcal/kg} \quad ...(i)$$

$$\text{NCV} = \text{GCV} - 0.09\%\ \text{H} \times 587 \text{ kcal/kg.} \quad ...(ii)$$

Substitute the value of GCV form equation (*i*)

$$\text{NCV} = \frac{1}{100}\left[8080 \times 87 + 34500\%\ \text{H} - 34500 \times \frac{4}{8} + 2240 \times 1\right] - 52.83\%\ \text{H}$$

$$8629 = 6879.5 + 345\ \%\text{H} - 52.83\ \%\text{H}$$

$$292.17\ \%H = 1749.5$$

$$\%H = 5.987$$

Now substitute the value of %H in equation (*i*)

$$GCV = \frac{1}{100}\left[8080 \times 87 + 34500\left(5.987 - \frac{4}{8}\right) + 2240 \times 1\right] \text{ kcal/kg.}$$

$$= \frac{1}{100}\ [702960 + 206551.5 - 17250 + 2240]$$

$$= 7029.60 + 2065.52 - 172.50 + 22.40$$

$$GCV = 8945.02 \text{ kcal/kg.}$$

Example 11.5. *A coal sample contains C = 90%, H = 6% and ash = 3%. When this coal sample was tested in the laboratory for its calorific value in a bomb calorimeter, the following data were obtained:*

Weight of coal burnt	*= 0.90 g*
Weight of water taken	*= 670 g*
Water equivalent of bomb calorimeter	*= 1927 g*
Rise in temperature	*= 2.12°C*
Fuse wire correction	*= 9.2 cal*
Acid correction	*= 60.8 cal*
Cooling correction	*= 0.04°C.*

Calculate the gross and net calorific value of the coal sample in cal/g. Assume the latent heat of condensation of steam as 587 cal/g.

Solution:

$$GCV = \frac{(W + w)(t_2 - t_1 + \text{cooling correction}) - (\text{acid correction} + \text{fuse wire correction})}{\text{weight of coal sample taken}}$$

$$GCV = \frac{(1927 + 670)(2.12 + 0.04) - (60.8 + 9.2)}{0.90}$$

$$= \frac{(2597)(2.16) - 70}{0.90} = \frac{5609.52 - 70}{0.90} = 6155.02 \text{ cal/gm.}$$

$$NCV = GCV - 0.09\ \%\ H \times 587 \text{ cal/gm.}$$

$$= 6155.02 - 0.09 \times 6 \times 587 = 6155.02 - 316.98$$

$$NCV = 5838.04 \text{ cal/gm.}$$

Example 11.6. *The temperature of 950.0 g of water increases from 25.5°C to 28.5°C on burning 0.75 g of a solid fuel in a bomb calorimeter. Water equivalent of calorimeter and latent heat of steam are 400.0 g and 587.0 cal/gm respectively. If the fuel contains 0.65 % of hydrogen, calculate its net calorific value.*

Solution: Given: Weight of water taken = 950.0 g

Weight of coal burnt = 0.75 g

Water equivalent of calorimeter = 400.0 g

Rise in temperature = 28.5 – 25.5 = 3°C

Latent heat of steam = 587 cal/gm.

$$\%H = 0.65.$$

$$NCV = GCV - 0.09\%H \times 587 \text{ cal/gm} \qquad ...(i)$$

So, we have to first find out GCV,

$$GCV = \frac{(W + w)(t_2 - t)}{\text{wt. of coal sample taken}} \qquad ...(ii)$$

$$= \frac{(400 + 950)\,(3)}{0.75} = \frac{4050}{0.75}$$

$$GCV = 5400 \text{ cal/gm.}$$

Substitute the value of GCV in equation (*i*)

$$NCV = 5400 - 0.09 \times 0.65 \times 587 \text{ cal/gm}$$

$$= 5400 - 34.34$$

$$= 5365.6 \text{ cal/gm.}$$

Example 11.7. *A liquid fuel weighing 0.98 g and containing 90.1% C, 8% H, have the following results in bomb calorimeter experiment:*

Amount of water taken in calorimeter = 1450 g

Water equivalent of calorimeter = 450 g

Rise in temperature of water = 1.8°C

If latent heat of steam is 587 cal/g, calculate gross and net calorific value.

Solution: $GCV = \dfrac{(W + w)(t_2 - t_1)}{\text{wt. of coal sample taken}}$

$$GCV = \frac{(450 + 1450)(1.8)}{0.98} = \frac{3420}{0.98}$$

$$GCV = 3489.8 \text{ cal/gm.}$$

$$NCV = GCV - 0.09\%\ H \times 587 \text{ cal/gm}$$

$$= 3489.8 - 0.09 \times 8 \times 587$$

$$= 3489.8 - 422.64$$

$$= 3067.16 \text{ cal/gm.}$$

Example 11.8. *The following data were obtained in a Boy's gas calorimeter experiment.*

Volume of gas used	*= 0.1 cubic meter of NTP*
Weight of water heated	*= 25 kg*
Temperature of inlet water	*= 20°C*
Temperature of outlet water	*= 33°C*
Weight of steam condensed	*= 0.025 kg.*

Calculate the higher and lower calorific values per m^3 at NTP assuming that the heat liberated in condensing water vapour and cooling the condensate is 580 kcal/kg.

Solution: Here,

$$V = 0.1\ m^3,\ W' = 0.025 \text{ kg}$$

$$W = 25 \text{ kg},\ t_2 - t_1 = 33 - 20 = 13°C$$

Latent heat of steam = 580 kcal/kg

$$\text{Now higher calorific value } (C) = \frac{W(t_2 - t_1)}{V} = \frac{25 \times 13}{0.1} = 3250 \text{ kcal/m}^3$$

$$\text{Again lower calorific value} = C - \frac{W' \times \text{Latent heat of steam}}{V}$$

$$= 3250 - \frac{0.025 \times 580}{0.1} = 3250 - 145 = 3105 \text{ kcal/m}^3.$$

Example 11.9. *During the determination of calorific value of a gaseous fuel by Boy's calorimeter, the following results were obtained.*

Volume of gaseous fuels burnt at NTP = *0.85 m^3*
Weight of water used for cooling the combustion products = *45 kg*
Weight of steam condensed = *0.045 kg*
Temperature of inlet water = *25°C*
Temperature of outlet water = *45°C*
Latent heat of condensation of steam = *587 kcal/kg.*

Find out the gross and net calorific value.

Solution: Given: $V = 0.085\ m^3$, $W = 45$ kg, $m = 0.045$ kg.

$$T_1 = 25°\text{C},\ T_2 = 45°\text{C}$$

$$\text{GCV} = \frac{W(T_2 - T_1)}{V} = \frac{45(45 - 25)}{0.085} = 10588.2 \text{ kcal/m}^3.$$

$$\text{NCV} = \text{GCV} - \left(\frac{m}{V} \times 587\right)$$

$$= 10588.2 - \left(\frac{0.045}{0.085} \times 587\right)$$

$$= 10588.2 - 310.76$$

$$\text{NCV} = 10277.4 \text{ kcal/m}^3.$$

Example 11.10. *A sample of coal was analysed as follows: Exactly 2.500 g was weighed into a silica crucible. After heating for one hour at 110°C, the residue weighed 2.415 g. The crucible next was covered with a vented lid and strongly heated for exactly 7 minutes at 950°C ± 20°C. The residue weighed 1.628 g. The crucible was then heated without the cover, until a constant weight was obtained. The last residue was found to weight 0.245 g. Calculate the proximate analysis of the above sample.*

Solution: We have to determine the % of moisture, volatile matter, ash and fixed carbon

1. $$\%\text{ of moisture} = \frac{\text{Weight of moisture}}{\text{Weight of coal taken}} \times 100$$

Weight of coal sample taken = 2.500 g
Weight after heating at 110°C = 2.415 g

Loss of weight = weight of moisture = 2.500 – 2.415 = 0.085 g.

$$\%\text{ moisture} = \frac{0.085}{2.500} \times 100 = 3.4\%$$

2. $$\% \text{ of volatile matter} = \frac{\text{Weight of volatile matter}}{\text{Weight of coal taken}} \times 100$$

Weight of residue after heating at $950 \pm 20°C = 1.628$

$$\text{Loss of weight} = \text{Weight of volatile matter} = 2.415 - 1.628 = 0.787$$

$$\% \text{ of volatile matter} = \frac{0.787}{2.500} \times 100 = 31.48\ \%$$

3. $$\% \text{ of ash} = \frac{\text{Weight of residue left}}{\text{Weight of coal taken}} \times 100$$

Weight of residue left = 0.245 g

$$\% \text{ of ash} = \frac{0.245}{2.500} \times 100 = 9.8\ \%$$

4. $$\% \text{ of fixed carbon} = 100 - \% \text{ of (moisture + volatile matter + ash)}$$

$$= 100 - (3.4 + 31.48 + 9.8)$$

$$\% \text{ of fixed carbon} = 55.32\%.$$

Example 11.11. *0.3 g of a coal sample was used in bomb calorimeter for the determination of calorific value. The ash formed in the bomb calorimeter was extracted with acid and the acid extract was heated with barium chloride solution and a precipitate of $BaSO_4$ was obtained. The precipitate was filtered, dried and weighed. The weight of precipitate was 0.025 g. Calculate the percentage of sulphur in the coal sample.*

Solution: $$\% \text{ of sulphur} = \frac{\text{Weight of } BaSO_4 \text{ ppt. obtained} \times 32 \times 100}{\text{Weight of coal sample taken in bomb} \times 233}$$

$$= \frac{0.025 \times 32 \times 100}{0.3 \times 233} = 1.1445\%.$$

Example 11.12. *2.32 g of a coal sample was used for estimation of nitrogen by Kjeldahl's method. The evolved ammonia was collected in 50 mL of $\frac{N}{10}$ sulphuric acid. After absorption, the excess (residual) acid required 10.5 mL of $\frac{N}{10}$ NaOH for exact neutralization. Determine the percentage of nitrogen in the coal sample.*

Solution: $$\% \text{ of nitrogen} = \frac{\text{Volume of acid consumed} \times \text{Normality of acid} \times 1.4}{\text{Weight of coal sample taken}}$$

Given : Weight of coal sample taken = 2.32 g

As 10.5 mL of $\frac{N}{10}$ NaOH is used for neutralization, hence excess acid will be

$$= 10.5 \text{ mL of } \frac{N}{10}\ H_2SO_4$$

$\therefore$ Volume of H_2SO_4 used to neutralize NH_3 evolved

$$= 50 \text{ mL of } \frac{N}{10}\ H_2SO_4 - 10.5 \text{ mL of } \frac{N}{10}\ H_2SO_4$$

$$= (50 - 10.5) \text{ mL of } \frac{N}{10}\ H_2SO_4 = 39.5 \text{ mL of } \frac{N}{10}\ H_2SO_4$$

$$= 39.5 \text{ mL of } 0.1 \text{ N } H_2SO_4$$

$$\% \text{ of nitrogen} = \frac{39.5 \times 0.1 \times 1.4}{2.32} = 2.38\%.$$

Example 11.13. *0.42 g of coal sample was Kjeldahlized and 37 mL of 0.1 N sulphuric acid was just sufficient to neutralize the evolved ammonia gas. Calculate the percentage of nitrogen in the coal sample.*

Solution: Given: Weight of coal sample = 0.42 g

Volume of sulphuric acid used = 37 mL

Normality of sulphuric acid used = 0.1 N

$$\% \text{ of nitrogen} = \frac{\text{Volume of } H_2SO_4 \text{ used} \times \text{Normality of } H_2SO_4 \times 1.4}{\text{Weigth of coal sample taken}}$$

$$= \frac{37 \times 0.1 \times 1.4}{0.42} = 12.33\%.$$

Example 11.14. *0.5 g of a coal sample was analysed by combustion method. The increase in weights of $CaCl_2$ tube and the KOH bulb at the end of the operation was found to be 0.30 g and 0.75 g respectively. Calculate the percentage of carbon and hydrogen in the coal sample.*

Solution: Given: Increase in weight of $CaCl_2$ tube = Weight of water = 0.30 g

Increase in weight of KOH bulb = weight of CO_2 = 0.75 g

$$\% \text{ of carbon} = \frac{12}{44} \times \frac{\text{Increase in weight of KOH}}{\text{Weight of coal smaple taken}} \times 100$$

$$= \frac{12}{44} \times \frac{0.75}{0.5} \times 100 = 40.9\%$$

$$\% \text{ of hydrogen} = \frac{2}{18} \times \frac{\text{Increase in weight of } CaCl_2}{\text{Weight of coal sample taken}} \times 100$$

$$= \frac{2}{18} \times \frac{0.30}{0.5} \times 100 = 6.67\%.$$

Example 11.15. *On analysis, an oil was found to have the following percentage composition: C = 84%, H = 12% and O = 4%. Calculate the weight of oxygen and air required for the complete burning of one kg of this oil (air contains 23% oxygen by weight).*

Solution: Here,

Weight of oil = 1 kg

Weight of carbon in it = 84/100 = 0.84 kg

Weight of hydrogen in it = 12/100 = 0.12 kg

Weight of oxygen in it = 4/100 = 0.04 kg

According to combustion equations

(*a*) $\underset{12 \text{ kg}}{C} + \underset{32 \text{ kg}}{O_2} \longrightarrow CO_2$ (*b*) $\underset{2 \times 2 \text{ kg}}{2H_2} + \underset{32 \text{ kg}}{O_2} \longrightarrow 2H_2O$

$\therefore$ Weight of oxygen required for the combustion of 0.84 kg of C $= \frac{32}{12} \times 0.84 = 2.24$ kg

Similarly, weight of O_2 required for the combustion of 0.12 kg of $H_2 = \frac{32}{4} \times 0.12 = 0.96$ kg

$\therefore$ Total weight of O_2 required = weight of O_2 required by C + weight of O_2 required by H_2

$$= 2.24 + 0.96 \text{ kg} = 3.20 \text{ kg}$$

But weight of O_2 already present = 0.04 kg

$\therefore$ Weight of O_2 required = 3.20 – 0.04 kg = 3.16 kg

Now since 23 kg of oxygen is present in 100 kg of air

$$3.16 \text{ kg of oxygen will be present} = \frac{100}{23} \times 3.16 = 13.74 \text{ kg.}$$

Example 11.16. *Calculate the weight and volume of air required for the combustion of 1 kg of carbon.*

Solution. According to the combustion equation

$$\underset{12}{C} + \underset{32}{O_2} \longrightarrow CO_2$$

Weight of oxygen required by 1 kg of carbon $= \frac{32}{12} \times 1 = 2.667$ kg

Now since 32 gm of oxygen occupies 22.4 litres at N.T.P.

$$2.667 \times 1000 \text{ gm of oxygen will occupy} = \frac{22.4 \times 2.667 \times 1000}{32} = 1866.9 \text{ litres}$$

$\therefore$ Weight of air (containing 23% oxygen) required $= \frac{100}{23} \times 2.667 = 11.59$ kg

Similarly volume of air (containing 21% oxygen) required

$$= \frac{100}{21} \times 1866.9 = 8890 \text{ litre} = 8.89 \text{ m}^3$$

Example 11.17. *Calculate the volume of air required for the complete combustion of 1m³ of the gaseous fuel having following composition by volume.*

$H_2 = 50\%$	$CH_4 = 36\%$	$N_2 = 1.5\%$
$CO = 6\%$	$C_2H_4 = 4\%$	H_2O *vapour* $= 2.5\%$

Air contains 21% oxygen by volume.

Solution. Given:

Volume of gaseous fuel = 1 m³, Volume of H_2 = 0.50 m³, Volume of CO = 0.06 m³

Volume of CH_4 = 0.36 m³. Volume of C_2H_4 = 0.04 m³. Volume of N_2 = 0.015 m³, Volume of H_2O = 0.025 m³.

Now since nitrogen and water vapours do not burn, they do not require any oxygen (air). The combustion equations for rest of the constituents may be written as below.

$$\underset{2\,m^2}{2H_2} + \underset{1\,m^3}{O_2} \longrightarrow 2H_2O \qquad \underset{2\,m^3}{2CO} + \underset{1\,m^3}{O_2} \longrightarrow 2CO_2$$

$$\underset{1\,m^3}{CH_4} + \underset{2\,m^3}{2O_2} \longrightarrow CO_2 + 2H_2O \qquad \underset{1\,m^3}{C_2H_4} + \underset{3\,m^3}{3O_2} \longrightarrow 2CO_2 + 2H_2O$$

$\therefore$ Volume of O_2 required by 0.50 m^3 of $H_2 = \frac{1}{2} \times 0.50 = 0.25$ m^3

Volume of O_2 required by 0.06 m^3 of $CO = \frac{1}{2} \times 0.06 = 0.03$ m^3

Volume of O_2 required by 0.36 m^3 of $CH_4 = \frac{2}{1} \times 0.36 = 0.72$ m^3

Volume of O_2 required by 0.04 m^3 of $C_2H_4 = \frac{3}{1} \times 0.04 = 0.12$ m^3

Hence total volume of O_2 required = 1.12 m^3

$\therefore$ Volume of air containing 21% oxygen required $= \frac{1.12 \times 100}{21} = 5.33$ m^3.

Example 11.18 *A sample of petrol was found to contain 15.4% hydrogen and 84.6% carbon by weight. Calculate the volume of oxygen at N.T.P. required for the complete combustion of 1kg of this fuel.*

Solution. Weight of petrol = 1 kg, Weight of carbon = 0.846 kg, Weight of hydrogen = 0.154 kg

According to combustion equations

$$\underset{12\text{ kg}}{C} + \underset{32\text{ kg}}{O_2} \longrightarrow CO_2 \qquad \underset{2\times 2\text{ kg}}{2H_2} + \underset{32\text{kg}}{O_2} \longrightarrow 2H_2O$$

$\therefore$ Weight of O_2 required by 0.846 kg of $C = \frac{32}{12} \times 0.846 = 2.256$ kg

Weight of O_2 required by 0.154 kg of $H_2 = \frac{32}{4} \times 0.154 = 1.232$ kg

$\therefore$ Total weight of O_2 required = 2.256 + 1.232 = 3.488 kg

Now since 32 gm of O_2 occupies volume of 22.4 litres at N.T.P.

3.488 × 1000 gm of O_2 will occupy $= \frac{22.4}{32} \times 3.488 \times 1000 = 2441.6$ litres.

Example 11.19. *A sample of a fuel on analysis gave the following results.*

C = 87%	*H = 4%*	*N = 1.2%*
S = 2%	*O = 4%*	*Ash = 18%.*

Calculate the minimum weight of air (containing 23% of oxygen of weight) required for the complete combustion of 500 gm of this fuel.

Solution: Weight of C = 0.87 kg, Weight of S = 0.02 kg, Weight of H = 0.04 kg,

Weight of O = 0.04 kg

Since nitrogen and ash are incombustible, they do not required oxygen.

$$C + O_2 \longrightarrow CO_2, \qquad S + O_2 \longrightarrow SO_2$$

According to combustion equations,

$$2H_2 + O_2 \longrightarrow 2H_2O$$

Weight of O_2 required by carbon $= \frac{32}{12} \times 0.87 = 2.37$ kg

Weight of oxygen required by sulphur $= \frac{32}{32} \times 0.02 = 0.02$ kg

$$\text{Weight of oxygen required by hydrogen} = \frac{32}{4} \times 0.04 = 0.32 \text{ kg}$$

Hence total weight of oxygen required = 2.66 kg

Weight of oxygen already present = 0.04 kg

$\therefore$ Weight of oxygen needed = 2.66 – 0.04 = 2.62 kg

$$\therefore \text{Weight of air (containing 23\% oxygen) required} = \frac{100}{23} \times 2.62 = 11.39 \text{ kg/kg of the fuel.}$$

$$\therefore \text{Weight of air required by 500 gm of the fuel} = \frac{11.39 \times 500}{1000} = 5.695 \text{ kg.}$$

Example 11.20. *Calculate the volume of air, containing 20% of oxygen by volume at 27°C and 760 mm pressure which will be required for the complete combustion of 1 kg of coal containing carbon = 80%, hydrogen = 15% and incombustible matter = 5%.*

Solution. Weight of coal = 1 kg, Weight of carbon = 0.80 kg, Weight of hydrogen = 0.15 kg
According to combustion reactions

$$\text{Weight of oxygen required by C} = \frac{32}{12} \times 0.80 = 2.133 \text{ kg}$$

$$\text{Weight of oxygen required by H} = \frac{32}{4} \times 0.15 = 1.200 \text{ kg}$$

Hence total weight of oxygen required = 2.133 + 1.200 = 3.333 kg

$$\text{or Total weight of oxygen required at N.T.P.} = \frac{22.4}{32} \times 3.333 \times 1000 = 2333.1 \text{ litres}$$

Calculation of volume of oxygen required at 27°C and 760 mm pressure

V_1 = 2333.1 litres V_2 = ?

P_1 = 760 mm P_2 = 760 mm

T_1 = 273 K T_2 = 273 + 27 = 300 K

Hence by gas equation, $\dfrac{P_1 V_1}{T_1} = \dfrac{P_2 V_2}{T_2}$

$$V_2 = \frac{P_1 \times V_1 \times T_2}{P_2 \times T_1} = \frac{760 \times 2333.1 \times 300}{760 \times 273} = 2563.85 \text{ litres}$$

Hence volume of air (containing 20% oxygen) required at 27°C and 760 mm pressure

$$= \frac{100}{20} \times 2563.85 = 12819.25 \text{ litres.}$$

Example 11.21. *A sample of petrol was found to contain 15.2% H and 84.8% C by weight. Calculate:*

(i) The weight of oxygen needed for the combustion of 1 kg of the fuel.

(ii) The volume composition of the products of combustion if 15% excess of oxygen is supplied.

Solution: Weight of petrol = 1 kg, Weight of carbon = 0.848 kg, Weight of hydrogen = 0.152 kg

$$\text{Weight of } O_2 \text{ required by C} = \frac{32}{12} \times 0.848 = 2.261 \text{ kg}$$

$$\text{Weight of } O_2 \text{ required by hydrogen} = \frac{32}{4} \times 0.152 = 1.216 \text{ kg}$$

Total weight of O_2 required = 2.261 + 1.216 = 3.477 kg

Weight of O_2 supplied when 15% excess oxygen is used $= \frac{3.477 \times 115}{100} = 3.999$ or 4 kg.

Calculation of volume of combustion products: The combustion products will consist of (*i*) CO_2 from *C*, (*ii*) oxygen from excess air supplied, and (*iii*) nitrogen from the air supplied.

(*i*) **Volume of CO_2.** From the combustion equation

$$\underset{12}{C} + O_2 \longrightarrow \underset{44}{CO_2}$$

12 kg of carbon gives 44 kg of CO_2

0.848 kg of carbon $= \frac{44}{12} \times 0.848 = 3.109$ kg of CO_2

44 gm of CO_2 occupies 22.4 litres at N.T.P.

3.109×1000 gm of $CO_2 = \frac{22.4 \times 3.109 \times 1000}{44} = 1583$ litres

(*ii*) **Volume of oxygen**

$$\text{Weight of oxygen} = \text{Minimum oxygen used} \times \text{excess oxygen \%}$$

$$= 3.477 \times \frac{15}{100} = 0.522 \text{ kg}$$

$$\therefore \quad \text{Volume of oxygen} = \frac{22.4 \times 0.522 \times 1000}{32} = 365.4 \text{ litres}$$

(*iii*) **Volume of nitrogen**

Since 100 kg of air contains 77 kg of N_2

$$4 \text{ kg of air will contain} = \frac{77}{100} \times 4 \text{ kg of } N_2 = 3.08 \text{ kg}$$

$$\text{Volume of nitrogen} = \frac{22.4 \times 3.08 \times 1000}{28} = 2464 \text{ litres.}$$

Example 11.22. *Calculate the weight of air required per kg of the oil if 20% excess of air is used for complete combustion. The oil contains 85% carbon and 15% hydrogen. Also calculate the percentage composition by weight of the dry products of combustion assuming air to be a mixture of 20% oxygen and 80% nitrogen by weight.*

Solution: Weight of the oil = 1 kg

Weight of carbon = 0.85 kg

Weight of hydrogen = 0.15 kg

$$\therefore \quad \text{Weight of } O_2 \text{ required by C} = \frac{32}{12} \times 0.85 = 2.267 \text{ kg}$$

$$\text{Weight of } O_2 \text{ required by } H_2 = \frac{32}{4} \times 0.15 = 1.200 \text{ kg}$$

$$\therefore \quad \text{Total weight of } O_2 \text{ required} = 2.267 + 1.200 = 3.467 \text{ kg}$$

Weight of air (containing 20% oxygen) required $= \frac{100}{20} \times 3.467 = 17.335$ kg

Actual quantity of air supplied is 20% excess to that of the required amount (17.335 kg).

$$\therefore \quad \text{Actual quantity of air supplied} = \frac{17.335 \times 120}{100} = 20.802 \text{ kg}$$

Calculation of weights of dry combustion products

The dry flue gases will consist of (*i*) CO_2 from C, (*ii*) oxygen from the excess air supplied, and (*iii*) nitrogen from the air supplied.

(*i*) **Weight of carbon dioxide**

From the combustion equation:

$$\underset{12}{C} + O_2 \longrightarrow \underset{44}{CO_2}$$

12 kg of carbon gives 44 kg of CO_2

0.85 kg of carbon will give = $\frac{44}{12} \times 0.85 = 3.117$ kg.

(*ii*) **Weight of nitrogen**

Since 100 kg of air contains 80 kg of N_2

20.802 kg of air will contain = $\frac{80}{100} \times 20.802 = 16.640$ kg

(*iii*) **Weight of excess oxygen** = Weight of minimum O_2 required × excess%

$$= 3.467 \times \frac{20}{100} = 0.693 \text{ kg}$$

Total weight of dry products = 3.117 + 16.640 + 0.693 = 20.450 kg

$$\therefore \quad \% \text{ of } CO_2 = \frac{3.117 \times 100}{20.450} = 15.23$$

$$\% \text{ of } N_2 = \frac{16.640 \times 100}{20.450} = 81.87$$

$$\% \text{ of } O_2 = \frac{0.693 \times 100}{20.450} = 3.40.$$

Example 11.23. *A gaseous fuel has the following composition:*

$H_2 = 50\%$ $\quad CH_4 = 30\%$ $\quad C_2H_6 = 6\%$

$CO = 8\%$ $\quad N_2 = 6\%$.

Calculate the volume of air required per cubic meter of the gas if 20% excess air is supplied for combustion. Also find out the percentage composition by volume of the dry products of combustion. (Assume air to be a mixture of 80% N_2 and 20% oxygen by volume).

Solution: Volume of the gaseous fuel = 1 m^3; Volume of H_2 = 0.50 m^3; Volume of CH_4 = 0.30 m^3; Volume of C_2H_6 = 0.06 m^3; Volume of CO = 0.08 m^3; Volume of N_2 = 0.06 m^3.

According to combustion equations

$$\underset{2\text{ m}^3}{2H_2} + \underset{1\text{ m}^3}{O_2} \longrightarrow H_2O \qquad \underset{2\text{ m}^3}{2CO} + \underset{1\text{ m}^3}{O_2} \longrightarrow \underset{2\text{ m}^3}{2CO_2}$$

$$\underset{1\text{ m}^3}{CH_4} + \underset{2\text{ m}^3}{2O_2} \longrightarrow \underset{1\text{ m}^3}{CO_2} + 2H_2O \qquad \underset{2\text{ m}^3}{2C_2H_6} + \underset{7\text{ m}^3}{7O_2} \longrightarrow \underset{4\text{ m}^3}{4CO_2} + 6H_2O$$

Volume of oxygen required by $H_2 = \frac{1}{2} \times 0.50 = 0.25$ m^3

Volume of oxygen required by $CH_4 = \frac{2}{1} \times 0.30 = 0.60$ m^3

$$\text{Volume of oxygen required by } C_2H_4 = \frac{7}{2} \times 0.06 = 0.21 \text{ m}^3$$

$$\text{Volume of oxygen required by CO} = \frac{1}{2} \times 0.08 = 0.04 \text{ m}^3$$

$$\text{Total volume of oxygen required} = 1.10 \text{ m}^3$$

$$\text{Volume of air (containing 20\% oxygen) required} = \frac{100}{20} \times 1.10 = 5.5 \text{ m}^3$$

$$20\% \text{ of } 5.5 \text{ m}^3 \text{ of air} = \frac{5.5 \times 20}{100} = 1.1 \text{ m}^3.$$

Hence the volume of air when 20% excess than required amount is used = 5.5 +1.1 = 6.6 m^3.

Calculation of volume of dry combustion products. The dry gases will consist of (*i*) CO_2 from CH_4, C_2H_6 and CO, (*ii*) nitrogen from the gaseous fuel and the air used, and (*iii*) oxygen from excess are supplied.

(*i*) $$\text{Volume of } CO_2 = \left[\text{Volume of } CH_4 \times \frac{1}{1}\right] + \left[\text{Volume of } C_2H_6 \times \frac{4}{2}\right] + \left[\text{Volume of CO} \times \frac{2}{2}\right]$$

$$= (0.30 \times 1) + (0.06 \times 2) + (0.08 \times 1)$$

$$= 0.30 + 0.12 + 0.08 = 0.50 \text{ m}^3.$$

(*ii*) Volume of N_2 = Volume of N_2 in fuel + Volume of N_2 in air used

$$= 0.06 + \text{Volume of air used} \times \text{\% of nitrogen in air}$$

$$= 0.06 + 6.6 \times \frac{80}{100} = 0.06 + 5.28 = 5.34 \text{ m}^3.$$

(*iii*) Volume of O_2 = Weight of minimum O_2 required × excess%

$$= \frac{1.10 \times 20}{100} = 0.22 \text{ m}^3$$

Total volume of dry products of combustion = 0.50 + 5.34 + 0.22 = 6.06 m^3

$$\therefore \quad \text{\% of } CO_2 = \frac{0.50 \times 100}{6.06} = 8.25\%$$

$$\text{\% of } N_2 = \frac{5.34 \times 100}{6.06} = 88.12\%$$

$$\text{\% of } O_2 = \frac{0.22 \times 100}{6.06} = 3.63\%.$$

Example 11.24. *The percentage composition of a sample of anthracite coal by weight was found to be C = 90.0 H = 3.3, O = 3.0, N = 0.8, S = 0.9 and ash = 2.0. Calculate the minimum weight of air required for the complete combustion of 1 kg of this fuel. If 50% excess of air is supplied, find the percentage composition of the dry flue gases by volume and the weight of carbon per kg of the dry flue gases.*

Solution:

Weight of coal	= 1 kg	Weight of carbon = 0.90 kg
Weight of nitrogen	= 0.033 kg	Weight of oxygen = 0.030 kg
Weight of nitrogen	= 0.008 kg	Weight of sulphur = 0.009 kg
Weight of ash	= 0.02 kg	

According to combustion equations:

$$\underset{12\,kg}{C} + \underset{32\,kg}{O_2} \longrightarrow \underset{44\,kg}{CO_2}\,;\ \underset{4\,kg}{2H_2} + \underset{32\,kg}{O_2} \longrightarrow \underset{36\,kg}{2H_2O}\,;\ \underset{32\,kg}{S} + \underset{32\,kg}{O_2} \longrightarrow \underset{64\,kg}{SO_2}$$

$$\text{Weight of oxygen required by C} = \frac{32}{12} \times 0.90 = 2.40 \text{ kg}$$

$$\text{Weight of oxygen required by } H_2 = \frac{32}{4} \times 0.033 = 0.264 \text{ kg}$$

$$\text{Weight of oxygen required by S} = \frac{32}{32} \times 0.09 = 0.009 \text{ kg}$$

Total weight of oxygen required = 2.673 kg

Weight of oxygen present in coal = 0.030 kg

∴ Net weight of oxygen required = 2.643 kg

$$\therefore \text{ Weight of air (containing 23\% oxygen) required} = \frac{2.643 \times 100}{23} = 11.5 \text{ kg}$$

$$\text{Weight of air when 50\% excess of it is supplied} = \frac{11.5 \times 150}{100} = 17.25 \text{ kg}$$

Calculation of weight of dry combustion products

$$\text{Weight of } CO_2 = \text{Weight of carbon} \times \frac{44}{12}$$

$$= \frac{0.900 \times 44}{12} = 3.3 \text{ kg}$$

$$\text{Weight of } N_2 = \text{Weight of } N_2 \text{ in fuel} + \text{Weight of } N_2 \text{ in air}$$

$$= 0.008 + 17.25 \times \frac{77}{100}$$

$$= 0.008 + 10.63 = 10.638 \text{ kg}$$

$$\text{Weight of excess of } O_2 = \text{Weight of oxygen used} \times \text{excess\%}$$

$$= \frac{2.643 \times 50}{100} = 1.3215 \text{ kg}$$

$$\text{Weight of } SO_2 = \text{Weight of S} \times \frac{64}{32} = 0.009 \times 2 = 0.018 \text{ kg}$$

Total weight of dry combustion products = 3.3 + 10.638 + 1.3215 + 0.018 = 15.2775 kg

Calculation of corresponding volumes of products

Proportional volume of the gases

$$= \frac{\text{Wt. of } CO_2}{\text{Mol. wt. of } CO_2} : \frac{\text{Wt. of } N_2}{\text{Mol. wt. of } N_2} : \frac{\text{Wt. of } O_2}{\text{Mol. wt. of } O_2} : \frac{\text{Wt. of } SO_2}{\text{Mol. wt. of } SO_2}$$

$$= \frac{3.3}{44} : \frac{10.638}{28} : \frac{1.3215}{32} : \frac{0.018}{64}$$

$$= 0.0750 : 0.380 : 0.00413 : 0.0002$$

Total volume of gases = 0.0750 + 0.380 + 0.00413 + 0.0002 = 0.45933

$$\% \text{ of } CO_2 \text{ by volume} = \frac{\text{Vol. of } CO_2}{\text{Total vol. gases}} \times 100 = \frac{0.0750}{0.4593} \times 100 = 16.33$$

$$\% \text{ of } N_2 \text{ by volume} = \frac{0.380}{0.4593} \times 100 = 82.73$$

$$\% \text{ of } O_2 \text{ by volume} = \frac{0.00413}{0.4593} \times 100 = 0.899$$

$$\% \; SO_2 \text{ by volume} = \frac{0.0002}{0.4593} \times 100 = 0.04$$

Calculation of weight of carbon/kg of dry flue gases

15.2775 kg of dry flue gases contain 3.3 kg of CO_2

$$1 \text{ kg of dry flue gases will contain} = \frac{3.3}{15.2775} \text{ kg of } CO_2$$

44 kg of CO_2 contain 12 kg of carbon

$$\frac{3.3}{15.2775} \text{ kg of } CO_2 \text{ will contain} = \frac{12}{44} \times \frac{3.3}{15.2775} \text{ kg of C} = 0.06 \text{ kg.}$$

Problems on the Determination of Composition of Gaseous Mixtures

The composition of a fuel having two gases can be determined by knowing the volume of oxygen used for the combustion of a known volume of the gaseous mixture. However, if the gaseous mixture contains more than two gases, the composition can be determined only when the volume of CO_2 produced during combustion is known. Two problems are solved for making the statement clear.

Example 11.25. *10 c.c. of a mixture of ethylene and acetylene require 29 c.c of oxygen for complete combustion. Determine the percentage composition of the mixture, all gases being measured at the same condition of temperature and pressure.*

Solution:

Volume of the mixture = 10 c.c.

Now let the volume of ethylene = x c.c.

∴ Volume of acetylene = $(10 - x)$ c.c.

Volume of oxygen required for combustion = 29 c.c.

Now according to combustion equations

$$\underset{1 \text{ vol.}}{C_2H_4} + \underset{3 \text{ vol.}}{3O_2} \longrightarrow 2CO_2 + 2H_2O$$

$$\underset{2 \text{ vol.}}{2C_2H_2} + \underset{5 \text{ vol.}}{5O_2} \longrightarrow 4CO_2 + 2H_2O$$

∴ Volume of oxygen required by x c.c. of C_2H_4 $= \frac{3}{1} \times x \text{ c.c} = 3x$ c.c.

Volume of O_2 required by $(10 - x)$ c.c. of C_2H_2 $= \frac{5}{2} (10 - x)$ c.c.

∴ Total volume of O_2 required $= 3x + \frac{5}{2} (10 - x)$

or

$$29 = 3x + \frac{5}{2} (10 - x)$$

$$29 = 3x + 25 - \frac{5x}{2}$$

$$3x - \frac{5x}{2} = 29 - 25$$

$$x = 8 \text{ mL}$$

$\therefore$ Volume of C_2H_4 = 8 mL

and Volume of C_2H_2 = 10 – 8 = 2 mL

$$\% \text{ of } C_2H_4 = \frac{8}{10} \times 100 = 80\%$$

$$\% \text{ of } C_2H_2 = \frac{2}{10} \times 100 = 20\%.$$

Example 11.26. *45 mL of a mixture of methane, ethylene and acetylene was exploded with 125 mL of oxygen. On adding caustic potash there was a reduction of 80 mL. The remaining gas measuring 10 mL was completely absorbed by alkaline pyrogallol. Find the composition of the mixture.*

Solution: Total volume of the mixture = 45 mL

Let Volume of $CH_4 = x$ mL

and Volume of $C_2H_4 = y$ mL

$\therefore$ Volume of $C_2H_2 = 45 - (x + y)$ mL

Total volume of oxygen exploded (taken) = 125 mL

Volume of remaining O_2 (absorbed by pyrogallol) = 10 mL

$\therefore$ Volume of oxygen consumed = 125 – 10 = 115 mL

Now according to combustion equations

$$\underset{1 \text{ vol.}}{CH_4} + \underset{2 \text{ vol.}}{2O_2} \longrightarrow \underset{1 \text{ vol.}}{CO_2} + 2H_2O$$

$$\underset{1 \text{ vol.}}{C_2H_4} + \underset{3 \text{ vol.}}{3O_2} \longrightarrow \underset{2 \text{ vol.}}{2CO_2} + 2H_2O$$

$$\underset{2 \text{ vol.}}{2C_2H_2} + \underset{5 \text{ vol.}}{5O_2} \longrightarrow \underset{4 \text{ vol.}}{4CO_2} + 2H_2O$$

$\therefore$ Volume of O_2 consumed by x mL of $CH_4 = \frac{2}{1} \times x = 2x$ mL.

$\therefore$ Volume of O_2 consumed by y mL of $CH_4 = \frac{3}{1} \times y = 3y$ mL.

Volume of O_2 consumed by $C_2H_4 = \frac{5}{2} \times [45 - (x + y)]$ mL.

$\therefore$ Total volume of O_2 consumed $= 2x + 3y + \frac{5}{2}[45 - (x + y)]$

or $$115 = 2x + 3y + \frac{5}{2}[45 - (x + y)] \quad ...(i)$$

Calculation of carbon dioxide produced

Total volume of CO_2 produced (absorbed by KOH) = 80 mL.

Volume of CO_2 produced by x mL of $CH_4 = \frac{1}{1} \times x = x$ mL.

Volume of CO_2 produced by y mL of $C_2H_4 = \frac{2}{1} \times y = 2y$ mL.

Volume of CO_2 produced by acetylene $= \frac{4}{2}$ $[45 - (x + y)]$

$\therefore$ Total volume of CO_2 produced $= x + 2y + 2\,[45 - (x + y)]$

or $80 = x + 2y + 2[45 - (x + y)]$

From equations (*i*) and (*ii*), we get

$$x = 10 \text{ and } y = 15$$

$\therefore$ Volume of CH_4 = 10 mL

Volume of C_2H_4 = 15 mL

and Volume of C_2H_2 = 45 – (15 + 10) = 20 mL.

EXERCISES

I. SHORT ANSWER TYPE QUESTIONS

1. Define and classify fuels. **(RGPV, 2003, 2007)**
2. Define fuel. Discuss various parameters under proximate analysis giving their significance. **(RGPV, 2019)**
3. How are fuels classified? Give examples for each of them. **(Anna Univ., 2019)**
4. Distinguish between thermal and catalytic cracking. **(RGPV, 2019, 2009)**
5. What is cracking? Explain advantages of catalytic cracking. **(RGPV, 2018, 2010; RTU, 2014, 2017)**
6. Discuss Dulong's formula for calculating calorific value of fuels. **(RGPV, 2018, 2004, RTU, 2017)**
7. How can you determine % of C and % of H in a coal sample. **(RGPV, 2018, 2006)**
8. What is knocking and octane number? Give names of two anti knocking substances. **(RTU, 2017)**
9. What are the advantages of gaseous fuels over solid and liquid fuel? Give one example of gaseous fuel with its calorific value. **(RTU, 2013, 2014, 2017)**
10. What is calorific value? Explain the determination of calorific value of solid fuels. **(RTU, 2017)**
11. What are net and gross calorific value of a fuel.
12. Explain the composition and uses of coal gas. **(RTU, 2017)**
13. What is oil gas? Give its synthesis, composition, calorific value and uses. **(RTU, 2019, 2017, 2016)**
14. What is knocking? How do you rate the quality of petrol and diesel? **(JNTU, 2018)**
15. Give the composition and uses of LPG and CNG. **(JNTU, 2018)**

16. Distinguish between: **(Anna Univ., 2017)**
    (*a*) High and low calorific value
    (*b*) Coal and coke **(RGPV, 2009)**
    (*c*) Proximate and ultimate analysis.
17. What is ultimate analysis of coal? Give its significance. **(Anna Univ., 2018, RTU, 2017)**
18. How is proximate analysis of coal carried out? Mention its significance. **(Anna Univ., 2019, JNTU, 2018, RTU, 2014, 2013, RGP, 2008, 2003)**
19. What is calorific value? What are its types? Explain. **(Anna Univ., 2019)**
20. Define fuel. What are the characteristics of a good fuel?
21. What is knocking? How will you increase the anti knocking properties of a fuel. **(RGPV, 2005)**
22. Differentiate between cracking and reforming.

II. LONG ANSWER TYPE QUESTIONS

1. What is fuel? How many types of fuel are there? What are the requirements of fuel to be used in an industry?
2. What do you understand by the calorific value of a fuel and how is it determined by Bomb calorimeter?
3. What do you understand by proximate and ultimate analysis of coal?
4. What is ultimate and proximate analysis of coal? Discuss their significance. How are ultimate and proximate analysis done?
5. Name the various solid fuels. Which of them is best suited for manufacture of metallurgical grade coke and why? How will you determine net and gross calorific value of a solid fuel?
6. What is difference between high and low temperature carbonization of coal? Discuss the by product coke oven process for the manufacture of coke and name the by products recovered.
7. Describe the high temperature carbonization process.
8. (*a*) With the help of a line diagram describe the fractional distillation of crude petroleum and name the various products obtained.
   (*b*) What is thermal cracking and how is it carried out?
9. How is synthetic gasoline prepared from coal by the Fisher Tropsh process? Why is this method not very commonly used? What is catalytic cracking?
10. What is difference in the composition of producer gas, water gas and carburetted water gas? Describe briefly Orsat gas analysis method for flue gases.
11. Give the name, diagram and working of the apparatus used for the analysis of flue gas. What conclusion will you be able to draw from this analysis?
12. Define calorific value of a fuel. Describe method to determine calorific value using Bomb calorimeter. **(RGPV, 2019, RTU, 2019, 2018, 2017)**
13. What is meant by knocking? What are its ill effects? Discuss the mechanism of knocking by giving relevant equations. **(VTU, 2018, 2019)**

14. What is cracking of petroleum? Describe the fluidized and catalytic cracking. **(VTU, 2018, 2019, RTU, 2016, RGPV, 2009)**

15. What is synthetic petrol? Explain the manufacturing of synthetic petrol by Bergius process. **(RTU, 2014)**

16. Define synthetic petrol. Describe Fischer Tropsch process with the help of diagram. **(RTU, 2017, 2015, 2013)**

17. What is carbonization of coal? Describe Otto. Hoffmann by product oven method of carbonization. **(RTU, 2018, 2017, 2016, 2015, RGPV, 2008, 2006, 2009)**

18. What is carbonization of coal? Explain Beehive coke oven method of carbonization **(RTU, 2017, 2014, RGPV, 2004)**

19. Neatly draw a schematic diagram of the Orsat apparatus and explain the steps involved in the flue gas analysis. **(AU, 2017)**

III. NUMERICAL PROBLEMS

1. In a bomb calorimeter experiment, the following data was obtained: Weight of coal = 0.95 g, weight of water taken in the calorimeter = 3000 g; water equivalent of the calorimeter = 550 g; observed rise in temperature = 2.15°C, cooling correction = 0.055°C, fuse wire correction = 6.4 calories, acid correction = 46.8 calories, cotton thread correction = 1.7 calories calculate gross and net calorific value of coal, if it contains 6% of hydrogen. **(RGPV, 2004)**

2. A sample of coal contains 92% C, 5% H and 3% ash. When this coal was tested for its calorific value in the bomb calorimeter, the following results were obtained: Weight of coal = 0.95 g, weight of water taken in the calorimeter = 700 g. Water equivalent of bomb calorimeter = 2000 g, increase in temperature = 2.48°C, acid correction = 60.0 cal, cooling correction = 0.02°C, fuse wire correction = 10.0 cal, calculate gross and net calorific values of coal. Given latent heat of condensation of steam = 587 cal/g. **(RGPV, 2010)**

3. On burning 0.83 g of a solid fuel in a bomb calorimeter, the temperature of 3600g of water increased from 26.5°C to 29.2°C. Water equivalent of calorimeter and latent heat of steam are 385.0 and 587.0 cal/g respectively. If the fuel contains 0.7% hydrogen, calculate its gross and net calorific value.

4. A coal sample contains C = 92%, H = 5% and Ash = 3%. When this coal sample was tested in laboratory for its calorific value in a bomb calorimeter , the following data were obtained; weight of coal burnt = 0.95 g, weight of water taken 600 g, water equivalent of bomb calorimeter = 2100 g, rise in temperature = 2.48°C, acid correction = 60.0 cal, fuse wire correction = 10.0 cal, cooling correction = 0.02°C. Calculate the gross and net calorific value of the coal sample in cal/g. (latent heat of condensation of steam = 580 cal/gm).

5. Calculate the gross and net calorific value of coal having the following composition – carbon = 85%, hydrogen = 8%, sulphur = 1 %, nitrogen = 2%, ash = 4%, latent heat of steam = 587 cal/g. **(Ravishanker, 98, KU, 99)**

6. On burning 0.83 g of a solid fuel in a bomb calorimeter, the temperature of 3500g of water increased from 26.5°C to 29.2°C. Water equivalent of calorimeter and latent heat of steam are 385.0 g and 587 cal/g respectively. If the fuel contains 0.7% hydrogen, calculate its gross and net calorific value. **(Kerala, 97)**

7. 1.05 g of the fuel on complete combustion in excess of oxygen increased the temperature of water in the calorimeter from 15°C to 18.5°C. The weight of water in calorimeter was found to be 1630 gm. Calculate the calorific value of fuel if the water equivalent of the calorimeter is 110 gm.

8. The determination of the calorific value of a coal sample gave the following data. Weight of coal sample = 0.9 gm, water equivalent of the calorimeter = 440gm, weight of water = 2560 gm, rise in temperature = 2.42°C, cooling correction = 0.052°C, fuse wire correction= 10.0 cal. Calculate the gross and net calorific values if the coal contains 6% hydrogen and assume latent heat of steam = 600 cal/gm.

9. A fuel has 80% carbon, 10% hydrogen and remaining 10% incombustible matter. What volume of air at N.T.P. is required to burn completely 1 kg of this fuel?

10. A sample of fuel on analysis gave the following results:

    C = 84%, H = 6%, N =3.2%, S = 4% and ash = 2.8%

    Calculate the minimum volume of air (containing 21% oxygen by volume) at 0°C and 1 atmospheric pressure required for the combustion of 1 kg of this fuel.

11. Calculate the weight and volume of air containing 20% oxygen and 80% nitrogen by volume, needed for the combustion of 1 kg of carbon. Give the composition of the combustion products.

12. A coal sample has the following composition:

    C = 82%, H = 4.2%, O = 4.8%, Ash = rest

    This coat was used in a boiler, the analysis of flue gases was CO_2 = 10%, CO = 1.5%, O_2 = 8%, N_2 = 80.5% Calculate.

    (*i*) The amount of excess air per kg of coal burnt

    (*ii*) Total mass of air supplied per kg of coal burnt

    (*iii*) Percentage of excess air supplied for combustion.

13. 0.28 g of a sample of coal was analyzed by combustion method. The increase in weights of $CaCl_2$ tube and the potash bulb at the end of the operation was found to be 0.17 g and 0.60 g respectively. Calculate the percentage of carbon and hydrogen in the coal sample.

14. 1.3 g of a coal sample was used in a bomb calorimeter for the determination of calorific value. Calorific value of coal was found to be 9000 cal/g. The ash formed in the bomb calorimeter was extracted with acid and the acid extract was heated with $BaCl_2$ solution and a precipitate of $BaSO_4$ was obtained. The precipitate was filtered, dried and weighed. The weight of precipitate was found to be 0.11g. Calculate the percentage of sulphur in the coal sample.

15. 1.5 g of a coal sample was used for nitrogen estimation by Kjeldahl method. The evolved ammonia was collected in 25 mL of 0.1 N sulphuric acid. To neutralize excess acid, 13 mL of 0.1 N NaOH were required. Determine the percentage of nitrogen in the given sample of coal.

16. A hydrocarbon fuel on combustion gave a flue gas of the following volume % composition: CO_2 = 13.53, N_2 = 82.91 and O_2 = 3.56. (*a*) Determine the composition of fuel by weight (*b*) % of air used in excess and (*c*) volume of air supplied per kg of the fuel.

(RGPV, 2008, 2009)

17. The percentage composition of petrol by weight was found to be C = 84% and H = 16%. Calculate (*a*) minimum air necessary for complete combustion of 1 kg of petrol (*b*)% composition by weight of dry products of combustion corresponding to minimum air per 1 kg of petrol burnt (*c*) calorific value of petrol.

18. A producer gas has the following composition by volume: CH_4 = 4%, CO = 25%, H_2 = 10%, CO_2 = 10.3%, N_2 = 50.7%. Calculate (*a*) minimum quantity of air required (*b*) % composition of dry products of combustion per cubic meter of the gas.

19. Find the volume of air required for complete combustion of 1 m^3 of acetylene and the weight of air necessary for the combustion of 1 kg of a fuel.

IV. MULTIPLE CHOICE QUESTIONS

1. The total amount of heat liberated when a unit mass (or volume) of a fuel is burnt completely is called as:

(*a*) Burning volume (*b*) Heat value
(*c*) Calorific value (*d*) Combustion value.

2. A good fuel should have

(*a*) Low moisture content (*b*) High calorific value
(*c*) Low ash content (*d*) All of the above.

3. The correct relationship between HCV and LCV is:

(*a*) GCV = NCV – 0.09% H × 587 (*b*) NCV = GCV – 0.09% H × 587
(*c*) GCV = NCV – 0.9% H × 58.7 (*d*) NCV = GCV – 0.9% H × 58.7.

4. In high temperature carbonization of coal compared to low temperature carbonization.

(*a*) Calorific value of the coke oven gas is lower
(*b*) Yield of ammonia is less
(*c*) Aromatic content of tar is low
(*d*) H_2 content in the coke oven gas is more.

5. KOG solution used in Orsat apparatus absorbs:

(*a*) CO_2 (*b*) SO_2
(*c*) Both (*a*) and (*b*) (*d*) Neither (*a*) nor (*b*).

6. Maximum coal producing state in India is:

(*a*) Assam (*b*) Jharkhand
(*c*) Orrisa (*d*) Chhattisgarh.

7. Bomb calorimeter can be used to determine the ——— of the coal

(*a*) Calorific value (*b*) Sulphur content
(*c*) Both (*a*) and (*b*) (*d*) Neither (*a*) nor (*b*).

8. Gross scalorific value will be equal to net calorific value for:

(*a*) C_2H_4 (*b*) C_2H_6
(*c*) H_2 (*d*) CO.

9. An example of primary fuel is:

(*a*) Coke (*b*) Coal gas
(*c*) Lignite (*d*) Charcoal.

10. A good metallurgical coke:

(*a*) should be brittle

(*b*) should have high porosity

(*c*) should have low fusion point of its ash

(*d*) must contain moderate quantities of ash, moisture, sulphur and volatile matters.

11. ——— present in coal is not determined by its ultimate analysis

(*a*) Fixed carbon (*b*) Total carbon

(*c*) Hydrogen (*d*) Nitrogen.

12. Producer gas is mainly composed of

(*a*) CO and H_2 (*b*) CO and N_2

(*c*) CO_2 and H_2 (*d*) CO_2 and N_2.

13. In flue gas analysis by Orsat's apparatus, CO is absorbed by

(*a*) Dilute potassium carbonate (*b*) Potassium hydroxide

(*c*) Cuprous chloride (*d*) Alkaline pyrogallol solution.

14. Fischer-Tropsch method is used for

(*a*) Synthesis of gasoline from water gas

(*b*) Hydrogenation of coal to produce gasoline

(*c*) Gasification of coal

(*d*) Analysis of flue gases.

15. Gobar gas is produced by the

(*a*) Fermentation of cow dung (*b*) Oxidation of cow dung

(*c*) Hydrogenation of cow dung (*d*) None of these.

16. Calorific value of both the solid and liquid fuels can be determined by using ——— calorimeter.

(*a*) Bomb (*b*) Junker's

(*c*) Boy's (*d*) All of the above.

17. Octane number of 2, 2, 4-trimethyl pentane is

(*a*) 0 (*b*) 100

(*c*) In between 0 and 100 (*d*) More than 100.

18. Gross and net calorific value of a fuel will be the same

(*a*) If its ash content is zero (*b*) If its hydrogen content is zero

(*c*) If its carbon content is low (*d*) Under no circumstances.

19. The process of breaking bigger hydrocarbons into simpler low boiling fractions in called

(*a*) Knocking (*b*) Cracking

(*c*) Reforming (*d*) Refining.

20. The quality of diesel fuel depends on

(*a*) Octane number (*b*) Steam number

(*c*) Cetane number (*d*) Saponification number.

21. Orsat flue gas apparatus is used for analysing

(*a*) SO_2, CO_2, N_2, O_2 (*b*) SO_2, O_2, CO_2, H_2O vapour

(*c*) CO_2, O_2, CO and N_2 (*d*) N_2, O_2, SO_2, Cl_2.

22. Power alcohol consist of

(*a*) Petrol and methyl alcohol (*b*) Petrol and ethyl alcohol

(*c*) Diesel and methyl alcohol (*d*) Diesel and ethyl alcohol.

23. Main constituent of LPG is:

(*a*) methane (*b*) propane

(*c*) benzene (*d*) butane.

24. Process which is used or direct hydrogenation of coal to produce liquid fuel

(*a*) Bergius (*b*) Fischer-Tropsch

(*c*) Cracking (*d*) Beehive.

25. Pyragallol used in Orsat apparatus can absorb

(*a*) Only O_2 (*b*) Both O_2 and CO

(*c*) Both O_2 and CO_2 (*d*) All O_2, CO and CO_2.

Answers

III. NUMERICAL PROBLEMS ANSWERS

1. (*i*) 8181.95 cal/gm (*ii*) 7864.97 cal/gm
2. GCV = 7031.58 cal/gm, NCV = 6767.43 cal/gm
3. GCV = 12638 cal/gm, NCV = 12601 cal/gm
4. GCV = 7031.57 cal/gm, NCV = 6770.57 cal/gm.
5. GCV = 9650.4 kcal/kg, NCV = 9227.8 kcal/kg.
6. GCV = 12638 cal/gm, NCV = 12601 cal/gm
7. 6380 cal/gm.
8. GCV= 8230 cal/gm, NCV = 7906 cal/gm.
9. 9777.8 litres
10. 9200 litres
11. Weight of air = 116 kg, Volume of air = 9333.5 litres, Volume of CO_2 = 1866.7 litres Volume of N_2 = 7466.8 litres
12. (*i*) 6.035 kg (*ii*) 16.79 kg (*iii*) (56.1%)
13. (*i*) % C = 58.44 (*ii*) % H = 6.74
14. % *S* = 1.16
15. %N = 1.12
16. (*a*) % C = 89.13, %H = 10.87 (*b*) 19.26 (*c*) 12.91 m^3/kg
17. (*a*) 15.304 kg (*b*) 100% (*c*) GCV= 12307.2 cal/gm, NCV = 11461.92 cal/gm.
18. (*a*) 1.214 m^3 (*b*) % CO_2 = 21.14, %N_2 = 78.86
19. Volume of air = 11.9 m^3, Weight of air = 13.378 kg.

IV. MULTIPLE CHOICE QUESTIONS

1. (*c*)	**2.** (*d*)	**3.** (*b*)	**4.** (*d*)	**5.** (*c*)	**6.** (*b*)	**7.** (*c*)	**8.** (*d*)	**9.** (*c*)	**10.** (*b*)
11. (*a*)	**12.** (*b*)	**13.** (*c*)	**14.** (*a*)	**15.** (*a*)	**16.** (*a*)	**17.** (*b*)	**18.** (*b*)	**19.** (*b*)	**20.** (*c*)
21. (*c*)	**22.** (*b*)	**23.** (*d*)	**24.** (*a*)	**25.** (*c*)					

Chapter 12 Liquid Crystals

12.1 INTRODUCTION

It is observed that many long chain organic molecules when heated undergo two sharp phase changes one after the other. They first fuse sharply giving turbid liquids (mesophases) and then again equally sharply at a higher temperature giving clear liquids. On cooling at the same temperature, these changes get reversed. These changes can be represented as

$$\underset{\text{Solid}}{A} \underset{}{\overset{145°C}{\rightleftharpoons}} \underset{\substack{\text{Liquid crystal}\\\text{(mesophase)}}}{A} \underset{}{\overset{178°C}{\rightleftharpoons}} \underset{\text{Liquid}}{A} \qquad A = p\text{-cholesteryl benzoate}$$

The first temperature at which solid changes into turbid liquid is called as **transition point** and the second temperature at which turbid liquid is converted into clear liquid is called as **melting point.**

The turbid liquid thus obtained exhibits double refraction and also gives interference pattern in polarized light. These properties are shown by anisotropic crystals. Hence, this turbid liquid is called as **liquid crystal.**

Lehmann proposed the name liquid crystals to these turbid liquids. The usage of this name (liquid crystals) is not satisfactory since the substances in this state do not have the arrangement like that of a crystal lattice. Except for few anisotropic properties like double refraction, they are more like liquids possessing viscosity, surface tension, ability to flow etc. Some other names have also been proposed like crystalline liquids, anisotropic liquids and para crystals but the term **mesomorphic state** (means 'intermediate form' in Greek) fits the best. However, the older term liquid crystals is frequently used.

Many compounds show this behaviour. Substances which shows this type of behaviour are all long chain organic compounds either having groups like —C ≡ N—, —N = NO—, —C = C— in the middle or terminating in groups like —OR, —COOR etc.

Cholesteryl benzoate (C_6H_5 $COOC_{27}$ H_{45}) was among the first solids discovered in 1988 to show this property of liquid crystals. We have seen earlier that it fuses sharply at 145°C to form liquid crystal which on further heating changes into clear liquid at 178°C.

Later on few other compounds were founds to show similar behaviour like *p*-azoxy anisole, *p*-azoxy phenetole, cholesteryl acetate, ammonium oleate etc.

An essential condition for molecules to exhibit mesomorphism is that the molecule must be anisotropic in shape like a rod or a disc. Depending on the molecular structure of compound, the system may pass through one or more mesophases before converting into clear isotopic liquid. Conversion into the intermediate state may be brought about by

- Thermotropic mesomorphism (conversion by thermal processes)
- Lyotropic mesomorphism (conversion by intervention of the solvent)

Examples of Liquid Crystals

Table 12.1: Examples of Liquid Crystals.

S. No.	Substance	Transition temperature (°C)	Melting point (°C)
1.	*p*-azoxyanisole	116	135
2.	*p*-azoxyphenetole	137	167
3.	*p*-methoxycinnamic acid	170	186
4.	Diethyl benzidine	115	120
5.	Mercury di (p-ethoxybenzal-aminophenyl)	204	272
6.	Anisaldazine	165	180

P.G. de Gennes, a French physicist, received the noble prize in physics in the year 1991 for his contribution to liquid crystals and polymers.

Table 12.2: Differences Between Crystalline Solid, Liquid Crystal and True Liquids

S. No.	Crystalline solids	Liquid crystals	True liquids
1.	The molecules in solid are rigid.	The molecules in liquid crystals are rigid.	The molecules liquid are not rigid.
2.	They have a definite shape.	They have a definite shape generally oblong or rod shaped.	They do not have a fixed shape. They take up the shape of the container in which they are kept.
3.	They cannot flow.	They can flow.	They can flow.
4.	They have regular arrangement of molecules.	They are not as disordered as liquids because they have some degree of alignment.	They do not have any regular arrangement.
5.	Crystalline solids are anisotropic.	Liquid crystals are anisotropic.	True liquids are isotropic.

12.2 VAPOUR PRESSURE-TEMPERATURE GRAPHS

The phase changes occurring during the transformation of an ordinary solid into vapour state through liquid can be represented as

$$\text{Solid} \rightleftharpoons \text{Liquid} \rightleftharpoons \text{Vapour}$$

Whereas, the phase transformation when a solid shows metamorphic behaviour can be represented as:

$$\text{Solid} \rightleftharpoons \text{Liquid crystal} \rightleftharpoons \text{Liquid} \rightleftharpoons \text{Vapour}$$

These transformations can be best represented by a vapour pressure-temperature curves as shown in Fig. 12.1.

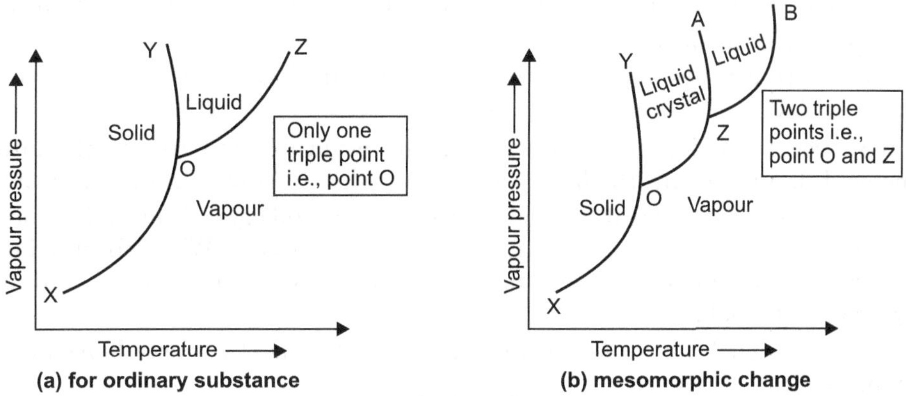

Fig. 12.1. Vapour Pressure-temperature curves.

In Fig. 12.1 (*a*), *XO* represents the vapour pressure curve of the substance in the solid state whereas *OZ* represents the vapour pressure curve in the liquid state. This shows that along *XO* curve, the solid phase is in equilibrium with the vapour phase (solid $\rightleftharpoons$ vapour), whereas along curve *OZ*, the liquid state is in equilibrium with the vapour state (liquid $\rightleftharpoons$ vapour). Point *O* (the melting point of the solid) is the triple point where all the three phases coexist. Curve *OY* represents the effect of varying pressure on the melting point of the substance.

In Fig. 12.1 (*b*), *XO* is the vapour pressure curve of the solid state. *OZ* is the vapour pressure curve of the liquid crystal and *ZB* is the vapour pressure curve of clear liquids.

At point *O*, solid crystal is converted into liquid crystal and point *Z* represents the melting point at which the liquid crystal changes into clear liquid. In this figure, there are tow triple points *O* and *Z*. At point *O*, the solid, liquid crystal and vapour phase coexist in equilibrium with each other. At point *Z*, the three phases liquid crystal, liquid and vapour phase coexist in equilibrium with each other. *OY* represents the effect of pressure on the transition temperature and *ZA* represents the effect of pressure on the melting point of the substance.

12.3 CLASSIFICATION OF LIQUID CRYSTALS

Depending upon the method by which the liquid crystalline phase is brought about, liquid crystals are classified into two types:

(*a*) Thermotropic liquid crystals (*b*) Lyotropic liquid crystals (c) Polymeric liquid crystals.

In thermotropic liquid crystals, the transformation to the liquid crystalline state depends on temperature while in lyotropic liquid crystals, the transformation depends on concentration of the solvent.

Thermotropic liquid crystals

Thermotropic liquid crystals find widespread application as display materials, information storage materials, optical couplers and many other technical uses while lyotrophic crystals find application in biological systems (such as membranes), nano technology etc.

Thermotropic crystals are of three types:

(*a*) Smectic (*b*) Nematic (*c*) Cholesteric.

(*a*) Smectic Liqauid Crystals: These liquid crystals do not flow as normal liquids but they flow in layers as if different sheets are sliding over one another. They have limited mobility and the distribution of velocity in different layers is different from that found in a true isotropic liquid. In short, the flow of smectic liquid crystals is non-Newtonion while that of true liquids is Newtonion (*i.e.* the viscosity of the liquid remains constant, when shear is applied).

Depending on the molecular arrangements within the layer, these liquid crystals are classified into different types according to the chronological order of their discovery and are designated as *A*, *B*, *C*.... .

The inter layer attraction sin these crystals are weak as compared to the lateral forces between molecules. As a result, the layers are able to slide over one another relatively easily.

These crystals also give X-ray diffraction patterns like solid crystals but it is in one direction only. Therefore, these crystals have complicated internal structure. When observed in polarised light, these crystals appear to have fan like structure. They are always uniaxial and are not affected by a magnetic field.

Examples: Soap such as cholesteryl oleyl carbonate, ethyl *p*-azoxy benzoate, *n*-octyl-*p*-azoxy cinnamate etc.

Fig. 12.2. Layer structure of smectic liquid crystal.

(*b*) Nematic Liquid Crystals (thread like crystals): These crystals show near normal flow behaviour of true liquids. They flow more readily than the smectic crystals. The flow of these crystals is Newtonian like that of true liquids. They have low viscosity than liquids. In other words, nematic crystals have liquid like character but being turbid and anisotropic, they are unlike true liquids.

In polarised light, these crystals appear to have thread like structures. They are uniaxial (like smectic crystal) but are affected by strong magnetic field. Thus, when observed in the direction of lines of force of a magnetic field, the turbid liquid seems quite clear. When the magnetic field is cut off. the turbidity of liquid reappears.

Examples: *p*-azoxy phenetole, *p*-azoxy anisole, anisaldazine, *p*-methoxycinnamic acid etc.

Fig. 12.3. Nematic liquid crystal.

(c) Cholesteric Liquid Crystals: It is observed that certain ling chain organic molecules are optically active showing characteristics of nematic liquid crystals but at the same time show strong colour effects in polarised light like the smectic phase. These crystals have layered structure (helical) similar to smectic liquid crystal but the layers are much thicker unlike smectic crystals.

Cholesteryl benzoate was the first substance to exhibit this type of behaviour. It shows transition point at 145°C and melting point at 178°C. They are also called as chiral nematic liquid as these crystals are characterized by very high optical rotation *i.e.* thousand times greater than the activity of a solid crystal such as quartz. Optical studies shows that these crystals exhibit non-Newtonian flow properties.

Examples: *l*-cholesteryl esters, solutions of certain polypeptides in organic solvents (like poly-γ-benzyl L-glutamate in dioxane spontaneous adopt cholesteric mesophase above a certain concentration) etc.

Fig. 12.4. Cholesteric liquid crystals.

Lyotropic liquid crystals:

Lyotropic liquid crystals are obtained when an appropriate concentration of material is dissolved in some solvent. The most common systems are those formed by water and amphiphilic molecules like soaps, detergents and lipids.

Lyotropic liquid crystals are soap like molecules with a hydrocarbon group at one end and a polar group at the other, form liquid crystals that change phase according to their concentration in water. At low concentrations, these molecules are randomly oriented but as the concentration increases, the molecules start arranging themselves. The hydrophobic heads point in one direction and their tails point in the other direction (Fig. 12.5).

Fig. 12.5. Chemical structure of soap forming micelles.

These crystals are very common in living systems. Common examples of such crystals are soaps and various phospholipids present in cell membranes.

Polymeric liquid crystals/liquid crystal polymers (LCPs)

There are relatively new class of high temperature polymers that have attracted a great deal of interest academically as well as industrially due to their outstanding mechanical properties at high temperature, excellent chemical resistance, good weatherability etc. They are exceptionally inert. They resist stress cracking in the presence of most chemicals at elevated temperature. They are polymers with the property of liquid crystal usually containing aromatic rings as mesogens. These molecules contain repeated monomer units which are connected to form extended chain like molecules. Most LCPs are characterised by a common basic structure consisting of three parts: a hydrophobic flexible linker on one end, a hydrophilic moiety on other end and a rigid mesogen core (Fig. 12.6).

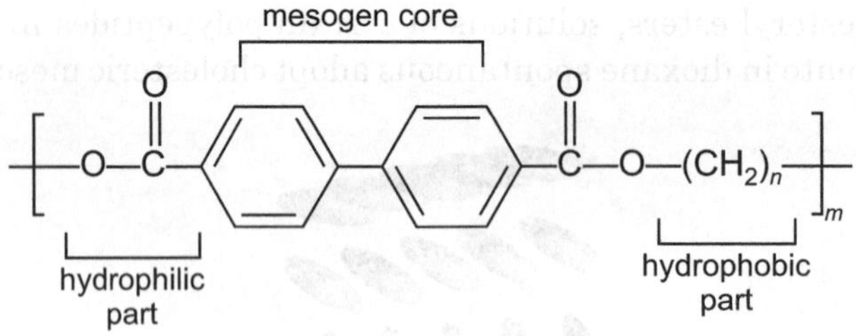

Fig. 12.6. Representation of LCP.

For example: Vectra (R) sumikasuper (R) etc. They have even been found in biological molecules including DNA and micelles.

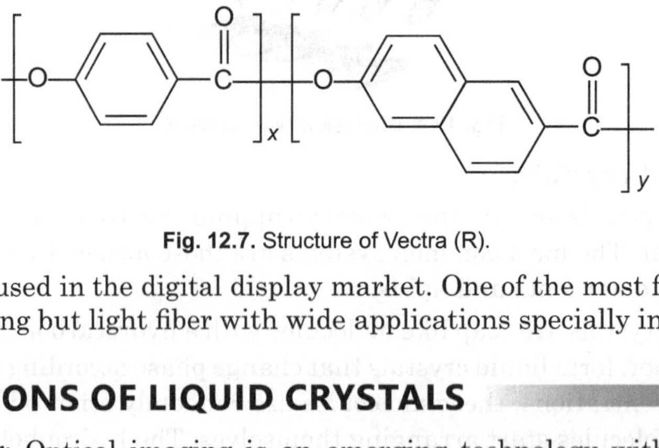

Fig. 12.7. Structure of Vectra (R).

They are widely used in the digital display market. One of the most famous application of LCP is Kevlar, a strong but light fiber with wide applications specially in bullet proof vests.

12.4 APPLICATIONS OF LIQUID CRYSTALS

1. Optical imaging: Optical imaging is an emerging technology with great potential for improving disease prevention, diagnosis and treatment in the medical office at the bedside or in the operating room. In this technique, a liquid crystal cell is placed between two layers of photoconductor. When light falls on the photoconductor, an electric field is developed in the liquid crystal corresponding to the intensity of light. The electric pattern can be transmitted by an electrode, which records the image. This technology is still being developing and is one of the promising areas of liquid crystal research.

2. Liquid crystal thermometer: A cholesteric liquid crystal reflects only one colour when light falls on it. If the temperature is changed, it reflects different colour light. So, such crystals are able to detect temperature just by looking at the colour of the thermometer. These crystals are able to detect very small temperature changes as small as 0.01°C. These thermometers are highly sensitive, hence, finds application in medical and electronic fields. In medical field, they are used to detect tumours which have a different temperature than the surrounding tissue. In electronic field, they are used to locate faults in circuit, condition of batteries etc. by detecting the characteristic higher temperature in the faulty regions.

3. Liquid crystal displays (LCD): The most common application of liquid crystal technology is liquid crystal displays (LCDs).

Principle: In recent years, the nematic and smectic type of crystals have been widely used in LCD devices. The orientation of molecules in a thin film of nematic liquid crystal is affected by pressure and electric field, which in turn affects the optical properties of the liquid crystal (film), causing the film to become opaque.

If we arrange electrodes in some pattern and apply an electric field, the patterns of the electrodes become visible. This principle is used in computer monitors, television, instrument panels and devices ranging from aircraft cockpit displays to everyday human need such as clocks, calculators and telephones.

Few features of LCD that make them more desirable for displays than other materials are lower power consumption and greater clarity of display in presence of bright light.

4. Drug delivery: Hexagonal and cubic liquid crystals are particularly of high interest in drug delivery field due to their exceptional potential as drug vehicles. They are highly investigated for their capability to control or sustain the release of both hydrophobic and hydrophilic drug moieties having wide range of atomic weights. Liquid crystals are non-toxic, biodegradable and bioadhesive which makes them highly significant in drug delivery through different routes of administration *e.g.* buccal, gastrointestinal, lung, nasal, intravenous, oral etc.

5. As a solvent in research work: Liquid crystals have been used in chromatographic separations as a solvent to direct the course of chemical reactions and to study kinetics and molecular arrangements. They are also used as an anisotropic solvent for UV-visible and IR spectroscopy of organic molecules.

Nematic liquid crystals are useful research tools for structure elucidation of organic compounds using NMR spectroscopy. Organic compounds dissolved in nematic liquid crystal solvents give a very highly resolved NMR spectrum exhibiting inter molecular dipole-dipole fine structures. The spectral analysis of molecules in liquid crystal solvents provide various information like anisotropy of chemical shifts, spin-spin coupling, dipole-dipole interaction, bond angle etc.

6. As polymer composite material: If a polymer is extruded in the liquid crystal phase the anisotropic ordering of molecules confers an extremely high strength to the polymer *e.g.*, kevlar. Kevlar is a high strength liquid crystal polymer used in bullet proof vests and car body panels.

7. Radiation and pressure sensors: The property of cholesteric crystals to change colour with temperature finds application in radiation and pressure sensors. When an invisible radiation falls on a device, it causes local changed in temperature which can be easily detected. This principle finds use in making sensors for detecting ultrasonic, microwave, IR, UV and other ionizing radiations. In the same way, pressure sensors can also be made.

8. Other applications: Liquid crystal also find applications in:

- **Pharmaceutical industry:** sustained release formulations, gels, cream, ointments, liposomes, transdermal patches etc.
- **Cosmetics as personal care products:** (nail paint removers, eye shadow, lipstic etc.)

- **IT industry:** liquid crystals having low molecular weight are used for making erasable optical discs, full colour electronic slides for computer aided drawing and light modulators for colour electronic imaging.
- **Biological systems:** liquid crystal compounds exists as lipid or sterol derivatives in various body parts like liver, kidney spleen, brain etc.

EXERCISES

I. SHORT ANSWER TYPE QUESTIONS

1. What are liquid crystals? Explain.
2. How does a liquid crystal differ from that of a solid and an isotropic liquid?
3. How are liquid crystals classified? Give an example in each case.
4. Write short notes on:
   (*a*) Thermotropic liquid crystals (*b*) Lyotropic liquid crystals.
5. Distinguish between nematic and smectic liquid crystals.
6. Explain the following:
   (*a*) Nematic liquid crystals (*b*) Smectic liquid crystals
   (*c*) Cholesteric liquid crystals.

II. LONG ANSWER TYPE QUESTIONS

1. Discuss the vapour pressure temperature curves for ordinary substance and liquid crystals.
2. Write various applications of liquid crystals in detail.

III. MULTIPLE CHOICE QUESTIONS

1. Liquid crystals are generally composed of:
   (*a*) Oval molecules (*b*) Circular molecules
   (*c*) Rod like molecules (*d*) All of the above.
2. The properties of liquid crystals are intermediate between
   (*a*) Solid-liquid state (*b*) Liquid-vapour state
   (*c*) Solid-vapour state (*d*) None of the above.
3. Melting point of cholesteryl benzoate is
   (*a*) 145°C (*b*) 165°C
   (*c*) 125°C (*d*) 178°C.
4. The point at which solid changes into turbid liquid (liquid crystal) is known as
   (*a*) Melting point (*b*) Transition point
   (*c*) Eutectic point (*d*) triple point
5. First liquid phase was discovered in
   (*a*) Cholesteryl benzoate (*b*) Cholesteryl propanoate
   (*c*) Cholesteryl ethanoate (*d*) Cholesteryl methanoate.

6. Liquid crystals which flow like near normal flow behaviour of liquids
   (*a*) Smectic liquid crystals (*b*) Nematic liquid crystals
   (*c*) Cholesteric liquid crystals (*d*) All of the above.
7. The appearance of nematic liquid crystals is
   (*a*) Gel like substance (*b*) Slippery (soapy) substance
   (*c*) Thread like substance (*d*) All of the above.
8. Chiral liquid crystals are
   (*a*) Smectic liquid crystals (*b*) nematic liquid crystals
   (*c*) Cholesteric liquid crystals (*d*) Lyotropic liquid crystals.
9. Which of the following is a thermotropic liquid crystal
   (*a*) Phospholipids (*b*) α-lecithin
   (*c*) Sodium laurate (*d*) *p*-azoxyanisole.
10. Lyotropic mesomorphism in a substance is introduced by
   (*a*) Adding solute (*b*) Adding solvent
   (*c*) Increasing temperature (*d*) Decreasing temperature.
11. The flow of cholesteric and smectic liquid crystals is respectively
   (*a*) Newtonian, Non-newtonian (*b*) Non newtonian, Newtonian
   (*c*) Both non-newtonian (*d*) Both newtonian.
12. Liquid thermometers use ________ liquid crystals
   (*a*) Smectic (*b*) Nematic
   (*c*) Cholesteric (*d*) Lyotropic.
13. The liquid crystal which shows colour change with temperature
   (*a*) Smectic (*b*) Nematic
   (*c*) Cholesteric (*d*) Lyotropic.
14. Liquid crystals in which the molecules are arranged parallel to each other in layers and the layers can slip over each other are
   (*a*) Smectic (*b*) Nematic
   (*c*) Lyotropic (*d*) Cholesteric.
15. Cholesteric mesophase are exhibited by ________ molecules.
   (*a*) Enantiomeric (*b*) Optically active
   (*c*) Optically inactive (*d*) Diastereomeric.
16. Helical or spiral structure are shown by ________ liquid crystals.
   (*a*) Cholesteric (*b*) Nematic
   (*c*) Smectic (*d*) Both (*b*) and (*c*).

Answers

MULTIPLE CHOICE QUESTIONS

1. (*c*)	**2.** (*a*)	**3.** (*a*)	**4.** (*b*)	**5.** (*a*)	**6.** (*b*)	**7.** (*c*)	**8.** (*c*)	**9.** (*d*)	**10.** (*b*)
11. (*c*)	**12.** (*c*)	**13.** (*c*)	**14.** (*a*)	**15.** (*b*)	**16.** (*a*)				

Chapter 13 Nanomaterials

13.1 INTRODUCTION

Nano materials are the cornerstone of nano science and nano technology. Nano science is a broad, interdisciplinary area of research and development that has been growing explosively all over the world in the past few years. It has the potential for revolutionizing the manner in which materials and products are designed and the range and nature of functionalities that can be assessed. It is already having a significant commercial impact which will definitely increase in the times to come.

One nano metre is equal to 1 billionth of a metre approximately 1,00,000 times smaller than the diameter of a human hair. The term nano technology refers to the engineered structures, devices and systems having length scale of 1 to 100 nm. Exact history of utilization of nano sized objects by humans is difficult to clarify. However, the history of their utilization is ancient, human beings used these particles a long time ago for various applications unknowningly for examples PbS nano particles was used by Egyptians 4000 years ago in a hair dyeing formula, humans exploited asbestos nano fibers for ceramic mixtures around 4500 years ago.

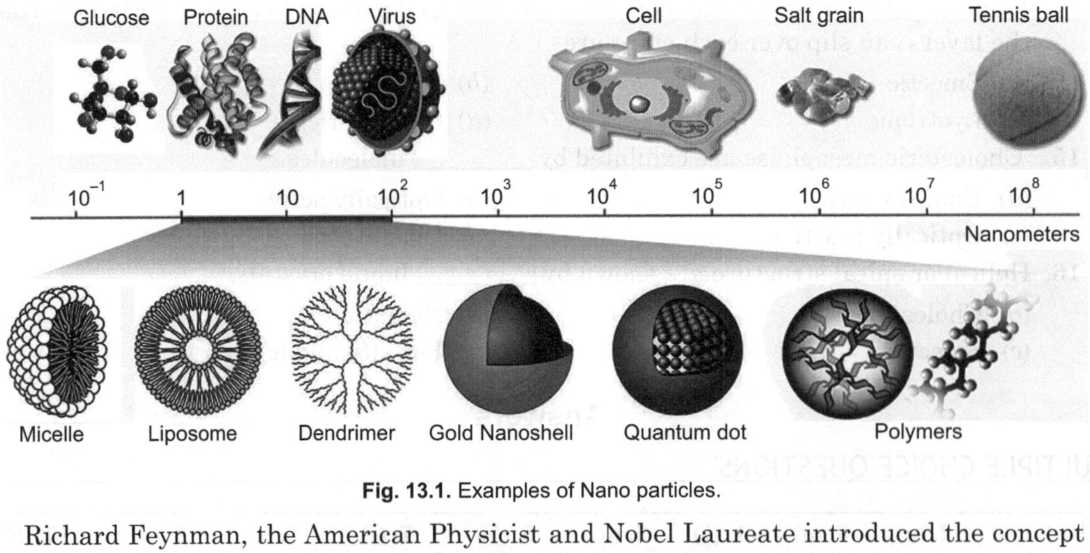

Fig. 13.1. Examples of Nano particles.

Richard Feynman, the American Physicist and Nobel Laureate introduced the concept of nano technology in the year 1959 while addressing an annual meeting of American physical society. In this meeting, he presented a lecture entitled "there is plenty of room at the bottom" in which he presented that "why can't we write the entire 24 volumes of the Encyclopedia

Britannica on the head of a pin". His idea was to develop smaller machines down to the molecular level. He is often considered as the father of modern nano technology. The term nano technology was first used by Norio Taniguchi in 1974. He stated "nano technology mainly consist of the processing of separation, consolidation and deformation of materials by one atom or one molecule.

Currently nano technology is rapidly evolving and becoming part of almost every field associated with material chemistry. Nano -materials find applications in electronics, cosmetics, surface coating, sports equipment, sensors, scratch free paints, energy storage devices etc.

13.2 CLASSIFICATION OF NANO PARTICLES

Nano particles can be divided on the basis of

A. Physical and Chemical properties, B. Number of dimensions

13.2.1 Physical and Chemical Properties

Nano particles are broadly divided into various categories depending on their physical and chemical properties. Few well known classes of nano particles are:

(*i*) Carbon based nano particles: (organic nano particles) *e.g.* fullerenes, carbon nano tutes etc.

(*ii*) Metal based nano particles: (Inorganic nano particles) *e.g.* nano particles of alkali and noble metals, nano particles of metal oxides etc.

(*iii*) Nano composites

(*iv*) Dendrimers

Carbon based Nano particles

These nano particles are completely made up of carbon and are called as carbon based nano particles. They can be classified into fullereness, graphene, carbon nano tubes (CNIs), carbon nano cones, carbon based quantum dots and many more.

Fullerenes

Fullerenes are an amazing isotope of carbon first discovered by Harold Kroto, Richard Smalley and Robert Curl in 1985. They are highly symmetrical cages of sp^2 hybridized carbon atoms. They occur in different sizes according to the number of carbon atoms joined together. For example, C_{60}, C_{70}, C_{72}, C_{76}, C_{84} and C_{100}. Out of all these available fullerenes, C_{60} is the most abundant and famous example. C_{60} fullerene consists of a hollow structure comprising of 12 pentagons and 20 hexagons made up of 60 carbon atoms which are held together by sp^2 hybridization (a design that resembles a football). It was named as **Buckminster fullerene** or **buckyball**. The name was chosen because the geodesic domes which were invented by Buckminster Fuller provided a clue that the atoms in a molecule can be arranged in the form of a hollow cage. C_{60} molecules are held together by weak Van der Waal's forces. They are insoluble in ionic solvents like water, ammonia, HCl as it is non-ionic. It is an organic molecule, therefore it is soluble in organic compounds like benzene. Fullerene is a good example of zero dimensional material (materials where all dimensions are at nano scale *i.e.* < 100 nm) due to its small, spherical and isotropic nature. The structure of Fullerene is shown in Fig. 13.2.

Applications of Fullerenes

1. Fullerenes are used as biological antioxidants.
2. They find potential medical applications because of their ability to bind specific antibiotics and target certain types of cancer cells.
3. They are used as catalysts in hydrogenation reactions.
4. Fullerenes and their derivatives find potential antiviral activity and may find application in the treatment of HIV infections.

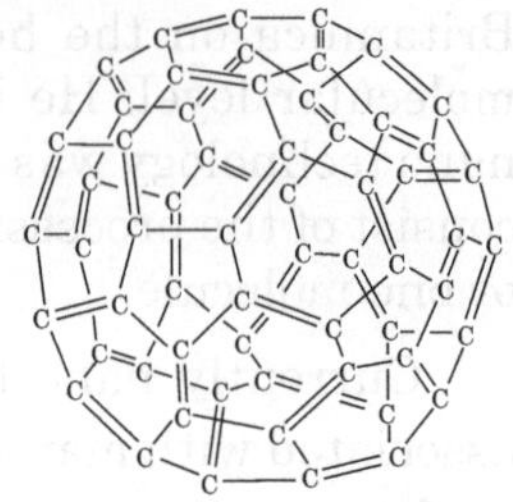

Fig. 13.2. Fullerene C_{60}.

Graphene

Graphene was first isolated by Geim and Novoselov at the university of Manchester in 2004. They received Noble prize in 2010 for their pioneering work. Graphene is an allotrope of carbon. Graphene is a hexagonal network of honeycomb lattice made up of sp^2-hybridized carbon atoms in a two dimensional planar structure. It is one of the thinnest known material which possesses excellent mechanical strength. It is transparent in nature and possesses exceptionally high surface area. The surface area of graphene is much higher as compared to fullerenes, graphite and carbon nano tubes. Due to higher surface area of graphene, it possesses high thermal conductivity. The structure of graphene is shown in Fig. 13.3.

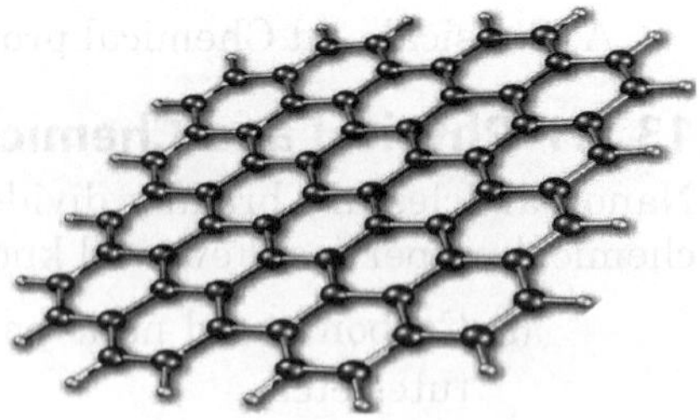

Fig. 13.3. Graphene.

Applications of Graphene

1. Graphene based nano materials have many promising applications in energy related areas.
   (*a*) It improves both charge rate and energy capacity in rechargeable batteries.
   (*b*) Graphene electrodes may find application in making solar cells which are inexpensive, lightweight and flexible.
   (*c*) Activated graphene makes superior supercapacitors for storing energy.
2. It is also used in building transperent light panels and touch screens.

Carbon Nano tubes (CNTs)

The carbon nano tubes (elongated form of fullerenes) were discovered in 1991 by a Japanese scientist, Iijima Sumio. CNTs are elongated, tubular structure, 1–2 nm in diameter. Structurally they resemble to graphite sheet rolling upon itself. The rolled graphene sheets can be single, double or multi walled and therefore, they are named as single walled (SWNTs), double walled (DWNTs) or multi-walled nano tubes (MWNTs) respectively. The diameter of SWNTs was found to be in the range of 0.4 to 2 nm. The inner wall distance between DWNTs was found to be in the range of 0.33 to 0.42 nm. For MWNTs, the inner wall distance is approximately 0.34 nm and the diameter is in the range of 2 – 100 nm. The structure of carbon nano tubes is shown in Fig. 13.4.

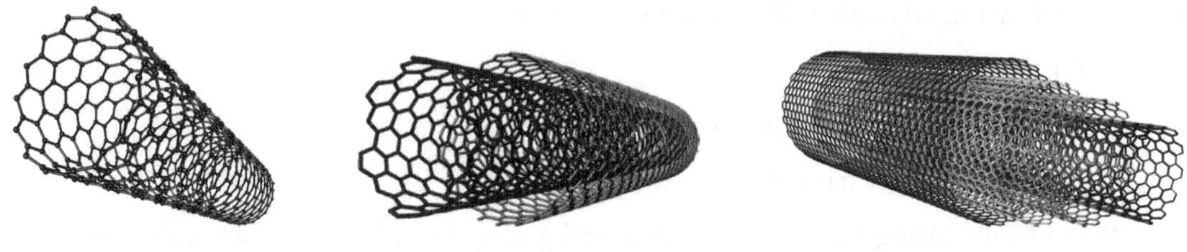

(a) Single walled (SWNT's) (b) DWNTs (c) MWNTs carbon nano tubes

Fig. 13.4. Carbon nano tubes.

Applications of Carbon Nano tubes

1. They are ideal reinforcing agents due to their high tensile strength and aspect ratio.
2. They are used in the design of electronic devices such as rectifying diode, single electron transistors, etc.
3. They are used in Lithium ion batteries, solar panels.
4. They find applications in various devices like energy storage, boat hulls, water filters, thin film electronic coatings etc.

Carbon Nano cones/Nano horns

Carbon nano horns (CNHs) are the conical shaped carbon nano structures sometimes also referred as carbon nano cones. They are first explored by Harris et al. from the waste product of shoot which is formed during synthesis of fullerene via arc discharge process. Single walled carbon nano horns (SWCNHs) are newly discovered aggregates of single wall carbon nano tubes with closed ends. However, SWCNHs differ considerably from SWNTs in that they have long cone shaped tips with cone angle of about 20° and large tube diameter of .2 – 5 nm and thousands of SWCNHs form spherical aggregates with diameters of 80 – 100 nm approximately. The structure of carbon nano cones is given in Fig. 13.5.

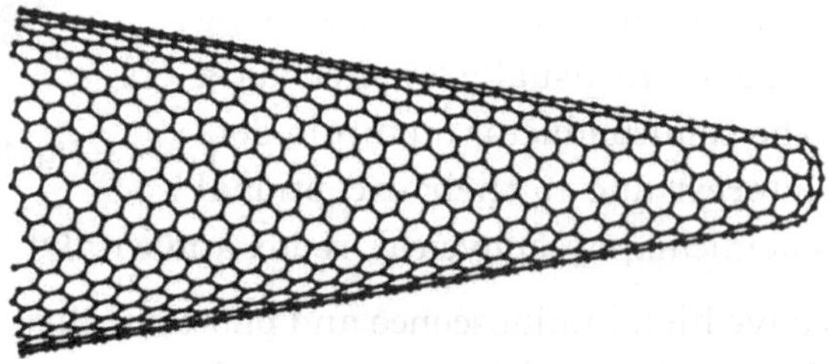

Fig. 13.5. Carbon nano horns/nano cones.

Applications of Carbon Nano horns/Nano cones

1. They have great potential for energy storage, electrochemiluminescence, adsorption, catalyst support, electrochemical sensing, drug delivery systems etc.

2. They have interesting applications in nano lithography.

Carbon based quantum dots: Carbon quantum dots were accidently formed during the electrophoretic purification of SWCTs in 2004. These nano particles are zero dimensional discrete and quasi spherical nano particles which are less than 10 nm in size. They possess several unique properties like:

(*i*) good water solubility due to rich oxygen containing groups.

(*ii*) excellent chemical stability

(*iii*) low toxicity, photobleaching resistance

(*iv*) biocompatability

(*v*) excellent optical properties

(*vi*) environment friendly.

Due to their strong luminescence properties they are also called as carbon nano lights.

Applications of Carbon Based Quantum Dots

1. Used in developing efficient sensors for detecting explosives like TNT.
2. Doped quantum dots are capable of biological imaging and also display advanced capacity for scavanging reactive oxygen species.
3. Find applications in the fields of nano medicine, solar cells, catalysis, light emitting diodes, drug delivery etc.

Inorganic Based Nano particles

Inorganic nano particles represent a new era in the nano particle field. They exhibit unique physical and chemical properties and find applications in various physical, biological, biomedical and pharmaceutical fields. Inorganic nano particles include metal nano particles, metal oxide nano particles, semiconductor quantum dots, silicon nano particles etc.

Fig. 13.6. Carbon quantum dots.

Gold nano particles are particularly used with photothermal agents in cancer therapy and biosensing whereas silica nano structures are usually applied as a support for drug loading. The semiconductor quantum dots have gained widespread interest due to their exceptional optical, electronic, electrochemical, photophysical, redox and catalytic properties.

Silicon nano particles have high luminescence and photostability properties therefore they are highly demanded in bioimaging and biosensor applications, especially in optical based sensors.

Metal oxide nano particles like iron oxide nano particles (Fe_2O_3, Fe_3O_4), gadolinium oxide nano particles (Gd_2O_3) and manganese oxide nano particles (MnO, Mn_3O_4) are the most frequently used magnetic nano particles that have find various applications in clinical MRI. To make these metal oxides biocompatible for biological applications, they are generally coated with various water soluble molecules like cationic polymers, cationic lipids and dendrimers.

Applications of Inorganic Nano particles

1. They find applications in drug delivery, cancer therepy and other therapeutic applications.
2. They are highly demanded in bioimaging and biosensor applications.

Nano composites

A nano composite combines two or more materials of which atleast one is a nano material with different physical and chemical properties. Nano composite materials are designed to exhibit properties that exceed sometimes drastically the capabilities of the sum of their constituent parts. Properties that showed considerable improvements:

- mechanical strength
- electrical and thermal conductivity
- reduce smoke generation
- increased chemical resistance
- resistance to corrosion.

Nano composites are manufactured by embedding materials (reinforcing phase) into another material (matrix phase). Either one or both phases can be nano materials. The reinforcing phase brings to the composite material its greater mechanical performance while the role of the matrix is to transmit to the fiber (a reinforcing phase) to the external mechanical load and protect it from external attack. Composites are generally classified on the basis of material used for the matrix phase like polymer matrix composites, metal matrix composites, ceramic matrix composites and carbon matrix composites. Among all these nano composites, polymer matrix composites are the most widely used nano composites.

Applications of nano composites: Nano composites are currently being used in a number of fields and new applications are being continuously developed. In the future, nano composites can be used to develop the wings of jets that could be as light as balsa wood yet stronger than the toughest metal alloys. Various applications of nano composites include:

(a) Producing batteries with greater power output.

(b) Speeding up the healing process for broken bones.

(c) Making light weight sensors with nano composites.

(d) Making flexible batteries

(e) Making tumors easier to see and remove

(f) They are used in aerospace automobile and marine applications. Recently, composite materials have been increasingly considered in civil engineering structures.

(g) Stents are made with steel and more recently with composite materials.

13.2.2 Number of Dimensions

According to Siegel, nano structured materials are classified as:

(*i*) zero-dimensional	(*ii*) one-dimensional
(*iii*) two-dimensional	(*iv*) three-dimensional.

(*i*) Zero-dimensional nano particles (0D): Nano materials wherein all the dimensions (x, y, z) are measured within the nano scale *i.e.* no dimensions are greater than 100 nm. For example, nano spheres and nano clusters (Fig. 13.7)

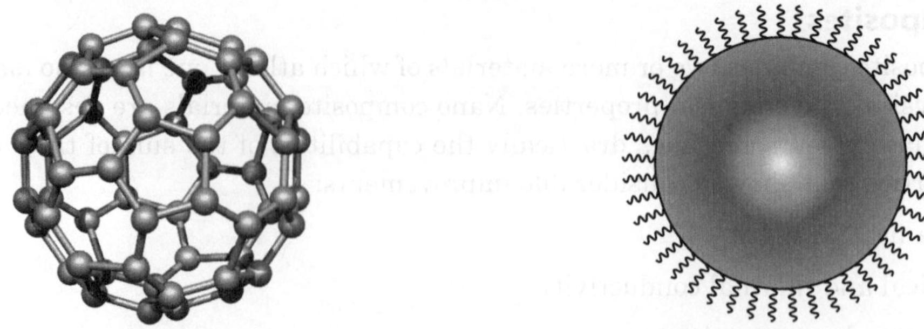

(a) Fullerenes (b) Gold nano particles

Fig. 13.7. Zero dimensional nano particles

(*ii*) **One-dimensional nano particles (1D):** Nano materials where in two dimensions are at nano scale and one dimension is outside the nano scale. This leads to needle shaped nano materials. For example, nano tubes, nano rods, nano fibres and nano wires (Fig. 13.8)

(*a*) Carbon nano tubes (*b*) gold nano wires

Fig. 13.8. One dimensional nano particles

(*iii*) **Two-dimensional nano particles (2D):** Nano materials wherein one dimension is at nano scale and two dimensions are outside the nano scale. 2-D nano materials exhibit plate like shapes. For example, nano films, nano coatings and nano layers (Fig. 13.9)

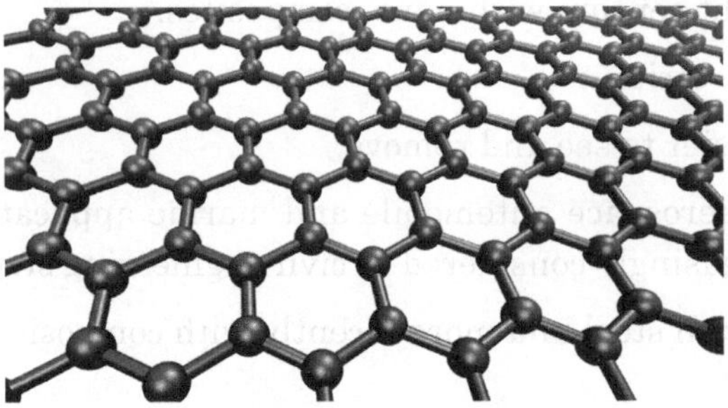

Graphene sheets.

Fig. 13.9. 2-D- nano particles.

(*iv*) **Three-dimensional nano particles (3D):** Nano materials that are not confined to the nano scale in any dimension. These nano materials are therefore, characterised by three arbitrarily dimensions above 100 nm. For example, bulk powders, dispersions of nano particles, bundles of nano wires and nano tubes (Fig. 13.10) as well as multi-monolayers wherein 0D, 1D, 2D structural elements are in close contact with each other and form interfaces.

Fig. 13.10. 3-D-nano particles.

13.3 SYNTHESIS OF NANO MATERIALS

There are two general approaches for the synthesis of nano material these are:

(*i*) Top down approach (*ii*) Bottom up approach

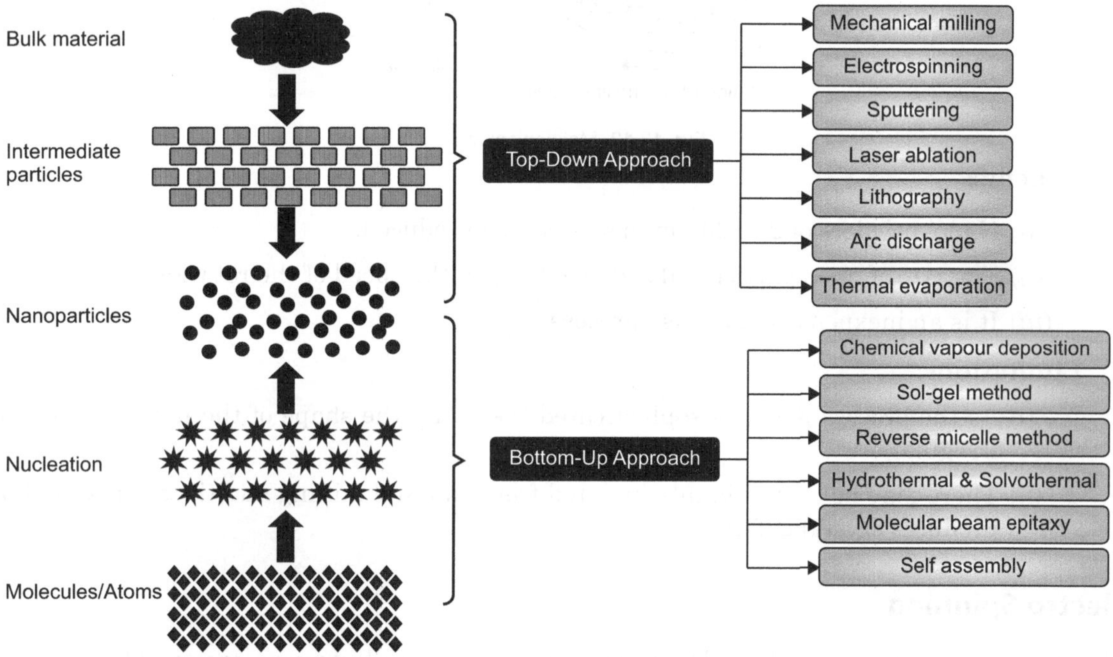

Fig. 13.11. Approaches for nano material synthesis.

13.3.1 Top Down Approach

This type of approach involve the breaking down of the bulk material into nano sized structures or particles. Top down approaches are inherently simpler and depend either on removal or division of bulk material or on miniaturization of bulk fabrication processes to produce the desired structure with suitable properties. Top down methods include mechanical milling, electro spinning, lithography, sputtering, arc discharge method and laser ablation.

Mechanical Milling

It is a cost effective method for producing blends of different phases and it is useful in the production of nano -composites. In mechanical milling, a suitable powder mixture is placed in a high energy mill alongwith the suitable milling medium. The purpose of milling is to reduce the particle size and blending of particles in new phases. The different types of ball milling can be used to synthesis nano particles in which ball impact upon the powder mixture. It takes approximately 100 to 150 hours to get uniform fine powder. It is used to produce wear resistant spray coatings, oxide and carbide strengthened aluminium alloys, Cu/Ni/Mg/Al- based nano alloys and many other nano composite materials.

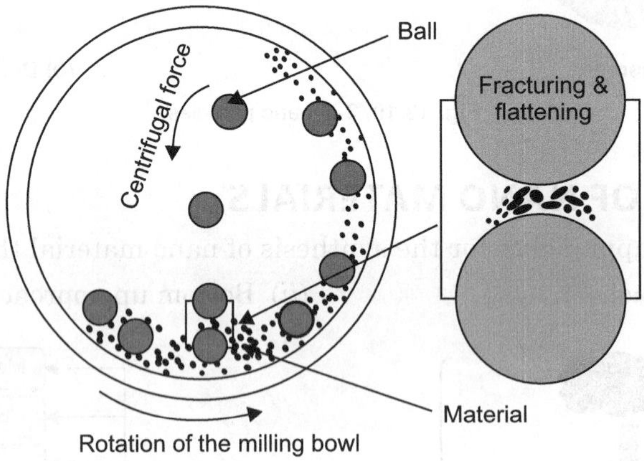

Fig. 13.12. Mechanical milling.

Benefits:

(*i*) Nano powders of 2 to 20 nm in size can be produced.

(*ii*) The size of nano particles also depends upon the speed of the rotation of the balls.

(*iii*) It is an inexpensive and easy process.

Limitations:

(*i*) As the process is not so sophisticated therefore, the shape of the nano material is irregular.

(*ii*) There may be contaminants inserted from ball and milling additives. This method produces crystal defects.

Electro Spinning

The electro spinning method is used to generate a nonwoven web of micro- or nano fibers. In this method, high voltage electricity is applied to the liquid solution and a collector, which lets the solution extrude from a nozzle forming a jet. The jet formed fibers during drying and deposited these on the collector. Electro spinning is a simple and versatile method for preparation of micro- or nano polymer fibers. Inorganic fibers can also be prepared by electro spinning with polymers incorporated in the precursor solution. Electro spinning is influenced by several parameters, such as the viscosity, the operating voltage, the temperature, the pressure, and the flow rate. Viscosity is a key parameter in electro spinning because it is related to the extent that the polymer molecule chain is entangled within the solution. Electro spinning finds use in several industries: life science, biotextiles, biomedical engineering, battery research, and the overall development, production and commercialization of nano fiber materials.

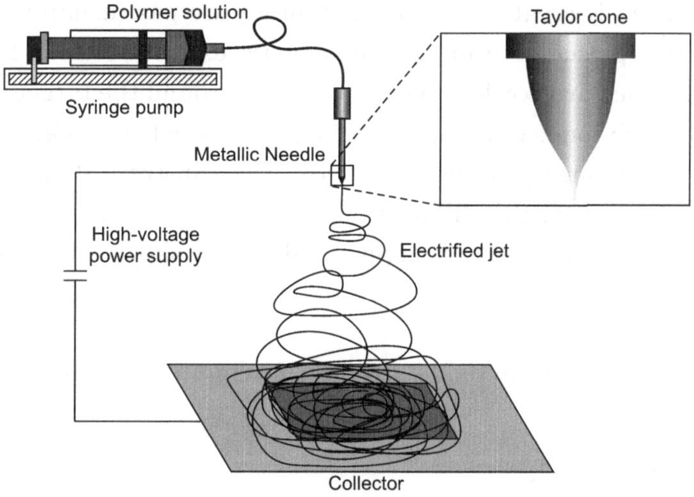

Fig. 13.13. Electro spinning process.

Benefits: The main advantages of electro spinning technique over other fabrication methods is its versatility to create fibers with multiple arrangements (ex. aligned fibers, random orientations, or their combinations) and morphological structures (ex. tubular scaffolds, flat surfaces, and asymmetrical configurations).

Limitations: The solution flow rate during the single-needle electro spinning process generally varies from 0.1 to 0.3 mL/h, which results in very low nano fiber production and seriously limits the large-scale production of electrospun nano fibers and the promotion of their products.

Sputtering

Sputtering is a technique to deposit thin films of different materials onto a surface. Materials such as metals, plastics and ceramics are deposited on a surface through different processes, and the sputtering process is one among them. It is a process used to produce nano -particles by bombarding solid surfaces with high energy particles like plasma or gas. The principle of sputtering is to use the energy of a plasma (partially ionized gas) on the surface of a target (cathode), to pull the atoms of the material one by one and deposit them on the substrate.

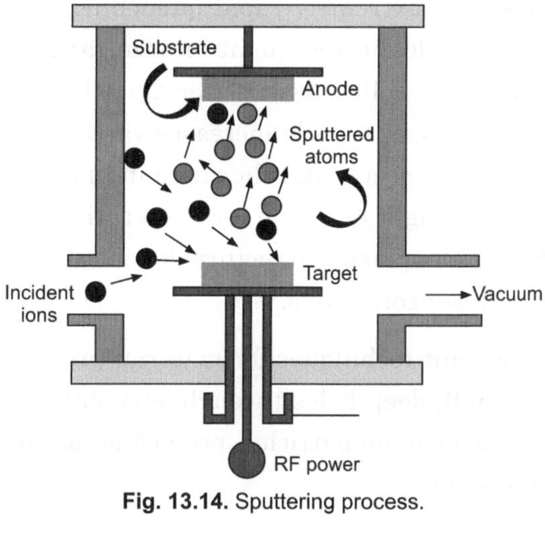

Fig. 13.14. Sputtering process.

To do this, a plasma is created by ionization of a pure gas (usually Argon) by means of a potential difference (pulsed DC) or electromagnetic excitation (MF, RF); this plasma is compoed of Ar^+ ions which are accelerated and confined around the target due to the presence of a magnetic field. Each ionized atom, by striking the target, transfers its energy and rips an atom, having enough energy to be projected to the substrate. It is considered to be an effective method for producing thin films of nano materials. It has been used to prepare Ag nano particles, WSe_2 layout nano films on SiO_2 and carbon paper substrates.

Benefits:

1. Insulators (*e.g.* aluminium oxide or boron nitride) and semiconductors can also be sputtered.
2. The substrate heats up less.
3. Due to the oscillating electrons, the sputtering rate at the same chamber pressure is about 10 times higher than with DC sputtering.

Limitations:

1. Relatively low coating rates.
2. The RF generation is more expensive than a DC voltage source.
3. For large rectangular cathodes (> 1 m), unevenness in the plasma density (layer thickness distribution) may occur.

Laser Ablation

Laser ablation is a method for fabricating various kinds of nano particles including semiconductor quantum dots, carbon nano tubes, nano wires and core shell nano particles. In this method, nano particles are generated by nucleation and growth of laser-vapourized species in a background gas. The extremely rapid quenching of vapour is advantageous in producing high purity nano particles in the quantum size range (< 10 nm). When the laser beam is focussed on the surface of a solid target material in the ambient media (gas or liquid) the temperature of the irradiated spot rapidly increases vapourizing the target material. The collisions between the evaporated species and the surrounding molecules result in excitation of the electron state coupled with light emission and generation of electrons and ions forming a laser induced plasma plume. The plasma structure depend on the target material, ambient media, ambient pressure and laser conditions.

It is one of the most important techniques for material processing. Laser ablation can be used for drilling extremely small, deep holes through very hard materials such as metals or diamonds, producing thin films or nano particles, preparing material surface in a micro- and nano -controlled fashion, and so on.

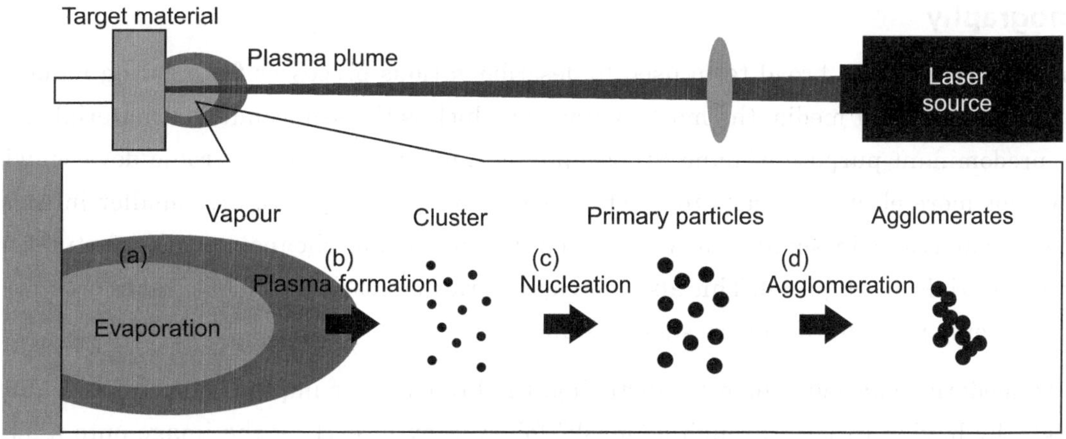

Fig. 13.15. Laser ablation.

Benefits:

1. Laser ablation uses a laser with appropriate power settings to heat and ablate an area. This makes it a non-contact process. As a result, laser ablation eliminates the need for the use of consumables (*e.g.*, drill bits) and reduces the operating costs of the manufacturing process.

2. Laser ablation also provides an effective way of cleaning the surface of the workpiece without using any chemicals. This prevents damage to surfaces and reduces the need for a robust drainage system, which again reduces manufacturing costs and environmental footprint.

3. Furthermore, laser cutters are CNC machines that can be easily automated to perform operations with high precision. This reduces the need for skilled labour and increases the repeatability of manufacturing operations.

Limitations:

1. Laser ablation involves the burning and vapourization of material, which can generate heavy fumes and requires a good exhaust system to extract the fumes from the work area.

2. Without proper fume extraction, the fumes might interfere with the laser beam and reduce the efficiency of the process.

3. Lasers are high-energy beams of light, capable of causing severe health and fire hazards.

4. Even though laser ablation has low operative costs, it has a higher start-up cost than most manufacturing techniques.

5. It is disadvantaged by high energy input and the smaller laser irradiating area for evaporating the target materials therefore, laser ablation application have been limited to exploring unique properties of new types of materials. They cannot be used for large scale production.

Lithography

Nano lithography is a broad term used to describe various processes for creating nano scale patterns on different media, the most common of which is the semiconductor material silicon. The predominant purpose of nano lithography is the shrinking of electronic devices, which allows for more electronic parts to be crammed into smaller spaces, *i.e.*, smaller integrated circuits that result in smaller devices, which are faster and cheaper to manufacture since fewer materials are required. This also increases performance and response times because the electrons only need to travel very short distances.

In modern semiconductor manufacturing, the lithographer imposes structure on a beam of light by having it pass through a "mask" followed by projecting the image onto a silicon wafer coated with a thin layer of material called resist (Fig. 13.16). The resist undergoes a chemical transformation when exposed to light. This transformation alters the solubility of the material so that when placed in a developer of an appropriate solvent the latent pattern image transforms into a patterned chemical stencil. This chemical stencil then serves as the template for further process steps. Deposition and etching tools add or remove material as needed through the openings in the chemical stencil. Another process step strips away the chemical stencil and a fresh layer of resist is applied. The process repeats until all of the device levels necessary to build a full device have been assembled. The enormous productivity of modern electronics is driven by the capability of a single lithographic machine to pattern features at a rate in excess of 100 trillion features per hour.

Some techniques used in nano lithography are as follows:

- **X-ray lithography:** Implemented through a proximity printing approach and relies on near-field X-rays in Fresnel diffraction. It is known to extend its optical resolution to 15 nm.
- **Double patterning:** A method used to increase the pitch resolution of a lithographic process by printing additional patterns between spaces of already printed patterns in the same layer.
- **Electron-beam direct-write (EBDW) lithography:** The most common process used in lithographic, which uses a beam of electrons to create patterns.
- **Extreme ultraviolet (EUV) lithogrphy:** A form of optical lithography that makes use of ultrashort light wavelengths of 13.5 nm.

This technology can be suitable to use in nano fabrication of various semiconductor integrated circuits (IC's), NEMS and for various applications in research. The modification in semiconductor chips at the nano level is also possible.

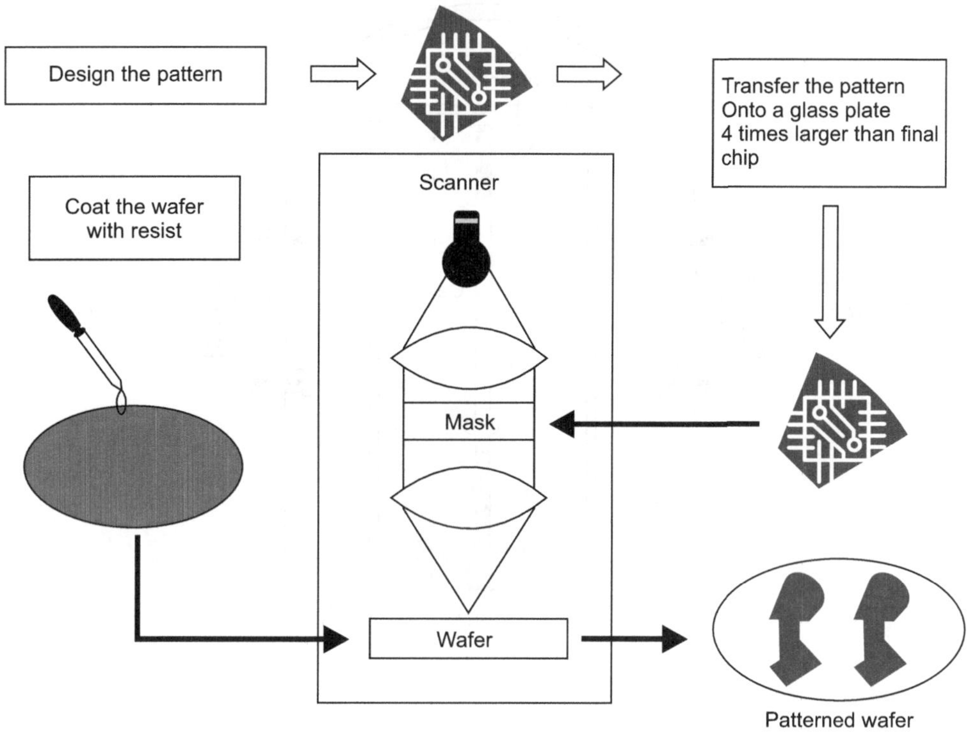

Fig. 13.16. Nano lithography.

Arc Discharge Method

The principle of this technique is to vapourize carbon in the presence of catalysts (iron, nickel, cobalt, yttrium, boron, gadolinium, etc. under reduced atmosphere of inert gas (argon or helium). In this method the graphite electrodes of high purity acts as cathode and anode and held at short distance apart under a Helium atmosphere. After the triggering of the arc between two electrodes, a plasma is formed consisting of the mixture of carbon vapour, the rare gas (helium or argon), and the vapours of catalysts. The vapourization is the consequence of the energy transfer from the arc to the anode made of graphite doped with catalysts. The anode erosion rate is more or less important depending on the power of the arc and also on the other experimental conditions. It is noteworthy that a high anode erosion does not necessarily lead to a high carbon nano tube production.

It consists of a cylinder of about 30 cm in diameter and about 1m in height, equipped with diametrically opposed sapphire windows located so that they face the plasma zone in view of observing the arc. The reactor possesses two valves, one for carrying out the primary evacuation (0.1 Pa) of the chamber, the other permitting it to fill with a rare gas up to the desired working pressure.

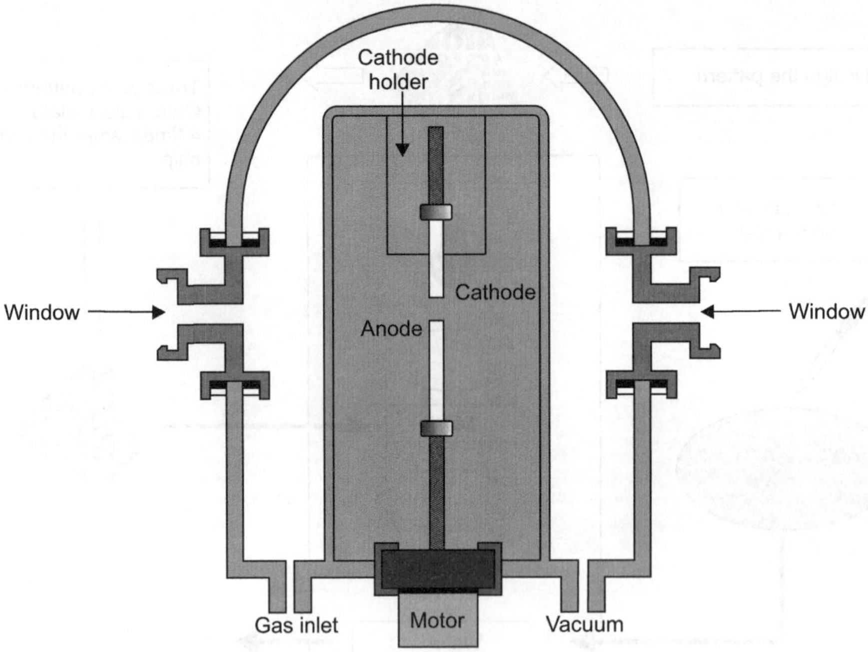

Fig. 13.17. Arc discharge method.

Benefits:

1. Arc discharges tend to produce narrower and shorter tubes than those obtained from laser ablation (up to 5 nm in diameter and around 1 mm long).
2. Simple and easy method producing few structural defect.

Limitations:

Short tubes of random sizes requiring high degree of purification.

Thermal Evaporation

Thermal evaporation is a well-known method for coating a thin layer in which the source material evaporates in a vacuum due to high temperature heating, which facilitates the vapour particles moving and directly reaching a substrate where these vapors again change to a solid state. In this method, a charge holding boat or resistive coil is used in the form of a powder or solid bar. In order to get the high melting points necessary for metals, the resistive boat/coil is exposed to a large direct current (DC), where the high vacuum (below 10^{-4} Pa) supports the evaporation of the metal and further carrying it to the substrate. This technique is specially applicable for material with low melting points.

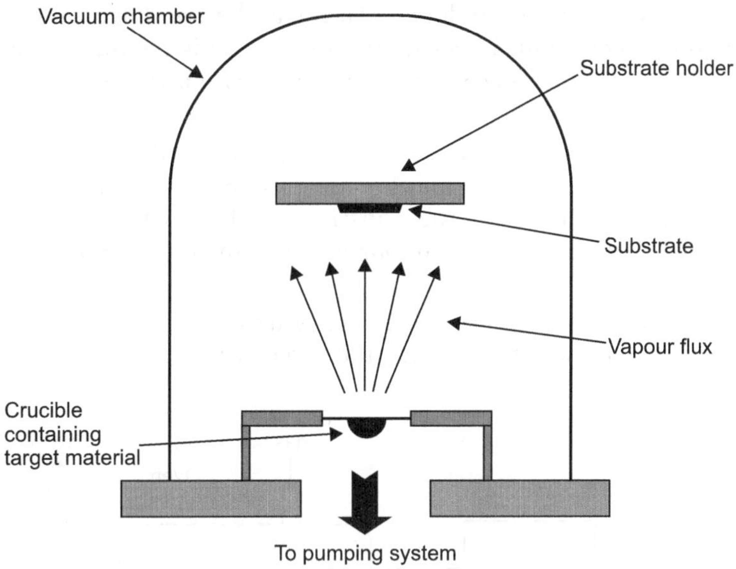

Fig. 13.18. Thermal evaporation.

Benefits:

1. One of the most salient advantages of thermal vacuum evaporation is that it enables fabrication of multilayer devices in which the thickness of each layer can be controlled easily.
2. Developed films have higher purity and good quality.
3. Little residual gas impurities in corporation due to high vacuum conditions.
4. Widely used to form metal contacts to the devices.

Limitations:

1. One of the disadvantages of thermal vapour deposition technique is the requirement of precise control of temperature during deposition as both precursor sources and the products have low thermal stability.
2. Materials with low vapour pressure are very difficult to deposit.
3. It covers limited steps and needs material heating.
4. Material stoichiometry in compounds and alloys deposition is difficult.

13.3.2 Bottom up Approach

Bottom up approach refers to the building up of a material from the bottom : atom by atom molecule by molecule or cluster by cluster. This process has the potential to create less waste and hence is more economical as compared to top down approaches.

Chemical Vapour Deposition (CVD)

It is a method to produce thin films by chemical reaction on the surface of substrate by using precursors like gaseous compounds, elemental substances containing thin film elements. For CVD, a suitable precursor is one which has adequate volatility, high chemical purity, low cost, good stability during evaporation, long shelf life and a non-hazardous nature. Moreover, it's decomposition should not result in residual impurity. This technique involves exposure of the substrate to precursors which decomposes the substrate and react with it to produce the desired deposit.

In this process, vapourized precursors are first adsorbed on to a substrate at high temperature and then react with one another or decompose and produce crystals. In this method nano sheets are produced on the substrate with or without the help of catalysts. However, the choice of catalyst place an important role in the morphology and type of nano material produced.

For example in the CVD based preparation of graphene, if copper catalyst is used it will produce monolayer graphene whereas nickel and cobalt catalyst result in formation of multi layer graphene.

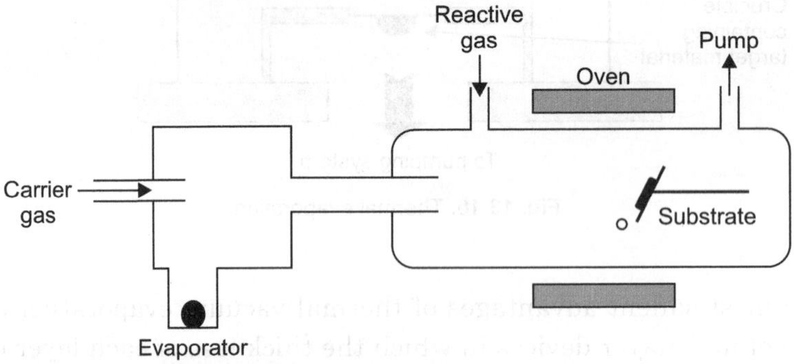

Fig. 13.19. Chemical vapour deposition.

Sol-gel Method

The sol-gel process is a more chemical method (wet chemical method) for the synthesis of various nano structures, especially metal oxide nano particles. In this method, the molecular precursor (usually metal alkoxide) is dissolved in water or alcohol and converted to gel by heating and stirring by hydrolysis/alcoholysis. Since the gel obtained from the hydrolysis/ alcoholysis process is wet or damp, it should be dried using appropriate methods depending on the desired properties and application of the gel. For example, if it is an alcoholic solution, the drying process is done by burning alcohol. After the drying stage, the produced gels are powdered and then calcined.

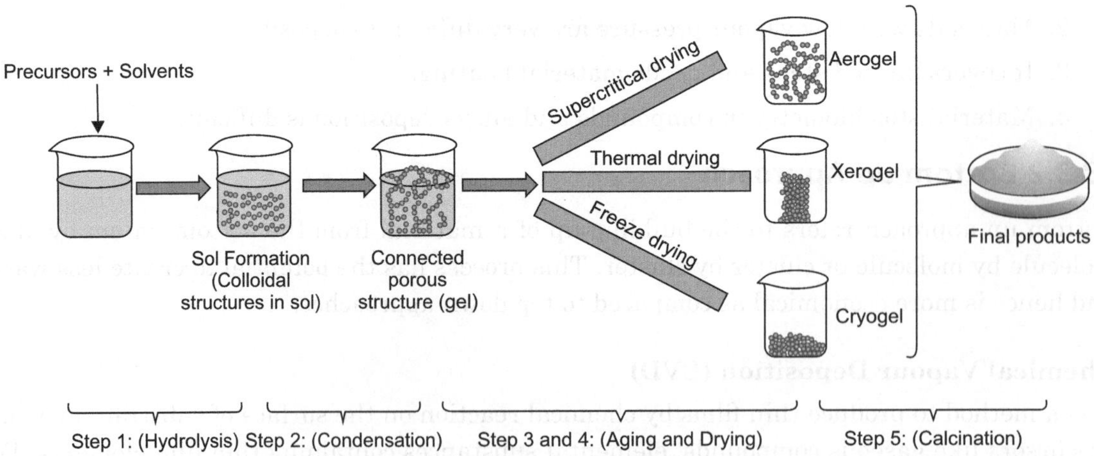

Fig. 13.20. Sol-gel method.

The basis of the sol-gel method is the production of a homogeneous sol from the precursors and its conversion into a gel. The solvent in the gel is then removed from the gel structure and the remaining gel is dried. The properties of the dried gel depend significantly on the drying method. In other words, the "removing solvent method" is selected according to the application in which the gel will be used. Dried gels in various ways are used in industries such as surface coating, building insulation and the production of special clothing. It is worth mentioning that by grinding the gel by special mills, it is possible to achieve nano particles.

The sol-gel method can be used in the process of making ceramics as a molding material and can be used as an intermediate between thin films of metal oxides in various applications. The materials obtained from the sol-gel method are used in various optical, electronic, energy, surface engineering, biosensors, pharmaceutics and separation technologies (such as chromatography).

Benefits:

1. The sol-gel method is a cost-effective method and due to the low reaction temperature there is good control over the chemical composition of the products.
2. It can produce a thin coating to ensure excellent adhesion between the substrate and the top layer.
3. It can produce a thick coating to provide protection against corrosion.
4. Capacity of sintering at low temperature between 200 to 600 degree centigrade.
5. It synthesizes high purity products because the organometallic precursor of ceramic oxide can be dissolved in a specified solvent and hydrolysed in a sol and subsequently a gel, the composition can be highly controllable.
6. It is a simple, economical and efficient method to produce high quality coverage.

Limitations:

1. The contradiction that occurs during processing.
2. The residual hydroxyl or carbon groups.
3. It has long processing time.
4. Use of organic solutions that can be toxic.

Reverse Micelle Method

Synthesis of nano materials with desired shape and size is very important for the potential applications. This technique is very useful for producing nano particles with desired shape and sizes.

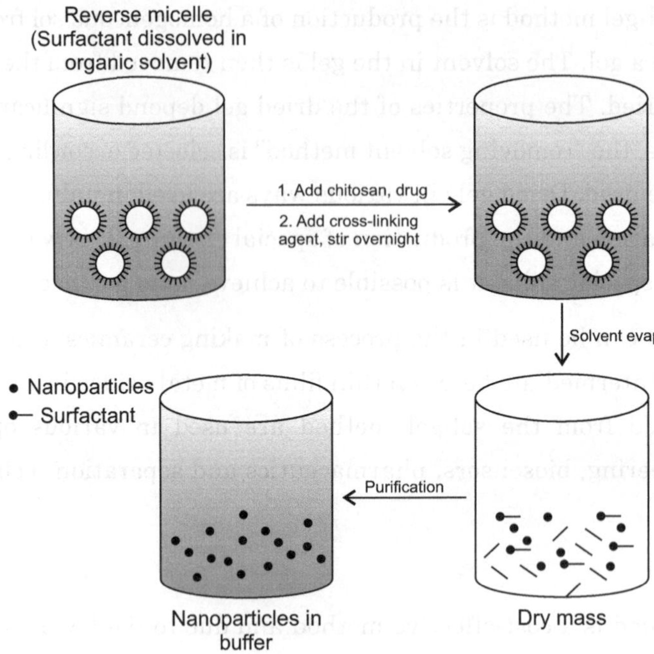

Fig. 13.21. Reverse micelle.

An oil in water in emulsion results in normal micelles where hydrophobic tails facing towards a core containing oil droplets within it. However, reverse micelle are formed in case of water in oily emulsion where hydrophyllic heads facing towards the core that contains water. It is the core of reverse micelle that acts as nano reactor for synthesis of nano particles. The size of nano particles can be controlled by varying the water to surfactant ratio. For synthesis of small nano particles, the concentration of water should be low.

Benefits:

Reverse micelles are also used as nano reactors for nano particle synthesis because they increase the reaction rate and the distribution of nano particles is more uniform.

Limitations:

The only disadvantage is the higher temperature required, which leads to enhanced inactivation.

Hydrothermal and Solvothermal Technique

This is the most common technique for the synthesis of nano particle. It is basically a solution reaction based approach. Solvothermal synthesis is generally defined as a chemical reaction taking place in a solvent (water, alcohol etc.) at temperatures above the boiling point and pressures above 1 bar. If the solvent used in this process is water, it is called as **hydrothermal process** while if solvent other than water like alcohol or any other organic or inorganic solvent, then it is called as **solvothermal process.**

This process is generally carried out in a sealed vessel known as **autoclave** which is made up of some strong alloy like steel so that it can tolerate the high pressure developed during the course of the reaction. The reactants are kept inside the autoclave which is then placed in a conventional oven at a particular temperature. The solvent are heated above their melting points and at high pressure so that it gets converted into a super critical fluid in which liquid and gas phases exist simultaneously. After the reaction is complete, the autoclave is cooled to room temperature and the products are washed to remove the unreacted reactants and other impurities from the solution.

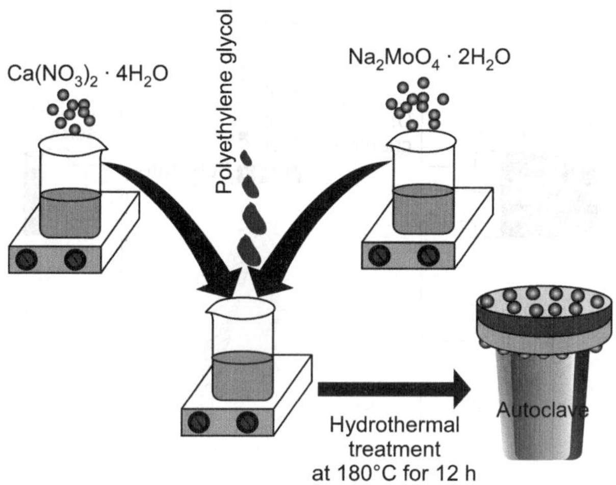

Fig. 13.22. Hydrothermal technique.

This process is used for the synthesis of crystalline ZnO nano rods, films of $PbTiO_3$, ZnO, $BaTiO_3$, TiO_2 etc.

Molecular Beam Epitaxy

Molecular beam epitaxy (MBE) is an experimental technique utilized for layer-by-layer growth of thin films of various quantum materials. Out of the variety of thin film growth techniques available, MBE is considered to be one of the cleanest, but also one of the most technically challenging and demanding, as MBE growth takes place in ultra-high vacuum (UHV) environment.

Typical MBE experimental setup consists of two or more **Knudsen effusion cells** (K-cells), located at the bottom of a UHV chamber and aligned towards the center of the chamber where a sample holder with a substrate is located (Fig. 13.23). Each individual K-cell contains a different element in ultra pure solid form (*i.e.* elemental 99.999% Selinum, Bismuth, etc.) which can be used in the thin film synthesis. The process of MBE growth starts by heating the K-cells to appropriate temperatures until the elements in each cell reach a sublimation point. Then, the shutters are opened and physical vapour from each K-cell diffuses though the chamber until it reaches the substrate where it gets deposited and the thin film gets formed. The final composition and stoichiometry of the film will depend on the temperature and surface atomic structure of the substrate as well as the flux ratios of individual components reaching the substrate. For more uniform growth, substrate can be continuously rotated at low rotation speeds (~1–2 rotations per minute) by utilizing a stepper motor attached to the magnetic manipulator.

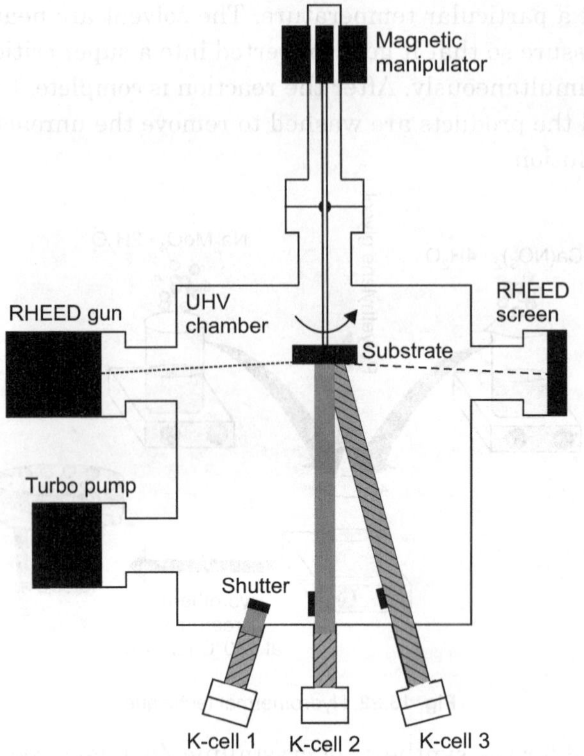

Fig. 13.23. Molecular Beam Epitaxy.

Self Assembly

Self assembly of nano particles refers to the organization of molecules or particles into well defined aggregates or structures without any external intervention. Moreover, nano particle self assembly is a significant bottom up synthetic methodology that involves the aggregation of colloidal nano particles into the final desired structure. This aggregation may occur chemically as a result of the complementary binding of organic molecules and supramolecules (molecular self assembly) or it may occur spontaneously (entropically) and as a result of thermodynamic minimum (energy minimization) restrictions.

The principle behind the self assembly process is the spontaneous physical or chemical aggregation of colloidal nano particles. The process of spontaneous self assembly takes advantage of the ability of mono dispersed nano or sub-micro colloidal spheres to organise into a face centred cubic lattice. The systems goal to reach at thermodynamically stable state is the driving force behind the process other than naturally occurring thermal self assembly. Complex 3D structures can also be created by applying gravitational, convective and electro-hydrodynamic process.

Chemical self assembly needs the attachment of a single molecule organic layer to the colloidal particles and the subsequent self assembly of these components into a complex structure *via* molecular recognition and binding

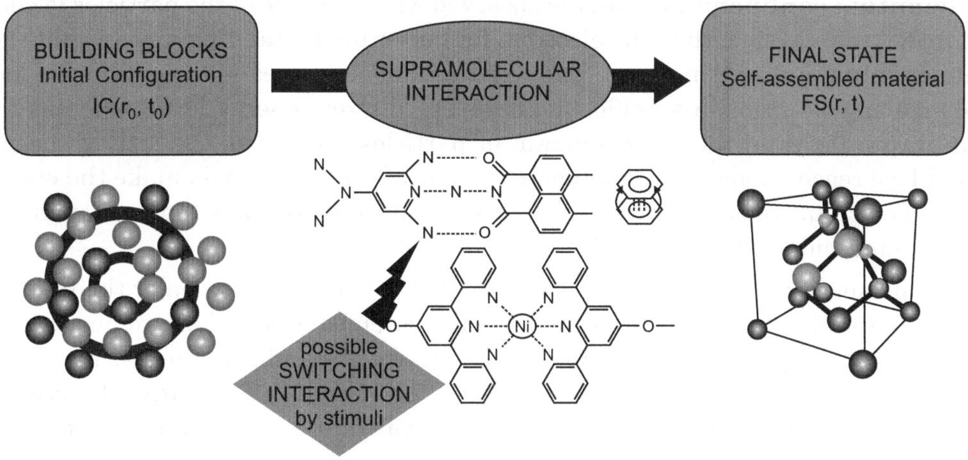

Fig. 13.24. Self-assembly.

Benefits:

1. Simple
2. Inexpensive
3. Versatile method
4. Capable of producing 2D nano structured metal oxides, such as nano sheets
5. Applicable in drug delivery
6. Application in biosensors, biomedical science, imaging techniques, photocatalysis and so on.

13.4 PROPERTIES OF NANO PARTICLES

As material get smaller, transforming from bulk phase to nano phase, their properties alter. Owing to their very small size, nano particles have a very large surface area which results in large surface area to volume ratio when compared to bulk material. This feature enables nano particles to possess unexpected optical, physical and chemical properties, as they are small enough to confine their electrons and produce quantum effect. Some properties of nano particles are explained below

(*i*) **Surface area:** The surface area of the nano particles are generally substantially high when compared to their bulk counter parts. This property is associated with all nano particles.

(*ii*) **Mechanical properties:** These properties include elastic modules, hardness, interfacial adhesion and friction, strength etc. The mechanical properties of nano particles increase with decrease in size. Smaller the size, lesser is the probability of finding imperfections like dislocations, vacancies, grain boundaries. Improvement in mechanical properties make nano materials ideal for a wide range of applications in aerospace and automotive industries, medicines, energy etc.

(*iii*) **Optical properties:** Optical properties of nano material include absorbance, luminosity, refractive index, scattering, transmittance. The reduction of material size has pronounced effect on these properties. Two factors, namely, increased energy level spacing (quantum confinement effect) and surface plasmon resonance profoundly contribute to the optical properties of nano materials.

The **quantum confinement effect** is observed when the size of the particles is very small as compared of the wavelength of the electron. for better understanding we can split the above term into quantum and confinement. The word confinement means to confine the motion of randomly moving electrons in specific energy levels (discrete energy level) whereas the term quantum throws light on the realm/domain of particles. Thus, as the size of the particles decrease till we reach a nano scale, the decrease in confining dimension make the energy level is discrete, as a result the band gap increases which ultimately leads to increase in band gap energy. *e.g.* semiconductor support quantum confinement.

Surface plasmon resonance (SPR) is the result of coherent excitation of the free electrons of the nano materials which are present in the conduction band and their in phase resonance oscillation with the applied light energy. Thus, unlike the bulk materials, nano materials can produce surface plasmon resonance. The intensity of such SPR is varies directly with the number of such excited electrons and the dielectric constant of the medium used, *e.g.* metals like Au, Ag, Al support SPR.

***(iv)* Magnetic Properties:** Magnetic properties of nano particles are used for targetted drug delivery, therapeutic treatment, contrast agents for MRI imaging, bioseparation, magnetic data storage media, catalysis (heterogeneous and homogeneous) and in vitro diagnostics. The nano particles shows superparamagnetism, (a property where magnetization can randomly flip direction under the influence of temperature) a property resulting from their tiny size. Superparamagnetic nano particles are not magnetic when located in a zero magnetic field but they quickly become magnetized when an external magnetic field is applied. When returned to a zero magnetic field, they quickly revert to a non-magnetized state.

***(v)* Thermal properties:** Metal nano particles are known to have higher thermal conductivities than those of fluids in solid form. For example, the thermal conductivity of copper is about 700 times higher that of water and about 3000 times higher than that of engine oil. Even alumina shows greater thermal conductivity as compared to water. Thus, the fluids containing suspended solid particles are expected to exhibit enhanced thermal conductivities as compared to conventional heat transfer fluids. The process of heat transfer takes place at the surface of particles which increases with the increase in surface area. Therefore, nano particles exhibit better thermal conductivity as compared to others. For example, nano fluids consisting of CuO or Al_2O_3 nano particles in water or ethylene exhibit excellent thermal conductivity.

13.5 APPLICATIONS OF NANO MATERIALS

In Medicine

- Early detection and prevention of various diseases like tumor due to their improved targeting strategies and long circulation life in blood.
- With the rapid development of nano technology and invention of nano particles like gold nano particles has made gene sequencing less difficult.
- Repairing and reproduction of damaged tissue.
- Revolutionization of organ transplantation/artificial implantation.
- They have the potential to deliver drugs in the optimum dosage range often resulting in improved therapeutic efficacy of the drugs, weakened side effects and improved patient compliance.

- Nano particles like quantum dots, gold nano particles etc. are useful in cancer diagnosis at the molecular level. Development of biomarkers can accurately and quickly detect the cancer. Fullerenes have high number of conjugated double bonds in the core structure, therefore they can be used as free radicals scavengers and this property of fullerenes can be used in cancer therapy.
- Nano particles have great potential as in vivo imaging tools and devices. Quantum dots when used for MRI create exceptional images of tumor sites.
- Liposomes are one of the promising drug delivery devices. The major limitation of liposome is its rapid degradation and clearance by the liver macrophages, thus reducing the duration of action of the drug it carries. This can be reduced to a certain extent with the advent of stealth liposomes where the liposomes are coated with materials like polyoxyethylene which prevents opsonisation of the liposome and their uptake by macrophages.

In Electronics

- In electronics, nano technology offers faster, smaller and more portable systems.
- Nano particles increases the efficiency of electronic devices, enhances the density of memory chips and reduces power consumption and the size of transistors used in integrated circuits.
- Nano particles form an important part of many electronic devices like laptops, computers, television, cell phones, digital cameras and also include nano films such as organic light emitting diodes (OLED's), sensors etc.
- They are also used in 3-D printing which allows the production of objects with shapes impossible to achieve by classical methods.

In Environmental Technologies

- Nano particles have the potential to improve current environmental protection measures and our understanding of the environment. Current research could create new emission control devices, develop new "green technology" that reduce the production of undesirable by-products and improve existing polluted water sources.
- Nano technology has the potential to remove the smallest pollutant from the air we breathe and the water we drink as well as to continuously measure and mitigate pollutants in the environment.
- Nano technology could also help in reducing and improving current waste, improves energy efficiency, create environment benign composite structures and conserve energy reserves. For example carbon nano tube membrane have the potential to reduce desalination costs. Similarly nano filters could be used to clean up groundwater or surface water contaminated with chemicals or hazardous substances.
- Nano filters could also be applied to automobile tale pipes and factories smoke stacks to separate out contaminants and prevent them from entering the atmosphere.
- Nano -sensors could be developed to detect water borne contaminants as well as toxic gas leaks at extremely low concentrations.

In Energy Harvesting

- Due to the increasing use of fossil fuels, they will not be available in the coming years. Therefore, scientists have shifted the research strategies to generate renewable energy from easily available sources at a cheaper rate. They found that nano particles are the best materials for this purpose because of their large surface area, optical properties and catalytic behaviour.
- Nano particles are widely used to generate energy from photoelectrochemical and electrochemical splitting of water. Apart from water splitting other options to generate energy are electrochemical carbon dioxide reduction to fuel precursors, solar cells and piezoelectric generators. Recently, nano generators have been developed which can convert mechanical energy to electrical energy with the use of piezoelectric.

In the Field of Mechanical Engineering

- Advances in nano engineering expand the mechanical engineer's toolbox. In comparison to naturally occurring materials, nano particles have enhanced properties biochemical sensitivity, electrical or thermal conductivity, mechanical strength, optical properties and selective transport. For example the strong, lightweight and high conductivity nature of carbon nano materials make them of high interest in space applications.
- Particles also offers many applications in industries like coating, lubrication and adhesive applications. Tribological properties of nano particles can be controlled by embedding them in the metal and polymer matrix to increase their mechanical strength. Nano particles also offer good sliding and delamination properties which results in low friction and wear and hence increase lubrication effect.
- Alumina, titania and carbon based nano particles are extensively used to get desired mechanical properties in coatings.
- Another important application of nano particles is for making self cleaning surfaces. For example, for the industrial mass production of self cleaning glass, TiO_2 nano particles are typically coated on the glass surface using chemical vapour deposition technique. Similarly for self cleaning ceramic and polymer surfaces, TiO_2 to nano particles are used. In the same way vanadium dioxide nano particles are ultra resistant to water and can also be used for self cleaning surfaces.

In Food Industry

- The application of nano technology in food industry ranges from food processing and food packaging to food nano sensing. In food processing, these nano structures can be used as food additives, anti microbial agents, career for smart delivery of nutrients, anticaking agents.
- They are also used as fillers for improving mechanical strength and durability of the packaging material. Nano sensors can be used to detect the presence of contaminants, mycotoxins and microorganisms in food products.
- Nano particles also increases the shelf life of food products. In various food product, where bioactive component often get degraded and becomes inactive due to adverse

environmental conditions, nano encapsulation of these bioactive components extend the shelf life of food product by slowing down the degradation or prevent degradation until the product is delivered at the specific site.

In Catalysis

- Nano particles are useful material for catalysis due to their high relative surface area. If a nano particle has the same volume as a bulk material its relative surface area is greater as compared to the bulk material. Hence, are promising homogeneous as well as heterogeneous catalysts.
- Nano catalysis improve the selectivity of the reactions by allowing reactions at a lower temperature, minimising side reactions, higher recycling rates and recovery of energy consumption. Hence, these catalysts are widely used in green chemistry, environmental remediation, efficient conversion of biomass and various other areas.
- Various processes where nano particles are used as catalyst are:
  - nano particles of Ag over carbon covered alumina are highly efficient in controlling microbes in water.
  - TiO_2 is considered to be the most efficient and environmentally benign photocatalyst that has been most widely used in photo degradation.
  - the solid based nano catalyst KF/CaO can be used to convert Chinese tallow seed oil to bio diesel with yield greater than 95%.
  - Fe and Co powders of 10 to 50 nm dimensions are used as catalysts for producing green diesel using Fischer-Tropsch process.

Textiles and Fabrics

- To make a piece of cloth wearable, wrinkle and odor-free across seasons, specialized fabrics with nano -sized silver and titanium particles are being used. It is used to develop desired textile characteristics, such as high tensile strength, unique surface structure, soft hand, durability, water repellency, fire retardancy, antimicrobial properties etc.
- This has led to the production of lightweight, thin and breathable fabrics. The other applications of nano technology in this industry include making fabrics stain-resistant and improving durability.
- The most widely recognized application is in the shark-skin suit worn during world-record breaking Olympic swimming championship. The suit, which includes a plasma layer enhanced by nano technology to repel water molecules is designed to help the swimmer glide through the water and has become a common feature of major swimming events as all competitors attempt to enhance their chances of winning.

Automobiles

- The automobile industry has seen a paradigm shift in the past decade. Every now and then, new four- and two-wheeler models are launched which work on extra-edge technology.
- Various polymer nano composites like natural rubber-organoclay have been used in tyres to make them abrasion-resistant. Furthermore, adding nano particles like tungsten nano spheres to car fluids has enhanced their mechanical properties.

- Nano technology could be applied to various body parts, including the chassis, tyres, windows, engines, etc., to enhance their performance and durability.
- Nano technology is used as a useful technology to provide protection for automobile bodies against corrosion and abrasion resistant. The coating with nano particles is an effective practice to enhance the protection and scratch resistance of automotive bodies.

Sporting Equipment and Goods

- Nano materials are used in sports equipments like racing bicycles, baseball bats, hockey sticks, tennis and badminton racquets, golf balls, archery arrows, skis, fly-fishing rods etc. to improve strength, stiffness, durability, abrasion resistance and to reduce weight.
- Polymers of different sizes and stiffness with different strength combined with different molecules are used as soft and hard bits for making the running shoes comfortable.
- Jeremy Wariner, using a new shoe design specifically for him using nano technology by Adidas, was able to win the silver medal in the men's 400 m race.

Space Science

- Another domain where the applications of nano technology is visible is space science and research. Apart from making the outer structure of satellites durable and lightweight using materials like CNT, research is also being done on how to send spacecraft with lesser fuel.
- Nano technology can contribute to the development of more efficient solar panels and energy storage devices, enabling spacecraft to generate and store more energy. This will increase the autonomy of spacecraft and reduce the need for frequent recharging or refueling.
- Using carbon nano tubes to make the cable needed for the space elevator, a system which could significantly reduce the cost of sending material into orbit.
- Deploying a network of nano sensors to search large areas of planets such as Mars for traces of water or other chemicals.

EXERCISES

I. SHORT ANSWER TYPE QUESTIONS

1. What are nano materials? List various methods of their synthesis.
2. Explain any three size dependent properties of nano materials.
3. Explain the synthesis of nano materials by chemical vapour deposition method.
4. Explain the synthesis of nano materials by sol-gel method.
5. What are carbon nano tubes? What are its applications? **(HMTU, 2016)**
6. Write a short note on dendrimers.
7. Write a short notes on uses of fullerenes.
8. Explain the optical properties of nano particles.

9. Write short note on:
   (*a*) Inorganic nano particles
   (*b*) Quantum dots
   (*c*) Carbon nano cones
   (*d*) Carbon nano tubes.
10. Write a note on organic nano particles and their applications.
11. Write the application of nano particles in medicine.
12. Write the application of nano particles in the field of electronics.
13. How many hexagonal and pentagonal faces are present in fullerene? **(HMTU, 2016)**

II. LONG ANSWER TYPE QUESTIONS

1. What are nano material? Give their synthesis by sol gel techniques. **(VTU Jan., 2020)**
2. Write a note on Graphenes. Mention their applications. **(VTU Jan., 2020)**
3. Write a note on fullerenes. Mention their applications. **(VTU Jan., 2020)**
4. Explain size dependent properties of nano materials. **(VTU July, 2019)**
   (*a*) Surface area
   (*b*) electrical properties
   (*c*) optical properties.
5. Define nano materials. Give their synthesis by bottom up approach.
6. Write down the various methods of the synthesis of nano materials. Explain any two of them.
7. Discuss in detail application of nano particles.
8. What are nano materials? Explain top down synthesis of nano particles.
9. Explain the properties of nano materials in detail.
10. Write a detailed note on soft and hard templating methods.
11. What are nano particles? Explain in detail classification of naoparticles.
12. What are nano materials? Discuss the preparation, properties and applications of carbon nano tubes. **(HMTU, 2016)**
13. What are fullerenes and nano -cones? Discuss their applications. **(HMTU, 2016)**

III. MULTIPLE CHOICE QUESTIONS

1. The statement "there is a plenty of room at the bottom" was given by
   (*a*) Eric Drexler
   (*b*) Issac Newton
   (*c*) Richard Feyman
   (*d*) Albert Einstein.
2. The term "nano technology" was first used by
   (*a*) Sumio Iijima
   (*b*) Eric Drexler
   (*c*) Nario Taniguchi
   (*d*) Richard Feyman.
3. The size of nano particles is between ____ nm.
   (*a*) 100 – 1000
   (*b*) 1 – 100
   (*c*) 0.1 – 10
   (*d*) 0.01 – 1.
4. Fullerene is made up of _____ number of carbon atoms.
   (*a*) 120
   (*b*) 25
   (*c*) 40
   (*d*) 60.

5. Egyptians were using _____ in hair drying.

(*a*) nano aluminium (*b*) nano lead

(*c*) nano gold (*d*) nano copper.

6. Which of the following does not apply to nano technology?

(*a*) It involves rearrangement of atoms

(*b*) It is a green technology

(*c*) It can be described by Newtonian mechanics

(*d*) It is a general purpose technology.

7. Spherical gold nano particles are ____ dimensional nano materials

(*a*) zero (*b*) one

(*c*) two (*d*) three.

8. The bottom up approach of synthesis of nano materials is:

(*a*) Sputtering (*b*) Lithography

(*c*) Mechanical milling (*d*) Chemical vapour deposition.

9. A closed cage structure of icosahedral symmetry with 20 hexagon and 12 pentagonal rings are called as ____.

(*a*) Graphene (*b*) Fullerene

(*c*) Carbon balls (*d*) Crystals.

10. Nano materials differs from bulk materials in their

(*a*) magnetic properties (*b*) Optical properties

(*c*) Electrical properties (*d*) All of the above.

11. Nano science can be studied with the help of

(*a*) newtonian mechanics (*b*) quantum mechanics

(*c*) macro dynamics (*d*) geophysics.

12. The procedure in top down fabrication method is:

(*a*) nano particle → bulk → powder (*b*) powder → bulk → nano particle

(*c*) nano particle → powder → bulk (*d*) bulk → powder → nano particle.

13. C_{60} is soluble in

(*a*) Water (*b*) Ammonia

(*c*) HCl (*d*) Benzene.

14. Carbon n anotubes were discovered by

(*a*) Sumio Iijima (*b*) Richard Feyman

(*c*) Eric Drexler (*d*) None of the above.

15. Carbon based quantum dots are _____ structures

(*a*) zero dimensional (*b*) one dimensional

(*c*) two dimensional (*d*) three dimensional.

16. The process used to produce nano particles by bombarding solid surfaces by gas is ______

(*a*) lithography (*b*) sputtering

(*c*) templating method (*d*) mechanical milling.

17. For milling operations _________ environment is preferred.

(*a*) acidic (*b*) basic

(*c*) inert (*d*) active.

18. CVD stands for

(*a*) chemical vapour deposition (*b*) carbon vapour deposition

(*c*) chemical vapour density (*d*) carbon vapour density.

19. _____________ are the typical precursors in sol-gel technique of the synthesis of nano particles.

(*a*) Metal oxides (*b*) Metal dioxides

(*c*) Metal alkoxides (*d*) Metal fluorides.

20. Fullerene molecule is

(*a*) a cluster of 60 carbon atoms, all bonded with sp^3 hybrids

(*b*) a shell of 60 carbon atoms, all bonded with sp^2 hybrids

(*c*) a complex of 60 carbon atoms bonded both with sp^2 and sp^3 hybrids

(*d*) a ball shape of 60 carbon atoms bonded with $2p$ valence electrons.

Answers

MULTIPLE CHOICE QUESTIONS

1. (*c*)	**2.** (*c*)	**3.** (*b*)	**4.** (*d*)	**5.** (*b*)	**6.** (*c*)	**7.** (*a*)	**8.** (*d*)	**9.** (*b*)	**10.** (*d*)
11. (*b*)	**12.** (*d*)	**13.** (*d*)	**14.** (*a*)	**15.** (*a*)	**16.** (*b*)	**17.** (*c*)	**18.** (*a*)	**19.** (*c*)	**20.** (*b*)

Chapter 14 Spectroscopic Methods of Analysis

14.1 INTRODUCTION

Chemists, physicist, biochemists and other scientists are deeply interested in knowing the structure of molecules. If one could actually see a molecule there would probably be little fun in investigating it further. However, these systems are of infinitesimal dimensions that it is not possible to see them, though some progress has of late been made in photographing these species. Our knowledge about molecular structure is derived indirectly from the technique known as spectroscopy. **Spectroscopy** deals with the transitions that a molecule undergoes between its energy levels upon absorption of suitable electromagnetic radiations determined by quantum mechanical selections rules. Thus, spectroscopy is defined as the study of interaction of electromagnetic radiations with matter.

Quantum mechanics tells us that the energy levels of all systems are quantised and are designated by appropriate quantum number. These energy levels are obtained by the solution of the time independent Schrödinger wave equation.

14.2 ELECTROMAGNETIC RADIATIONS

An electromagnetic radiation is a form of energy which is transmitted through space at very high velocity. According to quantum mechanics, the electromagnetic radiations exhibit dual character *i.e.* possess wave as well as particle behaviour. The wave nature of radiations suggest that the electromagnetic waves consist of oscillating electric and magnetic field. The electric and magnetic field oscillate perpendicular to each other which in turn are perpendicular to the direction of propagation of wave (Fig. 14.1).

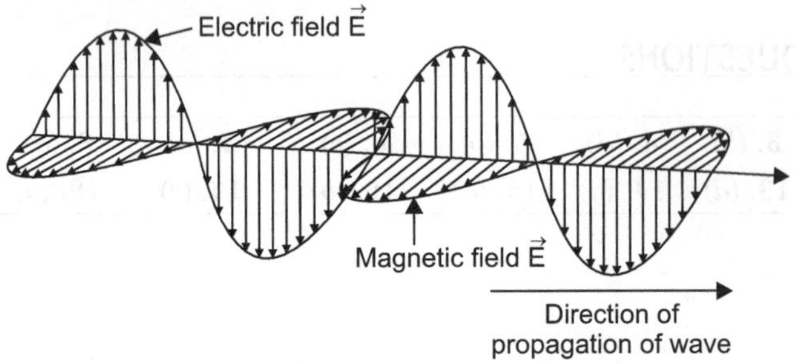

Fig. 14.1. Beam of electromagnetic waves.

Properties of Electromagnetic Radiations

- Electromagnetic waves are composed of oscillating electric and magnetic fields perpendicular to each other and both are perpendicular to the direction of the propagation of the wave.

- Em waves do not require any medium for propagation.
- In vacuum, all em waves travel with the same speed *i.e.,* the speed of light (3×10^8 m/s).
- Em waves have no mass.
- Em waves are not deflected by electric or magnetic fields.
- Em waves follow the lows of reflection and refraction.
- Energy of electromagnetic waves is directly proportional to its frequency.

14.3 SOME IMPORTANT CHARACTERISTICS OF WAVES

Every wave has some important characteristics which are described below:

1. **Wavelength (λ):** It is the distance between two neighbouring crests or troughs in a wave (Fig. 14.2).

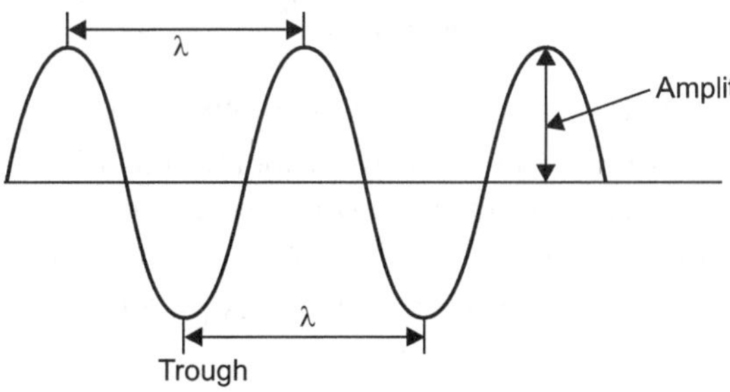

Fig. 14.2. Properties of electromagnetic radiations.

It is denoted by λ and is generally expressed in angstrom (1 Å = 10^{-10} m = 10^{-8} cm) nanometer (1 nm = 10^{-9} m = 10^{-7} cm) centimeter etc.

2. **Amplitude (*A*):** It is the height of a crest or the depth of a trough from base in a wave. It is expressed in centimeter (Fig. 14.2). It determines the brightness or intensity of the beam of em radiation/wave.

3. **Frequency (ν):** It is defined as the number of waves which can pass through a given point in one second. (Fig. 14.3) It is denoted by ν (nu) and is expressed in cycles per second or hertz (Hz).

$$1 \text{ Hz} = 1 \text{ cps (cycle per second)}$$

$\nu = \frac{C}{\lambda}$ where C = velocity of em wave (3×10^8 m/s = 3×10^{10} cm/s)

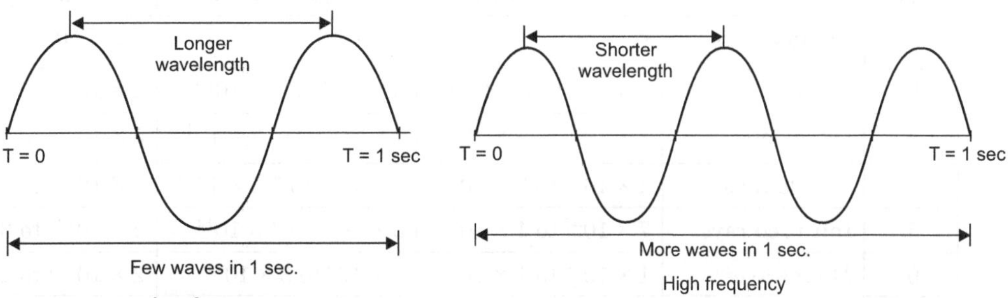

Fig. 14.3. Frequency of em radiations.

4. **Velocity (*C*):** The velocity of a wave is defined as the distance travelled by it in one second. It is denoted by *C* and is expressed in m/s or cm/s.
   All electromagnetic waves travels with a speed of 3×10^8 m/s in vacuum whatever may be their frequency or wavelength.
5. **Wavenumber ($\bar{\nu}$):** It is the reciprocal of wavelength. Wavenumber is defined as the total number of waves in a length of one centimeter of we can define it as number of wavelengths per centimeter. It is denoted by $\bar{\nu}$ and is expressed in cm^{-1}.

$$\bar{\nu} = \frac{1}{\lambda} = \frac{\nu}{C}$$

6. **Energy (*E*):** Electromagnetic radiations are made up of energy packets or bundles which are called as photons and each photon is associated with a fixed amount of energy. According to Planck's equation, the energy associated with a single photon is given by

$$E = h\nu = \frac{hC}{\lambda}$$

where *h* is the Planck's constant and its value is 6.626×10^{-34} Js or 6.628×10^{-27} ergs.

Thus, energy of any em radiation is directly proportional to its frequency and inversely proportional to its wavelength. To calculate energy associated with one mole of photons, we have to multiply the energy of single photon with the Avogadro's number.

$$E/\text{mole} = E\,N_A \qquad N_A = 6.023 \times 10^{23}.$$

14.4 ELECTROMAGNETIC SPECTRUM.

The electromagnetic spectrum is the arrangement of all types of electromagnetic radiation according to energy or wavelength. The sun, the earth and other bodies radiate electromagnetic radiations of varying wavelengths. However, the fact is that most of the light in the universe is invisible to our eyes. The only light that we can see represents a small portion of the electromagnetic spectrum *i.e.,* the visible portion of the light.

The entire electromagnetic spectrum from lowest to highest frequency or longest to shortest wavelength includes radio waves, infrared radiations, visible light, ultraviolet radiations, X-rays, gamma rays and cosmic radiations. Thus, comic rays have highest energy while radiowaves are least energetic. The various regions of electromagnetic spectrum along-with their frequency, wavelength and energy are given in Table. 14.1.

Table 14.1: Wavelength, frequency and Energy of Electromagnetic Radiations

S. No.	Region	Wavelength (*m*)	Frequency (Hz)	Energy (*J*)
1.	Gamma rays	$< 1\times 10^{-11}$	$> 3 \times 10^{19}$	$> 2 \times 10^{-14}$
2.	X-rays	1×10^{-11} to 1×10^{-8}	3×10^{16} to 3×10^{19}	2×10^{-17} to 2×10^{-14}
3.	Ultraviolet rays	1×10^{-8} to 4×10^{-7}	7.5×10^{14} to 3×10^{16}	5×10^{-19} to 2×10^{-17}
4.	Visible rays	4×10^{-7} to 7×10^{-7}	4×10^{14} to 7.5×10^{14}	3×10^{-19} to 5×10^{-19}
5.	Infra red rays	7×10^{-7} to 1×10^{-3}	3×10^{11} to 4×10^{14}	2×10^{-22} to 3×10^{-19}
6.	Microwaves	1×10^{-3} to 1×10^{-1}	3×10^{9} to 3×10^{11}	2×10^{-24} to 2×10^{-22}
7.	Radiowaves	$> 1 \times 10^{-1}$	$< 3 \times 10^{9}$	$< 2 \times 10^{-24}$

- In the radio-frequency region of spectrum, the NMR (Nuclear Magnetic Resonance) and ESR (Electron Spin Resonance) spectra are obtained.
- In the microwave region, the rotational spectra are obtained.
- In the infra red region, the vibrational spectra are obtained.
- In the visible and ultra violet regions, the electronic spectra are obtained.
- X-rays are produced from radioactive substances.
- Cosmic rays are present in outer space and continuously fall on the earth. The different em radiations in order of their increasing λ and decreasing ν are Cosmic rays > γ-rays > X-rays > UV rays > Visible rays > IR radiations > Microwaves > radiowaves. The different regions of the em spectrum from the region X-rays to those of micro and radio waves have been used to determine structures of atoms/molecules (Table. 14.2).

Table 14.2: Summary of Spectroscopic Techniques

S. No.	Spectroscopy	Effect on the molecule
1.	Ultraviolet (200 – 400 nm) and Visible (400 – 800 nm)	It causes changes in electronic energy levels within the molecule.
2.	Infra red (2.5 – 16 μm)	It brings about changes in vibrational and rotational movements of the molecule.
3.	Nuclear magnetic resonance (NMR) Radiowaves are used (60 – 500 MHz)	It induces changes in the magnetic properties of certain atomic nuclei.

14.5 BASICS OF SPECTROSCOPY

At the beginning of the twentieth century. Max Planck in 1901, gave a new theory known as quantum theory of radiation. According to this theory, radiant energy is not emitted or absorbed continuously but discontinuously in the form of small packets of energy called as **quanta**. Each such quanta is associated with a fixed amount of energy which is given by

$$E = h\nu$$

where h is the Planck's constant and ν is the frequency of electromagnetic radiation.

This theory was further extended to explain the atomic spectra of atoms. When atoms absorb energy, their valence electrons jump to excited energy levels and when they return to ground state energy level, they emit the energy equal to the difference between energies of two levels. This emission of radiation by an atom is recorded as its atomic spectra. In case of hydrogen atom, the spectrum consists of a number of lines which are grouped into five different series of lines, each being named after the name of its discoverer. These are Lyman series, Balmer series, Paschen series, Brackett series and Pfund series.

In contrast to atomic spectra which arise due to transitions of an electron between the atomic energy levels, the molecular spectra arise from three types of transitions – electronic, vibrational and rotational transitions depending on the amount of energy absorbed. The total energy of a molecule according to the Born-Oppenheimer approximation is give by

$$E = E_{el} + E_{vib} + E_{rot} + E_{tr}$$

Which means that the total energy of a molecule is the sum of electronic energy (E_{el}), Vibrational energy (E_{vib}), rotational energy (E_{rot}) and translational energy (E_{tr}). All these energies of the molecule are qauantised except translational energy. Also,

$$E_{el} >> E_{vib} >> E_{rot} >> E_{tr}$$

As the translational energy is negligibly small, we can rewrite the Born-Oppenheimer approximation as

$$E = E_{el} + E_{vib} + E_{rot}.$$

Thus, there are only discrete electronic, vibrational and rotational energy levels available to the molecule for excitation. These energy levels are also called as molecular energy levels and the transitions which a molecule undergoes between these energy levels on absorption of suitable radiation result in a molecular spectra. These molecular energy levels are designated by appropriate quantum numbers (Fig. 14.4).

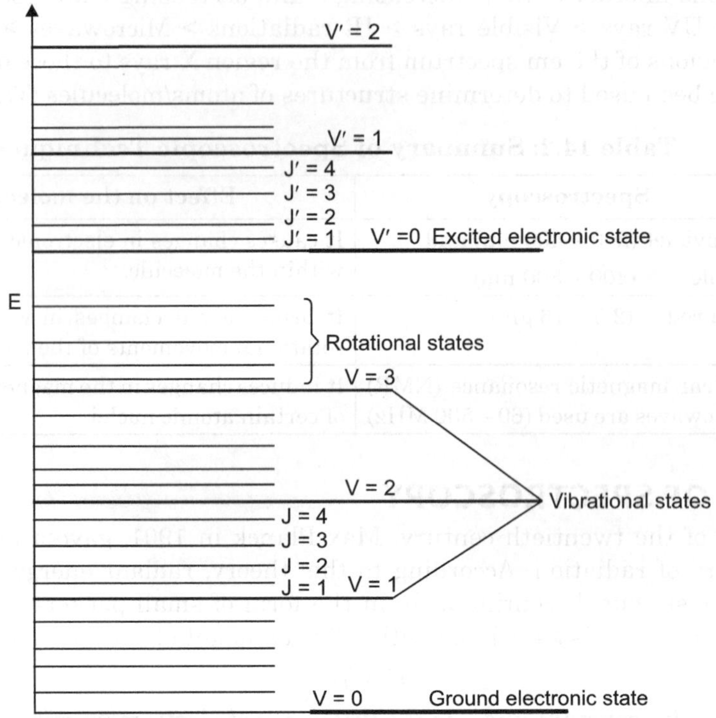

Fig. 14.4. Energy level diagram showing various molecular energy levels.

It is clear from the energy level diagram that each electronic energy level is associated with a series of vibrational energy levels (designated by vibrational quantum number; V = 0, 1, 2, 3...) and each vibrational energy level is associated with a series of rotational energy levels (designated by rotational quantum number, J = 0, 1, 2, ...) The lower energy levels are designated by V, J and higher energy levels are designated by single prime , V', J'.

The various types of spectra given by a molecule, the regions in which these spectra lie and the energy changes that take place in the molecule on absorption of radiation are given below:

1. **Pure rotational spectra:** The rotational spectra of a molecule are observed in the microwave region. These spectra are observed when the molecule undergoes transitions in rotational energy levels of a gaseous molecule on the absorption of suitable radiations. Molecules having permanent dipole moment exhibit rotational spectra, *e.g.* H_2O, heteronuclear diatomic molecules like HCl, CO, NO etc. Homonuclear diatomic molecules like H_2, Cl_2, N_2 etc. which does not exhibit permanent dipole moment do not give rotational spectra.

2. **Vibrational and Vibrational-rotational spectra:** Vibrational spectra are observed in the infrared region. Vibrational spectra are obtained by the transitions of molecule in vibrational energy levels. Since, vibrational transitions are also accompanied by the rotational transitions, these are also called as vibrational rotational spectra. Molecules in which vibrational motion is accompanied by a change in dipole moment exhibit IR spectra.
3. **Raman spectra:** Raman spectra are generally observed in visible region. Raman spectroscopy deals with the scattering of light and not with its absorption. When a beam of monochromatic radiation is passed through a sample, a small fraction of light is scattered at right angle to the incident radiation. Almost the entire scattered radiation has the same frequency as that of the incident radiation (called as Rayleigh scattering). However, later it was observed by Prof. C.V. Raman that some of the scattered light has different frequencies than the incident beam and this is called as Raman scattering / Raman effect.
4. **Electronic spectra:** Electronic spectra are observed in the ultraviolet or visible region. Electronic spectra arise from electronic transitions in a molecule. Since, electronic transitions in a molecule are invariably accompanied by vibrational and rotational transition, thus electronic spectra of molecules are quite complex.
5. **Nuclear Magnetic Resonance (NMR) Spectra:** NMR spectra are observed in radio waves region. NMR spectra result from transitions induced between the nuclear spin energy levels of a molecule in an applied magnetic field. Only those nuclei display the NMR phenomenon for which the spin quantum number, I is greater than zero (*e.g.* ^{1}H, ^{13}C, ^{19}F, ^{31}P etc.). Nuclei like ^{12}C, ^{16}O, ^{32}S have spin quantum number, I = O, therefore, these nuclei do not display NMR spectrum.
6. **Electron Spin Resonance (ESR) spectra:** ESR spectra are observed in microwave region. ESR spectra result from the transitions between the electron spin energy levels of a molecule in an external magnetic field. ESR spectra is shown by the systems which contain odd electrons (*i.e.* unpaired electrons).

Source of electromagnetic radiation: Various sources of electromagnetic radiations are tabulated below (Table 14.3).

Table 14.3: Various Sources of em Radiations

S. No.	Electromagnetic radiation	Source of radiation
1.	Ultraviolet radiations	Hydrogen discharge lamp and deuterium discharge lamp.
2.	Visible radiations	Tungsten filament lamp.
3.	Infrared radiations	Electrically heated rods of • Nernst glower (sintered mixture of rare earth oxides like Zr, Y, Er, etc.) • Globar (SiC) • Ceramic element
4.	Microwave radiations	Klystron value.
5.	Radiowaves	Magnet of stable field strength.

14.6 UV-VISIBLE SPECTROSCOPY/ELECTRONIC SPECTROSCOPY

Ultraviolet and visible spectroscopy is primarily used to measure the multiple bond or aromatic conjugation within molecules. The UV region extends from 100 – 400 nm and visible region from 400 – 800 nm. The ultraviolet region is further divided into near UV region (200 – 400 nm) and far or vacuum UV region (below 200 nm). The vacuum UV is so named because the air molecules absorb in this region and thus this region is accessible only with special vacuum equipment.

As the electronic transitions are accompanied by vibrational and rotational transitions, electronic spectra of molecules are generally very complex. The electronic spectra is produced when a molecule jumps from lower electronic level to higher electronic level by the absorption of energy. The total energy of the molecule in an electronic level is given by Born-Oppenheimer approximation.

Born-Oppenheimer Approximation

According to Born-Oppenheimer approximation, the total energy of a molecule in the ground state is given by

$$E = E_{el} + E_{vib} + E_{rot}$$

It shows that the electronic, vibrational and rotational energies of the molecule are independent of each other. Assuming that the Born-Oppenheimer approximation is valid in the excited state also, the energy of the molecule in the excited state is given by.

$$E' = E'_{el} + E'_{vib} + E'_{rot}$$

Thus, for an electronic transition, the change in energy is

$$\begin{aligned} \Delta E &= E' - E \\ &= (E'_{el} + E'_{vib} + E'_{rot}) - (E_{el} + E_{vib} + E_{rot}) \\ &= (E'_{el} - E_{el}) + (E'_{vib} - E_{vib}) + (E'_{rot} - E_{rot}) \\ \Delta E &= \Delta E_{el} + \Delta E_{vib} + \Delta E_{rot} \end{aligned}$$

This energy of electronic transition can be expressed in wavenumbers (cm^{-1}) as,

$$\bar{\nu} = \frac{\Delta E}{hc} = \frac{\Delta E_{el} + \Delta E_{vib} + \Delta E_{rot}}{hc}\ \text{cm}^{-1}.$$

This equation shows that electronic transition possess the vibrational and rotational fine structures. A very useful guiding principle for investigating the vibrational structure of electronic spectra is provided by the well known Frank-Condon principle.

Frank Condon Principle

It states that an electronic transition takes place so fast that a vibrating molecule does not change its internuclear distance appreciably during the transition. Since nucleus is much more massive that the electrons, therefore electrons move much faster than the nuclei, as a result the nuclei do not change their position during the electronic transition. Thus, an electronic transition can be represented by a vertical line on a potential energy diagram (potential energy versus internuclear distance) Fig. 14.5.

In the Fig. 14.5, two potential energy curves are drown– one for the molecule in the ground electronic state and the other for the excited electronic state. Since the bonding in the excited state is weaker that in the ground state (when electron goes to excited state *i.e.,* antibonding orbital or we can say that when an electron goes from ground state *i.e.,* bonding orbital to excited state *i.e.,* antibonding orbital, the bond order decreases B.O. = $\frac{N_b - N_a}{2}$ where N_b

and N_a are the number of electrons in bonding and antibonding orbital. As the bond order decreases, the internuclear distance increases), the minimum in potential energy curve for the excited electronic state occurs at a little greater internuclear distance than the corresponding minimum in the ground electronic state. Now, according to Frank Condon Principle, a transition occurs vertically because the internuclear distance remains the same. Thus, the most probable electronic transition takes place from $V = 0$ to $V' = 2$. The other transitions also occur but have very less probability and thus give weak intensity lines.

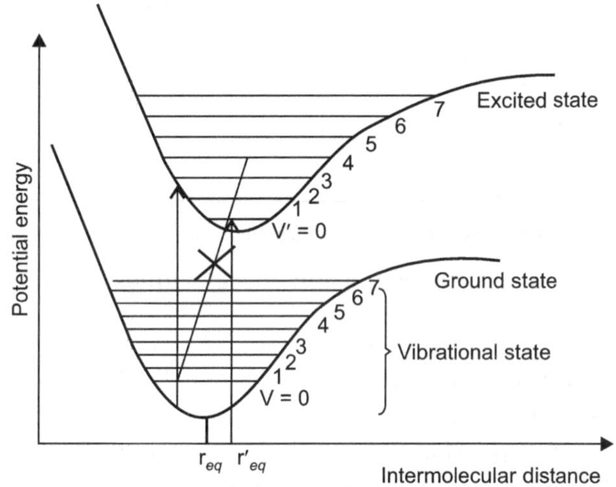

Fig. 14.5. Electronic transition in a diatonic molecule.

Lambert Beer's Law

According to this law, when a beam of monochromatic light is passed through a solution, the decrease in intensity of radiation with thickness of the absorbing material is directly proportional to the intensity of incident radiation as well as to the concentration of the solution. Mathematically,

$$A = \log \frac{I_o}{I} = \varepsilon c l$$

where

I = Intensity of light

ε = molar absorption coefficient

c = concentration of absorbing material

l = path length

Details of this law has been discussed in chapter 6 section 6.3.1.

14.7 ELECTRONIC TRANSITIONS

Energy absorbed by a molecule results in electronic transitions which involves valence electrons of the molecule. Three distinct types of electrons *viz.* σ, π and non-bonding electrons are involved in these transition. According to molecular orbital theory, when two atomic orbitals overlap one bonding M.O. and one antibonding M.O. are formed. Similarly when one σ (sigma) or π (pi) bond is formed, one bonding and other antibonding M.O. is formed. There is no antibonding level for non-bonding electrons as they do not form any bond.

Thus, the possible electronic levels in a molecule can be σ, π, *n*, σ* and π* and the only transitions that are allowed are σ – σ*, π – π*, *n* – σ* and *n* – π*.

The energy level scheme and various electronic transitions are shown in Fig. 14.6.

The antibonding molecular orbital is designated by an asterisk σ* and π*.

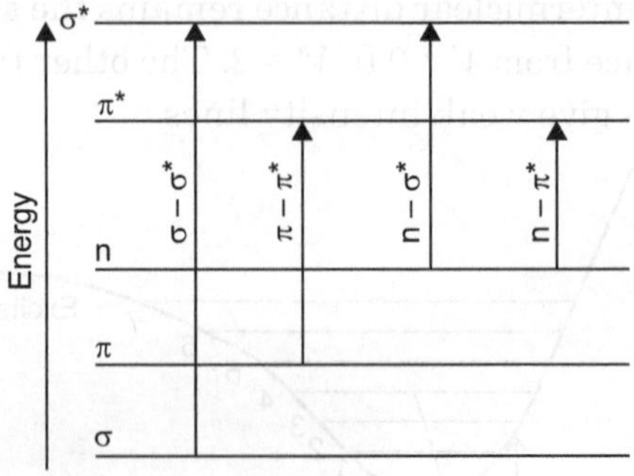

Fig. 14.6. Electronic energy levels and electronic transitions.

From the figure it is clear that the change in energy values for different transitions are in the following order:

$$\sigma - \sigma^* > n - \sigma^* > \pi - \pi^* > n - \pi^*$$

Transitions other than these are quantum mechanically forbidden. The main features of these transitions are discussed below:

1. **σ – σ* transition:** A transition of electron from a bonding sigma orbital to the higher energy antibonding sigma orbital is designated as σ – σ*. Such type of transitions can occur in compounds where all the electrons are involved in single bonds and there is no lone pair of electrons *e.g.* saturated hydrocarbons (methane, ethane etc.). Sigma bonds are very strong, therefore this is a high energy transition and hence require very short wavelengths *i.e.*, high energy ultraviolet radiations around 150 nm. For example,

   $CH_4 \rightarrow \lambda_{max} = 121.9$ nm
   $C_2H_6 \rightarrow \lambda_{max} = 135$ nm] corresponding to σ – σ* transition

   A study of such transitions is done in vacuum UV region since below 200 nm oxygen present in air begin to absorb. This transition is generally not observed in commercial spectrophotometers as they do not operate below 180 nm.

2. ***n* – σ* transition:** Saturated compounds with one hetero atom with lone pair (non-bonding) of electrons undergo *n* – σ* transition, *e.g.* saturated halides, alcohols, ethers, amines etc. These transitions require less energy as compared to σ – σ* transition. In saturated alkyl halides, the energy required for this transition decreases with increase in electro-negativity of the halogen atom. For example, energy required for *n* – σ* transition in CH_3Cl is more as compared to CH_3I because chlorine being more electronegative will hold its electrons tightly as compared to iodine as a result more energy will be required to excite electrons in CH_3Cl ($\lambda_{max} \simeq$ 175 nm) as compared to CH_3I ($\lambda_{max} \simeq 258$ nm).

   Also, these transitions are sensitive to hydrogen bonding. Hydrogen bonding of compound with the solvent molecules shifts the UV-absorption to shorter wavelengths. For example, alcohols form H-bond with the solvent molecules, as a result *n* – σ* transition requires higher energy and will absorb at shorter wavelengths (λ_{max} for CH_3OH – 174 nm).

3. **$\pi - \pi^*$ transition:** This type of transition occur in any molecule having unsaturated centres or π-electron system *e.g.* simple alkenes, alkynes, aromatics, carbonyl compounds, azo compounds, cyanides etc. This transition requires lesser energy than $n - \sigma^*$ transition. In alkenes, although several transitions are possible the lowest energy transition is $\pi - \pi^*$.

4. **$n - \pi^*$ transition:** This type of transitions are shown by unsaturated molecules which contains atleast one hetero atom such as oxygen, nitrogen, sulphur, halogen etc. Non-bonding electrons are weakly held, so energy required for excitation is much less. Infact this type of transition requires least amount of energy of all the possible electronic transitions. Hence, these transitions occur at longer wavelengths.

The spectra of carbonyl compounds exhibit two bands: One a more intense band at 180 – 200 nm due to $\pi - \pi^*$ transition and other a low intensity band around 280 nm due to $n - \pi^*$ transition. $n - \pi^*$ transitions are always less intense as the non bonding electrons are situated perpendicular to the plane of π bond and hence to the plane of π^* orbital. As a result, the probability of electronic transition from $n - \pi^*$ is very low, infact zero according to symmetry selection rules.

However, because of atomic vibrations and partial atomic orbital overlap, $n - \pi^*$ transition happens but to a limited extent. The more the probability of a particular transition, the more the ε value for that transition. For most molecules, absorptions corresponding to $\pi - \pi^*$ transition have higher ε values than $n - \pi^*$ transitions.

The Chromophore Concept

The part of the molecule containing the electrons involved in the electronic transition which gives rise to an absorption is called the chromophore. The wavelength of the maximum absorption is called as λ_{max} (lambda maximum). Absorption maximum (λ_{max}) of simple, non-conjugated chromophores in given in Table 14.4.

Table 14.4: Absorption Maximum (λ_{max}) of Simple, Non-conjugated Chromophores.

S. No.	Chromophore	λ_{max} (nm)	Transition
1.	—C = C— (isolated)	~ 175	$\pi - \pi^*$
2.	—C = O	~ 285	$n - \pi^*$
3.	R—NO_2	~ 200	$\pi - \pi^*$
4.	—N = N—	~ 340	$n - \pi^*$
5.	—C(=O)—OH	~ 200	$n - \pi^*$

Except $\sigma - \sigma^*$ transition of saturated alkyl systems, electronic transitions require either a lone pair or a π bond from which the electrons can be promoted. In fact, UV spectra are generally only of interest, if the system is unsaturated. Chromophores with the highest degree of unsaturation give the most intense absorptions.

Auxochrome

It is a saturated group with lone pair of electrons which does not itself act as a chromophore but when attached to a chromophore shifts the absorption maximum towards longer wavelength alongwith increase in intensity of absorption. For example, —OH, —OR, —NH_2, —Cl, —NHR, —NR_2 etc. Auxochrome does not impart the colour but only deepens the colour, therefore these groups are also called as colour enhancing groups. All auxochromes have one or more lone pair of electrons. The effect of an auxoochrome is due to its ability to extend the conjugation in a chromophore by sharing its lone pair of electrons.

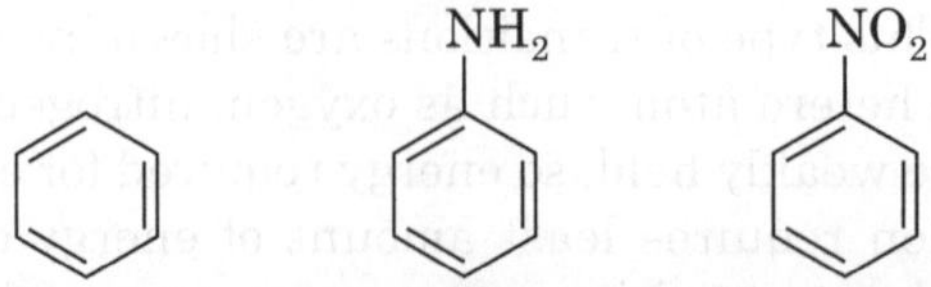

Benzene	Aniline	Nitrobenzene
λ_{max} = 255 nm	(NH_2 is an auxo chromic group)	(—NO_2 group is an auxo-chromic group)
	λ_{max} = 280 nm	λ_{max} = 280 nm

When an auxochrome —NH_2 or —NO_2 is attached to benzene ring its absorption changes from 255 nm in benzene to 280 nm (in Aniline) and —— (in nitrobenzene).

14.8 ABSORPTION AND INTENSITY SHIFTS

Changes in chemical structure or the environment of a molecule lead to the changes or shift in the absorption spectrum of molecules. Several terms are used to describe these changes:

1. **Bathochromic shift (Red shift):** The shifting of absorption maxima towards longer wavelength is called as bathochromic shift (Fig. 14.7). This is also called as **red shift** because the red colour has a longer wavelength than the other colours in the visible spectrum. The bathochromic shift may be produced due to presence of an auxochrome or change in polarity of the solvent (discussed in later section)

2. **Hypsochromic shift (Blue shift):** The shifting of absorption maxima towards shorter wavelength is called as hypsochromic shift (Fig. 14.7). This is also called as **blue shift** as the blue colour has a shorter wavelength than the other colours in the visible spectrum. Hypsochromic shift may be caused due to removal of conjugation or due to change in polarity of the solvent (discussed in later section).

3. **Hyperchromic shift:** This is an effect which leads to increase in intensity of absorption *i.e.* increase in ε_{max}. For example benzene shows B-band (benzenoid band which is a characteristic of aromatic compounds) at 256 nm and ε_{max} at 200, whereas aniline shows B-band at 280 nm and ε_{max} at 1430. The increase of 1230 in the value of ε_{max} of aniline in comparison to benzene is due to the hyperchromic effect of the —NH_2 auxochrome. Another example is the shifting of B-band from 257 nm and ε_{max} at 2750 in pyridine to 262 nm and ε_{max} at 3560 in 2-methyl pyridine.

4. **Hypochromic effect:** This is an effect which leads to decrease in intensity of absorption *i.e.*, decrease in ε_{max}. This is caused by the introduction of a group which distorts the geometry of the molecule. For example, biphenyl shows λ_{max} at 252 nm and ε_{max} at 19000, whereas 2-methyl biphenyl shows λ_{max} at 237 nm and ε_{max} at 10250. This decrease in the value of ε_{max} is due to the steric crowding of the methyl group which distort the chromophore by pushing/forcing the rings out of coplanarity which results in the loss of conjugation.

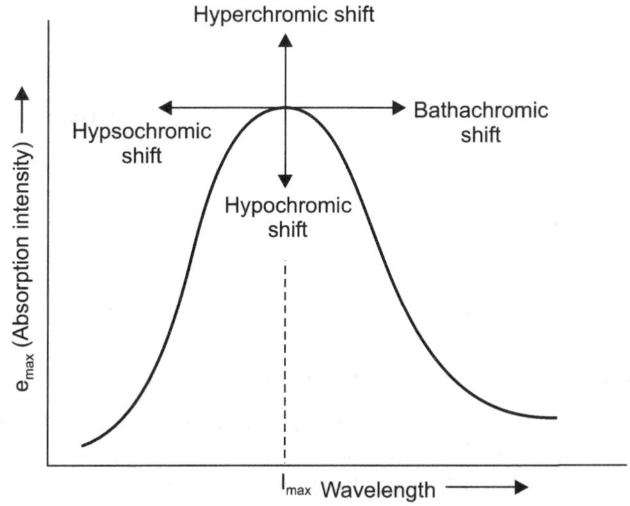

Fig. 14.7. Absorption and Intensity shifts.

14.9 FACTORS CAUSING SHIFTS IN UV-VISIBLE BANDS

Effect of Conjugation

Conjugation of a double bond with another double bond or a C=O group causes the absorption maxima to shift to longer wavelength with higher intensity (ε_{max}). Increased conjugation decreases the energy gap between the HOMO and the LUMO of a particular system, which means that less energy is required for an electronic transition in a conjugated system as compared to a non-conjugated system. As lower energy transitions appear at higher wavelength, it follows the general principle that the longer the chromophore, the longer the wavelength of the absorption maxima (Table 14.5). Increase in conjugation leads to bathochromic shift.

Table 14.5: Effect of Conjugation on UV-visible Bands ($\pi - \pi^*$ Transitions)

S. No.	Structure	λ_{max} (nm)	ε_{max}
1.	$CH_2{=}CH_2$	171	15,530
2.	$CH_2{=}CH—CH{=}CH_2$	217	21,000
3.	$CH_2{=}CH(H)C{=}C(H)CH{=}CH_2$	256	50,000
4.	$CH_2—C(=O)—CH_3$	187	900
5.	$CH_3—C(=O)—CH{=}CH_2$	219	3600

In ethylene, there are only two molecular orbitals *viz.* π bonding (ground state) and π^* antibonding (excited state). But in conjugated dienes, the π molecular orbitals of the two separate C = C group combine to form two new bonding orbitals (π_1 and π_2) and two new antibonding orbitals (π_3^* and π_4^*) Fig. 14.8.

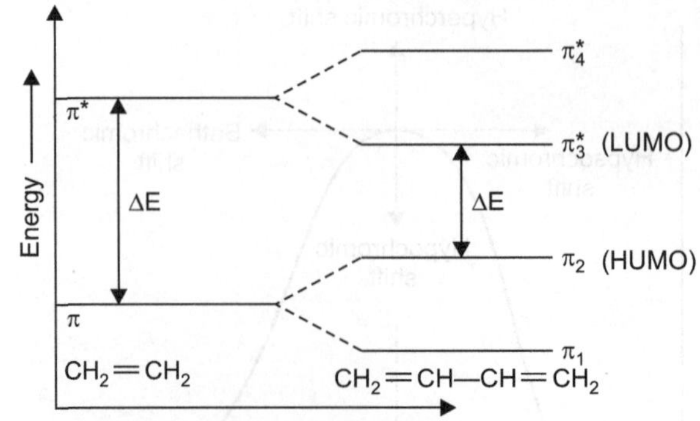

Fig. 14.8. Energy levels in conjugated and non-conjugated system.

It is clear from the above figure that as the number of conjugated double bonds increases, the gap between HOMO and LUMO decreases progressively. As a result the absorption maxima (λ_{max}) shifts to longer wavelength (bathochromic shift).

Sufficient conjugation shifts the absorption to wavelength that reach the visible region of the spectrum and the compound appears coloured. For example, β-carotene, an orange coloured pigment found in carrots has 11 conjugated double bonds which leads to much smaller energy gap between highest occupied π molecular orbitals and lowest unoccuppied π* molecular orbital than for an isolated double bond (Fig. 14.9).

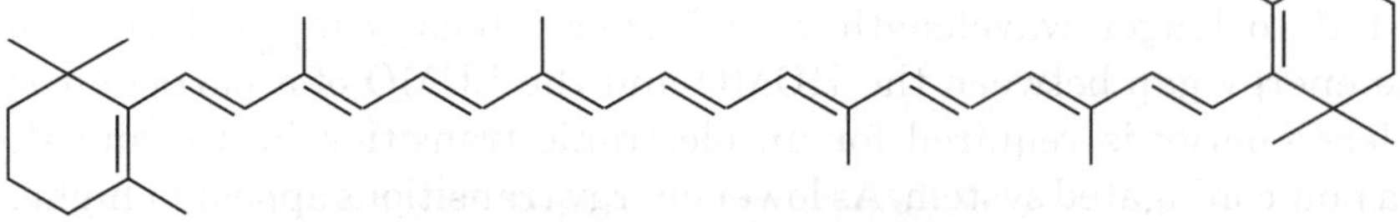

Fig. 14.9. β-carotene (λ_{max} = 455 nm).

Another example is lycopene, the pigment responsible for the red colour of tomatoes also has 11 conjugated double bonds (Fig. 14.10).

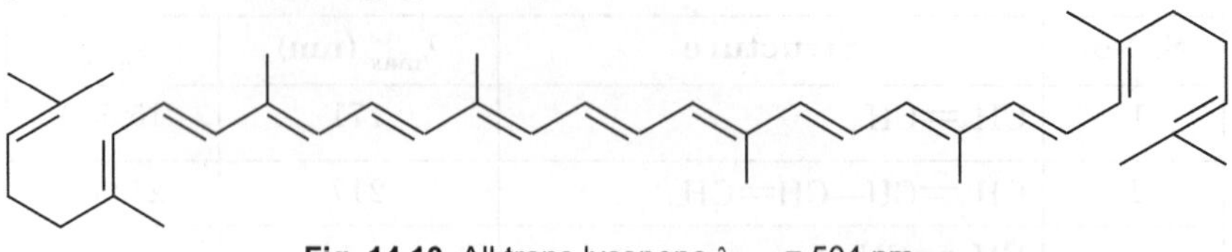

Fig. 14.10. All trans lycopene λ_{max} = 504 nm.

Also, as the number of condensed ring increases, the absorption maxima (λ_{max}) shifts progressively to higher wavelength. For example,

Benzene λ_{max} = 254 nm

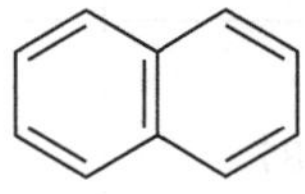

Naphthalene λ_{max} = 286 nm

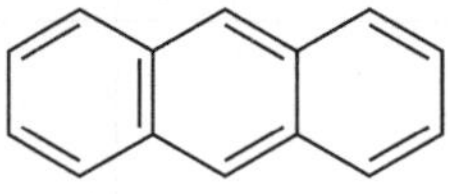

Anthracene λ_{max} = 375 nm

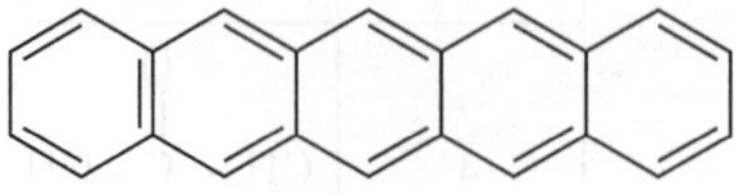

Pentacene λ_{max} = 580 nm (occurs in visible region)

Effect of Steric Hinderance

UV spectroscopy is highly sensitive to distortion of the chromophore whether it is brought about by ring strain or by steric hinderance. Thus, UV spectroscopic technique offers an advantage to detect any distortion if present in a molecule. This is reflected in a marked decrease in intensity and may also lead to either red or blue shift depending upon the nature of distortion.

The best example of steric hindrance to conjugation is found in biphenyl and its 2, 2′ - dimethyl analogues. Biphenyl system is completely planar and in 2,2′-dimethyl biphenyl, the two phenyl rings are pushed even further out of co-planarity resulting in the diminished π-orbital overlap. As a result the intensity (ε_{max}) and wavelegth (λ_{max}) of absorption maxima decreases.

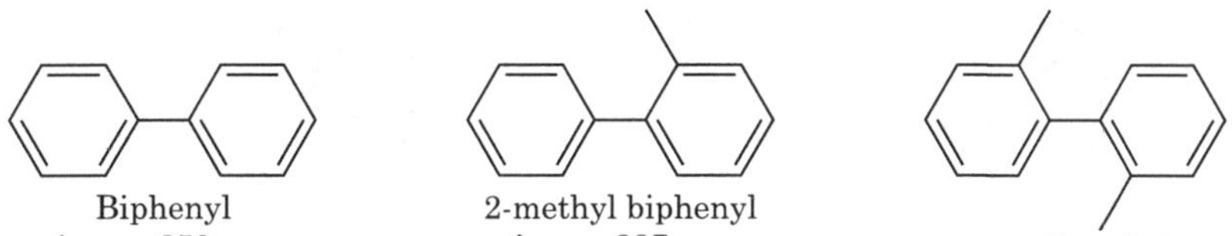

Biphenyl
λ_{max} = 250 nm
ε_{max} = 19000

2-methyl biphenyl
λ_{max} = 237 nm
ε_{max} = 10250

2,2′-dimethyl biphenyl (twist)
λ_{max} = 270 nm
ε_{max} = 800

Fig. 14.11

Similar trends can also be observed in compounds where geometrical isomerism is possible. It has been observed that *trans* isomers have higher λ_{max} with more intensity (ε_{max}) as compared to their *cis*-counterparts. For example, in Stilbene, the *trans* isomer absorbs at a higher wavelength with greater intensity than *cis*-isomer due to steric effect (Fig. 14.11). It is due to the more effective overlap of the π orbitals in *trans* isomer which results in achieving coplanarity of π system more readily than in *cis*-isomer.

Due to crowding/closeness of the bulky groups on the same side of double bond, planar geometry of *cis*-isomer is distorted as a result, it absorbs at shorter wavelength with less intensity.

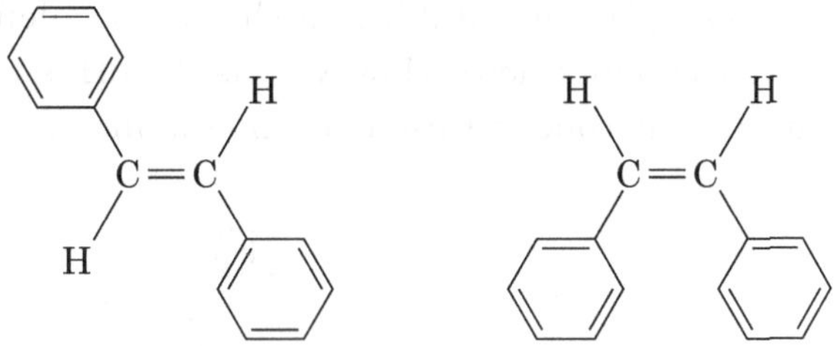

trans-Stilbene
λ_{max} = 295 nm
ε_{max} = 27000

cis-Stilbene
λ_{max} = 280 nm
ε_{max} = 13500

Fig. 14.12

Effect of Change in pH of the Solvent

Dramatic changes in the absorption spectra of some compounds, especially certain substituted aromatic compounds is observed with a change in the pH of the solvent.

Phenols and substituted phenols are acidic and display striking changes in their absorption on addition of a base. Removal of the phenolic proton yields phenoxide ion. In the phenoxide ion, the lone pairs of oxygen are delocalized over the entire π-system of the aromatic ring and increases the conjugation of the same. Due to extended conjugation, there is a decrease in the energy difference between the HOMO and LUMO, as a result bathochromic shift is observed alongwith an increase in the intensity of the absorption (Fig. 14.13).

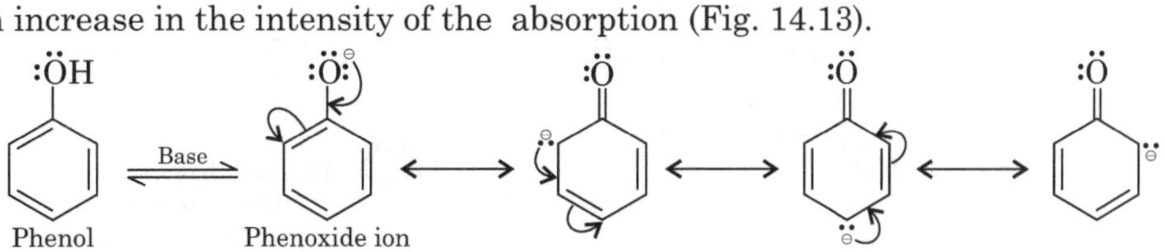

Phenol

Phenoxide ion

λ_{max} (H_2O) = 210 nm (ε_{max} = 6000)
= 270 nm (ε_{max} = 1500)

λ_{max} = 235 nm (ε_{max} = 9400)
= 287 nm (ε_{max} = 2600)

Fig. 14.13

In the similar fashion, when an aromatic amine is treated with an acid, it gets protonated to form anilinium ion. As a result the conjugation between the lone pair on nitrogen and the π system of aromatic ring gets disturbed. This results in a hypsochromic shift alongwith a decrease in intensity. (Fig. 14.14).

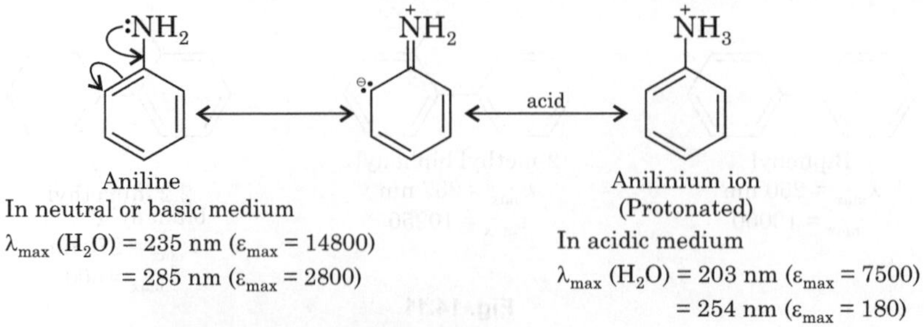

Fig. 14.14

Many pH indicators have their application due to their absorption in the visible region of the UV-Vis spectrum. Small changes in the pH lead to changes in the indicator charomophore and result in appreciable colour changes at predictable pH values. For example, phenolphthalein, an acid base indicator is a phenol which can be deprotonated at high pH value to give an anion (Fig. 14.15) extending the chromophore and leading to an appreciable bathochromic shift. As a result, the anion of phnolphthlein is deep magenta in colour while the non-ionized form is colourless. In neutral and acidic pH, the equilibrium shifts to the left and the concentration of anion is too low to observe the pink colour. However, as the pH is increased (basic pH), the equilibrium shifts to right and the concentration of anion is increased to an extent that the pink colour is observed.

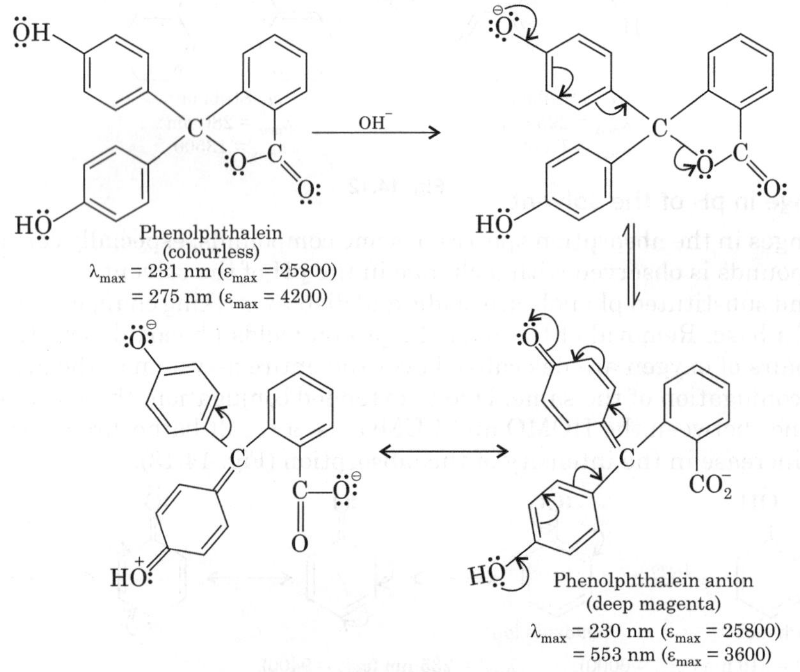

Fig. 14.15. Acid base equilibria of phenolphthalein.

Effect of the Solvent

All molecules absorb in the UV region. Therefore, the solvent used must be transparent within the wavelength range being examined. Most commonly used solvents and the minimum wavelength from which they can be used are given in Table 14.6.

Table 14.6: Commonly used Solvents in UV Spectroscopy

S. No.	Solvent	Minimum wavelength (nm)
1.	Water	190
2.	Cyclohexane	195
3.	Hexane, methanol, ethanol	200
4.	Ether	215
5.	Chloroform	240
6.	Carbon tetrachloride	265
7.	Benzene	280

The absorption spectrum depends on the solvent in which the solute/absorbing substance is dissolved. The position and intensity of absorption maxima for a particular chromophore can be shifted by changing the polarity of the solvent. Compounds like dienes and conjugated hydrocarbons do not experience any appreciable wavelength shift on changing the polarity of the solvent. Thus, in general the absorption maxima of non-polar compounds is same in polar as well as non-polar solvents. However, the absorption maxima of the polar compounds (like α-β unsaturated carbonyl compounds) is usually shifted on changing th polarity of the solvent. Polarity of solvent affect the $n - \pi^*$ and $\pi - \pi^*$ transition in a different manner. Let us discuss the effect of solvent polarity on these transitions one by one.

1. **$n \rightarrow \pi^*$ transitions:** In case of $n - \pi^*$ transitions of polar molecules like carbonyl compounds, the absorption maxima moves to shorter wavelength by increasing the polarity of the solvent. In these transitions, the ground state is more polar as compared to the excited state. As a result, the polar solvents form hydrogen bonds with the ground state of the polar molecules more readily than with their excited states and thereby decreases the energy of the ground state. Thus, the energy gap between the ground and the excited state increases which results in blue shift (shift towards shorter wavelength).
2. **$\pi - \pi^*$ transitions:** In case of $\pi - \pi^*$ transitions of an alkene, the absorption maxima shifts to longer wavelength by increasing the polarity of the solvent. In such transitions, the excited states are more polar than the ground state. If polar solvents are used, they form dipole-dipole interaction more with the excited state which reduces the energy of the excited state more than the ground state. Thus, the energy gap between the excited and the ground state decreases which results in red shift (shift towards longer wavelength).

14.10 APPLICATIONS OF UV-VISIBLE SPECTROSCOPY

Before NMR spectroscopy and mass spectrometry revolutionized the structural elucidation of organic compounds, UV spectroscopy was an important tool and was used to identify the key chromophore of an unknown compound. The application of UV is much diminished now-a-days, but is still retains its place in certain applications.

1. Qualitative Analysis

(*i*) **Structure elucidation of organic compounds:** UV spectroscopy is useful in structure elucidation of organic compounds, the presence or absence of unsaturation, conjugated double bonds, presence of hetero atoms etc.

(*ii*) **Determination of impurities:** UV spectroscopy is exploited for the detection of analytes in a number of separative analytical techniques like TLC and HPLC.

(*a*) **TLC (Thin layer chromatography):** TLC is commonly used for the rapid qualitative analysis of reaction mixtures. Many organic compounds used in research contain an aromatic ring or other UV absorbing moiety as an impurity which can be visualized on the TLC plate under a UV lamp.

(*b*) **HPLC (High performance liquid chromatography):** HPLC has transformed quality control in the pharmaceutical and other industries as it provides a rapid means of checking the sample purity. The majority of such systems use UV to detect the substance. UV detectors are usually of variable wavelength and can be used to detect molecules with absorption maxima (λ_{max}) above 210 nm by measuring the absorbance of the eluent. When a compound is eluted from the HPLC column, it absorbs UV radiation at the appropriate wavelength. The amount of absorbed UV radiation is directly proportional to the quantity of the particular substance that is passing through the column at that time.

2. Quantitative Analysis

(*i*) **Determination of concentration of a compound:** UV-visible spectroscopy can be used for the quantitative determination of compounds which absorb UV visible radiation. This determination is based on Lambert Beer Law which states that

$$A = \log_{10} \frac{I_0}{I} = \log \frac{I}{T} = -\log T = \varepsilon.c.l.$$

(*ii*) **Study of kinetics of chemical reaction:** UV-visible spectroscopy can be used to study the kinetics of chemical reaction by following the change in concentration of a product or a reactant with time at a fixed wavelength.

(*iii*) **Determination of dissociation constants of acids and bases:** The pK_a of *a* compound can be determined using UV-visible spectroscopy if either the acidic form or the basic form of the compound absorbs UV or visible light. The pK_a can be calculated by using Henderson-Hasselbalch equation:

$$\text{pH} = pK_a + \log [A]/[HA]$$

The ratio $[A]/[HA]$ can be determined from the graph plotted between absorbance and wavelength at different pH values and hence the pK_a value of the compound can be calculated.

3. Identification of Geometrical Isomers

Among *cis* and *trans* isomers, generally *trans* isomer absorbs at longer wavelength with more intensity (ε_{max}). This is due to steric hindrance in *cis* isomer as discussed (Fig. 14.12).

4. Study of Charge Transfer Complexes

Many inorganic species show charge transfer absorption and are called charge transfer complexes or EDA complexes (Electron donor acceptor complexes). For a complex to demonstrate charge transfer behaviour, one of its components must have electron donating properties and another component must be able to accept electrons. The evidence of the formation of these type of complexes is electronic spectroscopy. Such complexes generally display a spectrum which is different from the spectra of parent individual molecules. Charge transfer complexes are generally coloured as the first excited state of the complex is relatively close to the ground state, as a result the peak appears in the visible or near UV region. Typical examples of such complexes are the quinhydrone, benzene/iodine solution tertracyano ethylene and 1, 2, 4, 5-tetramethylbenzene complex etc. Hydroquinone is colourless and quinone is yellow but the quinhydrone crystals which are formed form hydroquinone and quinone are metallic green in colour. Similarly, benzene/iodine charge transfer complex shows absorption band at 3000 Å which has no counterpart in the spectrum of either benzene or iodine. Charge transfer spectra of tetracyanoethylene and 1, 2, 4, 5-tetra methyl benzene is shown in Fig. 14.16.

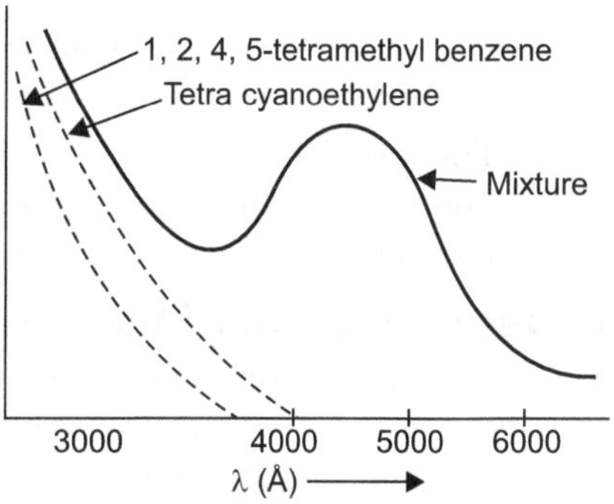

Fig. 14.16. Charge transfer spectrum.

5. Preference over two tautomeric forms:

UV spectroscopy can be used to detect the preference of one tautomeric form over the other. The tautomeric equilibrium between 2-hydroxy pyridine and pyridone-2 can be shown as

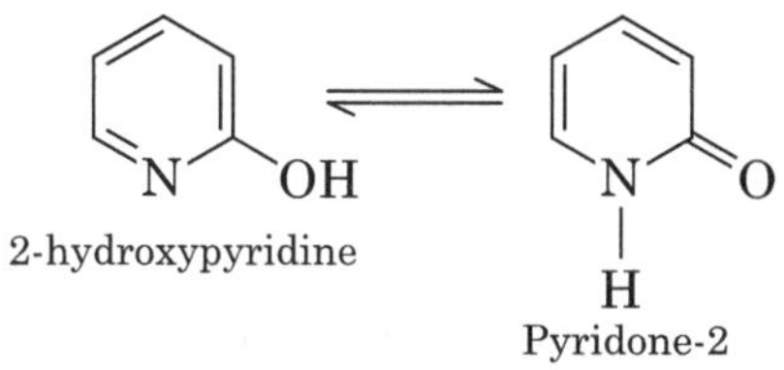

The spectra of these two compounds were found to favour 2-pyridone which contains a C=C—C=O moiety. The equilibrium is, therefore, shifted towards the right.

6. Distinction between equatorial and axial conformations

UV spectroscopy can also be used to differentiate between equatorial and axial conformations. Consider the following example:

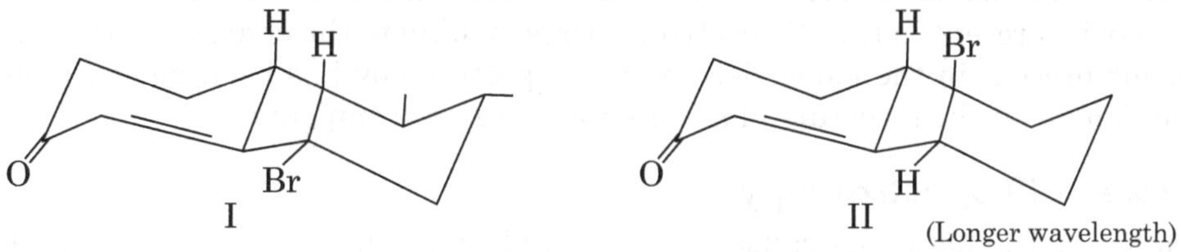

The $n - \pi^*$ transition (R band) which appears at longer wavelength is influenced by the presence of polar group in the γ-position. It has been observed that an axial γ-sustituent shifts the absorption to longer wavelength as compared to equatorial γ-substituent. Thus, the two diastereoisomeric compounds can be distinguished by comparing their λ_{max} values.

7. Distinction between conjugated and non-conjugated compounds

UV-vis spectroscopy can be used to distinguish between conjugated and non-conjugated compounds. Consider the following example:

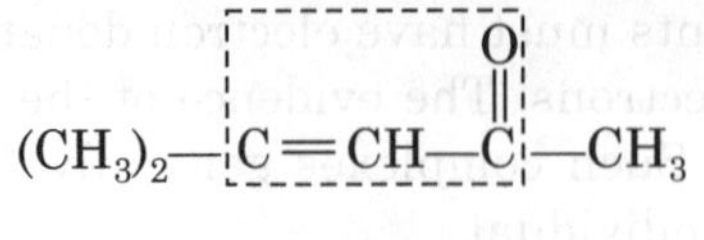

Conjugation

I

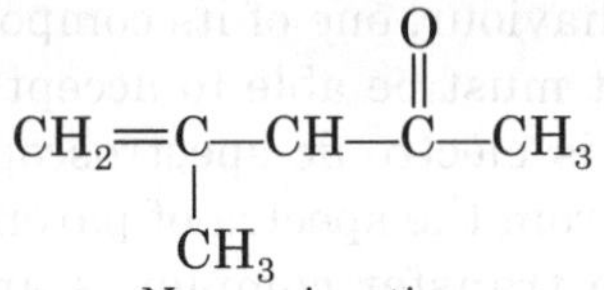

Non-conjugation

II

The $n - \pi^*$ band for the carbonyl group in compound I will appear at longer wavelength due to the presence of conjugation in it, while the same band appears at shorter wavelength in compound II.

8. Determination of the strength of *H*-bonding

Protic solvents form *H*-bonds with the *n*-electrons of carbonyl oxygen. As a result, the energy of *n*-electrons in the ground state is decreased depending upon the strength of *H*-bond. As the energy of *n*-electrons decreases, the energy gap between *n* level and π^* level increases and hence the $n - \pi^*$ transition will shift towards shorter wavelength. Therefore, by measuring the absorption maxima (λ_{max}) of a carbonyl compound in a polar protic solvent and non-polar solvent, the strength of *H*-bond can be determined.

14.11 INFRARED SPECTROSCOPY

Infrared radiations refer broadly to that part of the electromagnetic spectrum which lies between the visible and microwave regions. The IR region constitutes three parts as shown below:

Near IR – 0.8 μ to 2.5 μ

Middle IR – 2.5 μ to 15 μ

For IR – 15 μ to 200 μ

The IR region extends from 0.8 μ to 200 μ (12500 cm^{-1} to 50 cm^{-1}) but the most important region for an organic chemist is the region from 2.5 μ to 15 μ (4000 cm^{-1} to 667 cm^{-1}) in which molecular vibrations can be detected and measured.

Near IR is close to the visible region and has higher energy as compared to middle and far IR regions. Radiations in the infrared region are not energetic enough to cause electronic excitations as in UV spectroscopy. However, it does supply sufficient energy for bonds in the molecule to vibrate by stretching or bending. After absorption of IR radiation, the molecule thus gives close packed absorption bonds called as infrared absorption spectrum. A number of bands may be present in the IR spectrum corresponding to the characteristic functional group and bonds present in the molecule. Thus, IR spectroscopy has been most widely used to get information about the structure of an unknown organic compound.

Principle of IR Spectroscopy

Absorption of IR radiations causes excitation of molecule form lower to higher vibrational levels. As each vibrational level is associated with a number of closely spaced rotational levels therefore absorbed radiation causes transitions in its rotational energy levels also. Hence, IR spectroscopy is also called as vibrational rotational spectroscopy. Vibrational spectra appear as bands rather than as lines because a single vibrational transition is accompanied by a number of rotational transitions (Fig. 14.17). All the bonds in a molecule are not capable of

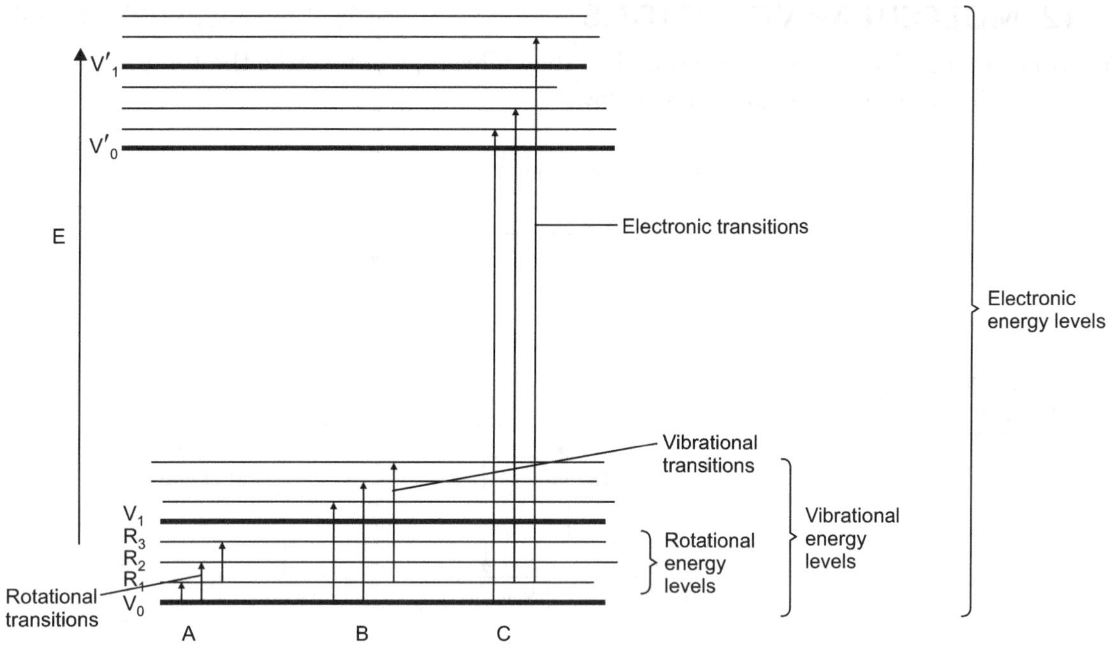

Fig. 14.17. Energy levels for a molecule and the possible transitions.

absorbing IR radiation but only those which are accompanied by a change in dipole moment will absorb in IR region. Thus, for a molecule to be IR active it must either possess a permanent dipole moment or its dipole moment must change during a vibration. Homonuclear diatomic molecules like N_2, O_2, Cl_2 etc. are thus IR inactive while heteronuclear diatomic molecules like CO, HCl, ICl etc. are IR active.

A typical IR spectra is shown in Fig. 14.18. Band positions in IR spectra are represented as wavenumber ($\bar{v}$) whose units are in cm^{-1}. On the other hand, intensities of the bands can be expressed either as transmittance (*T*) or absorbance.

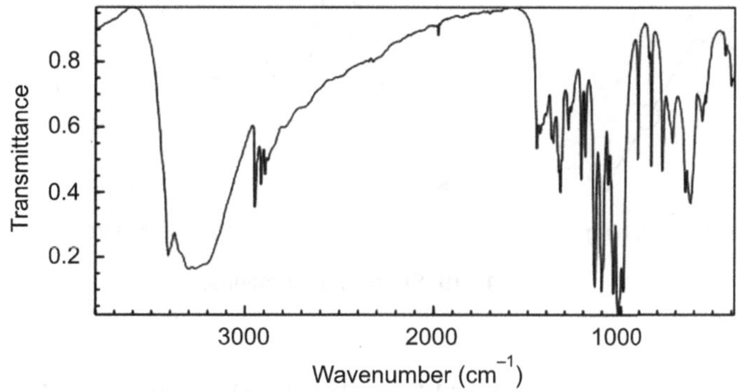

Fig. 14.18. A typical IR spectra.

14.12 MOLECULAR VIBRATIONS

The atoms in a molecule are never static but they vibrate, whatever be the temperature. The molecular vibrations are categorised as below:

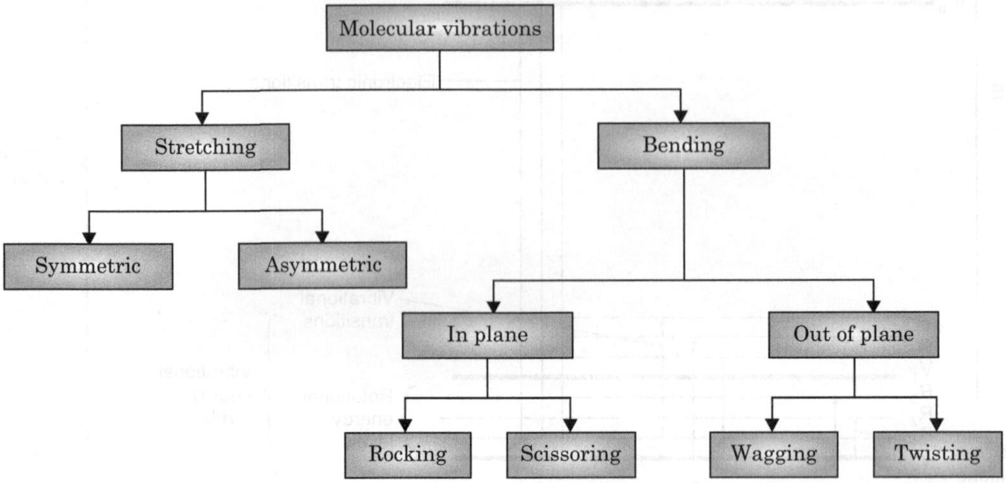

These molecular vibrations are also called as fundamental vibrations or normal modes of vibrations.

Stretching Vibrations

A stretching vibration is a rhythmical movement of the atoms essentially along the bond axis so that the bond length increases or decreases periodically. Stretching vibrations are of two types.

(*i*) **Symmetric stretching:** In this mode of vibration, the movement of the atoms with respect to a particular atom in a molecule is in the same direction (Fig. 14.19).

(*ii*) **Asymmetric stretching:** In this vibrational mode, one atom approaches the central atom while the other departs from it (Fig. 14.19)

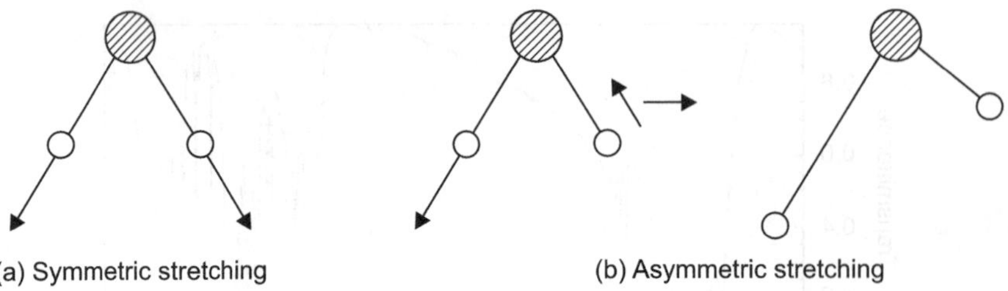

Fig. 14.19. Stretching Vibrations.

Bending Vibrations

When a three-atom systems is a part of big molecule, there is a possibility of occurrence of bending vibrations.

In this type of vibration, the distance between the atoms remains same while the position of atoms changes relative to the original bond axis (or it involves a change in bond angle between bonds with a common atom). We know that stretching of a spring requires more energy as compared to its bending, therefore, stretching vibrations require more energy and appear at higher frequencies as compared to bending vibrations of the same bond. Bending vibrations are of two types:

1. **In plane bending vibrations:** In this type of bending vibration, the atoms remain in the same plane as the nodal plane of the system. In plane bending vibrations one of two types:
   (*a*) **Scissoring vibrations:** In such of vibrations, the two atoms attached to a central atom move away from and towards each other like the two arms of scissors (Fig. 14.19).
   (*b*) **Rocking vibrations:** In rocking vibration, both the atoms attached to a central atom move in the same direction (Fig. 14.19).
2. **Out of plane bending vibrations:** In this type of bending vibrations, the atoms bend out of the nodal plane with respect to the central atom. These are again of two types:
   (*a*) **Wagging vibrations:** In this type of vibration, both the atoms move up and down the plane with respect to the central atom (Fig. 14.20).
   (*b*) **Twisting vibrations:** In this type of vibration, one of the atoms moves up the plane whereas the other atom moves down the plane with respect to the central atom.

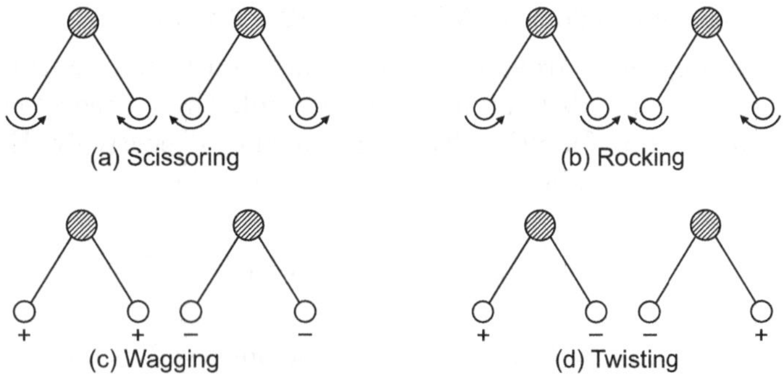

(+ and – sign shows movement of atoms up and down the plane)

Fig. 14.20. Bending vibrational modes.

14.13 NUMBER OF FUNDAMENTAL VIBRATIONS

A diatomic molecule has only one fundamental vibration which arises due to stretching or compression of the bond connecting two atoms like spring. Polyatomic molecules on the other hand, exhibit more than one fundamental vibrational absorption bands. The number of these fundamental bands is related to the degrees of freedom in a molecule.

A molecule has as many degrees of freedom as the total degrees of freedom of its individual atoms. Each atom has three degrees of freedom corresponding to the three Cartesian coordinates (x, y and z) necessary to locate its position relative to other atoms in the molecule. Hence, a molecule with N atoms will have total $3N$ degrees of freedom. A molecule with finite dimension will, thus, be made up of translation, rotational and vibrational degrees of freedom. Therefore,

$3N$ degrees of freedom = Translational + Rotational + Vibrational

The vibrational degrees of freedom can be calculated as follows:

For linear molecules:

Total degrees of freedom $= 3N$

Translational degrees of freedom $= 3$

Rotational degrees of freedom $= 2$

Vibrational degrees of freedom $= (3N - 3 - 2)$ $= 3N - 5$

(rotation about its axis of linearity does not change the position of atom $\therefore$ only 2 degrees of rotation)

For non-linear molecules, there are three degrees of rotation besides 3 translational degrees of freedom. Thus, for non-linear molecules.

Vibrational degrees of freedom $= (3N - 3 - 3) = 3N - 6$

For example, 1. SO_2 molecule: SO_2 is a non-linear molecule. Here,

$$N = 3$$

$\therefore$ Vibrational degrees of freedom $= 3N - 6 = 3 \times 3 - 6 = 3$

2. CO_2 molecule: CO_2 is a linear molecule. Here,

$$N = 3$$

$\therefore$ Vibrational degrees of freedom $= 3N - 5 = 3 \times 3 - 5 = 4$

3. C_6H_6 molecule: Benzene is a non-linear molecule. Here,

$$N = 12$$

$\therefore$ Vibrational degrees of freedom $= 3N - 6 = 3 \times 12 - 6 = 30$

As each vibrational degree of freedom corresponds to a fundamental vibration and each fundamental vibration corresponds to an absorption band. Thus, theoretically there should be 3, 4 and 30 fundamental bands for SO_2, CO_2 and benzene respectively. However, it has been observed that the theoretical number of fundamental vibrations are seldom obtained. This is due to the following reasons:

(*i*) The frequency of fundamental vibrations which fall outside the IR region of $4000 - 667\ cm^{-1}$.

(*ii*) Fundamental vibrations that are too weak to be observed as bands.

(*iii*) Fundamental bands which are so close that they overlap *i.e.* degenerate vibrations.

(*iv*) Certain vibrational bands do not appear due to lack of the required change in dipole moment of the molecule. Example, as in CO_2 molecule.

Vibrational Frequency

The stretching vibrations of two bonded atoms may be considered as the vibration of two balls connected by a spring, a situation for which Hooke's law applies. Therefore, an approximate value for the stretching vibrational frequency (ν) of a bond can be calculated using Hooke's law:

$$\nu = \frac{1}{2\pi}\sqrt{\frac{k}{\mu}}$$

where k is the force constant and μ is the reduced mass and is given by

$$\mu = \frac{m_1 m_2}{m_1 + m_2}$$

here m_1 and m_2 are the masses of the atoms (in grams) linked to a particular bond. The value of frequency can also be converted into wavenumber as follows:

$$\bar{\nu} = \frac{1}{2\pi C}\sqrt{\frac{k}{\mu}} \quad \text{where } C \text{ is the velocity of light } i.e.\ 2.998 \times 10^{10} \text{ cm s}^{-1}.$$

For a single C—C bond, the force constant k is approximately 5×10^5 gs^{-2} and it doubles and triples for double and triple bond respectively. The force constant is a measure of the strength of a bond.

The value of stretching frequency is directly proportional to the bond strength and inversely proportional to the reduced mass.

i.e.
$$\bar{\nu} \propto \sqrt{k}$$
$$\bar{\nu} \propto \sqrt{\frac{1}{\mu}}.$$

As the triple bonds are stronger than double bonds followed by single bond between the same two atoms, therefore, the vibrational frequency of these bonds follow the order

$$\underset{2150\ \text{cm}^{-1}}{\text{C}\equiv\text{C}} > \underset{1650\ \text{cm}^{-1}}{\text{C}=\text{C}} > \underset{1200\ \text{cm}^{-1}}{\text{C}-\text{C}}$$

⟶ force constant decreases
⟶ vibrational frequency decreases

Further, as the reduced mass increases, the vibrational frequency decreases. Thus,

$$\underset{3000\ \text{cm}^{-1}}{\text{C}-\text{H}} > \underset{1200\ \text{cm}^{-1}}{\text{C}-\text{C}} > \underset{1100\ \text{cm}^{-1}}{\text{C}-\text{O}} > \underset{750\ \text{cm}^{-1}}{\text{C}-\text{Cl}} > \underset{600\ \text{cm}^{-1}}{\text{C}-\text{Br}} > \underset{500\ \text{cm}^{-1}}{\text{C}-\text{I}}$$

⟶ reduced mass increses
⟶ vibrational frequency decreases

At ordinary temperatures the potential energy diagram of vibrating molecules approximates that of a harmonic oscillator. The potential energy diagram of simple harmonic oscillator or molecules at ordinary temperature is given by Fig. 14.21.

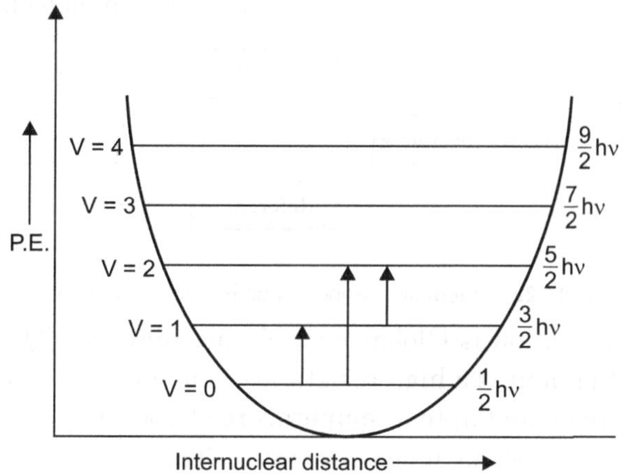

Fig. 14.21. Potential energy diagram of harmonic oscillator.

The vibrational energy of a chemical bond is given by the following expression:

$$E_{vib} = \left(V + \frac{1}{2}\right)h\nu$$

V = vibrational quantum number

h = Planck's constant

ν = frequency of vibration.

Transition from

(*i*) $V = 0$ to $V = 1$ are the most intense due to highly populated ground state and are called as fundamental bands.

(*ii*) $V = 0$ to $V = 2$ I overtone

$V = 0$ to $V = 3$ II overtone

$V = 0$ to $V = 4$ III overtone

Transitions from ground state to second, third, fourth or any other higher vibrational level give rise to weak bands called as overtones. These are weak because they are forbidden according to vibrational selection rules [*i.e.*, transitions can only take place between two vibrational levels if $\Delta V = \pm 1$, means change in vibrational energy level should be ±1].

(*iii*) $V = 1$ to $V = 2$ – I hot band (Hot bands are seen in IR spectum due to anharmonicity)

$V = 2$ to $V = 3$ – II hot band

The intensities of these hot bands are very small as compared to fundamental bands due to the fact that the population of $V = 1$ or $V = 2$ or $V = 3$ (from where hot bands arises) are very small as compared to $V = 0$ (from where fundamental band arises). This is because according to Maxwell Boltzmann distribution law, more the population of a particular state, more will be the intensity of the vibrational transition.

14.14 INSTRUMENTATION

A simplified working of the double beam IR spectrophotometer is shown in Fig. 14.22. One portion of the beam is passed through the sample cell while the other through the reference cell. Thus, the effect of solvent in the sample cell and the reference cell are cancelled out and the spectrum contains only the absorption bands of the sample molecule.

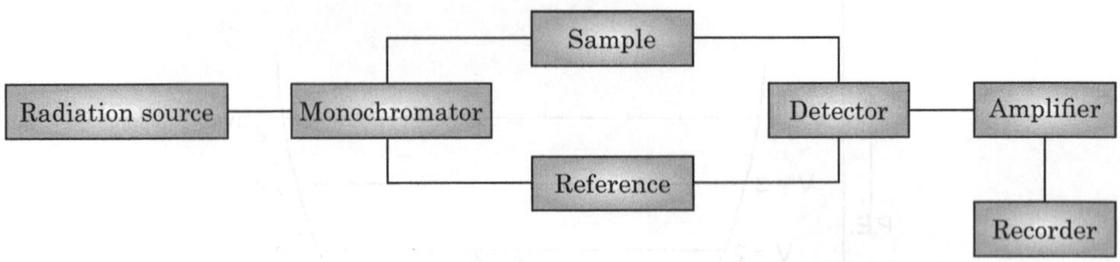

Fig. 14.22. Schematic diagram of an IR spectrophotometer.

- The source of IR radiation is Globar or a Nernst filament. The Globar is a rod of SiC while the Nernst filament is a high resistance element composed mainly of the oxides of rare earth elements heated upto a temperature of 1500°C.
- Prism or grating is used as monochromator. The dispersion of light by any prism material depends on its refractive index which changes with the frequency of light. Therefore, different prism materials are effective over different frequency range. NaCl prisms gives very good resolution in the 1300 – 650 cm^{-1} range and has acceptable resolution in the 1950 – 1600 cm^{-1} range but the dispersion is not satisfactory above 2000 cm^{-1}. Better resolutions are obtained with gratings as compared to prisms.

- The sample can be in any form *i.e.* solid, liquid, gas or solution.
- Commonly used solvents are CCl_4, CS_2, $CHCl_3$ etc. which absorb very less in the IR region.

14.15 INTERPRETATION OF IR SPECTRUM

IR spectrum is generally studied in two parts:

(*a*) **Functional group region (4000 – 1500 cm^{-1}):** The bands in this region are particularly helpful in identifying the functional groups present in the organic molecules. The characteristic stretching frequencies of all the important functional groups lie in this region, *e.g.* OH, NH_2, >C = O etc. The characteristic group frequencies are given in Table 14.7.

(*b*) **Finger print region (1500–667 cm^{-1}):** The absorption pattern in this region is complex and unique just like finger prints are characteristic to an individual. Stretching vibrations of C—C, C—O and C—N bonds and bending vibrations lie in this region. The overall pattern in the finger print region is characteristic of the compound as a whole because every compound shows a unique pattern in this region. For example, 2 pentanone and 3-pentanone have the same functional groups, so they show the same absorption bands in the functional group region but they differ in finger print region. So, a compound can be easily identified by comparing its finger print region with the finger print region of the actual spectrum of the compound.

Table 14.7: Functional Group Stretching Frequencies

Functional Group	Frequency (cm^{-1})
Alcohol O—H (free)	3640 – 3610
Alcohol O—H (H bonded)	3500 – 3200 (variable)
Amine N—H	3500 – 3300 (1° doublet, 2° singlet)
Terminal alkyne C—H	3315 – 3270
Olefinic and aromatic C—H	3080 – 3020
Aliphatic C—H	2990 – 2850
Aldehyde C—H	2900 – 2700
Nitrile —C≡N	2300 – 2200
Terminal —C≡C	2260 – 2210
Internal —C≡N	2140 – 2100 (weak)
Ester C=O	1750 – 1740
Aldehyde C=O	1740 – 1720
Ketone C=O	1700 – 1720
Amide C=O	1715 – 1650
Unsaturated ketone C=O	1680 – 1660
Alkene C=C	1675 – 1640
Aliphatic C—O	1280 – 1000 (strong)

Characteristic IR Bands

1. Hydrocarbons: Hydrocarbons show C—H and C—C stretching and bending vibrations.

Alkanes: A strong absorption band at 2850 – 3000 cm^{-1} represents sp^3 C—H stretching absorption (Fig. 14.23) and C—C stretching band appears at 800–1300 cm^{-1}.

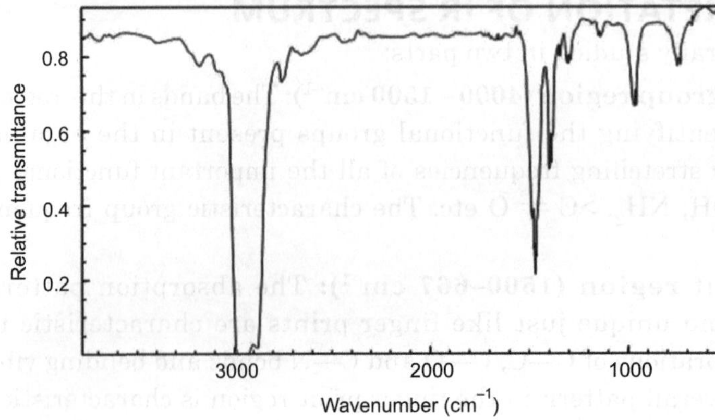

(a) Alkanes (Butane)

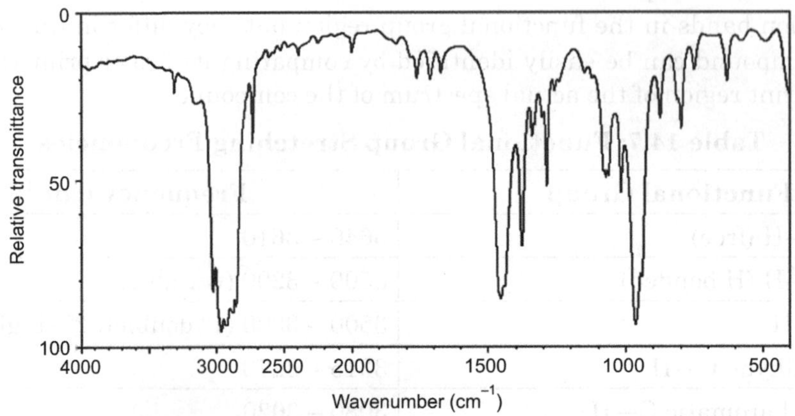

(b) Trans-alkene (trans-pent-2-ene)

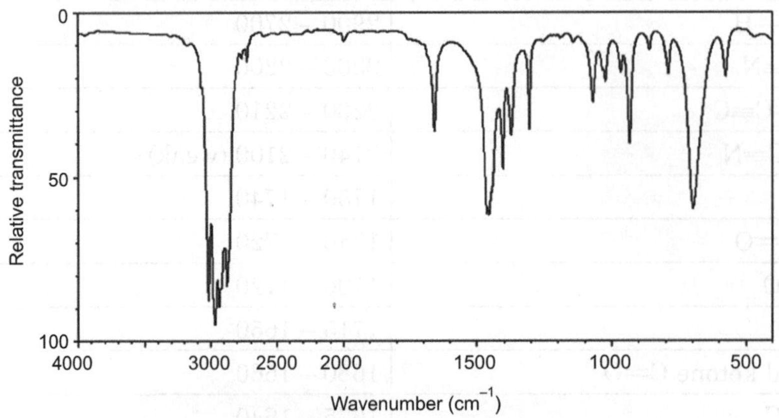

(c) Cis-alkene (cis-pent-2-ene)

Fig. 14.23. IR spectra.

Alkenes: Alkenes shows sp^2 C—H stretching absorption band at 3000 – 3100 cm^{-1} (Fig. 14.23) and C═C stretching band at 1600 – 1650 cm^{-1}. Also, for *trans* alkene C—H bending absorption occurs at 970 cm^{-1} and for *cis* alkene at 700 cm^{-1}. Thus, IR helps in distinguishing *cis* and *trans* alkenes.

Alkynes: Alkynes shows terminal sp^3 C—H stretching absorption band approximately at 3200 – 3300 cm^{-1} (Fig. 14.24) and C≡C stretching band at 2100 – 2140 cm^{-1}.

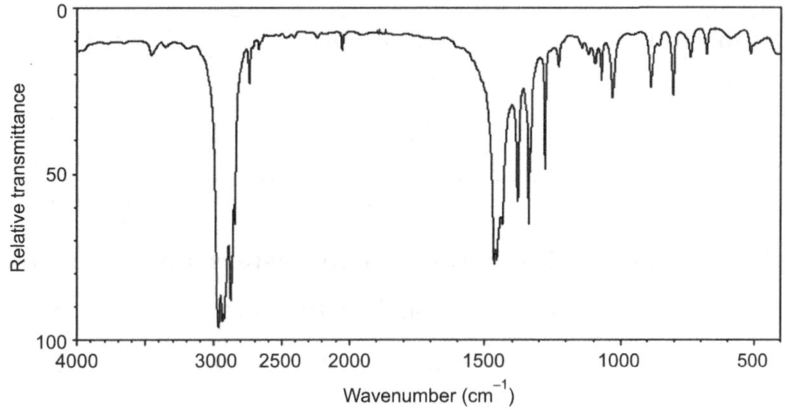

Fig. 14.24. IR spectra of alkyne.

2. Alcohols and Phenols: The characteristic bands observed in the spectrum of alcohols and phenols result from O—H stretching and C—O stretching. However, the O—H stretching is not a reliable indicator of the functional group present because the position of the O—H absorption is very sensitive to hydrogen bonding. In general, the more concentrated a solution, the greater the extent of hydrogen bonding. As hydrogen bonding weakens the O—H bond, the smaller the value of force constant and hence lower is frequency of vibration.

The free O—H group of alcohols and phenols absorb strongly at approximately 3650 cm^{-1} and this strong band is observed only in vapour phase or in very dilute solution in non-polar solvents. With increase in concentration of the solution, the extent of intermolecular hydrogen bonding increases and the strength of O—H bond decreases. As a result, an additional band starts appearing at around 3350 cm^{-1} at the expense of the free hydroxyl group (Fig. 14.25).

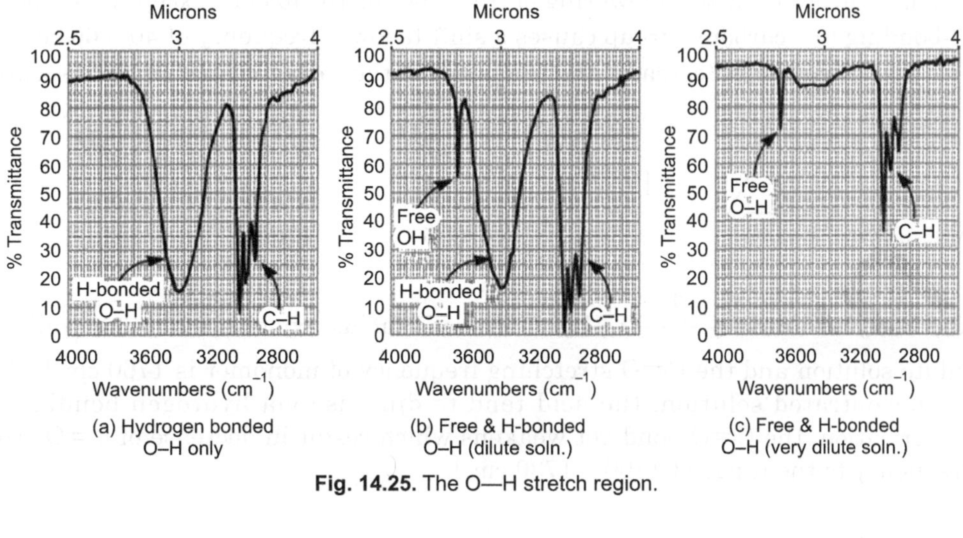

Fig. 14.25. The O—H stretch region.

The sharp C—O stretching vibrations are observed in the range from 1000 – 1260 cm^{-1}. However, the C—O stretching of phenols occur at relatively higher frequency as compared to alcohols because C—O bond in phenols exhibit some double bond character due to resonance. The O—H and C—H stretching frequencies are gives in table below (Table 14.8).

Table 14.8: O—H and C—O Stretching Vibrations in Phenols and Saturated Alcohols

Compound	O—H stretching	C—O stretching
1° alcohol	3640 cm^{-1}	1050 cm^{-1}
2° alcohol	3630 cm^{-1}	1100 cm^{-1}
3° alcohol	3620 cm^{-1}	1150 cm^{-1}
Phenol	3610 cm^{-1}	1220 cm^{-1}

3. Carbonyl group (aldehydes, ketones, acids, esters, amides, acid chlorides and anhydrides): The >C=O group absorbs strongly in the range of 1650 to 1850 cm^{-1}. The C=O stretching frequency is sensitive to attached atoms, therefore all the groups containing C=O moiety absorb at characteristic frequencies. The normal base values for the C=O stretching frequency of various functional groups are given below:

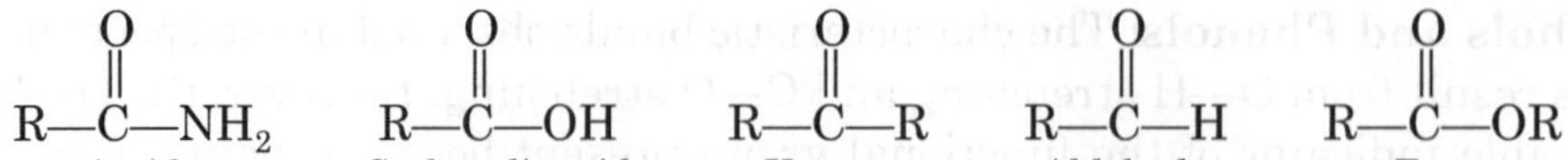

Amide 1675 cm^{-1} | Carboxylic acid 1710 cm^{-1} | Ketone 1715 cm^{-1} | Aldehyde 1725 cm^{-1} | Ester 1735 cm^{-1}

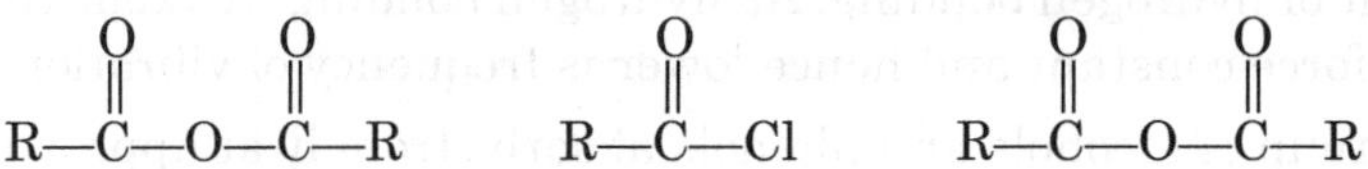

Anhydride 1760 cm^{-1} (Band 2) | Acid chloride 1800 cm^{-1} | Anhydride 1810 cm^{-1} (Band 1)

The position of C=O stretching frequency changes with the structural variation in the compound. Thus,

(*i*) α-β unsaturation causes a lowering of frequency of 15–40 cm^{-1} except in amides.

(*ii*) H-bonding to a carbonyl group causes a shift to lower frequency of 40 – 60 cm^{-1}.

(*iii*) Increase in ring size decreases the frequency of the carbonyl stretching absorption.

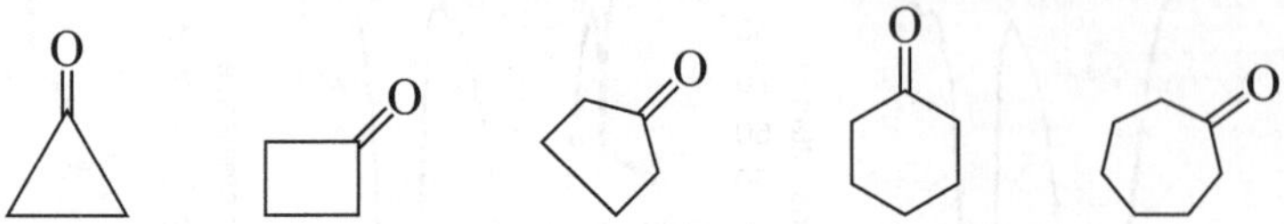

$\bar{\nu}_{c=o\ str}$ (cm^{-1}) 1850 1780 1745 1715 1705

(*iv*) **Carboxylic acids (—C(=O)—O—H):** Carboxylic acids exist as monomers only in very dilute solution and the C=O stretching frequency of monomer is 1760 cm^{-1}. However, in concentrated solution, the acid tend to dimerise via hydrogen bonding. Due to dimerisation, the C=O bond get weakens which result in decrease of C=O stretching frequency to the range of 1700 – 1730 cm^{-1}.

The other IR absorption characteristic of a carboxyl group is a very broad bond for O—H stretching in the range 2400 – 3400 cm^{-1}. It is a very broad band which is seen only with C=O band and it almost certainly indicates the presence of carboxylic acid group in the compound.

14.16 APPLICATIONS OF IR SPECTROSCOPY

IR spectroscopy is a simple and reliable technique widely used both in organic and inorganic analysis. Various applications of IR spectroscopy are discussed below:

1. Detection of functional groups: Each functional group has their characteristic fundamental vibration which gives rise to absorption at a certain frequency range in the spectrum. Thus, the presence or absence of absorptions at a certain frequency in the IR spectrum can be interpreted in terms of the presence or absence of a particular functional group in the compound. For example, compounds having $\rangle$C=O group like aldehydes, ketones, acids, anhydrides etc. give absorption band in the range 1650 – 1750 cm^{-1}. Absence of band in this range confirms the absence of $\rangle$C=O group in the compound.

2. Identification of substances: IR spectroscopy is very useful in identification of an unknown compound with a reference infrared spectrum. If all the bands of the unknown compound match the reference, the compound can be identified. In an IR spectrum, a large number of bands are observed and there is no possibility to have the *exactly* same IR spectrum of any two compounds (particularly in the finger print region). However, the IR spectra of two enantiomers are identical hence, IR spectroscopy fails to distinguish *enantiomers.*

3. Studying the progress of a reaction: Progress of a chemical reaction can be determined by examining IR spectra of small portions of the reaction mixture withdrawn from time to time. As the reaction progresses, some changes in the IR spectra occurs, like disappearance of a characteristic absorption band of the reactant group and/or the appearance of the characteristic absorption band of the product group because of product formation. For example, the gradual disappearance of the O—H stretching band around 3750 cm^{-1} and the appearance of C=O stretching band around 1725 cm^{-1} can be used to study the oxidation of alcohols to carbonyl compounds.

4. Testing the purity of a sample: It is possible to test the purity of a test sample by comparing its IR spectrum with that of the pure sample. Presence of any additional peaks in the spectrum is an indication of impurities in the sample. Sometimes detecting impurities by IR spectroscopy may be misleading because IR bands are generally not very intense and hence small amount of impurities remain undetected. However, the presence of impurities can be detected provided they absorb strongly in that region of the spectrum where the main component does not. For example, the impurity of cyclohexanone (a ketone) in cyclohexanol (an alcohol) can be easily detected on account of its intense C=O absorption band.

5. Detection of automobile pollutants: The exhaust from the poorly maintained automobiles contains hydrocarbons and carbon monoxide as two major pollutants. These pollutants can be detected by remote sensing which consists of an IR source on one side of the road for the intensity of absorption of hydrocarbons (2800 – 3000 cm^{-1}) and carbon monoxide (2170 cm^{-1}). The percentage of pollutants and hence, the extent of pollution can be detected by placing a detector, calibrator and a computer.

6. To ascertain hydrogen bonding in a molecule: IR spectroscopy is useful in distinguishing inter and intramolecular hydrogen bonding. This can be ascertained by taking a number of IR spectra of the compound at different dilutions. With increase in dilution the,

the absorption bond due to inter molecular hydrogen bonding shifts to lower frequency region whereas that due to intramolecular hydrogen bonding remains unchanged.

7. For determining alcohol level in blood: IR spectroscopy can be used to determine alcohol level in the blood of a suspected *drunken* driver. For this purpose, intoxilyser is used. It is an IR spectrometer that is specifically tuned to measure the intensity of the signals for the O—H stretching bands in alcohol. The diffusion of blood alcohol through the lung occurs into the blow of breath which is subjected to IR spectroscopy.

8. Study of Keto-enol tautomerism: IR spectroscopy is useful in determining the keto-enol tautomerism. β-diketones and α-ketoesters are known to exist as tautomeric mixtures and their IR spectra will show absorptions characteristic of both keto and enol forms *i.e.* a broad O—H stretching frequency (typical of alcohols) and a C═C stretching frequency are also observed in addition to the carbonyl stretching frequency.

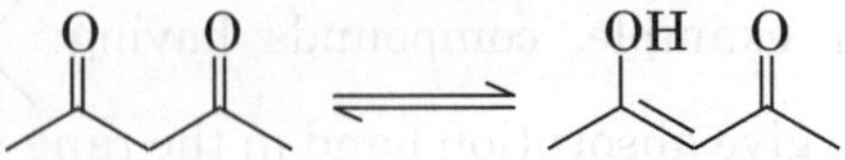

keto form
C = O → 1733 cm^{-1}
1710 cm^{-1}

enol form
C═O → 1645 cm^{-1}
C—O → 3300 cm^{-1}

The keto form has two carbonyl groups with different stretching frequencies, hence a doublet is observed in CCl_4. The enol form, on the other hand, has only one carbonyl group alongwith one O—H group.

9. IR spectroscopy is also useful in identification of ortho-, meta- and para-substitution in benzene rings.

10. IR spectroscopy is also helpful in identification of 1°, 2° and 3° amines.

11. IR spectroscopy is also useful to study the progress of chromatographic separations.

14.17 NUCLEAR MAGNETIC RESONANCE (NMR) SPECTROSCOPY

During the last seventy years or so, the use of spectroscopic technique has completely revolutionised the approach to structural problems and research in the field of chemistry. We have already studied ultraviolet and infrared spectroscopies. Nuclear magnetic resonance (NMR) spectroscopy is different from UV and IR spectroscopies in the sense that separation of energy levels exists only in the presence of externally applied magnetic field.

In the absence of externally applied magnetic field, the energy levels will be degenerate (*i.e.* all the energy levels have equal energy) and as a result there will be no transition and no spectra. NMR spectroscopy was discovered by Felix Bloch and Edward Purcell in 1946 and they received the Noble prize for physics in the year 1952.

NMR involves the absorption of radiation in the radiofrequency region and is concerned with the magnetic properties of certain atomic nuclei, notably the nucleus of the hydrogen atom (*i.e.* proton) and that of the carbon-13 isotope. The hydrogen nucleus is the most commonly studied nuclei by NMR spectroscopy because of its high natural abundance (99.98%) and presence in the majority of organic compounds. NMR, studies involving hydrogen atom are called as hydrogen or proton NMR spectroscopy (^{1}H-NMR or PMR). ^{1}H-NMR provides information about the number of different types of protons and also the chemical environment around it.

Carbon on the other hand is the main constituent of the organic molecules, therefore carbon-13 NMR is also very important in determining the structure of organic molecules. Carbon-12 isotope do not absorb radiofrequency energy (will be discussed in later sections) but the other isotope carbon-13 absorbs energy in radiofrequency region. Carbon-13 has a natural abundance of only 1%, hence, the sensitivity of ^{13}C is less as compared to ^{1}H NMR and requires longer time to record.

NMR active nuclei: The nuclei are made up of protons and neutrons each possessing an angular momentum due to its motion about the centre of the nucleus. Thus, the total angular momentum of a particular nucleus is the vector sum of the individual angular momentum of the constituent particles (*i.e.* protons and neutrons). The nuclear spin is characterised by a spin quantum number, ***I***. The value of I depends on the number of protons and neutrons present in the nucleus. Table 14.9 shows certain empirical rules which determine the net spin of a nucleus.

Table 14.9: Rules to determine Net Spin of a Nucleus

No. of protons	No. of neutrons	Spin quantum No. (I)	Examples	NMR activity
Even	Even	O	$^{12}_{6}C$, $^{16}_{8}O$, $^{32}_{16}S$ etc.	Inactive
Odd	Odd	Integral values (*e.g.*, 1, 2, 3....)	Deuterium (D or $^{2}_{1}H$), $^{10}_{5}B$, $^{14}_{7}N$	Active
Odd Even	Even Odd	Half integral values (*e.g.* 1/2, 3/2, 5/2,....)	$^{1}_{1}H$, $^{13}_{6}C$, $^{15}_{7}N$, $^{19}_{9}F$, $^{31}_{15}P$, $\left(I=\frac{1}{2}\right)$ $^{11}_{5}B$, $^{35}_{17}Cl$ $\left(I=\frac{3}{2}\right)$ $^{17}_{8}O$ $\left(I=\frac{5}{2}\right)$.	Active

* Important point to note here is that only those nuclei which have non-zero spin quantum number (I > O) can absorb or emit radiofrequency radiations (*i.e.* exhibit NMR spectra) and therefore, are NMR active nuclei. Nuclei like ^{12}C, ^{16}O, ^{32}S have spin quantum number equals zero, therefore these nuclei do not display NMR spectrum.

Principle of NMR Spectroscopy

It is very well known that a spinning charge generates a magnetic field. Since an atomic nucleus is also associated with electric charge (due to presence of +vely charged protons in it), therefore, like any other spinning charge, the spinning nucleus gives rise to a magnetic moment along the axis of rotation. Thus, a spinning nucleus acts like a tiny bar magnet.

In the absence of externally applied magnetic field (or field free space), the magnetic nuclei are oriented in a random fashion. But, when an external magnetic field is applied, the nuclei orient themselves either with or against the external magnetic field. When a magnetic field is applied to NMR active nuclei with spin quantum number I, the nuclei can adopt $(2I + 1)$ orientations in the field. Hence, for a nucleus with spin quantum number $I = \frac{1}{2}$ (such as ^{1}H, ^{13}C, ^{19}F etc.), there are two possible orientations $\left(2 \times \frac{1}{2} + 1 = 2\right)$: either the nuclei align themselves with the field (*i.e.*, parallel) or against the field (*i.e.*, antiparallel) the nuclei requires more energy to align themselves against the field than to align with the field. Therefore, nuclei which align with the field are more stable and hence are lower in energy (a state called as **α-spin state**), while the nuclei which align against the field are less stable and higher in energy (a state called as **β-spin state**).

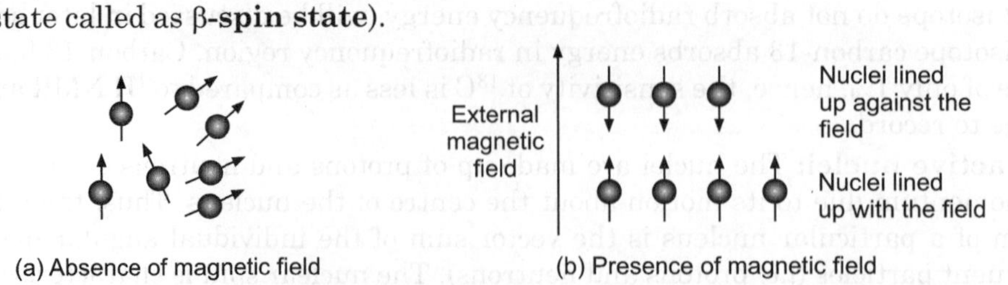

Fig. 14.26. Diagram showing arrangement of nuclei in presence and absence of magnetic field.

These two energetically different states provide the necessary condition for proton NMR spectroscopy. Energy is needed to flip the proton from its lower energy state (α-spin state) to the higher one (β-spin state). This energy is supplied by an electromagnetic radiation in the radio frequency region in an NMR spectrometer.

$\Delta E_2 > \Delta E_1$ *i.e.*, greater the strength of applied magnetic field, more is the energy difference between the two spin states.

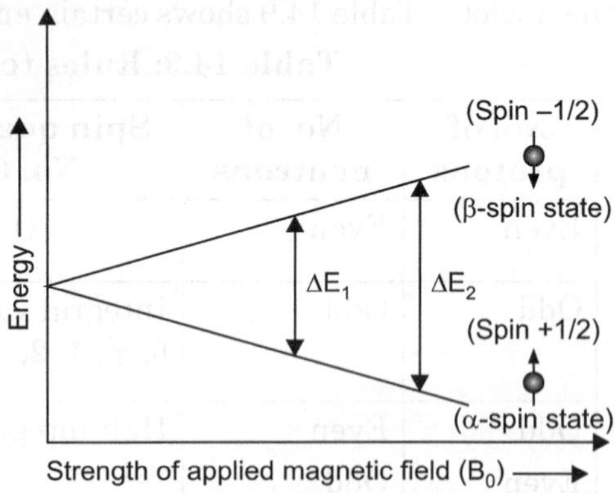

Fig. 14.27. Orientations for a nucleus with I = 1/2 in an applied magnetic field.

The energy difference between the two spin states is given by the following relationship:

$$\Delta E = h\nu = \frac{h\gamma B_0}{2\pi} \quad \text{and} \quad \nu = \frac{\gamma B_0}{2\pi} \quad i.e., \quad \nu \propto B_0$$

where h is the Planck's constant, γ is a nuclear constant, called as gyromagnetic ratio. It is the ratio of angular momentum of an atomic system to its magnetic momentum.

It has different values for different nuclei. B_0 is the external magnetic field strength.

*The unit for magnetic field strength commonly used is gauss but the SI unit is tesla and 1 Tesla = 10^4 gauss.

When an appropriate energy in radio frequency region is supplied to a nucleus, transition takes place from lower energy state (α-spin state) to higher energy state (β-spin state) and the nucleus is said to be in resonance with the external magnetic field. A typical NMR spectra is shown in Fig. 14.28.

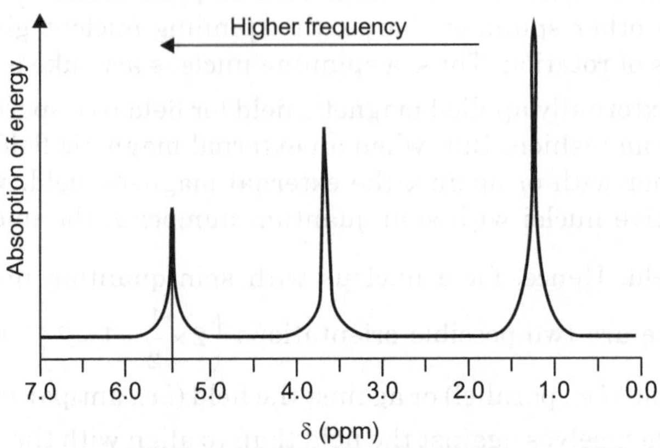

Fig. 14.28. ^{1}H-NMR spectrum.

14.18 INSTRUMENTATION

The first commercial NMR spectrometer came in 1953. The early instruments used permanent magnets or electromagnets with fields corresponding to 60, 80, 90 or 100 MHz. Now-a-days, 200–500 HMz instruments are widely used. All of the instruments above 100 MHz are based on helium-cooled superconducting magnets (solenoids) and operate in pulse Fourier Transform (FT) mode.

NMR spectrophotmeter consists of the following parts:

1. **Magnet:** A permanent magnet or an electromagnet is used to provide a powerful, stable and homogeneous magnetic field. The most common student spectrometer is equipped with a magnet providing magnetic field of 14,092 gauss.
2. **Sweep generator:** It is used to vary the strength of magnetic field over a small range by passing a variable direct current through coils that are coaxial with the direction of applied magnetic field.
3. **Sample holder:** NMR sample cell consists of a glass tube about 5 mm in diameter and 15–20 cm in length. The sample holder is placed between the pole faces of a magnet.
4. **Radio frequency oscillator and radio frequency source:** A signal from radio frequency source (ν = 60 megacycles s^{-1}) is made to fall on the sample by feeding energy from the radio frequency source into a coil around the sample tube.
5. **Signal detector:** It monitors the absorption of energy and amplifies the electronic signal.
6. **Recorder:**

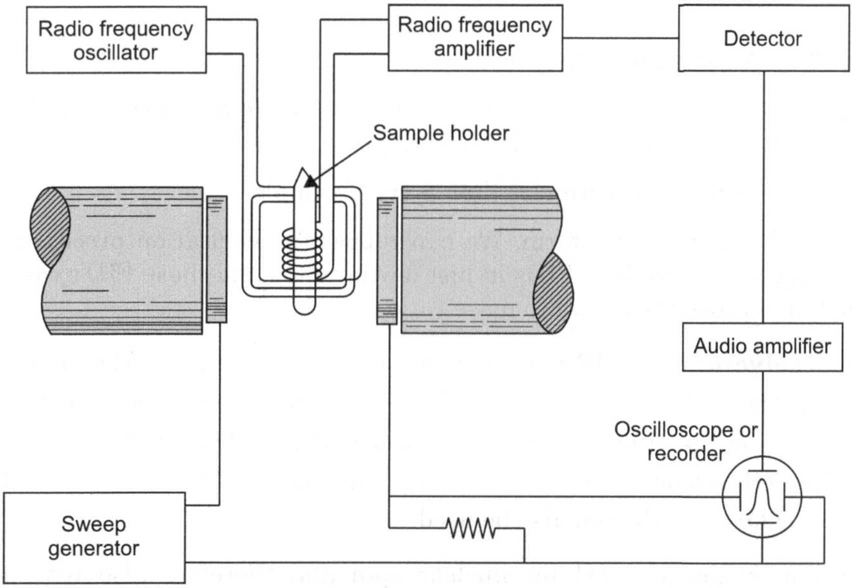

Fig. 14.29. NMR spectrometer.

NMR instruments are of two types: Continuous wave (CW) and Fourier transform (FT), let us discuss these one by one:

(*i*) **Continuous wave:** In CW spectrometer, the spectras can be obtained either by varying the external magnetic field keeping the frequency fixed or by varying the frequency keeping the field constant. The first approach is often preferred since technically it is difficult to very the frequency and holding the magnetic field constant.

The sample is dissolved in a suitable solvent and transferred in a sample tube which is then placed between the poles of a magnet. The sample tube is rotated about its long axis to average the molecules w.r.t. their position in the magnetic field. This increases the resolution of the spectrum.

When the field is varied and it reaches the correct strength for a given proton the nuclei absorbs energy and resonance occurs. As a result, a small electrical current starts flowing in the receiver coil surrounding the sample and displays it as a signal.

An important point to note in CW spectrometers is that each different type of proton is excited individually and its resonance peak is observed and recorded independently of all the other protons.

(*ii*) **Fourier transform (FT) NMR spectroscopy:** A fourier transform experiment is carried out by placing the sample tube in a magnetic field and by irradiating with a short pulse (broad spectrum i.e., rf pulse having all the frequencies) of radio frequency radiation. The result of this irradiation over such a broad range is that all the nuclei in the sample are excited at the same time. The spectrometer then detects the radiation given off by the sample as the nuclei "relax" back to their lower energy state and re-emit radio frequency radiation at their respective resonance frequencies and the net result is interfering wave patterns of differing frequency forming an interferogram or free induction decay (FID)—a plot of signal intensity versus time. The frequencies are then extracted from the FID by a mathematical process called as Fourier transform.

Advantages of FT-NMR over CW-NMR

(*i*) FT-NMR records a spectrum much faster (*i.e.*, 1–2 seconds) as compared to CW-NMR which takes 2–5 minutes to record a spectra.

(*ii*) FT-NMR can be obtained with less than 5 mg of sample.

(*iii*) Since, the FID is in digital form. We can repeat the excitation process a number of times to acquire hundreds of FIDs in just few minutes and these FID's can be added or averaged to improve the signal to noise ratio.

Selection of solvent: The NMR solvent is present in vast excess over the sample. Therefore ideally the solvent should be free of protons. Therefore, samples must be prepared using high quality deuterated solvents like deuterochloroform ($CDCl_3$), deutero diemethyl sulphoxide (CD_3SOCD_3), deuterobenzene, deuterated methanol, deuterated methylene chloride (CD_2Cl_2), deuterium oxide (D_2O) etc. CCl_4 can also be used.

The deuterium nuclei also exhibit nuclear spin and therefore also resonate but the resonating frequency of deuterium is quite different from that of the protons and the NMR instrument covers very narrow range of frequencies absorbed by protons only.

14.19 STUDY OF NMR SPECTRA

Number of signals: Equivalent and non-equivalent protons.

In a molecule, the proton with same environment absorb at the same applied field strength whereas protons with different environment absorb at a different applied field strength. A set of protons having same chemical environment are referred to as **equivalent protons** and all of them give rise to one signal. The protons with different chemical environment are called as **non-equivalent protons** and they give rise to different signals. Therefore, the number of signals in a ^{1}H-NMR spectrum indicates that how many different types of protons are present in a molecule. For example:

Compound	Number of signals
(*i*) 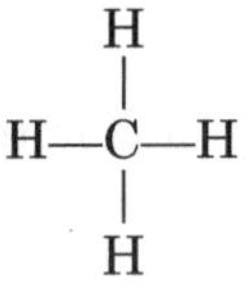	one signal (4 equivalent protons)
(*ii*) $\overset{a}{C}H_3—\overset{b}{O}H$	two signals
(*iii*) $\overset{a}{C}H_3—\overset{b}{C}H_2—Cl$	two signals
(*iv*) $CH_3—CBr_2—CH_3$	only one signal (6 equivalent protons)
(*v*) $\overset{b}{C}H_3—\overset{a}{C}HBr—\overset{b}{C}H_3$	two signals
(*vi*) $\overset{c}{C}H_3—\overset{b}{C}H_2—\overset{a}{C}H_2—Br$	three signals
(*vii*) 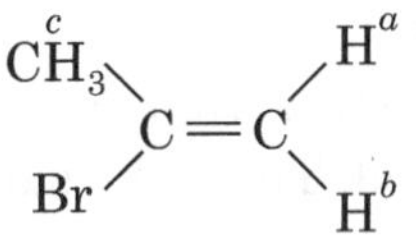	three signals
(*viii*) 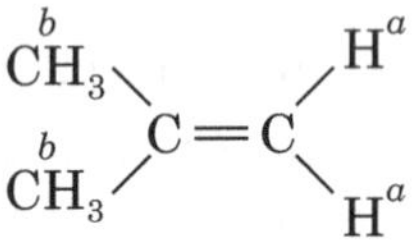	two signals
(*ix*) 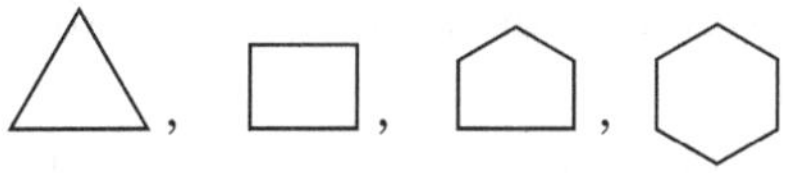	All will give only one signal (All protons are equivalent in all the four compounds)

Position of Signal-(Shielding and Deshielding)

We have seen in the previous section that the number of signals in an NMR spectrum tells us about the number of types of protons that a molecule has. The position of the signals in the spectrum reveals the nature of protons, i.e., aromatic, aliphatic, vinylic, hydroxyl, acetylenic adjacent to some electron attracting or electron releasing group etc.

When a molecule is placed in a magnetic field, its electron cloud tend to circulate and thus generates a secondary magnetic field (or inclined magnetic field) which may either reinforce or oppose the applied magnetic field. In case, the **induced magnetic field opposes the applied field**, the effective field strength experienced by the proton decreases and the proton is said to be **shielded**. As compared to naked proton, a shielded proton, requires a stronger magnetic field to produce an absorption signal and thus the proton is said to absorb **upfield**.

On the other hand, if the **induced magnetic field reinforces the applied field**, the effective field strength experienced by a proton increases and the proton is said to be **deshielded**. A deshielded proton requires a lower applied field to produce a signal and it is said to absorb **downfield**.

Whether the induced magnetic field opposes or reinforces the applied field depends upon the way in which π electrons circulate under the influence of applied field. For example, the induced field reinforces the applied field at the protons of benzene while it opposes the applied field at the acetylenic protons. As a result the aromatic protons get deshielded and absorb downfield whereas the acetylenic protons get shielded and absorb upfield.

The shifts in the position of NMR signals arising from the shielding or deshielding caused by electrons are called as **chemical shifts**.

Chemical Shift and Its Measurement

For measuring chemical shifts of various protons in a molecule, the signal for tetramethyl silane (TMS) is used as a reference.

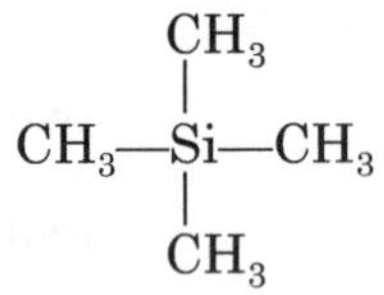

A small quantity of TMS is added to the sample under investigation. TMS protons resonate at exactly 60 MHz when the field strength is 1.4092 T and we can measure the position of other signals in reference to TMS. The shifts in the position of ^{1}H-NMR signals of different protons in a given sample with reference to TMS are called a chemical shifts.

TMS is used as a reference due to the following reasons:

1. It is chemically inert and has a very low boiling point (27°C) so that it can be easily removed by evaporation after the spectrum has been recorded. Thus, the sample under study can be easily recovered.
2. It has 12 equivalent protons, therefore its resonance is intense and sharp.
3. Si has very low electronegativity (1.8) as compared to carbon (2.5), therefore the shielding of equivalent protons in TMS is more than that of almost all the organic compounds. Consequently, almost all other signals appear in the downfield direction w.r.t. TMS signal.
4. It is soluble is most of the organic solvents and can be added to the sample solution as a reference.

NMR Scale

The most commonly used scale is delta (δ) scale. In this scale, the position of TMS is arbitrarily fixed at zero as most of the organic compounds resonate at lower field than the protons of TMS.

$$\delta_{sample} = \frac{\nu_{sample} - \nu_{TMS}}{\nu_0} \times 10^6$$

$$= \frac{\Delta\nu}{\nu_0} \times 10^6$$

ν_{sample} = resonating frequency of sample

ν_{TMS} = resonating frequency of TMS

where $\Delta\nu$ is the frequency shift in Hz and ν_0 is the operating frequency of the oscillator.

Greater is the deshielding of protons, larger will be the value of δ (and smaller τ).

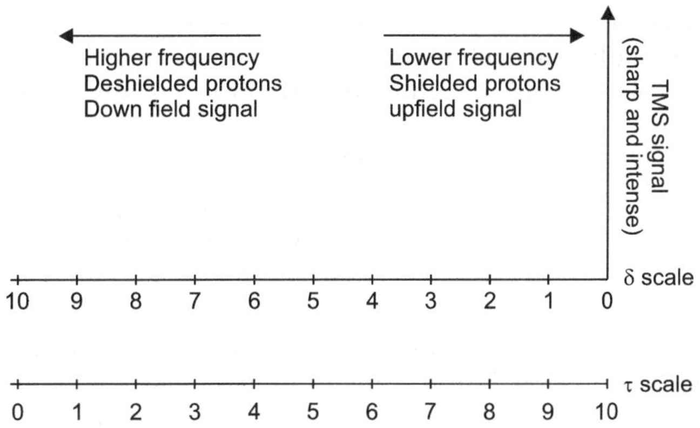

Fig. 14.30. Chemical shift.

For example, If a signal comes at 120 Hz down field w.r.t. TMS in an instrument using 60 MHz, it's δ value can be calculated as

$$\delta = \frac{120 - 0}{60 \times 10^6} \times 10^6 = \frac{120}{60} = 2 \text{ ppm.}$$

The ppm units are dimensionless and independent of the ratio frequency and the magnetic field used in the spectrometer.

Another scale for measurement is τ-scale (τ). On the τ scale, the position of TMS signal is assigned a value of 10 ppm. The two scales are related as follows:

$$\tau = 10 - \delta$$

Factors affecting chemical shifts: The main factors affecting chemical shifts are:

(*i*) Electronegativity effects (inductive effect)

(*ii*) Anisotropy effects

(*iii*) Hydrogen bonding.

Electronegativity Effects

Electronegative atoms like halogens, oxygen and nitrogen when attached to proton brings about its deshielding and therefore absorption takes place downfield. Greater is the electronegativity of the atom, greater is the deshielding of the proton and larger is the value of chemical shift. For example,

	CH_4	CH_3I	CH_3Br	CH_3Cl	CH_3F
δ(ppm)	1.0	2.2	2.7	3.1	4.3

With the increase in number of electronegative atoms attached to a particular carbon containing proton increases, the deshielding of proton also increases which results in increased value of chemical shift. For example,

	CH_4	CH_3Cl	CH_2Cl_2	$CHCl_3$
δ(ppm)	1.0	3.1	5.3	7.3

The inductive effect of eletronegative atoms weakens with increasing distance from a particular proton. As a result, the deshielding effect due to it also diminishes and therefore the farther proton from the electronegative atom appears at low δ value as compared to the closer protons. For example,

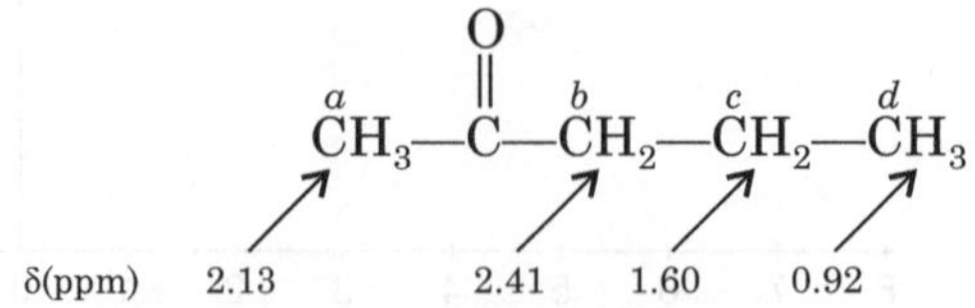

Here '*a*' and '*b*' protons are at the same distance from the carbonyl group, but the signal for '*b*' protons (—CH_2) appears farther downfield because methylenic protons appear farther downfield as compared to methyl protons in the same environment.

Anisotropic effects (π electron induced fields): Shielding and deshielding in unsaturated compounds depends upon the manner in which the π-electrons circulate under the influence of applied magnetic field. This effect is complex and produces different shift in different direction either downfield shifts called as **paramagnetic shift** or upfield shift called as **diamagnetic shift**. Let us consider few cases:

Alkene protons: An alkene in an external magnetic field is so oriented that the plane of the double bond is at right angle to the applied magnetic field. As a result, the circulation of π-electrons induces a magnetic field which is diamagnetic around the carbon atom and paramagnetic in the region of olefenic protons. Hence, olefenic protons experience greater field strength and appears downfield (or at higher value of chemical shift).

Alkyne protons: When placed in an external magnetic field, the orientation of alkyne molecule is such that the plane of the triple bond lies parallel to the direction of applied magnetic field. The circulation of π-electrons induces a magnetic field which is diamagnetic in the region of acetylenic protons. Hence, acetylenic protons are shielded and experience lower field strength and appears upfield (or at lower value of chemical shift).

Aromatic protons: In benzene, the π-electrons are delocalized cylindrically over the aromatic ring (above and below the plane of the ring). When a magnetic field is applied at right angle to the plane of the aromatic ring, the induced magnetic field is diamagnetic in the centre of the ring and paramagnetic outside the ring. Hence, the protons at the periphery of the aromatic ring experience greater field strength and appears downfield. On the other hand, the protons which are present above and below the plane of aromatic ring appears upfield.

Carbonyl protons: When placed in an external magnetic field, the orientation of carbonyl compounds is such that the plane of the carbon-oxygen double bond lies perpendicular to the applied field. The circulation of π-electrons induces a field which is in the direction of applied field at the aldehydic protons. Therefore, aldehydic protons experience greater field strength and appears downfield. Further, the high electronegativity of the oxygen atom also contributes to the higher δ value of the aldehydic proton.

Hydrogen bonding: If a hydrogen atom is involved in hydrogen bonding in a compound, it will get deshielded due to the strongly electronegative atom attached to it. As a result the absorption is shifted downfield (*i.e.* at high δ value). The downfield shift of the proton deepends on the strength of the hydrogen bonding. Greater is the strength of hydrogen bonding of proton, more is the deshielding of proton.

^{1}H-NMR spectroscopy can be used to distinguish between intermolecular and intramolecular hydrogen bonding. The intermolecular hydrogen bonding depends on the concentration of the sample and decreases on dilution while intramolecular hydrogen bonding does not depend on concentration and therefore shows no change in absorption on dilution.

Signal splitting (Spin-spin coupling): We have stated in the earlier sections that the number of signals in a ^{1}H-NMR system is equal to the number of type of protons present in a given molecule; there being one signal each for every type of equivalent protons. However, the actual spectra of the most of the compounds is much more complicated than expected on the basis of above statement. For example, $\overset{b}{C\text{H}}Cl_2—\overset{a}{C\text{H}}_3$ contains only two types of protons and hence, its ^{1}H-NMR spectrum may be expected to show two peaks, but in actual practice its spectrum consist of five peaks (Fig. 14.31).

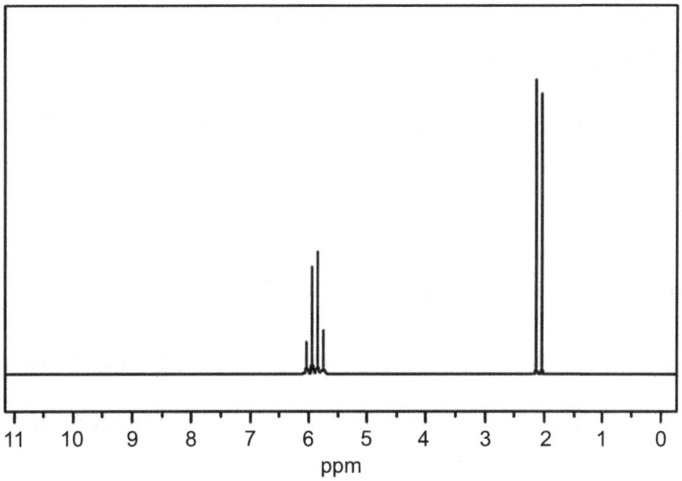

Fig. 14.31. ^{1}H-NMR spectrum of $CHCl_2—CH_3$.

In the similar fashion, ^{1}H-NMR spectra of other molecules also shows more number of peaks than expected on the basis of types of protons. This implies that the individual signal which we expect from a set of equivalent protons must be appearing as a group of peaks (*i.e.*, multiplet) and not a single peak (*i.e.*, singlet). This is known as **splitting of signals**.

The splitting of signals *i.e.*, number of peaks in a particular signal for a group of protons is not related to the number of protons in that group but is related to the number of protons in the neighbouring group. The splitting of the lines arises as a result of nuclear spin-spin interaction as discussed below:

$$CHCl_2—CH_3$$

Relative to a given proton in the CH_3 group, the proton of CH group can align itself in two different ways as shown:

	(1)	(2)
alignment of protons	$\uparrow$	$\downarrow$
degeneracy	1	1
net spin	$+\frac{1}{2}$	$-\frac{1}{2}$

This, there are two possible orientations of CH protons. Relative to a proton in the CH group, the three protons of the CH_3 group can align themselves in following ways:

	1	2	3	4	5	6	7	8
alignment of protons	↑↑↑	↑↑↓	↑↓↑	↓↑↑	↓↓↑	↓↑↓	↑↓↓	↓↓↓
Degeneracy	1		3			3		1
Net spin	+3/2	+1/2	+1/2	+1/2	−1/2	−1/2	−1/2	−3/2

Thus, the net spin combinations of protons in CH_3 group are four because some of the alignments are energetically equivalent (*i.e.*, 2, 3, 4 and 5, 6, 7).

The two possible orientations of CH group produces two different local fields at CH_3 protons, as a result the CH_3 absorption peak splits into a doublet (Fig. 14.26) *i.e.*, two lines/peaks of equal intensity. Similarly the four possible orientations of CH_3 protons produce 4 different local fields at CH protons, thus splitting the CH absorption peak into a quartet *i.e.*, four lines of relative intensity 1 : 3 : 3 : 1.

The magnitude of the splitting between the lines of a given multiplet is given by the spin-spin coupling constant (J). There are some general rules about spin-spin interaction which are helpful in predicting the number of lines in the NMR spectra. These are:

1. Splitting of a proton is caused mainly by the neighbouring protons which are not equivalent to the proton under consideration. For example:

   $\overset{b}{C}HCl_2—\overset{a}{C}H_2Cl$ – here, we have two types of protons, therefore splitting will occur.

   $CH_2Cl—CH_2Cl$ – here, there is no splitting as all the protons are equivalent to each other.

2. Splitting of one proton by another on the same carbon is very rare because such protons are usually equivalent to each other. For example:

   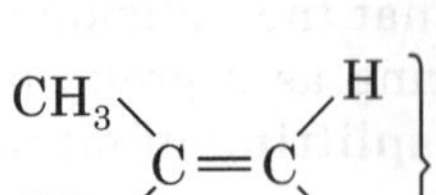

   Equivalent protons on same carbon (they will not cause splitting of one another)

   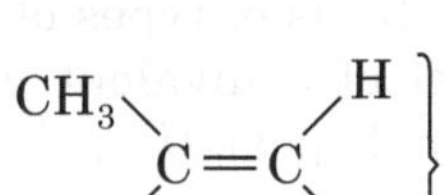

   Non-equivalent protons on same carbon (they will cause mutual splitting of each other)

3. The mutual splitting of protons which are separated by more than two atoms is generally not observed. For example:

   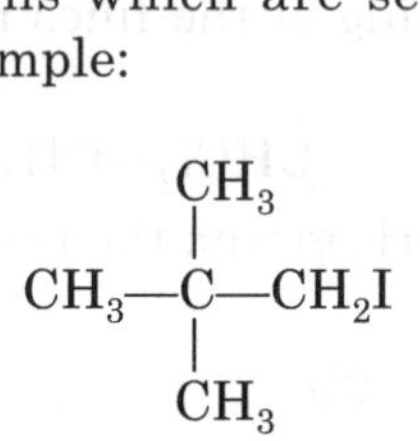

   There is no splitting of signals in this compound as the non-equivalent protons are separated by more than two C-atoms.

4. **(*n* + 1) rule:** The multiplicity of the peak of a group of equivalent protons is determined by the neighbouring protons. A general rule is that if '*n*' equivalent protons couple with the protons on adjacent C-atom, the signal splits into *n* + 1 peaks or lines. For example:

$\overset{a}{C}H_3—\overset{b}{C}HCl_2$

The signal of these three protons will split due to adjacent protons. Adjacent C-atom has only one proton *i.e.*, $n = 1$ hence according to splitting rule $(1 + 1 = 2)$, the signal would into two peaks *i.e.*, a doublet is obtained.

The signal of this proton will split due to 3 protons on adjacent carbon. Hence, the signal would split into $(3+ 1= 4)$ four peaks. Hence a quartet will be obtained.

5. When a group of protons have different chemical environment on both sides then a multiplet consisting of $(n + 1)(n' + 1)$ peaks is observed (n and n') are the number of protons on the adjacent C-atoms on both sides.
6. All the peaks of a given multiplet are not exactly of the same intensity. The intensity of these peaks is given by Pascal's triangle as shown below:

Number of protons on neighbouring carbon (n)	Number of NMR lines/peaks	Relative intensity (Pascal's triangle)										
0	1						1					
1	2					1		1				
2	3				1		2		1			
3	4			1		3		3		1		
4	5		1		4		6		4		1	
5	6	1		5		10		10		5		1

Applications of ¹H-NMR Spectroscopy

^{1}H-NMR spectroscopy provides the most informative tool in the study of organic chemistry. Some of its important applications are listed below:

1. **Determination of structure:** The following characteristics of ^{1}H-NMR spectrum provides a detailed information regarding the structure of an unknown compound:

   (*a*) the number of signals

   (*b*) position of signals (chemical shifts)

   (*c*) splitting pattern of the signals

   (*d*) coupling constant values etc.

   Certain other techniques like isotopic substitution, double resonance etc. are useful in analysing completely even the most complex ^{1}H-NMR spectra.

2. **Distinction between *cis* and *trans* isomers or geometrical isomers:** *cis* and *trans* isomers of a compound can be easily differentiated on the basis of their coupling constants. For example, the coupling constant lies between 7–11 Hz in the case of *cis*-protons and 13–18 Hz in the case of *trans*-protons.

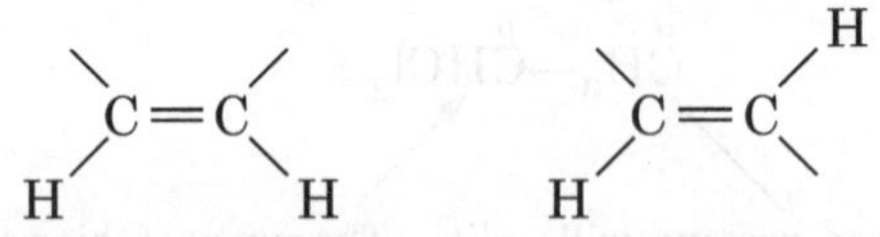

cis *trans*

3. **Identification of reaction products:** As the NMR spectrum helps to determine the presence or absence of various functional groups and other structural features in different substances, it can be used to identify the products of practically every reaction carried out in the laboratory. For example, the following reaction *i.e.*,

$$CH_3CH{=}CH_2 \xrightarrow{HBr} \underset{\text{I}}{CH_3CH_2CH_2Br} + \underset{\text{II}}{CH_3{-}\underset{|}{\underset{Br}{CH}}{-}CH_3}$$

either I or II can be obtained as a product. The spectrum of I would show 3 signals, II will show two signals. On interpretation of NMR spectrum, it was found that the product is identical with II. Hence, the product is $CH_3CHBrCH_3$ (according to Markownikoff's rule).

4. **Detection of hydrogen bonding:** Inter and intramolecular hydrogen bonding can also be detected by ^{1}H-NMR spectroscopy (as discussed in earlier sections).

5. **Magnetic resonance imaging (MRI) :** Medical practitioners use MRI, a multidimensional NMR imaging technique as a diagnostic tool for imaging soft tissues such as brain, heart and muscles. MRI is the image of the section of human body. It is helpful in detecting tumours in many organs.

6. **Study of proton exchange reactions:** There are certain processes which involve rapid chemical exchange like rapid exchange of O—H protons among the molecules of alcohol and of N—H protons among the molecules of an amine. Such exchange can be easily identified by taking the sample of the compound with excess of D_2O. The exchangeable protons in the sample are readily replaced by deutrons. We know that deutrons does not give a signal in ^{1}H-NMR spectrum. This implies that the signal of such protons (which are replaced by deutron) disappear from the spectrum. Hence, the comparison of the ^{1}H-NMR spectra of the original sample and the deuterated sample will enable us to identify proton that undergoes rapid exchange.

7. **Food chemistry:** ^{1}H-NMR can be used in the verification of the wine aging and authenticity as well as in the identification of the oil's fatty constituents.

8. **Quantitative analysis (determination of relative amount of tautomers):** The percentage of keto and enol tautomers in an equilibrium mixture can be determined quantitatively by using NMR spectroscopy. For example: Acetylacetone

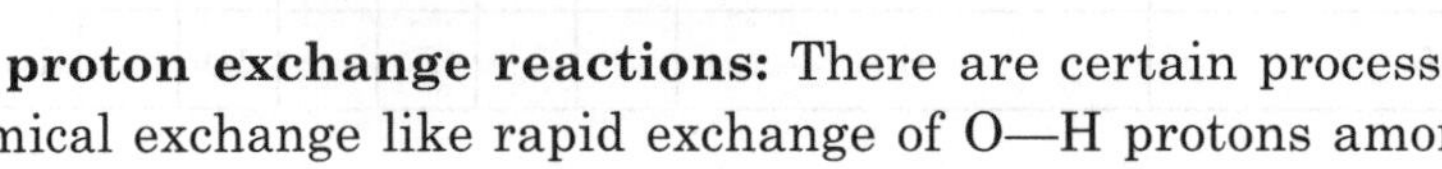

keto enol

The NMR spectrum of pure acetyl acetone shows signal for the following types of equivalent protons.

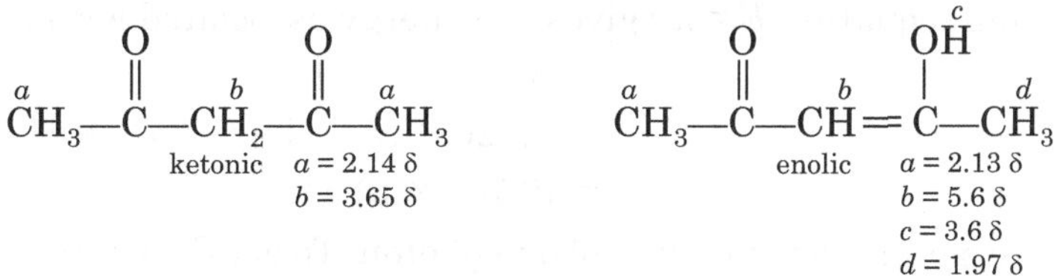

Ketonic form gives only two signals in ^{1}H-NMR while enolic form gives four signals. Quantitatively the number of keto protons relative to enol protons yields the following ratio:

keto protons : enol protons = 1 : 4 (This ratio can be obtained by comparing the areas under these signals).

Thus, we can say that the equilibrium mixture of acetylacetone contains 80% enol form and 20% keto form.

SOLVED EXAMPLES

Example 14.1. *The speed of a wave is 600 m/s in some medium. If 2400 waves are passing through a point in one minute, then calculate the wavelength of the wave.*

Solution: Given:

$$C = 600 \text{ m/s}$$

$$\nu = \text{Number of waves passing through a point in one second}$$

$$= \frac{2400}{60} = 40 \text{ wave/second}$$

$$\lambda = \frac{C}{\nu} = \frac{600}{40} = 15 \text{ m.}$$

Example 14.2. *For a light of wavelength 408 nm, determine*

(a) *the frequency*

(b) *the wavenumber*

(c) *the wavelength in Å*

(d) *the total energy in joules associated with one mole of photons*

Solution: Given: $\lambda = 408 \text{ nm} = 408 \times 10^{-9}$ m

We know $C = 3 \times 10^8$ m/s

(a) Frequency $\nu = \frac{C}{\nu} = \frac{3 \times 10^8}{408 \times 10^{-9} \text{ m}} = 7.35 \times 10^{14} \text{ s}^{-1}$

(b) Wavenumber $= \bar{\nu} = \frac{1}{\lambda} = \frac{1}{408 \times 10^{-9} \text{ m}} = 2.45 \times 10^6 \text{ m}^{-1}$

(c) Wavelength in Å (1 Å = 10^{-10} m)

$$\lambda = 408 \text{ nm } (1 \text{ nm} = 10^{-9} \text{ m})$$

$$1 \text{ nm} = 10 \text{ Å}$$

$$\therefore \quad \lambda = 4080 \text{ Å}$$

(*d*) The Einstein equation $E = h\nu$ gives the energy associated with a single photon.

$$E = h\nu$$
$$= (6.626 \times 10^{-34}\ \text{Js})\ (7.35 \times 10^{14}\ \text{s}^{-1})$$
$$= 48.701 \times 10^{-19}\ \text{J}$$

This is the energy per photon or energy of one photon. To get the energy per mole of photon, we need to multiply the obtained energy by Avogadro's number

$$\text{Energy/mole} = E \cdot N_A = 48.701 \times 6.023 \times 10^{23}\ \text{J/mole}$$
$$= 293.32\ \text{J/mole.}$$

Example 14.3. *Convert the following wavelengths in terms of wave numbers in cm*$^{-1}$*.*

(*a*) *12.5 μ* (*b*) *285 nm* (*c*) *1950 pm.*

Solution: (*a*) $\lambda = 12.5\ \mu = 12.5 \times 10^{-6}\ \text{m} = 12.5 \times 10^{-4}\ \text{cm}$

$$\bar{\nu} = \frac{1}{\lambda} = \frac{1}{12.5 \times 10^{-4}\ \text{cm}} = 0.8 \times 10^{4}\ \text{cm}^{-1} = 8000\ \text{cm}^{-1}$$

(*b*) $\lambda = 285\ \text{nm} = 285 \times 10^{-9}\ \text{m} = 285 \times 10^{-7}\ \text{cm}$

$$\bar{\nu} = \frac{1}{\lambda} = \frac{1}{285 \times 10^{-7}\ \text{cm}} = 0.00351 \times 10^{7}\ \text{cm}^{-1} = 3.51 \times 10^{4}\ \text{cm}^{-1}$$

(*c*) $\lambda = 1950\ \text{pm} = 1950 \times 10^{-12}\ \text{m} = 1950 \times 10^{-10}\ \text{cm}$

$$\bar{\nu} = \frac{1}{1950 \times 10^{-10}\ \text{cm}}$$
$$= 0.000513 \times 10^{10}\ \text{cm}^{-1}$$
$$= 5.13 \times 10^{6}\ \text{cm}^{-1}.$$

Example 14.4. *Calculate the wavenumber of stretching vibration of a C═C bond. Given force constant (k = 10 × 10*^{5} *dynes cm*$^{-1}$*).*

Solution: Wavenumber is given by

$$\bar{\nu} = \frac{1}{2\pi C}\sqrt{\frac{k}{\mu}}$$
$$C = 3 \times 10^{10}\ \text{cm s}^{-1}$$
$$k = 10 \times 10^{5}\ \text{dyne cm}^{-1} = 10 \times 10^{5}\ \text{gm sec}^{-2}$$
$$\mu = \frac{m_1 m_2}{m_1 + m_2} \text{ for C═C} \Rightarrow m_1 = m_2 = 12\ \text{amu}$$
$$= \frac{12 \times 12}{12 + 12} = \frac{144}{24} = 6\ \text{amu}$$

amu can be converted into gm by dividing it by Avogadro's number N_A (*i.e.*, 6.022 × 10^{23})

$$= \frac{6}{6.022 \times 10^{23}}\ \text{gm} = 9.96 \times 10^{-24}\ \text{gm}$$
$$\bar{\nu} = \frac{1}{2 \times 3.142 \times 3 \times 10^{10}}\sqrt{\frac{10 \times 10^{5}}{9.96 \times 10^{-24}}}\ \text{cm}^{-1}$$
$$= 1.680 \times 10^{3}\ \text{cm}^{-1} = 1680\ \text{cm}^{-1}.$$

Example 14.5. *Fundamental vibrational frequency of H_2 is 4401.21 cm^{-1}. Compute the fundamental vibrational frequency of D_2 assuming the same force constant.*

Solution: $\bar{\nu}_{H_2} = \frac{1}{2\pi C}\sqrt{\frac{k_{H_2}}{\mu_{H_2}}}$, $\bar{\nu}_{D_2} = \frac{1}{2\pi C}\sqrt{\frac{k_{D_2}}{\mu_{D_2}}}$, $k_{H_2} = k_{D_2} = k$

$$\frac{\bar{\nu}_{D_2}}{\bar{\nu}_{H_2}} = \frac{\frac{1}{2\pi C}\sqrt{\frac{k}{\mu_{D_2}}}}{\frac{1}{2\pi C}\sqrt{\frac{k}{\mu_{H_2}}}} = \sqrt{\frac{\mu_{H_2}}{\mu_{D_2}}}$$

$$\mu_{H_2} = \frac{1\times 1}{1+1} = \frac{1}{2}\text{ amu}$$

$$\mu_{D_2} = \frac{2\times 2}{2+2} = 1\text{ amu}$$

$$\bar{\nu}_{H_2} = 4401\text{ cm}^{-1}$$

$$\bar{\nu}_{D_2} = \bar{\nu}_{H_2}\sqrt{\frac{\mu_{H_2}}{\mu_{D_2}}} = 4401\sqrt{\frac{1}{2}}$$

$$= 4401 \times 0.707\text{ cm}^{-1}$$

$$\bar{\nu}_{D_2} = 3111.65\text{ cm}^{-1}.$$

Example 14.6. *The far IR spectrum of KCl has an intense line at 278 cm^{-1}. Calculate the force constant (atomic weights K = 38.964 amu and Cl = 34.969 amu).*

Solution:

$$\bar{\nu} = \frac{1}{2\pi C}\sqrt{\frac{k}{\mu}}$$

$$\mu = \frac{M_K M_{Cl}}{(M_K + M_{Cl})}$$

$$= \frac{38.964\times 34.969}{(38.964+34.969)} = \frac{1362.532}{73.933}\text{ amu}$$

$$= \frac{1362.532}{73.933}\times\frac{1}{N_A}\text{ gm}$$

$$= \frac{1362.532}{73.933}\times\frac{1}{6.022\times 10^{23}}$$

$$= 30.59 \times 10^{-24}\text{ g} = 30.59 \times 10^{-27}\text{ kg}$$

$$\bar{\nu} = 278\text{ cm}^{-1}$$

$$\therefore \quad \sqrt{k} = 2\pi C\bar{\nu}\sqrt{\mu}$$

$$k = (2\pi C\bar{\nu})^2\,\mu$$

$$= (2 \times 3.14 \times 3 \times 10^{10} \times 278)^2 \times 30.59 \times 10^{-27}\text{ Nm}^{-1}$$

$$= 83.94\text{ Nm}^{-1}.$$

Example 14.7. *How many proton signals would be expected in the ^1H-NMR spectra of the following compounds?*

(a) CH_2ClCH_2Cl *(b)* CH_3OCH_3 *(c)* $CH_3OCH_2CH_3$ *(d)* $(CH_3)_2C{=}C(CH_3)_2$

Solution:

(*a*) 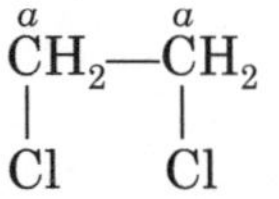 one signal (All protons are equivalent)

(*b*) $\overset{a}{C}H_3{-}O{-}\overset{a}{C}H_3$ one signal (All protons are equivalent)

(*c*) $\overset{a}{C}H_3{-}O{-}\overset{b}{C}H_2{-}\overset{c}{C}H_3$ three signals

(*d*) 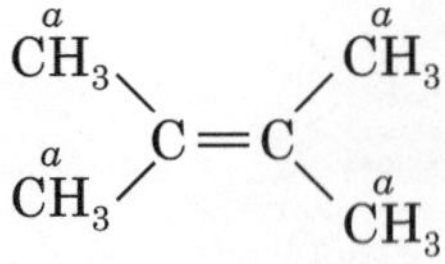 only one signal (All protons are equivalent)

Example 14.8. *How many PMR signals would you expect from the following?*

(*a*) 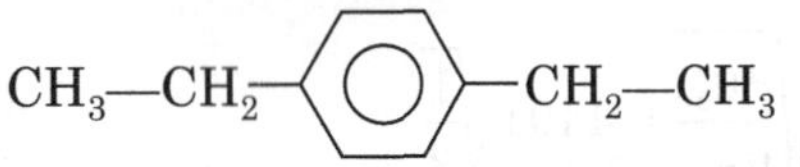 (*b*) $CH_3{-}CH_2{-}CHO$

(*c*) $CH_3{-}CH_2{-}CHCl{-}CH_3$ (*d*) $(CH_3)_2C{=}CH_2$

(*e*) 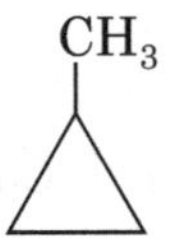

Solution:

(*a*) 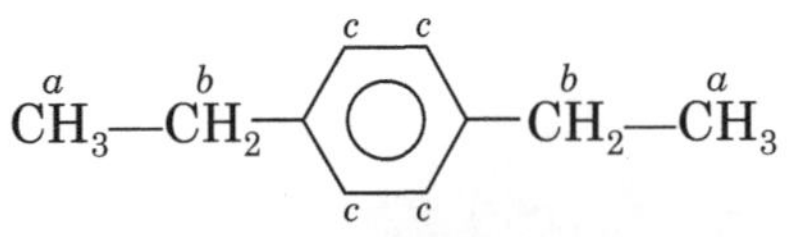 three signals

(*b*) $\overset{c}{C}H_3{-}\overset{b}{C}H_2{-}\overset{a}{C}HO$ three signals

(*c*) 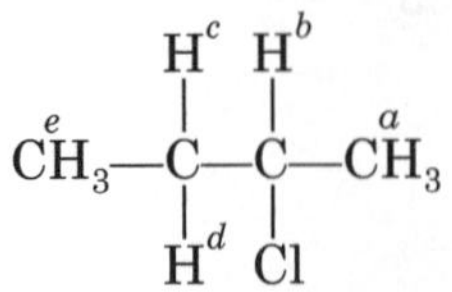 five signals

(*d*) 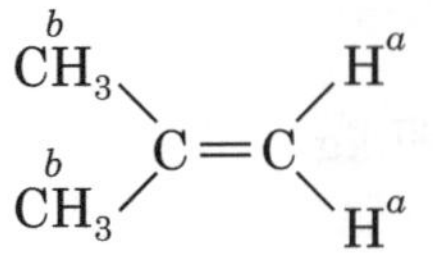 two signals

(*e*) 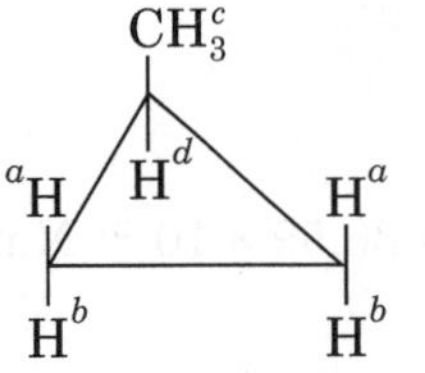 four signals

Example 14.9. *In a given organic compound two kinds of protons exhibit signals at 80 Hz and 210 Hz using a 60 MHz ^{1}H-NMR spectrometer. What will be their relative position using 90 MHz spectrometer? Also convert the position of signals into δ and τ units (in 60 MHz spectrometer).*

Solution: Chemical shifts are directly proportional to the frequency of the spectrometer. Thus,

60 MHz spectrometer will give signal at 80 Hz

90 MHz spectrometer will give signal at $\frac{80}{60} \times 90 = 120$ Hz.

Similarly, 210 Hz signal in 60 MHz spectrometer

$$= \frac{210}{60} \times 90 = 315 \text{ Hz in 90 MHz spectrometer}$$

Values in δ and τ scale:

(*i*) Signal at 80 Hz in 60 MHz spectrometer

$$\delta = \frac{80 \times 10^6}{60 \times 10^6} = 1.33 \text{ ppm}$$

$$\tau = 10 - 1.33 = 8.67 \text{ ppm}$$

(*ii*) Signal at 210 Hz using 60 MHz spectrometer

$$\delta = \frac{210 \times 10^6}{60 \times 10^6} = 3.5 \text{ ppm}$$

$$\tau = 10 - 3.5 = 6.5 \text{ ppm.}$$

Example 14.10. *PMR spectrum of an organic compound recorded on a 60 MHz instrument shows a signal at 84 Hz. Compute the position of the signal using 200 MHz spectrometer. What would be the position of the signals in δ units in each instrument?*

Solution: 60 MHz instrument shows signal at 84 Hz

∴ 200 MHz instrument will show signal at $\frac{84}{60} \times 200 = 280$ Hz

Position of the signal in δ units.

(*i*) 84 Hz in 60 MHz instrument

$$\delta = \frac{84 \times 10^6}{60 \times 10^6} \text{ ppm} = 1.4 \text{ ppm}$$

(*ii*) 280 Hz in 200 HMz instrument

$$\delta = \frac{280 \times 10^6}{200 \times 10^6} \text{ ppm} = 1.4 \text{ ppm.}$$

EXERCISES

I. SHORT ANSWER TYPE QUESTIONS

1. What is an electromagnetic radiation? Define the terms—wavelength, frequency, wave number and time period of a wave.

2. Why is UV-visible spectroscopy known as electronic spectroscopy? What is the absorption range?
3. What are auxochromes? Why and how do auxochrome increase the colouring power of a chromophore?
4. What are chromophores? Name some chromophores and explain how will you identify a particular chromophore in a compound.
5. What are the possible transitions that fall in UV-visible region? Discuss the effect of solvent polarity on $n \rightarrow \pi^*$ and $\pi - \pi^*$ transitions with suitable examples. **(HMTU, 2016)**
6. What type of electronic transitions do you expect from each of the following compounds?
   (*i*) Cyclopentane (*ii*) Propane (*iii*) Methanol (*iv*) Acetone
   (*v*) Vinyl chloride.
7. Explain the various transitions taking place in UV-visible spectroscopy. Discuss with suitable examples. **(HMTU, 2016)**
8. Which number of each pair absorbs UV-visible light at a longer wavelength than the other?
   (*i*) Hept-1-en-4-one and hep-2-en-4-one
   (*ii*) 1,3-pentadiene and 1,4-pentadiene
   (*iii*) *cis*-stilbene and *trans*-stilbene
   (*iv*) 1,2 dihydronaphthalene and 1, 4-dihydronaphthalene.
9. Define the following terms: **(HMTU, 2016)**
   (*i*) Chromophore (*ii*) Auxochrome
   (*iii*) Bathochromic shift (*iv*) Hypsochromic shift
   (*v*) Hyperchromic shift (*vi*) Hypochromic shift.
10. What is the importance of finger print region in IR spectroscopy? **(UP Tech. Univ., 2004)**
11. Define IR spectroscopy. Describe the various molecular vibrations in the technique. **(UP Tech. Univ., 2004)**
12. How do you determine the force constant of a bond by IR spectroscopy?
13. Write short notes on:
    (*a*) Fundamental frequency (*b*) Overtones
    (*c*) Hot bands (*d*) Degree of freedom
    (*e*) Molecular vibrations.
14. What is the effect of isotopes on IR spectra? Explain with the help of an example.
15. Explain the following:
    (*i*) Some fundamental vibrations are IR active whereas remaining are not.
    (*ii*) Band frequency decreases due to hydrogen bonding.
16. What is the principle of IR spectroscopy? Explain the effect of hydrogen bonding on the IR stretching frequency. **(HMTU, 2016)**

17. How many vibrational modes are there in a linear and non-linear molecule having *n* atoms? Explain with the help of degrees of freedom.

18. How will you distinguish between intermolecular and intramolecular hydrogen bonding by IR spectroscopy?

19. Explain the theory of NMR spectroscopy. What kind of nuclei exhibit NMR spectroscopy?

20. How many different kinds of protons are there in the PMR spectrum of each of the following compounds?

(*a*) $CH_3—O—CH_3$

(*b*) $CH_3CH_2CH_3$

(*c*) $CH_3—CH_2Cl$

(*d*) 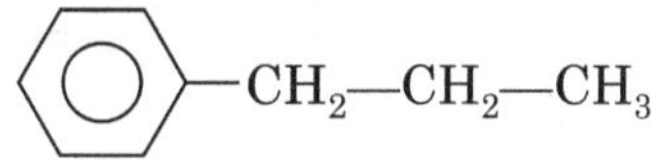

(*e*) $CH_3—CO—CH_2CH_3$

(*f*) 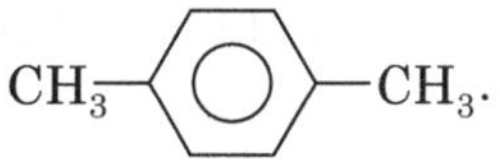

21. Describe in detail shielding and deshielding of protons with suitable examples.

22. What is chemical shift? Why TMS is chosen as a reference for NMR spectroscopy? **(HMTU, 2016)**

23. What is splitting of signals?

24. How many NMR signals would you expect for the following compounds? Explain

(*a*) 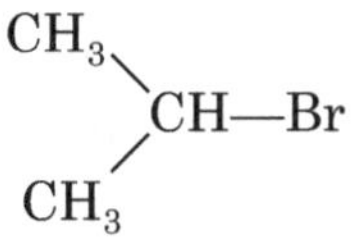 [**Hint:** 2 signals]

(*b*) 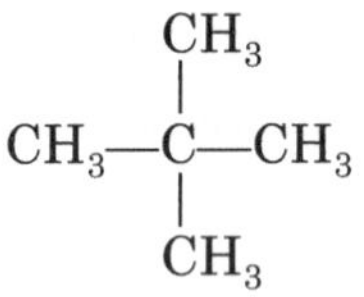 [**Hint:** 1 signal]

(*c*) 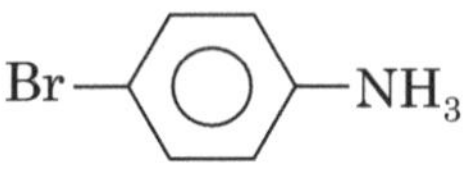 [**Hint:** 3 signals]

(*d*) 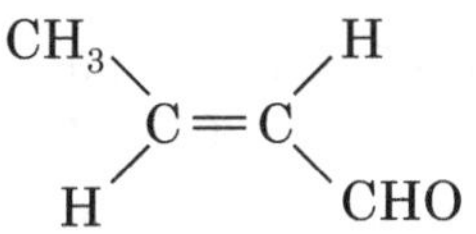 [**Hint:** 4 signals]

(*e*) $CH_3CH_2CH_2CH_2Br$ [**Hint:** 4 signals]

(*f*)  [**Hint:** 3 signals]

24. What is infra-red spectroscopy? Describe the various molecular vibrations in the technique. **(JNTU May, 2019)**

25. Explain with suitable example, the shielding effects involved in NMR spectroscopy.

26. State and explain Beer-Lambert's Law. Also derive its mathematical expression. **(RGPV, 2019, HMTU, 2021)**

27. Differentiate UV and IR spectroscopy. **(HMTU, 2021)**

28. Define molar absorptivity and absorptivity. **(HMTU, 2021)**

29. Why broad absorption bands are found in UV-visible spectrum instead of sharp peaks. **(HMTU, 2016)**

30. Explain fundamental vibration in IR spectroscopy. **(HMTU, 2016)**

31. What is coupling constant? How will you distinguish between a doublet and two peaks in NMR spectra? **(HMTU, 2016)**

32. Alkene chromophore is capable of exhibiting geometrical isomerism (*cis* and *trans*). *Trans* isomer displays longer wavelength absorption with higher intensity than corresponding *cis*-isomer. Why? **(HMTU, 2016)**

33. Compare the IR stretching frequency of C—H and C—D bonds with explanation. **(HMTU, 2016)**

34. What is bathochromic and hypsochromic shift? Explain with suitable example. **(HMTU, 2016)**

II. LONG ANSWER TYPE QUESTIONS

1. State the applications of UV-visible spectroscopy.

2. Give the principle of UV-visible spectroscopy. Explain different types of electronic transitions. **(RGPV, 2005) (JNTU May, 2019)**

3. What are the essential parts of UV-visible spectrometer? Explain important applications of UV spectroscopy. **(RGPV, 2010)**

4. Explain different types of absorption shifts in UV spectroscopy with the help of examples. Also draw the diagram showing various shifts.

5. Explain in detail the various factors affecting the vibrational frequency of the molecules.

6. Discuss the principle, instrumentation and applications of IR spectroscopy. **(RGPV, 2019)**

7. Define chemical shift. Describe the various factors affecting it.

8. With the help of well labelled diagram, explain the instrumentation of NMR spectroscopy.

9. What is the principle of NMR spectroscopy? What type of information may be obtained from NMR spectroscopy? **(JNTU May, 2019)**

10. What is NMR spectroscopy? How does it differ from other types of spectroscopies? What are the applications of NMR spectroscopy?

11. Explain splitting of the signals in NMR spectroscopy giving suitable examples.

12. Define the term bathochromic and hypsochromic shift. What structural features may produce a bathochromic or a hypsochromic shift in an organic compound?

13. Define chemical shift. Explain with suitable examples, the shielding and deshielding effects involved in NMR spectroscopy.

III. NUMERICAL PROBLEMS

1. Calculate the energy associated with a radiation having wavelength 4000 Å. Give answer in kcal mol^{-1} and also in kJ mol^{-1}.

2. Calculate the frequency of radiations having wavelength 5000 Å.

3. Calculate the energy associated with a radiation having wavelength 3000 Å. Give the answer in kcal/mol and kJ/mol.
4. Calculate energy per mole of light having wavelength (*a*) 85 nm, (*b*) 300 nm.
5. Calculate the energy associated with one quantum of radiation having wavelength 350 pm. Also compute its wavenumber.
6. Fundamental vibrational frequency of H_2 is 4401.31 cm^{-1}. Compute the fundamental vibrational frequency of HD assuming the same force constant.
7. The force constant of Br_2 is 240 Nm^{-1}. Calculate the fundamental vibrational frequency of Br_2 in cm^{-1} (Atomic mass of Br = 78.92 amu).
8. The infrared spectra of KCl has an intense line at 278 cm^{-1}. Calculate the period of vibration of KCl.
9. Calculate the approximate frequency of C—H stretching vibration from the following data:

   (*a*) force constant = 5×10^5 gm sec^{-1}

   (*b*) mass of carbon = 20×10^{-24} gm

   (*c*) mass of hydrogen = 1.6×10^{-24} gm.
10. Calculate the fundamental frequency for the C=C stretching vibration. (Given k = 9.77×10^5 dynes cm^{-1}; C = 3×10^{10} cm s^{-1}).
11. When the ^{1}H-NMR spectrum of acetone is recorded on 60 MHz spectrometer a sharp signal is observed at δ2.1. How many Hz downfield does this signal correspond to in this spectrometer?
12. The following PMR absorptions determined on a 60 MHz spectrometer downfield from TMS standard. Convert the following absorptions to δ units:

    (*a*) 150 Hz (*b*) 370 Hz (*c*) 560 Hz.
13. The C—H stretching bond in $CHCl_3$ appears at 3000 cm^{-1}. Assume that the force constant of C—H is identical to that of C—D bond, calculate the C—D stretching frequency in $CDCl_3$.
14. The OH signal in an NMR spectrum is observed at 144 Hz higher frequency then TMS. Calculate the chemical shift in terms of δ? (Operating frequency of the spectrometer is 60 MHz).
15. To wave number of the fundamental vibration of ^{79}Br—^{81}Br is 323.2 cm^{-1}. Determine the force constant of the bond. (Given: Mass of ^{79}Br = 78.9183 amu and ^{81}Br = 80.9163 amu).
16. A solution of thickness 3 cm transmits 30% incident light. Calculate the concentration of the solution. (Extinction coefficient ε = 4,000 dm^3 mol^{-1} cm^{-1}).

IV. MULTIPLE CHOICE QUESTIONS

1. Which of the following electronic transition requires minimum energy?

   (*a*) $\sigma \to \sigma^*$ (*b*) $n \to \sigma^*$ (*c*) $n \to \pi^*$ (*d*) $\pi \to \pi^*$.
2. In methyl alcohol, the following transition absorbs least energy

   (*a*) $\pi \to \pi^*$ (*b*) $n \to \sigma^*$ (*c*) $\sigma \to \sigma^*$ (*d*) $n \to \pi^*$.

3. Characteristic groups that are responsible for the colour of dyestuffs are called as

(*a*) chromosomes (*b*) diazogroups

(*c*) auxochromes (*d*) chromosphores.

4. Visible light lies between the wavelength range

(*a*) 3000–7000 Å (*b*) 4000–8000 Å (*c*) 2000–4000 Å (*d*) 6000–8000 Å.

5. One removal of conjugation, the spectra of a compound exhibit

(*a*) Bathochromic shift

(*b*) Hypsochromic shift

(*c*) No change in the position of absorption maxima

(*d*) None of the above.

6. Which of the following compounds will not undergo π–π^* transition?

(*a*) Azo compounds (*b*) Alkanes

(*c*) Alcohols (*d*) Cyanides.

7. The increasing order of frequency is

(*a*) X-ray, UV, IR, microwave (*b*) Microwave, UV, IR, X-ray

(*c*) UV, IR, X-ray, microwave (*d*) Microwave, IR, UV, X-ray.

8. UV-visible spectroscopic technique does not help in detecting

(*a*) Aromatic system

(*b*) Multiple bonds

(*c*) Conjugated system

(*d*) Nature of hydrogen bonding.

9. Which of the following is IR active?

(*a*) H_2 (*b*) F_2 (*c*) HCN (*d*) All of the above.

10. What is the number of vibrational degrees of freedom in toluene ($C_6H_5CH_3$)?

(*a*) 40 (*b*) 39 (*c*) 30 (*d*) 29.

11. Stretching is a vibration in which

(*a*) bond length changes (*b*) bond length does not change

(*c*) bond angle changes (*d*) both (*a*) and (*c*) are correct.

12. Which of the following regions belong to fingerprint region?

(*a*) 1650–2000 cm^{-1} (*b*) 2000–3500 cm^{-1}

(*c*) 1300–4000 cm^{-1} (*d*) 600–1300 cm^{-1}.

13. The expression for the fundamental vibration is:

(*a*) $\bar{\nu} = \frac{1}{2\pi}\sqrt{\frac{k}{\mu}}$ (*b*) $\bar{\nu} = \frac{1}{2\pi C}\sqrt{\frac{\mu}{k}}$ (*c*) $\bar{\nu} = \frac{1}{2\pi C}\sqrt{\frac{k}{\mu}}$ (*d*) $\bar{\nu} = \frac{1}{2\pi}\sqrt{\frac{\mu}{k}}$.

14. The value of force constant in a vibrational spectra is given by:

(*a*) $k = \pi^2 C^2 (\bar{\nu})^2 \mu$ (*b*) $k = \pi^2 C^2 (\bar{\nu})^2 \mu^2$ (*c*) $k = 4\pi^2 C^2 (\bar{\nu})^2 \mu$ (*d*) $k = 4\pi^2 C^2 (\bar{\nu})^2 \mu^2$.

15. The frequency of a transition is 5.4×10^{15} Hz. What is the corresponding wavelength?

(*a*) 5.6×10^{-6} m (*b*) 5.6×10^{-8} m (*c*) 560 nm (*d*) 5600 cm^{-1}.

16. The dichromate ion absorbs light of wavelength approximately 500 nm. Based on this information, what can you conclude?

(*a*) The dichromate ion absorbs in the UV region.

(*b*) Solutions of dichromate ion are colourless.

(*c*) The dichromate ion absorbs within the visible region.

(*d*) The dichromate ion absorbs outside the visible region.

17. Which of the following molecule will show IR spectrum?

$$H_2, HCl, CH_4, CO_2, H_2O_2$$

(*a*) H_2, HCl and CO_2 (*b*) H_2O_2, H_2 and HCl

(*c*) HCl, CO_2, CH_4 and H_2O_2 (*d*) CH_4, CO_2 and H_2.

18. Groups of nuclei which are ^1H NMR active:

(*a*) ^1_1H, $^{31}_{15}P$, $^{16}_8O$ (*b*) $^{13}_6C$, $^{32}_{16}S$, $^{19}_9F$

(*c*) $^{13}_6C$, $^{27}_{13}Al$, $^{19}_9F$ (*d*) ^1_1H, $^{12}_6C$, $^{19}_9F$.

19. Electromagnetic rays used for detection of NMR spectroscopy belongs to:

(*a*) Microwave region (*b*) γ-ray region

(*c*) X-ray region (*d*) Radio frequency region.

20. The chemical shift of a proton on delta scale (δ) is 6.9. The value of τ scale will be:

(*a*) 16.9 (*b*) 3.1 (*c*) 6.9 (*d*) 2.1.

21. The δ values of the methyl protons in methyl halides follow the order:

(*a*) $CH_3F > CH_3Cl > CH_3Br > CH_3I$ (*b*) $CH_3I > CH_3Br > CH_3Cl > CH_3F$

(*c*) $CH_3F > CH_3I > CH_3Br > CH_3Cl$ (*d*) $CH_3I > CH_3Cl > CH_3F > CH_3Br$.

22. The amount of energy available is radio frequency radiation is sufficient for which of the following?

(*a*) Excite an atom (*b*) Vibrate an atom

(*c*) Rotate a molecule (*d*) Affect the nuclear spin of an atom.

23. Coupling causes the peaks in ^1H NMR spectra to be split into

(*a*) two peaks

(*b*) multiple peaks equal to the number of surrounding C-atoms

(*c*) multiple peaks equal to the number of hydrogens on surrounding atoms

(*d*) multiple peaks equal to the number of hydrogens on surrounding atoms, plus one.

24. The nuclei that does not give NMR signal.

(*a*) ^{11}B (*b*) ^{15}N (*c*) ^{19}F (*d*) ^{31}P.

25. Splitting of signal in NMR arises from

(*a*) spin-spin coupling (*b*) rotation of nucleus

(*c*) spin-spin decoupling (*d*) shielding effect.

Answers

III. Numerical Problems

1. 71.6 kcal/mole and 299.5 kJ/mol [1 kcal = 4.184 kJ]
2. 6.0×10^{14} sec^{-1}
3. 95.4 kcal/mole and 399.15 kJ/mol
4. (*a*) 1.408×10^6 J/mol (*b*) 3.990×10^5 J/mol
5. $E = 5.678 \times 10^{-16}$ J, $\bar{\nu} = 2.857 \times 10^9$ m^{-1}
6. 3811.45 cm^{-1}
7. 321 cm^{-1}
8. 1.20×10^{-13} sec.
9. $\nu = 9.3 \times 10^{13}$ sec^{-1}
10. 1659 cm^{-1}
11. 126 Hz
12. (*a*) 2.5 (*b*) 6.2 (*c*) 9.3
13. 2190 cm^{-1}
14. 2.40 ppm
15. 246.095 Nm^{-1}
16. 4.35×10^{-5} mol dm^{-3}.

IV. Multiple Choice Questions

1. (*c*)	2. (*b*)	3. (*c*)	4. (*b*)	5. (*b*)	6. (*c*)	7. (*d*)	8. (*d*)	9. (*c*)	10. (*b*)
11. (*a*)	12. (*d*)	13. (*c*)	14. (*c*)	15. (*b*)	16. (*c*)	17. (*c*)	18. (*c*)	19. (*d*)	20. (*b*)
21. (*a*)	22. (*d*)	23. (*d*)	24. (*a*)	25. (*a*)					

Chapter 15 Surface Chemistry

15.1 INTRODUCTION

Surface Chemistry deals with phenomena that occur at the surfaces or interfaces (boundary of two different phases) like solid-solid, solid-liquid, solid-gas, liquid-liquid, liquid-solid, liquid-gas. Due to complete miscibility, there is no interface between the gases. Various phenomenona that occur at surface include adsorption, catalysis, corrosion, crystallization, colloidal properties etc. Hence, the study of the surface chemistry is of great importance as it has many applications in industry as well as in our daily life.

15.2 ADSORPTION

The phenomena of attracting and retaining the molecules of a substance on the surface of a liquid or a solid is called as *adsorption*. Adsorption is a surface phenomenon and is therefore a fairly rapid process. The substrate (solid substance) on which adsorption takes place is called the *adsorbent* while the adsorbed material (a gas or a liquid) is called *adsorbate*. The common surface between the two phases where the adsorbed molecule concentrate is called *interface*.

Good adsorbents are solids in a finely divided state while an adsorbate may be a gas or a liquid. For example, in the decolourization of sugar solution by activated charcoal-charcoal is the adsorbent while the colouring impurities in sugar solution are adsorbates. Similarly, in the refining of vegetable oils by Fuller's earth, fuller's earth is adsorbent while dissolved colouring impurities are adsorbates.

Adsorption arises at the surface of solids and liquids due to the presence of unbalanced forces at the surface (Fig. 15.1). In a solid or liquid, the molecules present in the bulk are

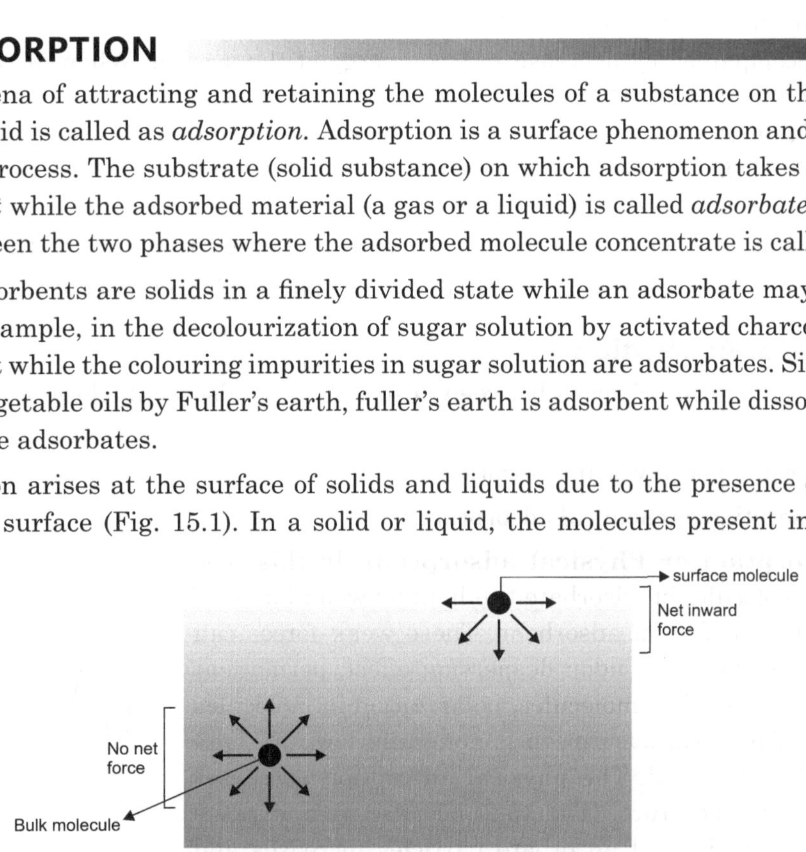

Fig. 15.1. Force acting on a solid or liquid substances.

attracted equally from all sides and the net force experienced by the molecule in the bulk is zero. However, the molecules present near the surface are being attracted only by the molecules below it as no molecules are present above it. Hence, a net downward force is experienced by the surface molecule. As a result of this downward force, the surface molecule tends to attract and retain other species. These species do not penetrate inside the molecule but remain on the surface. Therefore, concentration of species in higher on the surface as compared to bulk.

The term adsorption refers to the attraction and retention of the molecules of a substance only on the surface of the solid (surface phenomenon) while the term absorption refers to the passing of the substance through the surface into the bulk of the solid (bulk phenomenon).

Examples: (*i*) Ink is absorbed by the chalk.

(*ii*) When few drops of water are added to a lump of sugar, water is absorbed by the entire mass.

Since absorption involves diffusion into the interior of the mass, it is a slow process and the substance is uniformly distributed throughout the mass.

Sorption is a process where adsorption and absorption occur simultaneously i.e., in the first stage, the material appears on the surface of the adsorbent (*adsorption*) and then passes into the bulk of the adsorbent (*absorption*).

The reverse of sorption *i.e.* the release of adsorbed or absorbed substance into the surrounding medium is called as *desorption.* Characteristics of adsorption:

(*i*) It is specific and selective in nature.

(*ii*) It is accompanied by decrease in free energy of the system. When ΔG becomes zero, adsorption equilibrium is established.

(*iii*) Adsorption is a spontaneous process. Therefore, change in free energy (ΔG) for the process is negative. According to Gibb's Helmholtz equation

$$\Delta G = \Delta H - T\Delta S$$

ΔS is negative because adhering of gas molecules to the surface lowers the randomness.

$\therefore$ ΔG can be negative only when ΔH is negative. Hence, adsorption is always *exothermic.*

15.2.1 Types of Adsorption

Depending on the nature of forces between adsorbate and adsorbent, there are two types of adsorption.

(*i*) Physisorption or physical adsorption.

(*ii*) Chemisorption or chemical adsorption.

1. Physisorption or Physical adsorption: In this type of adsorption, molecules of adsorbate are held by weak forces of attraction on the surface of adsorbent. These weak forces can be van der Waal's forces, London despersion effect, permanent dipole moment in adsorbed molecules, polarization in molecules etc. Enthalpy of physical adsorption is generally low and is of the order of 20–40 kJ/mol. The physical adsorption decreases with increase in temperature (Fig. 15.2) because with increase in temperature, the K.E. of adsorbate particles increases and overcomes the weak forces of attraction. As a result, the adsorbate

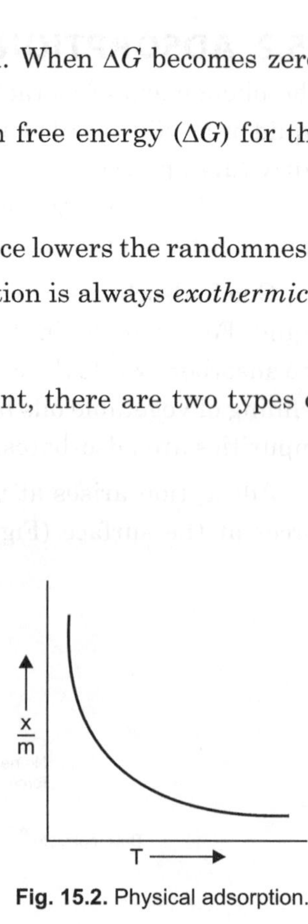

Fig. 15.2. Physical adsorption.

particles escapes from the surface of adsorbent. Physisorption is generally reversible in nature, as it can increased or decreased by increasing or decreasing the pressure, respectively.

Example: Adsorption of various gases by charcoal.

Chemisorption or Chemical adsorption: When a gas is held (adsorbed) onto the surface of a solid by forces similar to those of a chemical bond, the adsorption is called as chemical adsorption. The molar heat of adsorption is high of the order of 40–400 kJ/mol. Chemical adsorption first increases and then decreases with increase in temperature (Fig. 15.3). Initially the adsorption increases because the heat supplied acts as activation energy and more and more molecules of adsorbate gain energy and possess energy greater than activation energy. Hence, initially adsorption increases with increase in temperature. Further increase in temperature will increase the kinetic energy of adsorbed molecules which results in desorption as a result, adsorption decreases.

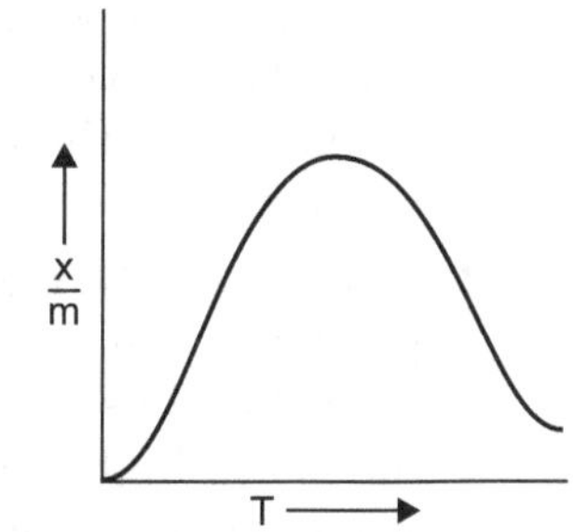

Fig. 15.3. Chemical adsorption.

Example: Adsorption of H_2 gas on surface of Ni, Pt or Pd, adsorption of oxygen on tungsten.

Table 15.1: Distinction between Physical Adsorption

S.No.	Physical Adsorption	Chemical Adsorption
1.	Adsorbate and adsorbent molecules are held together by weak physical forces of attraction like van der Waal's forces, London dispersion forces etc.	Adsorbate and adsorbent molecules are held together by strong chemical forces.
2.	Adsorption is multilayer.	Adsorption is only in the upper layer.
3.	Heat of adsorption is low (20–40 kJ/mol.).	Heat of adsorption is high (40–400 kJ/mol).
4.	The process is reversible *i.e.,* desorption of the gas occurs by decreasing the pressure or increasing the temperature.	The process is irreversible because molecules are tightly retained by adsorbent.
5.	It does not show specificity as it involves only physical forces between adsorbent and adsorbate.	It is highly specific as it involves bond formation between adsorbent and adsorbate.
6.	More easily liquifiable (*e.g.,* SO_2, NH_3, HCl, CO_2 etc.) and more soluble gas is adsorbed more readily.	As it involves bond formation, the extent of adsorption is independent of the ease of liquification.
7.	It decreases with increase in temperature.	It first increases and then decreases with increases in temperature.
8.	It does not require appreciable activation energy.	Activation energy is involved in the process.
9.	No surface compound is formed. Thc state of adsorbate does not change after adsorption. It is same as in the bulk.	Surface compounds are formed and the state of adsorbate on the surface may be different from that in the bulk.
10.	The rate of adsorption increases with increase in pressure or concentration of the adsorbate.	The rate of adsorption decreases with increase in pressure or concentration of the adsorbate.

15.2.2 Factors Affecting Adsorption

The adsorption of gases on solid surfaces is affected by following factors:

1. **Nature of the gas (adsorbate):** Easily liquifiable gases (such as HCl, NH_3, Cl_2, CO_2 etc.) are adsorbed more easily than permanent gases (such as H_2, N_2, O_2 etc.). The ease of liquefaction of a gas depends upon its critical temperature (T_C). The more the critical temperature, the more easily the gas is liquified and consequently, more readily it is adsorbed.
2. **Nature and surface area of adsorbent:** Under given conditions of temperature and pressure, the greater the surface area of the adsorbent, greater is its adsorption capacity. Thus, substances like charcoal and silica gel are excellent adsorbents because they have highly porous structures and hence large surface area. Adsorbing power of few adsorbents *e.g.* wood charcoal can be further increased by heating it in vacuum or some inert gas at 350 – 1000°C to remove hydrocarbons and other gases which will increase the surface available for adsorption.
3. **Effect of pressure:** The magnitude or extent of adsorption of a gas on a solid is expressed as x/m where 'x' denotes the number of moles of gas and 'm' denotes the mass of solid when a dynamic equilibrium is attained between free gas and adsorbed gas. The extent of adsorption (x/m) depends upon the pressure.

   The variation in the amount of gas adsorbed by the adsorbent with pressure at constant temperature can be expressed by means of a curve called as adsorption isotherm (Fig. 15.4).

   It is clear from the graph (15.4) that the extent of adsorption (x/m) increases with increase in pressure and becomes maximum corresponding to pressure, P_s (the equilibrium pressure or the saturation pressure). Adsorption is a reversible process and therefore, adsorption and desorption occur simultaneously. At pressure P_s, the amount of gas adsorbed becomes equal to the amount of gas absorbed. Hence, further increase in pressure does not affect the extent of adsorption.

   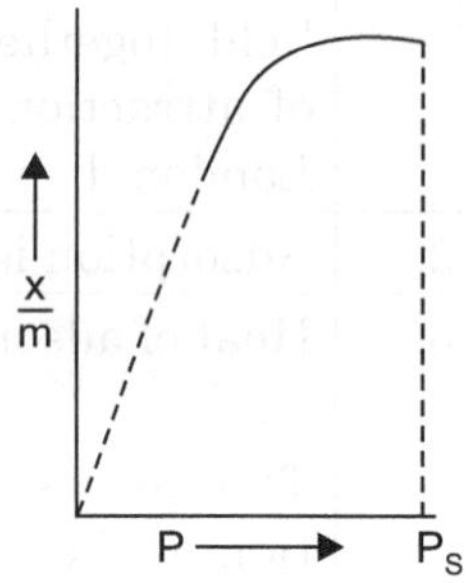

   Fig. 15.4. Adsorption isotherm.

4. **Effect of temperature: Adsorption isobar** is a graph plotted between magnitude of adsorption and temperature at constant pressure. Since adsorption is an exothermic process, therefore according to Le Chatliers principle, with increase in temperature, the extent of adsorption decreases. This is always true in case of physical adsorption (Fig. 15.2). However, in case of chemical adsorption, the extent of adsorption first increase and then decrease with rise in temperature (Fig. 15.3).
5. **Activation of adsorbent:** To increase the rate of adsorption, the adsorbing power of adsorbent is increased by activation. This can be done by:
   (*i*) Metallic adsorbents are activated by rubbing the surface.
   (*ii*) Subjecting to some chemical reactions for metallic adsorbents.
   (*iii*) Activity of adsorbents can be increased by taking it in powdered state because in powdered state surface area is maximum.
   (*iv*) Adsorbents can also be activated by heating with superheated steam . For example, charcoal is activated by heating between 650 K – 1330 K in vacuum, air or superheated steam.

15.3 ADSORPTION ISOTHERMS

Adsorption isotherm area of two types:

(*i*) Freundlich adsorption isotherm

(*ii*) Langmuir adsorption isotherm.

1. Freundlich adsorption isotherm: Freundlich in 1909 gave an empirical relationship between the quantity of gas adsorbed by unit mass of solid adsorbent and pressure at a particular temperature. Mathematically, the relationship can be expressed by the following relationship:

$$\frac{x}{m} = kp^{1/n} \qquad ...(15.1)$$

where x is the weight of the gas adsorbed on mass 'm' of the adsorbent at pressure P; thus $\frac{x}{m}$ represents the amount of gas adsorbed per gram of the adsorbent, k and n are constants and depends on the nature of the adsorbent and the gas at a particular temperature.

This relationship is generally represented in the form of a curve where x/m is plotted against P (Fig. 15.5).

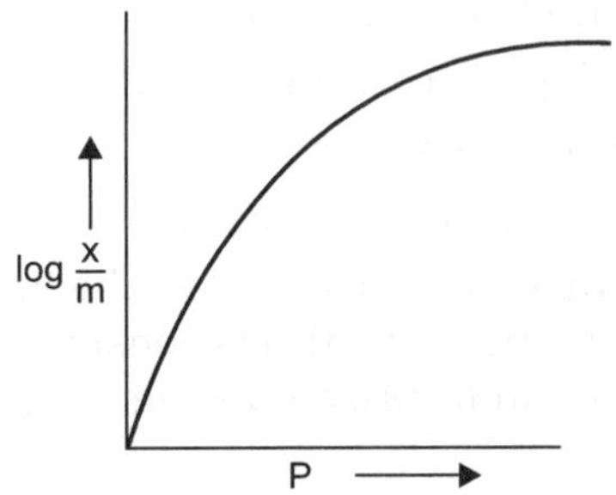

Fig. 15.5. Adsorption isotherm $\left(\frac{x}{m} \text{ Vs } P\right)$.

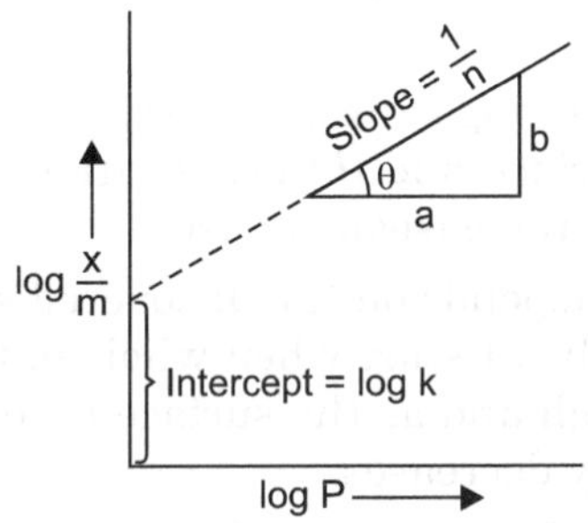

Fig. 15.6. Freundlich isotherm $\left(\log \frac{x}{m} \text{ Vs } \log P\right)$.

On taking logarithm of equation (15.1), we get

$$\log \frac{x}{m} = \log k + \frac{1}{n} \log P \qquad ...(15.2)$$

If a graph of $\log \frac{x}{m}$ is plotted against $\log P$, a straight line is observed (Fig. 15.6). The slope of the line gives the value of $\frac{1}{n}$ and the intercept on y axis gives the value of $\log k$.

From the adsorption isotherm (Fig. 15.5), the following observations can easily be made:

(*i*) At low pressure, the graph is almost a straight line which indicates that

$$\frac{x}{m} \propto P \text{ or } \frac{x}{m} = kP$$

(*ii*) At high pressure, the graph becomes almost parallel to x-axis which indicates that $\frac{x}{m}$ becomes independent of pressure

$$\frac{x}{m} = \text{Constant or } \frac{x}{m} \propto P^{\circ} \quad \text{or} \quad \frac{x}{m} = kP^{\circ}$$

(*iii*) At intermediate pressure, $\frac{x}{m}$ depends on 0 to 1 power of pressure as value of $n < 0$. This can be expressed as

$$\frac{x}{m} \propto P^{1/n} \quad \text{or} \quad \frac{x}{m} = kP^{1/2}$$

Limitations of Freundlich Isotherm:

1. This type of isotherm is purely empirical and has no theoretical basis.
2. The equation is valid only upto a certain pressure and invalid at high pressures.
3. The constants k and n are not temperature independent.
4. This type of isotherm fails if the concentration of the adsorbate is very high.

2. Langmuir adsorption isotherm: To overcome the limitations of Freundlich equation. Irving Langmuir in 1916 deduced a theoretical relationship which has been found to be more in agreement with many experimental facts over a wide range of pressure. Langmuir theory is based on following assumptions:

1. Adsorption takes place on the surface of the solid only till the whole of the surface is completely covered with a unimolecular layer of the adsorbed gas. Although multimolecular layer of adsorbed molecules is possible at high pressure, he considered only unimolecular layer.
2. Adsorption consists of two opposing processes, namely (*a*) condensation of the gas molecules on the solid surface and (*b*) evaporation (desorption) of the gas molecules from the surface back into the gaseous phase.
3. The rate of condensation depends on the uncovered surface of the adsorbent available for condensation. Naturally, at start when whole of the surface is uncovered, the rate of condensation is very high and as the surface is covered more and more, the rate of condensation progressively decreases.

   On the contrary, the rate of evaporation depends upon the covered surface and hence increases as more and more of the surface is covered. Ultimately an equilibrium will be set up at a stage when the rate of condensation becomes equal to the rate of evaporation (adsorption equilibrium).
4. Adsorption takes place on fixed sites and there is no interaction between adsorbed molecules and whole of surface.

Consider a surface on which the molecules of a gas are condensing and evaporating. Let θ = fraction of total surface covered at a particular instant, then $(1 - \theta)$ = fraction of the surface still uncovered. Then rate of condensation (r_1) is given by

$$r_1 = k_1 (1 - \theta)P \qquad ...(15.3)$$

where k_1 is the specific condensation rate constant and P is the pressure of the gas

$$\text{rate of evaporation } (r_2) = k_2\theta \quad ...(15.4)$$

At equilibrium $r_1 = r_2$

$$\therefore \quad k_1(1 - \theta)P = k_2\theta$$

$$\theta = \frac{k_1 P}{k_2 + k_1 P} = \frac{\frac{k_1}{k_2} P}{\frac{k_2}{k_2} + \frac{k_1}{k_2} P} = \frac{kP}{1 + kP} \quad ...(15.5)$$

where $k = k_1/k_2$.

But, the quantity of gas adsorbed per unit mass of the adsorbent (x/m) is proportional to the surface covered, *i.e.*,

$$\frac{x}{m} \propto \theta \quad ...(15.6)$$

or

$$\frac{x}{m} = K\theta \quad ...(15.7)$$

where K is another proportionality constant. Equation (15.6) shows that the amount of gas adsorbed per unit mass of the adsorbent is proportional to the fraction of the surface covered. On substituting the value of θ from equation (15.5), we get

$$\frac{x}{m} = K\frac{kP}{1 + kP} \quad ...(15.8)$$

or

$$\frac{1}{x/m} = \frac{1 + kP}{KkP} \quad \text{or} \quad \frac{P}{x/m} = \frac{1}{Kk} + \frac{P}{K} \quad ...(15.9)$$

Equation (15.9) is called as the Langmuir adsorption isotherm. A plot of $\frac{P}{x/m}$ against P, a straight line is observed (Fig. 15.7) equation is found to be valid in all cases.

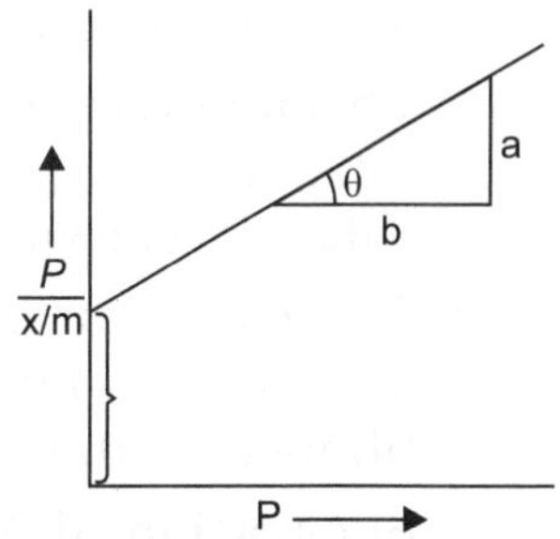

Fig. 15.7. A plot of $P/x/m$ Vs. P.

Case 1: At low pressure ($P << 1$) : At low pressure kP in equation (15.8) becomes negligible in comparison to unity. Hence, equation (15.8) reduces to

$$\frac{x}{m} = KkP$$

As K and k both are constants, therefore

$$\frac{x}{m} \propto P$$

Thus, the amount of gas adsorbed per unit quantity of the adsorbent is directly proportional to the pressure of the gas at low pressures.

Case 2: At very high pressure ($P >> 1$): At very high pressures, 1 can be ignored in comparison to kP in denominator. Hence, equation (15.8) reduces to

$$\frac{x}{m} = \frac{KkP}{kP} \quad \text{or} \quad \frac{x}{m} = KP^{\circ}$$

Thus, at high pressure, the extent of adsorption is independent of pressure of the gas because the surface becomes completely covered at high pressure.

Applications of Adsorption:

1. **Refining of petroleum, vegetable oils and sugar solution:** Refining of petroleum and vegetable oils with fuller's earth or decolorization of sugar solution with activated charcoal is due to adsorption of colouring material by these adsorbents.
2. **In preserving vacuum:** In Dewar flask, activated charcoal is placed between the walls of the flask, so that any gas which entered annular space is adsorbed.
3. **In gas mask:** The gas masks used as protective devices against poisonous gases such as methane, chlorine, sulphur dioxide etc. contain suitable adsorbents. The adsorbents preferentially adsorb poisonous gases and thus purify the air used for breathing. The common form of gas mask contains a layer of activated charcoal that adsorbs poisonous gases.
4. **Softening of hard water:** Hard water contains calcium and magnesium ions. In permutit process, the permutit adsorbs Ca^{2+} and Mg^{2+} ions present in hard water and thus the water coming through permutit is free from Ca^{2+} and Mg^{2+} ions.
5. **In heterogeneous catalysis:** Most heterogeneous catalytic reactions proceed through the adsorption of the gaseous reactant on the solid catalyst. For example,
   (*i*) Finely powdered Ni is used for the hydrogenation of oil.
   (*ii*) Finely divided vanadium pentaoxide (V_2O_5) is used in the contact process.
6. **In dyeing:** In dyeing, clothes are first kept dipped in a mordant usually alum and then in the solution of the dye. The mordant is first adsorbed on the clothes and then the dye is adsorbed on the mordant.
7. **During arsenic poisoning:** Colloidal $Fe(OH)_3$ is administered which adsorbs arsenic which in turn can be removed by vomiting.
8. **Chromatography:** Chromatography is based on selective adsorption of ions from solution using powdered adsorbents such as silica or alumina gel. It has several industrial and analytical applications.
9. **In adsorption indicators:** Various dyes such as fluorescein, eosin etc. are used as adsorption indicators in the precipitation titrations. For example, eosin during titration if KBr with $AgNO_3$.
10. **Separation of Noble gases:** A mixture of noble gases is usually separated by adsorbing them on activated charcoal. The separation is based on the difference in the degree of adsorption of these gases by charcoal.
11. **In pharmaceutical industry:** The germicidal action of drugs/medicines is based on the property of adsorption.
12. **For desiccation or Dehumidification:** Certain substances have a strong tendency to adsorb moisture. These substances can be used to remove or reduce water vapours present in air. Silica gel is used for removing moisture from electronic equipments.

15.4 COLLOIDAL STATE

Thomas Graham (1861) studied the rate of diffusion of liquids and solutions across the animal membranes and as a result of his experiments, he divided the soluble substances into two classes *viz.* crystalloids and colloids.

1. **Crystalloids:** These substances can easily be obtained in the crystalline form and their solution can diffuse rapidly through a vegetable or an animal membrane (*e.g.* parchment membrane); For example sugar, urea, salts, acids etc.
2. **Colloids:** These are generally amorphous and their solutions show little or no tendency to diffuse through the membrane; *e.g.* gelatin, albumin, glue, gum, starch etc.

   Graham's classification of substances into crystalloids and colloids was soon proved to be wrong. A crystalloid was found to behave as colloid under different set of conditions and vice versa. For example,

   (*i*) NaCl behaves as crystalloid when dissolved in water but behaves as a colloid in benzene.

   (*ii*) Soap behaves as crystalloid in benzene and colloid in water.

Further studies on the behaviour of these solutes have shown that the nature of the substances whether crystalloid or colloid depends upon the particle size. When the size of the particle is between 10^{-9} m to 10^{-7} m, it behaves like a colloid and when it is less than this range, it behaves like a crystalloid. Hence, colloid is not a substance but is a state of a substance which depends upon the particle size.

15.5 TRUE SOLUTION, COLLOIDAL SOLUTION AND SUSPENSION

True solution is a homogeneous solution in which molecules or ions are uniformly dispersed in the solvent (dispersion phase). The size of solute particles is < 1 nm. The solute particles are invisible and do not settle on standing. For example, sugar and salt solution in water.

Suspension is a heterogeneous solution containing suspended insoluble particles. The size of the particles is > 100 nm which can be visible either to a naked eye or under a microscope. The particles of suspension can neither pass through ordinary filter paper nor through animal membrane.

Colloidal solution is a heterogeneous solution which contains particles of dimensions between true solution and suspension *i.e.* 1 nm – 100 nm. These particles can pass through ordinary filter paper but cannot pass through animal membrane. The colloidal particles cannot be seen with naked eye but can be seen under an ultramicroscope.

Hence, colloidal particles are intermediate between true solution and suspension (Fig. 15.8). The main distinguishing features of these three type of solutions are given in Table 15.2.

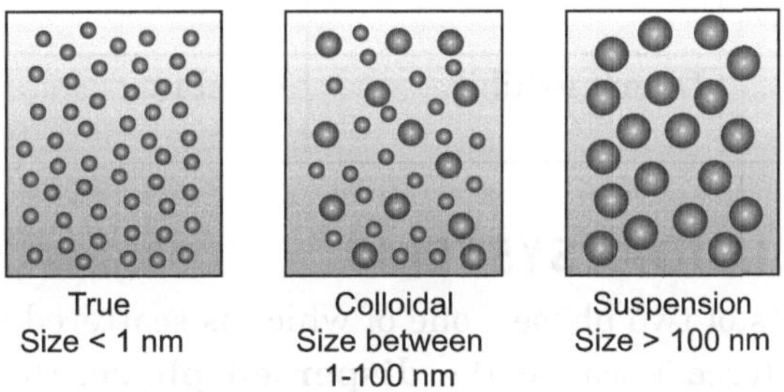

Fig. 15.8. Particle size based classification (True solution, colloidal solution and suspension).

Table 15.2: Distinguishing Features of True Solution, Colloidal Solution and Suspension

S. No.	Property	True solution	Colloidal solution	Suspension
1.	Appearance	Transparent	Translucent	Opaque
2.	Particle size	< 1 nm	1 nm – 100 nm	> 100 nm
3.	Visibility	Particles are invisible under all circumstances.	Although particles are invisible even under the most powerful microscope, light scattering effect by the particles can be observed under ultra-microscope.	Particles are visible under a microscope and sometimes even to a naked eye.
4.	Filtration	True solution passes easily through filter paper as well as parchment membrane.	Colloidal solution passes easily through filter paper but slowly through parchment membrane.	Suspension does not pass either through filter paper or parchment membrane.
5.	Tyndall effect	Does not show	Shows	Shows
6.	Settling of particles	Does not settle	Settle only on centrifugation	Settle under gravity
7.	Coagulation	They can be precipitated by addition of suitable electrolytes.	They can be coagulated by addition of suitable electrolytes.	They are not coagulated.
8.	Diffusion of particles	Diffuse rapidly	Diffuse very slowly	Do not diffuse.
9.	Nature	Homogeneous	Heterogeneous	Heterogeneous.
10.	Electrophoresis	Do not exhibit	Exhibit	Do not exhibit.
11.	Brownian movement	Do not exhibit	Exhibit	Do not exhibit.

15.6 TYPES OF COLLOIDAL SYSTEMS

A colloidal system consists of two phases, one of which is scattered or dispersed in the other. The phase which is scattered is called the **dispersed phase**, the **internal phase** or the **discontinuous** phase. The phase in which scattering or dispersion is done is called the

dispersion medium or the external phase or the **continuous phase**. This is the major phase of the system while dispersed phase constitutes a smaller fraction of the system. Each of the two phases may be solid, liquid or gas.

The colloids are classified on the basis of following criteria:

(*i*) Physical state of dispersed phase and dispersion medium.

(*ii*) Nature of interactions between dispersed phase and dispersion medium.

(*iii*) Based on electrical charge on the dispersed phase.

(*iv*) Size of particles of dispersed phase.

1. Depending on the physical state of dispersed phase and dispersion medium: Depending upon whether the dispersed phase and dispersion medium are solids, liquids or gases, eight types of colloidal systems are possible. The various types of colloidal systems alongwith examples are given in Table 15.3.

Table 15.3: Various Colloidal Systems

S.No.	Dispersed phase	Dispersion medium	Name	Examples
1.	Solid	Solid	Solid sol	Coloured glasses, coloured precious stones, rock salt, alloys.
2.	Solid	Liquid	Sol	Starch proteins, As_2S_3, gold solution, glue, paints, ink, muddy water, etc.
3.	Solid	Gas	Solid foam (Aerosol)	Smoke, dust, fumes.
4.	Liquid	Solid	Gel (Solid emulsion)	Curd, cheese, jellies $Fe(OH)_3$, $Al(OH)_3$, butter, boot polish
5.	Liquid	Liquid	Emulsion	Milk, cream, certain medicines, cod liver oil
6.	Liquid	Gas	Aerosol	Clouds, fog, mist, insecticide sprays
7.	Gas	Solid	Solid foam	Occluded gases in metals, pumice stone, bread, foam rubber
8.	Gas	Liquid	Foam	Froth, soap, whipped cream, beaten egg white, beer, shaving cream.

Out of various types of colloidal systems tabulated above, the most common are sols (solids in liquids), gels (liquids in solids) and emulsions (liquid in liquid). Further, depending upon the nature of dispersion medium, sols are sometimes given specific names. For example,

Dispersion medium	Name of the sol
Water	Aquasol or Hydrosol
Alcohol	Alcosol
Benzene	Benzosol
Gases (Air)	Aerosol

2. Based on the nature of interaction between dispersed phase and dispersion medium: Depending upon the nature of interaction between dispersed phase and dispersion medium, the colloidal solutions can be classified into

(*a*) Lyophilic colloids (*b*) Lyophobic colloids.

If water is the dispersion medium, the terms used are hydrophilic and hydrophobic.

(*a*) Lyophilic colloids: The colloidal solutions in which the particles of the dispersed phase have a great affinity for the dispersion medium are called as **lyophilic colloids**. Such colloids are obtained readily on simple warming or shaking the substance with suitable solvent (lyo-liquid; philic-love). For example, gelatin, starch, proteins, gum and rubber. Lyophilic colloids are also known as **reversible colloids** since on evaporating the dispersion medium (*e.g.* water), the residue can again be easily reconverted into colloidal state simply by addition of the liquid *i.e.* water. These sols are quite stable and cannot be easily precipitated.

(*b*) Lyophobic colloids: The colloidal solutions in which there is no affinity between the particles of the dispersed phase and the dispersion medium are called **Lyophobic colloids**. Such colloids are obtained with difficulty (Lyo-liquid; phobic - hate). Such colloids are formed by substances like $Fe(OH)_3$, As_2S_3, gold and other metals which are sparingly soluble and thus their molecules do not pass readily into colloidal state. Lyophobic colloids are also known as irreversible colloids since the residue (obtained by evaporating the dispersion medium) cannot readily be reconverted into sol by ordinary means. These sols are readily precipitated (or coagulated) on addition of small amounts of electrolytes, by heating or by shaking. Therefore, these are not stable.

The main points of difference between the lyophilic sols and lyophobic sols are given in Table 15.4.

Table 15.4: Difference between Lyophilic and Lyophobic Colloids

S.No.	Property	Lyophilic colloids	Lyophobic colloids
1.	Reversibility	These are reversible.	These are irreversible.
2.	Visibility	The particles cannot be readily detected even under ultra microscope.	The particles can be readily detected under ultramicroscope.
3.	Surface tension	Surface tension is usually lower than that of the dispersion medium.	Surface tension is of the same order as that of the dispersion medium.
4.	Viscosity	Viscosity is much higher than that of the dispersion medium.	Viscosity range is about the same as that of the dispersion medium.

5.	Action of electrolytes	Much large quantities of electrolytes are required to cause precipitation (coagulation).	Addition of small quantities of electrolytes causes precipitation.
6.	Influence of electric field	The particles may or may not migrate under the influence of electric field.	The particles migrate either to cathode or anode under the influence of electric field.
7.	Hydration	Owing to the presence of a number of polar groups in the molecules, the particles are appreciably hydrated.	The particles are not hydrated to an appreciable extent.
8.	Preparation	They can be prepared easily by merely shaking or warming with dispersion medium.	They are very difficult to prepare. They are prepared by special methods.
9.	Stability	They are self stabilized.	Stabilizers are added for their safety.
10.	Stability	They have high stability and are coagulated with difficulty.	They have low stability and are coagulated easily.
11.	Examples	Glycogen, albumin, rubber, starch etc.	Colloidal gold, colloidal silver, colloidal As_2S_3 etc.

3. Based on electrical charge on the dispersed phase: On the basis of electrical charge present on the dispersed phase, colloidal particles can be of two types: positive colloids and negative colloids.

Positive colloids: The colloids in which the dispersed phase carry a positive charge are known as positive colloids. For example, $Fe(OH)_3$, haemoglobin (blood), $Al(OH)_3$, $Cr(OH)_3$, TiO_2 solutions etc.

Negative colloids: The colloids in which the dispersed phase carry a negative charge are known as negative colloids for example, As_2S_3, sols of metals like Cu, Ag, Au etc.

4. Based on the size of particles of dispersed phase: Depending upon the size of particles of dispersed phase, the colloids are classified as:

(*a*) Multi-molecular colloids, (*b*) Macromolecular colloids, (*c*) Associated colloids.

(*a*) Multi-molecular colloids: When on dissolution, a large number of atoms or smaller molecules of a substance (having diameter less than 1 nm) aggregate together to form species having size in the colloidal range, the species so formed are called **multi-molecular colloids.** Thus, in these sols the dispersed phase consist of aggregates of atoms or molecules with molecular size less than 1 nm. In these colloids, particles are held together by weak van der Waal's forces. For example, gold sol, sulphur (S_8) sol etc.

(*b*) Macromolecular colloids: Colloids in which macromolecules (big size molecules) having large molecular masses are dissolved in a suitable liquid to form solution in which the dispersed phase particles have size in the colloidal range are called as **macromolecular colloids**. These macromolecules forming the dispersed phase are generally polymers with very high molecular masses. These macromolecules can be natural like cellulose, proteins, gelatin etc. or can be man made like nylon, polyethylene, polystyrene, synthetic rubber etc. The solutions of such colloids are quite stable and resemble true solutions in various aspects.

(c) Associated colloids or Micelles: The substances which when dissolved in a medium behaves a normal electrolytes at low concentration but behaves as colloidal particles at higher concentration due to the formation of aggregate particles are called as **associated colloids** and the aggregated particles thus formed are called as **micelles**. The micelle formation takes place only above a particular temperature (Kraft temperature T_k) and above a particular concentration (Critical Micelle Concentration CMC). The most common examples are soaps and detergents.

15.7 MECHANISM OF MICELLE FORMATION

Micelles are usually formed by the aggregation of several ions or molecules with lyophobic as well as lyophilic parts. For example, soap solution.

Soap is sodium salt of higher fatty acid and may be represented as $C_{17}H_{35}COONa$. In aqueous solution, it ionizes as

$$\underset{\text{Sodium stearate (soap)}}{C_{17}H_{35}COONa} \rightleftharpoons \underset{\text{Stearate ion}}{C_{17}H_{35}COO^-} + Na^+$$

The stearate ion ($C_{17}H_{35}COO^-$) consists of two parts *i.e.* long non-polar hydrocarbon chain ($C_{17}H_{35}$) called the tail which is hydrophobic (water repelling) and the polar group COO^- called the head which is hydrophilic (water loving).

The stearate ions $C_{17}H_{35}COO^-$ are therefore present on the surface with their COO^- groups in water and the hydrocarbon chains R staying away from it and remain on the surface (Fig. 15.9). However, at higher concentration (or at CMC), these ions do not remain on the surface but are pulled into the bulk of the solution and form an oily aggregate with their hydrocarbon chain (wavy lines in figure) pointing towards the centre and the COO^- part (solid circles in figure) outwards as shown in Fig. 15.9. An aggregate so formed is known as "Ionic Micelle". Each Micelle contain atleast 1000 molecules.

Similarly, in detergents *i.e.* sodium lauryl sulphate $C_{12}H_{25}SO_4^-Na^+$, the polar group is SO_4^{2-} alongwith a long hydrocarbon chain $C_{12}H_{25}$. The mechanism of micelle formation is similar to that of soaps.

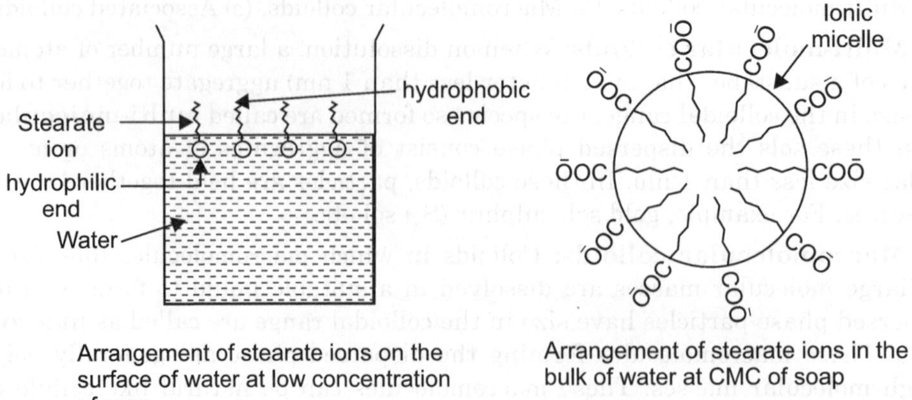

Arrangement of stearate ions on the surface of water at low concentration of soap

Arrangement of stearate ions in the bulk of water at CMC of soap

Fig. 15.9. Mechanism of micelle formation.

Table 15.5: Differences between Three Types of Colloids

S. No.	Multi-molecular colloids	Macromolecular colloids	Associated colloids
1.	These colloids are formed by the aggregation of a large number of atoms or molecules which generally have diameter less than 1 nm.	These colloids consists of large molecules (generally polymers).	These colloids are formed by the aggregation of a large number of ions in concentrated solution.
2.	Their atoms or molecules are held together by weak van der Waal's forces.	Due to long chain, the van der Waal's forces holding atoms and molecules are comparatively stronger.	Higher is the concentration, greater are the van der Waal's forces.
3.	Their molecular masses are not very high.	They have high molecular masses.	They generally have high molecular masses.
4.	They usually have lyophobic character.	They usually have lyophilic character.	Both lyophobic and lyophilic character can be seen in such colloids.

15.8 PREPARATION OF COLLOIDAL SOLUTIONS

Lyophilic colloids have strong affinity between the particles of dispersed phase and dispersion medium. Hence, these colloidal solutions can be prepared readily by simply mixing the dispersed phase and the dispersion medium under ordinary conditions. However, the preparation of colloidal solution of lyophobic colloids requires special methods which are grouped under two headings, *viz.* dispersion methods and condensation methods.

Dispersion or Disintegration Methods

In these methods, larger particles of a substance are broken into smaller particles of colloidal size. The following methods are generally employed.

(*i*) **Mechanical dispersion or disintegration method:** In this method the substance is first ground to coarse particles. It is then mixed with the dispersion medium to get a suspension. The suspension is farther grinded in a "colloidal mill" (Fig. 15.10). Colloidal suspensions of black ink, paints, varnishes, dyes etc. are obtained by this method.

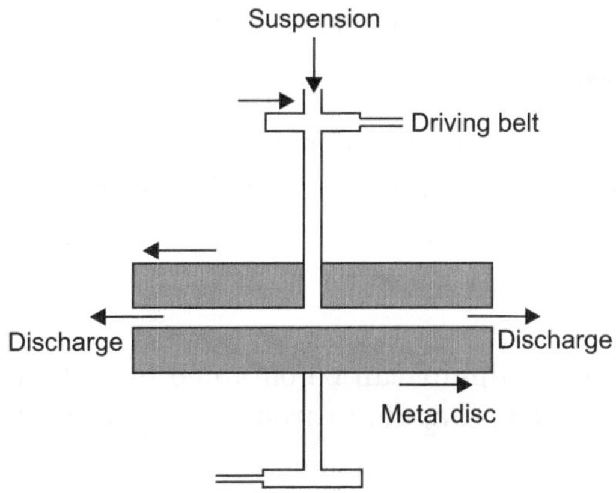

Fig. 15.10. Colloidal mill.

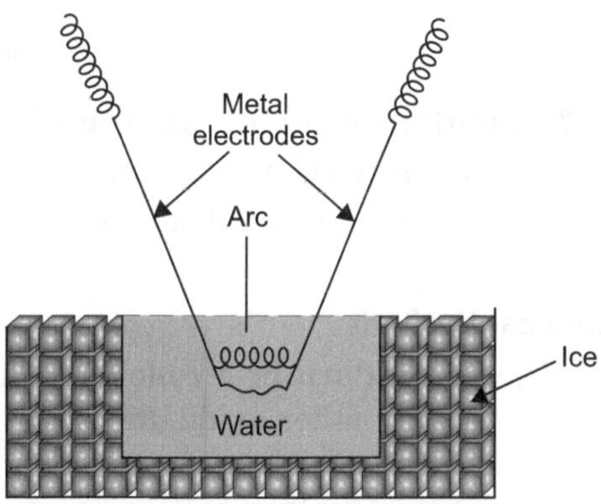

Fig. 15.11. Bredig's arc method.

(*ii*) **Electrical dispersion (Bredig's arc method):** This method is employed for obtaining colloidal solutions of metals like gold, silver, platinum etc. An electric arc is struck between two metallic electrodes suspended in a trough of water (Fig. 15.11). The tremendous heat generated by the arc converts the metals into vapours which are condensed immediately in the liquid to give colloidal solution. The colloidal solution is stabilized by adding a small amount of alkali.

(*iii*) **Peptization:** The process of converting a freshly prepared precipitate into colloidal form by the addition of a suitable electrolyte is called **peptization.** The electrolyte used for this purpose is called peptizing agent or dispersing agent. Few examples are given below:

(*a*) Freshly prepared $Fe(OH)_3$ can be peptized by adding small amount of $FeCl_3$.

(*b*) A solution of AgI can be peptized by shaking with a small amount of KI or $AgNO_3$.

(*c*) Freshly prepared $Al(OH)_3$ can be peptized by adding small amount of very dilute HCl solution.

(*d*) Stannic oxide can be peptized by adding a small amount of dilute HCl solution.

(*e*) Lamp black is peptized by gums to form Indian ink.

(*f*) Gelatin stabilizes the colloidal state of ice-cream.

Cause of peptization: When an electrolyte is added to a freshly prepared precipitate, the particles of the precipitate preferentially adsorb suitable ions from the electrolyte and get dispersed due to electrostatic repulsions. This forms particles of colloidal size (Fig. 15.12). For example, freshly prepared $Fe(OH)_3$ can be peptized by adding small amount of $FeCl_3$ and a reddish brown coloured colloidal solution is obtained. Here, Fe^{3+} ions from $FeCl_3$ are adsorbed by $Fe(OH)_3$ precipitate.

$$\underset{\text{Precipitate}}{Fe(OH)_3} + \underset{\substack{\text{(From } FeCl_3\\ \text{electrolyte)}}}{Fe^{3+}} \longrightarrow \underset{\text{Colloidal solution}}{Fe(OH)_3Fe^{3+}}$$

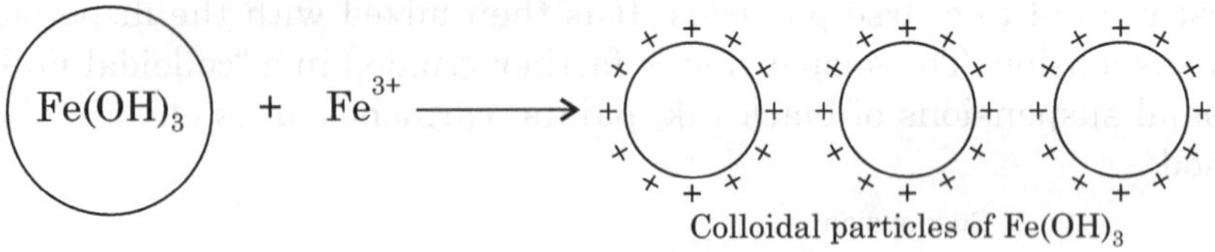

Fig. 15.12. Peptization.

2. Condensation or aggregation method: In these methods, smaller particles of dispersed phase condense or join together to form particles of colloidal size. The following chemical and physical methods can be used for condensation.

Chemical Methods

(*i*) **By oxidation:** A colloidal solution of sulphur can be obtained by bubbling oxygen (or any other oxidizing agent like HNO_3, Br_2 etc.) through a solution of hydrogen sulphide in water.

$$2H_2S + O_2 \text{ (or any other oxidising agent)} \longrightarrow 2H_2O + 2S$$

(*ii*) **By reduction:** A number of metals such as Ag, Au and Pt have been obtained in colloidal state by treating the aqueous solution of their salts with a suitable reducing agent such as formaldehyde, phenyl hydrazine, hydrogen peroxide, stannous chloride etc.

$$2AuCl_3 + 3SnCl_2 \longrightarrow 2SnCl_4 + \underset{\text{Gold sol}}{2\,Au}$$

(*iii*) **By hydrolysis:** Many salt solutions are rapidly hydrolyzed by boiling dilute solutions of their salts. For example, $Fe(OH)_3$ and $Al(OH)_3$ sols are obtained by boiling solutions of the corresponding chlorides

$$FeCl_3 + 3H_2O \longrightarrow \underset{\text{Colloidal sol}}{Fe(OH)_3} + 3HCl$$

Similarly, silicic acid sol is obtained by the hydrolysis of sodium silicate.

(*iv*) **By double decomposition:** A sol of arsenic sulphide is obtained by passing hydrogen sulphide through a cold solution of arsenious oxide in water

$$As_2O_3 + 3H_2S \longrightarrow \underset{\text{Colloidal sol.}}{As_2S_3} + 3H_2O$$

Physical Methods

(*i*) **By exchange of solvent:** Substances like sulphur and phosphorus are fairly soluble in alcohol but less soluble in water. If their alcohlic solutions are poured in water, colloidal solutions of sulphur and phosphorus are obtained.

(*ii*) **By excessive cooling:** A colloidal solution of ice in an organic solvent (*e.g.*, ether, chloroform etc.) can be prepared by freezing a solution of water in the solvent. The water molecules which can no longer be held in solution, separately combine to form colloidal particles.

(*iii*) **By change of physical state:** Colloidal solution of sulphur and mercury in water are prepared by passing their vapours in cold water containing a little stabilizer like ammonium salt or citrate.

15.9 PURIFICATION OF COLLOIDAL SOLUTIONS

The colloidal solutions prepared by the above methods generally contain impurities especially electrolytes which can destabilize the sols. Hence, their removal is essential for the stability of colloidal sols. The following methods are employed for purification of colloidal sols:

1. **Dialysis:** The process of separating a crystalloid from a colloid by diffusion or filtration through a fine membrane (parchment or animal membrane) is called as **dialysis**. The process is based on the fact that the colloidal particles cannot pass through a parchment membrane while the ions of the electrolyte can pass through it. The apparatus used for this process is called as **dialyser** (Fig. 15.13).

   Dialysis consists of a bag made of cellophone or parchment. The bag is filled with colloidal solution and is placed in running water in a trough. The soluble impurities gradually diffuse out leaving behind the pure colloidal solution. Dialysis is a slow process and it takes several hours and sometimes even days for complete purification of colloidal solution. The process of dialysis can be quickened by using hot water (hot dialysis) or by applying an electric field (electrodialysis).

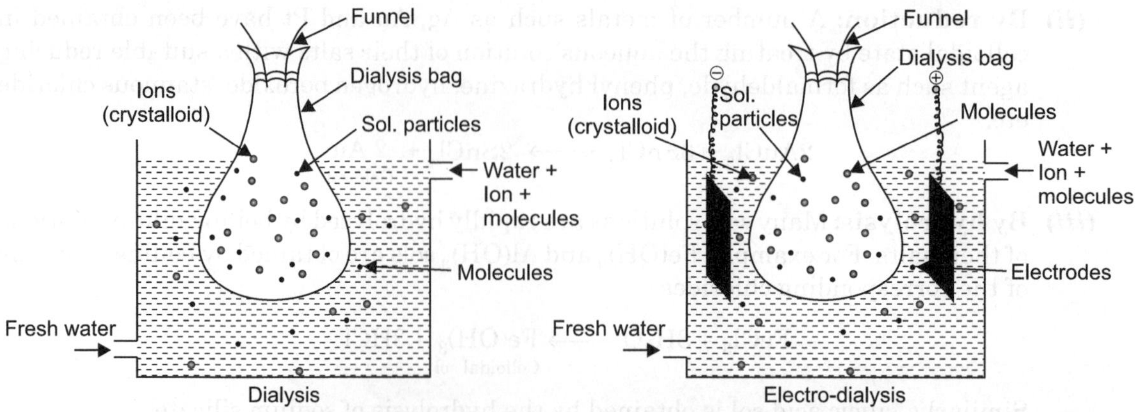

Fig. 15.13. Dialysis and electro-dialysis.

The most important application of dialysis is in the purification of blood in the artificial kidney machine.

2. **Ultrafiltration:** It is the process of removing the impurities from the colloidal solution by passing it through graded filter papers called **ultra filter papers.**

   Ordinary filter paper is permeable to colloidal particles as well as true solutions and thus cannot be used for filtering sols. However, if the pores of the ordinary filter paper are made smaller by soaking the filter paper in a solution of gelatin or collodion followed by its hardening by dipping in formaldehyde solution serves the purpose. Due to this treatment, the pore size of filter paper is reduced and the filter paper so obtained is called as ultra-filter paper. By using the impregnating solutions of different concentrations, a series of ultra filter papers can be prepared. The ions and molecules of impurities pass through these pores but colloidal particles are retained.

15.10 PROPERTIES OF COLLOIDAL SOLUTIONS

The main characteristic properties of colloidal solution are as follows:

1. **Heterogeneous character:** Colloidal solutions are heterogeneous in nature. These consist of two phases *viz.*, the dispersed phase and the dispersion medium. The phenomena of Tyndall effect, electrophoresis and electroosmosis confirm heterogeneity of colloidal systems.

2. **Filterability:** Due to very small size, the colloidal particles pass through an ordinary filter paper. Hence, ordinary filter paper cannot be used for removing the dispersed phase. However, they can be retained by animal membranes, cellophone membrane and ultrafilters.

3. **Visibility:** Although colloidal solutions are heterogeneous in nature yet the dispersed particles present in them are not visible to the naked eye and they appear homogeneous. This is because colloidal particles are too small to be visible to the naked eye.

4. **Stability:** Colloidal sols are quite stable and the dispersed particles present in them do not settle down even on keeping. However, on standing for a long time, a few colloidal particles of comparatively larger size may get sedimented slowly.

5. **Colour:** The colour of colloidal solution depends upon the size of colloidal particles present in it. Larger particles absorb the light of longer wavelength and therefore transmit light of shorter wavelength. For example, a silver sol having particles of size 150 nm appears violet, whereas that having particles of size 60 nm appears orange yellow.

6. **Colligative properties:** Colligative properties like osmotic pressure, depression in freezing point etc. depend upon the number of moles or number of particles present. Due to formation of associated molecules, they have high molecular masses. Hence, the number of particles per litre of the sol is relatively smaller than in a true solution. Therefore, they have low values of colligative properties.

   Colloidal solutions boil and freeze at almost the same temperature as the pure dispersion medium and lowering of vapour pressure is also negligible. However, the osmotic pressure of colloidal solutions, though smaller than true solution is the only colligative property which has been determined with a reasonable degree of accuracy and can be used to determine the average molecular masses of colloidal particles.

7. **Mechanical properties (Kinetic properties):**

   (*a*) **Brownian movement:** Robert Brown, an English botanist in 1827, observed that pollen grains in aqueous suspension were in constant motion. When colloidal solutions were examined under the ultramicroscope, it was found that the particles in these solutions were also in constant, random motion, traversing no definite set paths but travelling in zig-zag directions all over the field of view. This movement of colloidal particles is called **Brownian movement** (Fig. 15.14).

   The Brownian movement is due to the bombardment of colloidal particles by the molecules of the dispersion medium which are in constant motion like molecules in a gas. Since the colloidal particles are considerably heavier than the molecules of the dispersion medium, their movement is considerably slower than that of the medium molecules and hence can be observed under the ultramicroscope.

   The mass of particle of an ordinary suspension is so large that the bombardment of molecules of the dispersion medium produces little effect and thus ordinary suspension does not exhibit Brownian movement.

   (*b*) **Diffusion:** In a colloidal solution, colloidal particles move from a region of higher concentration to a region of lower concentration until uniformity is attained. But the diffusion process is slower than diffusion in true solution due to higher mass and lower speed of colloidal particles. Diffusion is used to separate colloidal particles of different size.

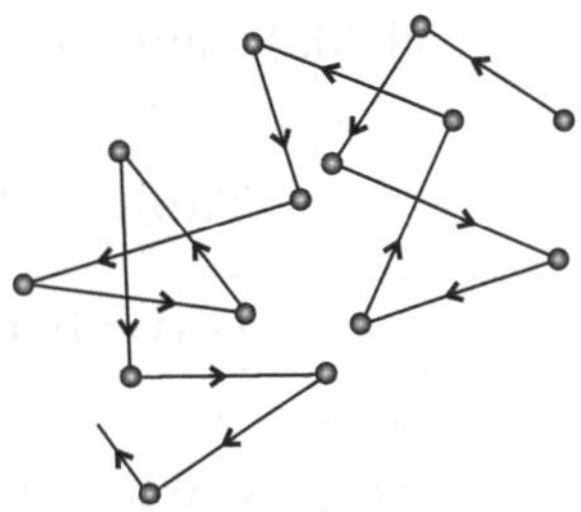

Fig. 15.14. Brownian movement of colloidal particles.

   (*c*) **Sedimentation:** Colloidal particles constantly exhibit Brownian motion and remain suspended in solution, thereby stabilizing the colloidal solution. Larger colloidal particles settle slowly by the effect of gravity and is called **sedimentation**.

8. **Optical properties or Tyndall effect:** When a strong beam of light is passed through a true solution in a dark room, the path of light is not visible. However, if the beam of light is passed through a colloidal solution, the path of light becomes illuminated due to the scattering of light by the colloidal particles. This phenomena is called **Tyndall effect** (Fig. 15.15) and illuminated path (streak of light) is known as Tyndall cone. The colloidal particles can be viewed through a microscope placed at right angles to the path of light.

   The appearance of dust particles in a semidarkened room when a sun beam enters or when a light is thrown from a projector in cinema hall are the well-known examples of Tyndall effect.

   The particles in true solution are too small in size to cause any scattering. Therefore, true solutions do not exhibit this phenomena. The Tyndall effect confirms the heterogeneous nature of colloidal solutions.

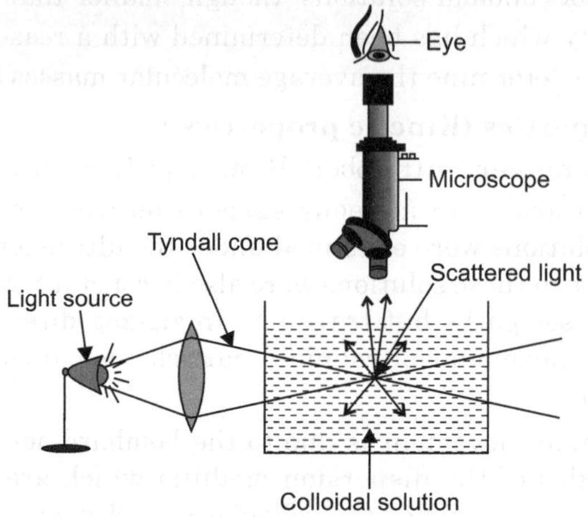

Fig. 15.15. Tyndall effect.

9. **Electrical properties:** Colloidal particles are electrically charged. All the particles of a colloidal system carry the same charge while the dispersion medium has an equal but opposite charge with the result the system as a whole is electrically neutral. The presence of equal and similar charge on colloidal particles is responsible in giving stability to the system. The colloidal particles, owing to the similar nature of the charge, repel each other and do not combine to form bigger particles and thus the colloidal solution is stable and particles do not settle down. Charge on some common sols is given in Table 15.6.

Table 15.6: Charge on Particles of Some Common Sols.

Positively charged sols	Negatively charged sols
Hydroxides like $Al(OH)_3$, $Ca(OH)_2$, $Fe(OH)_3$, $Cr(OH)_3$, etc.	Sulphides like As_2S_3, CdS, Sb_2S_3 etc.
Oxides like TiO_2 etc.	Metallic sols like Cu, Ag, Au, Pt etc.
Basic dye like methylene blue, crystal violet etc.	Acidic dyes like eosin, congo red etc.
Haemoglobin, protein in acid solution.	Organic sols like gelatin, starch etc.

15.11 ORIGIN OF CHARGE ON COLLOIDAL PARTICLES

Colloidal particles develop charge due to following reasons:

(*i*) Frictional electrification caused by the mutual rubbing of the colloidal particles with molecules of the dispersion medium.

(*ii*) Electron capture by particles from air and during electro-dispersion in Bredig's arc method.

(*iii*) **Dissociation of the surface molecules:** For example, an aqueous solution of soap ($RCOO^-Na^+$) which dissociates into ions $RCOO^-$ and Na^+. The cations (Na^+) pass into solution while the anions ($RCOO^-$) have a tendency to aggregate into cluster carrying negative charge. Hence, a negatively charged sol is obtained.

(*iv*) **Preferential adsorption of ions from solutions:** The particles of dispersed phase adsorb preferentially only those ions which are common with their own lattice ions. For example, when colloidal sol. of AgI is prepared by adding KI solution to $AgNO_3$ solution till KI is in slight excess, iodide ions (I^-) will be adsorbed on the surface of AgI particles hence giving them a negative charge.

$$AgI + \underset{\text{(from KI)}}{I^-} \longrightarrow \underset{\text{Negative sol}}{[(AgI)I^-]}$$

However, if the colloidal sol of AgI is prepared by adding $AgNO_3$ solution to KI till $AgNO_3$ is in slight excess, silver ions (Ag^+) will be adsorbed hence giving it a positive charge.

$$AgI + \underset{\text{(from AgNO}_3\text{)}}{Ag^+} \longrightarrow \underset{\text{positive sol}}{[(AgI)Ag^+]}$$

Similarly, ferric hydroxide sol ($Fe(OH)_3$) is positively charged due to preferential adsorption of Fe^{3+} ions on the surface of $Fe(OH)_3$.

Electrical properties of colloidal solutions are related to following phenomena:

(*a*) Electrophoresis or cataphoresis

(*b*) Electroosmosis.

(*a*) **Electrophoresis:** The presence of electrical charge on the sol particles can be determined with the help of electrophoresis or cataphoresis. The process involves the movement of colloidal particles towards one or the other electrode when placed under the influence of an electric field (Fig. 15.16).

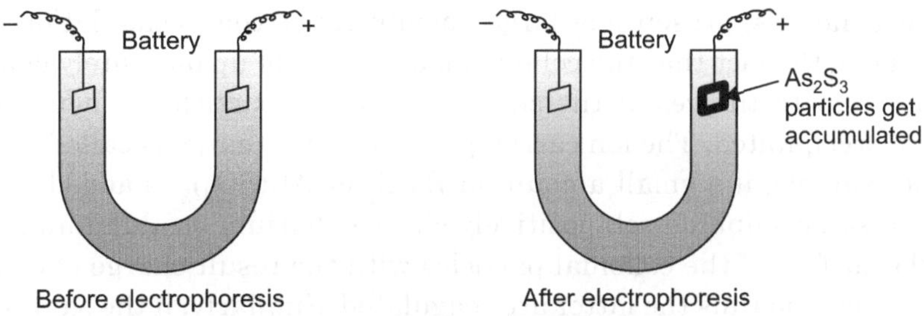

Fig. 15.16. Electrophoresis.

The phenomena of movement of colloidal particles under the influence of an applied electric field as called as **electrophoresis or cataphoresis**. To study the phenomena, a U-tube containing Pt electrodes in each limb is taken. As_2S_3 sol is taken in the U-tube and electric current is passed through it. The direction of movement of colloidal particles is decided by the nature of charge present on them. If the colloidal particles carry positive charge, they move towards cathode and vice versa. In the case of As_2S_3, the increase in charge accumulation can be seen near the positive electrode. Hence, it shows that the As_2S_3 sol bears a negative charge.

(*b*) **Electro-osmosis:** If in the set up of electrophoresis, a partition is made between the two electrodes using a parchment membrane so that the colloidal particles do not pass through it but there is movement of dispersion medium when the electric field is applied. Thus, electro-osmosis is the phenomenon of the movement of the molecules of the dispersion medium under the influence of electric field whereas colloidal particles are not allowed to move.

15.12 COAGULATION OR FLOCCULATION OF COLLOIDAL SOLUTIONS

As mentioned above, stability of the colloidal state is due to the existence of electrical charge on the particles. However, if the charge is lowered to a certain critical value or neutralized, the particles approach close enough to coalesce to form bigger particles of the suspension range. This phenomenon of the change of colloidal state to suspension state is known as **coagulation or flocculation of colloidal solutions**. It is generally brought about by the following ways:

(*i*) **By mutual precipitation:** When the two oppositely charged sols [*e.g.*, As_2S_3 and $Fe(OH)_3$ sols] are mixed in approximately equal proportions, the charge of one sol is neutralized by the opposite charge on the other sol, with the result the dispersed phase of both the sols are precipitated out.

(*ii*) **By prolonged dialysis:** As discussed earlier that the traces of electrolytes are always associated with the colloidal particles. So, if the colloidal system is subjected to prolonged dialysis, the electrolyte is completely removed and the colloidal system becomes unstable since the stability of colloidal system is due to the presence of traces of electrolytes.

(*iii*) **By electrophoresis:** This method is used for the coagulation of lyophobic colloids. Under the influence of electric field, the particles of dispersed phase move towards oppositely charge electrodes and get neutralized.

(*iv*) **By addition of electrolytes:** Although traces of an electrolyte are essential for stabilizing the sols, presence of large amount cause their coagulation or flocculation. This is due to the fact that the colloidal particles take up oppositely charged ions from electrolytes, with the result the charge on the sol particles is neutralized and thus these are precipitated. The ion carrying the opposite charge is called the **flocculating ion**. For example, if a small amount of $BaCl_2$ or $Al_2(SO_4)_3$ is added to the negatively charged arsenic sulphide sol, positively charged barium or aluminium ions are taken up on the surface of the colloidal particles with the result charge of colloidal particles is neutralized and thus the latter are coagulated. Similarly, if the same electrolytes are added to the positively charged ferric hydroxide sol, the negatively charged chloride or sulphate ions are taken up by the colloidal particles with the result the latter are neutralized and thus coagulated.

The amount of electrolyte required to coagulate a fixed amount of a sol depends upon the valency of the flocculating ion. In general, **greater the valency of the flocculating ion, the higher is its power to cause precipitation**. This is known as *Hardy Schulze rule*. Thus, the flocculating power of the cations for a negatively charged sol like As_2S_3 are in the order

$$Al^{3+} > Ba^{2+} > Na^+$$

The flocculating power of anions, for a positively charged sol like $Fe(OH)_3$ are in the order

$$[Fe(CN)_6]^{4-} > PO_4^{3-} > SO_4^{2-} > Cl^-$$

Flocculating cations and anions cause coagulation of the negatively and positively charged colloids respectively. The flocculation power of a trivalent ion is nearly 500 – 1000 times more than that of a monovalent ion; while that of a bivalent ion is about 100 – 500 times more than that of a univalent ion.

Coagulating Power and Coagulation Value

The minimum amount of the electrolyte in millimoles that must be added to one litre of the colloidal sol to bring about complete coagulation or flocculation is called the **coagulation or flocculation value** of the electrolyte. Thus, smaller is the flocculation value of an electrolyte, greater is its flocculating power. In short

$$\frac{\text{Coagulating power of electrolyte } A}{\text{Coagulating power of electrolyte } B} = \frac{\text{Coagulating value of electrolyte } B}{\text{Coagulating value of electrolyte } A}.$$

The flocculating values (in millimoles/litre) for the coagulation of positively charged sol $Fe(OH)_3$ and negatively charged sol As_2S_3 are given in Table 15.7.

Table 15.7: Flocculating values of common electrolytes in millimoles/litre

Ferric Hydroxide (+) Sol			Arsenic sulphide (–) Sol		
Electrolyte	**Active anion**	**Flocculating value**	**Electrolyte**	**Active cation**	**Flocculating value**
KCl	Cl^-	103	NaCl	Na^+	51
KBr	Br^-	138	KCl	K^+	50
K_2SO_4	SO_4^{2-}	0.210	$MgSO_4$	Mg^{2+}	0.72
$Na_2C_2O_4$	$C_2O_4^{2-}$	0.238	$BaCl_2$	Ba^{2+}	0.69
$K_3[Fe(CN)_6]$	$[Fe(CN)_6]^{3-}$	0.096	$AlCl_3$	Al^{3+}	0.093

- More the flocculating power less will be the flocculating value.

Note: Lyophobic sols are easily coagulated by small amounts of the electrolyte but lyophilic sols are not easily coagulated. They require large amount of electrolytes for their coagulation. This process of coagulation or precipitation of lyophilic sols is called as **salting out** while the term coagulation is used for lyophobic sols.

The salting out of lyophilic sols occurs due to hydration of particles of added electrolyte resulting into the dehydration of the dispersed particles thereby causing coagulation.

The salting out effect depends on the nature of the ion and not on the charge of the ion. The order of cation is

$$Mg^{2+} > Ca^{2+} > Sr^{2+} > Ba^{2+} > Na^{+} > K^{+} > Rb^{+} > Cs^{+}$$

and the order of anion is

$$\text{citrate}^{3-} > \text{tartarate}^{2-} > SO_4^{2-} > PO_4^{3-} > CH_3COO^{-} > Cl^{-} > NO_3^{-} > I^{-} > CNS^{-}$$

The above series is popularly known as **Hofmeister series** or more generally **Lyotropic series.**

Protective Action of Lyophilic Colloids

As mentioned earlier lyophilic colloids are much more stable than the lyophobic colloids. The extra stability of the former is due to the fact that they are extensively solvated.

The extra stability of lyophilic colloids impart them the property of protecting lyophobic colloids from precipitation by electrolytes. When a lyophilic sol is added to a lyophobic sol, the former particles provide envelopes around the latter particles and thus protect the latter from the action of electrolytes. Lyophilic colloids used for such purposes are known as **protective colloids**. Thus, the addition of gelatin (lyophilic colloid) to a gold sol (lyophobic colloid) protects the latter by the action of limited amount of sodium chloride.

The lyophilic colloids differ in their protective powers. **Zsigmondy** introduced the term gold number to measure the protective power of different colloids. He defined the **gold number** as the weight in milligram of a protective colloid which checks the coagulation of 10 mL of a given gold solution on adding 1 mL of a 10% solution of sodium chloride. Thus, smaller the gold number of a lyophilic colloid, greater is its protective power. The gold numbers of a few protective colloids are given below in Table 15.8.

Table 15.8: Gold Number of a Few Protective Colloids

Sol	Gold number	Reciprocal of gold number
Gelatin	0.005 – 0.01	200 – 100
Casein	0.01 – 0.02	100 – 50
Haemoglobin	0.03 – 0.07	33 – 14
Albumin	0.1 – 0.2	10 – 5
Gum arabic	0.15 – 0.25	7 – 4
Potato starch	20 – 25	0.5 – 0.4

Thus, according to above list, gelatin is the best protective colloid. The protective action of a lyophilic colloid is due to the formation of a protective layer around the lyophobic colloid (because of adsorption). The particles of electrolyte do not have enough potential to penetrate this protective layer easily. Hence, they are unable to neutralize charge on colloidal particles and bring about coagulation.

Ostwald introduced another term to express protective action of lyopilic colloid, **congo rubin number** which is defined as the amount of protective colloids in milligram which prevents colour change in 100 mL of 0.01% congo rubin dye to which 0.16 gm equivalent of KCl added.

Emulsions: Emulsions are those colloidal system in which the dispersed phase as well as dispersion medium are liquids. The two common examples are :

(*i*) Milk which consists of particles of liquid fat dispersed in water and

(*ii*) Cod liver oil in which particles of water are dispersed in oil.

An emulsion is prepared by vigorously shaking the mixture of two liquids or by passing the mixture through a colloid mill, called the **homogenizer**. The emulsions prepared in such a manner are usually not stable and the two liquids separate out on standing. Thus, to get a stable emulsion, small quantities of certain other substances are added during preparation. The substances that are added to stabilize the emulsions are called as **emulsifier** or **emulsifying agent**. Some commonly used emulsifying agents are soaps of various kinds, lyophilic colloids (gum, agar, protein etc.), long chain sulphonic acids etc.

In most of emulsions, the two liquid phases are oil and water and thus emulsions may be of following two types:

(*i*) Oil-in-water emulsion: In these emulsions, oil is the dispersed phase and water is the dispersion medium. Milk and vanishing cream are the two important examples of this type of emulsion.

(*ii*) Water-in-oil emulsion: In these emulsions, water is the dispersed phase and oil is the dispersion medium. For example, butter, cold cream etc.

Foams: Foams are colloidal dispersions of gas in liquid stabilized by soap or other surface active agents. Foams can be broken by anti-foaming agents, *e.g.*, castor oil, alcohol etc. Foams have a high absorptive capacity.

The most important industrial applications of foam are:

(*i*) In ore floatation.

(*ii*) In detergency (the washing action of soap is partly explained as adsorption of dirt to form bubbles).

(*iii*) In fire fighting etc.

Gels: A gel is a colloidal system in which a liquid is dispersed in a solid. Certain lyophobic sols *e.g.*, that of gelatin or agar-agar or gum-arabic etc. containing high concentration of the dispersed solid, on cooling change instantly into a semi-solid from *i.e.*, jelly like enclosing the entire liquid within it. The product so obtained is called as **gel** and the process of gel formation is called as **gelation**.

The most important applications of gels are:

(*i*) Silica gel is used as a dehydrating agent.

(*ii*) Some of the gels are edible like curd, jelly etc.

(*iii*) Boot polish also have a gel like structure.

(*iv*) Some gels are used in laboratories like gelatin, agar-agar.

15.13 APPLICATIONS OF COLLOIDS

Colloids play a very significant role in nature and in our daily life. Some of the important applications of colloids are listed below:

(*i*) Foodstuffs: Many of our foodstuffs are colloidal in nature. For example, milk is an emulsion of fat dispersed in water and stabilized by casein which itself is a lyophilic colloid and being a protein, is a nutrient of great value. Other foodstuffs colloidal in nature are eggs, fruit jellies, whipped cream, gelatin deserts, salad dressings etc. Bread is a dispersion of air in baked dough.

(ii) **Medicines:** A large number of medicinal and pharmaceutical preparations are emulsions, *e.g.,* emulsions of cod liver oil and halibut liver oil. It is believed that the emulsified oils are easily acted upon by the digestive juices in the stomach and hence are readily digested. Colloidal gold is given by injection to raise the vitality of the human system. The disinfectants such as phenyl, dettol produces emulsion of the oil in water type when poured into water. Colloidal sulphur is used as a germ killer especially in plants. Colloidal antimony (kajal) has been found effective in treating eye diseases. Antibiotics such as penicillin and streptomycin are produced in colloidal form suitable for injections.

(iii) **Non-drip or thixotropic paints:** All paints are colloidal dispersions of solid pigments in a liquid medium. The modern non-drip paints also contain long chain polymers. At rest, the chains of molecules are coiled and entrap much dispersion medium. Thus, the paint is a semisolid gel structure. On applying shearing stress with a plant brush, the coiled molecules straighten, as a result the entrapped medium is released. As soon as the brush is removed, the liquid paint reverts to the semisolid form. This renders the paint "non-drip".

(iv) **Smoke precipitation (Cottrell precipitator):** Smoke and dust are nuisance and pollute the atmosphere of the industrial areas. Actually smoke consists of electrically charged colloidal particles dispersed in air. These particles may be removed from the dispersing medium (air) by means of electrophoresis.

(v) **Clarification of municipal water:** The municipal water obtained from natural sources often contains colloidal particles as impurity. The process of coagulation is used to remove these impurities. The colloidal particles carry a negative charge and when potash alum or aluminium sulphate is added to water, a gelatinous precipitate of hydrated aluminium hydroxide (floc) is formed

$$Al^{3+} + 3H_2O \longrightarrow Al(OH)_3 + 3H^+$$
$$Al(OH)_3 + 4H_2O + H^+ \longrightarrow Al(OH)_3\,(H_2O)_4^+$$

The positively charged floc attracts negative sol particles which gels coagulated. The floc alongwith the impurities comes down, leaving the water clean.

(vi) **Delta formation:** River water contains colloidal particles of clay, sand and many other materials which carry negative charge. The sea water, on the other hand, contains positively charged ions such as Na^+, Mg^{2+}, Ca^{2+}. As the river water meets sea water, these ions discharge the sand or clay particles which are precipitated as delta.

(vii) **Blue colour of the sky:** This is an application of Tyndall effect. The upper atmosphere contains colloidal dust or ice particles dispersed in air. As the sun rays enters the atmosphere, these strike the colloidal particles. The particles absorb sunlight and scatter light of blue colour.

(viii) **Rubber plating and chrome tanning:** Several industrial processes such as rubber plating, chrome tanning, dyeing, lubrication etc. are of colloidal nature. Let us discuss the first two processes.

In rubber plating, the negatively charged particles of rubber (latex) are made to deposit on the wires on handle of various tools (in order to insulate them) by means of electrophoresis. The article on which rubber is to be deposited is made anode.

In tanning, the positively charged colloidal particles of hides and leather are coagulated by impregnating them in negatively charged tanning materials (present in the barks of trees). Among the tanning agents, chromium salts are most commonly used for the coagulation of the hide material and the process is called **chrome tanning**. The rate of chrome tanning can be increased by electrophoresis.

(ix) **Smoke screens:** Smoke screens are used in warfare for the purpose of concealment. These screens consist of very fine particles of titanium oxide dispersed in air. These are dropped from aeroplanes and since titanium oxide is very heavy, the smoke screens drops down rapidly as a curtain of dazzling whiteness.

(x) **Sewage disposal:** Sewage water contains particles of dirt, rubbish, mud etc. which are of colloidal size and carry electric charge and therefore do not settle down easily. These particles can be removed by the process of cataphoresis in which sewage water is passed through a tunnel fitted with metallic electrodes, maintained at high potential difference. The particles migrate to the oppositely charged electrodes, get neutralized and settle down (coagulated). The deposited matter (rubbish matter) is used as a manure and the clear water is used for irrigation purposes.

(xi) **Cleansing action of detergents:** This is due to emulsifying properties of the detergents. They form an emulsion with oil and dirt particles in water.

(xii) **Fire-foam:** Fire foam is a carbon dioxide **froth** made by mixing sodium carbonate solution and alum. The protective colloids like glue, **dextrin** or saponin is added to stabilize the foam and keep the bubbles in finely dispersed form.

(xiii) **Soils:** Good soils are colloidal in nature in which humus acts as a protective colloid. On account of their colloidal nature, they can retain more moisture for emergency and moreover, the nourishing materials are supplied to the plant by the process of adsorption.

(xiv) **Artificial rain:** Clouds are tiny droplets of water dispersed in air. Rain is caused by aggregation of these minute particles to form bigger drops of water which fall down under the action of gravity. Thus, artificial rain can be produced by throwing the electrified sand from an aeroplane and thus coagulating the mist hanging in air.

(xv) **Coagulation of blood:** Blood consists of negatively charged colloidal particles (albuminoid substance). The colloidal nature of blood explains why bleeding stops by applying a ferric chloride solution to the wound. Actually ferric chloride solution causes coagulation of blood to form a clot which stops further bleeding.

(xvi) **Industrial goods:** Soaps, detergents and wetting agents are colloidal electrolytes. Paints, varnishes, enamels, cellulose, resin, gums, glues and other adhesives, rayon, nylon, terylene, textiles, leather, paper etc. are all colloidal in nature. Later, from which rubber is obtained, is a suspension of negatively charged colloidal particles of rubber.

15.14 CATALYSIS

Catalyst

A catalyst may be defined as a substance which by its mere presence influences the rate of a chemical reaction without itself undergoing any permanent chemical change. Thus, a catalyst is not a reactant and recovered in a chemically unchanged state. A catalyst may be a single substance or a mixture of substances or a micro-particle (atom, ion or molecule). Transition metals and their compounds are the most efficient catalysts.

The action of a catalyst in changing the rate of a chemical reaction is called catalysis. Reactants on which catalyst operate are called *substrates.* Catalysts are generally written on the top of the arrow.

Positive and negative catalysts: *A catalyst which increases the rate of a reaction is called positive catalyst.* For example,

(*i*) $2KClO_3(s) \xrightarrow{MnO_2(s)} 2KCl(s) + 3O_2(g)\uparrow$

(*ii*) $N_2(g) + 3H_2(g) \xrightarrow{Fe_2O_3(s)} 2NH_3(g)$

(*iii*) $2SO_2(g) + O_2(g) \xrightarrow[\text{or } V_2O_5(s)]{Pt(s)} 2SO_3$

(*iv*) $2SO_2(g) + O_2(g) \xrightarrow{NO(g)} 2SO_3(g)$

(*v*) $CH_2 = CH_2(g) + H_2(g) \xrightarrow{Ni(s)} CH_3 - CH_3(g)$

(*vi*) $C_{12}H_{22}O_{11}(l) + H_2O(l) \xrightarrow{H_2SO_4(l)} C_6H_{12}O_6(l) + C_6H_{12}O_6(l)$

On the other hand, a catalyst which decreases the rate of a reaction is called a *negative catalyst, retarder* or *inhibitor.* For example, phosphoric acid retards the decomposition of H_2O_2, alcohol slows down the oxidation of chloroform, etc.

Homogeneous and heterogeneous catalysis: *When the reactants and catalyst are in the same phase, the catalysis is known as* ***homogeneous,*** *while when the reactants and catalyst are in different phases, the catalysis is known as* ***heterogeneous.***

Above mentioned (*i*), (*iv*) and (*vi*) are examples of homogeneous; while (*ii*), (*iii*) and (*v*) are examples of heterogeneous catalysis.

Characteristics of a Catalyst

1. Catalyst is unchanged chemically at the end of the reaction.
2. Small quantity of the catalyst is required.
3. The catalyst does not alter the position of equilibrium in a reversible reaction.
4. A catalyst speeds up the rate of forward and reverse reaction to the same degree.
5. Catalyst does not initiate a reaction that would not otherwise occur, i.e., they cannot make an impossible reaction to occur.
6. Every catalyst has its optimum temperature at which is efficiency is maximum.
7. The catalyst decreases the activation energy of the reaction and hence increases the rate of reaction.
8. The more finely divided the catalyst is, the more will be its catalytic activity.
9. Catalyst are very specific in respect of reaction, *e.g.,*

$$H_2O + CO \xleftarrow[\text{or } TiO_2]{Al_2O_3} HCOOH \xrightarrow[ZnO]{\text{Cu or}} CO_2 + H_2$$

Mode of Action of Catalysts: In *homogeneous catalysis,* catalyst combines with one or more of the reactants to form one or more *intermediate products* with low activation energy.

The intermediate compound(s) then decompose to form the products along with regeneration of the catalyst. For example, oxidation of SO_2 to SO_3 in presence of nitric oxide takes place in this way.

Ist step $\underset{\text{(reactant)}}{O_2} + \underset{\text{(catalyst)}}{2NO} \longrightarrow \underset{\text{(intermediate)}}{2NO_2}$

IInd step $\underset{\text{(intermediate)}}{2NO_2} + \underset{\text{(reactant)}}{2SO_2} \longrightarrow \underset{\text{(product)}}{2SO_3} + \underset{\text{(catalyst)}}{2NO}$

Overall reaction: $2SO_2 + O_2 \xrightarrow{NO} 2SO_3$

In a given number of molecules at a specific temperature, some have large amount of energy (*energy-rich molecules*), a few are poor-energy molecules and majority of these have normal energy. On collision, molecules with normal energy simply collide and rebound without reacting. On the other hand molecules having sufficiently high energy react. *The extra energy which the two molecules must possess in order to react is termed as the* ***activation energy*** of the reaction. In the absence of catalyst, since activation energy of the reaction is high, the reaction takes place only between small fraction of molecules with high energy and thus the reaction is quite slow. In the presence of catalyst, the activation energy of the reaction is comparatively lower and even molecules with lower energy can react with the result several molecules participate in the reaction which thus takes place faster.

In *heterogeneous catalysis*, the reactant molecules are *adsorbed* on the surface of the catalyst and the reaction take place on that surface. The adsorbed molecules are held to the surface of the catalyst by bonds similar in strength to those in chemical compounds (*chemisorption*). Now some bonds of the adsorbed molecules may be stretched, weakened and ultimately cleaved to form products.

Catalytic promoters or activators *are those which themselves are not catalysts but when present with some catalyst greatly enhance their action.* For example, in the Haber's synthesis of ammonia, the catalytic power of iron is increased by adding traces of molybdenum.

$$N_2 + 3H_2 \xrightarrow[\text{MO (catalytic promoter)}]{Fe_2O_3 \text{ (catalyst)}} 2NH_3$$

Catalytic poisons or anticatalysts *are those substances which decrease or inhibit the activity of catalysts.* For example, oxides of arsenic poison the catalytic power of platinum in the contact process for making sulphur trioxide from sulphur dioxide and oxygen (contact process for the manufacture of H_2SO_4).

Autocatalysis

Some reactions are slow at start but after some time they become quite rapid because one of the products formed during the reaction acts as a catalyst. Such reactions are called **autocatalyzed reactions** and the process is known as *autocatalysis.* A common example of autocatalysis is observed during the titration of $KMnO_4$ against acidified oxalic acid. When $KMnO_4$ solution is added to oxalic acid, the disappearance of pink colour is slow at start but as soon as some Mn^{2+} ions are formed the disappearance of colour becomes rapid.

$$2MnO_4^- + 5C_2O_4^{2-} + 16H^+ \longrightarrow 2Mn^{2+} + 10CO_2 + 8H_2O$$

Thus Mn^{2+} ions are acting as catalyst in this reaction. The fact that the rapid disappearance of colour is due to Mn^{2+} ions can be proved by the fact that if some $MnCl_2$ is added to oxalic acid solution at start, disappearance of pink colour will be rapid from the very beginning of titration.

Enzyme or biological catalysis

This type of reaction is common in body. Here the reactions are catalyzed by certain catalysts found in living tissues. These catalysts are proteinous in nature and called as *enzymes*. Catalysis brought about by the enzymes is called *enzyme catalysis*. Many of the life processes, *e.g.*, digestion of food, proceed by this type of catalysis. Enzyme catalysis may also be brought about outside the body, *e.g.*, manufacture of ethyl alcohol from molasses (alcoholic fermentation), hydrolysis of cane sugar, hydrolysis of starch etc.

$$\text{Sucrose} \xrightarrow{\text{Invertase}} \text{Glucose + Fructose}$$

$$\text{Glucose or Fructose} \xrightarrow{\text{Zymase}} \text{Ethyl alcohol} + CO_2$$

Enzymes are highly specific in their reactions.

The enzyme-catalyzed reactions are highly sensitive to temperature; the optimum temperature although depends upon the nature of individual enzyme for most of the body enzymes it is near the body temperature, *i.e.*, about 37°C. *The catalytic activity of enzymes is due to their capacity to lower the activation energy for a particular reaction.* The important enzymes involved in the digestion of food are given below:

	Source	Enzymes
(*i*)	Saliva	Salivary amylase (ptyalin) and mucin
(*ii*)	Gastric juice	Pepsin, rennin and gastric lipase
(*iii*)	Pancreatic juice	Trypsin, chymotrypsin, steapsin etc.

Catalysts in Industry

Some of the important industrial processes and their corresponding catalysts are listed below:

S.No.	Process	Catalyst
1.	Haber's process for synthesis of ammonia	Iron; Mo (promoter)
2.	Contact process for manufacture of H_2SO_4	Pt, V_2O_5
3.	Ostwald process for manufacture of HNO_3	Pt gauze
4.	Deacon's process for manufacture of Cl_2	Cu_2Cl_2
5.	Bosch process for manufacture of H_2	$Fe_2O_3 + Cr_2O_3$
6.	Manufacture of vegetable ghee	Ni
7.	Fischer-Tropsch process (synthesis of hydrocarbons) from H_2 and CO	Co,ThO_2
8.	Synthetic petrol from coal (Bergius process)	iron oxalate

9.	Manufacture of C_2H_5OH from sucrose	Invertase, zymase
10.	Manufacture of C_2H_5OH from starch	Diastase, maltase
11.	Phthalic acid from naphthalene	$HgSO_4$
12.	Methanol from H_2 and CO	ZnO and Cr_2O_3
13.	Dehydrogenation of alcohol to aldehyde	Copper
14.	Polymerization of alkenes	H_3PO_4 on kieselguhr
15.	Acetic acid from CH_3CHO by oxidation with air	V_2O_5
16.	Preparation of O_2 from $KClO_3$	MnO_2

EXERCISES

I. SHORT ANSWER TYPE QUESTIONS

1. What are physical and chemical adsorption?
2. What is the principle of separation of inert gases from their mixture?
3. Why silica and alumina gels are used for removing moisture and controlling humidity?
4. How is adsorption dependent on temperature?
5. What are dispersion phases and dispersion mediums?
6. What is the reason for the formation of a delta where the sea and river water meet?
7. Why is the process of physisorption reversible whereas chemisorption is not?
8. What are the types of adsorption?
9. What is Freundlich adsorption isotherm?
10. What happens when an electric field is applied to a colloidal solution?
11. How do emulsifying agents stabilise the emulsion?
12. Why does leather get hardened after tanning?
13. What is the role of adsorption in heterogeneous catalysis?
14. Write short notes on:
    (*i*) Electrophoresis (*ii*) Brownian movement
    (*iii*) Tyndall effect (*iv*) Coagulation
    (*v*) Adsorption isotherm (*vi*) Lyophilic and Lyophobic colloids
    (*vi*) Protective colloids (*viii*) Hardy schulze rule
    (*ix*) Dialysis (*x*) Peptization.
15. What is salting out? How is it different from coagulation?
16. If AgCl sol is prepared by peptization, under what conditions it will be (*i*) positively charged, (*ii*) negatively charged?
    What will be the charge on the dispersion medium?

17. What special names are given to the following colloidal dispersions and what are their dispersed phase and dispersion medium?

(*i*) coloured glasses, (*ii*) smoke, (*iii*) milk, (*iv*) fog, (*v*) whipped cream.

II. LONG ANSWER TYPE QUESTIONS

1. What is the difference between physisorption and chemisorption?

2. On what assumption did Langmuir derive his adsorption isotherm? Derive it and explain how it justified the experimental results of adsorption at different pressure.

3. What are colloids? Write in detail the various methods employed for their preparation.

4. Write in detail the applications of colloids in various fields.

5. Define colloids and classify them in detail.

6. What are lyophilic and lyophobic colloids? Describe the important point of difference between them in a tabular form.

7. Explain with suitable examples multimolecular, macromolecular and associated colloids. What do you mean by Critical Micellization Concentration (CMC)?

8. What do you understand by coagulation of colloidal sol. Briefly explain Hardy schulze law.

9. What are protective colloids? Explain gold number in detail.

10. Define coagulation. Write at least four ways by which coagulation of a colloidal sol can be brought about.

11. What are colloidal particles? Explain briefly five important properties of colloidal sols.

12. What is adsorption? Explain the factors affecting adsorption.

13. What is absorption isotherm? Derive the equation for Freundlich absorption isotherm and also mention the limitations of Freundlich isotherm.

14. What is absorption? Explain in detail the applications of absorption in different fields.

15. What is colloidal system? How colloids are classified on the basis of different criteria?

16. What are colloidal solutions? Explain various methods used for the purification of colloidal solutions.

17. Write a detailed note on origin of charge on colloidal particles.

III. MULTIPLE CHOICE QUESTIONS

1. Difference between colloids and crystalloids is of:

(*a*) diameter (*b*) radius

(*c*) particle size (*d*) solubility.

2. Size of colloidal particles is

(*a*) 1 mμ to 100 mμ (*b*) 10 μ to 20 μ

(*c*) 0.05 mμ to 0.1 mμ (*d*) 25 μ to 30 μ.

3. Colloidal solution of gold is prepared by

(*a*) Colloidal mill (*b*) Double decomposition method

(*c*) Bredig's method (*d*) Peptization.

4. Colloids can be purified by
   (*a*) Peptization (*b*) Coagulation
   (*c*) Dialysis (*d*) Bredig are method.
5. Smoke is an example of
   (*a*) Gas dispersed in liquid (*b*) Gas dispersed in solid
   (*c*) Solid dispersed in gas (*d*) Solid dispersed in solid.
6. Which of the following is not a method of preparation of colloidal solution?
   (*a*) Electrical dispersion (*b*) Peptization
   (*c*) Mechanical dispersion (*d*) Coagulation.
7. Butter is
   (*a*) A gel (*b*) A sol
   (*c*) An emulsion (*d*) None of these.
8. The extra stability of lyophilic colloids is due to
   (*a*) Charge on their particles
   (*b*) A layer of medium of dispersion on their particles
   (*c*) The smaller size of their particles
   (*d*) The larger size of their particles.
9. Which of the following electrolytes will have maximum flocculation value for $Fe(OH)_3$ sol?
   (*a*) NaCl (*b*) Na_2S
   (*c*) $(NH_4)_3PO_4$ (*d*) K_2SO_4.
10. The formation of colloid from suspension is called
    (*a*) peptization (*b*) condensation
    (*c*) sedimentation (*d*) fragmentation.
11. Tyndall phenomena is exhibited by
    (*a*) NaCl solution (*b*) Starch solution
    (*c*) Urea solution (*d*) $FeCl_3$ solution.
12. Which property of colloidal suspension is used to determine the nature of charge on the particles?
    (*a*) Dialysis (*b*) Electrophoresis
    (*c*) Sedimentation (*d*) Ultrafiltration.
13. The brownian motion is due to
    (*a*) Temperature fluctuation within the liquid phase
    (*b*) Attraction and repulsion between charges on the colloidal particles
    (*c*) Impact of molecules of the dispersion medium on the colloidal particles
    (*d*) Convective currents.
14. Among the electrolytes Na_2SO_4, $CaCl_2$, $Al_2(SO_4)_3$ and NH_4Cl, the most effective coagulating agent for Sb_2S_3 sol is
    (*a*) Na_2SO_4 (*b*) $CaCl_2$
    (*c*) $Al_2(SO_4)_3$ (*d*) NH_4Cl.

15. The ability of an ion to bring about coagulation of a given colloid depends upon

(*a*) Its size (*b*) The magnitude of its charge only

(*c*) The sign of its charge only (*d*) Both magnitude and sign of its charge.

16. The equation for Freundlich adsorption isotherm is

(*a*) $\log \frac{x}{m} = \log K + n \log P$ (*b*) $\log \frac{m}{x} = \log K + \frac{1}{n} \log P$

(*c*) $\log \frac{m}{x} = \log K + n \log P$ (*d*) $\log \frac{x}{m} = \log K + \frac{1}{n} \log P$

17. In physical adsorption, the forces associated are:

(*a*) Ionic (*b*) Covalent

(*c*) van der Waal (*d*) H-bonding.

18. Langmuir adsorption isotherm is deduced using the assumption

(*a*) The adsorbed molecules interact with each other

(*b*) The heat of adsorption varies with the coverage

(*c*) The adsorption takes place in multilayers

(*d*) The adsorption sites are equivalent in their ability to adsorb particles.

19. Which of the following statements is true?

(*a*) Chemisorption forms unimolecular layer

(*b*) Chemisorption is a reversible process

(*c*) Chemisorption is independent of pressure

(*d*) Chemisorption has low enthalpy change.

20. For the adsorption of a gas on a solid, the plot of log $\frac{x}{m}$ versus lot P is linear with slope equal to

(*a*) k (*b*) $\log k$

(*c*) n (*d*) $\frac{1}{n}$.

21. Which of the following is not correct?

(*a*) Enthalpy of physical adsorption is less as compared to that of chemical adsorption

(*b*) Milk is an example of emulsion

(*c*) Physical adsorption increases with the increase in temperature

(*d*) Smoke is an aerosol.

22. In Freundlich adsorption isotherm, the value of $\frac{1}{n}$ is:

(*a*) between 0 and 1 in all cases (*b*) between 2 and 4 in all cases

(*c*) 1 in case of physical adsorption (*d*) 1 in case of chemical adsorption.

23. Gold numbers of protective colloids A, B, C and D are 0.50, 0.01, 0.10 and 0.005 respectively. The correct order of their protective powers is

(*a*) $A < C < B < D$ (*b*) $B < D < A < C$

(*c*) $D < A < C < B$ (*d*) $C < B < D < A$

24. Gelatin is mostly used in making ice-creams in order to

(*a*) Prevent making of a colloid

(*b*) Stabilize the colloid and prevent crystallization

(*c*) Stabilize the mixture

(*d*) Enrich the aroma.

25. Alum helps in purifying water due to

(*a*) Formation of Si complex with clay particles

(*b*) Sulphate part which combines with the dirt and removes it

(*c*) Aluminium which coagulates the mud particles

(*d*) Making mud water soluble.

Answers

MULTIPLE CHOICE QUESTIONS

1. (*c*)	**2.** (*a*)	**3.** (*c*)	**4.** (*c*)	**5.** (*c*)	**6.** (*d*)	**7.** (*a*)	**8.** (*b*)	**9.** (*a*)	**10.** (*a*)
11. (*b*)	**12.** (*b*)	**13.** (*c*)	**14.** (*c*)	**15.** (*d*)	**16.** (*d*)	**17.** (*c*)	**18.** (*d*)	**19.** (*a*)	**20.** (*d*)
21. (*c*)	**22.** (*a*)	**23.** (*a*)	**24.** (*b*)	**25.** (*c*)					